FE

Rapid Preparation for the Mechanical
Fundamentals of Engineering Exam

MECHANICAL
REVIEW MANUAL

Pass The Exam—Guaranteed

Michael R. Lindeburg, PE

PPI®

PPI2PASS.COM
A **KAPLAN** COMPANY

Report Errors for This Book

PPI is grateful to every reader who notifies us of a possible error. Your feedback allows us to improve the quality and accuracy of our products. Report errata at **ppi2pass.com**.

FE MECHANICAL REVIEW MANUAL
First Edition

Current release of this edition: 9

Release History

date	edition number	revision number	update
Feb 2021	1	7	Minor corrections.
Oct 2021	1	8	Minor corrections.
Apr 2023	1	9	Minor corrections.

Printed in the United States of America.
PPI
ppi2pass.com

ISBN: 978-1-59126-441-5

PPI's Guarantee

This book is your best choice to prepare for the Fundamentals of Engineering (FE) examination. It is the only review that

- covers every FE exam knowledge area
- is based on the NCEES *FE Reference Handbook* (*NCEES Handbook*)
- provides example questions in true exam format
- provides instructional material for essentially every relevant equation, figure, and table in the *NCEES Handbook*
- can be accessed online at **ppi2pass.com**

PPI is confident that if you use this book conscientiously to prepare for the FE exam, following the guidelines described in the "How to Use This Book" section, you'll pass the exam. Otherwise, regardless of where you purchased this book, with no questions asked, we will refund the purchase price of your printed book (up to PPI's published website price).

To request a refund, you must provide the following items within three months of taking the exam:

1. A summary letter listing your name, email address, and mailing address
2. Your original packing slip, store sales receipt, or online order acknowledgment showing the price you paid (price must be individually listed on receipt)
3. A dated email, notification letter, or printout of your MyNCEES webpage showing that you did not pass the FE exam
4. Your book

To complete the return, contact PPI on our website, **ppi2pass.com** or call 650-593-9119.

This guarantee does not extend to web access books, other products, or books with invalid registration numbers.

Topics

Mathematics

Probability/ Statistics

Fluid Mechanics

Thermodynamics

Heat Transfer

Statics

Material Props./ Processing

Mechanics of Materials

Electricity/ Magnetism

Dynamics/ Vibrations

Mechanical/ Design/Analysis

Measurement/ Instrumentation

Computational Tools

Engineering Economics

Ethics/ Prof. Prac.

Table of Contents

Topic XI: Mechanical Design and Analysis

Topic XII: Measurement, Instrumentation, and Controls

Topic XIII: Computational Tools

Topic XIV: Engineering Economics

Topic XV: Ethics and Professional Practice

Preface

The purpose of this book is to prepare you for the National Council of Examiners for Engineering and Surveying (NCEES) fundamentals of engineering (FE) exam.

In 2014, the NCEES adopted revised specifications for the exam. The council also transitioned from a paper-based version of the exam to a computer-based testing (CBT) version. The FE exam now requires you to sit in front of a monitor, respond to questions served up by the CBT system, access an electronic reference document, and perform your scratch calculations on a reusable notepad. You may also use an on-screen calculator with which you will likely be unfamiliar. The experience of taking the FE exam will probably be unlike anything you have ever, or will ever again, experience in your career. Similarly, preparing for the exam will be unlike preparing for any other exam.

The CBT FE exam presented three new challenges to me when I began preparing instructional material for it. (1) The subjects in the testable body of knowledge are oddly limited and do not represent a complete cross section of the traditional engineering fundamentals subjects. (2) The NCEES *FE Reference Handbook* (*NCEES Handbook*) is poorly organized, awkwardly formatted, inconsistent in presentation, and idiomatic in convention. (3) Traditional studying, doing homework while working toward a degree, and working at your own desk as a career engineer are poor preparations for the CBT exam experience.

No existing exam review book overcomes all of these challenges. But, I wanted you to have something that does. So, in order to prepare you for the CBT FE exam, this book was designed and written from the ground up. In many ways, this book is as unconventional as the exam.

This book covers all of the knowledge areas listed in the NCEES Mechanical FE exam specifications. For all practical purposes, this book contains the equivalent of all of the equations, tables, and figures presented in the *NCEES Handbook*, ninth edition (September 2013 revision) that you will need for the Mechanical FE exam. And, with the exceptions listed in the "Variables" section, for better or worse, this book duplicates the terms, variables, and formatting of the *NCEES Handbook* equations.

NCEES has selected, what it believes to be, all of the engineering fundamentals important to an early-career, minimally-qualified engineer, and has distilled them into its single reference, the *NCEES Handbook*. Personally, I cannot accept the premise that engineers learn and use so little engineering while getting their degrees and during their first few career years. However, regardless of whether you accept the NCEES subset of engineering fundamentals, one thing is certain: In serving as your sole source of formulas, theory, methods, and data during the exam, the *NCEES Handbook* severely limits the types of questions that can be included in the FE exam.

The obsolete paper-based exam required very little knowledge outside of what was presented in the previous editions of the *NCEES Handbook*. That *NCEES Handbook* supported a plug-and-chug examinee performance within a constrained body of knowledge. Based on the current FE exam specifications and the *NCEES Handbook*, the CBT FE exam is even more limited than the old paper-based exam. The number (breadth) of knowledge areas, the coverage (depth) of knowledge areas, the number of questions, and the duration of the exam are all significantly reduced. If you are only concerned about passing and/or "getting it over with" before graduation, these reductions are all in your favor. Your only deterrents will be the cost of the exam and the inconvenience of finding a time and place to take it.

Accepting that "it is what it is," I designed this book to guide you through the exam's body of knowledge.

I have several admissions to make: (1) This book contains nothing magical or illicit. (2) This book, by itself, is only one part of a complete preparation. (3) This book stops well short of being perfect. What do I mean by those admissions?

First, this book does not contain anything magical. It's called a "review" manual, and you might even learn something new from it. It will save you time in assembling review material and questions. However, it won't learn the material for you. Merely owning it is not enough. You will have to put in the time to use it.

Similarly, there is nothing clandestine or unethical about this book. It does not contain any actual exam questions. It was written in a vacuum, based entirely on the NCEES Mechanical FE exam specifications. This book is not based on feedback from actual examinees.

Truthfully, I expect that many exam questions will be similar to the questions I have used because NCEES and I developed content with the same set of constraints. (If anything, NCEES is even more constrained when it comes to fringe, outlier, eccentric, or original topics.)

There are a finite number of ways that questions about Ohm's law ($V = IR$) and Newton's second law of motion ($F = ma$) can be structured. Any similarity between questions in this book and questions in the exam is easily attributed to the limited number of engineering formulas and concepts, the shallowness of the coverage, and the need to keep the entire solution process (reading, researching, calculating, and responding) to less than three minutes for each question.

Let me give an example to put some flesh on the bones. As any competent engineer can attest, in order to calculate the pressure drop in a pipe network, you would normally have to (1) determine fluid density and viscosity based on the temperature, (2) convert the mass flow rate to a volumetric flow rate, (3) determine the pipe diameter from the pipe size designation (e.g., pipe schedule), (4) calculate the internal pipe area, (5) calculate the flow velocity, (6) determine the specific roughness from the conduit material, (7) calculate the relative roughness, (8) calculate the Reynolds number, (9) calculate or determine the friction factor graphically, (10) determine the equivalent length of fittings and other minor losses, (11) calculate the head loss, and finally, (12) convert the head loss to pressure drop. Length, flow quantity, and fluid property conversions typically add even more complexity. (SSU viscosity? Diameter in inches? Flow rate in SCFM?) As reasonable and conventional as that solution process is, a question of such complexity is beyond the upper time limit for an FE exam question.

To make it possible to be solved in the time allowed, any exam question you see is likely to be more limited. In fact, most or all of the information you need to answer a question will be given to you in its question statement. If only the real world were so kind!

Second, by itself, this book is inadequate. It was never intended to define the entirety of your preparation activity. While it introduces essentially all of the exam knowledge areas and content in the *NCEES Handbook*, an introduction is only an introduction. To be a thorough review, this book needs augmentation.

By design, this book has three significant inadequacies.

1. This book has a limited number of pages, so it cannot contain enough of everything for everyone. The number of example questions that can fit in it is limited. The number of questions needed by you, personally, to come up to speed in a particular subject may be inadequate. For example, how many questions will you have to review in order to feel comfortable about divergence, curl, differential equations, and linear algebra? (Answer: Probably more than are in all the books you will ever own!) So, additional exposure is inevitable if

you want to be adequately prepared in every subject.

2. This book does not contain the *NCEES Handbook*, per se. This book is limited in helping you become familiar with the idiosyncratic sequencing, formatting, variables, omissions, and presentation of topics in the *NCEES Handbook*. The only way to remedy this is to obtain your own copy of the *NCEES Handbook* (available in printed format from PPI and as a free download from the NCEES website) and use it in conjunction with your review.

3. This book does not contain a practice examination (mock exam, sample exam, etc.). With the advent of the CBT format, any sample exam in printed format is little more than another collection of practice questions. The actual FE exam is taken sitting in front of a computer using an online reference book, so the only way to practice is to sit in front of a computer while you answer questions. Using an online reference is very different from the work environment experienced by most engineers, and it will take some getting used to.

Third, and finally, I reluctantly admit that I have never figured out how to write or publish a completely flawless first (or, even subsequent) edition. The PPI staff comes pretty close to perfection in the areas of design, editing, typography, and illustrating. Subject matter experts help immensely with calculation checking. And, beta testing before you see a book helps smooth out wrinkles. However, I still manage to muck up the content. So, I hope you will "let me have it" when you find my mistakes. PPI has established an easy way for you to report an error, as well as to review changes that resulted from errors that others have submitted. Just go to **ppi2pass.com/errata**. When you submit something, I'll receive it via email. When I answer it, you'll receive a response. We'll both benefit.

Best wishes in your examination experience. Stay in touch!

Michael R. Lindeburg, PE

Acknowledgments

Developing a book specific to the computerized Mechanical FE exam has been a monumental project. It involved the usual (from an author's and publisher's standpoint) activities of updating and repurposing existing content and writing new content. However, the project was made extraordinarily more difficult by two factors: (1) a new book design, and (2) the publication schedule.

Creating a definitive resource to help you prepare for the computerized FE exam was a huge team effort, and PPI's entire Product Development and Implementation (PD&I) staff was heavily involved. Along the way, they had to learn new skills and competencies, solve unseen technical mysteries, and exercise professional judgment in decisions that involved publishing, resources, engineering, and user utility. They worked long hours, week after week, and month after month, often into the late evening, to publish this book for examinees taking the exam.

PPI staff members have had a lot of things to say about this book during its development. In reference to you and other examinees being unaware of what PPI staff did, one of the often-heard statements was, "They will never know."

However, I want you to know, so I'm going to tell you.

Editorial project managers Chelsea Logan, Magnolia Molcan, and Julia White managed the gargantuan operation, with considerable support from Sarah Hubbard, director of PD&I. Production services manager Cathy Schrott kept the process moving smoothly and swiftly, despite technical difficulties that seemed determined to stall the process at every opportunity. Christine Eng, product development manager, arranged for all of the outside subject matter experts who were involved with this book. All of the content was eventually reviewed for consistency, PPI style, and accuracy by Jennifer Lindeburg King, associate editor-in-chief.

Though everyone in PD&I has a specialty, this project pulled everyone from his or her comfort zone. The entire staff worked on "building" the chapters of this book from scratch, piecing together existing content with new content. Everyone learned (with amazing speed) how to grapple with the complexities of XML and MathML while wrestling misbehaving computer code into submission. Tom Bergstrom, technical illustrator, and Kate Hayes, production associate, updated existing illustrations and created new ones. They also paginated and made corrections. Copy editors Tyler Hayes, Scott Marley, Connor Sempek, and Ian A. Walker copy edited, proofread, corrected, and paginated. Copy editors Alexander Ahn; Manuel Carreiro; Nicole Evans, EIT; Hilary Flood; and Heather Turbeville proofread and corrected. Scott's comments were particularly insightful. Nicole Evans, EIT; Prajesh Gongal, EIT; and Jumphol Somsaad assisted with content selection, problem writing, and calculation checking. Jeanette Baker, EIT; Scott Miller, EIT; Alex Valeyev, EIT; and Akira Zamudio, EIT, remapped existing PPI problems to the new NCEES Mechanical FE exam specifications. Staff engineer Phil Luna, PE, helped ensure the technical accuracy of the content.

Paying customers (such as you) shouldn't have to be test pilots. So, close to the end of the process, when content was starting to coalesce out of the shapelessness of the PPI content management system, several subject matter experts became crash car dummies "for the good of engineering." They pretended to be examinees and worked through all of the content, looking for calculation errors, references that went nowhere, and logic that was incomprehensible. These engineers and their knowledge area contributions are: C. Dale Buckner, PhD, PE, SECB (Statics); John C. Crepeau, PhD, PE (Dynamics, Kinematics, and Vibrations; Electricity and Magnetism; Heat Transfer; Mathematics; Measurements, Instrumentation, and Controls; Mechanical Design and Analysis; and Mechanics of Materials); Joshua T. Frohman, PE (Computational Tools and Transportation Engineering); David Hurwitz, PhD (Computational Tools and Probability and Statistics); Liliana M. Kandic, PE (Fluid Mechanics and Statics); Aparna Phadnis, PE (Engineering Economics); David To, PE (Dynamics, Kinematics, and Vibrations; Electricity and Magnetism; Fluid Mechanics; Heat Transfer; Mathematics; Measurements, Instrumentation, and Controls; Mechanical Design and Analysis; Mechanics of Materials; and Thermodynamics); and L. Adam Williamson, PE (Heat Transfer; Fluid Mechanics; Dynamics, Kinematics, and Vibrations; Material Properties and Processing; and Thermodynamics).

Consistent with the past 38 years, I continue to thank my wife, Elizabeth, for accepting and participating in a writer's life that is full to overflowing. Even though our children have been out on their own for a long time, we seem to have even less time than we had before. As a corollary to Aristotle's "Nature abhors a vacuum," I propose: "Work expands to fill the void."

To my granddaughter, Sydney, who had to share her Grumpus with his writing, I say, "I only worked when you were taking your naps. And besides, you hog the bed!"

I also appreciate the grant of permission to reproduce materials from several other publishers. In each case, attribution is provided where the material has been included. Neither PPI nor the publishers of the reproduced material make any representations or warranties as to the accuracy of the material, nor are they liable for any damages resulting from its use.

Thank you, everyone! I'm really proud of what you've accomplished. Your efforts will be pleasing to examinees and effective in preparing them for the Mechanical FE exam.

Michael R. Lindeburg, PE

Codes and References Used to Prepare This Book

This book is based on the NCEES *FE Reference Handbook* (*NCEES Handbook*), ninth edition (June 2015 revision). The other documents, codes, and standards that were used to prepare this book were the most current available at the time.

NCEES does not specifically tie the FE exam to any edition (version) of any code or standard. Rather than make the FE exam subject to the vagaries of such codes and standards as are published by the American Concrete Institute (ACI), the American Institute of Steel Construction (AISC), the American National Standards Institute (ANSI), the American Society of Civil Engineers (ASCE), the American Society of Heating, Refrigerating and Air-Conditioning Engineers (ASHRAE), the American Society of Mechanical Engineers (ASME), ASTM International (ASTM), the International Code Council (ICC), and so on, NCEES effectively writes its own "code," the *NCEES Handbook*.

Most surely, every standard- or code-dependent concept (e.g., bolt fits and limits) in the *NCEES Handbook* can be traced back to some section of some edition of a standard or code (e.g., ASME B4.2). So, it would be logical to conclude that you need to be familiar with everything (the limitations, surrounding sections, and commentary) in the code related to that concept.

However, that does not seem to be the case. The *NCEES Handbook* is a code unto itself, and you won't need to study the parent documents. Nor will you need to know anything pertaining to related, adjacent, similar, or parallel code concepts. For example, some HVAC topics are included in the *NCEES Handbook*, but ventilation, infiltration, and the crack method are no longer included. With the possible exception of some general information, knowledge of ASHRAE methods of determining ventilation cannot be expected.

Therefore, although methods and content in the *NCEES Handbook* can be ultimately traced back to some edition (version) of a relevant code, you don't need to know which. You don't need to know whether that content is current, limited in intended application, or relevant. You only need to use the content.

Introduction

PART 1: ABOUT THIS BOOK

This book is intended to guide you through the Mechanical Fundamentals of Engineering (FE) examination body of knowledge and the idiosyncrasies of the National Council of Examiners for Engineers and Surveyors (NCEES) *FE Reference Handbook* (*NCEES Handbook*). This book is not intended as a reference book, because you cannot use it while taking the FE examination. The only reference you may use is the *NCEES Handbook*. However, the *NCEES Handbook* is not intended as a teaching tool, nor is it an easy document to use. The *NCEES Handbook* was never intended to be something you study or learn from, or to have value as anything other than an exam-day compilation. Many of its features may distract you because they differ from what you were expecting, were exposed to, or what you currently use.

To effectively use the *NCEES Handbook*, you must become familiar with its features, no matter how odd they may seem. *FE Mechanical Review Manual* will help you become familiar with the format, layout, organization, and odd conventions of the *NCEES Handbook*. This book, which displays the *NCEES Handbook* material in blue for easy identification, satisfies two important needs: it is (1) something to learn from, and (2) something to help you become familiar with the *NCEES Handbook*.

Organization

This book is organized into topics (e.g., "Mechanical Design and Analysis") that correspond to the knowledge areas listed by NCEES in its Mechanical FE exam specifications. However, unlike the *NCEES Handbook*, this book arranges subtopics into chapters (e.g., "Machine Design") that build logically on one another. Each chapter contains sections (e.g., "Gear Sets and Gear Drives") organized around *NCEES Handbook* equations, but again, the arrangement of those equations is based on logical development, not the *NCEES Handbook*. Equations that are presented together in this book may actually be many pages apart in the *NCEES Handbook*.

The presentation of each subtopic or related group of equations uses similar components and follows a specific sequence. The components of a typical subtopic are:

- general section title
- background and developmental content
- equation name (or description) and equation number

- equation with *NCEES Handbook* formatting
- any relevant variations of the equation
- any values typically associated with the equation
- additional explanation and development
- worked quantitative example using the *NCEES Handbook* equation
- footnotes

Not all sections contain all of these features. Some features may be omitted if they are not needed. For example, "$g = 9.81$ m/s^2" would be a typical value associated with the equation $W = mg$. There would be no typical values associated with the equation $F = ma$.

Much of the information in this book and in the *NCEES Handbook* is relevant to more than one knowledge area or subtopic. For example, equations related to the Material Properties and Processing knowledge area also pertain to the subtopics of Mechanical Design and Analysis. Many Thermodynamics concepts correlate with Heat Transfer subtopics. The index will help you locate all information related to any of the topics or subtopics you wish to review.

Content

This book presents equations, figures, tables, and other data equivalent to those given in the *NCEES Handbook*. For example, the *NCEES Handbook* includes tables for conversion factors, material properties, and areas and centroids of geometric shapes, so this book provides equivalent tables. Occasionally, a redundant element of the *NCEES Handbook*, or some item having no value to examinees, has been omitted.

Some elements, primarily figures and tables, that were originally published by authoritative third parties (and for whom reproduction permission has been granted) have been reprinted exactly as they appear in the *NCEES Handbook*. Other elements have been editorially and artistically reformulated, but they remain equivalent in utility to the originals.

Colors

Due to the selective nature of topics included in the *NCEES Handbook*, coverage of some topics in the *NCEES Handbook* may be incomplete. This book aims to offer more comprehensive coverage, and so, it contains material that is not covered in the *NCEES Handbook*. This book uses color to differentiate between what is available to you during the exam, and what is supplementary content that makes a topic more interesting or easier to understand. Anything that closely parallels or duplicates the *NCEES Handbook* is printed in blue. Headings that introduce content related to *NCEES Handbook* equations are printed in blue. Titles of figures and tables that are essentially the same as in the *NCEES Handbook* are similarly printed in blue. Headings that introduce sections, equations, figures, and tables that are NOT in the *NCEES Handbook* are printed in **black**. The **black** content is background, preliminary and supporting material, explanations, extensions to theory, and application rules that are generally missing from the *NCEES Handbook*.

Numbering

The equations, figures, and tables in the *NCEES Handbook* are unnumbered. All equations, figures, and tables in this book include unique numbers provided to help you navigate through the content.

You will find many equations in this book that have no numbers and are printed in **black**, not blue. These equations represent instructional materials which are often missing pieces or interim results not presented in the *NCEES Handbook*. In some cases, the material was present in the eighth edition of the *NCEES Handbook*, but is absent in the ninth edition. In some cases, I included instruction in deleted content. (This book does not contain all of the deleted eighth edition *NCEES Handbook* content, however.)

Equation and Variable Names

This book generally uses the *NCEES Handbook* terminology and naming conventions, giving standard, normal, and customary alternatives within parentheses or footnotes. For example, the *NCEES Handbook* refers to what is commonly known as the Bernoulli equation as the "energy equation." This book acknowledges the *NCEES Handbook* terminology when introducing the equation, but uses the term "Bernoulli equation" thereafter.

Variables

This book makes every effort to include the *NCEES Handbook* equations exactly as they appear in the *NCEES Handbook*. While any symbol can be defined to represent any quantity, in many cases, the *NCEES Handbook*'s choice of variables will be dissimilar to what most engineers are accustomed to. For example, although there is no concept of weight in the SI system, the *NCEES Handbook* defines W as the symbol for weight with units of newtons. While engineers are comfortable with E, E_k, KE, and U representing kinetic energy, after introducing KE in its introductory pages,

the *NCEES Handbook* uses T (which is used sparingly by some scientists) for kinetic energy. The *NCEES Handbook* designates power as $\dot{W}$ instead of P. Because you have to be familiar with them, this book reluctantly follows all of those conventions.

This book generally follows the *NCEES Handbook* convention regarding use of italic fonts, even when doing so results in ambiguity. For example, as used by the *NCEES Handbook*, aspect ratio, AR, is indistinguishable from $A \times R$, area times radius. Occasionally, the *NCEES Handbook* is inconsistent in how it represents a particular variable, or in some sections, it drops the italic font entirely and presents all of its variables in roman font. This book maintains the publishing convention of showing all variables as italic.

There are a few important differences between the ways the *NCEES Handbook* and this book present content. These differences are intentional for the purpose of maintaining clarity and following PPI's publication policies.

- *pressure:* The *NCEES Handbook* primarily uses P for pressure, an atypical engineering convention. This book always uses p so as to differentiate it from P, which is reserved for power, momentum, and axial loading in related chapters.

- *velocity:* The *NCEES Handbook* uses v and occasionally Greek nu, ν, for velocity. This book always uses v to differentiate it from Greek upsilon, υ, which represents specific volume in some topics (e.g., thermodynamics), and Greek nu, ν, which represents absolute viscosity and Poisson's ratio.

- *specific volume:* The *NCEES Handbook* uses v for specific volume. This book always uses Greek upsilon, υ, a convention that most engineers will be familiar with.

- *units:* The *NCEES Handbook* and the FE exam generally do not emphasize the difference between pounds-mass and pounds-force. "Pounds" ("lb") can mean either force or mass. This book always distinguishes between pounds-force (lbf) and pounds-mass (lbm).

Distinction Between Mass and Weight

The *NCEES Handbook* specifies the unit weight of water, γ_w, as 9.810 kN/m^3. This book follows that convention but takes every opportunity to point out that there is no concept of weight in the SI system.

Equation Formatting

The *NCEES Handbook* writes out many multilevel equations as an awkward string of characters on a single line, using a plethora of parentheses and square and curly brackets to indicate the precedence of mathematical operations. So, this book does also. However, in examples using the equations, this book reverts to normal publication style after presenting the base equation styled as it is in the *NCEES Handbook*. The change in style will show you the equations as the *NCEES Handbook* presents them, while presenting the calculations in a normal and customary typographic manner.

Footnotes

I have tried to anticipate the kinds of questions about this book and the *NCEES Handbook* that an instructor would be asked in class. Footnotes are used in this book as the preferred method of answering those questions and of drawing your attention to features in the *NCEES Handbook* that may confuse, confound, and infuriate you. Basically, *NCEES Handbook* conventions are used within the body of this book, and any inconsistencies, oddities and unconventionalities, and occasionally, even errors, are pointed out in the footnotes.

If you know the NCEES knowledge areas backward as well as forward, many of the issues pointed out in the footnotes will seem obvious. However, if you have only a superficial knowledge of the knowledge areas, the footnotes will answer many of your questions. The footnotes are intended to be factual and helpful.

Indexed Terms

The print version of this book contains an index with thousands of terms. The index will help you quickly find just what you are looking for, as well as identify related concepts and content.

PART 2: HOW YOU CAN USE THIS BOOK

IF YOU ARE A STUDENT

In reference to Isaac Asimov's *Foundation and Empire* trilogy, you'll soon experience a Seldon crisis. Given all the factors (the exam you're taking, what you learned as a student, how much time you have before the exam, and your own personality), the behaviors (strategies made evident through action) required of you will be self-evident.

Here are some of those strategies.

Get the NCEES *FE Reference Handbook*

Get a copy of the *NCEES Handbook*. Use it as you read through this book. You will want to know the sequence of the sections, what data is included, and the approximate locations of important figures and tables in the *NCEES Handbook*. You should also know the terminology (words and phrases) used in the *NCEES Handbook* to describe equations or subjects, because those are the terms you will have to look up during the exam.

The *NCEES Handbook* is available both in printed and PDF format. The index of the print version may help you locate an equation or other information you are looking for, but few terms are indexed thoroughly. The PDF version includes search functionality that is similar to what you'll have available when taking the computer-based exam. In order to find something using the PDF search function, your search term will have to match the content exactly (including punctuation).

Diagnose Yourself

Use the diagnostic exams in this book to determine how much you should study in the various knowledge areas. You can use diagnostic exams (and other assessments) in two ways: take them before you begin studying to determine which subjects you should emphasize, or take them after you finish studying to determine if you are ready to move on.

Make a Schedule

In order to complete your review of all examination subjects, you must develop and adhere to a review schedule. If you are not taking a live review course (where the order of your preparation is determined by the lectures), you'll want to prepare your own schedule. If you want to pencil out a schedule on paper, a blank study schedule template is provided at the end of this Introduction.

The amount of material in each chapter of this book, and the number of questions in the corresponding chapter of *FE Mechanical Practice Problems*, were designed to fit into a practical schedule. You should be able to review one chapter in each book each day. There are 53 chapters and 15 diagnostic exams in this book, as well as corresponding chapters of practice problems in the companion book *FE Mechanical Practice Problems*. So, you need at least 68 study days. This requires you to treat every day the same and work through weekends.

If you'd rather take all the weekends off and otherwise stick with the one-chapter-per-study-day concept, you will have to begin approximately 99 days before the exam. Use the off days to rest, review, and study questions from other books. If you are pressed for time or get behind schedule, you don't have to take the days off. That will be your choice.

Near the exam date, give yourself a week to take a realistic practice exam, to remedy any weaknesses it exposes, and to recover from the whole ordeal.

Work Through Everything

NCEES has greatly reduced the number of subjects about which you are expected to be knowledgeable and has made nothing optional. Skipping your weakest subjects is no longer a viable preparation strategy. You should study all examination knowledge areas, not just your specialty areas. That means you study every chapter in this book and skip nothing. Do not limit the number of chapters you study in hopes of finding enough problems in your areas of expertise to pass the exam.

Be Thorough

Being thorough means really doing the work. Read the material, don't skim it. Solve each numerical example using your calculator. Read through the solution, and refer back to the equations, figures, and tables it references.

Don't jump into answering problems without first reviewing the instructional text in this book. Unlike reference books that you skim or merely refer to when needed, this book requires you to read everything. That reading is going to be your only review. Reading the instructional text is a "high value" activity. There isn't much text to read in the first place, so the value per word is high. There aren't any derivations or proofs, so the text is useful. Everything in blue titled sections is in the *NCEES Handbook*, so it has a high probability of showing up on the exam.

Work Problems

You have less than an average of three minutes to answer each question on the exam. You must be able to quickly recall solution procedures, formulas, and important data. You will not have time to derive solution methods—you must know them instinctively. The best way to develop fast recall is to work as many practice problems as you can find, including those in the companion book *FE Mechanical Practice Problems*.

Solve every example in this book and every problem in *FE Mechanical Practice Problems*. Don't skip any of them. All of the problems were written to illustrate key points.

Finish Strong

There will be physical demands on your body during the examination. It is very difficult to remain alert, focused, and attentive for six hours or more. Unfortunately, the more time you study, the less time you have to maintain your physical condition. Thus, most examinees arrive at the examination site in high mental condition but in deteriorated physical condition. While preparing for the FE exam is not the only good reason for embarking on a physical conditioning program, it can serve as a good incentive to get in shape.

Claim Your Reward

As Hari Seldon often said in Isaac Asimov's *Foundation and Empire* trilogy, the outcome of your actions will be inevitable.

IF YOU ARE AN INSTRUCTOR

CBT Challenges

The computer-based testing (CBT) FE exam format, content, and frequent administration present several challenges to teaching a live review course. Some of the challenges are insurmountable to almost all review courses. Live review courses cannot be offered year round, a different curriculum is required for each engineering discipline, and a hard-copy, in-class mock exam taken at the end of the course no longer prepares examinees for the CBT experience. The best that instructors can do is to be honest about the limitations of their courses, and to refer examinees to any other compatible resources.

Many of the standard, tried-and-true features of live FE review courses are functionally obsolete. These obsolete features include general lectures that cover "everything," complex numerical examples with more than two or three simple steps, instructor-prepared handouts containing notes and lists of reference materials, and a hard-copy mock exam. As beneficial as those features were in the past, they are no longer best commercial practice for the CBT FE exam. However, they may still be used and provide value to examinees.

This book parallels the content of the *NCEES Handbook* and, with the exceptions listed in this Introduction, uses the same terminology and nomenclature. The figures and tables are equivalent to those in the *NCEES Handbook*. You can feel confident that I had your students and the success of your course in mind when I designed this book.

Instruction for Multiple Exams

Since this book is intended to be used by those studying for the Mechanical FE exam, there is no easy way to use it as the basis for more than a Mechanical FE exam review course.

Historically, most commercial review courses (taken primarily by engineers who already have their degrees) prepared examinees for the Other Disciplines FE examination. That is probably the only logical (practical, sustainable, etc.) course of action, even now. Few commercial review course providers have the large customer base and diverse instructors needed to offer simultaneous courses for every discipline.

University review courses frequently combine students from multiple disciplines, focusing the review course content on the core overlapping concepts and the topics covered by the Other Disciplines FE exam. The change in the FE exam scope has made it more challenging than ever to adequately prepare a diverse student group.

If you are tasked with teaching a course to examinees taking more than one exam, refer to the guidelines and suggestions posted at **ppi2pass.com/instructor/resources**. The materials available to review course instructors (as well as for examinees) continue to evolve, and that site will reference the most current resources available.

Lectures

Your lectures should duplicate what the examinees would be doing in a self-directed review program. That means walking through each chapter in this book in its entirety. You're basically guiding a tour through the book. By covering everything in this book, you'll cover everything on the exam.

Handouts

Everything you do in a lecture should be tied back to the *NCEES Handbook*. You will be doing your students a great disservice if you get them accustomed to using your course handouts or notes to solve problems. They can't use your notes in the exam, so train them to use the only reference they are allowed to use.

NCEES allows that the exam may require broader knowledge than the *NCEES Handbook* contains. However, there are very few areas that require formulas not present in the *NCEES Handbook*. Therefore, you shouldn't deviate too much from the subject matter of each chapter.

Homework

Students like to see and work a lot of problems. They experience great reassurance in working exam-like problems and finding out how easy the problems are. Repetition and reinforcement should come from working additional problems, not from more lecture.

It is unlikely that your students will be working to capacity if their work is limited to what is in this book. You will have to provide or direct your students to more problems in order to help them effectively master the concepts you will be teaching.

Schedule

I have found that a 15-week format works best for a live FE exam review course that covers everything and is intended for working engineers who already have their degrees. This schedule allows for one 2 to 2½ hour lecture per week, with a 10-minute break each hour.

Table 1 outlines a typical format for a live commercial Mechanical FE review course. To some degree, the lectures build upon one another. However, a credible decision can be made to present the knowledge areas in the order they appear in the *NCEES Handbook*.

However, a 15-week course is too long for junior and senior engineering majors still working toward a degree. College students and professors don't have that much time. And, students don't need as thorough of a review as do working engineers who have forgotten more of the fundamentals. College students can get by with the most cursory of reviews in some knowledge areas, such as mathematics, fluid mechanics, and statics.

For college students, an 8-week course consisting of six weeks of lectures followed by two weeks of open questions seems appropriate. If possible, two 1-hour lectures per week are more likely to get students to attend than a single 2- or 3-hour lecture per week. The course consists of a comprehensive march through all knowledge areas except mathematics, with the major emphasis being on problem-solving rather than lecture. For current engineering majors, the main goals are to keep the students focused and to wake up their latent memories, not to teach the subjects.

Table 2 outlines a typical format for a live university review course. The sequence of the lectures is less important for a university review course than for a commercial course, because students will have recent experience in the subjects. Some may actually be enrolled in some of the related courses while you are conducting the review.

I strongly believe in the benefits of exposing all review course participants to a realistic sample examination. Unless you have made arrangements with **feprep.com** for your students to take an online exam, you probably cannot provide them with an experience equivalent to the actual exam. A written take-home exam is better than nothing, but since it will not mimic the exam experience, it must be presented as little more than additional problems to solve.

I no longer recommend an in-class group final exam. Since a review course usually ends only a few days before the real FE examination, it seems inhumane to make students sit for hours into the late evening for the final exam. So, if you are going to use a written mock exam, I recommend distributing it at the first meeting of the review course and assigning it as a take-home exercise.

PART 3: ABOUT THE EXAM

EXAM STRUCTURE

The FE exam is a computer-based test of 110 questions. It is closed-book and allows only the *NCEES Handbook* as an electronic reference.

Only one problem and its answer options are given on-screen at a time. The exam is not adaptive (i.e., your response to one problem has no bearing on the next problem you are given). Even if you answer the first five mathematics problems correctly, you'll still have to answer the sixth problem.

In essence, the FE exam is two separate, partial exams given in sequence. During either session, you cannot view or respond to problems in the other session.

Your exam will include a limited (unknown) number of problems (known as "pretest items") that will not be scored and will not have an impact on your results. NCEES does this to determine the viability of new

Table 1 *Recommended 15-Week Mechanical FE Exam Review Course Format for Commercial Review Courses*

week	FE Mechanical Review Manual chapter titles	FE Mechanical Review Manual chapter numbers
1	Analytic Geometry and Trigonometry; Algebra and Linear Algebra; Calculus; Differential Equations and Transforms; Numerical Methods	1–5
2	Probability and Statistics	6
3	Engineering Economics	50
4	Professional Practice; Ethics; Licensure	51–53
5	Systems of Forces and Moments; Trusses; Pulleys, Cables, and Friction; Centroids and Moments of Inertia	22–25
6	Kinematics; Kinetics; Kinetics of Rotational Motion; Energy and Work; Vibrations	37–41
7	Fluid Properties; Fluid Statics; Fluid Dynamics; Fluid Measurement and Similitude; Compressible Fluid Dynamics; Fluid Machines	7–12
8	Properties of Substances; Laws of Thermodynamics; Power Cycles and Entropy; Mixtures of Gases, Vapors, and Liquids; Combustion; Heating, Ventilating, and Air Conditioning (HVAC)	13–18
9	Conduction; Convection; Radiation	19–21
10	Material Properties and Testing; Engineering Materials; Manufacturing Processes	26–28
11	Stresses and Strains; Thermal, Hoop, and Torsional Stress; Beams; Columns	29–32
12	Fasteners; Machine Design; Hydraulic and Pneumatic Mechanisms; Pressure Vessels; Manufacturability, Quality, and Reliability	42–46
13	Electrostatics; Direct-Current Circuits; Alternating-Current Circuits; Rotating Machines	33–36
14	Measurement and Instrumentation; Controls	47–48
15	Computer Software	58

problems for future exams. You won't know which problems are pretest items. They are not identifiable and are randomly distributed throughout the exam.

EXAM DURATION

The exam is six hours long and includes a 2-minute nondisclosure agreement, an 8-minute tutorial, an optional 25-minute break, and a brief survey at the conclusion of the exam. The total time you'll have to actually answer the exam problems is 5 hours and 20 minutes. The problem-solving pace works out to slightly less than 3 minutes per problem. However, the exam does not pace you. You may spend as much time as you like on each problem. Although the on-screen navigational interface is slightly awkward, you may work through the problems (in that session) in any sequence. If you want to go back and check your answers before you submit a session for grading, you may. However, once you submit a section you are not able to go back and review it.

You can divide your time between the two sessions any way you'd like. That is, if you want to spend 4 hours on the first section, and 1 hour and 20 minutes on the second section, you could do so. Or, if you want to spend

2 hours and 10 minutes on the first section, and 3 hours and 10 minutes on the second section, you could do that instead. Between sessions, you can take a 25-minute break. (You can take less, if you would like.) You cannot work through the break, and the break time cannot be added to the time permitted for either session. Once each session begins, you can leave your seat for personal reasons, but the "clock" does not stop for your absence. Unanswered problems are scored the same as problems answered incorrectly, so you should use the last few minutes of each session to guess at all unanswered problems.

THE NCEES NONDISCLOSURE AGREEMENT

At the beginning of your CBT experience, a nondisclosure agreement will appear on the screen. In order to begin the exam, you must accept the agreement within two minutes. If you do not accept within two minutes, your CBT experience will end, and you will forfeit your appointment and exam fees. The CBT nondisclosure agreement is discussed in the section entitled "Subversion After the Exam." The nondisclosure agreement, as stated in the *NCEES Examinee Guide*, is as follows.

Table 2 *Recommended 8-Week Mechanical FE Exam Review Course Format for University Courses*

class	FE Mechanical Review Manual chapter titles	FE Mechanical Review Manual chapter numbers
1	Computer Software; Engineering Economics; Ethics	49–50, 52
2	Systems of Forces and Moments; Trusses; Pulleys, Cables, and Friction; Centroids and Moments of Inertia; Kinematics; Kinetics; Kinetics of Rotational Motion; Energy and Work; Vibrations	22–25, 37–41
3	Fluid Properties; Fluid Statics; Fluid Dynamics; Fluid Measurement and Similitude; Compressible Fluid Dynamics; Fluid Machines	7–12
4	Properties of Substances; Laws of Thermodynamics; Power Cycles and Entropy; Mixtures of Gases, Vapors, and Liquids; Combustion; Heating, Ventilating, and Air Conditioning (HVAC); Conduction; Convection; Radiation	13–21
5	Material Properties and Testing; Engineering Materials; Manufacturing Processes; Stresses and Strains; Thermal, Hoop, and Torsional Stress; Beams; Columns; Fasteners; Machine Design; Hydraulic and Pneumatic Mechanisms; Pressure Vessels; Manufacturability, Quality, and Reliability	26–32, 42–46
6	Electrostatics; Direct-Current Circuits; Alternating-Current Circuits; Rotating Machines; Measurement and Instrumentation; Controls	33–36, 47–48
7	open questions	–
8	open questions	–

This exam is confidential and secure, owned and copyrighted by NCEES and protected by the laws of the United States and elsewhere. It is made available to you, the examinee, solely for valid assessment and licensing purposes. In order to take this exam, you must agree not to disclose, publish, reproduce, or transmit this exam, in whole or in part, in any form or by any means, oral or written, electronic or mechanical, for any purpose, without the prior express written permission of NCEES. This includes agreeing not to post or disclose any test questions or answers from this exam, in whole or in part, on any websites, online forums, or chat rooms, or in any other electronic transmissions, at any time.

YOUR EXAM IS UNIQUE

The exam that you take will not be the exam taken by the person sitting next to you. Differences between exams go beyond mere sequencing differences. NCEES says that the CBT system will randomly select different, but equivalent, problems from its database for each examinee using a linear-on-the-fly (LOFT) algorithm. Each examinee will have a unique exam of equivalent difficulty. That translates into each examinee having a slightly different minimum passing score.

So, you may conclude either that many problems are static clones of others, or that NCEES has an immense database of trusted problems with supporting econometric data.[1,2] However, there is no way to determine exactly how NCEES ensures that each examinee is given an equivalent exam. All that can be said is that looking at your neighbor's monitor would be a waste of time.

THE EXAM INTERFACE

The on-screen exam interface contains only minimal navigational tools. On-screen navigation is limited to selecting an answer, advancing to the next problem, going back to the previous problem, and flagging the current problem for later review. The interface also includes a timer, the current problem number (e.g., 45 of 110), a pop-up scientific calculator, and access to an on-screen version of the *NCEES Handbook*.

During the exam, you can advance sequentially through the problems, but you cannot jump to any specific problem, whether or not it has been flagged. After you have completed the last problem in a session, however, the navigation capabilities change, and you are permitted to review problems in any sequence and navigate to flagged problems.

---

[1]The FE exam draws upon a simple database of finished problems. The CBT system does not construct each examinee's problems from a set of "master" problems using randomly generated values for each problem parameter constrained to predetermined ranges.

[2]Problems used in the now-obsolete paper-and-pencil exam were either 2-minute or 4-minute problems, based on the number of problems and time available in morning and afternoon sessions. Since all of the CBT exam problems are 3-minute problems, a logical conclusion is that 100% of the problems are brand new, or (more likely) that morning and afternoon problems are comingled within each subject.

THE *NCEES HANDBOOK* INTERFACE

Examinees are provided with a 24-inch computer monitor that will simultaneously display both the exam problems and a searchable PDF of the *NCEES Handbook*. The PDF's table of contents consists of live links. The search function is capable of finding anything in the *NCEES Handbook*, down to and including individual variables. However, the search function finds only precise search terms (e.g., "Hazenwilliams" will not locate "Hazen-Williams"). Like the printed version of the *NCEES Handbook*, the PDF also contains an index, but its terms and phrases are fairly limited and likely to be of little use.

WHAT IS THE REQUIRED PASSING SCORE?

Scores are based on the total number of problems answered correctly, with no deductions made for problems answered incorrectly. Raw scores may be adjusted slightly, and the adjusted scores are then scaled.

Since each problem has four answer options, the lower bound for a minimum required passing score is the performance generated by random selection, 25%. While it is inevitable that some examinees can score less than 25%, it is more likely that most examinees can score slightly more than 25% simply with judicious guessing and elimination of obvious incorrect options. So, the goal of all examinees should be to increase their scores from 25% to the minimum required passing score.

NCEES does not post minimum required passing scores for the CBT FE exam because the required passing score varies depending on the difficulty of the exam. While all exams have approximately equivalent difficulty, each exam has different problems, and so, minor differences in difficulty exist between the exam you take and the exam your neighbor will be taking. To account for these differences in difficulty, the exam's raw score is turned into a scaled score, and the scaled score is used to determine the passing rate.

For the CBT examination, each examinee will have a unique exam of approximately equivalent difficulty. This translates into a different minimum passing score for each examination. NCEES "accumulates" the passing score by summing each problem's "required performance value" (RPV).[3] The RPV represents the fraction of minimally qualified examinees that it

thinks will solve the problem correctly. In the past, RPVs for new problems were dependent on the opinions of experts that it polled with the question, "What fraction of minimally qualified examinees do you think should be able to solve this problem correctly?" For problems that have appeared in past exams, including the "pre-test" items that are used on the CBT exam, NCEES actually knows the fraction. Basically, out of all of the examinees who passed the FE exam (the "minimally qualified" part), NCEES knows how many answered a pre-test problem correctly (the "fraction of examinees" part). A particularly easy problem on Ohm's law might have an RPV of 0.88, while a more difficult problem on Bayes' theorem might have an RPV of 0.37. Add up all of the RPVs, and bingo, you have the basis for a passing score. What could be simpler?[4]

WHAT IS THE AVERAGE PASSING RATE?

For the sessions administered in July/August and October/November 2015, approximately 80% of first-time CBT test takers passed the Mechanical FE exam. The average failure rate was, accordingly, 20%. Some of those who failed the first time retook the FE exam, although the percentage of successful examinees declined precipitously with each subsequent attempt.

WHAT REFERENCE MATERIAL CAN I BRING TO THE EXAM?

Since October 1993, the FE exam has been what NCEES calls a "limited-reference exam." This means that nothing except what is supplied by NCEES may be used during the exam. Therefore, the FE exam is really an "NCEES-publication only" exam. NCEES provides its own searchable, electronic version of the *NCEES Handbook* for use during the exam. Computer screens are 24 inches wide so there is enough room to display the exam problems and the *NCEES Handbook* side-by-side. No printed books from any publisher may be used.

WILL THE *NCEES HANDBOOK* HAVE EVERYTHING I NEED DURING THE EXAM?

In addition to not allowing examinees to be responsible for their own references, NCEES also takes no responsibility for the adequacy of coverage of its own reference. Nor does it offer any guidance or provide examples as to

---

[3]NCEES does not actually use the term "required performance value," although it does use the method described.

[4]The flaw in this logic, of course, is that water seeks its own level. Deficient educational background and dependency on automation results in lower RPVs, which the NCEES process translates into a lower minimum passing score requirement. In the past, an "equating subtest" (a small number of problems in the exam that were associated with the gold standard of econometric data) was used to adjust the sum of RPVs based on the performance of the candidate pool. Though unmentioned in NCEES literature, that feature may still exist in the CBT exam process. However, the adjustment would still be based on the performance (good or bad) of the examinees.

what else you should know, study, or memorize. The following warning statement comes from the *NCEES Handbook* preface.

> The *FE Reference Handbook* does not contain all the information required to answer every question on the exam. Basic theories, conversions, formulas, and definitions examinees are expected to know have not been included.

As open-ended as that warning statement sounds, the exam does not actually expect much knowledge outside of what is covered in the *NCEES Handbook*. For all practical purposes, the *NCEES Handbook* will have everything that you need. For example, if the *NCEES Handbook* covers only copper resistivity, you won't be asked to demonstrate a knowledge of aluminum resistivity. If the *NCEES Handbook* covers only common-emitter circuits, you won't be expected to know about common-base or common-collector circuits.

That makes it pretty simple to predict the kinds of problems that will appear on the exam. If you take your preparation seriously, the *NCEES Handbook* is pretty much a guarantee that you won't waste any time learning subjects that are not on the FE exam.

WILL THE *NCEES HANDBOOK* HAVE EVERYTHING I NEED TO STUDY FROM?

Saying that you won't need to work outside of the content published in the *NCEES Handbook* is not the same as saying the *NCEES Handbook* is adequate to study from.

From several viewpoints, the *NCEES Handbook* is marginally adequate in organization, presentation, and consistency as an examination reference. The *NCEES Handbook* was never intended to be something you study or learn from, so it is most definitely inadequate for that purpose. Background, preliminary and supporting material, explanations, extensions to the theory, and application rules are all missing from the *NCEES Handbook*. Many subtopics (e.g., contract law) listed in the exam specifications are not represented in the *NCEES Handbook*.

That is why you will notice many equations, figures, and tables in this book that are not blue. You may, for example, read several paragraphs in this book containing various **black** equations before you come across a blue equation section. While the **black** material may be less likely to appear on the exam than the blue material, it provides background information that is essential to understanding the blue material. Although memorization of the **black** material is not generally required, this material should at least make sense to you.

MECHANICAL FE EXAM KNOWLEDGE AREAS AND QUESTION DISTRIBUTION

The following Mechanical FE exam specifications have been published by NCEES. Some of the topics listed are not covered in any meaningful manner (or at all) by the *NCEES Handbook*. The only conclusion that can be drawn is that the required knowledge of these subjects is shallow, qualitative, and/or nonexistent.

1. **mathematics (6–9 questions):** analytic geometry; calculus; linear algebra; vector analysis; differential equations; numerical methods

2. **probability and statistics (4–6 questions):** probability distributions; regression and curve fitting

3. **computational tools (3–5 questions):** spreadsheets; flow charts

4. **ethics and professional practice (3–5 questions):** codes of ethics; agreements and contracts; ethical and legal considerations; professional liability; public health, safety, and welfare

5. **engineering economics (3–5 questions):** time value of money; cost, including incremental, average, sunk, and estimating; economic analyses; depreciation

6. **electricity and magnetism (3–5 questions):** charge, current, voltage, power, and energy; current and voltage laws (Kirchhoff, Ohm); equivalent circuits (series, parallel); AC circuits; motors and generators

7. **statics (8–12 questions):** resultants of force systems; concurrent force systems; equilibrium of rigid bodies; frames and trusses; centroids; moments of inertia; static friction

8. **dynamics, kinematics, and vibrations (9–14 questions):** kinematics of particles; kinetic friction; Newton's second law for particles; work-energy of particles; impulse-momentum of particles; kinematics of rigid bodies; kinematics of mechanisms; Newton's second law for rigid bodies; work-energy of rigid bodies; impulse-momentum of rigid bodies; free and forced vibrations

9. **mechanics of materials (8–12 questions):** shear and moment diagrams; stress types (axial, bending, torsion, shear); stress transformations; Mohr's circle; stress and strain caused by axial loads; stress and strain caused by bending loads; stress and strain caused by torsion; stress and strain caused by shear; combined loading; deformations; columns

10. **material properties and processing (8–12 questions):** properties, including chemical, electrical, mechanical, physical, and thermal; stress-strain diagrams; engineered materials; ferrous metals;

nonferrous metals; manufacturing processes; phase diagrams; phase transformation, equilibrium, and heat treating; materials selection; surface conditions; corrosion mechanisms and control; thermal failure; ductile or brittle behavior; fatigue; crack propagation

11. **fluid mechanics (9–14 questions):** fluid properties; fluid statics; energy, impulse, and momentum; internal flow; external flow; incompressible flow; compressible flow; power and efficiency; performance curves; scaling laws for fans, pumps, and compressors

12. **thermodynamics (13–20 questions):** properties of ideal gases and pure substances; energy transfers; laws of thermodynamics; processes; performance of components; power cycles, thermal efficiency, and enhancements; refrigeration and heat pump cycles and coefficients of performance; nonreacting mixtures of gases; psychrometrics; heating, ventilating, and air-conditioning (HVAC) processes; combustion and combustion products

13. **heat transfer (9–14 questions):** conduction; convection; radiation; thermal resistance; transient processes; heat exchangers; boiling and condensation

14. **measurements, instrumentation, and controls (5–8 questions):** sensors; block diagrams; system response; measurement uncertainty

15. **mechanical design and analysis (9–14 questions):** stress analysis of machine elements; failure theories and analysis; deformation and stiffness; springs; pressure vessels; beams; piping; bearings; power screws; power transmission; joining methods; manufacturability; quality and reliability; hydraulic components; pneumatic components; electromechanical components

DOES THE EXAM REQUIRE LOOKING UP VALUES IN TABLES?

For some problems, you might have to look up a value, but in those cases, you must use the value in the *NCEES Handbook*. For example, you might know that the density of atmospheric air is 0.075 lbm/ft³ for all comfortable conditions. If you needed the density of air for a particle settling problem, you would find the official *NCEES Handbook* value is "0.0734 lbm/ft³ at 80°F." Whether or not using 0.075 lbm/ft³ will result in an (approximate) correct answer or an incorrect answer depends on whether the problem writer wants to reward you for knowing something or punish you for not using the *NCEES Handbook*.

However, in order to reduce the time required to solve problems, and to reduce the variability of answers caused by examinees using different starting values, problems generally provide all required information. Unless the problem is specifically determining whether you can read a table or figure, all relevant values (resistivity, permittivity, permeability, density, modulus of elasticity, viscosity, enthalpy, yield strength, etc.) needed to solve the problem are often included in the problem statement. NCEES does not want the consequences of using correct methods with ambiguous data.

DO PROBLEM STATEMENTS INCLUDE SUPERFLUOUS INFORMATION?

Particularly since all relevant information is provided in the problem statements, some problems end up being pretty straightforward. In order to obfuscate the solution method, some irrelevant, superfluous information will be provided in the problem statement. For example, when finding the capacitance from a given plate area and separation (i.e., $C = \varepsilon A/d$), the temperature and permeability of the surrounding air might be given. However, if you understand the concept, this practice will be transparent to you.

Problems in this book typically do not include superfluous information. The purpose of this book is to teach you, not confuse you.

REGISTERING FOR THE EXAM

The CBT exams are administered at approved Pearson VUE testing centers. Registration is open year-round and can be completed online through your MyNCEES account.[5] Registration fees may be paid online. Once you receive notification from NCEES that you are eligible to schedule your exam, you can do so online through your MyNCEES account. Select the location where you would like to take your exam, and select from the list of available dates. You will receive a letter from Pearson VUE (via email) confirming your exam location and date.

Whether or not applying for and taking the exam is the same as applying for an FE certificate from your state depends on the state. In most cases, you might take the exam without your state board ever knowing about it. In fact, as part of the NCEES online exam application process, you will have to agree to the following statement:

> Passage of the FE exam alone does not ensure certification as an engineer intern or engineer-in-training in any U.S. state or territory. To obtain certification, you must file an application with an engineering licensing board and meet that board's requirements.

---

[5]PPI is not associated with NCEES. Your MyNCEES account is not your PPI account.

After graduation, when you are ready to obtain your FE (EIT, IE, etc.) suitable-for-wall-hanging certificate, you can apply and pay an additional fee to your state. In some cases, you will be required to take an additional nontechnical exam related to professional practice in your state. Actual procedures will vary from state to state.

WHEN YOU CAN TAKE THE EXAM

The FE exam is administered throughout all 12 months of the year.

WHAT TO BRING TO THE EXAM

You do not need to bring much with you to the exam. For admission, you must bring a current, signed, government-issued photographic identification. This is typically a driver's license or passport. A student ID card is not acceptable for admittance. The first and last name on the photographic ID must match the name on your appointment confirmation letter. NCEES recommends that you bring a copy of your appointment confirmation letter in order to speed up the check-in process. Pearson VUE will email this to you once you create a MyNCEES account and register for the exam.

Earplugs, noise-cancelling headphones, and tissues are provided at the testing center. Additionally, all examinees are provided with a reusable, erasable notepad and compatible writing instrument to use for scratchwork during the exam.

Pearson VUE staff may visually examine any approved item without touching you or the item. In addition to the items provided at the testing center, the following items are permitted during the FE exam.[6]

- your ID (same one used for admittance to the exam)
- key to your test center locker
- NCEES-approved calculator without a case
- inhalers
- cough drops and prescription and nonprescription pills, including headache remedies, all unwrapped and not bottled, unless the packaging states they must remain in the packaging
- bandages, braces (for your neck, back, wrist, leg, or ankle), casts, and slings
- eyeglasses (without cases); eye patches; handheld, nonelectric magnifying glasses (without cases); and eyedrops[7]
- hearing aids

- medical/surgical face masks, medical devices attached to your body (e.g., insulin pumps and spinal cord stimulators), and medical alert bracelets (including those with USB ports)
- pillows and cushions
- light sweaters or jackets
- canes, crutches, motorized scooters and chairs, walkers, and wheelchairs

WHAT ELSE TO BRING TO THE EXAM

Depending on your situation, any of the following items may prove useful but should be left in your test center locker.

- calculator batteries
- contact lens wetting solution
- spare calculator
- spare reading glasses
- loose shoes or slippers
- extra set of car keys
- eyeglass repair kit, including a small screwdriver for fixing glasses (or removing batteries from your calculator)

WHAT NOT TO BRING TO THE EXAM

Leave all of these items in your car or at home: pens and pencils, erasers, scratch paper, clocks and timers, unapproved calculators, cell phones, pagers, communication devices, computers, tablets, cameras, audio recorders, and video recorders.

WHAT CALCULATORS ARE PERMITTED?

To prevent unauthorized transcription and distribution of the exam problems, calculators with communicating and text editing capabilities have been banned by NCEES. Get used to one of the calculators NCEES has approved. If you start using one of these approved calculators at the beginning of your review, you should be familiar enough with it by the time of the exam. Calculators permitted by NCEES are listed at **ppi2pass.com**. All of the listed calculators have sufficient engineering/ scientific functionality for the exam.

At the beginning of your review program, you should purchase or borrow a spare calculator. It is preferable, but not essential, that your primary and spare

---

[6]All items are subject to revision and reinterpretation at any time.
[7]Eyedrops can remain in their original bottle.

calculators be identical. If your spare calculator is not identical to your primary calculator, spend some time familiarizing yourself with its functions.

Examinees found using a calculator that is not approved by NCEES will be discharged from the testing center and charged with exam subversion by their states. (See the section "Exam Subversion.")

WHAT UNITS ARE USED ON THE EXAM?

You will need to learn the SI system if you are not already familiar with it. Contrary to engineering practice in the United States, the FE exam primarily uses SI units.

The *NCEES Handbook* generally presents only dimensionally consistent equations. (For example, $F = ma$ is consistent with units of newtons, kilograms, meters, and seconds. However, it is not consistent for units of pounds-force, pounds-mass, feet, and seconds.) Although pound-based data is provided parallel to the SI data in most tables, many equations cannot use the pound-based data without including the gravitational constant. After being mentioned in the first few pages, the gravitational constant ($g_c = 32.2$ ft-lbm/lbf-sec^2), which is necessary to use for equations with inconsistent U.S. units, is barely mentioned in the *NCEES Handbook* and does not appear in most equations.

Outside of the table of conversions and introductory material at its beginning, the *NCEES Handbook* does not consistently differentiate between pounds-mass and pounds-force. The labels "pound" and "lb" are used to represent both force and mass. Densities are listed in tables with units of lb/in^3.

Kips are always units of force that can be incorporated into ft-kips, units for moment, and ksi, units of stress or strength.

IS THE EXAM HARD AND/OR TRICKY?

Whether or not the exam is hard or tricky depends on who you talk to. Other than providing superfluous data (so as not to lead you too quickly to the correct formula) and anticipating common mistakes, the FE exam is not a tricky exam. The exam does not overtly try to get you to fail. The problems are difficult in their own right. NCEES does not need to provide you misleading or vague statements. Examinees manage to fail on a regular basis with perfectly straightforward problems.

Commonly made mistakes are routinely incorporated into the available answer choices. Thus, the alternative answers (known as distractors) will seem logical to many examinees. For example, if you forget to convert the pipe diameter from millimeters to meters, you'll find an answer option that is off by a factor of 1000. Perhaps that meets your definition of "tricky."

Problems are generally practical, dealing with common and plausible situations that you might encounter on the job. In order to avoid the complications of being too practical, the ideal or perfect case is often explicitly called for in the problem statement (e.g., "Assume an ideal gas."; "Disregard the effects of air friction."; or "The steam expansion is isentropic.").

You won't have to draw on any experiential knowledge or make reasonable assumptions. If a motor efficiency is required, it will be given to you. You won't have to assume a reasonable value. If a wire is to be sized to limit current density, the limit will be explicitly given to you. If a temperature increase requires a factor of safety, the factor of safety will be given to you.

IS THE EXAM SOPHISTICATED?

Considering the features available with computerized testing, the sophistication of the FE testing algorithm is relatively low. All of the problems are fixed and predefined; new problems are not generated from generic stubs. You will get the same number of problems in each knowledge area, regardless of how well or poorly you do on previous problems in that knowledge area; adaptive testing is not used. The testing software randomly selects problems from a limited database; it is possible to see some of the same problems if you take the exam a second time.

Only two levels of categorization are used in the database: discipline and knowledge area. For example, a problem would be categorized as "Electrical and Computer Discipline" and "Electronics." With problems randomly selected from the database, the variation (breadth) of coverage follows the variation of the database. Within the limitations imposed by the need for an equivalent exam, it is statistically possible for the testing program to present you with ten bipolar junction transistor problems or seventeen differential equation problems.

Although the overall difficulty level of the exam is intended to be equivalent for all examinees, the difficulty level within a particular knowledge area can vary significantly. For example, within the Probability and Statistics knowledge area, you might have to solve nine Bayes' theorem problems, while your friend may get nine coin flip problems. In order to keep the overall difficulty level the same, after calculating all of those conditional probabilities, you may be rewarded with nine simple $F = ma$ and $v = Q/A$ type problems, while your friend gets to work problems involving organic chemistry, entropy, and three-dimensional tripods.

GOOD-FAITH EFFORT

Let's be honest. Some examinees take the FE exam because they have to, not because they want to. This situation is usually associated with university degree programs that require taking the exam as a condition of graduation. In most cases, such programs require only that students take the exam, not pass it. Accordingly, some short-sighted students consider the exam to be a formality, and they give it only token attention.

NCEES uses several methods to determine if you have made a "good-faith effort" on the exam. Some of the criteria for determining that you haven't include marking all of the answer choices the same (all "A," all "B," etc.), using a repeating sequence of responses (e.g., "A, B, C, D" over and over), leaving the exam site significantly early, and achieving a raw score of less than 30%. These criteria may be used by themselves or together.

The test results of examinees who are deemed not to have given a "good-faith effort" are separated statistically from other test results. Releasing to the universities the names of specific examinees whose test results are in that category is at the discretion of NCEES, which has not yet formalized its policy.

WHAT DOES "MOST NEARLY" REALLY MEAN?

One of the more disquieting aspects of exam questions is that answer choices generally have only two or three significant digits, and the answer choices are seldom exact. An exam question may prompt you to complete the sentence, "The value is most nearly...", or may ask "Which answer choice is closest to the correct value?" A lot of self-confidence is required to move on to the next question when you don't find an exact match for the answer you calculated, or if you have had to split the difference because no available answer choice is close.

At one time, NCEES provided this statement regarding the use of "most nearly."

> Many of the questions on NCEES exams require calculations to arrive at a numerical answer. Depending on the method of calculation used, it is very possible that examinees working correctly will arrive at a range of answers. The phrase "most nearly" is used to accommodate all these answers that have been derived correctly but which may be slightly different from the correct answer choice given on the exam. You should use good engineering judgment when selecting your choice of answer. For example, if the question asks you to calculate an electrical current or determine the load on a beam, you should literally select the answer option that is most nearly what you calculated, regardless of whether it is more or less than your calculated value. However, if the question asks you to select a fuse or circuit breaker to protect against a calculated current or to size a beam to carry a load, you should select an answer option that will safely carry the current or load. Typically, this requires selecting a value that is closest to but larger than the current or load.

The difference is significant. Suppose you were asked to calculate "most nearly" the volumetric flow rate of pure water required to dilute a contaminated stream to an acceptable concentration. Suppose, also, that you calculated 823 gpm. If the answer choices were (A) 600 gpm, (B) 800 gpm, (C) 1000 gpm, and (D) 1200 gpm, you would go with answer choice (B), because it is most nearly what you calculated. If, however, you were asked to select a pump or pipe to provide the calculated capacities, you would have to go with choice (C). Got it? If not, stop reading until you understand the distinction.

WHEN DO I FIND OUT IF I PASSED?

You will receive an email notification that your exam results are ready for viewing through your MyNCEES account 7–10 days after the exam. That email will also include instructions that you can use to proceed with your state licensing board. If you fail, you will be shown your percentage performance in each knowledge area. The diagnostic report may help you figure out what to study before taking the exam again. Because each examinee answers different problems in each knowledge area, the diagnostic report probably should not be used to compare the performance of two examinees, to determine how much smarter than another examinee you are, to rate employees, or to calculate raises and bonuses.

If you fail the exam, you may take it again. NCEES's policy is that examinees may take the exam once per testing window, up to three times per 12-month period. However, you should check with your state board to see whether it imposes any restrictions on the number and frequency of retakes.

SUBVERSION DURING THE EXAM

With the CBT exam, you can no longer get kicked out of the exam room for not closing your booklet or putting down your pencil in time. However, there are still plenty of ways for you to run afoul of the rules imposed on you by NCEES, your state board, and Pearson VUE. For example, since communication devices are prohibited in the exam, occurrences as innocent as your cell phone ringing during the exam can result in the immediate invalidation of your exam.

The *NCEES Examinee Guide* gives the following statement regarding fraudulent and/or unprofessional behavior. Somewhere along the way, you will probably have to read and accept it, or something similar, before you can take the FE exam.

> Fraud, deceit, dishonesty, unprofessional behavior, and other irregular behavior in connection with taking any NCEES exam are strictly prohibited. Irregular behavior includes but is not limited to the following: failing to work independently; impersonating another individual or permitting such impersonation (surrogate testing); possessing

prohibited items; communicating with other examinees or any outside parties by way of cell phone, personal computer, the Internet, or any other means during an exam; disrupting other examinees; creating safety concerns; and possessing, reproducing, or disclosing nonpublic exam questions, answers, or other information regarding the content of the exam before, during, or after the exam administration. Evidence of an exam irregularity may be based on your performance on the exam, a report from an administrator or a third party, or other information.

The chief proctor is authorized to take appropriate action to investigate, stop, or correct any observed or suspected irregular behavior, including discharging you from the test center and confiscating any prohibited devices or materials. You must cooperate fully in any investigation of a suspected irregularity. NCEES reserves the right to pursue all available remedies for exam irregularities, including canceling scores and pursuing administrative, civil, and/or criminal remedies.

If you are involved in an exam irregularity, the following may occur: invalidation of results, notification to your licensing board, forfeiture of exam fees, and restrictions on future testing. Some violations may incur additional consequences, to be pursued at the discretion of NCEES.

Based on the grounds for dismissal used with previous exam administrations, you can expect harsh treatment for

- having a cell phone in your possession

- having a device with copying, recording, or communication capabilities in your possession. These include but are not limited to cameras, pagers, personal digital assistants (PDAs), radios, headsets, tape players, calculator watches, electronic dictionaries, electronic translators, transmitting devices, digital media players (e.g., iPods), and tablets (e.g., iPads, Kindles, or Nooks)

- having papers, books, or notes

- having a calculator that is not on the NCEES-approved list

- appearing to copy or actually copying someone else's work

- talking to another examinee during the exam

- taking notes or writing on anything other than your NCEES-provided reusable, erasable notepad

- removing anything from the exam area

- leaving the exam area without authorization

- violating any other restrictions that are cause for dismissal or exam invalidation (e.g., whistling while you work, chewing gum, or being intoxicated)

If you are found to be in possession of a prohibited item (e.g., a cell phone) after the exam begins, that item will be confiscated and sent to NCEES. While you will probably eventually get your cell phone back, you won't get a refund of your exam fees.

Cheating and what is described as "subversion" are dealt with quite harshly. Proctors who observe you giving or receiving assistance, compromising the integrity of the exam, or participating in any other form of cheating during an exam will require you to surrender all exam materials and leave the test center. You won't be permitted to continue with the exam. It will be a summary execution, carried out without due process and mercy.

Of course, if you arrive with a miniature camera disguised as a pen or eyeglasses, your goose will be cooked. Talk to an adjacent examinee, and your goose will be cooked. Use a mirror to look around the room while putting on your lipstick or combing your hair, and your goose will be cooked. Bring in the wrong calculator, and your goose will be cooked. Loan your calculator to someone whose batteries have died, and your goose will be cooked. Though you get the idea, many of the ways that you might inadvertently get kicked out of the CBT exam are probably (and, unfortunately) yet to be discovered. Based on this fact, you shouldn't plan on being the first person to bring a peppermint candy in a crackly cellophane wrapper.

And, as if being escorted with your personal items out of the exam room wasn't embarrassing enough, your ordeal still won't be over. NCEES and your state will bar you from taking any exam for one or more years. Any application for licensure pending an approval for exam will be automatically rejected. You will have to reapply and pay your fees again later. By that time, you probably will have decided that the establishment's response to a minor infraction was so out of proportion that licensure as a professional engineer isn't even in the cards.

SUBVERSION AFTER THE EXAM

The NCEES testing (and financial) model is based on reusing all of its problems forever. To facilitate such reuse, the FE (and PE) exams are protected by nondisclosure agreements and a history of aggressive pursuit of actual and perceived offenses. In order to be allowed to take its exams, NCEES requires examinees to agree to its terms.

Copyright protection extends to only the exact words, phrases, and sentences, and sequences thereof, used in problems. However, the intent of the NCEES nondisclosure agreement is to grant NCEES protection beyond what is normally available through copyright protection —to prevent you from even discussing a problem in general terms (e.g., "There was a problem on structural bolts that stumped me. Did anyone else think the problem was unsolvable?").

Most past transgressions have been fairly egregious.[8] In several prominent instances, NCEES has incurred substantial losses and expenses. In those cases, offenders have gotten what they deserved. But, even innocent public disclosures of the nature of "Hey, did anyone else have trouble solving that vertical crest curve problem?" have been aggressively pursued.

A restriction against saying anything at all to anybody about any aspect of a problem is probably too broad to be legally enforceable. Unfortunately, most examinees don't have the time, financial resources, or sophistication to resist what NCEES throws at them. Their only course of action is to accept whatever punishment is meted out to them by their state boards and by NCEES.

In the past, NCEES has used the U.S courts and aggressively pursued financial redress for loss of its intellectual property and violation of its copyright. It has administratively established a standard (accounting) value of thousands of dollars for each disclosed or compromised problem. You can calculate your own *pro forma* invoice from NCEES by multiplying this amount by the number of problems you discuss with others.

DOING YOUR PART, NCEES STYLE

NCEES has established a security tip line so that you can help it police the behavior of other examinees. Before, during, or after the exam, if you see any of your fellow examinees acting suspiciously, NCEES wants you to report them by phone or through the NCEES website. You'll have to identify yourself, but NCEES promises that the information you provide will be strictly confidential, and that your personal contact information will not be shared outside the NCEES compliance and security staff. Unless required by statute, rules of discovery, or a judge, of course.

PART 4: STRATEGIES FOR PASSING THE EXAM

A FEW DAYS BEFORE THE EXAM

There are a few things you should do a week or so before the examination date. For example, visit the exam site in order to find the testing center building, parking areas, examination room, and restrooms. You should also make arrangements for childcare and

transportation. Since your examination may not start or end exactly at the designated times, make sure that your childcare and transportation arrangements can allow for some flexibility.

Second in importance to your scholastic preparation is the preparation of your two examination kits. (See "What to Bring to the Exam" and "What Else to Bring to the Exam" in this Introduction.) The first kit includes items that can be left in your assigned locker (e.g., your admittance letter, photo ID, and extra calculator batteries). The second kit includes items that should be left in your car in case you need them (e.g., copy of your application, warm sweater, and extra snacks or beverages).

THE DAY BEFORE THE EXAM

If possible, take the day before the examination off from work to relax. Do not cram the last night. A good prior night's sleep is the best way to start the examination. If you live far from the examination site, consider getting a hotel room in which to spend the night.

Make sure your exam kits are packed and ready to go.

THE DAY OF THE EXAM

You should arrive at least 30 minutes before your scheduled start time. This will allow time for finding a convenient parking place, bringing your items to the testing center, and checking in.

DURING THE EXAM

Once the examination has started, observe the following suggestions.

Do not spend more than four minutes working a problem. (The average time available per problem is slightly less than three minutes.) If you have not finished a problem in that time, flag it for later review if you have time, and continue on.

Don't ask your proctors technical questions. Proctors are pure administrators. They don't know anything about the exam or its subjects.

Even if you do not discover them, errors in the exam (and in the *NCEES Handbook*) do occur. Rest assured that errors are almost always discovered during the scoring process, and that you will receive the performance credit for all flawed items.

---

[8]A candidate in Puerto Rico during the October 2006 Civil PE exam administration was found with scanning and transmitting equipment during the exam. She had recorded the entire exam, as well as the 2005 FE exam. The candidate pled guilty to two counts of fourth-degree aggravated fraud and was sentenced to six months' probation. All of the problems in both exams were compromised. NCEES obtained a civil judgment of over $1,000,000 against her.

However, NCEES has a form for reporting errors, and the test center should be able to provide it to you. If you encounter a problem with (a) missing information, (b) conflicting information, (c) no correct response from the four answer choices, or (d) more than one correct answer, use your provided reusable, erasable notepad to record the problem identification numbers. It is not necessary to tell your proctor during the exam. Wait until after the exam to ask your proctor about the procedure for reporting errors on the exam.

AFTER YOU PASS

[] Celebrate. Take someone out to dinner. Go off your diet. Get dessert.

[] Thank your family members and anyone who had to put up with your grouchiness before the exam.

[] Thank your old professors.

[] Tell everyone at the office.

[] Ask your employer for new business cards and a raise.

[] Tell your review course provider and instructors.

[] Tell the folks at PPI who were rootin' for you all along.

[] Start thinking about the PE exam.

Table 2

Sample Study Schedule (for Individuals)

Time required to complete study schedule:
    53 days for a "crash course," going straight through, with no rest and review days, no weekends, and no final exam
    73 days going straight through, taking off rest and review days, but no weekends
    99 days using only the five-day work week, taking off rest and review days, and weekends

Your examination date: _____

Number of days: _____

Latest day you can start: _____

day no.	date	chap. no.	knowledge area	subject
1	_____	Introduction	Mathematics	Introduction; Units
2	_____	1		Analytic Geometry and Trigonometry
3	_____	2		Algebra and Linear Algebra
4	_____	3		Calculus
5	_____	none		**rest; review**
6	_____	4		Differential Equations and Transforms
7	_____	5		Numerical Methods
8	_____	6	Probability and Statistics	Probability and Statistics
9	_____	none		**rest; review**
10	_____	7	Fluid Mechanics	Fluid Properties
11	_____	8		Fluid Statics
12	_____	9		Fluid Dynamics
13	_____	12		Fluid Machines
14	_____	11		Compressible Fluid Dynamics
15	_____	10		Fluid Measurement and Similitude
16	_____	none		**rest; review**
17	_____	13	Thermodynamics	Properties of Substances
18	_____	14		Laws of Thermodynamics
19	_____	16		Mixtures of Gases, Vapors, and Liquids
20	_____	15		Power Cycles and Entropy
21	_____	17		Combustion
22	_____	18		Heating, Ventilation, and Air Conditioning (HVAC)
23	_____	none		**rest; review**
24	_____	19	Heat Transfer	Conduction
25	_____	20		Convection
26	_____	21		Radiation
27	_____	none		**rest; review**
28	_____	22	Statics	Systems of Forces and Moments
29	_____	23		Trusses
30	_____	24		Pulleys, Cables, and Friction
31	_____	25		Centroids and Moments of Inertia
32	_____	none		**rest; review**
33	_____	26	Material Properties and Processing	Material Properties and Testing
34	_____	27		Engineering Materials
35	_____	28		Manufacturing Processes
36	_____	none		**rest; review**
37	_____	29	Mechanics of Materials; Mechanical Design and Analysis; Material Properties and Processing	Stresses and Strains
38	_____	30		Thermal, Hoop, and Torsional Stress
39	_____	31		Beams
40	_____	32		Columns
41	_____	none		**rest; review**

Table 2

day no.	date	chap. no.	knowledge area	subject
42	_____	42	Mechanical Design and Analysis	Fasteners
43	_____	43		Machine Design
44	_____	44		Hydraulic and Pneumatic Mechanisms
45	_____	45		Pressure Vessels
46	_____	46		Manufacturability, Quality, and Reliability
47	_____	none		**rest; review**
48	_____	37	Dynamics, Kinematics, and Vibrations	Kinematics
49	_____	38		Kinetics
50	_____	39		Kinetics of Rotational Motion
51	_____	40		Energy and Work
52	_____	41		Vibrations
53	_____	none		**rest; review**
54	_____	33	Electricity and Magnetism	Electrostatics
55	_____	34		Direct-Current Circuits
56	_____	35		Alternating-Current Circuits
57	_____	36		Rotating Machines
58	_____	none		**rest; review**
59	_____	47	Measurements, Instrumentation, and Controls	Measurement and Instrumentation
60	_____	48		Controls
61	_____	49	Computational Tools	Computer Software
62	_____	none		**rest; review**
63	_____	50	Engineering Economics	Engineering Economics
64	_____	51	Ethics and Professional Practice	Professional Practice
65	_____	52		Ethics
66	_____	53	none	Licensure
67	_____	none		**rest; review**
68–72	_____	none		Practice Examination
73	_____	none		FE Examination

Units

INTRODUCTION

The purpose of this chapter is to eliminate some of the confusion regarding the many units available for each engineering variable. In particular, an effort has been made to clarify the use of the so-called English systems, which for years have used the *pound* unit both for force and mass—a practice that has resulted in confusion for even those familiar with it.

It is expected that most engineering problems will be stated and solved in either English engineering or SI units. Therefore, a discussion of these two systems occupies the majority of this chapter.

COMMON UNITS OF MASS

The choice of a mass unit is the major factor in determining which system of units will be used in solving a problem. Obviously, you will not easily end up with a force in pounds if the rest of the problem is stated in meters and kilograms. Actually, the choice of a mass unit determines more than whether a conversion factor will be necessary to convert from one system to another (e.g., between the SI and English systems). An inappropriate choice of a mass unit may actually require a conversion factor *within* the system of units.

The common units of mass are the gram, pound, kilogram, and slug. There is nothing mysterious about these units. All represent different quantities of matter, as Fig. 1 illustrates. In particular, note that the pound and slug do not represent the same quantity of matter. One slug is equal to 32.1740 pounds-mass.

Figure 1 Common Units of Mass

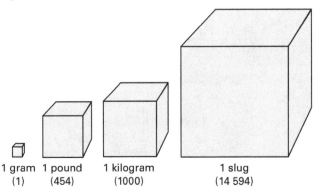

1 gram (1) 1 pound (454) 1 kilogram (1000) 1 slug (14 594)

MASS AND WEIGHT

The SI system uses kilograms for mass and newtons for weight (force). The units are different, and there is no confusion between the variables. However, for years, the term *pound* has been used for both mass and weight. This usage has obscured the distinction between the two: mass is a constant property of an object; weight varies with the gravitational field. Even the conventional use of the abbreviations *lbm* and *lbf* (to distinguish between pounds-mass and pounds-force) has not helped eliminate the confusion.

An object with a mass of one pound will have an earthly weight of one pound, but this is true only on the earth. The weight of the same object will be much less on the moon. Therefore, care must be taken when working with mass and force in the same problem.

The relationship that converts mass to weight is familiar to every engineering student.

$$W = mg$$

This equation illustrates that an object's weight will depend on the local acceleration of gravity as well as the object's mass. The mass will be constant, but gravity will depend on location. Mass and weight are not the same.

ACCELERATION OF GRAVITY

Gravitational acceleration on the earth's surface is usually taken as 32.2 ft/sec^2 or 9.81 m/s^2. These values are rounded from the more exact standard values of 32.1740 ft/sec^2 and 9.8066 m/s^2. However, the need for greater accuracy must be evaluated on a problem-by-problem basis. Usually, three significant digits are adequate, since gravitational acceleration is not constant anyway, but is affected by location (primarily latitude and altitude) and major geographical features.

CONSISTENT SYSTEMS OF UNITS

A set of units used in a calculation is said to be *consistent* if no conversion factors are needed. (The terms *homogeneous* and *coherent* are also used to describe a consistent set of units.) For example, a moment is calculated as the product of a force and a lever arm length.

$$M = dF$$

A calculation using the previous equation would be consistent if M was in newton-meters, F was in newtons, and d was in meters. The calculation would be inconsistent if M was in ft-kips, F was in kips, and d was in inches (because a conversion factor of 1/12 would be required).

The concept of a consistent calculation can be extended to a system of units. A *consistent system of units* is one in which no conversion factors are needed for any calculation. For example, Newton's second law of motion can be written without conversion factors. Newton's second law for an object with a constant mass simply states that the force required to accelerate the object is proportional to the acceleration of the object. The constant of proportionality is the object's mass.

$$F = ma$$

Notice that this relationship is $F = ma$, not $F = Wa/g$ or $F = ma/g_c$. $F = ma$ is consistent: It requires no conversion factors. This means that in a consistent system where conversion factors are not used, once the units of m and a have been selected, the units of F are fixed. This has the effect of establishing units of work and energy, power, fluid properties, and so on.

The decision to work with a consistent set of units is desirable but unnecessary, depending often on tradition and environment. Problems in fluid flow and thermodynamics are routinely solved in the United States with inconsistent units. This causes no more of a problem than working with inches and feet when calculating moments. It is necessary only to use the proper conversion factors.

THE ENGLISH ENGINEERING SYSTEM

Through common and widespread use, pounds-mass (lbm) and pounds-force (lbf) have become the standard units for mass and force in the *English Engineering System*.

There are subjects in the United States where the practice of using pounds for mass is firmly entrenched. For example, most thermodynamics, fluid flow, and heat transfer problems have traditionally been solved using the units of lbm/ft³ for density, Btu/lbm for enthalpy, and Btu/lbm-°F for specific heat. Unfortunately, some equations contain both lbm-related and lbf-related variables, as does the steady flow conservation of energy equation, which combines enthalpy in Btu/lbm with pressure in lbf/ft².

The units of pounds-mass and pounds-force are as different as the units of gallons and feet, and they cannot be canceled. A mass conversion factor, g_c, is needed to make the equations containing lbf and lbm dimensionally consistent. This factor is known as the *gravitational constant* and has a value of 32.1740 lbm-ft/lbf-sec². The numerical value is the same as the standard acceleration of gravity, but g_c is not the local gravitational acceleration, g. (It is acceptable, and recommended, that g_c be rounded to the same number of significant digits as g. Therefore, a value of 32.2 for g_c would typically be used.) g_c is a conversion constant, just as 12.0 is the conversion factor between feet and inches.

The English Engineering System is an inconsistent system, as defined according to Newton's second law. $F = ma$ cannot be written if lbf, lbm, and ft/sec² are the units used. The g_c term must be included.

$$F \text{ in lbf} = \frac{(m \text{ in lbm})\left(a \text{ in } \dfrac{\text{ft}}{\text{sec}^2}\right)}{g_c \text{ in } \dfrac{\text{lbm-ft}}{\text{lbf-sec}^2}}$$

g_c does more than "fix the units." Since g_c has a numerical value of 32.1740, it actually changes the calculation numerically. A force of 1.0 pound will not accelerate a 1.0 pound-mass at the rate of 1.0 ft/sec².

In the English Engineering System, work and energy are typically measured in ft-lbf (mechanical systems) or in British thermal units, Btu (thermal and fluid systems). One Btu is equal to approximately 778 ft-lbf.

Example

What is most nearly the weight in lbf of a 1.00 lbm object in a gravitational field of 27.5 ft/sec²?

(A)   0.85 lbf

(B)   1.2 lbf

(C)   28 lbf

(D)   32 lbf

Solution

The weight is

$$F = \frac{ma}{g_c}$$

$$= \frac{(1.00 \text{ lbm})\left(27.5 \dfrac{\text{ft}}{\text{sec}^2}\right)}{32.2 \dfrac{\text{lbm-ft}}{\text{lbf-sec}^2}}$$

$$= 0.854 \text{ lbf} \quad (0.85 \text{ lbf})$$

The answer is (A).

OTHER FORMULAS AFFECTED BY INCONSISTENCY

It is not a significant burden to include g_c in a calculation, but it may be difficult to remember when g_c should be used. Knowing when to include the gravitational constant can be learned through repeated exposure to the formulas in which it is needed, but it is safer to carry the units along in every calculation.

The following is a representative (but not exhaustive) list of formulas that require the g_c term.[1] In all cases, it is assumed that the standard English Engineering System units will be used.

- kinetic energy

$$KE = \frac{m\mathrm{v}^2}{2g_c} \quad \text{[in ft-lbf]}$$

- potential energy

$$PE = \frac{mgh}{g_c} \quad \text{[in ft-lbf]}$$

- pressure at a depth (fluid pressure)

$$p = \frac{\rho gh}{g_c} \quad \text{[in lbf/ft}^2\text{]}$$

- specific weight

$$SW = \frac{\rho g}{g_c} \quad \text{[in lbf/ft}^3\text{]}$$

- shear stress

$$\tau = \left(\frac{\mu}{g_c}\right)\left(\frac{d\mathrm{v}}{dy}\right) \quad \text{[in lbf/ft}^2\text{]}$$

Example

A rocket that has a mass of 4000 lbm travels at 27,000 ft/sec. What is most nearly its kinetic energy?

(A) 1.4×10^9 ft-lbf

(B) 4.5×10^{10} ft-lbf

(C) 1.5×10^{12} ft-lbf

(D) 4.7×10^{13} ft-lbf

Solution

The kinetic energy is

$$EK = \frac{m\mathrm{v}^2}{2g_c} = \frac{(4000 \text{ lbm})\left(27{,}000 \dfrac{\text{ft}}{\text{sec}}\right)^2}{(2)\left(32.2 \dfrac{\text{lbm-ft}}{\text{lbf-sec}^2}\right)}$$

$$= 4.53 \times 10^{10} \text{ ft-lbf} \quad (4.5 \times 10^{10} \text{ ft-lbf})$$

The answer is (B).

WEIGHT AND SPECIFIC WEIGHT

Weight is a force exerted on an object due to its placement in a gravitational field. If a consistent set of units is used, $W = mg$ can be used to calculate the weight of a mass. In the English Engineering System, however, the following equation must be used.

$$W = \frac{mg}{g_c}$$

Both sides of this equation can be divided by the volume of an object to derive the *specific weight* (*unit weight, weight density*), γ, of the object. The following equation illustrates that the weight density (in lbf/ft^3) can also be calculated by multiplying the mass density (in lbm/ft^3) by g/g_c.

$$\frac{W}{V} = \left(\frac{m}{V}\right)\left(\frac{g}{g_c}\right)$$

Since g and g_c usually have the same numerical values, the only effect of the following equation is to change the units of density.

$$\gamma = \frac{W}{V} = \left(\frac{m}{V}\right)\left(\frac{g}{g_c}\right) = \frac{\rho g}{g_c}$$

Weight does not occupy volume; only mass has volume. The concept of weight density has evolved to simplify certain calculations, particularly fluid calculations. For example, pressure at a depth is calculated from

$$p = \gamma h$$

Compare this to the equation for pressure at a depth.

---

[1]The NCEES *FE Reference Handbook* is not consistent in the variables it uses for these formulas. For example, T is used for kinetic energy and U is used for potential energy in the Dynamics knowledge area, and γ is used for specific weight in the Fluids knowledge area.

THE ENGLISH GRAVITATIONAL SYSTEM

Not all English systems are inconsistent. Pounds can still be used as the unit of force as long as pounds are not used as the unit of mass. Such is the case with the consistent *English Gravitational System*.

If acceleration is given in ft/sec^2, the units of mass for a consistent system of units can be determined from Newton's second law.

$$\text{units of } m = \frac{\text{units of } F}{\text{units of } a} = \frac{\text{lbf}}{\dfrac{\text{ft}}{\text{sec}^2}}$$

$$= \frac{\text{lbf-sec}^2}{\text{ft}}$$

The combination of units in this equation is known as a *slug*. g_c is not needed since this system is consistent. It would be needed only to convert slugs to another mass unit.

Slugs and pounds-mass are not the same, as Fig. 1 illustrates. However, both are units for the same quantity: mass. The following equation will convert between slugs and pounds-mass.

$$\text{no. of slugs} = \frac{\text{no. of lbm}}{g_c}$$

The number of slugs is not derived by dividing the number of pounds-mass by the local gravity. g_c is used regardless of the local gravity. The conversion between feet and inches is not dependent on local gravity; neither is the conversion between slugs and pounds-mass.

Since the English Gravitational System is consistent, the following equation can be used to calculate weight. Notice that the local gravitational acceleration is used.

$$W \text{ in lbf} = (m \text{ in slugs})\left(g \text{ in } \frac{\text{ft}}{\text{sec}^2}\right)$$

METRIC SYSTEMS OF UNITS

Strictly speaking, a *metric system* is any system of units that is based on meters or parts of meters. This broad definition includes *mks systems* (based on meters, kilograms, and seconds) as well as *cgs systems* (based on centimeters, grams, and seconds).

Metric systems avoid the pounds-mass versus pounds-force ambiguity in two ways. First, matter is not measured in units of force. All quantities of matter are specified as mass. Second, force and mass units do not share a common name.

The term *metric system* is not explicit enough to define which units are to be used for any given variable. For example, within the cgs system there is variation in how

certain electrical and magnetic quantities are represented (resulting in the ESU and EMU systems). Also, within the mks system, it is common engineering practice today to use kilocalories as the unit of thermal energy, while the SI system requires the use of joules. Thus, there is a lack of uniformity even within the metricated engineering community.

The "metric" parts of this book are based on the SI system, which is the most developed and codified of the so-called metric systems. It is expected that there will be occasional variances with local engineering custom, but it is difficult to anticipate such variances within a book that must be consistent.

SI UNITS (THE MKS SYSTEM)

SI units comprise an mks system (so named because it uses the meter, kilogram, and second as dimensional units). All other units are derived from the dimensional units, which are completely listed in Table 1. This system is fully consistent, and there is only one recognized unit for each physical quantity (variable).

Two types of units are used: base units and derived units. The *base units* (see Table 1) are dependent only on accepted standards or reproducible phenomena. The previously unclassified *supplementary units*, radian and steradian, have been classified as derived units. The *derived units* (see Table 2 and Table 3) are made up of combinations of base and supplementary units.

Table 1 *SI Base Units*

quantity	name	symbol
length	meter	m
mass	kilogram	kg
time	second	s
electric current	ampere	A
temperature	kelvin	K
amount of substance	mole	mol
luminous intensity	candela	cd

In addition, there is a set of non-SI units that may be used. This concession is primarily due to the significance and widespread acceptance of these units. Use of the non-SI units listed in Table 4 will usually create an inconsistent expression requiring conversion factors.

The units of force can be derived from Newton's second law.

$$\text{units of force} = (m \text{ in kg})\left(a \text{ in } \frac{\text{m}}{\text{s}^2}\right) = \frac{\text{kg·m}}{\text{s}^2}$$

This combination of units for force is known as a *newton*. Figure 2 illustrates common force units.

Table 2 *Some SI Derived Units with Special Names*

quantity	name	symbol	expressed in terms of other units
frequency	hertz	Hz	$1/s$
force	newton	N	$kg \cdot m/s^2$
pressure, stress	pascal	Pa	N/m^2
energy, work, quantity of heat	joule	J	$N \cdot m$
power, radiant flux	watt	W	J/s
quantity of electricity, electric charge	coulomb	C	
electric potential, potential difference, electromotive force	volt	V	W/A
electric capacitance	farad	F	C/V
electric resistance	ohm	Ω	V/A
electric conductance	siemen	S	A/V
magnetic flux	weber	Wb	$V \cdot s$
magnetic flux density	tesla	T	Wb/m^2
inductance	henry	H	Wb/A
luminous flux	lumen	lm	
illuminance	lux	lx	lm/m^2
plane angle	radian	rad	
solid angle	steradian	sr	

Table 3 *Some SI Derived Units*

quantity	description	expressed in terms of other units
area	square meter	m^2
volume	cubic meter	m^3
speed		
linear	meter per second	m/s
angular	radian per second	rad/s
acceleration		
linear	meter per second squared	m/s^2
angular	radian per second squared	rad/s^2
density, mass density	kilogram per cubic meter	kg/m^3
concentration (of amount of substance)	mole per cubic meter	mol/m^3
specific volume	cubic meter per kilogram	m^3/kg
luminance	candela per square meter	cd/m^2
absolute viscosity	pascal second	$Pa \cdot s$
kinematic viscosity	square meters per second	m^2/s
moment of force	newton meter	$N \cdot m$
surface tension	newton per meter	N/m
heat flux density, irradiance	watt per square meter	W/m^2
heat capacity, entropy	joule per kelvin	J/K
specific heat capacity, specific entropy	joule per kilogram kelvin	$J/kg \cdot K$
specific energy	joule per kilogram	J/kg
thermal conductivity	watt per meter kelvin	$W/m \cdot K$
energy density	joule per cubic meter	J/m^3
electric field strength	volt per meter	V/m
electric charge density	coulomb per cubic meter	C/m^3
surface density of charge, flux density	coulomb per square meter	C/m^2
permittivity	farad per meter	F/m
current density	ampere per square meter	A/m^2
magnetic field strength	ampere per meter	A/m
permeability	henry per meter	H/m
molar energy	joule per mole	J/mol
molar entropy, molar heat capacity	joule per mole kelvin	$J/mol \cdot K$
radiant intensity	watt per steradian	W/sr

Figure 2 *Common Force Units and Relative Sizes*

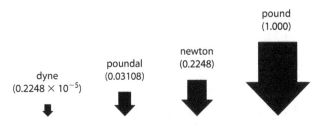

Energy variables in the SI system have units of N·m, or equivalently, $kg \cdot m^2/s^2$. Both of these combinations are known as a *joule*. The units of power are joules per second, equivalent to a *watt*.

Table 4 *Acceptable Non-SI Units*

quantity	unit name	symbol name	relationship to SI unit
area	hectare	ha	1 ha = 10 000 m²
energy	kilowatt-hour	kW·h	1 kW·h = 3.6 MJ
mass	metric ton[a]	t	1 t = 1000 kg
plane angle	degree (of arc)	°	1° = 0.017453 rad
speed of rotation	revolution per minute	r/min	1 r/min = 2π/60 rad/s
temperature interval	degree Celsius	°C	1°C = 1K (ΔT°C = ΔTK)
time	minute	min	1 min = 60 s
	hour	h	1 h = 3600 s
	day (mean solar)	d	1 d = 86 400 s
	year (calendar)	a	1 a = 31 536 000 s
velocity	kilometer per hour	km/h	1 km/h = 0.278 m/s
volume	liter[b]	L	1 L = 0.001 m³

[a]The international name for metric ton is *tonne*. The metric ton is equal to the *megagram* (Mg).

[b]The international symbol for liter is the lowercase l, which can be easily confused with the numeral 1. Several English-speaking countries have adopted the script ℓ and uppercase L as a symbol for liter in order to avoid any misinterpretation.

Example

A 10 kg block hangs from a cable. What is most nearly the tension in the cable? (Standard gravity equals 9.81 m/s².)

(A)   1.0 N

(B)   9.8 N

(C)   65 N

(D)   98 N

Solution

The tension is

$$F = mg$$
$$= (10 \text{ kg})\left(9.81 \ \frac{\text{m}}{\text{s}^2}\right)$$
$$= 98.1 \text{ kg·m/s}^2 \quad (98 \text{ N})$$

The answer is (D).

Example

A 10 kg block is raised vertically 3 m. What is most nearly the change in potential energy?

(A)   30 J

(B)   98 J

(C)   290 J

(D)   880 J

Solution

The change in potential energy is

$$\Delta\text{PE} = mg\Delta h$$
$$= (10 \text{ kg})\left(9.81 \ \frac{\text{m}}{\text{s}^2}\right)(3 \text{ m})$$
$$= 294 \text{ kg·m}^2/\text{s}^2 \quad (290 \text{ J})$$

The answer is (C).

RULES FOR USING THE SI SYSTEM

In addition to having standardized units, the SI system also has rigid syntax rules for writing the units and combinations of units. Each unit is abbreviated with a specific symbol. The following rules for writing and combining these symbols should be adhered to.

- The expressions for derived units in symbolic form are obtained by using the mathematical signs of multiplication and division; for example, units of velocity are m/s, and units of torque are N·m (not N-m or Nm).

- Scaling of most units is done in multiples of 1000.

- The symbols are always printed in roman type, regardless of the type used in the rest of the text. The only exception to this is in the use of the symbol for liter, where the use of the lowercase el (l) may be confused with the numeral one (1). In this case, "liter" should be written out in full, or the script ℓ or L should be used.

- Symbols are not pluralized: 1 kg, 45 kg (not 45 kgs).

- A period after a symbol is not used, except when the symbol occurs at the end of a sentence.

- When symbols consist of letters, there is always a full space between the quantity and the symbols: 45 kg (not 45kg). However, when the first character of a symbol is not a letter, no space is left: 32°C (not 32° C or 32 °C); or 42°12′45″ (not 42° 12′ 45″).

- All symbols are written in lowercase, except when the unit is derived from a proper name: m for meter; s for second; A for ampere, Wb for weber, N for newton, W for watt.

- Prefixes are printed without spacing between the prefix and the unit symbol (e.g., km is the symbol for kilometer). (See Table 5 for a list of SI prefixes.)

- In text, symbols should be used when associated with a number. However, when no number is involved, the unit should be spelled out: The area of the carpet is 16 m^2, not 16 square meters. Carpet is sold by the square meter, not by the m^2.

- A practice in some countries is to use a comma as a decimal marker, while the practice in North America, the United Kingdom, and some other countries is to use a period (or dot) as the decimal marker. Furthermore, in some countries that use the decimal comma, a dot is frequently used to divide long numbers into groups of three. Because of these differing practices, spaces must be used instead of commas to separate long lines of digits into easily readable blocks of three digits with respect to the decimal marker: 32 453.246 072 5. A space (half-space preferred) is optional with a four-digit number: 1 234 or 1234.

- Where a decimal fraction of a unit is used, a zero should always be placed before the decimal marker: 0.45 kg (not .45 kg). This practice draws attention to the decimal marker and helps avoid errors of scale.

- Some confusion may arise with the word "tonne" (1000 kg). When this word occurs in French text of Canadian origin, the meaning may be a ton of 2000 pounds.

CONVERSION FACTORS AND CONSTANTS

Commonly used equivalents are given in Table 6. Temperature conversions are given in Table 7. Table 8 gives commonly used constants in customary U.S. and SI units, respectively. Conversion factors are given in Table 9.

Table 5 SI Prefixes*

prefix	symbol	value
exa	E	10^{18}
peta	P	10^{15}
tera	T	10^{12}
giga	G	10^{9}
mega	M	10^{6}
kilo	k	10^{3}
hecto	h	10^{2}
deka	da	10^{1}
deci	d	10^{-1}
centi	c	10^{-2}
milli	m	10^{-3}
micro	μ	10^{-6}
nano	n	10^{-9}
pico	p	10^{-12}
femto	f	10^{-15}
atto	a	10^{-18}

*There is no "B" (billion) prefix. In fact, the word billion means 10^9 in the United States but 10^{12} in most other countries. This unfortunate ambiguity is handled by avoiding the use of the term billion.

Table 6 Commonly Used Equivalents

1 gal of water weighs	8.34 lbf
1 ft^3 of water weighs	62.4 lbf
1 in^3 of mercury weighs	0.491 lbf
The mass of 1 m^3 of water is	1000 kg
1 mg/L is	8.34 lbf/ Mgal

Table 7 Temperature Conversions

$$°F = 1.8(°C) + 32°$$
$$°C = \frac{°F - 32°}{1.8}$$
$$°R = °F + 459.69°$$
$$K = °C + 273.15°$$

Table 8 *Fundamental Constants*

quantity	symbol	customary U.S.	SI
Charge			
electron	e		-1.6022×10^{-19} C
proton	p		$+1.6021 \times 10^{-19}$ C
Density			
air [STP, 32°F, (0°C)]		0.0805 lbm/ft^3	1.29 kg/m^3
air [70°F, (20°C), 1 atm]		0.0749 lbm/ft^3	1.20 kg/m^3
earth [mean]		345 lbm/ft^3	5520 kg/m^3
mercury		849 lbm/ft^3	1.360×10^4 kg/m^3
seawater		64.0 lbm/ft^3	1025 kg/m^3
water [mean]		62.4 lbm/ft^3	1000 kg/m^3
Distance [mean]			
earth radius		2.09×10^7 ft	6.370×10^6 m
earth-moon separation		1.26×10^9 ft	3.84×10^8 m
earth-sun separation		4.89×10^{11} ft	1.49×10^{11} m
moon radius		5.71×10^6 ft	1.74×10^6 m
sun radius		2.28×10^9 ft	6.96×10^8 m
first Bohr radius	a_0	1.736×10^{-10} ft	5.292×10^{-11} m
Gravitational Acceleration			
earth [mean]	g	32.174 (32.2) ft/sec^2	9.807 (9.81) m/s^2
moon [mean]		5.47 ft/sec^2	1.67 m/s^2
Mass			
atomic mass unit	u	3.66×10^{-27} lbm	1.6606×10^{-27} kg
earth		1.32×10^{25} lbm	6.00×10^{24} kg
electron [rest]	m_e	2.008×10^{-30} lbm	9.109×10^{-31} kg
moon		1.623×10^{23} lbm	7.36×10^{22} kg
neutron [rest]	m_n	3.693×10^{-27} lbm	1.675×10^{-27} kg
proton [rest]	m_p	3.688×10^{-27} lbm	1.673×10^{-27} kg
sun		4.387×10^{30} lbm	1.99×10^{30} kg
Pressure, atmospheric		14.696 (14.7) lbf/in^2	1.0133×10^5 Pa
Temperature, standard		32°F (492°R)	0°C (273K)
Velocity			
earth escape (from surface, average)		3.67×10^4 ft/sec	1.12×10^4 m/s
light [vacuum]	c	9.84×10^8 ft/sec	2.99792 (3.00) $\times 10^8$ m/s
sound [air, STP]	a	1090 ft/sec	331 m/s
[air, 70°F (20°C)]		1130 ft/sec	344 m/s
Volume			
molar ideal gas [STP]	V_m	359 ft^3/lbmol	22.414 m^3/kmol
			22 414 L/kmol
Fundamental Constants			
Avogadro's number	N_A		6.0221 (6.022) $\times 10^{23}$ mol^{-1}
Bohr magneton	μ_B		9.2732×10^{-24} J/T
Boltzmann constant	k	5.65×10^{-24} ft-lbf/°R	1.3807×10^{-23} J/K
Faraday constant	F		96 485 C/mol
gravitational constant	g_c	32.174 (32.2) lbm-ft/lbf-sec^2	
gravitational constant	G	3.44×10^{-8} ft^4/lbf-sec^4	6.673×10^{-11} N·m^2/kg^2 (m^3/kg·s^2)
nuclear magneton	μ_N		5.050×10^{-27} J/T
permeability of a vacuum	μ_0		1.2566×10^{-6} N/A^2 (H/m)
permittivity of a vacuum	ϵ_0		8.854 (8.85) $\times 10^{-12}$ C^2/N·m^2 (F/m)
Planck's constant	h		6.6256×10^{-34} J·s
Rydberg constant	R_∞		1.097×10^7 m^{-1}
specific gas constant, air	R	53.3 ft-lbf/lbm-°R	287 J/kg·K
Stefan-Boltzmann constant	σ	1.71×10^{-9} Btu/ft^2-hr-°R^4	5.67×10^{-8} W/m^2·K^4
triple point, water		32.02°F, 0.0888 psia	0.01109°C, 0.6123 kPa
universal gas constant*	$\bar{R}$	1545 ft-lbf/lbmol-°R	8314 J/kmol·K
	$\bar{R}$	1.986 Btu/lbmol-°R	8.314 kPa·m^3/kmol·K
			0.08206 atm·L/mol·K

*The *NCEES Handbook* is inconsistent in its presentation of the universal gas constant. Although units of J/kmolK are used for the value of 8314, which in the *NCEES Handbook* includes a comma (8,314), units of kPa·m^3/kmolK are used for the value of 8.314. The comma is easily mistaken for a decimal point and so has not been used in this book.

Table 9 *Conversion Factors*

multiply	by	to obtain	multiply	by	to obtain
ac	43,560	ft^2	km	3281	ft
ampere-hr	3600	coulomb	km/h	0.621	mi/hr
angstrom	1×10^{-10}	m	kPa	0.145	lbf/in^2
atm	76.0	cm Hg	kW	1.341	hp
atm	29.92	in Hg	kW	737.6	ft-lbf/sec
atm	14.70	lbf/in^2 (psia)	kW	3413	Btu/hr
atm	33.90	ft water	kW·h	3413	Btu
atm	1.013×10^5	Pa	kW·h	1.341	hp-hr
bar	1×10^5	Pa	kW·h	3.6×10^6	J
bar	0.987	atm	kip	1000	lbf
barrels of oil	42	gallons of oil	kip	4448	N
Btu	1055	J	L	61.02	in^3
Btu	2.928×10^{-4}	kW·h	L	0.264	gal
Btu	778	ft-lbf	L	10×10^{-3}	m^3
Btu/hr	3.930×10^{-4}	hp	L/s	2.119	ft^3/min
Btu/hr	0.293	W	L/s	15.85	gal/min
Btu/hr	0.216	ft-lbf/sec	m	3.281	ft
cal (g-cal)	3.968×10^{-3}	Btu	m	1.094	yd
cal	1.560×10^{-6}	hp-hr	m	196.8	ft/min
cal (g-cal)	4.186	J	mi	5280	ft
cal/sec	4.184	W	mi	1.609	km
cm	3.281×10^{-2}	ft	mph	88.0	ft/min
cm	0.394	in	mph	1.609	kph
cP	0.001	Pa·s	mm of Hg	1.316×10^{-3}	atm
cP	1	g/m·s	mm of H$_2$O	9.678×10^{-5}	atm
cP	2.419	lbm/hr-ft	N	0.225	lbf
cSt	1×10^{-6}	m^2/s	N	1	kg·m/s^2
cfs	0.646371	MGD	N·m	0.7376	ft-lbf
ft^3	7.481	gal	N·m	1	J
m^3	1000	L	Pa	9.869×10^{-6}	atm
eV	1.602×10^{-19}	J	Pa	1	N/m^2
ft	30.48	cm	Pa·s	10	P
ft	0.3048	m	lbm	0.454	kg
ft-lbf	1.285×10^{-3}	Btu	lbf	4.448	N
ft-lbf	3.766×10^{-7}	kW·h	lbf-ft	1.356	N·m
ft-lbf	0.324	g-cal	lbf/in^2	0.068	atm
ft-lbf	1.35582	J	lbf/in^2	2.307	ft water
ft-lbf/sec	1.818×10^{-3}	hp	lbf/in^2	2.036	in Hg
gal	3.785	L	lbf/in^2	6895	Pa
gal	0.134	ft^3	radian	$180/\pi$	deg
gal water	8.3453	lbf water	stokes	1×10^{-4}	m^2/s
γ, Γ	1×10^{-9}	T	therm	10^5	Btu
gauss	1×10^{-4}	T	ton (metric)	1000	kg
gram	2.205×10^{-3}	lbm	ton (short)	2000	lbf
hectare	1×10^4	m^2	W	3.413	Btu/hr
hectare	2.47104	ac	W	1.341×10^{-3}	hp
hp	42.4	Btu/min	W	1	J/s
hp	745.7	W	Wb/m^2	10,000	gauss
hp	33,000	ft-lbf/min			
hp	550	ft-lbf/sec			
hp-hr	2545	Btu			
hp-hr	1.98×10^{-4}	ft-lbf			
hp-hr	2.68×10^{-4}	J			
hp-hr	0.746	kW·h			
in	2.54	cm			
in of Hg	0.0334	atm			
in of Hg	13.60	in of H$_2$O			
in of H$_2$O	0.0361	lbf/in^2			
in of H$_2$O	0.002458	atm			
J	9.478×10^{-4}	Btu			
J	0.7376	ft-lbf			
J	1	N·m			
J/s	1	W			
kg	2.205	lbm			
kgf	9.8066	N			

Atmospheres are standard; calories are gram-calories; gallons are U. S. liquid; miles are statute; pounds-mass are avoirdupois.)

Diagnostic Exam

Topic I: Mathematics

1. Which of the following equations correctly describes the shaded area of the x-y plane?

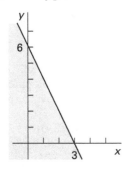

  (A) $2x - y \leq 6$

  (B) $2x + y \leq 6$

  (C) $2x - y \geq 6$

  (D) $x + 2y \geq 6$

2. What is most nearly the slope of the line tangent to the parabola $y = 12x^2 + 3$ at a point where $x = 5$?

  (A)   24

  (B)   120

  (C)   140

  (D)   300

3. What is most nearly the interior angle, θ, of a regular polygon with seven sides?

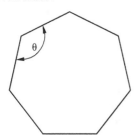

  (A) $51°$

  (B) $64°$

  (C) $120°$

  (D) $130°$

4. Which statement about a polynomial equation of the form $y(x) = ax^2 + bx + c$ is always true if the constants are all positive?

  (A)   It has two different roots.

  (B)   If one of its roots is real, the other root can be imaginary.

  (C)   The curve defined by the equation will pass through the y-axis.

  (D)   The curve defined by the equation will pass through the x-axis.

5. Four vector fields are shown.

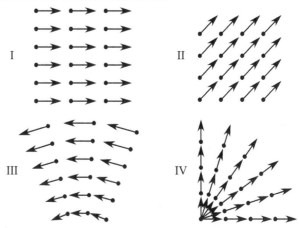

Which field has a positive vector curl?

  (A)   I

  (B)   II

  (C)   III

  (D)   IV

6. What are the coordinates of the point of intersection of the following lines?

$$y_1 = x + 2$$
$$y_2 = x^2 + 5x + 6$$

(A) $(-3, 0)$

(B) $(-2, 0)$

(C) $(-1, 1)$

(D) $(2, 0)$

7. $x = -2$ is one of the roots of the equation $x^3 + x^2 - 22x - 40 = 0$. What are the other two roots?

(A) -5 and 5

(B) -5 and 2

(C) -4 and 5

(D) -4 and 2

8. A vector originates at point $(2, 3, 11)$ and terminates at point $(10, 15, 20)$. What is the magnitude of the vector?

(A) 12

(B) 14

(C) 15

(D) 17

9. What is the unit vector of $\mathbf{R} = 12\mathbf{i} - 20\mathbf{j} - 9\mathbf{k}$?

(A) $0.25\mathbf{i} - 0.80\mathbf{j} - 0.54\mathbf{k}$

(B) $0.48\mathbf{i} - 0.80\mathbf{j} - 0.36\mathbf{k}$

(C) $0.54\mathbf{i} - 0.77\mathbf{j} - 0.35\mathbf{k}$

(D) $0.64\mathbf{i} - 0.64\mathbf{j} - 0.42\mathbf{k}$

10. Which of these vector identities is INCORRECT?

(A) $\mathbf{A} \cdot \mathbf{A} = 0$

(B) $\mathbf{A} \times \mathbf{A} = 0$

(C) $\mathbf{A} \cdot \mathbf{B} = \mathbf{B} \cdot \mathbf{A}$

(D) $\mathbf{A} \times \mathbf{B} = -\mathbf{B} \times \mathbf{A}$

SOLUTIONS

1. Find the slope given two points using the point-slope equation for two points.

$$P_1 = (3, 0)$$
$$P_2 = (0, 6)$$

Straight Line

$$m = (y_2 - y_1) / (x_2 - x_1)$$
$$= (6 - 0) / (0 - 3)$$
$$= -2$$

Using the standard form of a line equation and the slope, solve for the y-intercept by picking any one of the two points given and substitute into the equation.

$$P_1 = (3, 0)$$
$$m = -2$$

Straight Line

$$y = mx + b$$
$$b = y - mx = 0 - (-2)(3)$$
$$= 6$$

Alternatively,

$$P_2 = (0, 6)$$
$$m = -2$$

Straight Line

$$y = mx + b$$
$$b = y - mx = 6 - (-2)(0)$$
$$= 6$$

The standard form of the line that passes through both points is

$$y = -2x + 6$$

By rearranging the standard form of the line, the inequality representing the shaded area is a solid line represented by the less than or equal to symbol and verified by picking points within the shaded region to validate the inequality.

$$P_{\text{test}} = (0, 0)$$
$$2x + y \leq 6$$
$$(2)(0) + 0 \leq 6$$
$$0 \leq 6 \quad [\text{true}]$$

The equation describing the shaded area is $2x + y \leq 6$.

The answer is (B).

2. The slope of the line is the derivative of the parabola function evaluated at the point where $x = 5$.

$$m = \frac{dy}{dx}\bigg|_{x=5} = 24x$$
$$= (24)(5)$$
$$= 120$$

The answer is (B).

3. The interior angle is

$$\theta = \left[\frac{\pi(n-2)}{n}\right] = \pi\left(1 - \frac{2}{n}\right) = (180°)\left(1 - \frac{2}{7}\right)$$
$$= 128.6° \quad (130°)$$

The answer is (D).

4. The curve defined by a polynomial equation of the form $y(x) = ax^2 + bx + c$ with the constants positive is always a parabola that opens vertically. The parabola will always pass through the y-axis at some value of x, so option C is true. When the minimum or maximum point of the parabola is on the x-axis, the two roots are the same (a double root), so option A is false. The two roots must be both real or both imaginary, so option B is false. The parabola may open upward and be entirely above the x-axis, or open downward and be entirely below it, so option D is false.

The answer is (C).

5. Curl is a vector operator that describes a vector field's vorticity (rotation) at a point. Illustrations I and II are linear vector fields without rotation or accumulation (divergence). Illustration IV has divergence, but no rotation. Only Illustration III has rotation.

The answer is (C).

6. At the point where the two lines cross, the x- and y-values satisfy both equations.

$$y_1 = y_2$$
$$x + 2 = x^2 + 5x + 6$$
$$x^2 + 4x + 4 = 0$$

The roots of this quadratic equation are

$$x = \frac{-b \pm \sqrt{b^2 - 4ac}}{2a} = \frac{-4 \pm \sqrt{(4)^2 - (4)(1)(4)}}{(2)(1)}$$
$$= -2$$

The discriminant (the portion under the radical sign) is equal to zero, so the quadratic equation has one double root of –2. Inserting $x = -2$ into the original equations gives

$$y_1 = (-2) + 2 = 0$$
$$y_2 = (-2)^2 + 5(-2) + 6 = 0$$

The lines cross at $(x, y) = (-2, 0)$.

The answer is (B).

7. One root of the equation is given as –2. Divide both sides of the equation by $x + 2$ to get $x^2 - x - 20 = 0$, then use the quadratic formula to find the remaining two roots.

$$\begin{array}{r} x^2 - x - 20 \\ x + 2 \overline{\smash{\big)}\ x^3 + x^2 - 22x - 40} \\ \underline{x^3 + 2x^2} \\ -(x^2 - 22x) \\ \underline{-x^2 - 2x} \\ -(20x - 40) \\ \underline{-20x - 40} \\ 0 \end{array}$$

Quadratic Equation

$$x = \frac{-b \pm \sqrt{b^2 - 4ac}}{2a} = \frac{-(-1) \pm \sqrt{(-1)^2 - (4)(1)(-20)}}{(2)(1)}$$
$$= -4 \text{ and } 5$$

The answer is (C).

8. In three-dimensional space, the distance between two points is

$$d = \sqrt{(x_2 - x_1)^2 + (y_2 - y_1)^2 + (z_2 - z_1)^2}$$
$$= \sqrt{(10 - 2)^2 + (15 - 3)^2 + (20 - 11)^2}$$
$$= 17$$

The answer is (D).

9. The magnitude of $\mathbf{R} = a\mathbf{i} + b\mathbf{j} + c\mathbf{k}$ is

$$|\mathbf{R}| = \sqrt{a^2 + b^2 + c^2} = \sqrt{(12)^2 + (-20)^2 + (-9)^2}$$
$$= 25$$

Divide vector **R** by its magnitude to find the unit vector that is parallel with **R**.

$$\frac{\mathbf{R}}{|\mathbf{R}|} = \frac{12\mathbf{i} - 20\mathbf{j} - 9\mathbf{k}}{25} = 0.48\mathbf{i} - 0.80\mathbf{j} - 0.36\mathbf{k}$$

The answer is (B).

10. If the dot product of two vectors is zero, either one or both of the vectors is zero or the two vectors are perpendicular. The equation $\mathbf{A} \cdot \mathbf{A} = 0$ is, therefore, true only when $\mathbf{A} = 0$, and it is not an identity. The other three options are identities.

The answer is (A).

1 Analytic Geometry and Trigonometry

1. STRAIGHT LINES

Figure 1.1 is a straight line in two-dimensional space. The *slope* of the line is m, the y-intercept is b, and the x-intercept is a. A known point on the line is represented as (x_1, y_1).

Figure 1.1 *Straight Line*

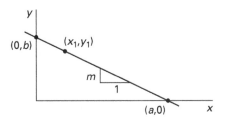

Equation 1.1: Slope

$$m = (y_2 - y_1)/(x_2 - x_1) \qquad 1.1$$

Description

Given two points on a straight line, (x_1, y_1) and (x_2, y_2), Eq. 1.1 gives the slope of the line. The slopes of two parallel lines are equal.

Example

Find the slope of the line that passes through points $(-3, 2)$ and $(5, -2)$.

(A) -2

(B) -0.5

(C) 0.5

(D) 2

Solution

Use Eq. 1.1.

$$m = (y_2 - y_1)/(x_2 - x_1) = \frac{-2 - 2}{5 - (-3)} = -0.5$$

The answer is (B).

Equation 1.2: Slopes of Perpendicular Lines

$$m_1 = -1/m_2 \qquad 1.2$$

Description

If two lines are perpendicular to each other, then their slopes, m_1 and m_2, are negative reciprocals of each other, as shown by Eq. 1.2. For example, if the slope of a line is 5, the slope of a line perpendicular to it is $-1/5$.

Example

A line goes through the point $(4, -6)$ and is perpendicular to the line $y = 4x + 10$. What is the equation of the line?

(A) $y = -\frac{1}{4}x - 20$

(B) $y = -\frac{1}{4}x - 5$

(C) $y = \frac{1}{5}x + 5$

(D) $y = \frac{1}{4}x + 5$

Solution

The slopes of two lines that are perpendicular are related by

$$m_1 = -\frac{1}{m_2}$$

The slope of the line perpendicular to the line with slope $m_1 = 4$ is

$$m_2 = -\frac{1}{m_1} = -1/4$$

The equation of the line is in the form $y = mx + b$. $m = -1/4$, and a known point is $(x, y) = (4, -6)$.

$$-6 = \left(-\frac{1}{4}\right)(4) + b$$

$$b = -6 - \left(-\frac{1}{4}\right)(4)$$

$$= -5$$

The equation of the line is

$$y = -\frac{1}{4}x - 5$$

The answer is (B).

Equation 1.3: Standard Form of the Equation of a Line

$$y = mx + b \qquad \text{1.3}$$

Description

The equation of a line can be represented in several forms. The procedure for finding the equation depends on the form chosen to represent the line. In general, the procedure involves substituting one or more known points on the line into the equation in order to determine the constants.

Equation 1.3 is the *standard form* of the equation of a line. This is also known as the *slope-intercept form* because the constants in the equation are the line's slope, m, and its y-intercept, b.

Example

What is the slope of the line defined by $y - x = 5$?

(A) -1

(B) $-1/5$

(C) $1/4$

(D) 1

Solution

The standard (or slope-intercept) form of the equation of a straight line is $y = mx + b$, where m is the slope and b is the y-intercept. Rearrange the given equation into standard form.

$$y - x = 5$$

$$y = x + 5$$

The slope, m, is the coefficient of x, which is 1.

The answer is (D).

Equation 1.4: General Form of the Equation of a Line

$$Ax + By + C = 0 \qquad \text{1.4}$$

Description

Equation 1.4 is the *general form* of the equation of a line.

Example

What is the general form of the equation for a line whose x-intercept is 4 and y-intercept is -6?

(A) $2x - 3y - 18 = 0$

(B) $2x + 3y + 18 = 0$

(C) $3x - 2y - 12 = 0$

(D) $3x + 2y + 12 = 0$

Solution

Find the slope of the line.

$$m = \frac{y_2 - y_1}{x_2 - x_1}$$

$$= \frac{-6 - 0}{0 - 4}$$

$$= 3/2$$

Write the equation of the line in standard (or slope-intercept) form, then arrange it in the form of Eq. 1.4.

$$y = mx + b$$

$$mx - y + b = 0$$

$$\frac{3}{2}x - y + (-6) = 0$$

$$3x - 2y - 12 = 0$$

The answer is (C).

Equation 1.5: Point-Slope Form of the Equation of a Line

$$y - y_1 = m(x - x_1) \qquad 1.5$$

Description

Equation 1.5 is the *point-slope form* of the equation of a line. This equation defines the line in terms of its slope, m, and one known point, (x_1, y_1).

Example

A circle with a radius of 5 is centered at the origin.

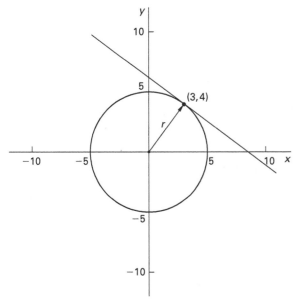

What is the standard form of the equation of the line tangent to this circle at the point $(3, 4)$?

(A) $x = \frac{-4}{3}y - \frac{25}{4}$

(B) $y = \frac{3}{4}x + \frac{25}{4}$

(C) $y = \frac{-3}{4}x + \frac{9}{4}$

(D) $y = \frac{-3}{4}x + \frac{25}{4}$

Solution

The slope of the radius line from point $(0, 0)$ to point $(3, 4)$ is $4/3$. Since the radius and tangent line are perpendicular, the slope of the tangent line is $-3/4$.

The point-slope form of a straight line with slope $m = -3/4$ and containing point $(x_1, y_1) = (3, 4)$ is

$$y - y_1 = m(x - x_1)$$
$$y - 4 = \left(\frac{-3}{4}\right)(x - 3)$$

Rearranging this into standard form gives

$$y = \frac{-3}{4}x + \left(\frac{9}{4} + 4\right)$$
$$= \frac{-3}{4}x + \frac{25}{4}$$

The answer is (D).

Equation 1.6: Angle Between Two Lines

$$\alpha = \arctan[(m_2 - m_1)/(1 + m_2 \cdot m_1)] \qquad 1.6$$

Description

Two intersecting lines in two-dimensional space are shown in Fig. 1.2.

Figure 1.2 *Two Lines Intersecting in Two-Dimensional Space*

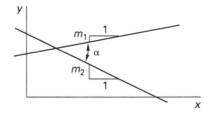

The slopes of the two lines are m_1 and m_2. The acute angle, α, between the lines is given by Eq. 1.6.[1]

Example

The angle between the line $y = -7x + 12$ and the line $y = 3x$ is most nearly

(A) $22°$

(B) $27°$

(C) $33°$

(D) $37°$

---

[1]Since the NCEES *FE Reference Handbook* (*NCEES Handbook*) does not specify an absolute value, Eq. 1.6 is sensitive to which slopes are designated m_1 and m_2. The slopes should be intuitively selected to avoid a negative arctan argument. Alternatively, since the tangent exhibits odd symmetry, if a negative angle is calculated, the negative sign can simply be disregarded.

Solution

Use Eq. 1.6.

$$\alpha = \arctan[(m_2 - m_1)/(1 + m_2 \cdot m_1)]$$
$$= \arctan\frac{-7 - 3}{1 + (-7)(3)} = \arctan 0.5$$
$$= 26.57° \quad (27°)$$

The answer is (B).

2. POLYNOMIAL FUNCTIONS

Equation 1.7 and Eq. 1.8: Quadratic Equations

$$ax^2 + bx + c = 0 \qquad 1.7$$

$$x = \frac{-b \pm \sqrt{b^2 - 4ac}}{2a} \qquad 1.8$$

Description

A *quadratic equation* is a second-degree polynomial equation with a single variable. A quadratic equation can be written in the form of Eq. 1.7, where x is the variable and a, b, and c are constants. (If a is zero, the equation is linear.)

The *roots*, x_1 and x_2, of a quadratic equation are the two values of x that satisfy the equation (i.e., make it true). These values can be found from the *quadratic formula*, Eq. 1.8.

The quantity under the radical in Eq. 1.8 is called the *discriminant*. By inspecting the discriminant, the types of roots of the equation can be determined.

- If $b^2 - 4ac > 0$, the roots are real and unequal.
- If $b^2 - 4ac = 0$, the roots are real and equal. This is known as a *double root.*
- If $b^2 - 4ac < 0$, the roots are complex and unequal.

Example

What are the roots of the quadratic equation $-7x + x^2 = -10$?

(A) −5 and 2

(B) −2 and 0.4

(C) 0.4 and 2

(D) 2 and 5

Solution

Rearrange the equation into the form of Eq. 1.7.

$$x^2 + (-7x) + 10 = 0$$

Use the quadratic formula, Eq. 1.8, with $a = 1$, $b = -7$, and $c = 10$.

$$x = \frac{-b \pm \sqrt{b^2 - 4ac}}{2a}$$
$$= \frac{-(-7) \pm \sqrt{(-7)^2 - (4)(1)(10)}}{(2)(1)}$$
$$= 2 \text{ and } 5$$

The answer is (D).

3. CONIC SECTIONS

A *conic section* is any of several kinds of curves that can be produced by passing a plane through a cone as shown in Fig. 1.3.

Equation 1.9: Eccentricity of a Cutting Plane

$$e = \cos\theta/(\cos\phi) \qquad 1.9$$

Description

If θ is the angle between the vertical axis and the cutting plane and ϕ is the *cone-generating angle*, then the *eccentricity*, e, of the conic section is given by Eq. 1.9.

Equation 1.10 Through Eq. 1.13: General Form and Normal Form of the Conic Section Equation

$$Ax^2 + Bxy + Cy^2 + Dx + Ey + F = 0 \qquad 1.10$$

$$x^2 + y^2 + 2ax + 2by + c = 0 \qquad 1.11$$

$$h = -a; \quad k = -b \qquad 1.12$$

$$r = \sqrt{a^2 + b^2 - c} \qquad 1.13$$

Description

All conic sections are described by second-degree (quadratic) polynomials with two variables. The *general form* of the conic section equation is given by Eq. 1.10. x and y are variables, and A, B, C, D, E, and F are constants.

Figure 1.3 *Conic Sections Produced by Cutting Planes*

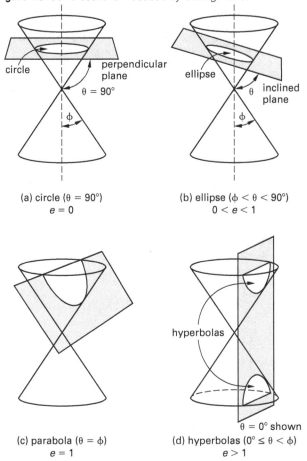

(a) circle ($\theta = 90°$)
$e = 0$

(b) ellipse ($\phi < \theta < 90°$)
$0 < e < 1$

(c) parabola ($\theta = \phi$)
$e = 1$

(d) hyperbolas ($0° \leq \theta < \phi$)
$e > 1$

h and k are the coordinates (h, k) of the conic section's center. r is a size parameter, usually the radius of a circle or a sphere. If $r = 0$, then the conic section describes a point.

If $A = C$, then B must be zero for a conic section. If $A = C = 0$, the conic section is a *line*, and if $A = C \neq 0$, the conic section is a *circle*. If $A \neq C$, then if

- $B^2 - 4AC < 0$, the conic section is an *ellipse*

- $B^2 - 4AC > 0$, the conic section is a *hyperbola*

- $B^2 - 4AC = 0$, the conic section is a *parabola*

The general form of the conic section equation can be applied when the conic section is at any orientation relative to the coordinate axes. Equation 1.11 is the *normal form* of the conic section equation. It can be applied when one of the principal axes of the conic section is parallel to a coordinate axis, thereby eliminating certain terms of the general equation and reducing the number of constants needed to three: a, b, and c.

Example

What kind of conic section is described by the following equation?

$$4x^2 - y^2 + 8x + 4y = 15$$

(A) circle

(B) ellipse

(C) parabola

(D) hyperbola

Solution

The general form of a conic section is given by Eq. 1.10 as

$$Ax^2 + Bxy + Cy^2 + Dx + Ey + F = 0$$

In this case, $A = 4$, $B = 0$, and $C = -1$. Since $A \neq C$, the conic section is not a circle or line.

Calculate the discriminant.

$$B^2 - 4AC = (0)^2 - (4)(4)(-1) = 16$$

This is greater than zero, so the section is a hyperbola.

The answer is (D).

Equation 1.14: Standard Form of the Equation of a Horizontal Parabola

$$(y - k)^2 = 2p(x - h) \quad \text{[center at } (h, k)\text{]} \qquad 1.14$$

Description

A *parabola* is the locus of points equidistant from the focus (point F in Fig. 1.4) and a line called the *directrix*. The constant p is the distance between the focus and the directrix.[2] The directrix is defined by the equation $x = h - (p/2)$. When the vertex of the parabola is at the origin, $h = k = 0$, and Eq. 1.15 and Eq. 1.16 apply.

A parabola is symmetric with respect to its *parabolic axis*. The line normal to the parabolic axis and passing through the focus is known as the *latus rectum*. The eccentricity of a parabola is equal to 1.

Equation 1.14 is the *standard form* of the equation of a horizontal parabola. It can be applied when the principal axes of the parabola coincide with the coordinate axes.

---

[2]There are two conventions used to define the parameters of a parabola. One convention, as used in the *NCEES Handbook*, is to define p as the distance from the focus to the directrix. This results in the $2p$ term in Eq. 1.14. Another convention, arguably more prevalent, is to define p as the distance from the focus to the vertex (i.e., the distance from the focus to the directrix is $2p$), which would result in a corresponding term of $4p$ in Eq. 1.14.

Figure 1.4 Parabola

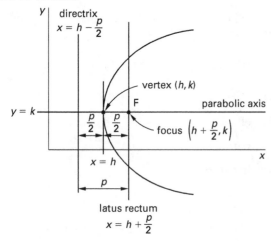

The equation for a vertical parabola is similar.

$$(x - h)^2 = 2p(y - k)$$

If p is positive, the parabola opens upward. If p is negative, the parabola opens downward.

Equation 1.15 and Eq. 1.16: Parabola with Vertex at the Origin

$$\text{focus: } (p/2, 0) \qquad\qquad 1.15$$

$$x = -p/2 \qquad\qquad 1.16$$

Description

The definitions in Eq. 1.15 and Eq. 1.16 apply when the vertex of the parabola is at the origin—that is, when $(h, k) = (0, 0)$.

The parabola opens to the right (points to the left) if $p > 0$, and it opens to the left (points to the right) if $p < 0$.

Example

What is the equation of a parabola with a vertex at $(4, 8)$ and a directrix at $y = 5$?

(A) $(x - 8)^2 = 12(y - 4)$

(B) $(x - 4)^2 = 12(y - 8)$

(C) $(x - 4)^2 = 6(y - 8)$

(D) $(y - 8)^2 = 12(x - 4)$

Solution

The directrix, described by $y = 5$, is parallel to the x-axis, so this is a vertical parabola. The vertex (at $y = 8$) is above the directrix, so the parabola opens upward.

The distance from the vertex to the directrix is

$$\frac{p}{2} = 8 - 5 = 3$$
$$p = 6$$

The focus is located a distance $p/2$ from the vertex. The focus is at $(4, 8 + 3)$ or $(4, 11)$.

The standard form equation for a parabola with vertex at (h, k) and opening upward is

$$(x - h)^2 = 2p(y - k)$$
$$(x - h)^2 = (2)(6)(y - 8)$$
$$(x - 4)^2 = 12(y - 8)$$

The answer is (B).

Equation 1.17: Standard Form of the Equation of an Ellipse

$$\frac{(x - h)^2}{a^2} + \frac{(y - k)^2}{b^2} = 1 \quad [\text{center at } (h, k)] \qquad 1.17$$

Description

An *ellipse* has two foci, F_1 and F_2, separated along the *major axis* by a distance $2c$. (See Fig. 1.5.) The line perpendicular to the major axis passing through the center of the ellipse is the *minor axis*. The lines perpendicular to the major axis passing through the foci are the *latera recta*. The distance between the two vertices is $2a$. The ellipse is the locus of points such that the sum of the distances from the two foci is $2a$. The eccentricity of the ellipse is always less than one. If the eccentricity is zero, the ellipse is a circle.

Figure 1.5 *Ellipse (with horizontal major axis)*

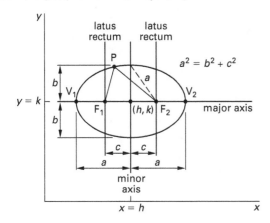

Equation 1.17 is the *standard form* of the equation of an ellipse with center at (h, k), *semimajor distance a*, and *semiminor distance b*. Equation 1.17 can be applied when the principal axes of the ellipse coincide with the coordinate axes and when the major axis is oriented vertically.

Example

What is the equation of the ellipse with center at $(0,0)$, with vertical major axis, and that passes through the points $(2,0), (0,3)$, and $(-2,0)$?

(A) $\dfrac{x^2}{9} - \dfrac{y^2}{4} = 1$

(B) $\dfrac{x^2}{4} - \dfrac{y^2}{9} = 1$

(C) $\dfrac{x^2}{9} + \dfrac{y^2}{4} = 1$

(D) $\dfrac{x^2}{4} + \dfrac{y^2}{9} = 1$

Solution

An ellipse has the standard form

$$\frac{(x-h)^2}{a^2} + \frac{(y-k)^2}{b^2} = 1$$

The center is at $(h, k) = (0,0)$.

$$\frac{(x-0)^2}{a^2} + \frac{(y-0)^2}{b^2} = 1$$

Substitute the known values of (x, y) to determine a and b.

For $(x, y) = (2, 0)$,

$$\frac{(2)^2}{a^2} + \frac{(0)^2}{b^2} = 1$$
$$a^2 = 4$$
$$a = 2$$

For $(x, y) = (0, 3)$,

$$\frac{(0)^2}{a^2} + \frac{(3)^2}{b^2} = 1$$
$$b^2 = 9$$
$$b = 3$$

This ellipse is oriented vertically since $b > a$.

Check: For $(x, y) = (-2, 0)$,

$$\frac{(-2)^2}{a^2} + \frac{(0)^2}{b^2} = 1$$
$$a^2 = 4$$
$$a = 2 \quad \begin{bmatrix} \text{This step is not necessary} \\ \text{as } a \text{ is determined} \\ \text{from the first point.} \end{bmatrix}$$

The equation of the ellipse is

$$\frac{x^2}{(2)^2} + \frac{y^2}{(3)^2} = 1$$
$$\frac{x^2}{4} + \frac{y^2}{9} = 1$$

The answer is (D).

Equation 1.18 Through Eq. 1.21: Ellipse with Center at the Origin

foci: $(\pm ae, 0)$	1.18
$x = \pm a/e$	1.19
$e = \sqrt{1 - (b^2/a^2)} = c/a$	1.20
$b = a\sqrt{1 - e^2}$	1.21

Description

When the center of the ellipse is at the origin ($h=k=0$), the foci are located at $(ae, 0)$ and $(-ae, 0)$, the directrices are located at $\pm x = a/e$, and the eccentricity and semiminor distance are given by Eq. 1.20 and Eq. 1.21, respectively. Each directrix is a vertical line located outside of the ellipse. The location of each directrix is such that the distance from a point on the ellipse to the nearest directrix is proportional to the distance from that point on the ellipse to the nearest focus.

Equation 1.22: Standard Form of the Equation of a Hyperbola

$$\frac{(x-h)^2}{a^2} - \frac{(y-k)^2}{b^2} = 1 \quad [\text{center at } (h,k)] \qquad 1.22$$

Description

As shown in Fig. 1.6, a *hyperbola* has two foci separated along the *transverse axis* by a distance $2c$. The two lines perpendicular to the transverse axis that pass through the foci are the *conjugate axes*. As the distance from the center increases, the hyperbola approaches two straight lines, called the *asymptotes*, that intersect at the hyperbola's center.

The distance from the center to either vertex is a. The distance from either vertex to either asymptote in a direction perpendicular to the transverse axis is b. The hyperbola is the locus of points such that the distances from any point to the two foci differ by $2a$. The distance from the center to either focus is c.

Equation 1.22 is the *standard form* of the equation of a hyperbola with center at (h, k) and opening horizontally.

Figure 1.6 *Hyperbola*

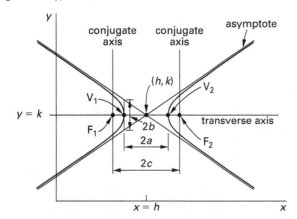

Equation 1.23 Through Eq. 1.26: Hyperbola with Center at the Origin

$$\text{foci: } (\pm ae, 0) \qquad 1.23$$

$$x = \pm a/e \qquad 1.24$$

$$e = \sqrt{1 + (b^2/a^2)} = c/a \qquad 1.25$$

$$b = a\sqrt{e^2 - 1} \qquad 1.26$$

Description

When the hyperbola is centered at the origin ($h=k=0$), the foci are located at $(ae, 0)$ and $(-ae, 0)$, the directrices are located at $x = a/e$ and $x = -a/e$, and the eccentricity, e, and distance b are given by Eq. 1.25 and Eq. 1.26, respectively.

Example

What is most nearly the eccentricity of the hyperbola shown?

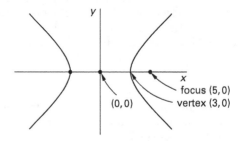

(A)   1.33

(B)   1.67

(C)   2.00

(D)   3.00

Solution

Use Eq. 1.25. a is the distance from the center to either vertex, and c is the distance from the center to either focus. The eccentricity is

$$e = c/a = \frac{5}{3} = 1.67$$

The answer is (B).

Equation 1.27 and Eq. 1.28: Standard Form of the Equation of a Circle

$$(x-h)^2 + (y-k)^2 = r^2 \qquad 1.27$$

$$r = \sqrt{(x-h)^2 + (y-k)^2} \qquad 1.28$$

Description

Equation 1.27 is the *standard form* (also called the *center-radius form*) of the equation of a circle with center at (h, k) and radius r. (See Fig. 1.7.) The radius is given by Eq. 1.28.

Figure 1.7 *Circle*

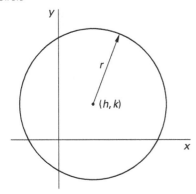

Example

What is the equation of the circle passing through the points $(0, 0)$, $(0, 4)$, and $(-4, 0)$?

(A) $(x - 2)^2 + (y - 2)^2 = \sqrt{8}$

(B) $(x - 2)^2 + (y - 2)^2 = 8$

(C) $(x + 2)^2 + (y - 2)^2 = 8$

(D) $(x + 2)^2 + (y + 2)^2 = \sqrt{8}$

Solution

From Eq. 1.27, the center-radius form of the equation of a circle is

$$(x - h)^2 + (y - k)^2 = r^2$$

Substitute the first two points, $(0, 0)$ and $(0, 4)$.

$$(0 - h)^2 + (0 - k)^2 = r^2$$
$$(0 - h)^2 + (4 - k)^2 = r^2$$

Since both are equal to the unknown r^2, set the left-hand sides equal. Simplify and solve for k.

$$h^2 + k^2 = h^2 + (4 - k)^2$$
$$k^2 = (4 - k)^2$$
$$k = 2$$

Substitute the third point, $(-4, 0)$, into the center-radius form.

$$(-4 - h)^2 + (0 - k)^2 = r^2$$

Set this third equation equal to the first equation. Simplify and solve for h.

$$(-4 - h)^2 + k^2 = h^2 + k^2$$
$$(-4 - h)^2 = h^2$$
$$h = -2$$

Now that h and k are known, substitute them into the first equation to determine r^2.

$$h^2 + k^2 = r^2$$
$$(-2)^2 + (2)^2 = 8$$

Substitute the known values of h, k, and r^2 into the center-radius form.

$$(x + 2)^2 + (y - 2)^2 = 8$$

The answer is (C).

Equation 1.29: Distance Between Two Points on a Plane

$$d = \sqrt{(y_2 - y_1)^2 + (x_2 - x_1)^2} \qquad \text{1.29}$$

Description

The distance, d, between two points (x_1, y_1) and (x_2, y_2) is given by Eq. 1.29.

Equation 1.30: Length of Tangent to Circle from a Point

$$t^2 = (x' - h)^2 + (y' - k)^2 - r^2 \qquad \text{1.30}$$

Description

The length, t, of a *tangent* to a circle from a point (x', y') in two-dimensional space is illustrated in Fig. 1.8 and can be found from Eq. 1.30.

Figure 1.8 *Tangent to a Circle from a Point*

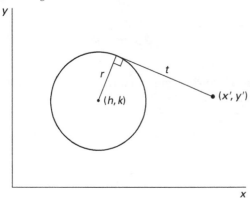

Example

What is the length of the line tangent from point $(7, 1)$ to the circle shown?

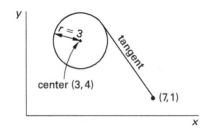

(A) 3

(B) 4

(C) 5

(D) 7

Solution

Use Eq. 1.30.

$$t^2 = (x' - h)^2 + (y' - k)^2 - r^2$$
$$= (7 - 3)^2 + (1 - 4)^2 - 3^2$$
$$= 16$$
$$t = 4$$

The answer is (B).

4. QUADRIC SURFACE (SPHERE)

Equation 1.31: Standard Form of the Equation of a Sphere

$$(x - h)^2 + (y - k)^2 + (z - m)^2 = r^2 \qquad \text{1.31}$$

Description

Equation 1.31 is the *standard form* of the equation of a sphere centered at (h, k, m) with radius r.

Example

Most nearly, what is the radius of a sphere with a center at the origin and that passes through the point $(8, 1, 6)$?

(A) 9.2

(B) $\sqrt{101}$

(C) 65

(D) 100

Solution

Use Eq. 1.31.

$$r^2 = (x - h)^2 + (y - k)^2 + (z - m)^2$$
$$r = \sqrt{(8 - 0)^2 + (1 - 0)^2 + (6 - 0)^2}$$
$$= \sqrt{101}$$

The answer is (B).

5. DISTANCE BETWEEN POINTS IN SPACE

Equation 1.32: Distance Between Two Points in Space

$$d = \sqrt{(x_2 - x_1)^2 + (y_2 - y_1)^2 + (z_2 - z_1)^2} \qquad \text{1.32}$$

Description

The distance between two points (x_1, y_1, z_1) and (x_2, y_2, z_2) in three-dimensional space can be found using Eq. 1.32.

Example

What is the distance between point P at $(1, -3, 5)$ and point Q at $(-3, 4, -2)$?

(A) $\sqrt{10}$

(B) $\sqrt{14}$

(C) 8

(D) $\sqrt{114}$

Solution

The distance between points P and Q is

$$d_{PQ} = \sqrt{(x_2 - x_1)^2 + (y_2 - y_1)^2 + (z_2 - z_1)^2}$$
$$= \sqrt{(-3-1)^2 + (4-(-3))^2 + (-2-5)^2}$$
$$= \sqrt{114}$$

The answer is (D).

6. DEGREES AND RADIANS

Degrees and *radians* are two units for measuring angles. One complete circle is divided into 360 degrees (written 360°) or 2π radians (abbreviated *rad*).[3] The conversions between degrees and radians are

multiply	by	to obtain
radians	$\dfrac{180}{\pi}$	degrees
degrees	$\dfrac{\pi}{180}$	radians

The number of radians in an angle, θ, corresponds to twice the area within a circular sector with arc length θ and a radius of one, as shown in Fig. 1.9. Alternatively, the area of a sector with central angle θ radians is $\theta/2$ for a *unit circle* (i.e., a circle with a radius of one unit).

Figure 1.9 *Radians and Area of Unit Circle*

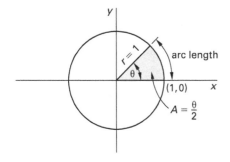

7. PLANE ANGLES

A *plane angle* (usually referred to as just an *angle*) consists of two intersecting lines and an intersection point known as the *vertex*. The angle can be referred to by a capital letter representing the vertex (e.g., B in Fig. 1.10), a letter representing the angular measure (e.g., B or β), or by three capital letters, where the middle letter is the vertex and the other two letters are two points on different lines, and either the symbol $\angle$ or $\sphericalangle$ (e.g., $\sphericalangle$ ABC).

Figure 1.10 *Angle*

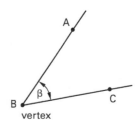

The angle between two intersecting lines generally is understood to be the smaller angle created.[4] Angles have been classified as follows.

- *acute angle:* an angle less than 90° ($\pi/2$ rad)
- *obtuse angle:* an angle more than 90° ($\pi/2$ rad) but less than 180° (π rad)
- *reflex angle:* an angle more than 180° (π rad) but less than 360° (2π rad)
- *related angle:* an angle that differs from another by some multiple of 90° ($\pi/2$ rad)
- *right angle:* an angle equal to 90° ($\pi/2$ rad)
- *straight angle:* an angle equal to 180° (π rad); that is, a straight line

Complementary angles are two angles whose sum is 90° ($\pi/2$ rad). *Supplementary angles* are two angles whose sum is 180° (π rad). *Adjacent angles* share a common vertex and one (the interior) side. Adjacent angles are supplementary if, and only if, their exterior sides form a straight line.

Vertical angles are the two angles with a common vertex and with sides made up by two intersecting straight lines, as shown in Fig. 1.11. Vertical angles are equal.

Angle of elevation and *angle of depression* are surveying terms referring to the angle above and below the horizontal plane of the observer, respectively.

Figure 1.11 *Vertical Angles*

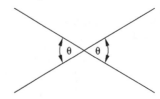

8. TRIANGLES

A *triangle* is a three-sided closed polygon with three angles whose sum is 180° (π rad). Triangles are identified by their vertices and the symbol $\triangle$ (e.g., $\triangle$ABC in Fig. 1.12). A side

---

[3]The abbreviation *rad* is also used to represent *radiation absorbed dose*, a measure of radiation exposure.
[4]In books on geometry, the term *ray* is used instead of *line*.

is designated by its two endpoints (e.g., AB in Fig. 1.12) or by a lowercase letter corresponding to the capital letter of the opposite vertex (e.g., c).

In *similar triangles*, the corresponding angles are equal and the corresponding sides are in proportion. (Since there are only two independent angles in a triangle, showing that two angles of one triangle are equal to two angles of the other triangle is sufficient to show similarity.) The symbol for similarity is $\sim$. In Fig. 1.12, $\triangle ABC \sim \triangle DEF$ (i.e., $\triangle ABC$ is similar to $\triangle DEF$).

Figure 1.12 *Similar Triangles*

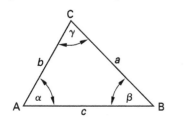 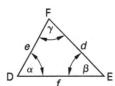

9. RIGHT TRIANGLES

A *right triangle* is a triangle in which one of the angles is $90°$ ($\pi/2$ rad), as shown in Fig. 1.13. Choosing one of the acute angles as a reference, the sides of the triangle are called the *adjacent side*, x, the *opposite side*, y, and the *hypotenuse*, r.

Figure 1.13 *Right Triangle*

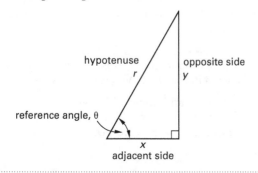

Equation 1.33 Through Eq. 1.38: Trigonometric Functions

$\sin\theta = y/r$	1.33
$\cos\theta = x/r$	1.34
$\tan\theta = y/x$	1.35
$\csc\theta = r/y$	1.36
$\sec\theta = r/x$	1.37
$\cot\theta = x/y$	1.38

Description

The trigonometric functions given in Eq. 1.33 through Eq. 1.38 are calculated from the sides of the right triangle.

The trigonometric functions correspond to the lengths of various line segments in a right triangle in a unit circle. Figure 1.14 shows such a triangle inscribed in a unit circle.

Figure 1.14 *Trigonometric Functions in a Unit Circle*

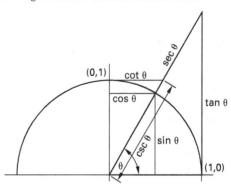

Example

The values of $\cos 45°$ and $\tan 45°$, respectively, are

(A) 1 and $\sqrt{2}/2$

(B) 1 and $\sqrt{2}$

(C) $\sqrt{2}/2$ and 1

(D) $\sqrt{2}$ and 1

Solution

For convenience, let the adjacent side of a $45°$ right triangle have a length of $x = 1$. Then the opposite side has a length of $y = 1$, and the hypotenuse has a length of $r = \sqrt{2}$.

Using Eq. 1.34 and Eq. 1.35,

$$\cos 45° = x/r = \frac{1}{\sqrt{2}} = \sqrt{2}/2$$

$$\tan 45° = y/x = \frac{1}{1} = 1$$

The answer is (C).

10. TRIGONOMETRIC IDENTITIES

Equation 1.39 through Eq. 1.41 are some of the most commonly used trigonometric identities.

Equation 1.39 Through Eq. 1.41: Reciprocal Functions

$$\csc \theta = 1/\sin \theta \qquad \textit{1.39}$$

$$\sec \theta = 1/\cos \theta \qquad \textit{1.40}$$

$$\cot \theta = 1/\tan \theta \qquad \textit{1.41}$$

Description

Three pairs of the trigonometric functions are reciprocals of each other. The prefix "co-" is not a good indicator of the reciprocal functions; while the tangent and cotangent functions are reciprocals of each other, two other pairs—the sine and cosine functions and the secant and cosecant functions—are not.

Example

Simplify the expression $\cos \theta \sec \theta / \tan \theta$.

 (A) 1

 (B) $\cot \theta$

 (C) $\csc \theta$

 (D) $\sin \theta$

Solution

Use the reciprocal functions given in Eq. 1.40 and Eq. 1.41.

$$\frac{\cos \theta \sec \theta}{\tan \theta} = \frac{\cos \theta \left(\dfrac{1}{\cos \theta} \right)}{\tan \theta}$$
$$= \frac{1}{\tan \theta}$$
$$= \cot \theta$$

The answer is (B).

Equation 1.42 Through Eq. 1.47: General Identities

$$\cos \theta = \sin(\theta + \pi/2) = -\sin(\theta - \pi/2) \qquad \textit{1.42}$$

$$\sin \theta = \cos(\theta - \pi/2) = -\cos(\theta + \pi/2) \qquad \textit{1.43}$$

$$\tan \theta = \sin \theta / \cos \theta \qquad \textit{1.44}$$

$$\sin^2 \theta + \cos^2 \theta = 1 \qquad \textit{1.45}$$

$$\tan^2 \theta + 1 = \sec^2 \theta \qquad \textit{1.46}$$

$$\cot^2 \theta + 1 = \csc^2 \theta \qquad \textit{1.47}$$

Description

Equation 1.42 through Eq. 1.47 give some general trigonometric identities.

Example

Which of the following expressions is equivalent to the expression $\csc \theta \cos^3 \theta \tan \theta$?

 (A) $\sin \theta$

 (B) $\cos \theta$

 (C) $1 - \sin^2 \theta$

 (D) $1 + \sin^2 \theta$

Solution

Simplify the expression using the trigonometric identities given in Eq. 1.39, Eq. 1.44, and Eq. 1.45.

$$\csc \theta \cos^3 \theta \tan \theta = \left(\frac{1}{\sin \theta} \right) \cos^3 \theta \left(\frac{\sin \theta}{\cos \theta} \right)$$
$$= \cos^2 \theta$$
$$= 1 - \sin^2 \theta$$

The answer is (C).

Equation 1.48 Through Eq. 1.51: Double-Angle Identities

$$\sin 2\alpha = 2 \sin \alpha \cos \alpha \qquad \textit{1.48}$$

$$\cos 2\alpha = \cos^2 \alpha - \sin^2 \alpha$$
$$= 1 - 2 \sin^2 \alpha \qquad \textit{1.49}$$
$$= 2 \cos^2 \alpha - 1$$

$$\tan 2\alpha = (2 \tan \alpha)/(1 - \tan^2 \alpha) \qquad \textit{1.50}$$

$$\cot 2\alpha = (\cot^2 \alpha - 1)/(2 \cot \alpha) \qquad \textit{1.51}$$

Description

The identities given in Eq. 1.48 through Eq. 1.51 show equivalent expressions of trigonometric functions of double angles.

Example

What is an equivalent expression for $\sin 2\alpha$?

(A) $-2\sin\alpha\cos\alpha$

(B) $\frac{1}{2}\sin\alpha\cos\alpha$

(C) $\dfrac{2\sin\alpha}{\sec\alpha}$

(D) $2\sin\alpha\cos\dfrac{\alpha}{2}$

Solution

Use Eq. 1.48, the double-angle formula for the sine function.

$$\sin 2\alpha = 2\sin\alpha\cos\alpha = \frac{2\sin\alpha}{\sec\alpha}$$

The answer is (C).

Equation 1.52 Through Eq. 1.59: Two-Angle Identities

$$\sin(\alpha+\beta) = \sin\alpha\cos\beta + \cos\alpha\sin\beta \qquad 1.52$$

$$\cos(\alpha+\beta) = \cos\alpha\cos\beta - \sin\alpha\sin\beta \qquad 1.53$$

$$\tan(\alpha+\beta) = (\tan\alpha+\tan\beta)/(1-\tan\alpha\tan\beta) \qquad 1.54$$

$$\cot(\alpha+\beta) = (\cot\alpha\cot\beta-1)/(\cot\alpha+\cot\beta) \qquad 1.55$$

$$\sin(\alpha-\beta) = \sin\alpha\cos\beta - \cos\alpha\sin\beta \qquad 1.56$$

$$\cos(\alpha-\beta) = \cos\alpha\cos\beta + \sin\alpha\sin\beta \qquad 1.57$$

$$\tan(\alpha-\beta) = (\tan\alpha-\tan\beta)/(1+\tan\alpha\tan\beta) \qquad 1.58$$

$$\cot(\alpha-\beta) = (\cot\alpha\cot\beta+1)/(\cot\beta-\cot\alpha) \qquad 1.59$$

Description

The identities given in Eq. 1.52 through Eq. 1.59 show equivalent expressions of two-angle trigonometric functions.

Example

Simplify the following expression.

$$\frac{\cos(\alpha+\beta)+\cos(\alpha-\beta)}{\cos\beta}$$

(A) $\cos\alpha/2$

(B) $2\cos\alpha$

(C) $\sin 2\alpha$

(D) $\sin^2\alpha$

Solution

Use Eq. 1.53 and Eq. 1.57.

$$\frac{\cos(\alpha+\beta)+\cos(\alpha-\beta)}{\cos\beta} = \frac{\left(\begin{array}{c}\cos\alpha\cos\beta\\-\sin\alpha\sin\beta\end{array}\right)+\left(\begin{array}{c}\cos\alpha\cos\beta\\+\sin\alpha\sin\beta\end{array}\right)}{\cos\beta}$$
$$= \frac{2\cos\alpha\cos\beta}{\cos\beta}$$
$$= 2\cos\alpha$$

The answer is (B).

Equation 1.60 Through Eq. 1.63: Half-Angle Identities

$$\sin(\alpha/2) = \pm\sqrt{(1-\cos\alpha)/2} \qquad 1.60$$

$$\cos(\alpha/2) = \pm\sqrt{(1+\cos\alpha)/2} \qquad 1.61$$

$$\tan(\alpha/2) = \pm\sqrt{(1-\cos\alpha)/(1+\cos\alpha)} \qquad 1.62$$

$$\cot(\alpha/2) = \pm\sqrt{(1+\cos\alpha)/(1-\cos\alpha)} \qquad 1.63$$

Description

The identities given in Eq. 1.60 through Eq. 1.63 show equivalent expressions of half-angle trigonometric functions.

Equation 1.64 Through Eq. 1.70: Miscellaneous Identities

$$\sin\alpha\sin\beta = (1/2)[\cos(\alpha-\beta)-\cos(\alpha+\beta)] \quad \text{1.64}$$

$$\cos\alpha\cos\beta = (1/2)[\cos(\alpha-\beta)+\cos(\alpha+\beta)] \quad \text{1.65}$$

$$\sin\alpha\cos\beta = (1/2)[\sin(\alpha+\beta)+\sin(\alpha-\beta)] \quad \text{1.66}$$

$$\sin\alpha+\sin\beta = 2\sin[(1/2)(\alpha+\beta)] \\ \times \cos[(1/2)(\alpha-\beta)] \quad \text{1.67}$$

$$\sin\alpha-\sin\beta = 2\cos[(1/2)(\alpha+\beta)] \\ \times \sin[(1/2)(\alpha-\beta)] \quad \text{1.68}$$

$$\cos\alpha+\cos\beta = 2\cos[(1/2)(\alpha+\beta)] \\ \times \cos[(1/2)(\alpha-\beta)] \quad \text{1.69}$$

$$\cos\alpha-\cos\beta = -2\sin[(1/2)(\alpha+\beta)] \\ \times \sin[(1/2)(\alpha-\beta)] \quad \text{1.70}$$

Description

The identities given in Eq. 1.64 through Eq. 1.70 show equivalent expressions of other trigonometric functions.

11. GENERAL TRIANGLES

The term *general triangle* refers to any triangle, including but not limited to right triangles. Figure 1.15 shows a general triangle.

Figure 1.15 *General Triangle*

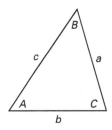

Equation 1.71: Law of Sines

$$\frac{a}{\sin A} = \frac{b}{\sin B} = \frac{c}{\sin C} \quad \text{1.71}$$

Description

For a general triangle, the *law of sines* relates the sines of the three angles A, B, and C and their opposite sides, a, b, and c, respectively.

Example

The angle of elevation to the top of a flagpole from point A on the ground is observed to be $37°11'$. The observer walks 17 m directly away from the flagpole from point A to point B and finds the new angle to be $25°43'$.

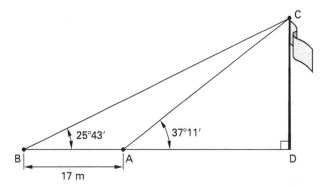

What is the approximate height of the flagpole?

(A)   10 m

(B)   22 m

(C)   82 m

(D)   300 m

Solution

The two observations lead to two triangles with a common leg, h.

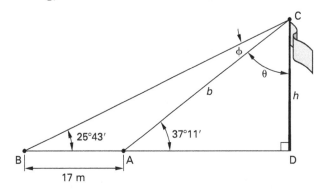

Find angle θ in triangle ADC.

$$37°11' + 90° + \theta = 180°$$
$$\theta = 52°49'$$

Find angle ϕ in triangle BAC.

$$25°43' + 90° + (52°49' + \phi) = 180°$$
$$\phi = 11°28'$$

Use the law of sines on triangle BAC to find side b.
[Law of Sines]

$$\frac{\sin 11^\circ 28'}{17 \text{ m}} = \frac{\sin 25^\circ 43'}{b}$$
$$b = 37.11 \text{ m}$$

Find the flagpole height, h, using triangle ADC.

$$\sin 37^\circ 11' = \frac{h}{b}$$
$$h = b \sin 37^\circ 11'$$
$$= (37.11 \text{ m}) \sin 37^\circ 11'$$
$$= 22.43 \text{ m} \quad (22 \text{ m})$$

The answer is (B).

Equation 1.72 Through Eq. 1.74: Law of Cosines

$$a^2 = b^2 + c^2 - 2bc \cos A \qquad 1.72$$

$$b^2 = a^2 + c^2 - 2ac \cos B \qquad 1.73$$

$$c^2 = a^2 + b^2 - 2ab \cos C \qquad 1.74$$

Variations

$$\cos A = \frac{b^2 + c^2 - a^2}{2bc}$$

$$\cos B = \frac{a^2 + c^2 - b^2}{2ac}$$

$$\cos C = \frac{a^2 + b^2 - c^2}{2ab}$$

Description

For a general triangle, the *law of cosines* relates the cosines of the three angles A, B, and C and their opposite sides, a, b, and c, respectively.

Example

Three circles of radii 110 m, 140 m, and 220 m are tangent to one another. What are the interior angles of the triangle formed by joining the centers of the circles?

(A) 34.2°, 69.2°, and 76.6°

(B) 36.6°, 69.1°, and 74.3°

(C) 42.2°, 62.5°, and 75.3°

(D) 47.9°, 63.1°, and 69.0°

Solution

The three circles and the triangle are shown.

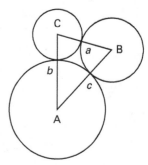

Calculate the length of each side of the triangle.

$$a = 110 \text{ m} + 140 \text{ m} = 250 \text{ m}$$
$$b = 110 \text{ m} + 220 \text{ m} = 330 \text{ m}$$
$$c = 140 \text{ m} + 220 \text{ m} = 360 \text{ m}$$

From Eq. 1.72,

$$a^2 = b^2 + c^2 - 2bc \cos A$$
$$\cos A = \frac{b^2 + c^2 - a^2}{2bc}$$
$$= \frac{(330 \text{ m})^2 + (360 \text{ m})^2 - (250 \text{ m})^2}{(2)(330 \text{ m})(360 \text{ m})}$$
$$= 0.7407$$
$$A = 42.2^\circ$$

From Eq. 1.73,

$$b^2 = a^2 + c^2 - 2ac \cos B$$
$$\cos B = \frac{a^2 + c^2 - b^2}{2ac}$$
$$= \frac{(250 \text{ m})^2 + (360 \text{ m})^2 - (330 \text{ m})^2}{(2)(250 \text{ m})(360 \text{ m})}$$
$$= 0.4622$$
$$B = 62.5^\circ$$

From Eq. 1.74,

$$c^2 = a^2 + b^2 - 2ab \cos C$$
$$\cos C = \frac{a^2 + b^2 - c^2}{2ab}$$
$$= \frac{(250 \text{ m})^2 + (330 \text{ m})^2 - (360 \text{ m})^2}{(2)(250 \text{ m})(330 \text{ m})}$$
$$= 0.2533$$
$$C = 75.3^\circ$$

The answer is (C).

12. MENSURATION OF AREAS

The dimensions, perimeter, area, and other geometric properties constitute the *mensuration* (i.e., the measurements) of a geometric shape.

Equation 1.75 and Eq. 1.76: Parabolic Segments

$$A = 2bh/3 \qquad \text{1.75}$$

$$A = bh/3 \qquad \text{1.76}$$

Description

Equation 1.75 and Eq. 1.76 give the area of a parabolic segment. (See Fig. 1.16.) Equation 1.75 gives the area within the curve of the parabola, and Eq. 1.76 gives the area outside the curve of the parabola.

Figure 1.16 Parabolic Segments

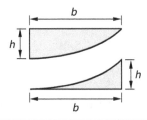

Equation 1.77 Through Eq. 1.80: Ellipses

$$A = \pi ab \qquad \text{1.77}$$

$$P_{\text{approx}} = 2\pi\sqrt{(a^2 + b^2)/2} \qquad \text{1.78}$$

$$P = \pi(a+b)\begin{bmatrix} 1 + (1/2)^2\lambda^2 + (1/2 \times 1/4)^2\lambda^4 \\ + (1/2 \times 1/4 \times 3/6)^2\lambda^6 \\ + (1/2 \times 1/4 \times 3/6 \times 5/8)^2\lambda^8 \\ + \left(\dfrac{1/2 \times 1/4 \times 3/6}{\times 5/8 \times 7/10}\right)^2 \lambda^{10} \\ + \cdots \end{bmatrix} \qquad \text{1.79}$$

$$\lambda = (a-b)/(a+b) \qquad \text{1.80}$$

Description

Equation 1.77 gives the area of an ellipse. (See Fig. 1.17.) a and b are the semimajor and semiminor axes, respectively. Equation 1.78 gives an approximation of the perimeter of an ellipse. Equation 1.79 expresses the perimeter exactly, but one factor is the sum of an infinite series in which λ is defined as in Eq. 1.80.

Figure 1.17 Ellipse

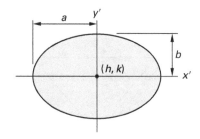

Example

An ellipse has a semimajor axis with length $a = 12$ and a semiminor axis with length $b = 3$. What is the approximate length of the perimeter of the ellipse?

(A) 24

(B) 47

(C) 55

(D) 180

Solution

Use Eq. 1.78.

$$P_{\text{approx}} = 2\pi\sqrt{(a^2 + b^2)/2} = 2\pi\sqrt{\frac{12^2 + 3^2}{2}}$$

$$= 54.96 \quad (55)$$

The answer is (C).

Equation 1.81 and Eq. 1.82: Circular Segments

$$A = [r^2(\phi - \sin\phi)]/2 \qquad \text{1.81}$$

$$\phi = s/r = 2\{\arccos[(r-d)/r]\} \qquad \text{1.82}$$

Description

A *circular segment* is a region bounded by a circular arc and a chord, as shown by the shaded portion in Fig. 1.18. The arc and chord are both limited by a central angle, ϕ. Use Eq. 1.81 to find the area of a circular segment when its central angle, ϕ, and the radius of the circle, r, are known; in Eq. 1.81, the central angle must be in radians. Use Eq. 1.82 to find the central angle when the radius of the circle and either the height of the circular segment, d, or the length of the arc, s, are known.

Figure 1.18 Circular Segment

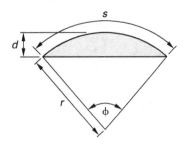

Example

Two 20 m diameter circles are placed so that the circumference of each just touches the center of the other.

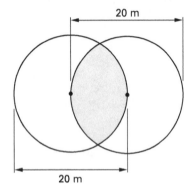

What is most nearly the area of the shared region?

(A)   62 m²

(B)   110 m²

(C)   120 m²

(D)   170 m²

Solution

The shared region can be thought of as two equal circular segments, each as shown in the illustration. The radius of each circle is $r = 10$ m. The height of each circular segment is half the radius, so $d = 5$ m.

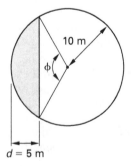

Use Eq. 1.82 to find the angle ϕ.

$$\phi = 2\{\arccos[(r-d)/r]\} = 2\arccos\left(\frac{10\ \text{m} - 5\ \text{m}}{10\ \text{m}}\right)$$

$$= 120°$$

Convert ϕ to radians.

$$\phi = (120°)\left(\frac{2\pi}{360°}\right) = 2.094\ \text{rad}$$

From Eq. 1.81, the area of a circular segment is

$$A = [r^2(\phi - \sin\phi)]/2$$

$$= \frac{(10\ \text{m})^2(2.094\ \text{rad} - \sin(2.094\ \text{rad}))}{2}$$

$$= 61.4\ \text{m}^2$$

The area of the shared region is twice this amount.

$$A_{\text{shared}} = 2A = (2)(61.4\ \text{m}^2)$$

$$= 122.8\ \text{m}^2 \quad (120\ \text{m}^2)$$

The answer is (C).

Equation 1.83 and Eq. 1.84: Circular Sectors

$$A = \phi r^2/2 = sr/2 \qquad \text{1.83}$$

$$\phi = s/r \qquad \text{1.84}$$

Description

A *circular sector* is a portion of a circle bounded by two radii and an arc, as shown in Fig. 1.19. Between the two radii is the central angle, ϕ. Use Eq. 1.83 to find the area of a circular sector when its radius, r, and either its central angle or the length of its arc, s, are known; the central angle must be in radians. Use Eq. 1.84 to find the central angle in radians when the arc length and radius are known.

Figure 1.19 Circular Sector

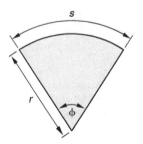

Example

A circular sector has an area of 3 m^2 and a central angle of 50°. What is most nearly the radius?

(A) 1.5 m

(B) 2.6 m

(C) 3.0 m

(D) 3.3 m

Solution

The central angle must be converted to radians.

$$\phi = (50°)\left(\frac{2\pi}{360°}\right) = 0.873 \text{ rad}$$

Use Eq. 1.83.

$$A = \phi r^2/2$$

$$r = \sqrt{\frac{2A}{\phi}} = \sqrt{\frac{(2)(3 \text{ m}^2)}{0.873 \text{ rad}}}$$

$$= 2.62 \text{ m} \quad (2.6 \text{ m})$$

The answer is (B).

Equation 1.85 Through Eq. 1.89: Parallelograms

$P = 2(a+b)$	1.85
$d_1 = \sqrt{a^2 + b^2 - 2ab(\cos\phi)}$	1.86
$d_2 = \sqrt{a^2 + b^2 + 2ab(\cos\phi)}$	1.87
$d_1^2 + d_2^2 = 2(a^2 + b^2)$	1.88
$A = ah = ab(\sin\phi)$	1.89

Description

Equation 1.85 is the formula for the perimeter of a parallelogram. (See Fig. 1.20.) Equation 1.86 and Eq. 1.87 give the diagonals of the parallelogram when its sides and acute included angle are known. Equation 1.88 relates the sides and the diagonals, and Eq. 1.89 gives the parallelogram's area. A parallelogram with all sides of equal length is called a *rhombus*.

Figure 1.20 *Parallelogram*

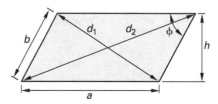

Equation 1.90 Through Eq. 1.94: Regular Polygons

$\phi = 2\pi/n$	1.90
$\theta = \left[\frac{\pi(n-2)}{n}\right] = \pi\left(1 - \frac{2}{n}\right)$	1.91
$P = ns$	1.92
$s = 2r[\tan(\phi/2)]$	1.93
$A = (nsr)/2$	1.94

Description

A *regular polygon* is a polygon with equal sides and equal angles. (See Fig. 1.21.) n is the number of sides. Equation 1.90 gives the central angle, ϕ, formed by two line segments drawn from the center to adjacent vertices. Equation 1.91 gives the measure of each interior angle, θ. Equation 1.92 gives the perimeter of the polygon (s is the length of one side).

Equation 1.93 can be used to find the length of one side when the polygon's central angle and apothem, r, are known. The *apothem* is a line segment drawn from the center of the polygon to the midpoint of one side; this is also the radius of a circle inscribed within the polygon. Equation 1.94 is the formula for the area of the polygon.

Figure 1.21 *Regular Polygon (n equal sides)*

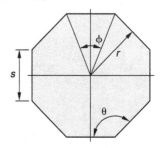

Example

A regular polygon has six sides, each with a length of 25 cm. What is most nearly the length of the apothem, r?

(A)   10 cm

(B)   15 cm

(C)   20 cm

(D)   22 cm

Solution

Use Eq. 1.90 to find the central angle.

$$\phi = 2\pi/n = \frac{2\pi \text{ rad}}{6} = 1.047 \text{ rad}$$

Convert radians to degrees.

$$\phi = (1.047 \text{ rad})\left(\frac{360°}{2\pi}\right) = 60.0°$$

Use Eq. 1.93 to find the length of the apothem.

$$s = 2r[\tan(\phi/2)]$$
$$r = \frac{s}{2\tan\dfrac{\phi}{2}} = \frac{25 \text{ cm}}{2\tan\dfrac{60°}{2}}$$
$$= 21.65 \text{ cm} \quad (22 \text{ cm})$$

The answer is (D).

13. MENSURATION OF VOLUMES

Equation 1.95: Prismoids

$$V = (h/6)(A_1 + A_2 + 4A) \qquad 1.95$$

Variation

$$h = \frac{6V}{A_1 + A_2 + 4A}$$

Description

A *polyhedron* is a three-dimensional solid whose faces are all flat and whose edges are all straight.

If all the vertices (corners) of the polyhedron are contained within two parallel planes, the solid is a *prismoid* (*prismatoid*). A simple example is a truncated pyramid whose top and bottom faces are parallel. Less obviously, a complete (not truncated) pyramid is also a prismoid;

one plane contains the bottom of the pyramid, while the other is parallel to the bottom and contains the single vertex at the top. Figure 1.22 shows an irregular prismoid with all vertices contained in the top and bottom planes.

Figure 1.22 Prismoid

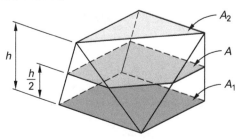

Use Eq. 1.95 to find the volume of a prismoid. h is the distance between the two parallel planes measured along a direction perpendicular to both. A_1 and A_2 are the areas of the faces contained within these two planes; if one of these planes contains only a single point (such as at the top vertex of a pyramid), the area is zero. A is the cross-sectional area of the solid halfway between the two parallel planes. Each vertex of this cross section is halfway between a vertex on the top face and another one on the bottom face, but A is not necessarily the average of A_1 and A_2.

Example

A prismoid has a volume of 100 cm³. The area of the bottom face is 20 cm², the area of the top face is 5 cm², and the cross-sectional area halfway between the top and bottom faces is 10 cm². What is the approximate height of the prismoid?

(A)   8.0 cm

(B)   9.2 cm

(C)   11 cm

(D)   13 cm

Solution

Use Eq. 1.95, the formula for the volume of a prismoid.

$$V = (h/6)(A_1 + A_2 + 4A)$$
$$h = \frac{6V}{A_1 + A_2 + 4A}$$
$$= \frac{(6)(100 \text{ cm}^3)}{20 \text{ cm}^2 + 5 \text{ cm}^2 + (4)(10 \text{ cm}^2)}$$
$$= 9.23 \text{ cm} \quad (9.2 \text{ cm})$$

The answer is (B).

Equation 1.96 and Eq. 1.97: Spheres

$$V = 4\pi r^3/3 = \pi d^3/6 \qquad \text{1.96}$$

$$A = 4\pi r^2 = \pi d^2 \qquad \text{1.97}$$

Description

Equation 1.96 and Eq. 1.97 are the formulas for the volume and surface area, respectively, of a sphere whose radius, r, or diameter, d, is known. (See Fig. 1.23.)

Figure 1.23 Sphere

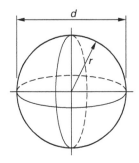

Example

A sphere has a radius of 10 cm. What is approximately the sphere's volume?

- (A) 3600 cm^3
- (B) 4000 cm^3
- (C) 4200 cm^3
- (D) 4800 cm^3

Solution

Use Eq. 1.96.

$$V = 4\pi r^3/3 = \frac{4\pi (10 \text{ cm})^3}{3}$$
$$= 4188.79 \text{ cm}^3 \quad (4200 \text{ cm}^3)$$

The answer is (C).

Equation 1.98 Through Eq. 1.100: Right Circular Cones

$$V = (\pi r^2 h)/3 \qquad \text{1.98}$$

$$A = \text{side area} + \text{base area} = \pi r \left(r + \sqrt{r^2 + h^2} \right) \qquad \text{1.99}$$

$$A_x : A_b = x^2 : h^2 \qquad \text{1.100}$$

Description

A *right circular cone* is a cone whose base is a circle and whose axis is perpendicular to the base. (See Fig. 1.24.) Equation 1.98 gives the volume of a right circular cone whose height, h, and base radius, r, are known. Equation 1.99 gives the cone's area. Equation 1.100 says that the cross-sectional area of the cone varies with the square of the distance from the apex.

Figure 1.24 Right Circular Cone

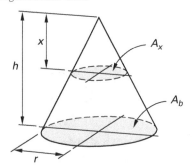

Example

A cone has a height of 100 cm. The cross section of the cone at a distance of 5 cm from the apex is a circle with an area of 20 cm^2. What is most nearly the area of the cone's base?

- (A) 5000 cm^2
- (B) 6000 cm^2
- (C) 8000 cm^2
- (D) 9000 cm^2

Solution

Use Eq. 1.100.

$$A_x : A_b = x^2 : h^2$$
$$A_b = \frac{h^2 A_x}{x^2} = \frac{(100 \text{ cm})^2 (20 \text{ cm}^2)}{(5 \text{ cm})^2}$$
$$= 8000 \text{ cm}^2$$

The answer is (C).

Equation 1.101 and Eq. 1.102: Right Circular Cylinders

$$V = \pi r^2 h = \frac{\pi d^2 h}{4} \qquad \text{1.101}$$

$$A = \text{side area} + \text{end areas} = 2\pi r (h + r) \qquad \text{1.102}$$

Description

A *right circular cylinder* is a cylinder whose base is a circle and whose axis is perpendicular to the base. (See Fig. 1.25.) Equation 1.101 gives the volume of a right circular cylinder, and Eq. 1.102 gives the total surface area.

Figure 1.25 *Right Circular Cylinder*

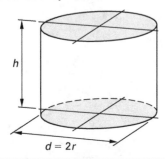

$d = 2r$

Equation 1.103: Paraboloids of Revolution

$$V = \frac{\pi d^2 h}{8} \qquad 1.103$$

Description

A *paraboloid of revolution* is the surface that is obtained by rotating a parabola around its axis. Equation 1.103 can be used to find the volume of a paraboloid of revolution if its height and diameter are known. (See Fig. 1.26.)

Figure 1.26 *Paraboloid of Revolution*

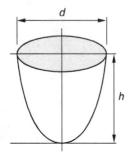

2 Algebra and Linear Algebra

1. LOGARITHMS

Logarithms can be considered to be exponents. In the equation $b^c = x$, for example, the exponent c is the logarithm of x to the base b. The two equations $\log_b x = c$ and $b^c = x$ are equivalent.

Equation 2.1 Through Eq. 2.3: Common and Natural Logarithms

$$\log_b(x) = c \quad [b^c = x] \qquad \text{2.1}$$

$$\ln x \quad [\text{base} = e] \qquad \text{2.2}$$

$$\log x \quad [\text{base} = 10] \qquad \text{2.3}$$

Description

Although any number may be used as a base for logarithms, two bases are most commonly used in engineering. The base for a *common logarithm* is 10. The notation used most often for common logarithms is *log*, although *log₁₀* is sometimes seen.

The base for a *natural logarithm* is 2.71828..., an irrational number that is given the symbol e. The most common notation for a natural logarithm is *ln*, but *logₑ* is sometimes seen.

Example

What is the value of $\log_{10} 1000$?

(A) 2

(B) 3

(C) 8

(D) 10

Solution

$\log_{10} 1000$ is the power of 10 that produces 1000. Use Eq. 2.1.

$$\log_b(x) = c \quad [b^c = x]$$
$$\log_{10} 1000 = c$$
$$10^c = 1000$$
$$c = 3$$

The answer is (B).

Equation 2.4 Through Eq. 2.10: Logarithmic Identities

$$\log_b b^n = n \qquad \text{2.4}$$

$$\log x^c = c \log x \qquad \text{2.5}$$

$$x^c = \text{antilog}(c \log x) \qquad \text{2.6}$$

$$\log xy = \log x + \log y \qquad \text{2.7}$$

$$\log_b b = 1 \qquad \text{2.8}$$

$$\log 1 = 0 \qquad \text{2.9}$$

$$\log x/y = \log x - \log y \qquad \text{2.10}$$

Description

Logarithmic identities are useful in simplifying expressions containing exponentials and other logarithms.

Mathematics

Example

Which of the following is equal to $(0.001)^{2/3}$?

(A) $\text{antilog}\left(\frac{3}{2}\log 0.001\right)$

(B) $\frac{2}{3}\text{antilog}(\log 0.001)$

(C) $\text{antilog}\left(\log \dfrac{0.001}{\frac{2}{3}}\right)$

(D) $\text{antilog}\left(\frac{2}{3}\log 0.001\right)$

Solution

Use Eq. 2.5 and Eq. 2.6.

$$\log x^c = c\log x$$
$$\log(0.001)^{2/3} = \tfrac{2}{3}\log 0.001$$
$$(0.001)^{2/3} = \text{antilog}\left(\tfrac{2}{3}\log 0.001\right)$$

The answer is (D).

Equation 2.11: Changing the Base

$$\log_b x = (\log_a x)/(\log_a b) \qquad 2.11$$

Variations

$$\log_{10} x = \ln x \, \log_{10} e$$

$$\ln x = \frac{\log_{10} x}{\log_{10} e}$$
$$\approx 2.302585 \, \log_{10} x$$

Description

Equation 2.11 is often useful for calculating a logarithm with any base quickly when the available resources produce only natural or common logarithms. Equation 2.11 can also be used to convert a logarithm to a different base, such as from a common logarithm to a natural logarithm.

Example

Given that $\log_{10} 5 = 0.6990$ and $\log_{10} 9 = 0.9542$, what is the value of $\log_5 9$?

(A)   0.2550

(B)   0.7330

(C)   1.127

(D)   1.365

Solution

Use Eq. 2.11.

$$\log_b x = (\log_a x)/(\log_a b)$$
$$\log_5 9 = \frac{\log_{10} 9}{\log_{10} 5} = \frac{0.9542}{0.6990}$$
$$= 1.365$$

The answer is (D).

2. COMPLEX NUMBERS

A *complex number* is the sum of a *real number* and an *imaginary number*. Real numbers include the *rational numbers* and the *irrational numbers*, while imaginary numbers represent the square roots of negative numbers. Every imaginary number can be expressed in the form ib, where i represents the square root of -1 and b is a real number. Another term for i is the *imaginary unit vector*.

$$i = \sqrt{-1}$$

j is commonly used to represent the imaginary unit vector in the fields of electrical engineering and control systems engineering to avoid confusion with the variable for current, i.[1]

$$j = \sqrt{-1}$$

When a complex number is expressed in the form $a + ib$, the complex number is said to be in *rectangular* or *trigonometric form*. In the expression $a + ib$, a is the real component (or real part), and b is the imaginary component (or imaginary part). (See Fig. 2.1.)

Figure 2.1 *Graphical Representation of a Complex Number*

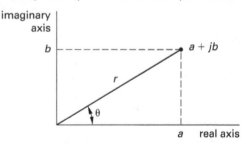

Most algebraic operations (addition, multiplication, exponentiation, etc.) work with complex numbers. When adding two complex numbers, real parts are added to real parts, and imaginary parts are added to imaginary parts.

$$(a + jb) + (c + jd) = (a + c) + j(b + d)$$

$$(a + jb) - (c + jd) = (a - c) + j(b - d)$$

---

[1]The NCEES *FE Reference Handbook* (*NCEES Handbook*) uses only j to represent the imaginary unit vector. This book uses both j and i.

Multiplication of two complex numbers in rectangular form uses the algebraic distributive law and the equivalency $j^2 = -1$.

$$(a + jb)(c + jd) = (ac - bd) + j(ad + bc)$$

Division of complex numbers in rectangular form requires use of the *complex conjugate*. The complex conjugate of a complex number $a + jb$ is $a - jb$. When both the numerator and the denominator are multiplied by the complex conjugate of the denominator, the denominator becomes the real number $a^2 + b^2$. This technique is known as *rationalizing the denominator*.

$$\frac{a + jb}{c + jd} = \frac{(a + jb)(c - jd)}{(c + jd)(c - jd)}$$
$$= \frac{(ac + bd) + j(bc - ad)}{c^2 + d^2}$$

Example

Which of the following is most nearly equal to $(7 + 5.2j)/(3 + 4j)$?

(A) $-0.3 + 1.8j$

(B) $1.7 - 0.5j$

(C) $2.3 - 1.2j$

(D) $2.3 + 1.3j$

Solution

When the numerator and denominator are multiplied by the complex conjugate of the denominator, the denominator becomes a real number.

$$\frac{a + jb}{c + jd} = \frac{(a + jb)(c - jd)}{(c + jd)(c - jd)}$$
$$= \frac{(ac + bd) + j(bc - ad)}{c^2 + d^2}$$
$$\frac{7 + 5.2j}{3 + 4j} = \frac{\big((7)(3) + (5.2)(4)\big) + j\big((5.2)(3) - (7)(4)\big)}{(3)^2 + (4)^2}$$
$$= 1.672 - 0.496j \quad (1.7 - 0.5j)$$

The answer is (B).

3. POLAR COORDINATES

Equation 2.12: Polar Form of a Complex Number

$$x + jy = r(\cos\theta + j\sin\theta) = re^{j\theta} \qquad 2.12$$

Variations

$$z \equiv r(\cos\theta + i\sin\theta)$$
$$z \equiv r\operatorname{cis}\theta$$
$$z = r\angle\theta$$

Description

A complex number can be expressed in the *polar form* $r(\cos\theta + j\sin\theta)$, where θ is the angle from the x-axis and r is the distance from the origin. r and θ are the *polar coordinates* of the complex number. Another notation for the polar form of a complex number is $re^{j\theta}$.

Equation 2.13 and Eq. 2.14: Converting from Polar Form to Rectangular Form

$$x = r\cos\theta \qquad 2.13$$
$$y = r\sin\theta \qquad 2.14$$

Description

The rectangular form of a complex number, $x + jy$, can be determined from the complex number's polar coordinates r and θ using Eq. 2.13 and Eq. 2.14.

Equation 2.15 and Eq. 2.16: Converting from Rectangular Form to Polar Form

$$r = |x + jy| = \sqrt{x^2 + y^2} \qquad 2.15$$
$$\theta = \arctan(y/x) \qquad 2.16$$

Description

The polar form of a complex number, $r(\cos\theta + j\sin\theta)$, can be determined from the complex number's rectangular coordinates x and y using Eq. 2.15 and Eq. 2.16.

Example

The rectangular coordinates of a complex number are $(4, 6)$. What are the complex number's approximate polar coordinates?

(A) $(4.0, 33°)$

(B) $(4.0, 56°)$

(C) $(7.2, 33°)$

(D) $(7.2, 56°)$

Solution

The radius and angle of the polar form can be determined from the x- and y-coordinates using Eq. 2.15 and Eq. 2.16.

$$r = \sqrt{x^2 + y^2} = \sqrt{(4)^2 + (6)^2} = 7.211 \quad (7.2)$$

$$\theta = \arctan(y/x) = \arctan\frac{6}{4}$$

$$= 56.3° \quad (56°)$$

The answer is (D).

Equation 2.17 and Eq. 2.18: Multiplication and Division with Polar Forms

$$[r_1(\cos\theta_1 + j\sin\theta_1)][r_2(\cos\theta_2 + j\sin\theta_2)]$$
$$= r_1 r_2[\cos(\theta_1 + \theta_2) + j\sin(\theta_1 + \theta_2)] \qquad \text{2.17}$$

$$\frac{r_1(\cos\theta_1 + j\sin\theta_1)}{r_2(\cos\theta_2 + j\sin\theta_2)} = \frac{r_1}{r_2}\left[\begin{array}{c}\cos(\theta_1 - \theta_2) \\ + j\sin(\theta_1 - \theta_2)\end{array}\right] \qquad \text{2.18}$$

Variations

$$z_1 z_2 = (r_1 r_2)\angle(\theta_1 + \theta_2)$$
$$\frac{z_1}{z_2} = \frac{r_1}{r_2}\angle(\theta_1 - \theta_2)$$

Description

The multiplication and division rules defined for complex numbers expressed in rectangular form can be applied to complex numbers expressed in polar form. Using the trigonometric identities, these rules reduce to Eq. 2.17 and Eq. 2.18.

Equation 2.19: de Moivre's Formula

$$(x + jy)^n = [r(\cos\theta + j\sin\theta)]^n$$
$$= r^n(\cos n\theta + j\sin n\theta) \qquad \text{2.19}$$

Description

Equation 2.19 is *de Moivre's formula*. This equation is valid for any real number x and integer n.

Equation 2.20 Through Eq. 2.23: Euler's Equations

$$e^{j\theta} = \cos\theta + j\sin\theta \qquad \text{2.20}$$

$$e^{-j\theta} = \cos\theta - j\sin\theta \qquad \text{2.21}$$

$$\cos\theta = \frac{e^{j\theta} + e^{-j\theta}}{2} \qquad \text{2.22}$$

$$\sin\theta = \frac{e^{j\theta} - e^{-j\theta}}{2j} \qquad \text{2.23}$$

Description

Complex numbers can also be expressed in exponential form. The relationship of the exponential form to the trigonometric form is given by *Euler's equations*, also known as *Euler's identities*.

Example

If $j = \sqrt{-1}$, which of the following is equal to j^j?

(A) j^2

(B) e^{2j}

(C) -1

(D) $e^{-\pi/2}$

Solution

j is the imaginary unit vector, so $r = 1$ and $\theta = 90°(\pi/2)$ in Fig. 2.1. From Eq. 2.19,[2]

$$(j)^n = (\cos\theta + j\sin\theta)^n$$

From Eq. 2.20,

$$e^{j\theta} = \cos\theta + j\sin\theta$$

Since $\theta = \pi/2$,

$$j^j = \left(e^{j\pi/2}\right)^j = e^{j^2\pi/2} = e^{-\pi/2}$$

The answer is (D).

4. ROOTS

Equation 2.24: *k*th Roots of a Complex Number

$$w = \sqrt[k]{r}\left[\cos\left(\frac{\theta}{k} + n\frac{360°}{k}\right) + j\sin\left(\frac{\theta}{k} + n\frac{360°}{k}\right)\right] \qquad \text{2.24}$$

Description

Use Eq. 2.24 to find the *k*th root of the complex number $z = r(\cos\theta + j\sin\theta)$. n can be any integer number.

---

[2]For non-integer values of n, de Moivre's formula produces one possible solution.

Example

What is the cube root of the complex number $8e^{j60°}$?

- (A) $2(\cos 60° + j\sin 60°)$
- (B) $2(j\cos 20° + \sin 20°)$
- (C) $2.7(\cos 20° + j\sin 20°)$
- (D) $2(\cos(20° + 120°n) + j\sin(20° + 120°n))$

Solution

From Eq. 2.24, the kth root of a complex number is

$$w = \sqrt[k]{r}\left[\cos\left(\frac{\theta}{k} + n\frac{360°}{k}\right) + j\sin\left(\frac{\theta}{k} + n\frac{360°}{k}\right)\right]$$

$$= \sqrt[3]{8}\left(\begin{array}{c}\cos\left(\dfrac{60°}{3} + n\left(\dfrac{360°}{3}\right)\right) \\[2ex] + j\sin\left(\dfrac{60°}{3} + n\left(\dfrac{360°}{3}\right)\right)\end{array}\right)$$

$$= 2\big(\cos(20° + 120°n) + j\sin(20° + 120°n)\big)$$

$$[n = 0, 1, 2, ...]$$

The answer is (D).

5. MATRICES

A *matrix* is an ordered set of *entries* (*elements*) arranged rectangularly and set off by brackets. The entries can be variables or numbers. A matrix by itself has no particular value; it is merely a convenient method of representing a set of numbers.

The size of a matrix is given by the number of rows and columns, and the nomenclature $m \times n$ is used for a matrix with m rows and n columns. For a square matrix, the numbers of rows and columns are the same and are equal to the *order of the matrix*.

Matrices are designated by bold uppercase letters. Matrix entries are designated by lowercase letters with subscripts, for example, a_{ij}. The term a_{23} would be the entry in the second row and third column of matrix $\mathbf{A}$. The matrix $\mathbf{C}$ can also be designated as (c_{ij}), meaning "the matrix made up of c_{ij} entries."

Equation 2.25: Addition of Matrices

$$\begin{bmatrix} A & B & C \\ D & E & F \end{bmatrix} + \begin{bmatrix} G & H & I \\ J & K & L \end{bmatrix} = \begin{bmatrix} A{+}G & B{+}H & C{+}I \\ D{+}J & E{+}K & F{+}L \end{bmatrix} \quad \text{2.25}$$

Variation

$$\mathbf{C} = \mathbf{A} + \mathbf{B}$$
$$\equiv (c_{ij}) \equiv (a_{ij} + b_{ij})$$

Description

Addition and subtraction of two matrices are possible only if both matrices have the same number of rows and columns. They are accomplished by adding or subtracting the corresponding entries of the two matrices.

Equation 2.26: Multiplication of Matrices

$$\mathbf{C} = \begin{bmatrix} A & B \\ C & D \\ E & F \end{bmatrix} \cdot \begin{bmatrix} H & I \\ J & K \end{bmatrix}$$

$$= \begin{bmatrix} (A{\cdot}H + B{\cdot}J) & (A{\cdot}I + B{\cdot}K) \\ (C{\cdot}H + D{\cdot}J) & (C{\cdot}I + D{\cdot}K) \\ (E{\cdot}H + F{\cdot}J) & (E{\cdot}I + F{\cdot}K) \end{bmatrix} \quad \text{2.26}$$

Variations

$$\mathbf{C} = \mathbf{AB}$$

$$\mathbf{C} = \mathbf{A} \times \mathbf{B}$$

$$\mathbf{C} \equiv (c_{ij})$$

$$= \left(\sum_{l=1}^{n} a_{il}b_{lj}\right)$$

Description

A matrix can be multiplied by another matrix, but only if the left-hand matrix has the same number of columns as the right-hand matrix has rows. *Matrix multiplication* occurs by multiplying the elements in each left-hand matrix row by the entries in each corresponding right-hand matrix column, adding the products, and placing the sum at the intersection point of the participating row and column.

The commutative law does not apply to matrix multiplication. That is, $\mathbf{A} \times \mathbf{B}$ is not equivalent to $\mathbf{B} \times \mathbf{A}$.

Mathematics

Example

What is the matrix product **AB** of matrices **A** and **B**?

$$\mathbf{A} = \begin{bmatrix} 2 & 1 \\ 1 & 0 \end{bmatrix} \qquad \mathbf{B} = \begin{bmatrix} 4 & 3 \\ 2 & 1 \end{bmatrix}$$

(A) $\begin{bmatrix} 10 & 4 \\ 7 & 3 \end{bmatrix}$

(B) $\begin{bmatrix} 11 & 4 \\ 5 & 2 \end{bmatrix}$

(C) $\begin{bmatrix} 8 & 3 \\ 2 & 0 \end{bmatrix}$

(D) $\begin{bmatrix} 10 & 7 \\ 4 & 3 \end{bmatrix}$

Solution

Use Eq. 2.26. Multiply the elements of each row in matrix **A** by the elements of the corresponding column in matrix **B**.

$$\mathbf{C} = \begin{bmatrix} A & B \\ C & D \\ E & F \end{bmatrix} \cdot \begin{bmatrix} H & I \\ J & K \end{bmatrix} = \begin{bmatrix} (A{\cdot}H + B{\cdot}J) & (A{\cdot}I + B{\cdot}K) \\ (C{\cdot}H + D{\cdot}J) & (C{\cdot}I + D{\cdot}K) \\ (E{\cdot}H + F{\cdot}J) & (E{\cdot}I + F{\cdot}K) \end{bmatrix}$$

$$= \begin{bmatrix} 2\times4 + 1\times2 & 2\times3 + 1\times1 \\ 1\times4 + 0\times2 & 1\times3 + 0\times1 \end{bmatrix}$$

$$= \begin{bmatrix} 10 & 7 \\ 4 & 3 \end{bmatrix}$$

The answer is (D).

Equation 2.27: Transposes of Matrices

$$\mathbf{A} = \begin{bmatrix} A & B & C \\ D & E & F \end{bmatrix} \qquad \mathbf{A}^T = \begin{bmatrix} A & D \\ B & E \\ C & F \end{bmatrix} \qquad 2.27$$

Variation

$$B = \mathbf{A}^T$$

Description

The *transpose*, $\mathbf{A}^T$, of an $m \times n$ matrix **A** is an $n \times m$ matrix constructed by taking the ith row and making it the ith column.

Example

What is the transpose of matrix **A**?

$$\mathbf{A} = \begin{bmatrix} 5 & 8 & 5 & 8 \\ 8 & 7 & 6 & 2 \end{bmatrix}$$

(A) $\begin{bmatrix} 8 & 7 & 6 & 2 \\ 5 & 8 & 5 & 8 \end{bmatrix}$

(B) $\begin{bmatrix} 2 & 6 & 7 & 8 \\ 8 & 5 & 8 & 5 \end{bmatrix}$

(C) $\begin{bmatrix} 8 & 5 \\ 7 & 8 \\ 6 & 5 \\ 2 & 8 \end{bmatrix}$

(D) $\begin{bmatrix} 5 & 8 \\ 8 & 7 \\ 5 & 6 \\ 8 & 2 \end{bmatrix}$

Solution

The transpose of a matrix is constructed by taking the ith row and making it the ith column.

The answer is (D).

Equation 2.28: Determinants of 2×2 Matrices

$$\begin{vmatrix} a_1 & a_2 \\ b_1 & b_2 \end{vmatrix} = a_1 b_2 - a_2 b_1 \qquad 2.28$$

Variation

$$|\mathbf{A}| = \begin{vmatrix} a_1 & a_2 \\ b_1 & b_2 \end{vmatrix} = a_1 b_2 - a_2 b_1$$

Description

A *determinant* is a scalar calculated from a square matrix. The determinant of matrix **A** can be represented as $D\{\mathbf{A}\}$, $Det(\mathbf{A})$, or $|\mathbf{A}|$. The following rules can be used to simplify the calculation of determinants.

- If **A** has a row or column of zeros, the determinant is zero.
- If **A** has two identical rows or columns, the determinant is zero.
- If **B** is obtained from **A** by adding a multiple of a row (column) to another row (column) in **A**, then $|\mathbf{B}| = |\mathbf{A}|$.
- If **A** is *triangular* (a square matrix with zeros in all positions above or below the diagonal), the determinant is equal to the product of the diagonal entries.
- If **B** is obtained from **A** by multiplying one row or column in **A** by a scalar k, then $|\mathbf{B}| = k|\mathbf{A}|$.

- If **B** is obtained from the $n \times n$ matrix **A** by multiplying by the scalar matrix k, then $|\mathbf{B}| = |\mathbf{k} \times \mathbf{A}| = k^n |\mathbf{A}|$.

- If **B** is obtained from **A** by switching two rows or columns in **A**, then $|\mathbf{B}| = -|\mathbf{A}|$.

Calculation of determinants is laborious for all but the smallest or simplest of matrices. For a 2×2 matrix, the formula used to calculate the determinant is easy to remember.

Example

What is the determinant of matrix **A**?

$$\mathbf{A} = \begin{bmatrix} 3 & 6 \\ 2 & 4 \end{bmatrix}$$

(A) 0

(B) 15

(C) 14

(D) 26

Solution

From Eq. 2.28, for a square 2×2 matrix,

$$\begin{vmatrix} a_1 & a_2 \\ b_1 & b_2 \end{vmatrix} = a_1 b_2 - a_2 b_1$$

$$\begin{vmatrix} 3 & 6 \\ 2 & 4 \end{vmatrix} = 3 \times 4 - 6 \times 2$$

$$= 0$$

The answer is (A).

Equation 2.29: Determinants of 3×3 Matrices

$$\begin{vmatrix} a_1 & a_2 & a_3 \\ b_1 & b_2 & b_3 \\ c_1 & c_2 & c_3 \end{vmatrix} = \begin{matrix} a_1 b_2 c_3 + a_2 b_3 c_1 + a_3 b_1 c_2 - a_3 b_2 c_1 \\ - a_2 b_1 c_3 - a_1 b_3 c_2 \end{matrix} \quad \text{2.29}$$

Variations

$$\mathbf{A} = \begin{bmatrix} a_1 & a_2 & a_3 \\ b_1 & b_2 & b_3 \\ c_1 & c_2 & c_3 \end{bmatrix}$$

$$|\mathbf{A}| = a_1 b_2 c_3 + a_2 b_3 c_1 + a_3 b_1 c_2 - a_3 b_2 c_1 - a_2 b_1 c_3 - a_1 b_3 c_2$$

Description

In addition to the formula-based method expressed as Eq. 2.29, two methods are commonly used for calculating the determinants of 3×3 matrices by hand. The first uses an augmented matrix constructed from the original matrix and the first two columns. The determinant is

calculated as the sum of the products in the left-to-right downward diagonals less the sum of the products in the left-to-right upward diagonals.

$$\text{augmented } \mathbf{A} = \begin{bmatrix} a_1 & a_2 & a_3 & a_1 & a_2 \\ b_1 & b_2 & b_3 & b_1 & b_2 \\ c_1 & c_2 & c_3 & c_1 & c_2 \end{bmatrix}$$

The second method of calculating the determinant is somewhat slower than the first for a 3×3 matrix but illustrates the method that must be used to calculate determinants of 4×4 and larger matrices. This method is known as *expansion by cofactors* (cofactors are explained in the following section). One row (column) is selected as the base row (column). The selection is arbitrary, but the number of calculations required to obtain the determinant can be minimized by choosing the row (column) with the most zeros. The determinant is equal to the sum of the products of the entries in the base row (column) and their corresponding cofactors.

$$\mathbf{A} = \begin{bmatrix} a_1 & a_2 & a_3 \\ b_1 & b_2 & b_3 \\ c_1 & c_2 & c_3 \end{bmatrix} \quad \begin{bmatrix} \text{first column chosen} \\ \text{as base column} \end{bmatrix}$$

$$|\mathbf{A}| = a_1 \begin{vmatrix} b_2 & b_3 \\ c_2 & c_3 \end{vmatrix} - b_1 \begin{vmatrix} a_2 & a_3 \\ c_2 & c_3 \end{vmatrix} + c_1 \begin{vmatrix} a_2 & a_3 \\ b_2 & b_3 \end{vmatrix}$$

$$= a_1(b_2 c_3 - b_3 c_2) - b_1(a_2 c_3 - a_3 c_2) + c_1(a_2 b_3 - a_3 b_2)$$

$$= a_1 b_2 c_3 - a_1 b_3 c_2 - b_1 a_2 c_3 + b_1 a_3 c_2 + c_1 a_2 b_3 - c_1 a_3 b_2$$

Example

For the following set of equations, what is the determinant of the coefficient matrix?

$$10x + 3y + 10z = 5$$
$$8x - 2y + 9z = 5$$
$$8x + y - 10z = 5$$

(A) 598

(B) 620

(C) 714

(D) 806

Solution

Calculate the determinant of the coefficient matrix.

$$|\mathbf{A}| = \begin{vmatrix} a_1 & a_2 & a_3 \\ b_1 & b_2 & b_3 \\ c_1 & c_2 & c_3 \end{vmatrix}$$

$$= a_1b_2c_3 + a_2b_3c_1 + a_3b_1c_2 - a_3b_2c_1$$
$$- a_2b_1c_3 - a_1b_3c_2$$
$$= (10)(-2)(-10) + (3)(9)(8) + (10)(8)(1)$$
$$- (8)(-2)(10) - (1)(9)(10)$$
$$- (-10)(8)(3)$$
$$= 806$$

The answer is (D).

Inverse of a Matrix

The *inverse*, $\mathbf{A}^{-1}$, of an invertible matrix, $\mathbf{A}$, is a matrix such that the product $\mathbf{AA}^{-1}$ produces a matrix with ones along its diagonal and zeros elsewhere (i.e., above and below the diagonal). Only square matrices have inverses, but not all square matrices are invertible (i.e., have inverses). The product of a matrix and its inverse produces an identity matrix. For 3×3 matrices,

$$\mathbf{AA}^{-1} = \mathbf{I} = \begin{bmatrix} 1 & 0 & 0 \\ 0 & 1 & 0 \\ 0 & 0 & 1 \end{bmatrix}$$

The inverse of a 2×2 matrix is easily determined by the following formula.

$$\mathbf{A} = \begin{bmatrix} a_1 & a_2 \\ b_1 & b_2 \end{bmatrix}$$

$$\mathbf{A}^{-1} = \frac{\begin{bmatrix} b_2 & -a_2 \\ -b_1 & a_1 \end{bmatrix}}{|\mathbf{A}|}$$

Equation 2.30: Identity Matrix

$$[\mathbf{A}][\mathbf{A}]^{-1} = [\mathbf{A}]^{-1}[\mathbf{A}] = [\mathbf{I}] \qquad 2.30$$

Variation

$$\mathbf{A} \times \mathbf{A}^{-1} = \mathbf{A}^{-1} \times \mathbf{A} = \mathbf{I}$$

Description

The product of a matrix $\mathbf{A}$ and its *inverse*, $\mathbf{A}^{-1}$, is the *identity matrix*, $\mathbf{I}$. A matrix has an inverse if and only if it is *nonsingular* (i.e., its determinant is nonzero).

Example

Using the property that $|\mathbf{AB}| = |\mathbf{A}||\mathbf{B}|$ for two square matrices, what is $|\mathbf{A}^{-1}|$ in terms of $|\mathbf{A}|$ for any invertible square matrix $\mathbf{A}$?

(A) $\dfrac{1}{|\mathbf{A}|}$

(B) $\dfrac{1}{|\mathbf{A}^{-1}|}$

(C) $\dfrac{|\mathbf{A}|}{|\mathbf{A}^{-1}|}$

(D) $\dfrac{|\mathbf{A}^{-1}|}{|\mathbf{A}|}$

Solution

Since $|\mathbf{AB}| = |\mathbf{A}||\mathbf{B}|$,

$$|\mathbf{AA}^{-1}| = |\mathbf{A}||\mathbf{A}^{-1}|$$

Solving for $|\mathbf{A}^{-1}|$,

$$|\mathbf{A}^{-1}| = \frac{|\mathbf{AA}^{-1}|}{|\mathbf{A}|}$$

But $|\mathbf{AA}^{-1}| = |\mathbf{I}| = 1$. Therefore,

$$|\mathbf{A}^{-1}| = \frac{|\mathbf{AA}^{-1}|}{|\mathbf{A}|} = \frac{1}{|\mathbf{A}|}$$

The answer is (A).

Cofactors

Cofactors are determinants of submatrices associated with particular entries in the original square matrix. The *minor* of entry a_{ij} is the determinant of a submatrix resulting from the elimination of the single row i and the single column j. For example, the minor corresponding to entry a_{12} in a 3×3 matrix $\mathbf{A}$ is the determinant of the matrix created by eliminating row 1 and column 2.

$$\text{minor of } a_{12} = \begin{vmatrix} a_{21} & a_{23} \\ a_{31} & a_{33} \end{vmatrix}$$

The cofactor of entry a_{ij} is the minor of a_{ij} multiplied by either $+1$ or -1, depending on the position of the entry (i.e., the cofactor either exactly equals the minor or it differs only in sign). The sign of the cofactor of a_{ij} is positive if $(i+j)$ is even, and it is negative if $(i+j)$ is odd. For a 3×3 matrix, the multipliers in each position are

$$\begin{bmatrix} +1 & -1 & +1 \\ -1 & +1 & -1 \\ +1 & -1 & +1 \end{bmatrix}$$

For example, the cofactor of entry a_{12} in a 3×3 matrix $\mathbf{A}$ is

$$\text{cofactor of } a_{12} = -\begin{vmatrix} a_{21} & a_{23} \\ a_{31} & a_{33} \end{vmatrix}$$

Equation 2.31: Classical Adjoint

$$\mathbf{B} = \mathbf{A}^{-1} = \frac{\text{adj}(\mathbf{A})}{|\mathbf{A}|} \qquad \text{2.31}$$

Description

The *classical adjoint*, or *adjugate*, is the transpose of the cofactor matrix. The resulting matrix can be designated as $\mathbf{A}_{\text{adj}}$, $\text{adj}\{\mathbf{A}\}$, or $\mathbf{A}^{\text{adj}}$.

For a 3×3 or larger matrix, the inverse is determined by dividing every entry in the classical adjoint by the determinant of the original matrix, as shown in Eq. 2.31.

Example

The cofactor matrix of matrix $\mathbf{A}$ is $\mathbf{C}$.

$$\mathbf{A} = \begin{bmatrix} 4 & 2 & 3 \\ 3 & 2 & 2 \\ 2 & 1 & 4 \end{bmatrix} \qquad \mathbf{C} = \begin{bmatrix} 6 & -8 & -1 \\ -5 & 10 & 0 \\ -2 & 1 & 2 \end{bmatrix}$$

What is the inverse of matrix $\mathbf{A}$?

(A) $\begin{bmatrix} 0.25 & 0 & 0 \\ 0 & 0.50 & 0 \\ 0 & 0 & 0.25 \end{bmatrix}$

(B) $\begin{bmatrix} 0.25 & 0.50 & 0.33 \\ 0.33 & 0.50 & 0.50 \\ 0.50 & 1.00 & 0.25 \end{bmatrix}$

(C) $\begin{bmatrix} 1.2 & -1.0 & -0.40 \\ -1.6 & 2.0 & 0.20 \\ -0.20 & 0 & 0.40 \end{bmatrix}$

(D) $\begin{bmatrix} 0.80 & 0.40 & -0.60 \\ 0.20 & -0.40 & 0.40 \\ -0.40 & 0.60 & 0.80 \end{bmatrix}$

Solution

The classical adjoint is the transpose of the cofactor matrix.

$$\text{adj}(\mathbf{A}) = \mathbf{C}^T = \begin{bmatrix} 6 & -5 & -2 \\ -8 & 10 & 1 \\ -1 & 0 & 2 \end{bmatrix}$$

Using Eq. 2.28, calculate the determinant of $\mathbf{A}$ by expanding along the top row.

$$\begin{aligned} |\mathbf{A}| &= (4)(8-2) - (2)(12-4) + (3)(3-4) \\ &= 24 - 16 - 3 \\ &= 5 \end{aligned}$$

Using Eq. 2.31, divide the classical adjoint by the determinant.

$$\begin{aligned} \mathbf{A}^{-1} &= \frac{\text{adj}(\mathbf{A})}{|\mathbf{A}|} \\ &= \frac{\begin{bmatrix} 6 & -5 & -2 \\ -8 & 10 & 1 \\ -1 & 0 & 2 \end{bmatrix}}{5} \\ &= \begin{bmatrix} 1.2 & -1.0 & -0.40 \\ -1.6 & 2.0 & 0.20 \\ -0.20 & 0 & 0.40 \end{bmatrix} \end{aligned}$$

The answer is (C).

6. WRITING SIMULTANEOUS LINEAR EQUATIONS IN MATRIX FORM

Matrices are used to simplify the presentation and solution of sets of simultaneous linear equations. For example, the following three methods of presenting simultaneous linear equations are equivalent:

$$\begin{aligned} a_{11}x_1 + a_{12}x_2 &= b_1 \\ a_{21}x_1 + a_{22}x_2 &= b_2 \end{aligned}$$

$$\begin{bmatrix} a_{11} & a_{12} \\ a_{21} & a_{22} \end{bmatrix} \begin{bmatrix} x_1 \\ x_2 \end{bmatrix} = \begin{bmatrix} b_1 \\ b_2 \end{bmatrix}$$

$$\mathbf{AX} = \mathbf{B}$$

In the second and third representations, $\mathbf{A}$ is known as the *coefficient matrix*, $\mathbf{X}$ as the *variable matrix*, and $\mathbf{B}$ as the *constant matrix*.

Not all systems of simultaneous equations have solutions, and those that do may not have unique solutions. The existence of a solution can be determined by calculating the determinant of the coefficient matrix. Solution-existence rules are summarized in Table 2.1.

- If the system of linear equations is homogeneous (i.e., **B** is a zero matrix) and $|\mathbf{A}|$ is zero, there are an infinite number of solutions.

- If the system is homogeneous and $|\mathbf{A}|$ is nonzero, only the trivial solution exists.

- If the system of linear equations is nonhomogeneous (i.e., **B** is not a zero matrix) and $|\mathbf{A}|$ is nonzero, there is a unique solution to the set of simultaneous equations.

- If $|\mathbf{A}|$ is zero, a nonhomogeneous system of simultaneous equations may still have a solution. The requirement is that the determinants of all substitutional matrices (mentioned in Sec. 2.7) are zero, in which case there will be an infinite number of solutions. Otherwise, no solution exists.

Table 2.1 *Solution Existence Rules for Simultaneous Equations*

	B $= 0$	**B** $\neq 0$
$|\mathbf{A}| = 0$	infinite number of solutions (linearly dependent equations)	either an infinite number of solutions or no solution at all
$|\mathbf{A}| \neq 0$	trivial solution only ($x_i = 0$)	unique nonzero solution

7. SOLVING SIMULTANEOUS LINEAR EQUATIONS WITH CRAMER'S RULE

Gauss-Jordan elimination can be used to obtain the solution to a set of simultaneous linear equations. The coefficient matrix is augmented by the constant matrix. Then, elementary row operations are used to reduce the coefficient matrix to canonical form. All of the operations performed on the coefficient matrix are performed on the constant matrix. The variable values that satisfy the simultaneous equations will be the entries in the constant matrix when the coefficient matrix is in canonical form.

Determinants are used to calculate the solution to linear simultaneous equations through a procedure known as *Cramer's rule*.

The procedure is to calculate determinants of the original coefficient matrix **A** and of the n matrices resulting from the systematic replacement of a column in **A** by the constant matrix **B** (i.e., the *substitutional matrices*). For a system of three equations in three unknowns, there are three substitutional matrices, $\mathbf{A}_1$, $\mathbf{A}_2$, and $\mathbf{A}_3$, as well as the original coefficient matrix, for a total of four matrices whose determinants must be calculated.

The values of the unknowns that simultaneously satisfy all of the linear equations are

$$x_1 = \frac{|\mathbf{A}_1|}{|\mathbf{A}|}$$

$$x_2 = \frac{|\mathbf{A}_2|}{|\mathbf{A}|}$$

$$x_3 = \frac{|\mathbf{A}_3|}{|\mathbf{A}|}$$

Example

Using Cramer's rule, what values of x, y, and z will satisfy the following system of simultaneous equations?

$$2x + 3y - 4z = 1$$
$$3x - y - 2z = 4$$
$$4x - 7y - 6z = -7$$

(A) $x = 1$, $y = -4$, $z = -1$

(B) $x = 1$, $y = 3$, $z = 1$

(C) $x = 3$, $y = -2$, $z = 4$

(D) $x = 3$, $y = 1$, $z = 2$

Solution

The determinant of the coefficient matrix is

$$|\mathbf{A}| = \begin{vmatrix} 2 & 3 & -4 \\ 3 & -1 & -2 \\ 4 & -7 & -6 \end{vmatrix} = 82$$

The determinants of the substitutional matrices are

$$|\mathbf{A}_1| = \begin{vmatrix} 1 & 3 & -4 \\ 4 & -1 & -2 \\ -7 & -7 & -6 \end{vmatrix} = 246$$

$$|\mathbf{A}_2| = \begin{vmatrix} 2 & 1 & -4 \\ 3 & 4 & -2 \\ 4 & -7 & -6 \end{vmatrix} = 82$$

$$|\mathbf{A}_3| = \begin{vmatrix} 2 & 3 & 1 \\ 3 & -1 & 4 \\ 4 & -7 & -7 \end{vmatrix} = 164$$

The values of x, y, and z that will satisfy the linear equations are

$$x = \frac{246}{82} = 3$$

$$y = \frac{82}{82} = 1$$

$$z = \frac{164}{82} = 2$$

The answer is (D).

8. VECTORS

A physical property or quantity can be a scalar, vector, or tensor. A *scalar* has only magnitude. Knowing its value is sufficient to define a scalar. Mass, enthalpy, density, and speed are examples of scalars.

Force, momentum, displacement, and velocity are examples of *vectors*. A vector is a directed straight line with a specific magnitude. A vector is specified completely by its direction (consisting of the vector's *angular orientation* and its *sense*) and magnitude. A vector's *point of application* (*terminal point*) is not needed to define the vector. Two vectors with the same direction and magnitude are said to be equal vectors even though their *lines of action* may be different.

Unit vectors are vectors with unit magnitudes (i.e., magnitudes of one). They are represented in the same notation as other vectors. Although they can have any direction, the standard unit vectors (i.e., the *Cartesian unit vectors*, **i**, **j**, and **k**) have the directions of the x-, y-, and z-coordinate axes, respectively, and constitute the *Cartesian triad*.

A *tensor* has magnitude in a specific direction, but the direction is not unique. A tensor in three-dimensional space is defined by nine components, compared with the three that are required to define vectors. These components are written in matrix form. Stress, dielectric constant, and magnetic susceptibility are examples of tensors.

Equation 2.32: Components of a Vector

$$\mathbf{A} = a_x\mathbf{i} + a_y\mathbf{j} + a_z\mathbf{k} \qquad 2.32$$

Description

A vector **A** can be written in terms of unit vectors and its components. (See Fig. 2.2.)

If a vector is based (i.e., starts) at the origin $(0, 0, 0)$, its magnitude (length) can be calculated as

$$|\mathbf{A}| = L_{\mathbf{A}}$$

$$= \sqrt{a_x^2 + a_y^2 + a_z^2}$$

Figure 2.2 Components of a Vector

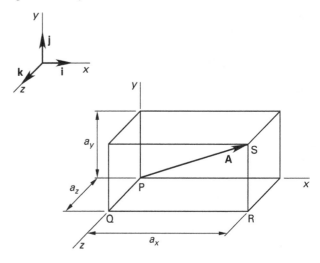

Example

Find the unit vector (i.e., the direction vector) associated with the origin-based vector $18\mathbf{i} + 3\mathbf{j} + 29\mathbf{k}$.

(A) $0.525\mathbf{i} + 0.088\mathbf{j} + 0.846\mathbf{k}$

(B) $0.892\mathbf{i} + 0.178\mathbf{j} + 0.416\mathbf{k}$

(C) $1.342\mathbf{i} + 0.868\mathbf{j} + 2.437\mathbf{k}$

(D) $6\mathbf{i} + \mathbf{j} + \frac{29}{3}\mathbf{k}$

Solution

The unit vector of a particular vector is the vector itself divided by its length.

$$\text{unit vector} = \frac{18\mathbf{i} + 3\mathbf{j} + 29\mathbf{k}}{\sqrt{(18)^2 + (3)^2 + (29)^2}}$$

$$= 0.525\mathbf{i} + 0.088\mathbf{j} + 0.846\mathbf{k}$$

The answer is (A).

Equation 2.33: Vector Addition

$$\mathbf{A} + \mathbf{B} = (a_x + b_x)\mathbf{i} + (a_y + b_y)\mathbf{j} + (a_z + b_z)\mathbf{k} \qquad 2.33$$

Description

Addition of two vectors by the *polygon method* is accomplished by placing the tail of the second vector at the head (tip) of the first. The sum (i.e., the *resultant vector*) is a vector extending from the tail of the first vector to the head of the second (see Fig. 2.3). Alternatively, the two vectors can be considered as two adjacent sides of a parallelogram, while the sum represents the diagonal. This is known as addition by the *parallelogram method*. The components of the resultant vector are the sums of the components of the added vectors.

Figure 2.3 *Addition of Two Vectors*

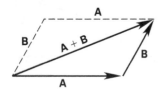

Example

What is the sum of the two vectors $5\mathbf{i} + 3\mathbf{j} - 7\mathbf{k}$ and $10\mathbf{i} - 12\mathbf{j} + 5\mathbf{k}$?

(A) $8\mathbf{i} - 7\mathbf{j} - \mathbf{k}$

(B) $10\mathbf{i} - 9\mathbf{j} + 3\mathbf{k}$

(C) $15\mathbf{i} - 9\mathbf{j} - 2\mathbf{k}$

(D) $15\mathbf{i} + 7\mathbf{j} - 3\mathbf{k}$

Solution

Use Eq. 2.33.

$$\begin{aligned}\mathbf{A} + \mathbf{B} &= (a_x + b_x)\mathbf{i} + (a_y + b_y)\mathbf{j} + (a_z + b_z)\mathbf{k} \\ &= (5 + 10)\mathbf{i} + (3 + (-12))\mathbf{j} + ((-7) + 5)\mathbf{k} \\ &= 15\mathbf{i} - 9\mathbf{j} - 2\mathbf{k}\end{aligned}$$

The answer is (C).

Equation 2.34: Vector Subtraction

$$\mathbf{A} - \mathbf{B} = (a_x - b_x)\mathbf{i} + (a_y - b_y)\mathbf{j} + (a_z - b_z)\mathbf{k} \qquad 2.34$$

Description

Vector subtraction is similar to vector addition, as shown by Eq. 2.34.

Equation 2.35 and Eq. 2.36: Vector Dot Product

$$\mathbf{A} \cdot \mathbf{B} = a_x b_x + a_y b_y + a_z b_z \qquad 2.35$$

$$\mathbf{A} \cdot \mathbf{B} = |\mathbf{A}| |\mathbf{B}| \cos \theta = \mathbf{B} \cdot \mathbf{A} \qquad 2.36$$

Variation

$$\theta = \arccos\left(\frac{\mathbf{A} \cdot \mathbf{B}}{|\mathbf{A}| |\mathbf{B}|}\right) = \arccos\left(\frac{a_x b_x + a_y b_y + a_z b_z}{|\mathbf{A}| |\mathbf{B}|}\right)$$

Description

The *dot product* (*scalar product*) of two vectors is a scalar that is proportional to the length of the projection of the first vector onto the second vector. (See Fig. 2.4.)

Use the variation to find the angle, θ, formed between two given vectors.

Figure 2.4 *Vector Dot Product*

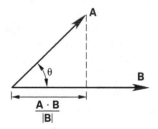

The dot product can be calculated in two ways, as Eq. 2.35 and Eq. 2.36 indicate. θ is limited to $180°$ and is the acute angle between the two vectors.

Example

What is the dot product, $\mathbf{A} \cdot \mathbf{B}$, of the vectors $\mathbf{A} = 2\mathbf{i} + 4\mathbf{j} + 8\mathbf{k}$ and $\mathbf{B} = -2\mathbf{i} + \mathbf{j} - 4\mathbf{k}$?

(A) $-4\mathbf{i} + 4\mathbf{j} - 32\mathbf{k}$

(B) $-4\mathbf{i} - 4\mathbf{j} - 32\mathbf{k}$

(C) -40

(D) -32

Solution

Use Eq. 2.35.

$$\begin{aligned}\mathbf{A} \cdot \mathbf{B} &= a_x b_x + a_y b_y + a_z b_z \\ &= (2)(-2) + (4)(1) + (8)(-4) \\ &= -32\end{aligned}$$

The answer is (D).

Equation 2.37 and Eq. 2.38: Vector Cross Product

$$\mathbf{A} \times \mathbf{B} = \begin{vmatrix} \mathbf{i} & \mathbf{j} & \mathbf{k} \\ a_x & a_y & a_z \\ b_x & b_y & b_z \end{vmatrix} = -\mathbf{B} \times \mathbf{A} \qquad 2.37$$

$$\mathbf{A} \times \mathbf{B} = |\mathbf{A}| |\mathbf{B}| \mathbf{n} \sin \theta \qquad 2.38$$

Description

The *cross product (vector product)*, $\mathbf{A} \times \mathbf{B}$, of two vectors is a vector that is orthogonal (perpendicular) to the plane of the two vectors. (See Fig. 2.5.) The unit vector representation of the cross product can be calculated as a third-order determinant. $\mathbf{n}$ is the unit vector in the direction perpendicular to the plane containing $\mathbf{A}$ and $\mathbf{B}$.

Figure 2.5 *Vector Cross Product*

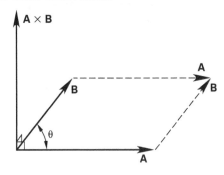

Example

What is the cross product, $\mathbf{A} \times \mathbf{B}$, of vectors $\mathbf{A}$ and $\mathbf{B}$?

$$\mathbf{A} = \mathbf{i} + 4\mathbf{j} + 6\mathbf{k}$$
$$\mathbf{B} = 2\mathbf{i} + 3\mathbf{j} + 5\mathbf{k}$$

(A) $\mathbf{i} - \mathbf{j} - \mathbf{k}$

(B) $-\mathbf{i} + \mathbf{j} + \mathbf{k}$

(C) $2\mathbf{i} + 7\mathbf{j} - 5\mathbf{k}$

(D) $2\mathbf{i} + 7\mathbf{j} + 5\mathbf{k}$

Solution

Use Eq. 2.37. The cross product of two vectors is the determinant of a third-order matrix as shown.

$$\mathbf{A} \times \mathbf{B} = \begin{vmatrix} \mathbf{i} & \mathbf{j} & \mathbf{k} \\ a_x & a_y & a_z \\ b_x & b_y & b_z \end{vmatrix} = \begin{vmatrix} \mathbf{i} & \mathbf{j} & \mathbf{k} \\ 1 & 4 & 6 \\ 2 & 3 & 5 \end{vmatrix}$$

$$= \mathbf{i}[(4)(5) - (6)(3)] - \mathbf{j}[(1)(5) - (6)(2)]$$
$$\quad + \mathbf{k}[(1)(3) - (4)(2)]$$
$$= 2\mathbf{i} + 7\mathbf{j} - 5\mathbf{k}$$

The answer is (C).

9. VECTOR IDENTITIES

Equation 2.39 Through Eq. 2.41: Dot Product Identities

$$\mathbf{A} \cdot \mathbf{B} = \mathbf{B} \cdot \mathbf{A} \qquad 2.39$$

$$\mathbf{A} \cdot (\mathbf{B} + \mathbf{C}) = \mathbf{A} \cdot \mathbf{B} + \mathbf{A} \cdot \mathbf{C} \qquad 2.40$$

$$\mathbf{A} \cdot \mathbf{A} = |\mathbf{A}|^2 \qquad 2.41$$

Description

The dot product for vectors is commutative and distributive, as shown by Eq. 2.39 and Eq. 2.40. Equation 2.41 gives the dot product of a vector with itself, the square of its magnitude.

Equation 2.42: Dot Product of Parallel Unit Vectors

$$\mathbf{i} \cdot \mathbf{i} = \mathbf{j} \cdot \mathbf{j} = \mathbf{k} \cdot \mathbf{k} = 1 \qquad 2.42$$

Description

As indicated in Eq. 2.42, the dot product of two parallel unit vectors is one.

Example

What is the dot product $\mathbf{A} \cdot \mathbf{B}$ of vectors $\mathbf{A} = 3\mathbf{i}$ and $\mathbf{B} = 2\mathbf{i}$?

(A) –6

(B) –5

(C) 5

(D) 6

Solution

Use Eq. 2.42.

$$\mathbf{A} \cdot \mathbf{B} = 3\mathbf{i} \cdot 2\mathbf{i} = (3 \cdot 2)\mathbf{i} \cdot \mathbf{i} = (6)(1) = 6$$

The answer is (D).

Equation 2.43: Dot Product of Orthogonal Vectors

$$\mathbf{i} \cdot \mathbf{j} = \mathbf{j} \cdot \mathbf{k} = \mathbf{k} \cdot \mathbf{i} = 0 \qquad 2.43$$

Description

The dot product can be used to determine whether a vector is a unit vector and to show that two vectors are orthogonal (perpendicular). As indicated in Eq. 2.43, the dot product of two non-null (nonzero) orthogonal vectors is zero.

Equation 2.44 Through Eq. 2.46: Cross Product Identities

$$\mathbf{A} \times \mathbf{B} = -\mathbf{B} \times \mathbf{A} \qquad 2.44$$

$$\mathbf{A} \times (\mathbf{B} + \mathbf{C}) = (\mathbf{A} \times \mathbf{B}) + (\mathbf{A} \times \mathbf{C}) \qquad 2.45$$

$$(\mathbf{B} + \mathbf{C}) \times \mathbf{A} = (\mathbf{B} \times \mathbf{A}) + (\mathbf{C} \times \mathbf{A}) \qquad 2.46$$

Description

The vector cross product is distributive, as demonstrated in Eq. 2.45 and Eq. 2.46. However, as Eq. 2.44 shows, it is not commutative.

Equation 2.47: Cross Product of Parallel Unit Vectors

$$\mathbf{i} \times \mathbf{i} = \mathbf{j} \times \mathbf{j} = \mathbf{k} \times \mathbf{k} = 0 \qquad 2.47$$

Description

If two non-null vectors are parallel, their cross product will be zero.

Equation 2.48 and Eq. 2.49: Cross Product of Normal Unit Vectors

$$\mathbf{i} \times \mathbf{j} = \mathbf{k} = -\mathbf{j} \times \mathbf{i} \qquad 2.48$$

$$\mathbf{k} \times \mathbf{i} = \mathbf{j} = -\mathbf{i} \times \mathbf{k} \qquad 2.49$$

Description

If two non-null vectors are normal (perpendicular), their vector cross product will be perpendicular to both vectors.

10. PROGRESSIONS AND SERIES

A *progression* or *sequence*, $\{\mathbf{A}\}$, is an ordered set of numbers a_i, such as 1, 4, 9, 16, 25, ... The *terms* in a sequence can be all positive, negative, or of alternating signs. l is the last term and is also known as the *general term* of the sequence.

$$\{\mathbf{A}\} = a_1, a_2, a_3, \ldots, l$$

A sequence is said to *diverge* (i.e., be *divergent*) if the terms approach infinity, and it is said to *converge* (i.e., be *convergent*) if the terms approach any finite value (including zero).

A *series* is the sum of terms in a sequence. There are two types of series: A *finite series* has a finite number of terms. An *infinite series* has an infinite number of terms, but this does not imply that the sum is infinite. The main tasks associated with series are determining the sum of the terms and determining whether the series

converges. A series is said to converge if the sum, S_n, of its terms exists. A finite series is always convergent. An infinite series may be convergent.

Equation 2.50 and Eq. 2.51: Arithmetic Progression

$$l = a + (n-1)d \qquad 2.50$$

$$S = n(a+l)/2 = n[2a+(n-1)d]/2 \qquad 2.51$$

Description

The *arithmetic progression* is a standard sequence that diverges. It has the form shown in Eq. 2.50.

In Eq. 2.50 and Eq. 2.51, a is the *first term*, d is a constant called the *common difference*, and n is the number of terms.

The difference of adjacent terms is constant in an arithmetic progression. The sum of terms in a finite arithmetic series is shown by Eq. 2.51.

Example

What is the sum of the following finite sequence of terms?

$$18, 25, 32, 39, \ldots, 67$$

(A) 181

(B) 213

(C) 234

(D) 340

Solution

Each term is 7 more than the previous term. This is an arithmetic sequence. The general mathematical representation for an arithmetic sequence is

$$l = a + (n-1)d$$

In this case, the difference term is $d = 7$. The first term is $a = 18$, and the last term is $l = 67$.

$$\begin{aligned} l &= a + (n-1)d \\ n &= \frac{l-a}{d} + 1 \\ &= \frac{67-18}{7} + 1 \\ &= 8 \end{aligned}$$

The sum of n terms is

$$S = n[2a + (n-1)d]/2$$
$$= \frac{(8)((2)(18) + (8-1)(7))}{2}$$
$$= 340$$

The answer is (D).

Equation 2.52 Through Eq. 2.55: Geometric Progression

$$l = ar^{n-1} \qquad 2.52$$

$$S = a(1 - r^n)/(1 - r) \quad [r \neq 1] \qquad 2.53$$

$$S = (a - rl)/(1 - r) \quad [r \neq 1] \qquad 2.54$$

$$\lim_{n \to \infty} S_n = a/(1 - r) \quad [|r| < 1] \qquad 2.55$$

Variations

$$S_n = \sum_{i=1}^{n} ar^{i-1} = \frac{a - rl}{1 - r} = \frac{a(1 - r^n)}{1 - r}$$

$$S_n = \sum_{i=1}^{\infty} ar^{i-1} = \frac{a}{1 - r}$$

Description

The *geometric progression* is another standard sequence. The quotient of adjacent terms is constant in a geometric progression. It converges for $-1 < r < 1$ and diverges otherwise.

In Eq. 2.52 through Eq. 2.55, a is the first term, and r is known as the *common ratio*.

The sum of a finite geometric series is given by Eq. 2.53 and Eq. 2.54. The sum of an infinite geometric series is given by Eq. 2.55.

Example

What is the sum of the following geometric sequence?

$$32, 80, 200, \ldots, 19{,}531.25$$

(A) 21,131.25

(B) 24,718.25

(C) 31,250.00

(D) 32,530.75

Solution

The common ratio is

$$r = \frac{80}{32} = \frac{200}{80} = 2.5$$

Since the ratio and both the initial and final terms are known, the sum can be found using Eq. 2.54.

$$S = (a - rl)/(1 - r) = \frac{32 - (2.5)(19{,}531.25)}{1 - 2.5}$$
$$= 32{,}530.75$$

The answer is (D).

Equation 2.56 Through Eq. 2.59: Properties of Series

$$\sum_{i=1}^{n} c = nc \qquad 2.56$$

$$\sum_{i=1}^{n} cx_i = c\sum_{i=1}^{n} x_i \qquad 2.57$$

$$\sum_{i=1}^{n}(x_i + y_i - z_i) = \sum_{i=1}^{n} x_i + \sum_{i=1}^{n} y_i - \sum_{i=1}^{n} z_i \qquad 2.58$$

$$\sum_{x=1}^{n} x = (n + n^2)/2 \qquad 2.59$$

Description

Equation 2.56 through Eq. 2.59 list some basic properties of series. The terms x_i, y_i, and z_i represent general terms in any series. Equation 2.56 describes the obvious result of n repeated additions of a constant, c. Equation 2.57 shows that the product of a constant, c, and a serial summation of series terms is distributive. Equation 2.58 shows that addition of series is associative. Equation 2.59 gives the sum of n consecutive integers. This is not really a property of series in general; it is the property of a special kind of arithmetic sequence. It is a useful identity for use with *sum-of-the-years' depreciation*.

Equation 2.60: Power Series

$$\sum_{i=0}^{\infty} a_i(x - a)^i \qquad 2.60$$

Variation

$$\sum_{i=1}^{n} a_i x^{i-1} = a_1 + a_2 x + a_3 x^2 + \cdots + a_n x^{n-1}$$

Description

A *power series* is a series of the form shown in Eq. 2.60. The *interval of convergence* of a power series consists of the values of x for which the series is convergent. Due to the exponentiation of terms, an infinite power series can only be convergent in the interval $-1 < x < 1$.

A power series may be used to represent a function that is continuous over the interval of convergence of the series. The *power series representation* may be used to find the derivative or integral of that function.

Power series behave similarly to polynomials: They may be added together, subtracted from each other, multiplied together, or divided term by term within the interval of convergence. They may also be differentiated and integrated within their interval of convergence. If $f(x) = \sum_{i=1}^{n} a_i x^i$, then over the interval of convergence,

$$f'(x) = \sum_{i=1}^{n} \frac{d(a_i x^i)}{dx}$$

$$\int f(x)\, dx = \sum_{i=1}^{n} \int a_i x^i\, dx$$

Equation 2.61: Taylor's Series

$$f(x) = f(a) + \frac{f'(a)}{1!}(x-a) + \frac{f''(a)}{2!}(x-a)^2$$
$$+ \cdots + \frac{f^{(n)}(a)}{n!}(x-a)^n + \cdots$$

2.61

Description

Taylor's series (*Taylor's formula*), Eq. 2.61, can be used to expand a function around a point (i.e., to approximate the function at one point based on the function's value at another point). The approximation consists of a series, each term composed of a derivative of the original function and a polynomial. Using Taylor's formula requires that the original function be continuous in the interval $[a, b]$. To expand a function, $f(x)$, around a point, a, in order to obtain $f(b)$, use Eq. 2.61.

If $a = 0$, Eq. 2.61 is known as a *Maclaurin series*.

To be a useful approximation, two requirements must be met: (1) Point a must be relatively close to point b, and (2) the function and its derivatives must be known or be easy to calculate.

Example

Taylor's series is used to expand the function $f(x)$ about $a = 0$ to obtain $f(b)$.

$$f(x) = \frac{1}{3x^3 + 4x + 8}$$

What are the first two terms of Taylor's series?

(A) $\dfrac{1}{16} + \dfrac{b}{8}$

(B) $\dfrac{1}{8} - \dfrac{b}{16}$

(C) $\dfrac{1}{8} + \dfrac{b}{16}$

(D) $\dfrac{1}{4} - \dfrac{b}{16}$

Solution

The first two coefficient terms of Taylor's series are

$$f(0) = \frac{1}{(3)(0)^3 + (4)(0) + 8}$$
$$= 1/8$$

$$f'(x) = \frac{-(9x^2 + 4)}{(3x^3 + 4x + 8)^2}$$

$$f'(0) = \frac{-((9)(0)^2 + 4)}{((3)(0)^3 + (4)(0) + 8)^2} = \frac{-4}{64} = -1/16$$

Using Eq. 2.61, find the first two complete terms of Taylor's series.

$$f(b) = f(a) + \frac{f'(a)}{1!}(b - a)$$

$$= \frac{1}{8} + \frac{\left(\dfrac{-1}{16}\right)(b - 0)}{1}$$

$$= \frac{1}{8} - \frac{b}{16}$$

The answer is (B).

3 Calculus

1. DERIVATIVES

In most cases, it is possible to transform a continuous function, $f(x_1, x_2, x_3 \ldots)$, of one or more independent variables into a derivative function. In simple two-dimensional cases, the *derivative* can be interpreted as the slope (tangent or rate of change) of the curve described by the original function.

Equation 3.1 Through Eq. 3.3: Definitions of the Derivative

$$y' = \underset{\Delta x \to 0}{\text{limit}} [(\Delta y)/(\Delta x)] \qquad 3.1$$

$$y' = \underset{\Delta x \to 0}{\text{limit}} \{ [f(x + \Delta x) - f(x)]/(\Delta x) \} \qquad 3.2$$

$$y' = \text{the slope of the curve } f(x) \qquad 3.3$$

Variation

$$f'(x) = \lim_{\Delta x \to 0} \left(\frac{f(x + \Delta x) - f(x)}{\Delta x} \right)$$

Description

Since the slope of a curve depends on x, the derivative function will also depend on x. The derivative, $f'(x)$, of a function $f(x)$ is defined mathematically by the variation given here. However, limit theory is seldom needed to actually calculate derivatives.

Equation 3.4 and Eq. 3.5: First Derivative

$$y = f(x) \qquad 3.4$$

$$D_x y = dy/dx = y' \qquad 3.5$$

Variations

$$f'(x), \ \frac{df(x)}{dx}, \ \mathbf{D}f(x), \ \mathbf{D}_x f(x)$$

Description

The derivative of a function $y = f(x)$, also known as the *first derivative*, is represented in various ways, as shown by the variations.

Example

What is the slope of the curve $y = 10x^2 - 3x - 1$ when it crosses the positive part of the x-axis?

(A) 3/20

(B) 1/5

(C) 1/3

(D) 7

Solution

The curve crosses the x-axis when $y = 0$. At this point,

$$10x^2 - 3x - 1 = 0$$

Use the quadratic equation or complete the square to determine the two values of x where the curve crosses the x-axis.

$$x^2 - 0.3x = 0.1$$
$$(x - 0.15)^2 = 0.1 + (0.15)^2$$
$$x = \pm 0.35 + 0.15$$
$$= -0.2, \ 0.5$$

Since x must be positive, $x = 0.5$. The slope of the function is the first derivative.

$$\frac{dy}{dx} = 20x - 3$$
$$= (20)(0.5) - 3$$
$$= 7$$

The answer is (D).

Equation 3.6 Through Eq. 3.32: Derivatives

$$dc/dx = 0 \qquad\qquad 3.6$$

$$dx/dx = 1 \qquad\qquad 3.7$$

$$d(cu)/dx = c\,du/dx \qquad\qquad 3.8$$

$$d(u + v - w)/dx = du/dx + dv/dx - dw/dx \qquad\qquad 3.9$$

$$d(uv)/dx = u\,dv/dx + v\,du/dx \qquad\qquad 3.10$$

$$d(uvw)/dx = uv\,dw/dx + uw\,dv/dx + vw\,du/dx \qquad\qquad 3.11$$

$$\frac{d(u/v)}{dx} = \frac{v\,du/dx - u\,dv/dx}{v^2} \qquad\qquad 3.12$$

$$d(u^n)/dx = nu^{n-1}du/dx \qquad\qquad 3.13$$

$$d[f(u)]/dx = \{d[f(u)]/du\}\,du/dx \qquad\qquad 3.14$$

$$du/dx = 1/(dx/du) \qquad\qquad 3.15$$

$$\frac{d(\log_a u)}{dx} = (\log_a e)\frac{1}{u}\frac{du}{dx} \qquad\qquad 3.16$$

$$\frac{d(\ln u)}{dx} = \frac{1}{u}\frac{du}{dx} \qquad\qquad 3.17$$

$$\frac{d(a^u)}{dx} = (\ln a)\,a^u\frac{du}{dx} \qquad\qquad 3.18$$

$$d(e^u)/dx = e^u du/dx \qquad\qquad 3.19$$

$$d(u^v)/dx = vu^{v-1}du/dx + (\ln u)u^v dv/dx \qquad\qquad 3.20$$

$$d(\sin u)/dx = \cos u\,du/dx \qquad\qquad 3.21$$

$$d(\cos u)/dx = -\sin u\,du/dx \qquad\qquad 3.22$$

$$d(\tan u)/dx = \sec^2 u\,du/dx \qquad\qquad 3.23$$

$$d(\cot u)/dx = -\csc^2 u\,du/dx \qquad\qquad 3.24$$

$$d(\sec u)/dx = \sec u \tan u\,du/dx \qquad\qquad 3.25$$

$$d(\csc u)/dx = -\csc u \cot u\,du/dx \qquad\qquad 3.26$$

$$\frac{d(\sin^{-1}u)}{dx} = \frac{1}{\sqrt{1-u^2}}\frac{du}{dx} \qquad\qquad 3.27$$
$$[-\pi/2 \le \sin^{-1}u \le \pi/2]$$

$$\frac{d(\cos^{-1}u)}{dx} = -\frac{1}{\sqrt{1-u^2}}\frac{du}{dx} \quad [0 \le \cos^{-1}u \le \pi] \qquad 3.28$$

$$\frac{d(\tan^{-1}u)}{dx} = \frac{1}{1+u^2}\frac{du}{dx} \qquad\qquad 3.29$$
$$[-\pi/2 < \tan^{-1}u < \pi/2]$$

$$\frac{d(\cot^{-1}u)}{dx} = -\frac{1}{1+u^2}\frac{du}{dx} \quad [0 < \cot^{-1}u < \pi] \qquad 3.30$$

$$\frac{d(\sec^{-1}u)}{dx} = \frac{1}{u\sqrt{u^2-1}}\frac{du}{dx} \qquad\qquad 3.31$$
$$[0 < \sec^{-1}u < \pi/2 \text{ or } -\pi \le \sec^{-1}u < -\pi/2]$$

$$\frac{d(\csc^{-1}u)}{dx} = -\frac{1}{u\sqrt{u^2-1}}\frac{du}{dx} \qquad\qquad 3.32$$
$$[0 < \csc^{-1}u \le \pi/2 \text{ or } -\pi < \csc^{-1}u \le -\pi/2]$$

Description

Formulas for the derivatives of some common functional forms are listed in Eq. 3.6 through Eq. 3.32.

Example

Evaluate dy/dx for the following expression.

$$y = e^{-x}\sin 2x$$

(A) $e^{-x}(2\cos 2x - \sin 2x)$

(B) $-e^{-x}(2\sin 2x + \cos 2x)$

(C) $e^{-x}(2\sin 2x + \cos 2x)$

(D) $-e^{-x}(2\cos 2x - \sin 2x)$

Solution

Use the product rule (Eq. 3.10) and the chain rule (Eq. 3.14).

$$\frac{d}{dx}(e^{-x}\sin 2x) = e^{-x}\frac{d}{dx}(\sin 2x)$$
$$+ (\sin 2x)\frac{d}{dx}(e^{-x})$$
$$= e^{-x}(\cos 2x)(2)$$
$$+ (\sin 2x)(e^{-x})(-1)$$
$$= e^{-x}(2\cos 2x - \sin 2x)$$

The answer is (A).

2. CRITICAL POINTS

Derivatives are used to locate the local *critical points*, that is, *extreme points* (also known as *maximum* and *minimum points*) as well as the *inflection points* (*points of contraflexure*) of functions of one variable. The plurals *extrema*, *maxima*, and *minima* are used without the word "points." These points are illustrated in Fig. 3.1. There is usually an inflection point between two adjacent local extrema.

Figure 3.1 *Critical Points*

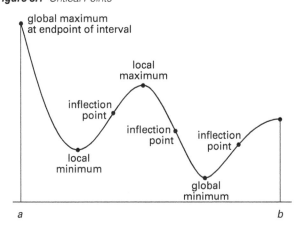

The first derivative, $f'(x)$, is calculated to determine where the critical points might be. The second derivative, $f''(x)$, is calculated to determine whether a located point is a maximum, minimum, or inflection point. With this method, no distinction is made between local and global extrema. The extrema should be compared to the function values at the endpoints of the interval.

Critical points are located where the first derivative is zero. This is a necessary, but not sufficient, requirement. That is, for a function $y = f(x)$, the point $x = a$ is a critical point if

$$f'(a) = 0$$

Equation 3.33 and Eq. 3.34: Test for a Maximum

$$f'(a) = 0 \qquad 3.33$$

$$f''(a) < 0 \qquad 3.34$$

Description

For a function $f(x)$ with an extreme point at $x = a$, if the point is a maximum, then the second derivative is negative.

Example

What is the maximum value of the function $f(x) = -x^2 - 8x + 1$?

(A) 1
(B) 4
(C) 8
(D) 17

Solution

Use Eq. 3.33 and Eq. 3.34.

$$f(x) = -x^2 - 8x + 1$$
$$f'(x) = -2x - 8$$
$$f''(x) = -2$$

$f'(x) = 0$ when x is equal to –4, and $f''(x)$ is less than zero, so $f(x)$ has its maximum value at $x = -4$.

$$f(x) = -x^2 - 8x + 1$$
$$= -(-4)^2 - (8)(-4) + 1$$
$$= 17$$

The answer is (D).

Equation 3.35 and Eq. 3.36: Test for a Minimum

$$f'(a) = 0 \qquad 3.35$$

$$f''(a) > 0 \qquad 3.36$$

Description

For a function $f(x)$ with a critical point at $x = a$, if the point is a minimum, then the second derivative is positive.

Mathematics

Example

What is the minimum value of the function $f(x) = 3x^2 + 3x - 5$?

- (A) -12.0
- (B) -8.0
- (C) -5.75
- (D) -5.00

Solution

Use Eq. 3.35 and Eq. 3.36.

$$f(x) = 3x^2 + 3x - 5$$
$$f'(x) = 6x + 3$$
$$f''(x) = 6$$

$f'(x) = 0$ when x is equal to -0.5, and $f''(x)$ is greater than zero, so $f(x)$ has its minimum value at $x = -0.5$.

$$f(x) = 3x^2 + 3x - 5$$
$$= (3)(-0.5)^2 + (3)(-0.5) - 5$$
$$= -5.75$$

The answer is (C).

Equation 3.37: Test for a Point of Inflection

$$f''(a) = 0 \qquad \text{3.37}$$

Description

For a function $f(x)$ with $f'(x) = 0$ at $x = a$, if the point is a point of inflection, then Eq. 3.37 is true.

3. PARTIAL DERIVATIVES

Derivatives can be taken with respect to only one independent variable at a time. For example, $f'(x)$ is the derivative of $f(x)$ and is taken with respect to the independent variable x. If a function, $f(x_1, x_2, x_3 \dots)$, has more than one independent variable, a *partial derivative* can be found, but only with respect to one of the independent variables. All other variables are treated as constants.

Equation 3.38 and Eq. 3.39: Partial Derivative

$$z = f(x, y) \qquad \text{3.38}$$

$$\frac{\partial z}{\partial x} = \frac{\partial f(x, y)}{\partial x} \qquad \text{3.39}$$

Variations

Symbols for a partial derivative of $f(x, y)$ taken with respect to variable x are $\partial f / \partial x$ and $f_x(x, y)$.

Description

The geometric interpretation of a partial derivative $\partial f / \partial x$ is the slope of a line tangent to the surface (a sphere, an ellipsoid, etc.) described by the function when all variables except x are held constant. In three-dimensional space with a function described by Eq. 3.38, the partial derivative $\partial f / \partial x$ (equivalent to $\partial z / \partial x$) is the slope of the line tangent to the surface in a plane of constant y. Similarly, the partial derivative $\partial f / \partial y$ (equivalent to $\partial z / \partial y$) is the slope of the line tangent to the surface in a plane of constant x.

Example

What is the partial derivative with respect to x of the following function?

$$z = e^{xy}$$

- (A) e^{xy}
- (B) $\dfrac{e^{xy}}{x}$
- (C) $\dfrac{e^{xy}}{y}$
- (D) ye^{xy}

Solution

Use Eq. 3.19 and Eq. 3.39. The partial derivative is

$$d(e^u)/dx = e^u \, du/dx$$
$$\frac{\partial z}{\partial x} = \frac{\partial e^{xy}}{\partial x} = e^{xy} \frac{\partial (xy)}{\partial x}$$
$$= ye^{xy}$$

The answer is (D).

4. CURVATURE

The sharpness of a curve between two points on the curve can be defined as the rate of change of the inclination of the curve with respect to the distance traveled along the curve. As shown in Fig. 3.2, the rate of change of the inclination of the curve is the change in the angle formed by the tangents to the curve at each point and the x-axis. The distance, s, traveled along the curve is the arc length of the curve between points 1 and 2.

Figure 3.2 Curvature

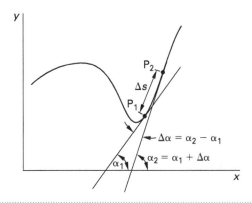

Equation 3.40: Curvature

$$K = \lim_{\Delta s \to 0} \frac{\Delta \alpha}{\Delta s} = \frac{d\alpha}{ds} \qquad 3.40$$

Description

On roadways, a "sharp" curve is one that changes direction quickly, corresponding to a small curve radius. The smaller the curve radius, the sharper the curve. Some roadway curves are circular, some are parabolic, and some are spiral. Not all curves are circular, but all curves described by polynomials have an instantaneous sharpness and radius of curvature. The sharpness, K, of a curve at a point is given by Eq. 3.40.

Equation 3.41 Through Eq. 3.43: Curvature in Rectangular Coordinates

$$K = \frac{y''}{[1 + (y')^2]^{3/2}} \qquad 3.41$$

$$x' = dx/dy \qquad 3.42$$

$$K = \frac{-x''}{[1 + (x')^2]^{3/2}} \qquad 3.43$$

Description

For an equation of a curve $f(x, y)$ given in rectangular coordinates, the curvature is defined by Eq. 3.41.

If the function $f(x, y)$ is easier to differentiate with respect to y instead of x, then Eq. 3.43 may be used.

Equation 3.44 and Eq. 3.45: Radius of Curvature

$$R = \frac{1}{|K|} \qquad [K \neq 0] \qquad 3.44$$

$$R = \left| \frac{[1 + (y')^2]^{3/2}}{|y''|} \right| \qquad [y'' \neq 0] \qquad 3.45$$

Description

The *radius of curvature*, R, of a curve describes the radius of a circle whose center lies on the concave side of the curve and whose tangent coincides with the tangent to the curve at that point. Radius of curvature is the absolute value of the reciprocal of the curvature.

Example

What is the approximate radius of curvature of the function $f(x)$ at the point $(x, y) = (8, 16)$?

$$f(x) = x^2 + 6x - 96$$

(A) 1.9×10^{-4}

(B) 9.8

(C) 96

(D) 5300

Solution

The first and second derivatives are

$$f'(x) = 2x + 6$$
$$f''(x) = 2$$

At $x = 8$,

$$f'(x) = (2)(8) + 6 = 22$$

From Eq. 3.45, the radius of curvature, R, is

$$R = \left| \frac{[1 + f'(x)^2]^{3/2}}{|f''(x)|} \right|$$

$$= \left| \frac{(1 + (22)^2)^{3/2}}{2} \right|$$

$$= 5340.5 \quad (5300)$$

The answer is (D).

5. LIMITS

A *limit* is the value a function approaches when an independent variable approaches a target value. For example, suppose the value of $y = x^2$ is desired as x approaches 5. This could be written as

$$y(5) = \lim_{x \to 5} x^2$$

The power of limit theory is wasted on simple calculations such as this one, but limit theory is appreciated when the function is undefined at the target value. The object of limit theory is to determine the limit without having to evaluate the function at the target. The general case of a limit evaluated as x approaches the target value a is written as

$$\lim_{x \to a} f(x)$$

It is not necessary for the actual value, $f(a)$, to exist for the limit to be calculated. The function $f(x)$ may be undefined at point a. However, it is necessary that $f(x)$ be defined on both sides of point a for the limit to exist. If $f(x)$ is undefined on one side, or if $f(x)$ is discontinuous at $x = a$, as in Fig. 3.3(c) and Fig. 3.3(d), the limit does not exist at $x = a$.

Figure 3.3 *Existence of Limits*

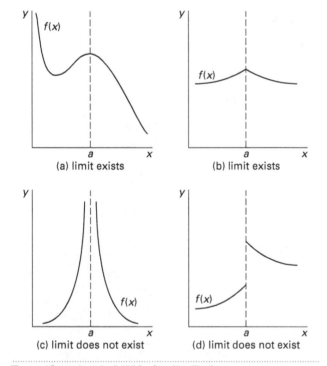

(a) limit exists

(b) limit exists

(c) limit does not exist

(d) limit does not exist

Equation 3.46: L'Hôpital's Rule

$$\lim_{x \to \alpha} \frac{f'(x)}{g'(x)}, \lim_{x \to \alpha} \frac{f''(x)}{g''(x)}, \lim_{x \to \alpha} \frac{f'''(x)}{g'''(x)} \qquad 3.46$$

Variation

$$\lim_{x \to a} \frac{f(x)}{g(x)} = \lim_{x \to a} \frac{f^k(x)}{g^k(x)}$$

Description

L'Hôpital's rule may be used only when the numerator and denominator of the expression are both indeterminate (i.e., are both zero or are both infinite) at the limit point. The first expression is equal to the second expression, which is not indeterminate. (This is shown in the variation.) $f^k(x)$ and $g^k(x)$ are the kth derivatives of the functions $f(x)$ and $g(x)$, respectively. L'Hôpital's rule can be applied repeatedly as required as long as the numerator and denominator are both indeterminate.

Example

Evaluate the following limit.

$$\lim_{x \to 0} \frac{1 - e^{3x}}{4x}$$

(A) $-\infty$

(B) $-3/4$

(C) 0

(D) $1/4$

Solution

This limit has the indeterminate form 0/0, so use L'Hôpital's rule.

$$\lim_{x \to \alpha} \frac{f(x)}{g(x)} = \lim_{x \to \alpha} \frac{f'(x)}{g'(x)}$$
$$\lim_{x \to 0} \frac{1 - e^{3x}}{4x} = \lim_{x \to 0} \frac{-3e^{3x}}{4}$$
$$= -3/4$$

The answer is (B).

6. INTEGRALS

Equation 3.47 Through Eq. 3.69: Indefinite Integrals

$$\int df(x) = f(x) \qquad 3.47$$

$$\int dx = x \qquad 3.48$$

$$\int a\, f(x)\, dx = a \int f(x)\, dx \qquad 3.49$$

$$\int [u(x) \pm v(x)]\, dx = \int u(x)\, dx \pm \int v(x)\, dx \qquad \text{3.50}$$

$$\int x^m dx = \frac{x^{m+1}}{m+1} \quad [m \neq -1] \qquad \text{3.51}$$

$$\int u(x)\, dv(x) = u(x)\, v(x) - \int v(x)\, du(x) \qquad \text{3.52}$$

$$\int \frac{dx}{ax+b} = \frac{1}{a}\ln|ax+b| \qquad \text{3.53}$$

$$\int \frac{dx}{\sqrt{x}} = 2\sqrt{x} \qquad \text{3.54}$$

$$\int a^x dx = \frac{a^x}{\ln a} \qquad \text{3.55}$$

$$\int \sin x\, dx = -\cos x \qquad \text{3.56}$$

$$\int \cos x\, dx = \sin x \qquad \text{3.57}$$

$$\int \sin^2 x\, dx = \frac{x}{2} - \frac{\sin 2x}{4} \qquad \text{3.58}$$

$$\int \cos^2 x\, dx = \frac{x}{2} + \frac{\sin 2x}{4} \qquad \text{3.59}$$

$$\int x \sin x\, dx = \sin x - x \cos x \qquad \text{3.60}$$

$$\int x \cos x\, dx = \cos x + x \sin x \qquad \text{3.61}$$

$$\int \sin x \cos x\, dx = (\sin^2 x)/2 \qquad \text{3.62}$$

$$\int \sin ax \cos bx\, dx = -\frac{\cos(a-b)x}{2(a-b)}$$
$$-\frac{\cos(a+b)x}{2(a+b)} \quad [a^2 \neq b^2] \qquad \text{3.63}$$

$$\int \tan x\, dx = -\ln|\cos x| = \ln|\sec x| \qquad \text{3.64}$$

$$\int \cot x\, dx = -\ln|\csc x| = \ln|\sin x| \qquad \text{3.65}$$

$$\int \tan^2 x\, dx = \tan x - x \qquad \text{3.66}$$

$$\int \cot^2 x\, dx = -\cot x - x \qquad \text{3.67}$$

$$\int e^{ax} dx = (1/a)\, e^{ax} \qquad \text{3.68}$$

$$\int x e^{ax} dx = (e^{ax}/a^2)(ax - 1) \qquad \text{3.69}$$

Description

Integration is the inverse operation of differentiation. There are two types of integrals: *definite integrals*, which are restricted to a specific range of the independent variable, and *indefinite integrals*, which are unrestricted. Indefinite integrals are sometimes referred to as *antiderivatives*.

Equation 3.70: Fundamental Theorem of Integral Calculus

$$\lim_{n\to\infty} \sum_{i=1}^{n} f(x_i)\Delta x_i = \int_a^b f(x)\, dx \qquad \text{3.70}$$

Description

The definition of a definite integral is given by the *fundamental theorem of integral calculus*. The right-hand side of Eq. 3.70 represents the area bounded by $f(x)$ above, $y = 0$ below, $x = a$ to the left, and $x = b$ to the right. This is commonly referred to as the "*area under the curve.*"

Example

What is the approximate total area bounded by $y = \sin x$ over the interval $0 \leq x \leq 2\pi$? (x is in radians.)

(A) 0

(B) $\pi/2$

(C) 2

(D) 4

Solution

The integral of $f(x)$ represents the area under the curve $f(x)$ between the limits of integration. However, since the value of $\sin x$ is negative in the range $\pi \leq x \leq 2\pi$, the total area would be calculated as zero if the integration was carried out in one step. The integral could be calculated over two ranges, but it is easier to exploit the symmetry of the sine curve.

$$A = \int_{x_1}^{x_2} f(x)\,dx = \int_0^{2\pi} |\sin x|\,dx = 2\int_0^{\pi} \sin x\,dx$$

$$= -2\cos x\Big|_0^{\pi}$$

$$= (-2)(-1-1)$$

$$= 4$$

The answer is (D).

7. CENTROIDS AND MOMENTS OF INERTIA

Applications of integration include the determination of the *centroid of an area* and various moments of the area, including the *area moment of inertia*.

The integration method for determining centroids and moments of inertia is not necessary for basic shapes. Formulas for basic shapes can be found in tables.

Equation 3.71 Through Eq. 3.74: Centroid of an Area

$$x_c = \frac{\int x\,dA}{A} \qquad \text{3.71}$$

$$y_c = \frac{\int y\,dA}{A} \qquad \text{3.72}$$

$$A = \int f(x)\,dx \qquad \text{3.73}$$

$$dA = f(x)\,dx = g(y)\,dy \qquad \text{3.74}$$

Description

The centroid of an area is analogous to the *center of gravity* of a homogeneous body. The location, (x_c, y_c), of the centroid of the area bounded by the x- and y-axis and the mathematical function $y = f(x)$ can be found from Eq. 3.71 through Eq. 3.74.

Example

What is most nearly the x-coordinate of the centroid of the area bounded by $y = 0$, $f(x)$, $x = 0$, and $x = 20$?

$$f(x) = x^3 + 7x^2 - 5x + 6$$

(A) 7.6

(B) 9.4

(C) 14

(D) 16

Solution

Use Eq. 3.71 and Eq. 3.74.

$$\int xf(x)\,dx = \int_0^{20} (x^4 + 7x^3 - 5x^2 + 6x)\,dx$$

$$= \frac{x^5}{5} + \frac{7x^4}{4} - \frac{5x^3}{3} + \frac{6x^2}{2}\Big|_0^{20}$$

$$= 907{,}867$$

From Eq. 3.73, the area under the curve is

$$A = \int_a^b f(x)\,dx = \int_0^{20} (x^3 + 7x^2 - 5x + 6)\,dx$$

$$= \tfrac{1}{4}x^4 + \tfrac{7}{3}x^3 - \tfrac{5}{2}x^2 + 6x\Big|_0^{20}$$

$$= \left(\frac{1}{4}\right)(20)^4 + \left(\frac{7}{3}\right)(20)^3 - \left(\frac{5}{2}\right)(20)^2 + (6)(20)$$

$$= 57{,}786.67 \quad (57{,}787)$$

Use Eq. 3.71 to find the x-coordinate of the centroid.

$$x_c = \frac{\int x\,dA}{A} = \frac{\int xf(x)\,dx}{A} = \frac{907{,}867}{57{,}787} = 15.71 \quad (16)$$

The answer is (D).

Equation 3.75 and Eq. 3.76: First Moment of the Area

$$M_y = \int x\,dA = x_c A \qquad \text{3.75}$$

$$M_x = \int y\,dA = y_c A \qquad \text{3.76}$$

Description

The quantity $\int x\,dA$ is known as the *first moment of the area* or *first area moment* with respect to the y-axis. Similarly, $\int y\,dA$ is known as the *first moment of the area* with respect to the x-axis. Equation 3.75 and Eq. 3.76 show that the first moment of the area can be calculated from the area and centroidal distance.

Equation 3.77 and Eq. 3.78: Moment of Inertia

$$I_y = \int x^2\,dA \qquad \text{3.77}$$

$$I_x = \int y^2\,dA \qquad \text{3.78}$$

Description

The *second moment of the area* or *moment of inertia, I,* of the area is needed in mechanics of materials problems. The symbol I_x is used to represent a moment of inertia with respect to the x-axis. Similarly, I_y is the moment of inertia with respect to the y-axis.

Example

What is most nearly the moment of inertia about the y-axis of the area bounded by $y = 0$, $x = 0$, $x = 20$, and $f(x) = x^3 + 7x^2 - 5x + 6$?

(A) 6.3×10^5

(B) 8.2×10^6

(C) 9.9×10^6

(D) 1.5×10^7

Solution

From Eq. 3.77, the moment of inertia about the y-axis is

$$I_y = \int x^2 \, dA = \int x^2 f(x) \, dx$$

$$= \int_0^{20} (x^5 + 7x^4 - 5x^3 + 6x^2) \, dx$$

$$= \frac{x^6}{6} + \frac{7x^5}{5} - \frac{5x^4}{4} + \frac{6x^3}{3} \Big|_0^{20}$$

$$= 1.5 \times 10^7$$

The answer is (D).

Equation 3.79 Through Eq. 3.82: Centroidal Moment of Inertia

$$I_{\text{parallel axis}} = I_c + d^2 A \qquad 3.79$$

$$J = \int r^2 dA = I_x + I_y \qquad 3.80$$

$$I_x' = I_{x_c} + d_y^2 A \qquad 3.81$$

$$I_y' = I_{y_c} + d_x^2 A \qquad 3.82$$

Description

Moments of inertia can be calculated with respect to any axis, not just the coordinate axes. The moment of inertia taken with respect to an axis passing through the area's centroid is known as the *centroidal moment of inertia, I_c.* The centroidal moment of inertia is the smallest possible moment of inertia for the area.

If the moment of inertia is known with respect to one axis, the moment of inertia with respect to another parallel axis can be calculated from the *parallel axis theorem,* also known as the *transfer axis theorem.* (See Eq. 3.79.) This theorem is also used to evaluate the moment of inertia of areas that are composed of two or more basic shapes. In Eq. 3.79, d is the distance between the centroidal axis and the second, parallel axis.

The parallel axis theorem is generalized into two dimensions in Fig. 3.4, where the surface area of the shape $\int dA$ with the centroid located at distance d_y from the x-axis and distance d_x from the y-axis has moments of inertia I_x' and I_y' about the x- and y-axes, as defined by Eq. 3.81 and Eq. 3.82.

Figure 3.4 Parallel Axis Theorem in Two Dimensions

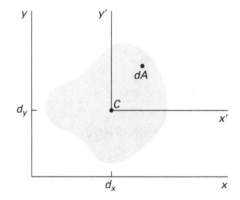

Example

The moment of inertia about the x'-axis of the cross section shown is $334\,000$ cm^4. The cross-sectional area is 86 cm^2, and the thicknesses of the web and the flanges are the same.

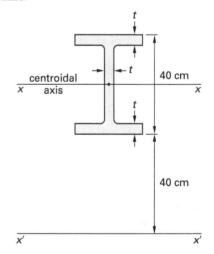

What is most nearly the moment of inertia about the centroidal axis?

(A) 2.4×10^4 cm^4

(B) 7.4×10^4 cm^4

(C) 2.0×10^5 cm^4

(D) 6.4×10^5 cm^4

Solution

Use Eq. 3.81. The moment of inertia around the centroidal axis is

$$I'_x = I_{x_c} + d_x^2 A$$

$$I_{x_c} = I'_x - d_x^2 A$$

$$= 334\,000 \text{ cm}^4 - (86 \text{ cm}^2)\left(40 \text{ cm} + \frac{40 \text{ cm}}{2}\right)^2$$

$$= 24\,400 \text{ cm}^4 \quad (2.4 \times 10^4 \text{ cm}^4)$$

The answer is (A).

8. GRADIENT, DIVERGENCE, AND CURL

The *vector del operator*, ∇, is defined as

$$\nabla = \frac{\partial}{\partial x}\mathbf{i} + \frac{\partial}{\partial y}\mathbf{j} + \frac{\partial}{\partial z}\mathbf{k}$$

Equation 3.83: Gradient of a Scalar Function

$$\nabla\phi = \left(\frac{\partial}{\partial x}\mathbf{i} + \frac{\partial}{\partial y}\mathbf{j} + \frac{\partial}{\partial z}\mathbf{k}\right)\phi \qquad 3.83$$

Variation

$$\nabla f(x,y,z) = \left(\frac{\partial f(x,y,z)}{\partial x}\right)\mathbf{i} + \left(\frac{\partial f(x,y,z)}{\partial y}\right)\mathbf{j}$$
$$+ \left(\frac{\partial f(x,y,z)}{\partial z}\right)\mathbf{k}$$

Description

A *scalar function* is a mathematical expression that returns a single numerical value (i.e., a *scalar*). The function may be of one or multiple variables (i.e., $f(x)$ or $f(x,y,z)$ or $f(x_1, x_2 \ldots x_n)$), but it must calculate a single number for each location. The *gradient vector field*, $\nabla\phi$, gives the maximum rate of change of the scalar function $\phi = \phi(x,y,z)$.

Equation 3.84: Divergence of a Vector Field

$$\nabla \cdot \mathbf{V} = \left(\frac{\partial}{\partial x}\mathbf{i} + \frac{\partial}{\partial y}\mathbf{j} + \frac{\partial}{\partial z}\mathbf{k}\right)\cdot(V_1\mathbf{i} + V_2\mathbf{j} + V_3\mathbf{k}) \qquad 3.84$$

Description

In three dimensions, $\mathbf{V}$ is a vector field with components V_1, V_2, and V_3. V_1, V_2, and V_3 may be specified as functions of variables, such as $P(x,y,z)$, $Q(x,y,z)$, and $R(x,y,z)$. The *divergence* of a vector field $\mathbf{V}$ is the scalar function defined by Eq. 3.84, the dot product of the del operator and the vector (i.e., the divergence is a scalar). The divergence of $\mathbf{V}$ can be interpreted as the *accumulation* of flux (i.e., a flowing substance) in a small region (i.e., at a point).

If $\mathbf{V}$ represents a flow (e.g., air moving from hot to cool regions), then $\mathbf{V}$ is incompressible if $\nabla \cdot \mathbf{V} = 0$, since the substance is not accumulating.

Example

What is the divergence of the following vector field?

$$\mathbf{V} = 2x\mathbf{i} + 2y\mathbf{j}$$

(A)   0

(B)   2

(C)   3

(D)   4

Solution

Use Eq. 3.84.

$$\nabla \cdot \mathbf{V} = \left(\frac{\partial}{\partial x}\mathbf{i} + \frac{\partial}{\partial y}\mathbf{j} + \frac{\partial}{\partial z}\mathbf{k}\right)\cdot(V_1\mathbf{i} + V_2\mathbf{j} + V_3\mathbf{k})$$
$$= \left(\frac{\partial}{\partial x}\mathbf{i} + \frac{\partial}{\partial y}\mathbf{j} + \frac{\partial}{\partial z}\mathbf{k}\right)\cdot(2x\mathbf{i} + 2y\mathbf{j} + 0\mathbf{k})$$
$$= \frac{\partial(2x)}{\partial x} + \frac{\partial(2y)}{\partial y} + \frac{\partial(0)}{\partial z}$$
$$= 2 + 2 + 0$$
$$= 4$$

The answer is (D).

Equation 3.85: Curl of a Vector Field

$$\nabla \times \mathbf{V} = \left(\frac{\partial}{\partial x}\mathbf{i} + \frac{\partial}{\partial y}\mathbf{j} + \frac{\partial}{\partial z}\mathbf{k}\right) \times (V_1\mathbf{i} + V_2\mathbf{j} + V_3\mathbf{k}) \qquad 3.85$$

Mathematics

Variation

$$\text{curl } \mathbf{V} = \nabla \times \mathbf{V}$$

$$= \begin{vmatrix} \mathbf{i} & \mathbf{j} & \mathbf{k} \\ \dfrac{\partial}{\partial x} & \dfrac{\partial}{\partial y} & \dfrac{\partial}{\partial z} \\ P(x,y,z) & Q(x,y,z) & R(x,y,z) \end{vmatrix}$$

Description

The *curl*, $\nabla \times \mathbf{V}$, of a vector field $\mathbf{V}(x, y, z)$ is the vector field defined by Eq. 3.85, the cross (vector) product of the del operator and vector. For any location, the curl vector has both magnitude and direction. That is, the curl vector determines how fast the flux is rotating and in what direction the flux is going. The curl of a vector field can be interpreted as the *vorticity* per unit area of flux (i.e., a flowing substance) in a small region (i.e., at a point). One of the uses of the curl is to determine whether flow (represented in direction and magnitude by $\mathbf{V}$) is rotational. Flow is irrotational if curl $\nabla \times \mathbf{V} = 0$.

Example

Determine the curl of the vector function $\mathbf{V}(x, y, z)$.

$$\mathbf{V}(x, y, z) = 3x^2 \mathbf{i} + 7e^x y \mathbf{j}$$

(A) $7e^x y$

(B) $7e^x y \mathbf{i}$

(C) $7e^x y \mathbf{j}$

(D) $7e^x y \mathbf{k}$

Solution

Using the variation of Eq. 3.85,

$$\text{curl } \mathbf{V} = \begin{vmatrix} \mathbf{i} & \mathbf{j} & \mathbf{k} \\ \dfrac{\partial}{\partial x} & \dfrac{\partial}{\partial y} & \dfrac{\partial}{\partial z} \\ 3x^2 & 7e^x y & 0 \end{vmatrix}$$

Expand the determinant across the top row.

$$\left(\frac{\partial}{\partial y} 0 - \frac{\partial}{\partial z} 7e^x y \right) \mathbf{i} - \left(\frac{\partial}{\partial x} 0 - \frac{\partial}{\partial z} 3x^2 \right) \mathbf{j}$$

$$+ \left(\frac{\partial}{\partial x} 7e^x y - \frac{\partial}{\partial y} 3x^2 \right) \mathbf{k}$$

$$= (0 - 0)\mathbf{i} - (0 - 0)\mathbf{j} + (7e^x y - 0)\mathbf{k}$$

$$= 7e^x y \mathbf{k}$$

The answer is (D).

Equation 3.86 Through Eq. 3.89: Vector Identities

$$\nabla^2 \phi = \nabla \cdot (\nabla \phi) = (\nabla \cdot \nabla)\phi \qquad 3.86$$

$$\nabla \times \nabla \phi = 0 \qquad 3.87$$

$$\nabla \cdot (\nabla \times \mathbf{A}) = 0 \qquad 3.88$$

$$\nabla \times (\nabla \times \mathbf{A}) = \nabla(\nabla \cdot \mathbf{A}) - \nabla^2 \mathbf{A} \qquad 3.89$$

Description

Equation 3.86 through Eq. 3.89 are identities associated with gradient, divergence, and curl.

Equation 3.90: Laplacian of a Scalar Function

$$\nabla^2 \phi = \frac{\partial^2 \phi}{\partial x^2} + \frac{\partial^2 \phi}{\partial y^2} + \frac{\partial^2 \phi}{\partial z^2} \qquad 3.90$$

Description

The *Laplacian* of a scalar function, $\phi = \phi(x, y, z)$, is the divergence of the gradient function. (This is essentially the second derivative of a scalar function.) A function that satisfies Laplace's equation $\nabla^2 = 0$ is known as a *potential function*. Accordingly, the operator ∇^2 is commonly written as $\nabla \cdot \nabla$ or Δ. The potential function quantifies the attraction of the flux to move in a particular direction. It is used in electricity (voltage potential), mechanics (gravitational potential), mixing and diffusion (concentration gradient), hydraulics (pressure gradient), and heat transfer (thermal gradient). The term Laplacian almost always refers to three-dimensional functions, and usually functions in rectangular coordinates. The term *d'Alembertian* is used when working with four-dimensional functions. The symbol $\Box^2$ (with four sides) is used in place of ∇^2. The d'Alembertian is encountered frequently when working with wave functions (including those involving relativity and quantum mechanics) of x, y, and z for location, and t for time.

Example

Determine the Laplacian of the scalar function $1/3x^3 - 9y + 5$ at the point $(3, 2, 7)$.

(A) 0

(B) 1

(C) 6

(D) 9

Solution

The Laplacian of the function is

$$\nabla^2 \phi = \frac{\partial^2 \phi}{\partial x^2} + \frac{\partial^2 \phi}{\partial y^2} + \frac{\partial^2 \phi}{\partial z^2}$$

$$\nabla^2 \left(\tfrac{1}{3}x^3 - 9y + 5 \right) = \frac{\partial^2 \left(\tfrac{1}{3}x^3 - 9y + 5 \right)}{\partial x^2}$$

$$+ \frac{\partial^2 \left(\tfrac{1}{3}x^3 - 9y + 5 \right)}{\partial y^2}$$

$$+ \frac{\partial^2 \left(\tfrac{1}{3}x^3 - 9y + 5 \right)}{\partial z^2}$$

$$= 2x + 0 + 0$$
$$= 2x$$

At $(3, 2, 7)$, $2x = (2)(3) = 6$.

The answer is (C).

Differential Equations and Transforms

1. INTRODUCTION TO DIFFERENTIAL EQUATIONS

A *differential equation* is a mathematical expression combining a function (e.g., $y = f(x)$) and one or more of its derivatives. The *order* of a differential equation is the highest derivative in it. *First-order differential equations* contain only first derivatives of the function, *second-order differential equations* contain second derivatives (and may contain first derivatives as well), and so on.

The purpose of solving a differential equation is to derive an expression for the function in terms of the independent variable. The expression does not need to be explicit in the function, but there can be no derivatives in the expression. Since, in the simplest cases, solving a differential equation is equivalent to finding an indefinite integral, it is not surprising that *constants of integration* must be evaluated from knowledge of how the system behaves. Additional data are known as *initial values*, and any problem that includes them is known as an *initial value problem*.

Equation 4.1: Linear Differential Equation with Constant Coefficients

$$b_n \frac{d^n y(x)}{dx^n} + \cdots + b_1 \frac{dy(x)}{dx} + b_0 y(x) = f(x) \qquad 4.1$$

$$[b_n, \ldots, b_i, \ldots, b_1, \text{ and } b_0 \text{ are constants}]$$

Description

A *linear differential equation* can be written as a sum of multiples of the function $y(x)$ and its derivatives. If the multipliers are scalars, the differential equation is said to have *constant coefficients*. Equation 4.1 shows the general form of a linear differential equation with constant coefficients. $f(x)$ is known as the forcing function. If the forcing function is zero, the differential equation is said to be *homogeneous*.

If the function $y(x)$ or one of its derivatives is raised to some power (other than one) or is embedded in another function (e.g., y embedded in $\sin y$ or e^y), the equation is said to be *nonlinear*.

Example

Which of the following is NOT a linear differential equation?

(A) $5\dfrac{d^2 y}{dt^2} - 8\dfrac{dy}{dt} + 16y = 4te^{-7t}$

(B) $5\dfrac{d^2 y}{dt^2} - 8t^2\dfrac{dy}{dt} + 16y = 0$

(C) $5\dfrac{d^2 y}{dt^2} - 8\dfrac{dy}{dt} + 16y = \dfrac{dy}{dy}$

(D) $5\left(\dfrac{dy}{dt}\right)^2 - 8\dfrac{dy}{dt} + 16y = 0$

Solution

A linear differential equation consists of multiples of a function, $y(t)$, and its derivatives, $d^n y / dt^n$. The multipliers may be scalar constants or functions, $g(t)$, of the independent variable, t. The forcing function, $f(t)$, (i.e., the right-hand side of the equation) may be 0, a constant, or any function of the independent variable, t. The multipliers cannot be higher powers of the function, $y(t)$.

The answer is (D).

2. LINEAR HOMOGENEOUS DIFFERENTIAL EQUATIONS WITH CONSTANT COEFFICIENTS

Each term of a *homogeneous differential equation* contains either the function or one of its derivatives. The forcing function is zero. That is, the sum of the function and its derivative terms is equal to zero.

$$b_n \frac{d^n y(x)}{dx^n} + \cdots + b_1 \frac{dy(x)}{dx} + b_0 y(x) = 0$$

Equation 4.2: Characteristic Equation

$$P(r) = b_n r^n + b_{n-1} r^{n-1} + \cdots + b_1 r + b_0 \qquad 4.2$$

Description

A *characteristic equation* can be written for a homogeneous linear differential equation with constant coefficients, regardless of order. This characteristic equation is simply the polynomial formed by replacing all derivatives with variables raised to the power of their respective derivatives. That is, all instances of $d^n y(x)/dx^n$ are replaced with r^n, resulting in an equation of the form of Eq. 4.2.

Equation 4.3: Solving Linear Differential Equations with Constant Coefficients

$$y_h(x) = C_1 e^{r_1 x} + C_2 e^{r_2 x} + \cdots + C_i e^{r_i x} + \cdots + C_n e^{r_n x} \qquad 4.3$$

Description

Homogeneous linear differential equations are most easily solved by finding the n roots of Eq. 4.2, the characteristic polynomial $P(r)$. If the roots of Eq. 4.2 are real and different, the solution is Eq. 4.3.

Equation 4.4 and Eq. 4.5: Homogeneous First-Order Linear Differential Equations

$$y' + ay = 0 \qquad 4.4$$

$$y = Ce^{-at} \qquad 4.5$$

Variations

$$\frac{dy}{dt} + ay = 0$$

$$f(t) = Ce^{-at}$$

Description

A homogeneous, first-order, linear differential equation with constant coefficients has the general form of Eq. 4.4.

The characteristic equation is $r + a = 0$ and has a root of $r = -a$. Equation 4.5 is the solution.

Example

Which of the following is the general solution to the differential equation and boundary conditions?

$$\frac{dy}{dt} - 5y = 0$$

$$y(0) = 3$$

(A) $-\frac{1}{3} e^{-5t}$

(B) $3e^{5t}$

(C) $5e^{-3t}$

(D) $\frac{1}{5} e^{-3t}$

Solution

This is a first-order, linear differential equation. The characteristic equation is $r - 5 = 0$. The root, r, is 5.

The solution is in the form of

$$y = Ce^{5t}$$

The initial condition is used to find C.

$$y(0) = Ce^{(5)(0)} = 3$$
$$C = 3$$
$$y = 3e^{5t}$$

The answer is (B).

Equation 4.6 Through Eq. 4.8: Homogeneous Second-Order Linear Differential Equations with Constant Coefficients

$$y'' + ay' + by = 0 \qquad 4.6$$

$$(r^2 + ar + b)Ce^{rx} = 0 \qquad 4.7$$

$$r^2 + ar + b = 0 \qquad 4.8$$

Description

A second-order, homogeneous, linear differential equation has the general form given by Eq. 4.6.

The characteristic equation is Eq. 4.8.

Depending on the form of the forcing function, the solutions to most second-order differential equations will contain sinusoidal terms (corresponding to oscillatory behavior) and exponential terms (corresponding to decaying or increasing unstable behavior). Behavior of real-world systems (electrical circuits, spring-mass-dashpot, fluid flow, heat transfer, etc.) depends on the amount of system *damping* (electrical resistance, mechanical friction, pressure drop, thermal insulation, etc.).

With *underdamping* (i.e., with "light" damping) without continued energy input (i.e., a free system without a forcing function), the transient behavior will gradually decay to the steady-state equilibrium condition. Behavior in underdamped free systems will be oscillatory with diminishing magnitude. The damping is known as underdamping because the amount of damping is less than the critical damping, and the *damping ratio*, ζ, is less than 1. The characteristic equation of underdamped systems has two complex roots.

With *overdamping* ("heavy" damping), damping is greater than critical, and the damping ratio is greater than 1. Transient behavior is a sluggish gradual decrease into the steady-state equilibrium condition without oscillations. The characteristic equation of overdamped systems has two distinct real roots (zeros).

With *critical damping*, the damping ratio is equal to 1. There is no overshoot, and the behavior reaches the steady-state equilibrium condition the fastest of the three cases, without oscillations. The characteristic equation of critically damped systems has two identical real roots (zeros).

Equation 4.9 Through Eq. 4.14: Roots of the Characteristic Equation

$$r_{1,2} = \frac{-a \pm \sqrt{a^2 - 4b}}{2} \qquad 4.9$$

$$y = C_1 e^{r_1 x} + C_2 e^{r_2 x} \qquad 4.10$$

$$y = (C_1 + C_2 x)e^{r_1 x} \qquad 4.11$$

$$y = e^{\alpha x}(C_1 \cos \beta x + C_2 \sin \beta x) \qquad 4.12$$

$$\alpha = -a/2 \qquad 4.13$$

$$\beta = \frac{\sqrt{4b - a^2}}{2} \qquad 4.14$$

Description

The roots of the characteristic equation are given by the quadratic equation, Eq. 4.9.

If $a^2 > 4b$, then the two roots are real and different, and the solution is overdamped, as shown in Eq. 4.10.

If $a^2 = 4b$, then the two roots are real and the same (i.e., are *double roots*), and the solution is critically damped, as shown in Eq. 4.11.

If $a^2 < 4b$, then the two roots are complex and of the form $(\alpha + i\beta)$ and $(\alpha - i\beta)$, and the solution is underdamped, as shown in Eq. 4.12.

Example

What is the general solution to the following homogeneous differential equation?

$$y'' - 8y' + 16y = 0$$

(A) $\quad y = C_1 e^{4x}$

(B) $\quad y = (C_1 + C_2 x)e^{4x}$

(C) $\quad y = C_1 e^{-4x} + C_2 e^{4x}$

(D) $\quad y = C_1 e^{2x} + C_2 e^{4x}$

Solution

Find the roots of the characteristic equation.

$$r^2 - 8r + 16 = 0$$
$$a = -8$$
$$b = 16$$

From Eq. 4.9,

$$\begin{aligned} r_{1,2} &= \frac{-a \pm \sqrt{a^2 - 4b}}{2} \\ &= \frac{-(-8) \pm \sqrt{(-8)^2 - (4)(16)}}{2} \\ &= 4, 4 \end{aligned}$$

Because $a^2 = 4b$, the characteristic equation has double roots. With $r = 4$, the solution takes the form

$$y = (C_1 + C_2 x)e^{rx} = (C_1 + C_2 x)e^{4x}$$

The answer is (B).

3. LINEAR NONHOMOGENEOUS DIFFERENTIAL EQUATIONS WITH CONSTANT COEFFICIENTS

In a nonhomogeneous differential equation, the sum of derivative terms is equal to a nonzero *forcing function* of the independent variable (i.e., $f(x)$ in Eq. 4.1 is non-zero). In order to solve a nonhomogeneous equation, it is often necessary to solve the homogeneous equation first. The homogeneous equation corresponding to a nonhomogeneous equation is known as the *reduced equation* or *complementary equation*.

Equation 4.15: Complete Solution to Nonhomogeneous Differential Equation

$$y(x) = y_h(x) + y_p(x) \qquad \text{4.15}$$

Description

The complete solution to the nonhomogeneous differential equation is shown in Eq. 4.15. The term $y_h(x)$ is the *complementary solution*, which solves the complementary (i.e., homogeneous) case. The *particular solution*, $y_p(x)$, is any specific solution to the nonhomogeneous Eq. 4.1 that is known or can be found. Initial values are used to evaluate any unknown coefficients in the complementary solution after $y_h(x)$ and $y_p(x)$ have been combined. The particular solution will not have any unknown coefficients.

Table 4.1: Method of Undetermined Coefficients

Table 4.1 Method of Undetermined Coefficients

form of $f(x)$	form of $y_p(x)$
A	B
$Ae^{\alpha x}$	$Be^{\alpha x}$, $\alpha \neq r_n$
$A_1 \sin \omega x + A_2 \cos \omega x$	$B_1 \sin \omega x + B_2 \cos \omega x$

Description

Two methods are available for finding a particular solution. The *method of undetermined coefficients*, as presented here, can be used only when $f(x)$ in Eq. 4.1 takes on one of the forms given in Table 4.1. $f(x)$ is known as the *forcing function*.

The particular solution can be read from Table 4.1 if the forcing function is one of the forms given. Of course, the coefficients A_i and B_i are not known—these are the *undetermined coefficients*. The exponent α is the smallest non-negative number (and will be zero, one, or two, etc.), which ensures that no term in the particular solution is also a solution to the complementary equation. α must be determined prior to proceeding with the solution procedure.

Once $y_p(x)$ (including s) is known, it is differentiated to obtain $dy_p(x)/dx$, $d^2y_p(x)/dx^2$, and all subsequent derivatives. All of these derivatives are substituted into the original nonhomogeneous equation. The resulting equation is rearranged to match the forcing function, $f(x)$, and the unknown coefficients are determined, usually by solving simultaneous equations.

The presence of an exponential of the form e^{rx} in the solution indicates that *resonance* is present to some extent.

Equation 4.16 Through Eq. 4.20: First-Order Linear Nonhomogeneous Differential Equations with Constant Coefficients, with Step Input

$$\tau \frac{dy}{dt} + y = Kx(t) \qquad \text{4.16}$$

$$x(t) = \begin{cases} A & t < 0 \\ B & t > 0 \end{cases} \qquad \text{4.17}$$

$$y(0) = KA \qquad \text{4.18}$$

$$y(t) = KA + (KB - KA)\left[1 - \exp\left(\frac{-t}{\tau}\right)\right] \qquad \text{4.19}$$

$$\frac{t}{\tau} = \ln\left[\frac{KB - KA}{KB - y}\right] \qquad \text{4.20}$$

Variation

$$b_1 \frac{dy(t)}{dt} + b_0 y(t) = u(t) \quad [u(t) = \text{unit step function}]$$

Description

As the variation equation for Eq. 4.16 implies, a first-order, linear, nonhomogeneous differential equation with constant coefficients is an extension of Eq. 4.1. Equation 4.16 builds on the differential equation of Eq. 4.1 in the context of a specific control system scenario. It also changes the independent variable from x to t and changes the notation for the forcing function used in Eq. 4.1.

The *time constant*, τ, is the amount of time a homogeneous system (i.e., one with a zero forcing function, $x(t)$) would take to reach $(e-1)/e$, or approximately 63.2% of its final value. This could also be described as the time required to grow to within 36.8% of the final value or as the time to decay to 36.8% of the initial value. The *system gain*, K, or *amplification ratio* is a scalar constant that gives the ratio of the output response to the input response at steady state.

Equation 4.16 describes a *step function*, a special case of a generic forcing function. The forcing function is some value, typically zero $(A = 0)$ until $t = 0$, at which time the forcing function immediately jumps to a constant value. Equation 4.19 gives the *step response*, the solution to Eq. 4.16.

Example

A spring-mass-dashpot system starting from a motionless state is acted upon by a step function. The response is described by the differential equation in which time, t, is given in seconds measured from the application of the step function.

$$\frac{dy}{dt} + 2y = 2u(0) \quad [y(0) = 0]$$

How long will it take for the system to reach 63% of its final value?

(A)   0.25 s

(B)   0.50 s

(C)   1.0 s

(D)   2.0 s

Solution

To fit this problem into the format used by Eq. 4.16, the coefficient of y must be 1. Dividing by 2,

$$0.5\frac{dy}{dt} + y = u(0)$$

$$\tau = 0.50 \text{ s}$$

The answer is (B).

4. FOURIER SERIES

Any periodic waveform can be written as the sum of an infinite number of sinusoidal terms (i.e., an infinite series), known as *harmonic terms*. Such a sum of sinusoidal terms is known as a *Fourier series*, and the process of finding the terms is *Fourier analysis*. Since most series converge rapidly, it is possible to obtain a good approximation to the original waveform with a limited number of sinusoidal terms.

Equation 4.21 and Eq. 4.22: Fourier's Theorem

$$f(t) = a_0 + \sum_{n=1}^{\infty} [a_n \cos(n\omega_0 t) + b_n \sin(n\omega_0 t)] \quad 4.21$$

$$T = 2\pi/\omega_0 \quad 4.22$$

Variation

$$\omega_0 = \frac{2\pi}{T} = 2\pi f$$

Description

Fourier's theorem is Eq. 4.21. The object of a Fourier analysis is to determine the *Fourier coefficients* a_n and b_n. The term a_0 can often be determined by inspection since it is the average value of the waveform.

ω_0 is the *natural (fundamental) frequency* of the waveform. It depends on the actual waveform *period*, T.

Equation 4.23 Through Eq. 4.25: Fourier Coefficients

$$a_0 = (1/T)\int_0^T f(t)\,dt \quad 4.23$$

$$a_n = (2/T)\int_0^T f(t)\cos(n\omega_0 t)\,dt \quad [n = 1, 2, ...] \quad 4.24$$

$$b_n = (2/T)\int_0^T f(t)\sin(n\omega_0 t)\,dt \quad [n = 1, 2, ...] \quad 4.25$$

Description

The *Fourier coefficients* are found from the relationships shown in Eq. 4.23 through Eq. 4.25.

Example

What are the first terms in the Fourier series of the repeating function shown?

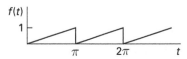

(A) $\dfrac{1}{2} - \cos 2t - \dfrac{1}{2}\cos 4t - \dfrac{1}{3}\cos 6t$

(B) $\dfrac{1}{2} - \dfrac{1}{\pi}\sin 2t - \dfrac{1}{2\pi}\sin 4t - \dfrac{1}{3\pi}\sin 6t$

(C) $\dfrac{1}{4} - \dfrac{1}{\pi}\left(\begin{array}{l}\cos 2t + \sin 2t + \cos 4t \\ \quad + \dfrac{1}{2}\sin 4t + \cos 6t + \dfrac{1}{3}\sin 6t\end{array}\right)$

(D) $\dfrac{1}{4} - \dfrac{1}{\pi}\left(\begin{array}{l}\dfrac{1}{\pi}\cos 2t + \sin 2t \\ \quad + \dfrac{1}{2\pi}\cos 4t + \dfrac{1}{2}\sin 4t \\ \quad + \dfrac{1}{3\pi}\cos 6t + \dfrac{1}{3}\sin 6t\end{array}\right)$

Solution

A Fourier series has the form given by Eq. 4.21.

$$f(t) = a_0 + \sum_{n=1}^{\infty} [a_n \cos(n\omega_0 t) + b_n \sin(n\omega_0 t)]$$

The constant term a_0 corresponds to the average of the function. The average is seen by observation to be $1/2$, so $a_0 = 1/2$.

In this problem, the triangular pulses are ramps, so $f(t)$ has the form of kt, where k is a scalar. A cycle is completed at $t = \pi$, so $T = \pi$, and $\omega_0 = 2\pi/T = 2$. Since $f(T) = 1$ (that is, $f(t) = 1$ at $t = \pi$), $f(t) = t/\pi$.

Calculate the general form of the a_n terms using Eq. 4.24.

$$a_n = (2/T) \int_0^T f(t)\cos(n\omega_0 t)\,dt$$

$$= \frac{2}{\pi^2} \int_0^\pi t \cos(2nt)\,dt$$

$$= \frac{1}{2n^2\pi^2} (\cos(2nt) + 2nt\sin(2nt)) \bigg|_0^\pi$$

$$= 0$$

There are no a_n terms in the series. From Eq. 4.21, there are no cosine terms in the expansion. There are only sine terms in the expansion.

Only choice (B) satisfies both of these requirements.

Alternatively, the values can be derived, though this would be a lengthy process.

The answer is (B).

Equation 4.26: Parseval Relation

$$F_N^2 = a_0^2 + (1/2) \sum_{n=1}^{N} (a_n^2 + b_n^2) \qquad \text{4.26}$$

Variation

$$F_{\text{rms}} = \sqrt{a_0^2 + \frac{a_1^2 + a_2^2 + \cdots + a_N^2 + b_1^2 + b_2^2 + \cdots + b_N^2}{2}}$$

Description

The *Parseval relation* (also known as *Parseval's equality*) calculates the root-mean-square (rms) value of a Fourier series that has been truncated after N terms. The rms value, F_{rms}, is the square root of Eq. 4.26.

5. FOURIER TRANSFORMS

Equation 4.27 Through Eq. 4.30: Fourier Transform Pairs

$$F(\omega) = \int_{-\infty}^{\infty} f(t) e^{-j\omega t}\,dt \qquad \text{4.27}$$

$$f(t) = [1/(2\pi)] \int_{-\infty}^{\infty} F(\omega) e^{j\omega t}\,d\omega \qquad \text{4.28}$$

$$X(f) = \int_{-\infty}^{+\infty} x(t) e^{-j2\pi ft}\,dt \qquad \text{4.29}$$

$$x(t) = \int_{-\infty}^{+\infty} X(f) e^{j2\pi ft}\,df \qquad \text{4.30}$$

Description

There are several useful ways to transform a complex, general equation of one variable into the summation of one or more relatively simple terms of another variable. Functions are transformed for convenience, as when it is necessary to solve exactly for one or more of their properties, and out of necessity, as when it is necessary to approximate the behavior of a waveform that has no exact mathematical expression. In engineering, it is common to use lowercase letters for the original function (of x or t), and to use uppercase letters for the *transform*. It is also necessary to change the variable so that position or time, x or t (known as the *spatial domain*) in the original is not confused with the transform's variable, s or ω (known as the *s-domain* or *frequency domain*). The original function, $f(t)$ and its transform, $F(s)$, constitute a *transform pair*. Although transforms can be determined mathematically from their functions, working with transforms is greatly facilitated by having tables of transform pairs. Extracting $f(t)$ from $F(s)$ is often described as finding the *inverse transform*.

The *Fourier transform*, Eq. 4.27, transforms a function of time, t, into a function of frequency, ω. Essentially, the Fourier transform replaces a function with a sum of simpler sinusoidal functions of a different frequency. Equation 4.28 calculates the inverse transform. Equation 4.29 and Eq. 4.30 are variations of Eq. 4.27 and Eq. 4.28.[1] While the limited number of Fourier transform pairs listed in Table 4.2 and Table 4.3 may not appear to simplify anything, in practice, the transformation is quite useful. Fourier transforms have a wide range of applications, including waveform and image analysis, filtering, reconstruction, and compression.

---

[1]Table 4.2 gives additional transform pairs that apply to Eq. 4.29 and Eq. 4.30.

Equation 4.31, Eq. 4.32, Table 4.2, and Table 4.3: Additional Fourier Transform Pairs

$$f(t) = 0 \quad [t < 0] \qquad \text{4.31}$$

$$\int_0^\infty |f(t)| \, dt < \infty \qquad \text{4.32}$$

Description

Table 4.3 gives some additional useful Fourier transform pairs.[2] Other pairs can be derived from the Laplace transform by replacing s in Table 4.2 with f, if the conditions given in Eq. 4.31 and Eq. 4.32 are met.

Table 4.2 Fourier Transform Pairs*

$x(t)$	$X(f)$
1	$\delta(f)$
$\delta(t)$	1
$u(t)$	$\dfrac{1}{2}\delta(f) + \dfrac{1}{j2\pi f}$
$\Pi(t/\tau)$	$\tau \operatorname{sinc}(\tau f)$
$\operatorname{sinc}(Bt)$	$\dfrac{1}{B}\Pi(f/B)$
$\Lambda(t/\tau)$	$\tau \operatorname{sinc}^2(\tau f)$
$e^{-at}u(t)$	$\dfrac{1}{a + j2\pi f} \quad [a > 0]$
$te^{-at}u(t)$	$\dfrac{1}{(a + j2\pi f)^2} \quad [a > 0]$
$e^{-a|t|}$	$\dfrac{2a}{a^2 + (2\pi f)^2} \quad [a > 0]$
$e^{-(at)^2}$	$\dfrac{\sqrt{\pi}}{a}e^{-(\pi f/a)^2}$
$\cos(2\pi f_0 t + \theta)$	$\dfrac{1}{2}[e^{j\theta}\delta(f - f_0) + e^{-j\theta}\delta(f + f_0)]$
$\sin(2\pi f_0 t + \theta)$	$\dfrac{1}{2j}[e^{j\theta}\delta(f - f_0) - e^{-j\theta}\delta(f + f_0)]$
$\displaystyle\sum_{n=-\infty}^{n=+\infty} \delta(t - nT_s)$	$f_s \displaystyle\sum_{k=-\infty}^{k=+\infty} \delta(f - kf_s) \quad \left[f_s = \dfrac{1}{T_s}\right]$

*Although not explicitly defined in the NCEES *FE Reference Handbook* (*NCEES Handbook*), sinc(x) is an abbreviation for $\sin(x)/x$.

Table 4.3 Fourier Transform Pairs

$f(t)$	$F(\omega)$
$\delta(t)$	1
$u(t)$	$\pi\delta(\omega) + 1/j\omega$
$u\left(t + \dfrac{\tau}{2}\right) - u\left(t - \dfrac{\tau}{2}\right) = r_{\text{rect}}\dfrac{t}{\tau}$	$\tau\dfrac{\sin(\omega\tau/2)}{\omega\tau/2}$
$e^{j\omega_0 t}$	$2\pi\delta(\omega - \omega_0)$

Example

The Fourier transform of an impulse $a^2\delta(t)$ of magnitude a^2 is equal to

(A) $\sqrt{a}$

(B) $a - 1$

(C) a

(D) a^2

Solution

The Fourier transform $X(f)$ of a given signal $x(t)$ is found from Eq. 4.29.

$$\begin{aligned}
X(f) &= \int_{-\infty}^{+\infty} x(t)e^{-j2\pi ft}\,dt \\
&= \int_{-\infty}^{+\infty} a^2\delta(t)e^{-j2\pi ft}\,dt \\
&= a^2\int_{-\infty}^{+\infty} \delta(t)e^{-j2\pi ft}\,dt
\end{aligned}$$

For $t = 0$, $x(t) = \delta(t) = 1$, and for all other values of t, $x(t) = 0$. This corresponds to the first line of Table 4.3.

$$\begin{aligned}
X(f) &= a^2\int_{-\infty}^{+\infty} \delta(t)e^{-j2\pi ft}\,dt \\
&= a^2(1) \\
&= a^2
\end{aligned}$$

The answer is (D).

---

[2]While any variable can be used to designate any quantity, the *NCEES Handbook* uses an uncommon Fourier transform notation that may be confusing to some. A spatial or temporal function is usually described as $f(x)$ or $f(t)$, where f designates the function, and x or t is the independent variable. In that case, the Fourier transform of $f(t)$ would be designated as $F(\omega)$, where ω is an independent variable from the imaginary frequency domain. However, in Eq. 4.29 and Eq. 4.30, the *NCEES Handbook* uses x and X to designate the function and its transform, and f to designate an independent variable from the frequency domain, where $\omega = 2\pi f$. What would commonly be shown as $F(\omega)$ is shown as $X(f)$.

Mathematics

Table 4.4: Fourier Transform Theorems

Table 4.4 Fourier Transform Theorems

theorem	function	transform
linearity	$ax(t) + by(t)$	$aX(f) + bY(f)$
scale change	$x(at)$	$\frac{1}{|a|}X\left(\frac{f}{a}\right)$
time reversal	$x(-t)$	$X(-f)$
duality	$X(t)$	$x(-f)$
time shift	$x(t - t_0)$	$X(f)e^{-j2\pi ft_0}$
frequency shift	$x(t)e^{j2\pi f_0 t}$	$X(f - f_0)$
modulation	$x(t)\cos 2\pi f_0 t$	$\frac{1}{2}X(f - f_0) + \frac{1}{2}X(f + f_0)$
multiplication	$x(t)y(t)$	$X(f)^* Y(f)$
convolution	$x(t)^* y(t)$	$X(f) Y(f)$
differentiation	$\frac{d^n x(t)}{dt^n}$	$(j2\pi f)^n X(f)$
integration	$\int_{-\infty}^{t} x(\lambda)\,d\lambda$	$\frac{1}{j2\pi f}X(f) + \frac{1}{2}X(0)\delta(f)$

Description

Determining the Fourier transform of a complex mathematical function is simplified by various Fourier theorems, which are summarized in Table 4.4. While all are important, the simplest are the addition, linearity, and scale change (commonly referred to as *similarity*) theorems. In Table 4.4, the addition theorem is combined with the linearity theorem. The addition theorem states, not surprisingly, that the transform of a sum of functions is the sum of the transforms of the individual functions. In Table 4.4's nomenclature and format, this would be designated as

$$x(t) + y(t) \qquad X(f) + Y(f) \qquad \text{[addition]}$$

The asterisk symbol * is used to designate the *convolution operation*, which is not the same as multiplication. The convolution of two functions $x(t)$ and $y(t)$ is a third function defined as the integral of the product of one of the functions and the other function shifted by some given distance, x_0. The convolution essentially determines the amount of overlap between the functions when the functions are separated by x_0.

$$x(t)^* y(t) = \int_{-\infty}^{+\infty} x(t)y(t_0 - t)\,dt$$

6. LAPLACE TRANSFORMS

Traditional methods of solving nonhomogeneous differential equations by hand are usually difficult and/or time consuming. *Laplace transforms* can be used to reduce many solution procedures to simple algebra.

Equation 4.33: Laplace Transform

$$F(s) = \int_0^\infty f(t)e^{-st}\,dt \qquad \text{4.33}$$

Description

Every mathematical function, $f(t)$, has a Laplace transform, written as $F(s)$ or $\mathcal{L}(s)$. The transform is written in the s-domain, regardless of the independent variable in the original function. The variable s is equivalent to a derivative operator, although it may be handled in the equations as a simple variable. Equation 4.33 converts a function into a Laplace transform.

Generally, it is unnecessary to actually obtain a function's Laplace transform by use of Eq. 4.33. Tables of these transforms are readily available (see Table 4.5).

Example

What is the Laplace transform of $f(t) = e^{-6t}$?

(A) $\dfrac{1}{s+6}$

(B) $\dfrac{1}{s-6}$

(C) e^{-6+s}

(D) e^{6+s}

Solution

The Laplace transform of a function, $F(s)$, can be calculated from the definition of a transform.

$$F(e^{-6t}) = \int_0^\infty e^{-(s+6)t}\,dt = -\frac{e^{-(s+6)t}}{s+6}\Bigg|_0^\infty = 0 - \left(-\frac{1}{s+6}\right)$$

$$= \frac{1}{s+6}$$

(This problem could have been solved more quickly by using a Laplace transform pair table, such as Table 4.5.)

The answer is (A).

Table 4.5: Laplace Transform Pairs

Table 4.5 Laplace Transforms

$f(t)$	$F(s)$
$\delta(t)$, impulse at $t = 0$	1
$u(t)$, step at $t = 0$	$1/s$
$t[u(t)]$, ramp at $t = 0$	$1/s^2$
$e^{-\alpha t}$	$1/(s+\alpha)$
$te^{-\alpha t}$	$1/(s+\alpha)^2$
$e^{-\alpha t}\sin \beta t$	$\beta/\left[(s+\alpha)^2 + \beta^2\right]$
$e^{-\alpha t}\cos \beta t$	$(s+\alpha)/[(s+\alpha)^2 + \beta^2]$
$\dfrac{d^n f(t)}{dt^n}$	$s^n F(s) - \displaystyle\sum_{m=0}^{n-1} s^{n-m-1}\dfrac{d^m f(0)}{dt^m}$
$\int_0^t f(\tau)\,d\tau$	$(1/s)F(s)$
$\int_0^t x(t-\tau)h(t)\,d\tau$	$H(s)X(s)$
$f(t-\tau)u(t-\tau)$	$e^{-\tau s}F(s)$

Description

Table 4.5 gives common Laplace transforms.

Example

What is the Laplace transform of the step function $f(t)$?

$$f(t) = u(t-1) + u(t-2)$$

(A) $\dfrac{1}{s} + \dfrac{2}{s}$

(B) $\dfrac{e^{-s} + e^{-2s}}{s}$

(C) $1 + \dfrac{e^{-2s}}{s}$

(D) $\dfrac{e^{s}}{s} + \dfrac{e^{2s}}{s}$

Solution

The notations $u(t{-}1)$ and $u(t{-}2)$ mean that a unit step input (a step of height 1) is applied at $t = 1$ and another unit step is applied at $t = 2$. (This function could be used to describe the terrain that a tracked robot would have to navigate to go up a flight of two stairs in a particular

interval.) Table 4.5 contains Laplace transforms for various input functions, including steps. For steps at $t = 0$, the Laplace transform is $1/s$. However, in this example, the steps are encountered at $t = 1$ and $t = 2$. Superposition can be used to calculate the Laplace transform of the summation as the sum of the two transforms. Use the last entry in Table 4.5, with $f(t{-}\tau){=}1$.

$$F(s) = F(u(t-1)) + F(u(t-2)) = \frac{e^{-s}}{s} + \frac{e^{-2s}}{s}$$
$$= \frac{e^{-s} + e^{-2s}}{s}$$

The answer is (B).

Equation 4.34: Inverse Laplace Transform

$$f(t) = \frac{1}{2\pi j} \int_{\sigma - j\infty}^{\sigma + j\infty} F(s)\, e^{st}\, dt \qquad 4.34$$

Description

Extracting a function from its transform is the *inverse Laplace transform* operation. Although Eq. 4.34 could be used and other methods exist, this operation is almost always done using a table, such as Table 4.5.

Equation 4.35: Initial Value Theorem

$$\lim_{s \to \infty} sF(s) \qquad 4.35$$

Description

Equation 4.35 shows the *initial value theorem* (IVT).

Equation 4.36: Final Value Theorem

$$\lim_{s \to 0} sF(s) \qquad 4.36$$

Description

Equation 4.36 shows the *final value theorem* (FVT).

7. DIFFERENCE EQUATIONS

Equation 4.37: Difference Equation

$$f(t) = y' = \frac{y_{i+1} - y_i}{t_{i+1} - t_i} \qquad 4.37$$

Description

Many processes can be accurately modeled by differential equations. However, exact solutions to these models may be difficult to obtain. In such cases, discrete versions of the original differential equations can be produced. These discrete equations are known as *finite difference equations* or just *difference equations*. Communication signal processing, heat transfer, and traffic flow are just a few of the applications of difference equations.

Difference equations are also ideal for modeling processes whose states or values are restricted to certain specified (equally spaced) points in time or space as is done with many simulation models.

A difference equation is a relationship between a function and its differences over some interval of integers. (This is analogous to a differential equation that is a relationship of functions and their derivatives over some interval of real numbers.) Any system with an input $v(t)$ and an output $y(t)$ defined only at the equally spaced intervals given by Eq. 4.37 can be described by a difference equation.

The *order* of the difference equation is the number of differences that are in the equation.

Although simple difference equations can be solved by hand, in practice, they are solved by computer using numerical analysis techniques.

Equation 4.38 and Eq. 4.39: First-Order Linear Difference Equation

$$\Delta t = t_{i+1} - t_i \qquad \text{4.38}$$

$$y_{i+1} = y_i + y'(\Delta t) \qquad \text{4.39}$$

Description

A *first-order difference equation* is a relationship between the values of some function at two consecutive points in time or space. The relationship can take on any form using any of the mathematical operators. For example, an additive relationship might be $y_{i+1} = y_i + 7$; a multiplicative relationship might be $y_{i+1} = 5y_i$; and an exponent relationship might be $y_{i+1} = y_i^2$. Equation 4.39 is a first-order linear difference equation that uses linear extrapolation to predict a subsequent curve point. For example, Eq. 4.39 can be interpreted as using the elevation of a projectile and slope of the path in one interval to predict the elevation reached by the projectile in the next interval.

Second-Order Difference Equation of the Fibonacci Sequence

A *second-order difference equation* is a relationship between the values of some function at three consecutive points in time or space. The relationship can take on

any form using any of the mathematical operators. For example, an additive relationship might be $y_{i+1} = y_i + y_{i-1} - 2$; a multiplicative relationship might be $y_{i+1} = 2y_i y_{i-1}$; and an exponent relationship might be $y_{i+1} = y_i^2 + 2y_{i-1}$. An additive second-order difference equation that describes the Fibonacci sequence (where each term is the sum of the previous two terms) is $F_{i+1} = F_i + F_{i-1}$.

$$y(k) = y(k-1) + y(k-2)$$

$$f(k+2) = f(k+1) + f(k) \quad [f(0) = 1 \text{ and } f(1) = 1]$$

5
Numerical Methods

1. INTRODUCTION TO NUMERICAL METHODS

Although the roots of second-degree polynomials are easily found by a variety of methods (by factoring, completing the square, or using the quadratic equation), easy methods of solving cubic and higher-order equations exist only for specialized cases. However, cubic and higher-order equations occur frequently in engineering, and they are difficult to factor. Trial and error solutions, including graphing, are usually satisfactory for finding only the general region in which the root occurs.

Numerical analysis is a general subject that covers, among other things, iterative methods for evaluating roots to equations. The most efficient numerical methods are too complex to present and, in any case, work by hand. However, some of the simpler methods are presented here. Except in critical problems that must be solved in real time, a few extra calculator or computer iterations will make no difference.[1]

2. ROOT EXTRACTION

Equation 5.1: Newton's Method

$$a^{j+1} = a^j - \left. \frac{f(x)}{\dfrac{df(x)}{dx}} \right|_{x=a^j} \qquad \textbf{5.1}$$

Description

Newton's method (also known as the *Newton-Raphson method*) is a particular form of *fixed-point iteration*. In this sense, "fixed point" is often used as a synonym for "root" or "zero."

All fixed-point techniques require a starting point. Preferably, the starting point will be close to the actual root.[2] And, while Newton's method converges quickly, it requires the function to be continuously differentiable.

At each iteration ($j = 0$, 1, 2, etc.), Eq. 5.1 estimates the root. The maximum error is determined by looking at how much the estimate changes after each iteration. If the change between the previous and current estimates (representing the magnitude of error in the estimate) is too large, the current estimate is used as the independent variable for the subsequent iteration.[3]

Example

Newton's method is being used to find the roots of the equation $f(x) = (x-2)^2 - 1$. What is the third approximation of the root if $x = 9.33$ is chosen as the first approximation?

(A) 1.0

(B) 2.0

(C) 3.0

(D) 4.0

Solution

Perform two iterations of Newton's method with an initial guess of 9.33.

$$
\begin{aligned}
f(x) &= (x-2)^2 - 1 \\
f'(x) &= (2)(x-2) \\
f(x_1) &= (9.33 - 2)^2 - 1 \\
&= 52.73 \\
f'(x_1) &= (2)(9.33 - 2) \\
&= 14.66
\end{aligned}
$$

---

[1]Most advanced handheld calculators have "root finder" functions that use numerical methods to iteratively solve equations.

[2]Theoretically, the only penalty for choosing a starting point too far away from the root will be a slower convergence to the root. However, for some nonlinear relations, the penalty will be nonconvergence.

[3]Actually, the theory defining the maximum error is more definite than this. For example, for a large enough value of j, the error decreases approximately linearly. The consecutive values of a^j converge linearly to the root as well.

From Eq. 5.1,

$$x^{j+1} = x^j - \frac{f(x)}{f'(x)}$$

$$x_2 = x_1 - \frac{f(x_1)}{f'(x_1)}$$

$$= 9.33 - \frac{f(9.33)}{f'(9.33)}$$

$$= 9.33 - \frac{52.73}{14.66}$$

$$= 5.73$$

$$f(x_2) = (5.73 - 2)^2 - 1 = 12.91$$
$$f'(x_2) = (2)(5.73 - 2) = 7.46$$
$$x_3 = x_2 - \frac{f(x_2)}{f'(x_2)} = 5.73 - \frac{f(5.73)}{f'(5.73)} = 5.73 - \frac{12.91}{7.46}$$

$$= 4.0$$

The answer is (D).

3. MINIMIZATION

Equation 5.2 Through Eq. 5.4: Newton's Method of Minimization

$$x_{k+1} = x_k - \left(\frac{\partial^2 h}{\partial x^2}\bigg|_{x=x_k}\right)^{-1} \frac{\partial h}{\partial x}\bigg|_{x=x_k} \qquad 5.2$$

$$\frac{\partial h}{\partial x} = \begin{bmatrix} \dfrac{\partial h}{\partial x_1} \\ \dfrac{\partial h}{\partial x_2} \\ \dots \\ \dots \\ \dfrac{\partial h}{\partial x_n} \end{bmatrix} \qquad 5.3$$

$$\frac{\partial^2 h}{\partial x^2} = \begin{bmatrix} \dfrac{\partial^2 h}{\partial x_1^2} & \dfrac{\partial^2 h}{\partial x_1 \partial x_2} & \dots & \dots & \dfrac{\partial^2 h}{\partial x_1 \partial x_n} \\ \dfrac{\partial^2 h}{\partial x_1 \partial x_2} & \dfrac{\partial^2 h}{\partial x_2^2} & \dots & \dots & \dfrac{\partial^2 h}{\partial x_2 \partial x_n} \\ \dots & \dots & \dots & \dots & \dots \\ \dots & \dots & \dots & \dots & \dots \\ \dfrac{\partial^2 h}{\partial x_1 \partial x_n} & \dfrac{\partial^2 h}{\partial x_2 \partial x_n} & \dots & \dots & \dfrac{\partial^2 h}{\partial x_n^2} \end{bmatrix} \qquad 5.4$$

Description

Newton's algorithm for minimization is given by Eq. 5.2. Equation 5.2 applies to a scalar value function, $h(\boldsymbol{x}) = h(x_1, x_2, \dots, x_n)$, and is used to calculate a vector, $\boldsymbol{x}^* \in R_n$, where $h(\boldsymbol{x}^*) \leq h(\boldsymbol{x})$ for all $\boldsymbol{x}$ values.

4. NUMERICAL INTEGRATION

Equation 5.5: Euler's Rule

$$\int_a^b f(x)\, dx \approx \Delta x \sum_{k=0}^{n-1} f(a + k\Delta x) \qquad 5.5$$

Description

Equation 5.5 is known as *Euler's rule* or the *forward rectangular rule*.

Equation 5.6 and Eq. 5.7: Trapezoidal Rule

$$\int_a^b f(x)\, dx \approx \Delta x \left[\frac{f(a) + f(b)}{2}\right] \quad [n = 1] \qquad 5.6$$

$$\int_a^b f(x)\, dx \approx \frac{\Delta x}{2}\left[f(a) + 2\sum_{k=0}^{n-1} f(a + k\Delta x) + f(b)\right] \qquad 5.7$$

$$[n > 1]$$

Variation

$$A = \frac{d}{2}\left(h_0 + 2\sum_{i=1}^{n-1} h_i + h_n\right)$$

Description

Areas of sections with irregular boundaries cannot be determined precisely, and approximation methods must be used. Figure 5.1 shows an example of an *irregular area*. If the irregular side can be divided into a series of n cells of equal width, and if the irregular side of each cell is fairly straight, the *trapezoidal rule* is appropriate. Equation 5.6 and Eq. 5.7 describe the trapezoidal rule for $n = 1$ and $n > 1$, respectively.

Figure 5.1 *Irregular Areas*

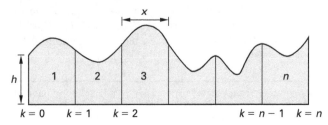

Example

For the irregular area under the curve shown, $a = 3$, and $b = 15$. The formula of the curve is

$$f(x) = (1-x)(x-30)$$

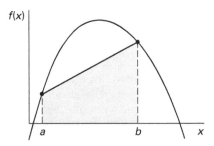

Most nearly, what is the approximate area using the trapezoidal rule?

(A) 1200

(B) 1300

(C) 1600

(D) 1900

Solution

Calculate Δx.

$$\Delta x = b - a = 15 - 3 = 12$$

Calculate $f(a)$ and $f(b)$.

$$f(a) = (1-a)(a-30) = (1-3)(3-30) = 54$$

$$f(b) = (1-b)(b-30) = (1-15)(15-30) = 210$$

This is a one-trapezoid integration (i.e., $n = 1$), so use Eq. 5.6. The area under the curve is

$$\text{area} = \Delta x \left[\frac{f(a) + f(b)}{2} \right]$$

$$= (12) \left(\frac{54 + 210}{2} \right)$$

$$= 1584 \quad (1600)$$

The answer is (C).

Equation 5.8 Through Eq. 5.10: Simpson's Rule

$$\int_a^b f(x)\, dx \approx \left(\frac{b-a}{6} \right) \left[f(a) + 4f\left(\frac{a+b}{2} \right) + f(b) \right] \qquad 5.8$$

$$[n = 2]$$

$$\int_a^b f(x)\, dx \approx \frac{\Delta x}{3} \left[\begin{array}{l} f(a) + 2 \displaystyle\sum_{k=2,4,6,\ldots}^{n-2} f(a + k\Delta x) \\[2ex] + 4 \displaystyle\sum_{k=1,3,5,\ldots}^{n-1} f(a + k\Delta x) + f(b) \end{array} \right] \qquad 5.9$$

$$[n \geq 4]$$

$$\Delta x = (b-a)/n \qquad 5.10$$

Variation

$$A = \frac{d}{3} \left(h_0 + 2 \sum_{\substack{i\,\text{even} \\ i=2}}^{n-2} h_i + 4 \sum_{\substack{i\,\text{odd} \\ i=1}}^{n-1} h_i + h_n \right)$$

Description

If the irregular side of each cell is curved (parabolic), *Simpson's rule* (*parabolic rule*) should be used. n must be even to use Simpson's rule.

The Simpson's rule equations for $n = 2$ and $n \geq 4$ are given by Eq. 5.8 and Eq. 5.9, respectively.

Example

For the irregular area under the curve shown, $a = 3$, and $b = 15$. The formula of the curve is

$$f(x) = (1-x)(x-30)$$

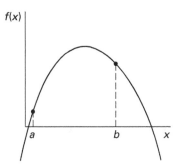

Most nearly, what is the approximate area using Simpson's rule?

(A) 1310

(B) 1870

(C) 1960

(D) 2000

Solution

Calculate $f(a)$, $f(b)$, and $f((a+b)/2)$.

$$f(a) = (1-a)(a-30) = (1-3)(3-30) = 54$$

$$f(b) = (1-b)(b-30) = (1-15)(15-30) = 210$$

$$\frac{a+b}{2} = \frac{3+15}{2} = 9$$

$$f\left(\frac{a+b}{2}\right) = f(9) = (1-9)(9-30) = 168$$

Calculate Δx, using the smallest even number of cells, $n = 2$, and Eq. 5.10.

$$\Delta x = (b-a)/n = \frac{15-3}{2} = 6$$

Using Eq. 5.8, the area is

$$\int_a^b f(x)\,dx \approx \left(\frac{b-a}{6}\right)\left[f(a) + 4f\left(\frac{a+b}{2}\right) + f(b)\right]$$

$$= \left(\frac{15-3}{6}\right)(54 + (4)(168) + 210)$$

$$= 1872 \quad (1870)$$

The answer is (B).

5. NUMERICAL SOLUTION OF ORDINARY DIFFERENTIAL EQUATIONS

Equation 5.11 Through Eq. 5.14: Euler's Approximation

$$x[(k+1)\Delta t] \cong x(k\Delta t) + \Delta t f[x(k\Delta t), k\Delta t] \qquad 5.11$$

$$x[(k+1)\Delta t] \cong x(k\Delta t) + \Delta t f[x(k\Delta t)] \qquad 5.12$$

$$x_{k+1} = x_k + \Delta t (dx_k/dt) \qquad 5.13$$

$$x_{k+1} = x + \Delta t[f(x(k), t(k))] \qquad 5.14$$

Description

Euler's approximation is a method for estimating the value of a function given the value and slope of the function at an adjacent location. The simplicity of the concept is illustrated by writing Euler's approximation in terms of the traditional two-dimensional x-y coordinate system.

$$y(x_2) = y(x_1) + (x_2 - x_1)y'(x_1)$$

As long as the derivative can be evaluated, Euler's method can be used to predict the value of any function whose values are limited to discrete, sequential points in time or space (e.g., a difference equation).

Euler's approximation applies to a differential equation of the form $f(x,t) = dx/dt$, where $x(0) = x_0$. Equation 5.11 applies to a general time $k\Delta t$. Equation 5.12 applies when $f(x) = dx/dt$ and can be expressed recursively as Eq. 5.13, or as Eq. 5.14.

The error associated with Euler's approximation is zero for linear systems. Euler's approximation can be used as a quick estimate for nonlinear systems as long as the presence of error is recognized. Figure 5.2 shows the geometric interpretation of Euler's approximation for a curvilinear function.

Figure 5.2 *Geometric Interpretation of Euler's Approximation*

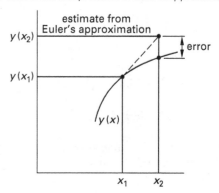

Diagnostic Exam

Topic II: Probability and Statistics

1. A fair coin is tossed three times. What is the approximate probability of heads appearing at least one time?

- (A) 0.67
- (B) 0.75
- (C) 0.80
- (D) 0.88

2. Samples of aluminum-alloy channels are tested for stiffness. Stiffness is normally distributed. The following frequency distribution is obtained.

stiffness	frequency
2480	23
2440	35
2400	40
2360	33
2320	21

What is the approximate probability that the stiffness of any given channel section is less than 2350?

- (A) 0.08
- (B) 0.16
- (C) 0.23
- (D) 0.36

3. Most nearly, what is the sample variance of the following data?

$$0.50, 0.80, 0.75, 0.52, 0.60$$

- (A) 0.015
- (B) 0.018
- (C) 0.11
- (D) 0.12

4. Two students are working independently on a problem. Their respective probabilities of solving the problem are 1/3 and 3/4. What is the probability that at least one of them will solve the problem?

- (A) 1/2
- (B) 5/8
- (C) 2/3
- (D) 5/6

5. Most nearly, what is the arithmetic mean of the following values?

$$9.5, 2.4, 3.6, 7.5, 8.2, 9.1, 6.6, 9.8$$

- (A) 6.3
- (B) 7.1
- (C) 7.8
- (D) 8.1

6. A normal distribution has a mean of 12 and a standard deviation of 3. If a sample is taken from the normal distribution, most nearly, what is the probability that the sample will be between 15 and 18?

- (A) 0.091
- (B) 0.12
- (C) 0.14
- (D) 0.16

7. A marksman can hit a bull's-eye from 100 m three times out of every four shots. What is the probability that he will hit a bull's-eye with at least one of his next three shots?

- (A) 3/4
- (B) 15/16
- (C) 31/32
- (D) 63/64

8. The final scores of students in a graduate course are distributed normally with a mean of 72 and a standard deviation of 10. Most nearly, what is the probability that a student's score will be between 65 and 78?

(A)   0.42

(B)   0.48

(C)   0.52

(D)   0.65

9. What is the sample standard deviation of the following 50 data points?

data value	frequency
1.5	3
2.5	8
3.5	18
4.5	12
5.5	9

(A)   1.12

(B)   1.13

(C)   1.26

(D)   1.28

10. 15% of a batch of mixed-color gumballs are green. Out of a random sample of 20 gumballs, what is the probability of getting two green balls?

(A)   0.12

(B)   0.17

(C)   0.23

(D)   0.46

SOLUTIONS

1. Calculate the probability of no heads, and then subtract that from 1 to get the probability of at least one head. If there are no heads, then all tosses must be tails.

$$P\left(\genfrac{}{}{0pt}{}{\text{three tails in}}{\text{three tosses}}\right) = P\left(\genfrac{}{}{0pt}{}{\text{one tail in}}{\text{one toss}}\right)^3 = \left(\frac{1}{2}\right)^3$$
$$= 0.125$$
$$P(E) = 1 - P(\text{not } E) = 1 - 0.125$$
$$= 0.875 \quad (0.88)$$

The answer is (D).

2. The probability can be found using the unit normal distribution chart. In order to use the unit normal distribution chart, the population mean and standard deviation must be found.

The arithmetic mean is an unbiased estimator of the population mean.

$$n = 23 + 35 + 40 + 33 + 21$$
$$= 152$$

$$\overline{X} = (1/n)\sum_{i=1}^{n} X_i$$
$$= \left(\frac{1}{152}\right)\left(\genfrac{}{}{0pt}{}{(2480)(23) + (2440)(35)}{\genfrac{}{}{0pt}{}{+(2400)(40) + (2360)(33)}{+(2320)(21)}}\right)$$
$$= 2402$$

The sample standard deviation is an unbiased estimator of the standard deviation.

$$s = \sqrt{[1/(n-1)]\sum_{i=1}^{n}(X_i - \overline{X})^2}$$
$$= \sqrt{\left(\frac{1}{152-1}\right)\left(\genfrac{}{}{0pt}{}{(23)(2480-2402)^2}{\genfrac{}{}{0pt}{}{+(35)(2440-2402)^2}{\genfrac{}{}{0pt}{}{+(40)(2400-2402)^2}{\genfrac{}{}{0pt}{}{+(33)(2360-2402)^2}{+(21)(2320-2402)^2}}}}\right)}$$
$$= 50.82$$

Find the standard normal variable corresponding to 2350.

$$Z = \frac{x - \mu}{\sigma} = \frac{2350 - 2402}{50.82}$$
$$= -1.0$$

Since the unit normal distribution is symmetrical about $x=0$, the probability of x being in the interval $[-\infty, -1]$ is the same as x being in the interval $[+1, +\infty]$.

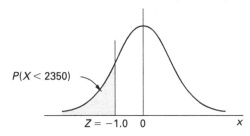

$$P(X < 2350) = P(Z < -1.0)$$
$$= R(1.0)$$
$$= 0.1587 \quad (0.16)$$

The answer is (B).

3. The arithmetic mean of the data is

$$\overline{X} = (1/n) \sum_{i=1}^{n} X_i$$
$$= \left(\frac{1}{5}\right)(0.50 + 0.80 + 0.75 + 0.52 + 0.60)$$
$$= 0.634$$

Use the mean to find the sample variance.

$$s^2 = [1/(n-1)] \sum_{i=1}^{n}(X_i - \overline{X})^2$$
$$= \left(\frac{1}{5-1}\right)\begin{pmatrix}(0.50 - 0.634)^2 + (0.80 - 0.634)^2 \\ +(0.75 - 0.634)^2 + (0.52 - 0.634)^2 \\ +(0.60 - 0.634)^2\end{pmatrix}$$
$$= 0.0183 \quad (0.018)$$

The answer is (B).

4. The probability that either or both of the students solve the problem is given by the laws of total and joint probability.

Since the two students are working independently, the joint probability of both students solving the problem is

$$P(A, B) = P(A)P(B)$$
$$= \left(\frac{1}{3}\right)\left(\frac{3}{4}\right)$$
$$= 1/4$$

The total probability is

$$P(A + B) = P(A) + P(B) - P(A, B)$$
$$= \frac{1}{3} + \frac{3}{4} - \frac{1}{4}$$
$$= 5/6$$

The answer is (D).

5. The arithmetic mean is the sum of the values divided by the total number of items.

$$\overline{X} = (1/n) \sum_{i=1}^{n} X_i$$
$$= \left(\frac{1}{8}\right)(9.5 + 2.4 + 3.6 + 7.5 + 8.2 + 9.1 + 6.6 + 9.8)$$
$$= 7.09 \quad (7.1)$$

The answer is (B).

6. Find the standard normal values for the minimum and maximum values.

$$Z_1 = \frac{x_1 - \mu}{\sigma} = \frac{15 - 12}{3} = 1$$
$$Z_2 = \frac{x_2 - \mu}{\sigma} = \frac{18 - 12}{3} = 2$$

Plot these values on a normal distribution curve.

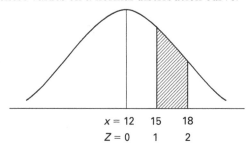

From the standard normal table, the probabilities are

$$P(Z < 1) = 0.8413$$
$$P(Z < 2) = 0.9772$$

The probability that the outcome will be between 15 and 18 is

$$P(15 < x < 18) = P(x < 18) - P(x < 15)$$
$$= P(Z < 2) - P(Z < 1)$$
$$= 0.9772 - 0.8413$$
$$= 0.1359 \quad (0.14)$$

The answer is (C).

7. Solving this problem requires calculating three probabilities.

$$P(\text{at least 1 hit in 3 shots}) = P(\text{1 hit in 3 shots})$$
$$+ P(\text{2 hits in 3 shots})$$
$$+ P(\text{3 hits in 3 shots})$$

An easier way to find the probability of making at least one hit is to solve for its complementary probability, that of making zero hits.

$$P(\text{miss}) = 1 - P(\text{hit}) = 1 - \frac{3}{4}$$
$$= 1/4$$
$$P(\text{at least one hit}) = 1 - P(\text{no hits})$$
$$= 1 - \begin{pmatrix} P(\text{miss}) \times P(\text{miss}) \\ \times P(\text{miss}) \end{pmatrix}$$
$$= 1 - \left(\frac{1}{4}\right)\left(\frac{1}{4}\right)\left(\frac{1}{4}\right)$$
$$= 63/64$$

The answer is (D).

8. Calculate standard normal values for the points of interest, 65 and 78.

Combinations of Random Variables

$$Z = \frac{x_0 - \mu}{\sigma}$$
$$Z_{65} = \frac{65 - 72}{10}$$
$$= -0.70$$
$$Z_{78} = \frac{78 - 72}{10}$$
$$= 0.60$$

The probability of a score falling between 65 and 78 is equal to the area under the unit normal curve between -0.70 and 0.60. Determine this area by subtracting $F(Z_{65})$ from $F(Z_{78})$. Although the $F(x)$ statistic is not tabulated for negative x values, the curve's symmetry allows the $R(x)$ statistic to be used instead. *[Unit Normal Distribution ($\mu=0$, $\sigma=1$)]*

$$F(-x) = R(x)$$
$$P(65 < X < 78) = F(0.60) - R(0.70)$$
$$= 0.7257 - 0.2420$$
$$= 0.4837 \quad (0.48)$$

The answer is (B).

9. The number of data points is given as 50. The arithmetic mean is

$$\overline{X} = (1/n)\sum_{i=1}^{n} X_i$$
$$= \left(\frac{1}{50}\right)\begin{pmatrix} (3)(1.5) + (8)(2.5) + (18)(3.5) \\ +(12)(4.5) + (9)(5.5) \end{pmatrix}$$
$$= 3.82$$

The sample standard deviation is

$$s = \sqrt{[1/(n-1)]\sum_{i=1}^{n}(X_i - \overline{X})^2}$$
$$= \sqrt{\left(\frac{1}{50-1}\right)\begin{pmatrix} (3)(1.5 - 3.82)^2 + (8)(2.5 - 3.82)^2 \\ +(18)(3.5 - 3.82)^2 \\ +(12)(4.5 - 3.82)^2 \\ +(9)(5.5 - 3.82)^2 \end{pmatrix}}$$
$$= 1.133 \quad (1.13)$$

The answer is (B).

10. Use the binomial distribution.

$$p = 0.15$$
$$P_{20}(2) = \frac{n!}{x!\,(n-x)!}p^x q^{n-x}$$
$$= \left(\frac{20!}{(2!)(20-2)!}\right)(0.15)^2(1-0.15)^{20-2}$$
$$= 0.229 \quad (0.23)$$

The answer is (C).

6 Probability and Statistics

1. SET THEORY

A *set* (usually designated by a capital letter) is a population or collection of individual items known as *elements* or *members*. The *null set*, $\varnothing$, is empty (i.e., contains no members). If A and B are two sets, A is a *subset* of B if every member in A is also in B. A is a *proper subset* of B if B consists of more than the elements in A. These relationships are denoted as follows.[1]

$$A \subseteq B \ \text{[subset]}$$

$$A \subset B \ \text{[proper subset]}$$

The *universal set*, U, is one from which other sets draw their members. If A is a subset of U, then $\bar{A}$ (also designated as A', A^{-1}, $\tilde{A}$, and $-A$) is the *complement* of A and consists of all elements in U that are not in A. This is illustrated in a *Venn diagram* in Fig. 6.1(a).

The *union of two sets*, denoted by $A \cup B$ and shown in Fig. 6.1(b), is the set of all elements that are either in A or B or both. The *intersection of two sets*, denoted by $A \cap B$ and shown in Fig. 6.1(c), is the set of all elements that belong to both A and B. If $A \cap B = \varnothing$, A and B are said to be *disjoint sets*.

Figure 6.1 Venn Diagrams

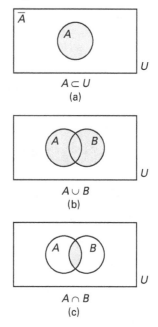

$A \subset U$
(a)

$A \cup B$
(b)

$A \cap B$
(c)

If A, B, and C are subsets of the universal set, the following laws apply.

Identity Laws

$$A \cup \varnothing = A$$

$$A \cup U = U$$

$$A \cap \varnothing = \varnothing$$

$$A \cap U = A$$

Idempotent Laws

$$A \cup A = A$$

$$A \cap A = A$$

---

[1]The *NCEES FE Reference Handbook* (*NCEES Handbook*) is inconsistent in its representation of sets, set members, matrices, matrix elements, and relations. Uppercase and lowercase, bold and not bold, italic, and not italic are all used interchangeably. For example, uppercase italic letters are used for set theory, while nonitalic letters are used in discrete math. In order to present these subjects in the same chapter, this book has adopted a consistent presentation style that may differ somewhat from the *NCEES Handbook*.

Complement Laws

$$A \cup \overline{A} = U$$

$$\overline{(\overline{A})} = A$$

$$A \cap \overline{A} = \varnothing$$

$$\overline{U} = \varnothing$$

Commutative Laws

$$A \cup B = B \cup A$$

$$A \cap B = B \cap A$$

Equation 6.1 and Eq. 6.2: Associative Laws

$$A \cup (B \cup C) = (A \cup B) \cup C \qquad 6.1$$

$$A \cap (B \cap C) = (A \cap B) \cap C \qquad 6.2$$

Equation 6.3 and Eq. 6.4: Distributive Laws

$$A \cup (B \cap C) = (A \cup B) \cap (A \cup C) \qquad 6.3$$

$$A \cap (B \cup C) = (A \cap B) \cup (A \cap C) \qquad 6.4$$

Equation 6.5 and Eq. 6.6: De Morgan's Laws

$$\overline{A \cup B} = \overline{A} \cap \overline{B} \qquad 6.5$$

$$\overline{A \cap B} = \overline{A} \cup \overline{B} \qquad 6.6$$

2. COMBINATIONS AND PERMUTATIONS

There are a finite number of ways in which n elements can be combined into distinctly different groups of r items. For example, suppose a farmer has a chicken, a rooster, a duck, and a cage that holds only two birds. The possible *combinations* of three birds taken two at a time are (chicken, rooster), (chicken, duck), and (rooster, duck). The birds in the cage will not remain stationary, so the combination (rooster, chicken) is not distinctly different from (chicken, rooster). That is, the combinations are not *order conscious*.

Equation 6.7: Combinations

$$C(n,r) = \frac{P(n,r)}{r!} = \frac{n!}{r!\,(n-r)!} \qquad 6.7$$

Description

The number of *combinations* of n items taken r at a time is written $C(n, r)$, C_r^n, nC_r, $_nC_r$, or $\binom{n}{r}$ (pronounced "n choose r"). It is sometimes referred to as the *binomial coefficient* and is given by Eq. 6.7.

Example

Six design engineers are eligible for promotion to pay grade G8, but only four spots are available. How many different combinations of promoted engineers are possible?

(A)   4

(B)   6

(C)   15

(D)   20

Solution

The number of combinations of $n = 6$ items taken $r = 4$ items at a time is

$$
\begin{aligned}
C(6,4) &= \frac{n!}{r!\,(n-r)!} = \frac{6!}{4!\,(6-4)!} \\
&= \frac{6 \times 5 \times 4 \times 3 \times 2 \times 1}{4 \times 3 \times 2 \times 1 \times 2 \times 1} \\
&= 15
\end{aligned}
$$

The answer is (C).

Equation 6.8: Permutations

$$P(n,r) = \frac{n!}{(n-r)!} \qquad 6.8$$

Description

An order-conscious subset of r items taken from a set of n items is the *permutation*, $P(n, r)$, also written P_r^n, $_nP_r$, and nP_r. A permutation is order conscious because the arrangement of two items (e.g., a_i and b_i) as $a_i b_i$ is different from the arrangement $b_i a_i$. The number of permutations is found from Eq. 6.8.

Example

An identification code begins with three letters. The possible letters are A, B, C, D, and E. If none of the letters are used more than once, how many different ways can the letters be arranged to make a code?

(A) 10

(B) 20

(C) 40

(D) 60

Solution

Since the order of the letters affects the identification code, determine the number of permutations of $n = 5$ items taken $r = 3$ items at a time using Eq. 6.8.

$$P(5, 3) = \frac{n!}{(n-r)!} = \frac{5!}{(5-3)!}$$
$$= \frac{5 \times 4 \times 3 \times 2 \times 1}{2 \times 1}$$
$$= 60$$

The answer is (D).

Equation 6.9: Permutations of Different Object Types

$$P(n; n_1, n_2, \ldots, n_k) = \frac{n!}{n_1! \, n_2! \ldots n_k!} \qquad 6.9$$

Description

Suppose n_1 objects of one type (e.g., color, size, shape, etc.) are combined with n_2 objects of another type and n_3 objects of yet a third type, and so on, up to k types. The collection of $n = n_1 + n_2 + \cdots + n_k$ objects forms a population from which arrangements of n items can be formed. The number of permutations of n objects taken n at a time from a collection of k types of objects is given by Eq. 6.9.

Example

An urn contains 13 marbles total: 4 black marbles, 2 red marbles, and 7 yellow marbles. Arrangements of 13 marbles are made. Most nearly, how many unique ways can the 13 marbles be ordered (arranged)?

(A) 800

(B) 1200

(C) 14,000

(D) 26,000

Solution

The marble colors represent different types of objects. The number of permutations of the marbles taken 13 at a time is

$$P(13; 4, 2, 7) = \frac{n!}{n_1! \, n_2! \ldots n_k!} = \frac{13!}{4! \, 2! \, 7!}$$

$$= \frac{\begin{array}{c}13 \times 12 \times 11 \times 10 \times 9 \times 8 \times 7 \\ \times 6 \times 5 \times 4 \times 3 \times 2 \times 1\end{array}}{\begin{array}{c}4 \times 3 \times 2 \times 1 \times 2 \times 1 \\ \times 7 \times 6 \times 5 \times 4 \times 3 \times 2 \times 1\end{array}}$$

$$= 25{,}740 \quad (26{,}000)$$

The answer is (D).

3. LAWS OF PROBABILITY

Probability theory determines the relative likelihood that a particular event will occur. An *event*, E, is one of the possible outcomes of a *trial*. The *probability* of E occurring is denoted as $P(E)$.

Probabilities are real numbers in the range of zero to one. If an event E is certain to occur, then the probability $P(E)$ of the event is equal to one. If the event is certain *not* to occur, then the probability $P(E)$ of the event is equal to zero. The probability of any other event is between zero and one.

The probability of an event occurring is equal to one minus the probability of the event not occurring. This is known as a *complementary probability*.

$$P(E) = 1 - P(\text{not } E)$$

Complementary probability can be used to simplify some probability calculations. For example, calculation of the probability of numerical events being "greater than" or "less than" or quantities being "at least" a certain number can often be simplified by calculating the probability of the complementary event.

Probabilities of multiple events can be calculated from the probabilities of individual events using a variety of methods. When multiple events are considered, those events can be either independent or dependent. The probability of an *independent event* does not affect (and is not affected by) other events. The assumption of independence is appropriate when sampling from infinite or very large populations, when sampling from finite populations with replacement, or when sampling from different populations (universes). For example, the outcome of a second coin toss is generally not affected by the outcome of the first coin toss. The probability of a *dependent event* is affected by what has previously happened. For example, drawing a second card from a deck of cards without replacement is affected by what was drawn as the first card.

Events can be combined in two basic ways, according to the way the combination is described. Events can be connected by the words "and" and "or." For example, the question, "What is the probability of event A and event B occurring?" is different than the question, "What is the probability of event A or event B occurring?" The combinatorial "and" is designated in various ways: AB, $A{\cdot}B$, $A \times B$, $A \cap B$, and A, B, among others. In this book, the probability of A and B both occurring is designated as $P(A, B)$.

The combinatorial "or" is designated as $A + B$ and $A \cup B$. In this book, the probability of A or B occurring is designated as $P(A + B)$.

Equation 6.10: Law of Total Probability

$$P(A + B) = P(A) + P(B) - P(A, B) \qquad 6.10$$

Description

Equation 6.10 gives the probability that either event A or B will occur. $P(A, B)$ is the probability that both A and B will occur.

Example

A deck of ten children's cards contains three fish cards, two dog cards, and five cat cards. What is the probability of drawing either a cat card or a dog card from a full deck?

- (A)   1/10
- (B)   2/10
- (C)   5/10
- (D)   7/10

Solution

The two events are mutually exclusive, so the probability of both happening, $P(A, B)$, is zero. The total probability of drawing either a cat card or a dog card is

$$P(A + B) = P(A) + P(B) - P(A, B)$$
$$= \frac{5}{10} + \frac{2}{10} - 0$$
$$= 7/10$$

The answer is (D).

Equation 6.11: Law of Compound (Joint) Probability

$$P(A, B) = P(A)P(B|A) = P(B)P(A|B) \qquad 6.11$$

Variation

$$P(A, B) = P(A)P(B) \quad \begin{bmatrix} \text{independent} \\ \text{events} \end{bmatrix}$$

Description

Equation 6.11, the *law of compound (joint) probability*, gives the probability that events A and B will both occur. $P(B|A)$ is the *conditional probability* that B will occur given that A has already occurred. Likewise, $P(A|B)$ is the conditional probability that A will occur given that B has already occurred. It is possible that the events come from different populations (universes, sample spaces, etc.), such as when one marble is drawn from one urn and another marble is drawn from a different urn. In that case, the events will be independent and won't affect each other. If the events are independent, then $P(B|A) = P(B)$ and $P(A|B) = P(A)$. Examples of dependent events for which the probability is conditional include drawing objects from a container or cards from a deck, without replacement.

Example

A bag contains seven orange balls, eight green balls, and two white balls. Two balls are drawn from the bag without replacing either of them. Most nearly, what is the probability that the first ball drawn is white and the second ball drawn is orange?

- (A)   0.036
- (B)   0.052
- (C)   0.10
- (D)   0.53

Solution

There is a total of 17 balls. There are 2 white balls. The probability of picking a white ball as the first ball is

$$P(A) = 2/17$$

After picking a white ball first, there are 16 balls remaining, 7 of which are orange. The probability of picking an orange ball second given that a white ball was chosen first is

$$P(B|A) = 7/16$$

The probability of picking a white ball first and an orange ball second is

$$P(A, B) = P(A)P(B|A)$$

$$= \left(\frac{2}{17}\right)\left(\frac{7}{16}\right)$$

$$= 0.05147 \quad (0.052)$$

The answer is (B).

Equation 6.12: Bayes' Theorem

$$P(B_j|A) = \frac{P(B_j)P(A|B_j)}{\displaystyle\sum_{i=1}^{n} P(A|B_i)P(B_i)} \qquad 6.12$$

Variation

$$P(B_j|A) = \frac{P(B \text{ and } A)}{P(A)}$$

Description

Given two dependent sets of events, A and B, the probability that event B will occur given the fact that the dependent event A has already occurred is written as $P(B_j|A)$ and is given by *Bayes' theorem*, Eq. 6.12.

Example

A medical patient exhibits a symptom that occurs naturally 10% of the time in all people. The symptom is also exhibited by all patients who have a particular disease. The incidence of that particular disease among all people is 0.0002%. What is the probability of the patient having that particular disease?

    (A)   0.002%

    (B)   0.01%

    (C)   0.3%

    (D)   4%

Solution

This problem is asking for a conditional probability: the probability that a person has a disease, D, given that the person has a symptom, S. Use Bayes' theorem to calculate the probability. The probability that a person has the symptom S given that they have the disease

D is $P(S|D)$ and is 100%. Multiply by 100% to get the answer as a percentage.

$$P(D|S) = \frac{P(D)P(S|D)}{P(S|D)P(D) + P(S|\text{not } D)P(\text{not } D)}$$

$$= \frac{(0.000002)(1.00)}{(1.00)(0.000002) + (0.10)(0.999998)}$$

$$= 0.00002 \quad (0.002\%)$$

The answer is (A).

4. MEASURES OF CENTRAL TENDENCY

It is often unnecessary to present experimental data in their entirety, either in tabular or graphic form. In such cases, the data and distribution can be represented by various parameters. One type of parameter is a measure of *central tendency*. The mode, median, and mean are measures of central tendency.

Mode

The *mode* is the observed value that occurs most frequently. The mode may vary greatly between series of observations; its main use is as a quick measure of the central value, since little or no computation is required to find it. Beyond this, the usefulness of the mode is limited.

Median

The *median* is the point in the distribution that partitions the total set of observations into two parts containing equal numbers of observations. It is not influenced by the extremity of scores on either side of the distribution. The median is found by counting from either end through an ordered set of data until half of the observations have been accounted for. If the number of data points is odd, the median will be the exact middle value. If the number of data points is even, the median will be the average of the middle two values.

Equation 6.13: Arithmetic Mean

$$\overline{X} = (1/n)(X_1 + X_2 + \cdots + X_n) = (1/n)\sum_{i=1}^{n} X_i \qquad 6.13$$

Variation

$$\overline{X} = \frac{\sum f_i X_i}{\sum f_i} \quad \begin{bmatrix} f_i \text{ are frequencies} \\ \text{of occurrence of} \\ \text{events } i \end{bmatrix}$$

Description

The *arithmetic mean* is the arithmetic average of the observations. The *sample mean*, $\overline{X}$, can be used as an unbiased estimator of the *population mean*, μ. The term *unbiased estimator* means that on the average, the sample mean is equal to the population mean. The mean may be found without ordering the data (as was necessary to find the mode and median) from Eq. 6.13.

Example

100 random samples were taken from a large population. A particular numerical characteristic of sampled items was measured. The results of the measurements were as follows.

- 45 measurements were between 0.859 and 0.900.

- 0.901 was observed once.

- 0.902 was observed three times.

- 0.903 was observed twice.

- 0.904 was observed four times.

- 45 measurements were between 0.905 and 0.958.

The smallest value was 0.859, and the largest value was 0.958. The sum of all 100 measurements was 91.170. Except those noted, no measurements occurred more than twice.

What are the (a) mean, (b) mode, and (c) median of the measurements, respectively?

(A) 0.908; 0.902; 0.902

(B) 0.908; 0.904; 0.903

(C) 0.912; 0.902; 0.902

(D) 0.912; 0.904; 0.903

Solution

(a) From Eq. 6.13, the arithmetic mean is

$$\overline{X} = (1/n) \sum_{i=1}^{n} X_i = \left(\frac{1}{100}\right)(91.170) = 0.9117 \quad (0.912)$$

(b) The mode is the value that occurs most frequently. The value of 0.904 occurred four times, and no other measurements repeated more than four times. 0.904 is the mode.

(c) The median is the value at the midpoint of an ordered (sorted) set of measurements. There were 100 measurements, so the middle of the ordered set occurs

between the 50th and 51st measurements. Since these measurements are both 0.903, the average of the two is 0.903.

The answer is (D).

Equation 6.14: Weighted Arithmetic Mean

$$\overline{X}_w = \frac{\sum w_i X_i}{\sum w_i} \qquad 6.14$$

Description

If some observations are considered to be more significant than others, a *weighted mean* can be calculated. Equation 6.14 defines a *weighted arithmetic mean*, $\overline{X}_w$, where w_i is the weight assigned to observation X_i.

Example

A course has four exams that compose the entire grade for the course. Each exam is weighted. A student's scores on all four exams and the weight for each exam are as given.

exam	student score	weight
1	80%	1
2	95%	2
3	72%	2
4	95%	5

What is most nearly the student's final grade in the course?

(A) 82%

(B) 85%

(C) 87%

(D) 89%

Solution

The student's final grade is the weighted arithmetic mean of the individual exam scores.

$$\overline{X}_w = \frac{\sum w_i X_i}{\sum w_i}$$
$$= \frac{(1)(80\%) + (2)(95\%) + (2)(72\%) + (5)(95\%)}{1 + 2 + 2 + 5}$$
$$= 88.9\% \quad (89\%)$$

The answer is (D).

Equation 6.15: Geometric Mean

$$\text{sample geometric mean} = \sqrt[n]{X_1 X_2 X_3 \dots X_n} \qquad \textit{6.15}$$

Description

The *geometric mean* of n nonnegative values is defined by Eq. 6.15. The geometric mean is the number that, when raised to the power of the sample size, produces the same result as the product of all samples. It is appropriate to use the geometric mean when the values being averaged are used as consecutive multipliers in other calculations. For example, the total revenue earned on an investment of C earning an effective interest rate of i_k in year k is calculated as $R = C(i_1 i_2 i_3 \dots i_k)$. The interest rate, i, is a multiplicative element. If a $100 investment earns 10% in year 1 (resulting in $110 at the end of the year), then the $110 earns 30% in year 2 (resulting in $143), and the $143 earns 50% in year 3 (resulting in $215), the average interest earned each year would not be the arithmetic mean of $(10\% + 30\% + 50\%)/3 = 30\%$. The average would be calculated as a geometric mean (24.66%).

Example

What is most nearly the geometric mean of the following data set?

$$0.820, 1.96, 2.22, 0.190, 1.00$$

(A)   0.79

(B)   0.81

(C)   0.93

(D)   0.96

Solution

The geometric mean of the data set is

$$\text{sample geometric mean} = \sqrt[n]{X_1 X_2 X_3 \dots X_n}$$
$$= \sqrt[5]{\begin{array}{c}(0.820)(1.96)(2.22) \\ \times (0.190)(1.00)\end{array}}$$
$$= 0.925 \quad (0.93)$$

The answer is (C).

Equation 6.16: Root-Mean-Square

$$\begin{array}{c}\text{sample root-mean-} \\ \text{square value}\end{array} = \sqrt{(1/n)\sum X_i^2} \qquad \textit{6.16}$$

Description

The *root-mean-square* (rms) value of a series of observations is defined by Eq. 6.16. The variable X_{rms} is often used to represent the rms value.

Example

The water level on a tank in a chemical plant is measured every six hours. The tank has a depth of 6 m. The water levels on the tank on a certain day were found to be 2.5 m, 4.2 m, 5.6 m, and 3.3 m. What is most nearly the root-mean-square value of water level for that day?

(A)   2.0 m

(B)   3.3 m

(C)   4.1 m

(D)   5.8 m

Solution

Use Eq. 6.16 to find the root-mean-square value of water level for the day.

$$X_{\text{rms}} = \sqrt{(1/n)\sum X_i^2}$$
$$= \sqrt{\left(\frac{1}{4}\right)\left(\begin{array}{c}(2.5 \text{ m})^2 + (4.2 \text{ m})^2 \\ + (5.6 \text{ m})^2 + (3.3 \text{ m})^2\end{array}\right)}$$
$$= 4.07 \text{ m} \quad (4.1 \text{ m})$$

The answer is (C).

5. MEASURES OF DISPERSION

Measures of dispersion describe the variability in observed data.

Equation 6.17 Through Eq. 6.21: Standard Deviation

$$\sigma_{\text{population}} = \sqrt{(1/N)\sum(X_i - \mu)^2} \qquad 6.17$$

$$\sigma_{\text{sum}} = \sqrt{\sigma_1^2 + \sigma_2^2 + \cdots + \sigma_n^2} \qquad 6.18$$

$$\sigma_{\text{series}} = \sigma\sqrt{n} \qquad 6.19$$

$$\sigma_{\text{mean}} = \frac{\sigma}{\sqrt{n}} \qquad 6.20$$

$$\sigma_{\text{product}} = \sqrt{A^2\sigma_b^2 + B^2\sigma_a^2} \qquad 6.21$$

Variation

$$\sigma = \sqrt{\frac{\sum f_i(X_i - \mu)^2}{\sum f_i}}$$

Description

One measure of dispersion is the *standard deviation*, defined in Eq. 6.17. N is the total population size, not the sample size, n. This implies that the entire population is measured.

Equation 6.17 can be used to calculate the standard deviation only when the entire population can be included in the calculation. When only a small subset is available, as when a sample is taken (see Eq. 6.22), there are two obstacles to its use. First, the population mean, μ, is not known. This obstacle is overcome by using the sample average, $\bar{X}$, which is an unbiased estimator of the population mean. Second, Eq. 6.17 is inaccurate for small samples.

When combining two or more data sets for which the standard deviations are known, the standard deviation for the combined data is found using Eq. 6.18. This equation is used even if some of the data sets are subtracted; subtracting one data set from another increases the standard deviation of the result just as adding the two data sets does.

When a series of samples is taken from the same population, the sum of the standard deviations for the series is calculated from Eq. 6.19, where σ is the population standard deviation and n is the number of samples. The standard deviation of the mean values of these samples is called the *standard deviation* (or *standard error*) *of the mean* and is found with Eq. 6.20.

The standard deviation of the product of two random variables is given by Eq. 6.21. A and B are the expected values of the two variables, and σ_a^2 and σ_b^2 are the population variances for the two variables.

Example

A cat colony living in a small town has a total population of seven cats. The ages of the cats are as shown.

age	number
7 yr	1
8 yr	1
10 yr	2
12 yr	1
13 yr	2

What is most nearly the standard deviation of the age of the cat population?

(A)   1.7 yr

(B)   2.0 yr

(C)   2.2 yr

(D)   2.4 yr

Solution

Using Eq. 6.13, the arithmetic mean of the ages is the population mean, μ.

$$\mu = (1/n)\sum_{i=1}^{n} X_i$$
$$= \left(\frac{1}{7}\right)\left(\begin{array}{c}(1)(7 \text{ yr}) + (1)(8 \text{ yr}) + (2)(10 \text{ yr}) \\ +(1)(12 \text{ yr}) + (2)(13 \text{ yr})\end{array}\right)$$
$$= 10.4 \text{ yr}$$

From Eq. 6.17, the standard deviation of the ages is

$$\sigma_{\text{population}} = \sqrt{(1/N)\sum(X_i - \mu)^2}$$
$$= \sqrt{\left(\frac{1}{7}\right)\left(\begin{array}{c}(7 \text{ yr} - 10.4 \text{ yr})^2 \\ +(8 \text{ yr} - 10.4 \text{ yr})^2 \\ +(2)(10 \text{ yr} - 10.4 \text{ yr})^2 \\ +(12 \text{ yr} - 10.4 \text{ yr})^2 \\ +(2)(13 \text{ yr} - 10.4 \text{ yr})^2\end{array}\right)}$$
$$= 2.19 \text{ yr} \quad (2.2 \text{ yr})$$

The answer is (C).

Equation 6.22: Sample Standard Deviation

$$s = \sqrt{[1/(n-1)]\sum_{i=1}^{n}(X_i - \overline{X})^2} \qquad 6.22$$

Description

The *standard deviation of a sample* (particularly a small sample) of n items calculated from Eq. 6.17 is a *biased estimator* of (i.e., on the average, it is not equal to) the population standard deviation. A different measure of dispersion, called the *sample standard deviation, s* (not the same as the standard deviation of a sample), is an unbiased estimator of the population standard deviation. The sample standard deviation can be found using Eq. 6.22.

Example

Samples of aluminum-alloy channels were tested for stiffness. The following distribution of results was obtained.

stiffness	frequency
2480	23
2440	35
2400	40
2360	33
2320	21

If the mean of the samples is 2400, what is the approximate standard deviation of the population from which the samples are taken?

- (A) 48.2
- (B) 49.7
- (C) 50.6
- (D) 50.8

Solution

The number of samples is

$$n = 23 + 35 + 40 + 33 + 21 = 152$$

The sample standard deviation, s, is the unbiased estimator of the population standard deviation, σ.

$$s = \sqrt{[1/(n-1)]\sum_{i=1}^{n}(X_i - \overline{X})^2}$$

$$= \sqrt{\left(\frac{1}{152-1}\right)\begin{pmatrix}(23)(2480-2400)^2 \\ +(35)(2440-2400)^2 \\ +(40)(2400-2400)^2 \\ +(33)(2360-2400)^2 \\ +(21)(2320-2400)^2\end{pmatrix}}$$

$$= 50.847 \quad (50.8)$$

The answer is (D).

Equation 6.23 Through Eq. 6.25: Variance and Sample Variance

$$\sigma^2 = (1/N)[(X_1 - \mu)^2 + (X_2 - \mu)^2 + \cdots + (X_N - \mu)^2] \qquad 6.23$$

$$\sigma^2 = (1/N)\sum_{i=1}^{N}(X_i - \mu)^2 \qquad 6.24$$

$$s^2 = [1/(n-1)]\sum_{i=1}^{n}(X_i - \overline{X})^2 \qquad 6.25$$

Description

The *variance* is the square of the standard deviation. Since there are two standard deviations, there are two variances. The *variance of the population* (i.e., the *population variance*) is σ^2, and the *sample variance* is s^2. The population variance can be found using either Eq. 6.23 or Eq. 6.24, both derived from Eq. 6.17, and the sample variance can be found using Eq. 6.25, derived from Eq. 6.22.

Example

Most nearly, what is the sample variance of the following data set?

$$2, 4, 6, 8, 10, 12, 14$$

- (A) 4.3
- (B) 5.2
- (C) 8.0
- (D) 19

Solution

Find the mean using Eq. 6.13.

$$\overline{X} = (1/n) \sum_{i=1}^{n} X_i = \left(\frac{1}{7}\right)(2 + 4 + 6 + 8 + 10 + 12 + 14)$$
$$= 8$$

From Eq. 6.25, the sample variance is

$$s^2 = [1/(n-1)] \sum_{i=1}^{n} (X_i - \overline{X})^2$$
$$= \left(\frac{1}{7-1}\right) \begin{pmatrix} (2-8)^2 + (4-8)^2 + (6-8)^2 \\ +(8-8)^2 + (10-8)^2 + (12-8)^2 \\ +(14-8)^2 \end{pmatrix}$$
$$= 18.67 \quad (19)$$

The answer is (D).

Equation 6.26: Sample Coefficient of Variation

$$CV = s/\overline{X} \qquad \text{6.26}$$

Description

The *relative dispersion* is defined as a measure of dispersion divided by a measure of central tendency. The *sample coefficient of variation*, *CV*, is a relative dispersion calculated from the sample standard deviation and the mean.

Example

The following data were recorded from a laboratory experiment.

$$20, 25, 30, 32, 27, 22$$

The mean of the data is 26. What is most nearly the sample coefficient of variation of the data?

    (A)   0.18

    (B)   1.1

    (C)   2.4

    (D)   4.6

Solution

Find the sample standard deviation of the data using Eq. 6.22.

$$s = \sqrt{[1/(n-1)] \sum_{i=1}^{n} (X_i - \overline{X})^2}$$
$$= \sqrt{\left(\frac{1}{6-1}\right) \begin{pmatrix} (20-26)^2 + (25-26)^2 \\ +(30-26)^2 + (32-26)^2 \\ +(27-26)^2 + (22-26)^2 \end{pmatrix}}$$
$$= 4.6$$

From Eq. 6.26, the sample coefficient of variation is

$$CV = s/\overline{X} = \frac{4.6}{26} = 0.177 \quad (0.18)$$

The answer is (A).

6. NUMERICAL EVENTS

A *discrete numerical event* is an occurrence that can be described by an integer. For example, 27 cars passing through a bridge toll booth in an hour is a discrete numerical event. Most numerical events are *continuously distributed* and are not constrained to discrete or integer values. For example, the resistance of a 10% 1 Ω resistor may be any value between 0.9 Ω and 1.1 Ω.

7. PROBABILITY DENSITY FUNCTIONS (DISCRETE)

Equation 6.27: Probability Mass Function

$$f(x_k) = P(X = x_k) \quad [k = 1, 2, \ldots, n] \qquad \text{6.27}$$

Description

A *discrete random variable*, *X*, can take on values from a set of discrete values, x_i. The set of values can be finite or infinite, as long as each value can be expressed as an integer. The *probability mass function*, defined by Eq. 6.27, gives the probability that a discrete random variable, *X*, is equal to each of the set's possible values, x_k. The probabilities of all possible outcomes add up to unity.

Equation 6.28: Probability Density Function

$$P(a \leq X \leq b) = \int_{a}^{b} f(x) \, dx \qquad \text{6.28}$$

Description

A *density function* is a nonnegative function whose integral taken over the entire range of the independent variable is unity. A *probability density function* (PDF) is a mathematical formula that gives the probability of a numerical event.

Various mathematical models are used to describe probability density functions. Figure 6.2 shows a graph of a continuous probability density function. The area under the probability density function is the probability that the variable will assume a value between the limits of evaluation. The total probability, or the probability that the variable will assume any value over the interval, is 1.0. The probability of an exact numerical event is zero. That is, there is no chance that a numerical event will be exactly a. It is possible to determine only the probability that a numerical event will be less than a, greater than b, or between the values of a and b.

Figure 6.2 *Probability Density Function*

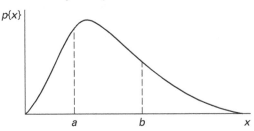

If a random variable, X, is continuous over an interval, then a nonnegative *probability density function* of that variable exists over the interval as defined by Eq. 6.28.

8. PROBABILITY DISTRIBUTION FUNCTIONS (CONTINUOUS)

A *cumulative probability distribution function*, $F(x)$, gives the probability that a numerical event will occur or the probability that the numerical event will be less than or equal to some value, x.

Equation 6.29: Cumulative Distribution Function: Discrete Random Variable

$$F(x_m) = \sum_{k=1}^{m} P(x_k) = P(X \leq x_m) \quad [m = 1, 2, \ldots, n] \quad \text{6.29}$$

Description

For a *discrete random variable*, X, the probability distribution function is the sum of the individual probabilities of all possible events up to and including event x_m. The *cumulative distribution function* (CDF) is a function that calculates the cumulative sum of all values up to and including a particular end point. For discrete probability density functions (PDFs), $F(x_m)$, the CDF can be calculated as a summation, as shown in Eq. 6.29.

Because calculating cumulative probabilities can be cumbersome, tables of values are often used. Table 6.1 at the end of this chapter gives values for cumulative binomial probabilities, where n is the number of trials, P is the probability of success for a single trial, and x is the maximum number of successful trials.

Equation 6.30: Cumulative Distribution Function: Continuous Random Variable

$$F(x) = \int_{-\infty}^{x} f(t)\, dt \qquad \text{6.30}$$

Description

For continuous functions, the CDF is calculated as an integral of the PDF from minus infinity to the limit of integration, as in Eq. 6.30. This integral corresponds to the area under the curve up to the limit of integration and represents the probability that a random variable, X, is less than or equal to the limit of integration. That is, $F(x) = P(X \leq x)$. A CDF has a maximum value of 1.0, and for a continuous probability density function, $F(x)$ will approach 1.0 asymptotically.

Example

For the probability density function shown, what is the probability of the random variable x being less than 1/3?

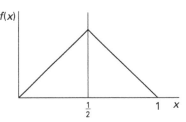

(A) 0.11

(B) 0.22

(C) 0.25

(D) 0.33

Solution

The total area under the probability density function is equal to 1. The area of two triangles is

$$A = (2)\left(\frac{1}{2}\right)bh = (2)\left(\frac{1}{2}\right)\left(\frac{1}{2}\right)h = 1$$

Therefore, the height of the curve at its peak is 2.

The equation of the line from $x = 0$ up to $x = 1/2$ is

$$f(x) = 4x \quad \left[0 \leq x \leq \frac{1}{2}\right]$$

The probability that $x < 1/3$ is equal to the area under the curve between 0 and 1/3. From Eq. 6.30,

$$F\left(0 < x < \frac{1}{3}\right) = \int_0^{1/3} f(x)\,dx = \int_0^{1/3} 4x\,dx = 2x^2 \big|_0^{1/3}$$

$$= (2)\left(\frac{1}{3}\right)^2 - 0$$

$$= 0.222 \quad (0.22)$$

The answer is (B).

9. EXPECTED VALUES

Equation 6.31: Expected Value of a Discrete Variable

$$\mu = E[X] = \sum_{k=1}^{n} x_k f(x_k) \qquad 6.31$$

Description

The *expected value*, E, of a discrete random variable, X, is given by Eq. 6.31. $f(x_k)$ is the probability mass function as defined in Eq. 6.27.

Example

The probability distribution of the number of calls, X, that a customer service agent receives each hour is shown.

x	$f(x)$
0	0.00
2	0.04
4	0.05
6	0.10
8	0.35
10	0.46

What is most nearly the average number of phone calls that a customer service agent expects to receive in an hour?

(A) 5
(B) 7
(C) 8
(D) 9

Solution

The expected number of received calls is

$$\mu = E[X] = \sum_{k=1}^{n} x_k f(x_k)$$

$$= (0)(0.00) + (2)(0.04) + (4)(0.05)$$
$$+ (6)(0.10) + (8)(0.35) + (10)(0.46)$$
$$= 8.28 \quad (8)$$

The answer is (C).

Equation 6.32: Variance of a Discrete Variable

$$\sigma^2 = V[X] = \sum_{k=1}^{n} (x_k - \mu)^2 f(x_k) \qquad 6.32$$

Description

Equation 6.32 gives the variance, σ^2, of a discrete function of variable X. To use Eq. 6.32, the population mean, μ, must be known, having been calculated from the total population of n values. The name "discrete" requires only that n be a finite number and all values of x be known. It does not limit the values of x to integers.

Equation 6.33 and Eq. 6.34: Expected Value (Mean) of a Continuous Variable

$$\mu = E[X] = \int_{-\infty}^{\infty} x f(x)\,dx \qquad 6.33$$

$$E[Y] = E[g(X)] = \int_{-\infty}^{\infty} g(x) f(x)\,dx \qquad 6.34$$

Description

Equation 6.33 calculates the population mean, μ, of a continuous variable, X, from the probability density function, $f(x)$. Equation 6.34 calculates the mean of any continuously distributed variable defined by $Y = g(X)$, whose values are observed according to the probabilities given by the probability density function (PDF) $f(x)$. Equation 6.34 is the general form of Eq. 6.33, where $g(x) = x$.

Equation 6.35: Variance of a Continuous Variable

$$\sigma^2 = V[X] = E[(X - \mu)^2] = \int_{-\infty}^{\infty} (x - \mu)^2 f(x)\,dx \qquad 6.35$$

Description

Equation 6.35 gives the variance of a continuous random variable, X. μ is the mean of X, and $f(x)$ is the density function of X.

Equation 6.36: Standard Deviation of a Continuous Variable

$$\sigma = \sqrt{V[X]} \qquad 6.36$$

Variation

$$\sigma = \sqrt{\sigma^2}$$

Description

The standard deviation is always the square root of the variance, as shown in the variation equation. Equation 6.36 gives the standard deviation for a continuous random variable, X.

Equation 6.37: Coefficient of Variation of a Continuous Variable

$$CV = \sigma/\mu \qquad 6.37$$

Description

The coefficient of variation of a continuous variable is calculated from Eq. 6.37.

10. PROBABILITY DISTRIBUTIONS

Equation 6.38 and Eq. 6.39: Binomial Distribution

$$P_n(x) = C(n, x)p^x q^{n-x}$$
$$= \frac{n!}{x!\,(n-x)!}p^x q^{n-x} \qquad 6.38$$

$$q = 1 - p \qquad 6.39$$

Description

The *binomial probability function* is used when all outcomes are discrete and can be categorized as either successes or failures. The probability of success in a single trial is designated as p, and the probability of failure is the complement, q, calculated from Eq. 6.39.

Equation 6.38 gives the probability of x successes in n independent successive trials. The quantity $C(n, x)$ is the *binomial coefficient*, identical to the number of combinations of n items taken x at a time. (See Eq. 6.7.)

Example

A cat has a litter of seven kittens. If the probability that any given kitten will be female is 0.52, what is the probability that exactly two of the seven will be male?

(A) 0.07

(B) 0.18

(C) 0.23

(D) 0.29

Solution

Since the outcomes are "either-or" in nature, the outcomes (and combinations of outcomes) follow a binomial distribution. A male kitten is defined as a success. The probability of a success is

$$p = 1 - 0.52 = 0.48 = P(\text{male kitten})$$
$$q = 0.52 = P(\text{female kitten})$$
$$n = 7 \text{ trials}$$
$$x = 2 \text{ successes}$$
$$P_n(x) = \frac{n!}{x!\,(n-x)!}p^x q^{n-x}$$
$$P_7(2) = \left(\frac{7!}{2!\,(7-2)!}\right)(0.48)^2(0.52)^{7-2}$$
$$= 0.184 \quad (0.18)$$

The answer is (B).

Equation 6.40 Through Eq. 6.43: Normal Distribution

$$f(x) = \frac{1}{\sigma\sqrt{2\pi}}e^{-\frac{1}{2}\left(\frac{x-\mu}{\sigma}\right)^2} \quad [-\infty \leq x \leq \infty] \qquad 6.40$$

$$f(x) = \frac{1}{\sqrt{2\pi}}e^{-x^2/2} \quad [-\infty \leq x \leq \infty] \qquad 6.41$$

$$Z = \frac{x - \mu}{\sigma} \qquad 6.42$$

$$F(-x) = 1 - F(x) \qquad 6.43$$

Description

The *normal distribution (Gaussian distribution)* is a symmetrical continuous distribution, commonly referred to as the *bell-shaped curve*, which describes the distribution of outcomes of many real-world experiments, processes, and phenomena. (See Fig. 6.3.)

Figure 6.3 *Normal Distribution*

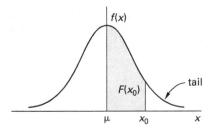

The probability density function for the normal distribution with population mean μ and population variance σ^2 is illustrated in Fig. 6.4 and is described by Eq. 6.40.

Figure 6.4 *Normal Curve with Mean μ and Standard Deviation σ*

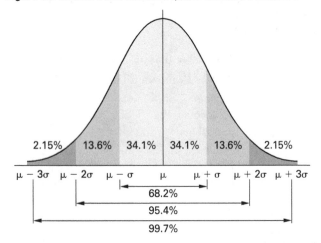

Since $f(x)$ is difficult to integrate (i.e., Eq. 6.40 is difficult to evaluate), Eq. 6.40 is seldom used directly, and a *unit normal table* is used instead. (See Table 6.2 at the end of this chapter.) The unit normal table (also called the *standard normal table*) is based on a normal distribution with a mean of zero and a standard deviation of one. The standard normal distribution is given by Eq. 6.41. In Table 6.2, $F(x)$ is the area under the curve from $-\infty$ to x, $R(x)$ is the area under the curve from x to ∞, and $W(x)$ is the area under the curve between $-x$ and x. The generic variable x used in Table 6.2 is the *standard normal variable*, Z, calculated in Eq. 6.42, not the actual measurement of the random variable, X. That is, the x used in Table 6.2 is not the x used in Eq. 6.42.

Since the range of values from an experiment or phenomenon will not generally correspond to the unit normal table, a value, x, must be converted to a standard normal variable, Z. In Eq. 6.42, μ and σ are the population mean and standard deviation, respectively, of the distribution from which x comes. The unbiased estimators for μ and σ are $\overline{X}$ and s, respectively, when a sample is used to estimate the population parameters. Both $\overline{X}$ and s approach the population values as the sample size, n, increases.

Example

The heights of several thousand fifth grade boys in Santa Clara County are measured. The mean of the heights is 1.20 m, and the variance is 25×10^{-4} m^2. Approximately what percentage of these boys is taller than 1.23 m?

(A)   27%

(B)   31%

(C)   69%

(D)   73%

Solution

To convert the normal distribution to unit normal distribution, the new variable, Z, is constructed from the height, x, mean, μ, and standard deviation, σ. The mean is known; the standard deviation is found from the variance and a variation of Eq. 6.36.

$$\sigma = \sqrt{\sigma^2} = \sqrt{25 \times 10^{-4} \text{ m}^2}$$
$$= 0.05 \text{ m}$$

For a height less than or equal to 1.23 m, from Eq. 6.42,

$$Z = \frac{x - \mu}{\sigma} = \frac{1.23 \text{ m} - 1.20 \text{ m}}{0.05 \text{ m}}$$
$$= 0.6$$

From Table 6.2, the cumulative distribution function at $Z = 0.6$ is $F(Z) = 0.7257$. The percentage of boys having height greater than 1.23 m is

percentage taller than 1.23 m $= 100\% - (0.7257)(100\%)$
$$= 27.43\% \quad (27\%)$$

The answer is (A).

Equation 6.44 and Eq. 6.45: Central Limit Theorem

$$\mu_{\bar{y}} = \mu \qquad \text{6.44}$$

$$\sigma_{\bar{y}} = \frac{\sigma}{\sqrt{n}} \qquad \text{6.45}$$

Description

The *central limit theorem* states that the distribution of a significantly large number of sample means of n items where all items are drawn from the same (i.e., parent) population will be normal. According to the central limit theorem, the mean of sample means, $\mu_{\bar{y}}$, is equal to the population mean of the parent distribution, μ, as shown in Eq. 6.44. The standard deviation of the sample means, $\sigma_{\bar{y}}$, is equal to the standard deviation of the parent population divided by the square root of the sample size, as shown in Eq. 6.45.

Equation 6.46 and Eq. 6.47: t-Distribution

$$f(t) = \frac{\Gamma\left(\frac{\nu+1}{2}\right)}{\sqrt{\nu\pi}\,\Gamma\left(\frac{\nu}{2}\right)}\left(1+\frac{t^2}{\nu}\right)^{-\frac{\nu+1}{2}} \quad [-\infty \le t \le \infty] \qquad 6.46$$

$$t = \frac{\bar{x}-\mu}{s/\sqrt{n}} \quad [-\infty \le t \le \infty] \qquad 6.47$$

Description

For the *t-distribution* (commonly referred to as *Student's t-distribution*), the probability distribution function with ν *degrees of freedom* (sample size of $n+1$) is given by Eq. 6.46. The t-distribution is tabulated in Table 6.4 at the end of this chapter, with t as a function of ν and α. In Table 6.4, the column labeled "ν" lists the degrees of freedom, one less than the sample size. Degrees of freedom is sometimes given the symbol "df."

In Eq. 6.47, x is the sample mean, μ is the population mean, n is the sample size, and s is the sample standard deviation.

Equation 6.48: Gamma Function

$$\Gamma(n) = \int_0^\infty t^{n-1}e^{-t}dt \quad [n > 0] \qquad 6.48$$

Description

The *gamma function*, $\Gamma(n)$, is an extension of the factorial function and is used to determine values of the factorial for complex numbers (other than negative integers).

Equation 6.49: Chi-Squared Distribution

$$\chi^2 = Z_1^2 + Z_2^2 + \ldots + Z_n^2 \qquad 6.49$$

Description

The sum of the squares of n independent normal random variables will be distributed according to the *chi-squared distribution* and will have n degrees of freedom. The chi-squared distribution is often used with hypothesis testing of variances. Chi-squared values, $\chi^2_{\alpha,n}$, for selected values of α and n can be found from Table 6.5 at the end of this chapter.

11. STUDENT'S t-TEST

Equation 6.50: Exceedance

$$\alpha = \int_{t_{\alpha,\nu}}^\infty f(t)\,dt \qquad 6.50$$

Description

The *t-test* is a method of comparing two variables, usually to test the significance of the difference between samples. For example, the t-test can be used to test whether the populations from which two samples are drawn have the same means.

The *exceedance* (i.e., the probability of being incorrect), α, is equal to the total area under the upper tail. (See Fig. 6.5.) For a *one-tail test*, $\alpha = 1 - C$. For a *two-tail test*, $\alpha = 1 - C/2$. Since the t-distribution is symmetric about zero, $t_{1-\alpha,n} = -t_{1-\alpha,n}$. As n increases, the t-distribution approaches the normal distribution.

α can be used to find the critical values of F, as listed in Table 6.6 at the end of this chapter.

Figure 6.5 Exceedance

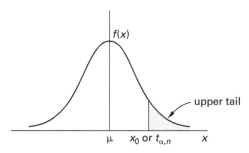

12. CONFIDENCE LEVELS

The results of experiments are seldom correct 100% of the time. Recognizing this, researchers accept a certain probability of being wrong. In order to minimize this probability, an experiment is repeated several times. The number of repetitions required depends on the level of confidence wanted in the results. For example, if the results have a 5% probability of being wrong, the *confidence level*, C, is 95% that the results are correct.

13. SUMS OF RANDOM VARIABLES

Equation 6.51: Sums of Random Variables

$$Y = a_1 X_1 + a_2 X_2 + \ldots + a_n X_n \qquad 6.51$$

Description

The sum of random variables, Y, is found from Eq. 6.51.

Equation 6.52: Expected Value of the Sum of Random Variables

$$\mu_y = E(Y) = a_1 E(X_1) + a_2 E(X_2) + \ldots + a_n E(X_n) \quad \text{6.52}$$

Description

The expected value of the sum of random variables, μ_y, is calculated using Eq. 6.52.

Equation 6.53 and Eq. 6.54: Variance of the Sum of Independent Random Variables

$$
\begin{aligned}
\sigma_y^2 &= V(Y) \\
&= a_1^2 V(X_1) + a_2^2 V(X_2) + \ldots + a_n^2 V(X_n)
\end{aligned}
\quad \text{6.53}
$$

$$\sigma_y^2 = a_1^2 \sigma_1^2 + a_2^2 \sigma_2^2 + \ldots + a_n^2 \sigma_n^2 \quad \text{6.54}$$

Description

The variance of the sum of independent random variables can be calculated from Eq. 6.53 and Eq. 6.54.

Equation 6.55: Standard Deviation of the Sum of Independent Random Variables

$$\sigma_y = \sqrt{\sigma_y^2} \quad \text{6.55}$$

Description

The standard deviation of the sum of independent random variables (see Eq. 6.51) is found from Eq. 6.55.

Equation 6.56: Standard Deviation of a Combination of Independent Random Variables

$$\sigma_Y = \sqrt{\left(\frac{\partial f}{\partial X_1}\sigma_{X_1}\right)^2 + \left(\frac{\partial f}{\partial X_2}\sigma_{X_2}\right)^2 + \ldots + \left(\frac{\partial f}{\partial X_n}\sigma_{X_n}\right)^2} \quad \text{6.56}$$

Description

When the sum of random variables, Y, is a combination of independent random variables, the standard deviation of Y, σ_Y, is found from Eq. 6.56.

14. SUMS AND DIFFERENCES OF MEANS

When two variables are sampled from two different standard normal variables (i.e., are independent), their sums will be distributed with mean $\mu_{new} = \mu_1 + \mu_2$ and variance $\sigma_{new}^2 = \sigma_1^2/n_1 + \sigma_2^2/n_2$. The sample sizes, n_1 and n_2, do not have to be the same. The relationships

for confidence intervals and hypothesis testing can be used for a new variable, $x_{new} = x_1 + x_2$, if μ is replaced by μ_{new} and σ is replaced by σ_{new}.

For the difference in two standard normal variables, the mean is the difference in two population means, $\mu_{new} = \mu_1 - \mu_2$, but the variance is the sum, as it was for the sum of two standard normal variables.

15. CONFIDENCE INTERVALS

Population properties such as means and variances must usually be estimated from samples. The sample mean, $\overline{X}$, and sample standard deviation, s, are unbiased estimators, but they are not necessarily precisely equal to the true population properties. For estimated values, it is common to specify an interval expected to contain the true population properties. The interval is known as a confidence interval because a confidence level, C (e.g., 99%), is associated with it. (There is still a $1 - C$ chance that the true population property is outside of the interval.) The interval will be bounded below by its *lower confidence limit* (LCL) and above by its *upper confidence limit* (UCL).

As a consequence of the *central limit theorem*, means of samples of n items taken from a distribution that is normally distributed with mean μ and standard deviation σ will be normally distributed with mean μ and variance σ^2/n. Therefore, the probability that any given average, $\overline{X}$, exceeds some value, L, is

$$p\{\overline{X} > L\} = p\left\{x > \left|\frac{L - \mu}{\frac{\sigma}{\sqrt{n}}}\right|\right\}$$

L is the *confidence limit* for the confidence level $1 - p\{\overline{X} > L\}$ (expressed as a percentage). Values of px are read directly from the unit normal table. (See Table 6.2.) As an example, $x = 1.645$ for a 95% confidence level since only 5% of the curve is above that x in the upper tail. This is known as a *one-tail confidence limit* because all of the exceedance probability is given to one side of the variation.

With *two-tail confidence limits*, the probability is split between the two sides of variation. There will be upper and lower confidence limits: UCL and LCL, respectively. This is appropriate when it is not specifically known that the calculated parameter is too high or too low. Table 6.3 at the end of this chapter lists standard normal variables and t values for two-tail confidence limits.

$$p\{\text{LCL} < \overline{X} < \text{UCL}\}$$

$$= p\left\{\frac{\text{LCL} - \mu}{\frac{\sigma}{\sqrt{n}}} < x < \frac{\text{UCL} - \mu}{\frac{\sigma}{\sqrt{n}}}\right\}$$

Equation 6.57 and Eq. 6.58: Confidence Limits and Interval for Mean of a Normal Distribution

$$\overline{X} - Z_{\alpha/2}\frac{\sigma}{\sqrt{n}} \leq \mu \leq \overline{X} + Z_{\alpha/2}\frac{\sigma}{\sqrt{n}} \quad \text{[known } \sigma] \quad \text{6.57}$$

$$\overline{X} - t_{\alpha/2}\frac{s}{\sqrt{n}} \leq \mu \leq \overline{X} + t_{\alpha/2}\frac{s}{\sqrt{n}} \quad \text{[unknown } \sigma] \quad \text{6.58}$$

Variations

$$\text{LCL} = \overline{X} - t_{\alpha/2,n-1}\left(\frac{s}{\sqrt{n}}\right)$$

$$\text{UCL} = \overline{X} + t_{\alpha/2,n-1}\left(\frac{s}{\sqrt{n}}\right)$$

Description

The *confidence limits for the mean*, μ, of a normal distribution can be calculated from Eq. 6.57 when the standard deviation, σ, is known.

If the standard deviation, σ, of the underlying distribution is not known, the confidence limits must be estimated from the sample standard deviation, s, using Eq. 6.58. Accordingly, the standard normal variable is replaced by the t-distribution parameter, $t_{\alpha/2}$, with $n - 1$ degrees of freedom, where n is the sample size. $\alpha = 1 - C$, and $\alpha/2$ is the t-distribution parameter since half of the exceedance is allocated to each confidence limit.

Equation 6.59 and Eq. 6.60: Confidence Limits for the Difference Between Two Means

$$\overline{X}_1 - \overline{X}_2 - Z_{\alpha/2}\sqrt{\frac{\sigma_1^2}{n_1} + \frac{\sigma_2^2}{n_2}}$$
$$\leq \mu_1 - \mu_2 \leq \overline{X}_1 - \overline{X}_2 \quad \text{6.59}$$
$$+ Z_{\alpha/2}\sqrt{\frac{\sigma_1^2}{n_1} + \frac{\sigma_2^2}{n_2}} \quad \text{[known } \sigma_1 \text{ and } \sigma_2]$$

$$\overline{X}_1 - \overline{X}_2 - t_{\alpha/2}\sqrt{\frac{\left(\dfrac{1}{n_1} + \dfrac{1}{n_2}\right)\left[\begin{matrix}(n_1-1)S_1^2 \\ +(n_2-1)S_2^2\end{matrix}\right]}{n_1 + n_2 - 2}}$$
$$\leq \mu_1 - \mu_2 \leq \overline{X}_1 - \overline{X}_2 \quad \text{6.60}$$
$$+ t_{\alpha/2}\sqrt{\frac{\left(\dfrac{1}{n_1} + \dfrac{1}{n_2}\right)\left[\begin{matrix}(n_1-1)S_1^2 \\ +(n_2-1)S_2^2\end{matrix}\right]}{n_1 + n_2 - 2}}$$
$$\text{[unknown } \sigma_1 \text{ and } \sigma_2]$$

Description

The difference in two standard normal variables will be distributed with mean $\mu_{\text{new}} = \mu_1 - \mu_2$. Use Eq. 6.59 to calculate the confidence interval for the difference between two means, μ_1 and μ_2, if the standard deviations σ_1 and σ_2 are known. If the standard deviations σ_1 and σ_2 are unknown, use Eq. 6.60. S_1 and S_2 are the sample standard deviations for the two sample sets. The t-distribution parameter, $t_{\alpha/2}$, has $n_1 + n_2 - 2$ degrees of freedom.

Example

100 resistors produced by company A and 150 resistors produced by company B are tested to find their limits before burning out. The test results show that the company A resistors have a mean rating of 2 W before burning out, with a standard deviation of 0.25 W, and the company B resistors have a 3 W mean rating before burning out, with a standard deviation of 0.30 W. What are the 95% confidence limits for the difference between the two means for the company A resistors and company B resistors (i.e., A − B)?

    (A)   −1.1 W; −1.0 W

    (B)   −1.1 W; −0.93 W

    (C)   −1.1 W; −0.90 W

    (D)   −1.0 W; −0.99 W

Solution

From Table 6.3, the value of the standard normal variable for a two-tail test with 95% confidence is 1.9600.

From Eq. 6.59, the confidence limits for the difference between the two means are

$$\text{LCL}(\mu_1 - \mu_2) = \overline{X}_1 - \overline{X}_2 - Z_{\alpha/2}\sqrt{\frac{\sigma_1^2}{n_1} + \frac{\sigma_2^2}{n_2}}$$
$$= 2 \text{ W} - 3 \text{ W}$$
$$-1.9600\sqrt{\frac{(0.25 \text{ W})^2}{100} + \frac{(0.30 \text{ W})^2}{150}}$$
$$= -1.0686 \text{ W} \quad (-1.1 \text{ W})$$

$$\text{UCL}(\mu_1 - \mu_2) = \overline{X}_1 - \overline{X}_2 + Z_{\alpha/2}\sqrt{\frac{\sigma_1^2}{n_1} + \frac{\sigma_2^2}{n_2}}$$
$$= 2 \text{ W} - 3 \text{ W}$$
$$+1.9600\sqrt{\frac{(0.25 \text{ W})^2}{100} + \frac{(0.30 \text{ W})^2}{150}}$$
$$= -0.9314 \text{ W} \quad (-0.93 \text{ W})$$

The answer is (B).

Equation 6.61: Confidence Limits and Interval for the Variance of a Normal Distribution

$$\frac{(n-1)s^2}{\chi^2_{\alpha/2,n-1}} \le \sigma^2 \le \frac{(n-1)s^2}{\chi^2_{1-\alpha/2,n-1}} \qquad 6.61$$

Description

Equation 6.61 gives the limits of a confidence interval (confidence $C = 1 - \alpha$) for an estimate of the population variance calculated as the sample variance from Eq. 6.25 with a sample size of n drawn from a normal distribution. Since the variance is a squared variable, it will be distributed as a chi-squared distribution with $n - 1$ degrees of freedom. Therefore, the denominators are the χ^2 values taken from Table 6.5 at the end of this chapter. (The values in Table 6.5 are already squared and should not be squared again.) Since the chi-squared distribution is not symmetrical, the table values for $\alpha/2$ and for $1 - (\alpha/2)$ will be different for the two confidence limits.

16. HYPOTHESIS TESTING

A *hypothesis test* is a procedure that answers the question, "Did these data come from [a particular type of] distribution?" There are many types of tests, depending on the distribution and parameter being evaluated. The most simple hypothesis test determines whether an average value obtained from n repetitions of an experiment could have come from a population with known mean μ and standard deviation σ. A practical application of this question is whether a manufacturing process has changed from what it used to be or should be. Of course, the answer (i.e., yes or no) cannot be given with absolute certainty—there will be a confidence level associated with the answer.

The following procedure is used to determine whether the average of n measurements can be assumed (with a given confidence level) to have come from a known normal population, or to determine the sample size required to make the decision with the desired confidence level.

Equation 6.62 Through Eq. 6.67: Test on Mean of Normal Distribution, Population Mean and Variance Known

step 1: Assume random sampling from a normal population.

The *null hypothesis* is

$$H_0: \mu = \mu_0 \qquad 6.62$$

The *alternative hypothesis* is

$$H_1: \mu = \mu_1 \qquad 6.63$$

A *type I error* is rejecting H_0 when it is true. The probability of a type I error is the *level of significance*.

$$\alpha = \text{probability(type I error)} \qquad 6.64$$

A *type II error* is accepting H_0 when it is false.

$$\beta = \text{probability(type II error)} \qquad 6.65$$

step 2: Choose the desired confidence level, C.

step 3: Decide on a one-tail or two-tail test. If the hypothesis being tested is that the average has or has not *increased* or has not *decreased*, use a one-tail test. If the hypothesis being tested is that the average has or has not *changed*, use a two-tail test.

step 4: Use Table 6.3 or the unit normal table to determine the x-value corresponding to the confidence level and number of tails.

step 5: Calculate the actual standard normal variable, Z, from Eq. 6.66. The relationship of the sample size, n, and the actual standard normal variable is illustrated in Eq. 6.67.

$$Z = \frac{\overline{X} - \mu_0}{\sigma/\sqrt{n}} \qquad 6.66$$

$$n = \left[\frac{Z_{\alpha/2}\sigma}{\overline{x} - \mu}\right]^2 \qquad 6.67$$

step 6: If $|Z| \ge x$, the average can be assumed (with confidence level C) to have come from a different distribution.

Equation 6.68 Through Eq. 6.75: Sample Size for Normal Distribution, α and β Known

$$H_0: \mu = \mu_0 \qquad 6.68$$

$$H_1: \mu \neq \mu_0 \qquad 6.69$$

$$\beta = \Phi\left(\frac{\mu_0 - \mu}{\sigma/\sqrt{n}} + Z_{\alpha/2}\right) - \Phi\left(\frac{\mu_0 - \mu}{\sigma/\sqrt{n}} - Z_{\alpha/2}\right) \qquad 6.70$$

$$n \simeq \frac{(Z_{\alpha/2} + Z_{\beta})^2 \sigma^2}{(\mu_1 - \mu_0)^2} \qquad 6.71$$

$$H_0 : \mu = \mu_0 \qquad 6.72$$

$$H_1 : \mu > \mu_0 \qquad 6.73$$

$$\beta = \Phi\left(\frac{\mu_0 - \mu}{\sigma/\sqrt{n}} + Z_{\alpha} \right) \qquad 6.74$$

$$n = \frac{(Z_{\alpha} + Z_{\beta})^2 \sigma^2}{(\mu_1 - \mu_0)^2} \qquad 6.75$$

Description

Equation 6.68 through Eq. 6.75 are used to determine the required sample size when the probabilities of type 1 and type 2 errors, α and β, respectively, are known. μ_1 is the assumed true mean. The notation $\Phi(z)$ designates the cumulative normal distribution function (i.e., the fraction of the normal curve from $-\infty$ up to z).[2] Equation 6.68 through Eq. 6.71 are used when the test is to determine if the sample mean is the same as the population mean, while Eq. 6.72 through Eq. 6.75 are used when the test is to determine if the sample mean is larger or smaller than the population mean.

Example

When it is operating properly, a chemical plant has a daily production rate that is normally distributed with a mean of 880 tons/day and a standard deviation of 21 tons/day. During an analysis period, the output is measured with random sampling on 50 consecutive days, and the mean output is found to be 871 tons/day. With a 95% confidence level, determine if the plant is operating properly.

(A) There is at least a 5% probability that the plant is operating properly.

(B) There is at least a 95% probability that the plant is operating properly.

(C) There is at least a 5% probability that the plant is not operating properly.

(D) There is at least a 95% probability that the plant is not operating properly.

Solution

Since a specific direction in the variation is not given (i.e., the example does not ask if the average has decreased), use a two-tail hypothesis test.

From Table 6.3, $x = 1.9600$.

Use Eq. 6.66 to calculate the actual standard normal variable.

$$\begin{aligned} Z &= \frac{\overline{X} - \mu}{\sigma/\sqrt{n}} \\ &= \frac{871 - 880}{\dfrac{21}{\sqrt{50}}} \\ |Z| &= -3.03 \end{aligned}$$

Since $|-3.03| > 1.9600$, the distributions are not the same. There is at least a 95% probability that the plant is not operating correctly.

The answer is (D).

17. LINEAR REGRESSION

Equation 6.76 Through Eq. 6.82: Method of Least Squares

If it is necessary to draw a straight line $(\hat{y} = \hat{a} + \hat{b}\,x)$ through n two-dimensional data points (x_1, y_1), (x_2, y_2), ..., (x_n, y_n), the following method based on the *method of least squares* can be used.

step 1: Calculate the following seven quantities.

$$\sum x_i \quad \sum x_i^2 \quad \left(\sum x_i\right)^2 \quad \sum x_i y_i$$

$$\sum y_i \quad \sum y_i^2 \quad \left(\sum y_i\right)^2$$

$$\overline{x} = (1/n)\left(\sum_{i=1}^{n} x_i\right) \qquad 6.76$$

$$\overline{y} = (1/n)\left(\sum_{i=1}^{n} y_i\right) \qquad 6.77$$

step 2: Calculate the slope, $\hat{b}$, of the line.

$$\hat{b} = S_{xy}/S_{xx} \qquad 6.78$$

---

[2]Not only is $\Phi(z)$ undefined in the *NCEES Handbook*, but it is the same as what the *NCEES Handbook* designated earlier as $F(x)$.

$$S_{xy} = \sum_{i=1}^{n} x_i y_i - (1/n)\left(\sum_{i=1}^{n} x_i\right)\left(\sum_{i=1}^{n} y_i\right) \qquad 6.79$$

$$S_{xx} = \sum_{i=1}^{n} x_i^2 - (1/n)\left(\sum_{i=1}^{n} x_i\right)^2 \qquad 6.80$$

step 3: Calculate the y-intercept, $\hat{a}$.

$$\hat{a} = \bar{y} - \hat{b}\,\bar{x} \qquad 6.81$$

The equation of the straight line is

$$y = \hat{a} + \hat{b}\,x \qquad 6.82$$

Example

The least squares method is used to plot a straight line through the data points $(1,6)$, $(2,7)$, $(3,11)$, and $(5,13)$. The slope of the line is most nearly

(A) 0.87

(B) 1.7

(C) 1.9

(D) 2.0

Solution

First, calculate the following values.

$$\sum x_i = 1 + 2 + 3 + 5 = 11$$
$$\sum y_i = 6 + 7 + 11 + 13 = 37$$
$$\sum x_i^2 = (1)^2 + (2)^2 + (3)^2 + (5)^2 = 39$$
$$\sum x_i y_i = (1)(6) + (2)(7) + (3)(11) + (5)(13) = 118$$

Find the value of S_{xy} using Eq. 6.79.

$$S_{xy} = \sum_{i=1}^{n} x_i y_i - (1/n)\left(\sum_{i=1}^{n} x_i\right)\left(\sum_{i=1}^{n} y_i\right)$$
$$= 118 - \left(\frac{1}{4}\right)(11)(37)$$
$$= 16.25$$

Find the value of S_{xx} from Eq. 6.80.

$$S_{xx} = \sum_{i=1}^{n} x_i^2 - (1/n)\left(\sum_{i=1}^{n} x_i\right)^2$$
$$= 39 - \left(\frac{1}{4}\right)(11)^2$$
$$= 8.75$$

From Eq. 6.78, the slope is

$$\hat{b} = S_{xy}/S_{xx}$$
$$= \frac{16.25}{8.75}$$
$$= 1.857 \quad (1.9)$$

The answer is (C).

Equation 6.83 and Eq. 6.84: Standard Error of Estimate

$$S_e^2 = \frac{S_{xx}S_{yy} - S_{xy}^2}{S_{xx}(n-2)} = MSE \qquad 6.83$$

$$S_{yy} = \sum_{i=1}^{n} y_i^2 - (1/n)\left(\sum_{i=1}^{n} y_i\right)^2 \qquad 6.84$$

Description

Equation 6.83 gives the *mean squared error*, S_e^2 or MSE, which estimates the likelihood of a value being close to an observed value by averaging the square of the errors (i.e., the difference between the estimated value and observed value). Small MSE values are favorable, as they indicate a smaller likelihood of error.

Equation 6.85 and Eq. 6.86: Confidence Intervals for Slope and Intercept

$$\hat{b} \pm t_{\alpha/2,n-2}\sqrt{\frac{MSE}{S_{xx}}} \qquad 6.85$$

$$\hat{a} \pm t_{\alpha/2,\,n-2}\sqrt{\left(\frac{1}{n} + \frac{\bar{x}^2}{S_{xx}}\right)MSE} \qquad 6.86$$

Description

The confidence intervals for calculated slope and intercept are calculated from the mean square error using Eq. 6.85 and Eq. 6.86, respectively.

Equation 6.87 and Eq. 6.88: Sample Correlation Coefficient

$$R = \frac{S_{xy}}{\sqrt{S_{xx}S_{yy}}} \qquad \text{6.87}$$

$$R^2 = \frac{S_{xy}^2}{S_{xx}S_{yy}} \qquad \text{6.88}$$

Description

Once the slope of the line is calculated using the least squares method, the *goodness of fit* can be determined by calculating the *sample correlation coefficient*, R. The goodness of fit describes how well the calculated regression values, plotted as a line, match actual observed values, plotted as points.

If $\hat{b}$ is positive, R will be positive; if $\hat{b}$ is negative, R will be negative. As a general rule, if the absolute value of R exceeds 0.85, the fit is good; otherwise, the fit is poor. R equals 1.0 if the fit is a perfect straight line.

Example

The least squares method is used to plot a straight line through the data points $(5, -5)$, $(3, -2)$, $(2, 3)$, and $(-1, 7)$. The correlation coefficient is most nearly

- (A) -0.97
- (B) -0.92
- (C) -0.88
- (D) -0.80

Solution

First, calculate the following values.

$$\sum x_i = 5 + 3 + 2 + (-1) = 9$$
$$\sum y_i = (-5) + (-2) + 3 + 7 = 3$$
$$\sum x_i^2 = (5)^2 + (3)^2 + (2)^2 + (-1)^2 = 39$$
$$\sum y_i^2 = (-5)^2 + (-2)^2 + (3)^2 + (7)^2 = 87$$
$$\sum x_i y_i = (5)(-5) + (3)(-2) + (2)(3) + (-1)(7) = -32$$

From Eq. 6.87, and substituting Eq. 6.79, Eq. 6.80, and Eq. 6.84 for S_{xy}, S_{xx}, and S_{yy}, respectively, the correlation coefficient is

$$R = \frac{S_{xy}}{\sqrt{S_{xx}S_{yy}}}$$

$$= \frac{\sum x_i y_i - (1/n)\left(\sum x_i\right)\left(\sum y_i\right)}{\sqrt{\left[\sum x_i^2 - (1/n)\left(\sum x_i\right)^2\right] \times \left[\sum y_i^2 - (1/n)\left(\sum y_i\right)^2\right]}}$$

$$= \frac{-32 - \left[\dfrac{1}{4}\right](9)(3)}{\sqrt{\left[39 - \left(\dfrac{1}{4}\right)(9)^2\right]\left[87 - \left(\dfrac{1}{4}\right)(3)^2\right]}}$$

$$= -0.972 \quad (-0.97)$$

The answer is (A).

Equation 6.89: Residuals

$$e_i = y_i - \hat{y}_i = y_i - \left(\hat{a} + \hat{b}\,x_i\right) \qquad \text{6.89}$$

Description

Residuals are calculated by taking the observed values of the dependent variable, y_i, and subtracting the estimated response from the statistical model (e.g., linear regression), $\hat{y}_i$. Model residuals should be normally distributed with a mean value of zero and constant variance, otherwise the statistical model is not reliable.

Statistics

Table 6.1 *Cumulative Binomial Probabilities P(X ≤ x)*

							P						
n	x	0.1	0.2	0.3	0.4	0.5	0.6	0.7	0.8	0.9	0.95	0.99
1	0	0.9000	0.8000	0.7000	0.6000	0.5000	0.4000	0.3000	0.2000	0.1000	0.0500	0.0100
2	0	0.8100	0.6400	0.4900	0.3600	0.2500	0.1600	0.0900	0.0400	0.0100	0.0025	0.0001
	1	0.9900	0.9600	0.9100	0.8400	0.7500	0.6400	0.5100	0.3600	0.1900	0.0975	0.0199
3	0	0.7290	0.5120	0.3430	0.2160	0.1250	0.0640	0.0270	0.0080	0.0010	0.0001	0.0000
	1	0.9720	0.8960	0.7840	0.6480	0.5000	0.3520	0.2160	0.1040	0.0280	0.0073	0.0003
	2	0.9990	0.9920	0.9730	0.9360	0.8750	0.7840	0.6570	0.4880	0.2710	0.1426	0.0297
4	0	0.6561	0.4096	0.2401	0.1296	0.0625	0.0256	0.0081	0.0016	0.0001	0.0000	0.0000
	1	0.9477	0.8192	0.6517	0.4752	0.3125	0.1792	0.0837	0.0272	0.0037	0.0005	0.0000
	2	0.9963	0.9728	0.9163	0.8208	0.6875	0.5248	0.3483	0.1808	0.0523	0.0140	0.0006
	3	0.9999	0.9984	0.9919	0.9744	0.9375	0.8704	0.7599	0.5904	0.3439	0.1855	0.0394
5	0	0.5905	0.3277	0.1681	0.0778	0.0313	0.0102	0.0024	0.0003	0.0000	0.0000	0.0000
	1	0.9185	0.7373	0.5282	0.3370	0.1875	0.0870	0.0308	0.0067	0.0005	0.0000	0.0000
	2	0.9914	0.9421	0.8369	0.6826	0.5000	0.3174	0.1631	0.0579	0.0086	0.0012	0.0000
	3	0.9995	0.9933	0.9692	0.9130	0.8125	0.6630	0.4718	0.2627	0.0815	0.0226	0.0010
	4	1.0000	0.9997	0.9976	0.9898	0.6988	0.9222	0.8319	0.6723	0.4095	0.2262	0.0490
6	0	0.5314	0.2621	0.1176	0.0467	0.0156	0.0041	0.0007	0.0001	0.0000	0.0000	0.0000
	1	0.8857	0.6554	0.4202	0.2333	0.1094	0.0410	0.0109	0.0016	0.0001	0.0000	0.0000
	2	0.9842	0.9011	0.7443	0.5443	0.3438	0.1792	0.0705	0.0170	0.0013	0.0001	0.0000
	3	0.9987	0.9830	0.9295	0.8208	0.6563	0.4557	0.2557	0.0989	0.0159	0.0022	0.0000
	4	0.9999	0.9984	0.9891	0.9590	0.9806	0.7667	0.5798	0.3446	0.1143	0.0328	0.0015
	5	1.0000	0.9999	0.9993	0.9959	0.9844	0.9533	0.8824	0.7379	0.4686	0.2649	0.0585
7	0	0.4783	0.2097	0.0824	0.0280	0.0078	0.0106	0.0002	0.0000	0.0000	0.0000	0.0000
	1	0.8503	0.5767	0.3294	0.1586	0.0625	0.0188	0.0038	0.0004	0.0000	0.0000	0.0000
	2	0.9743	0.8520	0.6471	0.4199	0.2266	0.0963	0.0288	0.0047	0.0002	0.0000	0.0000
	3	0.9973	0.9667	0.8740	0.7102	0.5000	0.2898	0.1260	0.0333	0.0027	0.0002	0.0000
	4	0.9998	0.9953	0.9712	0.9037	0.7734	0.5801	0.3529	0.1480	0.0257	0.0038	0.0000
	5	1.0000	0.9996	0.9962	0.9812	0.9375	0.8414	0.6706	0.4233	0.1497	0.0444	0.0020
	6	1.0000	1.0000	0.9998	0.9984	0.9922	0.9720	0.9176	0.7903	0.5217	0.3017	0.0679
8	0	0.4305	0.1678	0.0576	0.0168	0.0039	0.0007	0.0001	0.0000	0.0000	0.0000	0.0000
	1	0.8131	0.5033	0.2553	0.1064	0.0352	0.0085	0.0013	0.0001	0.0000	0.0000	0.0000
	2	0.9619	0.7969	0.5518	0.3154	0.1445	0.0498	0.0113	0.0012	0.0000	0.0000	0.0000
	3	0.9950	0.9437	0.8059	0.5941	0.3633	0.1737	0.0580	0.0104	0.0004	0.0000	0.0000
	4	0.9996	0.9896	0.9420	0.8263	0.6367	0.4059	0.1941	0.0563	0.0050	0.0004	0.0000
	5	1.0000	0.9988	0.9887	0.9502	0.8555	0.6846	0.4482	0.2031	0.0381	0.0058	0.0001
	6	1.0000	0.9999	0.9987	0.9915	0.9648	0.8936	0.7447	0.4967	0.1869	0.0572	0.0027
	7	1.0000	1.0000	0.9999	0.9993	0.9961	0.9832	0.9424	0.8322	0.5695	0.3366	0.0773
9	0	0.3874	0.1342	0.0404	0.0101	0.0020	0.0003	0.0000	0.0000	0.0000	0.0000	0.0000
	1	0.7748	0.4362	0.1960	0.0705	0.0195	0.0038	0.0004	0.0000	0.0000	0.0000	0.0000
	2	0.9470	0.7382	0.4628	0.2318	0.0889	0.0250	0.0043	0.0003	0.0000	0.0000	0.0000
	3	0.9917	0.9144	0.7297	0.4826	0.2539	0.0994	0.0253	0.0031	0.0001	0.0000	0.0000
	4	0.9991	0.9804	0.9012	0.7334	0.5000	0.2666	0.0988	0.0196	0.0009	0.0000	0.0000
	5	0.9999	0.9969	0.9747	0.9006	0.7461	0.5174	0.2703	0.0856	0.0083	0.0006	0.0000
	6	1.0000	0.9997	0.9957	0.9750	0.9102	0.7682	0.5372	0.2618	0.0530	0.0084	0.0001
	7	1.0000	1.0000	0.9996	0.9962	0.9805	0.9295	0.8040	0.5638	0.2252	0.0712	0.0034
	8	1.0000	1.0000	1.0000	0.9997	0.9980	0.9899	0.9596	0.8658	0.6126	0.3698	0.0865
10	0	0.3487	0.1074	0.0282	0.0060	0.0010	0.0001	0.0000	0.0000	0.0000	0.0000	0.0000
	1	0.7361	0.3758	0.1493	0.0464	0.0107	0.0017	0.0001	0.0000	0.0000	0.0000	0.0000
	2	0.9298	0.6778	0.3828	0.1673	0.0547	0.0123	0.0016	0.0001	0.0000	0.0000	0.0000
	3	0.9872	0.8791	0.6496	0.3823	0.1719	0.0548	0.0106	0.0009	0.0000	0.0000	0.0000
	4	0.9984	0.9672	0.8497	0.6331	0.3770	0.1662	0.0473	0.0064	0.0001	0.0000	0.0000
	5	0.9999	0.9936	0.9527	0.8338	0.6230	0.3669	0.1503	0.0328	0.0016	0.0001	0.0000
	6	1.0000	0.9991	0.9894	0.9452	0.8281	0.6177	0.3504	0.1209	0.0128	0.0010	0.0000
	7	1.0000	0.9999	0.9984	0.9877	0.9453	0.8327	0.6172	0.3222	0.0702	0.0115	0.0001
	8	1.0000	1.0000	0.9999	0.9983	0.9893	0.9536	0.8507	0.6242	0.2639	0.0861	0.0043
	9	1.0000	1.0000	1.0000	0.9999	0.9990	0.9940	0.9718	0.8926	0.6513	0.4013	0.0956

$$P$$

n	x	0.1	0.2	0.3	0.4	0.5	0.6	0.7	0.8	0.9	0.95	0.99
15	0	0.2059	0.0352	0.0047	0.0005	0.0000	0.0000	0.0000	0.0000	0.0000	0.0000	0.0000
	1	0.4590	0.1671	0.0353	0.0052	0.0005	0.0000	0.0000	0.0000	0.0000	0.0000	0.0000
	2	0.8159	0.3980	0.1268	0.0271	0.0037	0.0003	0.0000	0.0000	0.0000	0.0000	0.0000
	3	0.9444	0.6482	0.2969	0.0905	0.0176	0.0019	0.0001	0.0000	0.0000	0.0000	0.0000
	4	0.9873	0.8358	0.5155	0.2173	0.0592	0.0093	0.0007	0.0000	0.0000	0.0000	0.0000
	5	0.9978	0.9389	0.7216	0.4032	0.1509	0.0338	0.0037	0.0001	0.0000	0.0000	0.0000
	6	0.9997	0.9819	0.8689	0.6098	0.3036	0.0950	0.0152	0.0008	0.0000	0.0000	0.0000
	7	1.0000	0.9958	0.9500	0.7869	0.5000	0.2131	0.0500	0.0042	0.0000	0.0000	0.0000
	8	1.0000	0.9992	0.9848	0.9050	0.6964	0.3902	0.1311	0.0181	0.0003	0.0000	0.0000
	9	1.0000	0.9999	0.9963	0.9662	0.8491	0.5968	0.2784	0.0611	0.0022	0.0001	0.0000
	10	1.0000	1.0000	0.9993	0.9907	0.9408	0.7827	0.4845	0.1642	0.0127	0.0006	0.0000
	11	1.0000	1.0000	0.9999	0.9981	0.9824	0.9095	0.7031	0.3518	0.0556	0.0055	0.0000
	12	1.0000	1.0000	1.0000	0.9997	0.9963	0.9729	0.8732	0.6020	0.1841	0.0362	0.0004
	13	1.0000	1.0000	1.0000	1.0000	0.9995	0.9948	0.9647	0.8329	0.4510	0.1710	0.0096
	14	1.0000	1.0000	1.0000	1.0000	1.0000	0.9995	0.9953	0.9648	0.7941	0.5367	0.1399
20	0	0.1216	0.0115	0.0008	0.0000	0.0000	0.0000	0.0000	0.0000	0.0000	0.0000	0.0000
	1	0.3917	0.0692	0.0076	0.0005	0.0000	0.0000	0.0000	0.0000	0.0000	0.0000	0.0000
	2	0.6769	0.2061	0.0355	0.0036	0.0002	0.0000	0.0000	0.0000	0.0000	0.0000	0.0000
	3	0.8670	0.4114	0.1071	0.0160	0.0013	0.0000	0.0000	0.0000	0.0000	0.0000	0.0000
	4	0.9568	0.6296	0.2375	0.0510	0.0059	0.0003	0.0000	0.0000	0.0000	0.0000	0.0000
	5	0.9887	0.8042	0.4164	0.1256	0.0207	0.0016	0.0000	0.0000	0.0000	0.0000	0.0000
	6	0.9976	0.9133	0.6080	0.2500	0.0577	0.0065	0.0003	0.0000	0.0000	0.0000	0.0000
	7	0.9996	0.9679	0.7723	0.4159	0.1316	0.0210	0.0013	0.0000	0.0000	0.0000	0.0000
	8	0.9999	0.9900	0.8867	0.5956	0.2517	0.0565	0.0051	0.0001	0.0000	0.0000	0.0000
	9	1.0000	0.9974	0.9520	0.7553	0.4119	0.1275	0.0171	0.0006	0.0000	0.0000	0.0000
	10	1.0000	0.9994	0.9829	0.8725	0.5881	0.2447	0.0480	0.0026	0.0000	0.0000	0.0000
	11	1.0000	0.9999	0.9949	0.9435	0.7483	0.4044	0.1133	0.0100	0.0001	0.0000	0.0000
	12	1.0000	1.0000	0.9987	0.9790	0.8684	0.5841	0.2277	0.0321	0.0004	0.0000	0.0000
	13	1.0000	1.0000	0.9997	0.9935	0.9423	0.7500	0.3920	0.0867	0.0024	0.0000	0.0000
	14	1.0000	1.0000	1.0000	0.9984	0.9793	0.8744	0.5836	0.1958	0.0113	0.0003	0.0000
	15	1.0000	1.0000	1.0000	0.9997	0.9941	0.9490	0.7625	0.3704	0.0432	0.0026	0.0000
	16	1.0000	1.0000	1.0000	1.0000	0.9987	0.9840	0.8929	0.5886	0.1330	0.0159	0.0000
	17	1.0000	1.0000	1.0000	1.0000	0.9998	0.9964	0.9645	0.7939	0.3231	0.0755	0.0010
	18	1.0000	1.0000	1.0000	1.0000	1.0000	0.9995	0.9924	0.9308	0.6083	0.2642	0.0169
	19	1.0000	1.0000	1.0000	1.0000	1.0000	1.0000	0.9992	0.9885	0.8784	0.6415	0.1821

Montgomery, Douglas C., and George C. Runger, *Applied Statistics and Probability for Engineers*, 4th ed. Reproduced by permission of John Wiley & Sons, 2007.

Table 6.2 *Unit Normal Distribution*

x	$f(x)$	$F(x)$	$R(x)$	$2R(x)$	$W(x)$
0.0	0.3989	0.5000	0.5000	1.0000	0.0000
0.1	0.3970	0.5398	0.4602	0.9203	0.0797
0.2	0.3910	0.5793	0.4207	0.8415	0.1585
0.3	0.3814	0.6179	0.3821	0.7642	0.2358
0.4	0.3683	0.6554	0.3446	0.6892	0.3108
0.5	0.3521	0.6915	0.3085	0.6171	0.3829
0.6	0.3332	0.7257	0.2743	0.5485	0.4515
0.7	0.3123	0.7580	0.2420	0.4839	0.5161
0.8	0.2897	0.7881	0.2119	0.4237	0.5763
0.9	0.2661	0.8159	0.1841	0.3681	0.6319
1.0	0.2420	0.8413	0.1587	0.3173	0.6827
1.1	0.2179	0.8643	0.1357	0.2713	0.7287
1.2	0.1942	0.8849	0.1151	0.2301	0.7699
1.3	0.1714	0.9032	0.0968	0.1936	0.8064
1.4	0.1497	0.9192	0.0808	0.1615	0.8385
1.5	0.1295	0.9332	0.0668	0.1336	0.8664
1.6	0.1109	0.9452	0.0548	0.1096	0.8904
1.7	0.0940	0.9554	0.0446	0.0891	0.9109
1.8	0.0790	0.9641	0.0359	0.0719	0.9281
1.9	0.0656	0.9713	0.0287	0.0574	0.9426
2.0	0.0540	0.9772	0.0228	0.0455	0.9545
2.1	0.0440	0.9821	0.0179	0.0357	0.9643
2.2	0.0355	0.9861	0.0139	0.0278	0.9722
2.3	0.0283	0.9893	0.0107	0.0214	0.9786
2.4	0.0224	0.9918	0.0082	0.0164	0.9836
2.5	0.0175	0.9938	0.0062	0.0124	0.9876
2.6	0.0136	0.9953	0.0047	0.0093	0.9907
2.7	0.0104	0.9965	0.0035	0.0069	0.9931
2.8	0.0079	0.9974	0.0026	0.0051	0.9949
2.9	0.0060	0.9981	0.0019	0.0037	0.9963
3.0	0.0044	0.9987	0.0013	0.0027	0.9973
Fractiles					
1.2816	0.1755	0.9000	0.1000	0.2000	0.8000
1.6449	0.1031	0.9500	0.0500	0.1000	0.9000
1.9600	0.0584	0.9750	0.0250	0.0500	0.9500
2.0537	0.0484	0.9800	0.0200	0.0400	0.9600
2.3263	0.0267	0.9900	0.0100	0.0200	0.9800
2.5758	0.0145	0.9950	0.0050	0.0100	0.9900

Table 6.3 *Values of x for Various Two-Tail Confidence Intervals*

confidence interval level, C	two-tail limit, x $(Z_{\alpha/2})$
80%	1.2816
90%	1.6449
95%	1.9600
96%	2.0537
98%	2.3263
99%	2.5758

Table 6.4 *Student's t-Distribution (values of t for ν degrees of freedom (sample size n + 1); 1 – α confidence level)*

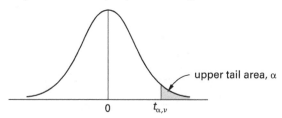

upper tail area, α

area under the upper tail

ν^*	$\alpha = 0.25$	$\alpha = 0.20$	$\alpha = 0.15$	$\alpha = 0.10$	$\alpha = 0.05$	$\alpha = 0.025$	$\alpha = 0.01$	$\alpha = 0.005$	ν^*
1	1.000	1.376	1.963	3.078	6.314	12.706	31.821	63.657	1
2	0.816	1.061	1.386	1.886	2.920	4.303	6.965	9.925	2
3	0.765	0.978	1.350	1.638	2.353	3.182	4.541	5.841	3
4	0.741	0.941	1.190	1.533	2.132	2.776	3.747	4.604	4
5	0.727	0.920	1.156	1.476	2.015	2.571	3.365	4.032	5
6	0.718	0.906	1.134	1.440	1.943	2.447	3.143	3.707	6
7	0.711	0.896	1.119	1.415	1.895	2.365	2.998	3.499	7
8	0.706	0.889	1.108	1.397	1.860	2.306	2.896	3.355	8
9	0.703	0.883	1.100	1.383	1.833	2.262	2.821	3.250	9
10	0.700	0.879	1.093	1.372	1.812	2.228	2.764	3.169	10
11	0.697	0.876	1.088	1.363	1.796	2.201	2.718	3.106	11
12	0.695	0.873	1.083	1.356	1.782	2.179	2.681	3.055	12
13	0.694	0.870	1.079	1.350	1.771	2.160	2.650	3.012	13
14	0.692	0.868	1.076	1.345	1.761	2.145	2.624	2.977	14
15	0.691	0.866	1.074	1.341	1.753	2.131	2.602	2.947	15
16	0.690	0.865	1.071	1.337	1.746	2.120	2.583	2.921	16
17	0.689	0.863	1.069	1.333	1.740	2.110	2.567	2.898	17
18	0.688	0.862	1.067	1.330	1.734	2.101	2.552	2.878	18
19	0.688	0.861	1.066	1.328	1.729	2.093	2.539	2.861	19
20	0.687	0.860	1.064	1.325	1.725	2.086	2.528	2.845	20
21	0.686	0.859	1.063	1.323	1.721	2.080	2.518	2.831	21
22	0.686	0.858	1.061	1.321	1.717	2.074	2.508	2.819	22
23	0.685	0.858	1.060	1.319	1.714	2.069	2.500	2.807	23
24	0.685	0.857	1.059	1.318	1.711	2.064	2.492	2.797	24
25	0.684	0.856	1.058	1.316	1.708	2.060	2.485	2.787	25
26	0.684	0.856	1.058	1.315	1.706	2.056	2.479	2.779	26
27	0.684	0.855	1.057	1.314	1.703	2.052	2.473	2.771	27
28	0.683	0.855	1.056	1.313	1.701	2.048	2.467	2.763	28
29	0.683	0.854	1.055	1.311	1.699	2.045	2.462	2.756	29
30	0.683	0.854	1.055	1.310	1.697	2.042	2.457	2.750	30
∞	0.674	0.842	1.036	1.282	1.645	1.960	2.326	2.576	∞

*The number of independent degrees of freedom, ν, is always one less than the sample size, n.

Table 6.5 *Critical Values of Chi-Squared Distribution*

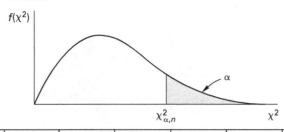

degrees of freedom, ν	$\chi^2_{0.995}$	$\chi^2_{0.990}$	$\chi^2_{0.975}$	$\chi^2_{0.950}$	$\chi^2_{0.900}$	$\chi^2_{0.100}$	$\chi^2_{0.050}$	$\chi^2_{0.025}$	$\chi^2_{0.010}$	$\chi^2_{0.005}$
1	0.0000393	0.0001571	0.0009821	0.0039321	0.0157908	2.70554	3.84146	5.02389	6.6349	7.87944
2	0.0100251	0.0201007	0.0506356	0.102587	0.21072	4.60517	5.99147	7.37776	9.21034	10.5966
3	0.0717212	0.114832	0.215795	0.351846	0.584375	6.25139	7.81473	9.3484	11.3449	12.8381
4	0.20699	0.29711	0.484419	0.710721	1.063623	7.77944	9.48773	11.1433	13.2767	14.8602
5	0.41174	0.5543	0.831211	1.145476	1.61031	9.23635	11.0705	12.8325	15.0863	16.7496
6	0.675727	0.872085	1.237347	1.63539	2.20413	10.6446	12.5916	14.4494	16.8119	18.5476
7	0.989265	1.239043	1.68987	2.16735	2.83311	12.017	14.0671	16.0128	18.4753	20.2777
8	1.344419	1.646482	2.17973	2.73264	3.48954	13.3616	15.5073	17.5346	20.0902	21.955
9	1.734926	2.087912	2.70039	3.32511	4.16816	14.6837	16.919	19.0228	21.666	23.5893
10	2.15585	2.55821	3.24697	3.9403	4.86518	15.9871	18.307	20.4831	23.2093	25.1882
11	2.60321	3.05347	3.81575	4.57481	5.57779	17.275	19.6751	21.92	24.725	26.7569
12	3.07382	3.57056	4.40379	5.22603	6.3038	18.5494	21.0261	23.3367	26.217	28.2995
13	3.56503	4.10691	5.00874	5.89186	7.0415	19.8119	22.3621	24.7356	27.6883	29.8194
14	4.07468	4.66043	5.62872	6.57063	7.78953	21.0642	23.6848	26.119	29.1413	31.3193
15	4.60094	5.22935	6.26214	7.26094	8.54675	22.3072	24.9958	27.4884	30.5779	32.8013
16	5.14224	5.81221	6.90766	7.96164	9.31223	23.5418	26.2962	28.8454	31.9999	34.2672
17	5.69724	6.40776	7.56418	8.67176	10.0852	24.769	27.5871	30.191	33.4087	35.7185
18	6.26481	7.01491	8.23075	9.39046	10.8649	25.9894	28.8693	31.5264	34.8053	37.1564
19	6.84398	7.63273	8.90655	10.117	11.6509	27.2036	30.1435	32.8523	36.1908	38.5822
20	7.43386	8.2604	9.59083	10.8508	12.4426	28.412	31.4104	34.1696	37.5662	39.9968
21	8.03366	8.8972	10.28293	11.5913	13.2396	29.6151	32.6705	35.4789	38.9321	41.401
22	8.64272	9.54249	10.9823	12.338	14.0415	30.8133	33.9244	36.7807	40.2894	42.7956
23	9.26042	10.19567	11.6885	13.0905	14.8479	32.0069	35.1725	38.0757	41.6384	44.1813
24	9.88623	10.8564	12.4011	13.8484	15.6587	33.1963	36.4151	39.3641	42.9798	45.5585
25	10.5197	11.524	13.1197	14.6114	16.4734	34.3816	37.6525	40.6465	44.3141	46.9278
26	11.1603	12.1981	13.8439	15.3791	17.2919	35.5631	38.8852	41.9232	45.6417	48.2899
27	11.8076	12.8786	14.5733	16.1513	18.1138	36.7412	40.1133	43.1944	46.963	49.6449
28	12.4613	13.5648	15.3079	16.9279	18.9392	37.9159	41.3372	44.4607	48.2782	50.9933
29	13.1211	14.2565	16.0471	17.7083	19.7677	39.0875	42.5569	45.7222	49.5879	52.3356
30	13.7867	14.9535	16.7908	18.4926	20.5992	40.256	43.7729	46.9792	50.8922	53.672
40	20.7065	22.1643	24.4331	26.5093	29.0505	51.805	55.7585	59.3417	63.6907	66.7659
50	27.9907	29.7067	32.3574	34.7642	37.6886	63.1671	67.5048	71.4202	76.1539	79.49
60	35.5346	37.4848	40.4817	43.1879	46.4589	74.397	79.0819	83.2976	88.3794	91.9517
70	43.2752	45.4418	48.7576	51.7393	55.329	85.5271	90.5312	95.0231	100.425	104.215
80	51.172	53.54	57.1532	60.3915	64.2778	96.5782	101.879	106.629	112.329	116.321
90	59.1963	61.7541	65.6466	69.126	73.2912	107.565	113.145	118.136	124.116	128.299
100	67.3276	70.0648	74.2219	77.9295	82.3581	118.498	124.342	129.561	135.807	140.169

Table 6.6 *Critical Values of F*

For a particular combination of numerator and denominator degrees of freedom, entry represents the critical values of F corresponding to a specified upper tail area (α).

$\alpha = 0.05$

$F(\alpha, df_1, df_2)$

numerator df_1

denominator df_2	1	2	3	4	5	6	7	8	9	10	12	15	20	24	30	40	60	120	∞
1	161.4	199.5	215.7	224.6	230.2	234.0	236.8	238.9	240.5	241.9	243.9	245.9	248.0	249.1	250.1	251.1	252.2	253.3	254.3
2	18.51	19.00	19.16	19.25	19.30	19.33	19.35	19.37	19.38	19.40	19.41	19.43	19.45	19.45	19.46	19.47	19.48	19.49	19.50
3	10.13	9.55	9.28	9.12	9.01	8.94	8.89	8.85	8.81	8.79	8.74	8.70	8.66	8.64	8.62	8.59	8.57	8.55	8.53
4	7.71	6.94	6.59	6.39	6.26	6.16	6.09	6.04	6.00	5.96	5.91	5.86	5.80	5.77	5.75	5.72	5.69	5.66	5.63
5	6.61	5.79	5.41	5.19	5.05	4.95	4.88	4.82	4.77	4.74	4.68	4.62	4.56	4.53	4.50	4.46	4.43	4.40	4.36
6	5.99	5.14	4.76	4.53	4.39	4.28	4.21	4.15	4.10	4.06	4.00	3.94	3.87	3.84	3.81	3.77	3.74	3.70	3.67
7	5.59	4.74	4.35	4.12	3.97	3.87	3.79	3.73	3.68	3.64	3.57	3.51	3.44	3.41	3.38	3.34	3.30	3.27	3.23
8	5.32	4.46	4.07	3.84	3.69	3.58	3.50	3.44	3.39	3.35	3.28	3.22	3.15	3.12	3.08	3.04	3.01	2.97	2.93
9	5.12	4.26	3.86	3.63	3.48	3.37	3.29	3.23	3.18	3.14	3.07	3.01	2.94	2.90	2.86	2.83	2.79	2.75	2.71
10	4.96	4.10	3.71	3.48	3.33	3.22	3.14	3.07	3.02	2.98	2.91	2.85	2.77	2.74	2.70	2.66	2.62	2.58	2.54
11	4.84	3.98	3.59	3.36	3.20	3.09	3.01	2.95	2.90	2.85	2.79	2.72	2.65	2.61	2.57	2.53	2.49	2.45	2.40
12	4.75	3.89	3.49	3.26	3.11	3.00	2.91	2.85	2.80	2.75	2.69	2.62	2.54	2.51	2.47	2.43	2.38	2.34	2.30
13	4.67	3.81	3.41	3.18	3.03	2.92	2.83	2.77	2.71	2.67	2.60	2.53	2.46	2.42	2.38	2.34	2.30	2.25	2.21
14	4.60	3.74	3.34	3.11	2.96	2.85	2.76	2.70	2.65	2.60	2.53	2.46	2.39	2.35	2.31	2.27	2.22	2.18	2.13
15	4.54	3.68	3.29	3.06	2.90	2.79	2.71	2.64	2.59	2.54	2.48	2.40	2.33	2.29	2.25	2.20	2.16	2.11	2.07
16	4.49	3.63	3.24	3.01	2.85	2.74	2.66	2.59	2.54	2.49	2.42	2.35	2.28	2.24	2.19	2.15	2.11	2.06	2.01
17	4.45	3.59	3.20	2.96	2.81	2.70	2.61	2.55	2.49	2.45	2.38	2.31	2.23	2.19	2.15	2.10	2.06	2.01	1.96
18	4.41	3.55	3.16	2.93	2.77	2.66	2.58	2.51	2.46	2.41	2.34	2.27	2.19	2.15	2.11	2.06	2.02	1.97	1.92
19	4.38	3.52	3.13	2.90	2.74	2.63	2.54	2.48	2.42	2.38	2.31	2.23	2.16	2.11	2.07	2.03	1.98	1.93	1.88
20	4.35	3.49	3.10	2.87	2.71	2.60	2.51	2.45	2.39	2.35	2.28	2.20	2.12	2.08	2.04	1.99	1.95	1.90	1.84
21	4.32	3.47	3.07	2.84	2.68	2.57	2.49	2.42	2.37	2.32	2.25	2.18	2.10	2.05	2.01	1.96	1.92	1.87	1.81
22	4.30	3.44	3.05	2.82	2.66	2.55	2.46	2.40	2.34	2.30	2.23	2.15	2.07	2.03	1.98	1.94	1.89	1.84	1.78
23	4.28	3.42	3.03	2.80	2.64	2.53	2.44	2.37	2.32	2.27	2.20	2.13	2.05	2.01	1.96	1.91	1.86	1.81	1.76
24	4.26	3.40	3.01	2.78	2.62	2.51	2.42	2.36	2.30	2.25	2.18	2.11	2.03	1.98	1.94	1.89	1.84	1.79	1.73
25	4.24	3.39	2.99	2.76	2.60	2.49	2.40	2.34	2.28	2.24	2.16	2.09	2.01	1.96	1.92	1.87	1.82	1.77	1.71
26	4.23	3.37	2.98	2.74	2.59	2.47	2.39	2.32	2.27	2.22	2.15	2.07	1.99	1.95	1.90	1.85	1.80	1.75	1.69
27	4.21	3.35	2.96	2.73	2.57	2.46	2.37	2.31	2.25	2.20	2.13	2.06	1.97	1.93	1.88	1.84	1.79	1.73	1.67
28	4.20	3.34	2.95	2.71	2.56	2.45	2.36	2.29	2.24	2.19	2.12	2.04	1.96	1.91	1.87	1.82	1.77	1.71	1.65
29	4.18	3.33	2.93	2.70	2.55	2.43	2.35	2.28	2.22	2.18	2.10	2.03	1.94	1.90	1.85	1.81	1.75	1.70	1.64
30	4.17	3.32	2.92	2.69	2.53	2.42	2.33	2.27	2.21	2.16	2.09	2.01	1.93	1.89	1.84	1.79	1.74	1.68	1.62
40	4.08	3.23	2.84	2.61	2.45	2.34	2.25	2.18	2.12	2.08	2.00	1.92	1.84	1.79	1.74	1.69	1.64	1.58	1.51
60	4.00	3.15	2.76	2.53	2.37	2.25	2.17	2.10	2.04	1.99	1.92	1.84	1.75	1.70	1.65	1.59	1.53	1.47	1.39
120	3.92	3.07	2.68	2.45	2.29	2.17	2.09	2.02	1.96	1.91	1.83	1.75	1.66	1.61	1.55	1.50	1.43	1.35	1.25
∞	3.84	3.00	2.60	2.37	2.21	2.10	2.01	1.94	1.88	1.83	1.75	1.67	1.57	1.52	1.46	1.39	1.32	1.22	1.00

Probability/ Statistics

Diagnostic Exam

Topic III: Fluid Mechanics

1. Oil flows through a 0.12 m diameter pipe at a velocity of 1 m/s. The density and the dynamic viscosity of the oil are 870 kg/m^3 and 0.082 N·s/m^2, respectively. If the pipe length is 100 m, the head loss due to friction is most nearly

(A) 1.2 m

(B) 1.5 m

(C) 1.8 m

(D) 2.1 m

2. A thin metal disc of mass 0.01 kg is kept balanced by a jet of air, as shown.

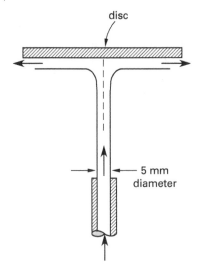

The diameter of the jet at the nozzle exit is 5 mm. Assuming atmospheric conditions at 101.3 kPa and 20°C, the velocity of the jet as it leaves the nozzle is most nearly

(A) 45 m/s

(B) 65 m/s

(C) 85 m/s

(D) 95 m/s

3. Water flows at 14 m^3/s in a 6 m wide rectangular open channel. The critical velocity is most nearly

(A) 0.82 m/s

(B) 1.8 m/s

(C) 2.8 m/s

(D) 14 m/s

4. To measure low flow rates of air, a laminar flow meter is used. It consists of a large number of small-diameter tubes in parallel. One design uses 4000 tubes, each with an inside diameter of 2 mm and a length of 25 cm. The pressure difference through the flow meter is 0.5 kPa, and the absolute viscosity (dynamic viscosity) of the air is 1.81×10^{-8} kPa·s. The flow rate of atmospheric air at 20°C is most nearly

(A) 0.1 m^3/s

(B) 0.2 m^3/s

(C) 0.4 m^3/s

(D) 0.5 m^3/s

5. Carbon tetrachloride has a specific gravity of 1.56. The height of a column of carbon tetracholoride that supports a pressure of 1 kPa is most nearly

(A) 0.0065 cm

(B) 6.5 cm

(C) 10 cm

(D) 64 cm

6. A model of a dam has been constructed so that the scale of dam to model is 15:1. The similarity is based on Froude numbers. At a certain point on the spillway of the model, the velocity is 5 m/s. At the corresponding point on the spillway of the actual dam, the velocity would most nearly be

(A) 6.7 m/s

(B) 7.5 m/s

(C) 15 m/s

(D) 19 m/s

7. A 10 cm diameter sphere floats half submerged in 20°C water. The density of water at 20°C is 998 kg/m³. The mass of the sphere is most nearly

(A) 0.26 kg

(B) 0.52 kg

(C) 0.80 kg

(D) 2.6 kg

8. From the illustration shown, what is most nearly the pressure difference between tanks A and B?

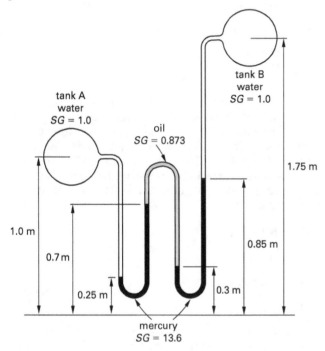

(A) 85 kPa

(B) 98 kPa

(C) 131 kPa

(D) 149 kPa

9. Water flows through a horizontal, frictionless pipe with an inside diameter of 20 cm as shown. A pitot-static meter measures the flow. The deflection of the mercury manometer attached to the pitot tube is 5 cm. The specific gravity of mercury is 13.6.

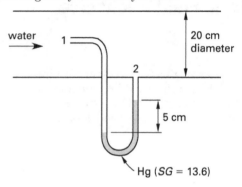

The flow rate in the pipe is most nearly

(A) 0.08 m³/s

(B) 0.1 m³/s

(C) 0.2 m³/s

(D) 0.3 m³/s

10. A horizontal pipe 10 cm in diameter carries 0.05 m³/s of water to a nozzle, through which the water exits to atmospheric pressure. The exit diameter of the nozzle is 4 cm. Friction energy losses through the nozzle and elevation changes are negligible. The pressure at the entrance to the nozzle is most nearly

(A) 420 kPa

(B) 560 kPa

(C) 680 kPa

(D) 770 kPa

SOLUTIONS

1. Dynamic viscosity is given in units of

$$\frac{N \cdot sec}{m^2}$$

The following is the conversion from the given unit to the units used to find the Reynolds number. Since a Newton is a unit of force, and $F=ma$,

$$\frac{N \cdot sec}{m^2} = \frac{\left(kg\,\frac{m}{sec^2}\right) \cdot sec}{m^2} = \frac{kg}{sec \cdot m}$$

The Reynolds number is

$$Re = \frac{vD\rho}{\mu} = \frac{\left(1\,\frac{m}{s}\right)(0.12\ m)\left(870\,\frac{kg}{m^3}\right)}{0.082\,\frac{kg}{s \cdot m}}$$

$$= 1273$$

Since Re < 2100, the flow is laminar.

$$f = \frac{64}{Re} = \frac{64}{1273}$$
$$= 0.05027$$

The head loss is

$$h_f = f\frac{L}{D}\frac{v^2}{2g} = (0.05027)\left(\frac{100\ m}{0.12\ m}\right)\left(\frac{\left(1\,\frac{m}{s}\right)^2}{(2)\left(9.81\,\frac{m}{s^2}\right)}\right)$$

$$= 2.135\ m \quad (2.1\ m)$$

The answer is (D).

2. Applying the momentum equation in the vertical direction, the weight of the disc is equal to the rate of change of momentum of the air jet.

$$mg = \rho A v^2$$

The specific gas constant for air is 0.2870 kJ/kg·K. The density of the air at the nozzle exit is

$$\rho = \frac{p}{RT}$$
$$= \frac{101.3\ kPa}{\left(0.2870\,\frac{kJ}{kg \cdot K}\right)(20°C + 273°)}$$
$$= 1.205\ kg/m^3$$

The velocity of the air jet is

$$v = \sqrt{\frac{mg}{\rho A}} = \sqrt{\frac{mg}{\rho\left(\frac{\pi D^2}{4}\right)}}$$

$$= \sqrt{\frac{(0.01\ kg)\left(9.81\,\frac{m}{s^2}\right)}{\left(1.205\,\frac{kg}{m^3}\right)\left(\frac{\pi(5\ mm)^2}{(4)\left(1000\,\frac{mm}{m}\right)^2}\right)}}$$

$$= 64.39\ m/s \quad (65\ m/s)$$

The answer is (B).

3. Find the critical depth.

Equation derivation from using NCEES formulas on pg. 295:

$$y_c = \left(\frac{q^2}{g}\right)^{1/3} \ and \ q = \frac{Q}{B}$$

$$y_c = \left(\frac{Q^2}{gB^2}\right)^{1/3}$$

$$= \sqrt[3]{\frac{\left(14\,\frac{m^3}{s}\right)^2}{\left(9.81\,\frac{m}{s^2}\right)(6\ m)^2}}$$

$$= 0.822\ m$$

The critical velocity is the velocity that makes the Froude number equal to one when the characteristic length, y_h, is equal to the critical depth.

$$\text{Fr} = \frac{\text{v}}{\sqrt{gy_h}} = \frac{\text{v}}{\sqrt{gy_c}} = 1$$

$$\text{v} = \sqrt{gy_c}$$

$$= \sqrt{\left(9.81 \ \frac{\text{m}}{\text{s}^2}\right)(0.822 \ \text{m})}$$

$$= 2.84 \ \text{m/s} \quad (2.8 \ \text{m/s})$$

The answer is (C).

4. For laminar flow in a circular pipe, the flow rate can be calculated with the Hagen-Poiseuille equation. The flow in one tube is

$$Q = \frac{\pi D^4 \Delta p_f}{128 \mu L}$$

The flow in N tubes, then, is

$$Q_N = \frac{\pi D^4 \Delta p_f N}{128 \mu L}$$

At 20°C and 1 atm (101.3 kPa), the density of the air is

$$Pv = n\bar{R}\,T = \frac{m}{mw}\bar{R}\,T = mRT \ ; \ \left(R_{gas\ specific} = \frac{\bar{R}_{universal}}{mw_{gas}}\right)$$

$$mw_{air} = 28.966 \ \frac{\text{g}}{\text{mol}}$$

$$R_{air} = \frac{8.314 \ \frac{\text{kPa} - \text{m}^3}{\text{kmol} - \text{k}}}{\left(28.966 \ \frac{\text{g}}{\text{mol}}\right)\left(\frac{1 \ \text{kg}}{1000 \ \text{g}}\right)\left(\frac{1000 \ \text{mol}}{1 \ \text{kmol}}\right)} = 0.2870 \ \frac{\text{kPa} - \text{m}^3}{\text{kg} - \text{K}}$$

$$\rho = \frac{P}{RT} = \frac{101.3 \ \text{kPa}}{\left(0.2870 \ \frac{\text{kPa} - \text{m}^3}{\text{kg} - \text{K}}\right)(20°C + 273°)} = 1.205 \ \frac{\text{kg}}{\text{m}^3}$$

The flow rate of the 20°C atmospheric air is

$$Q_N = \frac{\pi D^4 \Delta p_f N}{128 \mu L}$$

$$= \frac{\pi (2 \ \text{mm})^4 (0.5 \ \text{kPa})(4000)\left(100 \ \frac{\text{cm}}{\text{m}}\right)}{(128)(1.81 \times 10^{-8} \ \text{kPa·s})(25 \ \text{cm})\left(1000 \ \frac{\text{mm}}{\text{m}}\right)^4}$$

$$= 0.174 \ \text{m}^3/\text{s} \quad (0.2 \ \text{m}^3/\text{s})$$

To confirm that the flow is laminar, calculate the Reynolds number. The velocity of the airflow is

$$\text{v} = \frac{Q}{A} = \frac{Q}{N\left(\frac{\pi D_{tube}^2}{4}\right)}$$

$$= \frac{0.174 \ \frac{\text{m}^3}{\text{s}}}{(4000)\left[\frac{\pi (2 \ \text{mm})^2}{(4)\left(1000 \ \frac{\text{mm}}{\text{m}}\right)^2}\right]}$$

$$= 13.85 \ \text{m/s}$$

The Reynolds number is

$$\text{Re} = \frac{\text{v}D\rho}{\mu} = \frac{\left(13.85 \ \frac{\text{m}}{\text{s}}\right)(2 \ \text{mm})\left(1.205 \ \frac{\text{kg}}{\text{m}^3}\right)}{(1.81 \times 10^{-5} \ \text{Pa·s})\left(1000 \ \frac{\text{mm}}{\text{m}}\right)}$$

$$= 1844$$

The Reynolds number is less than 2300, so the flow is laminar, and the device is suitable to measure the flow. The calculated airflow rate, 0.2 m³/s, is correct.

The answer is (B).

5. Use the relationship between pressure, density, and fluid depth, and solve for the column height. *[The Pressure Field in a Static Liquid]*

$$p = \rho g h$$

$$h = \frac{p}{\rho g} = \frac{p}{SG\rho_{water}g} = \frac{\left(1000 \ \frac{\text{N}}{\text{m}^2}\right)\left(100 \ \frac{\text{cm}}{\text{m}}\right)}{(1.56)\left(1000 \ \frac{\text{kg}}{\text{m}^3}\right)\left(9.81 \ \frac{\text{m}}{\text{s}^2}\right)}$$

$$= 6.53 \ \text{cm} \quad (6.5 \ \text{cm})$$

The answer is (B).

6. The Froude numbers must be equal.

$$\text{Fr}_{\text{dam}} = \text{Fr}_{\text{model}}$$
$$\frac{v_{\text{dam}}}{\sqrt{gy_{h,\text{dam}}}} = \frac{v_{\text{model}}}{\sqrt{gy_{h,\text{model}}}}$$
$$v_{\text{dam}} = v_{\text{model}}\sqrt{\frac{y_{h,\text{dam}}}{y_{h,\text{model}}}} = \left(5\ \frac{\text{m}}{\text{s}}\right)\sqrt{\frac{15}{1}}$$
$$= 19.36 \text{ m/s} \quad (19 \text{ m/s})$$

The answer is (D).

7. The volume of the sphere is

Sphere

$$V_{\text{sphere}} = \frac{\pi D^3}{6} = \frac{\pi(10 \text{ cm})^3}{(6)\left(100\ \frac{\text{cm}}{\text{m}}\right)^3} = 0.0005236 \text{ m}^3$$

The buoyant force is equal to the weight of the entire sphere, and also equal to the weight of the displaced water.

$$F_b = W_{\text{sphere}} = W_{\text{displaced}}$$
$$m_{\text{sphere}}g = m_{\text{displaced}}g$$

Divide both weights by the gravitational acceleration, g. The mass of the sphere can be expressed in terms of the product of the density and volume of water that is displaced. *[Archimedes Principle and Buoyancy]*

$$m_{\text{sphere}} = m_{\text{displaced}}$$
$$= \rho_{\text{water}}V_{\text{displaced}}$$

The volume of the displaced water is equal to half the volume of the sphere.

$$V_{\text{displaced}} = \frac{V_{\text{sphere}}}{2}$$
$$m_{\text{sphere}} = \rho_{\text{water}}\left(\frac{V_{\text{sphere}}}{2}\right)$$
$$= \left(998\ \frac{\text{kg}}{\text{m}^3}\right)\left(\frac{0.0005236 \text{ m}^3}{2}\right)$$
$$= 0.262 \text{ kg} \quad (0.26 \text{ kg})$$

The answer is (A).

8. The pressures in tanks A and B are related by the equation

$$p_A + \gamma_w h_1 - \gamma_{\text{Hg}}h_2 + \gamma_{\text{oil}}h_3 - \gamma_{\text{Hg}}h_4 - \gamma_w h_5 = p_B$$

The heights are

$$h_1 = 1.0 \text{ m} - 0.25 \text{ m} = 0.75 \text{ m}$$
$$h_2 = 0.7 \text{ m} - 0.25 \text{ m} = 0.45 \text{ m}$$
$$h_3 = 0.7 \text{ m} - 0.3 \text{ m} = 0.4 \text{ m}$$
$$h_4 = 0.85 \text{ m} - 0.3 \text{ m} = 0.55 \text{ m}$$
$$h_5 = 1.75 \text{ m} - 0.85 \text{ m} = 0.90 \text{ m}$$

Also, $\gamma_w = \rho_w g$. Rearrange to solve for the differences in pressures.

The specific weight of the fluid is the specific gravity multiplied by the specific gravity of water, $\gamma = \gamma_w SG$. Substitute into the equation.

$$p_A - p_B = \rho_w g[(SG_w)(h_5 - h_1)$$
$$+ (SG_{\text{Hg}})(h_2 + h_4) - (SG_{\text{oil}})h_3]$$
$$= \left(1000\ \frac{\text{kg}}{\text{m}^3}\right)\left(9.8\ \frac{\text{m}}{\text{s}^2}\right)[(1.0)(0.90 \text{ m} - 0.75 \text{ m})$$
$$+ (13.6)(0.45 \text{ m} + 0.55 \text{ m}) - (0.873)(0.4 \text{ m})]$$
$$= 131{,}328 \text{ Pa} \quad (131 \text{ kPa})$$

The answer is (C).

9. As there is no head loss between location 1 and location 2,

$$\frac{p_2}{\rho_w} + \frac{v_2^2}{2} + z_2 g = \frac{p_1}{\rho_w} + \frac{v_1^2}{2} + z_1 g$$

The velocity at location 2 is zero, and the difference in elevations is negligible, so

$$v_1 = \sqrt{\frac{2(p_2 - p_1)}{\rho_w}} = \sqrt{\frac{2(\rho_{\text{Hg}} - \rho_w)g\Delta h}{\rho_w}}$$
$$= \sqrt{2(SG_{\text{Hg}} - SG_w)g\Delta h}$$
$$= \sqrt{(2)(13.6 - 1)\left(9.81\ \frac{\text{m}}{\text{s}^2}\right)\left(\frac{5 \text{ cm}}{100\ \frac{\text{cm}}{\text{m}}}\right)}$$
$$= 3.516 \text{ m/s}$$

The flow rate is

$$Q = A\mathrm{v} = \left(\frac{\pi D^2}{4}\right)\mathrm{v}$$

$$= \left(\frac{\pi(20\ \mathrm{cm})^2}{(4)\left(100\ \dfrac{\mathrm{cm}}{\mathrm{m}}\right)^2}\right)\left(3.516\ \frac{\mathrm{m}}{\mathrm{s}}\right)$$

$$= 0.11\ \mathrm{m^3/s} \quad (0.1\ \mathrm{m^3/s})$$

The answer is (B).

10. The areas of the nozzle entrance (location 1) and the nozzle exit (location 2) are

$$A_1 = \frac{\pi D^2}{4} = \frac{\pi(10\ \mathrm{cm})^2}{(4)\left(100\ \dfrac{\mathrm{cm}}{\mathrm{m}}\right)^2} = 0.007854\ \mathrm{m^2}$$

$$A_2 = \frac{\pi D^2}{4} = \frac{\pi(4\ \mathrm{cm})^2}{(4)\left(100\ \dfrac{\mathrm{cm}}{\mathrm{m}}\right)^2} = 0.001257\ \mathrm{m^2}$$

The velocities of the water at the nozzle entrance and exit are

Continuity Equation

$$\mathrm{v}_1 = \frac{Q}{A_1} = \frac{0.05\ \dfrac{\mathrm{m^3}}{\mathrm{s}}}{0.007854\ \mathrm{m^2}} = 6.366\ \mathrm{m/s}$$

$$\mathrm{v}_2 = \frac{Q}{A_2} = \frac{0.05\ \dfrac{\mathrm{m^3}}{\mathrm{s}}}{0.001257\ \mathrm{m^2}} = 39.78\ \mathrm{m/s}$$

Use the Bernoulli equation, and solve for the pressure at the entrance to the nozzle. The nozzle is horizontal, and the elevations at locations 1 and 2 are the same, so these terms cancel. The pressure energy (pressure head) at location 2 is discharging to atmosphere at a gage pressure of $P_2 = 0$ Pa.

Bernoulli Equation

$$\frac{P_2}{\gamma_w} + \frac{v_2^2}{2g} + z_2 = \frac{P_1}{\gamma_w} + \frac{v_1^2}{2g} + z_1$$

$$P_1 = P_2 + \frac{\gamma_w}{2g}(v_2^2 - v_1^2)$$

$$= 0\ Pa + \left(\frac{9.8\ \frac{kN}{m^3}}{(2)\left(9.81\ \frac{m}{s^2}\right)}\right)[(39.78\ \tfrac{m}{s})^2 - (6.366\ \tfrac{m}{s})^2]$$

$$= 770.2\ \mathrm{kPa} \quad (770\ \mathrm{kPa})$$

The answer is (D).

7 Fluid Properties

Nomenclature

A	area	m^2
d	diameter	m
F	force	N
g	gravitational acceleration, 9.81	m/s^2
h	height	m
K	power law consistency index	–
L	length	m
m	mass	kg
n	power law index	–
p	pressure	Pa
r	radius	m
SG	specific gravity	–
v	velocity	m/s
V	volume	m^3
W	weight	N

Symbols*

β	angle of contact	deg
γ	specific (unit) weight	N/m^3
δ	thickness of fluid	m
μ	absolute viscosity	Pa·s
ν	kinematic viscosity	m^2/s
ρ	density	kg/m^3
σ	surface tension	N/m
τ	stress	Pa
υ	specific volume	m^3/kg

*The NCEES *FE Reference Handbook* (*NCEES Handbook*) uses the symbol τ for both normal and shear stress. τ is almost universally interpreted in engineering practice as the symbol for shear stress. The use of τ stems from Cauchy stress tensor theory and the desire to use the same symbol for all nine stress directions. However, the stress tensor concept is not developed in the *NCEES Handbook*, and σ is used as the symbol for normal stress elsewhere, so the use of τ_n for normal stress and τ_t for tangential (shear) stress may be confusing. (This usage does avoid a symbol conflict with surface tension, σ, which is used in the *NCEES Handbook* in contexts unrelated to stress.)

Subscripts

n	normal
t	tangential (shear)
v	vapor
w	water

1. FLUIDS

A *fluid* is a substance in either the liquid or gas phase. Fluids cannot support shear, and they deform continuously to minimize applied shear forces.

In fluid mechanics, a fluid is modeled as a *continuum*—that is, a substance that can be divided into infinitesimally small volumes, with properties that are continuous functions over the entire volume. For the infinitesimally small volume ΔV, Δm is the infinitesimal mass, and ΔW is the infinitesimal weight.

Equation 7.1: Density

$$\rho = \lim_{\Delta V \to 0} \Delta m / \Delta V \qquad 7.1$$

Variation

$$\rho = \frac{m}{V}$$

Description

The *density*, ρ, also called *mass density*, of a fluid is its mass per unit volume. The density of a fluid in a liquid form is usually given, known in advance, or easily obtained from tables.

If ΔV is the volume of an infinitesimally small element, the density is given as Eq. 7.1. Density is typically measured in kg/m^3.

Specific Volume

Specific volume, υ, is the volume occupied by a unit mass of fluid.

$$\upsilon = \frac{1}{\rho}$$

Specific volume is the reciprocal of density and is typically measured in m^3/kg.

Equation 7.2 Through Eq. 7.4: Specific Weight

$$\gamma = \underset{\Delta V \to 0}{\text{limit}} \Delta W / \Delta V \qquad 7.2$$

$$\gamma = \underset{\Delta V \to 0}{\text{limit}} g \Delta m / \Delta V = \rho g \qquad 7.3$$

$$\gamma = \rho g \qquad 7.4$$

Variation

$$\gamma = \frac{W}{V} = \frac{mg}{V}$$

Description

Specific weight, γ, also known as *unit weight*, is the weight of substance per unit volume.

The use of specific weight is most often encountered in civil engineering work in the United States, where it is commonly called *density*. The usual units of specific weight are N/m^3. Specific weight is not an absolute property of a substance since it depends on the local gravitational field.

Example

The density of a gas is $1.5 \ kg/m^3$. The specific weight of the gas is most nearly

(A) $9.0 \ N/m^3$

(B) $15 \ N/m^3$

(C) $76 \ N/m^3$

(D) $98 \ N/m^3$

Solution

Use Eq. 7.4.

$$\gamma = \rho g = \left(1.5 \ \frac{kg}{m^3}\right)\left(9.81 \ \frac{m}{s^2}\right)$$
$$= 14.715 \ kg/s^2 m^2 \quad (15 \ N/m^3)$$

The answer is (B).

Equation 7.5: Specific Gravity

$$SG = \gamma / \gamma_w = \rho / \rho_w \qquad 7.5$$

Description

Specific gravity, SG, is the dimensionless ratio of a fluid's density to a standard reference density. For liquids and solids, the reference is the density of pure water, which is approximately $1000 \ kg/m^3$ over the normal ambient temperature range. The temperature at which water density

should be evaluated is not standardized, so some small variation in the reference density is possible. See Table 7.1 and Table 7.2 for the properties of water in SI and customary U.S. units, respectively.

Since the SI density of water is very nearly $1.000 \ g/cm^3$ ($1000 \ kg/m^3$), the numerical values of density in g/cm^3 and specific gravity are the same.

Example

A fluid has a density of $860 \ kg/m^3$. The specific gravity of the fluid is most nearly

(A) 0.63

(B) 0.82

(C) 0.86

(D) 0.95

Solution

Use Eq. 7.5. The specific gravity is

$$SG = \rho / \rho_w = \frac{860 \ \dfrac{kg}{m^3}}{1000 \ \dfrac{kg}{m^3}} = 0.86$$

The answer is (C).

2. PRESSURE

Fluid pressures are measured with respect to two pressure references: zero pressure and atmospheric pressure. Pressures measured with respect to a true zero pressure reference are known as *absolute pressures*. Pressures measured with respect to atmospheric pressure are known as *gage pressures*. To distinguish them, the word "gage" or "absolute" can be added to the measurement (e.g., 25.1 kPa absolute). Alternatively, the letter "g" can be added to the measurement for gage pressures (e.g., 15 kPag), and the pressure is assumed to be absolute otherwise.

Equation 7.6 and Eq. 7.7: Absolute Pressure

$$\text{absolute pressure} = \text{atmospheric pressure} \\ + \text{gage pressure reading} \qquad 7.6$$

$$\text{absolute pressure} = \text{atmospheric pressure} \\ - \text{vacuum gage pressure} \\ \text{reading} \qquad 7.7$$

Table 7.1 *Properties of Water (SI units)*

temperature (°C)	specific weight, γ (kN/m³)	density, ρ (kg/m³)	viscosity, $\mu \times 10^{-3}$ (Pa·s)	kinematic viscosity, $\nu \times 10^{-6}$ (m²/s)	vapor pressure, p_v (kPa)
0	9.805	999.8	1.781	1.785	0.61
5	9.807	1000.0	1.518	1.518	0.87
10	9.804	999.7	1.307	1.306	1.23
15	9.798	999.1	1.139	1.139	1.70
20	9.789	998.2	1.002	1.003	2.34
25	9.777	997.0	0.890	0.893	3.17
30	9.764	995.7	0.798	0.800	4.24
40	9.730	992.2	0.653	0.658	7.38
50	9.689	988.0	0.547	0.553	12.33
60	9.642	983.2	0.466	0.474	19.92
70	9.589	977.8	0.404	0.413	31.16
80	9.530	971.8	0.354	0.364	47.34
90	9.466	965.3	0.315	0.326	70.10
100	9.399	958.4	0.282	0.294	101.33

Table 7.2 *Properties of Water (customary U.S. units)*

temperature (°F)	specific weight, γ (lbf/ft³)	density, ρ (lbm-sec²/ft⁴)	viscosity, $\mu \times 10^{-5}$ (lbf-sec/ft²)	kinematic viscosity, $\nu \times 10^{-5}$ (ft²/sec)	vapor pressure, p_v (lbf/ft²)
32	62.42	1.940	3.746	1.931	0.09
40	62.43	1.940	3.229	1.664	0.12
50	62.41	1.940	2.735	1.410	0.18
60	62.37	1.938	2.359	1.217	0.26
70	62.30	1.936	2.050	1.059	0.36
80	62.22	1.934	1.799	0.930	0.51
90	62.11	1.931	1.595	0.826	0.70
100	62.00	1.927	1.424	0.739	0.95
110	61.86	1.923	1.284	0.667	1.24
120	61.71	1.918	1.168	0.609	1.69
130	61.55	1.913	1.069	0.558	2.22
140	61.38	1.908	0.981	0.514	2.89
150	61.20	1.902	0.905	0.476	3.72
160	61.00	1.896	0.838	0.442	4.74
170	60.80	1.890	0.780	0.413	5.99
180	60.58	1.883	0.726	0.385	7.51
190	60.36	1.876	0.678	0.362	9.34
200	60.12	1.868	0.637	0.341	11.52
212	59.83	1.860	0.593	0.319	14.70

Values

Standard atmospheric pressure is equal to 101.3 kPa or 29.921 inches of mercury.

Description

Absolute and gage pressures are related by Eq. 7.6. In this equation, "atmospheric pressure" is the actual atmospheric pressure that exists when the gage measurement is taken. It is not standard atmospheric pressure unless that pressure is implicitly or explicitly applicable. Also, since a barometer measures atmospheric pressure, *barometric pressure* is synonymous with atmospheric pressure.

A *vacuum* measurement is implicitly a pressure below atmospheric pressure (i.e., a negative gage pressure). It must be assumed that any measured quantity given as a vacuum is a quantity to be subtracted from the atmospheric pressure. (See Eq. 7.7.) When a condenser is operating with a vacuum of 4.0 inches of mercury, the absolute pressure is approximately $29.92 - 4.0 = 25.92$ inches of mercury (25.92 in Hg). Vacuums are always stated as positive numbers.

Example

A vessel is initially connected to a reservoir open to the atmosphere. The connecting valve is then closed, and a vacuum of 65.5 kPa is applied to the vessel. Assume standard atmospheric pressure. What is most nearly the absolute pressure in the vessel?

(A)   36 kPa

(B)   66 kPa

(C)   86 kPa

(D)   110 kPa

Solution

From Eq. 7.7, for vacuum pressures,

$$\begin{aligned} \text{absolute pressure} &= \text{atmospheric pressure} \\ &\quad -\text{vacuum gage pressure} \\ &\quad\text{reading} \\ &= 101.3 \text{ kPa} - 65.5 \text{ kPa} \\ &= 35.8 \text{ kPa} \quad (36 \text{ kPa}) \end{aligned}$$

The answer is (A).

3. STRESS

Stress, τ, is force per unit area. There are two primary types of stress, differing in the orientation of the loaded area: *normal stress* and *tangential* (or *shear*) *stress*. With *normal stress*, τ_n, the area is normal to the force carried. With *tangential* (or *shear*) *stress*, τ_t, the area is parallel to the force.

Ideal fluids that are inviscid and incompressible respond to normal stresses, but they cannot support shear, and they deform continuously to minimize applied shear forces.

Equation 7.8 and Eq. 7.9: Normal Stress[1]

$$\tau(1) = \lim_{\Delta A \to 0} \Delta F / \Delta A \qquad \text{7.8}$$

$$\tau_n = -p \qquad \text{7.9}$$

Description

At some arbitrary point 1, with an infinitesimal area, ΔA, subjected to a force, ΔF, the normal or shear stress is defined as in Eq. 7.8.

Normal stress is equal to the pressure of the fluid, as indicated by Eq. 7.9.

4. VISCOSITY

The *viscosity* of a fluid is a measure of that fluid's resistance to flow when acted upon by an external force, such as a pressure gradient or gravity.

The viscosity of a fluid can be determined with a *sliding plate viscometer* test. Consider two plates of area A separated by a fluid with thickness δ. The bottom plate is fixed, and the top plate is kept in motion at a constant velocity, v, by a force, F. (See Fig. 7.1.)

Figure 7.1 *Sliding Plate Viscometer*

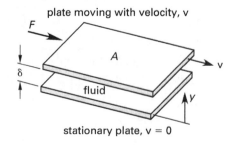

---

[1]Equation 7.8, as given in the *NCEES Handbook*, is vague. The *NCEES Handbook* calls $\tau(1)$ the "surface stress at point 1." Point 1 is undefined, and the term "surface stress" is used without explanation, although it apparently refers to both normal and shear stress. The format of using parentheses to designate the location of a stress is not used elsewhere in the *NCEES Handbook*.

Experiments with many fluids have shown that the force, F, that is needed to maintain the velocity, v, is proportional to the velocity and the area but is inversely proportional to the separation of the plates. That is,

$$\frac{F}{A} \propto \frac{\text{v}}{\delta}$$

The constant of proportionality needed to make this an equality for a particular fluid is the fluid's *absolute viscosity*, μ, also known as the *absolute dynamic viscosity*. Typical units for absolute viscosity are Pa·s (N·s/m²).

$$\frac{F}{A} = \mu\left(\frac{\text{v}}{\delta}\right)$$

F/A is the *fluid shear stress* (tangential stress), τ_t.

Equation 7.10 Through Eq. 7.12: Newton's Law of Viscosity

$$\text{v}(y) = \text{v}y/\delta \qquad\qquad 7.10$$

$$d\text{v}/dy = \text{v}/\delta \qquad\qquad 7.11$$

$$\tau_t = \mu(d\text{v}/dy) \quad \text{[one-dimensional]} \qquad 7.12$$

Variation

$$\tau_t = \frac{F}{A} = \mu\left(\frac{\text{v}}{\delta}\right)$$

Description

For a thin Newtonian fluid film, Eq. 7.10 and Eq. 7.11 describe the linear velocity profile. The quantity $d\text{v}/dy$ is known by various names, including *rate of strain*, *shear rate*, *velocity gradient*, and *rate of shear formation*.

Equation 7.12 is known as *Newton's law of viscosity*, from which Newtonian fluids get their name. (Not all fluids are Newtonian, although many are.) For a Newtonian fluid, strains are proportional to the applied shear stress (i.e., the stress versus strain curve is a straight line with slope μ). The straight line will be closer to the τ axis if the fluid is highly viscous. For low-viscosity fluids, the straight line will be closer to the $d\text{v}/dy$ axis. Equation 7.12 is applicable only to Newtonian fluids, for which the relationship is linear.

Equation 7.13: Power Law

$$\tau_t = K(d\text{v}/dy)^n \qquad\qquad 7.13$$

Values

fluid	power law index, n
Newtonian	1
non-Newtonian	
pseudoplastic	< 1
dilatant	> 1

Description

Many fluids are not Newtonian (i.e., do not behave according to Eq. 7.12). Non-Newtonian fluids have viscosities that change with shear rate, $d\text{v}/dt$. For example, *pseudoplastic fluids* exhibit a decrease in viscosity the faster they are agitated. Such fluids present no serious pumping difficulties. On the other hand, pumps for *dilatant fluids* must be designed carefully, since dilatant fluids exhibit viscosities that increase the faster they are agitated. The fluid shear stress for most non-Newtonian fluids can be predicted by the *power law*, Eq. 7.13. In Eq. 7.13, the constant K is known as the *consistency index*. The consistency index, also known as the *flow consistency index*, is actually the average fluid viscosity across the range of viscosities being modeled. For *pseudoplastic non-Newtonian fluids*, $n < 1$; for *dilatant non-Newtonian fluids*, $n > 1$. For Newtonian fluids, $n = 1$.

Equation 7.14: Kinematic Viscosity

$$\nu = \mu/\rho \qquad\qquad 7.14$$

Description

Another quantity with the name viscosity is the ratio of absolute viscosity to mass density. This combination of variables, known as *kinematic viscosity*, ν, appears often in fluids and other problems and warrants its own symbol and name. Kinematic viscosity is merely the name given to a frequently occurring combination of variables. Typical units are m²/s.

Example

32°C water flows at 2 m/s through a pipe that has an inside diameter of 3 cm. The viscosity of the water is 769×10^{-6} N·s/m², and the density of the water is 995 kg/m³. The kinematic viscosity of the water is most nearly

(A) 0.71×10^{-6} m²/s

(B) 0.77×10^{-6} m²/s

(C) 0.84×10^{-6} m²/s

(D) 0.92×10^{-6} m²/s

Fluid Mechanics

Fluid Mechanics

Solution

The kinematic viscosity is

$$\nu = \mu/\rho = \frac{769 \times 10^{-6} \; \dfrac{\text{N·s}}{\text{m}^2}}{995 \; \dfrac{\text{kg}}{\text{m}^3}}$$

$$= 0.773 \times 10^{-6} \; \text{m}^2/\text{s} \quad (0.77 \times 10^{-6} \; \text{m}^2/\text{s})$$

The answer is (B).

5. SURFACE TENSION AND CAPILLARITY

Equation 7.15: Surface Tension

$$\sigma = F/L \qquad \qquad 7.15$$

Description

The membrane or "skin" that seems to form on the free surface of a fluid is caused by intermolecular cohesive forces and is known as *surface tension*, σ. Surface tension is the reason that insects are able to sit on a pond and a needle is able to float on the surface of a glass of water, even though both are denser than the water that supports them. Surface tension also causes bubbles and droplets to form in spheres, since any other shape would have more surface area per unit volume.

Surface tension can be interpreted as the tensile force between two points a unit distance apart on the surface, or as the amount of work required to form a new unit of surface area in an apparatus similar to that shown in Fig. 7.2. Typical units of surface tension are N/m, J/m^2, and dynes/cm. (Dynes/cm are equivalent to mN/m.)

Figure 7.2 *Wire Frame for Stretching a Film*

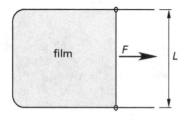

Surface tension is defined as a force, F, acting along a line of length L, as indicated by Eq. 7.15.

The apparatus shown in Fig. 7.2 consists of a wire frame with a sliding side that has been dipped in a liquid to form a film. Surface tension is determined by measuring the force necessary to keep the sliding side stationary against the surface tension pull of the film. However, since the film has two surfaces (i.e., two surface tensions), the surface tension is

$$\sigma = \frac{F}{2L} \quad \begin{bmatrix} \text{wire frame} \\ \text{apparatus} \end{bmatrix}$$

Surface tension can also be measured by measuring the force required to pull a *Du Nouy wire ring* out of a liquid, as shown in Fig. 7.3. Because the ring's inner and outer sides are both in contact with the liquid, the wetted perimeter is twice the circumference. The surface tension is therefore

$$\sigma = \frac{F}{4\pi r} \quad \begin{bmatrix} \text{Du Nouy ring} \\ \text{apparatus} \end{bmatrix}$$

Figure 7.3 *Du Nouy Ring Surface Tension Apparatus*

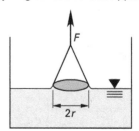

Equation 7.16: Capillary Rise or Depression

$$h = 4\sigma \cos\beta / \gamma d \qquad \qquad 7.16$$

Variation

$$h = \frac{4\sigma \cos\beta}{\rho g d_{\text{tube}}}$$

Description

Capillary action is the name given to the behavior of a liquid in a thin-bore tube. Capillary action is caused by surface tension between the liquid and a vertical solid surface. In water, the adhesive forces between the liquid molecules and the surface are greater than (i.e., dominate) the cohesive forces between the water molecules themselves. The adhesive forces cause the water to attach itself to and climb a solid vertical surface; the water rises above the general water surface level. (See Fig. 7.4.) This is called *capillary rise*, and the curved surface of the liquid within the tube is known as a *meniscus*.

Figure 7.4 *Capilarity of Liquids*

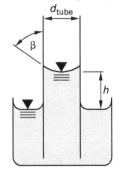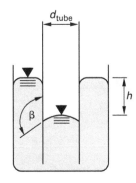

(a) adhesive force dominates (b) cohesive force dominates

For a few liquids, such as mercury, the molecules have a strong affinity for each other (i.e., the cohesive forces dominate). These liquids avoid contact with the tube surface. In such liquids, the meniscus will be below the general surface level, a state called *capillary depression.*

The *angle of contact*, β, is an indication of whether adhesive or cohesive forces dominate. For contact angles less than 90°, adhesive forces dominate. For contact angles greater than 90°, cohesive forces dominate. For water in a glass tube, the contact angle is zero; for mercury in a glass tube, the contact angle is 140°.

Equation 7.16 can be used to predict the capillary rise (if the result is positive) or capillary depression (if the result is negative) in a small-bore tube. Surface tension is a material property of a fluid, and contact angles are specific to a particular fluid-solid interface. Both may be obtained from tables.

Example

An open glass tube with a diameter of 1 mm contains mercury at 20°C. At this temperature, mercury has a surface tension of 0.519 N/m and a density of 13 600 kg/m^3. The contact angle for mercury in a glass tube is 140°. The capillary depression is most nearly

(A) 6.1 mm

(B) 8.6 mm

(C) 12 mm

(D) 17 mm

Solution

Use Eq. 7.4 and Eq. 7.16 to find the capillary depression (or negative rise).

$$h = 4\sigma \cos\beta/\gamma d = \frac{4\sigma \cos\beta}{\rho g d_{\text{tube}}}$$

$$= \frac{(4)\left(0.519 \ \dfrac{\text{N}}{\text{m}}\right)\cos 140° \left(1000 \ \dfrac{\text{mm}}{\text{m}}\right)}{\left(13\,600 \ \dfrac{\text{kg}}{\text{m}^3}\right)\left(9.81 \ \dfrac{\text{m}}{\text{s}^2}\right)(1 \ \text{mm})}$$

$$= -0.0119 \ \text{m} \quad (12 \ \text{mm})$$

The answer is (C).

Fluid Mechanics

Fluid Statics

Nomenclature

A	area	m^2
F	force	N
g	gravitational acceleration, 9.81	m/s^2
h	vertical depth or difference in vertical depth	m
I	moment of inertia	m^4
p	pressure	Pa
R	resultant force	N
SG	specific gravity	–
V	volume	m^3
y	distance	m
z	elevation	m

Symbols

α	angle	deg
γ	specific (unit) weight	N/m^3
θ	angle	deg
ρ	density	kg/m^3

Subscripts

0	atmospheric
atm	atmospheric
B	barometer fluid
C	centroid
CP	center of pressure
f	fluid
m	manometer
R	resultant
v	vapor
x	horizontal

1. HYDROSTATIC PRESSURE

Hydrostatic pressure is the pressure a fluid exerts on an immersed object or on container walls. The term *hydrostatic* is used with all fluids, not only with water.

Pressure is equal to the force per unit area of surface.

$$p = \frac{F}{A}$$

Hydrostatic pressure in a stationary, incompressible fluid behaves according to the following characteristics.

- Pressure is a function of vertical depth and density only. If density is constant, then the pressure will be the same at two points with identical depths.

- Pressure varies linearly with vertical depth. The relationship between pressure and depth for an incompressible fluid is given by the equation

$$p = \rho g h = \gamma h$$

Since ρ and g are constants, this equation shows that p and h are linearly related. One determines the other.

- Pressure is independent of an object's area and size, and of the weight (or mass) of water above the object. Figure 8.1 illustrates the *hydrostatic paradox*. The pressures at depth h are the same in all four columns because pressure depends only on depth, not on volume.

Figure 8.1 *Hydrostatic Paradox*

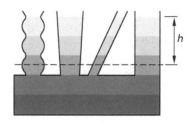

- Pressure at a point has the same magnitude in all directions (*Pascal's law*). Therefore, pressure is a scalar quantity.

- Pressure is always normal to a surface, regardless of the surface's shape or orientation. (This is a result of the fluid's inability to support shear stress.)

Equation 8.1: Pressure Difference in a Static Fluid[1]

$$p_2 - p_1 = -\gamma(z_2 - z_1) = -\gamma h = -\rho g h \qquad 8.1$$

Description

As pressure in a fluid varies linearly with depth, difference in pressure likewise varies linearly with difference in depth. This is expressed in Eq. 8.1. The variable z decreases with depth while the pressure increases with depth, so pressure and elevation have an inverse linear relationship, as indicated by the negative sign.

2. MANOMETERS

Manometers can be used to measure small pressure differences, and for this purpose, they provide good accuracy. A difference in manometer fluid surface heights indicates a pressure difference. When both ends of the manometer are connected to pressure sources, the name *differential manometer* is used. If one end of the manometer is open to the atmosphere, the name *open manometer* is used. An open manometer indicates gage pressure. It is theoretically possible, but impractical, to have a manometer indicate absolute pressure, since one end of the manometer would have to be exposed to a perfect vacuum.

Consider the simple manometer in Fig. 8.2. The pressure difference $p_2 - p_1$ causes the difference h_m in manometer fluid surface heights. Fluid column h_2 exerts a hydrostatic pressure on the manometer fluid, forcing the manometer fluid to the left. This increase must be subtracted out. Similarly, the column h_1 restricts the movement of the manometer fluid. The observed measurement must be increased to correct for this restriction. The typical way to solve for pressure differences in a manometer is to start with the pressure on one side, and then add or subtract changes in hydrostatic pressure at known points along the column until the pressure on the other side is reached.

$$p_2 = p_1 + \rho_1 g h_1 + \rho_m g h_m - \rho_2 g h_2$$
$$= p_1 + \gamma_1 h_1 + \gamma_m h_m - \gamma_2 h_2$$

Figure 8.2 *Manometer Requiring Corrections*

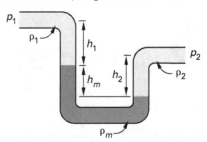

Equation 8.2 and Eq. 8.3: Pressure Difference in a Simple Manometer

$$p_0 = p_2 + \gamma_2 h_2 - \gamma_1 h_1 = p_2 + g(\rho_2 h_2 - \rho_1 h_1) \qquad 8.2$$

$$p_0 = p_2 + (\gamma_2 - \gamma_1)h = p_2 + (\rho_2 - \rho_1)gh$$
$$[h_1 = h_2 = h] \qquad 8.3$$

Description

Figure 8.3 illustrates an open manometer. Neglecting the air in the open end, the pressure difference is given by Eq. 8.2. $p_0 - p_2$ is the gage pressure in the vessel.

Figure 8.3 *Open Manometer*

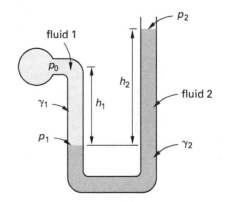

Equation 8.2 is a version of Eq. 8.1 as applied to an open manometer. Equation 8.3 is a simplified version that can be used only when h_1 is equal to h_2.[2]

Example

One leg of a mercury U-tube manometer is connected to a pipe containing water under a gage pressure of 100 kPa. The mercury in this leg stands 0.75 m below the water. The mercury in the other leg is open to the air.

---

[1] Although the variable y is used elsewhere in the NCEES *FE Reference Handbook* (*NCEES Handbook*) to represent vertical direction, the *NCEES Handbook* uses z to measure some vertical dimensions within fluid bodies. As referenced to a Cartesian coordinate system (a practice that is not continued elsewhere in the *NCEES Handbook*), Eq. 8.1 is academically correct, but it is inconsistent with normal practice, which measures z from the fluid surface, synonymous with "depth." The *NCEES Handbook* reverts to common usage of h, y, and z in its subsequent discussion of forces on submerged surfaces.

[2] h_1 and h_2 would be equal only in the most contrived situations.

The density of the water is 1000 kg/m³, and the specific gravity of the mercury is 13.6.

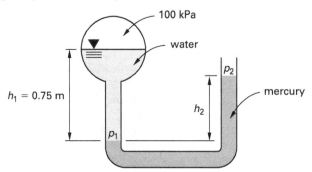

The height of the mercury in the open leg is most nearly

(A) 0.05 m

(B) 0.5 m

(C) 0.8 m

(D) 1 m

Solution

Find the specific weights of water, γ_1, and mercury, γ_2.

$$\gamma_1 = \rho_{\text{water}} g = \left(1000 \ \frac{\text{kg}}{\text{m}^3}\right)\left(9.81 \ \frac{\text{m}}{\text{s}^2}\right)$$

$$= 9810 \ \text{N/m}^3$$

$$\gamma_2 = \rho_{\text{Hg}} g = (\text{SG}_{\text{Hg}})\rho_{\text{water}} g$$

$$= (13.6)\left(1000 \ \frac{\text{kg}}{\text{m}^3}\right)\left(9.81 \ \frac{\text{m}}{\text{s}^2}\right)$$

$$= 133\,416 \ \text{N/m}^3$$

Use Eq. 8.2 to find the height of the mercury in the open leg. Since the 100 kPa pressure is a gage pressure, the atmospheric pressure, p_2, is zero.

$$p_0 = p_2 + \gamma_2 h_2 - \gamma_1 h_1$$

$$h_2 = \frac{p_0 + \gamma_1 h_1 - p_2}{\gamma_2}$$

$$= \frac{\begin{array}{c}(100 \ \text{kPa})\left(1000 \ \dfrac{\text{Pa}}{\text{kPa}}\right) \\[2mm] + \left(9810 \ \dfrac{\text{N}}{\text{m}^3}\right)(0.75 \ \text{m}) - 0 \ \text{Pa}\end{array}}{133\,416 \ \dfrac{\text{N}}{\text{m}^3}}$$

$$= 0.805 \ \text{m} \quad (0.8 \ \text{m})$$

The answer is (C).

3. BAROMETERS

The *barometer* is a common device for measuring the absolute pressure of the atmosphere. It is constructed by filling a long tube open at one end with mercury (alcohol or another liquid can also be used) and inverting the tube such that the open end is below the level of the mercury-filled container. The vapor pressure of the mercury in the tube is insignificant; if this is neglected, the fluid column is supported only by the atmospheric pressure transmitted through the container fluid at the lower, open end. (See Fig. 8.4.) In such a case, the atmospheric pressure is given by

$$p_{\text{atm}} = \rho g h$$

$$= \gamma h$$

Figure 8.4 Barometer

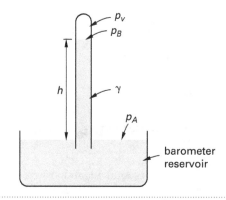

Equation 8.4: Vapor Pressure[3]

$$p_{\text{atm}} = p_A$$
$$= p_v + \gamma h$$
$$= p_B + \gamma h$$
$$= p_B + \rho g h$$

8.4

Variation

$$p_{\text{atm}} = p_v + (\text{SG})\rho_{\text{water}} g h$$

Description

When the vapor pressure of the barometer liquid is significant, as it is with alcohol or water, the vapor pressure effectively reduces the height of the fluid column, as Eq. 8.4 indicates.

---

[3]In Eq. 8.4, the *NCEES Handbook* uses A as a subscript to designate location A in Fig. 8.4, not to designate "atmosphere," which is inconsistently designated by the subscripts "atm" and "0." Figure 8.4 shows both p_v and p_B, although in fact, these two pressures are the same.

Example

A fluid with a vapor pressure of 0.2 Pa and a specific gravity of 12 is used in a barometer. If the fluid's column height is 1 m, the atmospheric pressure is most nearly

(A)   9.8 kPa

(B)   12 kPa

(C)   98 kPa

(D)   120 kPa

Solution

From Eq. 8.4,

$$p_{\text{atm}} = p_B + \rho g h$$
$$= p_v + (\text{SG})\rho_{\text{water}}gh$$
$$= 0.2 \text{ Pa} + (12)\left(1000 \ \frac{\text{kg}}{\text{m}^3}\right)\left(9.81 \ \frac{\text{m}}{\text{s}^2}\right)(1 \text{ m})$$
$$= 117\,720 \text{ Pa} \quad (120 \text{ kPa})$$

The answer is (D).

4. FORCES ON SUBMERGED PLANE SURFACES

The pressure on a horizontal plane surface is uniform over the surface because the depth of the fluid above is uniform. The resultant of the pressure distribution acts through the *center of pressure* of the surface, which corresponds to the centroid of the surface. (See Fig. 8.5.)

Figure 8.5 *Hydrostatic Pressure on a Horizontal Plane Surface*

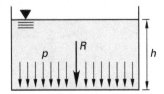

The total vertical force on the horizontal plane of area A is given by the equation

$$R = pA$$

It is not always correct to calculate the vertical force on a submerged surface as the weight of the fluid above it. Such an approach works only when there is no change in the cross-sectional area of the fluid above the surface. This is a direct result of the *hydrostatic paradox*. (See Fig. 8.1.) The two containers in Fig. 8.6 have the same distribution of pressure (or force) over their bottom surfaces.

Figure 8.6 *Two Containers with the Same Pressure Distribution*

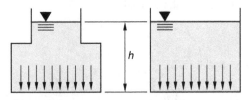

The pressure on a vertical rectangular plane surface increases linearly with depth. The pressure distribution will be triangular, as in Fig. 8.7(a), if the plane surface extends to the surface; otherwise, the distribution will be trapezoidal, as in Fig. 8.7(b).

Figure 8.7 *Hydrostatic Pressure on a Vertical Plane Surface*

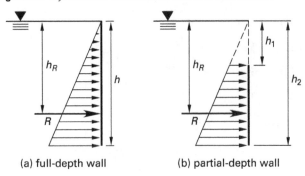

(a) full-depth wall   (b) partial-depth wall

The resultant force on a vertical rectangular plane surface is

$$R = \bar{p}A$$

$\bar{p}$ is the *average pressure*, which is also equal to the pressure at the centroid of the plane area. The average pressure is

$$\bar{p} = \tfrac{1}{2}(p_1 + p_2) = \tfrac{1}{2}\rho g(h_1 + h_2)$$
$$= \tfrac{1}{2}\gamma(h_1 + h_2)$$

Although the resultant is calculated from the average depth, the resultant does not act at the average depth. The resultant of the pressure distribution passes through the centroid of the pressure distribution. For the triangular distribution of Fig. 8.7(a), the resultant is located at a depth of $h_R = \tfrac{2}{3}h$. For the more general case, the center of pressure can be calculated by the method described in Sec. 8.5.

The average pressure and resultant force on an inclined rectangular plane surface are calculated in the same fashion as for the vertical plane surface. (See Fig. 8.8.) The pressure varies linearly with depth. The resultant is calculated from the average pressure, which, in turn, depends on the average depth.

Figure 8.8 *Hydrostatic Pressure on an Inclined Rectangular Plane Surface*

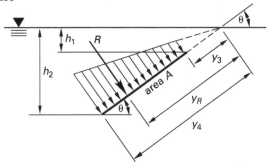

The resultant and average pressure on an inclined plane surface are given by the same equations as for a vertical plane surface.

$$R = \bar{p}A$$
$$\bar{p} = \tfrac{1}{2}(p_1 + p_2) = \tfrac{1}{2}\rho g(h_1 + h_2) = \tfrac{1}{2}\gamma(h_1 + h_2)$$

As with a vertical plane surface, the resultant acts at the centroid of the pressure distribution, not at the average depth.

5. CENTER OF PRESSURE

For the case of pressure on a general plane surface, the resultant force depends on the average pressure and acts through the *center of pressure*, CP. Figure 8.9 shows a nonrectangular plane surface of area A that may or may not extend to the liquid surface and that may or may not be inclined. The average pressure is calculated from the location of the plane surface's centroid, C, where y_C is measured parallel to the plane surface. That is, if the plane surface is inclined, y_C is an inclined distance.

The center of pressure is always at least as deep as the area's centroid. In most cases, it is deeper.

The pressure at the centroid is

$$p_C = \bar{p} = p_{\text{atm}} + \rho g y_C \sin\theta$$
$$= p_{\text{atm}} + \gamma y_C \sin\theta$$

Equation 8.5: Absolute Pressure on a Point[4]

$$p = p_0 + \rho g h \quad [h \geq 0] \qquad \text{8.5}$$

Description

Equation 8.5 gives the absolute pressure on a point at a vertical distance of h under the surface. Depth, h, must be greater than or equal to 0.[5]

Figure 8.9 *Hydrostatic Pressure on a Submerged Plane Surface**

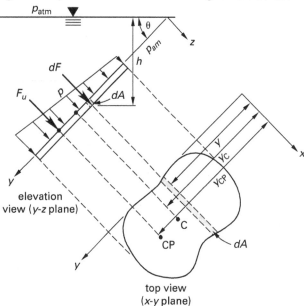

elevation view (*y-z* plane)

top view (*x-y* plane)

*The meaning of the inclined p_{am} in this figure as presented in the *NCEES Handbook* is ambient pressure. Its location implies that it is not the same as p_{atm} and is used to differentiate the pressures within different medium, i.e., air vs water.

Example

A closed tank with the dimensions shown contains water. The air pressure in the tank is 700 kPa. Point P is located halfway up the inclined wall.

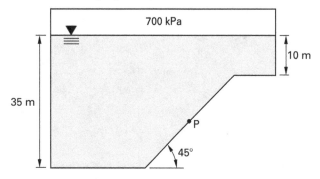

The pressure at point P is most nearly

(A)   920 kPa

(B)   1900 kPa

(C)   7200 kPa

(D)   8100 kPa

---

[4]The *NCEES Handbook* is inconsistent in how it designates atmospheric pressure. Although p_{atm} is used in Eq. 8.4 and in Fig. 8.9, Eq. 8.5 uses p_0.
[5]Equation 8.5 calculates the *absolute pressure* because it includes the atmospheric pressure. If the atmospheric pressure term is omitted, the *gauge pressure* (also known as *gage pressure*) will be calculated.

Solution

The tank and its geometry are shown.

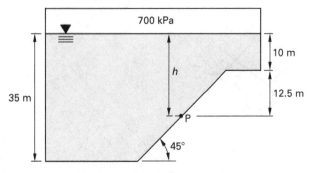

Point P is halfway up the inclined surface, so it is at a depth of

$$h = 10 \text{ m} + \frac{35 \text{ m} - 10 \text{ m}}{2} = 22.5 \text{ m}$$

The pressure at point P is

$$p = p_0 + \rho g h$$

$$= (700 \text{ kPa})\left(1000 \frac{\text{Pa}}{\text{kPa}}\right)$$

$$+ \left(1000 \frac{\text{kg}}{\text{m}^3}\right)\left(9.81 \frac{\text{m}}{\text{s}^2}\right)(22.5 \text{ m})$$

$$= 920\,725 \text{ Pa} \quad (920 \text{ kPa})$$

The answer is (A).

Equation 8.6 Through Eq. 8.8: Distance to Center of Pressure

$$y_{CP} = y_C + I_{xC}/y_C A \qquad 8.6$$

$$y_{CP} = y_C + \rho g \sin \theta I_{xC}/p_C A \qquad 8.7$$

$$y_C = h_C/\sin \alpha \qquad 8.8$$

Description

Equation 8.6 and Eq. 8.7 apply when the atmospheric pressure acts on the liquid surface and on the dry side of the submerged surface. The distance from the surface of the liquid to the center of pressure measured along the slanted surface, y_{CP}, is found from Eq. 8.6 and Eq. 8.7. Equation 8.7 is derived from Eq. 8.6 by using the pressure-height relationship $p_C = \rho g h_C = \rho g y_C \sin \theta$.[6] y_C is the distance from the surface of the liquid to the centroid of the area, C, calculated using Eq. 8.8. In Eq. 8.6 and Eq. 8.7, the subscript x refers to a horizontal (centroidal) axis parallel to the surface, which might not be obvious from Fig. 8.9, as presented in the *NCEES Handbook*.

Equation 8.9 and Eq. 8.10: Resultant Force

$$F_R = (p_0 + \rho g y_C \sin \theta) A \qquad 8.9$$

$$F_{R_{\text{net}}} = (\rho g y_C \sin \theta) A \qquad 8.10$$

Description

The resultant force, F_R, on the wetted side of the surface is found from Eq. 8.9. Equation 8.10 calculates the net resultant force when p_0 acts on both sides of the surface.[7]

6. BUOYANCY

Buoyant force is an upward force that acts on all objects that are partially or completely submerged in a fluid. The fluid can be a liquid or a gas. There is a buoyant force on all submerged objects, not only on those that are stationary or ascending. A buoyant force caused by displaced air also exists, although it may be insignificant. Examples include the buoyant force on a rock sitting at the bottom of a pond, the buoyant force on a rock sitting exposed on the ground (since the rock is "submerged" in air), and the buoyant force on partially exposed floating objects, such as icebergs.

Buoyant force always acts to cancel the object's weight (i.e., buoyancy acts against gravity). The magnitude of the buoyant force is predicted from *Archimedes' principle* (the *buoyancy theorem*), which states that the buoyant force on a submerged or floating object is equal to the weight of the displaced fluid. An equivalent statement of Archimedes' principle is that a floating object displaces liquid equal in weight to its own weight. In the situation of an object floating at the interface between two immiscible liquids of different densities, the buoyant force equals the sum of the weights of the two displaced fluids.

In the case of stationary (i.e., not moving vertically) floating or submerged objects, the buoyant force and object weight are in equilibrium. If the forces are not in equilibrium, the object will rise or fall until equilibrium is reached—that is, the object will sink until its remaining weight is supported by the bottom, or it will rise until the weight of liquid is reduced by breaking the surface.

The two forces acting on a stationary floating object are the *buoyant force* and the *object's weight*. The buoyant force acts upward through the centroid of the displaced volume (not the object's volume). This centroid is known as the *center of buoyancy*. The gravitational force on the object (i.e., the object's weight) acts downward through the entire object's center of gravity.

---

[6]p_C in Eq. 8.7 is defined as the "pressure at the centroid of the area," but it cannot be calculated from Eq. 8.5, because Eq. 8.5 calculates an absolute pressure. As used in Eq. 8.7, p_C is a gauge pressure, not an absolute pressure. $\sin \alpha$ in Eq. 8.8 is an error, and it should be $\sin \theta$.

[7]For all practical purposes, atmospheric pressure always acts on both sides of an object. It acts through the liquid on both sides of a submerged plate, it acts on both sides of a submerged gate, and it acts on both sides of a discharge gate/door. Except for objects in a vacuum, Eq. 8.9 is of purely academic interest.

Fluid Dynamics

Nomenclature

A	area	m^2
AR	aspect ratio	–
b	span	m
B	channel width	m
c	chord length	m
C	coefficient	–
$C_{D\infty}$	drag coefficient at zero lift	–
d	depth	m
d	diameter	m
D	diameter	m
E	specific energy	J/kg
f	friction factor	–
F	force	N
Fr	Froude number	–
g	gravitational acceleration, 9.81	m/s^2
h	head	m
h	height	m
I	impulse	N·s
k	conversion constant	–
k_1	constant of proportionality	–
K	constant	–
K	consistency index	–
L	length	m

m	mass	kg
$\dot{m}$	mass flow rate	kg/s
M	moment	N·m
n	Manning roughness coefficient	–
n	power law index	–
p	pressure	Pa
Δp_f	pressure drop due to friction	Pa
P	momentum	kg·m/s
q	unit discharge	$m^3/m \cdot s$
Q	flow rate	m^3/s
r	distance from centerline	m
R	radius	m
Re	Reynolds number (Newtonian fluid)	–
Re$'$	Reynolds number (non-Newtonian fluid)	–
S	slope of energy grade line	–
t	time	s
T	surface width	m
v	velocity	m/s
W	weight	N
$\mathcal{W}$	power	J/s
y	depth	m
y_h	hydraulic depth (characteristic length)	m
z	elevation	m

Symbols

α	angle	deg
α	geometric angle of attack	deg
α	kinetic energy correction factor	–
β	negative of angle of attack for zero lift	deg
γ	specific (unit) weight	N/m^3
ε	specific roughness	m
μ	absolute viscosity	Pa·s
ρ	density	kg/m^3
τ	shear stress	Pa
ν	kinematic viscosity	m^2/s

Fluid Mechanics

Subscripts

b	blade or bulk
c	critical
D	drag
f	friction
h	hydraulic
H	hydraulic
j	jet
L	lift or loss
max	maximum
M	moment
p	constant pressure, perpendicular, or plan
s	surface
t	total
v	constant volume or velocity
w	wall

1. INTRODUCTION

Fluid dynamics is the theoretical science of all fluids in motion. In a general sense, *hydraulics* is the study of the practical laws of incompressible fluid flow and resistance in pipes and open channels. Hydraulic formulas are often developed from experimentation, empirical factors, and curve fitting, without an attempt to justify why the fluid behaves the way it does.

2. CONSERVATION LAWS

Equation 9.1 Through Eq. 9.3: Continuity Equation

$$A_1 v_1 = A_2 v_2 \qquad 9.1$$

$$Q = A v \qquad 9.2$$

$$\begin{aligned} \dot{m} &= \rho Q \\ &= \rho A v \end{aligned} \qquad 9.3$$

Description

Fluid mass is always conserved in fluid systems, regardless of the pipeline complexity, orientation of the flow, and fluid. This single concept is often sufficient to solve simple fluid problems.

$$\dot{m}_1 = \dot{m}_2$$

When applied to fluid flow, the conservation of mass law is known as the *continuity equation*.

$$\rho_1 A_1 v_1 = \rho_2 A_2 v_2$$

If the fluid is incompressible, then $\rho_1 = \rho_2$. Equation 9.1 is the continuity equation for incompressible flow.

Volumetric flow rate, Q, is defined as the product of cross-sectional area and velocity, as shown in Eq. 9.2. From Eq. 9.1 and Eq. 9.2, it follows that

$$Q_1 = Q_2$$

Various units are used for volumetric flow rate. MGD (millions of gallons per day) and MGPCD (millions of gallons per capita day) are units commonly used in municipal water works problems. MMSCFD (millions of standard cubic feet per day) may be used to express gas flows.

Calculation of flow rates is often complicated by the interdependence between flow rate and friction loss. Each affects the other, so many pipe flow problems must be solved iteratively. Usually, a reasonable friction factor is assumed and used to calculate an initial flow rate. The flow rate establishes the flow velocity, from which a revised friction factor can be determined.

Example

An incompressible fluid flows through a pipe with an inner diameter of 10 cm at a velocity of 4 m/s. The pipe contracts to an inner diameter of 8 cm. What is most nearly the velocity of the fluid in the narrower section?

(A) 4.7 m/s

(B) 5.0 m/s

(C) 5.8 m/s

(D) 6.3 m/s

Solution

The cross-sectional areas of the two pipes are

$$A_1 = \frac{\pi D_1^2}{4} = \frac{\pi (10 \text{ cm})^2}{4} = 78.54 \text{ cm}^2$$

$$A_2 = \frac{\pi D_2^2}{4} = \frac{\pi (8 \text{ cm})^2}{4} = 50.27 \text{ cm}^2$$

Use Eq. 9.1.

$$A_1 v_1 = A_2 v_2$$

$$\begin{aligned} v_2 = \frac{A_1 v_1}{A_2} &= \frac{(78.54 \text{ cm}^2)\left(4 \dfrac{\text{m}}{\text{s}}\right)}{50.27 \text{ cm}^2} \\ &= 6.25 \text{ m/s} \quad (6.3 \text{ m/s}) \end{aligned}$$

The answer is (D).

Equation 9.4 and Eq. 9.5: Bernoulli Equation

$$\frac{p_2}{\gamma} + \frac{v_2^2}{2g} + z_2 = \frac{p_1}{\gamma} + \frac{v_1^2}{2g} + z_1 \qquad 9.4$$

$$\frac{p_2}{\rho} + \frac{v_2^2}{2} + z_2 g = \frac{p_1}{\rho} + \frac{v_1^2}{2} + z_1 g \qquad 9.5$$

Description

The *Bernoulli equation*, also known as the *field equation* or the *energy equation*, is an energy conservation equation that is valid for incompressible, frictionless flow. The Bernoulli equation states that the total energy of a fluid flowing without friction losses in a pipe is constant. The total energy possessed by the fluid is the sum of its pressure, kinetic, and potential energies. In other words, the Bernoulli equation states that the total head at any two points is the same.

Example

The diameter of a water pipe gradually changes from 5 cm at the entrance, point A, to 15 cm at the exit, point B. The exit is 5 m higher than the entrance. The pressure is 700 kPa at the entrance and 664 kPa at the exit. Friction between the water and the pipe walls is negligible. The water density is 1000 kg/m³.

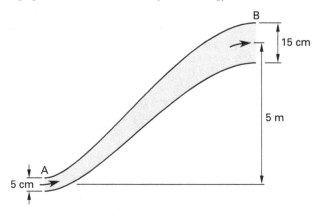

What is most nearly the rate of discharge at the exit?

(A) 0.0035 m³/s

(B) 0.0064 m³/s

(C) 0.010 m³/s

(D) 0.018 m³/s

Solution

Find the relationship between the entrance and exit velocities, v_1 and v_2, respectively. From Eq. 9.1 and substituting the pipe area equation,

$$A_1 v_1 = A_2 v_2$$

$$\left(\frac{\pi D_1^2}{4}\right) v_1 = \left(\frac{\pi D_2^2}{4}\right) v_2$$

$$v_1 = \left(\frac{D_2^2}{D_1^2}\right) v_2 = \left(\frac{(15\ \text{cm})^2 v_2}{(5\ \text{cm})^2}\right)$$

$$= 9 v_2$$

Use the Bernoulli equation, Eq. 9.5, to find the velocity at the exit.

$$\frac{p_2}{\rho} + \frac{v_2^2}{2} + z_2 g = \frac{p_1}{\rho} + \frac{v_1^2}{2} + z_1 g$$

$$= \frac{p_1}{\rho} + \frac{(9 v_2)^2}{2} + z_1 g$$

$$\frac{p_2 - p_1}{\rho} + g(z_2 - z_1) = \frac{81 v_2^2}{2} - \frac{v_2^2}{2}$$

$$v_2 = \sqrt{\frac{p_2 - p_1}{40\rho} + \frac{g(z_2 - z_1)}{40}}$$

$$= \sqrt{\frac{(664\ \text{kPa} - 700\ \text{kPa}) \times \left(1000\ \frac{\text{Pa}}{\text{kPa}}\right)}{(40)\left(1000\ \frac{\text{kg}}{\text{m}^3}\right)} + \frac{\left(9.81\ \frac{\text{m}}{\text{s}^2}\right)(5\ \text{m})}{40}}$$

$$= 0.571\ \text{m/s}$$

Multiply the velocity at the exit with the cross-sectional area to get the rate of flow.

$$Q = A_2 v_2 = \left(\frac{\pi D_2^2}{4}\right) v_2$$

$$= \left(\frac{\pi (15\ \text{cm})^2}{(4)\left(100\ \frac{\text{cm}}{\text{m}}\right)^2}\right)\left(0.571\ \frac{\text{m}}{\text{s}}\right)$$

$$= 0.0101\ \text{m}^3/\text{s} \quad (0.010\ \text{m}^3/\text{s})$$

The answer is (C).

Fluid Mechanics

3. REYNOLDS NUMBER

The *Reynolds number*, Re, is a dimensionless number interpreted as the ratio of inertial forces to viscous forces in the fluid.

The inertial forces are proportional to the flow diameter, velocity, and fluid density. (Increasing these variables will increase the momentum of the fluid in flow.) The viscous force is represented by the fluid's *absolute viscosity*, μ.

Equation 9.6: Reynolds Number, Newtonian Fluids

$$\mathrm{Re} = \mathrm{v} D \rho / \mu = \mathrm{v} D / \nu \qquad 9.6$$

Description

Since μ/ρ is the *kinematic viscosity*, ν, the equation can be simplified.

If all of the fluid particles move in paths parallel to the overall flow direction (i.e., in layers), the flow is said to be *laminar*. This occurs when the Reynolds number is less than approximately 2100. *Laminar flow* is typical when the flow channel is small, the velocity is low, and the fluid is viscous. Viscous forces are dominant in laminar flow.

Turbulent flow is characterized by a three-dimensional movement of the fluid particles superimposed on the overall direction of motion. A fluid is said to be in turbulent flow if the Reynolds number is greater than approximately 4000. (This is the most common case.)

The flow is said to be in the *critical zone* or *transition region* when the Reynolds number is between 2100 and 4000. These numbers are known as the lower and upper *critical Reynolds numbers*, respectively.

Example

The mean velocity of 40°C water in a 44.7 mm (inside diameter) tube is 1.5 m/s. The kinematic viscosity is $\nu = 6.58 \times 10^{-7}$ m²/s. What is most nearly the Reynolds number?

(A) 8.1×10^3

(B) 8.5×10^3

(C) 9.1×10^4

(D) 1.0×10^5

Solution

From Eq. 9.6,

$$\mathrm{Re} = \mathrm{v} D \rho / \mu = \mathrm{v} D / \nu$$

$$= \frac{\left(1.5 \; \dfrac{\mathrm{m}}{\mathrm{s}}\right)(44.7 \; \mathrm{mm})}{\left(6.58 \times 10^{-7} \; \dfrac{\mathrm{m}^2}{\mathrm{s}}\right)\left(1000 \; \dfrac{\mathrm{mm}}{\mathrm{m}}\right)}$$

$$= 1.02 \times 10^5 \quad (1.0 \times 10^5)$$

The answer is (D).

Equation 9.7: Reynolds Number, Non-Newtonian Fluids

$$\mathrm{Re}' = \frac{\mathrm{v}^{(2-n)} D^n \rho}{K \left(\dfrac{3n+1}{4n}\right)^n 8^{(n-1)}} \qquad 9.7$$

Description

Many fluids are not Newtonian (i.e., do not behave according to Eq. 7.12). Non-Newtonian fluids have viscosities that change with shear rate, $d\mathrm{v}/dt$. For example, *pseudoplastic fluids* exhibit a decrease in viscosity the faster they are agitated. Such fluids present no serious pumping difficulties. On the other hand, pumps for *dilatant fluids* must be designed carefully, since dilatant fluids exhibit viscosities that increase the faster they are agitated. For non-Newtonian fluids, *power law* parameters must be used when calculating the Reynolds number, Re'. In Eq. 9.7, the constant K is known as the *consistency index*. For *pseudoplastic non-Newtonian fluids*, $n < 1$; for *dilatant non-Newtonian fluids*, $n > 1$. For Newtonian fluids, $n = 1$, and Eq. 9.7 reduces to Eq. 9.6.

4. FLOW DISTRIBUTION

With laminar flow in a circular pipe or between two parallel plates, viscosity makes some fluid particles adhere to the wall. The closer to the wall, the greater the tendency will be for the fluid to adhere. In general, the fluid velocity will be zero at the wall and will follow a parabolic distribution away from the wall. The *average flow velocity* (also known as the *bulk velocity*) is found from the flow rate and cross-sectional area.

$$\mathrm{v} = \frac{Q}{A} \quad \text{[average]}$$

Because of the parabolic distribution, velocity will be maximum at the centerline, midway between the two walls (i.e., at the center of a pipe). (See Fig. 9.1.)

Figure 9.1 *Laminar and Turbulent Velocity Distributions*

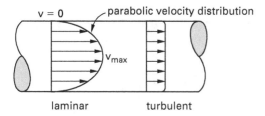

Equation 9.8 Through Eq. 9.11: Flow Velocity

$$v(r) = v_{max}\left[1 - \left(\frac{r}{R}\right)^2\right] \qquad 9.8$$

$$v_{max} = 2\bar{v} \quad \text{[laminar flow in circular pipe]} \qquad 9.9$$

$$v_{max} = 1.5\bar{v} \quad \text{[laminar flow between plates]} \qquad 9.10$$

$$v_{max} = 1.18\bar{v} \quad \text{[fully turbulent flow]} \qquad 9.11$$

Variation

$$\bar{v} = \frac{Q}{A}$$

Description

For flow through a pipe with diameter $2R$ or between parallel plates with separation distance $2R$, the velocity at any point a distance r from the centerline is given by Eq. 9.8. The value of v_{max} varies depending on the conditions of the flow. Equation 9.9 and Eq. 9.10 give the values of v_{max} for laminar flow in circular pipes and between plates, respectively.

With turbulent flow, a distinction between velocities of particles near the pipe wall or centerline is usually not made. All the fluid particles are assumed to flow at the bulk velocity. In reality, no flow is completely turbulent, and there is a slight difference between the centerline velocity and the average velocity. For fully turbulent flow (Re > 10 000), a good approximation of the average velocity is approximately 85% of the maximum velocity, as stated by Eq. 9.11.

Equation 9.12: Shear Stress

$$\frac{\tau}{\tau_w} = \frac{r}{R} \qquad 9.12$$

Description

Like flow velocity, the shear stress created by the flow also varies with location. The shear stress, τ, at any point a distance r from the centerline can be found from the shear stress at the wall, τ_w, using the relationship in Eq. 9.12.

5. STEADY INCOMPRESSIBLE FLOW IN PIPES AND CONDUITS

Equation 9.13 and Eq. 9.14: Energy Conservation Equation

$$\frac{p_1}{\gamma} + z_1 + \frac{v_1^2}{2g} = \frac{p_2}{\gamma} + z_2 + \frac{v_2^2}{2g} + h_f \qquad 9.13$$

$$\frac{p_1}{\rho g} + z_1 + \frac{v_1^2}{2g} = \frac{p_2}{\rho g} + z_2 + \frac{v_2^2}{2g} + h_f \qquad 9.14$$

Description

The *energy conservation (extended field) equation*, also known as the *steady-flow energy equation*, for steady incompressible flow is shown in Eq. 9.13 and Eq. 9.14. Equation 9.13 and Eq. 9.14 do not include the effects of *shaft devices* (so named because they have rotating shafts adding or extracting power) such as pumps, compressors, fans, and turbines. (Effects of shaft devices would be represented by *shaft work* terms.)

If the cross-sectional area of the pipe is the same at points 1 and 2, then $v_1 = v_2$ and $v_1^2/2g = v_2^2/2g$. If the elevation of the pipe is the same at points 1 and 2, then $z_1 = z_2$. When analyzing discharge from reservoirs and large tanks, it is common to use gauge pressures, so that $p_1 = 0$ at the surface. In addition, since the surface elevation changes slowly (or not at all) when drawing from a large tank or reservoir, $v_1 = 0$.

The *head loss due to friction* is denoted by the symbol h_f.

Example

An open reservoir with a water surface level at an elevation of 200 m drains through a 1 m diameter pipe with the outlet at an elevation of 180 m. The pipe outlet discharges to atmospheric pressure. The total head losses in the pipe and fittings are 18 m. Assume steady incompressible flow. The flow rate from the outlet is most nearly

(A) 4.9 m³/s

(B) 6.3 m³/s

(C) 31 m³/s

(D) 39 m³/s

Solution

Use the energy conservation equation, Eq. 9.14. Take point 1 at the reservoir surface and point 2 at the pipe outlet.

$$\frac{p_1}{\rho g} + z_1 + \frac{v_1^2}{2g} = \frac{p_2}{\rho g} + z_2 + \frac{v_2^2}{2g} + h_f$$

The pressure is atmospheric at the reservoir and the outlet, so $p_1 = p_2$. The velocity at the reservoir surface is $v_1 \approx 0 \text{ m/s}$, so the equation reduces to

$$z_1 = z_2 + \frac{v_2^2}{2g} + h_f$$

Solve for the velocity at the pipe outlet, v_2.

$$\begin{aligned} v_2 &= \sqrt{2g(z_1 - z_2 - h_f)} \\ &= \sqrt{\begin{array}{c}(2)\left(9.81\ \dfrac{\text{m}}{\text{s}^2}\right) \\ \times (200\ \text{m} - 180\ \text{m} - 18\ \text{m})\end{array}} \\ &= 6.26\ \text{m/s} \end{aligned}$$

The flow rate out of the pipe outlet is

$$\begin{aligned} Q &= v_2 A = v_2 \left(\frac{\pi D^2}{4}\right) \\ &= \left(6.26\ \frac{\text{m}}{\text{s}}\right)\left(\frac{\pi (1\ \text{m})^2}{4}\right) \\ &= 4.92\ \text{m}^3/\text{s} \quad (4.9\ \text{m}^3/\text{s}) \end{aligned}$$

The answer is (A).

Equation 9.15: Pressure Drop

$$p_1 - p_2 = \gamma h_f = \rho g h_f \qquad \text{9.15}$$

Description

For a pipe of constant cross-sectional area and constant elevation, the *pressure change* (*pressure drop*) from one point to another is given by Eq. 9.15.

6. FRICTION LOSS

Equation 9.16 Through Eq. 9.18: Darcy-Weisbach Equation[1]

$$h_f = f \frac{L}{D}\frac{v^2}{2g} \qquad \text{9.16}$$

$$h_f = (4f_{\text{Fanning}})\frac{Lv^2}{D2g} = \frac{2f_{\text{Fanning}}Lv^2}{Dg} \qquad \text{9.17}$$

$$f_{\text{Fanning}} = \frac{f}{4} \qquad \text{9.18}$$

Variation

$$h_f = \frac{fLv^2}{2Dg}$$

Values

See Table 9.1.

Description

The *Darcy-Weisbach equation* (*Darcy equation*) is one method for calculating the frictional energy loss for fluids. It can be used for both laminar and turbulent flow.

The *Darcy friction factor*, f, is one of the parameters that is used to calculate the friction loss. One of the advantages to using the Darcy equation is that the assumption of laminar or turbulent flow does not need to be confirmed if f is known. The friction factor is not constant, but decreases as the Reynolds number (fluid velocity) increases, up to a certain point, known as *fully turbulent flow*. Once the flow is fully turbulent, the friction factor remains constant and depends only on the relative roughness of the pipe surface and not on the Reynolds number. For very smooth pipes, fully turbulent flow is achieved only at very high Reynolds numbers.

The friction factor is not dependent on the material of the pipe, but is affected by its roughness. For example, for a given Reynolds number, the friction factor will be the same for any smooth pipe material (glass, plastic, smooth brass, copper, etc.).

The friction factor is determined from the *relative roughness*, ε/D, and the Reynolds number, Re. The relative roughness is calculated from the *specific roughness* of the material, ε, given in tables, and the inside diameter of the pipe. (See Table 9.1.)[2] The *Moody friction factor chart* (also

---

[1](1) The Weisbach frictional head loss equation is commonly presented as $h_f = fLv^2/2Dg$, as shown in the variation equation. The NCEES *FE Reference Handbook* (*NCEES Handbook*) separates out three terms, f, L/d, and $v^2/2g$, and changes the sequence of the denominator to show that the head loss is a multiple of velocity head. (2) The *Fanning friction factor* is primarily of interest to chemical engineers. Civil and mechanical engineers rarely encounter the Fanning friction factor and, to them, "friction factor" always refers to the Darcy friction factor.
[2]The information in Table 9.1 is presented as part of the Moody (Stanton) friction factor chart, Fig. 9.2.

known as the *Stanton diagram*), Fig. 9.2, presents the friction factor graphically. There are different lines for selected discrete values of relative roughness. Because of the complexity of this graph, it is easy to incorrectly locate the Reynolds number or use the wrong curve. Nevertheless, the Moody chart remains the most common method of obtaining the friction factor.

Table 9.1 *Specific Roughness of Typical Materials*

material	ε	
	ft	mm
asphalted cast iron	0.0002–0.0006	0.06–0.2
blasted rock tunnel	1.0–2.0	300–600
cast iron	0.0006–0.003	0.2–0.9
commercial steel or wrought iron	0.0001–0.0003	0.03–0.09
concrete	0.001–0.01	0.3–3.0
corrugated metal pipe	0.1–0.2	30–60
galvanized iron	0.0002–0.0008	0.06–0.2
glass, drawn brass, copper, or lead	smooth	smooth
concrete- or steel-lined large tunnel	0.002–0.004	0.6–1.2
riveted steel	0.003–0.03	0.9–9.0

Example

Water at 10°C is pumped through 300 m of steel pipe at a velocity of 2.3 m/s. The pipe has an inside diameter of 84.45 mm and a friction factor of 0.0195. The friction loss is most nearly

(A)   2.0 m

(B)   8.6 m

(C)   19 m

(D)   24 m

Solution

Use Eq. 9.16, the Darcy-Weisbach equation.

$$h_f = f\frac{L}{D}\frac{\mathrm{v}^2}{2g} = (0.0195)\left(\frac{300 \text{ m}}{\frac{84.45 \text{ mm}}{1000 \frac{\text{mm}}{\text{m}}}}\right)\left(\frac{\left(2.3 \frac{\text{m}}{\text{s}}\right)^2}{(2)\left(9.81 \frac{\text{m}}{\text{s}^2}\right)}\right)$$

$$= 18.7 \text{ m} \quad (19 \text{ m})$$

The answer is (C).

Equation 9.19: Hagen-Poiseuille Equation

$$Q = \frac{\pi R^4 \Delta p_f}{8\mu L}$$
$$= \frac{\pi D^4 \Delta p_f}{128\mu L}$$

9.19

Variation

$$\mathrm{v} = \frac{D^2 \Delta p_f}{32\mu L}$$

Description

If the flow is laminar and in a circular pipe, then the *Hagen-Poiseuille equation* can be used to calculate the flow rate. In Eq. 9.19, the Hagen-Poiseuille equation is presented in the form of a pressure drop, $\Delta p_f = \gamma h_f$.

Example

Water flows at 0.012 m/s through a horizontal pipe with an inner diameter of 8 cm. The absolute viscosity of the water is 0.001002 Pa·s. Assume the flow is laminar. What is most nearly the pressure drop after 60 m of pipe?

(A)   0.6 Pa

(B)   1.2 Pa

(C)   2.0 Pa

(D)   3.6 Pa

Solution

Use the Hagen-Poiseuille equation, Eq. 9.19.

$$Q = \frac{\pi D^4 \Delta p_f}{128\mu L}$$
$$\Delta p_f = \frac{128\mu L Q}{\pi D^4}$$
$$= \frac{32\mu L \mathrm{v}}{D^2}$$
$$= \frac{(32)(0.001002 \text{ Pa·s})(60 \text{ m})\left(0.012 \frac{\text{m}}{\text{s}}\right)\left(100 \frac{\text{cm}}{\text{m}}\right)^2}{(8 \text{ cm})^2}$$
$$= 3.61 \text{ Pa} \quad (3.6 \text{ Pa})$$

The answer is (D).

Figure 9.2 *Moody Friction Factor Chart*

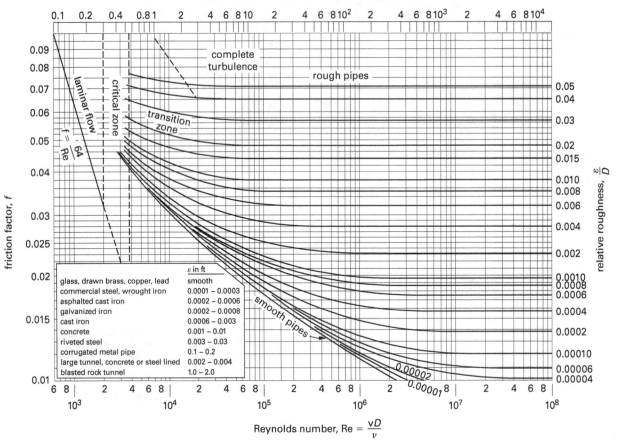

From *Friction Factor for Pipe Flow*, by L. F. Moody, copyright © 1944, by ASME. Reproduced with permission.

7. FLOW IN NONCIRCULAR CONDUITS

Equation 9.20: Hydraulic Radius

$$R_H = \frac{\text{cross-sectional area}}{\text{wetted perimeter}}$$
$$= \frac{D_H}{4} \qquad \qquad 9.20$$

Description

The *hydraulic radius* is defined as the cross-sectional area in flow divided by the *wetted perimeter*.

The area in flow is the cross-sectional area of the fluid flowing. When a fluid is flowing under pressure in a pipe (i.e., *pressure flow*), the area in flow will be the internal area of the pipe. However, the fluid may not completely fill the pipe and may flow simply because of a sloped surface (i.e., *gravity flow* or *open channel flow*).

The wetted perimeter is the length of the line representing the interface between the fluid and the pipe or channel. It does not include the *free surface* length (i.e., the interface between fluid and atmosphere).

For a circular pipe flowing completely full, the area in flow is πR^2. The wetted perimeter is the entire circumference, $2\pi R$. The hydraulic radius in this case is half the radius of the pipe.

$$R_H = \frac{\pi R^2}{2\pi R} = \frac{R}{2} = \frac{D}{4}$$

The hydraulic radius of a pipe flowing half full is also $R/2$, since the flow area and wetted perimeter are both halved.

Many fluid, thermodynamic, and heat transfer processes are dependent on the physical length of an object. The general name for this controlling variable is *characteristic dimension*. The characteristic dimension in evaluating fluid flow is the *hydraulic diameter*, D_H. The hydraulic diameter for a full-flowing circular pipe is simply its inside diameter. If the hydraulic radius of a noncircular duct is known, it can be used to calculate the hydraulic diameter.

$$D_H = 4R_H = 4 \times \frac{\text{area in flow}}{\text{wetted perimeter}}$$

The frictional energy loss by a fluid flowing in a rectangular, annular, or other noncircular duct can be calculated from the Darcy equation by using the hydraulic diameter, D_H, in place of the diameter, D. The friction factor, f, is determined in any of the conventional manners.

Example

The 8 cm × 12 cm rectangular flume shown is filled to three-quarters of its height.

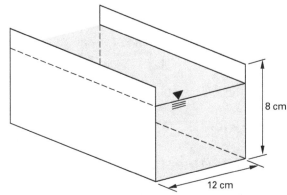

8 cm

12 cm

What is most nearly the hydraulic radius of the flow?

(A)   1.5 cm

(B)   2.5 cm

(C)   3.0 cm

(D)   5.0 cm

Solution

The hydraulic radius is

$$R_H = \frac{\text{cross-sectional area}}{\text{wetted perimeter}}$$

$$= \frac{(12 \text{ cm})\left(\dfrac{3}{4}\right)(8 \text{ cm})}{(2)\left(\dfrac{3}{4}\right)(8 \text{ cm}) + 12 \text{ cm}}$$

$$= 3.0 \text{ cm}$$

The answer is (C).

8. MINOR LOSSES IN PIPE FITTINGS, CONTRACTIONS, AND EXPANSIONS

In addition to the frictional energy lost due to viscous effects, friction losses also result from fittings in the line, changes in direction, and changes in flow area. These losses are known as *minor losses*, since they are usually much smaller in magnitude than the pipe wall frictional loss.

Equation 9.21 Through Eq. 9.25: Energy Conservation Equation[3]

$$\frac{p_1}{\gamma} + z_1 + \frac{v_1^2}{2g} = \frac{p_2}{\gamma} + z_2 + \frac{v_2^2}{2g} + h_f + h_{f,\text{fitting}} \qquad 9.21$$

$$\frac{p_1}{\rho g} + z_1 + \frac{v_1^2}{2g} = \frac{p_2}{\rho g} + z_2 + \frac{v_2^2}{2g} + h_f + h_{f,\text{fitting}} \qquad 9.22$$

$$h_{f,\text{fitting}} = C\frac{v^2}{2g} \qquad 9.23$$

$$\frac{v^2}{2g} = 1 \text{ velocity head} \qquad 9.24$$

$$h_{f,\text{fitting}} = 0.04v^2/2g \quad \begin{bmatrix} \text{gradual} \\ \text{contraction} \end{bmatrix} \qquad 9.25$$

Description

The energy conservation equation accounting for minor losses is Eq. 9.21 and Eq. 9.22.

The minor losses can be calculated using the *method of loss coefficients*. Each fitting has a *loss coefficient*, C, associated with it, which, when multiplied by the kinetic energy, gives the head loss. A loss coefficient is the minor head loss expressed in fractions (or multiples) of the velocity head.

Loss coefficients for specific fittings and valves must be known in order to be used. They cannot be derived theoretically.

Losses at pipe exits and entrances in tanks also fall under the category of minor losses. The values of C given in Fig. 9.3 account for minor losses in various exit and entrance conditions.

Figure 9.3 *C-Values for Head Loss*

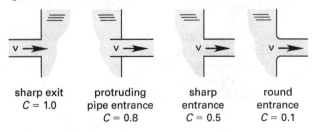

sharp exit
$C = 1.0$

protruding
pipe entrance
$C = 0.8$

sharp
entrance
$C = 0.5$

round
entrance
$C = 0.1$

Some fittings have specific loss values, which are generally provided in the problem statement. The nominal value for head loss, C, in well-streamlined gradual contractions is given by Eq. 9.25.

Example

Water exits a tank through a nozzle with a diameter of 5 cm located 5 m below the surface of the water. The water level in the tank is kept constant. The loss coefficient for the nozzle is 0.5.

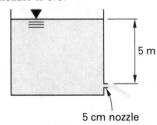

5 m

5 cm nozzle

The flow rate through the nozzle is most nearly

(A)   7.1 L/s

(B)   11 L/s

(C)   16 L/s

(D)   24 L/s

Solution

Use Eq. 9.22 and Eq. 9.23 to find the velocity through the nozzle, with location 1 at the surface of the water in the tank and location 2 at the nozzle exit.

$$\frac{p_1}{\rho g} + z_1 + \frac{v_1^2}{2g} = \frac{p_2}{\rho g} + z_2 + \frac{v_2^2}{2g} + h_f + h_{f,\text{fitting}}$$

$$= \frac{p_2}{\rho g} + z_2 + \frac{v_2^2}{2g} + h_f + C\frac{v_2^2}{2g}$$

The pressure is atmospheric at both locations, so the pressure terms cancel. The velocity at location 1 is zero. The head loss due to friction between locations 1 and 2 is zero. Rearrange to solve for v_2.

$$v_2 = \sqrt{\frac{2g(z_1 - z_2)}{C+1}} = \sqrt{\frac{(2)\left(9.81\ \frac{\text{m}}{\text{s}^2}\right)(5\ \text{m})}{0.5+1}}$$

$$= 8.087\ \text{m/s}$$

The flow rate is

$$Q = Av_2 = \left(\frac{\pi D^2}{4}\right)v_2$$

$$= \left(\frac{\pi(5\ \text{cm})^2}{(4)\left(100\ \frac{\text{cm}}{\text{m}}\right)^2}\right)\left(8.087\ \frac{\text{m}}{\text{s}}\right)\left(1000\ \frac{\text{L}}{\text{m}^3}\right)$$

$$= 15.88\ \text{L/s} \quad (16\ \text{L/s})$$

The answer is (C).

9. MULTIPATH PIPELINES

A *pipe loop* is a set of two pipes placed in parallel, both originating and terminating at the same junction. (See Fig. 9.4.) Adding a second pipe in parallel with the first is a standard method of increasing the capacity of a line.

Figure 9.4 *Parallel Pipe Loop System*

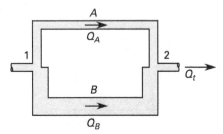

If the pipe diameters are known, the multipath flow equations can be solved simultaneously for the branch velocities. In such problems, it is common to neglect minor losses, the velocity head, and the variation in the friction factor, f, with velocity.

Equation 9.26 and Eq. 9.27: Head Loss and Flow Rate in Multipath Pipelines[4]

$$h_L = f_A \frac{L_A}{D_A} \frac{v_A^2}{2g} = f_B \frac{L_B}{D_B} \frac{v_B^2}{2g} \qquad 9.26$$

$$(\pi D^2/4)\,v = (\pi D_A^2/4)v_A + (\pi D_B^2/4)v_B \qquad 9.27$$

Description

The relationships between flow, velocity, and pipe diameter and length are illustrated in Fig. 9.5.

Figure 9.5 *Multipath Pipeline*

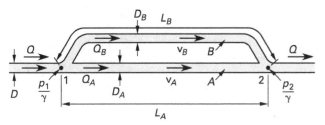

The flow divides in such a manner as to make the head loss in each branch the same.

$$h_{f,A} = h_{f,B}$$

The head loss between the two junctions is the same as the head loss in each branch.

$$h_{f,1-2} = h_{f,A} = h_{f,B}$$

The total flow rate is the sum of the flow rates in the two branches.

$$Q_t = Q_A + Q_B$$

Example

Water flows at 6 m³/s in a 1 m diameter pipeline, then divides into two branch lines that discharge to the atmosphere 1000 m from the junction. Branch A uses 0.75 m diameter pipe, and branch B uses 0.60 m diameter pipe. All branches are at the same elevation, and all pipes have the same friction factor of 0.0023. Friction losses from fittings are negligible. The flow rate in branch A is most nearly

(A) 3.5 m³/s

(B) 3.8 m³/s

(C) 4.1 m³/s

(D) 4.4 m³/s

Solution

The cross-sectional areas of the main and two branch pipes are

$$A_{\text{main}} = \frac{\pi D^2}{4}$$
$$= \frac{\pi (1 \text{ m})^2}{4}$$
$$= 0.785 \text{ m}^2$$
$$A_A = \frac{\pi D_A^2}{4}$$
$$= \frac{\pi (0.75 \text{ m})^2}{4}$$
$$= 0.442 \text{ m}^2$$
$$A_B = \frac{\pi D_B^2}{4}$$
$$= \frac{\pi (0.60 \text{ m})^2}{4}$$
$$= 0.283 \text{ m}^2$$

The velocity in the 1 m main pipe is

$$v_{\text{main}} = \frac{Q}{A_{\text{main}}}$$
$$= \frac{6 \ \dfrac{\text{m}^3}{\text{s}}}{0.785 \text{ m}^2}$$
$$= 7.64 \text{ m/s}$$

Find the relationship between v_A and v_B from Eq. 9.26.

$$f_A \frac{L_A}{D_A} \frac{v_A^2}{2g} = f_B \frac{L_B}{D_B} \frac{v_B^2}{2g}$$

$$(0.0023)\left(\frac{1000 \text{ m}}{0.75 \text{ m}}\right)\left(\frac{v_A^2}{2g}\right) = (0.0023)\left(\frac{1000 \text{ m}}{0.60 \text{ m}}\right)\left(\frac{v_B^2}{2g}\right)$$

$$v_B = v_A\sqrt{\frac{0.60 \text{ m}}{0.75 \text{ m}}}$$
$$= 0.894 v_A$$

---

[4]The *NCEES Handbook* is inconsistent in the symbol used for friction head loss. Head loss, h_L, used in Eq. 9.26 is no different than head loss due to friction, h_f, used in Eq. 9.16.

Find another relationship between v_A and v_B from Eq. 9.27, then solve for v_A.

$$Q = A_A v_A + A_B v_B$$

$$6 \frac{\text{m}^3}{\text{s}} = (0.442 \text{ m}^2)v_A + (0.283 \text{ m}^2)v_B$$

$$v_A = \frac{6 \frac{\text{m}^3}{\text{s}}}{0.442 \text{ m}^2} - 0.64v_B$$

$$= 13.58 \frac{\text{m}}{\text{s}} - (0.64)(0.894v_A)$$

$$= 8.637 \text{ m/s}$$

$$v_B = 0.894v_A = (0.894)\left(8.637 \frac{\text{m}}{\text{s}}\right)$$

$$= 7.725 \text{ m/s}$$

The flow rates in the two branches are

$$Q_A = A_A v_A$$

$$= (0.442 \text{ m}^2)\left(8.637 \frac{\text{m}}{\text{s}}\right)$$

$$= 3.816 \text{ m}^3/\text{s} \quad (3.8 \text{ m}^3/\text{s})$$

$$Q_B = A_B v_B$$

$$= (0.283 \text{ m}^2)\left(7.725 \frac{\text{m}}{\text{s}}\right)$$

$$= 2.184 \text{ m}^3/\text{s} \quad (2.2 \text{ m}^3/\text{s})$$

Calculate the total flow rate to check the calculation.

$$Q_t = Q_A + Q_B$$

$$= 3.8 \frac{\text{m}^3}{\text{s}} + 2.2 \frac{\text{m}^3}{\text{s}}$$

$$= 6 \text{ m}^3/\text{s}$$

The answer is (B).

10. OPEN CHANNEL AND PARTIAL-AREA PIPE FLOW

An *open channel* is a fluid passageway that allows part of the fluid to be exposed to the atmosphere. This type of channel includes natural waterways, canals, culverts, flumes, and pipes flowing under the influence of gravity (as opposed to pressure conduits, which always flow full). A *reach* is a straight section of open channel with uniform shape, depth, slope, and flow quantity.

Equation 9.28: Manning's Equation

$$v = (K/n)R_H^{2/3}S^{1/2} \qquad 9.28$$

Values

SI units	$K = 1$
customary U.S. units	$K = 1.486$

Description

Manning's equation has typically been used to estimate the velocity of flow in any open channel. It depends on the hydraulic radius, R_H, the slope of the energy grade line, S, and a dimensionless *Manning's roughness coefficient*, n. A conversion constant, K, modifies the equation for use with SI or customary U.S. units. The slope of the energy grade line is the terrain grade (slope) for uniform open-channel flow. The Manning roughness coefficient is typically taken as 0.013 for concrete.

Example

Water flows through the open concrete channel shown. Assume a Manning roughness coefficient of 0.013 for concrete.

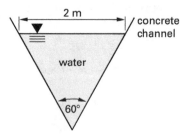

What is most nearly the minimum slope needed to maintain the flow at 3 m³/s?

(A) 0.00015

(B) 0.00052

(C) 0.0015

(D) 0.0052

Solution

The area of flow is that of an equilateral triangle 2 m on each side, so

$$A = \frac{\sqrt{3}\,a^2}{4} = \frac{\sqrt{3}\,(2 \text{ m})^2}{4} = 1.732 \text{ m}^2$$

The hydraulic radius is

$$R_H = \frac{\text{cross-sectional area}}{\text{wetted perimeter}} = \frac{1.732 \text{ m}^2}{2 \text{ m} + 2 \text{ m}} = 0.433 \text{ m}$$

The velocity needed is

$$v = \frac{Q}{A} = \frac{3 \frac{\text{m}^3}{\text{s}}}{1.732 \text{ m}^2} = 1.732 \text{ m/s}$$

Rearrange Manning's equation to solve for slope.

$$v = (K/n)R_H^{2/3}S^{1/2}$$

$$S = \left(\frac{vn}{KR_H^{2/3}}\right)^2$$

$$= \left(\frac{\left(1.732 \frac{\text{m}}{\text{s}}\right)(0.013)}{(1)(0.433 \text{ m})^{2/3}}\right)^2$$

$$= 0.001507 \quad (0.0015)$$

The answer is (C).

Equation 9.29: Hazen-Williams Equation

$$v = k_1 C R_H^{0.63} S^{0.54} \qquad \textbf{9.29}$$

Values

SI units	$k_1 = 0.849$
customary U.S. units	$k_1 = 1.318$

Description

Although Manning's equation can be used for circular pipes flowing less than full, the *Hazen-Williams equation* is used more often. A conversion constant, k_1, is used to modify the Hazen-Williams equation for use with SI or customary U.S. units.[5] The *Hazen-Williams roughness coefficient*, C, has a typical range of 100 to 130 for most materials as shown in Table 9.2, although very smooth materials can have higher values.

Example

Stormwater flows through a square concrete pipe that has a hydraulic radius of 1 m and an energy grade line

Table 9.2 *Values of Hazen-Williams Coefficient, C*

pipe material	C
ductile iron	140
concrete (regardless of age)	130
cast iron:	
new	130
5 yr old	120
20 yr old	100
welded steel, new	120
wood stave (regardless of age)	120
vitrified clay	110
riveted steel, new	110
brick sewers	100
asbestos-cement	140
plastic	150

slope of 0.8. Using the Hazen-Williams equation, the velocity of the water is most nearly

(A)   43 m/s

(B)   67 m/s

(C)   98 m/s

(D)   150 m/s

Solution

Use the Hazen-Williams equation, Eq. 9.29, to calculate the velocity. From Table 9.2, the Hazen-Williams roughness coefficient for concrete is 130.

$$v = k_1 C R_H^{0.63} S^{0.54} = (0.849)(130)(1 \text{ m})^{0.63}(0.8)^{0.54}$$

$$= 97.8 \text{ m/s} \quad (98 \text{ m/s})$$

The answer is (C).

Equation 9.30 Through Eq. 9.32: Circular Pipe Head Loss[6]

$$h_f = \frac{4.73L}{C^{1.852}D^{4.87}}Q^{1.852} \quad \text{[U.S. only]} \qquad \textbf{9.30}$$

$$p = \frac{4.52Q^{1.85}}{C^{1.85}D^{4.87}} \quad \text{[U.S. only]} \qquad \textbf{9.31}$$

$$p = \frac{6.05Q^{1.85}}{C^{1.85}D^{4.87}} \times 10^5 \quad \text{[SI only]} \qquad \textbf{9.32}$$

---

[5]There is no significance to the subscript or uppercase and lowercase usage in the conversion factor. While the *NCEES Handbook* chose to use K in Eq. 9.28 and Eq. 9.29, it could just as easily have chosen to use K_1 and K_2, or k_1 and k_2.
[6]The *NCEES Handbook* uses the exponents 1.852 and 1.85 interchangeably.

Description

Civil engineers commonly use the *Hazen-Williams equation* to calculate head loss. This method requires knowing the *Hazen-Williams roughness coefficient, C*. The advantage of using this equation is that C does not depend on the Reynolds number. The Hazen-Williams equation is empirical and is not dimensionally homogeneous.

Equation 9.30 gives the head loss expressed in feet. L is in feet, Q is in cubic feet per second, and D is in inches.[7]

Equation 9.31 and Eq. 9.32 give the head loss expressed as pressure in customary U.S. and SI units, respectively. In Eq. 9.31, p is in pounds per square inch per foot of pipe, Q is in gallons per minute, and D is in inches.[8] In Eq. 9.32, p is in bars per meter of pipe, Q is in liters per minute, and D is in millimeters.[9]

Equation 9.33: Specific Energy

$$E = \alpha \frac{\mathrm{v}^2}{2g} + y$$
$$= \frac{\alpha Q^2}{2gA^2} + y \qquad 9.33$$

Description

Specific energy, E, is a term used primarily with open channel flow. It is the total head with respect to the channel bottom. Because the channel bottom is the reference elevation for potential energy, potential energy does not contribute to specific energy; only kinetic energy and pressure energy contribute. α is the kinetic energy correction factor, which is usually equal to 1.0. The pressure head at the channel bottom is equal to the depth of the channel, y.

In *uniform flow* (flow with constant width and depth), total head decreases due to the frictional effects (e.g., elevation increase), but specific energy is constant. In nonuniform flow, total head also decreases, but specific energy may increase or decrease.

Equation 9.34 Through Eq. 9.36: Critical Depth

$$y_c = \left(\frac{q^2}{g} \right)^{1/3} \qquad 9.34$$

$$q = Q/B \qquad 9.35$$

$$\frac{Q^2}{g} = \frac{A^3}{T} \qquad 9.36$$

Description

For any channel, there is some depth of flow that will minimize the energy of flow. (The depth is not minimized, however.) This depth is known as the *critical depth, y_c*. The critical depth depends on the shape of the channel, but it is independent of the channel slope.

For rectangular channels, the critical depth can be found with Eq. 9.34. q in this equation is *unit discharge*, the flow per unit width. q is defined in Eq. 9.35 as the ratio of the flow rate, Q, to the channel width, B.

For channels with nonrectangular shapes (including trapezoidal channels), the critical depth can be found by trial and error from Eq. 9.36. T is the surface width. To use this equation, assume trial values of the critical depth, use them to calculate the dependent quantities in the equation, and then verify the equality.

Figure 9.6 illustrates how specific energy is affected by depth, and accordingly, how specific energy relates to critical depth.

Figure 9.6 Specific Energy Diagram

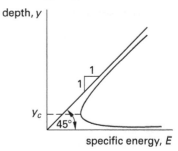

Equation 9.37 and Eq. 9.38: Froude Number

$$\mathrm{Fr} = \frac{\mathrm{v}}{\sqrt{gy_h}} \qquad 9.37$$

$$y_h = A/T \qquad 9.38$$

Description

Eq. 9.37 is the formula for the dimensionless *Froude number*, Fr, a convenient index of the flow regime. v is velocity. y_h is the *characteristic length*, also referred to as the *characteristic (length) scale, hydraulic depth,*

---

[7]In many expressions of the Hazen-Williams equation in engineering literature, including Eq. 9.31 in the *NCEES Handbook*, Q is in gallons per minute. Without an expressed statement, it is not possible to know which units are to be used.
[8]The *NCEES Handbook* is inconsistent in how it represents frictional pressure loss. p used in Eq. 9.31 is the same concept as Δp_f used in Eq. 9.19 except expressed on a per unit length basis. The units used in Eq. 9.31 are not the same as the units used in Eq. 9.30.
[9]Some of these units are traditional metric but not standard SI units. Without an expressed statement, it is not possible to know which units are to be used.

mean hydraulic depth, and others, depending on the channel configuration.[10] For a circular channel flowing half full, $y_h = \pi D/8$. For a rectangular channel, $y_h = d$, the depth corresponding to velocity v. For trapezoidal and semicircular channels, and in general, y_h is the area in flow divided by the top width.

The Froude number can be used to determine whether the flow is subcritical or supercritical. When the Froude number is less than one, the flow is subcritical. The depth of flow is greater than the critical depth, and the flow velocity is less than the critical velocity.

When the Froude number is greater than one, the flow is supercritical. The depth of flow is less than critical depth, and the flow velocity is greater than the critical velocity.

When the Froude number is equal to one, the flow is critical.[11]

Example

A 150 m long surface vessel with a speed of 40 km/h is modeled at a scale of 1:50. Similarity based on Froude numbers is appropriate for the modeling of surface vessels, so the model should travel at a speed of most nearly

(A) 0.22 m/s

(B) 1.6 m/s

(C) 2.2 m/s

(D) 16 m/s

Solution

The surface vessel and the model should have the same Froude numbers. From Eq. 9.37,

$$\text{Fr}_{\text{vessel}} = \text{Fr}_{\text{model}}$$
$$\frac{\text{v}_{\text{vessel}}}{\sqrt{gy_{h,\text{vessel}}}} = \frac{\text{v}_{\text{model}}}{\sqrt{gy_{h,\text{model}}}}$$
$$\text{v}_{\text{model}} = \text{v}_{\text{vessel}}\sqrt{\frac{y_{h,\text{model}}}{y_{h,\text{vessel}}}}$$
$$= \frac{\left(40\ \frac{\text{km}}{\text{h}}\right)\left(1000\ \frac{\text{m}}{\text{km}}\right)}{3600\ \frac{\text{s}}{\text{h}}}\sqrt{\frac{1}{50}}$$
$$= 1.57\ \text{m/s}\quad(1.6\ \text{m/s})$$

The answer is (B).

11. THE IMPULSE-MOMENTUM PRINCIPLE

The *momentum*, **P**, of a moving object is a vector quantity defined as the product of the object's mass and velocity.

$$\mathbf{P} = m\mathbf{v}$$

The *impulse*, **I**, of a constant force is calculated as the product of the force's magnitude and the length of time the force is applied.

$$\mathbf{I} = \mathbf{F}\Delta t$$

The *impulse-momentum principle* states that the impulse applied to a body is equal to the change in that body's momentum. This is one way of stating *Newton's second law*.

$$\mathbf{I} = \Delta\mathbf{P}$$

From this,

$$F\Delta t = m\Delta\text{v}$$
$$= m(\text{v}_2 - \text{v}_1)$$

For fluid flow, there is a mass flow rate, $\dot{m}$, but no mass per se. Since $\dot{m} = m/\Delta t$, the impulse-momentum equation can be rewritten as

$$F = \dot{m}\Delta\text{v}$$

Substituting for the mass flow rate, $\dot{m} = \rho A\text{v}$. The quantity $Q\rho\text{v}$ is the *rate of momentum*.

$$F = \rho A\text{v}\Delta\text{v}$$
$$= Q\rho\Delta\text{v}$$

Equation 9.39: Control Volume[12]

$$\sum F = Q_2\rho_2\text{v}_2 - Q_1\rho_1\text{v}_1 \qquad 9.39$$

Description

Eq. 9.39 results from applying the impulse-momentum principle to a control volume. $\sum F$ is the resultant of all external forces acting on the control volume. $Q_1\rho_1\text{v}_1$ and $Q_2\rho_2\text{v}_2$ represent the rate of momentum of the fluid entering and leaving the control volume, respectively, in the same direction as the force.

---

[10]The *NCEES Handbook* uses both H and h as subscripts to designate "hydraulic."
[11]The similarity of the Froude number to the Mach number used to classify gas flows is more than coincidental. The two bodies of knowledge employ parallel concepts.
[12]While any symbol can be used to represent any quantity, the use of bold letters is usually reserved for vector quantities. The *NCEES Handbook* uses bold *F* to designate force in its fluid dynamics section. While force can indeed be a vector quantity, the fluid equations in this section are not vector equations. *F* in text and **F** in illustrations should be interpreted as *F*, as it is presented in this book.

12. PIPE BENDS, ENLARGEMENTS, AND CONTRACTIONS

The impulse-momentum principle illustrates that fluid momentum is not always conserved when the fluid is acted upon by an external force. Examples of external forces are gravity (considered zero for horizontal pipes), gage pressure, friction, and turning forces from walls and vanes. Only if these external forces are absent is fluid momentum conserved.

When a fluid enters a pipe fitting or bend, as illustrated in Fig. 9.7, momentum is changed. Since the fluid is confined, the forces due to static pressure must be included in the analysis. The effects of gravity and friction are neglected.

Figure 9.7 *Forces on a Pipe Bend*

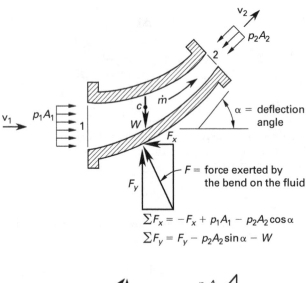

$$\sum F_x = -F_x + p_1A_1 - p_2A_2\cos\alpha$$
$$\sum F_y = F_y - p_2A_2\sin\alpha - W$$

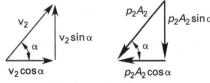

Equation 9.40 Through Eq. 9.43: Forces on Pipe Bends

$$p_1A_1 - p_2A_2\cos\alpha - F_x = Q\rho(v_2\cos\alpha - v_1) \qquad 9.40$$

$$F_y - W - p_2A_2\sin\alpha = Q\rho(v_2\sin\alpha - 0) \qquad 9.41$$

$$F = \sqrt{F_x^2 + F_y^2} \qquad 9.42$$

$$\theta = \tan^{-1}\frac{F_y}{F_x} \qquad 9.43$$

Variations

$$-F_x = p_2A_2\cos\alpha - p_1A_1 + Q\rho(v_2\cos\alpha - v_1)$$

$$F_y = (p_2A_2 + Q\rho v_2)\sin\alpha + m_{\text{fluid}}g \quad \begin{bmatrix} \text{fluid weight} \\ \text{included} \end{bmatrix}$$

Description

Applying Eq. 9.39 to the fluid in the pipe bend in Fig. 9.7 gives these equations for the force of the bend on the fluid. m_{fluid} and $W_{\text{fluid}} = m_{\text{fluid}}g$ are the mass and weight, respectively, of the fluid in the bend (often neglected). Equation 9.40 is the thrust equation for a pipe bend. The resultant force is calculated from Eq. 9.42. The value of the angle θ is found from Eq. 9.43.

Example

A 1 m penstock is anchored by a thrust block at a point where the flow makes a 20° change in direction. The water flow rate is 5.25 m³/s. The water pressure is 140 kPa everywhere in the penstock. If the initial flow direction is parallel to the x-direction, the magnitude of the force on the thrust block in the x-direction is most nearly

(A) 6.8 kN

(B) 8.3 kN

(C) 8.7 kN

(D) 9.2 kN

Solution

The pipe area is

$$A = \frac{\pi D^2}{4}$$
$$= \frac{\pi(1\ \text{m})^2}{4}$$
$$= 0.7854\ \text{m}^2$$

The velocity is

$$v = \frac{Q}{A}$$
$$= \frac{5.25\ \dfrac{\text{m}^3}{\text{s}}}{0.7854\ \text{m}^2}$$
$$= 6.68\ \text{m/s}$$

Use the thrust equation for a pipe bend, Eq. 9.40.

$$p_1 A_1 - p_2 A_2 \cos\alpha - F_x = Q\rho(v_2 \cos\alpha - v_1)$$
$$-F_x = p_2 A_2 \cos\alpha - p_1 A_1$$
$$+ Q\rho(v_2 \cos\alpha - v_1)$$
$$= (1.4 \times 10^5 \text{ Pa})(0.7854 \text{ m}^2)$$
$$\times (\cos 20° - 1)$$
$$+ \left(5.25 \ \frac{\text{m}^3}{\text{s}}\right)\left(1000 \ \frac{\text{kg}}{\text{m}^3}\right)$$
$$\times \left(6.68 \ \frac{\text{m}}{\text{s}}\right)$$
$$\times (\cos 20° - 1)$$
$$= -8748 \text{ N} \quad (8.7 \text{ kN})$$

The answer is (C).

13. JET PROPULSION[13]

A basic application of the impulse-momentum principle is *jet propulsion*. The velocity of a fluid jet issuing from an orifice in a tank can be determined by comparing the total energies at the free fluid surface and at the jet itself. (See Fig. 9.8.) At the fluid surface, $p_1 = 0$ (atmospheric) and $v_1 = 0$. The only energy the fluid has is potential energy. At the jet, $p_2 = 0$ and $z_2 = 0$. All of the potential energy difference has been converted to kinetic energy. The change in momentum of the fluid produces a force.

Impulse due to a constant force, F, acting over a duration Δt, is $F\Delta t$. The change in momentum of a constant mass is $m\Delta v$. The developed force can be derived from the impulse-momentum principle.

$$F\Delta t = m\Delta v$$
$$F = \frac{m}{\Delta t}\Delta v = \dot{m}v_2$$

Figure 9.8 Fluid Jet Issuing from a Tank Orifice

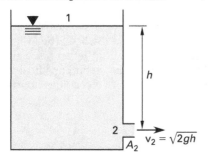

Equation 9.44 Through Eq. 9.47: Discharge from an Orifice

$$F = Q\rho(v_2 - 0) \qquad 9.44$$

$$F = 2\gamma h A_2 \qquad 9.45$$

$$Q = A_2\sqrt{2gh} \qquad 9.46$$

$$v_2 = \sqrt{2gh} \qquad 9.47$$

Description

The governing equations for reaction force due to discharge from an orifice are Eq. 9.44 and Eq. 9.45.

For the Bernoulli equation (see Eq. 9.4 and Eq. 9.5), it is easy to calculate the initial jet velocity (known as *Torricelli's speed of efflux*), Eq. 9.47.

14. DEFLECTORS AND BLADES

Equation 9.48 and Eq. 9.49: Fixed Blade

$$-F_x = Q\rho(v_2 \cos\alpha - v_1) \qquad 9.48$$

$$F_y = Q\rho(v_2 \sin\alpha - 0) \qquad 9.49$$

Description

Fig. 9.9 illustrates a fluid jet being turned through an angle, α, by a *fixed blade* (also called a *fixed* or *stationary vane*). It is common to assume that $|v_2| = |v_1|$, although this will not be strictly true if friction between the blade and fluid is considered. Since the fluid is both retarded (in the x-direction) and accelerated (in the y-direction), there will be two components of blade force on the fluid.

Figure 9.9 Open Jet on a Stationary Blade

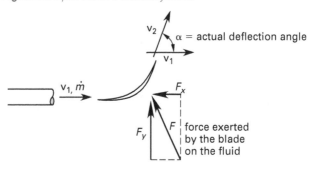

---

[13]"Jet propulsion" is probably too generic a description since this is a special case of a *reaction force* due to a liquid discharging from an orifice.

Equation 9.50 Through Eq. 9.53: Moving Blade

$$-F_x = Q\rho(v_{2x} - v_{1x}) \qquad 9.50$$

$$-F_x = -Q\rho(v_1 - v)(1 - \cos\alpha) \qquad 9.51$$

$$F_y = Q\rho(v_{2y} - v_{1y}) \qquad 9.52$$

$$F_y = +Q\rho(v_1 - v)\sin\alpha \qquad 9.53$$

Variation

$$F_y = \frac{Q\rho(v_1 - v)\sin\alpha}{g_c}$$

Description

If a blade is moving away at velocity v from the source of the fluid jet, only the *relative velocity difference* between the jet and blade produces a momentum change. Furthermore, not all of the fluid jet overtakes the moving blade. (See Fig. 9.10.)

Figure 9.10 Open Jet on a Moving Blade

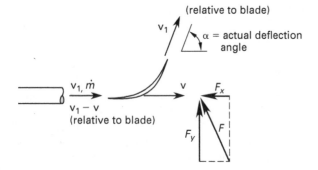

Example

A water jet impinges upon a retreating blade at a velocity of 10 m/s and mass rate of 1 kg/s, as shown.

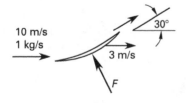

If the blade velocity is a constant 3 m/s, the magnitude of the force, F, that the blade imposes on the jet is most nearly

(A) 2.8 N

(B) 3.6 N

(C) 4.7 N

(D) 6.1 N

Solution

Using Eq. 9.51, find the x-component of the force.

$$
\begin{aligned}
-F_x &= -Q\rho(v_1 - v)(1 - \cos\alpha) \\
&= -\dot{m}(v_1 - v)(1 - \cos\alpha) \\
&= -\left(1 \ \frac{\text{kg}}{\text{s}}\right)\left(10 \ \frac{\text{m}}{\text{s}} - 3 \ \frac{\text{m}}{\text{s}}\right)(1 - \cos 30°) \\
&= -0.9378 \text{ N}
\end{aligned}
$$

Find the y-component of the force from Eq. 9.53.

$$
\begin{aligned}
F_y &= +Q\rho(v_1 - v)\sin\alpha \\
&= \dot{m}(v_1 - v)\sin\alpha \\
&= \left(1 \ \frac{\text{kg}}{\text{s}}\right)\left(10 \ \frac{\text{m}}{\text{s}} - 3 \ \frac{\text{m}}{\text{s}}\right)\sin 30° \\
&= 3.5 \text{ N}
\end{aligned}
$$

From Eq. 9.42, the magnitude of the force is

$$
\begin{aligned}
F &= \sqrt{F_x^2 + F_y^2} \\
&= \sqrt{(-0.9378 \text{ N})^2 + (3.5 \text{ N})^2} \\
&= 3.62 \text{ N} \quad (3.6 \text{ N})
\end{aligned}
$$

The answer is (B).

15. IMPULSE TURBINE

An *impulse turbine* consists of a series of blades (buckets or vanes) mounted around a wheel. (See Fig. 9.11.) The power transferred from a fluid jet to the blades of a turbine is calculated from the x-component of force on the blades. The y-component of force does no work. v is the tangential blade velocity.

Figure 9.11 *Impulse Turbine*

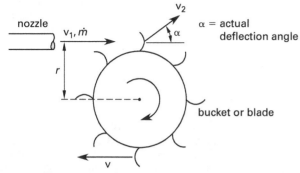

tangental blade velocity: $v = \dfrac{\text{rpm} \times 2\pi r}{60}$

Equation 9.54 Through Eq. 9.56: Power from an Impulse Turbine

$$\dot{W} = Q\rho(v_1 - v)(1 - \cos\alpha)v \qquad 9.54$$

$$\dot{W}_{max} = Q\rho(v_1^2/4)(1 - \cos\alpha) \qquad 9.55$$

$$\dot{W}_{max} = (Q\rho v_1^2)/2$$
$$= (Q\gamma v_1^2)/2g \quad [\alpha = 180°] \qquad 9.56$$

Description

The maximum theoretical tangential blade velocity is the velocity of the jet: $v = v_1$. This is known as the *runaway speed* and can only occur when the turbine is unloaded. If Eq. 9.54 is maximized with respect to v, however, the maximum power will be found to occur when the blade is traveling at half of the jet velocity: $v = v_1/2$. The power (force) is also affected by the deflection angle of the blade. Power is maximized when $\alpha = 180°$. Figure 9.12 illustrates the relationship between power and the variables α and v.

Equation 9.56 is a simplified version of Eq. 9.55, derived by substituting $\alpha = 180°$ and $v = v_1/2$.

Figure 9.12 *Turbine Power*

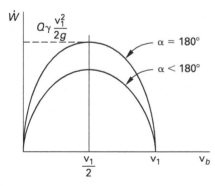

Example

A 200 kg/s stream of water leaves a nozzle and strikes a bucket whose angle is 120° from the horizontal. The total head as the water leaves the nozzle is 15 m, and the 25 cm diameter turbine runner is turning at 500 rpm. The power produced is most nearly

(A) 9.3 kW

(B) 14 kW

(C) 21 kW

(D) 32 kW

Solution

The radius of the turbine runner is

$$r = \frac{D}{2} = \frac{25 \text{ cm}}{(2)\left(100 \dfrac{\text{cm}}{\text{m}}\right)} = 0.125 \text{ m}$$

The blade velocity is

$$v = \frac{\text{rpm} \times 2\pi r}{60}$$
$$= \frac{\left(500 \dfrac{\text{rev}}{\text{min}}\right)2\pi(0.125 \text{ m})}{60 \dfrac{\text{s}}{\text{min}}}$$
$$= 6.54 \text{ m/s}$$

From Eq. 9.47, the velocity of the stream is

$$v_1 = \sqrt{2gh}$$
$$= \sqrt{(2)\left(9.81 \dfrac{\text{m}}{\text{s}^2}\right)(15 \text{ m})}$$
$$= 17.16 \text{ m/s}$$

Use Eq. 9.54 to find the power produced.

$$\dot{W} = Q\rho(v_1 - v)(1 - \cos\alpha)v$$
$$= \dot{m}(v_1 - v)(1 - \cos\alpha)v$$
$$= \left(200 \dfrac{\text{kg}}{\text{s}}\right)\left(17.16 \dfrac{\text{m}}{\text{s}} - 6.54 \dfrac{\text{m}}{\text{s}}\right)$$
$$\quad \times (1 - \cos 120°)\left(6.54 \dfrac{\text{m}}{\text{s}}\right)$$
$$= 20\,833 \text{ W} \quad (21 \text{ kW})$$

The answer is (C).

16. DRAG

Equation 9.57: Drag Force

$$F_D = \frac{C_D \rho v^2 A}{2} \qquad \text{9.57}$$

Description

Drag is a frictional force that acts parallel but opposite to the direction of motion. Drag is made up of several components (e.g., skin friction and pressure drag), but the total drag force can be calculated from a dimensionless *drag coefficient*, C_D. Dimensional analysis shows that the drag coefficient depends only on the Reynolds number.

In most cases, the area, A, to be used is the projected area (i.e., the frontal area) normal to the stream. This is appropriate for spheres, disks, and vehicles. It is also appropriate for cylinders and ellipsoids that are oriented such that their longitudinal axes are perpendicular to the flow. In a few cases (e.g., airfoils and flat plates parallel to the flow), the area is the projection of the object onto a plane parallel to the stream.

Equation 9.58 and Eq. 9.59: Drag Coefficients for Flat Plates Parallel with the Flow

$$C_D = 1.33/\text{Re}^{0.5} \quad [10^4 < \text{Re} < 5 \times 10^5] \qquad \text{9.58}$$

$$C_D = 0.031/\text{Re}^{1/7} \quad [10^6 < \text{Re} < 10^9] \qquad \text{9.59}$$

Description

Drag coefficients vary considerably with Reynolds numbers, often showing regions of distinctly different behavior. For that reason, the drag coefficient is often plotted. (Fig. 9.13 illustrates the drag coefficient for spheres and circular flat disks oriented perpendicular to the flow.) Semiempirical equations can be used to calculate drag coefficients as long as the applicable ranges of Reynolds numbers are stated. For example, for flat plates placed parallel to the flow, Eq. 9.58 and Eq. 9.59 can be used.

Equation 9.58 and Eq. 9.59 calculate the drag coefficient for one side of a plate. If the drag force for an entire plate is needed (the usual case), the drag force calculated from Eq. 9.57 would be doubled.

Equation 9.58 and Eq. 9.59 represent the average *skin friction coefficient* over an entire plate length, L, measured parallel to the flow moving with *far-field* (undisturbed) *velocity*, v_∞. The value of the local skin friction coefficient varies along the length of the plate.

Whether to use Eq. 9.58 or Eq. 9.59 depends on the length of the plate, which in turn affects the Reynolds number. In skin friction calculations, the laminar flow regime extends up to a Reynolds number of approximately 5×10^5. Equation 9.58 is valid for laminar flow, while Eq. 9.59 is valid for turbulent flow. For long plates, both regimes are present simultaneously with a *transition region* in between, although Eq. 9.59 takes that into consideration in its averaging.

$$\begin{aligned} \text{Re} &= \frac{\rho v_\infty L}{\mu} \\ &= \frac{v_\infty L}{\nu} \end{aligned}$$

Equation 9.60 and Eq. 9.61: Drag Coefficient for Airfoils

$$C_D = C_{D\infty} + \frac{C_L^2}{\pi AR} \qquad \text{9.60}$$

$$AR = \frac{b^2}{A_p} = \frac{A_p}{c^2} \qquad \text{9.61}$$

Variations

$$AR = \frac{b}{c}$$

$$A_p = bc$$

Description

Drag force also acts on airfoils parallel but opposite to the direction of motion. The drag coefficient for airfoils is approximated by Eq. 9.60. $C_{D\infty}$ is the *drag coefficient at zero lift*, also known as the *zero lift drag coefficient* and *infinite span drag coefficient*. C_L is the lift coefficient.[14] This value is determined by the type of object in motion.

The dimensions of an airfoil or wing are frequently given in terms of chord length and aspect ratio. The *chord length*, c, is the front-to-back dimension of the airfoil. The *aspect ratio*, AR, is the ratio of the *span* (wing length) to chord length.[15] The area, A_p, in Eq. 9.61 is the airfoil's area projected onto the plane of the chord. For a rectangular airfoil, $A_p = $ chord $\times$ span.

---

[14]The drag coefficient at zero lift is traditionally (and, almost universally) represented by the symbol $C_{D,0}$ or similar. The *NCEES Handbook* calls this the "infinite span drag coefficient" and uses the symbol $C_{D\infty}$, both practices of which are unusual and confusing. For an infinite span, the aspect ratio will be infinitely large, and Eq. 9.60 will reduce to an "infinite span drag coefficient" by definition. Since Eq. 9.60 is for an airfoil, the exclusion of the *wing span efficiency factor* (*Oswald efficiency factor*) without identifying the wing as having an elliptical shape is misleading.

[15]The nomenclature used by the *NCEES Handbook* for aspect ratio makes it difficult to distinguish AR from $A \times R$, except through context.

Figure 9.13 *Drag Coefficients for Spheres and Circular Flat Disks*

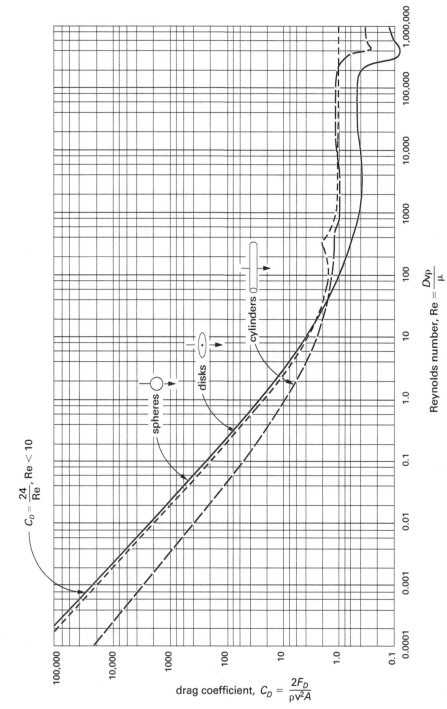

Note: Intermediate divisions are 2, 4, 6, and 8.

17. LIFT

Lift is a force that is exerted on an object (flat plate, airfoil, rotating cylinder, etc.) as the object passes through a fluid. Lift combines with drag to form the resultant force on the object, as shown in Fig. 9.14.

Figure 9.14 *Lift and Drag on an Airfoil*

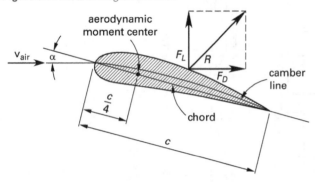

The generation of lift from air flowing over an airfoil is predicted by the Bernoulli equation. Air molecules must travel a longer distance over the top surface of the airfoil than over the lower surface, and, therefore, they travel faster over the top surface. Since the total energy of the air is constant, the increase in kinetic energy comes at the expense of pressure energy. The static pressure on the top of the airfoil is reduced, and a net upward force is produced.

Within practical limits, the lift produced can be increased at lower speeds by increasing the curvature of the wing. This increased curvature is achieved by the use of *flaps*. (See Fig. 9.15.) When a plane is traveling slowly (e.g., during takeoff or landing), its flaps are extended to create the lift needed.

Figure 9.15 *Use of Flaps in an Airfoil*

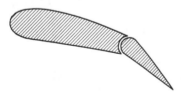

Equation 9.62: Lift Force

$$F_L = \frac{C_L \rho \mathrm{v}^2 A_p}{2} \qquad 9.62$$

Description

The lift produced, F_L, can be calculated from Eq. 9.62, whose use is not limited to airfoils.

Equation 9.63: Coefficient of Lift (Flat Plate)

$$C_L = 2\pi k_1 \sin(\alpha + \beta) \qquad 9.63$$

Description

The dimensionless *coefficient of lift*, C_L, is used to measure the effectiveness of the airfoil. The coefficient of lift depends on the shape of the airfoil and the Reynolds number. No simple relationship can be given for calculating the coefficient of lift for airfoils, but the theoretical coefficient of lift for a thin plate in two-dimensional flow at a low *angle of attack*, α, is given by Eq. 9.63.[16] Actual airfoils are able to achieve only 80–90% of this theoretical value. k_1 is a constant of proportionality, and β is the negative of the angle of attack for zero lift.[17]

For various reasons (primarily wingtip vortices), real airfoils of finite length generate a small amount of *downwash*. This downwash reduces the *geometric angle of attack* (or equivalently, reduces the coefficient of lift) slightly by the *induced (drag) angle of attack*, resulting in an *effective angle of attack*. Equation 9.63 conveys this reduction in angle of attack and is an important part of *Prandtl lifting-line theory*.[18]

$$\alpha_{\text{effective}} = \alpha_{\text{geometric}} - \alpha_{\text{induced}}$$

The coefficient of lift for an airfoil cannot be increased without limit merely by increasing α. Eventually, the *stall angle* is reached, at which point the coefficient of lift decreases dramatically. (See Fig. 9.16.)

Figure 9.16 *Typical Plot of Lift Coefficient*

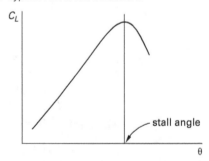

Equation 9.64: Aerodynamic Moment

$$M = \frac{C_M \rho \mathrm{v}^2 A_p c}{2} \qquad 9.64$$

Description

The *aerodynamic moment (pitching moment)*, M, is applied at the aerodynamic center of an airfoil. It is calculated at the quarter point using Eq. 9.64. C_M is the moment coefficient.

---

[16]The angle of attack is the geometric angle between the relative wind and the straight chord line, as shown in Fig. 9.14.
[17]k_1 in Eq. 9.63 in the *NCEES Handbook* is not the same as k_1 in Eq. 9.29.
[18]Rather than simply showing a subtraction operation, the *NCEES Handbook* combines the induced angle of attack with the mathematical operation by referring to it as "the negative of the angle of attack for zero lift."

10 Fluid Measurement and Similitude

Nomenclature

A	area	m^2
C	coefficient	–
Ca	Cauchy number	–
d	depth	m
D	diameter	m
E	specific energy	J/kg
F	force	N
Fr	Froude number	–
g	gravitational acceleration, 9.81	m/s^2
h	head	m
h	head loss	m
h	height	m
l	characteristic length	m
p	pressure	Pa
Q	flow rate	m^3/s
Re	Reynolds number	–
v	velocity	m/s
We	Weber number	–
z	elevation	m

Symbols

γ	specific (unit) weight	N/m^3
μ	absolute viscosity	Pa·s
ρ	density	kg/m^3
σ	surface tension	N/m

Subscripts

0	stagnation (zero velocity)
c	contraction
E	elastic
G	gravitational
I	inertial
m	manometer fluid or model
p	constant pressure or prototype
s	static
T	surface tension
v	velocity
v	constant volume

1. PITOT TUBE

A *pitot tube* is simply a hollow tube that is placed longitudinally in the direction of fluid flow, allowing the flow to enter one end at the fluid's *velocity of approach*. (See Fig. 10.1.) A pitot tube is used to measure velocity of flow.

Figure 10.1 Pitot Tube

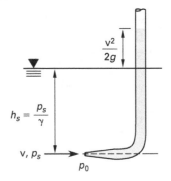

When the fluid enters the pitot tube, it is forced to come to a stop (at the *stagnation point*), and its kinetic energy is transformed into static pressure energy.

Equation 10.1: Fluid Velocity[1]

$$v = \sqrt{(2/\rho)(p_0 - p_s)} = \sqrt{2g(p_0 - p_s)/\gamma} \qquad 10.1$$

---

[1]As used in the NCEES *FE Reference Handbook* (*NCEES Handbook*), there is no significance to the inconsistent placement of the density terms in the two forms of Eq. 10.1.

Description

The Bernoulli equation can be used to predict the static pressure at the stagnation point. Since the velocity of the fluid within the pitot tube is zero, the upstream velocity can be calculated if the *static*, p_s, and *stagnation*, p_0, *pressures* are known.

$$\frac{p_s}{\rho} + \frac{v^2}{2} = \frac{p_0}{\rho}$$

$$\frac{p_s}{\gamma} + \frac{v^2}{2g} = \frac{p_0}{\gamma}$$

In reality, the fluid may be compressible. If the Mach number is less than approximately 0.3, Eq. 10.1 for incompressible fluids may be used.

Example

The density of air flowing in a duct is 1.15 kg/m³. A pitot tube is placed in the duct as shown. The static pressure in the duct is measured with a wall tap and pressure gage.

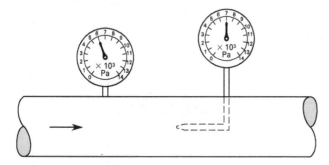

From the gage readings, the velocity of the air is most nearly

    (A)   42 m/s

    (B)   100 m/s

    (C)   110 m/s

    (D)   150 m/s

Solution

The static pressure is read from the first static pressure gage as 6000 Pa. The impact pressure is 7000 Pa. From Eq. 10.1,

$$v = \sqrt{(2/\rho)(p_0 - p_s)}$$

$$= \sqrt{\left(\frac{2}{1.15 \ \frac{\text{kg}}{\text{m}^3}}\right)(7000 \text{ Pa} - 6000 \text{ Pa})}$$

$$= 41.7 \text{ m/s} \quad (42 \text{ m/s})$$

The answer is (A).

2. VENTURI METER

Figure 10.2 illustrates a simple *venturi meter*. This flow-measuring device can be inserted directly into a pipeline. Since the diameter changes are gradual, there is very little friction loss. Static pressure measurements are taken at the throat and upstream of the diameter change. The difference in these pressures is directly indicated by a *differential manometer*.

The pressure differential across the venturi meter shown can be calculated from the following equations.

$$p_1 - p_2 = (\rho_m - \rho)gh_m = (\gamma_m - \gamma)h_m$$

$$\frac{p_1 - p_2}{\rho} = \left(\frac{\rho_m}{\rho} - 1\right)gh_m$$

$$\frac{p_1 - p_2}{\gamma} = \left(\frac{\gamma_m}{\gamma} - 1\right)h_m$$

Figure 10.2 Venturi Meter with Differential Manometer

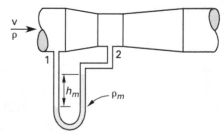

Equation 10.2: Flow Rate Through Venturi Meter

$$Q = \frac{C_v A_2}{\sqrt{1 - (A_2/A_1)^2}} \sqrt{2g\left(\frac{p_1}{\gamma} + z_1 - \frac{p_2}{\gamma} - z_2\right)} \qquad 10.2$$

Variation

$$Q = \frac{C_v A_2}{\sqrt{1 - \left(\frac{A_2}{A_1}\right)^2}} \sqrt{2\left(\frac{p_1}{\rho} + z_1 - \frac{p_2}{\rho} - z_2\right)}$$

Values

The *coefficient of velocity*, C_v, accounts for the small effect of friction and is very close to 1.0, usually 0.98 or 0.99.

Description

The flow rate, Q, can be calculated from venturi measurements using Eq. 10.2. For a horizontal venturi meter, $z_1 = z_2$. The quotients, p/γ, in Eq. 10.2 represent the heads of the fluid flowing through a venturi meter. Therefore, the specific weight, γ, of the fluid should be used, not the specific weight of the manometer fluid.

Example

A venturi meter is installed horizontally to measure the flow of water in a pipe. The area ratio of the meter, A_2/A_1, is 0.5, the velocity through the throat of the meter is 3 m/s, and the coefficient of velocity is 0.98. The pressure differential across the venturi meter is most nearly

(A)   1.5 kPa

(B)   2.3 kPa

(C)   3.5 kPa

(D)   6.8 kPa

Solution

From Eq. 10.2, for a venturi meter,

$$Q = \frac{C_v A_2}{\sqrt{1 - (A_2/A_1)^2}} \sqrt{2g\left(\frac{p_1}{\gamma} + z_1 - \frac{p_2}{\gamma} - z_2\right)}$$

Dividing both sides by the area at the throat, A_2, gives

$$\frac{Q}{A_2} = v_2 = \frac{C_v}{\sqrt{1 - \left(\frac{A_2}{A_1}\right)^2}} \sqrt{2g\left(\frac{p_1}{\gamma} + z_1 - \frac{p_2}{\gamma} - z_2\right)}$$

Since the venturi meter is horizontal, $z_1 = z_2$. Reducing and solving for the pressure differential gives

$$
\begin{aligned}
p_1 - p_2 &= \frac{v_2^2\left[1 - \left(\frac{A_2}{A_1}\right)^2\right]\gamma}{2gC_v^2} \\[2mm]
&= \frac{\left(3\ \frac{m}{s}\right)^2 (1 - (0.5)^2)\left(9.81\ \frac{kN}{m^3}\right)\left(1000\ \frac{N}{kN}\right)}{(2)\left(9.81\ \frac{m}{s^2}\right)(0.98)^2} \\[2mm]
&= 3514\ \text{Pa} \quad (3.5\ \text{kPa})
\end{aligned}
$$

The answer is (C).

3. ORIFICE METER

The *orifice meter* (or *orifice plate*) is used more frequently than the venturi meter to measure flow rates in small pipes. It consists of a thin or sharp-edged plate with a central, round hole through which the fluid flows.

As with the venturi meter, pressure taps are used to obtain the static pressure upstream of the orifice plate and at the *vena contracta* (i.e., at the point of minimum area and minimum pressure). A differential manometer connected to the two taps conveniently indicates the difference in static pressures. The pressure differential equations, derived for the manometer in Fig. 10.2, are also valid for the manometer configuration of the orifice shown in Fig. 10.3.

Figure 10.3 Orifice Meter with Differential Manometer

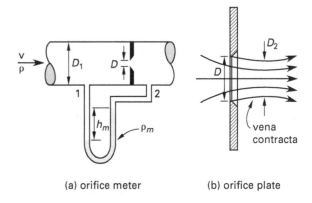

(a) orifice meter   (b) orifice plate

Fluid Mechanics

Equation 10.3: Orifice Area

$$A_2 = C_c A \qquad 10.3$$

Description

The area of the orifice is A, and the area of the pipeline is A_1. The area at the vena contracta, A_2, can be calculated from the orifice area and the *coefficient of contraction*, C_c, using Eq. 10.3.

Equation 10.4: Coefficient of the Meter (Orifice Plate)[2]

$$C = \frac{C_v C_c}{\sqrt{1 - C_c^2 (A_0/A_1)^2}} \qquad 10.4$$

Description

The *coefficient of the meter*, C, combines the coefficients of velocity and contraction in a way that corrects the theoretical discharge of the meter for frictional flow and for contraction at the vena contracta. The coefficient of the meter is also known as the *flow coefficient*.[3] Approximate orifice coefficients are listed in Table 10.1.

Table 10.1 *Approximate Orifice Coefficients for Turbulent Water*

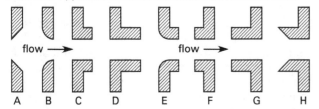

illustration	description	C	C_c	C_v
A	sharp-edged	0.61	0.62	0.98
B	round-edged	0.98	1.00	0.98
C	short tube (fluid separates from walls)	0.61	1.00	0.61
D	short tube (no separation)	0.80	1.00	0.80
E	short tube with rounded entrance	0.97	0.99	0.98
F	reentrant tube, length less than one-half of pipe diameter	0.54	0.55	0.99
G	reentrant tube, length 2–3 pipe diameters	0.72	1.00	0.72
H	Borda	0.51	0.52	0.98
(none)	smooth, well-tapered nozzle	0.98	0.99	0.99

Equation 10.5: Flow Through Orifice Plate

$$Q = C A_0 \sqrt{2g\left(\frac{p_1}{\gamma} + z_1 - \frac{p_2}{\gamma} - z_2\right)} \qquad 10.5$$

Variation

$$Q = C A_0 \sqrt{2\left(\frac{p_1}{\rho} + z_1 - \frac{p_2}{\rho} - z_2\right)}$$

Description

The flow rate through the orifice meter is given by Eq. 10.5. Generally, z_1 and z_2 are equal.

4. SUBMERGED ORIFICE

The flow rate of a jet issuing from a *submerged orifice* in a tank can be determined by modifying Eq. 10.5 in terms of the potential energy difference, or head difference, on either side of the orifice. (See Fig. 10.4.)

Figure 10.4 *Submerged Orifice*

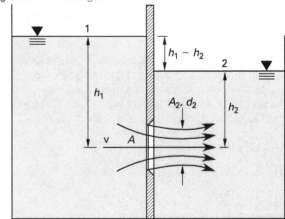

[2]The *NCEES Handbook*'s use of the symbol C for coefficient of the meter is ambiguous. In literature describing orifice plate performance, when C_d is not used, C is frequently reserved for the coefficient of discharge. The symbols C_M, C_F (for coefficient of the meter and *flow coefficient*), K, and F are typically used to avoid ambiguity.
[3]The *NCEES Handbook* lists "orifice coefficient" as a synonym for the "coefficient of the meter." However, this ambiguous usage should be avoided, as four orifice coefficients are attributed to an orifice: coefficient of contraction, coefficient of velocity, coefficient of discharge, and coefficient of resistance.

Equation 10.6 Through Eq. 10.8: Flow Through Submerged Orifice[4]

$$Q = A_2 v_2 = C_c C_v A \sqrt{2g(h_1 - h_2)} \qquad 10.6$$

$$Q = CA \sqrt{2g(h_1 - h_2)} \qquad 10.7$$

$$C = C_c C_v \qquad 10.8$$

Description

The coefficients of velocity and contraction can be combined into the *coefficient of discharge*, C, calculated from Eq. 10.8.

5. ORIFICE DISCHARGING FREELY INTO ATMOSPHERE

If the orifice discharges from a tank into the atmosphere, Eq. 10.7 can be further simplified. (See Fig. 10.5.)

Figure 10.5 Orifice Discharging Freely into the Atmosphere

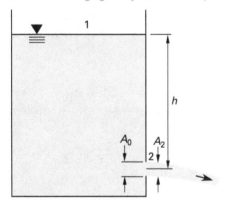

Equation 10.9: Orifice Flow with Free Discharge

$$Q = CA_0 \sqrt{2gh} \qquad 10.9$$

Variation

$$v_2 = \frac{Q}{A_2} = C_v \sqrt{2gh}$$

Description

A_0 is the orifice area. A_2 is the area at the vena contracta (see Eq. 10.3 and Fig. 10.5).

Example

Water under an 18 m head discharges freely into the atmosphere through a 25 mm diameter orifice. The orifice is round-edged and has a coefficient of discharge of 0.98.

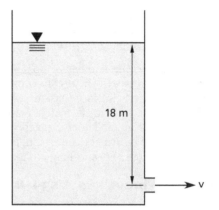

The velocity of the water as it passes through the orifice is most nearly

(A) 1.2 m/s

(B) 3.2 m/s

(C) 8.2 m/s

(D) 18 m/s

Solution

From Eq. 10.9, for an orifice discharging freely into the atmosphere,

$$Q = CA_0 \sqrt{2gh}$$

Dividing both sides by A_0 gives

$$
\begin{aligned}
v &= C\sqrt{2gh} \\
&= 0.98 \sqrt{(2)\left(9.81 \ \frac{m}{s^2}\right)(18 \ m)} \\
&= 18.4 \ m/s \quad (18 \ m/s)
\end{aligned}
$$

The answer is (D).

6. SIMILITUDE

Similarity considerations between a *model* (subscript m) and a full-size object (subscript p, for *prototype*) imply that the model can be used to predict the performance of the prototype. Such a model is said to be *mechanically similar* to the prototype.

---

[4]The *NCEES Handbook*'s use of the symbol C for both coefficient of discharge (submerged orifice) and coefficient of the meter (see Eq. 10.4) makes it difficult to determine the meaning of C.

Fluid Mechanics

Complete mechanical similarity requires geometric, kinematic, and dynamic similarity. *Geometric similarity* means that the model is true to scale in length, area, and volume. *Kinematic similarity* requires that the flow regimes of the model and prototype be the same. *Dynamic similarity* means that the ratios of all types of forces are equal for the model and the prototype. These forces result from inertia, gravity, viscosity, elasticity (i.e., fluid compressibility), surface tension, and pressure.

For dynamic similarity, the number of possible ratios of forces is large. For example, the ratios of viscosity/inertia, inertia/gravity, and inertia/surface tension are only three of the ratios of forces that must match for every corresponding point on the model and prototype. Fortunately, some force ratios can be neglected because the forces are negligible or are self-canceling.

Equation 10.10 Through Eq. 10.14: Dynamic Similarity[5]

$$\left[\frac{F_I}{F_p}\right]_p = \left[\frac{F_I}{F_p}\right]_m = \left[\frac{\rho \mathrm{v}^2}{p}\right]_p = \left[\frac{\rho \mathrm{v}^2}{p}\right]_m \qquad \textit{10.10}$$

$$\left[\frac{F_I}{F_V}\right]_p = \left[\frac{F_I}{F_V}\right]_m = \left[\frac{\mathrm{v}l\rho}{\mu}\right]_p = \left[\frac{\mathrm{v}l\rho}{\mu}\right]_m = [\mathrm{Re}]_p = [\mathrm{Re}]_m \qquad \textit{10.11}$$

$$\left[\frac{F_I}{F_G}\right]_p = \left[\frac{F_I}{F_G}\right]_m = \left[\frac{\mathrm{v}^2}{lg}\right]_p = \left[\frac{\mathrm{v}^2}{lg}\right]_m = [\mathrm{Fr}]_p = [\mathrm{Fr}]_m \qquad \textit{10.12}$$

$$\left[\frac{F_I}{F_E}\right]_p = \left[\frac{F_I}{F_E}\right]_m = \left[\frac{\rho \mathrm{v}^2}{E_v}\right]_p = \left[\frac{\rho \mathrm{v}^2}{E_v}\right]_m = [\mathrm{Ca}]_p = [\mathrm{Ca}]_m \qquad \textit{10.13}$$

$$\left[\frac{F_I}{F_T}\right]_p = \left[\frac{F_I}{F_T}\right]_m = \left[\frac{\rho l \mathrm{v}^2}{\sigma}\right]_p = \left[\frac{\rho l \mathrm{v}^2}{\sigma}\right]_m = [\mathrm{We}]_p = [\mathrm{We}]_m \qquad \textit{10.14}$$

Description

If Eq. 10.10 through Eq. 10.14 are satisfied for model and prototype, complete dynamic similarity will be achieved. In practice, it is rare to be able (or to even attempt) to demonstrate *complete similarity*. Usually, *partial similarity* is based on only one similarity law, and correlations, experience, and general rules of thumb are used to modify the results. For completely submerged objects (i.e., where there is no free surface), such as torpedoes in water and aircraft in the atmosphere, similarity is usually based on Reynolds numbers. For objects partially submerged and experiencing wave activity, such as surface ships, open channels, spillways, weirs, and hydraulic jumps, partial similarity is usually based on Froude numbers.

Example

A 200 m long submarine is being designed to travel underwater at 3 m/s. The corresponding underwater speed for a 6 m model is most nearly

   (A)   0.5 m/s

   (B)   2 m/s

   (C)   100 m/s

   (D)   200 m/s

Solution

The Reynolds numbers should be equal for model and prototype. From Eq. 10.11,

$$\left[\frac{F_I}{F_V}\right]_p = \left[\frac{F_I}{F_V}\right]_m = \left[\frac{\mathrm{v}l\rho}{\mu}\right]_p = \left[\frac{\mathrm{v}l\rho}{\mu}\right]_m = [\mathrm{Re}]_p = [\mathrm{Re}]_m$$

The density and absolute viscosity of the water will be the same for both prototype and model, so

$$\mathrm{v}_p l_p = \mathrm{v}_m l_m$$

$$\mathrm{v}_m = \frac{\mathrm{v}_p l_p}{l_m} = \frac{\left(3 \ \frac{\mathrm{m}}{\mathrm{s}}\right)(200 \ \mathrm{m})}{6 \ \mathrm{m}} = 100 \ \mathrm{m/s}$$

The answer is (C).

---

[5]The *NCEES Handbook* is inconsistent in its presentation and definition of the Froude number. While some equations use y_h as the symbol for *characteristic length*, Eq. 10.12 uses l. This leads to some potentially confusing and misleading conflicts.

11 Compressible Fluid Dynamics

Nomenclature

A	area	m^2
A^*	critical area	m^2
c	specific heat	J/kg·K
c	speed of sound	m/s
k	ratio of specific heats	–
m	mass	kg
Ma	Mach number	–
p	pressure	Pa
R	specific gas constant	J/kg·K
$\overline{R}$	universal gas constant, 8314	J/kmol·K
T	absolute temperature	K
v	velocity	m/s
V	volume	m^3

Symbols

ρ	density	kg/m^3
v	specific volume	m^3/kg

Subscripts

0	stagnation
p	constant pressure
v	constant volume

1. COMPRESSIBLE FLUID DYNAMICS

A *high-velocity gas* is defined as a gas moving with a velocity in excess of approximately 100 m/s. A high gas velocity is often achieved at the expense of internal energy. A drop in internal energy, u, is seen as a drop in enthalpy, h, since $h = u + pv$. Since the Bernoulli equation does not account for this conversion, it cannot be used to predict the thermodynamic properties of the gas. Furthermore, density changes and shock waves complicate the use of traditional evaluation tools such as energy and momentum conservation equations.

2. IDEAL GAS

Equation 11.1 and Eq. 11.2: Ideal Gas Law

$$pv = RT \qquad 11.1$$

$$pV = mRT \qquad 11.2$$

Variations

$$p = \left(\frac{m}{V}\right)RT = \rho RT$$

$$pv = p\left(\frac{V}{m}\right)$$

Description

The *ideal gas law* is an *equation of state* for ideal gases. An equation of state is a relationship that predicts the state (i.e., a property, such as pressure, temperature, volume, etc.) from a set of two other independent properties.

Equation 11.3: Specific Gas Constant

$$R = \frac{\overline{R}}{\text{mol. wt}} \qquad 11.3$$

Values

	customary U.S.	SI
universal gas constant, $\overline{R}$	1545 ft-lbf/lbmol-°R	8314 J/kmol·K
		8.314 kPa·m³/kmol·K
		0.08206 L·atm/mol·K
specific gas constant, R (dry air)	53.3 ft-lbf/lbm-°R	287 J/kg·K

Description

The *specific gas constant*, R, can be determined from the *molecular weight* of the substance, mol. wt, and the *universal gas constant*, $\overline{R}$.

The universal gas constant, $\bar{R}$, is "universal" (within a system of units), because the same value can be used for any gas. Its value depends on the units used for pressure, temperature, and volume, as well as on the units of mass.

Example

A vessel of air is kept at 97 kPa and 300K. The molecular weight of air is 29 kg/kmol. The density of the air in the vessel is most nearly

(A)   0.039 kg/m^3

(B)   0.53 kg/m^3

(C)   1.1 kg/m^3

(D)   3.2 kg/m^3

Solution

From Eq. 11.3, the specific gas constant for air is

$$R = \frac{\bar{R}}{\text{mol. wt}} = \frac{8314\ \dfrac{\text{J}}{\text{kmol·K}}}{29\ \dfrac{\text{kg}}{\text{kmol}}}$$

$$= 287\ \text{J/kg·K}$$

Use the equation of state for an ideal gas, Eq. 11.2.

$$pV = mRT$$
$$\rho = \frac{m}{V}$$
$$= \frac{p}{RT}$$
$$= \frac{(97\ \text{kPa})\left(1000\ \dfrac{\text{Pa}}{\text{kPa}}\right)}{\left(287\ \dfrac{\text{J}}{\text{kg·K}}\right)(300\text{K})}$$
$$= 1.128\ \text{kg/m}^3 \quad (1.1\ \text{kg/m}^3)$$

The answer is (C).

Equation 11.4: Boyle's Law

$$p_1 v_1 / T_1 = p_2 v_2 / T_2 \qquad 11.4$$

Variation

$$\frac{pv}{T} = \text{constant}$$

Description

The equation of state leads to another general relationship, as shown in Eq. 11.4. When temperature is held constant, Eq. 11.4 reduces to *Boyle's law*.

$$pv = \text{constant}$$

Equation 11.5: Ratio of Specific Heats

$$k = c_p/c_v \qquad 11.5$$

Values

For air, the ratio of specific heats is $k = 1.40$.

Description

There is no heat loss in an *adiabatic process*. An *isentropic process* is an adiabatic process in which there is no change in system *entropy* (i.e., the process is reversible). For such a process, the following equation is valid.

$$pv^k = \text{constant}$$

For gases, the *ratio of specific heats*, k, is defined by Eq. 11.5, in which c_p is the *specific heat at constant pressure* and c_v is the *specific heat at constant volume*. An implicit assumption (requirement) for ideal gases is that the ratio of specific heats is constant throughout all processes.

3. COMPRESSIBLE FLOW

Equation 11.6: Speed of Sound

$$c = \sqrt{kRT} \qquad 11.6$$

Values

Table 11.1 *Approximate Speeds of Sound (at one atmospheric pressure)*

material	speed of sound	
	(ft/sec)	(m/s)
air	1130 at 70°F	330 at 0°C
aluminum	16,400	4990
carbon dioxide	870 at 70°F	260 at 0°C
hydrogen	3310 at 70°F	1260 at 0°C
steel	16,900	5150
water	4880 at 70°F	1490 at 20°C

(Multiply ft/sec by 0.3048 to obtain m/s.)

Description

The *speed of sound*, *c*, in a fluid is a function of its bulk modulus, or equivalently, of its compressibility. Equation 11.6 gives the speed of sound in an ideal gas. The temperature, T, must be in degrees absolute (i.e., °R or K).

Approximate speeds of sound for various materials at 1 atm are given in Table 11.1.

Equation 11.7: Mach Number[1]

$$\text{Ma} \equiv \frac{\text{v}}{c} \qquad 11.7$$

Description

The *Mach number*, Ma, of an object is the ratio of the object's speed to the speed of sound in the medium through which the object is traveling.

The term *subsonic travel* implies Ma < 1.[2] Similarly, *supersonic travel* implies Ma > 1, but usually Ma < 5. Travel above Ma = 5 is known as *hypersonic travel*. Travel in the transition region between subsonic and supersonic (i.e., 0.8 < Ma < 1.2) is known as *transonic travel*. A *sonic boom* (a shock-wave phenomenon) occurs when an object travels at supersonic speed.

Example

Air at 300K flows at 1.0 m/s. The ratio of specific heats for air is 1.4, and the specific gas constant is 287 J/kg·K. The Mach number for the air is most nearly

(A)   0.003

(B)   0.008

(C)   0.02

(D)   0.07

Solution

Calculate the speed of sound in 300K air using Eq. 11.6.

$$c = \sqrt{kRT}$$
$$= \sqrt{(1.4)\left(287 \ \frac{\text{J}}{\text{kg·K}}\right)(300\text{K})}$$
$$= 347 \text{ m/s}$$

From Eq. 11.7, the Mach number is

$$\text{Ma} = \frac{\text{v}}{c}$$
$$= \frac{1.0 \ \dfrac{\text{m}}{\text{s}}}{347 \ \dfrac{\text{m}}{\text{s}}}$$
$$= 0.00288 \quad (0.003)$$

The answer is (A).

4. ISENTROPIC FLOW RELATIONSHIPS

If the gas flow is adiabatic and frictionless (that is, reversible), the entropy change is zero, and the flow is known as *isentropic flow*. As a practical matter, completely isentropic flow does not exist. However, some high-velocity, steady-state flow processes proceed with little increase in entropy and are considered to be isentropic. The irreversible effects are accounted for by various correction factors, such as nozzle and discharge coefficients.

Equation 11.8: Isentropic Flow

$$\frac{p_2}{p_1} = \left(\frac{T_2}{T_1}\right)^{\frac{k}{k-1}} = \left(\frac{\rho_2}{\rho_1}\right)^k \qquad 11.8$$

Description

Equation 11.8 gives the relationship between static properties for any two points in the flow. k is the ratio of specific heats, given by Eq. 11.5.

Example

Through an isentropic process, a piston compresses 2 kg of an ideal gas at 150 kPa and 35°C in a cylinder to a pressure of 300 kPa. The specific heat of the gas for constant pressure processes is 5 kJ/kg·K; for constant volume processes, the specific heat is 3 kJ/kg·K. The final temperature of the gas is most nearly

(A)   130°C

(B)   190°C

(C)   210°C

(D)   260°C

---

[1]The symbol ≡ means "is defined as." It is not a mathematical operator and should not be used in mathematical equations.
[2]In the language of compressible fluid flow, this is known as the *subsonic flow regime*.

Solution

Find the ratio of specific heats using Eq. 11.5.

$$k = \frac{c_p}{c_v}$$

$$= \frac{5 \dfrac{\text{kJ}}{\text{kg·K}}}{3 \dfrac{\text{kJ}}{\text{kg·K}}}$$

$$= 1.67$$

Use Eq. 11.8, converting Celsius to absolute temperature, and solve for the final temperature.

$$\frac{p_2}{p_1} = \left(\frac{T_2}{T_1}\right)^{\frac{k}{k-1}}$$

$$T_2 = T_1\left(\frac{p_2}{p_1}\right)^{(k-1)/k}$$

$$= (35°\text{C} + 273°)\left(\frac{300 \text{ kPa}}{150 \text{ kPa}}\right)^{(1.67-1)/1.67}$$

$$= 406.4\text{K}$$

Converting the result back to Celsius,

$$T_2 = 406.4\text{ K} - 273°$$

$$= 133.4°\text{C} \quad (130°\text{C})$$

The answer is (A).

Equation 11.9: Stagnation Temperature[3]

$$T_0 = T + \frac{\text{v}^2}{2 \cdot c_p} \qquad \text{11.9}$$

Description

In an ideal gas for an isentropic process, for a given point in the flow, *stagnation temperature* (also known as *total temperature*), T_0, is related to *static temperature*, T, as shown in Eq. 11.9.

Example

Air enters a straight duct at 300K and 300 kPa and with a velocity of 150 m/s. The specific heat of the air is 1004.6 J/kg·K. Assuming adiabatic flow and an ideal gas, the stagnation temperature is most nearly

(A) 310K

(B) 330K

(C) 350K

(D) 380K

Solution

The stagnation temperature is

$$T_0 = T + \frac{\text{v}^2}{2 \cdot c_p}$$

$$= 300\text{K} + \frac{\left(150 \dfrac{\text{m}}{\text{s}}\right)^2}{(2)\left(1004.6 \dfrac{\text{J}}{\text{kg·K}}\right)}$$

$$= 311.2\text{K} \quad (310\text{K})$$

The answer is (A).

Equation 11.10 Through Eq. 11.12: Isentropic Flow Factors[4]

$$\frac{T_0}{T} = 1 + \frac{k-1}{2} \cdot \text{Ma}^2 \qquad \text{11.10}$$

$$\frac{p_0}{p} = \left(\frac{T_0}{T}\right)^{\frac{k}{k-1}} = \left(1 + \frac{k-1}{2} \cdot \text{Ma}^2\right)^{\frac{k}{k-1}} \qquad \text{11.11}$$

$$\frac{\rho_0}{\rho} = \left(\frac{T_0}{T}\right)^{\frac{1}{k-1}} = \left(1 + \frac{k-1}{2} \cdot \text{Ma}^2\right)^{\frac{1}{k-1}} \qquad \text{11.12}$$

Description

In isentropic flow, total pressure, total temperature, and total density remain constant, regardless of the flow area and velocity. The instantaneous properties, known as *static properties*, do change along the flow path, however.[5] Eq. 11.10 through Eq. 11.12 predict these static properties as functions of the Mach number, Ma, and ratio of specific heats, k, for ideal gas flow. Therefore, the ratios can be easily tabulated. The numbers in such tables are known as *isentropic flow factors*.

---

[3]As used in the NCEES *FE Reference Handbook* (*NCEES Handbook*), there is no significance to the multiplication "dot" in Eq. 11.9 other than scalar multiplication. This is not a vector calculation.
[4]See Ftn. 3.
[5]The *static properties* are not the same as the *stagnation properties*.

Example

At the entry of a diverging section, the temperature of a gas is 27°C, and the Mach number is 1.5. The exit Mach number is 2.5. Assume isentropic flow of a perfect gas with a ratio of specific heats of 1.3. The temperature of the gas at exit is most nearly

(A)   –100°C

(B)   –85°C

(C)   –66°C

(D)   –31°C

Solution

Use Eq. 11.10 with the entrance conditions to find the stagnation temperature.

$$\frac{T_0}{T} = 1 + \frac{k-1}{2} \cdot \mathrm{Ma}^2$$

$$T_0 = \left[1 + \left(\frac{k-1}{2}\right)(\mathrm{Ma})^2\right]T$$

$$= \left[1 + \left(\frac{1.3-1}{2}\right)(1.5)^2\right](27°\mathrm{C} + 273°)$$

$$= 401.25\mathrm{K}$$

Total temperature does not change. Use Eq. 11.10 again, this time with the stagnation temperature just found and the exit Mach number, to find the temperature at the exit.

$$\frac{T_0}{T} = 1 + \frac{k-1}{2} \cdot \mathrm{Ma}^2$$

$$T = \frac{T_0}{1 + \left(\frac{k-1}{2}\right)(\mathrm{Ma})^2}$$

$$= \frac{401.25\mathrm{K}}{1 + \left(\frac{1.3-1}{2}\right)(2.5)^2} - 273°$$

$$= -65.90°\mathrm{C} \quad (-66°\mathrm{C})$$

The answer is (C).

5. CRITICAL AREA

In order to design a nozzle capable of expanding a gas to some given velocity or Mach number, it is sufficient to have an expression for the flow area versus Mach number. Since the reservoir cross-sectional area is an unrelated variable, it is not possible to use the stagnation area as a reference area and to develop the ratio $[A_0/A]$ as was done for temperature, pressure, and density. The

usual choice for a reference area is the *critical area*—the area at which the gas velocity is (or could be) sonic. This area is designated as A^*.

Equation 11.13: Critical Area

$$\frac{A}{A^*} = \frac{1}{\mathrm{Ma}}\left[\frac{1 + \frac{1}{2}(k-1)\mathrm{Ma}^2}{\frac{1}{2}(k+1)}\right]^{\frac{k+1}{2(k-1)}} \qquad 11.13$$

Description

Figure 11.1 is a plot of Eq. 11.13 versus the Mach number. As long as the Mach number is less than 1.0, the area must decrease in order for the velocity to increase. However, if the Mach number is greater than 1.0, the area must increase in order for the velocity to increase.

Figure 11.1 *A/A* versus Ma*

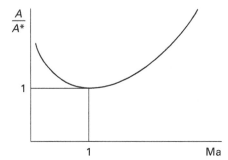

It is not possible to change the Mach number to any desired value over any arbitrary distance along the axis of a converging-diverging nozzle. If the rate of change, dA/dx, is too great, the assumptions of one-dimensional flow become invalid. Usually, the converging section has a steeper angle (known as the *convergent angle*) than the diverging section. If the diverging angle is too great, a normal shock wave may form in that part of the nozzle.

6. NORMAL SHOCK RELATIONSHIPS

A nozzle must be designed to the design pressure ratio in order to keep the flow supersonic in the diverging section of the nozzle. It is possible, though, to have supersonic velocity only in part of the diverging section. Once the flow is supersonic in a part of the diverging section, however, it cannot become subsonic by an isentropic process.

Therefore, the gas experiences a *shock wave* as the velocity drops from supersonic to subsonic. Shock waves are very thin (several molecules thick) and separate areas of radically different thermodynamic properties. Since the shock wave forms normal to the flow direction, it is known as a *normal shock wave*. The strength of a shock wave is measured by the change in Mach number across it. (See Fig. 11.2.)

Figure 11.2 *Normal Shock Relationships*

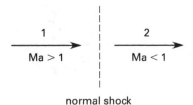

normal shock

The velocity always changes from supersonic to subsonic across a shock wave. Since there is no loss of heat energy, a shock wave is an adiabatic process, and total temperature is constant. However, the process is not isentropic, and total pressure decreases. Momentum is also conserved. Table 11.2 lists the property changes across a shock wave.

Table 11.2 *Property Changes Across a Normal Shock Wave*

property	change
total temperature	is constant
total pressure	decreases
total density	decreases
velocity	decreases
Mach number	decreases
pressure	increases
density	increases
temperature	increases
entropy	increases
internal energy	increases
enthalpy	is constant
momentum	is constant

Equation 11.14 Through Eq. 11.18: Properties Across a Normal Shock Wave

$$Ma_2 = \sqrt{\frac{(k-1)Ma_1^2 + 2}{2kMa_1^2 - (k-1)}} \quad 11.14$$

$$\frac{T_2}{T_1} = [2 + (k-1)Ma_1^2]\frac{2kMa_1^2 - (k-1)}{(k+1)^2 Ma_1^2} \quad 11.15$$

$$\frac{p_2}{p_1} = \frac{1}{k+1}[2kMa_1^2 - (k-1)] \quad 11.16$$

$$\frac{\rho_2}{\rho_1} = \frac{v_1}{v_2} = \frac{(k+1)Ma_1^2}{(k-1)Ma_1^2 + 2} \quad 11.17$$

$$T_{01} = T_{02} \quad 11.18$$

Description

Equation 11.14 through Eq. 11.18 give the relationships between downstream and upstream flow conditions for a normal shock wave.

12 Fluid Machines

Nomenclature

c	specific heat	J/kg·K
D	diameter	m
g	gravitational acceleration, 9.81	m/s²
h	enthalpy	J/kg
h	head	m
H	head	m
k	ratio of specific heats	–
KE	kinetic energy	J/kg
$\dot{m}$	mass flow rate	kg/s
N	rotational speed	rev/min
$NPSH$	net positive suction head	m
p	pressure	Pa or psi
Q	volumetric flow rate	L/s
R	specific gas constant	J/kg·K orft-lbf/ lbm-°R
T	absolute temperature	K
v	velocity	m/s
w	work per unit mass	J/kg
W	work	J
$\dot{W}$	power	W

Symbols

γ	specific (unit) weight	N/m³
η	efficiency	–
ρ	density	kg/m³

Subscripts

a	actual
A	available
c	compressor
comp	compressor
C	compressor
e	exit
es	exit after an isentropic process
f	fan or friction
H	hydraulic
i	inlet
p	constant pressure
R	required
s	isentropic or static
t	total
turb	turbine
T	turbine
v	constant volume

1. PUMPS AND COMPRESSORS

Pumps, compressors, fans, and *blowers* convert mechanical energy (i.e., work input) into fluid energy, increasing the total energy content of the fluid flowing through them. (See Fig. 12.1.) Pumps can be considered adiabatic devices because the fluid gains (or loses) very little heat during the short time it passes through them. If the inlet and outlet are the same size and at the same elevation, the kinetic and potential energy changes can be neglected.[1]

Figure 12.1 Compressor

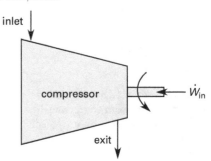

---

[1]Even if the pump inlet and outlet are different sizes and at different elevations, the kinetic and potential energy changes are small compared to the pressure energy increase.

2. PUMP POWER

Pumps convert mechanical energy into fluid energy, increasing the energy of the fluid. Pump power is known as *hydraulic power* or *water power*. Hydraulic power is the net power transferred to the fluid by the pump.

Horsepower is the unit of power used in the United States and other non-SI countries, which gives rise to the terms *hydraulic horsepower* and *water horsepower*. The unit of power in SI units is the watt.

Equation 12.1 and Eq. 12.2: Motor Input Power[2]

$$\dot{W} = Q\gamma h/\eta = Q\rho g h/\eta_t \qquad 12.1$$

$$\eta_t = \eta_{\text{pump}} \times \eta_{\text{motor}} \qquad 12.2$$

Description

A pump adds energy to a fluid flow. The increase in energy, ΔE, is manifested primarily by an increase in pressure, and to much lesser degrees, changes in velocity and, sometimes, elevation across the pump inlet and outlet. From the *work-energy principle*, the energy added is equal to the work, W, done on the fluid. The *rate of work done*, $\dot{W}$, is equal to the power. The power that is drawn in increasing the pressure is known as *hydraulic power* (*fluid power, hydraulic horsepower*, etc.). The hydraulic power is calculated from the head added to the fluid, h, and the fluid flow rate, Q.[3]

$$\dot{W}_H = Q\gamma h$$

A pump is a mechanical device, and some power delivered to it is lost due to friction between the fluid and the pump and friction in the pump bearings. This loss is accounted for by a *pump efficiency* term, η_{pump}. The power delivered to the pump is

$$\dot{W}_{\text{pump}} = \frac{\dot{W}_H}{\eta_{\text{pump}}}$$

A pump is usually driven by an electrical motor. The electrical power drawn from the power line is referred to as the *electrical power, consumed power*, or *purchased power*. Since the motor is an electromechanical device, some of the power delivered to it is lost due to frictional losses in the motor bearings, air windage, and electrical

heating. This loss is accounted for by a *motor efficiency* term, η_{motor}. The power delivered to the motor (purchased from the power line) is

$$\dot{W}_{\text{purchased}} = \frac{\dot{W}_{\text{pump}}}{\eta_{\text{motor}}}$$

Electrical motors are rated according to their output power. (So, a 2 horsepower motor would have a useful power of 2 horsepower.) Output power for any device is referred to as *brake power*.

Since the *total pump efficiency* (calculated from Eq. 12.2), η_t, is included, Eq. 12.1 calculates the power drawn by the motor (purchased). If the efficiency term were omitted, the power would be the hydraulic power. Since the hydraulic power is what is left over after losses, it is sometimes described as the *net power*.

Applying the continuity equation to Eq. 12.1,

$$\dot{W} = \frac{\dot{m}gh}{\eta}$$

Example

A pump with 70% efficiency moves water from ground level to a height of 5 m. The flow rate is 10 m³/s. Most nearly, what is the power delivered to the pump?

(A) 80 kW

(B) 220 kW

(C) 700 kW

(D) 950 kW

Solution

From Eq. 12.1,

$$\dot{W} = Q\rho g h/\eta_{\text{pump}}$$
$$= \frac{\left(10 \ \frac{\text{m}^3}{\text{s}}\right)\left(1000 \ \frac{\text{kg}}{\text{m}^3}\right)\left(9.81 \ \frac{\text{m}}{\text{s}^2}\right)(5 \ \text{m})}{0.70}$$
$$= 700\,714 \ \text{W} \quad (700 \ \text{kW})$$

The answer is (C).

---

[2]As used in the NCEES *FE Reference Handbook* (*NCEES Handbook*) in Eq. 12.1, the symbols η and η_t represent the same quantity, the *total pump efficiency*.
[3]The *NCEES Handbook* uses lowercase h to represent head added by a pump. While any symbol can be used to represent any quantity, the symbols used for head added by a pump are most commonly H, h_A, TH (for total head), and TDH (for total dynamic head).

Equation 12.3 Through Eq. 12.5: Centrifugal Pump Power[4]

$$\dot{W}_{\text{fluid}} = \rho g H Q \qquad \text{12.3}$$

$$\dot{W} = \frac{\rho g H Q}{\eta_{\text{pump}}} \qquad \text{12.4}$$

$$\dot{W}_{\text{purchased}} = \frac{\dot{W}}{\eta_{\text{motor}}} \qquad \text{12.5}$$

Values[5]

efficiency type	efficiency range
pump, η_{pump}	0–1
motor, η_{motor}	0–1

Description

The hydraulic power delivered by a centrifugal pump is calculated from Eq. 12.3. Brake (motor) power drawn by the pump can be found from Eq. 12.4, and *purchased power* is determined using Eq. 12.5. Efficiency ranges for pumps and motors are given in the values section. H is the increase in head delivered by the pump.

Example

Water at 10°C is pumped through smooth steel pipes from tank 1 to tank 2 as shown. The discharge rate is 0.1 m³/min. The pump efficiency is 80%.

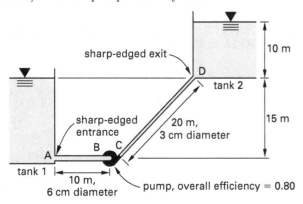

If the pump adds a total of 15 m of head, the pump motor's brake power is most nearly

(A) 19 W

(B) 32 W

(C) 200 W

(D) 310 W

Solution

From Eq. 12.4, the brake power is

$$\dot{W} = \frac{\rho g H Q}{\eta_{\text{pump}}} = \frac{\left(1000 \ \frac{\text{kg}}{\text{m}^3}\right)\left(9.81 \ \frac{\text{m}}{\text{s}^2}\right)(15 \ \text{m})\left(0.1 \ \frac{\text{m}^3}{\text{min}}\right)}{(0.80)\left(60 \ \frac{\text{s}}{\text{min}}\right)}$$

$$= 306.6 \ \text{W} \quad (310 \ \text{W})$$

The answer is (D).

Equation 12.6 Through Eq. 12.11: Pump and Compressor Power (Rate of Work)[6,7]

$$\dot{W}_{\text{comp}} = -\dot{m}(h_e - h_i) \quad \text{[adiabatic compressor]} \qquad \text{12.6}$$

$$\dot{W}_{\text{comp}} = -\dot{m}c_p(T_e - T_i) \quad \begin{bmatrix} \text{ideal gas; constant} \\ \text{specific heat} \end{bmatrix} \qquad \text{12.7}$$

$$w_{\text{comp}} = -c_p(T_e - T_i) \quad \text{[per unit mass]} \qquad \text{12.8}$$

$$\dot{W}_{\text{comp}} = -\dot{m}\left(h_e - h_i + \frac{\text{v}_e^2 - \text{v}_i^2}{2}\right)$$

$$= -\dot{m}\left(c_p(T_e - T_i) + \frac{\text{v}_e^2 - \text{v}_i^2}{2}\right) \quad \begin{bmatrix} \Delta KE \\ \text{included} \end{bmatrix} \qquad \text{12.9}$$

$$\dot{W}_{\text{comp}} = \frac{\dot{m}p_i k}{(k-1)\rho_i \eta_c}\left[\left(\frac{p_e}{p_i}\right)^{1-1/k} - 1\right] \quad \begin{bmatrix} \text{adiabatic} \\ \text{compression} \end{bmatrix} \qquad \text{12.10}$$

---

[4]The *NCEES Handbook* uses H for head added in Eq. 12.3 and Eq. 12.4, which is the same as h in Eq. 12.1.

[5]The values of efficiencies provided in the *NCEES Handbook* for pumps and motors are not particularly useful. All real devices fall into the range of 0–1. No efficiencies in the real universe are outside of those ranges.

[6]Although Eq. 12.6 through Eq. 12.11 are presented together in the *NCEES Handbook* and purport to calculate "compressor power," Eq. 12.10 is not the same quantity as the other equations. Equation 12.10 includes the compressor efficiency, and therefore, is the power drawn by (into) the compressor from its prime mover, before compressor losses. All of the other equations are based on working fluid properties, and therefore, represent the net power delivered to the fluid, after compressor losses. Only Eq. 12.10 calculates the input power shown in Fig. 12.1.

[7]The *NCEES Handbook* contains some inconsistencies in nomenclature and sign convention. Although M is used for molecular weight in Eq. 12.11, "mol. wt" is used elsewhere. (M does not represent "mass.") The subscript c used in η_c is the same as "comp" (compressor) used in Eq. 12.6 through Eq. 12.11 (and C used in Eq. 12.12). In keeping with the "standard" thermodynamic convention for systems that work (energy) is negative when work is done on a system, Eq. 12.6 through Eq. 12.9 have negative signs. This convention is not followed in Eq. 12.10 and Eq. 12.11.

$$\dot{W}_{comp} = \frac{\bar{R}\,T_i}{M\eta_c} \ln\frac{p_e}{p_i}\dot{m} \quad \text{[isothermal compression]} \qquad 12.11$$

Description

Equation 12.6 through Eq. 12.11 are used to calculate *compressor power*, referred to as a "rate of work," based on the fluid type and other appropriate assumptions.

The first form of Eq. 12.9 is the general equation, applicable to both vapors (such as steam) and real and ideal gases, while the second form of Eq. 12.9 is specifically only for ideal gases (for which specific heat is assumed to be constant). Equation 12.6 and Eq. 12.7 are simplifications of both forms of Eq. 12.9 that assume kinetic energy (velocity) changes are insignificant. Equation 12.8 is Eq. 12.7 restated on a per-mass basis. While Eq. 12.7 and the second form of Eq. 12.9 depend on temperature changes, Eq. 12.10 and Eq. 12.11 depend on the pressure changes. Equation 12.9 and Eq. 12.10 are strictly for ideal gases. Equation 12.10 calculates the input power, $\dot{W}_{in}$, shown in Fig. 12.1.

Example

15 kg/s of air are compressed from 1 atm and 300K (enthalpy of 300.19 kJ/kg) to 2 atm and 900K (enthalpy of 732.93 kJ/kg). Heat transfer is negligible. The power required to perform the air compression is most nearly

- (A)   5.6 MW
- (B)   6.5 MW
- (C)   7.6 MW
- (D)   8.9 MW

Solution

Heat transfer is negligible, so the compression process may be considered adiabatic. Use Eq. 12.6 to find the rate of work.[8]

$$\dot{W}_{comp} = -\dot{m}(h_e - h_i)$$

$$= -\left(15\ \frac{\text{kg}}{\text{s}}\right)\left(732.93\ \frac{\text{kJ}}{\text{kg}} - 300.19\ \frac{\text{kJ}}{\text{kg}}\right)$$

$$= 6491.1\ \text{kJ/s} \quad (6.5\ \text{MW})$$

The answer is (B).

Equation 12.12: Compressor Isentropic Efficiency

$$\eta_C = \frac{w_s}{w_a} = \frac{T_{es} - T_i}{T_e - T_i} \qquad 12.12$$

Description

The *isentropic efficiency* (*adiabatic efficiency*), η_C, of a compressor is the ratio of ideal (isentropic) energy extraction to actual energy extraction. Actual isentropic efficiencies vary from approximately 65% for 1 MW unit to over 90% for 100 MW and larger units.

3. TURBINES

Turbines can generally be thought of as pumps operating in reverse. A turbine extracts energy from the fluid, converting fluid energy into mechanical energy. These devices can be considered to be adiabatic because the fluid gains (or loses) very little heat during the short time it passes through them. The kinetic and potential energy changes can be neglected. (See Fig. 12.2.)

Figure 12.2 Turbine

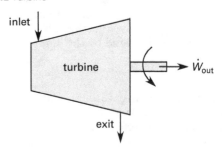

Equation 12.13 Through Eq. 12.16: Turbine Power (Rate of Work)[9]

$$\dot{W}_{turb} = \dot{m}(h_i - h_e) \quad \text{[adiabatic turbine]} \qquad 12.13$$

$$\dot{W}_{turb} = \dot{m}c_p(T_i - T_e) \quad \begin{bmatrix} \text{ideal gas; constant} \\ \text{specific heat} \end{bmatrix} \qquad 12.14$$

$$w_{turb} = c_p(T_i - T_e) \quad \text{[per unit mass]} \qquad 12.15$$

$$\dot{W}_{turb} = \dot{m}\left(h_e - h_i + \frac{v_e^2 - v_i^2}{2}\right)$$

$$= \dot{m}\left(c_p(T_e - T_i) + \frac{v_e^2 - v_i^2}{2}\right) \begin{bmatrix} \Delta KE \\ \text{included} \end{bmatrix} \qquad 12.16$$

---

[8]Negative power implies work is done on the air.
[9]Equation 12.13 through Eq. 12.16 can be used to calculate the output power, $\dot{W}_{out}$, in Fig. 12.2 only if the mechanical efficiency of the turbine is 100%.

Description

Equation 12.13 through Eq. 12.16 give the power (rate of work) for turbines. Since they are all based on actual fluid exit properties, these equations determine the actual energy extracted from the fluid. The first form of Eq. 12.16 is the general equation, applicable to both vapors (such as steam) and real and ideal gases, while the second form of Eq. 12.16 is specifically only for ideal gases (for which specific heat is assumed to be constant). Equation 12.13 and Eq. 12.14 are simplifications of both forms of Eq. 12.16 that assume kinetic energy (velocity) changes are insignificant. Equation 12.15 is Eq. 12.16 restated on a per-mass basis.

Example

Steam flows at 34 kg/s through a steam turbine. The steam decreases in temperature from 150°C to 145°C, while the specific heat of the steam remains constant at 2.1 kJ/kg·°C. Assume a negligible change in kinetic energy. The ideal power generated by the turbine is most nearly

- (A) 36 kW
- (B) 43 kW
- (C) 360 kW
- (D) 430 kW

Solution

Use Eq. 12.14 to determine the power developed by the turbine.

$$\dot{W}_{\text{turb}} = \dot{m}c_p(T_i - T_e)$$
$$= \left(34 \ \frac{\text{kg}}{\text{s}}\right)\left(2.1 \ \frac{\text{kJ}}{\text{kg·°C}}\right)(150°C - 145°C)$$
$$= 357 \ \text{kJ/s} \quad (360 \ \text{kW})$$

The answer is (C).

Equation 12.17: Turbine Isentropic Efficiency[10]

$$\eta_T = \frac{w_a}{w_s} = \frac{T_i - T_e}{T_i - T_{es}} \qquad \text{12.17}$$

Variation

$$\eta_T = \frac{h_i - h_e}{h_i - h_{es}}$$

Description

The definition of *isentropic efficiency (adiabatic efficiency)*, η_T, for a turbine is the inverse of what it is for a compressor. For a turbine, isentropic efficiency is the ratio of actual to ideal (isentropic) energy extraction. Actual isentropic efficiencies vary from approximately 65% for 1 MW unit to over 90% for 100 MW and larger units.

4. CAVITATION

Cavitation is a spontaneous vaporization of the fluid inside the pump, resulting in a degradation of pump performance. Wherever the fluid pressure is less than the vapor pressure, small pockets of vapor will form. These pockets usually form only within the pump itself, although cavitation slightly upstream within the suction line is also possible. As the vapor pockets reach the surface of the impeller, the local high fluid pressure collapses them. Noise, vibration, impeller pitting, and structural damage to the pump casing are manifestations of cavitation.

Cavitation can be caused by any of the following conditions.

- discharge head far below the pump head at peak efficiency
- high suction lift or low suction head
- excessive pump speed
- high liquid temperature (i.e., high vapor pressure)

5. NET POSITIVE SUCTION HEAD

The occurrence of cavitation is predictable. Cavitation will occur when the net pressure in the fluid drops below the vapor pressure. This criterion is commonly stated in terms of head: Cavitation occurs when the net positive suction head available is less than the net positive suction head required for satisfactory operation (e.g., $NPSH_A < NPSH_R$).

The minimum fluid energy required at the pump inlet for satisfactory operation (i.e., the required head) is known as the *net positive suction head required*, $NPSH_R$.[11] $NPSH_R$ is a function of the pump and will be given by the pump manufacturer as part of the pump performance data.[12] (See Fig. 12.3.) $NPSH_R$ is dependent on the flow rate.

---

[10]The subscript T in turbine isentropic efficiency, η_T, designates "turbine" and is the same as subscript "turb" used in Eq. 12.13 through Eq. 12.16.
[11]If $NPSH_R$ (a head term) is multiplied by the fluid specific weight, it is known as the *net inlet pressure required*, NIPR. Similarly, $NPSH_A$ can be converted to NIPA.
[12]It is also possible to calculate $NPSH_R$ from other information, such as suction specific speed. However, this still depends on information provided by the manufacturer.

Fluid Mechanics

Figure 12.3 Centrifugal Pump Characteristics

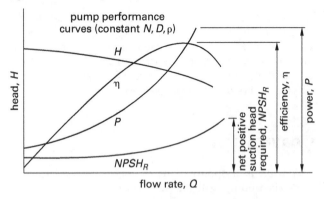

Equation 12.18: Net Positive Suction Head Available[13]

$$NPSH_A = \frac{p_{\text{atm}}}{\rho g} + H_s - H_f - \frac{v^2}{2g} - \frac{p_{\text{vapor}}}{\rho g} \qquad 12.18$$

Description

Net positive suction head available, $NPSH_A$, is the actual total fluid energy at the pump inlet. H_s is the static head at the pump inlet, and H_f is the friction loss between the fluid source and the pump inlet.

6. SIMILARITY (SCALING) LAWS

Equation 12.19 Through Eq. 12.23: Similarity (Scaling) Laws

$$\left(\frac{Q}{ND^3}\right)_2 = \left(\frac{Q}{ND^3}\right)_1 \qquad 12.19$$

$$\left(\frac{\dot{m}}{\rho ND^3}\right)_2 = \left(\frac{\dot{m}}{\rho ND^3}\right)_1 \qquad 12.20$$

$$\left(\frac{H}{N^2 D^2}\right)_2 = \left(\frac{H}{N^2 D^2}\right)_1 \qquad 12.21$$

$$\left(\frac{p}{\rho N^2 D^2}\right)_2 = \left(\frac{p}{\rho N^2 D^2}\right)_1 \qquad 12.22$$

$$\left(\frac{\dot{W}}{\rho N^3 D^5}\right)_2 = \left(\frac{\dot{W}}{\rho N^3 D^5}\right)_1 \qquad 12.23$$

Description

The performance of one pump can be used to predict the performance of a *dynamically similar (homologous)* pump. This can be done by using Eq. 12.19 through Eq. 12.23.

These *similarity laws* (also known as *scaling laws*) assume that both pumps

- operate in the turbulent region
- have the same pump efficiency
- operate at the same percentage of wide-open flow

These relationships assume that the efficiencies of the larger and smaller pumps are the same. In reality, larger pumps will be more efficient than smaller pumps. Therefore, extrapolations to much larger or much smaller sizes should be avoided.

Example

A 200 mm pump operating at 1500 rpm discharges 120 L/s of water. The capacity of a homologous 250 mm pump operating at the same speed is most nearly

(A)   150 L/s

(B)   180 L/s

(C)   200 L/s

(D)   230 L/s

Solution

Use Eq. 12.19, and solve for the flow rate of the second pump. The rotational speed, N, is unchanged.

$$\left(\frac{Q}{ND^3}\right)_2 = \left(\frac{Q}{ND^3}\right)_1$$

$$Q_2 = \left(\frac{Q_1}{D_1^3}\right) D_2^3$$

$$= \left(\frac{120 \, \dfrac{\text{L}}{\text{s}}}{(200 \text{ mm})^3}\right)(250 \text{ mm})^3$$

$$= 234.4 \text{ L/s} \quad (230 \text{ L/s})$$

The answer is (D).

---

[13]The *NCEES Handbook* is inconsistent in its nomenclature as it relates to $NPSH_A$. In Eq. 12.18, H_f is the same as h_f used elsewhere in the fluids sections; p_{vapor} corresponds to p_v used in Eq. 8.4; p_{atm} corresponds to p_0 in Eq. 8.5; H_s corresponds to h used in Eq. 8.1; and v corresponds to the inlet velocity, v_i, in Eq. 12.9.

7. FANS

There are two main types of fans: axial and centrifugal. Typical fan characteristics are given in Fig. 12.4.

Figure 12.4 Fan Characteristics

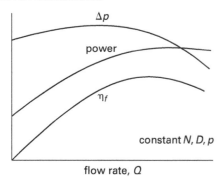

Axial-flow fans are essentially propellers mounted with small tip clearances in ducts. They develop static pressure by changing the airflow velocity. Axial flow fans are usually used when it is necessary to move large quantities of air (i.e., greater than 250 m³/s) against low static pressures (i.e., less than 3 kPa), although the pressures and flow rates are much lower at most installations. An axial-flow fan may be followed by a *diffuser* (i.e., an *evase*) to convert some of the kinetic energy to static pressure.

Compared with centrifugal fans, axial flow fans are more compact and less expensive. However, they run faster than centrifugals, draw more power, are less efficient, and are noisier. Axial flow fans are capable of higher velocities than centrifugal fans.

Centrifugal fans are used in installations moving less than 500 m³/s and pressures less than 15 kPa. Like centrifugal pumps, they develop static pressure by imparting a centrifugal force on the rotating air. Depending on the blade curvature, kinetic energy can be made greater (forward-curved blades) or less (backward-curved blades) than the tangential velocity of the impeller blades.

Forward-curved centrifugals (also called *squirrel cage fans*) are the most widely used centrifugals for general ventilation and packaged units. They operate at relatively low speeds, about half that of backward-curved fans. This makes them useful in high-temperature applications where stress due to rotation is a factor. Compared with backward-curved centrifugals, forward-curved blade fans have a greater capacity (due to their higher velocities) but require larger *scrolls*. However, since the fan blades are "cupped," they cannot be used when the air contains particles or contaminants. Efficiencies are the lowest of all centrifugals—between 70% and 75%.

Motors driving centrifugal fans with forward-curved blades can be overloaded if the duct losses are not calculated correctly. The power drawn increases rapidly with increases in the delivery rate. The motors are usually sized with some safety factor to compensate for the possibility that the actual system pressure will be less than the design pressure. For forward-curved blades, the maximum efficiency occurs near the point of maximum static pressure. Since their tip speeds are low, these fans are quiet. The fan noise is lowest at maximum pressure.

Radial fans (also called *straight-blade fans*, *paddle wheel fans*, and *shaving wheel fans*) have blades that are neither forward- nor backward-inclined. Radial fans are the workhorses of most industrial exhaust applications and can be used in material-handling and conveying systems where large amounts of bulk material pass through them. Such fans are low-volume, high-pressure (up to 15 kPa), high-noise, high-temperature, and low-efficiency (65–70%) units. *Radial tip fans* constitute a subcategory of radial fans. Their performance characteristics are between those of forward-curved and conventional radial fans.

Backward-curved centrifugals are quiet, medium- to high-volume and pressure, and high-efficiency units. They can be used in most applications with clean air below 540°C and up to about 10 kPa. They are available in three styles: flat, curved, and airfoil. Airfoil fans have the highest efficiency (up to 90%), while the other types have efficiencies between 80% and 90%. Because of these high efficiencies, power savings easily compensate for higher installation or replacement costs.

Equation 12.24: Backward-Curved Fan Power

$$\dot{W} = \frac{\Delta p Q}{\eta_f} \qquad 12.24$$

Description

Equation 12.24 is used to calculate the required power of a *fan motor* with backward-curved blades. η_f is the fan efficiency, and Δp is the rise in pressure. Power will be in watts if the pressure change is in pascals and the flow rate is in cubic meters per second. In heating, ventilating, and air conditioning work, pressure increase is often stated in centimeters of water. Heights of water must be converted to heights of air in order to determine the pressure rise.

$$\Delta p = \rho_{air} g h_{air}$$
$$= \rho_{air} g \left(\frac{\rho_{water}}{\rho_{air}} \right) h_{water}$$
$$= \rho_{water} g h_{water}$$

Diagnostic Exam

Topic IV: Thermodynamics

1. 2 m³ of an ideal gas is compressed from 100 kPa to 200 kPa. As a result of the process, the internal energy of the gas increases by 10 kJ, and 140 kJ of heat is lost to the surroundings. What is most nearly the work done by the gas during the process?

(A) −150 kJ

(B) −130 kJ

(C) −85 kJ

(D) −45 kJ

2. A cylinder fitted with a frictionless piston contains an ideal gas at temperature T and pressure p. The gas expands isothermally and reversibly until the pressure is $p/3$. Which statement is true regarding the work done by the gas during expansion?

(A) It is equal to the change in enthalpy of the gas.

(B) It is equal to the change in internal energy of the gas.

(C) It is equal to the heat absorbed by the gas.

(D) It is greater than the heat absorbed by the gas.

3. Consider the following balanced actual combustion reaction for propane.

$$C_3H_8 + 16.67(air) \rightarrow 4H_2O + 3CO_2 + 13.17N_2$$

Assume air is 21% oxygen and 79% nitrogen by volume. What is most nearly the percent theoretical air?

(A) 50%

(B) 60%

(C) 70%

(D) 80%

4. An airstream of 30,000 cfm needs to be sensibly cooled from 85°F dry-bulb temperature and 60% relative humidity to 75°F. The cooling load needed is most nearly

(A) 6200 Btu/hr

(B) 25,000 Btu/hr

(C) 370,000 Btu/hr

(D) 490,000 Btu/hr

5. Refrigerant HFC-134a at 0.8 MPa and 70°C is cooled and condensed at constant pressure in a steady-state process until it is a saturated liquid. Cooling water enters the condenser at 20°C and leaves at 30°C. If the mass flow rate of the refrigerant is 0.1 kg/s, the mass flow rate of the cooling water is most nearly

(A) 0.51 kg/s

(B) 0.65 kg/s

(C) 0.70 kg/s

(D) 0.75 kg/s

6. What is most nearly the melting temperature of sodium chloride, given that the latent heat of fusion is 30 kJ/mol, and the associated entropy change is 28 J/mol·K?

(A) 370K

(B) 880K

(C) 930K

(D) 1100K

7. Most nearly, what is the volume of 0.05 kg of refrigerant HFC-134a at 1.3 MPa with a quality of 37.5%?

(A) $9.6 \times 10^{-5} \text{ m}^3$

(B) $1.7 \times 10^{-4} \text{ m}^3$

(C) $3.1 \times 10^{-4} \text{ m}^3$

(D) $2.2 \times 10^{-3} \text{ m}^3$

8. The pressure of an ideal gas sample is increased linearly while the volume is kept constant. The temperature of the gas sample

(A) increases linearly

(B) increases exponentially

(C) decreases linearly

(D) decreases exponentially

9. 80 kg of water is sealed in a 0.5 m³ rigid container and is heated to 425°C. The critical temperature of steam is 647.1K, and the critical pressure of steam is 22.06 MPa. The specific gas constant for steam can be assumed to be 0.4615 kJ/(kg·K). Treating steam as a real gas, what is most nearly the pressure in the container?

(A) 20 MPa

(B) 33 MPa

(C) 40 MPa

(D) 52 MPa

10. A refrigerant is saturated at 312K and 0.9334 MPa. Under these saturated conditions, the specific volume of the saturated liquid is 0.000795 m³/kg, and the specific volume of the saturated gas is 0.01872 m³/kg. The quality is 0.02538. The total mass of the refrigerant is 400 kg. What is most nearly the volume of the liquid refrigerant?

(A) 0.16 m³

(B) 0.18 m³

(C) 0.31 m³

(D) 0.39 m³

SOLUTIONS

1. Use the first law of thermodynamics.

$$W = Q - \Delta U$$

Using the standard sign convention, heat transferred to the surroundings is negative.

$$W = -140 \text{ kJ} - 10 \text{ kJ}$$
$$= -150 \text{ kJ}$$

The minus sign indicates that work was done on the gas.
The answer is (A).

2. Use the first law of thermodynamics.

$$Q = \Delta U + W$$

Since the internal energy remains constant during an isothermal process, $\Delta U = 0$.

$$Q = W$$

The work done by the gas is equal to the heat absorbed by the gas.
The answer is (C).

3. Balance the combustion reaction equation for complete combustion.

$$C_3H_8 + a(\text{air}) \rightarrow bH_2O + dN_2 + eCO_2$$
$$C_3H_8 + a(0.21O_2 + 0.79N_2) \rightarrow bH_2O + dN_2 + eCO_2$$

From the hydrogen balance, 4 moles of water are produced. From the carbon balance, 3 moles of carbon dioxide are produced. Therefore 5 moles of oxygen are required to react 1 mole of propane.

$$5 = a(0.21)$$
$$a = 23.81$$

The percent theoretical air is

$$\frac{N_{\text{actual}}}{N_{\text{complete combustion}}} \times 100\% = \frac{16.67}{23.81 \text{ mol}} \times 100\%$$
$$= 70\%$$

The answer is (C).

4. Using the psychrometric chart, locate the state point 1 at 85°F dry-bulb temperature and 60% relative humidity to find the enthalpy, h_1, and specific volume, v_1. [Psychrometric Charts]

$$h_1 = 38.1 \text{ Btu/lbm}$$
$$v_1 = 14.08 \text{ ft}^3/\text{lbm}$$

During sensible cooling, the humidity ratio, W, remains unchanged. Locate state point 2 by drawing horizontal line from state point 1 to meet the line at temperature of 75°F. Find the enthalpy, h_2, at state point 2.

$$W_2 = W_1$$
$$h_2 = 35.2 \text{ Btu/lbm}$$

The cooling load required is

$$q = \dot{m}(h_1 - h_2) = \left(\frac{Q}{v_1}\right)(h_1 - h_2)$$

$$= \left(\frac{30{,}000 \dfrac{\text{ft}^3}{\text{min}}}{14.08 \dfrac{\text{ft}^3}{\text{lbm}}}\right)\left(60 \dfrac{\text{min}}{\text{hr}}\right)\left(38.1 \dfrac{\text{Btu}}{\text{lbm}} - 35.2 \dfrac{\text{Btu}}{\text{lbm}}\right)$$

$$= 370{,}700 \text{ Btu/hr} \quad (370{,}000 \text{ Btu/hr})$$

The answer is (C).

5. The inlet and exit enthalpies are found from the HFC-134a pressure-enthalpy diagram. The inlet and exit enthalpies are found using a pressure-enthalpy diagram for refrigerant 134a (see also NCEES *Handbook* diagram, "P-h Diagram for Refrigerant HFC-134a"). At 0.8 MPa and 70°C, the inlet enthalpy is 455.3 kJ/kg. At 0.8 MPa, the saturated exit enthalpy is 243.7 kJ/kg.

The inlet and exit enthalpies of water are found from steam tables. At 20°C, the saturated inlet enthalpy is 83.96 kJ/kg. At 30°C, the exit enthalpy is 125.79 kJ/kg.

The energy balance is

$$\dot{m}_{\text{HFC-134a}}(h_i - h_e)_{\text{HFC-134a}} = \dot{m}_{\text{water}}(h_e - h_i)_{\text{water}}$$

$$\left(0.1 \dfrac{\text{kg}}{\text{s}}\right)\left(455.3 \dfrac{\text{kJ}}{\text{kg}} - 243.7 \dfrac{\text{kJ}}{\text{kg}}\right)$$

$$= \dot{m}_{\text{water}}\left(125.79 \dfrac{\text{kJ}}{\text{kg}} - 83.96 \dfrac{\text{kJ}}{\text{kg}}\right)$$

$$\dot{m}_{\text{water}} = 0.506 \text{ kg/s} \quad (0.51 \text{ kg/s})$$

The answer is (A).

6. The NaCl will be in an equilibrium state when all of the substance is melted. At equilibrium, the change in Gibbs energy is zero.

$$\Delta g = \Delta h - T_m \Delta s = 0$$

$$T_m = \frac{\Delta h}{\Delta s} = \frac{\left(30 \dfrac{\text{kJ}}{\text{mol}}\right)\left(1000 \dfrac{\text{J}}{\text{kJ}}\right)}{28 \dfrac{\text{J}}{\text{mol·K}}}$$

$$= 1071\text{K} \quad (1100\text{K})$$

The answer is (D).

7. Use the HFC-134a pressure-enthalpy diagram. At 1.3 MPa, the specific volume of the saturated liquid (from the almost vertical broken line) is approximately 0.00090 m³/kg. Similarly, the specific volume of the saturated vapor is approximately 0.015 m³/kg.

The volume is

$$V = mv = m(v_f + xv_{fg}) = m(v_f + x(v_g - v_f))$$

$$= (0.05 \text{ kg})\left|\begin{array}{l} 0.00090 \dfrac{\text{m}^3}{\text{kg}} + (0.375) \\[2mm] \times\left(0.015 \dfrac{\text{m}^3}{\text{kg}} - 0.00090 \dfrac{\text{m}^3}{\text{kg}}\right) \end{array}\right|$$

$$= 3.094 \times 10^{-4} \text{ m}^3 \quad (3.1 \times 10^{-4} \text{ m}^3)$$

The answer is (C).

8. The relation between the temperature and the pressure of an ideal gas is given by the ideal gas law.

$$pV = mRT$$

The pressure and the temperature are directly proportional to each other, so if the other values remain constant, an increase or decrease in one will result in a proportional increase or decrease, respectively, in the other.

The answer is (A).

9. Use the ideal gas law to find the approximate pressure.

$$p \approx \frac{mRT}{V}$$

$$= \frac{(80 \text{ kg})\left(0.4615 \dfrac{\text{kJ}}{\text{kg·K}}\right)(425°\text{C} + 273°)}{(0.5 \text{ m}^3)\left(1000 \dfrac{\text{kPa}}{\text{MPa}}\right)}$$

$$= 51.54 \text{ MPa}$$

The reduced temperature and pressure for the real gas, respectively, are

$$T_r = \frac{T}{T_c} = \frac{425°C + 273°}{647.1K} = 1.08$$

$$p_r = \frac{p}{p_c} = \frac{51.54 \text{ MPa}}{22.06 \text{ MPa}} = 2.34$$

Use the generalized compressibility chart found in the *NCEES Handbook* section titled "Thermodynamics." At the reduced temperature and pressure, the compressibility factor is $Z \approx 0.38$. The generalized compressibility equation of state for a real gas is used to calculate the pressure and can be found in the *NCEES Handbook* section titled "Thermodynamics."

$$\begin{aligned} p' = Z\frac{mRT}{V} &= Zp \\ &= (0.38)(51.54 \text{ MPa}) \\ &= 19.59 \text{ MPa} \quad (20 \text{ MPa}) \end{aligned}$$

The answer is (A).

10. The mass of the liquid refrigerant is

$$\begin{aligned} m_f = (1 - x_2)m_{\text{total}} \\ &= (1 - 0.02538)(400 \text{ kg}) \\ &= 389.8 \text{ kg} \end{aligned}$$

The volume of the liquid refrigerant is

$$\begin{aligned} V_f = m_f v_f \\ &= (389.8 \text{ kg})\left(0.000795 \ \frac{\text{m}^3}{\text{kg}}\right) \\ &= 0.31 \text{ m}^3 \end{aligned}$$

The answer is (C).

13 Properties of Substances

Nomenclature

a	constant	–	–
a	Helmholtz function	Btu/lbm	kJ/kg
b	constant	–	–
c	specific heat	Btu/lbm	kJ/kg·K
$\bar{c}$	mean heat capacity	Btu/lbm	kJ/kg·K
C	heat	Btu	kJ
C	number of components in the system	–	–
F	number of independent variables	–	–
g	Gibbs function	Btu/lbm	kJ/kg
h	specific enthalpy	Btu/lbm	kJ/kg
H	enthalpy	Btu	kJ
J	Joule's constant, 778	ft-lbf/Btu	n.a.
k	ratio of specific heats	–	–
m	mass	lbm	kg
M	molecular weight	–	kg/kmol
N	number	–	–
p	pressure*	lbf/in^2	Pa
P	number of phases existing simultaneously	–	–
R	specific gas constant	ft-lbf/lbm-°R	kJ/kg·K
$\bar{R}$	universal gas constant, 1545 (8314)	ft-lbf/lbmol-°R	J/kmol·K
s	specific entropy	Btu/lbm-°R	kJ/kg·K
S	entropy	Btu/°R	kJ/K
T	absolute temperature	°R	K
u	specific internal energy	Btu/lbm	kJ/kg
U	internal energy	Btu	kJ
V	volume	ft^3	m^3
x	quality	–	–
z	compressibility factor	–	–
Z	compressibility factor	–	–

*With the exception of use as a subscript, the NCEES *FE Reference Handbook* (*NCEES Handbook*) uses uppercase P as the symbol for pressure. In contrast to the *NCEES Handbook*, this book generally uses lowercase p to represent pressure. The equations in this book involving pressure will differ slightly in appearance from the *NCEES Handbook*.

Symbols

ρ	density	lbm/ft^3	kg/m^3
υ	specific volume*	ft^3/lbm	m^3/kg
$\bar{\upsilon}$	molar specific volume	ft^3/lbmol	m^3/kmol

*The *NCEES Handbook* uses lowercase italic v for specific volume. This book uses Greek upsilon, υ, to avoid confusion with the symbol for velocity in kinetic energy calculations. The equations in this book involving specific volume will differ slightly in appearance from those in the *NCEES Handbook*.

Subscripts

c	critical
f	fluid
fg	liquid-to-gas (vaporization)
g	gas
p	constant pressure
r	reduced
T	constant temperature
υ	constant volume

1. PHASES OF A PURE SUBSTANCE

Thermodynamics is the study of a substance's energy-related properties. The properties of a substance and the procedures used to determine those properties depend on the state and the phase of the substance. The thermodynamic *state* of a substance is defined by two or more independent thermodynamic properties. For example, the temperature and pressure of a substance are two properties commonly used to define the state of a superheated vapor.

The common *phases* of a substance are solid, liquid, and gas. However, because substances behave according to different rules, it is convenient to categorize them into more than only these three phases.

Solid: A solid does not take on the shape or volume of its container.

Saturated liquid: A saturated liquid has absorbed as much heat energy as it can without vaporizing. Liquid water at standard atmospheric pressure and 212°F (100°C) is an example of a saturated liquid.

Subcooled liquid: If a liquid is not saturated (i.e., the liquid is not at its boiling point), it is said to be subcooled. Water at 1 atm and room temperature is subcooled, as it can absorb additional energy without vaporizing.

Liquid-vapor mixture: A liquid and vapor of the same substance can coexist at the same temperature and pressure. This is called a two-phase, liquid-vapor mixture.

Perfect gas: A perfect gas is an ideal gas whose specific heats (and hence ratio of specific heats) are constant.

Saturated vapor: A vapor (e.g., steam at standard atmospheric pressure and 212°F (100°C)) that is on the verge of condensing is said to be saturated.

Superheated vapor: A superheated vapor is one that has absorbed more energy than is needed merely to vaporize it. A superheated vapor will not condense when small amounts of energy are removed.

Ideal gas: A gas is a highly superheated vapor. If the gas behaves according to the ideal gas law, $pV = mRT$, it is called an ideal gas.

Real gas: A real gas does not behave according to the ideal gas laws.

Gas mixtures: Most gases mix together freely. Two or more pure gases together constitute a gas mixture.

Vapor-gas mixtures: Atmospheric air is an example of a mixture of several gases and water vapor.

It is theoretically possible to develop a three-dimensional surface that predicts a substance's phase based on the properties of pressure, temperature, and specific volume. Such a three-dimensional p-v-T diagram is illustrated in Fig. 13.1.

Figure 13.1 *Three-Dimensional p-v-T Phase Diagram*

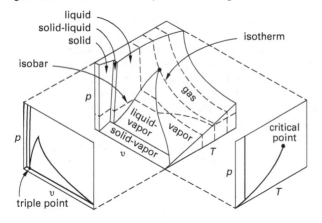

If one property is held constant during a process, a two-dimensional projection of the p-v-T diagram can be used. Figure 13.2 is an example of this projection, which is known as an *equilibrium diagram* or a *phase diagram*.

Figure 13.2 *Pressure-Volume Phase Diagram*

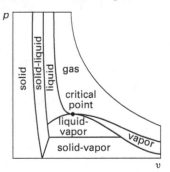

The most important part of a phase diagram is limited to the liquid-vapor region. A general phase diagram showing this region and the bell-shaped dividing line (known as the *vapor dome*) is shown in Fig. 13.3.

Figure 13.3 *Vapor Dome with Isobars*

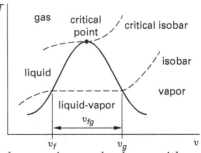

The vapor dome region can be drawn with many variables for the axes. For example, either temperature or pressure can be used for the vertical axis. Internal energy, enthalpy, specific volume, or entropy can be chosen for the horizontal axis. However, the principles presented here apply to all combinations.

The left-hand part of the vapor dome curve separates the liquid phase from the liquid-vapor phase. This part of the line is known as the *saturated liquid line*. Similarly, the right-hand part of the line separates the liquid-vapor phase from the vapor phase. This line is called the *saturated vapor line*.

Lines of constant pressure (*isobars*) can be superimposed on the vapor dome. Each isobar is horizontal as it passes through the two-phase region, verifying that both temperature and pressure remain unchanged as a liquid vaporizes.

There is no dividing line between liquid and vapor at the top of the vapor dome. Above the vapor dome, the phase is a gas.

The implicit dividing line between liquid and gas is the isobar that intersects the topmost part of the vapor dome. This is known as the *critical isobar*, and the highest point of the vapor dome is known as the *critical point*. This critical isobar also provides a way to distinguish between a vapor and a gas. A substance below the critical isobar (but to the right of the vapor dome) is a vapor. Above the critical isobar, it is a gas.

The *triple point* of a substance is a unique state at which solid, liquid, and gaseous phases can coexist. For instance, the triple point of water occurs at a pressure of 0.00592 atm and a temperature of 491.71°R (273.16K).

Figure 13.4 illustrates a vapor dome for which pressure has been chosen as the vertical axis and enthalpy has been chosen as the horizontal axis. The shape of the dome is essentially the same, but the lines of constant temperature (*isotherms*) have slopes of different signs than the isobars.

Figure 13.4 *Vapor Dome with Isotherms*

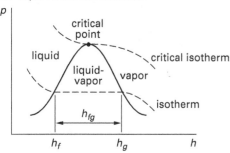

Figure 13.4 also illustrates the subscripting convention used to identify points on the saturation line. The subscript f (fluid) is used to indicate a saturated liquid. The subscript g (gas) is used to indicate a saturated vapor. The subscript fg is used to indicate the difference in saturation properties.

The vapor dome is a good tool for illustration, but it cannot be used to determine a substance's phase. Such a determination must be made based on the substance's pressure and temperature according to the following rules.

rule 1: A substance is a subcooled liquid if its temperature is less than the saturation temperature corresponding to its pressure.

rule 2: A substance is in the liquid-vapor region if its temperature is equal to the saturation temperature corresponding to its pressure.

rule 3: A substance is a superheated vapor if its temperature is greater than the saturation temperature corresponding to its pressure.

rule 4: A substance is a subcooled liquid if its pressure is greater than the saturation pressure corresponding to its temperature.

rule 5: A substance is in the liquid-vapor region if its pressure is equal to the saturation pressure corresponding to its temperature.

rule 6: A substance is a superheated vapor if its pressure is less than the saturation pressure corresponding to its temperature.

Equation 13.1: Gibbs' Phase Rule (Non-Reacting Systems)

$$P + F = C + 2 \qquad 13.1$$

Description

Gibbs' phase rule defines the relationship between the number of phases and components in a mixture at equilibrium.

P is the number of phases existing simultaneously; F is the number of independent variables, known as *degrees of freedom*; and C is the number of components in the system. Composition, temperature, and pressure are examples of degrees of freedom that can be varied.

For example, if water is to be stored such that three phases (solid, liquid, gas) are present simultaneously, then $P = 3$, $C = 1$, and $F = 0$. That is, neither pressure nor temperature can be varied independently. This state is exemplified by water at its triple point.

Example

How many phases can exist in equilibrium for a fixed proportion water-alcohol mixture held at constant pressure?

(A) 0

(B) 1

(C) 2

(D) 3

Solution

There are two components, water and alcohol, so $C = 2$. Normally, composition, pressure, and temperature can be varied (i.e., three degrees of freedom), but with a specific composition and pressure held constant, $F = 1$. From Gibbs' phase rule, Eq. 13.1, the number of phases, P, is

$$\begin{aligned} P + F &= C + 2 \\ P &= C + 2 - F \\ &= 2 + 2 - 1 \\ &= 3 \end{aligned}$$

The answer is (D).

2. STATE FUNCTIONS (PROPERTIES)

The thermodynamic state or condition of a substance is determined by its properties. *Intensive properties* are independent of the amount of substance present. Temperature, pressure, and stress are examples of intensive properties. *Extensive properties* are dependent on (i.e., are proportional to) the amount of substance present. Examples are volume, strain, charge, and mass.

In most books on thermodynamics, both lowercase and uppercase forms of the same characters are used to represent property variables. The two forms are used to distinguish between the units of mass. For example, lowercase h represents specific enthalpy (usually called "enthalpy") in units of Btu/lbm or kJ/kg. Uppercase H is used to represent the molar enthalpy in units of Btu/lbmol or kJ/kmol.

Properties of gases in tabulated form are useful or necessary for solving many thermodynamic problems. The properties of saturated and superheated steam are tabulated in Table 13.1[1] and Table 13.2, respectively, at the end of this chapter. A pressure-enthalpy (p-h) diagram for refrigerant HFC-134a in SI units is presented in Fig. 13.5 at the end of this chapter.[2]

Mass

The mass, m, of a substance is a measure of its quantity. Mass is independent of location and gravitational field strength. In thermodynamics, the customary U.S. and SI units of mass are pound-mass (lbm) and kilogram (kg), respectively.

Pressure

Customary U.S. pressure units are pounds per square inch (lbf/in^2). Standard SI pressure units are kPa or MPa, although bars are also used in tabulations of thermodynamic data. (1 bar = 1 atm = 10^5 Pa.)

Most pressure gauges read atmospheric pressures, but in general, thermodynamic calculations will be performed using absolute pressures. The values of a standard atmosphere in various units are given in Table 13.3.

Table 13.3 Standard Atmospheric Pressure

1.000 atm	(atmosphere)
14.696 psia	(pounds per square inch absolute)
2116.2 psfa	(pounds per square foot absolute)
407.1 in w.g.	(inches of water; inches water gage)
33.93 ft w.g.	(feet of water; feet water gage)
29.921 in Hg	(inches of mercury)
760.0 mm Hg	(millimeters of mercury)
760.0 torr	
1.013 bars	
1013 millibars	
1.013×10^5 Pa	(pascals)
101.3 kPa	(kilopascals)

Temperature

Temperature is a thermodynamic property of a substance that depends on energy content. Heat energy entering a substance will increase the temperature of that substance. Normally, heat energy will flow only

from a hot object to a cold object. If two objects are in *thermal equilibrium* (are at the same temperature), no heat energy will flow between them.

If two systems are in thermal equilibrium, they must be at the same temperature. If both systems are in equilibrium with a third system, then all three systems are at the same temperature. This concept is known as the *zeroth law of thermodynamics*.

The *absolute temperature scale* defines temperature independently of the properties of any particular substance. This is unlike the Celsius and Fahrenheit scales, which are based on the freezing point of water. The absolute temperature scale should be used for all thermodynamic calculations.

In the customary U.S. system, the absolute temperature scale is the *Rankine scale*.

$$T_{°R} = T_{°F} + 459.67°$$

$$\Delta T_{°R} = \Delta T_{°F}$$

The absolute temperature scale in SI is the *Kelvin scale*.

$$T_K = T_{°C} + 273.15°$$

$$\Delta T_K = \Delta T_{°C}$$

The relationships between the four temperature scales are illustrated in Fig. 13.6, which also defines the approximate *boiling point*, *triple point*, *ice point*, and *absolute zero* temperatures.

Figure 13.6 Temperature Scales

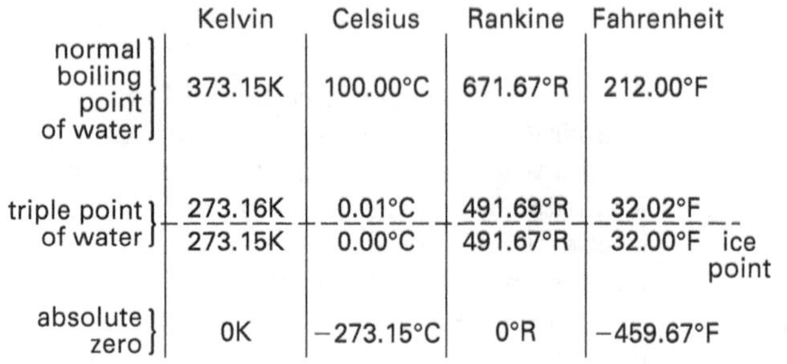

	Kelvin	Celsius	Rankine	Fahrenheit
normal boiling point of water	373.15K	100.00°C	671.67°R	212.00°F
triple point of water	273.16K	0.01°C	491.69°R	32.02°F
	273.15K	0.00°C	491.67°R	32.00°F ice point
absolute zero	0K	−273.15°C	0°R	−459.67°F

Equation 13.2: Specific Volume

$$v = V/m \qquad 13.2$$

Variation

$$v = \frac{1}{\rho}$$

---

[1]The *NCEES Handbook* is not consistent with how it uses zero in Table 13.1. There is no difference between "0.00" in the first line and "0" in the last line.
[2]The *NCEES Handbook* labels this figure as a *P-h* diagram, consistent with its convention to use uppercase *P* as the symbol for pressure.

Description

Specific volume, v, is the volume occupied by one unit mass of a substance. Customary U.S. units in tabulations of thermodynamic data are cubic feet per pound-mass (ft^3/lbm). Standard SI specific volume units are cubic meters per kilogram (m^3/kg). Molar specific volume has units of ft^3/lbmol (m^3/kmol) and is seldom tabulated. Specific volume is the reciprocal of density.

Example

A 1 m^3 volume of gas has a mass of 1.2 kg. What is most nearly the specific volume of the gas?

(A) 730 cm^3/g

(B) 830 cm^3/g

(C) 890 cm^3/g

(D) 940 cm^3/g

Solution

Use Eq. 13.2 to find the specific volume of the gas.

$$v = V/m = \frac{(1 \ m^3)\left(100 \ \frac{cm}{m}\right)^3}{(1.2 \ kg)\left(1000 \ \frac{g}{kg}\right)}$$

$$= 833 \ cm^3/g \quad (830 \ cm^3/g)$$

The answer is (B).

Equation 13.3: Specific Internal Energy

$$u = U/m \qquad \text{13.3}$$

Description

Internal energy accounts for all of the energy of the substance excluding pressure, potential, and kinetic energy. The internal energy is a function of the state of a system. Examples of internal energy are the translational, rotational, and vibrational energies of the molecules and atoms in the substance. Since the movement of atoms and molecules increases with temperature, internal energy is a function of temperature. It does not depend on the process or path taken to reach a particular temperature.

In the United States, the *British thermal unit*, Btu, is used in thermodynamics to represent the various forms of energy. (One Btu is approximately the energy given off by burning one wooden match.) Standard units of specific internal energy, u, are Btu/lbm and kJ/kg. The units of molar internal energy are Btu/lbmol and kJ/kmol. Equation 13.3 gives the relationship between the specific and system internal energy.[3]

Example

A system contains 1 kg of saturated steam vapor heated to 120°C. The specific internal energy of saturated steam vapor is 2529.3 kJ/kg. What is most nearly the total internal energy of the steam?

(A) 2525 kJ

(B) 2529 kJ

(C) 3525 kJ

(D) 3552 kJ

Solution

Use Eq. 13.3 to calculate the total internal energy.

$$u = U/m$$
$$U = mu$$
$$= (1 \ kg)\left(2529.3 \ \frac{kJ}{kg}\right)$$
$$= 2529.3 \ kJ \quad (2529 \ kJ)$$

The answer is (B).

Equation 13.4: Specific Enthalpy

$$h = u + pv$$
$$= H/m \qquad \text{13.4}$$

Description

Enthalpy represents the total useful energy of a substance. Useful energy consists of two parts: the specific internal energy, u, and the *flow energy* (also known as *flow work* and *p-V work*), pv. Therefore, enthalpy has the same units as internal energy.

Enthalpy is defined as useful energy because, ideally, all of it can be used to perform useful tasks. It takes energy to increase the temperature of a substance. If that internal energy is recovered, it can be used to heat something else (e.g., to vaporize water in a boiler). Also, it takes

---

[3]Some authorities use uppercase letters to represent the molar properties of a substance (e.g., H for molar enthalpy) and lowercase letters to represent the specific (i.e., per unit mass) properties (e.g., h for specific enthalpy). The *NCEES Handbook* uses uppercase letters to represent the total properties of the system, regardless of the amount of system substance. For example, V is the total volume of the substance in the system, U is the total internal energy of the substance in the system, and H is the total enthalpy of the substance in the system. Except for use with equations of state, the molar properties are not represented in the *NCEES Handbook*.

energy to increase pressure and volume (as in blowing up a balloon). If pressure and volume are decreased, useful energy is given up.

Strictly speaking, the customary U.S. units of Eq. 13.4 are not consistent, since flow work (as written) has units of ft-lbf/lbm, not Btu/lbm. (There is also a consistency problem if pressure is defined in lbf/ft² and given in lbf/in².) Eq. 13.4 should be written as

$$h = u + \frac{pv}{J}$$

The conversion factor, J, in the above equation is known as *Joule's constant*. It has a value of approximately 778 ft-lbf/Btu. (In SI units, Joule's constant has a value of 1.0 N·m/J and is unnecessary.) As in Eq. 13.4, Joule's constant is often omitted from the statement of generic thermodynamic equations, but it is always needed with customary U.S. units for dimensional consistency.

Example

Steam at 416 Pa and 166K has a specific volume of 0.41 m³/kg and a specific enthalpy of 29.4 kJ/kg. What is most nearly the internal energy per kilogram of steam?

(A)   28.5 kJ/kg

(B)   29.2 kJ/kg

(C)   30.2 kJ/kg

(D)   30.4 kJ/kg

Solution

From Eq. 13.4,

$$h = u + pv$$
$$u = h - pv$$

$$= 29.4 \ \frac{\text{kJ}}{\text{kg}} - \frac{(416 \ \text{Pa})\left(0.41 \ \dfrac{\text{m}^3}{\text{kg}}\right)}{1000 \ \dfrac{\text{Pa}}{\text{kPa}}}$$

$$= 29.2 \ \text{kJ/kg}$$

The answer is (B).

Equation 13.5: Specific Entropy

$$s = S/m \qquad \text{13.5}$$

Description

Entropy is a measure of the energy that is no longer available to perform useful work within the current environment. Other definitions (the "disorder of the system,"

the "randomness of the system," etc.) are frequently quoted. Although these alternate definitions cannot be used in calculations, they are consistent with the third law of thermodynamics (also known as the *Nernst theorem*). This law states that the absolute entropy of a perfect crystalline solid in thermodynamic equilibrium is (approaches) zero when the temperature is (approaches) absolute zero.

The units of specific entropy are Btu/lbm-°R and kJ/kg·K.

Equation 13.6: Gibbs Function

$$g = h - Ts \qquad \text{13.6}$$

Variation

$$g = u + pv - Ts$$

Description

The Gibbs function for a pure substance is defined by Eq. 13.6 and the variation equation. It is used in investigating latent heat changes and chemical reactions.

For a constant-temperature, constant-pressure, nonflow process that is approaching equilibrium, the Gibbs function approaches a minimum value.

$$(dg)_{T,p} < 0 \quad \text{[nonequilibrium]}$$

Once the minimum value is obtained, equilibrium is attained, and the Gibbs function is constant.

$$(dg)_{T,p} = 0 \quad \text{[equilibrium]}$$

The *Gibbs function of formation*, g^0, has been tabulated at the standard reference conditions of 25°C and 1 atm. A chemical reaction can occur spontaneously only if the change in Gibbs function is negative (i.e., the Gibbs function of formation for the products is less than the Gibbs function of formation for the reactants).

$$\sum_{\text{products}} Ng^0 < \sum_{\text{reactants}} Ng^0$$

Example

Water at 50°C and 1 atm has a specific enthalpy of 209.33 kJ/kg and a specific entropy of 0.7038 kJ/kgK. What is most nearly the Gibbs function for the water?

(A)   −18 kJ/kg

(B)   −3.0 kJ/kg

(C)   300 kJ/kg

(D)   440 kJ/kg

Solution

Use Eq. 13.6. The Gibbs function is

$$g = h - Ts$$

$$= 209.33 \ \frac{kJ}{kg} - (50°C + 273°)\left(0.7038 \ \frac{kJ}{kg \cdot K}\right)$$

$$= -17.997 \ kJ/kg \quad (-18 \ kJ/kg)$$

The answer is (A).

Equation 13.7: Helmholtz Function

$$a = u - Ts \qquad \qquad 13.7$$

Variation

$$a = h - pv - Ts$$

Description

The Helmholtz function for a pure substance is defined by Eq. 13.7. Like the Gibbs function, the Helmholtz function is used in investigating equilibrium conditions. For a constant-temperature, constant-volume nonflow process approaching equilibrium, the Helmholtz function approaches its minimum value.

$$(dA)_{T,V} < 0 \quad [\text{nonequilibrium}]$$

Once the minimum value is obtained, equilibrium is attained, and the Helmholtz function will be constant.

$$(dA)_{T,V} = 0 \quad [\text{equilibrium}]$$

The Helmholtz function is sometimes known as the *free energy of the system* because its change in a reversible isothermal process equals the maximum energy that can be "freed" and converted to mechanical work. The same term has also been used for the Gibbs function under analogous conditions. For example, the difference in standard Gibbs functions of reactants and products has often been called the "free energy difference."

Since there is a possibility for confusion, it is better to refer to the Gibbs and Helmholtz functions by their actual names.

Example

A superheated vapor has a specific internal energy of 2733.7 kJ/kg and a specific entropy of 8.0333 kJ/kg·K.

What is most nearly the Helmholtz free energy function of the superheated vapor at 250°C and 0.1 MPa?

- (A) −2700 kJ/kg
- (B) −1500 kJ/kg
- (C) 8.0 kJ/kg
- (D) 2700 kJ/kg

Solution

Use Eq. 13.7. The Helmholtz function is

$$a = u - Ts$$

$$= 2733.7 \ \frac{kJ}{kg} - (250°C + 273°)\left(8.0333 \ \frac{kJ}{kg \cdot K}\right)$$

$$= -1468 \ kJ/kg \quad (-1500 \ kJ/kg)$$

The answer is (B).

Equation 13.8 and Eq. 13.9: Specific Heat

$$c_p = \left(\frac{\partial h}{\partial T}\right)_p \quad [\text{at constant pressure}] \qquad 13.8$$

$$c_v = \left(\frac{\partial u}{\partial T}\right)_v \quad [\text{at constant volume}] \qquad 13.9$$

Variation

$$c = \frac{Q}{m\Delta T}$$

Values

Table 13.4 Approximate Specific Heats of Selected Liquids and Solids (at room temperature)

| | \multicolumn{2}{c}{c_p} | \multicolumn{2}{c}{density} |
substance	$\frac{kJ}{kg \cdot K}$	$\frac{Btu}{lbm\text{-}°R}$	$\frac{kg}{m^3}$	$\frac{lbm}{ft^3}$
liquids				
ammonia	4.80	1.146	602	38
mercury	0.139	0.033	13 560	847
water	4.18	1.000	997	62.4
solids				
aluminum	0.900	0.215	2700	170
copper	0.386	0.092	8900	555
ice (0°C; 32°F)	2.11	0.502	917	57.2
iron	0.450	0.107	7840	490
lead	0.128	0.030	11 310	705

Description

An increase in internal energy is needed to cause a rise in temperature. Different substances differ in the quantity of heat needed to produce a given temperature increase. The heat energy, Q, required to change the temperature of a mass, m, by an amount, ΔT, is called the *specific heat (heat capacity) of the substance*, c (see the variation equation). Because specific heats of solids and liquids are slightly temperature dependent, the mean specific heats are used for processes covering large temperature ranges.

For gases, the specific heat depends on the type of process during which the heat exchange occurs. Equation 13.8 defines the specific heats for constant-pressure processes, c_p, and Eq. 13.9 defines the specific heat for constant-volume processes, c_v.

c_p and c_v for solids and liquids are essentially the same and are given in Table 13.4. Approximate values of c_p and c_v for common gases are given in Table 13.5.

Example

The temperature-dependent molar heat capacity of nitrogen in units of kJ/kmol·K is

$$C_p = 39.06 - 512.79\,T^{-1.5} + 1072.7\,T^{-2} - 820.4\,T^{-3}$$

What is most nearly the change in enthalpy per kg of nitrogen when it is heated at constant pressure from 1000K to 1500K?

(A)   600 kJ/kg

(B)   700 kJ/kg

(C)   800 kJ/kg

(D)   900 kJ/kg

Solution

Use separation of variables with Eq. 13.8 to find the change in specific enthalpy. (Use uppercase letters to designate the molar quantities.)

$$C_p = \left(\frac{\partial H}{\partial T}\right)_p$$

$$\partial H = C_p\,\partial T$$

$$\Delta H = \int C_p\,dT$$

$$= \int_{1000K}^{1500K}\left(\begin{array}{l}39.06 - 512.79\,T^{-1.5}\\ +1072.7\,T^{-2} - 820.4\,T^{-3}\end{array}\right)dT$$

$$= 19\,524 \text{ kJ/kmol}$$

The molecular weight of nitrogen is 28 kg/kmol. The change in specific enthalpy is

$$\Delta h = \frac{\Delta H}{M} = \frac{19\,524\ \dfrac{\text{kJ}}{\text{kmol}}}{28\ \dfrac{\text{kg}}{\text{kmol}}}$$

$$= 697.3 \text{ kJ/kg}\quad (700 \text{ kJ/kg})$$

The answer is (B).

3. TWO-PHASE SYSTEMS: LIQUID-VAPOR MIXTURES

Equation 13.10: Quality

$$x = m_g/(m_g + m_f) \qquad \textit{13.10}$$

Description

Within the vapor dome, water is at its saturation pressure and temperature. When saturated, water can simultaneously exist in liquid and vapor phases in any proportion between 0 and 1. The *quality* is the fraction by weight of the total mass that is vapor.

Example

If the ratio of vapor mass to liquid mass in a mixture is 0.8, the quality of the mixture is most nearly

(A)   0.20

(B)   0.25

(C)   0.44

(D)   0.80

Solution

Write the mass of the vapor in terms of the mass of liquid.

$$\frac{m_g}{m_f} = 0.8$$

$$m_g = 0.8 m_f$$

From Eq. 13.10, the quality of the mixture is

$$x = m_g/(m_g + m_f) = \frac{0.8 m_f}{0.8 m_f + m_f}$$

$$= 0.44$$

The answer is (C).

Table 13.5 *Approximate Specific Heats of Selected Gases (at room temperature)*

gas	mol. wt	c_p kJ/kg·K	c_p Btu/lbm-°R	c_v kJ/kg·K	c_v Btu/lbm-°R	k	R kJ/kg·K
air	29	1.00	0.240	0.718	0.171	1.40	0.2870
argon	40	0.520	0.125	0.312	0.0756	1.67	0.2081
butane	58	1.72	0.415	1.57	0.381	1.09	0.1430
carbon dioxide	44	0.846	0.203	0.657	0.158	1.29	0.1889
carbon monoxide	28	1.04	0.249	0.744	0.178	1.40	0.2968
ethane	30	1.77	0.427	1.49	0.361	1.18	0.2765
helium	4	5.19	1.25	3.12	0.753	1.67	2.0769
hydrogen	2	14.3	3.43	10.2	2.44	1.40	4.1240
methane	16	2.25	0.532	1.74	0.403	1.30	0.5182
neon	20	1.03	0.246	0.618	0.148	1.67	0.4119
nitrogen	28	1.04	0.248	0.743	0.177	1.40	0.2968
octane vapor	114	1.71	0.409	1.64	0.392	1.04	0.0729
oxygen	32	0.918	0.219	0.658	0.157	1.40	0.2598
propane	44	1.68	0.407	1.49	0.362	1.12	0.1885
steam	18	1.87	0.445	1.41	0.335	1.33	0.4615

Equation 13.11 Through Eq. 13.18: Primary Thermodynamic Properties

$$v = xv_g + (1-x)v_f \qquad \text{13.11}$$

$$v = v_f + xv_{fg} \qquad \text{13.12}$$

$$u = xu_g + (1-x)u_f \qquad \text{13.13}$$

$$u = u_f + xu_{fg} \qquad \text{13.14}$$

$$h = xh_g + (1-x)h_f \qquad \text{13.15}$$

$$h = h_f + xh_{fg} \qquad \text{13.16}$$

$$s = xs_g + (1-x)s_f \qquad \text{13.17}$$

$$s = s_f + xs_{fg} \qquad \text{13.18}$$

Description

When the thermodynamic state of a substance is within the vapor dome, there is a one-to-one correspondence between the saturation temperature and saturation pressure. One determines the other. The thermodynamic state is uniquely defined by any two independent properties (temperature and quality, pressure and enthalpy, entropy and quality, etc.).

If the quality of a liquid-vapor mixture is known, it can be used to calculate all of the primary thermodynamic properties (specific volume, specific internal energy, specific enthalpy, and specific entropy). If a thermodynamic property has a value between the saturated liquid and saturated vapor values (e.g., h is between h_f and h_g), then Eq. 13.11 through Eq. 13.18 can be solved for the quality.

Each pair of equations (e.g., Eq. 13.11 and Eq. 13.12, Eq. 13.13 and Eq. 13.14, Eq. 13.15 and Eq. 13.16, and Eq. 13.17 and Eq. 13.18) is equivalent by the following relationships.

$$v_{fg} = v_g - v_f$$
$$u_{fg} = u_g - u_f$$
$$h_{fg} = h_g - h_f$$
$$s_{fg} = s_g - s_f$$

If temperatures are known, the quantities in the previous relationships can be obtained from *saturation tables* (or *steam tables* in the case of water). (See Table 13.1.)

Example

A saturated steam supply line is analyzed for specific internal energy. At 270°C, the internal energy of the steam is 2160.1 kJ/kg. The specific internal energy of the saturated liquid is 1178.1 kJ/kg. The specific internal energy of the saturated vapor is 2593.7 kJ/kg. What is most nearly the quality of the steam?

(A) 20%

(B) 50%

(C) 70%

(D) 80%

Solution

Solve Eq. 13.13 for the quality.

$$u = xu_g + (1-x)u_f$$

$$x = \frac{u - u_f}{u_g - u_f} = \frac{2160.1 \ \frac{m^3}{kg} - 1178.1 \ \frac{m^3}{kg}}{2593.7 \ \frac{m^3}{kg} - 1178.1 \ \frac{m^3}{kg}}$$

$$= 0.69 \quad (70\%)$$

The answer is (C).

4. PHASE RELATIONS

Equation 13.19: Clapeyron Equation (for Phase Transitions)

$$\left(\frac{dp}{dT}\right)_{sat} = \frac{h_{fg}}{Tv_{fg}} = \frac{s_{fg}}{v_{fg}} \qquad \textit{13.19}$$

Description

The change in enthalpy during a phase transition, although it cannot be measured directly, can be determined from the pressure, temperature, and specific volume changes through the *Clapeyron equation*, Eq. 13.19.[4] $(dp/dT)_{sat}$ is the slope of the vapor-liquid saturation line.

Equation 13.20: Clausius-Clapeyron Equation

$$\ln\left(\frac{p_2}{p_1}\right) = \frac{h_{fg}}{R} \cdot \frac{T_2 - T_1}{T_1 T_2} \qquad \textit{13.20}$$

Description

Under the assumptions that $v_{fg} = v_g$, the system behaves ideally, and h_{fg} is independent of temperature, Eq. 13.19 reduces to the Clausius-Clapeyron equation, Eq. 13.20.[5] Although more accurate methods exist (e.g., the *Antoine equation*), the Clausius-Clapeyron equation can be used to estimate the vapor pressure of pure solids and pure liquids. For solids, the heat of vaporization, h_{fg}, is replaced by the heat of sublimation.

Example

At 100°C, the heat of vaporization of water is 40.7 kJ/mol. What is the vapor pressure at 110°C?

(A) 0.71 atm

(B) 0.80 atm

(C) 0.88 atm

(D) 1.4 atm

Solution

A substance vaporizes when the pressure on it is reduced to its saturation pressure. Water boils at 100°C, so the saturation pressure at that temperature is 1.0 atm. (The steam table could also be used to determine $p_{sat,100°C}$.)

Use Eq. 13.20.

$$T_1 = 100°C + 273° = 373K$$
$$T_2 = 110°C + 273° = 383K$$

$$\ln\left(\frac{p_{v,383K}}{p_{v,373K}}\right) = \frac{h_{fg}}{R} \cdot \frac{T_2 - T_1}{T_1 T_2}$$

$$p_{v,383K} = p_{v,373K} e^{\frac{h_{fg}(T_2 - T_1)}{R(T_1 T_2)}}$$

$$= (1.0 \ atm) e^{\frac{\left(40.7 \ \frac{kJ}{mol}\right)\left(1000 \ \frac{J}{kJ}\right)(383K - 373K)}{\left(8.314 \ \frac{J}{mol \cdot K}\right)(383K)(373K)}}$$

$$= 1.4 \ atm$$

The answer is (D).

---

[4]The *NCEES Handbook* presents both forms of Eq. 13.19 as the Clapeyron equation, and both forms as equalities, which is not accurate. $(dp/dT)_{sat} = \Delta s/\Delta v$ is the actual Clapeyron equation, and it is thermodynamically exact, needing no approximations in its derivation. $(dp/dT)_{sat} \approx h_{fg}/Tv_{fg}$ is the differential form of the *two-point Clausius-Clapeyron equation* (presented separately as Eq. 13.20), and it is a thermodynamic approximation derived from $\Delta s \approx \Delta h/T$. In addition to being an approximation, Δs, Δh, and their ratio are not constant over the temperature range. Δh usually varies more slowly with temperature than Δs.
[5]In the *NCEES Handbook*, the natural logarithm is represented as $\ln_e$. The subscript e is a redundant notation, and so has been deleted from Eq. 13.20.

5. IDEAL GASES

A gas can be considered to behave ideally if its pressure is very low or the temperature is much higher than its critical temperature. (Otherwise, the substance is in vapor form.) Under these conditions, the molecule size is insignificant compared with the distance between molecules, and molecules do not interact. By definition, an ideal gas behaves according to the various ideal gas laws.

Equation 13.21: Specific Gas Constant

$$R = \frac{\overline{R}}{\text{mol. wt}} \qquad 13.21$$

Values

	customary U.S.	SI
universal gas constant, $\overline{R}$	1545 ft-lbf/lbmol-°R	8314 J/kmol·K
		0.08206 atm·L/mol·K
		287 J/kg·K

Description

R is the *specific gas constant*. It is specific because it is valid only for a gas with a particular molecular weight.[6]

$\overline{R}$, given in Eq. 13.21, is known as the *universal gas constant*. It is "universal" (within a system of units) because the same value can be used with any gas. Its value depends on the units used for pressure, temperature, and volume, as well as on the units of mass. Selected values of the universal gas constant in various units are given in the values section.

Example

Assume air to be an ideal gas with a molecular weight of 28.967 kg/kmol. What is most nearly the specific gas constant of air?

(A)   0.11 kJ/kg·K

(B)   0.29 kJ/kg·K

(C)   3.5 kJ/kg·K

(D)   8.3 kJ/kg·K

Solution

The universal gas constant is 8314 J/kmol·K. Use Eq. 13.21 to find the specific gas constant.

$$R = \frac{\overline{R}}{\text{mol. wt}} = \frac{8314 \ \dfrac{\text{J}}{\text{kmol·K}}}{\left(28.967 \ \dfrac{\text{kg}}{\text{kmol}}\right)\left(1000 \ \dfrac{\text{J}}{\text{kJ}}\right)}$$

$$= 0.2870 \ \text{kJ/kg·K} \quad (0.29 \ \text{kJ/kg·K})$$

The answer is (B).

Equation 13.22 Through Eq. 13.24: Ideal Gas Law

$$pv = RT \qquad 13.22$$

$$pV = mRT \qquad 13.23$$

$$p_1 v_1 / T_1 = p_2 v_2 / T_2 \qquad 13.24$$

Description

An *equation of state* is a relationship that predicts the state (i.e., a property, such as pressure, temperature, volume) from a set of two other independent properties.

Avogadro's law states that equal volumes of different gases at the same temperature and pressure contain equal numbers of molecules. For one mole of any gas, Avogadro's law can be stated as the equation of state for ideal gases, equivalent formulations of which are given by Eq. 13.22 through Eq. 13.24. Temperature, T, in Eq. 13.22 through Eq. 13.24 must be in degrees absolute.

Since R is constant for any ideal gas of a particular molecular weight, it follows that the quantity pv/T is constant for an ideal gas undergoing any process, as shown by Eq. 13.24.

Example

0.5 m³ of superheated steam has a pressure of 400 kPa and temperature of 300°C. What is most nearly the mass of the steam?

(A)   0.040 kg

(B)   0.76 kg

(C)   42 kg

(D)   55 kg

---

[6]The *NCEES Handbook* is inconsistent in the symbol it uses for molecular weight. In Eq. 13.21, "mol. wt" is used. In other thermodynamics equations, M is used.

Solution

Since the steam is superheated, consider it to be an ideal gas. The molecular weight of water is 18 kg/kmol. From Eq. 13.21, the specific gas constant is

$$R = \frac{\overline{R}}{\text{mol. wt}}$$

$$= \frac{8314 \ \frac{\text{J}}{\text{kmol·K}}}{\left(18 \ \frac{\text{kg}}{\text{kmol}}\right)\left(1000 \ \frac{\text{J}}{\text{kJ}}\right)}$$

$$= 0.4619 \ \text{kJ/kg·K}$$

Use the ideal gas law as given by Eq. 13.23 to find the mass of the steam.

$$pV = mRT$$

$$m = \frac{pV}{RT}$$

$$= \frac{(400 \ \text{kPa})\left(1000 \ \frac{\text{Pa}}{\text{kPa}}\right)(0.5 \ \text{m}^3)}{\left(0.4619 \ \frac{\text{kJ}}{\text{kg·K}}\right)\left(1000 \ \frac{\text{J}}{\text{kJ}}\right)(300°\text{C} + 273°)}$$

$$= 0.7557 \ \text{kg} \quad (0.76 \ \text{kg})$$

The answer is (B).

Equation 13.25 Through Eq. 13.27: Ideal Gas Criteria

$$c_p - c_v = R \qquad \qquad 13.25$$

$$\left(\frac{\partial h}{\partial p}\right)_T = 0 \qquad \qquad 13.26$$

$$\left(\frac{\partial u}{\partial v}\right)_T = 0 \qquad \qquad 13.27$$

Description

Specific enthalpy, and similarly specific internal energy, can be related to the equation of state for ideal gases (i.e., Eq. 13.22). Depending on the units chosen, a conversion factor may be needed.

$$h = u + pv = u + RT$$

$$u = h - pv = h - RT$$

Equation 13.25 through Eq. 13.27 can be derived from these relationships.

For an ideal gas, specific heats are related by the specific gas constant of the ideal gas, as shown by Eq. 13.25. Furthermore, some thermodynamic properties of ideal gases do not depend on other thermodynamic properties. In particular, the specific enthalpy of an ideal gas is independent of pressure for constant-temperature processes. That is, changes in pressure do not affect changes in specific enthalpy when temperature is constant, as shown by Eq. 13.26. Similarly, the specific internal energy of an ideal gas undergoing a constant-temperature process is independent of specific volume, as shown by Eq. 13.27.

Equation 13.28 Through Eq. 13.31: Changes in Thermodynamic Properties of Perfect Gases

$$\Delta u = c_v \Delta T \qquad \qquad 13.28$$

$$\Delta h = c_p \Delta T \qquad \qquad 13.29$$

$$\Delta s = c_p \ln(T_2/T_1) - R \ln(p_2/p_1) \qquad 13.30$$

$$\Delta s = c_v \ln(T_2/T_1) + R \ln(v_2/v_1) \qquad 13.31$$

Description

Some relations for determining property changes in an ideal gas do not depend on the type of process. This is particularly true for *perfect gases*, which are defined as ideal gases whose specific heats are constant.[7] For perfect gases, changes in enthalpy, internal energy, and entropy are independent of the process, as shown by Eq. 13.28 through Eq. 13.31. Equation 13.28 through Eq. 13.31 can be used for any process. Equation 13.28 does not require a constant-volume process. Similarly, Eq. 13.29 does not require a constant-pressure process.

Example

Nitrogen behaving as an ideal gas undergoes a temperature change from 260°C to 93°C. The specific heat at

---

[7]The *NCEES Handbook* introduces Eq. 13.28 through Eq. 13.31 with the statement, "...For cold air standard, heat capacities are assumed to be constant at their room temperature values. In that case, the following are true:" In truth, the four equations are valid for an ideal (perfect) gas at any temperature. The equations are not limited to cold air, nor are they limited to the simplified analysis of an air turbine or reciprocating internal combustion engine, which is where the *cold air standard*, or more commonly, just *air standard*, analysis is encountered.

constant pressure is 1.04 kJ/kg·K. What is most nearly the change in enthalpy per kilogram of nitrogen gas?

(A)   −200 kJ/kg

(B)   −170 kJ/kg

(C)   110 kJ/kg

(D)   170 kJ/kg

Solution

Specific heats of ideal (perfect) gases are defined to be constant. Therefore, Eq. 13.29 can be used to find the change in enthalpy.

$$\Delta h = c_p \Delta T$$
$$= \left(1.04 \; \frac{kJ}{kg \cdot K}\right)((93°C + 273°) - (260°C + 273°))$$
$$= -173.7 \; kJ/kg \quad (-170 \; kJ/kg)$$

The answer is (B).

Mean Heat Capacity

The *mean heat capacity*, $\bar{c}_p$ is to be used in Eq. 13.28 through Eq. 13.31 when heat capacities are temperature dependent (i.e., not constant). As the following equation shows, for most calculations, the average specific heat is either calculated as the average of the specific heats at the end-point temperatures, or is taken as the specific heat at the average temperature. A third approximation, used in linear processes (such as fluid flowing through a long pipe or heat exchanger), is to the specific heat at midpoint (mid-length) along the process. Similar equations can be used to calculate $\bar{c}_v$ for use with Eq. 13.28.

$$\bar{c}_p \approx \frac{c_{p,T_2} - c_{p,T_1}}{T_2 - T_1}$$
$$\approx c_{p,\frac{1}{2}(T_1 + T_2)}$$

Equation 13.32: Ratio of Specific Heats

$$k = c_p / c_v \qquad \text{13.32}$$

Values

For air, $k = 1.40$. For gases with monoatomic molecules (e.g., helium and argon) at standard conditions, $k \approx 1.67$. For diatomic gases (e.g., nitrogen and oxygen) at standard conditions, $k \approx 1.4$.

Description

Equation 13.32 is the *ratio of specific heats*. The value of that ratio of specific heats depends on the gas; and for maximum accuracy, the value also depends on other properties, such as temperature and pressure. The values primarily depend on the type of molecule formed by the gas.

6. REAL GASES

Real gases do not meet the basic assumptions defining an ideal gas. Specifically, the molecules of a real gas occupy a volume that is not negligible in comparison with the total volume of the gas. (This is especially true for gases at low temperatures.) Furthermore, real gases are subject to *van der Waals' forces*, which are attractive forces between gas molecules.

Equation 13.33 and Eq. 13.34: Theorem of Corresponding States

$$T_r = \frac{T}{T_c} \qquad \text{13.33}$$

$$p_r = \frac{p}{p_c} \qquad \text{13.34}$$

Description

The *theorem of corresponding states* says that the behavior (e.g., properties) of all liquid and gaseous substances can be correlated with "normalized" temperature and pressure. These so-called normalized characteristics are known as the *reduced temperature* (see Eq. 13.33) and *reduced pressure* (see Eq. 13.34), calculated from the *critical properties* of the substance. These are the properties at the critical point. A substance's thermodynamic *critical point* corresponds to the point at the top of the vapor dome in a plot of thermodynamic properties. (See Fig. 13.7 at the end of this chapter.) Above the critical point, liquid and vapor phases are indistinguishable, and the substance is a vapor that cannot be liquefied at any pressure. (However, the substance can be solidified at a high enough pressure.)

Equation 13.35 Through Eq. 13.37: Equations of State (Real Gas)[8]

$$p = \left(\frac{RT}{v}\right)Z \qquad \text{13.35}$$

$$p = \left(\frac{RT}{v}\right)\left(1 + \frac{B}{v} + \frac{C}{v^2} + \cdots\right) \qquad \text{13.36}$$

---

[8](1) Although the specific volume, v, with typical units of m³/kg, is typically used with Eq. 13.35 and the compressibility factor, almost every other real gas equation of state is correlated with the molar volume, with typical units of m³/kmol. The *NCEES Handbook* uses molar volume with Eq. 13.38, but presents Eq. 13.36 and Eq. 13.37 in terms of the variable it uses for specific volume. (2) In some engineering literature, molar volume is commonly designated ν, V, V_m, or $\hat{V}$. The *NCEES Handbook* uses $\bar{v}$ for molar volume to distinguish it from the symbol used for specific volume.

$$p = \frac{RT}{v-b} - \frac{a(T)}{(v+c_1 b)(v+c_2 b)} \qquad 13.37$$

Description

Equation 13.35 is the *generalized compressibility* equation of state, where Z is the *compressiblity factor*. Values of Z can be found using Fig. 13.7.[9] Eq. 13.35 can be used with any substance (solid, liquid, or gas) for which the compressibility factor is known.

Equation 13.36 is the *virial equation of state*, where B, C, and so on are the *virial coefficients*. Equation 13.36 can only be used with gases.

Equation 13.37 is the *cubic equation of state*, where a (T), c_1, and c_2 are species dependent.[10] Eq. 13.37 is primarily used with gases, although it can also be used with liquids since the molecular spacing is explicitly incorporated. The van der Waals' equation of state, Eq. 13.38, is one form of the cubic equation of state.

Equation 13.38 Through Eq. 13.40: Van der Waals' Equation of State (Real Gas)

$$\left(p + \frac{a}{\bar{v}^2}\right)(\bar{v} - b) = \bar{R} T \qquad 13.38$$

$$a = \left(\frac{27}{64}\right)\left(\frac{\bar{R}^2 T_c^2}{p_c}\right) \qquad 13.39$$

$$b = \frac{\bar{R} T_c}{8 p_c} \qquad 13.40$$

Description

One of the methods of accounting for real gas behavior is to modify the ideal gas equation of state with various empirical correction factors. Since the modifications are empirical, the resulting equations of state are known as *correlations*. One well-known correlation is *van der Waals' equation of state*, given by Eq. 13.38. In Eq. 13.39 and Eq. 13.40, T_c and p_c are the substance's *critical temperature* and *critical pressure*, respectively.

The van der Waals corrections are particularly accurate when a gas is above its critical temperature but is also useful when a low-pressure gas is below its critical temperature. For an ideal gas, the a and b terms are zero. When the spacing between molecules is close, as it would be at low temperatures, the molecules attract each other and reduce the pressure exerted by the gas. The pressure is then corrected by the $a/\bar{v}^2$ term, where $\bar{v}$ is the molar specific volume. b is a constant that accounts for the molecular volume in a dense state.

Example

Steam in a rigid 3 m³ vessel has a critical temperature of 647.1K and a critical pressure of 22.06 MPa. The steam is heated to 500°C and 10 MPa. Using the van der Waals' equation of state, what is most nearly the molar specific volume of the steam?

(A) 0.2 m³/kmol

(B) 0.6 m³/kmol

(C) 1 m³/kmol

(D) 10 m³/kmol

Solution

Calculate the van der Waals constants, a and b, from Eq. 13.39 and Eq. 13.40, respectively.

$$a = \left(\frac{27}{64}\right)\left(\frac{\bar{R}^2 T_c^2}{p_c}\right)$$

$$= \left(\frac{27}{64}\right)\left(\frac{\left(8314 \frac{J}{kmol \cdot K}\right)^2 (647.1K)^2}{(22.06 \text{ MPa})\left(1000 \frac{J}{kJ}\right)^2 \left(1000 \frac{kPa}{MPa}\right)}\right)$$

$$= 553.53 \text{ kPa·m}^6/\text{kmol}^2$$

---

[9](1) The compressibility factor is typically represented by uppercase Z, as it is in Eq. 13.35. As presented in the *NCEES Handbook*, the use of lowercase z in Fig. 13.7 is inconsistent. (2) The label "$z_e = 0.27$," which appears within Fig. 13.7, is a reference to the *critical compressibility factor*, the value of z at $p_r = T_r = 1.00$ (i.e., at the critical point). Although any symbol can be used to represent any variable, z_e is probably a typographic deviation from z_c. (3) Real values can be used to "fine-tune" the results derived from generalized graphs. The "$z_e = 0.27$" label means that the graph has been "calibrated" (adjusted) and drawn such that the compressibility factor has a minimum value of 0.27 at $p_r = T_r = 1.00$. (4) Without having additional information, the graph is most likely improperly labeled, since the critical compressibility factor has a graphed minimum value of approximately 0.23. (5) For well-behaved real gases, minimum values of z_c may deviate slightly from 0.27. The value ranges from 0.26 to 0.29 for common hydrocarbon gases and vapors, and essentially all well-behaved gases fall within the range of 0.20 to 0.30. (6) For well-behaved gases, the error in the compressibility factor may still be as high at 6% near the minimum value. Some elements and compounds, such as hydrogen, helium, and neon, as well as polar, nonspherical, and chain molecules, do not follow the two-parameter model (i.e., are not well-behaved) and require different methods.

[10](1) The *NCEES Handbook* presents the numerator of the second term of Eq. 13.37 as $a(T)$. This is intended to indicate that the constant, a, is a function of temperature and temperature only. (Other models may include a dependency on the *acentric factor*, which accounts for molecules with nonspherical shapes.) The product $a \times T$ is not the intended meaning. (2) Although Eq. 13.37 is presented in its common form, the dependency is actually on the reduced temperature, $T_r = T/T_c$, not specifically on the absolute temperature, T. (3) Since all of the constants in the real gas equations of state depend on some combination of properties and their ranges, it is unnecessary (and confusing) to show the dependency in Eq. 13.37.

$$b = \frac{\bar{R}\,T_c}{8p_c}$$

$$= \frac{\left(8314 \ \dfrac{J}{kmol \cdot K}\right)(647.1K)}{(8)(22.06 \ MPa)\left(1000 \ \dfrac{J}{kJ}\right)\left(1000 \ \dfrac{kPa}{MPa}\right)}$$

$$= 0.0305 \ m^3/kmol$$

From Eq. 13.38, the molar specific volume is

$$\left(p + \frac{a}{\bar{v}^2}\right)(\bar{v} - b) = \bar{R}\,T$$

$$\left(\begin{array}{c} (10 \ MPa)\left(1000 \ \dfrac{kPa}{MPa}\right) \\[2mm] + \dfrac{553.53 \ \dfrac{kPa \cdot m^6}{kmol^2}}{\bar{v}^2} \end{array} \right) = \frac{\left(8314 \ \dfrac{J}{kmol \cdot K}\right)}{\times (500°C + 273°)}{1000 \ \dfrac{J}{kJ}}$$

$$\times \left(\bar{v} - 0.0305 \ \frac{m^3}{kmol}\right)$$

$$10{,}000\bar{v}^3 - 6731.7\bar{v}^2 + 553.53\bar{v} - 16.88 = 0$$

This is a cubic equation.[11]

$$\bar{v} = 0.583 \ m^3/kmol \quad (0.6 \ m^3/kmol)$$

The answer is (B).

---

[11]For the FE exam, the easiest way to solve cubic equations is to substitute the four answer choices to determine which one solves the cubic equation.

Table 13.1 *Saturated Water—Temperature Table*

temp., T (°C)	sat. press., p_{sat} (kPa)	specific volume(m³/kg)		internal energy (kJ/kg)			enthalpy (kJ/kg)			entropy (kJ/kg·K)		
		sat. liquid, v_f	sat. vapor, v_g	sat. liquid, u_f	evap., u_{fg}	sat. vapor, u_g	sat. liquid, h_f	evap., h_{fg}	sat. vapor, h_g	sat. liquid, s_f	evap., s_{fg}	sat. vapor, s_g
0.01	0.6113	0.001 000	206.14	0.00	2375.3	2375.3	0.01	2501.3	2501.4	0.0000	9.1562	9.1562
5	0.8721	0.001 000	147.12	20.97	2361.3	2382.3	20.98	2489.6	2501.6	0.0761	8.9496	9.0257
10	1.2276	0.001 000	106.38	42.00	2347.2	2389.2	42.01	2477.7	2519.8	0.1510	8.7498	8.9008
15	1.7051	0.001 001	77.93	62.99	2333.1	2396.1	62.99	2465.9	2528.9	0.2245	8.5569	8.7814
20	2.339	0.001 002	57.79	83.95	2319.0	2402.9	83.96	2454.1	2538.1	0.2966	8.3706	8.6672
25	3.169	0.001 003	43.36	104.88	2304.9	2409.8	104.89	2442.3	2547.2	0.3674	8.1905	8.5580
30	4.246	0.001 004	32.89	125.78	2290.8	2416.6	125.79	2430.5	2556.3	0.4369	8.0164	8.4533
35	5.628	0.001 006	25.22	146.67	2276.7	2423.4	146.68	2418.6	2565.3	0.5053	7.8478	8.3531
40	7.384	0.001 008	19.52	167.56	2262.6	2430.1	167.57	2406.7	2574.3	0.5725	7.6845	8.2570
45	9.593	0.001 010	15.26	188.44	2248.4	2436.8	188.45	2394.8	2583.2	0.6387	7.5261	8.1648
50	12.349	0.001 012	12.03	209.32	2234.2	2443.5	209.33	2382.7	2592.1	0.7038	7.3725	8.0763
55	15.758	0.001 015	9.568	230.21	2219.9	2450.1	230.23	2370.7	2600.9	0.7679	7.2234	7.9913
60	19.940	0.001 017	7.671	251.11	2205.5	2456.6	251.13	2358.5	2609.6	0.8312	7.0784	7.9096
65	25.03	0.001 020	6.197	272.02	2191.1	2463.1	272.06	2346.2	2618.3	0.8935	6.9375	7.8310
70	31.19	0.001 023	5.042	292.95	2176.6	2569.6	292.98	2333.8	2626.8	0.9549	6.8004	7.7553
75	38.58	0.001 026	4.131	313.90	2162.0	2475.9	313.93	2321.4	2635.3	1.0155	6.6669	7.6824
80	47.39	0.001 029	3.407	334.86	2147.4	2482.2	334.91	2308.8	2643.7	1.0753	6.5369	7.6122
85	57.83	0.001 033	2.828	355.84	2132.6	2488.4	355.90	2296.0	2651.9	1.1343	6.4102	7.5445
90	70.14	0.001 036	2.361	376.85	2117.7	2494.5	376.92	2283.2	2660.1	1.1925	6.2866	7.4791
95	84.55	0.001 040	1.982	397.88	2102.7	2500.6	397.96	2270.2	2668.1	1.2500	6.1659	7.4159
	MPa											
100	0.101 35	0.001 044	1.6729	418.94	2087.6	2506.5	419.04	2257.0	2676.1	1.3069	6.0480	7.3549
105	0.120 82	0.001 048	1.4194	440.02	2072.3	2512.4	440.15	2243.7	2683.8	1.3630	5.9328	7.2958
110	0.143 27	0.001 052	1.2102	461.14	2057.0	2518.1	461.30	2230.2	2691.5	1.4185	5.8202	7.2387
115	0.169 06	0.001 056	1.0366	482.30	2041.4	2523.7	482.48	2216.5	2699.0	1.4734	5.7100	7.1833
120	0.198 53	0.001 060	0.8919	503.50	2025.8	2529.3	503.71	2202.6	2706.3	1.5276	5.6020	7.1296
125	0.2321	0.001 065	0.7706	524.74	2009.9	2534.6	524.99	2188.5	2713.5	1.5813	5.4962	7.0775
130	0.2701	0.001 070	0.6685	546.02	1993.9	2539.9	546.31	2174.2	2720.5	1.6344	5.3925	7.0269
135	0.3130	0.001 075	0.5822	567.35	1977.7	2545.0	567.69	2159.6	2727.3	1.6870	5.2907	6.9777
140	0.3613	0.001 080	0.5089	588.74	1961.3	2550.0	589.13	2144.7	2733.9	1.7391	5.1908	6.9299
145	0.4154	0.001 085	0.4463	610.18	1944.7	2554.9	610.63	2129.6	2740.3	1.7907	5.0926	6.8833
150	0.4758	0.001 091	0.3928	631.68	1927.9	2559.5	632.20	2114.3	2746.5	1.8418	4.9960	6.8379
155	0.5431	0.001 096	0.3468	653.24	1910.8	2564.1	653.84	2098.6	2752.4	1.8925	4.9010	6.7935
160	0.6178	0.001 102	0.3071	674.87	1893.5	2568.4	675.55	2082.6	2758.1	1.9427	4.8075	6.7502
165	0.7005	0.001 108	0.2727	696.56	1876.0	2572.5	697.34	2066.2	2763.5	1.9925	4.7153	6.7078
170	0.7917	0.001 114	0.2428	718.33	1858.1	2576.5	719.21	2049.5	2768.7	2.0419	4.6244	6.6663
175	0.8920	0.001 121	0.2168	740.17	1840.0	2580.2	741.17	2032.4	2773.6	2.0909	4.5347	6.6256
180	1.0021	0.001 127	0.194 05	762.09	1821.6	2583.7	763.22	2015.0	2778.2	2.1396	4.4461	6.5857
185	1.1227	0.001 134	0.174 09	784.10	1802.9	2587.0	785.37	1997.1	2782.4	2.1879	4.3586	6.5465
190	1.2544	0.001 141	0.156 54	806.19	1783.8	2590.0	807.62	1978.8	2786.4	2.2359	4.2720	6.5079
195	1.3978	0.001 149	0.141 05	828.37	1764.4	2592.8	829.98	1960.0	2790.0	2.2835	4.1863	6.4698
200	1.5538	0.001 157	0.127 36	850.65	1744.7	2595.3	852.45	1940.7	2793.2	2.3309	4.1014	6.4323
205	1.7230	0.001 164	0.115 21	873.04	1724.5	2597.5	875.04	1921.0	2796.0	2.3780	4.0172	6.3952
210	1.9062	0.001 173	0.104 41	895.53	1703.9	2599.5	897.76	1900.7	2798.5	2.4248	3.9337	6.3585
215	2.104	0.001 181	0.094 79	918.14	1682.9	2601.1	920.62	1879.9	2800.5	2.4714	3.8507	6.3221
220	2.318	0.001 190	0.086 19	940.87	1661.5	2602.4	943.62	1858.5	2802.1	2.5178	3.7683	6.2861
225	2.548	0.001 199	0.078 49	963.73	1639.6	2603.3	966.78	1836.5	2803.3	2.5639	3.6863	6.2503
230	2.795	0.001 209	0.071 58	986.74	1617.2	2603.9	990.12	1813.8	2804.0	2.6099	3.6047	6.2146
235	3.060	0.001 219	0.065 37	1009.89	1594.2	2604.1	1013.62	1790.5	2804.2	2.6558	3.5233	6.1791
240	3.344	0.001 229	0.059 76	1033.21	1570.8	2604.0	1037.32	1766.5	2803.8	2.7015	3.4422	6.1437
245	3.648	0.001 240	0.054 71	1056.71	1546.7	2603.4	1061.23	1741.7	2803.0	2.7472	3.3612	6.1083
250	3.973	0.001 251	0.050 13	1080.39	1522.0	2602.4	1085.36	1716.2	2801.5	2.7927	3.2802	6.0730
255	4.319	0.001 263	0.045 98	1104.28	1596.7	2600.9	1109.73	1689.8	2799.5	2.8383	3.1992	6.0375
260	4.688	0.001 276	0.042 21	1128.39	1470.6	2599.0	1134.37	1662.5	2796.9	2.8838	3.1181	6.0019
265	5.081	0.001 289	0.038 77	1152.74	1443.9	2596.6	1159.28	1634.4	2793.6	2.9294	3.0368	5.9662
270	5.499	0.001 302	0.035 64	1177.36	1416.3	2593.7	1184.51	1605.2	2789.7	2.9751	2.9551	5.9301
275	5.942	0.001 317	0.032 79	1202.25	1387.9	2590.2	1210.07	1574.9	2785.0	3.0208	2.8730	5.8938
280	6.412	0.001 332	0.030 17	1227.46	1358.7	2586.1	1235.99	1543.6	2779.6	3.0668	2.7903	5.8571
285	6.909	0.001 348	0.027 77	1253.00	1328.4	2581.4	1262.31	1511.0	2773.3	3.1130	2.7070	5.8199
290	7.436	0.001 366	0.025 57	1278.92	1297.1	2576.0	1289.07	1477.1	2766.2	3.1594	2.6227	5.7821
295	7.993	0.001 384	0.023 54	1305.2	1264.7	2569.9	1316.3	1441.8	2758.1	3.2062	2.5375	5.7437
300	8.581	0.001 404	0.021 67	1332.0	1231.0	2563.0	1344.0	1404.9	2749.0	3.2534	2.4511	5.7045
305	9.202	0.001 425	0.019 948	1359.3	1195.9	2555.2	1372.4	1366.4	2738.7	3.3010	2.3633	5.6643
310	9.856	0.001 447	0.018 350	1387.1	1159.4	2546.4	1401.3	1326.0	2727.3	3.3493	2.2737	5.6230
315	10.547	0.001 472	0.016 867	1415.5	1121.1	2536.6	1431.0	1283.5	2714.5	3.3982	2.1821	5.5804
320	11.274	0.001 499	0.015 488	1444.6	1080.9	2525.5	1461.5	1238.6	2700.1	3.4480	2.0882	5.5362
330	12.845	0.001 561	0.012 996	1505.3	993.7	2498.9	1525.3	1140.6	2665.9	3.5507	1.8909	5.4417
340	14.586	0.001 638	0.010 797	1570.3	894.3	2464.6	1594.2	1027.9	2622.0	3.6594	1.6763	5.3357
350	16.513	0.001 740	0.008 813	1641.9	776.6	2418.4	1670.6	893.4	2563.9	3.7777	1.4335	5.2112
360	18.651	0.001 893	0.006 945	1725.2	626.3	2351.5	1760.5	720.3	2481.0	3.9147	1.1379	5.0526
370	21.03	0.002 213	0.004 925	1844.0	384.5	2228.5	1890.5	441.6	2332.1	4.1106	0.6865	4.7971
374.14	22.09	0.003 155	0.003 155	2029.6	0	2029.6	2099.3	0	2099.3	4.4298	0	4.4298

Table 13.2 *Superheated Water Tables*

temperature, T (°C)	specific volume, v (m³/kg)	internal energy, u (kJ/kg)	enthalpy, h (kJ/kg)	entropy, s (kJ/kg·K)	specific volume, v (m³/kg)	internal energy, u (kJ/kg)	enthalpy, h (kJ/kg)	entropy, s (kJ/kg·K)
	$p=0.01$ MPa (45.81°C)				$p=0.05$ MPa (81.33°C)			
sat.	14.674	2437.9	2584.7	8.1502	3.240	2483.9	2645.9	7.5939
50	14.869	2443.9	2592.6	8.1749				
100	17.196	2515.5	2687.5	8.4479	3.418	2511.6	2682.5	7.6947
150	19.512	2587.9	2783.0	8.6882	3.889	2585.6	2780.1	7.9401
200	**21.825**	**2661.3**	**2879.5**	**8.9038**	**4.356**	**2659.9**	**2877.7**	**8.1580**
250	24.136	2736.0	2977.3	9.1002	4.820	2735.0	2976.0	8.3556
300	26.445	2812.1	3076.5	9.2813	5.284	2811.3	3075.5	8.5373
400	31.063	2968.9	3279.6	9.6077	6.209	2968.5	3278.9	8.8642
500	35.679	3132.3	3489.1	9.8978	7.134	3132.0	3488.7	9.1546
600	**40.295**	**3302.5**	**3705.4**	**10.1608**	**8.057**	**3302.2**	**3705.1**	**9.4178**
700	44.911	3479.6	3928.7	10.4028	8.981	3479.4	3928.5	9.6599
800	49.526	3663.8	4159.0	10.6281	9.904	3663.6	4158.9	9.8852
900	54.141	3855.0	4396.4	10.8396	10.828	3854.9	4396.3	10.0967
1000	58.757	4053.0	4640.6	11.0393	11.751	4052.9	4640.5	10.2964
1100	**63.372**	**4257.5**	**4891.2**	**11.2287**	**12.674**	**4257.4**	**4891.1**	**10.4859**
1200	67.987	4467.9	5147.8	11.4091	13.597	4467.8	5147.7	10.6662
1300	72.602	4683.7	5409.7	11.5811	14.521	4683.6	5409.6	10.8382
	$p=0.10$ MPa (99.63°C)				$p=0.20$ MPa (120.23°C)			
sat.	1.6940	2506.1	2675.5	7.3594	0.8857	2529.5	2706.7	7.1272
100	1.6958	2506.7	2676.2	7.3614				
150	1.9364	2582.8	2776.4	7.6134	0.9596	2576.9	2768.8	7.2795
200	2.172	2658.1	2875.3	7.8343	1.0803	2654.4	2870.5	7.5066
250	**2.406**	**2733.7**	**2974.3**	**8.0333**	**1.1988**	**2731.2**	**2971.0**	**7.7086**
300	2.639	2810.4	3074.3	8.2158	1.3162	2808.6	3071.8	7.8926
400	3.103	2967.9	3278.2	8.5435	1.5493	2966.7	3276.6	8.2218
500	3.565	3131.6	3488.1	8.8342	1.7814	3130.8	3487.1	8.5133
600	4.028	3301.9	3704.4	9.0976	2.013	3301.4	3704.0	8.7770
700	**4.490**	**3479.2**	**3928.2**	**9.3398**	**2.244**	**3478.8**	**3927.6**	**9.0194**
800	4.952	3663.5	4158.6	9.5652	2.475	3663.1	4158.2	9.2449
900	5.414	3854.8	4396.1	9.7767	2.705	3854.5	4395.8	9.4566
1000	5.875	4052.8	4640.3	9.9764	2.937	4052.5	4640.0	9.6563
1100	6.337	4257.3	4891.0	10.1659	3.168	4257.0	4890.7	9.8458
1200	**6.799**	**4467.7**	**5147.6**	**10.3463**	**3.399**	**4467.5**	**5147.5**	**10.0262**
1300	7.260	4683.5	5409.5	10.5183	3.630	4683.2	5409.3	10.1982
	$p=0.40$ MPa (143.63°C)				$p=0.60$ MPa (158.85°C)			
sat.	0.4625	2553.6	2738.6	6.8959	0.3157	2567.4	2756.8	6.7600
150	0.4708	2564.5	2752.8	6.9299				
200	0.5342	2646.8	2860.5	7.1706	0.3520	2638.9	2850.1	6.9665
250	0.5951	2726.1	2964.2	7.3789	0.3938	2720.9	2957.2	7.1816
300	**0.6548**	**2804.8**	**3066.8**	**7.5662**	**0.4344**	**2801.0**	**3061.6**	**7.3724**
350	0.7137	2884.6	3170.1	7.7324	0.4742	2881.2	3165.7	7.5464
400	0.7726	2964.4	3273.4	7.8985	0.5137	2962.1	3270.3	7.7079
500	0.8893	3129.2	3484.9	8.1913	0.5920	3127.6	3482.8	8.0021
600	1.0055	3300.2	3702.4	8.4558	0.6697	3299.1	3700.9	8.2674
700	**1.1215**	**3477.9**	**3926.5**	**8.6987**	**0.7472**	**3477.0**	**3925.3**	**8.5107**
800	1.2372	3662.4	4157.3	8.9244	0.8245	3661.8	4156.5	8.7367
900	1.3529	3853.9	4395.1	9.1362	0.9017	3853.4	4394.4	8.9486
1000	1.4685	4052.0	4639.4	9.3360	0.9788	4051.5	4638.8	9.1485
1100	1.5840	4256.5	4890.2	9.5256	1.0559	4256.1	4889.6	9.3381
1200	**1.6996**	**4467.0**	**5146.8**	**9.7060**	**1.1330**	**4466.5**	**5146.3**	**9.5185**
1300	1.8151	4682.8	5408.8	9.8780	1.2101	4682.3	5408.3	9.6906
	$p=0.80$ MPa (170.43°C)				$p=1.00$ MPa (179.91°C)			
sat.	0.2404	2576.8	2769.1	6.6628	0.194 44	2583.6	2778.1	6.5865
200	0.2608	2630.6	2839.3	6.8158	0.2060	2621.9	2827.9	6.6940
250	0.2931	2715.5	2950.0	7.0384	0.2327	2709.9	2942.6	6.9247
300	0.3241	2797.2	3056.5	7.2328	0.2579	2793.2	3051.2	7.1229
350	**0.3544**	**2878.2**	**3161.7**	**7.4089**	**0.2825**	**2875.2**	**3157.7**	**7.3011**
400	0.3843	2959.7	3267.1	7.5716	0.3066	2957.3	3263.9	7.4651
500	0.4433	3126.0	3480.6	7.8673	0.3541	3124.4	3478.5	7.7622
600	0.5018	3297.9	3699.4	8.1333	0.4011	3296.8	3697.9	8.0290
700	0.5601	3476.2	3924.2	8.3770	0.4478	3475.3	3923.1	8.2731
800	**0.6181**	**3661.1**	**4155.6**	**8.6033**	**0.4943**	**3660.4**	**4154.7**	**8.4996**
900	0.6761	3852.8	4393.7	8.8153	0.5407	3852.2	4392.9	8.7118
1000	0.7340	4051.0	4638.2	9.0153	0.5871	4050.5	4637.6	8.9119
1100	0.7919	4255.6	4889.1	9.2050	0.6335	4255.1	4888.6	9.1017
1200	0.8497	4466.1	5145.9	9.3855	0.6798	4465.6	5145.4	9.2822
1300	**0.9076**	**4681.8**	**5407.9**	**9.5575**	**0.7261**	**4681.3**	**5407.4**	**9.4543**

Figure 13.5 *p-h Diagram for Refrigerant HFC-134a (SI units)*

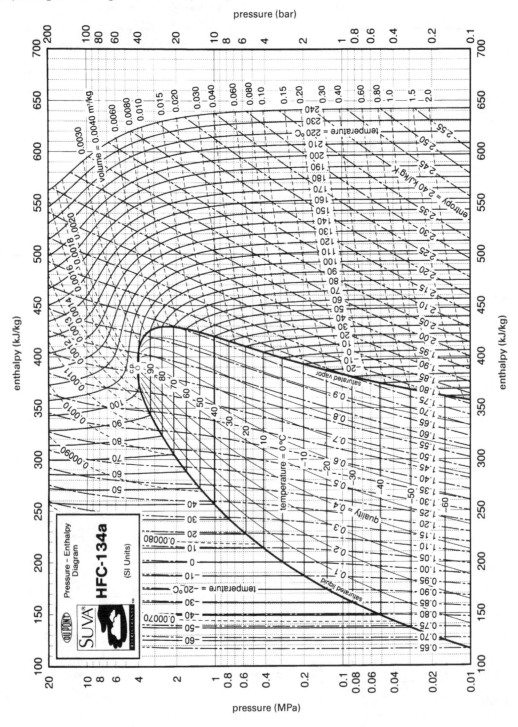

Reproduced with permission from the DuPont Company.

Figure 13.7 *Compressibility Factors*

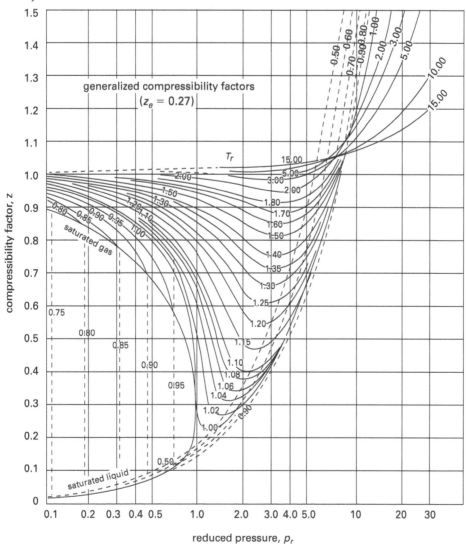

de Nevers, N. (2012) Appendix A: Useful Tables and Charts, in *Physical and Chemical Equilibrium for Chemical Engineers*, Second Edition, John Wiley & Sons, Inc., Hoboken, NJ.

14 Laws of Thermodynamics

Nomenclature

c	specific heat	kJ/kg·K
D	diameter	m
g	gravitational acceleration, 9.81	m/s^2
h	specific enthalpy	kJ/kg
H	total enthalpy	kJ
k	ratio of specific heats	–
KE	kinetic energy	kJ
L	length	m
m	mass	kg
$\dot{m}$	mass flow rate	kg/s
MW	molecular weight	kg/kmol
n	number of moles	–
n	polytropic exponent	–
p	pressure	Pa
PE	potential energy	kJ
q	heat energy	kJ/kg
Q	total heat energy	kJ
$\dot{Q}$	rate of heat transfer	kW
r	radius	m
R	specific gas constant	kJ/kg·K
s	specific entropy	kJ/kg·K
S	total entropy	kJ/K
T	absolute temperature	K
u	specific internal energy	kJ/kg
U	total internal energy	kJ
v	velocity	m/s
V	volume	m^3
w	specific work	kJ/kg
W	work	kJ
$\dot{W}$	rate of work (power)	kW
z	elevation*	m

*The NCEES *FE Reference Handbook* (*NCEES Handbook*) is inconsistent in the variable used to represent elevation above the datum in energy equations. For fluids subjects and in the Bernoulli equation, the *NCEES Handbook* uses z; for thermodynamics subjects, the *NCEES Handbook* uses Z. Since lowercase z is the most common symbol used in engineering practice, this book uses that convention. The equations in this book involving elevation above a datum will differ slightly in appearance from the *NCEES Handbook*.

Symbols

η	efficiency	–
υ	specific volume*	m^3/kg

*The *NCEES Handbook* uses lowercase italic v for specific volume. This book uses Greek upsilon, υ, to avoid confusion with the symbol for velocity in kinetic energy calculations. The equations in this book involving specific volume will differ slightly in appearance from those in the *NCEES Handbook*.

Subscripts

b	boundary
C	cold
e	exit
es	ideal (isentropic) exit state
f	fluid (liquid)
fg	liquid-to-gas (vaporization)
g	gas (vapor)
H	high or hot
i	in or inlet (entrance)
L	low
p	constant pressure
rev	reversible
s	isentropic
v	constant volume

1. SYSTEMS

A *thermodynamic system* is defined as the matter enclosed within an arbitrary but precisely defined *control volume*. Everything external to the system is defined as the *surroundings*, *environment*, or *universe*. The environment and system are separated by the *system boundaries.* The surface of the control volume is known as the *control surface.* The control surface can be real (e.g., piston and cylinder walls) or imaginary.

If mass flows through the system across system boundaries, the system is an *open system.* Pumps, heat exchangers, and jet engines are examples of open systems. An important type of open system is the *steady-flow open system* in which matter enters and exits at the same rate. Pumps, turbines, heat exchangers, and boilers are all steady-flow open systems.

If no mass crosses the system boundaries, the system is said to be a *closed system.* The matter in a closed system may be referred to as a *control mass.* Closed systems can have variable volumes. The gas compressed by a piston in a cylinder is an example of a closed system with a variable control volume.

In most cases, energy in the form of heat, work, or electrical energy can enter or exit any open or closed system. Systems closed to both matter and energy transfer are known as *isolated systems.*

2. TYPES OF PROCESSES

Changes in thermodynamic properties of a system often depend on the type of process experienced. This is particularly true for gaseous systems. The following list describes several common types of processes.

- *adiabatic process*—a process in which no heat crosses the system boundary. Adiabatic processes include isentropic and throttling processes.

- *isentropic process*—an adiabatic process in which there is no entropy production (i.e., it is reversible). Also known as a *constant entropy process.*

- *throttling process*—an adiabatic process in which there is no change in enthalpy, but for which there is a significant pressure drop.

- *constant pressure process*—also known as an *isobaric process.*

- *constant temperature process*—also known as an *isothermal process.*

- *constant volume process*—also known as an *isochoric* or *isometric process.*

- *polytropic process*—a process that obeys the polytropic equation of state (see Eq. 14.18). Gases always constitute the system in polytropic processes. n is the *polytropic exponent,* a property of the equipment, not of the gas.

A system that is in equilibrium at the start and finish of a process may or may not be in equilibrium during the process. A *quasistatic process (quasiequilibrium process)* is one that can be divided into a series of infinitesimal deviations (steps) from equilibrium. During each step,

the property changes are small, and all intensive properties are uniform throughout the system. The interim equilibrium at each step is often called *quasiequilibrium.*

A *reversible process* is one that is performed in such a way that, at the conclusion of the process, both the system and the local surroundings can be restored to their initial states. Quasiequilibrium processes are assumed to be reversible processes.

3. STANDARD SIGN CONVENTION

A standard sign convention is used in calculating work, heat, and property changes in systems. This sign convention takes the system (not the environment) as the reference. For example, a net heat gain, Q, would mean the system gained energy and the environment lost energy. Changes in enthalpy, entropy, and internal energy (ΔH, ΔS, and ΔU, respectively) are positive if these properties increase within the system. ΔU will be negative if the internal energy of the system decreases.

4. FIRST LAW OF THERMODYNAMICS

There is a basic principle that underlies all property changes as a system undergoes a process: All energy must be accounted for. Energy that enters a system must either leave the system or be stored in some manner, and energy cannot be created or destroyed. These statements are the primary manifestations of the *first law of thermodynamics:* The net energy crossing the system boundary is the change in energy inside the system.

The first law applies whether or not a process is reversible. So, the first law can also be stated as: The work done in an adiabatic process depends only on the system's endpoint conditions, not on the nature of the process.

Equation 14.1: Heat

$$q = Q/m \qquad 14.1$$

Description

Heat, Q, transferred due to a temperature difference is positive if heat flows into the system. In accordance with the standard sign convention, Q will be negative if the net heat exchange is a loss of heat to the surroundings.

Equation 14.2: Specific Work

$$w = W/m \qquad 14.2$$

Description

Work, W, is positive if the system does work on the surroundings. W will be negative if the surroundings do work on the system (e.g., a piston compressing gas in a cylinder).

5. CLOSED SYSTEMS

Equation 14.3: The First Law of Thermodynamics for Closed Systems

$$Q - W = \Delta U + \Delta KE + \Delta PE \qquad \text{14.3}$$

Variation

$$Q = \Delta U + W$$

Description

The first law of thermodynamics, as given by Eq. 14.3, states that the heat energy, Q, entering a closed system can either increase the temperature (increase U) or be used to perform work (increase W) on the surroundings. The Q term is understood to be the net heat entering the system, which is the heat energy entering the system less the heat energy lost to the surroundings. ΔKE is the change in kinetic energy, and ΔPE is the change in potential energy.[1]

In most cases, the changes in kinetic and potential energy can be disregarded and the first law of thermodynamics for closed systems can be written as in the variation equation.

Example

A half-cylinder tub is full of water at 30°C. The tub has a length of 1.5 m and a diameter of 0.8 m. The specific heat of water is 4.18 kJ/kg·K. What is most nearly the temperature of the water after 3 MJ of heat is added to the tub?

(A) 28°C

(B) 30°C

(C) 32°C

(D) 36°C

Solution

Find the volume of the tub.

$$V = \frac{\pi r^2 L}{2} = \frac{\pi D^2 L}{8} = \frac{\pi(0.8 \text{ m})^2(1.5 \text{ m})}{8}$$
$$= 0.377 \text{ m}^3$$

Find the mass of the water in the tub. The density of water at 30°C is 995.7 kg/m³.

$$m = \rho V$$
$$= \left(995.7 \ \frac{\text{kg}}{\text{m}^3}\right)(0.377 \text{ m}^3)$$
$$= 375.37 \text{ kg}$$

Since the only thing being added to the tub and water is heat, the tub and water constitute a closed system. Use Eq. 14.3 to find the final temperature. Because there is no work done by or on the system, the work, difference in potential energy, and difference in kinetic energy can be disregarded.

$$Q - W = \Delta U + \Delta KE + \Delta PE$$
$$Q = \Delta U$$

Solve for the temperature of the water after heat is added.

$$Q = \Delta U = mc_p \Delta T = mc_p(T_2 - T_1)$$
$$T_2 = \frac{Q + mc_p T_1}{mc_p}$$

$$= \frac{(3 \text{ MJ})\left(1000 \ \frac{\text{kJ}}{\text{MJ}}\right) + (375.37 \text{ kg})\left(4.18 \ \frac{\text{kJ}}{\text{kg·K}}\right)(30°C)}{(375.37 \text{ kg})\left(4.18 \ \frac{\text{kJ}}{\text{kg·K}}\right)}$$

$$= 31.9°C \quad (32°C)$$

The answer is (C).

Equation 14.4: Reversible Boundary Work

$$w_b = \int_{p_1}^{p_2} p \, dv \qquad \text{14.4}$$

Description

The work done by or on a closed system during a process, w_b, is calculated by the area under the curve in the p-V plane, and is called *reversible work, boundary work, p-V work,* or *flow work.*[2]

---

[1]The *NCEES Handbook* is inconsistent in the variables it uses to represent kinetic and potential energy. In its dynamics section, the *NCEES Handbook* uses T and U for kinetic and potential energy, respectively; for thermodynamics subjects, the *NCEES Handbook* uses KE and PE (presented in this book as KE and PE).
[2]Usually, the thermodynamic interpretation of the term "boundary work" is the work done on the entire boundary (i.e., on the entire system). The form of Eq. 14.4 calculates the "specific" boundary work (i.e., the work done per unit mass of the system). This is not explicitly stated in the *NCEES Handbook.*

Boundary work gets its name from the fact that the boundary of the system changes, resulting in a volume change. This volume change can be used to separate boundary work from other energy/work due to electrical, thermal, and mechanical sources. For example, a propeller within a closed volume can circulate and increase the kinetic energy of a gas, but this "shaft work" is not boundary work.

Equation 14.4 is defined as "reversible boundary work." If the system volume changes gradually (i.e., the boundary moves slowly), the process will be "quasistatic," achieving a continuum of equilibrium throughout. In that case, the work will be reversible. This would seem to imply that Eq. 14.4 is valid only for reversible processes. In fact, Eq. 14.4 can be used with irreversible processes as long as the total work performed is recognized as the sum of reversible and irreversible parts. Consider a heated gas expanding within a vertical cylinder with a rusty, heavy piston. To move the piston, the gas pressure has to overcome the weight of the piston (which might represent a reversible compression in some cases), and it also has to overcome the friction (which is not reversible). Equation 14.4 can be used to calculate the total of the two parts. However, the total isn't all reversible.

Values calculated from Eq. 14.4 will have signs that are derived from the definition of a definite integral. A negative boundary work will indicate that the volume has decreased. A negative sign is not related to the standard thermodynamic sign convention, which is arbitrary and independent of the definition of an integral. Equation 14.4 is defined as boundary work without specifying "on the system" or "by the system." Whether or not boundary work is positive or negative must be determined on a case-by-case basis, primarily depending on the context.[3]

Example

5 kmol of water vapor at 100°C and 1 atm are condensed from an initial volume of 153 L to a liquid state at 100°C. The molecular weight of water is 18.016 kg/kmol, and the specific volume of the liquid is 0.001044 m³/kg. What is most nearly the work done by the atmosphere on the water?

(A) 6.0 kJ

(B) 6.2 kJ

(C) 6.0 MJ

(D) 6.2 MJ

Solution

Calculate the initial and final volumes of the system.

$$V_1 = \frac{153 \text{ L}}{1000 \ \frac{\text{L}}{\text{m}^3}}$$

$$= 0.153 \text{ m}^3$$

$$V_2 = n(\text{MW})_{\text{H}_2\text{O}} v_f$$

$$= (5 \text{ kmol}) \left(18.016 \ \frac{\text{kg}}{\text{kmol}} \right) \left(0.001044 \ \frac{\text{m}^3}{\text{kg}} \right)$$

$$= 0.094 \text{ m}^3$$

As the vapor condenses, the total volume of water changes. The constant atmospheric pressure (p; 101 325 Pa) acts on the system boundary as the volume changes. Use Eq. 14.4 to calculate the work done. Use uppercase letters to designate the work done on the entire system.

$$W_b = \int_{V_1}^{V_2} p \, dV$$

$$= p(V_2 - V_1)$$

$$= \frac{(101\,325 \text{ Pa})(0.094 \text{ m}^3 - 0.153 \text{ m}^3)}{1000 \ \frac{\text{J}}{\text{kJ}}}$$

$$= -5.97 \text{ kJ} \quad (6.0 \text{ kJ})$$

The answer is (A).

6. SPECIAL CASE OF CLOSED SYSTEMS (FOR IDEAL GASES)

Equation 14.5 and Eq. 14.6: Constant Pressure Process (Charles' Law)

$$T/v = \text{constant} \qquad \qquad 14.5$$

$$w_b = p\Delta v \qquad \qquad 14.6$$

Description

A system whose pressure remains constant is known as an *isobaric system*.

The ideal gas law reduces to Eq. 14.5 and is known as *Charles' law*.[4] When pressure is constant in a closed system, Eq. 14.4 reduces to Eq. 14.6.

---

[3]Answers to the question, "How much work did you do today?" rarely include the word "negative." For that reason, boundary work is always positive in casual answers. The standard thermodynamic sign convention is relevant only when work is a component of an energy balance such as the first law.

[4]The *NCEES Handbook* uses "= constant" to mean "is constant," not to mean "a constant." There is no single number that describes the ratio T/v for all isobaric processes.

Example

A gas goes through the following thermodynamic processes.

A to B: constant-temperature compression
B to C: constant-volume cooling
C to A: constant-pressure expansion

The pressure and volume at state C are 140 kPa and 0.028 m³, respectively. The net work during the C-to-A process is 10.5 kJ.

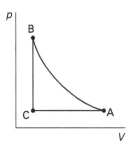

Most nearly, what is the volume at state A?

(A)   0.07 m³

(B)   0.10 m³

(C)   0.19 m³

(D)   0.24 m³

Solution

Since pressure is constant during the C-to-A process, use Eq. 14.6 to find the volume at A.

$$w_b = p\Delta v$$
$$w_{\text{C-A}} = p(v_A - v_C)$$
$$(10.5 \text{ kJ})\left(1000 \ \frac{\text{J}}{\text{kJ}}\right) = (140 \text{ kPa})\left(1000 \ \frac{\text{Pa}}{\text{kPa}}\right)$$
$$\times (v_A - 0.028 \text{ m}^3)$$
$$v_A = 0.103 \text{ m}^3 \quad (0.10 \text{ m}^3)$$

The answer is (B).

Equation 14.7 and Eq. 14.8: Constant Volume Process (Guy-Lussac's Law)

$$T/p = \text{constant} \qquad 14.7$$

$$w_b = 0 \qquad 14.8$$

Description

A system whose volume remains constant is known as an *isochoric system*.

The ideal gas law reduces to Eq. 14.7 and is known as *Guy-Lussac's law*. When the volume of a closed system is held constant, Eq. 14.4 reduces to Eq. 14.8.

Equation 14.9 and Eq. 14.10: Constant Temperature Process (Boyle's Law)

$$pv = \text{constant} \qquad 14.9$$

$$w_b = RT \ln(v_2/v_1) = RT \ln(p_1/p_2) \qquad 14.10$$

Description

A system whose temperature remains constant is known as an *isothermal system*.

The ideal gas law reduces to Eq. 14.9 and is known as *Boyle's law*. When the temperature of a closed system is held constant, Eq. 14.4 reduces to Eq. 14.10.

Example

A gas goes through the following thermodynamic processes.

A to B: constant-temperature compression
B to C: constant-volume cooling
C to A: constant-pressure expansion

The pressure and volume at state C are 140 kPa and 0.028 m³, respectively. The net work during the C-to-A process is 10.5 kJ. The volume at state A is 0.103 m³.

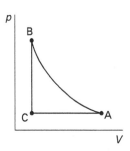

What is most nearly the work performed in the A-to-B process?

(A)   0 kJ

(B)   5.3 kJ

(C)   13 kJ

(D)   19 kJ

Solution

The pressure at state A is the same as the pressure at state C. By Eq. 14.10, the work in constant-temperature processes per unit mass is

$$w_{A\text{-}B} = RT_A \ln(v_B/v_A)$$

The mass of the gas (from the ideal gas law) is

$$m = \frac{p_A v_A}{RT_A}$$

The total work performed in the A-to-B process is

$$
\begin{aligned}
W_{A\text{-}B} &= m w_{A\text{-}B} \\
&= \left(\frac{p_A v_A}{RT_A}\right)\left(RT_A \ln \frac{v_B}{v_A}\right) \\
&= p_A v_A \ln \frac{v_B}{v_A} \\
&= \frac{(140 \text{ kPa})\left(10^3 \dfrac{\text{Pa}}{\text{kPa}}\right)}{1000 \dfrac{\text{J}}{\text{kJ}}} \\
&\quad \times (0.103 \text{ m}^3) \ln \frac{0.028 \text{ m}^3}{0.103 \text{ m}^3} \\
&= -18.8 \text{ kJ} \quad (19 \text{ kJ})
\end{aligned}
$$

The answer is (D).

Equation 14.11 Through Eq. 14.13: Isentropic Process

$$pv^k = \text{constant} \qquad 14.11$$

$$w = (p_2 v_2 - p_1 v_1)/(1-k) \qquad 14.12$$

$$w = R(T_2 - T_1)/(1-k) \qquad 14.13$$

Description

A process where the heat transfer (i.e., heat loss or heat gain) is zero is known as an *adiabatic process*. Since $\Delta s = Q/T_0$, if $Q = 0$, then entropy is unchanged. A process where entropy remains constant is known as an *isentropic process*, also known as a *reversible adiabatic process*.

Equation 14.11 describes the behavior of a closed, isentropic system. k is the ratio of specific heats (see Eq. 14.17). Equation 14.12 and Eq. 14.13 are related by the ideal gas law.

Equation 14.14 Through Eq. 14.17: Isentropic Process for Ideal Gases

$$\frac{p_2}{p_1} = \left(\frac{v_1}{v_2}\right)^k \qquad 14.14$$

$$\frac{T_2}{T_1} = \left(\frac{p_2}{p_1}\right)^{\frac{k-1}{k}} \qquad 14.15$$

$$\frac{T_2}{T_1} = \left(\frac{v_1}{v_2}\right)^{k-1} \qquad 14.16$$

$$k = c_p/c_v \qquad 14.17$$

Description

Equation 14.14 through Eq. 14.16 are valid for ideal gases undergoing *isentropic processes* (i.e., entropy is constant). The *ratio of specific heats*, k, is given by Eq. 14.17. For closed, isentropic systems, Eq. 14.4 reduces to Eq. 14.12 and Eq. 14.13.

Example

Air is compressed isentropically in a piston-cylinder arrangement to 1/10 of its initial volume. The initial temperature is 35°C, and the ratio of specific heats is 1.4. What is most nearly the final temperature?

(A)   350K

(B)   360K

(C)   620K

(D)   770K

Solution

Since the process is isentropic, use Eq. 14.16 to calculate the final temperature.

$$
\begin{aligned}
\frac{T_2}{T_1} &= \left(\frac{v_1}{v_2}\right)^{k-1} \\
T_2 &= T_1\left(\frac{v_1}{v_2}\right)^{k-1} \\
&= (35°\text{C} + 273°)\left(\frac{10}{1}\right)^{1.4-1} \\
&= 773.7\text{K} \quad (770\text{K})
\end{aligned}
$$

The answer is (D).

Thermodynamics

Equation 14.18 and Eq. 14.19: Polytropic Process

$$pv^n = \text{constant} \qquad 14.18$$

$$w = (p_2 v_2 - p_1 v_1)/(1 - n) \quad [n \neq 1] \qquad 14.19$$

Description

A process is polytropic if it satisfies Eq. 14.18 for some real number n, known as the *polytropic exponent*. Polytropic processes represent a larger class of processes. This is due to the fact that Eq. 14.18 reduces to other processes depending on the value of the polytropic exponent. Any process which is either constant-pressure, constant-temperature, constant-volume, or isentropic is also polytropic.

$n = 0$	[constant pressure process]
$n = 1$	[constant temperature process]
$n = k$	[isentropic process]
$n = \infty$	[constant volume process]

Processes with exponents other than 0, 1, k, and ∞ are typically found where the working fluid is acted upon by mechanical equipment (e.g., a reciprocating compressor). In a rotating device, the working fluid's pressure, temperature, and volume are determined by what the machine does, not what would occur naturally.

Example

0.5 m^3 of superheated steam at 400 kPa and 300°C is expanded behind a piston until the temperature is 210°C. The steam expands polytropically with a polytropic exponent of 1.3. The final volume and pressure of the steam are 0.884 m^3 and 190.7 kPa, respectively. What is most nearly the total work done during the expansion process?

(A) 24 kJ

(B) 100 kJ

(C) 330 kJ

(D) 420 kJ

Solution

The steam expands polytropically, so use Eq. 14.19 to find the work done during expansion. Use uppercase letters to distinguish the total work and total volume from their per unit mass counterparts.

$$
\begin{aligned}
W &= (p_2 V_2 - p_1 V_1)/(1 - n) \\
&= \frac{(190.7 \text{ kPa})(0.884 \text{ m}^3) - (400 \text{ kPa})(0.5 \text{ m}^3)}{1 - 1.3} \\
&= 104.7 \text{ kJ} \quad (100 \text{ kJ})
\end{aligned}
$$

The answer is (B).

7. OPEN THERMODYNAMIC SYSTEMS

In an *open system*, mass (the working fluid, substance, matter, etc.) crosses the system boundary. Water flowing through a pump and steam flowing through a turbine represent open systems. In a *steady-state open system*, the mass flow rates into and out of the system are the same.

The first law of thermodynamics can also be written for open systems, but more terms are required to account for the many energy forms. The first law formulation is essentially the *Bernoulli energy conservation equation* extended to nonadiabatic processes.

$$Q = \Delta U + \Delta \text{PE} + \Delta \text{KE} + W_{\text{rev}} + W_{\text{shaft}}$$

Q is the heat flow into the system, inclusive of any losses. It can be supplied from furnace flame, electrical heating, nuclear reaction, or other sources. If the system is adiabatic, Q is zero.

Equation 14.20: Reversible Flow Work

$$w_{\text{rev}} = -\int_{p_1}^{p_2} v \, dp + \Delta \text{KE} + \Delta \text{PE} \qquad 14.20$$

Description

At the boundary of an open system, there is pressure opposing fluid from entering the system. The work required to cause the flow into the system against the exit pressure is called reversible flow work, w_{rev} (also *p-V work*, *flow energy*, etc.), and is given by Eq. 14.20.[5] Since reversible flow work is work being done on the system, it is always negative.

Example

A boiler feedwater pump receives a steady flow of saturated liquid water at a temperature of 50°C and a pressure of 12.349 kPa. The pressure of the water

---

[5](1) The *NCEES Handbook* definition of Eq. 14.20 as "reversible flow work" implies that the equation is valid only for reversible processes. Equation 14.20 can be used with irreversible processes, and the flow work is understood as being the useful work performed after other energy losses. (2) Usually, the thermodynamic interpretation of the term "flow work" is the work done on all of the substance in the system. The form of Eq. 14.20 calculates the "specific" boundary work (i.e., the work done per unit mass of the system). This is not explicitly stated in the *NCEES Handbook*. (3) The inclusion of the kinetic and potential energy terms in the flow work is incorrect. Flow work is strictly $p_2 v_2 - p_1 v_1$. Flow work (power) is the work (power) needed to inject/eject mass into/out of the system: $\dot{m}(p_2 v_2 - p_1 v_1)$.

increases isentropically inside the boiler to 1000 kPa. At 50°C, the specific volume of the water is 0.001012 m³/kg. Changes in kinetic and potential energies are negligible. What is most nearly the work done on the water by the boiler?

(A)   0.64 kJ/kg

(B)   0.87 kJ/kg

(C)   1.0 kJ/kg

(D)   2.3 kJ/kg

Solution

From Eq. 14.20, the reversible flow work is

$$
\begin{aligned}
w_{\text{rev}} &= -\int v\, dp + \Delta\text{KE} + \Delta\text{PE} \\
&= -\int_{p_1}^{p_2} v\, dp \\
&= -v(p_2 - p_1) \\
&= \left(-0.001012\ \frac{\text{m}^3}{\text{kg}}\right) \\
&\quad \times (1000\ \text{kPa} - 12.349\ \text{kPa}) \\
&= -1.0\ \text{kJ/kg} \quad (1.0\ \text{kJ/kg})
\end{aligned}
$$

The answer is (C).

Equation 14.21: First Law of Thermodynamics for Open Systems

$$
\sum \dot{m}_i[h_i + v_i^2/2 + gz_i] - \sum \dot{m}_e[h_e + v_e^2/2 + gz_e] \\
+ \dot{Q}_{\text{in}} - \dot{W}_{\text{net}} = d(m_s u_s)/dt
$$

14.21

Description

The first law of thermodynamics applied to open systems has a simple interpretation: Work done on the substance flowing through the system results in pressure, kinetic or potential energy changes, a heat transfer, an energy storage, or a combination thereof.

Equation 14.21 is the first law of thermodynamics for open systems with multiple inlets and multiple outlets.[6] In the real world, there are seldom more than two inlets and/or two outlets. In Eq. 14.21, the entering and exiting mass flow rates may be different. If more mass enters the system than exits it, stationary mass will be stored within the system. A stationary stored mass also stores energy by virtue of its temperature (internal energy), pressure (flow energy), and elevation (potential energy). The rate of change in the energy storage within the control volume is represented by the $d(m_s u_s)/dt$ term in which m_s is the mass of fluid in the system, and u_s is the specific energy storage of the system.[7]

Most practical real-world processes do not have an accumulation of substance within them. If the mass flow rates are the same, Eq. 14.21 is known as the *steady-flow energy equation*. Specifically, there are several ways that work done on a steady-flow system can be manifested.

Heat loss:

$$
\dot{W}_{\text{in}} = \dot{Q}_{\text{in}}
$$

Change in pressure, volume, and/or temperature:

$$
\begin{aligned}
\frac{\dot{W}_{\text{in}}}{\dot{m}} &= h_i - h_e \\
&= p_i v_i + u_i - p_e v_e - u_e
\end{aligned}
$$

Change in velocity (kinetic energy):

$$
\frac{\dot{W}_{\text{in}}}{\dot{m}} = \frac{v_i^2}{2} - \frac{v_e^2}{2}
$$

Change in elevation (potential energy):

$$
\frac{\dot{W}_{\text{in}}}{\dot{m}} = gz_i - gz_e
$$

Example

The absolute pressure in a rigid, insulated tank is initially zero. The tank volume is 0.040 m³. The tank and steam inlet are at the same elevation. A valve is opened allowing 250°C and 600 kPa steam with

---

[6](1) Equation 14.21 is technically incomplete. By labeling the heat energy and work terms "in" and "net," respectively, the *NCEES Handbook* partially abandons the standard thermodynamic sign convention that was implicit in Eq. 14.3. In Eq. 14.3, the heat term, Q, implicitly represents $Q_{\text{in}} - Q_{\text{out}}$, and the work term, W, implicitly represents $W_{\text{out}} - W_{\text{in}}$. Equation 14.21 defines $\dot{Q}$ and $\dot{W}$ explicitly, but the equation is incomplete ($\dot{Q}_{\text{out}}$ has been omitted) and inconsistent ($\dot{W}_{\text{net}}$ appears, but not $\dot{Q}_{\text{net}}$; $\dot{W}_{\text{net}}$ in Eq. 14.21 is the same as W in Eq. 14.3). The standard thermodynamic sign convention applies only to the work term, $\dot{W}_{\text{net}}$. In order to properly use Eq. 14.21, the sign of the $\dot{Q}$ term must be changed based on the definitions (subscripts), not based on the standard thermodynamic sign convention. (2) The *NCEES Handbook* is inconsistent in the variable it uses to represent elevation above the datum in energy equations. For fluid subjects, the *NCEES Handbook* uses z in the Bernoulli equation; for thermodynamics subjects, the *NCEES Handbook* uses Z. Since lowercase z is the most common symbol used in engineering practice, this book uses that convention. The equations in this book involving elevation above a datum will differ slightly in appearance from those in the *NCEES Handbook*.

[7]For systems that accumulate mass, the right-hand side of Eq. 14.21 seems to imply that the energy storage within the control volume results in a change in internal energy (temperature) only. This is incorrect, as the energy can be stored in any of the forms represented by the terms in the equation. The correct representation for a rate of change in stored system energy would be $d E_{CV}/dt$ or similar.

negligible velocity to slowly fill the tank. Most nearly, what is the temperature of the steam in the tank after the tank is full?

(A) 250°C

(B) 300°C

(C) 350°C

(D) 400°C

Solution

Use Eq. 14.21. The control volume is the tank. Subscript s refers to the substance in the tank. Subscript i refers to the tank inlet, at the valve. The tank does not have an exit, so all subscript e variables are zero. Subscript 1 refers to what is initially in the tank. Since the tank is initially evacuated, it has no contents, so all subscript 1 variables are zero. Subscript 2 refers to the steam in the tank after filling. Since the tank is insulated, Q_{in} is zero. There is no work done on or by the steam, so W_{net} is zero. Although pressure does not appear explicitly in Eq. 14.21, the final pressure in the tank is $p_2 = p_i$.

$$\sum \dot{m}_i[h_i + v_i^2/2 + gz_i]$$
$$- \sum \dot{m}_e[h_e + v_e^2/2 + gz_e]$$
$$+ \dot{Q}_{in} - \dot{W}_{net} = d(m_s u_s)/dt$$
$$m_i h_i = m_2 u_2 - m_1 u_1$$
$$= m_2 u_2$$

Use a mass balance to relate m_i to m_2.

$$\sum m_i - \sum m_e = (m_2 - m_1)_{system}$$
$$m_i = m_2$$

Combine the two equations and solve for the internal energy of the system.

$$m_i h_i = m_2 u_2$$
$$u = h_i$$
$$= 2957.2 \text{ kJ/kg}$$

250°C, 600 kPa (0.6 MPa) steam is superheated. From the superheated steam table, its enthalpy is $h = 2957.2$ kJ/kg. Since this is the final internal energy of

the steam in the tank, interpolate between 2881.2 kJ/kg and 2962.1 kJ/kg, the internal energies of 350°C and 400°C steam, respectively.

$$\frac{u - u_1}{u_2 - u_1} = \frac{T - T_1}{T_2 - T_1}$$
$$T = \left(\frac{u - u_1}{u_2 - u_1}\right)$$
$$\times (T_2 - T_1) + T_1$$
$$= \left(\frac{2957.2 \frac{kJ}{kg} - 2881.2 \frac{kJ}{kg}}{2962.1 \frac{kJ}{kg} - 2881.2 \frac{kJ}{kg}}\right)$$
$$\times (400°C - 350°C) + 350°C$$
$$= 397.0°C \quad (400°C)$$

The answer is (D).

8. SPECIAL CASES OF OPEN SYSTEMS[8]

Equation 14.22: Constant Volume Process

$$w_{rev} = -v(p_2 - p_1) \qquad 14.22$$

Description

For an adiabatic, steady flow, constant volume (i.e., *isochoric*) process with negligible changes in potential and kinetic energy, Eq. 14.20 reduces to Eq. 14.22.

Example

Water flows steadily at a rate of 60 kg/min through a pump. The water pressure is increased from 50 kPa to 5000 kPa. The average specific volume of water is 0.001 m³/kg. Most nearly, what is the hydraulic power delivered to the water by the pump?

(A) 5 kW

(B) 60 kW

(C) 300 kW

(D) 500 kW

[8]The *NCEES Handbook* qualifies Eq. 14.22 through Eq. 14.31 with the title "Special Cases of Open Systems (with no change in kinetic or potential energy)." However, there are additional limitations. Since the heat term has been omitted, these equations are limited to adiabatic systems. Since the mass flow terms have been omitted, there is no possibility of accumulation within the system, so these equations are limited to steady-flow systems.

Solution

The pumping power is

$$\dot{W}_{rev} = -\dot{m}v(p_2 - p_1)$$

$$= \frac{-\left(60 \ \frac{kg}{min}\right)\left(0.001 \ \frac{m^3}{kg}\right)(5000 \ kPa - 50 \ kPa)}{60 \ \frac{s}{min}}$$

$$= -4.95 \ kW \quad (-5 \ kW)$$

The hydraulic power delivered to the water by the pump is 5 KW.

The answer is (A).

Equation 14.23: Constant Pressure Process

$$w_{rev} = 0 \qquad 14.23$$

Description

For an adiabatic, steady flow, constant pressure (i.e., *isobaric*) process with negligible changes in potential and kinetic energy, Eq. 14.20 reduces to Eq. 14.23.

Equation 14.24 and Eq. 14.25: Constant Temperature Process

$$pv = \text{constant} \qquad 14.24$$

$$w_{rev} = RT \ln(v_2/v_1) = RT \ln(p_1/p_2) \qquad 14.25$$

Description

For an adiabatic, steady flow, constant temperature (i.e., *isothermal*) process with negligible changes in potential and kinetic energy, Eq. 14.20 reduces to Eq. 14.25.

Equation 14.26 Through Eq. 14.29: Isentropic Systems

$$pv^k = \text{constant} \qquad 14.26$$

$$w_{rev} = k(p_2v_2 - p_1v_1)/(1 - k) \qquad 14.27$$

$$w_{rev} = kR(T_2 - T_1)/(1 - k) \qquad 14.28$$

$$w_{rev} = \frac{k}{k-1}RT_1\left[1 - \left(\frac{p_2}{p_1}\right)^{(k-1)/k}\right] \qquad 14.29$$

Values

k is the ratio of specific heats, equal to 1.4 for air.

Description

Equation 14.26 through Eq. 14.29 are for isentropic systems.

Equation 14.30 and Eq. 14.31: Polytropic Systems

$$pv^n = \text{constant} \qquad 14.30$$

$$w_{rev} = n(p_2v_2 - p_1v_1)/(1 - n) \qquad 14.31$$

Description

Equation 14.30 and Eq. 14.31 are for polytropic systems. n is the polytropic exponent described in Sec. 14.6. The work term given by Eq. 14.31 for steady flow polytropic systems is different from the corresponding work term given by Eq. 14.19 for closed system polytropic processes. This is because shaft work is calculated from $v \, dp$ (i.e., no change in volume), and boundary work is calculated from $p \, dv$ (i.e., with a change in volume). The derivations are different.

Example

The state of an ideal gas is changed in a steady-state open polytropic process from 400 kPa and 1.2 m³ to 300 kPa and 1.5 m³. The polytropic exponent is 1.3. Most nearly, what is the work performed?

(A) 130 kJ

(B) 930 kJ

(C) 1200 kJ

(D) 9000 kJ

Solution

The work for an open, polytropic process is

$$w_{rev} = n(p_2v_2 - p_1v_1)/(1 - n)$$

$$= \frac{(1.3)\left[\begin{array}{c}(300 \ kPa)(1.5 \ m^3) \\ -(400 \ kPa)(1.2 \ m^3)\end{array}\right]}{1 - 1.3}$$

$$= 130 \ kJ$$

The answer is (A).

9. STEADY-STATE SYSTEMS

Equation 14.32 and Eq. 14.33: Steady-Flow Energy Equation

$$\sum \dot{m}_i(h_i + \mathrm{v}_i^2/2 + gz_i) - \sum \dot{m}_e(h_e + \mathrm{v}_e^2/2 + gz_e)$$
$$+ \dot{Q}_{in} - \dot{W}_{out} = 0 \qquad \textit{14.32}$$

$$\sum \dot{m}_i = \sum \dot{m}_e \qquad \textit{14.33}$$

Description

If the mass flow rate is constant, the system is a *steady-flow system*, and the first law is known as the *steady-flow energy equation*, SFEE, given by Eq. 14.32.[9]

The subscripts i and e denote conditions at the in-point and exit of the control volume, respectively. $\mathrm{v}^2/2 + gz$ represents the sum of the fluid's kinetic and potential energies. Generally, these terms are insignificant compared with the thermal energy terms.

$\dot{W}_{out}$ is the rate of *shaft work* (i.e., *shaft power*)—work that the steady-flow device does on the surroundings. Its name is derived from the output shaft that serves to transmit energy out of the system. For example, turbines and internal combustion engines have output shafts. $\dot{W}_{out}$ can be negative, as in the case of a pump or compressor.[10]

The enthalpy, h, represents a combination of internal energy and reversible (flow) work ($pv + u$).

Example

An insulated reservoir has three inputs and one output. The first input is saturated water at 80°C with a mass flow rate of 1 kg/s. The second input is saturated water at 30°C with a mass flow rate of 2 kg/s. The output is water with a mass flow rate of 4 kg/s and a temperature of 60°C. The water level of the reservoir remains constant. Velocity and elevation changes are insignificant. What is most nearly the temperature of the third input?

(A) 60°C

(B) 70°C

(C) 80°C

(D) 100°C

Solution

Since the system is a steady-state system, the sum of the mass flow rates at the entrance is equal to the mass flow rate at the exit. Calculate the mass flow rate of the third input.

Use Eq. 14.33.

$$\sum \dot{m}_i = \sum \dot{m}_e$$
$$\dot{m}_1 + \dot{m}_2 + \dot{m}_3 = \dot{m}_e$$
$$\dot{m}_3 = \dot{m}_e - \dot{m}_1 - \dot{m}_2$$
$$= 4 \, \frac{\mathrm{kg}}{\mathrm{s}} - 2 \, \frac{\mathrm{kg}}{\mathrm{s}} - 1 \, \frac{\mathrm{kg}}{\mathrm{s}}$$
$$= 1 \, \mathrm{kg/s}$$

Use Eq. 14.32. Since the reservoir is insulated, the system is adiabatic, and $Q_{in} = 0$. Since the system does no work on the surroundings, $W_{out} = 0$. Since velocity and elevation changes are insignificant, the $\mathrm{v}^2/2$ and gz terms can be omitted.

$$\sum \dot{m}(h_i + \mathrm{v}_i^2/2 + gz_i)$$
$$- \sum \dot{m}_e(h_e + \mathrm{v}_e^2/2 + gz_e)$$
$$+ \dot{Q}_{in} - \dot{W}_{out} = 0$$
$$= \dot{m}_1 h_1 + \dot{m}_2 h_2 + \dot{m}_3 h_3 - \dot{m}_e h_e$$
$$h_3 = \frac{\dot{m}_e h_e - \dot{m}_1 h_1 - \dot{m}_2 h_2}{\dot{m}_3}$$

Although the enthalpies of saturated liquid water could be determined from the steam tables, it is not necessary to do so. All of the inputs and the output are liquid water, so the enthalpies, h, can be represented by $c_p T$.

---

[9]Equation 14.32 is technically incomplete. By labeling the heat energy and work terms "in" and "out," respectively, the *NCEES Handbook* abandons the standard thermodynamic sign convention that was implicit in Eq. 14.3. In Eq. 14.3, the heat term, Q, implicitly represents $Q_{in} - Q_{out}$, and the work term, W, implicitly represents $W_{out} - W_{in}$. Equation 14.32 defines $\dot{Q}$ and $\dot{W}$ explicitly, but the $\dot{Q}_{out}$ and $\dot{W}_{in}$ terms are omitted. In order to properly use Eq. 14.32, the signs of the $\dot{Q}$ and $\dot{W}$ terms must be changed based on the definitions (subscripts), not based on the standard thermodynamic sign convention.

[10]As already explained, Eq. 14.32 does not use the standard thermodynamic sign convention that was implicit in Eq. 14.3. In order to properly use Eq. 14.32, the signs of the Q and W terms must be changed based on the definitions (subscripts), not based on the standard thermodynamic sign convention.

And, since c_p is a common term and is essentially constant over the small temperature range involved, it can be omitted.

$$T_3 \approx \frac{\dot{m}_e T_e - \dot{m}_1 T_1 - \dot{m}_2 T_2}{\dot{m}_3}$$

$$= \frac{\left(4\,\dfrac{\text{kg}}{\text{s}}\right)(60°\text{C}) - \left(1\,\dfrac{\text{kg}}{\text{s}}\right)(80°\text{C}) -\left(2\,\dfrac{\text{kg}}{\text{s}}\right)(30°\text{C})}{1\,\dfrac{\text{kg}}{\text{s}}}$$

$$= 100°\text{C}$$

The answer is (D).

10. EQUIPMENT AND COMPONENTS

Equation 14.34 and Eq. 14.35: Nozzles and Diffusers

$$h_i + v_i^2/2 = h_e + v_e^2/2 \qquad \textit{14.34}$$

$$\text{isentropic efficiency} = \frac{v_e^2 - v_i^2}{2(h_i - h_{es})} \quad \text{[nozzle]} \qquad \textit{14.35}$$

Description

Since a flowing fluid is in contact with nozzle, orifice, and valve walls for only a very short period of time, flow through them is essentially adiabatic. No work is done on the fluid as it passes through. Since most of the fluid does not contact the nozzle walls, friction is minimal. A lossless adiabatic process is an isentropic process. If the potential energy changes are neglected, Eq. 14.32 reduces to Eq. 14.34.

The *nozzle efficiency* is defined as Eq. 14.35.[11] The subscript "*es*" refers to the exit condition for an isentropic (ideal) expansion.

Example

Steam enters an adiabatic nozzle at 1 MPa, 250°C, and 30 m/s. At one point in the nozzle, the enthalpy drops 40 kJ/kg from its inlet value. What is most nearly the velocity at that point?

(A)   31 m/s

(B)   110 m/s

(C)   250 m/s

(D)   280 m/s

Solution

Use Eq. 14.34.

$$h_i + v_i^2/2 = h_e + v_e^2/2$$

$$\begin{aligned} v_e &= \sqrt{2(h_i - h_e) + v_i^2} \\ &= \sqrt{(2)\left(40\,\frac{\text{kJ}}{\text{kg}}\right)\left(1000\,\frac{\text{J}}{\text{kJ}}\right) + \left(30\,\frac{\text{m}}{\text{s}}\right)^2} \\ &= 284 \text{ m/s} \quad (280 \text{ m/s}) \end{aligned}$$

The answer is (D).

Equation 14.36 Through Eq. 14.38: Turbines, Pumps, and Compressors

$$h_i = h_e + w \qquad \textit{14.36}$$

$$\text{isentropic efficiency} = \frac{h_i - h_e}{h_i - h_{es}} \quad \text{[turbine]} \qquad \textit{14.37}$$

$$\text{isentropic efficiency} = \frac{h_{es} - h_i}{h_e - h_i} \quad \text{[compressor, pump]} \qquad \textit{14.38}$$

Description

A *pump* or *compressor* converts mechanical energy into fluid energy, increasing the total energy content of the fluid flowing through it. *Turbines* can generally be thought of as pumps operating in reverse. A turbine extracts energy from the fluid, converting fluid energy into mechanical energy.

These devices can be considered to be adiabatic because the fluid gains (or loses) very little heat during the short time it passes through them.

---

[11]In its section on heat cycles, the *NCEES Handbook* uses the symbol η for (thermal) efficiency. However, it does not use any symbol for (isentropic) efficiency in Eq. 14.35 or in the equations for other components. Isentropic efficiency for nozzles and other components is commonly written as η_s.

Equation 14.36 assumes that the pump or turbine is capable of isentropic compression or expansion.[12] However, due to inefficiencies, the actual exit enthalpy will deviate from the ideal isentropic enthalpy, h_{es}. The isentropic efficiencies are given by Eq. 14.37 and Eq. 14.38.

Equation 14.37 for turbines is equivalent to the ratio $w_{out,actual}/w_{out,ideal}$, while Eq. 14.38 for pumps and compressors is equivalent to the ratio $w_{in,ideal}/w_{in,actual}$. For turbines, the ideal power generated (i.e., the denominator) is larger than the actual power generated. For pumps, the actual work input (the denominator) is larger than the ideal work input. Since these two expressions are essentially reciprocals, it is important to recognize that the larger quantity always is in the denominator.

Equation 14.37 and Eq. 14.38 both imply that it is necessary to know the ideal conditions when determining isentropic efficiencies. This often results in having to solve a problem twice: once with the ideal properties, and once with the actual properties. Actual properties are usually measured and are known. Ideal properties assume a process that has neither friction nor heat loss (i.e., is reversible and adiabatic). By definition, a reversible adiabatic process is isentropic. Two characteristics of isentropic processes are used to determine the ideal state properties: (1) Entropy does not change in an isentropic process (i.e., $\Delta s = 0$). (2) The final pressure is not changed by the inefficiency. For both pumps and turbines, the exit properties can be evaluated at the entrance entropy and the actual exit pressure.[13]

Example

A turbine produces 3 MW of power by expanding 500°C steam at 1 MPa to a saturated 30 kPa vapor. What is most nearly the isentropic efficiency of the turbine?

(A) 96.5%

(B) 98.2%

(C) 99.1%

(D) 99.7%

Solution

From the superheated water table, at 1 MPa and 500°C, the entering enthalpy is $h_i = 3478.5$ kJ/kg.

At the exit, the steam is saturated at 30 kPa. (This roughly corresponds to a saturation temperature of 70°C.) Interpolating from the saturated water table, the actual exit enthalpy is

$$h_e = h_{g,p_{sat}=p_e} = 2625.2 \text{ kJ/kg}$$

The actual enthalpy change (work) is

$$w_{actual} = h_i - h_e$$
$$= 3478.5 \text{ } \frac{kJ}{kg} - 2625.2 \text{ } \frac{kJ}{kg}$$
$$= 853.3 \text{ kJ/kg}$$

In order to calculate the turbine's isentropic efficiency, it is necessary to calculate the ideal exit enthalpy, h_{es}, that corresponds to isentropic expansion (i.e., the ideal case). The ideal exit enthalpy is calculated from the ideal quality, which in turn, is found from the ideal entropy. If the expansion had been isentropic, the entropy at the exit would have corresponded to the entropy at the entrance of the turbine. The exit pressure is unaffected by the isentropic efficiency.

At the initial state of 1 MPa and 500°C, the entropy is $s_i = 7.7622$ kJ/kg·K. At the final state, the pressure is 30 kPa, which roughly corresponds to a saturation temperature of 70°C. Interpolating from the saturated water table, the saturated liquid and vaporization entropies are $s_f = 0.9430$ kJ/kg·K and $s_{fg} = 6.827$ kJ/kg·K. For an isentropic (ideal) expansion, the ideal quality would have been

$$x_{es} = \frac{s_{es} - s_{f,p_{sat}=p_{es}}}{s_{fg,p_{sat}=p_{es}}}$$
$$= \frac{7.7622 \text{ } \frac{kJ}{kg \cdot K} - 0.9430 \text{ } \frac{kJ}{kg \cdot K}}{6.827 \text{ } \frac{kJ}{kg \cdot K}}$$
$$= 0.9989$$

---

[12]The *NCEES Handbook* is inconsistent in its subscripting for work terms. The standard thermodynamic sign convention is required to determine the sign of the work term, w, in Eq. 14.36. Work, w, can be either positive or negative. For turbines (when the system does work on the environment), the w term is positive. For pumps (where the environment does work on the system), the w term is negative. Algebraically, Eq. 14.36 is equivalent to $h_i - w = h_e$. Since, for pumps, w is negative, this is equivalent to $h_i + w_{in} = h_e$. For pump problems asking for the work per unit mass of fluid, answers derived rigorously from Eq. 14.36 would all need to be negative.

[13]The *NCEES Handbook* does not provide a "pressures" saturated water properties table (i.e., a table of properties presented with constant pressure increments). This makes solving pump and turbine problems (and, all steam power cycle problems) extremely inconvenient, as interpolation is almost always required. The inconvenience is particularly extreme when evaluating condenser performance, since the primary descriptive operating condition of a condenser is its pressure. Since interpolation takes more time than is normally available for a single problem on the FE exam, the logical interpretation is that accurate results are not required for these problems. It is probably sufficient to use the values that correspond to the closest pressure in the "temperatures" saturated water properties table.

Interpolating from the saturated water table, the saturated liquid and vaporization entropies are $h_f = 288.94$ kJ/kg and $h_{fg} = 2336.2$ kJ/kg. If the expansion had been isentropic, the enthalpy would have been

$$h_{es} = h_{f,p_{es}=p_{sat}} + x_{es}h_{fg,p_{es}=p_{sat}}$$
$$= 288.94 \ \frac{kJ}{kg} + (0.9989)\left(2336.2 \ \frac{kJ}{kg}\right)$$
$$= 2622.5 \ kJ/kg$$

The ideal work would have been

$$w_{ideal} = h_i - h_{es}$$
$$= 3478.5 \ \frac{kJ}{kg} - 2622.5 \ \frac{kJ}{kg}$$
$$= 856.0 \ kJ/kg$$

From Eq. 14.37, the isentropic efficiency of the turbine is

$$\text{isentropic efficiency} = \frac{h_i - h_e}{h_i - h_{es}}$$
$$= \frac{w_{actual}}{w_{ideal}}$$
$$= \frac{853.3 \ \frac{kJ}{kg}}{856.0 \ \frac{kJ}{kg}}$$
$$= 0.9968 \quad (99.7\%)$$

The answer is (D).

Equation 14.39: Throttling Valves and Throttling Processes

$$h_i = h_e \qquad \text{14.39}$$

Description

In a *throttling process*, there is no change in system enthalpy, but there is a significant pressure drop. The process is adiabatic, and Eq. 14.32 reduces to Eq. 14.39.

Equation 14.40: Boilers, Condensers, and Evaporators

$$h_i + q = h_e \qquad \text{14.40}$$

Description

An *evaporator* is a device that adds heat, q, to water at low (near atmospheric) pressure and produces saturated steam. A *boiler* adds heat to water (known as *feedwater*) and produces superheated steam. The superheating may occur in the boiler, or there may be a separate unit known as a *superheater*. Both evaporators and boilers add most, if not all, of the heat of vaporization, h_{fg}, to the water. Superheaters add additional energy known as the *superheat* or *superheat energy*.

A *condenser* is a device that removes heat, q, from saturated or superheated steam. Usually, all of the superheat energy is removed, leaving the steam as a saturated liquid. Some of the heat of vaporization may also be removed, resulting in a *subcooled liquid*. Heat removed from the steam is released (usually to the environment) after being carried away by cooling water or air.

Disregarding changes to kinetic and potential energies, Eq. 14.40 describes the operation of evaporators, boilers, and condensers.[14] For both adiabatic and nonadiabatic devices, q represents the change in water or steam energy.

Example

A simple Rankine cycle operates between 20°C and 100°C and uses water as the working fluid. The turbine has an isentropic efficiency of 100%, and the pump has an isentropic efficiency of 65%. The steam leaving the boiler and the water leaving the condenser are both saturated.

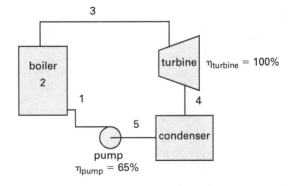

---

[14]The standard thermodynamic sign convention is required to determine the sign of the work term, q, in Eq. 14.40. Work, q, can be either positive or negative. For evaporators and boilers (where energy enters the system), the q term is positive. For condensers (where energy leaves the system), the q term is negative. Algebraically, Eq. 14.40 is equivalent to, $h_i = h_e - q$. Since, for condensers, q is negative, this is equivalent to $h_i = h_e + q_{out}$. For condenser problems asking for the energy removal per unit mass of steam, answers derived rigorously from Eq. 14.40 would all need to be negative.

The properties of steam at the two temperatures are as follows.

For a saturation temperature of 20°C,

pressure 2.339 kPa
specific volume
  fluid 0.001002 m³/kg
  gas 57.79 m³/kg
enthalpy
  fluid 83.95 kJ/kg
  fluid-to-gas 2454.1 kJ/kg
  gas 2538.1 kJ/kg
entropy
  fluid 0.2966 kJ/kg·K
  gas 8.6672 kJ/kg·K

For a saturation temperature of 100°C,

pressure 101.35 kPa
specific volume
  fluid 0.001044 m³/kg
  gas 1.6729 m³/kg
enthalpy
  fluid 419.04 kJ/kg
  fluid-to-gas 2257.0 kJ/kg
  gas 2676.1 kJ/kg
entropy
  fluid 1.3069 kJ/kg·K
  gas 7.3549 kJ/kg·K

The energy removed from each kilogram of steam in the condenser is most nearly

(A) 84 kJ/kg

(B) 420 kJ/kg

(C) 1500 kJ/kg

(D) 2100 kJ/kg

Solution

At state 3,

$$T_3 = 100°C \quad \text{[saturated]}$$
$$h_3 = h_g = 2676.1 \text{ kJ/kg}$$
$$s_3 = s_g = 7.3549 \text{ kJ/kg·K}$$

At state 4,

$$s_4 = s_3 = 7.3549 \text{ kJ/kg·K}$$
$$x = \frac{s - s_f}{s_{fg}} = \frac{s - s_f}{s_g - s_f}$$
$$= \frac{7.3549 \frac{\text{kJ}}{\text{kg·K}} - 0.2966 \frac{\text{kJ}}{\text{kg·K}}}{8.6672 \frac{\text{kJ}}{\text{kg·K}} - 0.2966 \frac{\text{kJ}}{\text{kg·K}}}$$
$$= 0.843$$
$$h_4 = h_f + x h_{fg}$$
$$= 83.95 \frac{\text{kJ}}{\text{kg}} + (0.843)\left(2454.1 \frac{\text{kJ}}{\text{kg}}\right)$$
$$= 2153 \text{ kJ/kg}$$

Use Eq. 14.40. The energy removed is

$$h_i + q = h_e$$
$$q_L = h_{e4} - h_{i5}$$
$$= 2153 \frac{\text{kJ}}{\text{kg}} - 83.95 \frac{\text{kJ}}{\text{kg}}$$
$$= 2069 \text{ kJ/kg} \quad (2100 \text{ kJ/kg})$$

The answer is (D).

Equation 14.41: Heat Exchangers

$$\dot{m}_1(h_{1i} - h_{1e}) = \dot{m}_2(h_{2e} - h_{2i}) \qquad 14.41$$

Description

A *heat exchanger* transfers heat energy from one fluid to another through a wall separating them. Heat exchangers have two working fluids, two entrances, and two exits. In Eq. 14.41, the hot and cold substances are identified by the numerical subscripts.[15]

No work is done within a heat exchanger, and the potential and kinetic energies of the fluids can be ignored. If the heat exchanger is well insulated (i.e., is adiabatic), Eq. 14.32 reduces to Eq. 14.41.

[15]Although there is no single unified convention on how to differentiate between the two working fluids, a common convention is to use the subscripts H and C to designate the hot and cold fluids, respectively. (The *NCEES Handbook* adopts that convention in equations involving the logarithmic mean temperature difference, LMTD.) This helps to avoid errors when assigning temperatures and other properties in equations.

Equation 14.42 and Eq. 14.43: Mixers, Separators, and Open or Closed Feedwater Heaters

$$\sum \dot{m}_i h_i = \sum \dot{m}_e h_e \qquad \text{14.42}$$

$$\sum \dot{m}_i = \sum \dot{m}_e \qquad \text{14.43}$$

Description

A *feedwater heater* uses steam to increase the temperature of water entering the steam generator. The steam can come from any waste steam source but is usually bled off from a turbine. In this latter case, the heater is known as an *extraction heater*. The water that is heated usually comes from the condenser.

Open heaters (also known as *direct contact heaters* and *mixing heaters*) physically mix the steam and water. A *closed feedwater heater* is a traditional closed heat exchanger that can operate at either high or low pressures. There is no mixing of the water and steam in the closed feedwater heater. The cooled stream leaves the feedwater heater as a liquid.

For adiabatic operation, Eq. 14.32 reduces to Eq. 14.42. Since some feedwater heaters have two or more input streams (e.g., a bleed steam input and a condenser liquid input), Eq. 14.42 and Eq. 14.43 are presented as summations.

11. SECOND LAW OF THERMODYNAMICS

The *second law of thermodynamics* can be stated in several ways. The second law can be described in terms of the environment ("The entropy of the environment always increases in real processes."), working fluid ("A substance can be brought back to its original state without increasing the entropy of the environment only in a reversible system."), or equipment ("A machine that returns the working fluid to its original state requires a heat sink." Or, "A machine rejects more energy than the useful work it performs."). The second law can also be used to define what kinds of processes can occur naturally (spontaneously).

A natural process that starts in one equilibrium state and ends in another will go in the direction that causes the entropy of the system and the environment to increase.

Equation 14.44 and Eq. 14.45: Change of Entropy

$$ds = (1/T)\delta q_{\text{rev}} \qquad \text{14.44}$$

$$s_2 - s_1 = \int_1^2 (1/T)\delta q_{\text{rev}} \qquad \text{14.45}$$

Description

Entropy is a measure of the energy that is no longer available to perform useful work within the current environment. An increase in entropy is known as *entropy production*. The total entropy in a system is equal to the integral of all entropy productions that have occurred over the life of the system.

Equation 14.44 defines the *exact differential* of entropy, ds, in terms of the *inexact differential* of heat, δq.[16] An inexact differential is path-dependent, while the exact differential is not.[17]

Since Eq. 14.44 is stated as an equality, the heat transfer process is implicitly reversible. (If the process is irreversible, an inequality is required.) Equation 14.44 and Eq. 14.45 are restatements of the *inequality of Clausius* (see Eq. 14.56) for reversible processes. Equation 14.45 purports to be the solution to Eq. 14.44.[18]

Equation 14.46 and Eq. 14.47: Entropy Change for Solids and Liquids

$$ds = c(dT/T) \qquad \text{14.46}$$

$$s_2 - s_1 = \int c(dT/T) = c_{\text{mean}} \ln(T_2/T_1) \qquad \text{14.47}$$

---

[16]The *NCEES Handbook* uses inexact differentials with Eq. 14.44, Eq. 14.45, Eq. 14.56, and Eq. 14.57, but probably nowhere else. Most notably, they are not used in first-law formulations such as Eq. 14.3, where a presentation consistent with the concept of inexact differentials would be $dU = \delta Q - \delta W$.

[17]*Inexact differentials* are also known as *imperfect differentials* and *incomplete differentials*. The distinction between exact and inexact differentials is unique to the field of thermodynamics. Rudolf Clausius, who formulated the concept of entropy (ca. 1850), recognized that entropy production was path-dependent, although the notational difference between the two types of differentials was apparently introduced only later by Carl Neuman (ca. 1875).

[18](1) The integral notation used by the *NCEES Handbook* in Eq. 14.45 is incorrect. There is no mathematical operation that "maps" an inexact entropy differential to an entropy change because the entropy production is path-dependent. From the (second part of the) fundamental theorem of calculus, a definite integral is defined by its endpoints, not its path. For example,

$$\int_a^b f(x)\,dx = F(b) - F(a)$$

That is not possible with an inexact differential. (2) The temperature, T, used in Eq. 14.44 and Eq. 14.45 is the temperature of the heat sink or heat source. It is the same as $T_{\text{reservoir}}$ used elsewhere in the *NCEES Handbook*.

Description

Since entropy production is related to heat transfer, it is logical to incorporate the calculation of thermal energy transfers into the calculation of entropy production. The general relationship between thermal energy and temperature difference for a unit mass is $q = c\Delta T$. The specific heat, c, of liquids and solids is essentially constant over fairly large temperature and pressure ranges. Equation 14.46 substitutes $c\,dT$ for δq in Eq. 14.44. Equation 14.47 substitutes $c\,dT$ for δq in Eq. 14.45.[19]

Equation 14.48: Entropy Production at Constant Temperature

$$\Delta S_{\text{reservoir}} = Q/T_{\text{reservoir}} \qquad \textit{14.48}$$

Description

Discussions of entropy and the second law invariably lead to use of the terms "heat source" and "heat sink." A *thermal reservoir* is an infinite mass with a constant temperature. When the thermal reservoir supplies energy, it is known as a *heat source*. When the reservoir absorbs energy, it is known as a *heat sink*. Since the reservoir has an infinite mass, its temperature, $T_{\text{reservoir}}$, does not change when energy is supplied or absorbed.[20]

Equation 14.48 defines the total change in reservoir entropy when heat is transferred to or from it.[21] This change is known as *entropy production*. Equation 14.48 is an equality because Q is explicitly the heat that enters the reservoir, regardless of how much heat was lost in transit.

Example

A large concrete bridge anchorage at 15°C receives 50 GJ of thermal energy from exposure to sunlight. The temperature of the anchorage does not change significantly. What is most nearly the change in entropy within the concrete?

(A) 97 MJ/K

(B) 170 MJ/K

(C) 1900 MJ/K

(D) 3300 MJ/K

Solution

The anchorage is essentially an infinite thermal sink. From Eq. 14.48, the entropy production is

$$\begin{aligned}
\Delta S_{\text{reservoir}} &= Q/T_{\text{reservoir}} \\
&= \frac{(50 \text{ GJ})\left(1000\,\dfrac{\text{MJ}}{\text{GJ}}\right)}{15°\text{C} + 273°} \\
&= 173.6 \text{ MJ/K} \quad (170 \text{ MJ/K})
\end{aligned}$$

The answer is (B).

Equation 14.49: Isothermal, Reversible Process

$$\Delta s = s_2 - s_1 = q/T \qquad \textit{14.49}$$

Variation

$$\begin{aligned}
\Delta S &= m\Delta s \\
&= S_2 - S_1 \\
&= \frac{Q}{T_{\text{reservoir}}}
\end{aligned}$$

---

[19](1) The *NCEES Handbook* presents Eq. 14.46 and Eq. 14.47 as equalities. The implication of this is the substance has been assumed to be completely incompressible (i.e., unaffected by pressure). (2) The *NCEES Handbook* presents the last form of Eq. 14.47 as an equality (i.e., as an engineering fact). However, there is no theoretical basis to using the mean specific heat. Using the mean specific heat is merely a computational convenience. If the last form of Eq. 14.47 is presented at all, it should be as an approximation and limited to small temperature changes. (3) The *NCEES Handbook* does not define c_{mean}. Three common definitions are used as simplifications of more rigorous methods: (a) the average of the specific heats at the beginning and ending temperatures, (b) the specific heat at the average temperature, and (c) the specific heat at the midpoint of a long pipe or other linear process.

[20]Although the *NCEES Handbook* identifies the reservoir temperature as $T_{\text{reservoir}}$, it is normal and customary in engineering thermodynamics to designate the environment temperature as T_0.

[21](1) It is important to recognize that Eq. 14.48 is written from the standpoint of the reservoir, not the process, machine, or substance that the reservoir is attached to. (2) The standard thermodynamic sign convention is required to determine the sign of the heat energy term, Q, in Eq. 14.48. Heat energy can be either positive or negative. For a heat sink, where energy enters the reservoir, Q is positive. For a heat source, where energy leaves the reservoir, Q is negative. (3) With a strict sign convention, it is important to recognize that ΔS is strictly defined as $S_2 - S_1$. If heat enters the reservoir (a positive Q), the final entropy will be greater than the initial entropy. (4) Since uppercase letters are used in Eq. 14.48, the intent is to calculate the entropy production in the entire reservoir from the entire heat transfer, not on a per unit mass basis. This is probably just as well, since the reservoir has an infinite mass.

Thermodynamics

Description

For a process taking place at a constant temperature, T (i.e., discharging energy to a constant-temperature reservoir at T), the entropy production in the reservoir depends on the amount of energy transfer.[22] The standard thermodynamic sign convention must be followed when using Eq. 14.49. If heat enters the system, q will be positive, and s_2 will be greater than s_1. Equation 14.49 can be written in terms of total properties, as the variation equation shows.

Example

An ideal gas undergoes a reversible isothermal expansion at 50°C. 200 kJ of heat enters the process. What is most nearly the change in air entropy at the end of the process?

(A)   0.62 kJ/K

(B)   0.72 kJ/K

(C)   0.90 kJ/K

(D)   1.0 kJ/K

Solution

The change in total entropy after the heat addition is

$$\Delta S = Q/T$$
$$= \frac{200 \text{ kJ}}{50°\text{C} + 273°}$$
$$= 0.619 \text{ kJ/K} \quad (0.62 \text{ kJ/K})$$

The answer is (A).

Equation 14.50 and Eq. 14.51: Isentropic Process

$$ds = 0 \qquad 14.50$$

$$\Delta s = 0 \qquad 14.51$$

Description

Isentropic means constant entropy. Entropy does not change in an isentropic process, as shown by Eq. 14.50 and Eq. 14.51.

Equation 14.52 and Eq. 14.53: Adiabatic Process

$$\delta q = 0 \qquad 14.52$$

$$\Delta s \geq 0 \qquad 14.53$$

Description

Equation 14.52 and Eq. 14.53 are for adiabatic processes. There is no heat gain or loss in an *adiabatic process*. Processes that are well insulated (or that occur quickly enough to preclude significant heat loss (e.g., supersonic flow through a nozzle)) are often assumed to be adiabatic. An adiabatic process is not necessarily reversible, however. So, even though $q = 0$, it is still possible that other losses may cause entropy to increase. For example, pumps, compressors, and turbines lose or gain negligible heat, but they are affected by fluid and bearing friction.

Example

Air at 80°C originally occupies 0.5 m^3 at 200 kPa. The gas is compressed reversibly and adiabatically to 1.20 MPa. What is most nearly the heat flow?

(A)   0 J

(B)   0.69 J

(C)   0.82 J

(D)   1.5 J

Solution

The gas is compressed adiabatically. So, by Eq. 14.52,

$$\delta q = 0 \quad (0 \text{ J})$$

The answer is (A).

Equation 14.54 and Eq. 14.55: Increase of Entropy Principle

$$\Delta s_{\text{total}} = \Delta s_{\text{system}} + \Delta s_{\text{surroundings}} \geq 0 \qquad 14.54$$

$$\Delta \dot{s}_{\text{total}} = \sum \dot{m}_{\text{out}} s_{\text{out}} - \sum \dot{m}_{\text{in}} s_{\text{in}} - \sum (\dot{q}_{\text{external}}/T_{\text{external}}) \geq 0 \qquad 14.55$$

[22](1) The variable T used by the *NCEES Handbook* in Eq. 14.49 is the same as $T_{\text{reservoir}}$ used elsewhere. This variable is commonly shown as T_0 to indicate the temperature of the environment. (2) It is important to recognize that, while Δs is defined as $s_2 - s_1$ (as it would be for any variable), $s_2 - s_1$ is not derived from a definite integral.

Description

The increase of entropy principle states that the change in total entropy (i.e., the entropy of the system and its surroundings) will be greater than or equal to zero.[23]

For all reversible processes, the equalities in Eq. 14.54 and Eq. 14.55 are valid.[24] For irreversible processes, the inequalities are valid.

Example

For an irreversible process, the total change in entropy of the system and surroundings is

(A) ∞

(B) 0

(C) greater than 0

(D) less than 0

Solution

For an irreversible process,

$$\Delta s_{\text{total}} = \Delta s_{\text{system}} + \Delta s_{\text{surroundings}} > 0$$

The answer is (C).

Kelvin-Planck Statement of Second Law (Power Cycles)

The *Kelvin-Planck statement of the second law* effectively says that it is impossible to build a cyclical engine that will have a thermal efficiency of 100%:

> No heat engine can operate in a cycle while transferring heat with a single thermal reservoir.

Figure 14.1(a) shows a violation of the second law in which a heat engine extracts heat from a high-temperature reservoir and converts that heat into an equivalent amount of work. There is no heat transfer to the low-temperature reservoir. (This is signified by the absence of an arrow going to the low-temperature reservoir.) In the real world, there are always losses (e.g., frictional heating) in the conversion of energy to work, and those losses cannot go back to a high-temperature reservoir. They must go to a low-temperature reservoir.

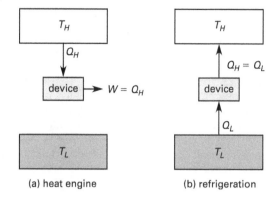

Figure 14.1 *Second Law Violations*

(a) heat engine   (b) refrigeration

Another statement that is equivalent is

> It is impossible to operate an engine operating in a cycle that will have no other effect than to extract heat from a reservoir and turn it into an equivalent amount of work.

This formulation is not a contradiction of the first law of thermodynamics. The first law does not preclude the possibility of converting heat entirely into work—it only denies the possibility of creating or destroying energy. The second law says that if some heat is converted entirely into work, some other energy must be rejected to a low-temperature reservoir (i.e., lost to the surroundings).

A corollary to this formulation of the second law is that the maximum possible efficiency of a heat engine operating between two thermal reservoirs is the Carnot cycle efficiency. It is possible to have a heat engine with a thermal efficiency higher than a particular Carnot cycle engine, but the temperatures of the heat engine would have to be different from the Carnot temperatures.

Equation 14.56 and Eq. 14.57: Inequality of Clausius

$$\oint (1/T)\delta q_{\text{rev}} \leq 0 \qquad \textit{14.56}$$

$$\int_1^2 (1/T)\delta q \leq s_2 - s_1 \qquad \textit{14.57}$$

---

[23]This is the principle that leads to the conclusion that the universe is winding down, and that its eventual demise will be as a chaotic collection of random, cold particles.

[24](1) Equation 14.54 is not a formula, per se. It is a symbolic formulation of the statement, "The total entropy change includes the entropy productions of the system and the surroundings." (2) The *NCEES Handbook* presents Eq. 14.54 with lowercase letters, representing entropy changes per unit mass. The sum of the per unit system entropy increase and the per unit surroundings entropy increase would be a meaningless quantity, because the masses are different. The implication that Δs_{total} could be multiplied by any total mass value is incorrect. (3) It is not obvious why the *NCEES Handbook* presents Eq. 14.54 in terms of entropy, while Eq. 14.55 uses entropy per unit time. While both equations are correct, Eq. 14.55 does not follow directly from Eq. 14.54, which appears to be the intention. (4) The subscript "external" has not been defined by the *NCEES Handbook*, although "environment" could be an intended interpretation. For the finite summation to be valid, however, all of the T_{external} terms would have to represent constant heat sink or heat source temperatures. In that case, T_{external} would be the same as the T and $T_{\text{reservoir}}$ variables used elsewhere in the *NCEES Handbook*.

Description

The *inequality of Clausius* is a mathematical statement of the second law of thermodynamics.

Equation 14.56 is the mathematical formulation of the inequality of Clausius, formulated as a *cyclic integral*, indicated by the symbol $\oint$. (A cyclic integral is a line integral evaluated over a closed path.) The left-hand side of Eq. 14.56 is a conceptual operation, not a mathematical operation or function. Equation 14.56 is interpreted as: "When a closed process is returned to its original condition in a cycle, after following the path taken by the substance in the process, the entropy production is, at best, zero, but otherwise, is less than zero."[25] Equation 14.57 purports to be the definition of entropy production.[26]

12. FINDING WORK AND HEAT GRAPHICALLY

Equation 14.58: Temperature-Entropy Diagrams

$$q_{\mathrm{rev}} = \int_1^2 T \, ds \qquad\qquad 14.58$$

Description

A process between two thermodynamic states can be represented graphically. The line representing the locus of quasiequilibrium states between the initial and final states is known as the *path* of the process.

It is convenient to plot the path on a T-s diagram. (See Fig. 14.2.) The amount of heat absorbed or released from a system can be determined as the area under the path on the T-s diagram, as given by Eq. 14.58 and shown in Fig. 14.2.

Figure 14.2 *Heat from T-s Diagram*

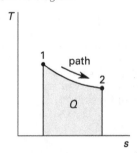

Pressure-Volume Diagrams

Similarly, the pressure and volume of a system can be plotted on a p-V diagram. Since $w = p\Delta v$, the work done by or on the system can be determined from that graph. (See Fig. 14.3.)

Figure 14.3 *Work from p-V Diagram*

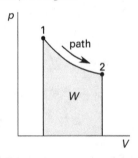

The variables p, V, T, and s are *point functions* because their values are independent of the path taken to arrive at the thermodynamic state. Work and heat (W and Q), however, are *path functions* because they depend on the path taken. For that reason, care should be taken when calculating work and heat by direct integration.[27]

---

[25]The *NCEES Handbook* states the inequality of Clausius incorrectly. The equality holds for the reversible case; the inequality holds for the irreversible case. If the inexact differential of heat were reversible, as indicated by the subscript, then the result would always be "= 0," not "< 0." The subscript "rev" should be omitted.

[26](1) The integral notation used by the *NCEES Handbook* in Eq. 14.56 and Eq. 14.57 is incorrect. There is no mathematical operation that "maps" an inexact entropy differential to an entropy change because the entropy production is path-dependent. From the (second part of the) fundamental theorem of calculus, a definite integral is defined by its endpoints, not its path. For example,

$$\int_a^b f(x) \, dx = F(b) - F(a)$$

That is not possible with an inexact differential. (2) Additionally, including the limits of integration strengthens the implication that an actual integration of the inexact differential is the intent. (3) Although the *NCEES Handbook* uses a cyclic integral for Eq. 14.56, it does not for Eq. 14.57. (4) The temperature, T, used in Eq. 14.56 and Eq. 14.57 is the temperature of the heat sink or heat source. It is the same as $T_{\mathrm{reservoir}}$ used elsewhere in the *NCEES Handbook*.

[27]As Fig. 14.2 and Fig. 14.3 show, the area under the curve depends on the path taken between points 1 and 2. The area does not merely depend on the values of T and p at points 1 and 2. This is the *de facto* definition of a path function. The calculation cannot involve a definite integral; it must involve a *line integral* (also known as a *path integral*, *contour integral*, or *curve integral*).

15 Power Cycles and Entropy

Nomenclature

B	width	m
c	specific heat	kJ/kg·K
COP	coefficient of performance	–
F	force	N
h	enthalpy	kJ/kg
HV	heating value	J/kg
I	process irreversibility	kJ/kg
k	ratio of specific heats	–
m	mass	kg
$\dot{m}$	mass flow rate	kg/s
mep	mean effective pressure	Pa
n	number	–
N	number	–
p	pressure	Pa
q	heat energy	kJ
$\dot{q}$	heat energy flow rate	kJ/s
Q	total heat energy	kJ
$\dot{Q}$	rate of heat transfer	kW
r	volumetric compression ratio	–
R	radius	m
s	specific entropy	kJ/kg·K
S	length of stroke	m
S	total entropy	kJ/K
sfc	specific fuel consumption	kg/J
T	absolute temperature	K
T	torque	N·m
u	specific internal energy	kJ/kg
v	velocity	m/s
V	volume	m³
w	specific work	kJ/kg
W	total work	kJ
$\dot{W}$	rate of work (power)	kW
z	elevation	m

Symbols

η	efficiency	–
υ	specific volume	m³/kg
ϕ	closed-system availability	kJ/kg
Ψ	open-system availability	kJ/kg

Subscripts

a	actual
b	brake
c	Carnot cycle, clearance, compression, or cylinders
d	displacement
f	fuel
H	high
HP	heat pump
L	low
ref	refrigerator
rev	reversible
s	stroke
t	total
T	turbine

1. BASIC CYCLES

It is convenient to show a source of energy as an infinite constant-temperature reservoir. Figure 15.1 illustrates a source of energy known as a *high-temperature reservoir* or *source* reservoir. By convention, the reservoir temperature is designated T_H (or T_{in}), and the heat transfer from it is Q_H (or Q_{in}). The energy derived from such a theoretical source might actually be supplied by combustion, electrical heating, or nuclear reaction.

Similarly, energy is released (i.e., is "rejected") to a low-temperature reservoir known as a *sink reservoir* or *energy sink*. The most common practical sink is the local environment. T_L and Q_L (or T_{out} and Q_{out}) are used to represent the reservoir temperature and energy absorbed. It is common to refer to Q_L as the "rejected energy" or "energy rejected to the environment."

Although heat can be extracted and work can be performed in a single process, a *cycle* is necessary to obtain work in a useful quantity and duration. A cycle is a series of processes that eventually brings the system back to its original condition. Most cycles are continuously repeated.

Figure 15.1 *Energy Flow in Basic Cycles*

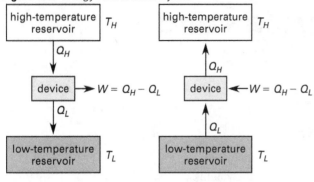

(a) power generation   (b) refrigeration

A cycle is completely defined by the working substance, the high- and low-temperature reservoirs, the means of doing work on the system, and the means of removing energy from the system. (The Carnot cycle depends only on the source and sink temperatures, not on the working fluid. However, most practical cycles depend on the working fluid.)

A cycle will appear as a closed curve when plotted on p-V and T-s diagrams. The area within the p-V and T-s curves represents both the net work and net heat.

2. POWER CYCLES

A *power cycle* is a cycle that takes heat and uses it to do work on the surroundings. The *heat engine* is the equipment needed to perform the cycle.

Equation 15.1: Thermal Efficiency

$$\eta = W/Q_H = (Q_H - Q_L)/Q_H \qquad \text{15.1}$$

Description

The *thermal efficiency* of a power cycle is defined as the ratio of useful work output to the supplied input energy. W in Eq. 15.1 is the net work, since some of the gross output work may be used to run certain parts of the cycle.[1] For example, a small amount of turbine output power may run boiler feed pumps.

Equation 15.1 shows that obtaining the maximum efficiency requires minimizing the Q_L term. Equation 15.1 also shows that $W_{\text{net}} = Q_{\text{net}}$. This follows directly from the first law of thermodynamics.

Example

350 MJ of heat are transferred into a system during each power cycle. The heat transferred out of the system is 297.5 MJ per cycle. Most nearly, what is the thermal efficiency of the cycle?

    (A)   1.0%

    (B)   5.0%

    (C)   7.5%

    (D)   15%

Solution

From Eq. 15.1, the thermal efficiency is

$$\eta = (Q_H - Q_L)/Q_H$$
$$= \frac{350 \text{ MJ} - 297.5 \text{ MJ}}{350 \text{ MJ}}$$
$$= 0.15 \quad (15\%)$$

The answer is (D).

Equation 15.2 and Eq. 15.3: Carnot Cycle

$$\eta_c = (T_H - T_L)/T_H \qquad \text{15.2}$$

$$\eta = 1 - \frac{T_L}{T_H} \qquad \text{15.3}$$

Description

The most efficient power cycle possible is the Carnot cycle. The thermal efficiency of the entire cycle is given by Eq. 15.2.[2] Temperature must be expressed in the absolute scale. Equation 15.2 is easily derived from Eq. 15.1 since $Q = T_{\text{reservoir}}\Delta S$. Figure 15.2 shows that the entropy change, ΔS, is the same for the two heat transfer processes.

The *Carnot cycle* is an ideal power cycle that is impractical to implement. However, its theoretical work output sets the maximum attainable from any heat engine, as evidenced by the isothermal (reversible) processes between states (4 and 1) and (2 and 3) and the adiabatic (reversible) processes between states (1 and 2) and (3 and 4) in Fig. 15.2. The working fluid in a Carnot cycle is irrelevant.

---

[1](1) The NCEES *FE Reference Handbook* (*NCEES Handbook*) presents the net work differently from the net heat. *Net heat* is the difference between the heat added in the boiler and the heat lost in the condenser. This is shown as $Q_H - Q_L$. In a steam power cycle, for example, the *net work* is the difference between the work done by the turbine and the work used by the feed pumps. Although the pump work is small, it is not zero, and the symmetry of Eq. 15.1 is lost by writing W instead of $W_H - W_L$ or similar. (2) From Eq. 15.1, it is obvious that $Q_H - Q_L = W_H - W_L$ and $Q_{\text{net}} = W_{\text{net}}$.

[2](1) Although "diesel cycle" is rarely capitalized in writing, "Carnot cycle" and "Otto cycle" usually are. The *NCEES Handbook* uses a subscripted lowercase c to designate "Carnot." (2) η in Eq. 15.3 is the same as η_c in Eq. 15.2, although these two equations are separated by several pages in the *NCEES Handbook*.

Figure 15.2 *Carnot Power Cycle*

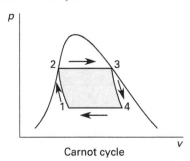

Carnot cycle

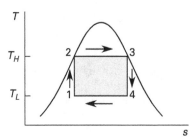

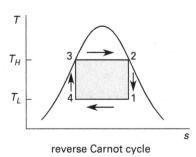

reverse Carnot cycle

Example

A Carnot engine operates on steam between 65°C and 425°C. What is most nearly the efficiency?

(A) 19%

(B) 48%

(C) 52%

(D) 81%

Solution

Although the denominator of Eq. 15.2 must be expressed as an absolute temperature, the numerator is a temperature difference. The offset temperatures (e.g., 273° for SI temperatures) cancel. The efficiency is

$$\eta_c = (T_H - T_L)/T_H$$
$$= \frac{425°C - 65°C}{425°C + 273°}$$
$$= 0.516 \quad (52\%)$$

The answer is (C).

Equation 15.4: Rankine Cycle

$$\eta = \frac{(h_3 - h_4) - (h_2 - h_1)}{h_3 - h_2} \qquad 15.4$$

Variation

$$\eta = \frac{W_{out} - W_{in}}{Q_{in}}$$
$$= \frac{Q_{in} - Q_{out}}{Q_{in}}$$
$$= \frac{(h_3 - h_2) - (h_4 - h_1)}{h_3 - h_2}$$

Description

The *Rankine cycle* is similar to the Carnot cycle except that the compression process occurs in the liquid region. (See Fig. 15.3.) The Rankine cycle is closely approximated in steam turbine plants. The thermal efficiency of the Rankine cycle is lower than that of a Carnot cycle operating between the same temperature limits because the mean temperature at which heat is added to the system is lower than T_H.

Figure 15.3 *Rankine Cycle*

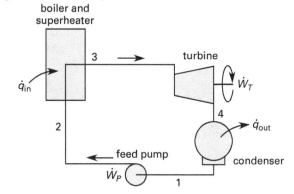

boiler and
superheater

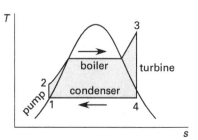

The thermal efficiency of the entire cycle is given by Eq. 15.4 and the variation equations. The enthalpy differences in the numerator of Eq. 15.4 represent work terms between the locations identified by the subscripts. Since $W_{net} = Q_{net}$, the equation could also be stated in

Thermodynamics

terms of heat transfers, as is done in the variation equation. The two formulations are rearrangements of the same terms.

Superheating occurs when heat in excess of that required to produce saturated vapor is added to the water. Superheat is used to raise the vapor above the critical temperature, to raise the mean effective temperature at which heat is added, and to keep the expansion primarily in the vapor region to reduce wear on the turbine blades.

Example

A Rankine steam cycle operates between the pressure limits of 600 kPa and 10 kPa. The turbine inlet temperature is 300°C. The liquid water leaving the condenser is saturated. (The enthalpies of the steam at the various points on the cycle are shown in the illustration.) Most nearly, what is the thermal efficiency of the cycle?

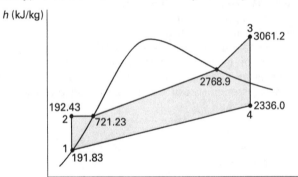

(A) 19%

(B) 25%

(C) 32%

(D) 48%

Solution

Using Eq. 15.4, the thermal efficiency of the Rankine cycle is

$$\eta = \frac{(h_3 - h_4) - (h_2 - h_1)}{h_3 - h_2}$$

$$= \frac{\left(3061.2\ \dfrac{kJ}{kg} - 2336.0\ \dfrac{kJ}{kg}\right) - \left(192.43\ \dfrac{kJ}{kg} - 191.83\ \dfrac{kJ}{kg}\right)}{3061.2\ \dfrac{kJ}{kg} - 192.43\ \dfrac{kJ}{kg}}$$

$$= 0.2526 \quad (25\%)$$

The answer is (B).

Equation 15.5 and Eq. 15.6: Otto Cycle

$$\eta = 1 - r^{1-k} \qquad \text{15.5}$$

$$r = v_1/v_2 \qquad \text{15.6}$$

Description

Combustion power cycles differ from vapor power cycles in that the combustion products cannot be returned to their initial conditions for reuse. Due to the computational difficulties of working with mixtures of fuel vapor and air, combustion power cycles are often analyzed as air-standard cycles.

An *air-standard cycle* is a hypothetical closed system using a fixed amount of ideal air as the working fluid. In contrast to a combustion process, the heat of combustion is included in the calculations without consideration of the heat source or delivery mechanism (i.e., the combustion process is replaced by a process of instantaneous heat transfer from high-temperature surroundings). Similarly, the cycle ends with an instantaneous transfer of waste heat to the surroundings. All processes are considered to be internally reversible. Because the air is assumed to be ideal, it has a constant specific heat.

Actual engine efficiencies for internal combustion engine cycles may be as much as 50% lower than the efficiencies calculated from air-standard analyses. Empirical corrections must be applied to theoretical calculations based on the characteristics of the engine. However, the large amount of excess air used in turbine combustion cycles results in better agreement (in comparison to reciprocating cycles) between actual and ideal performance.

The *air-standard Otto cycle* consists of the following processes and is illustrated in Fig. 15.4.

1 to 2:	isentropic compression ($q = 0$, $\Delta s = 0$)
2 to 3:	constant volume heat addition
3 to 4:	isentropic expansion ($q = 0$, $\Delta s = 0$)
4 to 1:	constant volume heat rejection

Figure 15.4 Air-Standard Otto Cycle

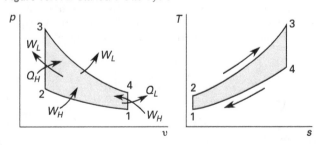

The Otto cycle is a four-stroke cycle because four separate piston movements (strokes) are required to accomplish all of the processes: the intake, compression, power, and exhaust strokes. Two complete crank revolutions are required for these four strokes. Therefore, each cylinder contributes one power stroke every other revolution.

The ideal thermal efficiency for the Otto cycle, Eq. 15.5, can be calculated from the *compression ratio, r*, Eq. 15.6.

Example

What is the ideal efficiency of an air-standard Otto cycle with a compression ratio of 6:1?

- (A) 17%
- (B) 19%
- (C) 49%
- (D) 51%

Solution

The ratio of specific heats for air is $k = 1.4$. From Eq. 15.5,

$$\eta = 1 - r^{1-k}$$
$$= 1 - (6)^{1-1.4}$$
$$= 0.512 \quad (51\%)$$

The answer is (D).

3. INTERNAL COMBUSTION ENGINES

The performance characteristics (e.g., horsepower) of internal combustion engines can be reported with or without the effect of power-reducing friction and other losses. A value of a property that includes the effect of friction is known as a *brake value*. If the effect of friction is removed, the property is known as an *indicated value*.[3]

Engine power can be measured by a *Prony brake* (also known as a *de Prony brake* and *absorption dynamometer*), which is basically a device that provides rotational resistance that the engine has to overcome. (See Fig. 15.5.) The engine's output shaft is connected to a rotating hub (wheel, disk, roller, etc.) in such a way that the engine (or, resisting) torque can be adjusted and measured. The resistance torque can be calculated as the product of the applied force and the moment arm, $T = FR$. The term "brake power" is derived from the

Prony brake apparatus, since the only power available to turn the rotating hub is what is left over after frictional and windage losses.

Figure 15.5 Brake Power

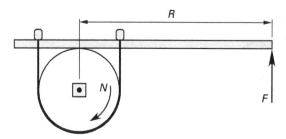

Equation 15.7 Through Eq. 15.13: Brake and Indicated Properties

$$\dot{W}_b = 2\pi TN = 2\pi FRN \qquad 15.7$$

$$\dot{W}_i = \dot{W}_b + \dot{W}_f \qquad 15.8$$

$$\text{mep} = \frac{\dot{W} n_s}{V_d n_c N} \qquad 15.9$$

$$V_d = \frac{\pi B^2 S}{4} \qquad 15.10$$

$$V_t = V_d + V_c \qquad 15.11$$

$$r_c = V_t / V_c \qquad 15.12$$

$$\text{sfc} = \frac{\dot{m}_f}{\dot{W}} = \frac{1}{\eta \text{HV}} \qquad 15.13$$

Description

Common brake properties are *brake power*, $\dot{W}_b$ (see Eq. 15.7 and Fig. 15.5); *fuel consumption rate*, $\dot{m}_f$; and *brake mean effective pressure*, mep (see Eq. 15.9). *Displacement volume*, V_d, is needed to calculate mep, and is found from Eq. 15.10. B is the diameter of the *cylinder bore*, and S is the length of the *stroke*. Total volume, V_t (see Eq. 15.11), is the sum of displacement volume and *clearance volume*, V_c. Dividing the total volume by the clearance volume yields the *compression ratio*, r_c (see Eq. 15.12).

Common indicated properties are *indicated power*, $\dot{W}_i$ (see Eq. 15.8); *indicated specific fuel consumption*, isfc; and *indicated mean effective pressure*, imep.

---

[3]It may be helpful to think of the *i* in "indicated" as meaning "ideal."

Specific fuel consumption, sfc (see Eq. 15.13), is the fuel usage rate divided by the power generated.

The brake and indicated powers differ by the *friction power*, $\dot{W}_f$.

Example

An electric motor is tested in a brake that uses a Kevlar belt to apply frictional resistance to a 22 cm radius hub. The tight side tension is measured by spring scale A as 30 N. The slack side tension is measured by spring scale B as 10 N. The motor turns at 1725 rpm.

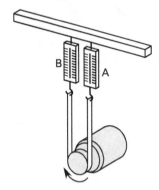

Most nearly, what is the motor horsepower?

(A) 0.17 hp

(B) 0.50 hp

(C) 0.80 hp

(D) 1.1 hp

Solution

The power is

$$\dot{W} = 2\pi TN = 2\pi FRN$$

$$= \frac{2\pi(30 \text{ N} - 10 \text{ N})(22 \text{ cm})\left(1725 \dfrac{\text{rev}}{\text{min}}\right)\left(1.341 \dfrac{\text{hp}}{\text{kW}}\right)}{\left(100 \dfrac{\text{cm}}{\text{m}}\right)\left(60 \dfrac{\text{s}}{\text{min}}\right)\left(1000 \dfrac{\text{W}}{\text{kW}}\right)}$$

$$= 1.07 \text{ hp} \quad (1.1 \text{ hp})$$

The answer is (D).

Equation 15.14 Through Eq. 15.17: Engine Efficiencies

$$\eta_b = \frac{\dot{W}_b}{\dot{m}_f(HV)} \qquad \text{15.14}$$

$$\eta_i = \frac{\dot{W}_i}{\dot{m}_f(HV)} \qquad \text{15.15}$$

$$\eta_i = \frac{\dot{W}_b}{\dot{W}_i} = \frac{\eta_b}{\eta_i} \qquad \text{15.16}$$

$$\eta_v = \frac{2\dot{m}_a}{\rho_a V_d n_c N} \quad \text{[four-stroke cycles only]} \qquad \text{15.17}$$

Description

The *brake thermal efficiency*, η_b (see Eq. 15.14), is found from the brake power, fuel consumption rate, and the *heating value* of the fuel, HV. The *indicated thermal efficiency* (see Eq. 15.15) is found from the indicated power, fuel consumption rate, and the heating value of the fuel. *Mechanical efficiency* (see Eq. 15.16) is the ratio of brake thermal efficiency to indicated thermal efficiency.

Because of friction in the intake system, the presence of expanding exhaust gases, valve timing, and air inertia, a reciprocating engine will not take in as much air as is calculated from the displacement. The *volumetric efficiency* (see Eq. 15.17) is the ratio of the actual amount of air taken in during each intake stroke to the *displacement volume*. This can be calculated from per-stroke characteristics or (as in the case of Eq. 15.17) from per unit time characteristics. In Eq. 15.17, $\dot{m}_a$ is the actual mass of air taken in per unit time for all cylinders; and, the denominator represents the theoretical mass of air based on the atmospheric density outside the engine and the displacement volume. n_c is the number of cylinders in the engine. In a four-stroke engine, where there is one intake stroke for every two revolutions, the rotational speed is divided by 2 to get the number of intake strokes per unit time. That is the source of the "2" in the numerator of Eq. 15.17.

4. REFRIGERATION CYCLES

In contrast to heat engines, in refrigeration cycles, heat is transferred from a low-temperature area to a high-temperature area. Since heat flows spontaneously only from high- to low-temperature areas, refrigeration needs an external energy source to force the heat transfer to occur. This energy source is a pump or compressor that does work in compressing the refrigerant. It is necessary to perform this work on the refrigerant in order to get it to discharge energy to the high-temperature area.

In a power (heat engine) cycle, heat from combustion is the input and work is the desired effect. Refrigeration cycles, though, are power cycles in reverse, and work is the input, with cooling the desired effect. (For every power cycle, there is a corresponding refrigeration cycle.) In a refrigerator, the heat is absorbed from a low-temperature area and is rejected to a high-temperature area. The pump work is also rejected to the high-temperature area.

General refrigeration devices consist of a coil (the evaporator) that absorbs heat, a condenser that rejects heat, a compressor, and a pressure-reduction device (the expansion valve or throttling valve).

In operation, liquid refrigerant passes through the evaporator where it picks up heat from the low-temperature area and vaporizes, becoming slightly superheated. The vaporized refrigerant is compressed by the compressor and in so doing, increases even more in temperature. The high-pressure, high-temperature refrigerant passes through the condenser coils, and because it is hotter than the high-temperature environment, it loses energy. Finally, the pressure is reduced in a throttling process in the expansion valve, where some of the liquid refrigerant also flashes into a vapor.

If the low-temperature area from which the heat is being removed is occupied space (i.e., air is being cooled), the device is known as an *air conditioner*. If the heat is being removed from water, the device is known as a *chiller*. An air conditioner produces cold air; a chiller produces cold water.

Rate of refrigeration (i.e., the rate at which heat is removed) is measured in *tons*. A ton of refrigeration corresponds to 200 Btu/min (12,000 Btu/hr) and 3516 W. The ton is derived from the heat flow required to melt a ton of ice in 24 hours.

Heat pumps also operate on refrigeration cycles. Like standard refrigerators, they transfer heat from low-temperature areas to high-temperature areas. The device shown in Fig. 15.1(b) could represent either a heat pump or a refrigerator. There is no significant difference in the mechanisms or construction of heat pumps and refrigerators; the only difference is the purpose of each.

The main function of a refrigerator is to cool the low-temperature area. The useful energy transfer of a refrigerator is the heat removed from the cold area. A heat pump's main function is to warm the high-temperature area. The useful energy transfer is the heat rejected to the high-temperature area.

Equation 15.18 and Eq. 15.19: Coefficient of Performance

$$\text{COP} = Q_H/W \quad \text{[heat pumps]} \qquad 15.18$$

$$\text{COP} = Q_L/W \quad \begin{bmatrix} \text{refrigerators and} \\ \text{air conditioners} \end{bmatrix} \qquad 15.19$$

Variation

$$\text{COP}_{\text{heat pump}} = \text{COP}_{\text{refrigerator}} + 1$$

Values

multiply	by	to obtain
tons of refrigeration	200	Btu/min
tons of refrigeration	12,000	Btu/hr
tons of refrigeration	3516	W

Description

The concept of thermal efficiency is not used with devices operating on refrigeration cycles. Rather, the *coefficient of performance* (COP) is defined as the ratio of useful energy transfer to the work input. The higher the coefficient of performance, the greater the effect for a given work input will be. Since the useful energy transfer is different for refrigerators and heat pumps, the coefficients of performance will also be different.

Example

A refrigeration cycle has a coefficient of performance of 2.2. The cycle exchanges heat between two infinite thermal reservoirs. For each 6 kW of cooling, what is most nearly the power input required?

(A) 1.4 kW

(B) 2.7 kW

(C) 5.5 kW

(D) 8.1 kW

Solution

From Eq. 15.19, the coefficient of performance of a refrigeration cycle is

$$
\begin{aligned}
\text{COP} &= Q_L/W \\
W &= \frac{Q_L}{\text{COP}} \\
&= \frac{6 \text{ kW}}{2.2} \\
&= 2.73 \text{ kW} \quad (2.7 \text{ kW})
\end{aligned}
$$

The answer is (B).

Equation 15.20 and Eq. 15.21: Carnot Refrigeration Cycle

$$\text{COP}_c = T_H/(T_H - T_L) \quad \text{[heat pumps]} \qquad 15.20$$

$$\text{COP}_c = T_L/(T_H - T_L) \quad \text{[refrigeration]} \qquad 15.21$$

Description

The *Carnot refrigeration cycle* is a Carnot power cycle running in reverse. Because it is reversible, the Carnot refrigeration cycle has the highest coefficient of performance for any given temperature limits of all the refrigeration cycles. As shown in Fig. 15.6, all processes occur within the vapor dome. The coefficients of performance for a Carnot refrigeration cycle, as given by Eq. 15.20 and Eq. 15.21, establish the upper limit of the COP.

As with Carnot power cycles, Eq. 15.20 and Eq. 15.21 are easily derived from Eq. 15.1 since $Q = T_{reservoir} \Delta S$ and ΔS are the same for the two heat transfer processes.

Figure 15.6 *Carnot Refrigeration Cycle*

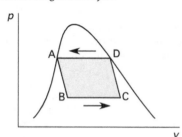

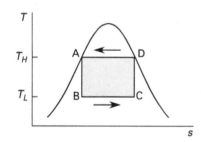

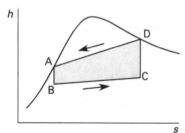

Example

A heat pump takes heat from groundwater at 7°C and maintains a room at 21°C. What is most nearly the maximum coefficient of performance possible for this heat pump?

(A) 1.4

(B) 2.8

(C) 5.6

(D) 21

Solution

The upper limit for the COP of a heat pump is set by the COP of a Carnot heat pump, as given by Eq. 15.20.

$$
\begin{aligned}
COP_c &= T_H/(T_H - T_L) \\
&= \frac{21°C + 273°}{(21°C + 273°) - (7°C + 273°)} \\
&= 21
\end{aligned}
$$

The answer is (D).

Equation 15.22 and Eq. 15.23: Vapor Refrigeration

$$
COP_{ref} = \frac{h_1 - h_4}{h_2 - h_1} \qquad \text{15.22}
$$

$$
COP_{HP} = \frac{h_2 - h_3}{h_2 - h_1} \qquad \text{15.23}
$$

Description

The components and processes of a *vapor refrigeration cycle*, also known as a *vapor compression cycle*, are shown in Fig. 15.7.[4] The coefficient of performance for the cycle used as refrigeration and as a heat pump are given by Eq. 15.22 and Eq. 15.23, respectively.[5]

Referring to Fig. 15.7, in the vapor compression cycle, cold liquid refrigerant in a saturated state passes through the *evaporator* and is vaporized while absorbing heat from the environment. In a refrigerator, this is referred to as the *cooling effect*, and it represents the useful energy transfer for a refrigerator. The vaporized refrigerant is then compressed, usually in a reciprocating compressor. This is the process in which work, w_c, is performed on the refrigerant.[6] The refrigerant is heated by the compression, and this heat is removed in a

---

[4]The *NCEES Handbook* refers to the vapor refrigeration cycle as a "reversed rankine" cycle. Although any power cycle can theoretically be reversed to create a refrigeration cycle, a reversed Rankine steam refrigeration cycle is not even a theoretical likelihood. The Rankine steam cycle and the vapor refrigeration cycle both involve vaporization and condensation of the working fluid. Beyond that, however, the working fluids, equipment, magnitudes of heat transfers, and physical sizes are very different.

[5](1) The *NCEES Handbook* is inconsistent in its capitalization of subscripts, which can lead to confusion. (2) A high-pressure (or topping) turbine is usually referred to as an *HP turbine*. Although clear from context, the subscripts "ref" and "HP" in Eq. 15.22 and Eq. 15.23, respectively, are abbreviations for "refrigerator" and "heat pump," not "reference" and "high pressure."

[6]The *NCEES Handbook* designates the compression power as $\dot{w}_c$. In this case, the subscript c refers to "compression," not to "Carnot" as it did in Eq. 15.20 and Eq. 15.21.

condenser. The heat removed comes from two sources: (1) the heat absorbed in the low-temperature region, and (2) the work of compression.

Figure 15.7 *Vapor Refrigeration Cycle*

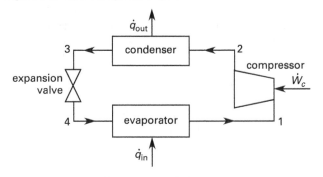

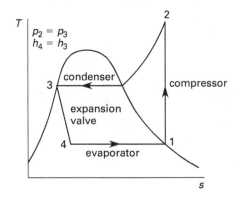

For a heat pump, the heat rejected is the useful energy transfer. This is referred to as the *heating effect*. Finally, the pressure of the cooled vapor is reduced by throttling through an *expansion valve* (*throttling valve*). In the throttling process, pressure decreases, but enthalpy remains constant. Of course, the entropy increases in the throttling process.

Equation 15.24 and Eq. 15.25: Two-Stage Refrigeration Cycle

$$\text{COP}_{\text{ref}} = \frac{\dot{Q}_{\text{in}}}{\dot{W}_{\text{in},1} + \dot{W}_{\text{in},2}} = \frac{h_5 - h_8}{h_2 - h_1 + h_6 - h_5} \qquad \text{15.24}$$

$$\text{COP}_{\text{HP}} = \frac{\dot{Q}_{\text{out}}}{\dot{W}_{\text{in},1} + \dot{W}_{\text{in},2}} = \frac{h_2 - h_3}{h_2 - h_1 + h_6 - h_5} \qquad \text{15.25}$$

Description

In a two-stage refrigeration cycle, the condenser heat from the low-temperature cycle evaporates a (usually different) refrigerant in the evaporator of the high-temperature cycle. Among other advantages, a two-cycle refrigerator can operate with a greater temperature difference between the hot and cold reservoirs.

A plot of a *two-stage refrigeration cycle* on a *T-s* diagram is shown in Fig. 15.8.[7] The coefficient of performance of a two-stage refrigeration cycle and the heat pump shown are given by Eq. 15.24 and Eq. 15.25, respectively.[8]

Figure 15.8 *Two-Stage Refrigeration Cycle*

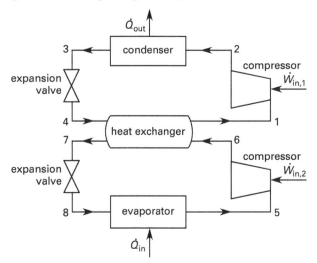

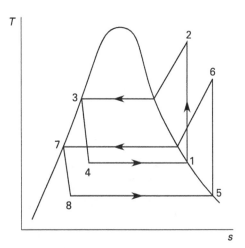

---

[7]The *NCEES Handbook* is not consistent in its representation of work and heat terms in power cycle and refrigeration cycle diagrams. For power cycles, the work and heat transfer terms are shown as lowercase w and q, while in refrigeration cycles, the same quantities are represented by W and Q. The same concepts are intended.

[8](1) The two forms of *NCEES Handbook* Eq. 15.24 and Eq. 15.25 are not entirely parallel. While the ratios yield the same numerical result, the numerators and denominators of each form do not refer to the same parameters. Since the numerator and denominator of the first term represent the total heat and work of a cycle, they are total properties with units of kJ (per second). The numerator and denominator of the second term represent the heat and work per unit mass of refrigerant. Based on the *NCEES Handbook*'s convention to use uppercase letters as variables for total properties and lowercase letters as variables for specific properties, it would be incorrect to assume that $\dot{Q}_{\text{in}} = h_5 - h_8$ as Eq. 15.24 suggests. (2) Furthermore, the first form of each equation is a ratio of energy per unit time, while the second form is a ratio of energy. Again, the ratios are numerically the same, but the numerators and denominators represent different parameters.

Thermodynamics

Equation 15.26 and Eq. 15.27: Air-Refrigeration Cycle

$$\text{COP}_{\text{ref}} = \frac{h_1 - h_4}{(h_2 - h_1) - (h_3 - h_4)} \qquad \textit{15.26}$$

$$\text{COP}_{\text{HP}} = \frac{h_2 - h_3}{(h_2 - h_1) - (h_3 - h_4)} \qquad \textit{15.27}$$

Description

An *air-refrigeration cycle* is essentially a *Brayton gas turbine cycle* operating in reverse.

An air-refrigeration cycle is shown in Fig. 15.9. The coefficient of performance of an air-refrigeration cycle and the heat pump shown are given by Eq. 15.26 and Eq. 15.27, respectively.

Figure 15.9 *Air-Refrigeration Cycle*

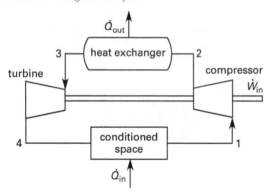

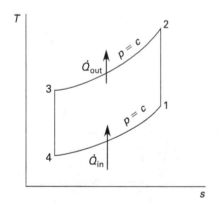

5. AVAILABILITY AND IRREVERSIBILITY

Consider some quantity of an "energized" substance. The potential for the substance to release its energy depends not only on the properties of the environment. For example, a hot billet of steel can give off its heat energy, but it can only cool to the temperature of the environment. Similarly, compressed air in a tire can only expand to the pressure of the atmosphere. A heated billet will release energy that is equal to its change in internal energy, and pressurized air will perform boundary work. If the processes that release energy are reversible (that is, are without friction and heat losses), all of the energy released will all be available for useful work. This will be the maximum possible usefulness for the substance in the local environment.

Exergy is the term that describes energy release all the way down to the local environmental conditions. "Exergy" is synonymous with "availability." An equation used to calculate exergy is known as an *availability function.*

Equation 15.28 and Eq. 15.29: Closed-System Exergy (Availability) Function

$$\phi = (u - u_L) - T_L(s - s_L) + p_L(v - v_L) \qquad \textit{15.28}$$

$$w_{\text{max}} = w_{\text{rev}} = \phi_1 - \phi_2 \qquad \textit{15.29}$$

Description

The maximum possible work that can be obtained from a substance is known as the *availability*, ϕ. Availability is independent of the device but is dependent on the temperature of the local environment. Both the first and second law of thermodynamics must be applied to determine availability.

The availability function of a closed system per unit mass is defined by Eq. 15.28.[9] The subscript L refers to the temperature (and pressure) of the low-temperature reservoir (i.e., often, but not necessarily, the local environment), which define the limits of cooling and expansion.[10] Eq. 15.29 calculates the maximum useful work from the starting and ending availability functions when the starting and ending conditions are not the local environment. For a process that reduces properties to the local environment (i.e., the final state is condition L), the reversible (i.e., maximum) work is simply the availability calculated in Eq. 15.28, and Eq. 15.29 is not needed.

---

[9]The *NCEES Handbook* sometimes uses extraneous parentheses in its equations. As presented in the *NCEES Handbook*, there is no significance to the parentheses around the first two terms of Eq. 15.28, nor around the first two terms of Eq. 15.30.

[10]The *NCEES Handbook* says that the subscript L "designates environmental conditions...," which is misleading. The properties of the substance, not the environment, are to be used. In Eq. 15.28, u_L represents the internal energy of the substance at the temperature of the low temperature reservoir. It does not mean the internal energy of the low temperature reservoir substance. For steam exhausting to atmospheric pressure, u_L would not represent the internal energy of the atmosphere.

The availability of a closed system is the same as the change in Helmholtz function, without the effect of boundary work.

Equation 15.30 and Eq. 15.31: Open-System Exergy (Availability) Function

$$\Psi = (h - h_L) - T_L(s - s_L) + v^2/2 + gz \qquad 15.30$$

$$w_{\max} = w_{rev} = \Psi_1 - \Psi_2 \qquad 15.31$$

Description

For an open system, the steady-state availability function, Ψ, is given by Eq. 15.30. Equation 15.30 incorporates terms for kinetic and potential energy which cannot be extracted in a closed system. Equation 15.30 also combines the internal energy and flow work into an enthalpy term, since $h = u + pv$. The subscript L refers to the temperature (and pressure) of the low-temperature reservoir (i.e., often the local environment), which define the limits of cooling and expansion. Equation 15.31 calculates the maximum useful work from the starting and ending availability functions when the starting and ending conditions are not the local environment. For a device (e.g., a turbine) that is discharging directly to the local environment (i.e., the final state is condition L), the reversible (i.e., maximum) work is simply the availability calculated in Eq. 15.30, and Eq. 15.31 is not needed. The availability of a closed system is the same as the change in Helmholtz function, without the effect of boundary work.

The availability of an open system is the same as the change in Gibbs function, without the effects of kinetic and potential energies.

Equation 15.32: Irreversibility

$$I = w_{rev} - w_{actual} = T_L \Delta s_{total} \qquad 15.32$$

Description

To achieve the maximum work output, both the process within the control volume and the energy transfers between the system and environment must be reversible. The difference between the maximum and the actual work output is known as the *process irreversibility*, I. Δs_{total} in Eq. 15.32 represents the net entropy production, considering both the substance and the environment. For example, if heat energy were lost from a high-temperature substance, the entropy of that substance would decrease, but the entropy of the environment would increase by an even greater amount. The total would be a net increase in total entropy.

16 Mixtures of Gases, Vapors, and Liquids

Nomenclature

a	Helmholtz function	kJ/kg
$\hat{a}$	activity	–
A	molar Helmholtz function	kJ/kmol
c	specific heat	kJ/kg·K
C	number of components	–
C	molar heat	kJ/kg·kmol
f^L	fugacity of pure liquid	–
$\hat{f}^L$	fugacity in liquid phase	–
f^V	fugacity of pure vapor	–
$\hat{f}^V$	fugacity in vapor phase	–
F	degrees of freedom	–
g	Gibbs function	kJ/kg
G	molar Gibbs function	kJ/kmol
h	specific enthalpy	kJ/kg
h	Henry's law constant	atm
H	molar enthalpy	kJ/kmol
k	constant	–
K	chemical equilibrium constant	–
m	mass	kg
M	molecular weight	kg/kmol
N	number of moles	–
p	absolute pressure	Pa
P	number of phases	–
R	specific gas constant	kJ/kg·K
$\overline{R}$	universal gas constant, 8314	J/kmol·K
s	specific entropy	kJ/kg·K
S	molar entropy	kJ/kmol·K
T	absolute temperature	K
u	specific internal energy	kJ/kg
U	molar internal energy	kJ/kmol
v	stoichiometric coefficient	kmol
V	volume	m³
x	mole fraction	–
x	volumetric fraction	–
y	mass fraction	–

Symbols

γ	activity coefficient	–
ξ	extent	mol
υ	specific volume	m³/kg
ϕ	relative humidity	%
Φ	fugacity coefficient	–
ω	humidity ratio	–

Subscripts

a	dry air
db	dry bulb
dp	dew point
fg	liquid-to-gas (vaporization)
g	saturation
i	component i
p	constant pressure
sat	saturation
v	constant volume
v	water vapor
wb	wet bulb
*	pure component

1. IDEAL GAS MIXTURES

Equation 16.1 Through Eq. 16.3: Mass Fraction

$$y_i = m_i/m \qquad 16.1$$

$$m = \sum m_i \qquad 16.2$$

$$\sum y_i = 1 \qquad 16.3$$

Description

An ideal gas mixture consists of a mixture of ideal gases, each behaving as if it alone occupied the space.

The *mass fraction*, y_i (also known as the *gravimetric fraction* and *weight fraction*), of a component i in a mixture of components $i = 1, 2, ..., n$ is the ratio of the component's mass to the total mixture mass.[1]

Example

A 2 L container holds a mixture of three inert gases. The pressure inside the container is measured at 1.5 atm at a temperature of 293K (room temperature). Two of the three inert gases are known. The first gas, krypton, has a mass fraction of 0.352. The second gas, argon, has a mass fraction of 0.2799. The combined mass of argon and krypton in the container is 5.630 g. What is most nearly the mass of the third gas?

(A) 2.5 g

(B) 3.1 g

(C) 3.3 g

(D) 5.6 g

Solution

The mass fractions of the three gases are related by $\sum y_i = 1$. This can be used to find the mass fraction of the third gas.

$$y_{Ar} + y_{Kr} + y_3 = 1$$
$$0.2799 + 0.352 + y_3 = 1$$
$$y_3 = 0.3681$$

The total mass can be found from the definition of mass fraction ($y_i = m_i/m$) and the combined masses of argon and krypton.

$$\frac{m_{Ar}}{m} + \frac{m_{Kr}}{m} = y_{Ar} + y_{Kr}$$

$$m = \frac{m_{Ar} + m_{Kr}}{y_{Ar} + y_{Kr}}$$

$$= \frac{5.630 \text{ g}}{0.2799 + 0.352}$$

$$= 8.910 \text{ g}$$

The mass of the third gas is

$$m_3 = y_3 m$$
$$= (0.3681)(8.910 \text{ g})$$
$$= 3.280 \text{ g} \quad (3.3 \text{ g})$$

The answer is (C).

Equation 16.4 Through Eq. 16.6: Mole Fractions

$$x_i = N_i / N \qquad 16.4$$

$$N = \sum N_i \qquad 16.5$$

$$\sum x_i = 1 \qquad 16.6$$

Description

The *mole fraction*, x_i, of a liquid component i is the ratio of the number of moles of substance i to the total number of moles of all substances in the mixture.

Since equal numbers of moles of any ideal gas occupy the same volume (i.e., approximately 22.4 L/mol at standard conditions), the mole fraction of a gas in a mixture of ideal gases is equal to its volumetric fraction. For chemical reactions that involve all gaseous components, the coefficients of the molecular species represent the number of molecules taking place in the reaction. Since each coefficient is some definite proportion of Avogadro's number, the coefficients also represent the numbers of moles (and, accordingly), the number of volumes of that gas taking part in the reaction.

Example

A 10 mole mixture of three gases is stored in a container. There are 2 moles of helium and 3 moles of nitrogen in the mixture. What is most nearly the mole fraction of the third gas in the mixture?

(A) 0.20

(B) 0.30

(C) 0.50

(D) 0.75

---

[1]In its thermodynamics section, the NCEES *FE Reference Handbook* (*NCEES Handbook*) uses the variable y to mean both mass fraction and mole fraction. It is common in engineering practice to designate mass fraction as w, g, G, M, and sometimes even x. In chemical engineering unit operations (mass transfer), it is common to use x and y both as mole fractions. In fact, the *NCEES Handbook* does this in its coverage of the thermodynamics of vapor-liquid equilibrium. Since the *NCEES Handbook* uses the same variable for two similar fractions, care must be observed when using equations (e.g., Henry's law) that use mass, volume, and mole fractions.

Solution

Use Eq. 16.5 to find the number of moles of the unknown gas in the mixture.

$$N_{\text{mixture}} = \sum N_i$$
$$= N_{\text{He}} + N_{\text{N}_2} + N_i$$
$$N_i = N_{\text{mixture}} - N_{\text{He}} - N_{\text{N}_2}$$
$$= 10 \text{ mol} - 2 \text{ mol} - 3 \text{ mol}$$
$$= 5 \text{ mol}$$

Use Eq. 16.4 to solve for the mole fraction of the unknown gas in the mixture.

$$x_i = \frac{N_i}{N_{\text{mixture}}}$$
$$= \frac{5 \text{ mol}}{10 \text{ mol}}$$
$$= 0.50$$

The answer is (C).

Equation 16.7 Through Eq. 16.9: Converting Between Mass and Mole Fractions

$$y_i = \frac{x_i M_i}{\sum x_i M_i} \qquad \text{16.7}$$

$$x_i = \frac{y_i / M_i}{\sum (y_i / M_i)} \qquad \text{16.8}$$

$$M = m/N = \sum x_i M_i \qquad \text{16.9}$$

Description

It is possible to convert from mole fraction to mass fraction (see Eq. 16.7) through the molecular weight of the component, M_i (see Eq. 16.9). Similarly, it is possible to convert from mass fraction to mole fraction (see Eq. 16.8).

Example

A gas mixture consisting of 4 moles of N_2, 2.5 moles of CO_2, and an unknown amount of CO is held at two times atmospheric pressure in a container with a volume of 0.13 m³. The total number of moles in the mixture is

8.5. The temperature of the mixture is 100°C. What is most nearly the mass fraction of CO in the mixture?

(A) 0.10

(B) 0.20

(C) 0.48

(D) 0.53

Solution

Rearrange the equation for total moles in a mixture to find the number of moles of CO in the mixture.

$$N = \sum N_i = N_{\text{N}_2} + N_{\text{CO}_2} + N_{\text{CO}}$$
$$N_{\text{CO}} = N - N_{\text{N}_2} - N_{\text{CO}_2}$$
$$= 8.5 \text{ mol} - 4 \text{ mol} - 2.5 \text{ mol}$$
$$= 2 \text{ mol}$$

Find the mole fraction of each compound in the mixture.

$$x_i = N_i / N$$
$$x_{\text{N}_2} = \frac{4 \text{ mol}}{8.5 \text{ mol}}$$
$$= 0.471$$
$$x_{\text{CO}_2} = \frac{2.5 \text{ mol}}{8.5 \text{ mol}}$$
$$= 0.294$$
$$x_{\text{CO}} = \frac{2 \text{ mol}}{8.5 \text{ mol}}$$
$$= 0.235$$

Use Eq. 16.7 to find the mass fraction of CO in the mixture.

$$y_i = \frac{x_i M_i}{\sum x_i M_i}$$

$$y_{\text{CO}} = \frac{x_{\text{CO}} M_{\text{CO}}}{x_{\text{N}_2} M_{\text{N}_2} + x_{\text{CO}_2} M_{\text{CO}_2} + x_{\text{CO}} M_{\text{CO}}}$$

$$= \frac{(0.235)\left(28 \frac{\text{g}}{\text{mol}}\right)}{(0.471)\left(28 \frac{\text{g}}{\text{mol}}\right) + (0.294)\left(44 \frac{\text{g}}{\text{mol}}\right) + (0.235)\left(28 \frac{\text{g}}{\text{mol}}\right)}$$

$$= 0.201 \quad (0.20)$$

The answer is (B).

Equation 16.10 and Eq. 16.11: Partial Pressure and Dalton's Law

$$p_i = \frac{m_i R_i T}{V} \qquad \text{16.10}$$

$$p = \sum p_i \qquad \text{16.11}$$

Description

The *partial pressure*, p_i, of gas component i in a mixture of nonreacting gases $i = 1, 2, ..., n$ is the pressure gas i alone would exert in the total volume at the temperature of the mixture (see Eq. 16.10).

According to *Dalton's law of partial pressures*, the total pressure of a gas mixture is the sum of the partial pressures (see Eq. 16.11).

Example

Three identical rigid containers each store a separate element. The first container holds helium at 90 kPa, the second container holds neon at 120 kPa, and the third container holds xenon at 150 kPa. The contents of the neon and xenon containers are then pumped into the helium container. After the temperature has stabilized, what is most nearly the pressure of the mixture inside the helium container?

(A) 90 kPa

(B) 120 kPa

(C) 150 kPa

(D) 360 kPa

Solution

The partial pressure is the pressure a gas would have if it occupied the container by itself. Using Dalton's law of partial pressures, Eq. 16.11, solve for the total pressure of the mixture inside the container.

$$\begin{aligned} p &= \sum p_i \\ &= p_{He} + p_{Ne} + p_{Xe} \\ &= 90 \text{ kPa} + 120 \text{ kPa} + 150 \text{ kPa} \\ &= 360 \text{ kPa} \end{aligned}$$

The answer is (D).

Equation 16.12 Through Eq. 16.14: Partial Volume and Amagat's Law

$$V_i = \frac{m_i R_i T}{p} \qquad \text{16.12}$$

$$V = \sum V_i \qquad \text{16.13}$$

$$x_i = p_i/p = V_i/V \qquad \text{16.14}$$

Description

The *partial volume*, V_i, of gas i in a mixture of nonreacting gases is the volume that gas i alone would occupy at the temperature and pressure of the mixture (see Eq. 16.12).

Amagat's law (also known as *Amagat-Leduc's rule*) states that the total volume of a mixture of nonreacting gases is equal to the sum of the partial volumes (see Eq. 16.13).

For mixtures of nonreacting ideal gases, the mole fraction, x_i, partial pressure ratio, and volumetric fraction are the same (see Eq. 16.14).

Example

1 g of oxygen and 2 g of helium are mixed in a gas sampling bag. The gases are at 50°C and atmospheric pressure. What is most nearly the volume of the bag?

(A) 0.002 m³

(B) 0.007 m³

(C) 0.012 m³

(D) 0.014 m³

Solution

Find the partial volume of each component.

$$\begin{aligned} \overline{R} &= \frac{8314 \, \frac{\text{J}}{\text{kmol·K}}}{1000 \, \frac{\text{J}}{\text{kJ}}} \\ &= 8.314 \, \frac{\text{kJ}}{\text{kmol·K}} \end{aligned}$$

$$\begin{aligned} V_i &= \frac{m_i R_i T}{p} \\ &= \frac{m_i \overline{R} T}{p M_i} \end{aligned}$$

$$\begin{aligned} V_{O_2} &= \frac{(1 \text{ g})\left(8.314 \, \frac{\text{kJ}}{\text{kmol·K}}\right)(50°\text{C} + 273°)}{(101.3 \text{ kPa})\left(32 \, \frac{\text{kg}}{\text{kmol}}\right)\left(1000 \, \frac{\text{g}}{\text{kg}}\right)} \\ &= 8.28 \times 10^{-4} \text{ m}^3 \end{aligned}$$

$$\begin{aligned} V_{He} &= \frac{(2 \text{ g})\left(8.314 \, \frac{\text{kJ}}{\text{kmol·K}}\right)(50°\text{C} + 273°)}{(101.3 \text{ kPa})\left(4.00 \, \frac{\text{kg}}{\text{kmol}}\right)\left(1000 \, \frac{\text{g}}{\text{kg}}\right)} \\ &= 1.33 \times 10^{-2} \text{ m}^3 \end{aligned}$$

Use Amagat's law to calculate the total volume of the bag.

$$V = \sum V_i$$
$$= V_{O_2} + V_{He}$$
$$= 8.28 \times 10^{-4}~\text{m}^3 + 1.33 \times 10^{-2}~\text{m}^3$$
$$= 0.0141~\text{m}^3 \quad (0.014~\text{m}^3)$$

The answer is (D).

Equation 16.15 Through Eq. 16.17: Gibbs' Theorem

$$u = \sum y_i u_i \qquad \textbf{16.15}$$

$$h = \sum y_i h_i \qquad \textbf{16.16}$$

$$s = \sum y_i s_i \qquad \textbf{16.17}$$

Description

Equation 16.15 through Eq. 16.17 are mathematical formulations of *Gibbs' theorem* (also known as *Gibbs' rule*). This theorem states that the total property (e.g., u, h, or s) of a mixture of ideal gases is the sum of the properties that the individual gases would have if each occupied the total mixture volume alone at the same temperature. Equation 16.17 is stated as an equality, and this requires the mixing of components to be isentropic (i.e., adiabatic and reversible). Each component's entropy must be evaluated at the temperature of the mixture and its partial pressure.[2]

While the *specific* mixture properties (i.e., u, h, s, c_p, c_v, and R) are all gravimetrically weighted, the *molar* properties are not. Molar U, H, S, C_p, and C_v, as well as the molecular weight and mixture density, are all volumetrically weighted.

Example

A mixture contains 50 g of nitrogen and 25 g of carbon dioxide. The gases are stored in a container at 500K. At this temperature, the molar enthalpy of the nitrogen is 5912 J/mol, and the molar enthalpy of the carbon dioxide is 8314 J/mol. What is most nearly the total enthalpy of the mixture?

(A) 5.7 kJ

(B) 8.3 kJ

(C) 11 kJ

(D) 15 kJ

Solution

Although Eq. 16.16 could be used, it would be necessary to calculate the specific enthalpies ($h = H/M$). It is easier to recognize that molar properties of mixtures are volumetrically weighted, and that volumetric fractions of ideal gases are the same as mole fractions. The numbers of moles are

$$N_i = \frac{m_i}{M_i}$$

$$N_{N_2} = \frac{50~\text{g}}{28~\dfrac{\text{g}}{\text{mol}}}$$
$$= 1.79~\text{mol}$$

$$N_{CO_2} = \frac{25~\text{g}}{44~\dfrac{\text{g}}{\text{mol}}}$$
$$= 0.57~\text{mol}$$

The mole (volumetric) fractions are

$$x_{N_2} = \frac{N_{N_2}}{N_{N_2} + N_{CO_2}}$$
$$= \frac{1.79~\text{mol}}{1.79~\text{mol} + 0.57~\text{mol}}$$
$$= 0.759$$
$$x_{CO_2} = 1 - x_{N_2}$$
$$= 1 - 0.759$$
$$= 0.241$$

The molar enthalpy of the mixture is weighted by the mole (volumetric) fractions.

$$H = \sum x_i H_i$$
$$= (0.759)\left(5912~\frac{\text{J}}{\text{mol}}\right) + (0.241)\left(8314~\frac{\text{J}}{\text{mol}}\right)$$
$$= 6492~\text{J/mol}$$

---

[2]The *NCEES Handbook* states that u_i and h_i are evaluated "…at T," referring to the temperature of the mixture, while s_i is evaluated "…at T and p_i." Internal energy is indeed a function of only temperature. However, enthalpy depends on the pressure, also, since $h = u + pv$. For a fixed mass of gas occupying a fixed volume, specifying the temperature is sufficient to establish the pressure. So, although the value of pressure is needed to determine enthalpy, it is necessary only to specify temperature if the volume is known. Pressure can be calculated from the equation of state.

The total enthalpy of the mixture is

$$H_{\text{total}} = NH$$

$$= \frac{(1.79 \text{ mol} + 0.57 \text{ mol})\left(6492 \dfrac{\text{J}}{\text{mol}}\right)}{1000 \dfrac{\text{J}}{\text{kJ}}}$$

$$= 15.3 \text{ kJ} \quad (15 \text{ kJ})$$

The answer is (D).

2. VAPOR-LIQUID MIXTURES[3]

Equation 16.18: Henry's Law at Constant Temperature

$$p_i = py_i = hx_i \qquad \text{16.18}$$

Description

Henry's law states that the partial pressure of a slightly soluble gas above a liquid is proportional to the amount (i.e., mole fraction, x_i) of the gas dissolved in the liquid. This law applies separately to each gas to which the liquid is exposed, as if each gas were present alone. The algebraic form of Henry's law is given by Eq. 16.18, in which h is the *Henry's law constant* with units of pressure.[4]

It is important to recognize that, in Eq. 16.18, x_i is the mole fraction of the gas (solute) in the liquid (solvent), while y_i is the mole fraction of the gas (solute) in the gas mixture above the liquid.

Equation 16.19: Raoult's Law for Vapor-Liquid Equilibrium

$$p_i = x_i p_i^* \qquad \text{16.19}$$

Description

Vapor pressure is the pressure exerted by the solvent's vapor molecules when they are in equilibrium with the liquid. The symbol for the vapor pressure of a pure vapor over a pure solvent at a particular temperature is p_i^*. Vapor pressure increases with increasing temperature.

Raoult's law, given by Eq. 16.19, states that the vapor pressure, p_i, of a solvent is proportional to the mole fraction of that substance in the solution.

According to Raoult's law, the partial pressure of a solution component will increase with increasing temperature (as p_i^* increases) and with increasing mole fraction of that component in the solution. Raoult's law applies to each of the substances in the solution. By *Dalton's law* (see Eq. 16.11) the total vapor pressure above the liquid is equal to the sum of the vapor pressures of each component.

Example

A nonvolatile, nonelectrolytic liquid is combined with a solid to form a solution that just boils at 1 atm pressure. The vapor pressure of the pure liquid is 850 torr. Most nearly, what is the molar percentage of the liquid in the solution?

(A) 64%

(B) 79%

(C) 86%

(D) 89%

Solution

A liquid boils when its vapor pressure equals the pressure of its surroundings. The vapor pressure of the solution is 1 atm or 760 torr. From Raoult's law,

$$p_i = x_i p_i^*$$

$$x_{\text{solvent}} = \frac{p_{\text{solution}}}{p_{\text{pure solvent}}} = \frac{760 \text{ torr}}{850 \text{ torr}} = 0.894 \quad (89\%)$$

The answer is (D).

Equation 16.20 Through Eq. 16.23: Vapor-Liquid Equilibrium

$$\widehat{f}_i^V = \widehat{f}_i^L \qquad \text{16.20}$$

$$\widehat{f}_i^L = x_i \gamma_i f_i^L \qquad \text{16.21}$$

$$\widehat{f}_i^L = x_i k_i \qquad \text{16.22}$$

---

[3]In comparison to the thousands of important and practical thermodynamics facts, principles, laws, and applications, fugacity and the related concept of activity are too esoteric, and the nomenclature sufficiently obtuse, to warrant much attention.

[4](1) *Henry's law* has four different practical formulations, with four different definitions (and values) of Henry's law constant. All of these formulations are in engineering use. It is important to use the Henry's law constant that has units matching the form of the law. (2) The *NCEES Handbook* presents Eq. 16.18 as Henry's law. In fact, only the $p_i = hx_i$ part is Henry's law. The $p_i = y_i p_{\text{total}}$ part is not Henry's law, although it is easily derived from the ideal gas laws. If it is associated with anything, $p_i = y_i p_{\text{total}}$ is usually presented in conjunction with *Dalton's law of partial pressures* ($p_{\text{total}} = \sum p_i = \sum x_i p_{\text{total}}$, where x is traditionally used to designate the mole fraction).

$$\widehat{f}_i^{\,V} = y_i \widehat{\Phi}_i p \qquad 16.23$$

Description

Fugacity, sometimes called *actual fugacity*, is an effective pressure which replaces the actual pressure of a real gas in precise chemical equilibrium computations.[5] If real substances (primarily gases) behaved ideally, fugacity would not be required. But, just as the ideal equation of state is replaced with corrected equations for pressure-volume-temperature problems, fugacity replaces actual pressure in vapor-liquid equilibrium calculations. Fugacity can also be used to derive the real gas compressibility factor, although that is not its primary function.

Fugacity, f, is calculated from the actual pressure and the *fugacity coefficient*, Φ. A "hat" (e.g., $\widehat{f}$) is used when the component is in a mixture, while the "unhatted" character designates a pure substance.

$$f = \Phi p_{\text{actual}}$$

For any actual pressure, the corresponding fugacity will produce calculated results that match observed results. The specific parameter that fugacity is designed to match (preserve, ensure, obtain, produce, etc.) is the *chemical potential*, μ. Chemical potential is an abstract concept based on Gibbs free energy, another abstract concept. Using the superscript "0" to indicate the standard reference condition of 25°C and either 1 atm (101.325 kPa), 1 bar (100 kPa), or 760 torr, a practical formula that is used to represent chemical potential is

$$\mu = \mu^0 + RT \ln \frac{p}{p^0}$$

Fugacity values, f, of pure substances are experimentally derived such that the parallel formula results in the same chemical potential.

$$\mu^0 + RT \ln \frac{f}{f^0} = \mu^0 + RT \ln \frac{p}{p^0}$$

A multicomponent vapor-liquid system is in equilibrium if the fugacities of each component's liquid and vapor phase are equal (see Eq. 16.20). The fugacity of liquid and vapor components can usually be calculated using Eq. 16.21 and Eq. 16.23, respectively. f represents the fugacity of a pure substance, while $\widehat{f}$ represents the fugacity of the substance in a mixture. $\widehat{f}^{\,L}$ represents the fugacity of the substance in a mixture in the liquid phase, and $\widehat{f}^{\,V}$ represents the fugacity of the substance in a vapor phase.

For slightly soluble gases, the fugacity of the liquid phase of a component can be calculated using Eq. 16.22. The *activity coefficient* of component i, γ_i, in a multicomponent system is a correction factor for non-ideal behavior of a component in the liquid phase.

Equation 16.24 and Eq. 16.25: Activity Coefficients of a Two-Component System

$$\ln \gamma_1 = A_{12}\left(1 + \frac{A_{12}x_1}{A_{21}x_2}\right)^{-2} \qquad 16.24$$

$$\ln \gamma_2 = A_{21}\left(1 + \frac{A_{21}x_2}{A_{12}x_1}\right)^{-2} \qquad 16.25$$

Description

Equation 16.24 and Eq. 16.25 are derived from the *van Laar model* and can be used to calculate the *activity coefficients* for a two-component system.[6] The constants A_{12} and A_{21} are determined empirically in practice.

Equation 16.26 and Eq. 16.27: Fugacity of a Pure Liquid

$$f_i^L = \Phi_i^{\text{sat}} p_i^{\text{sat}} \exp\{v_i^L(p - p_i^{\text{sat}})/(RT)\} \qquad 16.26$$

$$f_i^L \cong p_i^{\text{sat}} \qquad 16.27$$

Description

The fugacity of a pure liquid component, f_i^L, is given by Eq. 16.26.[7] Similar to the activity coefficient, the *fugacity coefficient* of component i, Φ_i, is an empirically determined value used to correct non-ideal behavior of the vapor-phase component. If pressures are near atmospheric, then the fugacity of a pure liquid component can often be approximated by Eq. 16.27.

---

[5]For all of its complexity and elegance, fugacity is just the pressure you have to use in certain kinds of problems in order to get the correct answer. It is an ideal (partial) pressure that has been corrected for real partial pressure behavior. The corrections are empirical, based on experimentation. For that reason, fugacity (like an equation of state for a real gas) is basically a fancy correlation, not a basic engineering principle.

[6]The van Laar model is one of many correlations that are used for fitting observed data into activity coefficients. As with all correlations, the form of the equation has been selected to provide the best data fit. As such, Eq. 16.24 and Eq. 16.25 are useful, but they are correlations, not engineering fundamentals.

[7]The saturation pressure that is represented by p^{sat} in Eq. 16.26 is the same as p_{sat} throughout the rest of the *NCEES Handbook*.

3. PSYCHROMETRICS

The study of the properties and behavior of atmospheric air is known as *psychrometrics*. Properties of air are seldom evaluated from theoretical thermodynamic principles, however. Specialized techniques and charts have been developed for that purpose.

Equation 16.28: Total Atmospheric Pressure

$$p = p_a + p_v \qquad 16.28$$

Description

Air in the atmosphere contains small amounts of moisture and can be considered to be a mixture of two ideal gases—dry air and water vapor. All of the thermodynamic rules relating to the behavior of nonreacting gas mixtures apply to atmospheric air. From Dalton's law, for example, the total atmospheric pressure is the sum of the dry air partial pressure and the water vapor pressure. (See Eq. 16.28.)

Example

An air-water vapor mixture is stored in a fixed-volume container at a temperature of 45°C. The total atmospheric pressure of the mixture is 1.13 atm, and the relative humidity of the mixture is 0.22. The partial pressure of the water vapor is 2.110 kPa. What is most nearly the partial pressure of the dry air in the mixture?

(A) 103 kPa

(B) 105 kPa

(C) 108 kPa

(D) 110 kPa

Solution

Rearrange Eq. 16.28 for total atmospheric pressure to find the partial pressure of the dry air.

$$p = p_a + p_v$$
$$p_a = p - p_v$$
$$= (1.13 \text{ atm})\left(101.325 \ \frac{\text{kPa}}{\text{atm}}\right) - 2.110 \text{ kPa}$$
$$= 112.4 \text{ kPa} \quad (110 \text{ kPa})$$

The answer is (D).

Equation 16.29: Dew-Point Temperature

$$T_{dp} = T_{sat} \quad [p_g = p_v] \qquad 16.29$$

Description

Psychrometrics uses three different definitions of temperature. These three terms are *not* interchangeable.

- *dry-bulb temperature*, T_{db}: This is the temperature that a regular thermometer measures if exposed to air.

- *wet-bulb temperature*, T_{wb}: This is the temperature of air that has gone through an adiabatic saturation process. It is measured with a thermometer that is covered with a water-saturated cotton wick.

- *dew-point temperature*, T_{dp}: This is the dry-bulb temperature at which water starts to condense when moist air is cooled in a constant pressure process. The dew-point temperature is equal to the saturation temperature (read from steam tables) for the partial pressure of the vapor.

For every temperature, there is a unique equilibrium vapor pressure of water, p_g, called the *saturation pressure*. If the vapor pressure equals the saturation pressure, the air is said to be saturated. *Saturated air* is a mixture of dry air and water vapor at the saturation pressure. When the air is saturated, all three temperatures are equal.

Unsaturated air is a mixture of dry air and superheated water vapor. When the air is unsaturated, the dew-point temperature will be less than the wet-bulb temperature.

$$T_{dp} < T_{wb} < T_{db} \quad [\text{unsaturated}]$$

Equation 16.30 and Eq. 16.31: Specific Humidity (Humidity Ratio, Absolute Humidity)

$$\omega = m_v / m_a \qquad 16.30$$

$$\omega = 0.622 p_v / p_a = 0.622 p_v / (p - p_v) \qquad 16.31$$

Description

The amount of water in atmospheric air is specified by the *humidity ratio* (also known as the *specific humidity*), ω. The humidity ratio is the mass ratio of water vapor to dry air. If both masses are expressed in pounds (kilograms), the units of ω are lbm/lbm (kg/kg). However, since there is so little water vapor, the water vapor mass is often reported in *grains* or grams. (There are 7000 grains per pound.) Accordingly, the humidity ratio may have the units of grains per pound or grams per kg. The humidity ratio is expressed as Eq. 16.30 or Eq. 16.32.

The humidity ratio is expressed per pound of dry air, not per pound of the total mixture. Equation 16.31 is derived from the ideal gas law, and 0.622 is the ratio of the specific gas constants for air and water vapor.

Example

One method of removing moisture from air is to cool the air so that the moisture condenses out. What is most nearly the temperature to which air at 100 atm must be cooled at constant pressure in order to obtain a humidity ratio of 0.0001?

(A) −6.0°C

(B) 2.0°C

(C) 8.0°C

(D) 14°C

Solution

Water vapor will condense when it is cooled to its dew-point temperature, which is the same as its saturation temperature. Rearranging Eq. 16.31,

$$\omega = 0.622 p_v/(p - p_v)$$

$$p_v = \left(\frac{\omega}{0.622}\right)(p - p_v)$$

$$= \frac{\dfrac{\omega p}{0.622}}{1 + \dfrac{\omega}{0.622}}$$

$$= \frac{(0.0001)(100 \text{ atm})\left(101.35 \dfrac{\text{kPa}}{\text{atm}}\right)}{0.622}}{1 + \dfrac{0.0001}{0.622}}$$

$$= 1.629 \text{ kPa}$$

From the steam tables, at 1.629 kPa,

$$T_{\text{sat}} \approx 14°C$$

The answer is (D).

Equation 16.32: Relative Humidity Ratio

$$\phi = p_v/p_g \qquad\qquad 16.32$$

Description

The *relative humidity*, ϕ, is a second index of moisture content of air. The relative humidity is the partial pressure of the water vapor divided by the saturation pressure at the dry-bulb temperature.

Example

Atmospheric air at 21°C has a relative humidity of 50%. What is most nearly the dew-point temperature?

(A) 7.0°C

(B) 10°C

(C) 17°C

(D) 24°C

Solution

At 21°C, the saturation pressure of water is

$$p_g = 2.505 \text{ kPa}$$

From Eq. 16.32, the vapor pressure is

$$\phi = p_v/p_g$$
$$p_v = \phi p_g$$
$$= (0.5)(2.505 \text{ kPa})$$
$$= 1.2525 \text{ kPa}$$

The dew-point temperature is the saturation temperature corresponding to the vapor pressure conditions. From the steam tables at 1.2525 kPa,

$$T_{\text{sat}} = T_{\text{dp}} \approx 10°C$$

The answer is (B).

4. PSYCHROMETRIC CHART

It is possible to develop mathematical relationships for enthalpy and specific volume (the two most useful thermodynamic properties) for atmospheric air. However, these relationships are almost never used. Rather, psychrometric properties are read directly from psychrometric charts, as illustrated in Fig. 16.1 and Fig. 16.2.

A psychrometric chart is easy to use, despite the multiplicity of scales. The thermodynamic state (i.e., the position on the chart) is defined by specifying the values of any two parameters on intersecting scales (e.g., dry-bulb and wet-bulb temperature, or dry-bulb temperature and relative humidity). Once the state has been located on the chart, all other properties can be read directly.

Figure 16.1 *ASHRAE Psychrometric Chart No. 1 (SI units)*

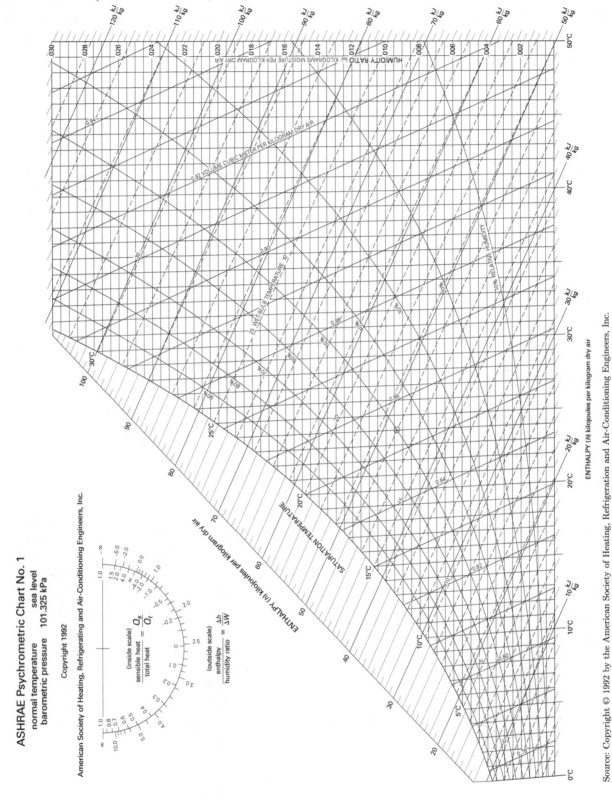

ASHRAE Psychrometric Chart No. 1
normal temperature   sea level
barometric pressure   101.325 kPa

Copyright 1992

American Society of Heating, Refrigerating and Air-Conditioning Engineers, Inc.

Source: Copyright © 1992 by the American Society of Heating, Refrigeration and Air-Conditioning Engineers, Inc.

Figure 16.2 *ASHRAE Psychrometric Chart No. 1 (customary U.S. units)*

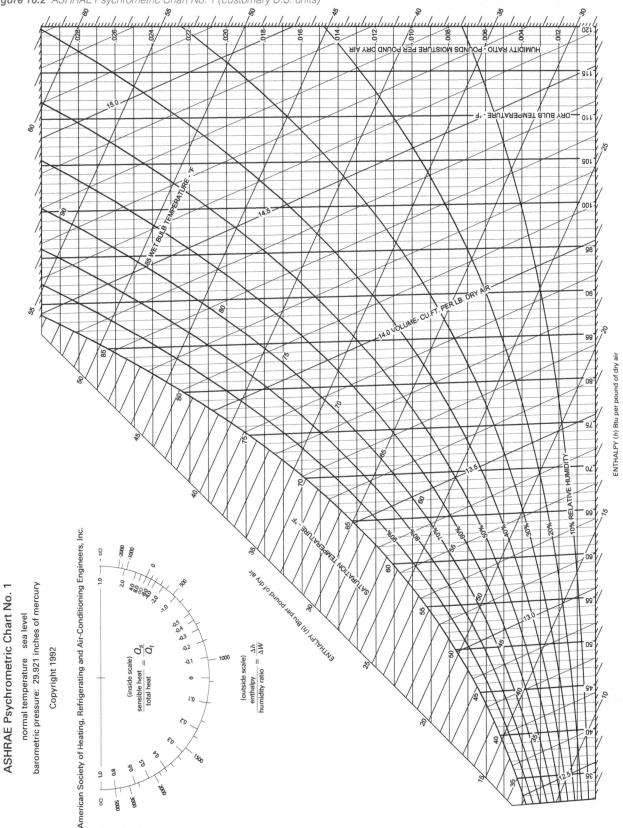

Source: Copyright © 1992 by the American Society of Heating, Refrigeration and Air-Conditioning Engineers, Inc.

Thermodynamics

Equation 16.33: Enthalpy of Dry Air

$$h = h_a + \omega h_v \qquad\qquad 16.33$$

Variation

$$h_{\text{total}} = m_a h \quad \begin{bmatrix} \text{for any mass} \\ \text{of dry air} \end{bmatrix}$$

Description

Enthalpy of an air-vapor mixture is the sum of the enthalpies of the air and water vapor. Enthalpy of the mixture per pound of dry air can be read from the psychrometric chart. Equation 16.33 computes enthalpy per pound of dry air. The variation equation illustrates an important point: In psychrometrics, the basis for the total enthalpy of air (an air-water vapor mixture) is the mass of the dry air only (i.e., $h_{\text{total}} = hm_{\text{air}}$), not the total air mass (i.e., not $h_{\text{total}} = h(m_{\text{air}} + m_{\text{vapor}})$).

Example

Atmospheric air has a humidity ratio of 0.008 kg/kg and a dry-bulb temperature of 30°C. What is most nearly the enthalpy of the air?

(A) 15 kJ/kg

(B) 22 kJ/kg

(C) 30 kJ/kg

(D) 50 kJ/kg

Solution

Using Fig. 16.1, locate the humidity ratio of 0.008 kg/kg along the vertical axis on the right side of the diagram. Move left along the horizontal grid line until the line for the humidity ratio intersects with the vertical grid line for a dry-bulb temperature of 30°C. Find the diagonal line for enthalpy that intersects with this point. The enthalpy of the air is approximately 50 kJ/kg.

The answer is (D).

5. CHEMICAL REACTION EQUILIBRIA

Reversible reactions are capable of going in either direction and do so to varying degrees (depending on the concentrations and temperature) simultaneously. These reactions are characterized by the simultaneous presence of all reactants and all products. For example, the chemical equation for the exothermic formation of ammonia from nitrogen and hydrogen is

$$N_2 + 3H_2 \rightleftharpoons 2NH_3 \quad (\Delta H = -92.4 \text{ kJ})$$

At *chemical equilibrium*, reactants and products are both present. Concentrations of the reactants and products do not change after equilibrium is reached.

Not all of a reactant may actually participate in a chemical reaction. There may be thermodynamic reasons, or too much of a reactant may simply be introduced. The *conversion* (*conversion ratio, conversion fraction,* etc.) of a reaction is the molar ratio of a reacted component to the component in the feed.

$$\text{conversion fraction} = X = \frac{N_{\text{reacted}}}{N_{\text{feed}}}$$

If the amount of products is limited by the amount of one of the reactants, that reactant is known as the *limiting reactant.*

The reaction may not produce as much product as the stoichiometric reaction equation predicts. There may be thermodynamic reasons, or limiting reactants, or other unexpected chemical losses. The amount of a specific product produced in a reaction is described by its yield. *Yield* (*yield ratio, yield fraction,* etc.) is the molar ratio of what is actually produced to the expected (ideal) production.

$$\text{yield fraction} = Y = \frac{N_{\text{obtained}}}{N_{\text{expected}}}$$

The products are not always what are expected, and the reaction may produce undesirable products. There may be limiting reactants (e.g., limited oxygen in a combustion reaction, resulting in the formation of carbon monoxide), or there may be impurities in the feed. The *selectivity* (*selectivity ratio, selectivity fraction*) is the molar ratio of desired and undesired products. A selectivity of 1.0 means that there are as many moles of undesired product as there are desired product.

$$\text{selectivity fraction} = S_{DU} = \frac{N_{\text{desired}}}{N_{\text{undesired}}}$$

Equation 16.34: Reversible Reactions

$$\text{moles}_{i,\text{out}} = \text{moles}_{i,\text{in}} + v_i \xi \qquad\qquad 16.34$$

Description

Equation 16.34 has a logical development. From the conservation of mass, all of a substance that goes into a reaction must either come out or be used. Consider the reaction of hydrogen and oxygen to form water vapor: $2H_2 + O_2 \rightarrow 2H_2O$. The stoichiometric coefficients 2, 1, and 2 represent the stoichiometric numbers of molecules taking part in the reaction. The coefficients also represent the number of moles and, if the components are gaseous, number of volumes. Since (for reactions with gaseous products and reactants) they are volumes, the stoichiometric coefficients can be given the symbol v. The molar balance is

$$N_{H_2,in} = N_{H_2,out} + v_{H_2}$$

Suppose 3 moles of hydrogen gas and 1 mole of oxygen gas are introduced and the reaction proceeds to completion. Oxygen will be the limiting reactant. 3 moles of hydrogen gas go in, 2 moles will be used up, and 1 mole will come out. The molar balance could be written as

$$N_{H_2,out} = N_{H_2,in} - v_{H_2}$$
$$1 = 3 - 2$$

For reversible reactions, this simple concept is complicated by the fact that the reactions do not necessarily use up all of the limiting reactant. Compared to the stoichiometric quantity, the actual molar fraction utilized or produced is known as the *extent*, ξ. By definition, extent has units of moles, while the stoichiometric constants have no units. Also by definition, the *stoichiometric coefficients*, v_i, are negative for reactants and positive for products.

$$\xi = \frac{\Delta N_{actual}}{\Delta N_{stoichiomeric}} = \frac{\Delta N_{actual}}{v}$$

Suppose 3 moles of hydrogen gas and 1 mole of oxygen gas are combined in a reactor. Further, suppose that some of the hydrogen does not react, and after equilibrium has been established, there are 1.5 moles of hydrogen gas remaining. The hydrogen's extent is

$$\xi_{H_2} = \frac{\Delta N_{H_2,actual}}{v_{H_2}}$$
$$= \frac{N_{H_2,ending} - N_{H_2,starting}}{v_{H_2}}$$
$$= \frac{1.5 \text{ mol} - 3 \text{ mol}}{-2}$$
$$= 0.75 \text{ mol}$$

Example

A fuel gas is 60% hydrogen (H_2) and 40% carbon monoxide (CO) by volume. 2.5 volumes of fuel gas and 1 volume of oxygen gas (O_2) are combined in a chemical reactor. The reaction goes to completion. For every mole of oxygen in the feed, the effluent consists of 1 mole of water vapor (H_2O), 1 mole of carbon

dioxide (CO_2), and ½ mole of hydrogen. Most nearly, what is the hydrogen's extent of reaction?

(A) 0.33

(B) 0.50

(C) 0.67

(D) 0.75

Solution

Volumetric ratios and mole ratios are numerically the same (for reactions with gaseous products and reactants). The actual reaction occurring is

$$2.5(0.6H_2 + 0.4CO) + O_2 \rightarrow H_2O + CO_2 + 0.5H_2$$
$$1.5H_2 + CO + O_2 \rightarrow H_2O + CO_2 + 0.5H_2$$

The limiting component is oxygen (since there is no oxygen in the products). With stoichiometric oxygen, the reaction would have been

$$1.5H_2 + CO + 1.25O_2 \rightarrow 1.5H_2O + CO_2$$

Based on the actual reaction, the hydrogen conversion fraction is

$$X_{H_2} = \frac{N_{H_2,reacted}}{N_{H_2,feed}} = \frac{1.5 \text{ mol} - 0.5 \text{ mol}}{1.5 \text{ mol}} = 0.667$$

Based on the actual and stoichiometric reactions, the water vapor yield fraction is

$$Y_{H_2O} = \frac{N_{H_2O,obtained}}{N_{H_2O,expected}} = \frac{1 \text{ mol}}{1.5 \text{ mol}} = 0.667$$

The hydrogen's extent is

$$\xi_{H_2} = \frac{\Delta N_{actual}}{v} = \frac{0.5 - 1.5}{-1.5}$$
$$= 0.667 \quad (0.67)$$

The answer is (C).

6. EQUILIBRIUM CONSTANT

Equation 16.35 Through Eq. 16.39: Equilibrium Constant for Liquids and Solids

$$\widehat{a}_i = \frac{\widehat{f}_i}{f_i^0} \qquad \qquad 16.35$$

$$\Delta G^0 = -RT \ln K_a \qquad 16.36$$

$$K_a = \frac{(\hat{a}_C^c)(\hat{a}_D^d)}{(\hat{a}_A^a)(\hat{a}_B^b)} = \prod_i (\hat{a}_i)^{v_i} \qquad 16.37$$

$$\hat{a}_i = 1 \quad \text{[solids]} \qquad 16.38$$

$$\hat{a}_i = x_i \gamma_i \quad \text{[liquids]} \qquad 16.39$$

Description

In a reversible reaction, the products and reactants will all be present simultaneously at equilibrium. (See Eq. 16.40.) The chemical *equilibrium constant*, K_a, is derived from an equation of state and is the value that minimizes the Gibbs standard energy change, ΔG^0, in Eq. 16.36.

The equilibrium constant is, essentially, a molar ratio of concentrations of products and reactants. The more the reaction goes towards completion, the larger the equilibrium constant and the greater the concentrations of products. Referring to Eq. 16.40 and denoting the molar concentration of species S as $[S]$, the traditional formula for calculating the equilibrium constant is

$$K_c = \frac{[C]^c [D]^d}{[A]^a [B]^b}$$

The effective concentration of a component (i.e., $[S]$ for component S) in a mixture is known as the *activity*, $\hat{a}$. Then, the equilibrium constant can be written as Eq. 16.37.[8] The equilibrium constant is the ratio of activities of products to reactants.

The concept of activity is related to *fugacity*. (Fugacity is not limited to substances in a gaseous state.) Equation 16.35 shows the relationship of the activity to the component's actual fugacity, $\hat{f}$, and standard state fugacity, f^0, in a mixture.[9]

Special rules are used to define the *activity* (i.e., the concentration) of solid and liquid components. Equation 16.38 ($\hat{a} = 1$) removes the concentrations of any pure solid and/or liquid components from the calculation of the equilibrium constant. Equation 16.39 calculates the activity of a liquid in a mixture as the product of the mole fraction and the experimental (empirical) *activity coefficient*, γ.

Equation 16.40 Through Eq. 16.42: Equilibrium Constant for Mixtures of Ideal Gases

$$aA + bB \rightleftharpoons cC + dD \qquad 16.40$$

$$K_a = K_p = \frac{(p_C^c)(p_D^d)}{(p_A^a)(p_B^b)} = p^{c+d-a-b} \frac{(y_C^c)(y_D^d)}{(y_A^a)(y_B^b)} \qquad 16.41$$

$$\hat{f}_i = y_i p = p_i \qquad 16.42$$

Description

For a reversible reaction with gaseous reactants, an equilibrium can be maintained only if the reactants remain gaseous. (See Eq. 16.40.) If the concentrations are molar, the equilibrium constant for gaseous reversible reactions is designated as K_c. A different equilibrium constant can also be calculated as a ratio of the components' partial pressures, as in Eq. 16.41, in which case, the equilibrium constant is designated as K_p.[10]

The second form of Eq. 16.41 relates the equilibrium constant to the total pressure, $p = \sum p_i$. Equation 16.42 relates the partial pressure to the actual fugacity.[11]

Equation 16.43: Variation of Equilibrium Constant with Temperature

$$\frac{d \ln K}{dT} = \frac{\Delta H^0}{RT^2} \qquad 16.43$$

As Eq. 16.36 shows, the equilibrium constant is related to the equation of state. Since the equation of state contains a temperature term, anything derived from the

[8](1) There is no mathematical significance to the parentheses used in Eq. 16.37. It is normal and customary in engineering to designate liquid molecular concentrations and gaseous molar concentrations used in the calculation of (liquid) equilibrium constants with square brackets (e.g., [A]). Parentheses have no such specific meaning. (2) The second form of Eq. 16.37 is an attempt to reduce the first form into the fewest characters. The exponent, v, is the coefficient of the chemical species in the chemical reaction, just as it is in Eq. 16.40. In order to use the second form, the same sign convention for v as is used with Eq. 16.40 must be imposed: v is positive for products and negative for reactants. Although the intent may have been an elegant simplification, nothing except complexity is gained by adding the second form of Eq. 16.37.
[9]The *NCEES Handbook* defines f^0 as the "unit pressure, often 1 bar." This is incorrect. f^0 is the fugacity at the standard state pressure. It is not the standard state pressure itself.
[10](1)The *NCEES Handbook* presents Eq. 16.41 as "$K_a = K_p$," which is incorrect. The numerical values of K_a and K_p are not the same, although they are related. (2) There is no mathematical significance to the parentheses used in Eq. 16.41. To avoid the appearance of using molecular or molar concentrations, it is normal and customary in engineering not to use either square brackets or parentheses with partial pressures in the formulas for gaseous equilibrium constants.
[11]The *NCEES Handbook* is incorrect in writing "$\hat{f}_i = \cdots = p_i$." Just as fugacity for real gases is not the same as the actual pressure, the fugacity of a gaseous component is not the same as its partial pressure. The fugacity is used in place of the partial pressure. If the numerical values were the same, there would be no need for fugacities.

equation of state depends on temperature. The equilibrium constant's dependency on temperature is given by Eq. 16.43, where ΔH^0 is the standard molar enthalpy of reaction.[12] Although the equilibrium constant varies considerably with temperature, ΔH^0 is reasonably insensitive to the temperature. When integrated, Eq. 16.43 is essentially the same as the Clausius-Clapeyron equation (and the Arrhenius equation for the temperature dependence of reaction rate constants), and is known as the *van't Hoff equation.*

$$\ln \frac{K_2}{K_1} = \left(\frac{\Delta H^0}{\overline{R}} \right) \left(\frac{T_2 - T_1}{T_1 T_2} \right)$$

---

[12]The *NCEES Handbook* refers to ΔH^0 as the "standard enthalpy change of reaction." This, and the similar "standard enthalpy change of combustion," should be avoided.

17 Combustion

Nomenclature

A/F	mass air-fuel ratio	–
$\overline{A/F}$	molar air-fuel ratio	–
c_p	molar heat capacity	J/mol·K
H	molar enthalpy	kcal/mol
m	mass	kg
M	molecular weight	g
N	number of moles	–
T	temperature	°C
v	stoichiometric coefficient	–

Symbols

η	efficiency	–

Subscripts

f	formation or fuel
i	indicated
r	reaction
ref	reference

1. HEATS OF REACTION

The *heating value* of a fuel is the energy that is given off when the fuel is burned (usually in atmospheric air). Heating value can be specified per unit mass, per unit volume, per unit liquid volume (e.g., kJ per liter), and per mole. In engineering practice, the heating value is always stated per measurable unit. The heating value will be specified in kJ/kg for coal, and in kJ/L for oil. Heating values of fuel gases may be given in kJ/m³ at a specified temperature and pressure that are approximately equal to normal atmospheric conditions (i.e., "room temperature"). However, fuel gases are seldom purchased by volume. In academia, heating values per mole are popular because for conditions close to room temperature, they can be derived from basic chemical and thermodynamic principles, as well as from tables of molar standard *enthalpies of formation* or *heats of formation*, ΔH_f. However, molar basis is rarely encountered outside of academia.

The enthalpy of formation of a compound is the energy absorbed during the formation of one (gram) mole of the compound from pure elements. The enthalpy of formation is defined as zero for elements (including diatomic gases such as H_2 and O_2) in their free states at standard conditions. Any deviation in temperature or phase of an element will change the value from zero. Compounds (combinations of elements) rarely have enthalpies of formation equal to zero.

When a heating value is derived from an enthalpy of formation, it is referred to as an *enthalpy of reaction* or *heat of reaction*, ΔH_r. (The general term, *heat of combustion*, is also used.) When compiled into tables, enthalpies of formation are standardized to some reference condition known as the *thermodynamic superscript, standard reference state*, or *reference state*, usually 25°C (298K) and 1 atm (1 bar, 100 torr). Standard enthalpies of reaction that are based on the standard enthalpies of formation are designated as ΔH_r^0.[1]

Enthalpies of reaction can also be determined in a bomb calorimeter. Since the energy given off is determined in a fixed volume, enthalpies of reaction are constant-volume values. This fact is rarely needed, however.

Chemical (including combustion) reactions that give off energy have negative enthalpies of reaction and are known as *exothermic reactions*. Many exothermic reactions begin spontaneously and/or are self-sustaining. *Endothermic reactions* absorb energy and have positive enthalpies for reaction. Endothermic reactions will continue only as long as they have energy sources.

Equation 17.1: Hess' Law

$$(\Delta H_r^0) = \sum_{\text{products}} v_i (\Delta H_f^0)_i - \sum_{\text{reactants}} v_i (\Delta H_f^0)_i \qquad 17.1$$

---

[1]The NCEES *FE Reference Handbook* (*NCEES Handbook*) uses a degree symbol to designate standard state. In practice, there is considerable variation in designating standard state (e.g., the subscript "std," a stroked lowercase letter o, a superscript zero, or a circle with a horizontal bar that either does extend outside of the circle or does not. Since the intent of the symbol is to designate a zero-energy condition, this book uses a superscripted zero to designate the standard state.

Description

Hess' law (*Hess' law of energy summation*) is used to calculate the enthalpy of reaction from the enthalpies of formation. The enthalpy of reaction is the sum of the enthalpies of formation of the products less the sum of the enthalpies of formation of the reactants. This is illustrated by Eq. 17.1.[2]

Enthalpy of formation is tabulated on a per mole basis. Since number of moles is proportional to the number of molecules, each molecule of a reactant or product will contribute its enthalpy of formation to the overall reaction. The multiplicity of contributions is accounted for in Eq. 17.1 by the coefficient terms, v_i.[3] These terms are the species coefficients in the stoichiometric chemical reaction equation.

Example

Standard enthalpies of formation for some gases are given.

$C_2H_5OH(l)$	−228 kJ/mol
CO	−111 kJ/mol
CO_2	−394 kJ/mol
$H_2O(g)$	−242 kJ/mol
$H_2O(l)$	−286 kJ/mol
NO	+30 kJ/mol

Most nearly, what is the standard enthalpy of reaction for the complete combustion of ethanol, C_2H_5OH?

(A) −1400 kJ/mol

(B) −1300 kJ/mol

(C) −1100 kJ/mol

(D) −910 kJ/mol

Solution

The balanced combustion reaction is

$$C_2H_5OH + 3O_2 \rightarrow 2CO_2 + 3H_2O$$

The standard enthalpy of reaction is evaluated at 25°C, so the water vapor will be in liquid form.

Use Hess' law, Eq. 17.1. The enthalpy of reaction is

$$(\Delta H_r^0) = \sum_{products} v_i(\Delta H_f^0)_i - \sum_{reactants} v_i(\Delta H_f^0)_i$$

$$= v_{CO_2}\Delta H_{f,CO_2}^0 + v_{H_2O}\Delta H_{f,H_2O}^0$$

$$-(v_{C_2H_5OH}\Delta H_{f,C_2H_5OH}^0 + v_{O_2}\Delta H_{f,O_2}^0)$$

$$= (2)\left(-394 \ \frac{kJ}{mol}\right) + (3)\left(-286 \ \frac{kJ}{mol}\right)$$

$$-\left[(1)\left(-228 \ \frac{kJ}{mol}\right) + (3)\left(0 \ \frac{kJ}{mol}\right)\right]$$

$$= -1418 \ kJ/mol \quad (-1400 \ kJ/mol)$$

The answer is (A).

Equation 17.2 and Eq. 17.3: Enthalpy of Reaction

$$\Delta H_r^0(T) = \Delta H_r^0(T_{ref}) + \int_{T_{ref}}^{T} \Delta c_p dT \qquad 17.2$$

$$\Delta c_p = \sum_{products} v_i c_{p,i} - \sum_{reactants} v_i c_{p,i} \qquad 17.3$$

Description

Enthalpies of formations are temperature dependent. For example, 286 kJ/mol of energy is released for each (gram) mole of 25°C liquid water produced. However, less energy is released when the water is formed at 50°C. Based on the equation $\Delta h = c_p\Delta T$ (which is good for any substance in any state), the molar enthalpy difference is $\Delta H = Mc_p\Delta T$, where c_p is a constant or mean specific heat, and M is the molecular weight.

Since enthalpies of formation are temperature dependent, enthalpies of reaction are temperature dependent. Equation 17.2, known as *Kirchhoff's law*, illustrates how the enthalpy of reaction at any temperature, T, is modified from the standard enthalpy of reaction.[4] Eq. 17.3 calculates Δc_p, the *aggregate molar heat capacity*, from the molar heat capacities of all of the reactants and products.[5]

---

[2](1) The *NCEES Handbook* sometimes uses extraneous parentheses in its equations. There is no mathematical or thermodynamic significance to the parentheses used in Eq. 17.1. As used in the *NCEES Handbook*, the parentheses around the left-hand side are particularly unnecessary. (2) Since the summations are shown to be over all of the "products" and "reactants," the increment variable, i, is not necessary. (3) Since the number of reactants is not the same as the number of products, the *NCEES Handbook's* use of variable i for both is misleading.

[3]The *NCEES Handbook* is inconsistent in the variable it uses to represent the stoichiometric coefficients. In Eq. 17.1, the *NCEES Handbook* uses Greek upsilon, v. In the material on the thermodynamics of chemical reaction equilibria, the *NCEES Handbook* uses lowercase italic v. This book uses Greek upsilon, v, for specific volume, and it uses lowercase italic v for stoichiometric coefficients.

[4](1) Although the *NCEES Handbook* frequently uses parentheses to separate multiplicative terms in equations, the parentheses used with (T) and (T_{ref}) in Eq. 17.2 mean "at that temperature." They do not mean multiplication by T and T_{ref}. (2) The use of the delta symbol for the molar aggregate heat capacity, Δc_p, within the integral is traditional to this subject. (3) Standard enthalpies of formation are always per unit mole, so the last term must also be on a molar basis. Although c_p is subsequently defined as a molar heat capacity, the symbol for specific heat capacity (unit mass basis) is used in Eq. 17.2 and Eq. 17.3. (4) The integral in Eq. 17.2 implies that the heat capacity varies with temperature. In practice, it may be approximated by a polynomial correlation that can be integrated. (5) Eq. 17.2 is insufficient when a substance experiences a change of phase while cooling or heating.

[5]Some of the comments regarding other equations apply to Eq. 17.3. (1) Although c_p is defined as a molar heat capacity, the symbol for specific heat capacity (unit mass basis) is used. (2) Since the summations are shown to be over all of the "products" and "reactants," the increment variable, i, is not necessary. (3) Since the number of reactants is not the same as the number of products, the *NCEES Handbook's* use of variable i for both is misleading.

Example

The standard (25°C) heat of combustion for hydrogen fuel in a bomb calorimeter is -285.8 kJ/mol. The mean specific heat of liquid water between the temperatures of 25°C and 50°C is 4.179 kJ/kg·°C. Most nearly, what is the molar heat of combustion if the combustion products in a 25°C bomb calorimeter are cooled at 50°C instead of the normal 25°C?

(A) -295 kJ/mol

(B) -288 kJ/mol

(C) -284 kJ/mol

(D) -280 kJ/mol

Solution

The stoichiometric chemical reaction equation for the combustion of hydrogen is

$$H_2(g) + \frac{1}{2}O_2(g) \rightarrow H_2O(l)$$

One mole of hydrogen produces one mole of water. Roughly based on Eq. 17.2, the molar heat of combustion at 50°C is

$$\Delta H_{r,T} = \Delta H_r^0 + Mc_p(T - T^0)$$

$$= -285.8 \ \frac{kJ}{mol}$$

$$+ \frac{\left(18 \ \frac{g}{mol}\right)\left(4.179 \ \frac{kJ}{kg \cdot °C}\right)(50°C - 25°C)}{1000 \ \frac{g}{kg}}$$

$$= -283.9 \ kJ/mol \quad (-284 \ kJ/mol)$$

The answer is (C).

2. COMBUSTION

Combustion reactions involving organic compounds and oxygen take place according to standard stoichiometric principles. *Stoichiometric air (ideal air)* is the exact quantity of air necessary to provide the oxygen required for complete combustion of the fuel. Stoichiometric

oxygen volumes can be determined from the balanced chemical reaction equation. Table 17.1 contains some of the more common chemical reactions.

As Table 17.1 shows, the products of complete combustion of a hydrocarbon fuel are carbon dioxide (CO_2) and water vapor (H_2O).[6] When sulfur is present in the fuel, sulfur dioxide (SO_2) is the normal product. When there is insufficient oxygen for complete combustion, carbon monoxide (CO) will be formed. Atmospheric nitrogen does not, under normal combustion conditions, dissociate and form oxides.

Table 17.1 *Ideal Combustion Reactions*

fuel	formula	reaction equation (excluding nitrogen)
carbon (to CO)	C	$2C + O_2 \rightarrow 2CO$
carbon (to CO_2)	C	$C + O_2 \rightarrow CO_2$
sulfur (to SO_2)	S	$S + O_2 \rightarrow SO_2$
sulfur (to SO_3)	S	$2S + 3O_2 \rightarrow 2SO_3$
carbon monoxide	CO	$2CO + O_2 \rightarrow 2CO_2$
methane	CH_4	$CH_4 + 2O_2 \rightarrow CO_2 + 2H_2O$
acetylene	C_2H_2	$2C_2H_2 + 5O_2 \rightarrow 4CO_2 + 2H_2O$
ethylene	C_2H_4	$C_2H_4 + 3O_2 \rightarrow 2CO_2 + 2H_2O$
ethane	C_2H_6	$2C_2H_6 + 7O_2 \rightarrow 4CO_2 + 6H_2O$
hydrogen	H_2	$2H_2 + O_2 \rightarrow 2H_2O$
hydrogen sulfide	H_2S	$2H_2S + 3O_2 \rightarrow 2H_2O + 2SO_2$
propane	C_3H_8	$C_3H_8 + 5O_2 \rightarrow 3CO_2 + 4H_2O$
n-butane	C_4H_{10}	$2C_4H_{10} + 13O_2 \rightarrow 8CO_2 + 10H_2O$
octane	C_8H_{18}	$2C_8H_{18} + 25O_2 \rightarrow 16CO_2 + 18H_2O$
olefin series	C_nH_{2n}	$2C_nH_{2n} + 3nO_2 \rightarrow 2nCO_2 + 2nH_2O$
paraffin series	C_nH_{2n+2}	$2C_nH_{2n+2} + (3n+1)O_2 \rightarrow 2nCO_2 + (2n+2)H_2O$

(Multiply oxygen volumes by 3.773 to get nitrogen volumes.)

[6](1) In a discussion of heat of reaction, the *NCEES Handbook* states about combustion, "The principal products [of combustion] are $CO_2(g)$ and H_2O (*l*)." *g* represents a substance in gaseous form, and *l* represents a substance in liquid form. While this may be correct for some entries in a heat of reaction tabulation that are derived from bomb calorimetry, this is patently in error for industrial and commercial combustion. The heat of combustion ensures that any water formed will, at least initially, appear in the stack (flue) gas as a vapor. In order to avoid the corrosive effects of high temperature liquid water (and sulfuric acid), great efforts are made to ensure that water remains in a vapor state throughout the stack/flue system. (2) From the standpoint of calculating heats of combustion, using the enthalpy of formation of liquid water includes the heat of vaporization in the heat of combustion. This is the definition of *higher heat of combustion*, which is not achievable in boilers, furnaces, and incinerators. Since water vapor is not permitted to condense out, only the lower heat of combustion is available in a combustion (burner/boiler/flue) system. (3) It is standard typographical notation to represent "(*g*)" and "(*l*)" with italic letters to avoid confusion with the chemical species.

Thermodynamics

Equation 17.4 and Eq. 17.5: Air-Fuel Ratios[7]

$$\overline{A/F} = \frac{\text{no. of moles of air}}{\text{no. of moles of fuel}} \qquad 17.4$$

$$A/F = \frac{\text{mass of air}}{\text{mass of fuel}}$$
$$= (\overline{A/F})\left(\frac{M_{\text{air}}}{M_{\text{fuel}}}\right) \qquad 17.5$$

Description

Stoichiometric air requirements are usually stated in units of mass (kilograms) of air for solid and liquid fuels, and in units of volume (cubic meters) of air for gaseous fuels. When stated in terms of mass, the ratio of air to fuel masses is known as the *air-fuel ratio, A/F*, given by Eq. 17.5. The molar air-fuel ratio is of academic interest. Since numbers of moles and numbers of volumes are proportional, the molar air-fuel ratio and volumetric air-fuel ratio are the same.[8]

Atmospheric Air for Combustion

Atmospheric air is a mixture of oxygen, nitrogen, and small amounts of carbon dioxide, water vapor, argon, and other inert gases. If all constituents except oxygen are grouped with the nitrogen, the air composition is as given in Table 17.2. It is helpful in many combustion problems to know the effective molecular weight of air, M_{air}, which is approximately 28.84 g/mol.[9]

Table 17.2 Composition of Dry Air[a]

component	percent by weight	percent by volume
oxygen	23.15	20.95
nitrogen/inerts	76.85	79.05
ratio of nitrogen to oxygen	3.320	3.773[b]
ratio of air to oxygen	4.320	4.773

[a]Inert gases and CO_2 are included as N_2.

[b]The value is also reported by various sources as 3.76, 3.78, and 3.784.

Stoichiometric air includes atmospheric nitrogen. For each volume (or mole) of oxygen, 3.773 volumes (or moles) of nitrogen and other atmospheric gases pass unchanged through the reaction. In combustion reaction equations, it is traditional to use a volumetric (or molar) ratio of 3.76, since that is the ratio based on a rounded air composition of 79% nitrogen and 21% oxygen. For example, the combustion of methane in air would be written as

$$CH_4 + 2O_2 + 2(3.76)N_2 \rightarrow CO_2 + 2H_2O + 7.52N_2$$

Example

In a stoichiometric octane (C_8H_{18}) combustion reaction, what is most nearly the air-fuel ratio?

- (A) 12.0
- (B) 12.5
- (C) 14.7
- (D) 15.1

Solution

Find the number of moles of air needed for complete combustion of octane.

$$C_8H_{18} + x(O_2 + 3.76N_2) \rightarrow 8CO_2 + 9H_2O + x(3.76N_2)$$
$$C_8H_{18} + 12.5(O_2 + 3.76N_2)$$
$$\rightarrow 8CO_2 + 9H_2O + 12.5(3.76N_2)$$

The total number of moles of air to fully combust 1 mole of octane is $(12.5)(1 + 3.76) = 59.5$ mol. Find the mass of air and mass of octane.

$$m_{\text{octane}} = NM$$
$$= (1 \text{ mol})\left(114 \ \frac{g}{\text{mol}}\right)$$
$$= 114 \text{ g}$$
$$m_{\text{air}} = (59.5 \text{ mol})\left(29 \ \frac{g}{\text{mol}}\right)$$
$$= 1725.5 \text{ g}$$

Use Eq. 17.5 to find the A/F ratio.

$$A/F = \frac{\text{mass of air}}{\text{mass of fuel}}$$
$$= \frac{1725.5 \text{ g}}{114 \text{ g}}$$
$$= 15.1$$

The answer is (D).

---

[7]The *NCEES Handbook* presents the definition of the air-fuel ratio under the heading "Incomplete Combustion." The value of the ratio is dependent on the amount of air, but the definition is not. Equation 17.4 and Eq. 17.5 can be used with stoichiometric air and excess air, as well as insufficient air.

[8]As stated, the molar air-fuel ratio is an academic concept. In practice, "air-fuel ratio" always means a ratio of masses. If anything else is intended, the term "air-fuel ratio" should never be used in spoken or written communications without including "molar" or some other qualification.

[9]In its table of thermodynamic properties of gases, the *NCEES Handbook* rounds this number to 29. Depending on the type of problem, this may or may not be sufficiently precise.

Equation 17.6: Percent Theoretical Air

$$\text{percent theoretical air} = \frac{(A/F)_{\text{actual}}}{(A/F)_{\text{stoichiometric}}} \times 100\% \qquad 17.6$$

Description

Complete combustion occurs when all of the fuel is burned. If there is inadequate oxygen, there will be *incomplete combustion*, and some carbon will appear as carbon monoxide in the products of combustion. As shown in Eq. 17.6, the *percent theoretical air* is the actual air-fuel ratio as a percentage of the theoretical air-fuel ratio calculated from the stoichiometric combustion equation.

Example

Assume air is 21% oxygen and 79% nitrogen. What is most nearly the percent theoretical air for the following balanced combustion reaction?

$$CH_4 + (7.14)\text{air} \rightarrow (2)H_2O + CO + (5.64)N_2$$

(A) 50%

(B) 66%

(C) 68%

(D) 75%

Solution

Find the actual air-fuel ratio.

$$
\begin{aligned}
(A/F)_{\text{actual}} &= \frac{\text{mass of air}}{\text{mass of fuel}} \\
&= \frac{N_{\text{air}}M_{\text{air}}}{N_{\text{fuel}}M_{\text{fuel}}} \\
&= \frac{(7.14)\begin{bmatrix}(0.21 \text{ mol})(32 \text{ g}) \\ +(0.79 \text{ mol})(28 \text{ g})\end{bmatrix}}{(1 \text{ mol})(16 \text{ g})} \\
&= 12.87
\end{aligned}
$$

Balance the following equation to find the number of moles of air for complete combustion.

$$CH_4 + (a)\text{air} \rightarrow (b)H_2O + (d)N_2 + (e)CO_2$$
$$CH_4 + (a)((0.21)O_2 + (0.79)N_2) \rightarrow (b)H_2O + (d)N_2 + (e)CO_2$$

From a hydrogen balance, 2 moles of water are produced. From a carbon balance, 1 mole of carbon dioxide is produced. Therefore, 2 moles of oxygen are required to react 1 mole of carbon.

$$2 = a(0.21)$$
$$a = 9.52$$

Calculate the stoichiometric air-fuel ratio.

$$
\begin{aligned}
(A/F)_{\text{stoichiometric}} &= \frac{\text{mass of air for complete combustion}}{\text{mass of fuel}} \\
&= \frac{N_{\text{air,combustion}}M_{\text{air,combustion}}}{N_{\text{fuel}}M_{\text{fuel}}} \\
&= \frac{(9.52 \text{ mol})\left(28.84 \frac{\text{g}}{\text{mol}}\right)}{(1 \text{ mol})\left(16 \frac{\text{g}}{\text{mol}}\right)} \\
&= 17.17
\end{aligned}
$$

Use Eq. 17.6 to find the percent theoretical air.

$$
\begin{aligned}
\text{percent theoretical air} &= \frac{(A/F)_{\text{actual}}}{(A/F)_{\text{stoichiometric}}} \times 100\% \\
&= \frac{12.87}{17.17} \times 100\% \\
&= 75\%
\end{aligned}
$$

The answer is (D).

Equation 17.7: Percent Excess Air

$$\text{percent excess air} = \frac{(A/F)_{\text{actual}} - (A/F)_{\text{stoichiometric}}}{(A/F)_{\text{stoichiometric}}} \times 100\% \qquad 17.7$$

Description

Usually 10–50% excess air is required for complete combustion to occur. *Excess air* is expressed as a percentage of the stoichiometric air requirements, as shown in Eq. 17.7. Excess air appears as oxygen and nitrogen along with the products of combustion.

Example

The stoichiometric air requirement for complete combustion of a unit of fuel is 75.2 mol, and the actual air provided is 95.4 mol. What is most nearly the percent excess air?

(A) 4.5%

(B) 6.0%

(C) 21%

(D) 27%

Solution

Use Eq. 17.7 to calculate the percent excess air.

$$
\begin{aligned}
\text{percent excess air} &= \frac{(A/F)_{\text{actual}} - (A/F)_{\text{stoichiometric}}}{(A/F)_{\text{stoichiometric}}} \times 100\% \\
&= \frac{95.4 \text{ mol air} - 75.2 \text{ mol air}}{75.2 \text{ mol air}} \times 100\% \\
&= 26.9\% \quad (27\%)
\end{aligned}
$$

The answer is (D).

Thermodynamics

18 Heating, Ventilating, and Air Conditioning (HVAC)

Nomenclature

A	area	ft^2	m^2
c_p	specific heat	Btu/lbm-°F	kJ/kg·°C
C	thermal conductance	Btu/hr-ft^2-°F	W/m^2·°C
CLF	cooling load factor	–	–
CLTD	cooling load temperature difference	°F	°C
h	specific enthalpy	Btu/lbm	kJ/kg
h	surface heat transfer coefficient	Btu/hr-ft^2-°F	W/m^2·°C
k	thermal conductivity	Btu-ft/hr-ft^2-°F	W·m/m^2·°C
L	length	ft	m
LF	latent factor	–	–
$\dot{m}$	mass flow rate	lbm/hr	kg/h
$\dot{Q}$	heat transfer rate	hp	W
R	thermal resistance	hr-ft^2-°F/Btu	m^2·°C/W
SC	shading coefficient	–	–
SCL	solar cooling load factor	Btu/hr-ft^2	W/m^2
SHR	sensible heat ratio	–	–
T	temperature	°F	°C
U	overall coefficient of heat transfer	Btu/hr-ft^2-°F	W/m^2·°C
V	volume	ft^3	m^3
$\dot{V}$	volumetric flow rate	ft^3/min	m^3/s

Symbols

ω	humidity ratio	lbm/lbm	kg/kg

Subscripts

c	cooling
fg	vaporization
i	inside design
id	indoor design
l	latent
m	mean
o	outside design
p	people or primary
s	sensible

1. HEATING

Heating Load

A building's *heating load* is the maximum heat loss (typically expressed in Btu/hr or kW) during the heating season. The *maximum heating load* occurs when the outside temperature is the lowest. The maximum heating load corresponds to the minimum furnace size, even though the lowest temperature occurs only a few times each year. The *average heating load* can be derived from the maximum heating load and is used to determine the annual fuel requirements.

Heating load consists of heat to make up for transmission and infiltration losses. Determining transmission losses is essentially a heat transfer problem. *Transmission loss* is heat lost through the walls, roof, and floor. *Infiltration loss* is heat required to warm ventilation and infiltration air. Though no "credit" for solar heat gain is taken in heating load calculations, reliable sources of internal heating are considered. Modifications for thermal inertia due to high-mass walls and ceilings are generally not made in calculations of heating load. When thermal inertia is considered, the approach taken is simplistic.

Design Conditions

For the purposes of initial heating load calculations for residences and office spaces, the *inside design temperature* is generally taken to be between 21.1°C and 22.2°C.

The outside temperature and average wind speed (for infiltration) are needed to determine heating load.

Walls and Ceilings

Each material used in constructing a wall, ceiling, and so on, contributes resistance to heat flow. This resistance can be specified in a variety of ways. *Total resistance*, R (with units of m^2·°C/W), is the total resistance to heat flow through the entire thickness of the material. *Unit resistance* (with units of m^2·°C/W·cm) is the resistance per unit thickness of the material. The total

Thermodynamics

resistance is the product of the resistivity and the material thickness. *Conductance*, *C*, and *conductivity*, *k*, are the reciprocals of total resistance and unit resistance, respectively.

$$R = \frac{1}{C}$$

$$k = \frac{L}{R}$$

The heat transfer through walls, doors, windows, and ceilings is calculated from the traditional heat transfer equation. The *overall coefficient of heat transfer*, *U*, can be calculated for each transmission path from the conductivities and resistances of the individual components in that path, or it can be obtained from tabulations of typical wall/ceiling construction.

$$\dot{Q} = UA(T_i - T_o)$$

$$U = \frac{1}{\sum R_i} = \frac{1}{\dfrac{1}{h_i} + \sum \dfrac{L}{k} + \sum \dfrac{1}{C} + \dfrac{1}{h_o}}$$

2. VENTILATING

Introduction

Ventilation primarily refers to air that is necessary to satisfy the needs of occupants. The term may mean the air that is introduced into an occupied space, or it may refer to the new air that is deliberately drawn in from the outside and mixed with return air. Ventilation, however, does not normally include unintentional infiltration through cracks and openings. Ventilation air is provided to the occupied space primarily to remove heat and moisture generated in the space. Heat and moisture can both be generated metabolically as well as by equipment and processes.

Humidification

Ventilation provides humidification to the occupied space, particularly during the winter. Air should not be completely dry when it enters an occupied space. Air that is too dry will cause discomfort and susceptibility to respiratory ailments. Also, some pathogenic bacteria that survive in low- and high-humidity air will die very quickly in air with midrange humidities.

Some manufacturing and materials handling processes require specific humidity for efficient operation. *Hygroscopic materials*, such as wood, paper, textiles, leather, and many food and chemical products, readily absorb moisture. A constant humidity level is required to obtain consistent manufacturing conditions with such products.

Dry air prevents static electricity from dissipating (into the air). Therefore, dry air can cause intermittent electrical/electronic failures; affect the handling of static-prone materials such as paper, films, and plastics; and ignite potentially explosive atmospheres of dust and gases.

Humidification can be provided by evaporating water in the occupied space (the *evaporative pan method*) or by injecting water (the *water spray method*) or steam into the duct flow. Most commercial humidification is accomplished by placing one or more steam manifolds in the air distribution duct. *Booster humidification* (*spot humidification*) from a separate, independent source is required when a higher humidity is needed in a limited area within a larger controlled space. Steam flow is controlled by humidistats placed downstream of the steam manifold.

Sensible and Latent Heat

Metabolic heat contains both sensible and latent components. *Sensible heat* is pure thermal energy that increases the air's dry-bulb temperature. *Latent heat* is moisture that increases air's humidity ratio.

Ventilation for Heat Removal

Ventilation requirements can be calculated from sensible heat and/or moisture (i.e., latent heat) generation rates. In the following equation, T_{in} is the dry-bulb temperature of the air entering the room.

$$\dot{Q}_s = \dot{m}c_p(T_{id} - T_{in})$$
$$= \dot{V}\rho c_p(T_{id} - T_{in})$$

The previous equation can be written in terms of the number of air changes per hour, ACH, and the temperature of the ventilation air, T_{out}.

$$\dot{Q} = \frac{\rho c_p V_{room}(\text{ACH})(T_{in} - T_{out})}{60 \, \dfrac{\text{min}}{\text{hr}}}$$

In ventilation work, volumetric flow rates are traditionally given in m³/min or L/s. The constant 0.02 in the following equation is the product of an air density of 1.2 kg/m³, a specific heat of 1.0 kJ/kg·°C, and the factor 60 s/min.

$$\dot{V}_{\text{m}^3/\text{min}} = \frac{\dot{Q}_{s,\text{kW}}}{\left(0.02 \, \dfrac{\text{kJ·min}}{\text{m}^3\text{·s·°C}}\right)(T_{id,\text{°C}} - T_{in,\text{°C}})}$$

The sensible heat loads will usually be more significant than the latent load, and ventilation will be determined solely on that basis. When large moisture sources are present, however, the latent loads may control.

$$\dot{Q}_l = \dot{m}_{\text{water}} h_{fg} = \dot{m}_{\text{air}} \Delta \omega h_{fg}$$
$$= \dot{V} \rho \Delta \omega h_{fg}$$

The constant 49.36 in the following equation is the product of the air density of 1.2 kg/m^3, a latent heat of vaporization at the approximate partial pressure of the water vapor in the air of 2468 kJ/kg, and the factor 60 s/min.

$$\dot{V}_{\text{m}^3/\text{min}} = \frac{\dot{Q}_{l,\text{kW}}}{\left(49.36 \; \dfrac{\text{kJ} \cdot \text{min}}{\text{m}^3 \cdot \text{s}}\right) \Delta \omega_{\text{kg/kg}}}$$

3. AIR CONDITIONING

Types of Air Conditioning Systems

Depending on the medium delivered to the conditioned space, air conditioning systems are categorized as all-air, air-and-water, all-water, and unitary. *All-air systems* maintain the temperature by distributing only air, and most systems rely on internal loads for heating, sending only cold air to the space. Most central units are *single-duct*, which means that the cooling and heating coils are in series. In *dual-duct* units, the heating and cooling coils are in parallel ducts.

In *air-and-water systems*, air and water are both distributed to the conditioned space. In *all-water systems*, the cooling and heating effects are provided solely by cooled and/or heated water pumped to the conditioned space. With *unitary equipment*, the fan, condenser, and cooling and heating coils are combined in a standalone unit for window and through-the-wall installation.

Cooling Load

The procedure for finding the *cooling load* (also referred to as the *air conditioning load*) is similar in some respects to the procedure for finding the heating load. The aspects of determining inside and outside design conditions, heat transfer from adjacent spaces, ventilation air requirements, and internal heat gains are the same as for heating load calculations and are not covered in this chapter.

However, the calculation of cooling load is complicated considerably by the thermal lag of the exterior surfaces (i.e., walls and roof). Depending on construction, the solar energy absorbed by exterior surfaces can take hours to appear as an interior cooling load. Further complicating the determination of cooling load are the direct transmission of solar energy through windows and the facts that the delay is different for each surface,

the solar energy absorbed changes with time of day, and instantaneous heat gain into the room contributes to instantaneous and delayed cooling loads.

It is important to distinguish between three terms. The *instantaneous heat absorption* is the solar energy that is absorbed at a particular moment. The *instantaneous heat gain* is the energy that enters the conditioned space at that moment. Due to solar lag, the heat gain is a complex combination of heat absorptions from previous hours. The *instantaneous cooling load* is a portion (i.e., is essentially the convective portion) of the instantaneous heat gain.

Source of Cooling

Once the cooling load is determined, the source and size of the cooling unit must be considered. Cooling normally comes from liquefied refrigerant passing through a cooling coil. Some or all of the airflow passes across the cooling coil. The refrigerant is continuously vaporized in the coil as part of a complete refrigeration cycle. Alternatively, cold water may be used in the coil to cool the airflow. In such cases, the water is cooled in a *chiller* running its own refrigeration cycle.

An *economizer* is an electromechanical system that changes a portion of the cooling process in order to decrease cost, usually by taking advantage of cold ambient air. A *water-side economizer* substitutes natural cooling from a cooling tower for the chiller's more expensive refrigeration cycle when the ambient air temperature drops below the desired coil temperature. An *air-side economizer* increases the amount of outside air that is brought into a space when the ambient air characteristics (temperature, humidity, or enthalpy) are better than the return airflow. The outside air may still be conditioned by passing through coils, but less change will be required. Use of cold ambient air by either type of economizer is known as *free cooling*.

Instantaneous Cooling Load from Walls and Roofs

The only modern method of calculating the cooling load suitable for quick (manual) analysis is the *cooling load temperature difference method*, CLTD, using the related *solar cooling load factor*, SCL, and *cooling load factor*, CLF. For exterior surfaces, the cooling load is calculated by the following equation. Tables of CLTD values are needed. Values depend on time of year, location and orientation, type, configuration, and orientation of the surface, as well as other factors. Using the CLTD/SCL/CLF method, the instantaneous cooling load for conduction through opaque walls and roofs is

$$\dot{Q}_c = UA(\text{CLTD}_{\text{corrected}})$$

The base conditions used to calculate the values of CLTD are

- a clear sky on July 21

- exposed, sunlit, flat roofs

- time of maximum temperature of 3:00 p.m.

- walls at 40°N latitude based on roof and wall construction and orientation

- an indoor temperature of 25.5°C (78°F)

- an outdoor maximum temperature of 35°C (95°F) with a mean temperature of 29.4°C (85°F)

- a daily temperature range of 11.6°C (21°F)

These base conditions generally don't coincide precisely with actual conditions during the study period, so CLTD is corrected according to the following equation. T_i is the indoor design temperature, and T_m is the mean outdoor temperature.

$$\text{CLTD}_{\text{corrected}} = \text{CLTD}_{\text{table}} + (25.5°C - T_i) \\ + (T_m - 29.4°C)$$

$$T_m = T_{\text{outdoor,max}} - \tfrac{1}{2}(\text{daily range})$$

Instantaneous Cooling Load from Windows

Using the CLTD/SCL/CLF method, the cooling load due to solar energy received through windows is calculated in two parts. The first is an immediate conductive part; the second is a radiant part. Appropriate tables are needed to evaluate the *shading coefficient*, SC, and the SCL for the radiant portions.

$$\dot{Q}_c = \dot{Q}_{\text{conductive}} + \dot{Q}_{\text{radiant}} \\ = UA(\text{CLTD}_{\text{corrected}}) + A(\text{SC})(\text{SCL})$$

Cooling Load from Internal Heat Sources

Latent loads (including metabolic latent loads) are considered instantaneous cooling loads. Only a portion, given by the CLF, of the sensible heat sources show up as instantaneous cooling load. The CLF is a function of time and depends on zone type, occupancy period, interior and exterior shading, and other factors. Although tables are usually necessary to evaluate the CLF, there are some cases where the CLF is assumed to be 1.0. These include when the cooling system is shut down during the night, when there is a high occupant density (as in theaters and auditoriums), and when lights and other sources are operated for 24 hours a day.

$$\dot{Q}_{c,\text{internal sources}} = \dot{Q}_l + \dot{Q}_s(\text{CLF})$$

Latent and Sensible Loads

Latent loads increase the cooling load. The main sources of residential latent loads are infiltration, perspiration and exhalation by occupants, cooking, laundry, showering, and bathing. The often quoted rule of thumb is that residential latent load is 30% of the total load, although the actual latent load varies widely depending on infiltration rate, climate, and occupancy.

The *sensible heat ratio*, SHR (also known as the *sensible heat factor*, SHF), is the sensible load divided by the total load (including the latent load). The *latent factor*, LF, is the reciprocal of the SHR. Most air conditioning equipment is designed to operate at a sensible heat ratio in the range of 0.70–0.75. According to ASHRAE, a latent factor of 1.3 or a sensible heat ratio of 0.77 matches the performance of typical residential vapor compression cooling systems.

$$\text{SHR} = \frac{1}{\text{LF}} = \frac{\dot{Q}_{\text{sensible}}}{\dot{Q}_{\text{sensible}} + \dot{Q}_{\text{latent}}}$$

Diagnostic Exam

Topic V: Heat Transfer

1. Liquid nitrogen at 77K is stored in an uninsulated 1.0 m radius spherical tank. The tank is exposed to ambient air at 285K. The thermal resistance of the tank material is negligible. The convective heat transfer coefficient of the tank exterior is 30 W/m^2·K. The initial heat transfer from the air to the tank is most nearly

(A) 4.9 kW

(B) 9.8 kW

(C) 16 kW

(D) 78 kW

2. The exterior walls of a house are 3 m high, 0.14 m thick, and 40 m in total length. The thermal conductivity of the walls is 0.038 W/m·°C. The interior of the walls is maintained at 20°C when the exterior (outdoor) wall temperature is 0°C. Neglecting corner effects, most nearly, what is the heat transfer through the walls?

(A) 0.023 kW

(B) 0.065 kW

(C) 0.23 kW

(D) 0.65 kW

3. A stainless steel tube (3 cm inside diameter and 5 cm outside diameter) is covered with 4 cm thick insulation. The thermal conductivities of stainless steel and the insulation are 20 W/m·K and 0.06 W/m·K, respectively.

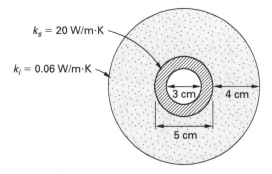

k_s = 20 W/m·K

k_i = 0.06 W/m·K

3 cm   4 cm

5 cm

If the inside wall temperature of the tube is 500K and the outside temperature of the insulation is 50K, what is most nearly the heat loss per meter of tube length?

(A) 120 W/m

(B) 140 W/m

(C) 160 W/m

(D) 180 W/m

4. A concrete wall is 20 cm thick and has an overall thermal resistance of 0.2 m^2·°C/W. The temperature difference between the two wall surfaces is 5°C. What is most nearly the heat transfer through the wall?

(A) 1.5 W/m^2

(B) 2.5 W/m^2

(C) 13 W/m^2

(D) 25 W/m^2

5. 50°C water flows through a 1.5 m long copper pipe. The thermal conductivity of the copper is 350 W/m·°C. The internal diameter of the pipe is 20 mm, and the pipe wall is 5 mm thick. The temperature outside of the pipe is 20°C. What is most nearly the heat transfer through the pipe?

(A) 140 kW

(B) 160 kW

(C) 240 kW

(D) 440 kW

6. A parallel flow tubular heat exchanger cools water from 90°C to 70°C. The coolant increases in temperature from 0°C to 35°C. The log mean temperature difference is most nearly

(A) 28°C

(B) 32°C

(C) 58°C

(D) 62°C

7. A fan moves 25°C air over a 25 W resistive electrical device that has a uniform surface temperature of 100°C.

The forced convection heat transfer coefficient is 50 W/m^2·°C. If the cooling fan fails and the device is cooled by natural convection (heat transfer coefficient of 10 W/m^2·°C), the resulting surface temperature of the device will be most nearly

(A) 100°C

(B) 375°C

(C) 400°C

(D) 625°C

8. Two large parallel plates are maintained electrically at uniform temperatures. Plate 1 has a surface temperature of 900K and an emissivity of 0.5. Plate 2 has a surface temperature of 650K and an emissivity of 0.8. The facing surfaces of both plates constitute opaque, diffuse gray radiators. A thin aluminum radiation shield is placed between the plates. The space between the plates is evacuated so that convective effects are negligible. The emissivity of both sides of the radiation shield is 0.15. In steady state, what is most nearly the net heat flux from plate 1 to plate 2?

(A) 940 W/m^2

(B) 1500 W/m^2

(C) 1900 W/m^2

(D) 2600 W/m^2

9. Air at 300K flows at 0.45 m/s over the surface of a 1 m × 1 m flat plate. The average kinematic viscosity of the air is 20.92 × 10^{-6} m^2/s, the Prandtl number is 0.7, and the thermal conductivity is 30 × 10^{-3} W/m·K. If the surface temperature of the plate is 400K, the average heat transfer coefficient is most nearly

(A) 2.6 W/m^2·K

(B) 5.0 W/m^2·K

(C) 7.5 W/m^2·K

(D) 8.2 W/m^2·K

10. A metal sphere at 750°C with a diameter of 2 cm is enclosed in a vacuum container. The temperature of the surroundings is −20°C. 12 W of power is needed to maintain the sphere's temperature. What is most nearly the emissivity of the sphere?

(A) 0.15

(B) 0.20

(C) 0.25

(D) 0.28

SOLUTIONS

1. The heat transfer from the tank to the atmosphere is

$$\dot{Q} = hA(T_w - T_\infty) = h4\pi r^2(T_w - T_\infty)$$

$$= \frac{\left(30 \ \frac{\text{W}}{\text{m}^2 \cdot \text{K}}\right)4\pi(1 \ \text{m})^2(77\text{K} - 285\text{K})}{1000 \ \frac{\text{W}}{\text{kW}}}$$

$$= 78.4 \ \text{kW}$$

The heat transfer from the air to the tank is 78.4 kW (78 kW).

The answer is (D).

2. Calculate the area.

$$A = Lh = (40 \ \text{m})(3 \ \text{m}) = 120 \ \text{m}^2$$

The heat transfer due to conduction is

$$\dot{Q} = \frac{kA(T_1 - T_2)}{\Delta x}$$

$$= \frac{\left(0.038 \ \frac{\text{W}}{\text{m} \cdot °\text{C}}\right)(120 \ \text{m}^2)(20°\text{C} - 0°\text{C})}{(0.14 \ \text{m})\left(1000 \ \frac{\text{W}}{\text{kW}}\right)}$$

$$= 0.651 \ \text{kW} \quad (0.65 \ \text{kW})$$

The answer is (D).

3. The radius of the inside of the tube is

$$r_1 = \frac{D_i}{2} = \frac{3 \ \text{cm}}{2} = 1.5 \ \text{cm}$$

The radius of the outside of the tube is

$$r_2 = \frac{D_o}{2} = \frac{5 \ \text{cm}}{2} = 2.5 \ \text{cm}$$

The outer radius of the insulation is

$$r_3 = r_2 + t = 2.5 \ \text{cm} + 4 \ \text{cm} = 6.5 \ \text{cm}$$

The heat transfer through the tube is

$$\dot{Q} = \frac{2\pi k_s L(T_1 - T_2)}{\ln \frac{r_2}{r_1}}$$

The temperature between the tube and insulation is

$$T_2 = T_1 - \frac{\dot{Q} \ln \dfrac{r_2}{r_1}}{2\pi k_s L}$$

The heat transfer through the insulation is

$$\dot{Q} = \frac{2\pi k_i L (T_2 - T_3)}{\ln \dfrac{r_3}{r_2}}$$

From this, the temperature between the tube and insulation is also

$$T_2 = \frac{\dot{Q} \ln \dfrac{r_3}{r_2}}{2\pi k_i L} + T_3$$

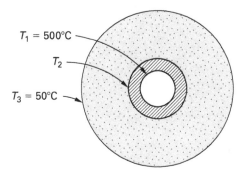

$T_1 = 500°C$

T_2

$T_3 = 50°C$

Equate the two expressions for the temperature between the tube and boundary.

$$T_1 - \frac{\dot{Q} \ln \dfrac{r_2}{r_1}}{2\pi k_s L} = \frac{\dot{Q} \ln \dfrac{r_3}{r_2}}{2\pi k_i L} + T_3$$

Solve for the heat transfer per unit length.

$$\frac{\dot{Q}}{L} = \frac{2\pi (T_1 - T_3)}{\dfrac{\ln \dfrac{r_2}{r_1}}{k_s} + \dfrac{\ln \dfrac{r_3}{r_2}}{k_i}}$$

$$= \frac{2\pi (500\text{ K} - 50\text{ K})}{\dfrac{\ln \dfrac{2.5\text{ cm}}{1.5\text{ cm}}}{20 \dfrac{\text{W}}{\text{m·K}}} + \dfrac{\ln \dfrac{6.5\text{ cm}}{2.5\text{ cm}}}{0.06 \dfrac{\text{W}}{\text{m·K}}}}$$

$$= 177.3\text{ W/m} \quad (180\text{ W/m})$$

The answer is (D).

4. Find the heat transfer per unit area.

$$\dot{Q} = \frac{A \Delta T}{R}$$

$$\dot{q} = \frac{\dot{Q}}{A} = \frac{\Delta T}{R}$$

$$= \frac{5°C}{0.2 \dfrac{\text{m}^2 \cdot °C}{\text{W}}}$$

$$= 25\text{ W/m}^2$$

The answer is (D).

5. Solve for rate of heat transfer, $\dot{Q}$, through the pipe using the equation from FE Handbook section, "Conduction Through a Cylindrical Wall.".

$$\dot{Q} = \frac{2\pi k L (T_1 - T_2)}{\ln\left(\dfrac{r_2}{r_1}\right)}$$

Find inner and outer radius.

$$r_1 = \frac{D}{2} = \frac{20\text{ mm}}{2} = 10\text{ mm}$$

$$r_2 = \text{inner radius} + \text{wall thickness}$$

$$= 10\text{ mm} + 5\text{ mm} = 15\text{ mm}$$

Plug in the radii values in the heat transfer equation.

$$\dot{Q} = \frac{(2\pi)\left(350 \dfrac{\text{W}}{\text{m·}°C}\right)(1.5\text{ m})(50°C - 20°C)}{\left(\ln\left(\dfrac{15\text{ mm}}{10\text{ mm}}\right)\right)\left(1000 \dfrac{\text{W}}{\text{kW}}\right)}$$

$$= 243.94\text{ kW} \quad (240\text{ kW})$$

The answer is (C).

6. Calculate the log mean temperature difference for parallel flow in tubular heat exchangers.

$$\Delta T_{\text{lm}} = \frac{(T_{\text{Ho}} - T_{\text{Co}}) - (T_{\text{Hi}} - T_{\text{Ci}})}{\ln\left(\dfrac{T_{\text{Ho}} - T_{\text{Co}}}{T_{\text{Hi}} - T_{\text{Ci}}}\right)}$$

$$= \frac{(70°C - 35°C) - (90°C - 0°C)}{\ln\left(\dfrac{70°C - 35°C}{90°C - 0°C}\right)}$$

$$= 58.23°C \quad (58°C)$$

The answer is (A).

7. Use Newton's law of cooling. At state 1, the fan is operating, and at state 2, the fan has failed.

$$\dot{Q} = hA(T_w - T_\infty)$$

$$\frac{\dot{Q}}{A} = h_1(T_{w,1} - T_\infty) = h_2(T_{w,2} - T_\infty)$$

Solve for the surface temperature of the device after the fan fails.

$$T_{w,2} = \left(\frac{h_1}{h_2}\right)(T_{w,1} - T_\infty) + T_\infty$$

$$= \left(\frac{50\ \frac{\text{W}}{\text{m}^2 \cdot ^\circ\text{C}}}{10\ \frac{\text{W}}{\text{m}^2 \cdot ^\circ\text{C}}}\right)(100^\circ\text{C} - 25^\circ\text{C}) + 25^\circ\text{C}$$

$$= 400^\circ\text{C}$$

The answer is (C).

8. The net heat transfer is

$$\dot{q}_{12} = \frac{\dot{Q}_{12}}{A}$$

$$= \frac{\sigma(T_1^4 - T_2^4)}{A\left(\dfrac{1 - \varepsilon_1}{\varepsilon_1 A_1} + \dfrac{1}{A_1 F_{13}} + \dfrac{1 - \varepsilon_{3,1}}{\varepsilon_{3,1} A_3} + \dfrac{1 - \varepsilon_{3,2}}{\varepsilon_{3,2} A_3} + \dfrac{1}{A_3 F_{32}} + \dfrac{1 - \varepsilon_2}{\varepsilon_2 A_2}\right)}$$

Since the plates are parallel, $A = A_1 = A_2 = A_3$. Since the plates are large, $F_{13} = F_{32} = 1$. Since the emissivity of the shield is the same on both sides, $\varepsilon_{3,1} = \varepsilon_{3,2} = \varepsilon_3$.

$$\dot{q}_{12} = \frac{\sigma(T_1^4 - T_2^4)}{\left(\frac{1-\varepsilon_1}{\varepsilon_1} + \frac{1}{F_{13}} + \frac{1-\varepsilon_{3,1}}{\varepsilon_{3,1}} + \frac{1-\varepsilon_{3,2}}{\varepsilon_{3,2}} + \frac{1}{F_{32}} + \frac{1-\varepsilon_2}{\varepsilon_2}\right)}$$

$$= \frac{\sigma(T_1^4 - T_2^4)}{\left(\frac{1}{\varepsilon_1} - \frac{\varepsilon_1}{\varepsilon_1} + \frac{1}{F_{13}} + \frac{1}{\varepsilon_{3,1}} - \frac{\varepsilon_{3,1}}{\varepsilon_{3,1}} + \frac{1}{\varepsilon_{3,2}} - \frac{\varepsilon_{3,2}}{\varepsilon_{3,2}} + \frac{1}{F_{3,2}} + \frac{1}{\varepsilon_2} - \frac{\varepsilon_2}{\varepsilon_2}\right)}$$

$$= \frac{\sigma(T_1^4 - T_2^4)}{\left(\frac{1}{\varepsilon_1} - 1 + 1 + \frac{1}{\varepsilon_3} - 1 + \frac{1}{\varepsilon_3} - 1 + 1 + \frac{1}{\varepsilon_2} - 1\right)}$$

$$= \frac{\sigma(T_1^4 - T_2^4)}{\left(\frac{1}{\varepsilon_1} + \frac{2}{\varepsilon_3} + \frac{1}{\varepsilon_2} - 2\right)}$$

$$= \frac{\left(5.67 \times 10^{-8}\ \frac{\text{W}}{\text{m}^2 \cdot \text{K}^4}\right)[(900\,\text{K})^4 - (650\,\text{K})^4]}{\left(\frac{1}{0.5} + \frac{2}{0.15} + \frac{1}{0.8} - 2\right)}$$

$$= 1856.9\ \text{W/m}^2 \quad (1900\ \text{W/m}^2)$$

The answer is (C).

9. The Reynolds number is

$$\text{Re}_L = \frac{\rho u_\infty L}{\mu} = \frac{u_\infty L}{\nu}$$

$$= \frac{\left(0.45\ \frac{\text{m}}{\text{s}}\right)(1\ \text{m})}{20.92 \times 10^{-6}\ \frac{\text{m}^2}{\text{s}}}$$

$$= 2.15 \times 10^4$$

Since Re_L is less than 10^5, the flow over the flat plate is laminar. Use a Nusselt correlation.

$$\overline{\text{Nu}}_L = \frac{\bar{h}L}{k} = 0.6640\,\text{Re}_L^{1/2}\text{Pr}^{1/3}$$

$$= (0.6640)(2.15 \times 10^4)^{1/2}(0.7)^{1/3}$$

$$= 86.47$$

$$\bar{h} = \overline{\text{Nu}}_L\left(\frac{k}{L}\right)$$

$$= (86.47)\left(\frac{30 \times 10^{-3}\ \frac{\text{W}}{\text{m}\cdot\text{K}}}{1\ \text{m}}\right)$$

$$= 2.59\ \text{W/m}^2\cdot\text{K} \quad (2.6\ \text{W/m}^2\cdot\text{K})$$

The answer is (A).

10. Calculate the absolute temperatures of the sphere and the surroundings.

$$T_1 = 750^\circ\text{C} + 273^\circ = 1023\text{K}$$
$$T_2 = -20^\circ\text{C} + 273^\circ = 253\text{K}$$

Use the equation for net energy exchange between two bodies when the body is small compared to its surroundings.

$$\dot{Q}_{12} = \varepsilon\sigma A(T_1^4 - T_2^4)$$

The surface area of a sphere is

$$A = 4\pi r^2 = \pi d^2$$

Heat Transfer

Solve for the emissivity of the sphere.

$$\varepsilon = \frac{\dot{Q}_{12}}{\sigma A (T_1^4 - T_2^4)} = \frac{\dot{Q}_{12}}{\sigma \pi d^2 (T_1^4 - T_2^4)}$$

$$= \frac{(12 \ \text{W}) \left(100 \ \dfrac{\text{cm}}{\text{m}} \right)^2}{\left(5.67 \times 10^{-8} \ \dfrac{\text{W}}{\text{m}^2 \cdot \text{K}^4} \right) \pi (2 \ \text{cm})^2}$$

$$\times \left((1023\text{K})^4 - (253\text{K})^4 \right)$$

$$= 0.154 \quad (0.15)$$

The answer is (A).

Heat Transfer

19 Conduction

Nomenclature

A	area	m^2
Bi	Biot number	–
c_p	specific heat	J/kg·K
G	heat generation rate	W/m^3
h	coefficient of heat transfer	W/m^2·K
h	enthalpy	kJ/kg
k	thermal conductivity	W/m·K
L	thickness	m
m	factor for fins equal to $\sqrt{hP/kA_c}$	1/m
m	mass	kg
P	perimeter	m
$\dot{q}$	heat transfer per unit area	W/m^2
Q	heat energy	J
$\dot{Q}$	rate of heat transfer	W
r	radius	m
R	thermal resistance	K/W
t	thickness	m
t	time	s
T	temperature	K
U	overall coefficient of heat transfer	W/m^2·K
V	volume	m^3
w	width	m
x	distance	m

Symbols

β	decay constant (reciprocal of time constant)	1/s
ρ	mass density	kg/m^3
τ	time constant	s

Subscripts

0	initial
1	inner
2	outer
b	base
c	cross section or corrected
cr	critical
i	initial, inner, or i^{th} layer
m	mean
o	outside
p	pressure
s	solids or surface
th	thermal
∞	bulk fluid

1. INTRODUCTION TO CONDUCTIVE HEAT TRANSFER

Conduction is the flow of heat through solids or stationary fluids. Thermal conductance in metallic solids is due to molecular vibrations within the metallic crystalline lattice and movement of free valence electrons through the lattice. Insulating solids, which have fewer free electrons, conduct heat primarily by the agitation of adjacent atoms vibrating about their equilibrium positions. This vibrational mode of heat transfer is several orders of magnitude less efficient than conduction by free electrons.

In stationary liquids, heat is transmitted by longitudinal vibrations, similar to sound waves. The *net transport theory* explains heat transfer through gases. Hot molecules move faster than cold molecules. Hot molecules travel to cold areas with greater frequency than cold molecules travel to hot areas.

Determining heat transfer by conduction can be an easy task if sufficient simplifying assumptions are made. Major discrepancies can arise, however, when the simplifying assumptions are not met. The following assumptions are commonly made in simple problems.

- The heat transfer is steady-state.

- The heat path is one-dimensional. (Objects are infinite in one or more directions and do not have any end effects.)

- The heat path has a constant area.

- The heat path consists of a homogeneous material with constant conductivity.

- The heat path consists of an isotropic material.[1]

- There is no internal heat generation.

Many real heat transfer cases violate one or more of these assumptions. Unfortunately, problems with closed-form solutions (suitable for working by hand) are in the minority. More complex problems must be solved by appropriate iterative, graphical, or numerical methods.[2]

Equation 19.1: Fourier's Law of Conduction

$$\dot{Q} = -kA\frac{dT}{dx} \qquad 19.1$$

Values

Table 19.1 Typical Thermal Conductivities at 0°C

substance	k W/m·K
silver	419
copper	388
aluminum	202
brass	97
steel (1% C)	47
lead	35
ice	2.2
glass	1.1
concrete	0.87
water	0.55
fiberglass	0.052
cork	0.043
air	0.024

Description

The steady-state heat transfer by conduction through a flat slab is specified by *Fourier's law*, Eq. 19.1. Fourier's law is written with a minus sign to indicate that the heat flow is opposite the direction of the thermal gradient.

The *thermal conductivity* (also known as the *thermal conductance*), k, is a measure of the rate at which a substance transfers thermal energy through a unit thickness.[3] Units of thermal conductivity are W/m·K or W·cm/m²·K. The conductivity of a substance should not be confused with the *overall conductivity*, U, of an object. Table 19.1 lists representative thermal conductivities for commonly encountered substances.

2. THERMAL RESISTANCE

Equation 19.2: Thermal Resistance, Plane Wall

$$R = \frac{L}{kA} \qquad 19.2$$

Description

For a plane wall, the thermal resistance depends on the thickness (path length), L, and the thermal conductivity, k. Thermal resistance is usually expressed per unit of exposed surface area, as Eq. 19.2 indicates.

Example

Concrete has a thermal conductivity of 1.4 W/m·°C. What is most nearly the thermal resistance of a 20 cm thick concrete wall with an exposed face area of 1 m²?

(A) 0.14 °C/W

(B) 0.28 °C/W

(C) 1.4 °C/W

(D) 7.0 °C/W

Solution

Use Eq. 19.2.

$$R = \frac{L}{kA} = \frac{0.2 \text{ m}}{\left(1.4 \ \frac{\text{W}}{\text{m·°C}}\right)(1 \text{ m}^2)}$$
$$= 0.143 \text{ °C/W} \quad (0.14 \text{ °C/W})$$

The answer is (A).

Equation 19.3 and Eq. 19.4: Resistance in Series

$$\dot{Q} = \frac{\Delta T}{R_{\text{total}}} \qquad 19.3$$

$$R_{\text{total}} = \sum R \qquad 19.4$$

Variation

$$\dot{Q} = \frac{T_1 - T_{n+1}}{R_{\text{total}}} = \frac{A(T_1 - T_{n+1})}{\displaystyle\sum_{i=1}^{n} \frac{L_i}{k_i}}$$

---

[1]Examples of *anisotropic materials*, materials whose heat transfer properties depend on the direction of heat flow, are crystals, plywood and other laminated sheets, and the core elements of some electrical transformers.
[2]Finite-difference methods are commonly used.
[3]Another (less-encountered) meaning for *conductivity* is the reciprocal of thermal resistance (conductivity = kA/L).

Description

For heat transfer through multiple layers (for example, a layered wall or cylinder with several layers of different insulation), each layer is considered a series resistance. The sum of the individual thermal resistances is the total thermal resistance. For example, in Fig. 19.1, the total thermal resistance is given by the sum of the two individual resistances. Typical units are K/W.

Figure 19.1 Composite Slab (Plane) Wall

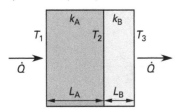

Equation 19.5: Thermal Resistance, Cylindrical Wall

$$R = \frac{\ln\left(\dfrac{r_2}{r_1}\right)}{2\pi k L} \qquad 19.5$$

Description

Equation 19.5 gives the thermal resistance for a cylindrical wall.

Example

A 0.5 m long cast iron pipe has an inner diameter of 6 cm and an outer diameter of 6.5 cm. The thermal conductivity of cast iron is 80 W/m·K. The thermal resistance of the pipe is most nearly

(A) 0.000080 K/W

(B) 0.00032 K/W

(C) 0.00064 K/W

(D) 0.0010 K/W

Solution

The thermal resistance is calculated using Eq. 19.5.

$$R = \frac{\ln\left(\dfrac{r_2}{r_1}\right)}{2\pi k L} = \frac{\ln\dfrac{6.5 \text{ cm}}{6 \text{ cm}}}{(2\pi)\left(80 \dfrac{\text{W}}{\text{m·K}}\right)(0.5 \text{ m})}$$

$$= 0.000318 \text{ K/W} \quad (0.00032 \text{ K/W})$$

The answer is (B).

Equation 19.6: Thermal Resistance, Film

$$R = \frac{1}{hA} \qquad 19.6$$

Description

Heat conducted through solids (walls) to an exposed surface is usually transferred to and removed by a moving fluid. For example, heat transmitted through a heat exchanger wall is removed by a moving coolant. Unless the fluid is extremely turbulent, the fluid molecules immediately adjacent to the exposed surface move much slower than molecules farther away. Molecules immediately adjacent to the wall may be stationary altogether. The fluid molecules that are affected by the exposed surface constitute a layer known as a *film*. The film has a thermal resistance just like any other layer.

Because the film thickness is not easily determined, the thermal resistance of a film is given by a *film coefficient* (*convective heat transfer coefficient* or *unit conductance*), h, with units of W/m²·K.

If the fluid is extremely turbulent, the thermal resistance will be small (that is, h will be very large). In such cases, the wall temperature is essentially the same as the fluid temperature.

Example

A wall has a film coefficient of 3500 W/m²·°C. What is most nearly the thermal resistance of a 1 m² area of the wall?

(A) 0.29 °C/kW

(B) 0.33 °C/kW

(C) 0.68 °C/kW

(D) 3.5 °C/kW

Solution

The thermal resistance is

$$R = \frac{1}{hA} = \frac{(1)\left(1000 \dfrac{\text{W}}{\text{kW}}\right)}{\left(3500 \dfrac{\text{W}}{\text{m}^2\text{·°C}}\right)(1 \text{ m}^2)}$$

$$= 0.286 \text{ °C/kW} \quad (0.29 \text{ °C/kW})$$

The answer is (A).

Heat Transfer

3. STEADY CONDUCTION THROUGH A PLANE WALL

Equation 19.7: Fourier's Law, Plane Wall

$$\dot{Q} = \frac{-kA(T_2 - T_1)}{L} \qquad 19.7$$

Variations

$$q_{12} = \frac{-k(T_2 - T_1)}{L} = \frac{k(T_1 - T_2)}{L}$$

$$Q_{12} = q_{12}A = \frac{kA(T_1 - T_2)}{L}$$

Description

On its own, heat always flows from a higher temperature to a lower temperature. The heat transfer from high-temperature point 1 to lower-temperature point 2 through an infinite plane of thickness L and homogeneous conductivity, k, is given by Eq. 19.7. (See Fig. 19.2.)

Figure 19.2 Plane Wall

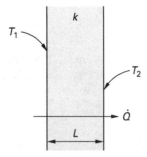

The temperature difference $T_2 - T_1$ is the *temperature gradient* or *thermal gradient*. Heat transfer is always positive. The minus sign in Eq. 19.7 indicates that the heat flow direction is opposite that of the thermal gradient. The direction of heat flow is obvious in most problems, so the minus sign is usually omitted, and the temperature difference is written as $T_1 - T_2$.[4]

Example

A 4 cm thick insulator ($k = 2 \times 10^{-4}$ cal/cm·s·°C) has an area of 1000 cm². If the temperatures on its two sides are 170°C and 50°C, and films are neglected, what is most nearly the heat transfer by conduction?

(A) 0.10 cal/s

(B) 1.2 cal/s

(C) 6.0 cal/s

(D) 30 cal/s

Solution

Use Eq. 19.7.

$$\dot{Q} = \frac{-kA(T_2 - T_1)}{L}$$

$$= \frac{-\left(2 \times 10^{-4}\ \dfrac{\text{cal}}{\text{cm·s·°C}}\right) \times (1000\ \text{cm}^2)(50°\text{C} - 170°\text{C})}{4\ \text{cm}}$$

$$= 6.0\ \text{cal/s}$$

The answer is (C).

Equation 19.8: Temperature at Intermediate Locations

$$\dot{Q} = \frac{T_1 - T_2}{R_A} = \frac{T_2 - T_3}{R_B} \qquad 19.8$$

Description

The temperature at any point on or within a simple or complex wall can be found if the heat transfer, q or Q, is known. The procedure is to calculate the thermal resistance up to the point of unknown temperature and then to solve for the temperature difference. Since one of the temperatures is known, the unknown temperature is found from the temperature difference.

4. CONDUCTION THROUGH A CYLINDRICAL WALL

The Fourier equation is based on a uniform path length and a constant cross-sectional area. If the heat flow is through an area that is not constant, the *logarithmic mean area*, A_m, should be used in place of the regular area. The log mean area should be used with heat transfer through thick pipe and cylindrical tank walls. (See Fig. 19.3.)

---

[4]The NCEES *FE Reference Handbook* (*NCEES Handbook*) is inconsistent in its inclusion of the minus sign. After Eq. 19.7, the *NCEES Handbook* abandons the convention for all subsequent heat transfer equations.

Figure 19.3 *Cylindrical Wall*

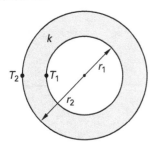

Equation 19.9: Fourier's Law, Cylindrical Wall

$$\dot{Q} = \frac{2\pi k L(T_1 - T_2)}{\ln\left(\dfrac{r_2}{r_1}\right)} \qquad 19.9$$

Variation

$$\dot{Q} = q A_m = \frac{k A_m (T_1 - T_2)}{r_2 - r_1}$$

Description

The overall radial heat transfer through an uninsulated hollow cylinder without films is given by Eq. 19.9. This equation disregards heat transfer from the ends and assumes that the length is sufficiently large so that the heat transfer is radial at all locations.

Example

An 8 m long pipe of 15 cm outside diameter is covered with 2 cm of insulation with a thermal conductivity of 0.09 W/m·K.

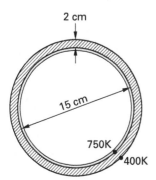

If the inner and outer temperatures of the insulation are 750K and 400K, respectively, what is most nearly the heat loss from the pipe?

(A) 4.5 kW

(B) 6.7 kW

(C) 8.5 kW

(D) 10 kW

Solution

Use Eq. 19.9.

$$
\begin{aligned}
\dot{Q} &= \frac{2\pi k L(T_1 - T_2)}{\ln\left(\dfrac{r_2}{r_1}\right)} \\[2mm]
&= \frac{(2\pi)\left(0.09\ \dfrac{\text{W}}{\text{m·K}}\right)(8\ \text{m})(750\text{K} - 400\text{K})}{\left(\ln\dfrac{9.5\ \text{cm}}{7.5\ \text{cm}}\right)\left(1000\ \dfrac{\text{W}}{\text{kW}}\right)} \\[2mm]
&= 6.698\ \text{kW} \quad (6.7\ \text{kW})
\end{aligned}
$$

The answer is (B).

Equation 19.10: Critical Insulation Radius

$$r_{\text{cr}} = \frac{k_{\text{insulation}}}{h_\infty} \qquad 19.10$$

Description

The addition of insulation to a bare pipe or wire increases the surface area. (See Fig. 19.4.) Adding insulation to a small-diameter pipe may actually increase the heat loss above bare-pipe levels. Adding insulation up to the *critical thickness* is dominated by the increase in surface area. Only adding insulation past the critical thickness will decrease heat loss.[5] The *critical radius* is usually very small (a few millimeters), and it is most relevant in the case of insulating thin wires. The critical radius, measured from the center of the pipe or wire, is given by Eq. 19.10. (See Fig. 19.5.) h_∞ is the film coefficient representing resistance to convective heat transfer.

---

[5]There is another, less commonly used, meaning for the term *critical thickness*: the thickest required insulation. In situations where the required insulation thickness is different for energy conservation, condensation control, personnel protection, and process temperature control, the "critical" thickness is the thickness that controls the design.

Figure 19.4 *Composite Cylinder (insulated pipe)*

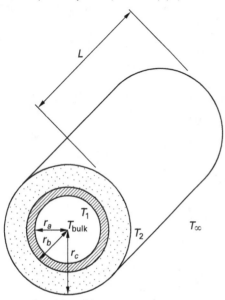

Figure 19.5 *Insulation Radius*

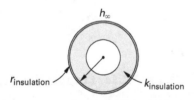

5. TRANSIENT CONDUCTION USING THE LUMPED CAPACITANCE MODEL

If the internal thermal resistance of a body is small in comparison to the external thermal resistance, the *lumped parameter method*, also known as the *lumped capacitance model*, can be used to approximate the transient (time-dependent) heat flow. This method is also referred to as *Newton's method*. Figure 19.6 shows the variables used in the lumped capacitance model.

Figure 19.6 *Variables Used in Transient Conduction*

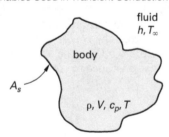

Equation 19.11: Biot Number

$$\mathrm{Bi} = \frac{hV}{kA_s} \ll 1 \qquad \text{19.11}$$

Variation

$$\mathrm{Bi} = \frac{hL_c}{k}$$

Description

The *Biot number*, Bi (also known as the *Biot modulus* and *transient modulus*), is a comparison of the internal thermal resistance to the external resistance of a body. If the Biot number is small (less than 0.1), the internal thermal resistance will be small, and the body temperature will be essentially uniform throughout, during heating or cooling. The length used to calculate the Biot number is the *characteristic length*, L_c, not an external body dimension.

$$L_c = \frac{V}{A_s}$$

Equation 19.12 Through Eq. 19.15: Constant Environment Temperature[6]

$$\dot{Q} = hA_s(T - T_\infty) = -\rho V c_p\left(\frac{dT}{dt}\right) \qquad \text{19.12}$$

$$T - T_\infty = (T_i - T_\infty)e^{-\beta t} \qquad \text{19.13}$$

$$\beta = \frac{hA_s}{\rho V c_p} \qquad \text{19.14}$$

$$\beta = \frac{1}{\tau} \qquad \text{19.15}$$

Description

Equation 19.12 gives the instantaneous heat transfer at a particular moment when the body temperature is known. Equation 19.13 gives the temperature of the body as a function of time. The time variable, t, starts at zero. Equation 19.15 shows that the factor β, known as the *decay constant* or *exponential frequency*, is the reciprocal of the time constant, τ.[7] As with many other engineering subjects, the *time constant* is the length of time required to vary (relax) the property (initial

---

[6]The *NCEES Handbook* refers to the case of a constant environment temperature as the "constant fluid temperature" case. This makes sense in the context of Fig. 19.6. The fluid is the substance surrounding the cooling body. Fluids include gases and are not necessarily liquids.

[7]τ is the time constant. As the reciprocal of the time constant, β has no other interpretation, and its significance is not explained in the *NCEES Handbook*. Equation 19.13 could have been written in terms of the time constant, rather than β. The most common symbol for the decay constant for all subjects is λ. Other symbols (e.g., b, k, r) are used, but the use of β is uncommon.

temperature differential in this case) by approximately 63.2%. Stated another way, the instantaneous temperature gradient will be approximately 36.8% of the initial temperature gradient after a duration equal to the time constant.

Equation 19.16: Total Heat Transferred

$$Q_{\text{total}} = \rho V c_p (T_i - T) \qquad \text{19.16}$$

Description

Although the rate of heat transfer varies with time in a transient condition, the energy change can be determined from the starting and ending conditions, independent of duration (time). Equation 19.16 calculates the total energy (heat) change as a function of the initial temperature, T_i, and final temperature, T. Since $T_i - T$ is a temperature difference, temperature can be expressed in any consistent scale. Absolute temperatures are not required.[8]

Example

A hot solid iron sphere (15 cm diameter) is placed in a bath of cold water. The initial temperature of the sphere is 433K. The sphere is cooled to 303K. The density of iron is 7.874 g/cm³, and the specific heat capacity of iron is 0.45 kJ/kg·K. The total heat transferred from the sphere to the water is most nearly

(A) 190 kJ

(B) 810 kJ

(C) 1000 kJ

(D) 1800 kJ

Solution

The volume of the iron sphere is

$$V = \frac{4}{3}\pi r^3$$
$$= \left(\frac{4}{3}\pi\right)\left(\frac{15 \text{ cm}}{2}\right)^3$$
$$= 1767.1 \text{ cm}^3$$

Use Eq. 19.16 to calculate the total heat transferred from the iron sphere to the water.

$$Q_{\text{total}} = \rho V c_p (T_i - T)$$

$$= \frac{\left(7.874 \ \dfrac{\text{g}}{\text{cm}^3}\right)(1767.1 \text{ cm}^3)\left(0.45 \ \dfrac{\text{kJ}}{\text{kg·K}}\right)}{1000 \ \dfrac{\text{g}}{\text{kg}}} \times (433\text{K} - 303\text{K})$$

$$= 814 \text{ kJ} \quad (810 \text{ kJ})$$

The answer is (B).

6. FINS

Fins (*extended surfaces*) are features that receive and move thermal energy by conduction along their lengths and widths prior to (in most cases) convective and radiative heat removal. They include simple fins, fin tubes, finned channels, and heat pipes. Some simple features (e.g., long wires) can be considered and evaluated as fins even though that is not their intended function.

Equation 19.17 Through Eq. 19.23: Heat Transfer, Fins

$$\dot{Q} = \sqrt{hPkA_c}\,(T_b - T_\infty)\tanh(mL_c) \qquad \text{19.17}$$

$$m = \sqrt{\frac{hP}{kA_c}} \qquad \text{19.18}$$

$$L_c = L + \frac{A_c}{P} \qquad \text{19.19}$$

$$P = 2w + 2t \quad \text{[rectangular]} \qquad \text{19.20}$$

$$A_c = wt \quad \text{[rectangular]} \qquad \text{19.21}$$

$$P = \pi D \quad \text{[pin]} \qquad \text{19.22}$$

$$A_c = \frac{\pi D^2}{4} \quad \text{[pin]} \qquad \text{19.23}$$

Heat Transfer

---

[8]The *NCEES Handbook* specifies that the initial body temperature is in kelvins. However, while use of absolute temperatures is an option, it is not a requirement.

Description

An external fin is attached at its base to a source of thermal energy at temperature T_b. The temperature across the face of the fin at any point along its length is assumed to be constant. The far-field temperature of the surrounding environment is T_∞. For *rectangular fins* (also known as *straight fins* or *longitudinal fins*), the cross-sectional area, A_c, is uniform and is given by Eq. 19.21.[9] (See Fig. 19.7.) For a *pin fin* (i.e., a fin with a circular cross section), cross-sectional area, A_c, is given by Eq. 19.23. (See Fig. 19.8.)

Figure 19.7 Rectangular Fin

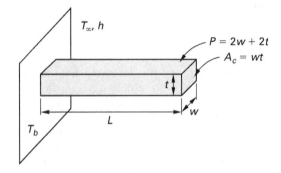

Figure 19.8 Pin Fin

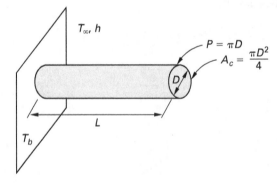

Most equations for heat transfer from a fin disregard the small amount of heat transfer from the exposed end. For that reason, the fin is assumed to possess an *adiabatic tip* or *insulated tip*. A simple approximation to the exact solution of a nonadiabatic tip can be obtained by replacing the actual fin length with a corrected length, as given in Eq. 19.19.[10]

Example

The base of a 1.2 cm × 1.2 cm × 25 cm long rectangular rod is maintained at 150°C by an electrical heating element. The conductivity of the rod is 140 W/m·K. The ambient air temperature is 27°C, and the average film coefficient is 9.4 W/m²·K. The fin has an adiabatic tip. What is most nearly the energy input required to maintain the base temperature?

(A) 0.10 W

(B) 1.7 W

(C) 9.7 W

(D) 100 W

Solution

From Eq. 19.20, the perimeter length is

$$2w + 2t = \frac{(2)(1.2 \text{ cm}) + (2)(1.2 \text{ cm})}{100 \ \dfrac{\text{cm}}{\text{m}}} = 0.048 \text{ m}$$

The cross-sectional area of the fin is

$$A_c = wt = \frac{(1.2 \text{ cm})(1.2 \text{ cm})}{\left(100 \ \dfrac{\text{cm}}{\text{m}}\right)^2}$$
$$= 0.000144 \text{ m}^2$$

Use Eq. 19.18.

$$m = \sqrt{\frac{hP}{kA_c}}$$
$$= \sqrt{\frac{\left(9.4 \ \dfrac{\text{W}}{\text{m}^2 \cdot \text{K}}\right)(0.048 \text{ m})}{\left(140 \ \dfrac{\text{W}}{\text{m} \cdot \text{K}}\right)(0.000144 \text{ m}^2)}}$$
$$= 4.73 \ 1/\text{m}$$

At steady state, the energy input is equal to the energy loss. Since the tip is adiabatic, it is not necessary to replace the actual length with the corrected length from Eq. 19.19.

---

[9](1) The *NCEES Handbook* refers to the substrate from which the fin extends as the "base," designated by subscript b. In common usage, the area or temperature of the "base of the fin" would refer to the fin. In NCEES usage, "base" refers to the substrate, not the fin at its attachment point. (2) The *NCEES Handbook* uses the subscript c to designate the kind of area (i.e., cross-sectional area, as differentiated from surface area) rather than the object (e.g., f for fin or b for the fin base).

[10]The *NCEES Handbook* is not consistent in its use of subscripts in Eq. 19.19. While c in A_c stands for "cross," c in L_c stands for "corrected."

From Eq. 19.17, the total heat loss is

$$\dot{Q} = \sqrt{hPkA_c}\ (T_b - T_\infty)\tanh(mL_c)$$

$$= \sqrt{\begin{array}{l}\left(9.4\ \dfrac{\text{W}}{\text{m}^2 \cdot \text{K}}\right)(0.048\ \text{m}) \\[2mm] \times\left(140\ \dfrac{\text{W}}{\text{m}\cdot\text{K}}\right)(0.000144\ \text{m}^2)\end{array}}$$

$$\times(150°\text{C} - 27°\text{C})\tanh\left(\left(4.73\ \dfrac{1}{\text{m}}\right)\left(\dfrac{25\ \text{cm}}{100\ \dfrac{\text{cm}}{\text{m}}}\right)\right)$$

$$= 9.72\ \text{W}\quad(9.7\ \text{W})$$

The answer is (C).

Heat Transfer

20 Convection

Nomenclature

A	area	m^2
B	separation distance	m
c_p	specific heat	J/kg·K
C	constant	–
C	heat capacity rate	W/K
D	diameter[a]	m
F	correction factor for mean temperature difference	–
g	gravitational acceleration, 9.81[b]	m/s^2
Gr	Grashof number	–
h	film coefficient	$W/m^2 \cdot K$
h_{fg}	latent heat of vaporization	J/kg
k	thermal conductivity	W/m·K
L	characteristic length	m
m	exponent	–
n	exponent	–
NTU	number of transfer units	–
Nu	Nusselt number	–
Pr	Prandtl number	–
$\dot{q}$	heat transfer per unit area	W/m^2
$\dot{Q}$	heat transfer rate[c]	W
R	thermal resistance	$m^2 \cdot K/W$
Ra	Rayleigh number	–
Re	Reynolds number	–
T	temperature	K
U	overall coefficient of heat transfer	$W/m^2 \cdot K$

v	velocity	m/s
x	distance	m

[a]The *NCEES FE Reference Handbook* (*NCEES Handbook*) uses the symbol D to designate both inside (see Eq. 20.9) and outside (see Eq. 20.2, Eq. 20.6, and Eq. 20.8) diameters. The context must be evaluated to determine the exact meaning.
[b]g also has a value of 1.27×10^8 m/h^2.
[c]The *NCEES Handbook* designates the heat transfer "rate" as $\dot{Q}$, with the top dot used to designate a rate per unit time. (This is known as *Newton's notation*.) While it is not a universal practice, modern usage dispenses with both the "rate" term in the name and the top dot in the symbol.

Symbols

α	thermal diffusivity	m^2/s
β	coefficient of volumetric expansion	1/K
ε	heat exchanger effectiveness	–
θ	angle	deg
μ	absolute viscosity*	kg/s·m
ν	kinematic viscosity	m^2/s
ρ	mass density	kg/m^3
σ	surface tension	N/m

*(1) The use of mass units in viscosity values is typical in the subject of convective heat transfer. (2) Most data compilations give fluid viscosity in units of seconds. In the United States, heat transfer is traditionally given on a per hour basis. Therefore, a conversion factor of 3600 is needed when calculating dimensionless numbers from table data. (3) The units kg/s·m are equivalent to N·s/m^2 or Pa·s.

Subscripts

b	boiling or bulk
c	cold or condensing
C	cooling
Ci	cold, in
Co	cold, out
D	diameter
e	excess
f	fluid, fowling, or friction
H	hot or hydraulic
Hi	hot, in
Ho	hot, out
i	inside
l	liquid
L	length
lm	log mean
m	mean
o	outside

Heat Transfer

r	radiation
s	surface
sat	saturated
v	vapor
w	wall or wire
∞	at infinity or free stream

1. INTRODUCTION TO CONVECTION

Convection is the removal of heat from a surface by a fluid. *Forced convection* is the removal of heat from a surface by a fluid resulting from external surface forces, such as a pump or fan. *Natural convection* (also known as *free convection*) is the removal of heat from a surface by a fluid that moves vertically under the influence of a density gradient.

Equation 20.1: Newton's Law of Cooling

$$\dot{Q} = hA(T_w - T_\infty) \qquad 20.1$$

Variation

$$\dot{Q} = \dot{q}A = hA(T_s - T_\infty)$$

Description

Equation 20.1, Newton's law of cooling, is the basic equation used to calculate the steady-state convective heat transfer in both heating and cooling configurations. The *film coefficient* (*heat transfer coefficient*), h, is seldom known to great accuracy.[1] (See Table 20.1.) The average film coefficient, $\bar{h}$, is used where there are variations over the heat transfer surface.[2]

In Eq. 20.1, T_∞ is the *bulk temperature* of the environment (air, gas, surrounding liquid, etc.), and T_w is the instantaneous temperature of the cooling body's surface.[3]

Values

Table 20.1 *Typical Film Coefficients for Natural Convection**

	h (W/m²·K)
no change in phase	
still air	5.0–25.0
condensing	
steam	
horizontal surface	9600–24 400
vertical	4000–11 300
organic solvents	850–2800
ammonia	2800–5700
evaporating	
water	4500–11 300
organic solvents	550–1700
ammonia	1100–2300

*Values outside these ranges have been observed. However, these ranges are typical of those encountered in industrial processes.

Example

An object is cooled by a circulating water bath. At a particular moment, the surface temperature of the body is 373K, while the bulk temperature of the water bath is 353K. The convective film coefficient is 350 W/m²·K. The object has an exposed surface area of 1 m². Most nearly, what is the instantaneous rate of heat transfer from the object?

(A) 3.5 kW

(B) 5.0 kW

(C) 7.0 kW

(D) 8.2 kW

Solution

Using Eq. 20.1, the rate of heat transfer is

$$\dot{Q} = hA(T_w - T_\infty)$$
$$= \frac{\left(350 \; \dfrac{\text{W}}{\text{m}^2 \cdot \text{K}}\right)(1 \; \text{m}^2)(373\,\text{K} - 353\text{K})}{1000 \; \dfrac{\text{W}}{\text{kW}}}$$
$$= 7.0 \; \text{kW}$$

The answer is (C).

---

[1]An error of up to 25% can be expected.

[2]Though $\bar{h}$ has traditionally been used in books on the subject of heat transfer and is used in the *NCEES Handbook*, most modern books use the symbol h. The fact that the film coefficient is an inaccurate, average value is implicit.

[3]The *NCEES Handbook* uses the subscript w to designate "wall." However, Newton's law of cooling does not primarily apply to heat transfer through a wall or even heat transfer from a surface. Newton's law of cooling applies to a cooling (body) object. The "wall" designation might also imply that the temperature is constant. However, the body temperature changes with time. Such is the entire purpose of Newton's law of cooling: to specify the heat transfer and temperature as functions of time. It is common to designate the body temperature at a particular moment in time simply with the variable T. If the temperature of the body is not uniform throughout, the symbol T_s can be used to designate a surface temperature.

2. NUSSELT NUMBER

Equation 20.2: Nusselt Number, Cylinder in Crossflow

$$\overline{\mathrm{Nu}}_D = \frac{\bar{h}D}{k} = C\mathrm{Re}_D^n \mathrm{Pr}^{1/3} \qquad \textit{20.2}$$

Values

Table 20.2 Values of C and n for a Known Reynolds Number, Re_D

Re_D	C	n
1–4	0.989	0.330
4–40	0.911	0.385
40–4000	0.683	0.466
4000–40,000	0.193	0.618
40,000–250,000	0.0266	0.805

Description

The *Nusselt number*, Nu, is defined by Eq. 20.2. The subscript D indicates that the correlation is based on the outside diameter of the cylinder, not some other characteristic dimension. The Nusselt number is sometimes written with a subscript (e.g., Nu_h or Nu_f) to indicate that the fluid properties are evaluated at the film temperature. Since the flow velocity, heat transfer rate, film resistance, and other fluid properties are not the same everywhere around the periphery of the cylinder, the overbars are used to designate average values.

For a cylinder (for example, a tube or wire) in crossflow, Eq. 20.2 can be used with any fluid to calculate the film coefficient.[4] The fluid properties are evaluated at the film temperature. The entire surface area of the tube is used when calculating the heat transfer.

Equation 20.2 can be simplified for air since $\mathrm{Pr}^{1/3} \approx 1.00$. This modified equation is known as the *Hilbert-Morgan equation*.

Values of C and n are found from Table 20.2 when Re_D is known.

Example

Water at 25°C flows perpendicularly over a long, hot pipe of 2.9 cm outside diameter. The water has an average convection film coefficient of 4900 W/m²·K and a thermal conductivity of 610×10^{-3} W/m·K. The Nusselt number is most nearly

(A) 230

(B) 290

(C) 350

(D) 410

Solution

The Nusselt number can be calculated with Eq. 20.2.

$$\overline{\mathrm{Nu}}_D = \frac{\bar{h}D}{k}$$

$$= \frac{\left(4900 \ \dfrac{\mathrm{W}}{\mathrm{m}^2 \cdot \mathrm{K}}\right)(2.9 \ \mathrm{cm})}{\left(610 \times 10^{-3} \ \dfrac{\mathrm{W}}{\mathrm{m} \cdot \mathrm{K}}\right)\left(100 \ \dfrac{\mathrm{cm}}{\mathrm{m}}\right)}$$

$$= 232.95 \quad (230)$$

The answer is (A).

3. PRANDTL NUMBER

Equation 20.3: Prandtl Number

$$\mathrm{Pr} = \frac{c_p \mu}{k} \qquad \textit{20.3}$$

Description

The dimensionless *Prandtl number*, Pr, is defined by Eq. 20.3. It represents the ratio of momentum diffusion to thermal diffusion. For gases, the values used in calculating the Prandtl number do not vary significantly with temperature, and so neither does the Prandtl number itself. The values used are for the fluid, not for the surface material.

Example

For air at a temperature of 42°C, the heat capacity is 990 J/kg·K, the viscosity is 1.9×10^{-5} kg/s·m, and the thermal conductivity is 0.028 W/m·K. What is most nearly the Prandtl number?

(A) 0.59

(B) 0.67

(C) 0.75

(D) 0.83

---

[4]There are more sophisticated correlations.

Solution

Using Eq. 20.3, the Prandtl number is

$$\mathrm{Pr} = \frac{c_p \mu}{k}$$

$$= \frac{\left(990 \ \frac{\mathrm{J}}{\mathrm{kg \cdot K}}\right)\left(1.9 \times 10^{-5} \ \frac{\mathrm{kg}}{\mathrm{s \cdot m}}\right)}{0.028 \ \frac{\mathrm{W}}{\mathrm{m \cdot K}}}$$

$$= 0.67$$

The answer is (B).

4. RAYLEIGH NUMBER

The dimensionless *Rayleigh number* is the product of the Grashof and Prandtl numbers.[5] It is used as an indicator of the primary heat transfer mechanism. When the Rayleigh number is less than some critical value (specific to the fluid, and usually determined by experimentation), heat transfer is primary by conduction. When the Rayleigh number is more than the critical value, heat transfer is primarily by convection. (The convective flow can be either laminar or turbulent.) The symbol can be written with a subscripted variable (e.g., Ra_L) designating the characteristic dimension with which the critical values have been correlated. For example, the length of a plate (see Eq. 20.4) is generally used, rather than its width. For a cylinder (see Eq. 20.6), the diameter is used.

Equation 20.4 and Eq. 20.5: Rayleigh Number, Flat Plate, Natural Convection

$$\mathrm{Ra}_L = \frac{g\beta(T_s - T_\infty)L^3}{\nu^2}\mathrm{Pr} \qquad 20.4$$

$$\beta = \frac{2}{T_s + T_\infty} \qquad 20.5$$

Variation

$$\mathrm{Ra} = \frac{L^3 g\beta\rho^2(T_s - T_\infty)c_p}{k\mu}$$

Description

Equation 20.4 gives the Rayleigh number for a vertical flat plate in a stationary fluid[6] with *characteristic length, L*.[7] The *coefficient of volumetric expansion, β*, for ideal gases is the reciprocal of the absolute film temperature. Gravitational acceleration, g, and viscosity, ν, must have the same unit of time in order to make Eq. 20.4 dimensionless.

For an ideal gas, the *coefficient of thermal expansion, β* (also known as the *volumetric coefficient of expansion*), can be found using Eq. 20.5. The temperatures used in Eq. 20.5 must be absolute temperatures.[8]

Equation 20.6: Rayleigh Number, Cylinder, Natural Convection

$$\mathrm{Ra}_D = \frac{g\beta(T_s - T_\infty)D^3}{\nu^2}\mathrm{Pr} \qquad 20.6$$

Description

For a horizontal cylinder in a stationary fluid, the Rayleigh number can be found using Eq. 20.6.

Example

A horizontal pipe has a diameter of 0.21 m and an outer surface temperature of 350K. The pipe is surrounded by stationary water with a bulk temperature of 300K. For water at 300K, the kinematic viscosity is 1.6×10^{-5} m²/s. The coefficient of thermal expansion is 0.0028 K⁻¹, and the Prandtl number is 0.72. What is most nearly the Rayleigh number?

(A) 2.2×10^7

(B) 2.9×10^7

(C) 3.3×10^7

(D) 3.6×10^7

---

[5](1) In Eq. 20.4, the *NCEES Handbook* recognizes the Prandtl number but not the *Grashof number*. Rather than define the Grashof number (as it did with the Reynolds, Nusselt, Prandtl, and Rayleigh numbers), the *NCEES Handbook* elects to present a combination of variables, $g\beta(T_s-T_\infty)L^3/\nu^2$. This is equivalent to, and generally presented as, the Grashof number, Gr. (2) The Grashof number relates the buoyancy and viscosity of the fluid, while the Prandtl number relates the momentum diffusivity and thermal diffusivity.
[6]The *NCEES Handbook* is not consistent in its designation for "surface." While the subscript w is used in Eq. 20.1 for the surface of an object (wall), Eq. 20.4 and Eq. 20.5 use subscript s.
[7]The length of the side of a square, the mean length of a rectangle, and 90% of the diameter of a circle have historically been used as the *characteristic length*. However, the ratio of surface area to perimeter gives better agreement with experimental data.
[8]The *NCEES Handbook* is not explicit about the temperature at which β, ν, and Pr are evaluated. Since β is the reciprocal of the film temperature, Eq. 20.5 implicitly defines the *film temperature* as the average of the surface and bulk fluid temperatures. This also implicitly identifies the temperature at which other properties are evaluated. Since the *NCEES Handbook* does not provide sufficient tables, it is logical to conclude that the film temperature is irrelevant, because on the exam, all necessary fluid data will be provided within a problem.

Solution

The Rayleigh number can be calculated using Eq. 20.6.

$$\mathrm{Ra}_D = \frac{g\beta(T_s - T_\infty)D^3}{\nu^2}\mathrm{Pr}$$

$$= \left(\frac{\left(9.81\ \dfrac{\mathrm{m}}{\mathrm{s}^2}\right)\left(0.0028\ \dfrac{1}{\mathrm{K}}\right)}{\times(350\mathrm{K} - 300\mathrm{K})(0.21\ \mathrm{m})^3}{\left(1.6 \times 10^{-5}\ \dfrac{\mathrm{m}^2}{\mathrm{s}}\right)^2}\right)(0.72)$$

$$= 3.577 \times 10^7 \quad (3.6 \times 10^7)$$

The answer is (D).

5. REYNOLDS NUMBER

The Reynolds number is used to determine which of the three flow regimes is applicable. Laminar flow over smooth flat plates occurs for Reynolds numbers up to approximately 2×10^5; turbulent flow exists for Reynolds numbers greater than approximately 3×10^6.[9] Transition flow is in between. The distance from the leading edge at which turbulent flow is initially experienced is determined from the *critical Reynolds number*, commonly taken as $\mathrm{Re} = 5 \times 10^5$ for smooth flat plates, though the actual value is highly dependent on surface roughness. Distance, x, is measured from the leading edge.

The free-stream velocity is always zero with natural convection, so the traditional Reynolds number is also always zero. The Grashof and Rayleigh numbers take the place of determining whether flow is laminar or turbulent.[10] The film Reynolds number is used to determine whether condensation is turbulent.

Equation 20.7: Reynolds Number, Flat Plate

$$\mathrm{Re}_L = \frac{\rho \mathrm{v}_\infty L}{\mu} \qquad \text{20.7}$$

Description

Use Eq. 20.7 to find the Reynolds number for a flat plate of length L in parallel flow.[11]

Example

20°C air flows at 0.75 m/s over and parallel to a wide flat plate 1.7 m long. At 20°C, the density of air is 1.2 kg/m³, and the absolute viscosity is 1.8×10^{-5} kg/m·s. What is most nearly the Reynolds number for the purpose of forced convection?

(A) 12 000

(B) 23 000

(C) 47 000

(D) 85 000

Solution

The Reynolds number can be calculated using Eq. 20.7.

$$\mathrm{Re}_L = \frac{\rho \mathrm{v}_\infty L}{\mu}$$

$$= \frac{\left(1.2\ \dfrac{\mathrm{kg}}{\mathrm{m}^3}\right)\left(0.75\ \dfrac{\mathrm{m}}{\mathrm{s}}\right)(1.7\ \mathrm{m})}{1.8 \times 10^{-5}\ \dfrac{\mathrm{kg}}{\mathrm{m}\cdot\mathrm{s}}}$$

$$= 85\,000$$

The answer is (D).

Equation 20.8: Reynolds Number, Cylinder

$$\mathrm{Re}_D = \frac{\rho \mathrm{v}_\infty D}{\mu} \qquad \text{20.8}$$

Description

Use Eq. 20.8 to calculate the Reynolds number for a cylinder of outside diameter D in crossflow.

Example

Water with a bulk temperature of 27°C flows over and across a long, hot pipe of 4 cm diameter at a velocity of 1.2 m/s. At 27°C, the density of water is 1.0×10^3 kg/m³,

---

[9]Turbulent flow can begin at Reynolds numbers less than 3×10^5 if the plate is rough. This discussion assumes the plate is smooth.

[10]Rising air nevertheless has a velocity. The critical Reynolds number for laminar flow of air is approximately 550 (corresponding to a Grashof number of 10^9).

[11]The *NCEES Handbook* is inconsistent in the variable used for velocity in the definition of Reynolds number. The *NCEES Handbook* uses lowercase roman v in the Fluid Mechanics section, uppercase roman V in the Moody diagram, lowercase italic v in the Environmental Engineering section, and uppercase italic V in the Chemical Engineering section. Inconsistent with any of those, the *NCEES Handbook*'s verison of Eq. 20.7, adopts the (common heat transfer) convention of using u_∞ as yet another velocity variable for the Reynolds number. This book uses lowercase roman v for velocity.

and the absolute viscosity is 850×10^{-6} kg/s·m. What is most nearly the Reynolds number?

(A) 44 000

(B) 51 000

(C) 56 000

(D) 61 000

Solution

The Reynolds number can be calculated using Eq. 20.8.

$$\mathrm{Re}_D = \frac{\rho \mathrm{v}_\infty D}{\mu}$$

$$= \frac{\left(1.0 \times 10^3 \; \frac{\mathrm{kg}}{\mathrm{m}^3}\right)\left(1.2 \; \frac{\mathrm{m}}{\mathrm{s}}\right)(4 \; \mathrm{cm})}{\left(850 \times 10^{-6} \; \frac{\mathrm{kg}}{\mathrm{s \cdot m}}\right)\left(100 \; \frac{\mathrm{cm}}{\mathrm{m}}\right)}$$

$$= 56\,471 \quad (56\,000)$$

The answer is (C).

Equation 20.9: Reynolds Number, Internal Flow

$$\mathrm{Re}_D = \frac{\rho \mathrm{v}_m D}{\mu} \qquad \text{20.9}$$

Description

Equation 20.9 is the traditional definition of the Reynolds number for internal flow within a circular channel. D is the internal diameter. v_m is defined as the average (mean) fluid velocity. The average velocity is essentially equal to the bulk velocity if the flow is fully turbulent. If the flow is fully developed laminar, the average velocity is 50% of the maximum velocity.

Example

Water at 25°C flows at 3.6 m/s in a pipe with an internal diameter of 0.10 m. The water has a density of 1.0×10^3 kg/m^3 and an absolute viscosity of 850×10^{-6} kg/s·m. What is most nearly the Reynolds number?

(A) 35 000

(B) 87 000

(C) 260 000

(D) 420 000

Solution

The Reynolds number for internal flow can be calculated using Eq. 20.9.

$$\mathrm{Re}_D = \frac{\rho \mathrm{v}_m D}{\mu}$$

$$= \frac{\left(1.0 \times 10^3 \; \frac{\mathrm{kg}}{\mathrm{m}^3}\right)\left(3.6 \; \frac{\mathrm{m}}{\mathrm{s}}\right)(0.10 \; \mathrm{m})}{850 \times 10^{-6} \; \frac{\mathrm{kg}}{\mathrm{s \cdot m}}}$$

$$= 423\,529 \quad (420\,000)$$

The answer is (D).

6. NATURAL CONVECTION

Natural convection (also known as *free convection*) is the removal of heat from a surface by a fluid that moves vertically under the influence of a density gradient. As a fluid warms, it becomes lighter and rises from the heating surface. The fluid is acted on by buoyant and gravitational forces. The fluid does not have a component of motion parallel to the surface.[12]

Heat transfer by natural convection is attractive from an engineering design standpoint because no motors, fans, pumps, or other equipment with moving parts are required. However, the transfer surface must be much larger than it would be with forced convection.[13]

7. NUSSELT EQUATION

The *Nusselt equation* and correlations of its form are often used to find the film coefficients for convective heating and cooling.

Equation 20.10: Nusselt Equation, Vertical Flat Plate or Cylinder

$$\bar{h} = C\left(\frac{k}{L}\right)\mathrm{Ra}_L^n \qquad \text{20.10}$$

Variation

$$\mathrm{Nu} = \frac{\bar{h}L}{k} = C\mathrm{Ra}^n$$

---

[12]Rotating spheres and cylinders and vertical plane walls are special categories of convective heat transfer where the fluid has a component of relative motion parallel to the heat transfer surface.

[13]Natural convection requires approximately 2 to 10 times more surface area than does forced convection.

Values

Table 20.3 *Values of C and n for Vertical Plate or Cylinder in Natural Convection*

range of Ra_L	C	n
10^4–10^9	0.59	1/4
10^9–10^{13}	0.10	1/3

Description

For a vertical flat plate or a large diameter vertical cylinder in a stationary fluid, the film coefficient can be found using Eq. 20.10.

For laminar convection $(1000 < Ra < 10^9)$, n has a value of approximately $1/4$. For turbulent convection $(Ra > 10^9)$, n is approximately $1/3$. For sublaminar convection $(Ra < 1000)$, n is less than $1/4$ (typically taken as $1/5$), and graphical solutions are commonly used.

The values of the dimensionless empirical constants C and n can be used with all fluids and any consistent systems of units. Table 20.3 is limited in application to single heat transfer surfaces (for example, a single tube or a single plate).

The thermal conductivity, k, in Eq. 20.10 is for the transfer fluid, not for the surface (wall), and it is evaluated at the film temperature.

Example

The Rayleigh number for a large diameter vertical pipe 1.7 m high is 1.4×10^5. Natural convection occurs in the laminar regime. The thermal conductivity of the pipe is 0.028 W/m·K. What is most nearly the average heat transfer coefficient?

(A) 0.10 W/m²·K

(B) 0.13 W/m²·K

(C) 0.19 W/m²·K

(D) 0.27 W/m²·K

Solution

Natural convection in the laminar regime is characterized by a Rayleigh number less than 10^9. From Table 20.3, $C = 0.59$, and $n = 1/4$ (0.25).

Using Eq. 20.10, the average heat transfer coefficient is

$$\bar{h} = C\left(\frac{k}{L}\right)Ra_L^n$$

$$= (0.59)\left(\frac{0.028 \ \frac{W}{m\cdot K}}{1.7 \ m}\right)(1.4 \times 10^5)^{0.25}$$

$$= 0.1880 \ W/m^2\cdot K \quad (0.19 \ W/m^2\cdot K)$$

The answer is (C).

Equation 20.11: Nusselt Equation, Horizontal Cylinder

$$\bar{h} = C\left(\frac{k}{D}\right)Ra_D^n \qquad 20.11$$

Values

Table 20.4 *Values of C and n for Horizontal Cylinder in Natural Convection*

Ra_D	C	n
10^{-3}–10^2	1.02	0.148
10^2–10^4	0.850	0.188
10^4–10^7	0.480	0.250
10^7–10^{12}	0.125	0.333

Description

For a horizontal cylinder in a stationary fluid, the film coefficient can be found using Eq. 20.11. Values of C and n are found from Table 20.4.

8. CONDENSING VAPOR

When a vapor condenses on a cooler surface, the condensate forms a thin layer on the surface. This layer insulates the surface and creates a thermal resistance. However, if the condensate falls or flows from the surface (as it would from a horizontal tube), the condensate also removes thermal energy from the surface. Film coefficients are relatively high (on the order of 11.5 kW/m²·K to 22.7 kW/m²·K).[14]

Filmwise condensation occurs when the condensing surface is smooth and free from impurities.[15] A continuous film of condensate covers the entire surface. The film flows smoothly down over the surface under the action of gravity and eventually falls off. However, if the surface contains

---

[14]A film coefficient of 11.5 kW/m²·K is routinely assumed as a first estimate for condensation of steam on the outside of tubes.
[15]Filmwise condensation can always be expected with clean steel and aluminum tubes under ordinary conditions, as well as with heavily contaminated tubes. Dropwise condensation generally requires smooth surfaces with minute amounts of contamination, rather than rough surfaces. Since dropwise condensation can be expected only under carefully controlled conditions, the assumption of filmwise condensation is generally warranted.

impurities or irregularities that prevent complete wetting, the film will be discontinuous, a condition known as *dropwise condensation*.[16]

Equation 20.12: Condensation, Outside Horizontal Tubes

$$\overline{\mathrm{Nu}}_D = \frac{\bar{h}D}{k} = 0.729 \left[\frac{\rho_l^2 g h_{fg} D^3}{\mu_l k_l (T_{\mathrm{sat}} - T_s)} \right]^{0.25} \qquad 20.12$$

Description

Equation 20.12, based on Nusselt's theoretical work, predicts film coefficients for the laminar filmwise condensation of a pure saturated vapor on the outside of a horizontal tube with a diameter between 2.5 cm and 7.6 cm. Eq. 20.12 is in fair agreement with experimental data, with calculated values generally being low.[17] Proper units must be observed in order to keep the argument of exponentiation unitless.

Using Nusselt correlations for condensing vapor depends on determining several properties of the resulting condensate. Since the properties of the condensing vapor vary with temperature, these liquid properties are evaluated (by convention) at the average of the saturation and surface temperatures.[18] This implicitly defines the *film temperature*.

$$T_{\mathrm{film}} = \frac{T_s + T_{\mathrm{sat}}}{2}$$

The actual surface temperature is often unknown in initial studies. However, for steam, condensation frequently occurs with a temperature difference of $T_{\mathrm{sat}} - T_s$ between 3°C and 22°C.

Equation 20.13: Condensation, Vertical Surfaces

$$\overline{\mathrm{Nu}}_L = \frac{\bar{h}L}{k_l} = 0.943 \left[\frac{\rho_l^2 g h_{fg} L^3}{\mu_l k_l (T_{\mathrm{sat}} - T_s)} \right]^{0.25} \qquad 20.13$$

Description

Filmwise condensation of pure saturated vapors on vertical surfaces (including the insides and outsides of tubes) is predicted by Eq. 20.13. Equation 20.13 cannot be used for condensation on inclined tubes. The film flow is not parallel with the longitudinal axis of an inclined tube, resulting in an effective inclination angle that varies with location along the tube.[19] As with condensation on horizontal surfaces, the latent heat of condensation is evaluated at the vapor temperature, while the remaining fluid properties are evaluated at the film temperature. The characteristic length, L, in Eq. 20.13 is the surface length.

9. INTRODUCTION TO FORCED CONVECTION

As with natural convection, *forced convection* depends on the movement of a fluid to remove heat from a surface. With forced convection, a fan, a pump, or relative motion causes the fluid motion. If the flow is over a flat surface, the fluid particles near the surface will flow more slowly due to friction with the surface. The *boundary layer* of slow-moving particles comprises the major thermal resistance. The thermal resistance of the tube and other heat exchanger components is often disregarded.

Newton's law of convection, Eq. 20.1, gives the heat transfer for Newtonian fluids in forced convection over exterior surfaces.[20] The film coefficient, h, is also known as the *coefficient of forced convection*. T_∞ is the *free-stream temperature*.

10. FLOW OVER FLAT PLATES

The boundary layer of a fluid flowing over a flat plate is assumed to have a parabolic velocity distribution.[21] The layer has three distinct regions: laminar, transition, and turbulent. From the leading edge, the layer is laminar and the thickness increases gradually until the transition region where the thickness increases dramatically. Thereafter, the boundary layer is turbulent. The

---

[16]Film coefficients for dropwise condensation can be 4 to 8 times larger than for filmwise condensation because the film is thinner and the thermal resistance is smaller.

[17](1) The ρ_l^2 term in the numerator is a simplification. Nusselt's theoretical work correlated heat transfer with the quantity $\rho_l(\rho_l - \rho_v)$. The quantity ρ_l^2 in the *NCEES Handbook* results from assuming the vapor density, ρ_v, is zero. The *NCEES Handbook* does not invoke this simplification for the material presented on boiling and evaporation. (2) The more precise value of the constant 0.729 is often reported as 0.725, which was the value originally derived from a numerical analysis. In practice, highly precise estimates are illusionary, as actual values are found within the range between the two values.

[18]The *NCEES Handbook* gives the guidance, "Evaluate all liquid properties at the average temperature..." However, this guidance does not apply to the latent heat, h_{fg}, which is a property of the vapor. The latent heat should be evaluated at the saturation temperature and pressure.

[19](1) Equation 20.13 was derived by Nusselt with a coefficient of 0.943. However, ripples in the laminar film appear at condensation Reynolds numbers as low as 30 or 40. Experimental data show actual film coefficients are approximately 20% higher than the theoretical. A coefficient of 1.13 in place of 0.943 reflects this increase. Retaining the 0.943 value, however, yields a conservative value. (2) Eq. 20.13 can be used to find the condensing film coefficient on a vertical tube when the total condensation is less than 460 kg/h.

[20](1) Newton's law of convection is the same for natural and forced convection. Only the methods used to evaluate the film coefficient are different. (2) The results of this chapter do not generally apply to non-Newtonian fluids.

[21]The velocity distribution does not have to be parabolic. In *Couette flow*, there are two closely spaced parallel surfaces, one which is stationary and the other moving with constant velocity. The velocity gradient is assumed to be linear between the plates.

laminar region is always present, though its length decreases as velocity increases. Turbulent flow may not develop at all with short plates.

Equation 20.14 and Eq. 20.15: Flat Plate

$$\overline{\mathrm{Nu}}_L = \frac{\bar{h}L}{k} = 0.6640\mathrm{Re}_L^{1/2}\mathrm{Pr}^{1/3} \quad [\mathrm{Re}_L < 10^5] \quad 20.14$$

$$\overline{\mathrm{Nu}}_L = \frac{\bar{h}L}{k} = 0.0366\mathrm{Re}_L^{0.8}\mathrm{Pr}^{1/3} \quad [\mathrm{Re}_L > 10^5] \quad 20.15$$

Description

Equation 20.14 and Eq. 20.15 give the Nusselt number for a flat plate in parallel flow. The Reynolds number is used to determine whether the flow regime is laminar ($\mathrm{Re}_L < 100\,000$) or turbulent ($\mathrm{Re}_L > 100\,000$). The Reynolds number is calculated using the length of the plate as the characteristic length.

Example

Air at 40°C flows at 0.65 m/s over a square flat plate 1.5 m on each side. The Reynolds number is 56 000. The Prandtl number is 0.71. What is most nearly the average Nusselt number?

(A) 140

(B) 180

(C) 320

(D) 560

Solution

Since $\mathrm{Re}_L = 56\,000 < 10^5$, Eq. 20.14 can be used to calculate the average Nusselt number.

$$\overline{\mathrm{Nu}}_L = 0.6640\mathrm{Re}_L^{1/2}\mathrm{Pr}^{1/3}$$
$$= (0.6640)(56\,000)^{1/2}(0.71)^{1/3}$$
$$= 140$$

The answer is (A).

11. FLOW INSIDE TUBES

Laminar flow in smooth tubes occurs at Reynolds numbers less than 2300. As with flow over a flat plate, the velocity distribution is parabolic, but the extent of the parabola is limited to the tube radius. In the *entrance region*, the parabola does not extend to the centerline. Further on, a point is reached where the parabolic distribution is complete, and the flow is said to be *fully developed* laminar flow.[22] At that point, the average velocity is one-half of the maximum (centerline) velocity.

Equation 20.16: Laminar Flow Inside Tubes with Uniform Heat Flux

$$\mathrm{Nu}_D = 4.36 \quad [\text{uniform heat flux}] \quad 20.16$$

Variation

$$\mathrm{Nu}_D = \frac{\bar{h}D}{k}$$

Description

Equation 20.16 correlates the Nusselt number in the case of laminar flow inside a circular channel with uniform heat flux along the length of flow. Laminar flow is appropriate when $\mathrm{Re}_D < 2300$. Equation 20.16 provides an effective means of determining the average film coefficient for this situation. Since the heat flux passing through the tube wall into the fluid is constant along the length of flow, the length of the tube is not relevant.

Equation 20.17: Laminar Flow Inside Tubes with Constant Surface Temperature

$$\mathrm{Nu}_D = 3.66 \quad \begin{bmatrix}\text{constant surface}\\ \text{temperature}\end{bmatrix} \quad 20.17$$

Variation

$$\mathrm{Nu}_D = \frac{\bar{h}D}{k}$$

Description

Equation 20.17 correlates the Nusselt number in the case of laminar flow inside a circular channel with constant surface temperature along the length of flow. Laminar flow is appropriate when $\mathrm{Re}_D < 2300$. Equation 20.17 provides an effective means of determining the average film coefficient for this situation. Since the temperature along the tube length is constant along the length of flow, the length of the tube is not relevant.

Equation 20.18: Laminar Flow Inside Tubes with Constant Wall Temperature

$$\mathrm{Nu}_D = 1.86\left(\frac{\mathrm{Re}_D\mathrm{Pr}}{\frac{L}{D}}\right)^{1/3}\left(\frac{\mu_b}{\mu_s}\right)^{0.14} \quad 20.18$$

---

[22]The term *fully developed* is also used when referring to full turbulence. In this section, it is understood that the flow is laminar.

Description

The *Sieder-Tate equation* (also known as *Sieder-Tate correlation*), Eq. 20.18, predicts the average film coefficient along the entire length of laminar flow. In Eq. 20.18, μ_b is the absolute viscosity of the fluid at the bulk temperature, and μ_s is the absolute viscosity of the fluid at the tube's surface (wall) temperature. All of the other fluid properties are evaluated at the bulk temperature.

Example

A fluid flows through a 0.30 m diameter circular tube 2.1 m in length. The following properties have been calculated.

$$\mathrm{Re}_D = 2100$$
$$\mathrm{Pr} = 0.71$$
$$\mu_b = 850 \text{ kg/s·m}$$
$$\mu_s = 860 \text{ kg/s·m}$$

What is most nearly the Nusselt number?

(A) 11

(B) 56

(C) 460

(D) 890

Solution

Since the Reynolds number is less than 2300, flow is laminar. Use Eq. 20.18 to calculate the Nusselt number.

$$\mathrm{Nu}_D = 1.86 \left(\frac{\mathrm{Re}_D \mathrm{Pr}}{\frac{L}{D}} \right)^{1/3} \left(\frac{\mu_b}{\mu_s} \right)^{0.14}$$

$$= (1.86) \left(\frac{(2100)(0.71)}{\frac{2.1 \text{ m}}{0.30 \text{ m}}} \right)^{1/3} \left(\frac{850 \frac{\text{kg}}{\text{s·m}}}{860 \frac{\text{kg}}{\text{s·m}}} \right)^{0.14}$$

$$= 11$$

The answer is (A).

Equation 20.19: Turbulent Flow Inside Straight Tubes

$$\mathrm{Nu}_D = 0.023 \mathrm{Re}_D^{0.8} \mathrm{Pr}^{1/3} \left(\frac{\mu_b}{\mu_s} \right)^{0.14} \qquad 20.19$$

Description

If there is a large change in viscosity during the heat transfer process, as there would be with oils and other viscous fluids heated in a long tube, the *Sieder-Tate equation* for turbulent flow, Eq. 20.19, should be used instead of the Nusselt equation. Equation 20.19 can be used with both the case of uniform surface temperature and the case of uniform heat flux but is limited to $\mathrm{Re}_D > 10\,000$ and $\mathrm{Pr} > 0.7$.[23]

All fluid properties in Eq. 20.19 are evaluated at the bulk temperature, except for μ_s, which is evaluated at the surface temperature.

Example

A fluid flows through a long circular tube with uniform surface temperature. The following properties have been calculated.

$$\mathrm{Re}_D = 2.2 \times 10^4$$
$$\mathrm{Pr} = 0.75$$
$$\mu_b = 840 \text{ kg/s·m}$$
$$\mu_s = 850 \text{ kg/s·m}$$

What is most nearly the Nusselt number?

(A) 53

(B) 62

(C) 320

(D) 1500

Solution

Since the Reynolds number is greater than 10 000, and the Prandtl number is greater than 0.7, Eq. 20.19 may be used. The Nusselt number is

$$\mathrm{Nu}_D = 0.023 \mathrm{Re}_D^{0.8} \mathrm{Pr}^{1/3} \left(\frac{\mu_b}{\mu_s} \right)^{0.14}$$

$$= (0.023)(2.2 \times 10^4)^{0.8}(0.75)^{1/3} \left(\frac{840 \frac{\text{kg}}{\text{s·m}}}{850 \frac{\text{kg}}{\text{s·m}}} \right)^{0.14}$$

$$= 62$$

The answer is (B).

---

[23]Although the *NCEES Handbook* specifies a lower limit for the Prandtl number, it does not specify an upper limit. The upper limit is reported by various researchers as 700, 16 700, and 17 000.

Equation 20.20 and Eq. 20.21: Turbulent Liquid Metal Flow in Tubes

$$\mathrm{Nu}_D = 7.0 + 0.025\mathrm{Re}_D^{0.8}\mathrm{Pr}^{0.8}$$

$$\begin{bmatrix} \text{constant surface} \\ \text{temperature} \end{bmatrix} \quad 20.20$$

$$\mathrm{Nu}_D = 6.3 + 0.0167\mathrm{Re}_D^{0.85}\mathrm{Pr}^{0.93}$$

$$[\text{uniform heat flux}] \quad 20.21$$

Description

When the surface (wall) temperature is constant, Eq. 20.20 can be used to calculate the average film coefficient for liquid metals (for example, mercury, sodium, and lead-bismuth alloys) experiencing fully developed turbulent flow inside tubes.[24] Fluid properties are evaluated at the mean bulk temperature.

With a constant heat flux, Eq. 20.21 can be used to calculate the average film coefficient for liquid metals with fully developed turbulent flow inside tubes.

Equation 20.20 and Eq. 20.21 are both limited to $0.003 < \mathrm{Pr} < 0.05$.

Example

Liquid metal flows through a tube with constant surface temperature. The Reynolds number is 2700, and the Prandtl number is 0.04. What is most nearly the Nusselt number?

(A) 2.5

(B) 6.6

(C) 8.1

(D) 9.7

Solution

For liquid metal flow with constant surface temperature, the Nusselt number can be calculated using Eq. 20.20.

$$\begin{aligned} \mathrm{Nu}_D &= 7.0 + 0.025\mathrm{Re}_D^{0.8}\mathrm{Pr}^{0.8} \\ &= 7.0 + (0.025)(2700)^{0.8}(0.04)^{0.8} \\ &= 8.06 \quad (8.1) \end{aligned}$$

The answer is (C).

12. FLOW THROUGH NONCIRCULAR DUCTS

Equation 20.22: Hydraulic Diameter

$$D_H = \frac{4 \times \text{cross-sectional area}}{\text{wetted perimeter}} \quad 20.22$$

Description

A *duct* is any closed channel through which a fluid flows. Tubes and pipes are examples of round ducts. "Ducts" are not limited to air conditioning ducts.

Dimensional analysis shows that a *characteristic length* is required in the Nusselt number, but it does not identify the length to be used. It has been common practice to correlate empirical pressure drop and heat transfer data with the *hydraulic diameter*, D_H, of noncircular (e. g., rectangular, square, elliptical, polygonal) ducts.

Though an approximation, empirical data supports using the hydraulic diameter in most cases. Notable exceptions are flow through ducts with narrow angles (for example, an equilateral triangle with a narrow vertex angle) and flow *parallel* to banks of tubes.

Equation 20.23: Hydraulic Diameter, Annulus

$$D_H = D_o - D_i \quad 20.23$$

Description

Annular flow is the flow of fluid through an annulus. Fluid flow is annular in simple tube-in-tube heat exchangers.[25] For an annulus, Eq. 20.23 gives the hydraulic diameter.

13. FLOW OVER SPHERES

Spheres have the smallest surface area-to-volume ratio, so spherical tanks are used where heat transfer is to be minimized. When a sphere experiences motion relative to a surrounding fluid, heat transfer to and from the fluid is predicted by a Nusselt number correlation.

Equation 20.24: Nusselt Number, Flow Over Spheres

$$\overline{\mathrm{Nu}}_D = \frac{\bar{h}D}{k} = 2.0 + 0.60\mathrm{Re}_D^{1/2}\mathrm{Pr}^{1/3}$$

$$\begin{bmatrix} 1 < \mathrm{Re}_D < 70\,000; \\ 0.6 < \mathrm{Pr} < 400 \end{bmatrix} \quad 20.24$$

Heat Transfer

---

[24]The term *fully developed* is also used when referring to full laminar flow. In this section it is understood that the flow is turbulent.
[25]Flow is not annular through shell and tube heat exchangers.

Description

The Nusselt correlation for fluid flow over a sphere is given by Eq. 20.24. Fluid properties should be evaluated at the film temperature.

Example

The Reynolds number for air flowing over a sphere is 62 000. The Prandtl number is 0.81. What is most nearly the average Nusselt number?

(A) 110

(B) 140

(C) 450

(D) 670

Solution

The average Nusselt number can be calculated using Eq. 20.24.

$$\overline{\mathrm{Nu}}_D = 2.0 + 0.6\mathrm{Re}_D^{1/2}\mathrm{Pr}^{1/3}$$
$$= 2.0 + (0.6)(62\,000)^{1/2}(0.81)^{1/3}$$
$$= 141.27 \quad (140)$$

The answer is (B).

14. BOILING

The temperature at which a liquid boils is known as its *saturation temperature*. Boiling will occur when a liquid is heated to its saturation temperature. A common method of boiling a liquid is to heat it in a vessel (pan, tank, etc.). Boiling will occur when the surface temperature, T_s, is greater than the saturation temperature, T_{sat}.

The behavior of a liquid that is just beginning to boil (i.e., when vapor bubbles start forming on the heated surface) is different from the behavior in a rolling boil. The boiling behavior is affected by the difference in temperature of the surface and the saturation temperature, as well as the roughness of the heated surface. Boiling behavior is also affected by the presence of external agitation. Boiling behavior is categorized in a number of ways. These boiling regimes are illustrated by a *boiling curve*, such as Fig. 20.1 for water at atmospheric pressure.

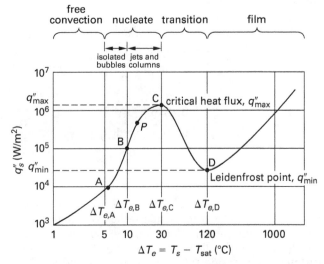

Figure 20.1 *Typical Boiling Curve*

Typical boiling curve for water at one atmosphere: surface heat flux q_s'' as a function of excess temperature, $\Delta T_e = T_s - T_{\mathrm{sat}}$

Source: Incropera, Frank P. and David P. DeWitt, *Fundamentals of Heat and Mass Transfer*, 3rd ed., Wiley, 1990.

In *forced convection boiling*, the fluid is moved or agitated by a stirrer or paddle. In *flow boiling*, the fluid is moved through a tube by a pump.

In *pool boiling*, the liquid pool is relatively calm (i.e., quiet, quiescent). Fluid motion near the heated surface is induced by free convection and bubble movement but does not significantly affect the free liquid surface.[26]

In *sub-cooled boiling*, the bulk temperature of the liquid is less than the saturation temperature. Vapor bubbles forming on the heated surface may condense back into liquid form. Fluid movement is induced by the density differences.

In *saturated boiling*, the liquid temperature exceeds the saturation temperature only slightly. Vapor bubbles forming on the heated surface rise into the liquid under the influence of buoyancy.

In *free convection boiling*, the liquid is at the saturation temperature, but there is insufficient heat transfer to cause vapor bubbles to form.[27] With an increasing surface temperature and increasing heat transfer, bubbles begin to form. This regime ends with the formation of isolated bubbles, a state known as the *onset of nucleate boiling* (ONB) or *bubble nucleation*.

In *nucleate boiling*, individual bubbles form on the heated surface and rise essentially vertically in succession. The rising vapor progresses from isolated bubbles to streams (jets or slugs) of bubbles. The bubbles rise vertically and follow direct paths until the bubbles

---

[26]In its description of boiling regimes, the *NCEES Handbook* repeatedly refers to "the surface." Since there are two surfaces (the heated surface and the liquid surface), care must be taken in interpreting the *NCEES Handbook*'s descriptions.

[27]The *NCEES Handbook* describes this regime as "Insufficient vapor is in contact with the liquid phase..." While there is insufficient vapor to transfer heat to the liquid, the root cause of free convection boiling is insufficient thermal energy transfer due to a low excess temperature.

become large enough to combine and the liquid begins to move ("roll") and disrupt direct vertical movement. The end of nucleate boiling marks the point where heat transfer (i.e., heat flux) is maximum. This defines the *critical heat flux*, commonly abbreviated as CHF.

In *transition boiling*, the vapor bubbles begin to combine within the liquid, and the liquid movement intermittently interrupts direct vapor bubble movement. The boiling regime oscillates between nucleate boiling and film boiling. The beginning of transition boiling is known as the *departure from nucleate boiling* (DNB) point. The end of the transition boiling regime is known as the *Leidenfrost point*, the minimum heat flux for film boiling.

In *film boiling* (also known as *filmwise boiling*), the heated surface is completely covered by a layer (blanket) of vapor. A significant fraction of the heat flux is via radiation through the vapor layer.

Equation 20.25 Through Eq. 20.30: Heat Flux

$$q'' = h(T_s - T_{sat}) = h\Delta T_e \qquad 20.25$$

$$\dot{q}_{nucleate} = \mu_l h_{fg}\left[\frac{g(\rho_l - \rho_v)}{\sigma}\right]^{1/2}\left[\frac{c_{pl}(T_s - T_{sat})}{C_{sf}h_{fg}\Pr_l^n}\right]^3 \qquad 20.26$$

$$\dot{q}_{max} = C_{cr}h_{fg}[\sigma g\rho_v^2(\rho_l - \rho_v)]^{1/4} \qquad 20.27$$

$$\dot{q}_{min} = 0.09\rho_v h_{fg}\left[\frac{\sigma g(\rho_l - \rho_v)}{(\rho_l + \rho_v)^2}\right]^{1/4} \qquad 20.28$$

$$\dot{q}_{film} = C_{film}\left[\frac{gk_v^3\rho_v(\rho_l - \rho_v)\times[h_{fg} + 0.4c_{pv}(T_s - T_{sat})]}{\mu_v D(T_s - T_{sat})}\right]^{1/4} \times (T_s - T_{sat}) \qquad 20.29$$

$$C_{film} = \begin{Bmatrix}0.62 \text{ for horizontal cylinders}\\0.67 \text{ for spheres}\end{Bmatrix} \qquad 20.30$$

Values

Table 20.5 *Values of the Coefficient C_{cr} for Maximum Heat Flux (dimensionless parameter $L^* = L(g(\rho_l - \rho_v)/\sigma)^{1/2})$*

heater geometry	C_{cr}	charac. dimension of heater, L	range of L^*
large horizontal flat heater	0.149	width or diameter	$L^* > 27$
small horizontal flat heater*	$18.9K_1$	width or diameter	$9 < L^* < 20$
large horizontal cylinder	0.12	radius	$L^* > 1.2$
small horizontal cylinder	$0.12L^{*-0.25}$	radius	$0.15 < L^* < 1.2$
large sphere	0.11	radius	$L^* > 4.26$
small sphere	$0.227L^{*-0.5}$	radius	$0.15 < L^* < 4.26$

*$K_1 = \sigma/(g(\rho_l - \rho_v)A_{heater})$

Description

Equation 20.25 is the general calculation of heat flux (i.e., $\dot{Q}/A$, the heat transfer per unit area).[28] In Eq. 20.25, ΔT_e is the *excess temperature*, defined as the difference between the surface temperature and the saturation temperature.

$$\Delta T_e = T_s - T_{sat}$$

Equation 20.26 is the *Rohsenow's correlation* for heat flux in nucleate boiling. C_{sf} is an empirical constant dependent on the fluid and heated surface. The exponent, n, on the Prandtl number is also empirical. The liquid and vapor properties are evaluated at the saturation temperature. Tables of heat-transfer-specific properties are usually used. Since the vapor density, ρ_v, is small, it can be omitted from first approximations.

Equation 20.27 calculates the critical (maximum, peak, etc.) heat flux (CHF) corresponding to the end of nucleate boiling. As Eq. 20.27 shows, the heat flux is proportional to the heat (enthalpy) of vaporization, h_{fg}. When maximum heat flux from a surface is desired, liquid (such as water) with large heats of vaporization should be used. C_{cr} is an empirical constant that depends on the type and orientation of the heating element used.

[28]The use of double-primed q (i.e., q'') to designate heat flux is colloquial in the subject of boiling heat transfer. The number of primes indicates the number of length units to be included. Thus, q would have units of W, q' would have units of W/m, and q'' would have units of W/m². After introducing this convention, the *NCEES Handbook* subsequently abandons it and uses $\dot{q}$ as the symbol for surface heat flux in every subsequent equation.

For large, flat heaters (e.g., the bottom of a pan on a stove), C_{cr} is approximately 0.15. (See Table 20.5.) The critical heat flux increases as pressure increases up to approximately one-third of the substance's critical pressure, after which it decreases, reaching zero at the critical pressure.

Equation 20.28, known as the *Zuber equation*, calculates the minimum heat flux corresponding to the beginning of film boiling (i.e., the *Leidenfrost point*).

Many industrial boilers contain tubular resistance (electrical) or hot fluid heaters. Equation 20.29, known as the *Bromley equation*, calculates the heat flux in film boiling for horizontal cylinders and spheres. Equation 20.29 cannot be used directly for heating from flat, horizontal plates.[29] The values of the empirical constant, C_{film}, for film boiling are given by Eq. 20.30.

Example

A horizontal cylindrical heater is used to boil water at a constant temperature of 90°C. The density of the liquid water is 965 kg/m³, and the density of the water vapor is 0.424 kg/m³. The surface tension between the liquid and vapor is 0.070 N/m. Most nearly, what is the peak heat flux with nucleate boiling?

(A) 740 kW/m²

(B) 860 kW/m²

(C) 910 kW/m²

(D) 1100 kW/m²

Solution

From the steam tables, at a temperature of 90°C, the enthalpy of evaporation is 2283.2 kJ/kg. From Table 20.5, $C_{cr} = 0.12$ for a large horizontal cylinder.

Use Eq. 20.27 to calculate the peak heat flux in the nucleate pool.

$$
\begin{aligned}
\dot{q}_{max} &= C_{cr}h_{fg}[\sigma g\rho_v^2(\rho_l - \rho_v)]^{1/4} \\
&= (0.12)\left(2283.2\ \frac{\text{kJ}}{\text{kg}}\right) \\
&\quad \times \left[\left(0.070\ \frac{\text{N}}{\text{m}}\right)\left(9.81\ \frac{\text{m}}{\text{s}^2}\right)\left(0.424\ \frac{\text{kg}}{\text{m}^3}\right)^2\right.^{1/4} \\
&\qquad \left. \times \left(965\ \frac{\text{kg}}{\text{m}^3} - 0.424\ \frac{\text{kg}}{\text{m}^3}\right)\right] \\
&= 905\ \text{kW/m}^2 \quad (910\ \text{kW/m}^2)
\end{aligned}
$$

The answer is (C).

15. HEAT EXCHANGERS

In a typical application, two fluids flow through or over a heat exchanger.[30] Heat from the hot fluid passes through the exchanger walls to the cold fluid.[31] The heat transfer mechanism is essentially completely forced convection.

Heat exchangers are categorized into simple *tube-in-tube heat exchangers* (also known as *jacketed pipe heat exchangers*), single-pass shell and tube heat exchangers, multiple-pass shell and tube heat exchangers, and crossflow heat exchangers.[32] *Shell and tube heat exchangers*, also known as *sathes* and *S & T heat exchangers*, consist of a large housing, the *shell*, with many smaller tubes running through it. The *tube fluid* passes through the tubes, while the *shell fluid* passes through the shell and around tubes.[33]

In a *single-pass heat exchanger*, each fluid is exposed to the other fluid only once. Operation is known as *parallel flow* (same as *cocurrent flow*) if both fluids flow in the same direction along the longitudinal axis of the exchanger and *counterflow* (same as *counter current flow*) if the fluids flow in opposite directions.[34] Counterflow is more efficient, and the heat transfer area required is less than that with parallel flow since the temperature gradient is more constant.

For increased efficiency, most exchangers are *multiple-pass heat exchangers*. The tubes pass through the shell more than once, and the shell fluid is routed around baffles.

---

[29](1) The *NCEES Handbook* gives the heat flux equation for cylinders and spheres, but not for flat horizontal plates, a common configuration (e.g., heating a pan on the stove). (2) Equation 20.29 can also be used for vertical flat plates by using the value of $C_{film} = 0.62$.

[30]These fluids do not have to be liquids. *Air-cooled exchangers* reduce water consumption in traditional cooling applications.

[31]A *recuperative heat exchanger*, typified by the traditional shell and tube exchanger, maintains separate flow channels for each of the fluids. A *regenerative heat exchanger* has only one flow path, to which the two fluids are exposed on an alternating basis.

[32]Fin coil heat exchangers are a special case of crossflow heat exchangers.

[33]Tubular heat exchangers are also known as *shell and tube heat exchangers*.

[34](1) Flow through shell and tube heat exchangers is neither purely parallel nor purely counterflow. Thus, these exchangers are sometimes designated as *parallel counterflow exchangers*. (2) The designation *cocurrent* is not an abbreviation for *counter current*.

Equation 20.31: Heat Transfer

$$\dot{Q} = UAF\Delta T_{\mathrm{lm}} \qquad\qquad 20.31$$

Description

Equation 20.31 calculates the steady-state heat transfer (also known as the *heat duty* and *heat load*) in a heat exchanger or feedwater heater.[35] F is a correction factor that depends on the configuration (i.e., crossflow, parallel flow, number of passes, etc.) and corrects the LMTD value for the effectiveness of the heat exchanger.[36] $F = 1$ when one fluid is condensing or evaporating (i.e., when the temperature of the fluid changing phase does not change in the heat exchanger). Values of F are often read from widely available graphs.[37] Equation 20.31 embodies the *LMTD method*, also known as the *F-factor method*, of accounting for heat exchanger effectiveness. The LMTD method is easily applied to problems when both outlet temperatures are known, such as when calculating the required heat transfer area. When both outlet temperatures are unknown, the NTU method must generally be used.

The *overall heat transfer coefficient*, U, also known as the *overall conductance* and the *overall coefficient of heat transfer*, can be specified for use with either the outside or inside tube areas. The heat transfer is independent of whether the outside or inside area is used. It is more common (and preferred) to use the outside tube area because the outside tube diameter is more easily measured.

In reality, it is very difficult to predict the heat transfer coefficient for most types of commercial heat exchangers. Values can be predicted by comparison with similar units, or "tried-and-true" rules of thumb can be used. One such rule of thumb for baffled shell and tube heat exchangers predicts the clean, average heat transfer coefficient as 60% of the value for the same arrangement of tubes in pure crossflow.

Equation 20.32: Overall Heat Transfer Coefficient

$$\frac{1}{UA} = \frac{1}{h_i A_i} + \frac{R_{fi}}{A_i} + \frac{\ln\!\left(\dfrac{D_o}{D_i}\right)}{2\pi kL} + \frac{R_{fo}}{A_o} + \frac{1}{h_o A_o} \qquad 20.32$$

Description

Equation 20.32 calculates the overall heat transfer coefficient, U, for concentric tube and shell and tube heat exchangers from the film coefficients and the tube material conductivities.

The area, A, on the left-hand side of Eq. 20.32 can be either the inside area of the tubing (i.e., based on the inside diameter) or the outside area (i.e., based on the outside diameter). The outside diameter is easier to measure in the field, so that convention is preferred. It is important to specify whether an overall heat transfer coefficient is to be used with the inside or outside area. The *fouling factors*, R_{fi} and R_{fo}, represent the thermal resistance of any accumulations, scale, deposits, and even living biological organisms (e.g., Zebra mussels).

Example

A pipe has a thermal conductivity of 0.25 W/m·K and a length of 10 m. The inside diameter of the pipe is 1.2 cm, and the outside diameter of the pipe is 2.0 cm. The outside convective heat transfer coefficient is 10 W/m²·K, and the inside convective heat transfer coefficient is 150 W/m²·K. The fouling factor for the inside of the pipe is 0.0005 m²·K/W, and the fouling factor for the outside of the pipe is negligible. What is most nearly the overall heat transfer coefficient based on the outside surface area?

(A) 2.4 W/m²·K

(B) 3.2 W/m²·K

(C) 7.6 W/m²·K

(D) 9.6 W/m²·K

Solution

Calculate the inside surface area of the pipe.

$$A_i = \pi D_i L = \frac{\pi (1.2 \text{ cm})(10 \text{ m})}{100 \,\dfrac{\text{cm}}{\text{m}}} = 0.3770 \text{ m}^2$$

Calculate the outside surface area of the pipe.

$$A_o = \pi D_o L = \frac{\pi (2.0 \text{ cm})(10 \text{ m})}{100 \,\dfrac{\text{cm}}{\text{m}}} = 0.6283 \text{ m}^2$$

---

[35](1) *Closed feedwater heaters* are heat exchangers whose purpose is to heat water with condensing steam. (2) There are three heat loads referred to in heat exchanger specifications: the *specific heat load*, which is the design heat transfer; the heat released by the hot fluid; and the heat absorbed by the cold fluid. All three would be the same if operation was adiabatic, but due to practical losses, they are not. If they differ by more than 10%, the cause of the discrepancy should be evaluated.

[36]The *NCEES Handbook* calls F the *configuration correction factor*. The actual name is the *mean temperature difference correction factor*.

[37]As published by Tubular Exchanger Manufacturers Association, Inc. (TEMA).

Use Eq. 20.32.

$$\frac{1}{UA} = \frac{1}{h_i A_i} + \frac{R_{fi}}{A_i} + \frac{\ln\left(\dfrac{D_o}{D_i}\right)}{2\pi k L} + \frac{R_{fo}}{A_o} + \frac{1}{h_o A_o}$$

$$UA = \left(\frac{1}{h_i A_i} + \frac{R_{fi}}{A_i} + \frac{\ln\left(\dfrac{D_o}{D_i}\right)}{2\pi k L} + \frac{R_{fo}}{A_o} + \frac{1}{h_o A_o}\right)^{-1}$$

$$= \left(\frac{1}{\left(150\ \dfrac{\text{W}}{\text{m}^2\cdot\text{K}}\right)(0.3770\ \text{m}^2)} + \frac{0.0005\ \dfrac{\text{m}^2\cdot\text{K}}{\text{W}}}{0.3770\ \text{m}^2} + \frac{\ln\dfrac{2.0\ \text{cm}}{1.2\ \text{cm}}}{(2\pi)\left(0.25\ \dfrac{\text{W}}{\text{m}\cdot\text{K}}\right)(10\ \text{m})} + 0 + \frac{1}{\left(10\ \dfrac{\text{W}}{\text{m}^2\cdot\text{K}}\right)(0.6283\ \text{m}^2)}\right)^{-1}$$

$$= 4.746\ \text{W/K}$$

Based on the outside surface area, the overall heat transfer coefficient is

$$U = \frac{UA}{A_o} = \frac{4.746\ \dfrac{\text{W}}{\text{K}}}{0.6283\ \text{m}^2}$$
$$= 7.55\ \text{W/m}^2\cdot\text{K}\quad(7.6\ \text{W/m}^2\cdot\text{K})$$

The answer is (C).

16. LOGARITHMIC TEMPERATURE DIFFERENCE

The temperature difference between two fluids is not constant in a heat exchanger. When calculating the heat transfer for a tube whose temperature difference changes along its length, the *logarithmic mean temperature difference*, ΔT_{lm} or LMTD, is used.[38] In the equation shown, ΔT_A and ΔT_B are the temperature differences at ends A and B, respectively, regardless of whether the fluid flow is parallel or counterflow.[39]

$$\Delta T_{\text{lm}} = \frac{\Delta T_A - \Delta T_B}{\ln\dfrac{\Delta T_A}{\Delta T_B}}$$

Equation 20.33: Logarithmic Temperature Difference, Counterflow

$$\Delta T_{\text{lm}} = \frac{(T_{\text{Ho}} - T_{\text{Ci}}) - (T_{\text{Hi}} - T_{\text{Co}})}{\ln\left(\dfrac{T_{\text{Ho}} - T_{\text{Ci}}}{T_{\text{Hi}} - T_{\text{Co}}}\right)} \qquad 20.33$$

Description

For counterflow tubular heat exchangers, the logarithmic temperature difference can be found using Eq. 20.33.

Equation 20.34: Logarithmic Temperature Difference, Parallel Flow

$$\Delta T_{\text{lm}} = \frac{(T_{\text{Ho}} - T_{\text{Co}}) - (T_{\text{Hi}} - T_{\text{Ci}})}{\ln\left(\dfrac{T_{\text{Ho}} - T_{\text{Co}}}{T_{\text{Hi}} - T_{\text{Ci}}}\right)} \qquad 20.34$$

Description

For parallel flow tubular heat exchangers, the logarithmic temperature difference can be found using Eq. 20.34.

---

[38](1) An exception occurs in HVAC calculations where ΔT at midlength has traditionally been used to calculate the heat transfer in air conditioning ducts. Considering the imprecise nature of HVAC calculations, the added sophistication of using the logarithmic mean temperature difference is probably unwarranted. (2) The symbol ΔT_m is also widely used for the log-mean temperature difference. However, this can also be interpreted as the arithmetic mean temperature. (3) The logarithmic temperature difference is used even with change of phase (e.g., boiling liquid or condensing vapor) and the temperature is constant in one tube.

[39](1) It doesn't make any difference which end is A and which is B. If the numerator is negative, the denominator will also be negative. (2) As ΔT_A and ΔT_B become equal, the equation becomes indeterminate, even though the correct relationship is $\Delta T_{\text{lm}} = \Delta T_A = \Delta T_B$. Also, the first derivative, used in some calculations, is undefined when ΔT_A and ΔT_B are equal, even though the correct value is 0.5. A replacement expression (Underwood, 1933) that avoids these difficulties with (generally) less than a 0.3% error is

$$\Delta T_{\text{lm}} \approx \left(\frac{\Delta T_A^{1/3} + \Delta T_B^{1/3}}{2}\right)^3$$

Example

A parallel flow heat exchanger is used to cool oil from 120°C to 60°C. The cooling water enters at 20°C and leaves at 55°C. What is most nearly the log mean temperature difference?

(A) 25°C

(B) 32°C

(C) 140°C

(D) 280°C

Solution

Using Eq. 20.34, the log mean temperature difference for a parallel heat exchanger is

$$
\Delta T_{lm} = \frac{(T_{Ho} - T_{Co}) - (T_{Hi} - T_{Ci})}{\ln\left(\dfrac{T_{Ho} - T_{Co}}{T_{Hi} - T_{Ci}}\right)}
$$

$$
= \frac{(60°C - 55°C) - (120°C - 20°C)}{\ln\dfrac{60°C - 55°C}{120°C - 20°C}}
$$

$$
= 31.7°C \quad (32°C)
$$

The answer is (B).

17. NTU METHOD

Some heat exchanger analysis problems, such as where both outlet temperatures are unknown, appear to be unsolvable or solvable only by trial and error using the traditional F-method.[40] However, the *number of transfer units* (NTU) *method* (also known as the *efficiency method* and *effectiveness method*) can be used to handle these problems more easily.[41] The steps in the NTU method depend on whether or not both exit temperatures are known.

Equation 20.35 Through Eq. 20.38: Heat Exchanger Effectiveness

$$
\varepsilon = \frac{\dot{Q}}{\dot{Q}_{max}} = \frac{\text{actual heat transfer rate}}{\text{maximum possible heat transfer rate}} \qquad 20.35
$$

$$
C = \dot{m}c_p \qquad 20.36
$$

$$
\varepsilon = \frac{C_H(T_{Hi} - T_{Ho})}{C_{min}(T_{Hi} - T_{Ci})} \qquad 20.37
$$

$$
\varepsilon = \frac{C_C(T_{Co} - T_{Ci})}{C_{min}(T_{Hi} - T_{Ci})} \qquad 20.38
$$

Description

The *heat exchanger effectiveness*, ε, is defined as the ratio of the actual heat transfer to the maximum possible heat transfer.[42] This ratio is generally not known in advance.

The first step in the NTU method is to calculate the *thermal capacity rates*, C, for the two fluids, given by Eq. 20.36. It is possible for the two capacity rates to be equal, but usually they are not. The smaller capacity rate is designated C_{min}. The larger is designated C_{max}. The fluid with the smaller capacity rate, C_{min}, will experience the larger temperature change. If the cold fluid has the minimum capacity rate (that is, $C_{min} = C_{cold}$), the effectiveness is given by Eq. 20.38. If the hot fluid has the minimum capacity rate (that is, $C_{min} = C_{hot}$), the effectiveness is given by Eq. 20.37.

Equation 20.39 Through Eq. 20.43: Number of Transfer Units

$$
C_r = \frac{C_{min}}{C_{max}} \qquad 20.39
$$

$$
NTU = \frac{UA}{C_{min}} \qquad 20.40
$$

$$
NTU = \frac{1}{C_r - 1}\ln\left(\frac{\varepsilon - 1}{\varepsilon C_r - 1}\right) \qquad 20.41
$$
$$
\begin{bmatrix} \text{counterflow,} \\ \text{concentric; } C_r < 1 \end{bmatrix}
$$

$$
NTU = \frac{\varepsilon}{1 - \varepsilon} \quad \begin{bmatrix} \text{counterflow, concentric;} \\ C_r = 1 \end{bmatrix} \qquad 20.42
$$

$$
NTU = -\frac{\ln[1 - \varepsilon(1 + C_r)]}{1 + C_r} \qquad 20.43
$$
$$
\text{[parallel flow, concentric]}
$$

---

[40]Actually, any shell and tube heat exchanger with an even number of tube passes has a closed-form analytical solution for the outlet temperature. However, the mathematics are laborious and the form of the solution varies with the type of flow and heat exchanger design.

[41]The names *number of thermal units* (NTU), *heat transfer units* (HTU), and *temperature ratio* (TR) are synonymous with *number of transfer units* (NTU).

[42](1) The maximum possible transfer can occur only if the heat exchanger has an infinite length. (2) Other names used in the literature to define the effectiveness are *efficiency*, *thermodynamic efficiency*, *temperature efficiency*, and *performance parameter*. The symbol P is also used in place of ε.

Description

Once the heat capacity ratio is found, Eq. 20.41 through Eq. 20.43 can be used to find the number of transfer units for heat exchangers operating under specific conditions. The number of transfer units for a single-pass counterflow heat exchanger with a heat capacity ratio less than 1 is found from Eq. 20.41. The number of transfer units for a single-pass counterflow heat exchanger with a heat capacity ratio of 1 is found from Eq. 20.42. The number of transfer units for a single-pass parallel flow heat exchanger is found from Eq. 20.43.

Example

A single-pass counterflow heat exchanger is used to cool lubricating oil with cooling water. The exchanger has an effective heat transfer rate of 280 W/m²·K based on an effective heat transfer area of 16 m². The thermal capacity rate of lubricating oil is 9.1 kW/K, and the thermal capacity rate of cooling water is 5.2 kW/K. What is most nearly the number of transfer units?

(A)   0.71

(B)   0.86

(C)   0.94

(D)   1.3

Solution

Since 5.2 kW /K< 9.1 kW/K,

$$C_{min} = C_{water} = 5.2 \text{ kW/K} \quad (5.2 \times 10^3 \text{ W/K})$$

Use Eq. 20.40.

$$
\begin{aligned}
\text{NTU} &= \frac{UA}{C_{min}} \\
&= \frac{\left(280 \ \frac{\text{W}}{\text{m}^2 \cdot \text{K}}\right)(16 \text{ m}^2)}{5.2 \times 10^3 \ \frac{\text{W}}{\text{K}}} \\
&= 0.8615 \quad (0.86)
\end{aligned}
$$

The answer is (B).

Equation 20.44 Through Eq. 20.46: Heat Exchanger Effectiveness, Counterflow and Parallel Flow

$$\varepsilon = \frac{1 - \exp[-\text{NTU}(1 - C_r)]}{1 - C_r \exp[-\text{NTU}(1 - C_r)]} \quad \text{20.44}$$

$$\begin{bmatrix} \text{counterflow,} \\ \text{concentric; } C_r < 1 \end{bmatrix}$$

$$\varepsilon = \frac{\text{NTU}}{1 + \text{NTU}} \quad \begin{bmatrix} \text{counterflow, concentric;} \\ C_r = 1 \end{bmatrix} \quad \text{20.45}$$

$$\varepsilon = \frac{1 - \exp[-\text{NTU}(1 + C_r)]}{1 + C_r} \quad \text{20.46}$$

$$[\text{parallel flow, concentric}]$$

Description

If a single-pass counterflow heat exchanger has a heat capacity ratio less than 1, the effectiveness of the exchanger is found from Eq. 20.44.

If a single-pass counterflow heat exchanger has a heat capacity ratio of 1, the effectiveness of the exchanger is found from Eq. 20.45.

For a single-pass parallel flow heat exchanger, the effectiveness of the exchanger is found from Eq. 20.46.

Example

For a counterflow concentric tube heat exchanger, if the number of transfer units is 0.76 and $C_r = 1$, what is most nearly the heat exchanger effectiveness?

(A)   0.27

(B)   0.38

(C)   0.43

(D)   0.67

Solution

Since $C_r = 1$, Eq. 20.45 can be used to calculate the effectiveness.

$$
\begin{aligned}
\varepsilon &= \frac{\text{NTU}}{1 + \text{NTU}} = \frac{0.76}{1 + 0.76} \\
&= 0.4318 \quad (0.43)
\end{aligned}
$$

The answer is (C).

21 Radiation

Nomenclature

A	area	m^2
F	factor	–
N	number of radiating surfaces	–
P	power	–
$\dot{q}$	unit heat transfer rate	W/m^2
$\dot{Q}$	heat transfer rate	W
T	temperature	K

Symbols

α	absorptivity	–
ε	emissivity	–
ρ	reflectivity	–
σ	Stefan-Boltzmann constant, 5.67×10^{-8}	$W/m^2 \cdot K^4$
τ	transmissivity	–

Subscripts

12	from body 1 to body 2
13	from body 1 to body 3
21	from body 2 to body 1
32	from body 3 to body 2
i	inner or i^{th} surface
j	j^{th} surface
R	reradiating

1. THERMAL RADIATION

Thermal radiation is electromagnetic radiation with wavelengths in the $0.1 \ \mu m$ to $100 \ \mu m$ range. All bodies, even "cold" ones, radiate thermal radiation. Thermal radiation incident to a body can be absorbed, reflected, or transmitted.

Equation 21.1: Radiation Conservation Law

$$\alpha + \rho + \tau = 1 \quad \text{[always]} \qquad 21.1$$

Description

A body in the path of thermal radiation energy can absorb the energy, reflect the energy, or pass the energy through (i.e., transmit the energy). All of the incident energy is accounted for by this requirement. Equation 21.1, written in terms of fractions of the incident energy, is the *radiation conservation law* (*energy conservation law for radiation*). α is the fraction of energy absorbed (the *absorptivity*), ρ is the fraction reflected (the *reflectivity*), and τ is the fraction transmitted (the *transmissivity*).

Example

Based on the radiation conservation law, if the absorptivity of a body is 48%, and the reflectivity is 36%, what is most nearly the transmissivity?

(A) 16%

(B) 36%

(C) 48%

(D) 84%

Solution

The transmissivity can be found by solving Eq. 21.1.

$$\begin{aligned} \alpha + \rho + \tau &= 1 \\ \tau &= 1 - \alpha - \rho \\ &= 1 - 0.48 - 0.36 \\ &= 0.16 \quad (16\%) \end{aligned}$$

The answer is (A).

Equation 21.2: Radiation Conservation Law for an Opaque Body

$$\alpha + \rho = 1 \quad \text{[opaque]} \qquad 21.2$$

Description

For an opaque body, transmissivity is zero. The radiation conservation law is Eq. 21.2.

Example

For an opaque body, if 62% of the incident energy is reflected, what is most nearly the percentage of energy absorbed?

(A) 19%

(B) 38%

(C) 46%

(D) 62%

Solution

Use Eq. 21.2 to find the absorptivity.

$$\alpha + \rho = 1$$
$$\alpha = 1 - \rho$$
$$= 1 - 0.62$$
$$= 0.38 \quad (38\%)$$

The answer is (B).

2. BLACK, REAL, AND GRAY BODIES

A body will naturally radiate thermal energy into its local environment. The ratio of the actual emitted energy to the ideal emitted power is known as the *emissivity*, ε.

$$\varepsilon = \frac{P_{actual}}{P_{ideal}}$$

When a body (or surface) is in thermal equilibrium, any energy it receives by radiation (or other means) is also lost (transmitted). The rates of absorbed and transmitted energies must be the same.[1] Therefore, at thermal equilibrium, the emissivity of a body equals its absorptivity. This statement is known as *Kirchhoff's radiation law*. Kirchhoff's law has a corollary: Emissivity cannot exceed 1.0. Since absorptivity is part of the radiation conservation law, absorptivity cannot exceed 1.0. And, at thermal equilibrium, emissivity equals absorptivity. Therefore, emissivity cannot exceed 1.0.

The emissivity (and, therefore, the emissive power) usually depends on the temperature of the body.[2] A body that emits at constant emissivity, regardless of wavelength, is known as a *gray body*. *Real bodies* are frequently approximated as gray bodies. *Real bodies* do not radiate at the ideal level.

Since absorptivity, α, cannot exceed 1.0, Kirchhoff's radiation law places an upper limit on emissive power. Bodies that radiate at this upper limit ($\alpha = 1$) are known as *black bodies* or *ideal radiators*. A black body emits the maximum possible radiation for its temperature and absorbs all incident energy.[3]

Equation 21.3: Radiant Heat Transfer

$$\dot{Q} = \varepsilon \sigma A T^4 \qquad \text{21.3}$$

Values

$$\sigma = 5.67 \times 10^{-8} \text{ W/m}^2 \cdot \text{K}^4$$

Description

Radiant heat transfer is the name given to heat transferred by way of thermal radiation. The energy radiated by a hot body at absolute temperature, T, is given by the *Stefan-Boltzmann law*, also known as the *fourth-power law*. In Eq. 21.3, σ is the *Stefan-Boltzmann constant*.

Example

A 17 m^2 plate with an emissivity of 0.26 is suspended vertically in a large room. If the absolute temperature is 430K, what is most nearly the radiation emitted?

(A) 2.6 kW

(B) 3.5 kW

(C) 6.7 kW

(D) 8.6 kW

Solution

Using Eq. 21.3, the radiation emitted by a body is

$$\dot{Q} = \varepsilon \sigma A T^4$$
$$= \frac{(0.26)\left(5.67 \times 10^{-8} \ \dfrac{\text{W}}{\text{m}^2 \cdot \text{K}^4}\right) \times (17 \text{ m}^2)(430\text{K})^4}{1000 \ \dfrac{\text{W}}{\text{kW}}}$$
$$= 8.568 \text{ kW} \quad (8.6 \text{ kW})$$

The answer is (D).

Equation 21.4: Black Body

$$\alpha = \varepsilon = 1 \quad \text{[black body]} \qquad \text{21.4}$$

---

[1]In the most general form of Kirchhoff's radiation law, energy must be integrated over all wavelengths and angles.
[2]This is equivalent to saying the emissivity depends on the wavelength of the radiation.
[3]Black-body performance can be approximated but not achieved in practice.

Description

For a black body, both emissivity and absorptivity are 1.

Equation 21.5 and Eq. 21.6: Gray Body

$$\alpha = \varepsilon \quad [0 < \alpha < 1; 0 < \varepsilon < 1] \qquad 21.5$$

$$\varepsilon + \rho = 1 \quad [\text{opaque gray body}] \qquad 21.6$$

Description

For a gray body, the reflectivity is constant. (See Eq. 21.6.)

Example

If 55% of energy from a gray body is reflected, what is most nearly the emissivity of the body?

(A) 15%

(B) 25%

(C) 45%

(D) 55%

Solution

Solve Eq. 21.6 for emissivity.

$$\varepsilon + \rho = 1$$
$$\varepsilon = 1 - \rho$$
$$= 1 - 0.55$$
$$= 0.45 \quad (45\%)$$

The answer is (C).

3. RECIPROCITY THEOREM FOR RADIATION

Equation 21.7: Reprocity Theorem

$$A_i F_{ij} = A_j F_{ji} \quad [0 \le F_{ij} \le 1] \qquad 21.7$$

Variation

$$A_1 F_{12} = A_2 F_{21}$$

Description

Equation 21.7 is known as the *reciprocity theorem for radiation*. A_i is the surface area (m^2) of surface i. F_{ij} is the *shape factor* (*view factor, configuration factor*), which is the fraction of the radiation leaving surface i that is intercepted by surface j.

Equation 21.8: View Conservation Rule

$$\sum_{j=1}^{N} F_{ij} = 1 \qquad 21.8$$

Description

The thermal energy radiated from a body (surface) must go someplace. For a transmitting body that is completely surrounded by N other distinct receiving bodies (surfaces), it is logical that the total energy intercepted by the receiving bodies will equal the transmitted energy. This logic is repeated for each of the bodies in the collection. Since the shape factor, F_{ij}, is defined as the fraction of the radiation leaving surface i that is intercepted by surface j, Eq. 21.8 represents this logic.[4]

4. NET RADIATION HEAT TRANSFER

When two bodies can "see each other," each will radiate energy to and absorb energy from the other. The net radiant heat transfer between the two bodies is given by

$$\dot{Q}_{12} = \sigma A_1 F_{12}(T_1^4 - T_2^4)$$

F_{12} is the *shape factor*, or *configuration factor*, which depends on the shapes, emissivities, and orientations of the two bodies. If body 1 is small and completely enclosed by body 2, then $F_{12} = \varepsilon_1$.

Equation 21.9: Net Radiation Heat Transfer, Small Body

$$\dot{Q}_{12} = \varepsilon \sigma A (T_1^4 - T_2^4) \qquad 21.9$$

Description

Where body 1 is small and completely enclosed by body 2, the net heat transfer due to radiation is given by Eq. 21.9.

---

[4](1) This is a *conservation rule*, not a "summation rule" as the NCEES *FE Reference Handbook* (*NCEES Handbook*) refers to it. (2) The summation is shown over N surfaces, but there are $N+1$ surfaces, counting the radiating surface. Only the "other" surfaces (i.e., the intercepting surfaces) are included in the summation. Alternatively, if there were N total surfaces, the summation limit would be $N-1$. (3) Not immediately obvious from Eq. 21.8 as presented in the *NCEES Handbook* is that index variable i is held constant during the summation. The summation is not over all combinations of all surfaces.

Heat Transfer

Example

An ideal radiator is maintained at 550K. It is enclosed in a tank with a temperature of 290K. The radiator is small compared to the tank. What is most nearly the net heat transfer between them per unit area of radiator?

- (A) 2.9 kW/m^2
- (B) 3.5 kW/m^2
- (C) 4.8 kW/m^2
- (D) 5.4 kW/m^2

Solution

Equation 21.9 can be used to determine the heat transfer per unit area. $\varepsilon = 1$ for an ideal radiator.

$$\dot{Q}_{12} = \varepsilon \sigma A (T_1^4 - T_2^4)$$

$$\frac{\dot{Q}_{12}}{A} = \varepsilon \sigma (T_1^4 - T_2^4)$$

$$= \frac{(1.0)\left(5.67 \times 10^{-8} \ \frac{\text{W}}{\text{m}^2 \cdot \text{K}^4}\right)\left((550\text{K})^4 - (290\text{K})^4\right)}{1000 \ \frac{\text{W}}{\text{kW}}}$$

$$= 4.787 \text{ kW/m}^2 \quad (4.8 \text{ kW/m}^2)$$

The answer is (C).

Equation 21.10: Net Radiation Heat Transfer, Black Bodies

$$\dot{Q}_{12} = A_1 F_{12} \sigma (T_1^4 - T_2^4) \qquad \text{21.10}$$

Description

The net heat transfer due to radiation between two black bodies is given by Eq. 21.10.

Example

A 15 cm thick furnace wall has a 8 cm square inspection port. The interior of the furnace is at 1200°C. The surrounding air temperature is 20°C. The shape factor, F_{12},

is 0.4. The heat loss due to radiation when the inspection port is open is most nearly

- (A)   150 W
- (B)   440 W
- (C)   680 W
- (D)   2700 W

Solution

The absolute temperatures are

$$T_{\text{furnace}} = 1200°\text{C} + 273° = 1473\text{K}$$
$$T_\infty = 20°\text{C} + 273° = 293\text{K}$$

The radiation heat loss is

$$\dot{Q} = A F_{12} \sigma (T_{\text{furnace}}^4 - T_\infty^4)$$

$$= \frac{(8 \text{ cm})^2 (0.4)\left(5.67 \times 10^{-8} \ \frac{\text{W}}{\text{m}^2 \cdot \text{K}^4}\right)}{\left(100 \ \frac{\text{cm}}{\text{m}}\right)^2}$$

$$\times \left((1473\text{K})^4 - (293\text{K})^4\right)$$

$$= 682.3 \text{ W} \quad (680 \text{ W})$$

The answer is (C).

Equation 21.11: Net Radiation Heat Transfer, Diffuse Gray Surfaces

$$\dot{Q}_{12} = \frac{\sigma(T_1^4 - T_2^4)}{\dfrac{1 - \varepsilon_1}{\varepsilon_1 A_1} + \dfrac{1}{A_1 F_{12}} + \dfrac{1 - \varepsilon_2}{\varepsilon_2 A_2}} \qquad \text{21.11}$$

Description

The net heat transfer due to radiation between two diffuse gray surfaces is given by Eq. 21.11. Equation 21.11 applies to two bodies (surfaces), each of which is completely covered (enclosed) by the other. This configuration is known as a *two-surface enclosure* and is shown in Fig. 21.1.[5] Either body can be designated as body 1, and either can be designated as body 2. Each body radiates to the other; each body receives energy from the other. The emissivities of the two bodies are not necessarily the same. Although the bodies are completely enclosed, this does not necessarily mean that the view factor, F_{12},

---

[5]The interpretation and application of Fig. 21.1 as presented in the *NCEES Handbook* are not obvious. There are two generalized cases shown. (The *NCEES Handbook* does not include the (a) and (b) designations, and so it appears that something is going on between the left-hand and right-hand sides.) Part (a) shows a radiating flat gray surface that is covered (enclosed) by a dome, which is also a radiation gray surface. Since the dome connects to the surface everywhere along the periphery, the two surfaces "form an enclosure" (as the *NCEES Handbook* phrases it). This constitutes the traditional *two surface enclosure*. In the case of part (b), radiating gray body 1 is completely enclosed by radiating gray body 2. It is not intuitive how the enclosed body 1 of part (b) "forms" an enclosure, as the *NCEES Handbook* phrases it. Nevertheless, Eq. 21.11 applies to both cases.

is equal to 1.0. The enclosure may not be sufficiently convex to enable all parts of the surfaces to see all other parts of the surfaces. There may be blind spots caused by shadowing.[6] Parallel plates, concentric cylinders, and concentric spheres, however, are *convex hulls* (*convex envelopes*), so $F_{12} = F_{21} = 1.0$.

Figure 21.1 *Radiation Between Two Diffuse Gray Surfaces*

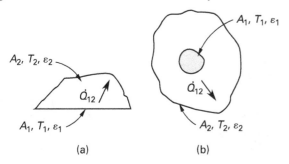

(a)   (b)

Example

Two plane radiating surfaces separated by a vacuum face each other. Each radiating surface has an emissivity of 0.02. The areas of the two surfaces are large and equal. One surface is at 400K, and the other is at 300K. The view factor, F_{12}, for the 400K surface is 1.0. Most nearly, what is the net heat transfer per unit area from the 400K surface?

(A) 4 W/m^2

(B) 6 W/m^2

(C) 8 W/m^2

(D) 10 W/m^2

Solution

Use Eq. 21.11 with $A_1 = A_2$ and $F_{12} = 1.0$.

$$\dot{Q}_{12} = \frac{\sigma(T_1^4 - T_2^4)}{\dfrac{1-\varepsilon_1}{\varepsilon_1 A_1} + \dfrac{1}{A_1 F_{12}} + \dfrac{1-\varepsilon_2}{\varepsilon_2 A_2}}$$

$$\dot{q} = \frac{Q_{12}}{A_1} = \frac{\sigma(T_1^4 - T_2^4)}{\dfrac{1-\varepsilon_1}{\varepsilon_1} + \dfrac{1}{1} + \dfrac{1-\varepsilon_2}{\varepsilon_2}} = \frac{\sigma(T_1^4 - T_2^4)}{\dfrac{1}{\varepsilon_1} + \dfrac{1}{\varepsilon_2} - 1}$$

$$= \frac{\left(5.67 \times 10^{-8} \dfrac{\text{W}}{\text{m}^2 \cdot \text{K}^4}\right)\left((400\text{K})^4 - (300\text{K})^4\right)}{\dfrac{1}{0.02} + \dfrac{1}{0.02} - 1}$$

$$= 10.02 \text{ W/m}^2 \quad (10 \text{ W/m}^2)$$

The answer is (D).

Equation 21.12: Net Radiation Heat Transfer, Parallel Plates

$$\dot{Q}_{12} = \frac{\sigma(T_1^4 - T_2^4)}{\dfrac{1-\varepsilon_1}{\varepsilon_1 A_1} + \dfrac{1}{A_1 F_{13}} + \dfrac{1-\varepsilon_{3,1}}{\varepsilon_{3,1} A_3} + \dfrac{1-\varepsilon_{3,2}}{\varepsilon_{3,2} A_3} + \dfrac{1}{A_3 F_{32}} + \dfrac{1-\varepsilon_2}{\varepsilon_2 A_2}} \quad \textit{21.12}$$

Description

Figure 21.2 illustrates two parallel plates that are separated by a thin internal shield.[7] The significance of the shield thickness is that a thin shield has no mass and cannot store any thermal energy. The significance of being a low-emissivity shield is that the corresponding reflectivity is high. Most of the energy intercepted by the shield is reflected back to the source. The thermal radiation that the shield does receive is re-emitted, some back to the source plate, and some through to the opposite parallel plate. The lower the emissivity of the shield, the higher its contribution will be to thermal resistance. Equation 21.12 calculates the net heat transfer from plate 1 to plate 2.

Heat Transfer

---

[6]In a convex hull, every point on the boundary can see every other point on the boundary. A simple visualization of a *convex hull* is the space (envelope) that is obtained by wrapping a rubber band around the vertices or other line intersection points defining the extent of the boundary.
[7]This configuration models thermal shielding of cryogenic vessels and temperature sensors.

Figure 21.2 Radiation Shield Between Parallel Plates

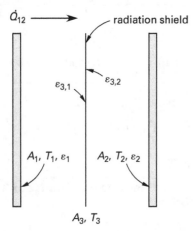

5. RADIATION WITH REFLECTION/ RERADIATION

Surfaces that reradiate absorbed thermal radiation are known as *refractory materials* or *refractories*. (Furnace walls that reradiate almost all of the thermal energy they receive from combustion flames back to boiler tubes are examples of refractories.)

Equation 21.13: Reradiating Surface

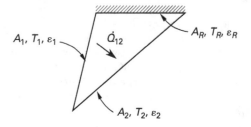

$$\dot{Q}_{12} = \cfrac{\sigma(T_1^4 - T_2^4)}{\cfrac{1-\varepsilon_1}{\varepsilon_1 A_1} + \cfrac{1}{A_1 F_{12} + \left[\left(\dfrac{1}{A_1 F_{1R}}\right) + \left(\dfrac{1}{A_2 F_{2R}}\right)\right]^{-1}} + \cfrac{1-\varepsilon_2}{\varepsilon_2 A_2}} \qquad 21.13$$

Description

Equation 21.13 gives the rate of heat transfer between two surfaces with an adjacent third reradiating surface. Reradiating surfaces are considered insulated (adiabatic). (See Fig. 21.3.)

Figure 21.3 Reradiating Surface

A_1, T_1, ε_1 $\dot{Q}_{12}$ A_R, T_R, ε_R

A_2, T_2, ε_2

Heat Transfer

Diagnostic Exam

Topic VI: Statics

1. A 100 kg block rests on an incline. The coefficient of static friction between the block and the ramp is 0.2. The mass of the cable is negligible, and the pulley at point C is frictionless.

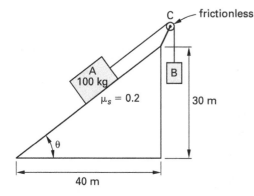

What is the smallest block B mass that will start the 100 kg block moving up the incline?

(A)   44 kg

(B)   65 kg

(C)   76 kg

(D)   92 kg

2. A 10 m long ladder rests against a frictionless wall. The coefficient of static friction between the ladder and the floor is 0.4. The combined weight of the ladder and an individual can be idealized as an 800 N force applied at point B, as shown.

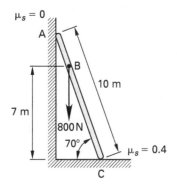

What is most nearly the horizontal frictional force between the ladder and floor?

(A)   180 N

(B)   220 N

(C)   270 N

(D)   320 N

3. A 100 kg block rests on a frictionless incline. Forces are applied to the block as shown.

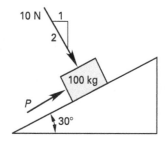

What is the minimum force, P, such that no downward motion occurs?

(A)   50 N

(B)   200 N

(C)   490 N

(D)   850 N

4. Two spheres, one with a mass of 7.5 kg and the other with a mass of 10.0 kg, are in equilibrium as shown.

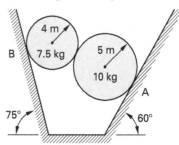

If all surfaces are frictionless, what is most nearly the magnitude of the reaction at point B?

(A) 170 N

(B) 200 N

(C) 210 N

(D) 240 N

5. An area is given as shown.

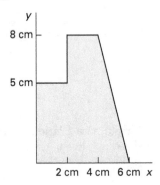

Most nearly, what are the x- and y-coordinates of the area's centroid?

(A) (2.5 cm, 3.4 cm)

(B) (2.8 cm, 3.3 cm)

(C) (3.2 cm, 4.2 cm)

(D) (3.4 cm, 3.7 cm)

6. The cantilever truss shown supports a vertical force of 600 000 N applied at point G.

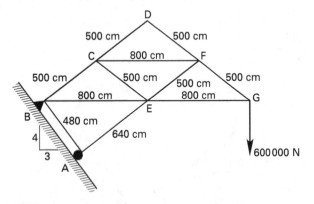

What is most nearly the force in member CF?

(A) 0.96 MN

(B) 1.2 MN

(C) 1.6 MN

(D) 2.3 MN

7. A sign has a mass of 150 kg. The sign is attached to the wall by a pin at point B and is supported by a cable between points A and C.

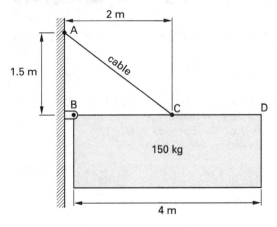

Determine the approximate force in the cable.

(A) 1900 N

(B) 2500 N

(C) 3800 N

(D) 5000 N

8. An inclined force, F, is applied to a block of mass m. There is no movement due to sliding.

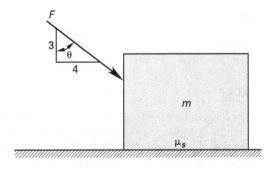

What is the minimum coefficient of static friction between the block and the ramp surface such that no motion occurs?

(A) $\dfrac{4F}{3F+5mg}$

(B) $\dfrac{F\tan\theta}{mg}$

(C) $\dfrac{3F}{4F+5mg}$

(D) $\dfrac{F}{mg}$

9. A rope supporting a mass passes over a horizontal tree branch. The mass exerts a force of 1000 N on the rope. The radius of the branch is 75 mm. The coefficient

Statics

of static friction between the rope and all the surfaces it contacts is 0.3, and the angle of contact is 300°. What is most nearly the minimum force necessary to hold the mass in position?

(A)   0.0 N

(B)   210 N

(C)   790 N

(D)   1200 N

10. The weight of a 500 kg homogenous crate is supported by three wall-mounted cables, as shown.

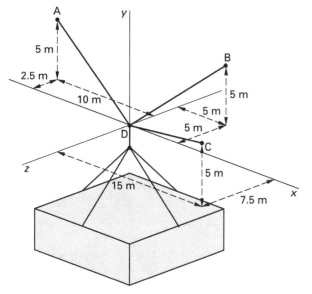

If the force in cable AD is 5950 N, most nearly, what is the sum of the x-components in cables BD and CD?

(A)   4700 N

(B)   5200 N

(C)   5900 N

(D)   6500 N

SOLUTIONS

1. Choose coordinate axes parallel and perpendicular to the incline.

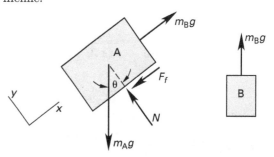

If the block is at rest, all forces are in equilibrium, so the sum of the forces must be zero.

$$\sum F_x = 0$$
$$= m_B g - m_A g(\sin\theta + \mu_s \cos\theta)$$

The smallest mass of block B that will start the block moving is

$$m_B = m_A(\sin\theta + \mu_s \cos\theta) = (100 \text{ kg})\left[\frac{3}{5} + (0.2)\left(\frac{4}{5}\right)\right]$$
$$= 76 \text{ kg}$$

(Note that the frictional force serves to increase, not decrease, the force required to accelerate the block.)

The answer is (C).

2. Draw the free-body diagram.

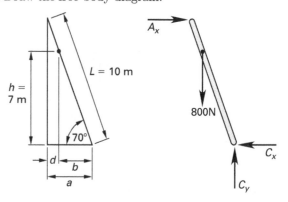

Since the wall is frictionless, the floor must support all of the vertical force.

$$\sum F_y = 0$$
$$= C_y - 800 \text{ N}$$
$$C_y = 800 \text{ N}$$

By trigonometry,

$$a = L\cos\theta = (10 \text{ m})\cos 70°$$
$$= 3.42 \text{ m}$$

$$b = \frac{h}{\tan\theta} = \frac{7 \text{ m}}{\tan 70°}$$
$$= 2.55 \text{ m}$$

$$d = a - b = 3.42 \text{ m} - 2.55 \text{ m}$$
$$= 0.87 \text{ m}$$

Sum moments about point A.

$$\sum M_A = 0$$
$$= (800 \text{ N})d - C_y a + C_x L \sin 70°$$
$$= (800 \text{ N})(0.87 \text{ m}) - (800 \text{ N})(3.42 \text{ m})$$
$$+ C_x(10 \text{ m})\sin 70°$$
$$C_x = \frac{(800 \text{ N})(3.42 \text{ m}) - (800 \text{ N})(0.87 \text{ m})}{(10 \text{ m})\sin 70°}$$
$$= 216.9 \text{ N} \quad (220 \text{ N})$$

($C_x < \mu_s N$ since motion is not impending.)

The answer is (B).

3. Choose coordinate axes that are parallel and perpendicular to the incline.

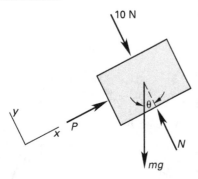

For no downward motion to occur, the forces must be in equilibrium, which means the sum of all forces must be zero. The force required to maintain equilibrium is

Equilibrium Requirements

$$\sum F_x = 0 = P - mg \sin\theta$$
$$P = mg \sin\theta$$
$$= (100 \text{ kg})\left(9.81 \ \frac{\text{m}}{\text{s}^2}\right)\sin 30°$$
$$= 490 \text{ N}$$

The answer is (C).

4. Draw the free-body diagram.

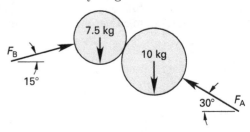

If the forces are in equilibrium, the sum of the forces must be zero.

$$\sum F_x = 0$$
$$= F_B \cos 15° - F_A \cos 30°$$
$$F_A = F_B\left(\frac{\cos 15°}{\cos 30°}\right)$$
$$= 1.12 F_B$$
$$\sum F_y = 0$$
$$= F_B \sin 15° + F_A \sin 30° - (7.5 \text{ kg})\left(9.81 \ \frac{\text{m}}{\text{s}^2}\right)$$
$$-(10.0 \text{ kg})\left(9.81 \ \frac{\text{m}}{\text{s}^2}\right)$$
$$= F_B \sin 15° + 1.12 F_B \sin 30° - 172 \text{ N}$$
$$= 0.816 F_B - 172 \text{ N}$$

The reaction force at point B if the system is in equilibrium is

$$F_B = 210.3 \text{ N} \quad (210 \text{ N})$$

The answer is (C).

5. Divide the shape into regions. Calculate the area and locate the centroid for each region.

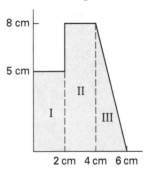

For region I (rectangular),

$$A = (2 \text{ cm})(5 \text{ cm}) = 10 \text{ cm}^2$$

$$x_c = \frac{2 \text{ cm}}{2} = 1 \text{ cm}$$

$$y_c = \frac{5 \text{ cm}}{2} = 2.5 \text{ cm}$$

For region II (rectangular),

$$A = (2 \text{ cm})(8 \text{ cm}) = 16 \text{ cm}^2$$

$$x_c = \frac{2 \text{ cm} + 4 \text{ cm}}{2} = 3 \text{ cm}$$

$$y_c = \frac{8 \text{ cm}}{2} = 4 \text{ cm}$$

For region III (triangular),

$$A = \left(\frac{1}{2}\right)(2 \text{ cm})(8 \text{ cm}) = 8 \text{ cm}^2$$

$$x_c = 4 \text{ cm} + \left(\frac{1}{3}\right)(2 \text{ cm}) = 4.67 \text{ cm}$$

$$y_c = \frac{8 \text{ cm}}{3} = 2.67 \text{ cm}$$

Calculate the centroidal x- and y-coordinates.

$$x_c = \frac{M_{ay}}{A_i} = \frac{\sum x_{c,i} A_i}{\sum A_i}$$

$$= \frac{\begin{array}{c}(1 \text{ cm})(10 \text{ cm}^2) + (3 \text{ cm})(16 \text{ cm}^2) \\ + (4.67 \text{ cm})(8 \text{ cm}^2)\end{array}}{10 \text{ cm}^2 + 16 \text{ cm}^2 + 8 \text{ cm}^2}$$

$$= 2.80 \text{ cm} \quad (2.8 \text{ cm})$$

$$y_c = \frac{M_{ax}}{A_i} = \frac{\sum y_{c,i} A_i}{\sum A_i}$$

$$= \frac{\begin{array}{c}(2.5 \text{ cm})(10 \text{ cm}^2) + (4 \text{ cm})(16 \text{ cm}^2) \\ + (2.67 \text{ cm})(8 \text{ cm}^2)\end{array}}{10 \text{ cm}^2 + 16 \text{ cm}^2 + 8 \text{ cm}^2}$$

$$= 3.25 \text{ cm} \quad (3.3 \text{ cm})$$

The answer is (B).

6. Draw the free-body diagram for the truss.

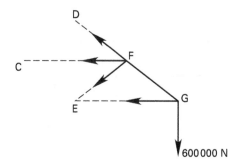

Equilibrium of pin D requires that the forces in members CD and DF are zero.

Use the method of sections. Sum moments about joint E. Clockwise moments are positive. From geometry, the vertical distance between member CF and point E is the moment arm for the force in member CF, and is equal to 300 cm.

Equilibrium Requirements

$$\sum M_{\mathrm{E}} = 0$$
$$= (600\,000 \text{ N})(800 \text{ cm}) - \mathrm{CF}(300 \text{ cm})$$
$$\mathrm{CF} = \frac{(600\,000 \text{ N})(800 \text{ cm})}{300 \text{ cm}}$$
$$= 1\,600\,000 \text{ N} \quad (1.6 \text{ MN})$$

The answer is (C).

7. Draw the free-body diagram.

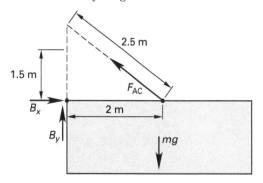

Find the length of the cable.

$$L_{\mathrm{AC}} = \sqrt{(1.5 \text{ m})^2 + (2 \text{ m})^2}$$
$$= 2.5 \text{ m}$$

The vertical component of the force in the cable is

$$F_{\mathrm{AC},y} = \left(\frac{1.5 \text{ m}}{2.5 \text{ m}}\right) F_{\mathrm{AC}}$$
$$= 0.6 F_{\mathrm{AC}}$$

Statics

Sum moments about point B. *[Equilibrium Requirements]*

$$\sum M_{\mathrm{B}} = mg(2\text{ m}) - F_{AC,y}(2\text{ m})$$
$$= 0$$
$$= (150\text{ kg})\left(9.81\ \frac{\text{m}}{\text{s}^2}\right)(2\text{ m})$$
$$\qquad -(0.6)F_{AC}(2\text{ m})$$
$$= 0$$
$$F_{AC} = \frac{(150\text{ kg})\left(9.81\ \dfrac{\text{m}}{\text{s}^2}\right)(2\text{ m})}{1.2\text{ m}}$$
$$= 2452.5\text{ N} \quad (2500\text{ N})$$

The answer is (B).

8. Draw the free-body diagram.

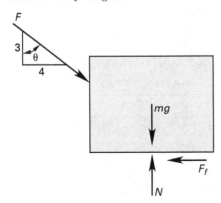

If no motion occurs, the forces are in equilibrium. The equilibrium equations are

$$\sum F_y = 0$$
$$= N - F\cos\theta - mg$$
$$N = F\cos\theta + mg$$
$$\sum F_x = 0$$
$$= F\sin\theta - F_f$$
$$= F\sin\theta - \mu_s N$$
$$\mu_s = \frac{F\sin\theta}{N}$$
$$= \frac{F\sin\theta}{F\cos\theta + mg}$$
$$= \frac{F\left(\dfrac{4}{5}\right)}{F\left(\dfrac{3}{5}\right) + mg}$$
$$= \frac{4F}{3F + 5mg}$$

The answer is (A).

9. The angle of contact must be expressed in radians.

$$\theta = \frac{(300°)2\pi}{360°}$$
$$= 5.24\text{ rad}$$

From the Equation for belt friction, the force necessary to hold the mass in position is

Belt Friction

$$F_1 = F_2 e^{\mu\theta}$$
$$F_2 = \frac{F_1}{e^{\mu\theta}} = \frac{1000\text{ N}}{e^{(0.3)(5.24\text{ rad})}}$$
$$= 208\text{ N} \quad (210\text{ N})$$

The answer is (B).

10. The length of cable AD is

$$L_{AD} = \sqrt{x_A^2 + y_A^2 + z_A^2}$$
$$= \sqrt{(-10\text{ m})^2 + (5\text{ m})^2 + (-2.5\text{ m})^2}$$
$$= 11.456\text{ m}$$

The x-component of force in member AD is found from the x-direction cosine.

$$\begin{aligned}
\mathrm{AD}_x &= \left(\frac{x_{\mathrm{A}}}{L_{\mathrm{AD}}}\right)\mathrm{AD} \\
&= \left(\frac{-10}{11.456 \text{ m}}\right)(5950 \text{ N}) \\
&= -5194 \text{ N}
\end{aligned}$$

The equilibrium requirement is

Equilibrium Requirements

$$\sum F_x = 0$$

The sum of the x-components is

$$\mathrm{BD}_x + \mathrm{CD}_x = -\mathrm{AD}_x = 5194 \text{ N} \quad (5200 \text{ N})$$

The answer is (B).

22 Systems of Forces and Moments

Nomenclature

d	distance	m
F	force	N
M	moment	N·m
r	distance	m
r	radius	m
R	resultant	N

Subscripts

θ	angle	deg

1. FORCES

Statics is the study of rigid bodies that are stationary. To be stationary, a rigid body must be in static equilibrium. In the language of statics, a stationary rigid body has no *unbalanced forces* acting on it.

Force is a push or a pull that one body exerts on another, including gravitational, electrostatic, magnetic, and contact influences. Force is a vector quantity, having a magnitude, direction, and point of application.

Strictly speaking, actions of other bodies on a rigid body are known as *external forces*. If unbalanced, an external force will cause motion of the body. *Internal forces* are the forces that hold together parts of a rigid body. Although internal forces can cause deformation of a body, motion is never caused by internal forces.

Forces are frequently represented in terms of unit vectors and force components. A *unit vector* is a vector of unit length directed along a coordinate axis. Unit vectors are used in vector equations to indicate direction without affecting magnitude. In the rectangular coordinate system, there are three unit vectors, $\mathbf{i}$, $\mathbf{j}$, and $\mathbf{k}$.

Equation 22.1: Vector Form of a Two-Dimensional Force

$$\mathbf{F} = F_x \mathbf{i} + F_y \mathbf{j} \qquad \text{22.1}$$

Description

The vector form of a two-dimensional force is described by Eq. 22.1.

Equation 22.2 and Eq. 22.3: Resultant of Two-Dimensional Forces

$$F = \left[\left(\sum_{i=1}^{n} F_{x,i} \right)^2 + \left(\sum_{i=1}^{n} F_{y,i} \right)^2 \right]^{1/2} \qquad \text{22.2}$$

$$\theta = \arctan\left(\sum_{i=1}^{n} F_{y,i} \middle/ \sum_{i=1}^{n} F_{x,i} \right) \qquad \text{22.3}$$

Description

The *resultant*, or sum, F, of n two-dimensional forces is equal to the sum of the components. The angle of the resultant with respect to the x-axis is calculated from Eq. 22.3.

Equation 22.4 Through Eq. 22.9: Components of Force

$$F_x = F \cos \theta_x \qquad \text{22.4}$$

$$F_y = F \cos \theta_y \qquad \text{22.5}$$

$$F_z = F \cos \theta_z \qquad \text{22.6}$$

$$\cos \theta_x = F_x / F \qquad \text{22.7}$$

$$\cos \theta_y = F_y / F \qquad \text{22.8}$$

$$\cos \theta_z = F_z / F \qquad \text{22.9}$$

Description

The components of a two- or three-dimensional force can be found from its *direction cosines*, the cosines of the true angles made by the force vector with the x-, y-, and z-axes. (See Fig. 22.1.)

Figure 22.1 *Components and Direction Angles of a Force*

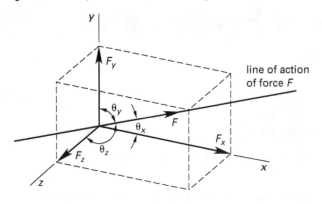

Example

What is most nearly the x-component of the 300 N force at point D on the member shown?

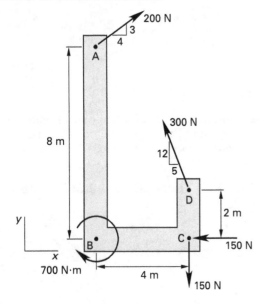

(A) 120 N

(B) 130 N

(C) 180 N

(D) 240 N

Solution

Use the Pythagorean theorem to calculate the hypotenuse of the inclined force triangle. (Alternatively, recognize that this is a 5-12-13 triangle.)

$$\sqrt{(12)^2 + (5)^2} = 13$$

The x-component of the force is

$$F_x = F \cos \theta_x = (300 \text{ N})\left(\frac{5}{13}\right)$$

$$= 115.4 \text{ N} \quad (120 \text{ N})$$

The answer is (A).

Equation 22.10 Through Eq. 22.13: Resultant Force

$R = \sqrt{x^2 + y^2 + z^2}$	22.10
$F_x = (x/R)F$	22.11
$F_y = (y/R)F$	22.12
$F_z = (z/R)F$	22.13

Description

When the x, y, and z components of a force are known, the resultant force is given by Eq. 22.10.

Example

Two forces of 20 N and 30 N act at right angles.

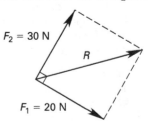

What is most nearly the magnitude of the resultant force?

(A) 7.0 N

(B) 36 N

(C) 50 N

(D) 75 N

Solution

Define the x-axis parallel to force F_1. From Eq. 22.10, the magnitude of the resultant force is

$$R = \sqrt{x^2 + y^2 + z^2} = \sqrt{(20 \text{ N})^2 + (30 \text{ N})^2 + (0 \text{ N})^2}$$

$$= 36 \text{ N}$$

The answer is (B).

2. MOMENTS

Moment is the name given to the tendency of a force to rotate, turn, or twist a rigid body about an actual or assumed pivot point. (Another name for moment is *torque*, although torque is used mainly with shafts and other power-transmitting machines.) When acted upon by a moment, unrestrained bodies rotate. However, rotation is not required for the moment to exist. When a restrained body is acted upon by a moment, there is no rotation.

An object experiences a moment whenever a force is applied to it. Only when the line of action of the force passes through the center of rotation (i.e., the actual or assumed pivot point) will the moment be zero. (The moment may be zero, as when the moment arm length is zero, but there is a trivial moment nevertheless.)

Moments have primary dimensions of length × force. Typical units are foot-pounds, inch-pounds, and newton-meters. To avoid confusion with energy units, moments may be expressed as pound-feet, pound-inches, and newton-meters.

Equation 22.14: Moment Vector

$$M = r \times F \qquad 22.14$$

Variation

$$M_O = |M_O| = |r||F|\sin\theta = d|F| \quad [\theta \leq 180°]$$

Description

Moments are vectors. The moment vector due to a vector force, F, applied at a point P, about an axis passing through point O, is designated as M_O. The moment also depends on the *position vector*, r, from point O to point P. The moment is calculated as the cross product, $r \times F$. The axis of the moment will be perpendicular to the plane containing vectors F and r. Any point could be chosen for point O, although it is usually convenient to select point O as the origin, and to put P in the horizontal x-y plane. In that case, M_O will be a moment about the vertical z-axis. The scalar product $|r|\sin\theta$, shown in the variation equation, is known as the *moment arm, d*.

Example

What is most nearly the magnitude of the moment about the x-axis produced by a force of $F = 10i - 20j + 40k$ acting at the point $(2, 1, 1)$ with coordinates in meters?

(A) 30 N·m

(B) 40 N·m

(C) 50 N·m

(D) 60 N·m

Solution

The x-, y-, and z-axes are being used, so point O corresponds to the origin. Work in meters and newtons. Equation 22.14 calculates the moment about the vertical z-axis. The cross product can be calculated as a determinant.

$$\begin{aligned} M_O &= r \times F \\ &= (r_y F_z - r_z F_y)i + (r_z F_x - r_x F_z)j \\ &\quad + (r_x F_y - r_y F_x)k \\ &= (2i + j + k) \times (10i - 20j + 40k) \\ &= ((1\text{ m})(40\text{ N}) - (1\text{ m})(-20\text{ N}))i \\ &\quad + ((1\text{ m})(10\text{ N}) - (2\text{ m})(40\text{ N}))j \\ &\quad + ((2\text{ m})(-20\text{ N}) - (1\text{ m})(10\text{ N}))k \\ &= 60i - 70j - 50k \text{ N·m} \end{aligned}$$

M_O is the moment about the origin, not the x-axis as requested. The moment about the x-axis is found as the projection of M_O onto the x-axis, which is the dot product operation.

$$\begin{aligned} M_{O,x} &= i \cdot M_O \\ &= (1\text{ m})(60\text{ N}) + (0\text{ m})(-70\text{ N}) + (0\text{ m})(-50\text{ N}) \\ &= 60\text{ N·m} \end{aligned}$$

The answer is (D).

Right-Hand Rule

The line of action of the moment vector is normal to the plane containing the force vector and the position vector. The sense (i.e., the direction) of the moment is determined from the *right-hand rule*. (See Fig. 22.2.)

> *Right-hand rule:* Place the position and force vectors tail to tail. Close your right hand and position it over the pivot point. Rotate the position vector into the force vector and position your hand such that your fingers curl in the same direction as the position vector rotates. Your extended thumb will coincide with the direction of the moment.

Figure 22.2 Right-Hand Rule

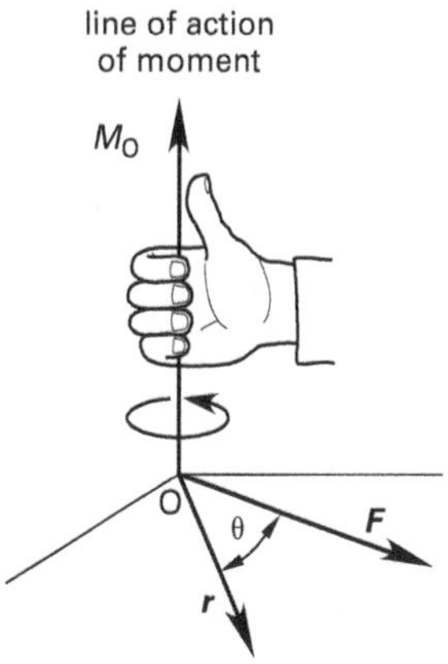

Equation 22.15 Through Eq. 22.17: Components of a Moment

$$M_x = yF_z - zF_y \qquad 22.15$$

$$M_y = zF_x - xF_z \qquad 22.16$$

$$M_z = xF_y - yF_x \qquad 22.17$$

Variations

$$M_x = M\cos\theta_x$$

$$M_y = M\cos\theta_y$$

$$M_z = M\cos\theta_z$$

Description

Equation 22.15, Eq. 22.16, and Eq. 22.17 can be used to determine the components of the moment from the component of a force applied at point (x, y, z) referenced to an origin at $(0, 0, 0)$. The resultant moment magnitude can be reconstituted from its components.

$$M = \sqrt{M_x^2 + M_y^2 + M_z^2}$$

The direction cosines of a force can be used to determine the components of the moment about the coordinate axes, as shown in the variation equations.

Example

What is most nearly the magnitude of the moment about the x-axis produced by a force of $\boldsymbol{F} = 10\mathbf{i} - 20\mathbf{j} + 40\mathbf{k}$ N acting at the point $(2, 1, 1)$ with coordinates in meters?

(A) 30 N·m

(B) 40 N·m

(C) 50 N·m

(D) 60 N·m

Solution

This is the same as the previous example. Use Eq. 22.15.

$$M_x = yF_z - zF_y = (1\text{ m})(40\text{ N}) - (1\text{ m})(-20\text{ N})$$
$$= 60\text{ N·m}$$

The answer is (D).

Couples

Any pair of equal, opposite, and parallel forces constitutes a *couple*. A couple is equivalent to a single moment vector. Since the two forces are opposite in sign, the x-, y-, and z-components of the forces cancel out. Therefore, a body is induced to rotate without translation. A couple can be counteracted only by another couple. A couple can be moved to any location without affecting the equilibrium requirements. (Such a moment is known as a *free moment, moment of a couple*, or *coupling moment*.)

In Fig. 22.3, the equal but opposite forces produce a moment vector, $\boldsymbol{M}_O$, of magnitude Fd. The two forces can be replaced by this moment vector that can be moved to any location on a body.

$$\boldsymbol{M}_O = 2rF\sin\theta = Fd$$

Figure 22.3 Couple

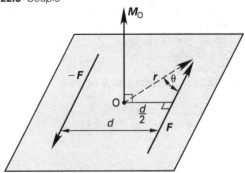

If a force, F, is moved a distance, d, from the original point of application, a couple, M, of magnitude Fd must be added to counteract the induced couple. The combination of the moved force and the couple is known as a *force-couple system*. Alternatively, a force-couple system can be replaced by a single force located a distance $d = M/F$ away.

3. SYSTEMS OF FORCES

Any collection of forces and moments in three-dimensional space is statically equivalent to a single resultant force vector plus a single resultant moment vector. (Either or both of these resultants can be zero.)

Equation 22.18 and Eq. 22.19[1]

$$\boldsymbol{F} = \sum \boldsymbol{F}_n \qquad 22.18$$

$$\boldsymbol{M} = \sum (\boldsymbol{r}_n \times \boldsymbol{F}_n) \qquad 22.19$$

---

[1]The NCEES *FE Reference Handbook* (*NCEES Handbook*) uses both n and i for summation variables. Though i is traditionally used to indicate summation, n appears to be used as the summation variable in order to indicate that the summation is over all n of the forces and all n of the position vectors that make up the system (i.e., $i = 1$ to n).

Description

The x-, y-, and z-components of the resultant force, given by Eq. 22.18, are the sums of the x-, y-, and z-components of the individual forces, respectively.

The resultant moment vector, given by Eq. 22.19, is more complex. It includes the moments of all system forces around the reference axes plus the components of all system moments.

Variations

$$\boldsymbol{R} = \sum \boldsymbol{F}_i$$
$$= \boldsymbol{i} \sum_{i=1}^{n} F_{x,i} + \boldsymbol{j} \sum_{i=1}^{n} F_{y,i} + \boldsymbol{k} \sum_{i=1}^{n} F_{z,i} \quad \begin{bmatrix} \text{three-} \\ \text{dimensional} \end{bmatrix}$$

$$\boldsymbol{M} = \sum \boldsymbol{M}_i$$

$$M_x = \sum_i (yF_z - zF_y)_i + \sum_i (M\cos\theta_x)_i$$

$$M_y = \sum_i (zF_x - xF_z)_i + \sum_i (M\cos\theta_y)_i$$

$$M_z = \sum_i (xF_y - yF_x)_i + \sum_i (M\cos\theta_z)_i$$

Equation 22.20 and Eq. 22.21: Equilibrium Requirements

$$\sum \boldsymbol{F}_n = 0 \qquad \text{22.20}$$

$$\sum \boldsymbol{M}_n = 0 \qquad \text{22.21}$$

Description

An object is static when it is stationary. To be stationary, all of the forces and moments on the object must be in *equilibrium*. For an object to be in equilibrium, the resultant force and moment vectors must both be zero.

The following equations follow directly from Eq. 22.20 and Eq. 22.21.

$$\sum F_x = 0$$

$$\sum F_y = 0$$

$$\sum F_z = 0$$

$$\sum M_x = 0$$

$$\sum M_y = 0$$

$$\sum M_z = 0$$

These equations seem to imply that six simultaneous equations must be solved in order to determine whether a system is in equilibrium. While this is true for general three-dimensional systems, fewer equations are necessary for most problems.

Concurrent Forces

A *concurrent force system* is a category of force systems where all of the forces act at the same point.

If the forces on a body are all concurrent forces, then only force equilibrium is necessary to ensure complete equilibrium.

In two dimensions,

$$\sum F_x = 0$$

$$\sum F_y = 0$$

In three dimensions,

$$\sum F_x = 0$$

$$\sum F_y = 0$$

$$\sum F_z = 0$$

Two- and Three-Force Members

Members limited to loading by two or three forces in the same plane are special cases of equilibrium. A *two-force member* can be in equilibrium only if the two forces have the same line of action (i.e., are collinear) and are equal but opposite.

In most cases, two-force members are loaded axially, and the line of action coincides with the member's longitudinal axis. By choosing the coordinate system so that one axis coincides with the line of action, only one equilibrium equation is needed.

A *three-force member* can be in equilibrium only if the three forces are concurrent or parallel. Stated another way, the force polygon of a three-force member in equilibrium must close on itself. If the member is in equilibrium and two of the three forces are known, the third can be determined.

Statics

4. PROBLEM-SOLVING APPROACHES

Determinacy

When the equations of equilibrium are independent, a rigid body force system is said to be *statically determinate*. A statically determinate system can be solved for all unknowns, which are usually reactions supporting the body. Examples of determinate beam types are illustrated in Fig. 22.4.

Figure 22.4 *Types of Determinate Systems*

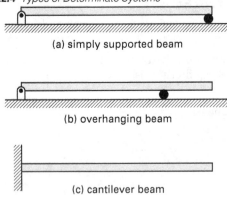

(a) simply supported beam

(b) overhanging beam

(c) cantilever beam

When the body has more supports than are necessary for equilibrium, the force system is said to be *statically indeterminate*. In a statically indeterminate system, one or more of the supports or members can be removed or reduced in restraint without affecting the equilibrium position. Those supports and members are known as *redundant supports* and *redundant members*. The number of redundant members is known as the *degree of indeterminacy*. Figure 22.5 illustrates several common indeterminate structures.

A body that is statically indeterminate requires additional equations to supplement the equilibrium equations. The additional equations typically involve deflections and depend on mechanical properties of the body or supports.

Free-Body Diagrams

A *free-body diagram* is a representation of a body in equilibrium, showing all applied forces, moments, and reactions. Free-body diagrams do not consider the internal structure or construction of the body, as Fig. 22.6 illustrates.

Since the body is in equilibrium, the resultants of all forces and moments on the free body are zero. In order to maintain equilibrium, any portions of the body that are conceptually removed must be replaced by the forces and moments those portions impart to the body. Typically, the body is isolated from its physical supports in order to help evaluate the reaction forces. In other cases, the body may be sectioned (i.e., cut) in order to determine the forces at the section.

Figure 22.5 *Examples of Indeterminate Systems*

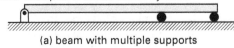

(a) beam with multiple supports

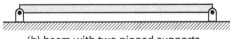

(b) beam with two pinned supports

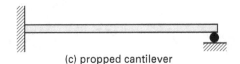

(c) propped cantilever

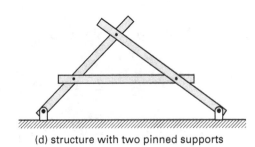

(d) structure with two pinned supports

Figure 22.6 *Bodies and Free Bodies*

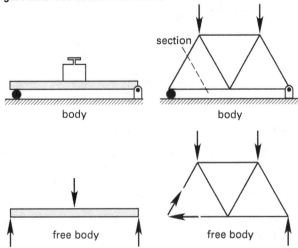

Reactions

The first step in solving most statics problems, after drawing the free-body diagram, is to determine the reaction forces (i.e., the *reactions*) supporting the body. The manner in which a body is supported determines the type, location, and direction of the reactions. Common support types are shown in Table 22.1.

For beams, the two most common types of supports are the roller support and the pinned support. The *roller support*, shown as a cylinder supporting the beam, supports vertical forces only. Rather than support a horizontal force, a roller support simply rolls into a new equilibrium position. Only one equilibrium equation (i.e., the sum of vertical forces) is needed at a roller support. Generally, the terms *simple support* and *simply supported* refer to a roller support.

The *pinned support*, shown as a pin and clevis, supports both vertical and horizontal forces. Two equilibrium equations are needed.

Generally, there will be vertical and horizontal components of a reaction when one body touches another. However, when a body is in contact with a *frictionless surface*, there is no frictional force component parallel to the surface, so the reaction is normal to the contact surfaces. The assumption of frictionless contact is particularly useful when dealing with systems of spheres and cylinders in contact with rigid supports. Frictionless contact is also assumed for roller and rocker supports.

The procedure for finding determinate reactions in two-dimensional problems is straightforward. Determinate structures will have either a roller support and pinned support or two roller supports.

step 1: Establish a convenient set of coordinate axes. (To simplify the analysis, one of the coordinate directions should coincide with the direction of the forces and reactions.)

step 2: Draw the free-body diagram.

step 3: Resolve the reaction at the pinned support (if any) into components normal and parallel to the coordinate axes.

step 4: Establish a positive direction of rotation (e.g., clockwise) for purposes of taking moments.

step 5: Write the equilibrium equation for moments about the pinned connection. (By choosing the pinned connection as the point about which to take moments, the pinned connection reactions do not enter into the equation.) This will usually determine the vertical reaction at the roller support.

step 6: Write the equilibrium equation for the forces in the vertical direction. Usually, this equation will have two unknown vertical reactions.

step 7: Substitute the known vertical reaction from step 5 into the equilibrium equation from step 6. This will determine the second vertical reaction.

step 8: Write the equilibrium equation for the forces in the horizontal direction. Since there is a minimum of one unknown reaction component in the horizontal direction, this step will determine that component.

step 9: If necessary, combine the vertical and horizontal force components at the pinned connection into a resultant reaction.

Table 22.1 *Types of Two-Dimensional Supports*

type of support	reactions and moments	number of unknowns*
simple, roller, rocker, ball, or frictionless surface	reaction normal to surface, no moment	1
cable in tension, or link	reaction in line with cable or link, no moment	1
frictionless guide or collar	reaction normal to rail, no moment	1
built-in, fixed support	two reaction components, one moment	3
frictionless hinge, pin connection, or rough surface	reaction in any direction, no moment	2

*The number of unknowns is valid for two-dimensional problems only.

Statics

23 Trusses

Nomenclature

F	force	N
M	moment	N·m

1. STATICALLY DETERMINATE TRUSSES

A *truss* or *frame* is a set of pin-connected *axial members* (i.e., *two-force members*). The connection points are known as *joints*. Member weights are disregarded, and truss loads are applied only at joints. A *structural cell* consists of all members in a closed loop of members. For the truss to be a table (i.e., to be a *rigid truss*), all of the structural cells must be triangles. Figure 23.1 identifies *chords*, *end posts*, *panels*, and other elements of a typical *bridge truss*.

Figure 23.1 *Parts of a Bridge Truss*

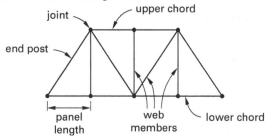

Several types of trusses have been given specific names. Some of the more common named trusses are shown in Fig. 23.2.

Truss loads are considered to act only in the plane of a truss, so trusses are analyzed as two-dimensional structures. Forces in truss members hold the various truss parts together and are known as *internal forces*. The internal forces are found by drawing free-body diagrams.

Although free-body diagrams of truss members can be drawn, this is not usually done. Instead, free-body diagrams of the pins (i.e., the joints) are drawn. A pin in compression will be shown with force arrows pointing toward the pin, away from the member. Similarly, a pin in tension will be shown with force arrows pointing away from the pin, toward the member.

Figure 23.2 *Special Types of Trusses*

Pratt roof truss (gabled)

Pratt bridge truss (flat or through)

Howe roof truss (gabled)

Howe bridge truss (flat or through)

Fink roof truss

Fink roof truss (with cambered bottom chord)

scissors roof truss

Warren bridge truss

K bridge truss

With typical bridge trusses supported at the ends and loaded downward at the joints, the upper chords are almost always in compression, and the end panels and lower chords are almost always in tension.

Since truss members are axial members, the forces on the truss joints are concurrent forces. Only force equilibrium needs to be enforced at each pin; the sum of the forces in each of the coordinate directions equals zero.

Forces in truss members can sometimes be determined by inspection. One of these cases is *zero-force members*. A third member framing into a joint already connecting two collinear members carries no internal force unless there is a load applied at that joint. Similarly, both members forming an apex of the truss are zero-force members unless there is a load applied at the apex. (See Fig. 23.3.)

Figure 23.3 *Zero-Force Members*

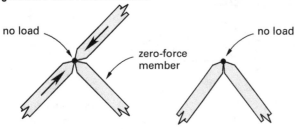

A truss will be *statically determinate* if

$$\text{no. of members} = (2)(\text{no. of joints}) - 3$$

If the left-hand side of the equation is greater than the right-hand side (i.e., there are *redundant members*), the truss is statically indeterminate. If the left-hand side is less than the right-hand side, the truss is unstable and will collapse under certain types of loading.

2. PLANE TRUSS

A *plane truss* (*planar truss*) is a rigid framework where all truss members are within the same plane and are connected at their ends by frictionless pins. External loads are in the same plane as the truss and are applied at the joints only.

Equation 23.1 and Eq. 23.2: Equations of Equilibrium[1]

$$\sum F_n = 0 \qquad\qquad 23.1$$

$$\sum M_n = 0 \qquad\qquad 23.2$$

Description

A plane truss is statically determinate if the truss reactions and member forces can be determined using the equations of equilibrium. If not, the truss is considered statically indeterminate.

Example

Most nearly, what are reactions F_1 and F_2 for the truss shown?

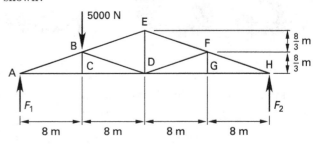

(A) $F_1 = 1000$ N; $F_2 = 4000$ N

(B) $F_1 = 1300$ N; $F_2 = 3800$ N

(C) $F_1 = 2500$ N; $F_2 = 2500$ N

(D) $F_1 = 3800$ N; $F_2 = 1300$ N

Solution

Calculate the reactions from Eq. 23.1 and Eq. 23.2. Let clockwise moments be positive.

$$\sum M_A = 0 = (5000\text{ N})(8\text{ m}) - F_2(32\text{ m})$$
$$F_2 = 1250\text{ N} \quad (1300\text{ N}) \quad [\text{upward}]$$
$$\sum F_y = 0 = F_1 + 1250\text{ N} - 5000\text{ N}$$
$$F_1 = 3750\text{ N} \quad (3800\text{ N}) \quad [\text{upward}]$$

The answer is (D).

3. METHOD OF JOINTS

The *method of joints* is one of the methods that can be used to find the internal forces in each truss member. This method is useful when most or all of the truss member forces are to be calculated. Because this method advances from joint to adjacent joint, it is inconvenient when a single isolated member force is to be calculated.

The method of joints is a direct application of the equations of equilibrium in the x- and y-directions. Traditionally, the method begins by finding the reactions supporting the truss. Next the joint at one of the reactions is evaluated, which determines all the member forces framing into the joint. Then, knowing one or more of the member forces from the previous step, an adjacent joint is analyzed. The process is repeated until all the unknown quantities are determined.

---

[1]The NCEES *FE Reference Handbook* (*NCEES Handbook*) uses both n and i for summation variables. Though i is traditionally used to indicate summation, n appears to be used as the summation variable in order to indicate that the summation is over all n of the forces and all n of the position vectors that make up the system (i.e., $i = 1$ to n).

At a joint, there may be up to two unknown member forces, each of which can have dependent x- and y-components. Since there are two equilibrium equations, the two unknown forces can be determined. Even though determinate, however, the sense of a force will often be unknown. If the sense cannot be determined by logic, an arbitrary decision can be made. If the incorrect direction is chosen, the force will be negative.

Occasionally, there will be three unknown member forces. In that case, an additional equation must be derived from an adjacent joint.

4. METHOD OF SECTIONS

The *method of sections* is a direct approach to finding forces in any truss member. This method is convenient when only a few truss member forces are unknown.

As with the previous method, the first step is to find the support reactions. Then, a cut is made through the truss, passing through the unknown member. (Knowing where to cut the truss is the key part of this method. Such knowledge is developed only by repeated practice.) Finally, all three conditions of equilibrium are applied as needed to the remaining truss portion. Since there are three equilibrium equations, the cut cannot pass through more than three members in which the forces are unknown.

Example

A truss is loaded as shown. The support reactions have already been determined.

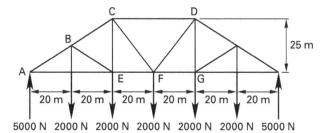

Most nearly, what is the force in member CE?

(A) 1000 N

(B) 2000 N

(C) 3000 N

(D) 4000 N

Solution

Cut the truss as shown.

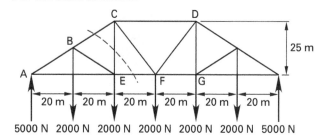

Draw the free body.

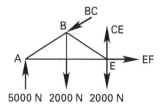

Taking moments about point A will eliminate all of the unknown forces except CE. Let clockwise moments be positive.

$$\sum M_A = 0$$
$$(2000 \text{ N})(20 \text{ m}) + (2000 \text{ N})(40 \text{ m}) - CE(40 \text{ m}) = 0$$
$$CE = 3000 \text{ N}$$

The answer is (C).

24 Pulleys, Cables, and Friction

Nomenclature

d	inside diameter	m
D	outside diameter	m
F	force	N
g	gravitational acceleration, 9.81	m/s^2
m	mass	kg
M	moment	N·m
n	number	–
N	normal force	N
p	pitch	m
P	power	W
r	radius	m
T	torque	N·m
v	velocity	m/s
W	weight	N

Symbols

α	pitch angle	deg
η	efficiency	–
θ	angle of wrap	radians
μ	coefficient of friction	–
ϕ	angle	deg

Subscripts

f	friction
k	kinetic
m	mechanical
s	static
t	tangential

1. PULLEYS

A *pulley* (also known as a *sheave*) is used to change the direction of an applied tensile force. A series of pulleys working together (known as a *block and tackle*) can also provide *pulley advantage* (i.e., *mechanical advantage*). (See Fig. 24.1.)

Figure 24.1 *Mechanical Advantage of Rope-Operated Machines*

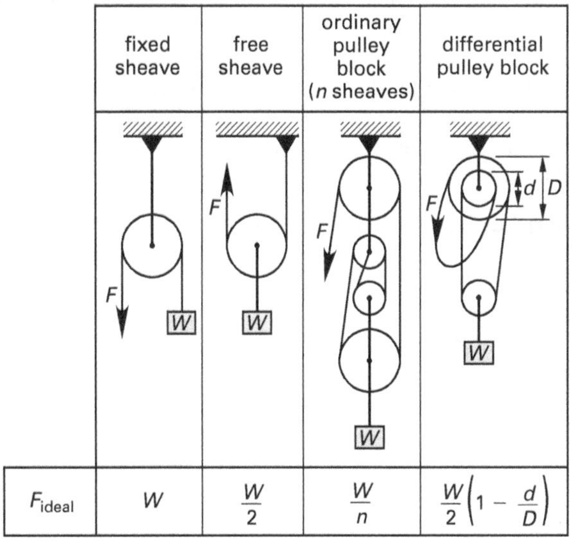

	fixed sheave	free sheave	ordinary pulley block (*n* sheaves)	differential pulley block
F_{ideal}	W	$\dfrac{W}{2}$	$\dfrac{W}{n}$	$\dfrac{W}{2}\left(1 - \dfrac{d}{D}\right)$

If the pulley is attached by a bracket to a fixed location, it is said to be a *fixed pulley*. If the pulley is attached to a load, or if the pulley is free to move, it is known as a *free pulley*.

Most simple problems disregard friction and assume that all ropes (fiber ropes, wire ropes, chains, belts, etc.) are parallel. In such cases, the pulley advantage is equal to the number of ropes coming to and going from the load-carrying pulley. The diameters of the pulleys are not factors in calculating the pulley advantage.

2. CABLES

An *ideal cable* is assumed to be completely flexible, massless, and incapable of elongation; it acts as an axial tension member between points of concentrated loading. The term *tension* or *tensile force* is commonly used in place of member force when dealing with cables.

The methods of joints and sections used in truss analysis can be used to determine the tensions in cables carrying concentrated loads. (See Fig. 24.2.) After separating the reactions into x- and y-components, it is particularly useful to sum moments about one of the reaction points. All cables will be found to be in tension, and (with vertical loads only) the horizontal tension component will be the same in all cable segments. Unlike the case of a rope passing over a series of pulleys, however, the total tension in the cable will not be the same in every cable segment.

Statics

Figure 24.2 *Cable with Concentrated Load*

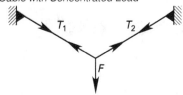

3. FRICTION

Friction is a force that always resists motion or impending motion. It always acts parallel to the contacting surfaces. The frictional force, F, exerted on a stationary body is known as *static friction, Coulomb friction,* and *fluid friction.* If the body is moving, the friction is known as *dynamic friction* and is less than the static friction.

Equation 24.1 Through Eq. 24.4: Frictional Force[1]

$$F \le \mu_s N \qquad \text{24.1}$$

$$\boldsymbol{F} < \mu_s \boldsymbol{N} \quad \text{[no slip occurring]} \qquad \text{24.2}$$

$$\boldsymbol{F} = \mu_s \boldsymbol{N} \quad \text{[point of impending slip]} \qquad \text{24.3}$$

$$\boldsymbol{F} = \mu_k \boldsymbol{N} \quad \text{[slip occurring]} \qquad \text{24.4}$$

Values

$$\mu_k \approx 0.75 \mu_s$$

Description

The actual magnitude of the frictional force depends on the *normal force*, N, and the *coefficient of friction*, μ, between the body and the surface. The coefficient of kinetic friction, μ_k, is approximately 75% of the coefficient of static friction, μ_s.

Equation 24.1 is a general expression of the laws of friction. Several specific cases exist depending on whether slip is occurring or impending. Use Eq. 24.2 when no slip is occurring. Equation 24.3 is valid at the point of impending slip (or slippage), and Eq. 24.4 is valid when slip is occurring.

For a body resting on a horizontal surface, the normal force is the weight of the body.

$$N = mg$$

If a body rests on a plane inclined at an angle ϕ from the horizontal, the normal force is

$$N = mg \, \cos\phi$$

Example

A 35 kg block resting on the 30° incline is shown.

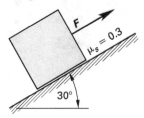

What is most nearly the frictional force at the point of impending slippage?

(A) 37 N

(B) 52 N

(C) 89 N

(D) 100 N

Solution

From Eq. 24.3, the frictional force is

$$\boldsymbol{F} = \mu_s \boldsymbol{N} = \mu_s(mg \, \cos\phi)$$
$$= (0.3)\left((35 \text{ kg})\left(9.81 \, \frac{\text{m}}{\text{s}^2}\right)\cos 30°\right)$$
$$= 89.2 \text{ N} \quad (89 \text{ N})$$

The answer is (C).

4. BELT FRICTION

Friction between a belt, rope, or band wrapped around a pulley or sheave is responsible for the transfer of torque. Except when stationary, one side of the belt (the tight side) will have a higher tension than the other (the slack side). (See Fig. 24.3.)

Figure 24.3 *Belt Friction*

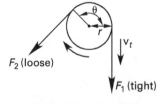

Equation 24.5: Belt Tension Relationship

$$F_1 = F_2 e^{\mu\theta} \qquad \text{24.5}$$

---

[1]Although the NCEES *FE Reference Handbook* (*NCEES Handbook*) uses bold, Eq. 24.2 through Eq. 24.4 are not vector equations.

Description

The basic relationship between the belt tensions and the coefficient of friction neglects centrifugal effects and is given by Eq. 24.5. F_1 is the tension on the tight side (direction of movement); F_2 is the tension on the other side. The *angle of wrap*, θ, must be expressed in radians.

The net transmitted torque is

$$T = (F_1 - F_2)r$$

The power transmitted to a belt running at tangential velocity v_t is

$$P = (F_1 - F_2)v_t$$

Example

A rope passes over a fixed sheave, as shown. The two rope ends are parallel. A fixed load on one end of the rope is supported by a constant force on the other end. The coefficient of friction between the rope and the sheave is 0.30.

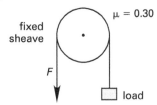

What is most nearly the maximum ratio of tensile forces in the two rope ends?

(A) 1.1

(B) 1.2

(C) 1.6

(D) 2.6

Solution

The angle of wrap, θ, is 180°, but it must be expressed in radians.

$$\theta = (180°)\left(\frac{2\pi \text{ rad}}{360°}\right) = \pi \text{ rad}$$

$$F_1 = F_2 e^{\mu\theta}$$

$$\frac{F_1}{F_2} = e^{(0.30)(\pi \text{ rad})}$$

$$= 2.57 \quad (2.6)$$

Either side could be the tight side. Therefore, the restraining force could be 2.6 times smaller or larger than the load tension.

The answer is (D).

5. SQUARE SCREW THREADS

A *power screw* changes angular position into linear position (i.e., changes rotary motion into traversing motion). The linear positioning can be horizontal (as in vices and lathes) or vertical (as in a jack). Square, Acme, and 10-degree modified screw threads are commonly used in power screws. A square screw thread is shown in Fig. 24.4.

Figure 24.4 *Square Screw Thread*

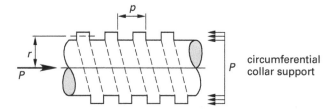

A square screw thread is designated by a mean radius, r, pitch, p, and *pitch angle*, α. The *pitch*, p, is the distance between corresponding points on a thread. The *lead* is the distance the screw advances each revolution. Often, double- and triple-threaded screws are used. The lead is one, two, or three times the pitch for single-, double-, and triple-threaded screws, respectively.

$$P = 2\pi r \tan\alpha$$

Equation 24.6 and Eq. 24.7: Coefficient of Friction and External Moment

$$\mu = \tan\phi \qquad 24.6$$

$$M = Pr\tan(\alpha \pm \phi) \qquad 24.7$$

Description

The coefficient of friction, μ, between the threads can be designated directly or by way of a *thread friction angle*, ϕ.

The torque or external moment, M, required to turn a square screw in motion against an axial force, P (i.e., "raise" the load), is found from Eq. 24.7.

r is the mean thread radius, M is the torque on the screw, and P is the tensile or compressive force in the screw (i.e., is the load being raised or lowered). The angles are added for tightening operations; they are subtracted for loosening. This equation assumes that all of the torque is used to raise or lower the load.

In Eq. 24.7, the "+" is used for screw tightening (i.e., when the load force is opposite in direction of the screw movement). The "−" is used for screw loosening (i.e., when the load force is in the same direction as the screw movement). If the torque is zero or negative (as it would be if the lead is large or friction is low), then the screw is not self-locking and the load will lower by itself, causing the screw to spin (i.e., it will "overhaul"). The screw will be self-locking when $\tan \alpha \leq \mu$.

The torque calculated in Eq. 24.7 is required to overcome thread friction and to raise the load (i.e., axially compress the screw). Typically, only 10–15% of the torque goes into axial compression of the screw. The remainder is used to overcome friction. The mechanical efficiency of the screw is the ratio of torque without friction to the torque with friction. The torque without friction can be calculated from Eq. 24.7 (or the variation equation, depending on the travel direction) using $\phi = 0$.

$$\eta_m = \frac{M_{f=0}}{M}$$

In the absence of an antifriction ring, an additional torque will be required to overcome friction in the collar. Since the collar is generally flat, the normal force is the jack load for the purpose of calculating the frictional force.

$$M_{\text{collar}} = N\mu_{\text{collar}} r_{\text{collar}}$$

Example

The nuts on a collar are each tightened to 18 N·m torque. 17% of this torque is used to tension the bolt. The bolts have a nominal diameter of 10 mm. The threads are a simple square cut with a pitch angle of 15°. The coefficient of friction in the threads is 0.10.

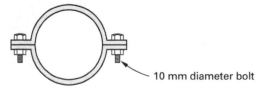

10 mm diameter bolt

Most nearly, what is the approximate tensile force in each bolt?

(A)   130 N

(B)   200 N

(C)   410 N

(D)   1600 N

Solution

The friction angle, ϕ, is

$$\begin{aligned} \phi &= \arctan\mu = \arctan 0.10 \\ &= 5.71° \end{aligned}$$

Use Eq. 24.7. Only 17% of the applied torque contributes to the tensile force in the bolt. The force in the bolt is

$$\begin{aligned} P &= \frac{M}{r\tan(\alpha + \phi)} \\ &= \frac{(0.17)(18 \text{ N·m})}{\left(\dfrac{0.01 \text{ m}}{2}\right)\tan(15° + 5.71°)} \\ &= 1619 \text{ N} \quad (1600 \text{ N}) \end{aligned}$$

The answer is (D).

25 Centroids and Moments of Inertia

Nomenclature

a	subarea	m^2
a	length or radius	m
A	area	m^2
b	base	m
d	distance	m
h	height	m
I	moment of inertia	m^4
I_{xy}	product of inertia	m^4
J	polar moment of inertia	m^4
l	length	m
L	total length	m
m	mass	kg
M	statical moment	m^3
r	radius or radius of gyration	m
v	volume	m^3
V	volume	m^3

Symbols

θ	angle	deg

Subscripts

a	area
c	centroidal
deg	degrees
l	line
o	origin
p	polar
rad	radians
v	volume

1. CENTROIDS

The *centroid* of an area is often described as the point at which a thin, homogeneous plate would balance. This definition, however, combines the definitions of centroid and center of gravity, and implies gravity is required to identify the centroid, which is not true. Nonetheless, this definition provides some intuitive understanding of the centroid.

Centroids of continuous functions can be found by the methods of integral calculus. For most engineering applications, though, the functions to be integrated are regular shapes such as the rectangular, circular, or composite rectangular shapes of beams. For these shapes, simple formulas are readily available and should be used.

Equation 25.1 and Eq. 25.2: First Moment of an Area in the x-y Plane[1]

$$M_{ay} = \sum x_n a_n \qquad \text{25.1}$$

$$M_{ax} = \sum y_n a_n \qquad \text{25.2}$$

Variations

$$M_y = \int x \, dA = \sum x_i A_i$$

$$M_x = \int y \, dA = \sum y_i A_i$$

Description

The quantity $\sum x_n a_n$ is known as the *first moment of the area* or *first area moment* with respect to the y-axis. Similarly, $\sum y_n a_n$ is known as the first moment of the area with respect to the x-axis. Equation 25.1 and Eq. 25.2 apply to regular shapes with subareas a_n.

The two primary applications of the first moment are determining centroidal locations and shear stress distributions. In the latter application, the first moment of the area is known as the *statical moment*.

---

[1]The NCEES *FE Reference Handbook* (*NCEES Handbook*) deviates from conventional notation in several ways. Q is the most common symbol for the first area moment (then referred to as the *statical moment*), although symbols S and M are also encountered. To avoid confusion with the moment of a force, the subscript a is used to designate the moment of an area. The *NCEES Handbook* uses a lowercase a to designate the area of a subarea (instead of A_i). The *NCEES Handbook* uses n as a summation variable (instead of i), probably to indicate that the moment has to be calculated from all n of the subareas that make up the total area.

Centroid of Line Segments in the *x-y* Plane

For a composite line of total length L, the location of the centroid of a line is defined by the following equations.

$$x_c = \frac{\int x \, dL}{L} = \frac{\sum x_i L_i}{\sum L_i}$$

$$y_c = \frac{\int y \, dL}{L} = \frac{\sum y_i L_i}{\sum L_i}$$

Using the *NCEES Handbook* notation, the equations would be written as

$$L = \sum l_n$$

$$x_{lc} = \frac{\sum x_n l_n}{L}$$

$$y_{lc} = \frac{\sum y_n l_n}{L}$$

Example

Find the approximate *x*- and *y*-coordinates of the centroid of wire ABC.

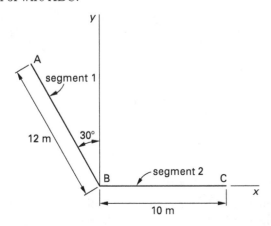

(A) 0.43 m; 1.3 m

(B) 0.64 m; 2.8 m

(C) 2.7 m; 1.5 m

(D) 3.3 m; 2.7 m

Solution

The total length of the line is

$$\sum L_i = 12 \text{ m} + 10 \text{ m} = 22 \text{ m}$$

The coordinates of the centroid of the line are

$$x_c = \frac{\sum x_i L_i}{\sum L_i}$$

$$= \frac{\left(\dfrac{(-12 \text{ m})\sin 30^\circ}{2}\right)(12 \text{ m}) + \left(\dfrac{10 \text{ m}}{2}\right)(10 \text{ m})}{22 \text{ m}}$$

$$= 0.64 \text{ m}$$

$$y_c = \frac{\sum y_i L_i}{\sum L_i}$$

$$= \frac{\left(\dfrac{(12 \text{ m})\cos 30^\circ}{2}\right)(12 \text{ m}) + (0 \text{ m})(10 \text{ m})}{22 \text{ m}}$$

$$= 2.83 \text{ m} \qquad (2.8 \text{ m})$$

The answer is (B).

Equation 25.3 Through Eq. 25.5: Centroid of an Area in the *x-y* Plane[2]

$$A = \sum a_n \qquad \qquad 25.3$$

$$x_{ac} = M_{ay}/A = \sum x_n a_n / A \qquad 25.4$$

$$y_{ac} = M_{ax}/A = \sum y_n a_n / A \qquad 25.5$$

Variations

$$x_c = \frac{\int x \, dA}{A} = \frac{\sum x_{c,i} A_i}{A}$$

$$y_c = \frac{\int y \, dA}{A} = \frac{\sum y_{c,i} A_i}{A}$$

---

[2]In Eq. 25.4 and Eq. 25.5, the subscript a is used to designate the centroid of an area, but this convention is largely omitted throughout the rest of the *NCEES Handbook*.

Description

The centroid of an area A composed of subareas a_n (see Eq. 25.3) is located using Eq. 25.4 and Eq. 25.5. The location of the centroid of an area depends only on the geometry of the area, and it is identified by the coordinates (x_{ac}, y_{ac}), or, more commonly, (x_c, y_c).

Example

What are the approximate x- and y-coordinates of the centroid of the area shown?

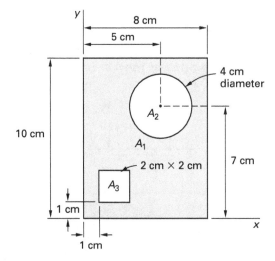

(A)   3.4 cm; 5.6 cm

(B)   3.5 cm; 5.5 cm

(C)   3.9 cm; 4.4 cm

(D)   3.9 cm; 4.8 cm

Solution

Calculate the total area.

$$A = \sum a_n$$
$$= (8 \text{ cm})(10 \text{ cm}) - \frac{\pi(4 \text{ cm})^2}{4}$$
$$\quad -(2 \text{ cm})(2 \text{ cm})$$
$$= 63.43 \text{ cm}^2$$

Find the first moments about the x-axis and y-axis.

$$M_{ax} = \sum y_n a_n$$
$$= (5 \text{ cm})(80 \text{ cm}^2) + \left(-\pi\left(\frac{4 \text{ cm}}{2}\right)^2 (7 \text{ cm})\right)$$
$$\quad +(-(2 \text{ cm})(4 \text{ cm}^2))$$
$$= 304.03 \text{ cm}^3$$

$$M_{ay} = \sum x_n a_n$$
$$= (4 \text{ cm})(80 \text{ cm}^2) + \left(-(5 \text{ cm})\left(\frac{\pi}{4}\right)(4 \text{ cm})^2\right)$$
$$\quad +(-(2 \text{ cm})(4 \text{ cm}^2))$$
$$= 249.17 \text{ cm}^3$$

The x-coordinate of the centroid is

$$x_c = M_{ay}/A$$
$$= \frac{249.17 \text{ cm}^3}{63.43 \text{ cm}^2}$$
$$= 3.93 \text{ cm} \quad (3.9 \text{ cm})$$

The y-coordinate of the centroid is

$$y_c = M_{ax}/A$$
$$= \frac{304.03 \text{ cm}^3}{63.43 \text{ cm}^2}$$
$$= 4.79 \text{ cm} \quad (4.8 \text{ cm})$$

The answer is (D).

Equation 25.6 Through Eq. 25.9: Centroid of a Volume[3]

$$V = \sum v_n \qquad \text{25.6}$$

$$x_{vc} = \left(\sum x_n v_n\right)/V \qquad \text{25.7}$$

$$y_{vc} = \left(\sum y_n v_n\right)/V \qquad \text{25.8}$$

$$z_{vc} = \left(\sum z_n v_n\right)/V \qquad \text{25.9}$$

Statics

---

[3]The *NCEES Handbook* uses lowercase v to designate the area of a subvolume (instead of V_i). In Eq. 25.7 through Eq. 25.9, the subscript v is used to designate the centroid of a volume, but this convention is largely omitted throughout the rest of the *NCEES Handbook*.

Description

The centroid of a volume V composed of subvolumes v_n (see Eq. 25.6) is located using Eq. 25.7 through Eq. 25.9, which are analogous to the equations used for centroids of areas and lines.

A solid body will have both a center of gravity and a centroid, but the locations of these two points will not necessarily coincide. The earth's attractive force, which is called *weight*, can be assumed to act through the *center of gravity* (also known as the *center of mass*). Only when the body is homogeneous will the *centroid of a volume* coincide with the center of gravity.

Example

The structure shown is formed of three separate solid aluminum cylindrical rods, each with a 1 cm diameter.

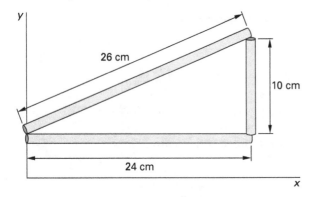

What is the approximate x-coordinate of the centroid of the structure?

   (A)   14.0 cm

   (B)   15.2 cm

   (C)   15.9 cm

   (D)   16.0 cm

Solution

Use Eq. 25.7.

$$V_1 = \left(\frac{\pi}{4}\right)(1\text{ cm})^2(24\text{ cm}) = 18.85\text{ cm}^3$$

$$V_2 = \left(\frac{\pi}{4}\right)(1\text{ cm})^2(10\text{ cm})$$

$$= 7.85\text{ cm}^3$$

$$V_3 = \left(\frac{\pi}{4}\right)(1\text{ cm})^2(26\text{ cm})$$

$$= 20.42\text{ cm}^3$$

$$V = 18.85\text{ cm}^3 + 7.85\text{ cm}^3 + 20.42\text{ cm}^3$$

$$= 47.12\text{ cm}^3$$

$$x_n = \left(\sum x_{vc}v_n\right)/V$$

$$= \frac{\left(\dfrac{24\text{ cm}}{2}\right)(18.85\text{ cm}^3) + (24\text{ cm})(7.85\text{ cm}^3)}{47.12\text{ cm}^3}$$

$$+ \left(\dfrac{24\text{ cm}}{2}\right)(20.42\text{ cm}^3)$$

$$= 14.0\text{ cm}$$

(The $\pi/4$ and area terms all cancel and could have been omitted.)

The answer is (A).

Equation 25.10 Through Eq. 25.50: Centroid and Area Moments of Inertia for Right Triangles

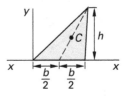

area and centroid

$A = bh/2$	25.10
$x_c = 2b/3$	25.11
$y_c = h/3$	25.12

area moment of inertia

$I_{x_c} = bh^3/36$	25.13
$I_{y_c} = b^3h/36$	25.14
$I_x = bh^3/12$	25.15
$I_y = b^3h/4$	25.16

(radius of gyration)^2

$r_{x_c}^2 = h^2/18$	25.17
$r_{y_c}^2 = b^2/18$	25.18
$r_x^2 = h^2/6$	25.19
$r_y^2 = b^2/2$	25.20

product of inertia

$$I_{x_c y_c} = Abh/36 = b^2 h^2/72 \qquad 25.21$$

$$I_{xy} = Abh/4 = b^2 h^2/8 \qquad 25.22$$

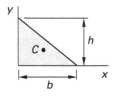

product of inertia

$$I_{x_c y_c} = -Abh/36 = -b^2 h^2/72 \qquad 25.34$$

$$I_{xy} = Abh/12 = b^2 h^2/24 \qquad 25.35$$

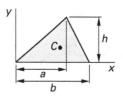

area and centroid

$$A = bh/2 \qquad 25.23$$

$$x_c = b/3 \qquad 25.24$$

$$y_c = h/3 \qquad 25.25$$

area and centroid

$$A = bh/2 \qquad 25.36$$

$$x_c = (a+b)/3 \qquad 25.37$$

$$y_c = h/3 \qquad 25.38$$

area moment of inertia

$$I_{x_c} = bh^3/36 \qquad 25.26$$

$$I_{y_c} = b^3 h/36 \qquad 25.27$$

$$I_x = bh^3/12 \qquad 25.28$$

$$I_y = b^3 h/12 \qquad 25.29$$

area moment of inertia

$$I_{x_c} = bh^3/36 \qquad 25.39$$

$$I_{y_c} = [bh(b^2 - ab + a^2)]/36 \qquad 25.40$$

$$I_x = bh^3/12 \qquad 25.41$$

$$I_y = [bh(b^2 + ab + a^2)]/12 \qquad 25.42$$

(radius of gyration)^2

$$r_{x_c}^2 = h^2/18 \qquad 25.30$$

$$r_{y_c}^2 = b^2/18 \qquad 25.31$$

$$r_x^2 = h^2/6 \qquad 25.32$$

$$r_y^2 = b^2/6 \qquad 25.33$$

(radius of gyration)^2

$$r_{x_c}^2 = h^2/18 \qquad 25.43$$

$$r_{y_c}^2 = (b^2 - ab + a^2)/18 \qquad 25.44$$

$$r_x^2 = h^2/6 \qquad 25.45$$

$$r_y^2 = (b^2 + ab + a^2)/6 \qquad 25.46$$

Statics

product of inertia

$$I_{x_c y_c} = [Ah(2a - b)]/36 \qquad 25.47$$

$$I_{x_c y_c} = [bh^2(2a - b)]/72 \qquad 25.48$$

$$I_{xy} = [Ah(2a + b)]/12 \qquad 25.49$$

$$I_{xy} = [bh^2(2a + b)]/24 \qquad 25.50$$

Description

Equation 25.10 through Eq. 25.50 give the areas, centroids, and moments of inertia for triangles.

The traditional moments of inertia, I_x and I_y (i.e., the second moments of the area), are always positive. However, the *product of inertia*, $I_{x_c y_c}$, listed in Eq. 25.34, is negative. Since the product of inertia is calculated as $I_{xy} = \sum x_i y_i A_i$, where the x_i and y_i are distances from the composite centroid to the subarea A_i, and since these distances can be either positive or negative depending on where the centroid is located, the product of inertia can be either positive or negative.

Example

If a triangle has a base of 13 cm and a height of 8 cm, what is most nearly the vertical distance between the centroid and the radius of gyration about the x-axis?

(A) 0.5 cm

(B) 0.6 cm

(C) 0.7 cm

(D) 0.8 cm

Solution

From Eq. 25.38, the y-component of the centroidal location is

$$y_c = h/3 = \frac{8 \text{ cm}}{3} = 2.667 \text{ cm}$$

From Eq. 25.45, the radius of gyration about the x-axis is

$$r_x = \sqrt{\frac{h^2}{6}} = \sqrt{\frac{(8 \text{ cm})^2}{6}} = 3.266 \text{ cm}$$

The vertical separation between these two points is

$$r_x - y_c = 3.266 \text{ cm} - 2.667 \text{ cm}$$
$$= 0.599 \text{ cm} \quad (0.6 \text{ cm})$$

The answer is (B).

Equation 25.51 Through Eq. 25.62: Centroid and Area Moments of Inertia for Rectangles

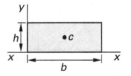

area and centroid

$$A = bh \qquad 25.51$$

$$x_c = b/2 \qquad 25.52$$

$$y_c = h/2 \qquad 25.53$$

area moment of inertia

$$I_x = bh^3/3 \qquad 25.54$$

$$I_{x_c} = bh^3/12 \qquad 25.55$$

$$J = [bh(b^2 + h^2)]/12 \qquad 25.56$$

(radius of gyration)^2

$$r_x^2 = h^2/3 \qquad 25.57$$

$$r_{x_c}^2 = h^2/12 \qquad 25.58$$

$$r_y^2 = b^2/3 \qquad 25.59$$

$$r_p^2 = (b^2 + h^2)/12 \qquad 25.60$$

product of inertia

$$I_{x_c y_c} = 0 \qquad 25.61$$

$$I_{xy} = Abh/4 = b^2 h^2/4 \qquad 25.62$$

Description

Equation 25.51 through Eq. 25.62 give the area, centroids, and moments of inertia for rectangles.

Example

A 12 cm wide $\times$ 8 cm high rectangle is placed such that its centroid is located at the origin, $(0, 0)$. What is the percentage change in the product of inertia if the rectangle is rotated 90° counterclockwise about the origin?

- (A)   –32% (decrease)
- (B)   0%
- (C)   32% (increase)
- (D)   64% (increase)

Solution

The product of inertia is zero whenever one or more of the reference axes are lines of symmetry. In this case, both axes are lines of symmetry before and after the rotation. From Eq. 25.61, $I_{x_c y_c} = 0$.

The answer is (B).

....

Equation 25.63 Through Eq. 25.68: Centroid and Area Moments of Inertia for Trapezoids

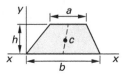

area and centroid

$$A = h(a + b)/2 \qquad \text{25.63}$$

$$y_c = \frac{h(2a + b)}{3(a + b)} \qquad \text{25.64}$$

area moment of inertia

$$I_{x_c} = \frac{h^3(a^2 + 4ab + b^2)}{36(a + b)} \qquad \text{25.65}$$

$$I_x = \frac{h^3(3a + b)}{12} \qquad \text{25.66}$$

(radius of gyration)²

$$r_{x_c}^2 = \frac{h^2(a^2 + 4ab + b^2)}{18(a + b)} \qquad \text{25.67}$$

$$r_x^2 = \frac{h^2(3a + b)}{6(a + b)} \qquad \text{25.68}$$

Description

Equation 25.63 through Eq. 25.68 give the area, centroids, and moments of inertia for trapezoids.

Example

What are most nearly the area and the y-coordinate, respectively, of the centroid of the trapezoid shown?

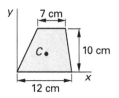

- (A)   95 cm²; 4.6 cm
- (B)   110 cm²; 5.4 cm
- (C)   120 cm²; 6.1 cm
- (D)   140 cm²; 7.2 cm

Solution

The area of the trapezoid is

$$A = h(a + b)/2 = \frac{(10 \text{ cm})(7 \text{ cm} + 12 \text{ cm})}{2}$$

$$= 95 \text{ cm}^2$$

From Eq. 25.64, the y-coordinate of the centroid of the trapezoid is

$$y_c = \frac{h(2a + b)}{3(a + b)}$$

$$= \frac{(10 \text{ cm})((2)(7 \text{ cm}) + 12 \text{ cm})}{(3)(7 \text{ cm} + 12 \text{ cm})}$$

$$= 4.56 \text{ cm} \quad (4.6 \text{ cm})$$

The answer is (A).

Statics

Equation 25.69 Through Eq. 25.80: Centroid and Area Moments of Inertia for Rhomboids

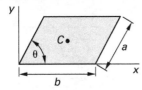

Description

Equation 25.69 through Eq. 25.80 give the area, centroids, and moments of inertia for rhomboids.

Equation 25.81 Through Eq. 25.116: Centroid and Area Moments of Inertia for Circles[4]

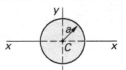

area and centroid

$$A = ab\sin\theta \qquad 25.69$$

$$x_c = (b + a\cos\theta)/2 \qquad 25.70$$

$$y_c = (a\sin\theta)/2 \qquad 25.71$$

area moment of inertia

$$I_{x_c} = (a^3 b\sin^3\theta)/12 \qquad 25.72$$

$$I_{y_c} = [ab\sin\theta(b^2 + a^2\cos^2\theta)]/12 \qquad 25.73$$

$$I_x = (a^3 b\sin^3\theta)/3 \qquad 25.74$$

$$I_y = [ab\sin\theta(b + a\cos\theta)^2]/3 \\ -(a^2 b^2 \sin\theta\cos\theta)/6 \qquad 25.75$$

(radius of gyration)²

$$r_{x_c}^2 = (a\sin\theta)^2/12 \qquad 25.76$$

$$r_{y_c}^2 = (b^2 + a^2\cos^2\theta)/12 \qquad 25.77$$

$$r_x^2 = (a\sin\theta)^2/3 \qquad 25.78$$

$$r_y^2 = (b + a\cos\theta)^2/3 - (ab\cos\theta)/6 \qquad 25.79$$

product of inertia

$$I_{x_c y_c} = (a^3 b\sin^2\theta\cos\theta)/12 \qquad 25.80$$

area and centroid

$$A = \pi a^2 \qquad 25.81$$

$$x_c = a \qquad 25.82$$

$$y_c = a \qquad 25.83$$

area moment of inertia

$$I_{x_c} = I_{y_c} = \pi a^4/4 \qquad 25.84$$

$$I_x = I_y = 5\pi a^4/4 \qquad 25.85$$

$$J = \pi r^4/2 \qquad 25.86$$

(radius of gyration)²

$$r_{x_c}^2 = r_{y_c}^2 = a^2/4 \qquad 25.87$$

$$r_x^2 = r_y^2 = 5a^2/4 \qquad 25.88$$

$$r_p^2 = a^2/2 \qquad 25.89$$

product of inertia

$$I_{x_c y_c} = 0 \qquad 25.90$$

$$I_{xy} = Aa^2 \qquad 25.91$$

[4]In Eq. 25.81 through Eq. 25.116, the *NCEES Handbook* designates the radius of a circle or circular segment as *a*, rather than as the conventional *r* or *R*, which are used almost everywhere else in the *NCEES Handbook*.

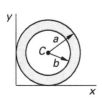

area and centroid

$$A = \pi(a^2 - b^2) \qquad 25.92$$

$$x_c = a \qquad 25.93$$

$$y_c = a \qquad 25.94$$

area moment of inertia

$$I_{x_c} = I_{y_c} = \pi(a^4 - b^4)/4 \qquad 25.95$$

$$I_x = I_y = \frac{5\pi a^4}{4} - \pi a^2 b^2 - \frac{\pi b^4}{4} \qquad 25.96$$

$$J = \pi(r_a^4 - r_b^4)/2 \qquad 25.97$$

(radius of gyration)²

$$r_{x_c}^2 = r_{y_c}^2 = (a^2 + b^2)/4 \qquad 25.98$$

$$r_x^2 = r_y^2 = (5a^2 + b^2)/4 \qquad 25.99$$

$$r_p^2 = (a^2 + b^2)/2 \qquad 25.100$$

product of inertia

$$I_{x_c y_c} = 0 \qquad 25.101$$

$$I_{xy} = Aa^2 \qquad 25.102$$

$$I_{xy} = \pi a^2 (a^2 - b^2) \qquad 25.103$$

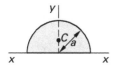

area and centroid

$$A = \pi a^2/2 \qquad 25.104$$

$$x_c = a \qquad 25.105$$

$$y_c = 4a/(3\pi) \qquad 25.106$$

area moment of inertia

$$I_{x_c} = \frac{a^4(9\pi^2 - 64)}{72\pi} \qquad 25.107$$

$$I_{y_c} = \pi a^4/8 \qquad 25.108$$

$$I_x = \pi a^4/8 \qquad 25.109$$

$$I_y = 5\pi a^4/8 \qquad 25.110$$

(radius of gyration)²

$$r_{x_c}^2 = \frac{a^2(9\pi^2 - 64)}{36\pi^2} \qquad 25.111$$

$$r_{y_c}^2 = a^2/4 \qquad 25.112$$

$$r_x^2 = a^2/4 \qquad 25.113$$

$$r_y^2 = 5a^2/4 \qquad 25.114$$

product of inertia

$$I_{x_c y_c} = 0 \qquad 25.115$$

$$I_{xy} = 2a^4/3 \qquad 25.116$$

Description

Equation 25.81 through Eq. 25.116 give the area, centroids, and moments of inertia for circles.

Example

The center of a circle with a radius of 7 cm is located at $(x, y) = (3 \text{ cm}, 4 \text{ cm})$. Most nearly, what is the minimum distance that the origin of the x- and y-axes would have

Statics

to be moved in order to reduce the product of inertia to its smallest absolute value?

(A)   3 cm

(B)   4 cm

(C)   5 cm

(D)   7 cm

Solution

The product of inertia of a circle can be a positive value, a negative value, or zero, depending on the location of the axes. The absolute value is zero (i.e., is minimized) when at least one of the axes coincides with a line of symmetry. Although this can be accomplished by moving the origin to the center of the circle (a distance of 5 cm recognizing that this is a 3-4-5 triangle), a shorter move results when the y-axis is moved 3 cm to the right. Then, the y-axis passes through the centroid, which is sufficient to reduce the product of inertia to zero.

The answer is (A).

Equation 25.117 Through Eq. 25.125: Centroid and Area Moments of Inertia for Circular Sectors

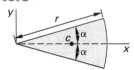

area and centroid

$$A = a^2\theta \qquad 25.117$$

$$x_c = \frac{2a}{3}\frac{\sin\theta}{\theta} \qquad 25.118$$

$$y_c = 0 \qquad 25.119$$

area moment of inertia

$$I_x = a^4(\theta - \sin\theta\cos\theta)/4 \qquad 25.120$$

$$I_y = a^4(\theta + \sin\theta\cos\theta)/4 \qquad 25.121$$

(*radius of gyration*)^2

$$r_x^2 = \frac{a^2}{4}\frac{(\theta - \sin\theta\cos\theta)}{\theta} \qquad 25.122$$

$$r_y^2 = \frac{a^2}{4}\frac{(\theta + \sin\theta\cos\theta)}{\theta} \qquad 25.123$$

product of inertia

$$I_{x_cy_c} = 0 \qquad 25.124$$

$$I_{xy} = 0 \qquad 25.125$$

Description

Equation 25.117 through Eq. 25.125 give the area, centroids, and moments of inertia for circular sectors. In order to incorporate θ into the calculations, as is done for some of the circular sector equations, the angle must be expressed in radians.

$$\theta_{rad} = \theta_{deg}\left(\frac{2\pi}{360°}\right)$$

Example

A grassy parcel of land shaped like a rhombus has sides measuring 120 m with a 65° included angle. A small, straight creek runs between the opposing acute corners. A goat is humanely tied to the bank of the creek at one of the acute corners by a 40 m long rope. Without crossing the creek, most nearly, on what area of grass can the goat graze?

(A)   450 m^2

(B)   710 m^2

(C)   910 m^2

(D)   26 000 m^2

Solution

The creek bisects the 65° angle. The goat sweeps out a circular sector with a 40 m radius.

$$\theta = \frac{\text{swept angle}}{2} = \left(\frac{\frac{65°}{2}}{2}\right)\left(\frac{2\pi}{360°}\right) = 0.2836 \text{ rad}$$

Use Eq. 25.117. The swept area is

$$A = a^2\theta = (40 \text{ m})^2(0.2836 \text{ rad}) = 453.8 \text{ m}^2 \quad (450 \text{ m}^2)$$

The answer is (A).

Statics

Equation 25.126 Through Eq. 25.134: Centroid and Area Moments of Inertia for Circular Segments

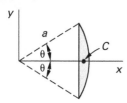

area and centroid

$$A = a^2\left[\theta - \frac{\sin 2\theta}{2}\right] \qquad 25.126$$

$$x_c = \frac{2a}{3}\frac{\sin^3\theta}{\theta - \sin\theta\cos\theta} \qquad 25.127$$

$$y_c = 0 \qquad 25.128$$

area moment of inertia

$$I_x = \frac{Aa^2}{4}\left[1 - \frac{2\sin^3\theta\cos\theta}{3\theta - 3\sin\theta\cos\theta}\right] \qquad 25.129$$

$$I_y = \frac{Aa^2}{4}\left[1 + \frac{2\sin^3\theta\cos\theta}{\theta - \sin\theta\cos\theta}\right] \qquad 25.130$$

(radius of gyration)²

$$r_x^2 = \frac{a^2}{4}\left[1 - \frac{2\sin^3\theta\cos\theta}{3\theta - 3\sin\theta\cos\theta}\right] \qquad 25.131$$

$$r_y^2 = \frac{a^2}{4}\left[1 + \frac{2\sin^3\theta\cos\theta}{\theta - \sin\theta\cos\theta}\right] \qquad 25.132$$

product of inertia

$$I_{x_c y_c} = 0 \qquad 25.133$$

$$I_{xy} = 0 \qquad 25.134$$

Description

Equation 25.126 through Eq. 25.134 give the area, centroids, and moments of inertia for circular segments.

Equation 25.135 Through Eq. 25.145: Centroid and Area Moments of Inertia for Parabolas

area and centroid

$$A = 4ab/3 \qquad 25.135$$

$$x_c = 3a/5 \qquad 25.136$$

$$y_c = 0 \qquad 25.137$$

area moment of inertia

$$I_{x_c} = I_x = 4ab^3/15 \qquad 25.138$$

$$I_{y_c} = 16a^3b/175 \qquad 25.139$$

$$I_y = 4a^3b/7 \qquad 25.140$$

(radius of gyration)²

$$r_{x_c}^2 = r_x^2 = b^2/5 \qquad 25.141$$

$$r_{y_c}^2 = 12a^2/175 \qquad 25.142$$

$$r_y^2 = 3a^2/7 \qquad 25.143$$

product of inertia

$$I_{x_c y_c} = 0 \qquad 25.144$$

$$I_{xy} = 0 \qquad 25.145$$

Description

Equation 25.135 through Eq. 25.145 give the area, centroids, and moments of inertia for parabolas.

Example

The entrance freeway to a city passes under a decorative parabolic arch with a 28 m base and a 200 m height. A famous illusionist contacts the city with a plan to make the city disappear from behind a curtain draped down from the arch. If the drape spans the entire width and height of the opening, and if seams and reinforcement increase the material requirements by 15%, most nearly, how much drapery fabric will be needed?

(A) 3700 m^2

(B) 4300 m^2

(C) 7500 m^2

(D) 8600 m^2

Solution

b is half of the width of the arch.

$$b = \frac{28 \text{ m}}{2}$$
$$= 14 \text{ m}$$

Use Eq. 25.135. Including the allowance for seams and reinforcement, the required area is

$$A = (1 + \text{allowance})\frac{4ab}{3}$$
$$= (1 + 0.15)\left(\frac{(4)(200 \text{ m})(14 \text{ m})}{3}\right)$$
$$= 4293 \text{ m}^2 \quad (4300 \text{ m}^2)$$

The answer is (B).

Equation 25.146 Through Eq. 25.153: Centroid and Area Moments of Inertia for Semiparabolas

area and centroid

$$A = 2ab/3 \qquad \text{25.146}$$

$$x_c = 3a/5 \qquad \text{25.147}$$

$$y_c = 3b/8 \qquad \text{25.148}$$

area moment of inertia

$$I_x = 2ab^3/15 \qquad \text{25.149}$$

$$I_y = 2ba^3/7 \qquad \text{25.150}$$

(radius of gyration)^2

$$r_x^2 = b^2/5 \qquad \text{25.151}$$

$$r_y^2 = 3a^2/7 \qquad \text{25.152}$$

product of inertia

$$I_{xy} = Aab/4 = a^2b^2 \qquad \text{25.153}$$

Description

Equation 25.146 through Eq. 25.153 give the area, centroids, and moments of inertia for semiparabolas.

Example

What is most nearly the area of the shaded section above the parabolic curve shown?

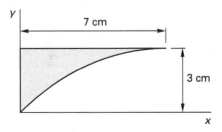

(A) 7 cm^2

(B) 9 cm^2

(C) 11 cm^2

(D) 14 cm^2

Solution

From Eq. 25.146, the semiparabolic area below the curve is

$$A_{\text{below}} = 2ab/3 = \frac{(2)(3 \text{ cm})(7 \text{ cm})}{3}$$
$$= 14 \text{ cm}^2$$

The shaded area above the parabolic curve is

$$A_{\text{above}} = A - A_{\text{below}} = (7 \text{ cm})(3 \text{ cm}) - 14 \text{ cm}^2$$
$$= 7 \text{ cm}^2$$

The answer is (A).

Equation 25.154 Through Eq. 25.160: Centroid and Area Moments of Inertia for General Spandrels (*n*th Degree Parabolas)

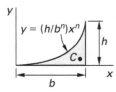

area and centroid

$$A = bh/(n+1) \qquad \text{25.154}$$

$$x_c = \frac{n+1}{n+2}b \qquad \text{25.155}$$

$$y_c = \frac{h}{2}\frac{n+1}{2n+1} \qquad \text{25.156}$$

area moment of inertia

$$I_x = \frac{bh^3}{3(3n+1)} \qquad \text{25.157}$$

$$I_y = \frac{hb^3}{n+3} \qquad \text{25.158}$$

(radius of gyration)^2

$$r_x^2 = \frac{h^2(n+1)}{3(3n+1)} \qquad \text{25.159}$$

$$r_y^2 = \frac{n+1}{n+3}b^2 \qquad \text{25.160}$$

Description

Equation 25.154 through Eq. 25.160 give the area, centroids, and moments of inertia for general spandrels.

Example

For the curve $y = x^3$, what are the approximate coordinates of the centroid of the shaded area between $x = 0$ and $x = 3$ cm?

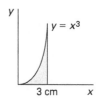

- (A) 1.6 cm; 7.8 cm
- (B) 1.8 cm; 5.8 cm
- (C) 2.0 cm; 18 cm
- (D) 2.4 cm; 7.7 cm

Solution

Treat x as the base and y as the height. n is 3 for this spandrel. The height is $h = x^3 = (3)^3 = 27$ cm. The x- and y-coordinates, respectively, are

$$x_c = \left(\frac{n+1}{n+2}\right)b = \left(\frac{3+1}{3+2}\right)(3 \text{ cm}) = 2.4 \text{ cm}$$

$$y_c = \left(\frac{h}{2}\right)\left(\frac{n+1}{2n+1}\right) = \left(\frac{27 \text{ cm}}{2}\right)\left(\frac{3+1}{(2)(3)+1}\right)$$

$$= 7.714 \text{ cm} \quad (7.7 \text{ cm})$$

The answer is (D).

Equation 25.161 Through Eq. 25.167: Centroids and Area Moments of Inertia for *n*th Degree Parabolas

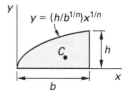

area and centroid

$$A = \frac{n}{n+1}bh \qquad \text{25.161}$$

$$x_c = \frac{n+1}{2n+1}b \qquad \text{25.162}$$

$$y_c = \frac{n+1}{2(n+2)}h \qquad \text{25.163}$$

area moment of inertia

$$I_x = \frac{n}{3(n+3)}bh^3 \qquad \text{25.164}$$

$$I_y = \frac{n}{3n+1}b^3h \qquad \text{25.165}$$

(radius of gyration)^2

$$r_x^2 = \frac{n+1}{3(n+1)}h^2 \qquad \text{25.166}$$

$$r_y^2 = \frac{n+1}{3n+1}b^2 \qquad \text{25.167}$$

Description

Equation 25.161 through Eq. 25.167 give the area, centroids, and moments of inertia for nth degree parabolas.

Equation 25.168: Centroid of a Volume

$$\mathbf{r}_c = \sum m_n \mathbf{r}_n \Big/ \sum m_n \qquad \text{25.168}$$

Description

Equation 25.168 provides a convenient method of locating the centroid of an object that consists of several isolated component masses. The masses do not have to be contiguous and can be distributed throughout space. It is implicit that the vectors that terminate at the submasses' centroids are based at the origin, $(0,0,0)$. These vectors have the form of $r_x\mathbf{i} + r_y\mathbf{j} + r_z\mathbf{k}$. The end result is a vector, but since the vector is based at the origin, the vector components can be interpreted as coordinates, (r_{cx}, r_{cy}, r_{cz}).

2. MOMENT OF INERTIA

The *moment of inertia*, I, of an area is needed in mechanics of materials problems. It is convenient to think of the moment of inertia of a beam's cross-sectional area as a measure of the beam's ability to resist bending. Given equal loads, a beam with a small moment of inertia will bend more than a beam with a large moment of inertia.

Since the moment of inertia represents a resistance to bending, it is always positive. Since a beam can be asymmetric in cross section (e.g., a rectangular beam) and be stronger in one direction than another, the moment of inertia depends on orientation. A reference axis or direction must be specified.

The symbol I_x is used to represent a moment of inertia with respect to the x-axis. Similarly, I_y is the moment of inertia with respect to the y-axis. I_x and I_y do not combine and are not components of some resultant moment of inertia.

Any axis can be chosen as the reference axis, and the value of the moment of inertia will depend on the reference selected. The moment of inertia taken with respect to an axis passing through the area's centroid is known as the *centroidal moment of inertia*, I_{x_c} or I_{y_c}. The centroidal moment of inertia is the smallest possible moment of inertia for the area.

Equation 25.169 and Eq. 25.170: Second Moment of the Area

$$I_y = \int x^2 dA \qquad \text{25.169}$$

$$I_x = \int y^2 dA \qquad \text{25.170}$$

Description

Integration can be used to calculate the moment of inertia of a function that is bounded by the x- and y-axes and a curve $y = f(x)$. From Eq. 25.169 and Eq. 25.170, it is apparent why the moment of inertia is also known as the *second moment of the area* or *second area moment*.

Equation 25.171 and Eq. 25.172: Perpendicular Axis Theorem

$$I_z = J = I_y + I_x = \int (x^2 + y^2) dA \qquad \text{25.171}$$

$$I_z = r_p^2 A \qquad \text{25.172}$$

Variation

$$J_c = I_{x_c} + I_{y_c}$$

Description

The *polar moment of inertia*, J or I_z, is required in torsional shear stress calculations. It can be thought of as a measure of an area's resistance to torsion (twisting). The definition of a polar moment of inertia of a two-dimensional area requires three dimensions because the reference axis for a polar moment of inertia of a plane area is perpendicular to the plane area.

The polar moment of inertia can be found using Eq. 25.171.

It is often easier to use the perpendicular axis theorem to quickly calculate the polar moment of inertia.

Perpendicular axis theorem: The moment of inertia of a plane area about an axis normal to the plane is equal to the sum of the moments of inertia about any two mutually perpendicular axes lying in the plane and passing through the given axis.

Since the two perpendicular axes can be chosen arbitrarily, it is most convenient to use the centroidal moments of inertia, as shown in the variation equation.

Example

For the composite plane area made up of two circles as shown, the moment of inertia about the y-axis is 4.7 cm^4, and the moment of inertia about the x-axis is 23.5 cm^4.

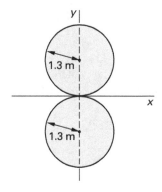

What is the approximate polar moment of inertia of the area taken about the intersection of the x- and y-axes?

- (A) 0 cm^4
- (B) 14 cm^4
- (C) 28 cm^4
- (D) 34 cm^4

Solution

Use the perpendicular axis theorem, as given by Eq. 25.171.

$$J = I_y + I_x$$
$$= 4.7 \text{ cm}^4 + 23.5 \text{ cm}^4$$
$$= 28.2 \text{ cm}^4 \quad (28 \text{ cm}^4)$$

The answer is (C).

Equation 25.173 and Eq. 25.174: Parallel Axis Theorem

$$I_x' = I_{x_c} + d_y^2 A \qquad \text{25.173}$$

$$I_y' = I_{y_c} + d_x^2 A \qquad \text{25.174}$$

Description

If the moment of inertia is known with respect to one axis, the moment of inertia with respect to another, parallel axis can be calculated from the *parallel axis theorem*, also known as the *transfer axis theorem*. This theorem is used to evaluate the moment of inertia of areas that are composed of two or more basic shapes. d is the distance between the centroidal axis and the second, parallel axis.

The second term in Eq. 25.173 and Eq. 25.174 is often much larger than the first term in each equation, since areas close to the centroidal axis do not affect the moment of inertia considerably. This principle is exploited in the design of structural steel shapes that derive bending resistance from *flanges* located far from the centroidal axis. The *web* does not contribute significantly to the moment of inertia. (See Fig. 25.1.)

Figure 25.1 *Structural Steel Shape*

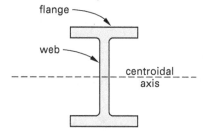

Example

The moment of inertia about the x'-axis of the cross section shown is 334 000 cm^4. The cross-sectional area is 86 cm^2, and the thicknesses of the web and the flanges are the same.

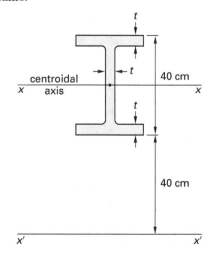

What is most nearly the moment of inertia about the centroidal axis?

(A) $2.4 \times 10^4 \text{ cm}^4$

(B) $7.4 \times 10^4 \text{ cm}^4$

(C) $2.0 \times 10^5 \text{ cm}^4$

(D) $6.4 \times 10^5 \text{ cm}^4$

Solution

Use Eq. 25.173. The moment of inertia around the centroidal axis is

$$I_x' = I_{x_c} + d_x^2 A$$
$$I_{x_c} = I_x' - d_x^2 A$$
$$= 334\,000 \text{ cm}^4 - (86 \text{ cm}^2)\left(40 \text{ cm} + \frac{40 \text{ cm}}{2}\right)^2$$
$$= 24\,400 \text{ cm}^4 \quad (2.4 \times 10^4 \text{ cm}^4)$$

The answer is (A).

....

Equation 25.175 Through Eq. 25.177: Radius of Gyration

$r_x = \sqrt{I_x/A}$	25.175
$r_y = \sqrt{I_y/A}$	25.176
$r_p = \sqrt{J/A}$	25.177

Variations

$$I = r^2 A$$
$$r_p^2 = r_x^2 + r_y^2$$

Description

Every nontrivial area has a centroidal moment of inertia. Usually, some portions of the area are close to the centroidal axis, and other portions are farther away. The *radius of gyration*, *r*, is an imaginary distance from the centroidal axis at which the entire area can be assumed to exist without changing the moment of inertia. Despite the name "radius," the radius of gyration is not limited to circular shapes or polar axes. This concept is illustrated in Fig. 25.2.

The radius of gyration, *r*, is given by Eq. 25.175 and Eq. 25.176. The analogous quantity in the polar system is calculated using Eq. 25.177.

Figure 25.2 Radius of Gyration of Two Equivalent Areas

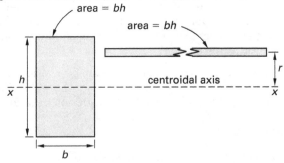

Just as the polar moment of inertia, *J*, can be calculated from the two rectangular moments of inertia, the polar radius of gyration can be calculated from the two rectangular radii of gyration, as shown in the second variation equation.

Example

For the shape shown, the centroidal moment of inertia about an axis parallel to the *x*-axis is 57.9 cm^4.

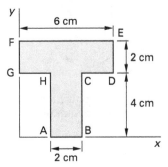

What is the approximate radius of gyration about a horizontal axis passing through the centroid?

(A) 0.86 cm

(B) 1.7 cm

(C) 2.3 cm

(D) 3.7 cm

Solution

The area is

$$A = (2 \text{ cm})(4 \text{ cm}) + (2 \text{ cm})(6 \text{ cm})$$
$$= 20 \text{ cm}^2$$

By definition, the radius of gyration is calculated with respect to the centroidal axis. From Eq. 25.175,

$$r_x = \sqrt{I_{x_c}/A}$$
$$= \sqrt{\frac{57.9 \text{ cm}^4}{20 \text{ cm}^2}}$$
$$= 1.70 \text{ cm} \quad (1.7 \text{ cm})$$

The answer is (B).

Equation 25.178 and Eq. 25.179: Product of Inertia

$$I_{xy} = \int xy\, dA \qquad\qquad 25.178$$

$$I'_{xy} = I_{x_c y_c} + d_x d_y A \qquad\qquad 25.179$$

Description

The *product of inertia*, I_{xy}, of a two-dimensional area is found by multiplying each differential element of area by its x- and y-coordinate and then summing over the entire area.

The product of inertia is zero when either axis is an axis of symmetry. Since the axes can be chosen arbitrarily, the area may be in one of the negative quadrants, and the product of inertia may be negative.

The transfer theorem for products of inertia is given by Eq. 25.179. (Both axes are allowed to move to new positions.) d_x and d_y are the distances to the centroid in the new coordinate system, and I_{xyc} is the centroidal product of inertia in the old system.

Diagnostic Exam

Topic VII: Material Properties and Processing

1. The results of a tensile test on a round specimen of a given material are shown.

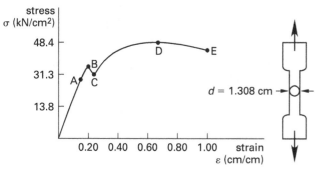

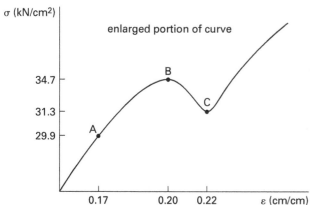

What is most nearly the yield stress?

(A) 14 kN/cm²

(B) 26 kN/cm²

(C) 35 kN/cm²

(D) 48 kN/cm²

2. The activation energy for creep is 161 kJ/mol for a given alloy. If the applied stress is fixed and the stress sensitivity remains the same, by approximately what factor does the creep rate change when the temperature increases from 350°C to 450°C?

(A) 2.2

(B) 3.0

(C) 74

(D) 220

3. Using the phase diagram given, what is most nearly the percentage of liquid remaining at 600°C that results from the equilibrium cooling of an alloy containing 5% silicon and 95% aluminum?

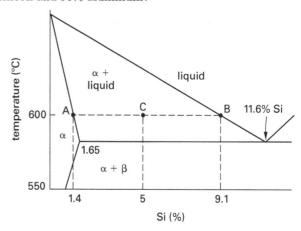

(A) 0.0%

(B) 47%

(C) 53%

(D) 67%

4. The stress-strain curve for a nonlinear, perfectly elastic material is shown. A sample of the material is loaded until the stress reaches the value at point B. Then, the material is unloaded to zero stress.

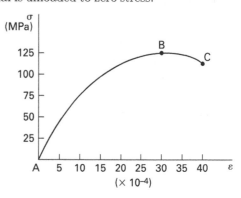

What is most nearly the permanent set in the material?

(A) 0

(B) 0.001

(C) 0.002

(D) 0.003

5. Which statement is FALSE?

(A) The amount or percentage of cold work cannot be obtained from information about change in the area or thickness of a metal.

(B) The process of applying force to a metal at temperatures below the temperature of crystallization in order to plastically deform the metal is called cold working.

(C) Annealing eliminates most of the defects caused by the cold working of a metal.

(D) Annealing reduces the hardness of the metal.

6. Which statement is most accurate regarding the two materials represented in the stress-strain diagrams?

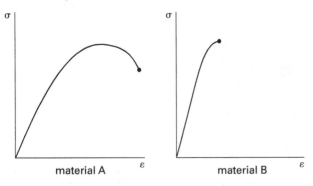

(A) Material B is more ductile and has a lower modulus of elasticity than material A.

(B) Material B would require more total energy to fracture than material A.

(C) Material A will withstand more stress before plastically deforming than material B.

(D) Material B will withstand a higher load than material A but is more likely to fracture suddenly.

7. Which statement is true?

(A) Low-alloy steels are a minor group and are rarely used.

(B) There are two basic types of stainless steels: martensitic and austenitic.

(C) The addition of small amounts of silicon to steel can cause a marked decrease in the yield strength of steel.

(D) The addition of small amounts of molybdenum to low-alloy steels makes it possible to harden and strengthen thick pieces of the metal by heat treatment.

8. The simplified phase diagram of an alloy of components A and B is shown.

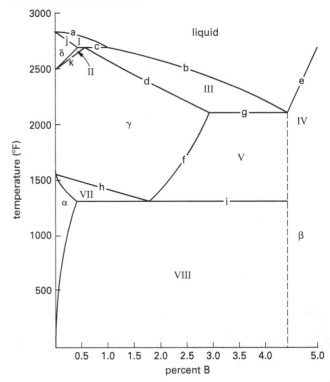

What is most nearly the percentage of solid alloy that will be present at 2300°F if the mixture is 3.0% B and 97% A?

(A) 32%

(B) 40%

(C) 51%

(D) 63%

9. All of the following metals will corrode if immersed in fresh water EXCEPT

(A) copper

(B) nickel

(C) chromium

(D) iron

10. The results of a tensile test on a round specimen of a given material are shown.

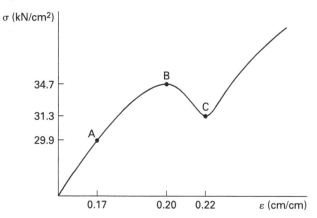

What is most nearly the elastic limit of the material?

(A) 30 kN/cm^2

(B) 31 kN/cm^2

(C) 35 kN/cm^2

(D) 52 kN/cm^2

SOLUTIONS

1. For this material, the stress required to continue the deformation drops markedly at yield.

$$\sigma_y = 35 \text{ kN/cm}^2$$

The answer is (C).

2. The absolute temperatures are

$$T_1 = 350°\text{C} + 273° = 623\text{K}$$
$$T_2 = 450°\text{C} + 273° = 723\text{K}$$

If the applied stress, σ, and the stress sensitivity, n, are fixed, the creep rate increases by a factor of

$$\frac{e^{(-Q/RT_2)}}{e^{(-Q/RT_1)}} = e^{\left(\left(\frac{-Q}{R}\right)\left(\frac{1}{T_2} - \frac{1}{T_1}\right)\right)}$$

$$= e^{\left(\left(\frac{-\left(161 \frac{\text{kJ}}{\text{mol}}\right)\left(1000 \frac{\text{J}}{\text{kJ}}\right)}{8.314 \frac{\text{J}}{\text{mol·K}}}\right) \times \left(\frac{1}{723\text{K}} - \frac{1}{623\text{K}}\right)\right)}$$

$$= 73.6 \quad (74)$$

The answer is (C).

3. Use the lever rule. At point A, there is 1.4% Si and no liquid, while at point B there is 9.1% Si and all liquid.

$$\% \text{ liquid} = \frac{\text{Si}_C - \text{Si}_A}{\text{Si}_B - \text{Si}_A} \times 100\% = \frac{5\% - 1.4\%}{9.1\% - 1.4\%} \times 100\%$$
$$= 46.75\% \quad (47\%)$$

The answer is (B).

4. A perfectly elastic material exhibits no permanent deformation upon unloading.

The answer is (A).

5. The percentage of cold work can be calculated directly from the reduction in thickness or area of the metal.

The answer is (A).

6. The slope of material B's curve is steeper, so it has the higher modulus of elasticity.

Material A's ultimate strain is greater, so material A is more ductile. Option A is incorrect.

The area under the curve represents the energy (work) required to deform the material, which is the definition of toughness. The area under material A's curve is greater, so material A is tougher. Option B is incorrect.

Material B has no clearly defined yield strength, so compare the stresses reached for any arbitrary amount (e.g., 0.002) of strain. For any strain, material B has a higher stress. Option C is incorrect.

Material B follows the classic stress-strain curve of a brittle material which can fracture suddenly. Option D is correct.

The answer is (D).

7. Low-alloy steels are one of the most commonly used classes of structural steels, so option A is false. There are only three basic types of stainless steels: magnetic (martensitic), non-magnetic (austenitic), and ferric. Option B is false. The addition of small amounts of silicon to steel increases both the yield strength and tensile strength. Option C is false. The addition of small amounts of molybdenum to low-alloy steels makes it possible to harden and strengthen thick pieces of the metal by heat treatment. Option D is true.

The answer is (D).

8. Draw the horizontal tie line at 2300°F between line d and line b. Use the horizontal boron (B) scale for convenience. The tie line intersects line d (100% solid γ phase) at approximately $B_{solid} = 2.1\%$ B. The tie line intersects line b (100% liquid phase) at approximately $B_{liquid} = 3.6\%$ B. The percentage of solid with $B_{actual} = 3.0\%$ B is

$$
\begin{aligned}
\% \text{ solid} &= \frac{B_{liquid} - B_{actual}}{B_{liquid} - B_{solid}} \times 100\% \\
&= \frac{3.6\% - 3.0\%}{3.6\% - 2.1\%} \times 100\% \\
&= 0.40 \quad (40\%)
\end{aligned}
$$

The answer is (B).

9. Copper pipes are used extensively in residential water service. In a table of oxidation potentials, copper is higher (i.e., more anodic) than the standard hydrogen reaction, while nickel, chromium, and iron are below the standard hydrogen reaction. Copper is considered a noble metal in the standard electrode potential series, while nickel, chromium, and iron are considered active metals. There is no galvanic driving potential for the copper ions to go into solution, so copper will not corrode in fresh water.

The answer is (A).

10. Point A is the proportionality limit. The elastic limit is very close to the yield point, point B.

$$\sigma_{\text{elastic limit}} = 34.7 \text{ kN/cm}^2 \quad (35 \text{ kN/cm}^2)$$

The answer is (C).

26 Material Properties and Testing

Nomenclature

a	crack length	m
A	area	m^2
A	constant	–
BHN	Brinell hardness number	–
c	specific heat	J/kg·°C
C	capacitance	F
C	molar specific heat	J/mol·°C
C_V	impact energy	J
d	diameter	m
d	distance	m
D	diameter	m
E	energy	eV
E	modulus of elasticity	MPa
F	force	N
F	load	N
g	gravitational acceleration, 9.81	m/s^2
G	modulus of rigidity	GPa
J	flux	$1/m^2 \cdot s$
k	reduction factor	–
K_{IC}	fracture toughness	MPa·$\sqrt{m}$
L	length	m
m	mass	kg
n	stress sensitivity exponent	–

N	number of cycles	–
P	load	N
q	charge	C
q	reduction in area	–
Q	activation energy	J/mol
Q	heat	J
R	resistance	Ω
R	universal gas constant, 8.314	J/mol·K
S	strength	MPa
S_e'	endurance limit	MPa
t	thickness	m
t	time	s
T	temperature	K
TS	tensile strength	MPa
V	voltage	V
V	volume	m^3
w	width	m
Y	geometrical factor	–

Symbols

α	thermal expansion coefficient	1/°C
γ	conductivity	W/m·K
δ	deformation	m
ε	engineering strain	–
ε	permittivity	F/m or C^2/N·m^2
ε_0	permittivity of a vacuum, 8.85×10^{-12}	F/m or C^2/N·m^2
κ	dielectric constant	–
λ	conductivity	W/m·K
μ	ductility	–
ν	Poisson's ratio	–
ρ	density	kg/m^3
ρ	resistivity	Ω·m
σ	engineering stress	MPa
ϕ	work function	eV

Subscripts

0	initial
a	activation or surface
b	size
c	conduction, critical, or load

d	diffusion or temperature
e	effects or endurance
eff	effective
f	failure, final, or fracture
g	gap or glass transition
i	intrinsic
I	intensity
o	original
p	constant pressure or particular
t	tensile or total
T	total or true
u	ultimate
ut	ultimate tensile
v	valence
v	constant volume
y	yield

1. MATERIALS SELECTION

Materials selection is the process of selecting materials used to design and manufacture a part or product. Materials selection is an important component in the design process, as materials must be carefully selected with product performance and manufacturing processes in mind. The goal of materials selection is to meet product performance goals (e.g., strength, ductility, safety) while minimizing costs and waste.

Materials selection typically begins by considering the ideal properties the material would exhibit based on the product's specifications. Then, materials that best exemplify those needs are selected, and a comparison of the selected materials, including costs, is performed. Because many kinds of materials are available, the process often starts by considering broad categories of materials before zeroing in on a specific choice. These general types of materials include

- *ceramics:* glass ceramics, glasses, graphite, and diamond
- *composites:* reinforced plastics, metal-matrix composites, and honeycomb structures
- *ferrous metals:* carbon, alloy, stainless steel, and tool and die steels
- *nonferrous metals and alloys:* aluminum, magnesium, copper, nickel, titanium, superalloys, refractory metals, beryllium, zirconium, low-melting alloys, and precious metals
- *plastics:* thermoplastics, thermosets, and elastomers

The materials selection process is often iterative; selections and comparisons may be done multiple times before finding the optimal material for a given use.

2. MATERIALS SCIENCE

Materials science is the study of materials to understand their properties, limits, and uses. *Material properties* are key characteristics of a material commonly classified into five main categories: chemical, electrical, mechanical, physical, and thermal.

Mechanical properties describe the relationship between properties and mechanical (i.e., physical) forces, such as stresses, strains, and applied force. Examples of mechanical properties include strength, toughness, ductility, hardness, fatigue, and creep.

Thermal properties are properties that are observed when heat energy is applied to a material. Examples of thermal properties include thermal conductivity, thermal diffusivity, the heat of fusion, and the glass transition temperature.

Electrical properties define the reaction of a material to an electric field. Typical electrical properties are dielectric strength, conductivity, permeability, permittivity, and electrical resistance.

Chemical properties are properties that are evident only when a substance is changed chemically. Common chemical properties include corrosivity, toxicity, and flammability.

Unlike chemical properties, *physical properties* can be observed without altering the material or its structure. Common physical properties include density, melting point, and specific heat.

Some common properties of various materials are given in Table 26.1 and Table 26.2. Additional mechanical properties are given in Table 26.5.

3. ELECTRICAL PROPERTIES

Equation 26.1 Through Eq. 26.3: Capacitance

$$q = CV \qquad 26.1$$

$$C = \frac{\varepsilon A}{d} \qquad 26.2$$

$$\varepsilon = \kappa \varepsilon_0 \qquad 26.3$$

Value

$\varepsilon_0 = 8.85 \times 10^{-12} \text{ F/m}$ (same as $\text{C}^2/\text{N·m}^2$)

Description

A *capacitor* is a device that stores electric charge. A capacitor is constructed as two conducting surfaces separated by an insulator, such as oiled paper, mica, or air.

Table 26.1 *Typical Material Properties**

material	modulus of elasticity, E (Mpsi (GPa))	modulus of rigidity, G (Mpsi (GPa))	Poisson's ratio, ν	coefficient of thermal expansion, α (10^{-6}/°F (10^{-6}/°C))	density, ρ (lbm/in^3 (Mg/m^3))
steel	29.0 (200.0)	11.5 (80.0)	0.30	6.5 (11.7)	0.282 (7.8)
aluminum	10.0 (69.0)	3.8 (26.0)	0.33	13.1 (23.6)	0.098 (2.7)
cast iron	14.5 (100.0)	6.0 (41.4)	0.21	6.7 (12.1)	0.246–0.282 (6.8–7.8)
wood (fir)	1.6 (11.0)	0.6 (4.1)	0.33	1.7 (3.0)	–
brass	14.8–18.1 (102–125)	5.8 (40)	0.33	10.4 (18.7)	0.303–0.313 (8.4–8.7)
copper	17 (117)	6.5 (45)	0.36	9.3 (16.6)	0.322 (8.9)
bronze	13.9–17.4 (96–120)	6.5 (45)	0.34	10.0 (18.0)	0.278–0.314 (7.7–8.7)
magnesium	6.5 (45)	2.4 (16.5)	0.35	14 (25)	0.061 (1.7)
glass	10.2 (70)	–	0.22	5.0 (9.0)	0.090 (2.5)
polystyrene	0.3 (2)	–	0.34	38.9 (70.0)	0.038 (1.05)
polyvinyl chloride (PVC)	<0.6 (<4)	–	–	28.0 (50.4)	0.047 (1.3)
alumina fiber	58 (400)	–	–	–	0.141 (3.9)
aramide fiber	18.1 (125)	–	–	–	0.047 (1.3)
boron fiber	58 (400)	–	–	–	0.083 (2.3)
beryllium fiber	43.5 (300)	–	–	–	0.069 (1.9)
BeO fiber	58 (400)	–	–	–	0.108 (3.0)
carbon fiber	101.5 (700)	–	–	–	0.083 (2.3)
silicon carbide fiber	58 (400)	–	–	–	0.116 (3.2)

*Use these values if the specific alloy and temper are not listed in Table 26.5.

A *parallel plate capacitor* is a simple type of capacitor constructed as two parallel plates. If the plates are connected across a voltage potential, charges of opposite polarity will build up on the plates and create an electric field between the plates. The amount of charge, q, built up is proportional to the applied voltage, V, as shown in Eq. 26.1. The constant of proportionality, C, is the *capacitance* in farads (F) and depends on the capacitor construction. Capacitance represents the ability to store charge; the greater the capacitance, the greater the charge stored.

Equation 26.2 gives the capacitance of two parallel plates of equal area A separated by distance d. ε is the permittivity of the medium separating the plates. The permittivity may also be expressed as the product of the *dielectric constant (relative permittivity)*, κ, and the *permittivity of a vacuum* (also known as the *permittivity of free space*), ε_0, as shown in Eq. 26.3.

Table 26.2 *Properties of Metals*

metal	symbol	atomic weight	density, ρ (kg/m³) water = 1000	melting point (°C)	melting point (°F)	specific heat (J/kg·K)	electrical resistivity (10^{-8} Ω·m) at 0°C (273.2K)[a]	heat conductivity,[b] λ (W/m·K) at 0°C (273.2K)
aluminum	Al	26.98	2698	660	1220	895.9	2.5	236
antimony	Sb	121.75	6692	630	1166	209.3	39	25.5
arsenic	As	74.92	5776	subl. 613	subl. 1135	347.5	26	–
barium	Ba	137.33	3594	710	1310	284.7	36	–
beryllium	Be	9.012	1846	1285	2345	2051.5	2.8	218
bismuth	Bi	208.98	9803	271	519	125.6	107	8.2
cadmium	Cd	112.41	8647	321	609	234.5	6.8	97
caesium	Cs	132.91	1900	29	84	217.7	18.8	36
calcium	Ca	40.08	1530	840	1544	636.4	3.2	–
cerium	Ce	140.12	6711	800	1472	188.4	7.3	11
chromium	Cr	52	7194	1860	3380	406.5	12.7	96.5
cobalt	Co	58.93	8800	1494	2721	431.2	5.6	105
copper	Cu	63.54	8933	1084	1983	389.4	1.55	403
gallium	Ga	69.72	5905	30	86	330.7	13.6	41
gold	Au	196.97	19 281	1064	1947	129.8	2.05	319
indium	In	114.82	7290	156	312	238.6	8	84
iridium	Ir	192.22	22 550	2447	4436	138.2	4.7	147
iron	Fe	55.85	7873	1540	2804	456.4	8.9	83.5
lead	Pb	207.2	11 343	327	620	129.8	19.2	36
lithium	Li	6.94	533	180	356	4576.2	8.55	86
magnesium	Mg	24.31	1738	650	1202	1046.7	3.94	157
manganese	Mn	54.94	7473	1250	2282	502.4	138	8
mercury	Hg	200.59	13 547	−39	−38	142.3	94.1	7.8
molybdenum	Mo	95.94	10 222	2620	4748	272.1	5	139
nickel	Ni	58.69	8907	1455	2651	439.6	6.2	94
niobium	Nb	92.91	8578	2425	4397	267.9	15.2	53
osmium	Os	190.2	22 580	3030	5486	129.8	8.1	88
palladium	Pd	106.4	11 995	1554	2829	230.3	10	72
platinum	Pt	195.08	21 450	1772	3221	134	9.81	72
potassium	K	39.09	862	63	145	753.6	6.1	104
rhodium	Rh	102.91	12 420	1963	3565	242.8	4.3	151
rubidium	Rb	85.47	1533	38.8	102	330.7	11	58
ruthenium	Ru	101.07	12 360	2310	4190	255.4	7.1	117
silver	Ag	107.87	10 500	961	1760	234.5	1.47	428
sodium	Na	22.989	966	97.8	208	1235.1	4.2	142
strontium	Sr	87.62	2583	770	1418	–	20	–
tantalum	Ta	180.95	16 670	3000	5432	150.7	12.3	57
thallium	Tl	204.38	11 871	304	579	138.2	10	10
thorium	Th	232.04	11 725	1700	3092	117.2	14.7	54
tin	Sn	118.69	7285	232	449	230.3	11.5	68
titanium	Ti	47.88	4508	1670	3038	527.5	39	22
tungsten	W	183.85	19 254	3387	6128	142.8	4.9	177
uranium	U	238.03	19 050	1135	2075	117.2	28	27
vanadium	V	50.94	6090	1920	3488	481.5	18.2	31
zinc	Zn	65.38	7135	419	786	393.5	5.5	117
zirconium	Zr	91.22	6507	1850	3362	284.7	40	23

[a]This is a rounded value. In its Units and Environmental Engineering sections, the NCEES *FE Reference Handbook* (*NCEES Handbook*) correctly lists the offset between degrees Celsius and kelvins as 273.15°.

[b]In this table, the *NCEES Handbook* uses lambda, λ, as the symbol for thermal (heat) conductivity. While this usage is not unheard of, it is less common than the use of k, and it is inconsistent with the symbol k used elsewhere in the *NCEES Handbook*.

Example

Two square parallel plates ($0.04 \text{ m} \times 0.04 \text{ m}$) are separated by a 0.1 cm thick insulator with a dielectric constant of 3.4. What is most nearly the capacitance?

(A) $1.2 \times 10^{-12} \text{ F}$

(B) $1.4 \times 10^{-11} \text{ F}$

(C) $4.8 \times 10^{-11} \text{ F}$

(D) $1.1 \times 10^{-10} \text{ F}$

Solution

From Eq. 26.2 and Eq. 26.3, the capacitance is

$$
\begin{aligned}
C &= \frac{\varepsilon A}{d} \\
&= \frac{\kappa \varepsilon_0 A}{d} \\
&= \frac{(3.4)\left(8.85 \times 10^{-12} \frac{\text{F}}{\text{m}}\right)(0.04 \text{ m})^2 \left(100 \frac{\text{cm}}{\text{m}}\right)}{0.1 \text{ cm}} \\
&= 4.814 \times 10^{-11} \text{ F} \quad (4.8 \times 10^{-11} \text{ F})
\end{aligned}
$$

The answer is (C).

Equation 26.4: Resistivity and Resistance

$$ R = \frac{\rho L}{A} \qquad 26.4 $$

Description

Resistance, R (measured in ohms, Ω), is the property of a circuit or circuit element to oppose current flow. A circuit with zero resistance is a *short circuit*, whereas an *open circuit* has infinite resistance.

Resistors are usually constructed from carbon compounds, ceramics, oxides, or coiled wire. Resistance depends on the *resistivity*, ρ (in $\Omega \cdot$m), which is a material property, and the length and cross-sectional area of the resistor. (The resistivities of metals at 0°C are given in Table 26.2.) Resistors with larger cross-sectional areas have more free electrons available to carry charge and have less resistance. Each of the free electrons has a limited ability to move, so the electromotive force must overcome the limited mobility for the entire length of the resistor. The resistance increases with the length of the resistor.

Resistivity depends on temperature. For most conductors, it increases with temperature. For most semiconductors, resistivity decreases with temperature.

Example

A standard copper wire has a diameter of 1.6 mm. What is most nearly the resistance of 150 m of wire at 0°C?

(A) $0.91 \ \Omega$

(B) $1.2 \ \Omega$

(C) $1.5 \ \Omega$

(D) $1.7 \ \Omega$

Solution

From Table 26.2, the resistivity of copper at 0°C is $1.55 \times 10^{-8} \ \Omega \cdot$m. From Eq. 26.4, the resistance is

$$
R = \frac{\rho L}{A} = \frac{(1.55 \times 10^{-8} \ \Omega \cdot \text{m})(150 \text{ m})\left(1000 \frac{\text{mm}}{\text{m}}\right)^2}{\left(\frac{\pi}{4}\right)(1.6 \text{ mm})^2}
$$

$$ = 1.156 \ \Omega \quad (1.2 \ \Omega) $$

The answer is (B).

Semiconductors

Conductors or *semiconductors* are materials through which charges flow more or less easily. When a semiconductor is pure, it is called an *intrinsic semiconductor*. When minor amounts of impurities called *dopants* are added, the materials are termed *extrinsic semiconductors*. The solubility of a dopant determines how well the dopant can *diffuse* (move into areas with low dopant concentration) within the material.

The electrical conductivity of semiconductor materials is affected by temperature, light, electromagnetic field, and the concentration of dopants (impurities). The *solubility of dopant atoms* (i.e., the concentration, typically given in atoms/cm³) increases very slightly with increasing temperature, reaching a relatively constant maximum in the 1000°C to 1200°C range. Higher concentrations result in precipitation of the doping element into a solid phase. Table 26.3 lists maximum values of dopant solubility. However, there may be limited value in achieving the maximum values, since some of the dopant atoms may not be electrically active. For example, arsenic (As) has a maximum solubility in p-type silicon of approximately 5×10^{-20} atoms/cm³, but the maximum useful electrical solubility is approximately 2×10^{-20} atoms/cm³. As calculated from *Fick's first law of diffusion*, the concentration gradient, dC/dx, is a major factor in determining the *electrical flux* (i.e., current), J.

$$ J = -D\frac{dC}{dx} $$

Table 26.3 *Some Extrinsic, Elemental Semiconductors*

element	dopant	periodic table group of dopant	maximum solid solubility of dopant (atoms/m³)
Si	B	III A	600×10^{24}
	Al	III A	20×10^{24}
	Ga	III A	40×10^{24}
	P	V A	1000×10^{24}
	As	V A	2000×10^{24}
	Sb	V A	70×10^{24}
Ge	Al	III A	400×10^{24}
	Ga	III A	500×10^{24}
	In	III A	4×10^{24}
	As	V A	80×10^{24}
	Sb	V A	10×10^{24}

Reprinted with permission from Charles A. Harper, ed., *Handbook of Materials and Processes for Electronics*, copyright © 1970, by The McGraw-Hill Companies, Inc.

Electrons in semiconductors may be bonded or free. Bonding electrons occupy states in the atoms' *valence bands*. Free electrons occupy states in the *conduction bands*. *Holes* are empty states in the valence band. Both holes and electrons can move around, so both are known as *carriers* or *charge carriers*.

Often, a small amount of energy (usually available thermally or provided electrically) is required to fill an *energy gap*, E_g, in order to initiate carrier movement through a semiconductor. The energy gap, often referred to as an *ionization energy*, is the difference in energy between the highest point in the valence band, E_v, and the lowest point in the conduction band, E_c. (The valence band energy may be referred to as the *intrinsic band* energy, and be given the symbol E_i.) The energy gap in insulators is relatively large compared to conductor or semiconductor materials.

$$E_g = E_v - E_c$$

Intrinsic semiconductors are those that occur naturally. When an electron in an intrinsic semiconductor receives enough energy, it can jump to the conduction band and leave behind a hole, a process known as *electron-hole pair production*. For an intrinsic material, electrons and holes are always created in pairs. Therefore, the *activation energy* is half of the energy gap.[1]

$$E_a = \frac{1}{2} E_g \quad \text{[intrinsic]}$$

An *extrinsic semiconductor* is created by artificially introducing dopants into otherwise "perfect" crystals. The analysis of energy levels is similar, except that the dopant energies are within the energy band gap, effectively reducing the energy required to overcome the gap. The valence band energy of the dopants may be referred to as a *donor level* (for *n*-type semiconductors) or an *acceptor level* (for *p*-type semiconductors).

At high temperatures, the carrier density approaches the intrinsic carrier concentration. Therefore, for extrinsic semiconductors at high temperatures, the activation energy (ionization energy) is the same as for intrinsic semiconductors, half of the difference in ionization energies. At low temperatures, including normal room temperatures, the carrier density is dominated by the ionization of the donors. At lower temperatures, the activation energy is equal to the difference in ionization energies.

$$E_a = \frac{1}{2}(E_g - E_d)$$
$$\approx \frac{1}{2}(E_v - E_c) \quad \text{[extrinsic, high temperatures]}$$

$$E_a = E_g - E_d \quad \text{[extrinsic, low temperatures]}$$

Table 26.4 lists ionization energy differences, $E_g - E_d$, and activation energies, E_a, for various extrinsic semiconductors.

Table 26.4 *Impurity Energy Levels for Extrinsic Semiconductors*

semiconductor	dopant	$E_g - E_d$ (eV)	E_a (eV)
Si	P	0.044	–
	As	0.049	–
	Sb	0.039	–
	Bi	0.069	–
	B	–	0.045
	Al	–	0.057
	Ga	–	0.065
	In	–	0.160
	Tl	–	0.260
Ge	P	0.012	–
	As	0.013	–
	Sb	0.096	–
	B	–	0.010
	Al	–	0.010
	Ga	–	0.010
	In	–	0.011
	Tl	–	0.010
GaAs	Se	0.005	–
	Te	0.003	–
	Zn	–	0.024
	Cd	–	0.021

Reprinted with permission from Charles A. Harper, ed., *Handbook of Materials and Processes for Electronics*, copyright © 1970, by The McGraw-Hill Companies, Inc.

---

[1]The *NCEES Handbook* is inconsistent in the symbols used for activation energy. E_a in Table 26.4 is the same as Q in Eq. 26.19. A common symbol used in practice for diffusion activation energy is Q_d, where the subscript clarifies that the activation energy is for diffusion.

Material Props./ Processing

Photoelectric Effect

The *work function*, ϕ, is a measure of the energy required to remove an electron from the surface of a metal. It is usually given in terms of electron volts, eV. It is specifically the minimum energy necessary to move an electron from the *Fermi level* of a metal (an energy level below which all available energy levels are filled, and above which all are empty, at 0K) to infinity, that is, the vacuum level. This energy level must be reached in order to move electrons from semiconductor devices into the metal conductors that constitute the remainder of an electrical circuit. It is also the energy level of importance in the design of optical electronic devices.

In photosensitive electronic devices, an incoming photon provides the energy to release an electron and make it available to the circuit, that is, free it so that it may move under the influence of an electric field. This phenomenon whereby a short wavelength photon interacts with an atom and releases an electron is called the *photoelectric effect*.

Transduction Principles

The *transduction* principle of a given *transducer* (a device that converts a signal to a different energy form) determines nearly all its other characteristics. There are three *self-generating* transduction types: photovoltaic, piezoelectric, and electromagnetic. All other types require the use of an external excitation power source.

In *photovoltaic transduction* (*photoelectric transduction*), light is directed onto the junction of two dissimilar metals, generating a voltage. This type of transduction is used primarily in optical sensors. It can also be used with the measured quantity (known as the *measurand*) controlling a mechanical-displacement shutter that varies the intensity of the built-in light source. *Piezoelectric transduction* occurs because certain crystals generate an electrostatic charge or potential when mechanical forces are applied to the material (i.e., the material is placed in compression or tension or bending forces are applied to it). In *electromagnetic transduction*, the measured quantity is converted into a voltage by a change in magnetic flux that occurs when magnetic material moves relative to a coil with a ferrous core. These self-generating types of transduction are illustrated in Fig. 26.1.

Figure 26.1 *Self-Generating Transducers*

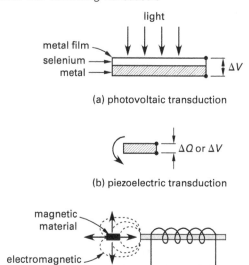

(a) photovoltaic transduction

(b) piezoelectric transduction

(c) electromagnetic transduction

4. THERMAL PROPERTIES

Equation 26.5 and Eq. 26.6: Specific Heat

$$Q = C_p \Delta T \quad \text{[constant pressure]} \qquad 26.5$$

$$Q = C_v \Delta T \quad \text{[constant volume]} \qquad 26.6$$

Description

An increase in internal energy is needed to cause a rise in temperature. Different substances differ in the quantity of heat needed to produce a given temperature increase.

The *specific heat* (known as the *specific heat capacity*), c, of a substance is the heat energy, q, required to change the temperature of one unit mass of the substance by one degree. The *molar specific heat*, conventionally designated by C, is the heat energy, Q, required to change the temperature of one mole of the substance by one degree. Specific heat capacity can be presented on a volume basis (e.g., J/m$^3 \cdot$°C), but a *volumetric heat capacity* is rarely encountered in practice outside of composite materials.[2] Even then, values of the volumetric heat capacity must usually be calculated from specific heats (by mass) and densities. The total heat energy required, Q_t, depends on the total mass or total number of moles.[3]

---

[2]The *NCEES Handbook* introduces C_v in reference to "constant volume," then follows it closely with a statement that "the heat capacity of a material can be reported as energy per degree per unit mass or per unit volume." The volumetric heat capacity is not related to C_v and is so rarely encountered that it doesn't have a common differentiating symbol other than "VHC."

[3]The *NCEES Handbook* describes Eq. 26.5 and Eq. 26.6 as the "...amount of heat required to raise the temperature of something..." "Something" here means "an entire object" as opposed to "some material." Without a definition of "something," the equations are ambiguous and misleading, as they are implicitly valid otherwise only for one unit mass or one mole.

Material Props./ Processing

Because specific heats of solids and liquids are slightly temperature dependent, the mean specific heats are used for processes covering large temperature ranges.

$$Q_t = mc\Delta T$$

$$c = \frac{Q_t}{m\Delta T}$$

The lowercase c implies that the units are J/kg·K. The molar specific heat, designated by the symbol C, has units of J/kmol·K.

$$C = \text{MW} \times c$$

For gases, the specific heat depends on the type of process during which the heat exchange occurs. Molar specific heats for constant-volume and constant-pressure processes are designated by C_v and C_p, respectively.

There are more thermal properties than those listed.

Equation 26.7: Coefficient of Thermal Expansion

$$\alpha = \frac{\varepsilon}{\Delta T} \qquad \text{26.7}$$

Variation

$$\alpha = \frac{\Delta L}{L_0 \Delta T}$$

Description

If the temperature of an object is changed, the object will experience length, area, and volume changes. The magnitude of these changes will depend on the *thermal expansion coefficient (coefficient of linear thermal expansion)*, α, calculated from the engineering strain, ε, and the change in temperature, ΔT.

5. MECHANICAL PROPERTIES

Mechanical properties are those that describe how a material will react to external forces. Materials are commonly classified by their mechanical properties, including strength, hardness, and roughness. Typical design values of various mechanical properties are given in Table 26.5. Various mechanical properties are covered in the following sections.

6. CLASSIFICATION OF MATERIALS

When used to describe engineering materials, the terms "strong" and "tough" are not synonymous. Similarly, "weak," "soft," and "brittle" have different engineering meanings. A *strong material* has a high ultimate strength, whereas a *weak material* has a low ultimate strength. A *tough material* will yield greatly before breaking, whereas a *brittle material* will not. (A brittle material is one whose strain at fracture is less than approximately 0.5%.) A *hard material* has a high modulus of elasticity, whereas a *soft material* does not. Figure 26.2 illustrates some of the possible combinations of these classifications, comparing the material's stress, σ, and strain, ε.

Figure 26.2 *Types of Engineering Materials*

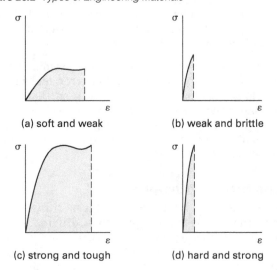

(a) soft and weak   (b) weak and brittle

(c) strong and tough   (d) hard and strong

7. ENGINEERING STRESS AND STRAIN

Figure 26.3 shows a *load-elongation curve* of *tensile test* data for a ductile ferrous material (e.g., low-carbon steel or other body-centered cubic (BCC) transition metal). In this test, a prepared material sample (i.e., a *specimen*) is axially loaded in tension, and the resulting elongation, ΔL, is measured as the load, F, increases.

Figure 26.3 *Typical Tensile Test of a Ductile Material*

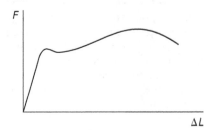

When elongation is plotted against the applied load, the graph is applicable only to an object with the same length and area as the test specimen. To generalize the test results, the data are converted to stresses and strains.

Table 26.5 Average Mechanical Properties of Typical Engineering Materials (customary U.S. units) [a,b]

materials		specific weight, γ (lbf/in³)	modulus of elasticity, E (10³ ksi)	modulus of rigidity, G (10³ ksi)	yield strength, σ_y (ksi)[c]			ultimate strength, σ_u (ksi)[c]			% elongation in 2 in specimen	Poisson's ratio, ν	coefficient of thermal expansion, α (10⁻⁶)/°F
					tens.	comp.	shear	tens.	comp.	shear			
metallic													
aluminum wrought alloys	2014-T6	0.101	10.6	3.9	60	60	25	68	68	42	10	0.35	12.8
	6061-T6	0.098	10.0	3.7	37	37	19	42	42	27	12	0.35	13.1
cast iron alloys	gray ASTM 20	0.260	10.0	3.9	–	–	–	26	97	–	0.6	0.28	6.70
	malleable ASTM A197	0.263	25.0	9.8	–	–	–	40	83	–	5	0.28	6.60
copper alloys	red brass C83400	0.316	14.6	5.4	11.4	11.4	–	35	35	–	35	0.35	9.80
	bronze C86100	0.319	15.0	5.6	50	50	–	95	95	–	20	0.34	9.60
magnesium alloy	Am 1004-T61	0.066	6.48	2.5	22	22	–	40	40	22	1	0.30	14.3
steel alloys	structural A36	0.284	29.0	11.0	36	36	–	58	58	–	30	0.32	6.60
	stainless 304	0.284	28.0	11.0	30	30	–	75	75	–	40	0.27	9.60
	tool L2	0.295	29.0	11.0	102	102	–	116	116	–	22	0.32	6.50
titanium alloy	Ti-6Al-4V	0.160	17.4	6.4	134	134	–	145	145	–	16	0.36	5.20
nonmetallic													
concrete	low strength	0.086	3.20	–	–	–	1.8	–	–	–	–	0.15	6.0
	high strength	0.086	4.20	–	–	–	5.5	–	–	–	–	0.15	6.0
plastic reinforced	Kevlar 49	0.0524	19.0	–	–	–	–	104	70	10.2	2.8	0.34	–
	30% glass	0.0524	10.5	–	–	–	–	13	19	–	–	0.34	–
wood select structural grade	Douglas Fir	0.017	1.90	–	–	–	–	0.30[d]	3.78[e]	0.90[e]	–	0.29[f]	–
	White Spruce	0.130	1.40	–	–	–	–	0.36[d]	5.18[e]	0.97[e]	–	0.31[f]	–

[a]Use these values for the specific alloys and temper listed. For all other materials, refer to Table 26.1.

[b]Specific values may vary for a particular material due to alloy or mineral composition, mechanical working of the specimen, or heat treatment. For a more exact value, reference books for the material should be consulted.

[c]The yield and ultimate strengths for ductile materials can be assumed to be equal for both tension and compression.

[d]Measured perpendicular to the grain.

[e]Measured parallel to the grain.

[f]Deformation measured perpendicular to the grain when the load is applied along the grain.

Source: Hibbeler, R. C., *Mechanics of Materials*, 4th ed., Prentice Hall, 2000.

Equation 26.8 and Eq. 26.9: Engineering Stress and Strain

$$\sigma = \frac{F}{A_0} \qquad \text{26.8}$$

$$\varepsilon = \frac{\Delta L}{L_0} \qquad \text{26.9}$$

Description

Equation 26.8 describes *engineering stress*, σ (usually called *stress*), which is the load per unit original area. Typical units of engineering stress are MPa.

Equation 26.9 describes *engineering strain*, ε (usually called *strain*), which is the elongation of the test specimen expressed as a percentage or decimal fraction of the original length. The units m/m are also sometimes used for strain.[4]

If the stress-strain data are plotted, the shape of the resulting line will be essentially the same as the force-elongation curve, although the scales will differ.

Example

A 100 mm gage length is marked on an aluminum rod. The rod is strained so that the gage marks are 109 mm apart. The strain is most nearly

(A)   0.001

(B)   0.01

(C)   0.1

(D)   1.0

Solution

From Eq. 26.9, the strain is

$$\varepsilon = \frac{\Delta L}{L_0} = \frac{109 \text{ mm} - 100 \text{ mm}}{100 \text{ mm}} = 0.09 \quad (0.1)$$

The answer is (C).

Equation 26.10 Through Eq. 26.12: True Stress and Strain

$$\sigma_T = \frac{F}{A} \qquad \text{26.10}$$

$$\varepsilon_T = \frac{dL}{L} \qquad \text{26.11}$$

$$\varepsilon_T = \ln(1 + \varepsilon) \qquad \text{26.12}$$

Description

As the stress increases during a tensile test, the length of a specimen increases, and the area decreases. The engineering stress and strain are not *true stress and strain parameters*, σ_T and ε_T, which must be calculated from instantaneous values of length, L, and area, A.[5]

Figure 26.4 illustrates engineering and true stresses and strains for a ferrous alloy. Although true stress and strain are more accurate, most engineering work has traditionally been based on engineering stress and strain, which is justifiable for two reasons: (1) design using ductile materials is limited to the elastic region where engineering and true values differ little, and (2) the reduction in area of most parts at their service stresses is not known; only the original area is known.

Figure 26.4 True and Engineering Stresses and Strains for a Ferrous Alloy

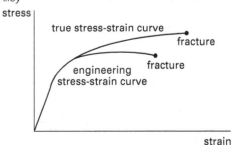

8. STRESS-STRAIN CURVES

Equation 26.13: Hooke's Law

$$\sigma = E\varepsilon \qquad \text{26.13}$$

Variation

$$E = \frac{F/A_0}{\Delta L/L_0} = \frac{FL_0}{A_0 \Delta L}$$

Description

Segment OA in Fig. 26.5 is a straight line. The relationship between the stress and the strain in this linear region is given by *Hooke's law*, Eq. 26.13.

Figure 26.5 Typical Stress-Strain Curve for Steel

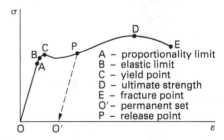

The slope of the line segment OA is the *modulus of elasticity*, E, also known as *Young's modulus* or the *elastic modulus*. Table 26.5 lists approximate values of the

---

[4]In the NCEES *FE Reference Handbook* (*NCEES Handbook*), strain, ε, is the same as creep but is unrelated to permittivity. All three share the same symbol in this section.

[5]The *NCEES Handbook* is inconsistent in representing change in length. ΔL in Eq. 26.9 is the same as dL in Eq. 26.11.

modulus of elasticity for materials at room temperature. The modulus of elasticity will be lower at higher temperatures.

Example

A test specimen with a circular cross section has an initial gage length of 500 mm and an initial diameter of 60 mm. The specimen is placed in a tensile test apparatus. When the instantaneous tensile force in the specimen is 50 kN, the specimen has a longitudinal elongation of 0.16 mm and a lateral decrease in diameter of 0.01505 mm. What is most nearly the modulus of elasticity?

(A) 30×10^9 Pa

(B) 46×10^9 Pa

(C) 55×10^9 Pa

(D) 70×10^9 Pa

Solution

The area of the 60 mm bar is

$$A_0 = \frac{\pi d_0^2}{4} = \frac{\pi \left(\dfrac{60 \text{ mm}}{1000 \frac{\text{mm}}{\text{m}}} \right)^2}{4} = 2.827 \times 10^{-3} \text{ m}^2$$

Using Eq. 26.13 and its variation, the modulus of elasticity is

$$\sigma = E\varepsilon$$

$$E = \frac{\sigma}{\varepsilon} = \frac{FL_0}{A_0 \Delta L} = \frac{(50 \text{ kN})\left(1000 \frac{\text{N}}{\text{kN}}\right)(500 \text{ mm})}{(2.827 \times 10^{-3} \text{ m}^2)(0.16 \text{ mm})}$$

$$= 55.26 \times 10^9 \text{ N/m}^2 \quad (55 \times 10^9 \text{ Pa})$$

The answer is (C).

9. POINTS ALONG THE STRESS-STRAIN CURVE

The stress at point A in Fig. 26.5 is known as the *proportionality limit* (i.e., the maximum stress for which the linear relationship is valid). Strain in the *proportional region* is called *proportional* (or *linear*) *strain*.

The *elastic limit*, point B in Fig. 26.5, is slightly higher than the proportionality limit. As long as the stress is kept below the elastic limit, there will be no *permanent set* (*permanent deformation*) when the stress is removed. Strain that disappears when the stress is removed is known as *elastic strain*, and the stress is said to be in the *elastic region*. When the applied stress is removed, the *recovery* is 100%, and the material follows the original curve back to the origin.

If the applied stress exceeds the elastic limit, the recovery will be along a line parallel to the straight line portion of the curve, as shown in the line segment PO′. The strain that results (line OO′) is permanent set (i.e., a permanent deformation). The terms *plastic strain* and *inelastic strain* are used to distinguish this behavior from the elastic strain.

For steel, the *yield point*, point C, is very close to the elastic limit. For all practical purposes, the *yield strength* or *yield stress*, S_y, can be taken as the stress that accompanies the beginning of plastic strain. Yield strengths are reported in MPa.

Most nonferrous materials, such as aluminum, magnesium, copper, and other face-centered cubic (FCC) and hexagonal close-packed (HCP) metals, do not have well-defined yield points. In such cases, the yield point is usually taken as the stress that will cause a 0.2% *parallel offset* (i.e., a plastic strain of 0.002), shown in Fig. 26.6. However, the yield strength can also be defined by other offset values or by total strain characteristics.

Figure 26.6 *Yield Strength of a Nonferrous Metal*

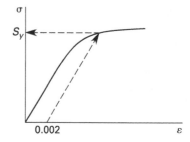

The *ultimate strength* or *tensile strength*, S_u, point D in Fig. 26.5, is the maximum stress the material can support without failure. This property is seldom used in the design of ductile material, since stresses near the ultimate strength are accompanied by large plastic strains.

The *breaking strength* or *fracture strength*, S_f, is the stress at which the material actually fails (point E in Fig. 26.5). For ductile materials, the breaking strength is less than the ultimate strength, due to the necking down in cross-sectional area that accompanies high plastic strains.

10. ALLOWABLE STRESS DESIGN

Once an actual stress has been determined, it can be compared to the *allowable stress*. In engineering design, the term "allowable" always means that a factor of safety has been applied to the governing material strength.

$$\text{allowable stress} = \frac{\text{material strength}}{\text{factor of safety}}$$

For ductile materials, the material strength used is the yield strength. For steel, the factor of safety, FS, ranges from 1.5 to 2.5, depending on the type of steel and the application. Higher factors of safety are seldom necessary in normal, noncritical applications, due to steel's predictable and reliable performance.

$$\sigma_a = \frac{S_y}{\text{FS}} \quad \text{[ductile]}$$

For brittle materials, the material strength used is the ultimate strength. Since brittle failure is sudden and unpredictable, the factor of safety is high (e.g., in the 6 to 10 range).

$$\sigma_a = \frac{S_u}{\text{FS}} \quad \text{[brittle]}$$

If an actual stress is less than the allowable stress, the design is considered acceptable. This is the principle of the *allowable stress design method*, also known as the *working stress design method*.

$$\sigma_{\text{actual}} \le \sigma_a$$

11. ULTIMATE STRENGTH DESIGN

The allowable stress method has been replaced in most structural work by the *ultimate strength design method*, also known as the *load factor design method*, *plastic design method*, or just *strength design method*. This design method does not use allowable stresses at all. Rather, the member is designed so that its actual *nominal strength* exceeds the required ultimate strength.[6]

The *ultimate strength* (i.e., the required strength) of a member is calculated from the actual *service loads* and multiplicative factors known as *overload factors* or *load factors*. Usually, a distinction is made between dead loads and live loads.[7] For example, the required ultimate moment-carrying capacity in a concrete beam designed according to the American Concrete Institute's *Building Code Requirements for Structural Concrete* (ACI 318) would be[8]

$$M_u = 1.2 M_{\text{dead load}} + 1.6 M_{\text{live load}}$$

The *nominal strength* (i.e., the actual ultimate strength) of a member is calculated from the dimensions and materials. A *capacity reduction factor*, ϕ, of 0.70 to 0.90

is included in the calculation to account for typical workmanship and increase required strength. The moment criteria for an acceptable design is

$$M_n \ge \frac{M_u}{\phi}$$

12. DUCTILE AND BRITTLE BEHAVIOR

Ductility is the ability of a material to yield and deform prior to failure.[9] Not all materials are ductile. *Brittle materials*, such as glass, cast iron, and ceramics, can support only small strains before they fail catastrophically, without warning. As the stress is increased, the elongation is linear, and Hooke's law can be used to predict the strain. Failure occurs within the linear region, and there is very little, if any, *necking down* (i.e., a localized decrease in cross-sectional area). Since the failure occurs at a low strain, brittle materials are not ductile.

Figure 26.7 illustrates typical stress-strain curves for ductile and brittle materials.

Figure 26.7 *Stress-Strain Curves for Ductile and Brittle Materials*

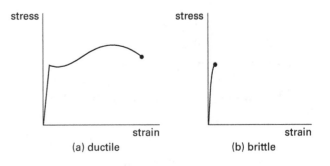

(a) ductile (b) brittle

Ductility, μ, is a ratio of two quantities—one of which is related to catastrophic failure (i.e., collapse), and the other related to the loss of serviceability (i.e., yielding). For example, a building's ductility might be the ratio of earthquake energy it takes to collapse the building to the earthquake energy that just causes the beams and columns to buckle or doorframes to warp.

$$\mu = \frac{\text{energy at collapse}}{\text{energy at loss of serviceability}}$$

---

[6]It is a characteristic of the ultimate strength design method that the term "strength" actually means load, shear, or moment. Strength seldom, if ever, refers to stress. Therefore, the nominal strength of a member might be the load (in newtons) or moment (in N·m) that the member supports at plastic failure.

[7]*Dead load* is an inert, inactive load, primarily due to the structure's own weight. *Live load* is the weight of all nonpermanent objects, including people and furniture, in the structure.

[8]ACI 318 has been adopted as the source of concrete design rules in the United States.

[9]The *NCEES Handbook* gives an incorrect and misleading statement when it says "Ductility (also called percent elongation) [is the] permanent engineering strain after failure." Ductility is a ratio of two quantities, not a percentage. Although there are many measures of ductility, none of them involve the permanent (snapped-back) set of a failed member. Percent elongation at failure might be used to categorize a ductile material, but it is not the same as ductility.

In contrast to the ductility of an entire building, various measures of ductility are calculated from test specimens for engineering materials. Definitions based on length, area, and the volume of the test specimen are in use. If ductility is to be based on test specimen length, the following definition might be used.

$$\mu = \frac{L_u}{L_y} = \frac{\varepsilon_u}{\varepsilon_y}$$

Equation 26.14: Percent Elongation

$$\% \text{ elongation} = \left(\frac{\Delta L}{L_o}\right) \times 100\% \qquad 26.14$$

Variation

$$\% \text{ elongation} = \frac{L_f - L_0}{L_0} \times 100\% = \varepsilon_f \times 100\%$$

Description

In contrast to ductility, the *percent elongation at failure* is based on the fracture length, as in Eq. 26.14, or fracture strain, ε_f, shown in Fig. 26.8 and the variation of Eq. 26.14. Percent elongation at failure might be used to categorize a ductile material, but it is not ductility. Since ductility is a ratio of energy absorbed at two points on the loading curve (as represented by the area under the curve), the ultimate length (area, volume, etc.) is measured just prior to fracture, not after. The ultimate length is not the same as what is commonly referred to as "fracture length." The *fracture length* is the length obtained after failure by measuring the two pieces of the failed specimen placed together end-to-end. This length includes the permanent, plastic strain but does not include the recovered elastic strain. The work (energy) required to elastically strain the failed member is not considered with this measure of fracture length.

If area is the measured parameter, the term *reduction in area*, q, is used. At failure, the reduction in area due to necking down will be 50% or greater for ductile materials and less than 10% for brittle materials. Reduction in area can be used to categorize a ductile material, but it is not ductility.

$$q_f = \frac{A_0 - A_f}{A_0}$$

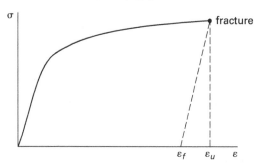

Figure 26.8 *Fracture and Ultimate Strain*

13. CRACK PROPAGATION IN BRITTLE MATERIALS

If a material contains a crack, stress is concentrated at the tip or tips of the crack. A crack in the surface of the material will have one tip (i.e., a stress concentration point); an internal crack in the material will have two tips. This increase in stress can cause the crack to propagate (grow) and can significantly reduce the material's ability to bear loads. Other things being equal, a crack in the surface of a material has a more damaging effect.

There are three modes of *crack propagation*, as illustrated by Fig. 26.9.

Figure 26.9 *Crack Propagation Modes*

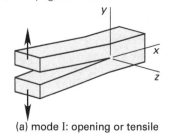

(a) mode I: opening or tensile

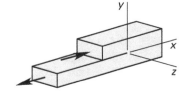

(b) mode II: in-plane shear or sliding

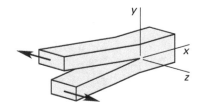

(c) mode III: out-of-plane shear or pushing (pulling)

- *opening or tensile:* forces act perpendicular to the crack, which pulls the crack open, as shown in Fig. 26.9(a). This is known as mode I.

- *in-plane shear or sliding:* forces act parallel to the crack, which causes the crack to slide along itself, as shown in Fig. 26.9(b). This is known as mode II.

- *out-of-plane shear or pushing (pulling):* forces act perpendicular to the crack, tearing the crack apart, as shown in Fig. 26.9(c). This is known as mode III.

Equation 26.15: Fracture Toughness

$$K_{IC} = Y\sigma\sqrt{\pi a} \qquad 26.15$$

Values

crack location	geometrical factor, Y
internal	1.0
surface (exterior)	1.1

Description

Fracture toughness is the amount of energy required to propagate a preexisting flaw. Fracture toughness is quantified by a *stress intensity factor*, K, a measure of energy required to grow a thin crack. For a mode I crack (see Fig. 26.9(a)), the stress intensity factor for a crack is designated K_{IC} or K_{Ic}. The stress intensity factor can be used to predict whether an existing crack will propagate through the material. When K_{IC} reaches a critical value, *fast fracture* occurs. The crack suddenly begins to propagate through the material at the speed of sound, leading to catastrophic failure. This critical value at which fast fracture occurs is called *fracture toughness*, and it is a property of the material.

The stress intensity factor is calculated from Eq. 26.15. σ is the nominal stress. a is the crack length. For a surface crack, a is measured from the crack tip to the surface of the material, as shown in Fig. 26.10(a). For an internal crack, a is half the distance from one tip to the other, as shown in Fig. 26.10(b). Y is a dimensionless factor that is dependent on the location of the crack, as shown in the values section.

Figure 26.10 *Crack Length*

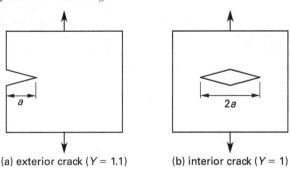

(a) exterior crack ($Y = 1.1$)   (b) interior crack ($Y = 1$)

When a is measured in meters and σ is measured in MPa, typical units for both the stress intensity factor and fracture toughness are MPa·$\sqrt{m}$, equivalent to MN/m$^{3/2}$. Typical values of fracture toughness for various materials are given in Table 26.6.

Table 26.6 *Representative Values of Fracture Toughness*

material	K_{IC} (MPa·$\sqrt{m}$)	K_{IC} (ksi·$\sqrt{in}$)
Al 2014-T651	24.2	22
Al 2024-T3	44	40
52100 steel	14.3	13
4340 steel	46	42
alumina	4.5	4.1
silicon carbide	3.5	3.2

Example

An aluminum alloy plate containing a 2 cm long crack is 10 cm wide and 0.5 cm thick. The plate is pulled with a uniform tensile force of 10 000 N.

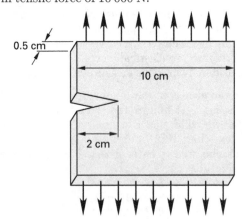

What is most nearly the stress intensity factor at the end of the crack?

- (A) 2.1 MPa·$\sqrt{m}$
- (B) 5.5 MPa·$\sqrt{m}$
- (C) 12 MPa·$\sqrt{m}$
- (D) 21 MPa·$\sqrt{m}$

Solution

From Eq. 26.8, the nominal stress is

$$\sigma = \frac{F}{A_0}$$

$$= \frac{(10\,000 \text{ N})\left(100 \; \dfrac{\text{cm}}{\text{m}}\right)^2}{(10 \text{ cm})(0.5 \text{ cm})}$$

$$= 20 \times 10^6 \text{ N/m}^2 \quad (20 \text{ MPa})$$

Since this is an exterior crack, $Y = 1.1$. Using Eq. 26.15, the stress intensity factor is

$$K_{IC} = Y\sigma\sqrt{\pi a}$$

$$= (1.1)(20 \text{ MPa})\sqrt{\pi\left(\frac{2 \text{ cm}}{100 \; \dfrac{\text{cm}}{\text{m}}}\right)}$$

$$= 5.51 \text{ MPa·}\sqrt{\text{m}} \quad (5.5 \text{ MPa·}\sqrt{\text{m}})$$

The answer is (B).

14. FATIGUE

A material can fail after repeated stress loadings even if the stress level never exceeds the ultimate strength, a condition known as *fatigue failure*.

The behavior of a material under repeated loadings is evaluated by an *endurance test* (or *fatigue test*). A specimen is loaded repeatedly to a specific stress amplitude, S, and the number of applications of that stress required to cause failure, N, is counted. *Rotating beam tests* that load the specimen in bending, as shown in Fig. 26.11, are more common than alternating deflection and push-pull tests, but are limited to round specimens. The *mean stress* is zero in rotating beam tests.

Figure 26.11 Rotating Beam Test

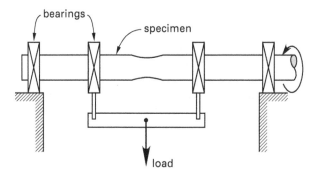

This procedure is repeated for different stresses using different specimens. The results of these tests are graphed on a semi-log plot, resulting in the *S-N curve* shown in Fig. 26.12.

Figure 26.12 Typical S-N Curve for Steel

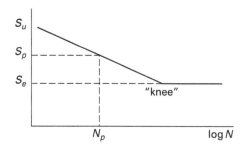

For a particular stress level, such as S_p in Fig. 26.12, the number of cycles required to cause failure, N_p, is the *fatigue life*. S_p is the *fatigue strength* corresponding to N_p.

For steel that is subjected to fewer than approximately 10^3 loadings, the fatigue strength approximately equals the ultimate strength. (Although *low-cycle fatigue theory* has its own peculiarities, a part experiencing a small number of cycles can usually be designed or analyzed as for static loading.) The curve is linear between 10^3 and approximately 10^6 cycles if a logarithmic N-scale is used. Above 10^6 cycles, there is no further decrease in strength.

Below a certain stress level, called the *endurance limit*, *endurance stress*, or *fatigue limit*, S_e', the material will withstand an almost infinite number of loadings without experiencing failure. This is characteristic of steel and titanium. If a dynamically loaded part is to have an infinite life, the stress must be kept below the endurance limit.

The yield strength is an irrelevant factor in cyclic loading. Fatigue failures are fracture failures, not yielding failures. They start with microscopic cracks at the material surface. Some of the cracks are present initially; others form when repeated cold working reduces the ductility in strain-hardened areas. These cracks grow minutely with each loading. Since cracks start at the location of surface defects, the endurance limit is increased by proper treatment of the surface. Such treatments include polishing, surface hardening, shot peening, and filleting joints.

Equation 26.16 Through Eq. 26.18: Endurance Limit Modifying Factors

$$S_e = k_a k_b k_c k_d k_e S_e' \qquad \text{26.16}$$

$$k_a = a S_{ut}^b \qquad \text{26.17}$$

$$k_b = 1.189 d_{eff}^{-0.097} \quad [8 \text{ mm} \leq d \leq 250 \text{ mm}] \qquad \text{26.18}$$

Description

The endurance limit is not a true property of the material since the other significant influences, particularly surface finish, are never eliminated. However, representative values of S_e' obtained from ground and polished specimens provide a baseline to which other factors can be applied to account for the effects of surface finish, temperature, stress concentration, notch sensitivity, size, environment, and desired reliability. These other influences are accounted for by *endurance limit modifying factors* that are used to calculate a working endurance strength, S_e, for the material.

The *surface factor*, k_a, is calculated from Eq. 26.17 using values of the factors a and b found from Table 26.7.

Table 26.7 Factors for Calculating k_a

surface finish	a		b
	(kpsi)	(MPa)	
ground	1.34	1.58	–0.085
machined or cold-drawn (CD)	2.70	4.51	–0.265
hot rolled	14.4	57.7	–0.718
as forged	39.9	272.0	–0.995

The *size factor*, k_b, and *load factor*, k_c, are determined for axial loadings from Table 26.8 and for bending and torsion from Table 26.9. For bending and torsion where the diameter, d, is between 8 mm and 250 mm, k_b is calculated from Eq. 26.18.

As the size gets larger, the endurance limit decreases due to the increased number of defects in a larger volume. Since the endurance strength, S_e', is derived from a circular specimen with a diameter of 7.6 mm, the size modification factor is 1.0 for bars of that size.[10] d_{eff} is the effective dimension.[11] Simplistically, for noncircular cross-sections, the smallest cross-sectional dimension should be used, and for a solid circular specimen in rotating bending, $d_{\text{eff}} = d$. For a nonrotating or noncircular cross section, d_{eff} is obtained by equating the area of material stressed above 95% of the maximum stress to the same area in the rotating-beam specimen of the same length. That area is designated $A_{0.95\sigma}$. For a nonrotating solid rectangular section with width w and thickness t, the effective dimension is

$$d_{\text{eff}} = 0.808\sqrt{wt}$$

Table 26.8 Endurance Limit Modifying Factors for Axial Loading

size factor, k_b	1
load factor, k_c	
$S_{\text{ut}} \leq 1520$ MPa	0.923
$S_{\text{ut}} < 1520$ MPa	1

Table 26.9 Endurance Limit Modifying Factors for Bending and Torsion

size factor, k_b	
$d \leq 8$ mm	1
8 mm $\leq d \leq$ 250 mm	use Eq. 26.18
$d > 250$ mm	between 0.6 and 0.75
load factor, k_c	
bending	1
torsion	0.577

Values of the *temperature factor*, k_d, and the *miscellaneous effects factor*, k_e, are found from Table 26.10. The miscellaneous effects factor is used to account for various factors that reduce strength, such as corrosion, plating, and residual stress.

Table 26.10 Additional Endurance Limit Modifying Factors

temperature factor, k_d	1 $[T \leq 450°C]$
miscellaneous effects factor, k_e	1, unless otherwise specified

Example

A 25 mm diameter machined bar is exposed to a fluctuating bending load in a 200°C environment. The bar is made from ASTM A36 steel, which has a yield strength of 250 MPa, an ultimate tensile strength of 400 MPa, and a density of 7.8 g/cm³. The endurance limit is determined to be 200 MPa. What is most nearly the endurance strength of the steel?

(A) 95 MPa

(B) 130 MPa

(C) 160 MPa

(D) 200 MPa

Solution

Determine the endurance limit modifying factors.

From Table 26.7, since the surface is machined, $a = 4.51$ MPa, and $b = -0.265$. From Eq. 26.17, the surface factor is

$$\begin{aligned} k_a &= aS_{\text{ut}}^b \\ &= (4.51 \text{ MPa})(400 \text{ MPa})^{-0.265} \\ &= 0.9218 \end{aligned}$$

---

[10]In Table 26.9, the *NCEES Handbook* gives the limits for the use of Eq. 26.18 as "8 mm < d ≤ 250 mm." This should be "8 mm ≤ d ≤ 250 mm" so as to be unambiguous at $d = 8$ mm.

[11]The *NCEES Handbook* does not give any explanation or guidance in determining the effective dimension.

Since the diameter is between 8 mm and 250 mm, the size factor is calculated from Eq. 26.18.

$$k_b = 1.189 d_{\text{eff}}^{-0.097}$$
$$= (1.189)(25 \text{ mm})^{-0.097}$$
$$= 0.8701$$

From Table 26.9, $k_c = 1$ for bending stress. From Table 26.10, the temperature is less than 450°C, so $k_d = 1$. $k_e = 1$ since it was not specified otherwise.

Using Eq. 26.16, the approximate endurance strength is

$$S_e = k_a k_b k_c k_d k_e S_e'$$
$$= (0.9218)(0.8701)(1)(1)(1)(200 \text{ MPa})$$
$$= 160.4 \text{ MPa} \quad (160 \text{ MPa})$$

The answer is (C).

15. TOUGHNESS

Toughness is a measure of a material's ability to yield and absorb highly localized and rapidly applied stress. A tough material will be able to withstand occasional high stresses without fracturing. Products subjected to sudden loading, such as chains, crane hooks, railroad couplings, and so on, should be tough. One measure of a material's toughness is the *modulus of toughness*, which is the *strain energy* or work per unit volume required to cause fracture. This is the total area under the stress-strain curve. Another measure is the *notch toughness*, which is evaluated by measuring the *impact energy* that causes a notched sample to fail. At 21°C, the energy required to cause failure ranges from 60 J for carbon steels to approximately 150 J for chromium-manganese steels.

16. CHARPY TEST

In the *Charpy test* (*Charpy V-notch test*), which is popular in the United States, a standardized beam specimen is given a 45° notch. The specimen is then centered on simple supports with the notch down. (See Fig. 26.13.) A falling pendulum striker hits the center of the specimen. This test is performed several times with different heights and different specimens until a sample fractures.

Figure 26.13 Charpy Test

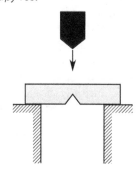

The kinetic energy expended at impact, equal to the initial potential energy, is calculated from the height. It is designated C_V and is expressed in joules (J). The energy required to cause failure is a measure of toughness. Without a notch, the specimen would experience uniaxial stress (tension and compression) at impact. The notch allows triaxial stresses to develop. Most materials become more brittle under triaxial stresses than under uniaxial stresses.

17. DUCTILE-BRITTLE TRANSITION

As temperature is reduced, the toughness of a material decreases. In BCC metals, such as steel, at a low enough temperature the toughness will decrease sharply. The transition from high-energy ductile failures to low-energy brittle failures begins at the *fracture transition plastic* (FTP) *temperature*.

Since the transition occurs over a wide temperature range, the *transition temperature* (also known as the *ductility transition temperature*) is taken as the temperature at which an impact of 20 J will cause failure. (See Table 26.11.) This occurs at approximately −1°C for low-carbon steel.

Table 26.11 Approximate Ductile Transition Temperatures

type of steel	ductile transition temperature (°C)
carbon steel	−1
high-strength, low-alloy steel	−18 to −1
heat-treated, high-strength, carbon steel	−32
heat-treated, construction alloy steel	−40 to −62

The appearance of the fractured surface is also used to evaluate the transition temperature. The fracture can be fibrous (from shear fracture) or granular (from cleavage fracture), or a mixture of both. The fracture planes are studied, and the percentages of ductile failure are plotted against temperature. The temperature at which the failure is 50% fibrous and 50% granular is known as *fracture appearance transition temperature* (FATT).

Not all materials have a ductile-brittle transition. Aluminum, copper, other face-centered cubic (FCC) metals, and most hexagonal close-packed (HCP) metals do not lose their toughness abruptly. Figure 26.14 illustrates the failure energy curves for several materials.

Figure 26.14 *Failure Energy versus Temperature*

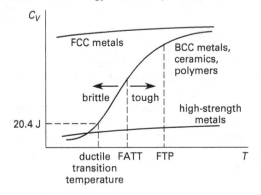

18. CREEP TEST

Creep or *creep strain* is the continuous yielding of a material under constant stress. For metals, creep is negligible at low temperatures (i.e., less than half of the absolute melting temperature), although the usefulness of nonreinforced plastics as structural materials is seriously limited by creep at room temperature.

During a *creep test*, a low tensile load of constant magnitude is applied to a specimen, and the strain is measured as a function of time. The *creep strength* is the stress that results in a specific creep rate, usually 0.001% or 0.0001% per hour. The *rupture strength*, determined from a *stress-rupture test*, is the stress that results in a failure after a given amount of time, usually 100, 1000, or 10,000 hours.

If strain is plotted as a function of time, three different curvatures will be apparent following the initial elastic extension.[12] (See Fig. 26.15.) During the first stage, the *creep rate* ($d\varepsilon/dt$) decreases since strain hardening (dislocation generation and interaction with grain boundaries and other barriers) is occurring at a greater rate than annealing (annihilation of dislocations, climb, cross-slip, and some recrystallization). This is known as *primary creep*.

Figure 26.15 *Stages of Creep*

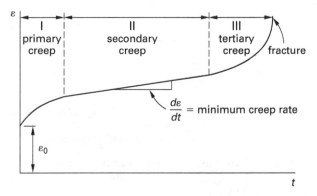

During the second stage, the creep rate is constant, with strain hardening and annealing occurring at the same rate. This is known as *secondary creep* or *cold flow*. During the third stage, the specimen begins to neck down, and rupture eventually occurs. This region is known as *tertiary creep*.

The secondary creep rate is lower than the primary and tertiary creep rates. The secondary creep rate, represented by the slope (on a log-log scale) of the line during the second stage, is temperature and stress dependent. This slope increases at higher temperatures and stresses. The creep rate curve can be represented by the following empirical equation, known as *Andrade's equation*.

$$\varepsilon = \varepsilon_0 (1 + \beta t^{1/3}) e^{kt}$$

Dislocation climb (glide and creep) is the primary creep mechanism, although diffusion creep and grain boundary sliding also contribute to creep on a microscopic level. On a larger scale, the mechanisms of creep involve slip, subgrain formation, and grain-boundary sliding.

Equation 26.19: Creep

$$\frac{d\varepsilon}{dt} = A\sigma^n e^{-Q/RT} \qquad 26.19$$

Value

$\overline{R} = 8314 \text{ J/kmol·K}$

Description

Equation 26.19 calculates creep from the strain, ε; time, t; a constant, A; universal gas constant, $\overline{R}$; absolute temperature, T; applied stress, σ; activation energy, Q; and stress sensitivity, n.[13] The activation energy and

---

[12]In Great Britain, the initial elastic elongation, ε_0, is considered the first stage. Therefore, creep has four stages in British nomenclature.
[13]The *NCEES Handbook* is inconsistent in the variable it uses for the universal gas constant. R in Eq. 26.19 is the same as $\overline{R}$ in its Units section and used almost everywhere in the *NCEES Handbook*.

stress sensitivity are dependent on the material type and glass transition temperature, T_g, as shown in Table 26.12. The exponent $-Q/\overline{R}T$ is unitless.

Table 26.12 Creep Parameters

material	n	Q
polymer		
$< T_g$	2–4	$\geq 100 \text{ kJ/mol}$
$> T_g$	6–10	approx. 30 kJ/mol
metals and ceramics	3–10	80–200 kJ/mol

19. HARDNESS TESTING

Hardness tests measure the capacity of a surface to resist deformation. The main use of hardness testing is to verify heat treatments, an important factor in product service life. Through empirical correlations, it is also possible to predict the ultimate strength and toughness of some materials.

Equation 26.20 and Eq. 26.21: Brinell Hardness Test

$$\text{TS}_{\text{MPa}} \approx 3.5(\text{BHN}) \qquad 26.20$$

$$\text{TS}_{\text{psi}} \approx 500(\text{BHN}) \qquad 26.21$$

Description

The *Brinell hardness test* is used primarily with iron and steel castings, although it can be used with softer materials. The *Brinell hardness number*, BHN (or HB or H_B), is determined by pressing a hardened steel ball into the surface of a specimen. The diameter of the resulting depression is correlated to the hardness. The standard ball is 10 mm in diameter and loads are 500 kg and 3000 kg for soft and hard materials, respectively.

The Brinell hardness number is the load per unit contact area. If a load, P (in kilograms), is applied through a steel ball of diameter, D (in millimeters), and produces a depression of diameter, d (in millimeters), and depth, t (in millimeters), the Brinell hardness number can be calculated from

$$\begin{aligned}\text{BHN} &= \frac{P}{A_{\text{contact}}} = \frac{P}{\pi D t} \\ &= \frac{2P}{\pi D(D - \sqrt{D^2 - d^2})}\end{aligned}$$

For heat-treated plain-carbon and medium-alloy steels, the ultimate tensile strength, TS, can be approximately calculated from the steel's Brinell hardness number, as shown in Eq. 26.20 and Eq. 26.21.

Other Hardness Tests

The *scratch hardness test*, also known as the *Mohs test*, compares the hardness of the material to that of minerals. Minerals of increasing hardness are used to scratch the sample. The resulting *Mohs scale* hardness can be used or correlated to other hardness scales.

The *file hardness test* is a combination of the cutting and scratch tests. Files of known hardness are drawn across the sample. The file ceases to cut the material when the material and file hardnesses are the same.

The *Rockwell hardness test* is similar to the Brinell test. A steel ball or diamond spheroconical penetrator (known as a *brale indenter*) is pressed into the material. The machine applies an initial load (60 kgf, 100 kgf, or 150 kgf) that sets the penetrator below surface imperfections.[14] Then, a significant load is applied. The Rockwell hardness, R (or HR or H_R), is determined from the depth of penetration and is read directly from a dial.

Although a number of Rockwell scales (A through G) exist, the B and C scales are commonly used for steel. The *Rockwell B scale* is used with a steel ball for mild steel and high-strength aluminum. The *Rockwell C scale* is used with the brale indentor for hard steels having ultimate tensile strengths up to 2 GPa. The *Rockwell A scale* has a wide range and can be used with both soft materials (such as annealed brass) and hard materials (such as cemented carbides).

Other penetration hardness tests include the *Meyer*, *Vickers*, *Meyer-Vickers*, and *Knoop* tests.

---

[14]Other Rockwell tests use 15 kgf, 30 kgf, and 45 kgf. The use of kgf units is traditional, and even modern test equipment is calibrated in kgf. Multiply kgf by 9.80665 to get newtons.

27
Engineering Materials

Nomenclature

c	specific heat	kJ/kg·K
C	number of components	–
D	diffusion coefficient	m²/s
D	distance	m
D_o	proportionality constant	m²/s
DP	degree of polymerization	–
E	energy	kJ
E	modulus of elasticity	GPa
E_o	oxidation potential	V
f	volumetric fraction	–
f_r	modulus of rupture	MPa
f_c'	compressive strength	MPa
F	degrees of freedom	–
L	length	m
m	mass	kg
M	Martensite transformation temperature	°C
MC	moisture content	–
MW	molecular weight	kg/kmol
n	grain size	–
n	number	–
N	number of grains per unit area	1/m²

P	number of phases	–
P_L	points per unit length	1/m
Q	activation energy	kJ/kmol
R	universal gas constant, 8314	J/kmol·K
R_C	Rockwell hardness (C-scale)	–
S_V	surface area per unit volume	1/m
T	absolute temperature	K
W	water content	%
x	gravimetric fraction	–

Symbols

ρ	density	kg/m³
σ	stress	MPa

Subscripts

a	activation
ave	average
c	composite
d	diffusion
f	finish
g	glass
i	individual
m	melting
o	original or oxidation
qe	quenched end
s	start

1. CHARACTERISTICS OF METALS

Metals are the most frequently used materials in engineering design. Steel is the most prevalent engineering metal because of the abundance of iron ore, simplicity of production, low cost, and predictable performance. However, other metals play equally important parts in specific products.

Metallurgy is the subject that encompasses the procurement and production of metals. *Extractive metallurgy* is the subject that covers the refinement of pure metals from their ores. Most metals are characterized by the properties in Table 27.1.

Table 27.1 *Properties of Most Metals and Alloys*

high thermal conductivity (low thermal resistance)

high electrical conductivity (low electrical resistance)

high chemical reactivity[a]

high strength

high ductility[b]

high density

high radiation resistance

highly magnetic (ferrous alloys)

optically opaque

electromagnetically opaque

[a]Some alloys, such as stainless steel, are more resistant to chemical attack than pure metals.
[b]Brittle metals, such as some cast irons, are not ductile.

2. UNIFIED NUMBERING SYSTEM

The *Unified Numbering System* (UNS) was introduced in the mid-1970s to provide a consistent identification of metals and alloys for use throughout the world. The UNS designation consists of one of seventeen single uppercase letter prefixes followed by five digits. Many of the letters are suggestive of the family of metals, as Table 27.2 indicates.

3. FERROUS METALS

Steel and Alloy Steel Grades

The properties of steel can be adjusted by the addition of *alloying ingredients*. Some steels are basically mixtures of iron and carbon. Other steels are produced with a variety of ingredients.

The simplest and most common grades of steel belong to the group of *carbon steels*. Carbon is the primary noniron element, although sulfur, phosphorus, and manganese can also be present. Carbon steel can be subcategorized into *plain carbon steel (nonsulfurized carbon steel)*, *free-machining steel (resulfurized carbon steel)*, and *resulfurized and rephosphorized carbon steel*. Plain carbon steel is subcategorized into *low-carbon steel* (less than 0.30% carbon), *medium-carbon steel* (0.30% to 0.70% carbon), and *high-carbon steel* (0.70% to 1.40% carbon).

Low-carbon steels are used for wire, structural shapes, and screw machine parts. Medium-carbon steels are used for axles, gears, and similar parts requiring medium to high hardness and high strength. High-carbon steels are used for drills, cutting tools, and knives.

Table 27.2 *UNS Alloy Prefixes*

A	aluminum
C	copper
E	rare-earth metals
F	cast irons
G	AISI and SAE carbon and alloy steels
H	AISI and SAE H-steels
J	cast steels (except tool steels)
K	miscellaneous steels and ferrous alloys
L	low-melting metals
M	miscellaneous nonferrous metals
N	nickel
P	precious metals
R	reactive and refractory metals
S	heat- and corrosion-resistant steels (stainless and valve steels and superalloys)
T	tool steels (wrought and cast)
W	welding filler metals
Z	zinc

Low-alloy steels (containing less than 8.0% total alloying ingredients) include the majority of steel alloys but exclude the high-chromium content *corrosion-resistant (stainless) steels*. Generally, low-alloy steels will have higher strength (e.g., double the yield strength) of plain carbon steel. *Structural steel*, *high-strength steel*, and *ultrahigh-strength steel* are general types of low-alloy steel.[1]

High-alloy steels contain more than 8.0% total alloying ingredients.

Table 27.3 lists typical alloying ingredients and their effects on steel properties. The percentages represent typical values, not maximum solubilities.

Tool Steel

Each grade of *tool steel* is designed for a specific purpose. As such, there are few generalizations that can be made about tool steel. Each tool steel exhibits its own blend of the three main performance criteria: toughness, wear resistance, and hot hardness.[2]

[1]The ultrahigh-strength steels, also known as *maraging steels*, are very low-carbon (less than 0.03%) steels, with 15–25% nickel and small amounts of cobalt, molybdenum, titanium, and aluminum. With precipitation hardening, ultimate tensile strengths up to 2.8 GPa, yield strengths up to 1.7 GPa, and elongations in excess of 10% are achieved. Maraging steels are used for rocket motor cases, aircraft and missile turbine housings, aircraft landing gear, and other applications requiring high strength, low weight, and toughness.
[2]The ability of a steel to resist softening at high temperatures is known as *hot hardness* and *red hardness*.

Table 27.3 *Steel Alloying Ingredients*

ingredient	range (%)	purpose
aluminum	–	deoxidation
boron	0.001–0.003	increase hardness
carbon	0.1–4.0	increase hardness and strength
chromium	0.5–2	increase hardness and strength
	4–18	increase corrosion resistance
copper	0.1–0.4	increase atmospheric corrosion resistance
iron sulfide	–	increase brittleness
manganese	0.23–0.4	reduce brittleness, combine with sulfur
	> 1.0	increase hardness
manganese sulfide	0.8–0.15	increase machinability
molybdenum	0.2–5	increase dynamic and high-temperature strength and hardness
nickel	2–5	increase toughness, increase hardness
	12–20	increase corrosion resistance
	> 30	reduce thermal expansion
phosphorus	0.04–0.15	increase hardness and corrosion resistance
silicon	0.2–0.7	increase strength
	2	increase spring steel strength
	1–5	improve magnetic properties
sulfur	–	(see *iron sulfide* and *manganese sulfide*)
titanium	–	fix carbon in inert particles; reduce martensitic hardness
tungsten	–	increase high-temperature hardness
vanadium	0.15	increase strength

Some of the generalizations possible are listed as follows.

- An increase in carbon content increases wear resistance and reduces toughness.
- An increase in wear resistance reduces toughness.
- Hot hardness is independent of toughness.
- Hot hardness is independent of carbon content.

Group A steels are air-hardened, medium-alloy cold-work tool steels. Air-hardening allows the tool to develop a homogeneous hardness throughout, without distortion. This hardness is achieved by large amounts of alloying elements and comes at the expense of wear resistance.

Group D steels are high-carbon, high-chromium tool steels suitable for cold-working applications. These steels are high in abrasion resistance but low in machinability and ductility. Some steels in this group are air hardened, while others are oil quenched. Typical uses are blanking and cold-forming punches.

Group H steels are hot-work tool steels, capable of being used in the 600–1100°C range. They possess good wear resistance, hot hardness, shock resistance, and resistance to surface cracking. Carbon content is low, between 0.35% and 0.65%. This group is subdivided according to the three primary alloying ingredients: chromium, tungsten, or molybdenum. For example, a particular steel might be designated as a "chromium hot-work tool steel."

Group M steels are molybdenum high-speed steels. Properties are very similar to the group T steels, but group M steels are less expensive since one part molybdenum can replace two parts tungsten. For that reason, most high-speed steel in common use is produced from group M. Cobalt is added in large percentages (5–12%) to increase high-temperature cutting efficiency in heavy-cutting (high-pressure cutting) applications.

Group O steels are oil-hardened, cold-work tool steels. These high-carbon steels use alloying elements to permit oil quenching of large tools and are sometimes referred to as *nondeforming steels*. Chromium, tungsten, and silicon are typical alloying elements.

Group S steels are shock-resistant tool steels. Toughness (not hardness) is the main characteristic, and either water or oil may be used for quenching. Group S steels contain chromium and tungsten as alloying ingredients. Typical uses are hot header dies, shear blades, and chipping chisels.

Group T steels are tungsten high-speed tool steels that maintain a sharp hard cutting edge at temperatures in excess of 550°C. The ubiquitous 18-4-1 grade T1 (named after the percentages of tungsten, chromium, and vanadium, respectively) is part of this group. Increases in hot hardness are achieved by simultaneous increases in carbon and vanadium (the key ingredient in these tool steels) and special, multiple-step heat treatments.[3]

Group W steels are water-hardened tool steels. These are plain high-carbon steels (modified with small amounts of vanadium or chromium, resulting in high surface hardness but low hardenability). The combination of high surface hardness and ductile core makes group W steels ideal for rock drills, pneumatic tools, and cold header dies. The limitation on this tool steel group is the loss of hardness that begins at temperatures above 150°C and is complete at 300°C.

Stainless Steel

Adding chromium improves steel's corrosion resistance. Moderate corrosion resistance is obtained by adding 4–6% chromium to low-carbon steel. (Other elements, specifically less than 1% each of silicon and molybdenum, are also usually added.)

For superior corrosion resistance, larger amounts of chromium are needed. At a minimum level of 12% chromium, steel is *passivated* (i.e., an inert film of chromic oxide forms over the metal and inhibits further oxidation). The formation of this protective coating is the basis of the corrosion resistance of *stainless steel.*[4]

Passivity is enhanced by oxidizers and aeration but is reduced by abrasion that wears off the protective oxide coating. An increase in temperature may increase or decrease the passivity, depending on the abundance of oxygen.

Stainless steels are generally categorized into ferritic, martensitic (heat-treatable), austenitic, duplex, and high-alloy stainless steels.[5]

Ferritic stainless steels contain more than 10% to 27% chromium. The body-centered cubic (BCC) ferrite structure is stable (i.e., does not transform to austenite, a face-centered cubic (FCC) structure) at all temperatures. For this reason, ferritic steels cannot be hardened significantly. Since ferritic stainless steels contain no nickel, they are less expensive than austenitic steels. Turbine blades are typical of the heat-resisting products manufactured from ferritic stainless steels.

The so-called *superferritics* are highly resistant to chloride pitting and crevice corrosion. Superferritics have been incorporated into marine tubing and heat exchangers for power plant condensers. Like all ferritics, however, superferritics experience embrittlement above 475°C.

The *martensitic (heat-treatable) stainless steels* contain no nickel and differ from ferritic stainless steels primarily in higher carbon contents. Cutlery and surgical instruments are typical applications requiring both corrosion resistance and hardness.

The *austenitic stainless steels* are commonly used for general corrosive applications. The stability of the austenite (a face-centered cubic structure) depends primarily on 4–22% nickel as an alloying ingredient. The basic composition is approximately 18% chromium and 8% nickel.

The so-called *superaustenitics* achieve superior corrosion resistance by adding molybdenum (typically up to about 7%) or nitrogen (typically up to about 14%).

Cast Iron and Wrought Iron

Cast iron is a general name given to a wide range of alloys containing iron, carbon, and silicon, and to a lesser extent, manganese, phosphorus, and sulfur. Generally, the carbon content will exceed 2%. The properties of cast iron depend on the amount of carbon present, as well as the form (i.e., graphite or carbide) of the carbon.

The most common type of cast iron is *gray cast iron.* The carbon in gray cast iron is in the form of graphite flakes. Graphite flakes are very soft and constitute points of weakness in the metal, which simultaneously improve machinability and decrease ductility. Compressive strength of gray cast iron is three to five times the tensile strength.

Magnesium and cerium can be added to improve the ductility of gray cast iron. The resulting *nodular cast iron* (also known as *ductile cast iron*) has the best tensile and yield strengths of all the cast irons. It also has good ductility (typically 5%) and machinability. Because of these properties, it is often used for automobile crankshafts.

White cast iron has been cooled quickly from a molten state. No graphite is produced from the cementite, and the carbon remains in the form of a carbide, Fe_3C.[6] The carbide is hard and is the reason that white cast iron is difficult to machine. White cast iron is used primarily in the production of malleable cast iron.

Malleable cast iron is produced by reheating white cast iron to between 800°C and 1000°C for several days, followed by slow cooling. During this treatment, the carbide is partially converted to nodules of graphitic

---

[3]For example, the 18-4-1 grade is heated to approximately 550°C for two hours, air cooled, and then heated again to the same temperature. The term *double-tempered steel* is used in reference to this process. Most heat treatments are more complex.

[4]Stainless steels are corrosion resistant in oxidizing environments. In reducing environments (such as with exposure to hydrochloric and other halide acids and salts), the steel will corrode.

[5](1) There is a fifth category, that of *precipitation-hardened stainless steels*, widely used in the aircraft industry. (Precipitation hardening is also known as *age hardening.*) (2) The *sigma phase* structure that appears at very high chromium levels (e.g., 24–50%) is usually undesirable in stainless steels because it reduces corrosion resistance and impact strength. A notable exception is in the manufacture of automobile engine valves.

[6]White and gray cast irons get their names from the coloration at a fracture.

carbon known as *temper carbon*. The tensile strength is increased to approximately 380 MPa, and the elongation at fracture increases to approximately 18%.

Mottled cast iron contains both cementite and graphite and is between white and gray cast irons in composition and performance.

Compacted graphitic iron (CGI) is a unique form of cast iron with worm-shaped graphite particles. The shape of the graphite particles gives CGI the best properties of both gray and ductile cast iron: twice the strength of gray cast iron and half the cost of aluminum. The higher strength permits thinner sections. (Some engine blocks are 25% lighter than gray iron castings.) Using computer-controlled refining, volume production of CGI with the consistency needed for commercial applications is possible.

Wrought iron is low-carbon (less than 0.1%) iron with small amounts (approximately 3%) of slag and gangue in the form of fibrous inclusions. It has good ductility and corrosion resistance. Prior to the use of steel, wrought iron was the most important structural metal.

4. NONFERROUS METALS

Aluminum and Its Alloys

Aluminum satisfies applications requiring low weight, corrosion resistance, and good electrical and thermal conductivities. Its corrosion resistance derives from the oxide film that forms over the raw metal, inhibiting further oxidation. The primary disadvantages of aluminum are its cost and low strength.

In pure form, aluminum is soft, ductile, and not very strong. Except for use in electrical work, most aluminum is alloyed with other elements. Copper, manganese, magnesium, and silicon can be added to increase its strength, at the expense of other properties, primarily corrosion resistance.[7] Aluminum is hardened by the *precipitation hardening* (*age hardening*) process.

Silicon occurs as a normal impurity in aluminum, and in natural amounts (less than 0.4%), it has little effect on properties. If moderate quantities (above 3%) of silicon are added, the molten aluminum will have high fluidity, making it ideal for castings. Above 12%, silicon improves the hardness and wear resistance of the alloy. When combined with copper and magnesium (as Mg_2Si and AlCuMgSi) in the alloy, silicon improves age hardenability. Silicon has negligible effect on the corrosion resistance of aluminum.

Copper improves the age hardenability of aluminum, particularly in conjunction with silicon and magnesium. Therefore, copper is a primary element in achieving high mechanical strength in aluminum alloys at elevated temperatures. Copper also increases the conductivity of aluminum, but decreases its corrosion resistance.

Magnesium is highly soluble in aluminum and is used to increase strength by improving age hardenability. Magnesium improves corrosion resistance and may be added when exposure to saltwater is anticipated.

Copper and Its Alloys

Zinc is the most common alloying ingredient in copper. It constitutes a significant part (up to 40% zinc) in brass.[8] (Brazing rod contains even more, approximately 45% to 50%, zinc.) Zinc increases copper's hardness and tensile strength. Up to approximately 30%, it increases the percent elongation at fracture. It decreases electrical conductivity considerably. *Dezincification*, a loss of zinc in the presence of certain corrosive media or at high temperatures, is a special problem that occurs in brasses containing more than 15% zinc.

Tin constitutes a major (up to 20%) component in most bronzes. Tin increases fluidity, which improves casting performance. In moderate amounts, corrosion resistance in saltwater is improved. (*Admiralty metal* has approximately 1%; *government bronze* and *phosphorus bronze* have approximately 10% tin.) In moderate amounts (less than 10%), tin increases the alloy's strength without sacrificing ductility. Above 15%, however, the alloy becomes brittle. For this reason, most bronzes contain less than 12% tin. Tin is more expensive than zinc as an alloying ingredient.

Lead is practically insoluble in solid copper. When present in small to moderate amounts, it forms minute soft particles that greatly improve machinability (2–3% lead) and wearing (bearing) properties (10% lead).

Silicon increases the mechanical properties of copper by a considerable amount. On a per unit basis, silicon is the most effective alloying ingredient in increasing hardness. *Silicon bronze* (96% copper, 3% silicon, 1% zinc) is used where high strength combined with corrosion resistance is needed (e.g., in boilers).

If aluminum is added in amounts of 9–10%, copper becomes extremely hard. Therefore, *aluminum bronze* (as an example) trades an increase in brittleness for increased wearing qualities. Aluminum in solution with the copper makes it possible to precipitation harden the alloy.

Beryllium in small amounts (less than 2%) improves the strength and fatigue properties of copper. These properties make precipitation-hardened *copper-beryllium*

---

[7]One ingenious method of having both corrosion resistance and strength is to produce a composite material. *Alclad* is the name given to aluminum alloy that has a layer of pure aluminum bonded to the surface. The alloy provides the strength, and the pure aluminum provides the corrosion resistance.
[8]*Brass* is an alloy of copper and zinc. *Bronze* is an alloy of copper and tin. Unfortunately, brasses are often named for the color of the alloys, leading to some very misleading names. For example, *nickel silver*, *commercial bronze*, and *manganese bronze* are all brasses.

(*beryllium-copper*, *beryllium bronze*, etc.) ideal for small springs. These alloys are also used for producing non-sparking tools.

Nickel and Its Alloys

Like aluminum, nickel is largely hardened by precipitation hardening. Nickel is similar to iron in many of its properties, except that it has higher corrosion resistance and a higher cost. Also, nickel alloys have special electrical and magnetic properties.

Copper and iron are completely miscible with nickel. Copper increases formability. Iron improves electrical and magnetic properties markedly.

Some of the better-known nickel alloys are *monel metal* (30% copper, used hot-rolled where saltwater corrosion resistance is needed), *K-monel metal*[9] (29% copper, 3% aluminum, precipitation-hardened for use in valve stems), *inconel* (14% chromium, 6% iron, used hot-rolled in gas turbine parts), and *inconel-X* (15% chromium, 7% iron, 2.5% titanium, aged after hot rolling for springs and bolts subjected to corrosion). *Hastelloy* (22% chromium) is another well-known nickel alloy.

Nichrome (15–20% chromium) has high electrical resistance, high corrosion resistance, and high strength at red heat temperatures, making it useful in resistance heating. *Constantan* (40% to 60% copper, the rest nickel) also has high electrical resistance and is used in thermocouples.

Alnico (14% nickel, 8% aluminum, 24% cobalt, 3% copper, the rest iron) and *cunife* (20% nickel, 60% copper, the rest iron) are two well-known nickel alloys with magnetic properties ideal for permanent magnets. Other magnetic nickel alloys are *permalloy* and *permivar*.

Invar, *Nilvar*, and *Elinvar* are nickel alloys with low or zero thermal expansion and are used in thermostats, instruments, and surveyors' measuring tapes.

Refractory Metals

Reactive and *refractory metals* include alloys based on titanium, tantalum, zirconium, molybdenum, niobium (also known as columbium), and tungsten. These metals are used when superior properties (i.e., corrosion resistance) are needed. They are most often used where high-strength acids are used or manufactured.

5. AMORPHOUS MATERIALS

Amorphous materials are materials that lack a crystalline structure like liquids, but are rigid and maintain their shape like solids. Glass is a distinct kind of amorphous material that exhibits a glass transition (see

Sec. 27.8). Figure 27.1 illustrates the difference between amorphous and crystalline solids over the glass transition temperature, T_g, and melting temperature, T_m.

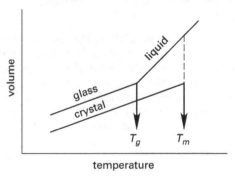

Figure 27.1 Volume-Temperature Curve for Amorphous Materials

6. POLYMERS

Natural Polymers

A *polymer* is a large molecule in the form of a long chain of repeating units. The basic repeating unit is called a *monomer* or just *mer*. (A large molecule with two alternating mers is known as a *copolymer* or *interpolymer*. Vinyl chloride and vinyl acetate form one important family of copolymer plastics.)

Many of the natural organic materials (e.g., rubber and asphalt) are polymers. (Polymers with elastic properties similar to rubber are known as *elastomers*.) Natural rubber is a polymer of the *isoprene latex* mer (formula $[C_5H_8]_n$, repeating unit of $CH_2{=}CCH_3{-}CH{=}CH_2$, systematic name of 2-methyl-1,3-butadiene). The strength of natural polymers can be increased by causing the polymer chains to cross-link, restricting the motion of the polymers within the solid.

Cross-linking of natural rubber is known as *vulcanization*. Vulcanization is accomplished by heating raw rubber with small amounts of sulfur. The process raises the tensile strength of the material from approximately 2.1 MPa to approximately 21 MPa. The addition of carbon black as a reinforcing *filler* raises this value to approximately 31 MPa and provides tear resistance and toughness.

The amount of cross-linking between the mers determines the properties of the solid. Figure 27.2 shows how sulfur joins two adjacent isoprene (natural rubber) mers in *complete cross-linking*.[10] If sulfur does not replace both of the double carbon bonds, *partial cross-linking* is said to have occurred.

---

[9]K-monel is one of four special forms of monel metal. There are also H-monel, S-monel, and R-monel forms.
[10]A tire tread may contain 3–4% sulfur. Hard rubber products, which do not require flexibility, may contain as much as 40–50% sulfur.

Material Props./ Processing

Figure 27.2 *Vulcanization of Natural Rubber*

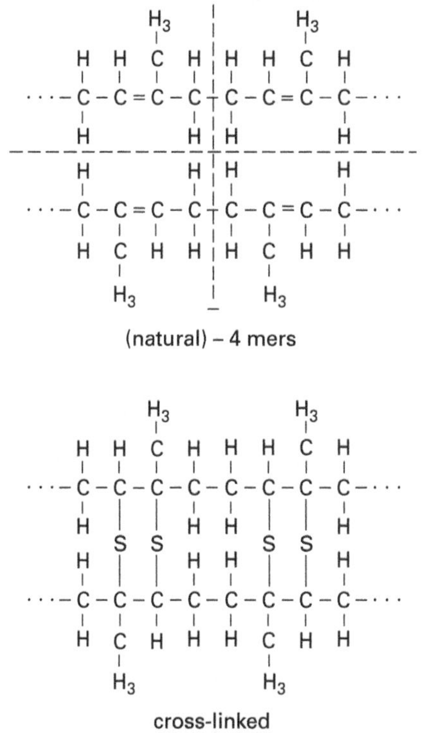

(natural) – 4 mers

cross-linked

Degree of Polymerization

The *degree of polymerization*, DP, is the average number of mers in the molecule, typically several hundred to several thousand.[11] (In general, compounds with degrees of less than ten are called *telenomers* or *oligomers*.) The degree of polymerization can be calculated from the mer and polymer molecular weights, MW.

$$DP = \frac{MW_{polymer}}{MW_{mer}}$$

A polymer batch usually will contain molecules with different length chains. Therefore, the degree of polymerization will vary from molecule to molecule, and an average degree of polymerization is reported.

The stiffness and hardness of polymers vary with their degrees. Polymers with low degrees are liquids or oils. With increasing degree, they go through waxy to hard resin stages. High-degree polymers have hardness and strength qualities that make them useful for engineering applications. Tensile strength and melting (softening) point also increase with increasing degree of polymerization.

Synthetic Polymers

Table 27.4 lists some of the common mers. Polymers are named by adding the prefix "poly" to the name of the basic mer. For example, C_2H_4 is the chemical formula for ethylene. Chains of C_2H_4 are called polyethylene.

Table 27.4 *Names of Common Mers*

name	repeating unit	combined formula
ethylene	CH_2CH_2	C_2H_4
propylene	$CH_2(HCCH_3)$	C_3H_6
styrene	$CH_2CH(C_6H_5)$	C_8H_8
vinyl acetate	$CH_2CH(C_2H_3O_2)$	$C_4H_6O_2$
vinyl chloride	CH_2CHCl	C_2H_3Cl
isobutylene	$CH_2C(CH_3)_2$	C_4H_8
methyl methacrylate	$CH_2C(CH_3)$ $(COOCH_3)$	$C_5H_8O_2$
acrylonitrile	CH_2CHCN	C_3H_3N
epoxide (ethoxylene)	CH_2CH_2O	C_2H_4O
amide (nylon)	$CONH_2$ or $CONH$	$CONH_2$ or $CONH$

Polymers are able to form when double (covalent) bonds break and produce reaction sites. The number of bonds in the mer that can be broken open for attachment to other mers is known as the *functionality* of the mer.

Vinyl polymers are a class of polymers where a different element or molecule, R, has been substituted for one of the hydrogen atoms in the repeating units (i.e., $-[CH_2-CHR]-$). For example, the repeating unit of polyethylene is $-[CH_2]-$ or $-[CH_2-CH_2]-$, but the repeating unit of polyvinyl chloride is $-[CH_2-CHCl]-$. *Copolymers* contain two repeating units (i.e., *comonomers*). One of the units may alternate with the other, or it may appear on a regular basis (i.e., periodically) according to some specific statistic or structure. In an *addition polymer*, all of the atoms in the combining molecules appear in the resulting polymer molecule. In a *condensation polymer*, the resulting structure has fewer atoms than the monomers from which it was created. (The missing atoms or fragments "condense out.") Usually, some energy source (e.g., heat) is required to form condensation polymers.

Example

Polyester repeating unit $-[CO(CH_2)_4CO-OCH_2CH_2O]-$ is formed by combining the two repeating units

---

[11]Degrees of polymerization for commercial plastics are usually less than 1000.

$-[HO_2C-(CH_2)_4-CO_2H]-$ and $-[HO-CH_2CH_2-OH]-$. Most accurately, what type of polymer is the polyester?

(A) addition polymer

(B) comonomer polymer

(C) condensation polymer

(D) vinyl polymer

Solution

Count the number of each atom in the combining and polyester molecules.

element	atoms in combining units	atoms in polyester repeating unit	discrepancy
carbon (C)	$6 + 2 = 8$	8	0
hydrogen (H)	$10 + 6 = 16$	12	4
oxygen (O)	$4 + 2 = 6$	4	2

Four hydrogen atoms and two oxygen atoms (the equivalent of two water molecules) are missing from the resulting polymer unit. Polyester is a condensation polymer.

The answer is (C).

Thermosetting and Thermoplastic Polymers

Most polymers can be softened and formed by applying heat and pressure. These are known by various terms, including *thermoplastics*, *thermoplastic resins*, and *thermoplastic polymers*. Thermoplastics may be either semicrystalline or amorphous. Polymers that are resistant to heat (and that actually harden or "kick over" through the formation of permanent cross-linking upon heating) are known as *thermosetting plastics*. Table 27.5 lists the common polymers in each category. Thermoplastic polymers retain their chain structures and do not experience any chemical change (i.e., bonding) upon repeated heating and subsequent cooling. Thermoplastics can be formed in a cavity mold, but the mold must be cooled before the product is removed. Thermoplastics are particularly suitable for injection molding. The mold is kept relatively cool, and the polymer solidifies almost instantly.

Figure 27.3 illustrates the relationship between temperature and the strength, σ, or modulus of elasticity, E, of thermoplastics.

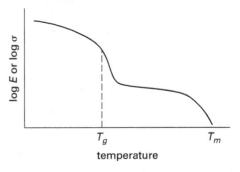

Figure 27.3 *Temperature Dependent Strength or Modulus for Thermoplastic Polymers*

Thermosetting polymers form complex, three-dimensional networks. Thus, the complexity of the polymer increases dramatically, and a product manufactured from a thermosetting polymer may be thought of as one big molecule. Thermosetting plastics are rarely used with injection molding processes.

Thermosetting compounds are purchased in liquid form, which makes them easy to combine with additives. Thermoplastic materials are commonly purchased in granular form. They are mixed with additives in a *muller* (i.e., a bulk mixer) before transfer to the feed hoppers. Thermoplastic materials can also be molded into small pellets called *preforms* for easier handling in subsequent melting operations. Common additives for plastics include

- *plasticizers:* vegetable oils, low molecular weight polymers or monomers

- *fillers:* talc, chopped glass fibers

- *flame retardants:* halogenated paraffins, zinc borate, chlorinated phosphates

- *ultraviolet or visible light resistance:* carbon black

- *oxidation resistance:* phenols, aldehydes

Fluoropolymers

Fluoropolymers (*fluoroplastics*) are a class of paraffinic, thermoplastic polymers in which some or all of the hydrogens have been replaced by fluorine.[12] There are seven major types of fluoropolymers, with overlapping characteristics and applications. They include the fully fluorinated fluorocarbon polymers of Teflon® polytetrafluoroethylene (PTFE), fluorinated ethylene propylene (FEP), and perfluoroalkoxy (PFA), as well as the partially fluorinated polymers of polychloro-trifluoroethylene (PCTFE), ethylene tetrafluoroethylene (ETFE), ethylene chlorotrifluoroethylene (ECTFE), and polyvinylidene fluoride (PVDF).

---

[12]*Fluoroelastomers* are uniquely different from fluoropolymers. They have their own areas of application.

Table 27.5 *Thermosetting and Thermoplastic Polymers*

thermosetting

    epoxy

    melamine

    natural rubber (polyisoprene)

    phenolic (phenol formaldehyde, Bakelite®)

    polyester (DAP)

    silicone

    urea formaldehyde

thermoplastic

    acetal

    acrylic

    acrylonitrile-butadiene-styrene (ABS)

    cellulosics (e.g., cellophane)

    polyamide (nylon)

    polyarylate

    polycarbonate

    polyester (PBT and PET)

    polyethylene

    polymethyl-methacrylate (Plexiglas®, Lucite®)

    polypropylene

    polystyrene

    polytetrafluoroethylene (Teflon®)

    polyurethane

    polyvinyl chloride (PVC)

    synthetic rubber (Neoprene®)

    vinyl

Bakelite® is a trademark of Momentive Specialty Chemicals Inc. Plexiglas® is a trademark of Altuglas International. Lucite® is a trademark of Lucite International. Teflon® and Neoprene® are trademarks of DuPont.

Fluoropolymers compete with metals, glass, and other polymers in providing corrosion resistance. Choosing the right fluoropolymer depends on the operating environment, including temperature, chemical exposure, and mechanical stress.

PTFE, the first available fluoropolymer, is probably the most inert compound known. It has been used extensively for pipe and tank linings, fittings, gaskets, valves, and pump parts. It has the highest operating temperature—approximately 260°C. Unlike the other fluoropolymers, however, it is not a melt-processed polymer. Like a powdered metallurgy product, PTFE is processed by compression and isostatic molding, followed by sintering. PTFE is also the weakest of all the fluoropolymers.

7. WOOD

Woods are classified broadly as softwoods or hardwoods, although it is difficult to define these terms exactly. *Softwoods* contain tube-like fibers (*tracheids*) oriented with the longitudinal axis (grain) and cemented together with *lignin*. *Hardwoods* contain more complex structures (e.g., storage cells) in addition to longitudinal fibers. Fibers in hardwoods are also much smaller and shorter than those in softwoods.

The mechanical properties of woods are influenced by moisture content and grain orientation. (Strengths of dry woods are approximately twice those of wet or green woods. Longitudinal strengths may be as much as 40 times higher than cross-grain strengths.) *Moisture content*, MC, is defined by

$$ \text{MC} = \frac{m_{\text{wet}} - m_{\text{oven-dry}}}{m_{\text{oven-dry}}} $$

Wood is considered to be green if its moisture content is above 19%. Wood is considered to be dry when it has reached its *equilibrium moisture content*, generally between 12% and 15% moisture. Therefore, moisture is not totally absent in dry wood.[13]

8. GLASS

Glass is a term used to designate any material that has a volumetric expansion characteristic similar to Fig. 27.4. Glasses are sometimes considered to be *supercooled liquids* because their crystalline structures solidify in random orientation when cooled below their melting points. It is a direct result of the high liquid viscosities of oxides, silicates, borates, and phosphates that the molecules cannot move sufficiently to form large crystals with cleavage planes. Glass is considered an amorphous material.

Material Props./ Processing

---

[13]Oven-dry lumber is not used in construction.

Figure 27.4 *Behavior of a Glass*

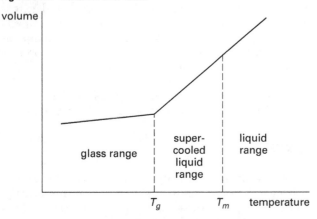

As a liquid glass is cooled, its atoms develop more efficient packing arrangements. This leads to a rapid decrease in volume (i.e., a steep slope on the temperature-volume curve). Since no crystallization occurs, the liquid glass simply solidifies without molecular change when cooled below the melting point. (This is known as *vitrification*.) The more efficient packing continues past the point of solidification.

At the *glass transition temperature* (*fictive temperature*), T_g, the glass viscosity increases suddenly by several orders of magnitude. Since the molecules are more restrained in movement, efficient atomic rearrangement is curtailed, and the volume-temperature curve changes slope. This temperature also divides the region into flexible and brittle regions. At the glass transition temperature, there is a 100-fold to 1000-fold increase in stiffness (modulus of elasticity).

Both organic and inorganic compounds may behave as glasses. *Common glasses* are mixtures of SiO_2, B_2O_3, and various other compounds to modify performance.[14]

9. CERAMICS

Ceramics are compounds of metallic and nonmetallic elements. Ceramics form crystalline structures but have no free valence electrons. All electrons are shared ionically or in covalent bonds. Common examples include brick, portland cement, refractories, and abrasives. (Glass is also considered a ceramic even though it does not crystallize.)

Although perfect ceramic crystals have extremely high tensile strengths (e.g., some glass fibers have ultimate strengths of 700 MPa), the multiplicity of cracks and other defects in natural crystals reduces their tensile strengths to near-zero levels.

Due to the absence of free electrons, ceramics are typically poor conductors of electrical current, although some (e.g., magnetite, Fe_3O_4) possess semiconductor

properties. Other ceramics, such as $BaTiO_3$, SiO_2, and $PbZrO_3$, have *piezoelectric* (*ferroelectric*) *qualities* (i.e., generate a voltage when compressed).

Polymorphs are compounds that have the same chemical formula but have different physical structures. Some ceramics, of which *silica* (SiO_2) is a common example, exhibit *polymorphism*. At room temperature, silica is in the form of *quartz*. At 875°C, the structure changes to *tridymite*. A change to a third structure, that of *cristobalite*, occurs at 1470°C.

Ferrimagnetic materials (*ferrites*, *spinels*, or *ferrispinels*) are ceramics with valuable magnetic qualities. Advances in near-room-temperature superconductivity have been based on *lanthanum barium copper oxide* ($La_{2-x}Ba_xCuO_4$), a ceramic oxide, as well as compounds based on yttrium (Y-Ba-Cu-O), bismuth, thallium, and others.

10. CONCRETE

Concrete (*portland cement concrete*) is a mixture of cementitious materials, aggregates, water, and air. The cement paste consists of a mixture of portland cement and water. The paste binds the coarse and fine aggregates into a rock-like mass as the paste hardens during the chemical reaction (*hydration*). Table 27.6 lists the approximate volumetric percentage of each ingredient.

Table 27.6 *Typical Volumetric Proportions of Concrete Ingredients*

component	air-entrained	non-air-entrained
coarse aggregate	31%	31%
fine aggregate	28%	30%
water	18%	21%
portland cement	15%	15%
air	8%	3%

Cementitious Materials

Cementitious materials include portland cement, blended hydraulic cements, expansive cement, and other cementitious additives, including fly ash, pozzolans, silica fume, and ground granulated blast-furnace slag.

Portland cement is produced by burning a mixture of lime and clay in a rotary kiln and grinding the resulting mass. Cement has a specific weight (density) of approximately 3120 kg/m^3 and is packaged in standard sacks (bags) weighing 40 kg.

Aggregate

Because aggregate makes up 60–75% of the total concrete volume, its properties influence the behavior of freshly mixed concrete and the properties of hardened concrete. Aggregates should consist of particles with

---

[14]This excludes lead-alkali glasses that contain 30–60% PbO.

sufficient strength and resistance to exposure conditions such as freezing and thawing cycles. Also, they should not contain materials that will cause the concrete to deteriorate.

Most sand and rock aggregate has a specific weight of approximately 2640 kg/m³ corresponding to a specific gravity of 2.64.

Water

Water in concrete has three functions: (1) Water reacts chemically with the cement. This chemical reaction is known as *hydration*. (2) Water wets the aggregate. (3) The water and cement mixture, which is known as *cement paste*, lubricates the concrete mixture and allows it to flow.

Water has a standard specific weight of 1000 kg/m³. 1000 L of water occupy 1 m³.

Potable water that conforms to ASTM C1602 and that has no pronounced odor or taste can be used for producing concrete. (With some quality restrictions, the American Concrete Institute (ACI) code also allows nonpotable water to be used in concrete mixing.) Impurities in water may affect the setting time, strength, and corrosion resistance. Water used in mixing concrete should be clean and free from injurious amounts of oils, acids, alkalis, salt, organic materials, and other substances that could damage the concrete or reinforcing steel.

Admixtures

Admixtures are routinely used to modify the performance of concrete. Advantages include higher strength, durability, chemical resistance, and workability; controlled rate of hydration; and reduced shrinkage and cracking. Accelerating and retarding admixtures fall into several different categories, as classified by ASTM C494.

Type A: water-reducing

Type B: set-retarding

Type C: set-accelerating

Type D: water-reducing and set-retarding

Type E: water-reducing and set-accelerating

Type F: high-range water-reducing

Type G: high-range water-reducing and set-retarding

Slump

The four basic concrete components (cement, sand, coarse aggregate, and water) are mixed together to produce a homogeneous concrete mixture. The *consistency* and *workability* of the mixture affect the concrete's ability to be placed, consolidated, and finished without segregation or bleeding. The slump test is commonly used to determine consistency and workability.

The *slump test* consists of completely filling a slump cone mold in three layers of about one-third of the mold volume. Each layer is rodded 25 times with a round, spherical-nosed steel rod of 16 mm diameter. When rodding the subsequent layers, the previous layers beneath are not penetrated by the rod. After rodding, the mold is removed by raising it carefully in the vertical direction. The slump is the difference in the mold height and the resulting concrete pile height. Typical values are 25–100 mm.

Concrete mixtures that do not slump appreciably are known as *stiff mixtures*. Stiff mixtures are inexpensive because of the large amounts of coarse aggregate. However, placing time and workability are impaired. Mixtures with large slumps are known as *wet mixtures* (*watery mixtures*) and are needed for thin castings and structures with extensive reinforcing. Slumps for concrete that is machine-vibrated during placement can be approximately one-third less than for concrete that is consolidated manually.

Density

The density, also known as *weight density*, *unit weight*, and *specific weight*, of normal-weight concrete varies from about 2240 kg/m³ to 2560 kg/m³, depending on the specific gravities of the constituents. For most calculations involving normal-weight concrete, the density may be taken as 2320 kg/m³ to 2400 kg/m³. Lightweight concrete can have a density as low as 1450 kg/m³. Although steel has a density of more than three times that of concrete, due to the variability in concrete density values and the relatively small volume of steel, the density of steel-reinforced concrete is typically taken as 2400 kg/m³ without any refinement for exact component contributions.

Compressive Strength

The concrete's *compressive strength*, f_c', is the maximum stress a concrete specimen can sustain in compressive axial loading. It is also the primary parameter used in ordering concrete. When one speaks of "6000 psi concrete," the compressive strength is being referred to. Compressive strength is expressed in psi or MPa. SI compressive strength may be written as "Cxx" (e.g., "C20"), where xx is the compressive strength in MPa. (MPa is equivalent to N/mm², which is also commonly quoted.)

Typical compressive strengths range from 4000 psi to 6000 psi for traditional structural concrete, though concrete for residential slabs-on-grade and foundations will be lower in strength (e.g., 3000 psi). 6000 psi concrete is used in the manufacture of some concrete pipes, particularly those that are jacked in.

Cost is approximately proportional to concrete's compressive strength—a rule that applies to high-performance concrete as well as traditional concrete. For example, if 5000 psi concrete costs $100 per cubic yard, then 14,000 psi concrete will cost approximately $280 per cubic yard.

Compressive strength is controlled by selective proportioning of the cement, coarse and fine aggregates, water, and various admixtures. However, the compressive strength of traditional concrete is primarily dependent on the mixture's water-cement ratio. (See Fig. 27.5.) Provided that the mix is of a workable consistency, strength varies directly with the water-cement ratio. (This is *Abrams' strength law*, named after Dr. Duff Abrams, who formulated the law in 1918.)

Figure 27.5 Water-Cement (W/C) Ratio*

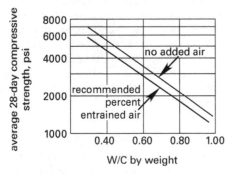

*Concrete strength decreases with increases in water-cement ratio for concrete with and without entrained air.

Concrete Manual, 8th ed., U.S. Bureau of Reclamation, 1975.

Compressive strength is normally measured on the 28th day after the specimens are cast. Since the strength of concrete increases with time, all values of f_c' must be stated with respect to a known age. If no age is given, a strength at a standard 28-day age is assumed.

The effect of the water-cement ratio on compressive strength (i.e., the more water the mix contains, the lower the compressive strength will be) is a different issue than the use of large amounts of surface water to cool the concrete during curing (i.e., *moist-curing*). (See Fig. 27.6.) The strength of newly poured concrete can be increased significantly (e.g., doubled) if the concrete is kept cool during part or all of curing. This is often accomplished by covering new concrete with wet burlap or by spraying with water. Although best results occur when the concrete is moist-cured for 28 days, it is seldom economical to do so. A substantial strength increase can be achieved if the concrete is kept moist for as little as three days. Externally applied curing retardants can also be used.

Stress-Strain Relationship

The stress-strain relationship for concrete is dependent on its strength, age at testing, rate of loading, nature of the aggregates, cement properties, and type and size of specimens. Typical stress-strain curves for concrete specimens loaded in compression at 28 days of age under a normal rate of loading are shown in Fig. 27.7.

Figure 27.6 Concrete Compressive Strength*

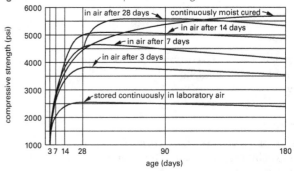

*Concrete compressive strength varies with moist-curing conditions. Mixes tested had a water-cement ratio of 0.50, a slump of 3.5 in, cement content of 556 lbf/yd³, sand content of 36%, and air content of 4%.

Figure 27.7 Typical Concrete Stress-Strain Curves

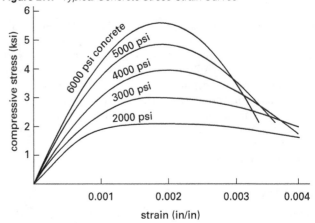

Modulus of Elasticity

The *modulus of elasticity* (also known as *Young's modulus*) is defined as the ratio of stress to strain in the elastic region. Unlike steel, the modulus of elasticity of concrete varies with compressive strength. Since the slope of the stress-strain curve varies with the applied stress, there are several ways of calculating the modulus of elasticity. Figure 27.8 shows a typical stress-strain curve for concrete with the *initial modulus*, the *tangent modulus*, and the *secant modulus* indicated.

Figure 27.8 Concrete Moduli of Elasticity

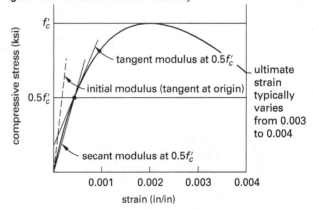

Splitting Tensile Strength

The extent and size of cracking in concrete structures are affected to a great extent by the tensile strength of the concrete. Lightweight concrete has a lower tensile strength than normal weight concrete, even if both have the same compressive strength.

Modulus of Rupture

The tensile strength of concrete in flexure is known as the *modulus of rupture*, f_r, and is an important parameter for evaluating cracking and deflection in beams. The tensile strength of concrete is relatively low, about 10–15% (and occasionally up to 20%) of the compressive strength.

Shear Strength

Concrete's true *shear strength* is difficult to determine in the laboratory because shear failure is seldom pure and is typically affected by other stresses in addition to the shear stress. Reported values of shear strength vary greatly with the test method used, but they are a small percentage (e.g., 25% or less) of the ultimate compressive strength.

Poisson's Ratio

Poisson's ratio is the ratio of the lateral strain to the axial strain. It varies in concrete from 0.11 to 0.23, with typical values being from 0.17 to 0.21.

11. COMPOSITE MATERIALS

There are many types of modern composite material systems, including dispersion-strengthened, particle-strengthened, and fiber-strengthened materials. High-performance composites are generally produced by dispersing large numbers of particles or whiskers of a strengthening component in a lightweight binder. (Steel-reinforced concrete and steel-plate-on-wood systems are also composite systems. However, these are designed and analyzed according to various building codes rather than to the theoretical methods presented in this section.)

Assuming a well-dispersed, well-bonded, and homogeneous mixture of components, the mechanical and thermal properties of a composite material can be predicted as volumetrically weighted fractions $(0 < f_i < 1.0)$ of the properties of the individual components. This is known as the *rule of mixtures*.

Table 27.7 lists properties of common components used in producing composite materials.

Table 27.7 *Properties of Components of Composite Materials*

	density, ρ (Mg/m³)	modulus of elasticity, E (GPa)	E/ρ (N·m/g)
binders/matrix			
polystyrene	1.05	2	2700
polyvinyl chloride	1.3	< 4	3500
strengtheners			
alumina fiber	3.9	400	100 000
aluminum	2.7	70	26 000
aramide fiber	1.3	125	100 000
BeO fiber	3.0	400	130 000
beryllium fiber	1.9	300	160 000
boron fiber	2.3	400	170 000
carbon fiber	2.3	700	300 000
glass	2.5	70	28 000
magnesium	1.7	45	26 000
silicon carbide fiber	3.2	400	120 000
steel	7.8	205	26 000

Equation 27.1 Through Eq. 27.5: Properties of a Composite Material

$$\rho_c = \sum f_i \rho_i \qquad 27.1$$

$$C_c = \sum f_i c_i \qquad 27.2$$

$$\left[\sum \frac{f_i}{E_i}\right]^{-1} \le E_c \le \sum f_i E_i \qquad 27.3$$

$$\sigma_c = \sum f_i \sigma_i \qquad 27.4$$

$$(\Delta L/L)_1 = (\Delta L/L)_2 \qquad 27.5$$

Description

Equation 27.1 gives the density of a composite material, ρ_c, typically expressed in units of kg/m³. f_i is the volumetric fraction of each individual material, and ρ_i is the density of each material.

The heat capacity of a composite material per unit volume, C_c, is calculated from Eq. 27.2.[15]

Equation 27.3 is used to calculate the *modulus of elasticity (Young's modulus)* of a composite material, E_c, calculated from the volumetric fraction of each material, f_i, and modulus of elasticity of each material, E_i.

---

[15]Normally, lowercase c is used to represent specific heat capacity on a per unit mass basis, and uppercase C is used for molar specific heat. In Eq. 27.2, the NCEES *FE Reference Handbook* (*NCEES Handbook*) uses both uppercase and lowercase to represent specific heat capacity. However, it is more common to use c_c for the composite specific heat for clarity. Equation 27.2 is valid only for the composite *volumetric heat capacity* (VHC) based on component VHCs. This equation cannot be used to calculate the specific heat on a per unit mass basis because a gravimetric fraction (not volumetric fraction) would be needed.

The ultimate tensile strength of a composite material parallel to the fiber direction, σ_c, is calculated from Eq. 27.4.[16]

Assuming perfect bonding, the strain in two adjacent components (e.g., strengthening whiskers and the supporting matrix) will be the same. This is expressed in Eq. 27.5.

Example

A composite material is 57% resin (density of 2.3 g/cm³) and 43% unidirectionally placed carbon fibers (1.05 g/cm³) by volume. The material has a composite modulus of elasticity of 400 GPa parallel to the carbon fibers. What is most nearly the density of the composite material?

(A) 1.3 g/cm³

(B) 1.8 g/cm³

(C) 1.9 g/cm³

(D) 2.2 g/cm³

Solution

Using Eq. 27.1, the density of the composite material is

$$\rho_c = \sum f_i \rho_i$$
$$= (0.57)\left(2.3 \ \frac{g}{cm^3}\right) + (0.43)\left(1.05 \ \frac{g}{cm^3}\right)$$
$$= 1.763 \ g/cm^3 \quad (1.8 \ g/cm^3)$$

The answer is (B).

12. CORROSION

Corrosion is an undesirable degradation of a material resulting from a chemical or physical reaction with the environment. *Galvanic action* results from a difference in oxidation potentials of metallic ions. The greater the difference in oxidation potentials, the greater the galvanic corrosion will be. If two metals with different oxidation potentials are placed in an *electrolytic medium* (e.g., seawater), a *galvanic cell* (*voltaic cell*) will be created. The more electropositive metal will act as an anode and will corrode. The metal with the lower potential, being the cathode, will be unchanged.

A galvanic cell is a device that produces electrical current by way of an oxidation-reduction reaction—that is, chemical energy is converted into electrical energy. Galvanic cells typically have the following characteristics.

- The oxidizing agent is separate from the reducing agent.
- Each agent has its own electrolyte and metallic electrode, and the combination is known as a *half-cell*.
- Each agent can be in solid, liquid, or gaseous form, or can consist simply of the electrode.
- The ions can pass between the electrolytes of the two half-cells. The connection can be through a porous substance, salt bridge, another electrolyte, or other method.

The amount of current generated by a half-cell depends on the electrode material and the oxidation-reduction reaction taking place in the cell. The current-producing ability is known as the *oxidation potential*, *reduction potential*, or *half-cell potential*. *Standard oxidation potentials* have a zero reference voltage corresponding to the potential of a *standard hydrogen electrode*.

To specify their tendency to corrode, metals are often classified according to their position in the galvanic series listed in Table 27.8. As expected, the metals in this series are in approximately the same order as their half-cell potentials. However, alloys and proprietary metals are also included in the series.

It is not necessary that two dissimilar metals be in contact for corrosion by galvanic action to occur. Different regions within a metal may have different half-cell potentials. The difference in potential can be due to different phases within the metal (creating very small galvanic cells), heat treatment, cold working, and so on.

In addition to corrosion caused by galvanic action, there is also *stress corrosion*, *fretting corrosion*, and *cavitation*. Conditions within the crystalline structure can accentuate or retard corrosion. In one extreme type of intergranular corrosion, *exfoliation*, open endgrains separate into layers.

Table 27.9 gives the oxidation potentials for common corrosion reactions.

Equation 27.6 Through Eq. 27.9: Oxidation-Reduction Corrosion Reactions

$M^o \rightarrow M^{n+} + ne^-$ [at the anode]	27.6
$\frac{1}{2}O_2 + 2e^- + H_2O \rightarrow 2OH^-$ [at the cathode]	27.7
$\frac{1}{2}O_2 + 2e^- + 2H_3O^+ \rightarrow 3H_2O$ [at the cathode]	27.8
$2e^- + 2H_3O^+ \rightarrow 2H_2O + H_2$ [at the cathode]	27.9

---

[16]Although the term "strength" is correctly used in reference to the ultimate tensile strength, the common symbol for stress, σ, is unfortunately used. The ultimate tensile strength can indeed be predicted by the rule of mixtures, although the composite strength will be greatly optimistic. Stress is generally weighted by area (or a combination of area and modulus of elasticity).

Table 27.8 *Galvanic Series in Seawater (top to bottom anodic (sacrificial, active) to cathodic (noble, passive))*

magnesium

zinc

Alclad 3S

cadmium

2024 aluminum alloy

low-carbon steel

cast iron

stainless steels (active)

    no. 410

    no. 430

    no. 404

    no. 316

Hastelloy A

lead

lead-tin alloys

tin

nickel

brass (copper-zinc)

copper

bronze (copper-tin)

90/10 copper-nickel

70/30 copper-nickel

Inconel

silver solder

silver

stainless steels (passive)

Monel metal

Hastelloy C

titanium

graphite

gold

Description

In an oxidation-reduction reaction, such as corrosion, one substance is oxidized and the other is reduced. The oxidized substance loses electrons and becomes less negative; the reduced substance gains electrons and becomes more negative.

Oxidation occurs at the *anode* (positive terminal) in an electrolytic reaction. Equation 27.6 shows the oxidation reaction (or *anode reaction*) of a typical metal, M. The superscript "o" is used to designate the standard, natural state of the atom.

Reduction occurs at the *cathode* (negative terminal) in an electrolytic reaction. Equation 27.7 through Eq. 27.9 list some reduction reactions (or *cathode reactions*) involving hydrogen and oxygen.

13. DIFFUSION OF DEFECTS

Real crystals possess a variety of imperfections and defects that affect *structure-sensitive properties*. Such properties include electrical conductivity, yield and ultimate strengths, creep strength, and semiconductor properties. Most imperfections can be categorized into *point*, *line*, and *planar* (*grain boundary*) imperfections. As shown in Fig. 27.9, *point defects* include vacant lattice sites, ion vacancies, substitutions of foreign atoms into lattice points or interstitial points, and occupation of interstitial points by atoms. *Line defects* consist of imperfections that are repeated consistently in many adjacent cells and have extension in a particular direction. *Grain boundary defects* are the interfaces between two or more crystals. This interface is almost always a mismatch in crystalline structures.

Figure 27.9 *Point Defects*

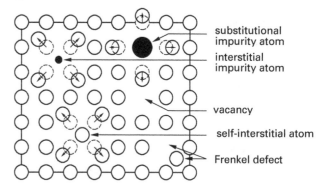

All point defects can move individually and independently from one position to another through *diffusion*. The *activation energy* for such diffusion generally comes from heat and/or strain (i.e., bending or forming). In the absence of the activation energy, the defect will move very slowly, if at all.

Diffusion of defects is governed by *Fick's laws*.

Equation 27.10: Diffusion Coefficient

$$D = D_o e^{-Q/(RT)} \hspace{2cm} 27.10$$

Values

$\overline{R} = 8314 \text{ J/kmol·K}$

Table 27.9 *Standard Oxidation Potentials for Corrosion Reactions*

corrosion reaction	potential, E_o (volts), versus normal hydrogen electrode
$Au \rightarrow Au^{3+} + 3e^-$	-1.498
$2H_2O \rightarrow O_2 + 4H^+ + 4e^-$	-1.229
$Pt \rightarrow Pt^{2+} + 2e^-$	-1.200
$Pd \rightarrow Pd^{2+} + 2e^-$	-0.987
$Ag \rightarrow Ag^+ + e^-$	-0.799
$2Hg \rightarrow Hg_2^{2+} + 2e^-$	-0.788
$Fe^{2+} \rightarrow Fe^{3+} + e^-$	-0.771
$4(OH)^- \rightarrow O_2 + 2H_2O + 4e^-$	-0.401
$Cu \rightarrow Cu^{2+} + 2e^-$	-0.337
$Sn^{2+} \rightarrow Sn^{4+} + 2e^-$	-0.150
$H_2 \rightarrow 2H^+ + 2e^-$	0.000
$Pb \rightarrow Pb^{2+} + 2e^-$	+0.126
$Sn \rightarrow Sn^{2+} + 2e^-$	+0.136
$Ni \rightarrow Ni^{2+} + 2e^-$	+0.250
$Co \rightarrow Co^{2+} + 2e^-$	+0.277
$Cd \rightarrow Cd^{2+} + 2e^-$	+0.403
$Fe \rightarrow Fe^{2+} + 2e^-$	+0.440
$Cr \rightarrow Cr^{3+} + 3e^-$	+0.744
$Zn \rightarrow Zn^{2+} + 2e^-$	+0.763
$Al \rightarrow Al^{3+} + 3e^-$	+1.662
$Mg \rightarrow Mg^{2+} + 2e^-$	+2.363
$Na \rightarrow Na^+ + e^-$	+2.714
$K \rightarrow K^+ + e^-$	+2.925

*Measured at 25°C. Reactions are written as anode half-cells. Arrows are reversed for cathode half-cells.
NOTE: In some chemistry texts, the reactions and the signs of the values (in this table) are reversed; for example, the half-cell potential of zinc is given as –0.763 V for the reaction $Zn^{2+} + 2e^- \rightarrow Zn$. When the potential E_o is positive, the reaction proceeds spontaneously as written.

Description

Equation 27.10 is used to determine the *diffusion coefficient*, D (also known as the *diffusivity*), expressed in units of square meters per second. The diffusion coefficient is dependent on the material, activation energy, and temperature. It is calculated from the proportionality constant, D_o, the activation energy, Q, the universal gas constant, $\overline{R}$, and the absolute temperature, T.[17] Since $e^{-Q/(RT)}$ is a number less than 1.0, the proportionality constant is actually the maximum possible value of the diffusion coefficient, which would occur at an infinite temperature.[18] The exponent $-Q/(\overline{R}\,T)$ in Eq. 27.10 must be unitless.

Example

The activation energy, Q, for aluminum in a copper solvent at 575°C is 1.6×10^5 kJ/kmol. What is most nearly the diffusion coefficient, D, if the proportionality constant, D_o, is 7×10^{-6} m²/s?

(A) 4.0×10^{-47} m²/s

(B) 2.0×10^{-20} m²/s

(C) 9.8×10^{-16} m²/s

(D) 2.3×10^{-5} m²/s

Solution

The absolute temperature is

$$T = 575°C + 273° = 848K$$

To use Eq. 27.10, the units in the exponent must cancel. Since the universal gas constant, $\overline{R}$, is given in units of joules per kmol, the activation energy, Q, must also have those units.

$$Q = \left(1.6 \times 10^5 \; \frac{kJ}{kmol}\right)\left(1000 \; \frac{J}{kJ}\right)$$
$$= 1.6 \times 10^8 \; J/kmol$$

The diffusion coefficient is

$$D = D_o e^{-Q/(RT)}$$
$$= \left(7 \times 10^{-6} \; \frac{m^2}{s}\right)$$
$$\times e^{-\left(1.6 \times 10^8 \; J/kmol / (8314 \; J/kmol\cdot K)(848K)\right)}$$
$$= 9.753 \times 10^{-16} \; m^2/s \quad (9.8 \times 10^{-16} \; m^2/s)$$

The answer is (C).

---

[17](1) The *NCEES Handbook* is inconsistent in the variable it uses for the universal gas constant. R in Eq. 27.10 is the same as $\overline{R}$ defined in its *Units* section and used almost everywhere in the *NCEES Handbook*. (2) There is no mathematical significance to the parentheses around the denominator of the exponent in Eq. 27.10.

[18](1) The *NCEES Handbook* uses a subscript letter o for the proportionality constant, which should be interpreted as the subscript zero, 0, normally used in references. (2) The *NCEES Handbook* is inconsistent in the symbols used for activation energy. Q in Eq. 27.10 is the same as $E_g - E_d$ and E_a in Table 26.4. A common symbol used in practice for diffusion activation energy is Q_d, where the subscript clarifies that the activation energy is for diffusion.

14. BINARY PHASE DIAGRAMS

Most engineering materials are not pure elements but are alloys of two or more elements. Alloys of two elements are known as *binary alloys*. Steel, for example, is an alloy of primarily iron and carbon. Usually one of the elements is present in a much smaller amount, and this element is known as the *alloying ingredient*. The primary ingredient is known as the *host ingredient, base metal*, or *parent ingredient*.

Sometimes, such as with alloys of copper and nickel, the alloying ingredient is 100% soluble in the parent ingredient. Nickel-copper alloy is said to be a *completely miscible alloy* or a *solid-solution alloy*.

The presence of the alloying ingredient changes the thermodynamic properties, notably the freezing (or melting) temperatures of both elements. Usually the freezing temperatures decrease as the percentage of alloying ingredient is increased. Because the freezing points of the two elements are not the same, one of them will start to solidify at a higher temperature than the other. For any given composition, the alloy might consist of all liquid, all solid, or a combination of solid and liquid, depending on the temperature.

A *phase* of a material at a specific temperature will have a specific composition and crystalline structure and distinct physical, electrical, and thermodynamic properties. (In metallurgy, the word "phase" refers to more than just solid, liquid, and gas phases.)

The regions of an *equilibrium diagram*, also known as a *phase diagram*, illustrate the various alloy phases. The phases are plotted against temperature and composition. The composition is usually a gravimetric fraction of the alloying ingredient. Only one ingredient's gravimetric fraction needs to be plotted for a binary alloy.

It is important to recognize that the equilibrium conditions do not occur instantaneously and that an equilibrium diagram is applicable only to the case of slow cooling.

Figure 27.10 is an equilibrium diagram for a copper-nickel alloy. (Most equilibrium diagrams are much more complex.) The *liquidus line* is the boundary above which no solid can exist. The *solidus line* is the boundary below which no liquid can exist. The area between these two lines represents a mixture of solid and liquid phase materials.

Figure 27.10 Copper-Nickel Phase Diagram

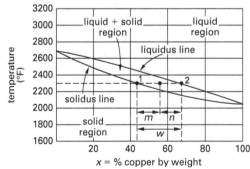

Just as only a limited amount of salt can be dissolved in water, there are many instances where a limited amount of the alloying ingredient can be absorbed by the solid mixture. The elements of a binary alloy may be completely soluble in the liquid state but only partially soluble in the solid state.

When the alloying ingredient is present in an amount above the maximum solubility percentage, the alloying ingredient precipitates out. In aqueous solutions, the precipitate falls to the bottom of the container. In metallic alloys, the precipitate remains suspended as pure crystals dispersed throughout the primary metal.

In chemistry, a *mixture* is different from a *solution*. Salt in water forms a solution. Sugar crystals mixed with salt crystals form a mixture.

Figure 27.11 is typical of an equilibrium diagram for ingredients displaying a limited solubility.

Figure 27.11 Equilibrium Diagram of a Limited Solubility Alloy

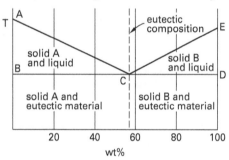

In Fig. 27.11, the components are perfectly miscible at point C only. This point is known as the *eutectic composition*. A *eutectic alloy* is an alloy having the composition of its eutectic point. The material in the region ABC consists of a mixture of solid component A crystals in a liquid of components A and B. This liquid is known as the *eutectic material*, and it will not solidify until the line BD (the *eutectic line, eutectic point*, or *eutectic temperature*)—the lowest point at which the eutectic material can exist in liquid form—is reached.

Since the two ingredients do not mix, reducing the temperature below the eutectic line results in crystals (layers or plates) of both pure ingredients forming. This is the microstructure of a solid eutectic alloy: alternating pure crystals of the two ingredients. Since two solid substances are produced from a single liquid substance, the process could be written in chemical reaction format as liquid → solid α + solid β. (Alternatively, upon heating, the reaction would be solid α + solid β → liquid.) For this reason, the phase change is called a *eutectic reaction*.

There are similar reactions involving other phases and states. Table 27.10 and Fig. 27.12 illustrate these.

Table 27.10 Types of Equilibrium Reactions

reaction name	type of reaction upon cooling
eutectic	liquid → solid α + solid β
peritectic	liquid + solid α → solid β
eutectoid	solid γ → solid α + solid β
peritectoid	solid α + solid γ → solid β

Figure 27.12 Typical Appearance of Equilibrium Diagram at Reaction Points

reaction name	phase reaction	phase diagram
eutectic	$L \rightarrow \alpha(s) + \beta(s)$ cooling	
peritectic	$L + \alpha(s) \rightarrow \beta(s)$ cooling	
eutectoid	$\gamma(s) \rightarrow \alpha(s) + \beta(s)$ cooling	
peritectoid	$\alpha(s) + \gamma(s) \rightarrow \beta(s)$ cooling	

Example

A binary solution with the characteristics and composition of point P is cooled.

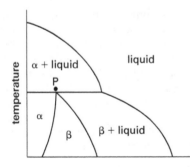

What type of alloy will result?

(A) eutectic

(B) eutectoid

(C) peritectic

(D) peritectoid

Solution

Dropping straight down from point P on the illustration, corresponding to cooling, the α solid and liquid transform into the β solid. This corresponds to the definition of a peritectic reaction. A peritectic alloy will form.

The answer is (C).

15. LEVER RULE

Within a liquid-solid region, the percentage of solid and liquid phases is a function of temperature and composition. Near the liquidus line, there is very little solid phase. Near the solidus line, there is very little liquid phase. The *lever rule* is an interpolation technique used to find the relative amounts of solid and liquid phase at any composition. These percentages are given in fraction (or percent) by weight.

Figure 27.10 shows an alloy with an average composition of 55% copper at 2300°F. (A horizontal line representing different conditions at a single temperature is known as a *tie line*.) The liquid composition is defined by point 2, and the solid composition is defined by point 1. Referring to Fig. 27.10, the gravimetric fraction of solid and liquid can be determined from the lever rule using the line segment lengths m, n, and $w = m + n$ in a method that is analogous to determining steam quality.

$$\text{fraction solid} = 1 - \text{fraction liquid} = \frac{n}{m+n} = \frac{n}{w}$$

$$\text{fraction liquid} = 1 - \text{fraction solid} = \frac{m}{m+n} = \frac{m}{w}$$

Equation 27.11 and Eq. 27.12: Gravimetric Component Fraction

$$\text{wt\% } \alpha = \frac{x_\beta - x}{x_\beta - x_\alpha} \times 100\% \qquad 27.11$$

$$\text{wt\% } \beta = \frac{x - x_\alpha}{x_\beta - x_\alpha} \times 100\% \qquad 27.12$$

Description

Referring to Fig. 27.13, from the lever rule, the gravimetric fractions of solid and liquid phases depend on the lengths of the lines $x - x_\alpha$ and $x_\beta - x$, along with the separation, $x_\beta - x_\alpha$, which may be measured using any convenient scale. (Although the distances can be measured in millimeters or tenths of an inch, it is more convenient to use the percentage alloying ingredient scale.) Then, the fractions of solid and liquid can be calculated from Eq. 27.11 and Eq. 27.12.

Figure 27.13 Two-Phase System Phase Diagram

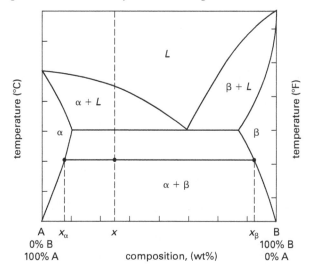

The lever rule and method of determining the composition of the two components are applicable to any solution or mixture, liquid or solid, in which two phases are present.

Example

Consider the Ag-Cu phase diagram given.

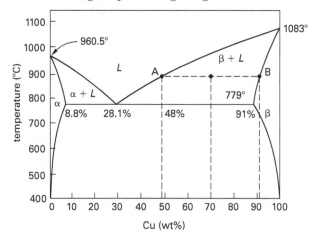

What is most nearly the equilibrium percentage of β in an alloy of 30% Ag, 70% Cu at 900°C?

(A) 0.0%

(B) 22%

(C) 51%

(D) 59%

Solution

Draw the horizontal tie line at 900°C between the liquid, L, phase at point A and the solid, β, at point B. Draw the

vertical line that identifies the alloy at $x = 70\%$ Cu. Rather than measure the lengths of the lines, use the horizontal Cu percentage scale. Point A is located at $x_L = 48\%$ Cu, and point B is located at $x_\beta = 91\%$ Cu. Use Eq. 27.12.

$$\text{wt\% } \beta = \frac{x - x_L}{x_\beta - x_L} \times 100\% = \frac{70\% - 48\%}{91\% - 48\%} \times 100\%$$
$$= 51.2\% \quad (51\%)$$

The answer is (C).

16. IRON-CARBON PHASE DIAGRAM

The iron-carbon phase diagram (see Fig. 27.14) is much more complex than idealized equilibrium diagrams due to the existence of many different phases. Each of these phases has a different microstructure and different mechanical properties. By treating the steel in such a manner as to force the occurrence of particular phases, steel with desired wear and endurance properties can be produced.

Allotropes have the same composition but different atomic structures (microstructures), volumes, electrical resistances, and magnetic properties. *Allotropic changes* are reversible changes that occur at the *critical points* (i.e., *critical temperatures*).

Iron exists in three primary allotropic forms: alpha-iron, delta-iron, and gamma-iron. The changes are brought about by varying the temperature of the iron. Heating pure iron from room temperature changes its structure from body-centered cubic (BCC) *alpha-iron* (−273–970°C), also known as *ferrite*, to face-centered cubic (FCC) *gamma-iron* (910–1400°C), to BCC *delta-iron* (above 1400°C).

Iron-carbon mixtures are categorized into *steel* (less than 2% carbon) and *cast iron* (more than 2% carbon) according to the amounts of carbon in the mixtures.

The most important eutectic reaction in the iron-carbon system is the formation of a solid mixture of austenite and cementite at approximately 1129°C. *Austenite* is a solid solution of carbon in gamma-iron. It is nonmagnetic, decomposes on slow cooling, and does not normally exist below 723°C, although it can be partially preserved by extremely rapid cooling.

Cementite (Fe_3C), also known as *carbide* or *iron carbide*, has approximately 6.67% carbon. Cementite is the hardest of all forms of iron, has low tensile strength, and is quite brittle.

The most important eutectoid reaction in the iron-carbon system is the formation of *pearlite* from the decomposition of austenite at approximately 723°C. Pearlite is actually a mixture of two solid components, ferrite and cementite, with the common *lamellar* (*layered*) *appearance*.

Ferrite is essentially pure iron (less than 0.025% carbon) in BCC alpha-iron structure. It is magnetic and has properties complementary to cementite, since it has low hardness, high tensile strength, and high ductility.

Figure 27.14 *Iron-Carbon Diagram*

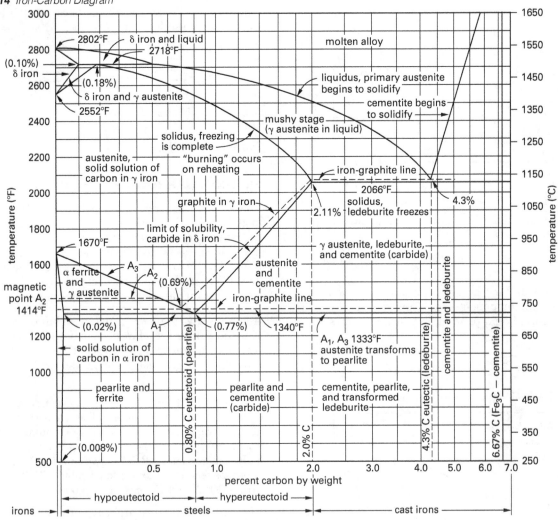

17. EQUILIBRIUM MIXTURES

Equation 27.13: Gibbs' Phase Rule

$$P + F = C + 2 \qquad 27.13$$

Variation

$$P + F = C + 1 \Big|_{\substack{\text{constant pressure,} \\ \text{constant temperature,} \\ \text{or constant composition}}}$$

Description

Gibbs' phase rule defines the relationship between the number of phases and elements in an equilibrium mixture. For such an equilibrium mixture to exist, the alloy must have been slowly cooled and thermodynamic equilibrium must have been achieved along the way.

At equilibrium, and considering both temperature and pressure to be independent variables, Gibbs' phase rule is Eq. 27.13.

P is the number of phases existing simultaneously; F is the number of independent variables, known as *degrees of freedom*; and C is the number of elements in the alloy. Composition, temperature, and pressure are examples of degrees of freedom that can be varied.

For example, if water is to be stored in a condition where three phases (solid, liquid, gas) are present simultaneously, then $P = 3$, $C = 1$, and $F = 0$. That is, neither pressure nor temperature can be varied. This state corresponds to the *triple point* of water.

If pressure is constant, then the number of degrees of freedom is reduced by one, and Gibbs' phase rule can be rewritten as shown in the variation.

If Gibbs' rule predicts $F = 0$, then an alloy can exist with only one composition.

Example

A system consisting of an open bucket containing a mixture of ice and water is to be warmed from 0°C to 20°C. How many degrees of freedom does the system have?

    (A) 0

    (B) 1

    (C) 2

    (D) 3

Solution

Degrees of freedom and the system properties are instantaneous values. What is happening and what is going to happen to the system are not relevant. Only the current, instantaneous equilibrium properties are relevant. In this case, the system consists of an open bucket containing ice and water, so the number of phases is $P = 2$. The only substance in the system is water, so the number of components is $C = 1$.

$$P + F = C + 2$$
$$F = C + 2 - P = 1 + 2 - 2$$
$$= 1$$

The answer is (B).

18. THERMAL PROCESSING

Thermal processing, including hot working, heat treating, and quenching, is used to obtain a part with desirable mechanical properties.

Cold and hot working are both forming processes (rolling, bending, forging, extruding, etc.). The term *hot working* implies that the forming process occurs above the *recrystallization temperature*. (The actual temperature depends on the rate of strain and the cooling period, if any.) *Cold working* (also known as *work hardening* and *strain hardening*) occurs below the recrystallization temperature.

Above the recrystallization temperature, almost all of the internal defects and imperfections caused by hot working are eliminated. In effect, hot working is a "self-healing" operation. A hot-worked part remains softer and has a greater ductility than a cold-worked part. Large strains are possible without strain hardening. Hot working is preferred when the part must go through a series of forming operations (passes or steps), or when large changes in size and shape are needed.

The hardness and toughness of a cold-worked part will be higher than that of a hot-worked part. Because the part's temperature during the cold working is uniform, the final microstructure will also be uniform. There are many times when these characteristics are desirable,

and hot working is not always the preferred forming method. In many cases, cold working will be the final operation after several steps of hot working.

Once a part has been worked, its temperature can be raised to slightly above the recrystallization temperature. This *heat treatment* operation is known as *annealing* and is used to relieve stresses, increase grain size, and recrystallize the grains. Stress relief is also known as *recovery*.

Quenching is used to control the microstructure of steel by preventing the formation of equilibrium phases with undesirable characteristics. The usual desired result is hard steel, which resists plastic deformation. The quenching can be performed with gases (usually air), oil, water, or brine. Agitation or spraying of these fluids during the quenching process increases the severity of the quenching.

Time-temperature-transformation (TTT) *curves* are used to determine how fast an alloy should be cooled to obtain a desired microstructure. Although these curves show different phases, they are not equilibrium diagrams. On the contrary, they show the microstructures that are produced with controlled temperatures or when quenching interrupts the equilibrium process.

TTT curves are determined under ideal, isothermal conditions. However, the curves are more readily available than experimentally determined *controlled-cooling-transformation* (CCT) *curves*. Both curves are similar in shape, although the CCT curves are displaced downward and to the right from TTT curves.

Figure 27.15 shows a TTT diagram for a high-carbon (0.80% carbon) steel. Curve 1 represents extremely rapid quenching. The transformation begins at 216°C, and continues for 8–30 seconds, changing all of the austenite to martensite. The martensitic transformation does not depend on diffusion. Since martensite has almost no ductility, martensitic microstructures are used in applications such as springs and hardened tools where a high elastic modulus and low ductility are needed.

Figure 27.15 *TTT Diagram for High-Carbon Steel*

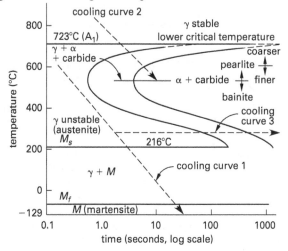

Curve 2 represents a slower quench that converts all of the austenite to fine pearlite.

A horizontal line below the critical temperature is a *tempering* process. If the temperature is decreased rapidly along curve 1 to 270°C and is then held constant along cooling curve 3, bainite is produced. This is the principle of *austempering*. Bainite is not as hard as martensite, but it does have good impact strength and fairly high hardness. Performing the same procedure at 180–200°C is *martempering*, which produces *tempered martensite*, a soft and tough steel.

19. HARDNESS AND HARDENABILITY

Hardness is the measure of resistance a material has to plastic deformation. Various *hardness tests* (e.g., Brinell, Rockwell, Meyer, Vickers, and Knoop) are used to determine hardness. These tests generally measure the depth of an impression made by a hardened penetrator set into the surface by a standard force.

Hardenability is a relative measure of the ease by which a material can be hardened. Some materials are easier to harden than others. See Fig. 27.16 for sample hardenability curves for steel.

Figure 27.16 Jominy Hardenability Curves for Six Steel Alloys

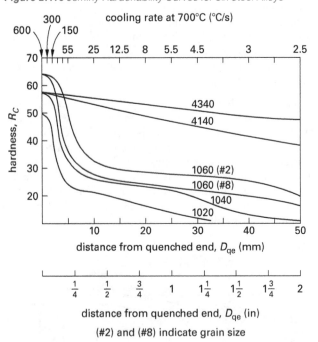

(#2) and (#8) indicate grain size

Van Vlack, L., *Elements of Materials Science and Engineering*, Addison-Wesley, 1989.

The hardness obtained also depends on the hardening method (e.g., cooling in air, other gases, water, or oil) and rate of cooling. For example, see Fig. 27.17 and

Figure 27.17 Cooling Rates for Bars Quenched in Agitated Water

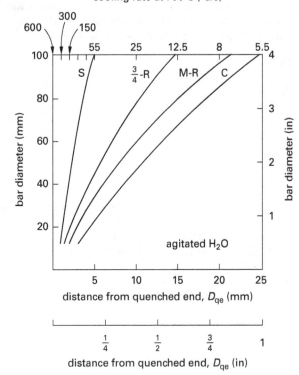

Van Vlack, L., *Elements of Materials Science and Engineering*, Addison-Wesley, 1989.

Fig. 27.18. Since the hardness obtained depends on the material, hardening data is often presented graphically. There are a variety of curve types used for this purpose.

Hardenability is not the same as hardness. *Hardness* refers to the ability to resist deformation when a load is applied, whereas *hardenability* refers to the ability to be hardened to a particular depth.

In the *Jominy end quench test*, a cylindrical steel specimen is heated long enough to obtain a uniform grain structure. Then, one end of the specimen is cooled ("quenched") in a water spray, while the remainder of the specimen is allowed to cool by conduction. The cooling rate decreases with increasing distance from the quenched end. When the specimen has entirely cooled, the hardness is determined at various distances from the quenched end. The hardness at the quenched end corresponds to water cooling, while the hardness at the opposite end corresponds to air cooling. The same test can be performed with different alloys. *Rockwell hardness* (C-scale) (also known as *Rockwell C hardness*), R_C, is plotted on the vertical axis, while distance from the quenched end, D_{qe}, is plotted on the horizontal scale.[19] The horizontal scale can also be correlated to and calibrated as *cooling rate*. The *Jominy hardenability curves* are used to

---

[19]In ASTM A255, "Standard Test Methods for Determining Hardenability of Steel," the distance from the quenched end is given the symbol J and is referred to as the *Jominy distance*. Rockwell C hardness is given the standard symbol "HRC." The *initial hardness* at the $J = \frac{1}{16}$ in position is given the symbol "IH."

Figure 27.18 Cooling Rates for Bars Quenched in Agitated Oil

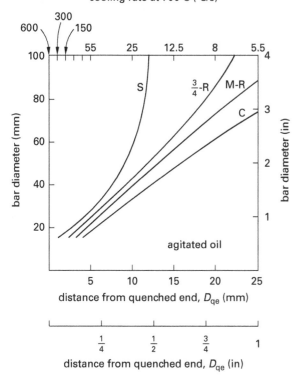

Van Vlack, L., *Elements of Materials Science and Engineering*, Addison-Wesley, 1989.

Figure 27.19 Bar Positions

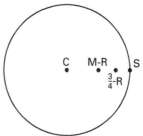

select an alloy and heat treatment that minimizes distortion during manufacturing. Figure 27.16 illustrates the results of Jominy hardenability tests of six steel alloys.

The position within the bar (see Fig. 27.19) is indicated by the following nomenclature.

- C = center of the bar

- M-R = halfway between the center of the bar and the surface of the bar

- $\frac{3}{4}$-R = three-quarters (75%) of the distance between C and S

- S = surface of the bar

20. METAL GRAIN SIZE

One of the factors affecting hardness and hardenability is the average metal *grain size*. Grain size refers to the diameter of a three-dimensional spherical grain as determined from a two-dimensional micrograph of the metal.

The size of the grains formed depends on the number of nuclei formed during the solidification process. If there are many nuclei, as would occur when cooling is rapid, there will be many small grains. However, if cooling is slow, a smaller number of larger grains will be produced. Fast cooling produces fine-grained material, and slow cooling produces coarse-grained material.

At moderate temperatures and strain rates, fine-grained materials deform less (i.e., are harder and tougher) while coarse-grained materials deform more. For ease of cold-formed manufacturing, coarse-grained materials may be preferred. However, appearance and strength may suffer.

It is difficult to measure grain size because the grains are varied in size and shape and because a two-dimensional image does not reveal volume. Semi-empirical methods have been developed to automatically or semi-automatically correlate grain size with the number of intersections observed in samples. ASTM E112, "Determining Average Grain Size" (and the related ASTM E1382), describes a planimetric procedure for metallic and some nonmetallic materials that exist primarily in a single phase.

Equation 27.14 Through Eq. 27.16: ASTM Grain Size, *n*

$$\frac{N_{\text{actual}}}{\text{actual area}} = \frac{N}{0.0645 \text{ mm}^2} \qquad 27.14$$

$$N_{(0.0645 \text{ mm}^2)} = 2^{(n-1)} \qquad 27.15$$

$$S_V = 2P_L \qquad 27.16$$

Description

Data on grain size is obtained by counting the number of grains in any small two-dimensional area. The number of grains, N, in a standard area (0.0645 mm^2) can be extrapolated from the observations using Eq. 27.14.

The standard number of grains, N, is the number of grains per square inch in an image of a polished specimen magnified 100 times. Equation 27.15 calculates the ASTM *grain size number* (also known as the ASTM *grain size*), n, from the standard number of grains, N, as the nearest integer greater than 1.

$$n = \frac{\log N + \log 2}{\log 2}$$

The grain-boundary surface area per unit volume, S_V, is taken as twice the number of points of intersection per unit length between the line and boundaries, P_L, as shown by

Eq. 27.16. If a random line (any length, any orientation) is drawn across a 100× magnified image (i.e., a *photomicrograph*) of grains, the line will cross some number of grains, say N. For each grain, the line will cross over two grain boundaries, so for a line of length L, the average grain diameter will be

$$D_{ave} = \frac{L}{2N} = \frac{1}{S_V}$$

Example

Eight grains are observed in a 0.0645 mm^2 area of a polished metal surface. What is most nearly the number of grains in an area of 710 mm^2?

(A)   16 grains

(B)   120 grains

(C)   1100 grains

(D)   88 000 grains

Solution

From Eq. 27.14, and rearranging to solve for N_{actual}, the number of grains in an area of 710 mm^2 is

$$\frac{N_{actual}}{actual\ area} = \frac{N}{0.0645\ mm^2}$$

$$N_{actual} = (actual\ area)\left(\frac{N}{0.0645\ mm^2}\right)$$

$$= (710\ mm^2)\left(\frac{8\ grains}{0.0645\ mm^2}\right)$$

$$= 88\,062\ grains\quad (88\,000\ grains)$$

The answer is (D).

28 Manufacturing Processes

Nomenclature

C	Taylor wear constant	–
d	depth of cut	m
f	tool feed rate	m/rev
n	constant	–
r	chip thickness ratio	–
t	thickness	m
T	tool life	min
v	cutting speed	m/min

Symbols

α	angle	

1. CHIP FORMATION

One of the most common ways that a workpiece can be shaped is by removing material through chip-forming operations such as turning, drilling, multitooth operations (e.g., milling, broaching, sawing, and filing), and specialized processes, such as thread and gear cutting.

The toughness of a workpiece can be determined from the nature of the chips produced. Brittle materials produce discrete fragments, known as *discontinuous chips*, *segmented chips*, or *type-one chips*. Some crispy brittle materials are known as *chocolate chips*. Ductile materials form long, helix-coiled string chips, known as *continuous chips* or *type-two chips*.[1] *Chip-breaker* grooves are often ground in the cutting tool face to cause long chips to break into shorter, more manageable pieces. Chip formation is optimum when chips are produced in the shapes of sixes and nines.

2. CUTTING TOOL SPEEDS AND FORCES

Figure 28.1 shows a chip produced during *orthogonal cutting* (i.e., two-dimensional cutting). Cutting involves both compressive and shear stresses. The chip expands from its undeformed thickness, t_o, to t_c (due to the release of compressive stress) as it slides over the cutting tool. The *chip thickness ratio*, $r = t_o/t_c$, is typically around 0.5.

Figure 28.1 *Tool-Workpiece-Chip Geometry*

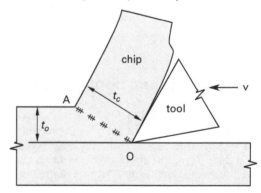

---

[1]There is also a *type-three chip*, a continuous chip with a *built-up edge* (BUE), which is not discussed here.

3. TOOL MATERIALS

Carbon tool steel is plain carbon steel with approximately 0.9% to 1.3% carbon, which has been hardened and tempered. It can be given a good edge but is restricted to use below 200°C to 300°C to prevent further tempering.

High-speed steel (HSS) contains tungsten or chromium and retains its hardness up to approximately 600°C, a property known as *red hardness*. The common 18-4-1 formulation contains 18% tungsten, 4% chromium, and 1% vanadium. Other categories include *molybdenum high-speed steels* and *superhigh-speed steels*. Tools made with these steels can be run approximately twice as fast as carbon steel tools.

Cast nonferrous cutting tools have similar characteristics to carbides and are used in an as-cast condition. A common composition contains 45% cobalt, 34% chromium, 18% tungsten, and 2% carbon. Cast nonferrous tools are brittle but can be used up to approximately 925°C and operate at speeds twice that of HSS tools.

Sintered carbides are produced through powder metallurgy from nonferrous metals (e.g., tungsten carbide and titanium carbide with some cobalt). *Carbide tools* are commonly of the throw-away type. They are very hard, can be used up to 1200°C, and operate at cutting speeds two to five times as fast as HSS tools. However, they are less tough and cannot be used where impact forces are significant.

Ceramic tools manufactured from aluminum oxide have the same expected life as carbide tools but can operate at speeds from two to three times higher. They operate below 1100°C.

Diamonds and diamond dust are used in specific cases, usually in finishing operations.

In addition to speed and temperature considerations, there should be no possibility of welding between the chip and tool material. Diamonds, for example, are soluble in the presence of high-temperature iron. Also, aluminum oxide tools are not satisfactory for machining aluminum.

4. TEMPERATURE AND COOLING FLUIDS

Friction is greatly reduced in *free-machining steels* that have had sulfur added as an alloying ingredient. However, only approximately 25% of the heat developed in cutting is due to friction between the tool and the workpiece. The remainder results from compression and shear stresses. Only 20% to 40% of this heat is removed by the tool and workpiece. The remainder must be removed by the chips and cooling fluids.

Cutting fluids are used to reduce friction, remove heat, remove chips, and protect against corrosion. Gases, such as air, carbon dioxide, and water vapor, can be used, but they do not remove heat well, cannot be reused, and may require an exhaust system. Water is a good heat remover, but it promotes rust. (Addition of *sal soda* to water produces an efficient, inexpensive cutting fluid that does not promote rusting.)

Straight-cutting oils (i.e., petroleum-based nonsoluble oils) reduce friction and do not cause rust but are less efficient at heat removal than water. Therefore, emulsions of water and oil or water-miscible fluids (soluble oils) are often used with steel. Kerosene lubricants are commonly used with aluminum.

Chlorinated or sulfurized oils are used to decrease friction.[2] Other additives are used to inhibit rust, clean the workpiece, soften water, promote film formation, and inhibit bacterial growth.

5. TOOL LIFE

Tools wear and fail through abrasion, loss of hardness, and fracture. Three common types of failure are *flank wear*, *crater wear*, and *nose failure*.

Equation 28.1: Taylor Tool Life Equation

$$\mathrm{v}T^n = C \qquad\qquad 28.1$$

Values

tool-workpiece setup	typical values of n (T in min; v in m/s)
high-speed steel	0.1
carbides	0.2
ceramics	0.4

Description

The life of a tool, T (expressed in minutes), is the length of time it will cut satisfactorily before requiring resharpening and depends on the conditions of use. The *tool life equation*, also known as *Taylor's equation*, relates cutting speed, v, and tool life, T, for a particular combination of tool and workpiece.[3] (The equation is not dimensionally consistent.)

The tool life exponent n is an empirical constant that must be determined for each tool-workpiece setup, as shown in the values. Since the equation is empirical and not dimensionally consistent, the units for velocity and

---

[2]Chlorine and sulfur form metallic chlorides and sulfides at cutting temperatures. These compounds have low shear strength, and therefore, friction is reduced. Chlorinated oils work better at low speeds, whereas sulfurized oils work better under severe conditions.
[3]The NCEES *FE Reference Handbook* (*NCEES Handbook*) uses uppercase *V* for velocity, which is consistent with many formulations of Taylor's tool life equation. To distinguish velocity from volume, and for consistency with other sections and chapters, this book uses lowercase v for velocity.

time must be specified when values of n are quoted. Feed rate and time are typically specified on a per minute basis.

Since the tool feed rate, f, and depth of cut, d, are also important parameters affecting tool life, Taylor's equation has been expanded into the following equation. (The depth of cut, d, is the same as the chip thickness, t_o, shown in Fig. 28.1.)

$$\text{v}\,T^n d^x f^y = \text{constant}$$

Example

Experimentation with a sintered carbide cutting tool at a 3.2 mm depth of cut has shown the Taylor wear constant, C, to be 522 and the tool life exponent, n, to be 0.25 for feed rate in m/min and time in min. What is most nearly the tool life at a cutting speed of 250 m/min?

(A) 0.20 min

(B) 1.0 min

(C) 20 min

(D) 200 min

Solution

Rearrange the Taylor Tool Life Equation to solve for the tool's lifespan, T.

$$\text{v}\,T^n = C$$

$$T = \left(\frac{C}{\text{v}}\right)^{1/n} = \left(\frac{522}{250\,\dfrac{\text{m}}{\text{min}}}\right)^{1/0.25}$$

$$= 19.01 \text{ min} \quad (20 \text{ min})$$

The answer is (A).

6. ABRASIVES AND GRINDING

Grinding (i.e., *abrasive machining*) is used as a finishing operation since very fine and dimensionally accurate surface finishes can be produced. However, grinding is also used for gross material removal. In fact, grinding is the only economical way to cut hardened steel.

Most modern grinding wheels are produced from aluminum oxide. However, grinding wheels can be produced from either *natural abrasives* or *synthetic abrasives*, as described in Table 28.1.

Table 28.1 *Types of Grinding Wheel Abrasives*

natural abrasives
   sandstone
   solid quartz
   emery (50% to 60% Al_2O_3 plus iron oxide)
   corundum (75% to 90% Al_2O_3 plus iron oxide)
   garnet
   diamond
synthetic abrasives
   silicon carbide, SiC
   aluminum oxide, Al_2O_3
   boron carbide

Abrasive grit size is measured by the smallest standard-size screen through which the grains will pass. *Coarse grits*, for example, will pass through no. 6 (i.e., having six uniform openings per inch) to no. 24 screens, inclusive, but will be retained on any finer screen. Table 28.2 summarizes the abrasive size designations.

Table 28.2 *Abrasive Grit Sizes*

	screen sizes	
designations	English	metric (mm)
coarse	no. 6–no. 24	4.23–1.06
medium	no. 30–no. 60	0.847–0.423
fine**	no. 70–no. 600	0.363–0.042

(Multiply mm by 0.03937 to obtain in.)

*Sizes no. 240 through no. 600 are also known as *flour grit*.

Snagging describes very rough grinding, such as that performed in foundries to remove gates, fins, and risers from castings.

Honing is grinding in which very little material, 0.025 mm to 0.13 mm is removed. Its purpose is to size the workpiece, to remove tool marks from a prior operation, and to produce very smooth surfaces. Coolants, such as sulfurized mineral-base oils and kerosene, are used to cool the workpiece and to flush away small chips. Because the stones are moved with an oscillatory pattern, honing leaves a characteristic cross-hatch pattern.

Lapping is used to produce dimensionally accurate surfaces by removing less than 0.025 mm. Parts are lapped to produce a close fit and to correct minor surface imperfections.

After any cutting or standard grinding operation, the surface of a workpiece will consist of *smear metal* (a fragmented, noncrystalline surface). *Superfinishing* or *ultrafinishing* using light pressure, short but fast oscillations of the stone, and copious amounts of lubricant-coolant, removes the smear metal and leaves a solid crystalline metal surface. The operation is similar to honing, but the stone moves with a different motion. There is essentially no dimensional change in the workpiece.

Material Props./ Processing

Other nonprecision methods of abrasion can be used to improve the surface finish and to remove burrs, scale, and oxides. Such methods include buffing, wire brushing, tumbling (i.e., barrel finishing), polishing, and vibratory finishing.

Centerless grinding is a method of grinding that does not require clamping, chucking, or holding round workpieces. The workpiece is supported between two abrasive wheels by a work-rest blade. One wheel rotates at the normal speed and does the actual grinding. The other wheel, the *regulating wheel*, is mounted at a slight offset angle and turns more slowly. Its purpose is to rotate and position the workpiece. (See Fig. 28.2.)

Figure 28.2 *Centerless Grinding*

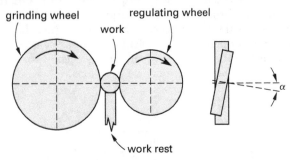

7. CHIPLESS (NONTRADITIONAL) MACHINING

Electrical discharge machining (EDM), also known as *electrodischarge machining, electrospark machining,* and *electronic erosion*, uses high-energy electrical discharges (i.e., sparks) to shape an electrically conducting workpiece. Thousands of controlled sparks are generated per second between a cutting head and the workpiece, while a servomechanism controls the separating gap. EDM requires the cutting to be performed in a dielectric liquid. The final cut surface consists of small craters melted by the arcs.

EDM can be used with all conductive metals, regardless of melting point, toughness, and hardness. Since there is no contact between the tool and the workpiece, delicate and intricate cutting is possible. However, the metal removal rate is low. Also, the tool material is lost much faster than the workpiece material. Wear ratios for the tool and workpiece vary between 20:1 for common brass tools to 4:1 for expensive tool materials.

Electrochemical machining (ECM) removes metal by electrolysis in a high-current deplating operation. Current densities up to 500 A/cm^2 are used, though most machining occurs at less than 250 A/cm^2. Depending on the desired material removal rate, even low current densities (i.e., less than 20 A/cm^2) are useful. A tool electrode (the cathode) with the approximate profile desired to be given to the workpiece (the anode) is brought close to the workpiece. The separation is maintained by a servomechanism. A water-based electrolyte

(e.g., sodium chlorate solution) is forced between the tool and workpiece. The electrolyte completes the circuit and removes the free ions.

ECM shapes and cuts metal of any hardness or toughness. Relatively high (compared with EDM) metal removal rates are possible. Unlike EDM, the tool is not consumed or changed in shape. The *current efficiency* is defined as the volume of metal removed per unit energy used. Typical units are cubic inches per 1000 ampere-minutes.

Electrochemical grinding (ECG), also known as *electrolytic grinding*, a variant of electrochemical machining, is used to shape and sharpen carbide cutting tools. It uses a rotating metal disk electrode with diamond dust (typically) bonded on the surface. Less than 1% of the workpiece material is removed by conventional grinding. The remainder is removed by electrolysis.

Chemical milling (*chem-milling*), typically used in the manufacture of printed circuit boards, is the selective removal of material not protected by a mask. Some masks are scribed and removed by hand, but most are *photosensitive resists*. When photosensitive resists are used, the workpiece is coated with a light-sensitive emulsion. The emulsion is then exposed through a negative and developed, which removes the unexposed emulsion. Finally, the workpiece is placed in a *reagent* (the *etchant*), which removes only unmasked workpiece metal.

Chemical milling works with almost any metal, such as copper, aluminum, magnesium, and steel. Although the removal rate is low, very large areas can be processed. For highly accurate work, the tendency of the etchant to undercut the mask must be known and compensated for. The *etching radius* (*etch factor*) is one method of quantifying this tendency.

Ultrasonic machining (USM) or *ultrasonic impact machining* works with metallic and nonmetallic materials of any hardness. USM can be used to shape hard and brittle materials such as glass, ceramics, crystals, and gemstones, as well as tool steel and other metals. Ultrasonic energy with a frequency between 15,000 Hz and 30,000 Hz is generated in a *transducer* through magnetostrictive and piezoelectric effects. Wear of the transducer is minimal.

The transducer is separated from the workpiece by a slurry of abrasive particles. The ultrasonic energy generated is used to hurl fine abrasive particles against the workpiece at ultrasonic velocities. The same abrasives used for grinding wheels are used with USM: aluminum oxide, silicon carbide, and boron carbide. Grit sizes of 280 mesh or finer are common.

Laser machining is used to cut or burn very small holes in the workpiece with high dimensional accuracy.

8. COLD- AND HOT-WORKING OPERATIONS

Whether a workpiece is considered cold worked or hot worked depends on whether the working temperature is below or above the recrystallization temperature, respectively. Table 28.3 categorizes most common forming operations.

Table 28.3 *Cold- and Hot-Working Operations*

cold working
  bending
  coining
  cold forging
  cold rolling
  cutting
  drawing
  drilling
  extruding
  grinding
  hobbing
  peening and burnishing
  riveting and staking
  rolling
  shearing, trimming, blanking, and piercing
  sizing
  spinning
  squeezing (e.g., swaging)
  thread rolling
hot working
  bending
  extruding and drawing (bar and wire)
  hot forging
  hot rolling
  piercing
  pipe welding
  spinning and shear forming
  swaging

9. PRESSWORK

Presswork is a general term used to denote the blanking, bending and forming, and shearing of thin-gage metals. *Presses* (also known as *brakes*) are used with dies and punches to form the workpieces. Press forces are very high, and *press capacities* (known as *tonnage*) are often quoted in tons.

With *progressive dies*, the workpiece advances through a sequence of operations. Each of the press operations is performed at a *station*. Progressive dies can be of the *strip die* or *transfer die* varieties.

Shearing operations (blanking, punching, notching, etc.) cut pieces from flat plates, strips, and coil stock.

The distinction between blanking and punching is relative. *Blanking* produces usable pieces (i.e., *blanks*), leaving the source piece behind as scrap. *Punching* is the operation of removing scrap blanks from the workpiece, leaving the source piece as the final product.

Bending and forming operations are often considered in the same category. *Bending dies* are used in press brakes to bend along a straight axis. *Forming dies* bend and form the blank along a curved axis and may incorporate other operations (e.g., notching, piercing, lancing, and cut-offs). There is little or no metal flow in a die-forming operation. The tension and compression on opposite surfaces of the blank are approximately equal.

Spring-back, bend allowance, and bending pressure can be calculated for bending and forming operations. However, it is generally necessary to make test runs to determine these values under realistic conditions.

Drawing is a cold-forming process that converts a flat blank into a hollow vessel (e.g., beverage cans). Drawing sheet metal blanks results in plastic metal flow along a curved axis. Double-acting presses may be required to accomplish deep draws.

Coining, as used in the production of coins, is a severe operation requiring high tonnage, due to the fact that the metal flow is completely confined within the die cavity. Because of this, coining is used mainly to form small parts.

Embossing forms shallow raised letters or other designs in relief on the surface of sheet metal blanks. It differs from coining in that the workpiece is not confined.

Swaging operations reduce the workpiece area by cold flowing the metal into a die cavity by a high compressive force or impact. It is applicable to small parts requiring close finishes. *Sizing* and *cold heading* of bolts and rivets are related operations.

10. FORGING

Forging is the repeated hammering of a workpiece to obtain the desired shape. Forging can be a cold-work process, but it is commonly considered to be a hot-work process when the term forging is used. Hot-work forging is carried out above the recrystallization temperature to produce a strain-free product. Table 28.4 lists the approximate temperatures for hot forging.

Table 28.4 *Approximate Hot-Forging Temperatures*

material	temperature	
	°F	°C
steel	2000–2300	1100–1250
copper alloys	1400–1700	750–925
magnesium alloys	600	300
aluminum alloys	700–850	375–450

The oldest form of forging is similar to what is done by blacksmiths. Commercial *hammer forging*, *smith forging*, or *open die forging* consists of repeatedly hammering the workpiece (known as the *stock*) in a powered forge. Accuracy is low since the shape is not defined by dies, and considerable operator skill is required.

Drop forging (*closed-die forming*) relies on closed-impression dies to produce the desired shape. One-half of the die set is stationary; the other half is attached to the hammer. The metal flows plastically into the die upon impact by the forge hammer. The forging blows are repeated at the rate of several times a minute (for *gravity drop hammers*, also known as *board hammers*) to more than 300 times a minute (for *powered hammers*).[4] Progressive forging operations are used to significantly change the shape of a part over several steps.

In *impactor forging* or *counterblow forging*, the workpiece is held in position while the dies are hammered horizontally into it from both sides. *Upset forming* involves holding and applying pressure to round heated blanks. The part is progressively formed from one end to the other and, characteristic of upset forming, becomes shorter in length but larger in diameter.

With *press forging*, the part is shaped by a slow squeezing action, rather than rapid impacts. This allows more forging energy to be used in shaping rather than in transmission to the machine and foundation. The pressing action can be obtained through screw or hydraulic action.

Following forging, the part will have a thin projection of excess metal known as *flash* at the *parting line*. The flash is trimmed off by *trimmer dies* in a subsequent operation. Also, since the hot-worked part will be covered with scale, the part is cleaned in acid (an operation known as *pickling*). Additional processing may include shotpeening, tumbling, and heat treatment.

11. SAND MOLDING

With *sand molding*, a mold is produced by packing sand around a pattern. After the pattern is removed, the remaining cavity has the desired shape. To facilitiate the removal of the pattern, all surfaces parallel to the direction of withdrawal are slightly tapered. This taper is called *draft*. After molten metal is poured into the mold, the sand is removed, exposing the completed cast part.

Various types of foundry sand are used, including green (moist) sand, dry (baked) sand, and carbon dioxide process sands. Carbon dioxide process sands contain approximately 4% silicate of soda (Na_2SiO_3), which hardens upon exposure to carbon dioxide. Pure, dry silica sand has no binding capacity and is not suited for molding. Various types of clay can be added to dry sand to improve its bonding characteristics (*cohesiveness*).

Other additives permit gases to escape during casting (*permeability*) and enhance the sand's heat resistance (*refractoriness*). Small amounts of organic matter can be added to the sand to enhance its *collapsibility*. The organic matter burns out when exposed to the hot metal, permitting the mold to be easily removed.

12. GRAVITY MOLDING

With *gravity molding* (*tilt pouring*, *gravity die casting*, or *permanent molding*), molten metal is poured into a metal or graphite mold. Pressure is not used to fill the mold.[5] The mold may be coated prior to filling to prevent the casting from sticking to the mold's interior. Both ferrous and nonferrous metals (including magnesium, aluminum, and copper alloys) can be gravity molded. This method has the advantage (over sand casting) that a new mold is not required for each casting.

13. DIE CASTING

Die casting (*pressure die casting*) is suitable for creating parts of zinc, aluminum, copper, magnesium, and lead/tin alloys. (More than 75% of all die casting uses zinc alloys.) Molten metal is forced under pressure into a permanent metallic mold known as a *die*. Dies that produce one part per injection are known as *single cavity dies*. Dies that produce more than one part per injection are known as *multiple cavity dies*. The metal can be introduced by a plunger or compressed air, but never by gravity alone. The casting pressure is maintained until solidification is complete.

Dies for zinc, tin, and lead alloys are usually made from high-carbon and alloy steels, although low-carbon steel can be used for zinc casting dies. Dies for aluminum, magnesium, and copper alloys (which melt at higher temperatures) are made out of heat-resisting alloy steel.

---

[4]Steam or compressed air can be used to lift the gravity drop hammer back into place, but the hammer is not powered during its downward travel.
[5]There is limited application of strength-, strain-, and safety-critical components (e.g., the production of railway wheels and some steel ingots) of a process known as *pressure pouring*, in which the molten metal is forced into the mold by air pressure, or drawn into the mold by a vacuum, or both (as in the case of counter-pressure casting). Pressure pouring differs from die casting in that ferrous alloys are used, typically magnesium ferrosilicon-treated ductile iron (MgFeSi iron).

Hot-chamber die casting and *cold-chamber die casting* are the two main variations of die casting. The hot-chamber method is limited to alloys (e.g., zinc, tin, and lead) that have melting temperatures below 550°C and that do not attack the injection apparatus. The injection apparatus (the *gooseneck*) is submerged in the molten metal, and low temperatures limit corrosion.

Brass (and other copper alloys), aluminum, and magnesium have high melting temperatures and require higher injection pressures. They also corrode ferrous machine parts and become contaminated by the iron they pick up. Brass and bronze, with their 875°C to 1050°C melting temperatures, particularly attack the steel in die casting machines. These alloys are usually melted in a separate furnace and ladled into the plunger cavity. This is the principle of the *cold-chamber method*.

After solidification, the sprues, gates, runners, and overflows are cut off in *trimming dies*. Die castings will typically be harder on the outside than on the inside due to the chilling action of the die. Also, gases may have been trapped inside the part, making the interior of the casting porous. Porous castings are brittle and subject to fracture.

14. CENTRIFUGAL CASTING

If the mold is rapidly rotated, the molten metal will be forced into the mold by centripetal action while the metal solidifies. This process is known as *centrifugal casting* or *centrifuging*. This method is particularly useful in producing objects with round and symmetrical (e.g., hexagonal) outer surfaces such as gun barrels and brake drums.

15. INVESTMENT CASTING

Casting methods that produce a molding cavity from a wax pattern are known as *investment casting*, *precision casting*, or the *lost-wax process*. These methods are suited to small, complex shapes and casting of precious metals.

A positive image of the part to be cast is created from wax.[6] The image is coated with the *investment material*, which can be finely ground refractory, plaster of paris or another ceramic material, or rubber, which becomes the mold. The mold is heated, and the liquid wax is poured out. The mold is then filled with molten metal. Centrifuging may be used to ensure complete filling. After the metal solidifies, the mold is broken off.

If more than one image is to be cast, a *master pattern* is made out of wood, steel, or plastic. The master pattern is used to make a *master die*. The wax patterns are then made in the master die.

16. CONTINUOUS CASTING

Any process in which molten material is continuously poured into a mold is known as *continuous casting*. This method can be used to produce sheets of glass, copper slabs, and brass or bronze bars. Continuous casting of bars is similar to extrusion, except that a cooling apparatus is included as part of the extrusion head.

17. PLASTIC MOLDING

Thermosetting compounds are purchased in liquid form, which makes them easy to combine with additives. Thermoplastic materials are commonly purchased in granular form. They are mixed with additives in a *muller* (i.e., a bulk mixer) before transfer to the feed hoppers. Thermoplastic materials can also be molded into small pellets called *preforms* for easier handling in subsequent melting operations. Common additives for plastics are color pigments and tints, stabilizers, plasticizers, fillers, and resins.

The *hot compression molding* process is the oldest plastic forming process but is used extensively only for thermosetting polymers. (Compression molding is similar to the coining process for metals.) A measured amount of plastic material is placed in the open cavity of a heated mold. The mold is closed, and pressure is applied. The plastic flows into the mold, taking on its shape. Compression molding of thermoplastic resins is not very practical.[7]

Some plastic parts can be produced by *cold molding*. In this process, the part is simply cold pressed in a mold and then heated outside the press to fuse the particles.

The main method of forming thermoplastic resins is *injection molding*. The plastic molding compound is gravity fed into a heating chamber, where it is plasticized. Heating and metering is done by the *torpedo*, illustrated in Fig. 28.3. The molten plastic is injected under pressure into a water-cooled mold, where it solidifies almost immediately. (The mold temperature is constant.)

Figure 28.3 Injection Molding Equipment

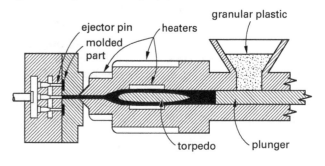

---

[6]Other variations of this process use plastics with low melting points, lead, and even frozen mercury (which freezes at 4°C).

[7]Unless a mold is cooled before the part is removed, distortion of thermoplastics can result.

Transfer molding involves the heating of thermosetting plastic powder or preforms under pressure outside the mold cavity. The molten plastic is then forced from the transfer chamber through the gate and runner system into the mold cavity. The plastic is cured in the mold by maintaining the pressure and temperature. This method differs from injection molding in that the mold is kept heated and the plastic part is ejected while it is still hot.

Blow molding and *vacuum forming* both rely on an air-pressure differential to draw a heated thermoplastic sheet around a pattern or into a mold. The plastic retains the shape of the mold after cooling.

Most thermoplastics can be *extrusion-formed* into shapes (including sheets) of any length.[8] Solid plastic in granulated or powdered form is fed by a screw-feed mechanism into a heating chamber and then extruded through a die. The plastic is cooled by contact with air or water after extrusion. (See Fig. 28.4.)

Figure 28.4 Extrusion Process

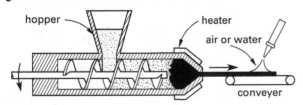

18. POWDER METALLURGY

Useful parts can be made by compressing a metal powder into shape and bonding the particles with heat—the principle of *powder metallurgy*. Typical powder metallurgy products include tungsten carbide cutting tools, copper motor brushes, bronze porous bearings, auto connecting rods and transmission parts, iron magnets, and filters.

Compared with machined products, parts made by powder metallurgy are relatively weak and expensive. However, the process is used for parts that cannot be easily produced in other manners. These are porous products, parts with complex shapes, items made from materials that are difficult to machine (e.g., tungsten carbide), and products that require the characteristics of two materials (e.g., copper/graphite electrical contacts).

The two most common types of powders are *iron-based powders* and *copper-based powders*. However, aluminum, nickel, tungsten, and other metals are also used. Bronze powders are regularly used to produce porous bearings; brass and iron are applicable to small machine parts where strength is important.

Metallic powders must be very fine. Most metal powders are produced by *atomizing* (i.e., using a jet of air to break up a fine stream of molten metal). Other methods include reduction of oxides, electrolytic deposition, and precipitation from a liquid or gas.

Pure metal powders are often mixed to improve manufacturing or performance characteristics. Graphite improves lubricating qualities and is added to powders used for bearings and electrical contacts. Cobalt and other metals are added to tungsten carbide to improve bonding.

Powders can be pressed into their final shape with a punch and die. The ejected shape is known as a *briquette* or *green compact*. With *isostatic molding*, hydraulic pressure is applied in all directions to the powder. Other methods of forming the green compact are centrifuging, *slip casting* (i.e., slurry casting), extrusion, and rolling. Due to internal friction, the density of a powder metallurgy part will not be consistent throughout but will be higher at the surface.

Sintering is heating to 70% to 90% of the melting point of the metal. The temperature is maintained for up to three hours, although the duration is commonly less than an hour. Typical sintering temperatures are 875°C for copper, 1120°C for iron, 1175°C for stainless steel, and 1475°C for tungsten carbide. To prevent the formation of metallic oxides, sintering must be performed in an inert or reducing gas (e.g., nitrogen) atmosphere.

19. HIGH ENERGY RATE FORMING

High energy rate forming (HERF), also known as *high velocity forming* (HVF), is the name given to several processes that plastically deform metals with blasts of high-pressure shock waves. Although these processes have traditionally been used to form thin metals, they are also applicable to other manufacturing needs such as powder metallurgy, forging, and welding.

The most common HERF method is *explosive forming*, as illustrated in Fig. 28.5. A small amount of low- or high-explosive is detonated. The resulting shock waves travel through the surrounding medium and force the metal into a shape determined by the dies. The medium can be either gas or liquid.

Figure 28.5 Explosive Forming

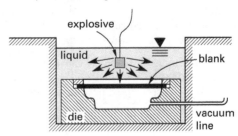

---

[8]Thermosetting plastics harden too quickly to be extruded.

Another process using explosives is *explosive bonding*. A detonation is used to drive two similar metals together. When used with explosives in sheet form, this method has been successful in producing combinations of two metallic sheets (i.e., *cladding*). The resulting bond is almost metallurgically complete.

With *electro-hydraulic forming* (also known as *electro-spark forming*), the forming pressure is obtained from the discharge of massive amounts of stored electricity. The electrical energy is built up in a capacitor bank. The energy used can be changed by adding or removing capacitors from the circuit. The discharge is across a spark gap between two electrodes in a nonconducting medium. Upon discharge, the electrical energy is converted directly into work. The usual medium is liquid.

Magnetic forming (*magnetic pulse forming*) is another example of the direct conversion of electrical energy into work. (See Fig. 28.6.) As with electrospark forming, a large amount of electrical energy is built up in a capacitor bank. A special expendable forming coil is placed around a part to be compressed or within a part to be expanded. (Magnetic forming can also be used for embossing if the workpiece is placed between the forming coil and the embossing die.) When the capacitor bank discharges, the current in the forming coil induces a current and a force in the workpiece. This force stresses the workpiece beyond its elastic limit.

Figure 28.6 Magnetic Forming

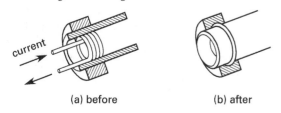

(a) before   (b) after

20. GAS WELDING

With *welding*, two metals are fused (i.e., melted) together by localized heat or pressure. This is known as *fusion* or *coalescence*. A welding rod of similar metal can be used to fill large voids between the two pieces but is not always necessary. The main types of welds are the *bead*, *groove*, *fillet*, and *plug* (*spot*) *welds* shown in Fig. 28.7.

Figure 28.7 Types of Fusion Welds

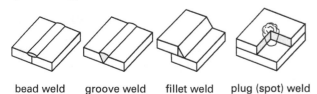

bead weld   groove weld   fillet weld   plug (spot) weld

In *gas welding processes*, a combustible fuel and oxidizing gas are combined in a *torch* (*blowpipe*). Although natural gas and hydrogen can be used as fuels, *acetylene gas* (C_2H_2) is most common. Oxygen gas is the oxidizer, hence the names *oxyhydrogen welding* and *oxyacetylene welding*. The maximum welding temperature with oxyhydrogen welding is approximately 2800°C, and with oxyacetylene welding, it is approximately 3300°C.

MAPP gas (*methyacetylene propadiene*) is also extensively used. It is safer to store, is more dense, and provides more energy per unit volume than acetylene.

The proportions of oxygen and acetylene can be adjusted to obtain three different welding conditions: reducing, neutral, and oxidizing flames. Figure 28.8 illustrates the reactions that occur with a *neutral flame*, which is obtained when the oxygen:acetylene proportions are approximately 1:1 by volume. The inner luminous cone of the flame is distinctly blue in color and is the hottest part of the flame. The outer envelope is only slightly luminous and may be difficult to see. Oxygen for the combustion of the outer envelope comes from the atmosphere.

Figure 28.8 Neutral Oxyacetylene Flame

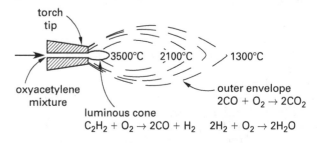

If the gas proportions are adjusted to an excess of acetylene, the flame is known as a *reducing flame* or *carburizing flame*. This process is used to weld many nonferrous metals (including Monel metal and nickel alloys as well as some alloy steels) and in applying several types of hard surfacing materials.

An *oxidizing flame* requires an excess of oxygen. Oxidizing fusion has some application to brass and bronze but is generally undesirable.[9]

21. ARC WELDING

Temperatures of up to 5550°C can be obtained from *arc welding* using either DC or AC electrical current. The arc is created by first touching the electrode to the workpiece, establishing the current flow, and then moving the electrode slightly away. The current flow is maintained by the arc, and the electrical energy is converted to heat, which melts the metal.

---

[9]An oxyacetylene *cutting torch* uses oxygen to cut steel, but the process is different from regular welding. A cutting torch uses a neutral flame to heat the steel. The oxygen used to oxidize (cut) the metal issues from a separate orifice in the torch and does not participate in the combustion of the acetylene.

If a *carbon electrode* is used to create an arc, a welding rod must be used to supply the filler material. Alternatively, in *metal electrode welding*, the electrode is itself melted by the arc and becomes the filler material.

Electrodes can be bare, but most have coatings known as *flux* that melt into slag and improve other welding characteristics.[10] The molten slag floats on and covers the molten metal, inhibiting the high temperature formation of oxides that weaken most welds. Welding with coated electrodes is known as *shielded metal arc welding* (SMAW). Most coatings have a significant amount of SiO_2 and/or TiO_2, plus small amounts of oxides of other metals. Hardened slag is chipped away after the weld has cooled.

In the United States, welding rods are classified according to the tensile strength (in ksi—thousands of lbf/in^2) of the deposited material. Thus, an E70 welding rod will produce a bead with a minimum nonstress relieved tensile strength of 70,000 lbf/in^2.

With *submerged-arc welding*, the flux is granular and is dispensed from a feed tube ahead of the welding process. The tip of the electrode and the arc are buried in the granular flux. The arc melts the granular flux, forming a coating that protects against oxidation.

Another method of protecting the molten weld metal from oxidation is by shielding with an inert gas. This is done when welding magnesium, aluminum, stainless steels, and some other steels. Argon gas is commonly used, although helium and argon-helium mixtures are also used. (Carbon dioxide gas can be used to shield the weld when working with plain-carbon and low-alloy steels.) This is the principle of *inert gas shielded arc welding*. With *TIG welding* (*tungsten inert gas*), the arc issues from an air- or water-cooled, nonconsumable tungsten electrode. (See Fig. 28.9(a).)

MIG welding (*metal inert gas*) is similar to TIG welding except that a consumable wire is used as the electrode. (See Fig. 28.9(b).) This method is also known as the *GMAW* (*gas metal arc welding*) process.

Figure 28.9 *TIG and MIG Welding Processes*

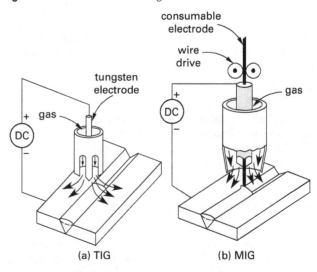

(a) TIG   (b) MIG

22. SOLDERING AND BRAZING

Soldering and *brazing* both use a molten dissimilar metal as glue between the two pieces. Generally, soldering uses a lead-tin filler with melting points below 425°C, whereas brazing uses copper-zinc or silver-based alloys with melting points above 425°C. Soldering is not a fusion process, since parts do not melt. Since some alloying occurs, brazing is considered to be a fusion process.

Usually, the solder or brazing material is drawn into the space separating the pieces by capillary action. However, a chemical flux can be used to remove oxides from the surfaces, inhibit additional oxidation, and improve cohesion of the filler material.

23. ADHESIVE BONDING

Both thermoplastic and thermosetting polymers are used as structural adhesives. Polymers of both types are sometimes combined to obtain the performance characteristics of both. A low-viscosity primer may be used to prepare the bonding surface for the adhesive. Almost all adhesive bonds are of the *lap-joint variety*.

Structural adhesives can be used to join any similar or dissimilar materials. However, even structural adhesives are limited to low-strength and low-temperature (e.g., less than 250°C) applications.[11]

Thermoplastic adhesives, such as polyamides, vinyls, and nonvulcanized neoprene rubbers, soften when heated and cannot be used for elevated temperatures. They are generally used for nonstructural applications.

---

[10]In addition to providing a protection from oxidation, the next most important function of the coating is to stabilize the arc (i.e., reduce the effect of variations in the separation of electrode and workpiece). Other functions include reducing weld metal splatter, adding alloying ingredients, changing the weld bead shape, improving overhead and vertical weldability, and providing additional filler material.
[11]Certain *ceramic adhesives* have useful ranges up to 550°C.

Thermosetting adhesives (e.g., epoxies, isocyanate, phenolic rubbers and vinyls, vulcanized rubbers, and neoprene) are used as structural adhesives. They must be used with elevated temperatures and where creep is unacceptable. Heat, pressure, ultraviolet radiation, and/or chemical hardeners must be used to activate the curing process.

The performance of an adhesive is determined by its toughness, tensile strength, peel strength, and temperature resistance. Adhesives with high tensile and shear strengths are usually hard and brittle and have low *peel strengths*. Adhesives with high peel strengths are usually more ductile and have fair tensile and shear strengths.

24. MANUFACTURE OF METAL PIPE

Pipes and tubes can be either seamed or seamless. Seamless pipe is made by piercing, whereas seamed pipe is made by forming and butt- or lap-welding the joined edges.

Thin-wall pipe can be formed by drawing a heated flat skelp through a welding bell. Prior to forming, the edges of the skelp are heated by flame or induction to the forging temperature, and joining occurs spontaneously in the welding bell, as shown in Fig. 28.10.

Figure 28.10 Butt-Welding in a Welding Bell

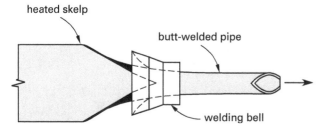

Pipes with larger diameters and wall thicknesses are formed with *roll forming* and *electric butt-welding*, in which the skelp is cold-rolled into circular shape by a series of roller pairs. One of the last rolling operations incorporates induction heating to bring the pipe edges up to forging temperature before they are pressed together. The flash is subsequently removed from the inside and outside of the pipe.

The skelp of *lap-welded pipe* passes through rollers that overlap the edges. Unlike roll forming, however, a fixed mandrel is placed inside the pipe. The heated skelp is rolled between the roller and mandrel at high pressure, which welds the heated edges together.

Seamless pipe is manufactured by heating a solid round bar known as a *billet* to forging temperature and piercing it with a mandrel. (See Fig. 28.11.) Subsequent operations with rollers strengthen, size, and finish the pipe.

Figure 28.11 Production of Seamless Pipe

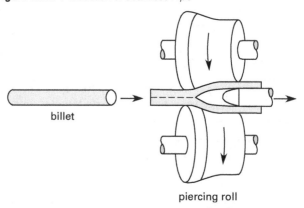

25. SURFACE FINISHING AND COATINGS

Finishes protect and improve the appearance of surfaces. Some processes involve material removal, and others involve material addition. Some of the common finishing methods and coating systems are listed as follows.

- *abrasive cleaning:* shooting sand (i.e., *sand blasting*), steel grit, or steel shot against workpieces to remove casting sand, scale, and oxidation.

- *anodizing:* an electroplating-acid bath oxidation process for aluminum and magnesium. The workpiece is the anode in the electrical circuit.

- *barrel finishing (tumbling):* rotating parts in a barrel filled with an abrasive or nonabrasive medium. Widely used to remove burrs, flash, scale, and oxides.

- *buffing:* a fine finishing operation, similar to polishing, using a very fine polishing compound (e.g., *rouge*).

- *burnishing:* a fine grinding or peening operation designed to leave a characteristic pattern on the surface of the workpiece.

- *calorizing:* the diffusing of aluminum into a steel surface, producing an aluminum oxide that protects the steel from high-temperature corrosion.

- *electroplating:* the electro-deposition of a coating onto the workpiece. Electrical current is used to drive ions in solution to the part. The workpiece is the cathode in the electrical circuit.

- *galvanizing:* a zinc coating applied to low-carbon steel to improve corrosion resistance. The coating can be applied in a hot dip bath, by electroplating, or by dry tumbling (*sheradizing*).

- *hard surfacing:* the creation (by spraying, plating, fusion welding, or heat treatment) of a hard metal surface in a softer product.

- *honing:* a grinding operation using stones moving in a reciprocating pattern. Leaves a characteristic cross-hatch pattern.

- *lapping:* a fine grinding operation used to obtain exact fit and dimensional accuracy.

- *metal spraying:* the spraying of molten metal onto a product. Methods include *metallizing, metal powder spraying,* and *plasma flame spraying.*

- *organic finishes:* the covering of surfaces with an organic film of paint, enamel, or lacquer.

- *painting:* see *organic finishes.*

- *parkerizing:* application of a thin phosphate coating on steel to improve corrosion resistance. This process is known as *bonderizing* when used as a primer for paints.

- *pickling:* a process in which metal is dipped in dilute acid solutions to remove dirt, grease, and oxides.

- *polishing:* abrasion of parts against wheels or belts coated with polishing compounds.

- *sheradizing:* a specific method of zinc galvanizing in which parts are tumbled in zinc dust at high temperatures.

- *superfinishing:* a super-fine grinding operation used to expose nonfragmented, crystalline base metal.

- *tin-plating:* a hot-dip or electroplate application of tin to steel.

Diagnostic Exam

Topic VIII: Mechanics of Materials

1. A 25 mm diameter, 1 m long aluminum rod is loaded axially in tension as shown. Aluminum has a modulus of elasticity of 69 GPa and a Poisson's ratio of 0.35.

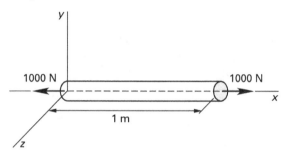

What is the approximate decrease in diameter of the rod due to the applied load?

(A) −260 nm

(B) −170 nm

(C) −73 nm

(D) −30 nm

2. A steel pipe fixed at one end is subjected to a torque of 100 000 N·m. Steel has a modulus of elasticity of 2.1×10^{11} Pa and a Poisson's ratio of 0.3.

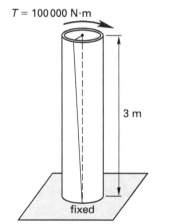
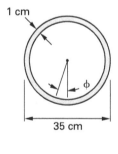

What is most nearly the resulting angle of twist, ϕ, of the pipe?

(A) 0.012°

(B) 0.12°

(C) 0.69°

(D) 0.95°

3. A beam has a triangular cross section as shown. The beam carries a uniformly distributed load of 80 N/m along its entire length.

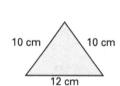
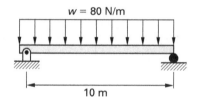

What is most nearly the maximum compressive stress in the beam?

(A) 7.8 MPa

(B) 16 MPa

(C) 23 MPa

(D) 31 MPa

4. A 10 m × 5 m rectangular steel plate is loaded in compression by two opposing triangular distributed loads as shown. Steel has a modulus of elasticity of 2.1×10^{11} Pa and a Poisson's ratio of 0.3. Buckling may be disregarded.

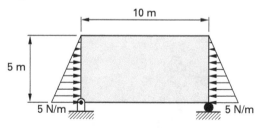

What is most nearly the shear stress, τ, in the direction of principal stress?

(A) −6.3 Pa

(B) 0 Pa

(C) 3.1 Pa

(D) 6.3 Pa

5. A thin-walled pressure vessel is constructed by rolling a 6 mm thick steel sheet into a cylindrical shape, welding the seam along line A-B, and capping the ends. The vessel is subjected to an internal pressure of 1.25 MPa and has an average diameter of 45 cm.

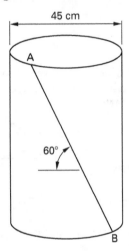

What is most nearly the maximum principal stress in the vessel?

(A) 23 MPa

(B) 29 MPa

(C) 41 MPa

(D) 47 MPa

6. A 50 mm diameter, 0.5 m long aluminum rod is loaded axially in tension as shown. Aluminum has a modulus of elasticity of 69 GPa and a Poisson's ratio of 0.35.

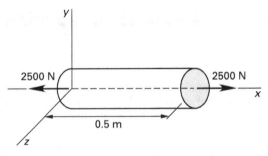

If the rod decreases in diameter by an average of 323 nm while the length increases, what is most nearly the percent change in the volume of the rod?

(A) −0.055% (decrease)

(B) −0.00055% (decrease)

(C) 0.00055% (increase)

(D) 0.055% (increase)

7. A 5 m long steel bar with a cross-sectional area of 0.01 m² is connected to a compression spring as shown. The spring has a stiffness of 2×10^8 N/m and is initially undeformed. The bar is fixed at its base. The temperature of the bar is increased by 70°C. Steel has a modulus of elasticity of 210 GPa and a coefficient of thermal expansion of 11.7×10^{-6} 1/°C.

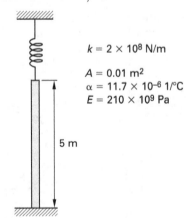

$k = 2 \times 10^8$ N/m

$A = 0.01$ m²
$\alpha = 11.7 \times 10^{-6}$ 1/°C
$E = 210 \times 10^9$ Pa

5 m

What is most nearly the resulting force in the spring?

(A) 550 kN

(B) 820 kN

(C) 1600 kN

(D) 1700 kN

8. Disregarding thermal roller strain, in which of the steel structures shown would a temperature change produce internal stresses?

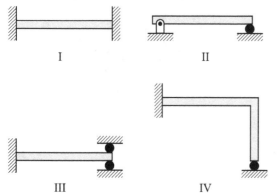

I

II

III

IV

(A) I only

(B) I and III

(C) I and IV

(D) II, III, and IV

9. For the beam and loading shown, which of the options best represents the shape of the shear diagram?

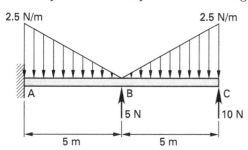

(A)

(B)

(C)

(D)

10. A 32 mm diameter, 2 m long aluminum rod is loaded axially in tension as shown. Aluminum has a modulus of elasticity of 69 GPa and a Poisson's ratio of 0.35.

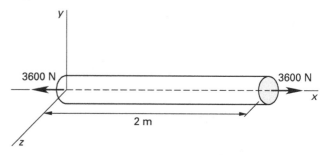

What is most nearly the total stored strain energy in the rod as a result of the loading?

(A) 0.12 J

(B) 0.23 J

(C) 0.46 J

(D) 0.58 J

SOLUTIONS

1. The axial stress is

$$\sigma_x = \frac{P}{A} = \frac{P}{\frac{\pi}{4}d^2} = \frac{4P}{\pi d^2}$$

$$= \frac{(4)(1000 \text{ N})\left(1000 \frac{\text{mm}}{\text{m}}\right)^2}{\pi(25 \text{ mm})^2}$$

$$= 2.037 \times 10^6 \text{ Pa}$$

The radial strain is

$$\varepsilon_y = \varepsilon_z = -\nu\varepsilon_x = \frac{-\nu\sigma_x}{E}$$

$$= \frac{-(0.35)(2.037 \times 10^6 \text{ Pa})}{(69 \text{ GPa})\left(10^9 \frac{\text{Pa}}{\text{GPa}}\right)}$$

$$= -1.033 \times 10^{-5} \text{ m/m}$$

The decrease in diameter of the rod is

$$\delta_d = \varepsilon_y d$$

$$= \left(-1.033 \times 10^{-5} \frac{\text{m}}{\text{m}}\right)\left(\frac{25 \text{ mm}}{1000 \frac{\text{mm}}{\text{m}}}\right)$$

$$= -2.58 \times 10^{-7} \text{ m} \quad (-260 \text{ nm})$$

The answer is (A).

2. Calculate the polar moment of inertia of the column.

$$J = \frac{\pi(a^4 - b^4)}{2} = \frac{\pi\left(\left(\frac{d_{outer}}{2}\right)^4 - \left(\frac{d_{inner}}{2}\right)^4\right)}{2}$$

$$= \frac{\pi(d_{outer}^4 - d_{inner}^4)}{32}$$

$$= \frac{\pi}{32}\left(\left(\frac{35 \text{ cm}}{100 \frac{\text{cm}}{\text{m}}}\right)^4 - \left(\frac{33 \text{ cm}}{100 \frac{\text{cm}}{\text{m}}}\right)^4\right)$$

$$= 3.0896 \times 10^{-4} \text{ m}^4$$

The shear modulus can be calculated from the modulus of elasticity and Poisson's ratio.

$$G = \frac{E}{2(1 + \nu)}$$

$$= \frac{2.1 \times 10^{11} \text{ Pa}}{(2)(1 + 0.3)}$$

$$= 8.0769 \times 10^{10} \text{ Pa}$$

The angle of twist is

$$\phi = \frac{TL}{GJ}$$

$$= \frac{(100\,000 \text{ N·m})(3 \text{ m})}{(8.0769 \times 10^{10} \text{ Pa})(3.0896 \times 10^{-4} \text{ m}^4)} \times \frac{360°}{2\pi}$$

$$= 0.689° \quad (0.69°)$$

The answer is (C).

3. Due to symmetry of the applied load, the two vertical reactions are equal. Each vertical reaction is half of the total vertical load.

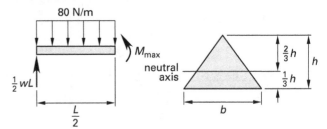

$$R = \frac{1}{2}wL$$

The maximum moment on a simply supported beam with a uniformly distributed load occurs at the center of the span.

$$M_{max} = \frac{1}{2}wL\left(\frac{L}{2}\right) - w\left(\frac{L}{2}\right)\left(\frac{L}{4}\right)$$

$$= \frac{1}{8}wL^2$$

The centroidal moment of inertia of the triangular cross section is given by

$$I = \frac{bh^3}{36}$$

The neutral axis for this cross section is at $h/3$ from the bottom of the beam. The maximum compressive stress will occur at the top of the beam, a distance of $2h/3$ from the neutral axis.

Mechanics of Materials

The maximum stress in the beam can be computed as

$$\sigma = \frac{Mc}{I} = \frac{\frac{1}{8}wL^2\left(\frac{2h}{3}\right)}{\frac{bh^3}{36}} = \frac{3wL^2}{bh^2}$$

$$= \frac{(3)\left(80\ \frac{\text{N}}{\text{m}}\right)(10\ \text{m})^2\left(100\ \frac{\text{cm}}{\text{m}}\right)^3}{(12\ \text{cm})(8\ \text{cm})^2}$$

$$= 3.125 \times 10^7\ \text{Pa} \quad (31\ \text{MPa})$$

The answer is (D).

4. The plate is loaded in pure compression. Loading is one-dimensional, so the compressive stress is the principal stress. Shear stress is zero in the direction of the principal stress.

The answer is (B).

5. In a thin-walled vessel, use of the inner, mean, and outer radii yields comparable stress values. The tensile tangential (hoop) stress is

Cylindrical Pressure Vessel

$$\sigma_t = \frac{pr}{t} = \frac{(1.25\ \text{MPa})\left(10^6\ \frac{\text{Pa}}{\text{MPa}}\right)\left(\frac{45\ \text{cm}}{2}\right)\left(1000\ \frac{\text{mm}}{\text{m}}\right)}{(6\ \text{mm})\left(100\ \frac{\text{cm}}{\text{m}}\right)}$$

$$= 4.688 \times 10^7\ \text{Pa} \quad (47\ \text{MPa})$$

The tangential and axial stresses in a pressurized vessel are the principal stresses. In the absence of torsion, these stresses do not combine. Since the tangential stress is twice as large as the axial stress, it is the maximum normal stress in the vessel.

The answer is (D).

6. The change in length of the rod is

Uniaxial Loading and Deformation

$$\delta_L = \frac{PL}{AE} = \frac{PL}{\frac{\pi}{4}d^2E} = \frac{4PL}{\pi d^2E}$$

$$= \frac{(4)(2500\ \text{N})(0.5\ \text{m})}{\pi\left(\frac{50\ \text{mm}}{1000\ \frac{\text{mm}}{\text{m}}}\right)^2(69\ \text{GPa})\left(10^9\ \frac{\text{Pa}}{\text{GPa}}\right)}$$

$$= 9.23 \times 10^{-6}\ \text{m}$$

The percent change in volume of the rod is

$$\%\frac{\delta_V}{V_o} = \frac{V - V_o}{V_o} \times 100\%$$

$$= \left|\frac{\left(\frac{\pi}{4}\right)(d-\delta_d)^2(L+\delta_L) - \frac{\pi}{4}d^2L}{\frac{\pi}{4}d^2L}\right| \times 100\%$$

$$= \left|\frac{(d-\delta_d)^2(L+\delta_L) - d^2L}{d^2L}\right| \times 100\%$$

$$= \left|\frac{\left(\frac{50\ \text{mm}}{1000\ \frac{\text{mm}}{\text{m}}} - 3.23 \times 10^{-7}\ \text{m}\right)^2 \times (0.5\ \text{m} + 9.23 \times 10^{-6}\ \text{m}) - \left(\frac{50\ \text{mm}}{1000\ \frac{\text{mm}}{\text{m}}}\right)^2(0.5\ \text{m})}{\left(\frac{50\ \text{mm}}{1000\ \frac{\text{mm}}{\text{m}}}\right)^2(0.5\ \text{m})}\right| \times 100\%$$

$$= 0.00055\% \quad [\text{increase}]$$

The answer is (C).

7. If the spring were not present, the bar would elongate by

$$\delta_L = \alpha L \Delta T$$

Under the action of the spring force alone, the bar would contract by

$$\delta_P = \frac{PL}{AE}$$

The net deformation of the bar must equal the deformation in the spring, P/k.

By superposition,

$$\alpha L \Delta T - \frac{PL}{AE} = \frac{P}{k}$$

$$P\left(\frac{1}{k} + \frac{L}{AE}\right) = \alpha L \Delta T$$

$$
P = \frac{\alpha L \Delta T}{\dfrac{1}{k} + \dfrac{L}{AE}}
$$

$$
= \frac{\left(11.7 \times 10^{-6}\,\dfrac{1}{°C}\right)(5\ \text{m})(70°C)}{\dfrac{1}{2 \times 10^{8}\,\dfrac{\text{N}}{\text{m}}} + \dfrac{5\ \text{m}}{(0.01\ \text{m}^2)(210 \times 10^{9}\ \text{Pa})}}
$$

$$= 554\,806\ \text{N} \quad (550\ \text{kN})$$

The answer is (A).

8. Thermal changes can only produce stresses in structures that are constrained against movement. Structure I cannot expand axially. Structure IV cannot flex upward (i.e., bend).

The answer is (C).

9. Solve for the vertical reaction at point A.

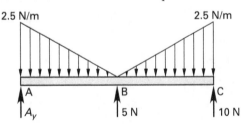

2.5 N/m   2.5 N/m

A   B   C

A_y 5 N   10 N

Equilibrium Requirements

$$\sum F_y = 0$$

$$A_y - (2)\left(\frac{1}{2}\right)\left(2.5\ \frac{\text{N}}{\text{m}}\right)(5\ \text{m}) + 5\ \text{N} + 10\ \text{N} = 0$$

$$A_y = -2.5\ \text{N} \quad [\text{downward}]$$

The shear force just to the right of the support is equal and opposite to the vertical reaction at point A.

Just to the left of point B, the shear force is

$$\sum F_y = 0$$

$$A_y - \left(\frac{1}{2}\right)\left(2.5\ \frac{\text{N}}{\text{m}}\right)(5\ \text{m}) - V = 0$$

$$V = A_y - \left(\frac{1}{2}\right)\left(2.5\ \frac{\text{N}}{\text{m}}\right)(5\ \text{m})$$

$$= -2.5\ \text{N} - \left(\frac{1}{2}\right)\left(2.5\ \frac{\text{N}}{\text{m}}\right)(5\ \text{m})$$

$$= -8.75\ \text{N}$$

Because the load varies linearly between points A and B, the shear force will vary parabolically between these points. And since the load is decreasing, the shear diagram, when drawn according to the sign convention, will be concave between these points.

The shear diagram is discontinuous at the location of a concentrated load.

Just to the right of point B, the shear force is

$$\sum F_y = 0$$

$$A_y - \left(\frac{1}{2}\right)\left(2.5\ \frac{\text{N}}{\text{m}}\right)(5\ \text{m}) + P - V = 0$$

$$V = A_y - \left(\frac{1}{2}\right)\left(2.5\ \frac{\text{N}}{\text{m}}\right)(5\ \text{m}) + P$$

$$= -2.5\ \text{N} - \left(\frac{1}{2}\right)\left(2.5\ \frac{\text{N}}{\text{m}}\right)(5\ \text{m}) + 5\ \text{N}$$

$$= -3.75\ \text{N}$$

Just to the left of point C, the shear force is equal to

$$\sum F_y = 0$$

$$A_y - \left(2.5\ \frac{\text{N}}{\text{m}}\right)(5\ \text{m}) + 5\ \text{N} - V = 0$$

$$V = A_y - \left(2.5\ \frac{\text{N}}{\text{m}}\right)(5\ \text{m}) + 5\ \text{N}$$

$$= -2.5\ \text{N} - \left(2.5\ \frac{\text{N}}{\text{m}}\right)(5\ \text{m}) + 5\ \text{N}$$

$$= -10\ \text{N}$$

Because the load varies linearly between points B and C, the shear force will vary parabolically between these points. And since the load is increasing, the shear diagram, when drawn according to the sign convention, will be convex between these points.

As a final check, note that the shear just to the left of point C is equal to the concentrated load at point C.

The answer is (D).

10. The total stored strain energy in the rod is

Elastic Strain Energy

$$U = \frac{1}{2}P\delta_L = \frac{1}{2}P\frac{PL}{AE} = \frac{1}{2}\left(\frac{P^2L}{AE}\right)$$

$$= \frac{\frac{1}{2}P^2L}{\frac{\pi}{4}d^2E}$$

$$= \frac{2P^2L}{\pi d^2 E}$$

$$= \frac{(2)(3600 \text{ N})^2(2 \text{ m})}{\pi\left(\dfrac{32 \text{ mm}}{1000 \ \frac{\text{mm}}{\text{m}}}\right)^2 (69 \text{ GPa})\left(10^9 \ \dfrac{\text{Pa}}{\text{GPa}}\right)}$$

$$= 0.23 \text{ J}$$

The answer is (B).

29 Stresses and Strains

Nomenclature

A	area	m^2
C	stress at center of Mohr's circle	MPa
d	diameter	m
E	modulus of elasticity	MPa
F	force	N
FS	factor of safety	–
g	gravitational acceleration, 9.81	m/s^2
G	shear modulus	MPa
k	stress concentration factor	–
L	length	m
P	force	N
R	radius	m
S	strength	MPa
u	strain energy per unit volume	MPa
U	energy	Nm
W	work	Nm

Symbols

γ	shear strain	–
δ	deformation	m
δ	elongation	m
ε	linear strain	–
θ	angle	rad
ν	Poisson's ratio	–
σ	normal stress	MPa
τ	shear stress	MPa

Subscripts

a	allowable or alternating
b	bending
e	endurance
eff	effective
f	final
m	mean
r	range
s	shear
t	tension
u	ultimate
y	yield

1. DEFINITIONS

Mechanics of materials deals with the elastic behavior of materials and the stability of members. Mechanics of materials concepts are used to determine the stress and deformation of axially loaded members, connections, torsional members, thin-walled pressure vessels, beams, eccentrically loaded members, and columns.

Equation 29.1: Stress

$$\sigma = \frac{P}{A} \qquad 29.1$$

Variation

$$\tau = \frac{P_{\text{parallel to area}}}{A}$$

Description

Stress is force per unit area. Typical units of stress are lbf/in^2, ksi, and MPa. There are two primary types of stress: *normal stress* and *shear stress*. With normal stress, σ, the force is normal to the surface area. With shear stress, τ, the force is parallel to the surface area.

Equation 29.1 describes the normal stress. Shear stress is given by the variation equation.

In mechanics of materials, stresses have a specific *sign convention*. Tensile stresses make a part elongate in the direction of application; tensile stresses are given a positive sign. Compressive stresses make a part shrink in the direction of application; compressive stresses are given a negative sign.

Example

A steel bar with a cross-sectional area of 6 cm² is subjected to axial tensile forces of 50 kN applied at each end of the bar. What is most nearly the stress in the bar?

(A) 67 MPa

(B) 78 MPa

(C) 83 MPa

(D) 94 MPa

Solution

From Eq. 29.1,

$$\sigma_{axial} = \frac{P}{A}$$

$$= \frac{(50\ \text{kN})\left(1000\ \dfrac{\text{N}}{\text{kN}}\right)\left(100\ \dfrac{\text{cm}}{\text{m}}\right)^2}{6\ \text{cm}^2}$$

$$= 8.33 \times 10^7\ \text{Pa} \quad (83\ \text{MPa})$$

The answer is (C).

Equation 29.2: Linear Strain

$$\varepsilon = \delta/L \qquad 29.2$$

Description

Linear strain (normal strain, longitudinal strain, axial strain, engineering strain), ε, is a change of length per unit of length. Linear strain may be listed as having units of in/in, mm/mm, percent, or no units at all. *Shear strain*, γ, is an angular deformation resulting from shear stress. Shear strain may be presented in units of radians, percent, or no units at all.

Equation 29.2 shows the relationship between engineering strain, ε, and elongation, δ.

Example

A 200 m cable is suspended vertically. At any point along the cable, the strain is proportional to the length of the cable below that point. If the strain at the top of the cable is 0.001, what is most nearly the total elongation of the cable?

(A) 0.05 m

(B) 0.10 m

(C) 0.15 m

(D) 0.20 m

Solution

Since the strain is proportional to the cable length, it varies from 0 at the end to the maximum value of 0.001 at the supports. The average engineering strain is

$$\varepsilon_{ave} = \frac{\varepsilon_{max}}{2}$$

$$= \frac{0.001}{2}$$

$$= 0.0005$$

From Eq. 29.2, the total elongation is

$$\varepsilon = \delta/L$$
$$\delta = \varepsilon_{ave}L$$
$$= (0.0005)(200\ \text{m})$$
$$= 0.10\ \text{m}$$

The answer is (B).

Equation 29.3: Hooke's Law

$$E = \sigma/\varepsilon = \frac{P/A}{\delta/L} \qquad 29.3$$

Variation

$$\sigma = E\varepsilon$$

Values

material	units*	steel	aluminum	cast iron	wood (fir)
modulus of	Mpsi	29	10	14.5	1.6
elasticity, E	GPa	200	69	100	11

*Mpsi = millions of pounds per square inch

Description

Hooke's law is a simple mathematical statement of the relationship between elastic stress and strain: stress is proportional to strain. For normal stress, the constant of proportionality is the *modulus of elasticity (Young's modulus)*, E.

An *isotropic material* has the same properties in all directions. For example, steel is generally considered to be isotropic, and its modulus of elasticity is invariant with respect to the direction of loading. The properties of an *anisotropic material* vary with the direction of loading.

Example

A 2 m long aluminum bar (modulus of elasticity = 69 GPa) is subjected to a tensile stress of 175 MPa. What is most nearly the elongation?

(A) 4 mm

(B) 5 mm

(C) 8 mm

(D) 9 mm

Solution

From Hooke's law,

$$E = \sigma/\varepsilon = \frac{P/A}{\delta/L}$$

$$\delta = \frac{\sigma L}{E}$$

$$= \frac{(175 \text{ MPa})\left(10^6 \dfrac{\text{Pa}}{\text{MPa}}\right)(2 \text{ m})}{(69 \text{ GPa})\left(10^9 \dfrac{\text{Pa}}{\text{GPa}}\right)}$$

$$= 0.00507 \text{ m} \quad (5 \text{ mm})$$

The answer is (B).

Equation 29.4: Poisson's Ratio

$$\nu = -(\text{lateral strain})/(\text{longitudinal strain}) \qquad 29.4$$

Variation

$$\nu = -\frac{\varepsilon_{\text{lateral}}}{\varepsilon_{\text{axial}}}$$

Values

Theoretically, Poisson's ratio could vary from 0 to 0.5; *typical values* are shown.

material	steel	aluminum	cast iron	wood (fir)
Poisson's ratio, ν	0.30	0.33	0.21	0.33

Description

Poisson's ratio, ν, is a constant that relates the lateral strain to the axial (longitudinal) strain for axially loaded members.

Example

A 1 m × 1 m × 0.01 m square steel plate (modulus of elasticity = 200 GPa) is loaded in tension parallel to one of its long edges. The resulting 30 MPa stress is uniform across the 1 m × 0.01 m cross section. Poisson's ratio of steel is 0.29. Neglecting the change in plate thickness, the new dimensions of the plate are most nearly

(A) 1000.15 mm × 999.852 mm

(B) 1000.15 mm × 999.957 mm

(C) 1000.15 mm × 1000.05 mm

(D) 1000.20 mm × 1000.50 mm

Solution

Use Eq. 29.3. The elongation in the direction of the tensile stress is

$$E = \sigma/\varepsilon = \frac{P/A}{\delta/L}$$

$$\delta_{\text{axial}} = \frac{\sigma L_{\text{axial}}}{E}$$

$$= \frac{(30 \text{ MPa})\left(10^6 \dfrac{\text{Pa}}{\text{MPa}}\right)(1 \text{ m})\left(1000 \dfrac{\text{mm}}{\text{m}}\right)}{(200 \text{ GPa})\left(10^9 \dfrac{\text{Pa}}{\text{GPa}}\right)}$$

$$= 0.15 \text{ mm}$$

Use Eq. 29.2 and the variation of Eq. 29.4. The elongation perpendicular to the tensile stress is

$$\delta_{\text{lateral}} = L_{\text{lateral}}\varepsilon_{\text{lateral}} = -L_{\text{lateral}}\nu\varepsilon_{\text{axial}}$$

$$= -L_{\text{lateral}}\nu\left(\frac{\delta_{\text{axial}}}{L_{\text{axial}}}\right)$$

Since the plate is square, $L_{\text{lateral}} = L_{\text{axial}}$.

$$\delta_{\text{lateral}} = -\nu\delta_{\text{axial}} = -(0.29)(0.15 \text{ mm})$$

$$= -0.0435 \text{ mm}$$

The dimensions of the plate under stress are

$$\left[(1 \text{ m})\left(1000 \frac{\text{mm}}{\text{m}}\right) + 0.15 \text{ mm}\right]$$

$$\times\left[(1 \text{ m})\left(1000 \frac{\text{mm}}{\text{m}}\right) - 0.0435 \text{ mm}\right]$$

$$= 1000.15 \text{ mm} \times 999.957 \text{ mm}$$

The answer is (B).

Equation 29.5: Shear Strain

$$\gamma = \tau / G \qquad 29.5$$

Values

material	units*	steel	aluminum	cast iron	wood (fir)
modulus of rigidity, G	Mpsi	11.5	3.8	6.0	0.6
	GPa	80.0	26.0	41.4	4.1

*Mpsi = millions of pounds per square inch

Description

Hooke's law applies also to a plane element in pure shear. For such an element, the shear stress is linearly related to the shear strain, γ, by the *shear modulus* (also known as the *modulus of rigidity*), G. Shear strain is a deflection angle measured from the vertical. In effect, a cubical element is deformed into a rhombohedron. In Eq. 29.5, shear strain is measured in radians.

Example

Given a shear stress, τ, of 12 000 kPa and a shear modulus, G, of 87 GPa, the shear strain is most nearly

(A) 0.73×10^{-5} rad

(B) 1.4×10^{-4} rad

(C) 2.5×10^{-4} rad

(D) 5.5×10^{-4} rad

Solution

The shear strain is

$$\gamma = \tau / G = \frac{12\,000 \text{ kPa}}{(87 \text{ GPa})\left(10^6 \frac{\text{kPa}}{\text{GPa}}\right)}$$

$$= 1.38 \times 10^{-4} \text{ rad} \quad (1.4 \times 10^{-4} \text{ rad})$$

The answer is (B).

Equation 29.6: Shear Modulus

$$G = \frac{E}{2(1+\nu)} \qquad 29.6$$

Description

For an elastic, isotropic material, the modulus of elasticity, shear modulus, and Poisson's ratio are related by Eq. 29.6.

Example

What is most nearly the shear modulus for a material with a modulus of elasticity of 25.55 GPa and a Poisson's ratio of 0.25?

(A) 10.07 GPa

(B) 10.09 GPa

(C) 10.11 GPa

(D) 10.22 GPa

Solution

From Eq. 29.6,

$$G = \frac{E}{2(1+\nu)} = \frac{25.55 \text{ GPa}}{(2)(1+0.25)} = 10.22 \text{ GPa}$$

The answer is (D).

2. UNIAXIAL LOADING AND DEFORMATION

Equation 29.7: Deformation

$$\delta = \frac{PL}{AE} \qquad 29.7$$

Variations

$$\delta = L\varepsilon = L\left(\frac{\sigma}{E}\right)$$

$$\delta = \frac{mgL}{AE}$$

$$\delta = \sum \frac{PL}{AE} = P\sum \frac{L}{AE} \quad \begin{bmatrix} \text{segments differing in} \\ \text{cross-sectional} \\ \text{area or composition} \end{bmatrix}$$

$$\delta = \int \frac{PdL}{AE} = P\int \frac{dL}{AE} \quad \begin{bmatrix} \text{one variable varies} \\ \text{continuously} \\ \text{along the length} \end{bmatrix}$$

Description

The deformation, δ, of an axially loaded member of original length L can be derived from Hooke's law. Tension loading is considered to be positive; compressive loading is negative. The sign of the deformation will be the same as the sign of the loading.

When an axial member has distinct sections differing in cross-sectional area or composition, superposition is used to calculate the total deformation as the sum of individual deformations.

Mechanics of Materials

Example

A 10 kg mass is supported axially by an aluminum alloy pipe with an outside diameter of 10 cm and an inside diameter of 9.6 cm. The pipe is 1.2 m long. The modulus of elasticity for the aluminum alloy is 7.5×10^4 MPa. Approximately how much does the pipe compress?

(A) 0.00025 mm

(B) 0.0025 mm

(C) 0.11 mm

(D) 25 mm

Solution

The modulus of elasticity is

$$E = (7.5 \times 10^4 \text{ MPa})\left(10^6 \, \frac{\text{Pa}}{\text{MPa}}\right) = 7.5 \times 10^{10} \text{ Pa}$$

Calculate the pipe's deformation using Eq. 29.7.

$$\delta = \frac{PL}{AE} = \frac{mgL}{AE}$$

$$= \frac{(10 \text{ kg})\left(9.81 \, \frac{\text{m}}{\text{s}^2}\right)(1.2 \text{ m})}{\left(\frac{\pi}{4}\right)\left(\left(\frac{10 \text{ cm}}{100 \, \frac{\text{cm}}{\text{m}}}\right)^2 - \left(\frac{9.6 \text{ cm}}{100 \, \frac{\text{cm}}{\text{m}}}\right)^2\right)(7.5 \times 10^{10} \text{ Pa})}$$

$$= 2.5 \times 10^{-6} \text{ m} \quad (0.0025 \text{ mm})$$

The answer is (B).

Equation 29.8 and Eq. 29.9: Strain Energy

$$U = W = P\delta/2 \qquad \text{29.8}$$

$$u = U/AL = \sigma^2/2E \qquad \text{29.9}$$

Variations

$$\text{work per volume} = \int \frac{P dL}{AL}$$

$$W = \int \sigma \, d\varepsilon$$

$$U = \frac{P^2 L}{2AE}$$

Description

Strain energy, also known as *internal work*, is the energy per unit volume stored in a deformed material. The strain energy is equivalent to the work done by the applied force. Simple work is calculated as the product of a force moving through a distance. For an axially loaded member below the proportionality limit, the total strain energy depends on the average force $(P/2)$ and is given by Eq. 29.8.

Work per unit volume corresponds to the area under the stress-strain curve. Units are N·m/m³, usually written as Pa (N/m²).

The strain energy per unit volume is given by Eq. 29.9.

Example

A 25 cm long piece of elastic material is placed under a 25 000 N tensile force and elongated by 0.01 m. The material is stressed within its proportional limit. What is most nearly the elastic strain energy stored in the steel?

(A) 130 J

(B) 150 J

(C) 180 J

(D) 250 J

Solution

From Eq. 29.8, the strain energy is

$$U = W = P\delta/2 = \frac{(25\,000 \text{ N})(0.01 \text{ m})}{2}$$

$$= 125 \text{ J} \quad (130 \text{ J})$$

The answer is (A).

3. TRIAXIAL AND BIAXIAL LOADING

Triaxial loading on an infinitesimal solid element is illustrated in Fig. 29.1.

Loading is rarely confined to a single direction. All real members are three dimensional, and most experience *triaxial loading* (see Fig. 29.1). Most problems can be analyzed with two dimensions because the normal stresses in one direction are either zero or negligible. This two-dimensional loading of the member is called *plane stress* or *biaxial loading*. Positive stresses are defined as shown (see Fig. 29.2).

Biaxial loading on an infinitesimal element is illustrated in Fig. 29.2.

Mechanics of Materials

Figure 29.1 *Sign Conventions for Positive Stresses in Three Dimensions*

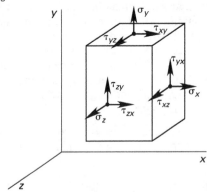

Figure 29.2 *Sign Conventions for Positive Stresses in Two Dimensions*

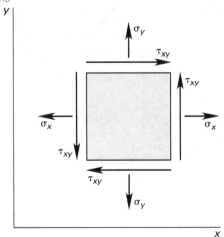

4. PRINCIPAL STRESSES

For any point in a loaded specimen, a plane can be found where the shear stress is zero. The normal stresses associated with this plane are known as the *principal stresses*, σ_a and σ_b, which are the maximum and minimum normal stresses acting at that point.

Equation 29.10 and Eq. 29.11: Maximum and Minimum Normal Stresses (Biaxial Loading)[1]

$$\sigma_a, \sigma_b = \frac{\sigma_x + \sigma_y}{2} \pm \sqrt{\left(\frac{\sigma_x - \sigma_y}{2}\right)^2 + \tau_{xy}^2} \qquad \text{29.10}$$

$$\sigma_c = 0 \qquad \text{29.11}$$

Variations

$$\sigma_a, \sigma_b = \frac{\sigma_x + \sigma_y}{2} \pm \frac{1}{2}\sqrt{(\sigma_x - \sigma_y)^2 + (2\tau_{xy})^2}$$

$$\sigma_a, \sigma_b = \tfrac{1}{2}(\sigma_x + \sigma_y) \pm \tau_{\max}$$

Description

The maximum and minimum normal stresses may be found from Eq. 29.10. The maximum and minimum shear stresses (on a different plane) may be found from

$$\tau_1, \tau_2 = \pm\sqrt{\left(\frac{\sigma_x - \sigma_y}{2}\right)^2 + \tau_{xy}^2} = \pm\frac{\sigma_1 - \sigma_2}{2}$$

The angles of the planes on which the principal stresses act are given by

$$\theta_{\sigma_1, \sigma_2} = \tfrac{1}{2} \arctan \frac{2\tau_{xy}}{\sigma_x - \sigma_y}$$

θ is measured from the x-axis, clockwise if positive. This equation will yield two angles, 90° apart.

Example

For the element of plane stress shown, what are most nearly the principal stresses?

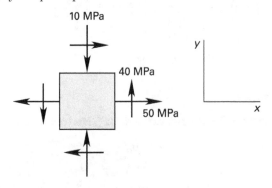

(A) $\sigma_{\max} = 35$ MPa, $\sigma_{\min} = -25$ MPa

(B) $\sigma_{\max} = 45$ MPa, $\sigma_{\min} = 55$ MPa

(C) $\sigma_{\max} = 70$ MPa, $\sigma_{\min} = -30$ MPa

(D) $\sigma_{\max} = 85$ MPa, $\sigma_{\min} = 15$ MPa

Solution

The stresses on the element are $\sigma_x = 50$ MPa (tensile), $\sigma_y = -10$ MPa (compressive), and $\tau_{xy} = 40$ MPa (positive because the direction of stress is consistent with Fig. 29.2).

---

[1]The NCEES *FE Reference Handbook* (*NCEES Handbook*) is inconsistent in its subscripting for principal stresses. In Eq. 29.10, Eq. 29.11, Eq. 29.14, and Eq. 29.15, lowercase letters are used (e.g., σ_a, σ_b, and σ_c). In Eq. 29.16, numbers are used (e.g., σ_1, σ_2, and σ_3). In Eq. 29.28, uppercase letters are used (e.g., σ_A, σ_B, and σ_C). In Eq. 29.31 and Eq. 29.33, the subscript a refers to an alternating stress, not to a principal stress.

From Eq. 29.10,

$$\sigma_a, \sigma_b = \frac{\sigma_x + \sigma_y}{2} \pm \sqrt{\left(\frac{\sigma_x - \sigma_y}{2}\right)^2 + \tau_{xy}^2}$$

$$= \frac{50 \text{ MPa} + (-10 \text{ MPa})}{2}$$

$$\pm \sqrt{\left(\frac{50 \text{ MPa} - (-10 \text{ MPa})}{2}\right)^2 + (40 \text{ MPa})^2}$$

$$= 20 \text{ MPa} \pm 50 \text{ MPa}$$

$$= 70 \text{ MPa or} -30 \text{ MPa}$$

The answer is (C).

5. MOHR'S CIRCLE

Mohr's circle can be constructed to graphically determine the principal normal and shear stresses. (See Fig. 29.3.) In some cases, this procedure may be faster than using the preceding equations, but a solely graphical procedure is less accurate. By convention, tensile stresses are positive; compressive stresses are negative. Clockwise shear stresses are positive; counterclockwise shear stresses are negative.

step 1: Determine the applied stresses: σ_x, σ_y, and τ_{xy}. Observe the correct sign conventions.

step 2: Draw a set of σ-τ axes.

step 3: Locate the center of the circle, point C, using Eq. 29.12.

step 4: Locate the point $\mathrm{p}_1 = (\sigma_x - \tau_{xy})$. (Alternatively, locate p_1' at $(\sigma_y + \tau_{xy})$.)

step 5: Draw a line from point p_1 through the center, C, and extend it an equal distance above the σ-axis to p_1'. This is the diameter of the circle.

step 6: Using the center, C, and point p_1, draw the circle. An alternative method is to draw a circle of radius R about point C (see Eq. 29.13).

step 7: Point p_2 defines the smaller principal stress, σ_b. Point p_3 defines the larger principal stress, σ_a.

step 8: Determine the angle θ as half of the angle 2θ on the circle. This angle corresponds to the larger principal stress, σ_a. On Mohr's circle, angle 2θ is measured from the $\mathrm{p}_1 - \mathrm{p}_1'$ line to the horizontal axis. θ (measured from the x-axis to the plane of principal stress) is in the same direction as 2θ (measured from line $\mathrm{p}_1 - \mathrm{p}_1'$ to the σ-axis).

step 9: The top and bottom of the circle define the largest and smallest shear stresses.

Figure 29.3 Mohr's Circle for Stress

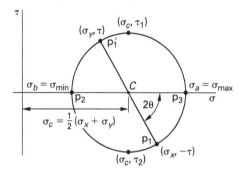

Equation 29.12 Through Eq. 29.16: Mohr's Circle Equations[2]

$$C = \frac{\sigma_x + \sigma_y}{2} \qquad \text{29.12}$$

$$R = \sqrt{\left(\frac{\sigma_x - \sigma_y}{2}\right)^2 + \tau_{xy}^2} \qquad \text{29.13}$$

$$\sigma_a = C + R \qquad \text{29.14}$$

$$\sigma_b = C - R \qquad \text{29.15}$$

$$\tau_{\max} = \frac{\sigma_1 - \sigma_3}{2} \qquad \text{29.16}$$

Variation

$$R = \sqrt{\tfrac{1}{4}(\sigma_x - \sigma_y)^2 + \tau_{xy}^2}$$

Description

C is the stress at the center of the circle and is found from Eq. 29.12. The radius, R, about the center C is calculated from Eq. 29.13.

Equation 29.14 and Eq. 29.15 determine the principal stresses, and Eq. 29.16 determines the maximum shear stress.

---

[2]In defining the normal stress at point C, the *NCEES Handbook* confuses the identifier of the point, C, with the stress at the point. After referring to the component stresses σ_x and σ_y, in Eq. 29.12, the *NCEES Handbook* refers to the stress at point C as C, rather than as σ_C.

Mechanics of Materials

Example

A plane element has an axial stress of $\sigma_x = \sigma_y = 100$ MPa and shear stress of $\tau_{xy} = 50$ MPa. What are most nearly the (x, y) coordinates for the center of the Mohr's circle in MPa?

(A) $(0, 100)$

(B) $(50, 0)$

(C) $(100, 0)$

(D) $(100, 50)$

Solution

The coordinates for the center of Mohr's circle for stress are (C, τ). The shear stress at the center of the circle is $\tau = 0$.

From Eq. 29.12, the stress at the center of the circle, C, is

$$C = \frac{\sigma_x + \sigma_y}{2}$$
$$= \frac{100\,\text{MPa} + 100\,\text{MPa}}{2}$$
$$= 100\,\text{MPa}$$

The answer is (C).

6. GENERAL STRAIN (THREE-DIMENSIONAL STRAIN)

Equation 29.17 Through Eq. 29.27

$$\varepsilon_x = (1/E)[\sigma_x - \nu(\sigma_y + \sigma_z)] \qquad 29.17$$

$$\varepsilon_x = (1/E)(\sigma_x - \nu\sigma_y) \qquad 29.18$$

$$\varepsilon_y = (1/E)[\sigma_y - \nu(\sigma_z + \sigma_x)] \qquad 29.19$$

$$\varepsilon_y = (1/E)(\sigma_y - \nu\sigma_x) \qquad 29.20$$

$$\varepsilon_z = (1/E)[\sigma_z - \nu(\sigma_x + \sigma_y)] \qquad 29.21$$

$$\varepsilon_z = -(1/E)(\nu\sigma_x + \nu\sigma_y) \qquad 29.22$$

$$\gamma_{xy} = \tau_{xy}/G \qquad 29.23$$

$$\gamma_{yz} = \tau_{yz}/G \qquad 29.24$$

$$\gamma_{zx} = \tau_{zx}/G \qquad 29.25$$

$$\begin{Bmatrix} \sigma_x \\ \sigma_y \\ \tau_{xy} \end{Bmatrix} = \frac{E}{1-\nu^2} \begin{bmatrix} 1 & \nu & 0 \\ \nu & 1 & 0 \\ 0 & 0 & \frac{1-\nu}{2} \end{bmatrix} \begin{Bmatrix} \varepsilon_x \\ \varepsilon_y \\ \gamma_{xy} \end{Bmatrix} \qquad 29.26$$

uniaxial case $(\sigma_y = \sigma_z = 0) : \sigma_x = E\varepsilon_x$ or

$$\sigma = E\varepsilon \qquad 29.27$$

Description

Hooke's law, previously defined for axial loads and for pure shear, can be extended to three-dimensional stress-strain relationships and written in terms of the three elastic constants, E, G, and ν. Equation 29.17 through Eq. 29.27 can be used to find the stresses and strains on the differential element in Fig. 29.1.

Example

The plane element shown is acted upon by combined stresses. The material has a modulus of elasticity of 200 GPa and a Poisson's ratio of 0.27.

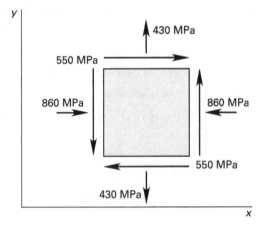

What is the approximate strain in the y-direction?

(A) -4.9×10^{-3}

(B) 0.58×10^{-3}

(C) 0.99×10^{-3}

(D) 3.3×10^{-3}

Solution

The normal stress in the y-direction is tensile, so σ_y is positive. The normal stress in the x-direction is compressive, so σ_x is negative.

The modulus of elasticity is

$$E = (200\,\text{GPa})\left(1000\,\frac{\text{MPa}}{\text{GPa}}\right) = 2 \times 10^5\,\text{MPa}$$

Use Eq. 29.19. The axial strain is

$$\varepsilon_y = (1/E)[\sigma_y - \nu(\sigma_z + \sigma_x)]$$

$$= \left(\frac{1}{2 \times 10^5 \text{ MPa}}\right)\left(\begin{array}{l}430 \text{ MPa} \\ -(0.27)\left(\begin{array}{l}0 \text{ MPa} \\ -860 \text{ MPa}\end{array}\right)\end{array}\right)$$

$$= 3.31 \times 10^{-3} \quad (3.3 \times 10^{-3})$$

The answer is (D).

7. FAILURE THEORIES

Maximum Normal Stress Theory

The *maximum normal stress theory* predicts the failure stress reasonably well for brittle materials under static biaxial loading. Failure is assumed to occur if the largest tensile principal stress, σ_1, is greater than the ultimate tensile strength, or if the largest compressive principal stress, σ_2, is greater than the ultimate compressive strength. Brittle materials generally have much higher compressive than tensile strengths, so both tensile and compressive stresses must be checked.

Stress concentration factors are applicable to brittle materials under static loading. The *factor of safety*, FS, is the ultimate strength, S_u, divided by the actual stress, σ. Where a factor of safety is known in advance, the *allowable stress*, S_a, can be calculated by dividing the ultimate strength by FS.

$$\text{FS} = \frac{S_u}{\sigma}$$

$$S_a = \frac{S_u}{\text{FS}}$$

The failure criterion is

$$\sigma > \frac{S_u}{\text{FS}}$$

Maximum Shear Stress Theory

For ductile materials (e.g., steel) under static loading (the conservative *maximum shear stress theory*), shear stress can be used to predict yielding (i.e., failure). Despite the theory's name, however, loading is not limited to shear and torsion. Loading can include normal stresses as well as shear stresses. According to the maximum shear stress theory, yielding occurs when the maximum shear stress exceeds the yield strength in shear. It is implicit in this theory that the yield strength in shear is half of the tensile yield strength.

$$S_{ys} = \frac{S_{yt}}{2}$$

The maximum shear stress, $\tau_{\max}$, is the maximum of the three combined shear stresses. (For biaxial loading, only the equation for τ_{12} is used.)

$$\tau_{12} = \frac{\sigma_1 - \sigma_2}{2}$$

$$\tau_{23} = \frac{\sigma_2 - \sigma_3}{2}$$

$$\tau_{31} = \frac{\sigma_3 - \sigma_1}{2}$$

$$\tau_{\max} = \max(\tau_{12}, \tau_{23}, \tau_{31})$$

The failure criterion is

$$\tau_{\max} > S_{ys}$$

The factor of safety with the maximum shear stress theory is

$$\text{FS} = \frac{S_{yt}}{2\tau_{\max}} = \frac{S_{ys}}{\tau_{\max}}$$

Equation 29.28 Through Eq. 29.30: von Mises Stress Equations

$$\sigma' = (\sigma_A^2 - \sigma_A\sigma_B + \sigma_B^2)^{1/2} \quad \text{29.28}$$

$$\sigma' = (\sigma_x^2 - \sigma_x\sigma_y + \sigma_y^2 + 3\tau_{xy}^2)^{1/2} \quad \text{29.29}$$

$$\left[\frac{(\sigma_1 - \sigma_2)^2 + (\sigma_2 - \sigma_3)^2 + (\sigma_1 - \sigma_3)^2}{2}\right]^{1/2} \geq S_y \quad \text{29.30}$$

Description

Whereas the maximum shear stress theory is conservative, the *distortion energy theory* is commonly used to accurately predict tensile and shear failure in steel and other ductile parts subjected to static loading.

The *von Mises stress* (also known as the *effective stress*), σ', is calculated for biaxial loading from the principal stresses using Eq. 29.28 or Eq. 29.29. The von Mises stress for triaxial loading is calculated from Eq. 29.30. The failure criterion is given by Eq. 29.30.

The factor of safety is

$$\text{FS} = \frac{S_{yt}}{\sigma'}$$

If the loading is pure torsion at failure (as with a shaft loaded purely in torsion), then $\sigma_1 = \sigma_2 = \pm\tau_{\max}$, and $\sigma_3 = 0$. If $\tau_{\max}$ is substituted for σ in Eq. 29.29 (with $\sigma_3 = 0$), an expression for the yield strength in shear is derived. The following equation predicts a larger yield strength in shear than did the maximum shear stress theory ($0.5S_{yt}$).

$$S_{ys} = \tau_{\text{max,failure}} = \frac{S_{yt}}{\sqrt{3}} = 0.577 S_{yt}$$

8. VARIABLE LOADING FAILURE THEORIES

Equation 29.31 and Eq. 29.32: Modified Goodman Theory

$$\frac{\sigma_a}{S_e} + \frac{\sigma_m}{S_{ut}} \geq 1 \quad [\sigma_m \geq 0] \qquad \textit{29.31}$$

$$\frac{\sigma_{\text{max}}}{S_y} \geq 1 \qquad \textit{29.32}$$

Description

Many parts are subjected to a combination of static and reversed loadings, as illustrated in Fig. 29.4 for sinusoidal loadings. For these parts, failure cannot be determined solely by comparing stresses with the yield strength or endurance limit. The combined effects of the average stress and the amplitude of the reversal must be considered. This is done graphically on a diagram that plots the mean stress versus the alternating stresses.

Figure 29.4 *Sinusoidal Fluctuating Stress*

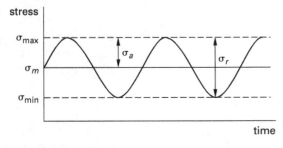

The *mean stress* is

$$\sigma_m = \frac{\sigma_{\text{max}} + \sigma_{\text{min}}}{2}$$

The *alternating stress* is half of the *range stress*.

$$\sigma_r = \sigma_{\text{max}} - \sigma_{\text{min}}$$

$$\sigma_a = \tfrac{1}{2}\sigma_r = \tfrac{1}{2}(\sigma_{\text{max}} - \sigma_{\text{min}})$$

Under the modified Goodman theory, fatigue failure will occur whenever the conditions given in Eq. 29.31 and Eq. 29.32 occur.

Equation 29.33: Soderberg Theory

$$\frac{\sigma_a}{S_e} + \frac{\sigma_m}{S_y} \geq 1 \quad [\sigma_m \geq 0] \qquad \textit{29.33}$$

Description

Under the Soderberg theory, fatigue failure will occur whenever the conditions given in Eq. 29.33 are true.

30 Thermal, Hoop, and Torsional Stress

Nomenclature

A	area	m^2
d	diameter	m
E	modulus of elasticity	MPa
F	force	N
g	gravitational acceleration, 9.81	m/s^2
G	shear modulus	MPa
J	polar moment of inertia	m^4
k	spring constant	N/m
L	length	m
p	pressure	MPa
q	shear flow	N/m
r	radius	m
t	thickness	m
T	temperature	°C
T	torque	Nm

Symbols

α	coefficient of linear thermal expansion	1/°C
δ	deformation	m
ε	axial strain	–
ρ	density	kg/m^3
σ	normal stress	MPa
τ	shear stress	MPa
	angle of twist	rad

Subscripts

0	initial
a	axial
i	inner
m	mean
o	initial or outer
t	tangential, thermal, or total
th	thermal

1. THERMAL STRESS

Equation 30.1: Coefficient of Linear Thermal Expansion[1]

$$\delta_t = \alpha L(T - T_o) \qquad 30.1$$

Values

Table 30.1 Average Coefficients of Linear Thermal Expansion

substance	1/°F	1/°C
aluminum	13.1	23.6
cast iron	6.7	12.1
steel	6.5	11.7
wood (fir)	1.7	3.0

(Multiply all values by 10^{-6}.)

Description

If the temperature of an object is changed, the object will experience length, area, and volume changes. The magnitude of these changes will depend on the *coefficient of linear thermal expansion*, α. (See Table 30.1.) The change in length in any direction is given by Eq. 30.1.

Changes in temperature affect all dimensions the same way. An increase in temperature will cause an increase in the dimensions, and likewise, a decrease in temperature will cause a decrease in the dimensions. It is a common misconception that a hole in a plate will decrease in size when the plate is heated (because the surrounding material squeezes in on the hole). In this case, the circumference of the hole is a linear dimension that follows Eq. 30.1. As the circumference increases, the hole area also increases. (See Fig. 30.1.)

If Eq. 30.1 is rearranged, an expression for the *thermal strain* is obtained.

$$\varepsilon_t = \frac{\delta_t}{L} = \alpha(T - T_0)$$

---

[1]The NCEES *FE Reference Handbook* (*NCEES Handbook*) uses two variables in Eq. 30.1 that are easily confused with related topics. In Eq. 30.1, T_o indicates the temperature at time zero (i.e., the initial temperature), not the outer temperature. Equation 30.1 is used to calculate the thermally induced elongation, δ_t, which is the same variable used to represent the total or tangential elongation in this subject.

Mechanics of Materials

Figure 30.1 *Thermal Expansion of an Area*

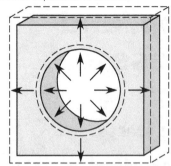

Thermal strain is handled in the same manner as strain due to an applied load. For example, if a bar is heated but is not allowed to expand, the *thermal stress* can be calculated from the thermal strain and Hooke's law.

$$\sigma_t = E\varepsilon_t$$

Low values of the coefficient of expansion, such as with Pyrex™ glassware, result in low thermally induced stresses and insensitivity to temperature extremes. Intentional differences in the coefficients of expansion of two materials are used in *bimetallic elements*, such as thermostatic springs and strips.

Example

A 30 cm long rod ($E = 3 \times 10^7$ N/cm^2, $\alpha = 6 \times 10^{-6}$ cm/cm·°C) with a 2 cm^2 cross section is fixed at both ends. If the rod is heated to 60°C above the neutral temperature, what is most nearly the stress?

   (A)   110 N/cm^2

   (B)   11 000 N/cm^2

   (C)   36 000 N/cm^2

   (D)   57 000 N/cm^2

Solution

From Eq. 30.1,

$$\delta_t = \alpha L(T - T_o)$$

$$\varepsilon_t = \frac{\delta_t}{L} = \alpha(T - T_o)$$

$$= \left(6 \times 10^{-6} \ \frac{\text{cm}}{\text{cm·°C}}\right)(60°\text{C} - 0°\text{C})$$

$$= 0.00036$$

$$\sigma_t = E\varepsilon_t = \left(3 \times 10^7 \ \frac{\text{N}}{\text{cm}^2}\right)(0.00036)$$

$$= 10\,800 \ \text{N/cm}^2 \quad (11\,000 \ \text{N/cm}^2)$$

The answer is (B).

Equation 30.2: Thermally Induced Normal Strain

$$\varepsilon_x = \frac{1}{E}[\sigma_x - \nu(\sigma_y + \sigma_z)] + \alpha(T_f - T_i) \qquad \text{30.2}$$

Description

Materials that are linearly elastic and isotropic produce only normal strain, ε, when a temperature change is applied. Equation 30.2 is the generalized equation of Hooke's law in three dimensions for normal stresses when a temperature change is applied. Equation 30.2 can be rearranged for strain in the y- and z- directions. The modulus of elasticity, E; Poisson's ratio, ν; and coefficient of linear thermal expansion, α, are elastic constants that represent physical properties of the material. These relationships are valid within the linear region of the material's stress-strain response. For triaxial deformation, tension is considered positive and compression is considered negative.

Example

A steel block is subjected to triaxial loading with uniformly distributed stress equal to 20 MPa tension in the x-direction, 5 MPa compression in the y-direction, and 10 MPa compression in the z-direction. The steel has a modulus of elasticity of 200 000 MPa, a Poisson's ratio of 0.30, and a coefficient of linear thermal expansion of 11.7×10^{-6} 1/°C. Most nearly, what is the strain in the x-direction if the steel block experiences a temperature drop of 30°C?

   (A)   −0.000229

   (B)   −0.000274

   (C)   −0.000582

   (D)   −0.000651

Solution

For triaxial deformation, tension is considered positive and compression is considered negative. Using the values given and Eq. 30.2, the strain is

$$= \left(\frac{1}{200000 \ \text{MPa}}\right)\Big(20 \ \text{MPa} - (0.30)(-5 \ \text{MPa} + (-10 \ \text{MPa}))\Big)$$

$$+ \left(0.0000117 \ \frac{1}{°\text{C}}\right)(-30°\text{C})$$

$$= -0.0002285 \quad (-0.000229)$$

The answer is (A).

2. CYLINDRICAL THIN-WALLED TANKS

Cylindrical tanks under internal pressure experience circumferential, longitudinal, and radial stresses. (See Fig. 30.2.) If the wall thickness is small, the radial stress component is negligible and can be disregarded. A cylindrical tank can be assumed to be a *thin-walled tank* if the ratio of thickness-to-internal radius is less than approximately 0.1.

$$\frac{t}{r_i} < 0.1 \quad \text{[thin-walled]}$$

A cylindrical tank with a wall thickness-to-radius ratio greater than 0.1 should be considered a *thick-walled pressure vessel*. In thick-walled tanks, radial stress is significant and cannot be disregarded, and for this reason, the radial and circumferential stresses vary with location through the tank wall.

Tanks under external pressure usually fail by buckling, not by yielding. For this reason, thin-wall equations cannot be used for tanks under external pressure.

Figure 30.2 *Stresses in a Thin-Walled Tank*

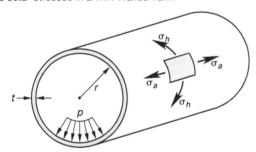

Equation 30.3 and Eq. 30.4: Hoop Stress

$$\sigma_t = \frac{p_i r}{t} \qquad 30.3$$

$$r = \frac{r_i + r_o}{2} \qquad 30.4$$

Variation

$$\sigma_t = \frac{pd}{2t}$$

Description

The *hoop stress*, σ_t, also known as *circumferential stress* and *tangential stress*, for a cylindrical thin-walled tank under internal pressure, p, is derived from the free-body diagram of a cylinder. If the cylinder tank is truly thin walled, it is not important which radius, r (e.g., inner,

mean, or outer), is used in Eq. 30.3. Although the inner diameter is used by common convention, the mean diameter will provide more accurate values as the wall thickness increases. The hoop stress is given by Eq. 30.3, where r is the radius as given by Eq. 30.4.

Example

The pressure gauge in an air cylinder reads 850 kPa. The cylinder is constructed of 6 mm rolled plate steel with an internal radius of 0.175 m. What is most nearly the tangential stress in the tank?

- (A)   2.1 MPa
- (B)   12 MPa
- (C)   17 MPa
- (D)   25 MPa

Solution

Tangential stress is the same as hoop stress. Use Eq. 30.3.

$$\sigma_t = \frac{p_i r}{t}$$

$$= \frac{(850 \text{ kPa})\left(10^3 \frac{\text{Pa}}{\text{kPa}}\right)\left(10^3 \frac{\text{mm}}{\text{m}}\right)(0.175 \text{ m})}{6 \text{ mm}}$$

$$= 2.479 \times 10^7 \text{ Pa} \quad (25 \text{ MPa})$$

The answer is (D).

Equation 30.5: Axial Stress

$$\sigma_a = \frac{p_i r}{2t} \qquad 30.5$$

Variation

$$\sigma_a = \frac{F}{A} = \frac{pd}{4t}$$
$$= \frac{\sigma_t}{2}$$

Description

When the cylindrical tank is closed at the ends like a soft drink can, the axial force on the ends produces a stress directed along the longitudinal axis known as the *longitudinal*, *long*, or *axial stress*, σ_a.

Mechanics of Materials

Example

A small cylindrical pressure tank has an internal gauge pressure of 1600 Pa. The inside diameter is 69 mm, and the wall thickness is 3 mm. What is most nearly the axial stress of the tank?

(A) 7700 Pa

(B) 9200 Pa

(C) 11 000 Pa

(D) 18 000 Pa

Solution

Check the ratio of wall thickness to radius.

$$\frac{t}{r} \approx \frac{3 \text{ mm}}{\dfrac{69 \text{ mm}}{2}} = 0.087$$

Since $t/r < 0.1$, this can be evaluated as a thin-walled tank.

The axial tensile stress is

$$\sigma_a = \frac{p_i r}{2t} = \frac{(1600 \text{ Pa})\left(\dfrac{69 \text{ mm}}{2}\right)}{(2)(3 \text{ mm})}$$

$$= 9200 \text{ Pa}$$

The answer is (B).

Principal Stresses in Tanks

The hoop and axial stresses are the principal stresses for pressure vessels when internal pressure is the only loading. It is not necessary to use the combined stress equations. If a three-dimensional portion of the shell is considered, the stress on the outside surface is zero. For this reason, the largest shear stress in three dimensions is $\sigma_h/2$ and is oriented at 45° to the surface.

Thin-Walled Spherical Tanks

Because of symmetry, the surface (tangential) stress of a spherical tank is the same in all directions.

$$\sigma = \frac{pd}{4t} = \frac{pr}{2t}$$

3. THICK-WALLED PRESSURE VESSELS

A thick-walled cylinder has a wall thickness-to-radius ratio greater than 0.1. In thick-walled tanks, radial stress is significant and cannot be disregarded. In *Lame's solution*, a thick-walled cylinder is assumed to

be made up of thin laminar rings. This method shows that the radial and tangential (circumferential or hoop) stresses vary with location within the tank wall.

At every point in the cylinder, the tangential, radial, and longitudinal stresses are the principal stresses. Unless an external torsional shear stress is added, it is not necessary to use the combined stress equations.

The maximum radial, tangential, and shear stresses occur at the inner surface for both internal and external pressurization. (The terms *tangential stress* and *circumferential stress* are preferred over *hoop stress* when dealing with thick-walled cylinders.) Compressive stresses are negative.

Equation 30.6 Through Eq. 30.8: Thick-Walled Cylinder with Internal Pressurization

$$\sigma_t = p_i \frac{r_o^2 + r_i^2}{r_o^2 - r_i^2} \qquad \text{30.6}$$

$$\sigma_r = -p_i \qquad \text{30.7}$$

$$\sigma_a = p_i \frac{r_i^2}{r_o^2 - r_i^2} \qquad \text{30.8}$$

Variation

$$\sigma_{\text{axial}} = \frac{F}{A}$$

$$= \frac{p_i \pi r_i^2}{\pi(r_o^2 - r_i^2)}$$

Description

Use Eq. 30.6 and Eq. 30.7 to calculate stresses in thick-walled cylinders under internal pressurization. Cylinders under internal pressurization will also experience an axial stress in the direction of the end caps (see Eq. 30.8 and the variation equation). This axial stress is calculated as the axial force divided by the annular area of the wall material.

Equation 30.9 and Eq. 30.10: Thick-Walled Cylinder with External Pressurization

$$\sigma_t = -p_o \frac{r_o^2 + r_i^2}{r_o^2 - r_i^2} \qquad \text{30.9}$$

$$\sigma_r = -p_o \qquad \text{30.10}$$

Description

Equation 30.9 and Eq. 30.10 are used for cylinders with external pressurization.

THERMAL, HOOP, AND TORSIONAL STRESS **30-5**

4. TORSIONAL STRESS

Equation 30.11 Through Eq. 30.13: Shafts

$$\tau = \frac{Tr}{J} \quad [t > 0.1r] \qquad 30.11$$

$$J = \pi r^4/2 \qquad 30.12$$

$$J = \pi(r_a^4 - r_b^4)/2 \qquad 30.13$$

Variations

$$J = \frac{\pi d^4}{32} \quad [\text{solid}]$$

$$J = \frac{\pi}{32}(d_o^4 - d_i^4) \quad [\text{hollow}]$$

Description

Shear stress occurs when a shaft is placed in *torsion*. The shear stress at the outer surface of a bar of radius r, which is torsionally loaded by a torque, T, is calculated from Eq. 30.11.

The *polar moment of inertia*, J, of a solid round shaft is found from Eq. 30.12. For a hollow shaft, use Eq. 30.13.

Example

A solid steel shaft of 200 mm diameter experiences a torque of 135.6 kN·m. What is most nearly the maximum shear stress in the shaft?

(A) 86 MPa

(B) 110 MPa

(C) 160 MPa

(D) 190 MPa

Solution

Calculate the maximum shear stress using Eq. 30.11.

$$\tau = \frac{Tr}{J} = \frac{Tr}{\pi r^4/2} = \frac{2T}{\pi r^3}$$

$$= \frac{(2)(135.6 \text{ kN·m})}{\pi \left(\dfrac{200 \text{ mm}}{(2)\left(1000 \dfrac{\text{mm}}{\text{m}}\right)} \right)^3}$$

$$= 86\,326 \text{ kPa} \quad (86 \text{ MPa})$$

The answer is (A).

Equation 30.14 and Eq. 30.15: Angle of Twist

$$\phi = \int_0^L \frac{T}{GJ} dz = \frac{TL}{GJ} \qquad 30.14$$

$$T = G(d\phi/dz)\int_A r^2 dA = GJ(d\phi/dz) \qquad 30.15$$

Description

If a shaft of length L carries a torque T, the angle of twist (in radians) can be found from Eq. 30.14.

Example

An aluminum bar 17 m long and 0.6 m in diameter is acted upon by an 11 kN·m torque. The shear modulus of elasticity, G, is 26 GPa. Neglect bending.

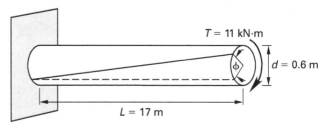

What is most nearly the angle of twist, ϕ, for the aluminum bar?

(A) 0.000 57°

(B) 0.0057°

(C) 0.032°

(D) 0.082°

Solution

From Eq. 30.14, and using the relationship $J = \pi d^4/32$ for a solid shaft, the angle of twist is

$$\phi = \frac{TL}{GJ}$$

$$= \frac{TL}{G\left(\dfrac{\pi d^4}{32}\right)}$$

$$= \frac{(11 \text{ kN·m})\left(10^3 \dfrac{\text{N}}{\text{kN}}\right)(17 \text{ m})\left(\dfrac{180°}{\pi \text{ rad}}\right)}{(26 \text{ GPa})\left(10^9 \dfrac{\text{Pa}}{\text{GPa}}\right)\left(\dfrac{\pi(0.6 \text{ m})^4}{32}\right)}$$

$$= 0.032°$$

The answer is (C).

P P I • **p p i 2 p a s s . c o m**

Equation 30.16: Torsional Stiffness

$$k_t = GJ/L \qquad \textit{30.16}$$

Variation

$$k_t = \frac{T}{\phi}$$

Description

The *torsional stiffness* (*torsional spring constant* or *twisting moment per radian of twist*) is given by Eq. 30.16.

Equation 30.17: Torsion in Hollow, Thin-Walled Shells

$$\tau = \frac{T}{2A_m t} \qquad \textit{30.17}$$

Description

Shear stress due to torsion in a thin-walled, noncircular shell (also known as a *closed box*) acts around the perimeter of the tube, as shown in Fig. 30.3. A_m is the area enclosed by the centerline of the shell. The shear stress, τ, is given by Eq. 30.17.

Figure 30.3 *Torsion in Thin-Walled Shells*

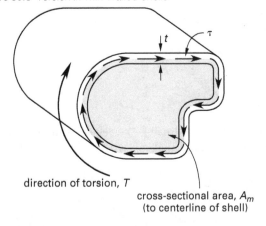

direction of torsion, T

cross-sectional area, A_m
(to centerline of shell)

The shear stress at any point is not proportional to the distance from the centroid of the cross section. Rather, the *shear flow*, q, around the shell is constant, regardless of whether the wall thickness is constant or variable. The shear flow is the shear per unit length of the centerline path. At any point where the shell thickness is t,

$$q = \tau t = \frac{T}{2A_m} \quad \text{[constant]}$$

Example

A hollow, thin-walled shell has a wall thickness of 12.5 mm. The shell is acted upon by a 280 N·m torque.

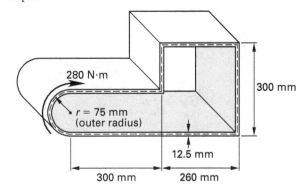

Find the approximate torsional shear stress in the shell's wall.

(A) 14 kPa

(B) 44 kPa

(C) 59 kPa

(D) 92 kPa

Solution

The enclosed area to the centerline of the shell is

$$A_m = \frac{\begin{aligned}&(300 \text{ mm} - 12.5 \text{ mm})\left(260 \text{ mm} - \frac{12.5 \text{ mm}}{2}\right)\\&\quad +\Big((2)(75 \text{ mm}) - 12.5 \text{ mm}\Big)(300 \text{ mm})\\&\quad +\left(\frac{\pi}{2}\right)\left(75 \text{ mm} - \frac{12.5 \text{ mm}}{2}\right)^2\end{aligned}}{\left(1000 \dfrac{\text{mm}}{\text{m}}\right)^2}$$

$$= 0.1216 \text{ m}^2$$

The torsional shear stress is

$$\begin{aligned}\tau &= \frac{T}{2A_m t}\\[2mm]&= \frac{280 \text{ N·m}}{(2)(0.1216 \text{ m}^2)\left(\dfrac{12.5 \text{ mm}}{1000 \dfrac{\text{mm}}{\text{m}}}\right)}\\[2mm]&= 92\,084 \text{ Pa} \quad (92 \text{ kPa})\end{aligned}$$

The answer is (D).

31
Beams

Nomenclature

A	area	m^2
b	width	m
c	distance from neutral axis to extreme fiber	m
C	couple	N·m
d	depth	m
d	distance	m
e	eccentricity	m
E	modulus of elasticity	MPa
F	force	N
g	gravitational acceleration, 9.81	m/s^2
h	height	m
I	moment of inertia	m^4
L	length	m
m	mass per unit length	kg/m
M	moment	N·m
n	modular ratio	–
P	load	N
q	shear flow	N/m
Q	statical moment	m^3
r	radius	m
s	elastic section modulus	m^3
t	thickness	m
v	deflection	m
V	shear	N
w	load	N
w	load per unit length	N/m
x	distance	m
y	deflection	m
y	depth	m
y'	slope	–

Symbols

ε	axial strain	–
θ	angle	deg
ρ	radius of curvature	m
σ	normal stress	MPa
τ	shear stress	MPa
ϕ	angle	deg

Subscripts

b	bending
c	centroidal
o	original
t	transformed
T	transformed
x	in x-direction
y	in y-direction

1. SHEARING FORCE AND BENDING MOMENT

Sign Conventions

The internal *shear* at a section is the sum of all shearing (e.g., vertical) forces acting on an object up to that section. It has units of pounds, kips, newtons, and so on. Shear is not the same as shear stress, since the area of the object is not considered.

The most typical application is shear, V, at a section on a horizontal beam defined as the sum of all vertical forces between the section and one of the ends. The direction (i.e., to the left or right of the section) in which the summation proceeds is not important. Since the values of shear will differ only in sign for summation to the left and right ends, the direction that results in the fewest calculations should be selected.

$$V = \sum_{\substack{\text{[section to]} \\ \text{[one end]}}} F_i$$

For beams, shear is positive when there is a net upward force to the left of a section, and it is negative when there is a net downward force to the left of the section. (See Fig. 31.1.)

Mechanics of Materials

Mechanics of Materials

Figure 31.1 Shear Sign Conventions

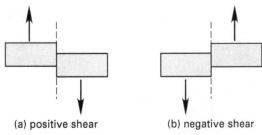

(a) positive shear   (b) negative shear

(Arrows show resultant of forces to
the left and right of the section.)

The *moment, M,* will be the algebraic sum of all moments and couples located between the section and one of the ends.

$$M = \underbrace{\sum F_i x_i}_{\substack{[\text{section to}] \\ [\text{one end}]}} + \underbrace{\sum C_i}_{\substack{[\text{section to}] \\ [\text{one end}]}}$$

Moments in a beam are positive when the upper surface of the beam is in compression and the lower surface is in tension. Positive moments cause lengthening of the lower surface and shortening of the upper surface. A useful image with which to remember this convention is to imagine the beam smiling when the moment is positive. (See Fig. 31.2.)

Figure 31.2 Bending Moment Sign Conventions

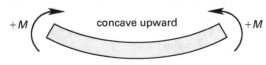

(a) positive bending moment

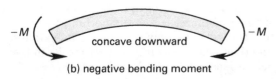

(b) negative bending moment

Equation 31.1 and Eq. 31.2: Change in Shear Magnitude

$$V_2 - V_1 = \int_{x_1}^{x_2} [-w(x)]\,dx \qquad 31.1$$

$$w(x) = -\frac{dV(x)}{dx} \qquad 31.2$$

Description

The change in magnitude of the shear between two points is the integral of the *load function, w(x),* or the area under the load diagram between those points.

Equation 31.3 and Eq. 31.4: Change in Moment Magnitude

$$M_2 - M_1 = \int_{x_1}^{x_2} V(x)\,dx \qquad 31.3$$

$$V = \frac{dM(x)}{dx} \qquad 31.4$$

Description

The change in magnitude of the moment between two points is equal to the integral of the *shear function, V(x),* or the area under the shear diagram between those points.

Shear and Moment Diagrams

Both shear and moment can be described mathematically for simple loadings, but the formulas become discontinuous as the loadings become more complex. It is more convenient to describe complex shear and moment functions graphically. Graphs of shear and moment as functions of position along the beam are known as *shear and moment diagrams.* The following guidelines and conventions should be observed when constructing a *shear diagram.*

- The shear at any section is equal to the sum of the loads and reactions from the section to the left end.

- The magnitude of the shear at any section is equal to the slope of the moment function at that section.

- Loads and reactions acting upward are positive.

- The shear diagram is straight and sloping for uniformly distributed loads.

- The shear diagram is straight and horizontal between concentrated loads.

- The shear is undefined at points of concentrated loads.

The following guidelines and conventions should be observed when constructing a *moment diagram.* By convention, the moment diagram is drawn on the compression side of the beam.

- The moment at any section is equal to the sum of the moments and couples from the section to the left end.

- The change in magnitude of the moment at any section is the integral of the shear diagram, or the area under the shear diagram. A concentrated moment will produce a jump or discontinuity in the moment diagram.

- The maximum or minimum moment occurs where the shear is either zero or passes through zero.

- The moment diagram is parabolic and is curved downward (i.e., is convex) for downward uniformly distributed loads.

Example

The shear diagram for a simply supported beam is as shown.

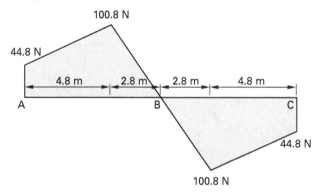

What is most nearly the maximum moment in the beam?

- (A) 100 N·m
- (B) 430 N·m
- (C) 490 N·m
- (D) 740 N·m

Solution

The maximum moment occurs at point B where the shear is zero.

$$M_B = (44.8 \text{ N})(4.8 \text{ m})$$
$$+ \left(\frac{1}{2}\right)(100.8 \text{ N} - 44.8 \text{ N})(4.8 \text{ m})$$
$$+ \left(\frac{1}{2}\right)(100.8 \text{ N})(2.8 \text{ m})$$
$$= 491 \text{ N·m} \quad (490 \text{ N·m})$$

The answer is (C).

2. STRESSES IN BEAMS

Equation 31.5 Through Eq. 31.8: Bending Stress[1]

$$\sigma_x = -My/I \qquad 31.5$$

$$\sigma_{x,\text{max}} = \pm Mc/I \qquad 31.6$$

$$s = I/c \qquad 31.7$$

$$\sigma_{x,\text{max}} = -M/s \qquad 31.8$$

Description

Normal stress is distributed triangularly in a bending beam as shown in Fig. 31.3. Although it is a normal stress, the term *bending stress* or *flexural stress* is used to indicate the source of the stress. For a positive bending moment, the lower surface of the beam experiences tensile stress while the upper surface of the beam experiences compressive stress. The bending stress distribution passes through zero at the centroid, or *neutral axis*, of the cross section. The distance from the neutral axis is y, and the distance from the neutral axis to the *extreme fiber* (i.e., the top or bottom surface most distant from the neutral axis) is c.

Figure 31.3 Bending Stress Distribution at a Section in a Beam

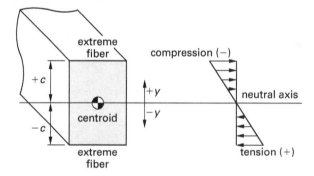

Bending stress varies with location (depth) within the beam. It is zero at the neutral axis, and increases linearly with distance from the neutral axis, as predicted by Eq. 31.5. In Eq. 31.5, I is the centroidal area moment of inertia of the beam. The negative sign in Eq. 31.5, required by the convention that compression is negative, is commonly omitted.

Since the maximum stress will govern the design, y can be set equal to c to obtain the extreme fiber stress. Equation 31.6 shows that the maximum bending stress will occur at the section where the moment is maximum.

For standard structural shapes, I and c are fixed. For design, the *elastic section modulus*, s, given by Eq. 31.7, is often used.

---

[1]The NCEES *FE Reference Handbook* (*NCEES Handbook*) presents Eq. 31.6 as "σ_x" without "max." While the moment on the beam can vary with the location, x, the maximum stress for any particular location will be derived when y is maximum (i.e., when $y = c$).

Example

For the beam shown, the moment, M, at the cross section is 15.7 N·m, and the moment of inertia, I, is 1.91×10^{-4} m^4.

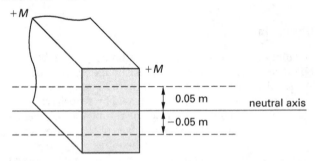

The bending stress that the beam experiences 0.05 m above the neutral axis is most nearly

(A)   −0.0051 MPa

(B)   −0.0041 MPa

(C)   −0.041 MPa

(D)   −0.051 MPa

Solution

Using Eq. 31.5, the bending stress is

$$\sigma_x = -My/I$$
$$= -\frac{(15.7 \text{ N·m})(0.05 \text{ m})}{(1.91 \times 10^{-4} \text{ m}^4)\left(10^6 \dfrac{\text{Pa}}{\text{MPa}}\right)}$$
$$= -0.0041 \text{ MPa} \quad \text{[compression]}$$

The answer is (B).

Stresses in Beams

Hooke's law is valid for any point within a beam, and any distance y from the neutral axis.

$$\sigma = E\varepsilon$$

At any point, x, a loaded beam that is oriented with its longitudinal axis parallel to the x-direction will have an instantaneous radius of curvature of ρ and an instantaneous strain in the x-direction of ε_x.

$$\varepsilon_x = -y/\rho$$
$$\sigma_x = -Ey/\rho$$
$$\frac{1}{\rho} = \frac{\varepsilon_{\text{max}}}{c} = \frac{d^2y}{dx^2} = \frac{d\theta}{dx} = \frac{M}{EI}$$

$$\varepsilon_{\text{max}} = \frac{c}{\rho}$$

Example

At a particular point within a beam, the longitudinal strain is 0.000284 and Poisson's ratio is 0.29. The modulus of elasticity of the beam is 200 MPa. What is most nearly the longitudinal normal stress at that point within the beam?

(A)   0.042 MPa

(B)   0.057 MPa

(C)   0.16 MPa

(D)   0.20 MPa

Solution

The longitudinal normal stress is

$$\sigma = E\varepsilon$$
$$= (200 \text{ MPa})(0.000284)$$
$$= 0.0568 \text{ MPa} \quad (0.057 \text{ MPa})$$

The answer is (B).

Equation 31.9: Centroidal Moment of Inertia

$$I_{x_c} = bh^3/12 \qquad \textit{31.9}$$

Description

Equation 31.9 is the centroidal moment of inertia for a rectangular $b \times h$ section. The section modulus for a rectangular $b \times h$ section is

$$s_{\text{rectangular}} = \frac{bh^2}{6}$$

Example

What is most nearly the moment of inertia of a rectangular 46 cm × 61 cm beam installed in its strongest vertical orientation?

(A) 4.9×10^{-3} m^4

(B) 6.1×10^{-3} m^4

(C) 8.7×10^{-3} m^4

(D) 3.5×10^{-2} m^4

Solution

Using Eq. 31.9,

$$I_{x_c} = bh^3/12$$
$$= \frac{(46 \text{ cm})(61 \text{ cm})^3}{(12)\left(100 \; \dfrac{\text{cm}}{\text{m}}\right)^4}$$
$$= 8.7 \times 10^{-3} \text{ m}^4$$

The answer is (C).

Equation 31.10: Shear Stress

$$\tau_{xy} = VQ/Ib \qquad \qquad 31.10$$

Variations

$$\tau_{\text{max,rectangular}} = \frac{3V}{2A} = \frac{3V}{2bh}$$
$$= 1.5\tau_{\text{ave}}$$

$$\tau_{\text{max,circular}} = \frac{4V}{3A} = \frac{4V}{3\pi r^2}$$

$$\tau_{\text{ave}} = \frac{V}{A_{\text{web}}} = \frac{V}{dt_{\text{web}}} \quad \begin{bmatrix} \text{web shear stress; steel beam} \\ \text{with web thickness} \\ t_{\text{web}} \text{ and depth } d \end{bmatrix}$$

Description

The shear stresses in a vertical section of a beam consist of both horizontal and transverse (vertical) shear stresses.

The exact value of shear stress is dependent on the location, y, within the depth of the beam. The shear stress distribution is given by Eq. 31.10. The shear stress is zero at the top and bottom surfaces of the beam. For a regular shaped beam, the shear stress is maximum at the neutral axis. (See Fig. 31.4.)

Figure 31.4 Dimensions for Shear Stress Calculations

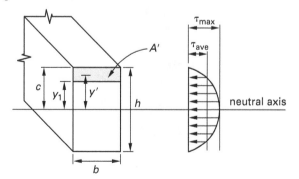

In Eq. 31.10, I is the area moment of inertia, and b is the width or thickness of the beam at the depth, y, within the beam where the shear stress is to be found.

The variation equations give simplifications of Eq. 31.10 for rectangular beams, beams with circular cross sections, and steel beams with web thicknesses and depths shown in Fig. 31.5, respectively.

Figure 31.5 Dimensions of a Steel Beam

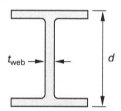

Equation 31.11: Moment of the Area

$$Q = A'\overline{y'} \qquad \qquad 31.11$$

Variation

$$Q = \int_{y_1}^{c} y\,dA \quad \begin{bmatrix} \text{first moment of the area with} \\ \text{respect to neutral axis} \end{bmatrix}$$

Description

The *first* (or *statical*) *moment of the area* of the beam with respect to the neutral axis, Q, is defined by the variation equation.

For rectangular beams, $dA = b\,dy$. Then, the moment of the area, A', above layer y is equal to the product of the area and the distance from the centroidal axis to the centroid of the area.

Example

A composite cross section is made up of two identical members—horizontally oriented member A and vertically oriented member B—as shown. The neutral axis passes through member B.

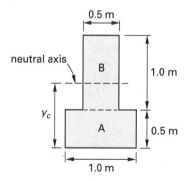

What is most nearly the first moment of the area for member A?

(A) 0.12 m^3

(B) 0.19 m^3

(C) 0.24 m^3

(D) 0.31 m^3

Solution

Determine the location of the neutral axis.

$$y_c = \frac{\sum y_i A_i}{\sum A_i}$$

$$= \frac{\left(\dfrac{0.5 \text{ m}}{2}\right)(1.0 \text{ m})(0.5 \text{ m}) + \left(0.5 \text{ m} + \dfrac{1.0 \text{ m}}{2}\right)(0.5 \text{ m})(1.0 \text{ m})}{(2)(0.5 \text{ m})(1.0 \text{ m})}$$

$$= 0.625 \text{ m}$$

Use Eq. 31.11. The moment of the area is

$$Q = A'\overline{y'}$$

$$= (1.0 \text{ m})(0.5 \text{ m})\left(0.625 \text{ m} - \frac{0.5 \text{ m}}{2}\right)$$

$$= 0.1875 \text{ m}^3 \quad (0.19 \text{ m}^3)$$

The answer is (B).

Equation 31.12: Shear Flow

$$q = VQ/l \qquad \qquad 31.12$$

Description

The *shear flow*, q, is the shear per unit length. In Eq. 31.12, the vertical shear, V, is a function of location, x, along the beam, generally designated as V_x. This shear is resisted by the entire cross section, although the shear stress depends on the distance from the neutral axis. The shear stress is usually considered to be vertical (i.e., in the y-direction), in line with the shearing force, but the same shear stress that acts in the y-z plane also acts on the x-z plane.

Example

An I-beam is made of three planks, each 20 mm × 100 mm in cross section, nailed together with a single row of nails on top and bottom as shown.

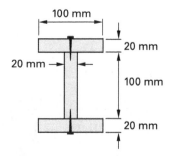

If the longitudinal spacing between the nails is 25 mm, and the vertical shear force acting on the cross section is 600 N, what is most nearly the shear per nail?

(A)   56 N

(B)   76 N

(C)   110 N

(D)   160 N

Solution

The statical moment of each flange is

$$Q = A'\overline{y'} = (100 \text{ mm})(20 \text{ mm})\left(\frac{100 \text{ mm}}{2} + \frac{20 \text{ mm}}{2}\right)$$

$$= 120\,000 \text{ mm}^3$$

The moment of inertia is

$$I = \frac{bh^3}{12}$$

$$= \left(\frac{1}{12}\right)(100 \text{ mm})(140 \text{ mm})^3$$

$$\quad - (2)\left(\frac{1}{12}\right)(40 \text{ mm})(100 \text{ mm})^3$$

$$= 16.2 \times 10^6 \text{ mm}^4$$

The shear force per unit distance along the beam's longitudinal axis is

$$q = VQ/I = \frac{(600 \text{ N})(120\,000 \text{ mm}^3)}{16.2 \times 10^6 \text{ mm}^4}$$

$$= 4.44 \text{ N/mm}$$

The shear per nail spaced at d is

$$F = qd = \left(4.44 \ \frac{\text{N}}{\text{mm}}\right)(25 \text{ mm})$$

$$= 111 \text{ N} \quad (110 \text{ N})$$

The answer is (C).

3. DEFLECTION OF BEAMS

Equation 31.13 Through Eq. 31.15: Deflection and Slope Relationships

$$EI\frac{d^2y}{dx^2} = M \qquad \text{31.13}$$

$$EI\frac{d^3y}{dx^3} = dM(x)/dx = V \qquad \text{31.14}$$

$$EI\frac{d^4y}{dx^4} = dV(x)/dx = -w \qquad \text{31.15}$$

Variations

$$y' = \frac{dy}{dx} = \text{slope}$$

$$y'' = \frac{d^2y}{dx^2} = \frac{M(x)}{EI}$$

$$y''' = \frac{d^3y}{dx^3} = \frac{V(x)}{EI}$$

$$y'''' = \frac{d^4y}{dx^4} = \frac{w(x)}{EI}$$

Description

The deflection, y, and slope, y', of a loaded beam are related to the moment $M(x)$, shear $V(x)$, and load $w(x)$ by Eq. 31.13 through Eq. 31.15 and the variation equations.

Equation 31.16 and Eq. 31.17: Deflection on a Beam Section

$$EI(dy/dx) = \int M(x)\,dx \qquad \text{31.16}$$

$$EIy = \int \left[\int M(x)\,dx\right]dx \qquad \text{31.17}$$

Description

If the moment function, $M(x)$, is known for a section of the beam, the deflection at any point on that section can be found from Eq. 31.16. The constants of integration are determined from the beam boundary conditions shown in Table 31.1.

Table 31.1 *Beam Boundary Conditions*

end condition	y	y'	y''	V	M
simple support	0				0
built-in support	0	0			
free end			0	0	0
hinge					0

Example

A beam of length L carries a concentrated load, P, at point C.

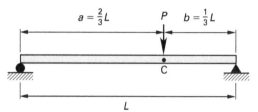

Determine the deflection at point C in terms of P, L, E, and I, where E is the modulus of elasticity, and I is the moment of inertia.

(A) $\quad -\dfrac{2PL^3}{243EI}$

(B) $\quad -\dfrac{4PL^3}{243EI}$

(C) $\quad -\dfrac{PL^3}{27EI}$

(D) $\quad -\dfrac{PL^3}{9EI}$

Solution

The equation for bending moment in the beam is

$$EI\frac{d^2y}{dx^2} = M$$

Computing M for the different beam sections,

$$EI\frac{d^2y}{dx^2} = \frac{Pbx}{L} \qquad [0 \le x \le a]$$

$$EI\frac{d^2y}{dx^2} = \frac{Pbx}{L} - P(x-a) \qquad [a \le x \le L]$$

Mechanics of Materials

Integrating each equation twice gives

$$EIy = \frac{Pbx^3}{6L} + C_1x + C_3 \quad [0 \le x \le a]$$

$$EIy = \frac{Pbx^3}{6L} - \frac{P(x-a)^3}{6}$$
$$+ C_2x + C_4 \quad [a \le x \le L]$$

The constants are determined by the following conditions: (1) at $x = a$, the slopes dy/dx and deflections y are equal; (2) at $x = 0$ and $x = L$, the deflection $y = 0$. These conditions give

$$C_1 = C_2$$
$$= \frac{-Pb(L^2 - b^2)}{6L}$$
$$C_3 = C_4 = 0$$

Evaluating the equation for $(0 \le x \le a)$ at $x = a = \frac{2}{3}L$ and $b = \frac{1}{3}L$,

$$EIy = \left[\frac{P\left(\frac{1}{3}L\right)\left(\frac{2}{3}L\right)}{6L} \right]\left[L^2 - \left(\frac{L}{3}\right)^2 - \left(\frac{2L}{3}\right)^2 \right]$$

$$y = -\frac{4PL^3}{243EI}$$

The answer is (B).

....

Equation 31.18 Through Eq. 31.41: Simply Supported Beam Slopes and Deflections[2]

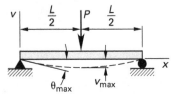

slope

$$\theta_{\max} = \frac{-PL^2}{16EI} \qquad 31.18$$

deflection

$$v_{\max} = \frac{-PL^3}{48EI} \qquad 31.19$$

elastic curve

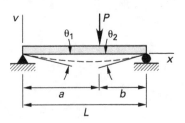

$$v = \frac{-Px}{48EI}(3L^2 - 4x^2) \qquad 31.20$$
$$[0 \le x \le L/2]$$

slope

$$\theta_1 = \frac{-Pab(L+b)}{6EIL} \qquad 31.21$$

$$\theta_2 = \frac{Pab(L+a)}{6EIL} \qquad 31.22$$

deflection

$$v \big|_{x=a} = \frac{-Pba}{6EIL}(L^2 - b^2 - a^2) \qquad 31.23$$

elastic curve

$$v = \frac{-Pbx}{6EIL}(L^2 - b^2 - x^2) \qquad [0 \le x \le a] \qquad 31.24$$

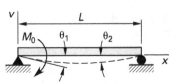

slope

$$\theta_1 = \frac{-M_0L}{3EI} \qquad 31.25$$

$$\theta_2 = \frac{M_0L}{6EI} \qquad 31.26$$

---

[2]Deflection in the vertical direction in the *NCEES Handbook* beam deflection table (see Eq. 31.18 Through Eq. 31.41) is given a new symbol, v. This is the same quantity that the *NCEES Handbook* refers to as y in other places. The deflection angles in Eq. 31.18 through Eq. 31.41, referred to as θ, have units of radians, and so are more conveniently thought of as slopes, corresponding to y' or $\tan \theta$ if variables consistent with the rest of the chapter are used.

deflection

$$v_{\max} = \frac{-M_0 L^2}{\sqrt{243}\, EI} \qquad \text{31.27}$$

elastic curve

$$v = \frac{-M_0 x}{6EIL}(x^2 - 3Lx + 2L^2) \qquad \text{31.28}$$

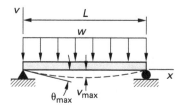

slope

$$\theta_{\max} = \frac{-wL^3}{24EI} \qquad \text{31.29}$$

deflection

$$v_{\max} = \frac{-5wL^4}{384EI} \qquad \text{31.30}$$

elastic curve

$$v = \frac{-wx}{24EI}(x^3 - 3Lx^2 + L^3) \qquad \text{31.31}$$

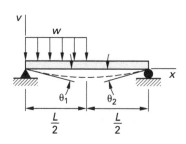

slope

$$\theta_1 = \frac{-3wL^3}{128EI} \qquad \text{31.32}$$

$$\theta_2 = \frac{7wL^3}{384EI} \qquad \text{31.33}$$

deflection

$$v\,\big|_{x=L/2} = \frac{-5wL^4}{768EI} \qquad \text{31.34}$$

$$v_{\max} = -0.006563\frac{wL^4}{EI} \qquad \text{31.35}$$
$$[\text{at } x = 0.4598L]$$

elastic curve

$$v = \frac{-wx}{384EI}(16x^3 - 24Lx^2 + 9L^3) \qquad \text{31.36}$$
$$[0 \le x \le L/2]$$

$$v = \frac{-wL}{384EI}(8x^3 - 24Lx^2 + 17L^2x - L^3) \qquad \text{31.37}$$
$$[L/2 \le x < L]$$

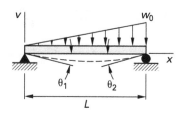

slope

$$\theta_1 = \frac{-7w_0 L^3}{360EI} \qquad \text{31.38}$$

$$\theta_2 = \frac{w_0 L^3}{45EI} \qquad \text{31.39}$$

deflection

$$v_{\max} = -0.00652\frac{w_0 L^4}{EI} \qquad \text{31.40}$$
$$[\text{at } x = 0.5193]$$

elastic curve

$$v = \frac{-w_0 x}{360EIL}(3x^4 - 10L^2x^2 + 7L^4) \qquad \text{31.41}$$

Description

Commonly used beam deflection formulas are given in Eq. 31.18 through Eq. 31.41. These formulas never need to be derived and should be used whenever possible.

Superposition

When multiple loads act simultaneously on a beam, all of the loads contribute to deflection. The principle of *superposition* permits the deflections at a point to be calculated as the sum of the deflections from each individual load acting singly. Superposition can also be used to calculate the shear and moment at a point and to draw the shear and moment diagrams. This principle is valid as long as the normal stress and strain are related by the modulus of elasticity, E (i.e., as long as Hooke's law is valid). Generally, this is true when the deflections are not excessive and all stresses are kept less than the yield point of the beam material.

Equation 31.42 Through Eq. 31.61: Cantilevered Beam Slopes and Deflections

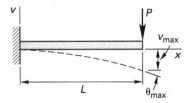

slope

$$\theta_{max} = \frac{-PL^2}{2EI} \qquad \text{31.42}$$

deflection

$$v_{max} = \frac{-PL^3}{3EI} \qquad \text{31.43}$$

elastic curve

$$v = \frac{-Px^2}{6EI}(3L - x) \qquad \text{31.44}$$

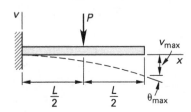

slope

$$\theta_{max} = \frac{-PL^2}{8EI} \qquad \text{31.45}$$

deflection

$$v_{max} = \frac{-5PL^3}{48EI} \qquad \text{31.46}$$

elastic curve

$$v = \frac{-Px^2}{6EI}\left(\frac{3}{2}L - x\right) \quad [0 \leq x \leq L/2] \qquad \text{31.47}$$

$$v = \frac{-PL^2}{24EI}\left(3x - \frac{1}{2}L\right) \quad [L/2 \leq x \leq L] \qquad \text{31.48}$$

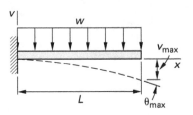

slope

$$\theta_{max} = \frac{-wL^3}{6EI} \qquad \text{31.49}$$

deflection

$$v_{max} = \frac{-wL^4}{8EI} \qquad \text{31.50}$$

elastic curve

$$v = \frac{-wx^2}{24EI}(x^2 - 4Lx + 6L^2) \qquad \text{31.51}$$

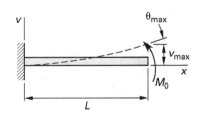

slope

$$\theta_{max} = \frac{M_0 L}{EI} \qquad 31.52$$

deflection

$$v_{max} = \frac{M_0 L^2}{2EI} \qquad 31.53$$

elastic curve

$$v = \frac{M_0 x^2}{2EI} \qquad 31.54$$

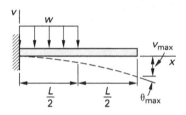

slope

$$\theta_{max} = \frac{-wL^3}{48EI} \qquad 31.55$$

deflection

$$v_{max} = \frac{-7wL^4}{384EI} \qquad 31.56$$

elastic curve

$$v = \frac{-wx^2}{24EI}\left(x^2 - 2Lx + \tfrac{3}{2}L^2\right) \qquad 31.57$$
$$[0 \le x \le L/2]$$

$$v = \frac{-wL^3}{192EI}(4x - L/2) \quad [L/2 \le x \le L] \qquad 31.58$$

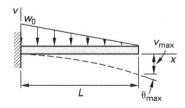

slope

$$\theta_{max} = \frac{-w_0 L^3}{24EI} \qquad 31.59$$

deflection

$$v_{max} = \frac{-w_0 L^4}{30EI} \qquad 31.60$$

elastic curve

$$v = \frac{-w_0 x^2}{120EIL}\left(10L^3 - 10L^2 x + 5Lx^2 - x^3\right) \qquad 31.61$$

Description

Commonly used cantilevered beam slopes and deflections are compiled into Eq. 31.42 through Eq. 31.61.

Example

The unloaded propped cantilever shown is fixed at one end and simply supported at the other end. The beam has a mass of 30.6 kg/m. The modulus of elasticity of the beam is 210 GPa; the moment of inertia is 2880 cm⁴.

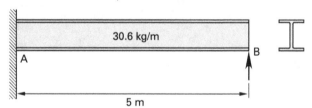

What is most nearly the reaction at the simply supported end?

- (A)   72 N
- (B)   510 N
- (C)   560 N
- (D)   770 N

Solution

Propped cantilevers are statically indeterminate and must be solved using criteria (usually equal deflections at some known point) other than equilibrium.

The deflection at the supported end is known to be zero. Therefore, the deflection due to the distributed self-weight load combined with the deflection due to the concentrated reaction load must sum to zero.

The deflection for a distributed load is found from Eq. 31.50.

$$v_1 = \frac{-wL^4}{8EI} \quad \text{[downward]}$$

The deflection due to a concentrated load (i.e., the reaction at point B) is found from Eq. 31.43, with $x = L$.

$$v_2 = \frac{-PL^3}{3EI} \quad \text{[upward]}$$

Since $v_1 + v_2 = 0$,

$$\frac{wL^4}{8EI} = \frac{PL^3}{3EI}$$

$$P = \frac{3wL}{8} = \frac{3mgL}{8} = \frac{(3)\left(30.6 \ \frac{\text{kg}}{\text{m}}\right)\left(9.81 \ \frac{\text{m}}{\text{s}^2}\right)(5 \ \text{m})}{8}$$

$$= 562.8 \ \text{N} \quad (560 \ \text{N})$$

The answer is (C).

Equation 31.62 Through Eq. 31.66: Fixed-Supported Beam Slopes and Deflections[3]

reactions

$$R_1 = R_2 = \frac{wL}{2} \qquad \textit{31.62}$$

moments

$$M_1 = M_2 = \frac{wL^2}{12} \qquad \textit{31.63}$$

slope

$$|\theta_{\max}| = 0.008 \frac{wL^3}{24EI} \quad \left[\text{at } x = \frac{1}{2} \pm \frac{L}{\sqrt{12}}\right] \qquad \textit{31.64}$$

deflection

$$|v_{\max}| = \frac{wL^4}{384EI} \quad \left[\text{at } x = \frac{L}{2}\right] \qquad \textit{31.65}$$

elastic curve

$$v(x) = \frac{wx^2}{24EI}(L^2 - 2Lx + x^2) \qquad \textit{31.66}$$

Description

A beam is rigidly fixed when the slope at both ends is zero and moments develop at the supports. Figure 31.6 shows a beam fixed at both end supports with a uniformly distributed load. Reactions, fixed end moments, maximum slope, deflection, and elastic curve are given by Eq. 31.62 through Eq. 31.66.

Figure 31.6 Beam Fixed at Both Ends

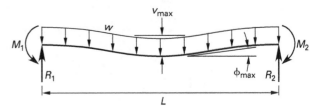

Example

A steel beam is shown.

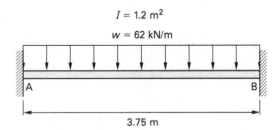

Most nearly, what is the moment at support B?

(A)   65 kN·m

(B)   73 kN·m

(C)   80 kN·m

(D)   87 kN·m

Solution

From Eq. 31.63,

$$M_A = M_B = \frac{wL^2}{12} = \frac{\left(62 \ \frac{\text{kN}}{\text{m}}\right)(3.75 \ \text{m})^2}{12}$$

$$= 73 \ \text{kN·m}$$

The answer is (B).

---

[3]The *NCEES Handbook* uses the term "piping segment" instead of "fixed-supported beam." However, given the equations and diagram used, the term "fixed supported beam" is more appropriate, so that term is used throughout this section.

4. COMPOSITE BEAMS

A *composite structure* is one in which two or more different materials are used. Each material carries part of the applied load. Examples of composite structures include steel-reinforced concrete and timber beams with bolted-on steel plates.

Most simple composite structures can be analyzed using the *method of consistent deformations*, also known as the *transformation method*. This method assumes that the strains are the same in both materials at the interface between them. Although the strains are the same, the stresses in the two adjacent materials are not equal, since stresses are proportional to the moduli of elasticity.

The transformation method starts by determining the modulus of elasticity for each (usually two in number) of the materials in the composite beam and then calculating the *modular ratio*, n. E_{weaker} is the smaller modulus of elasticity.

$$n = \frac{E}{E_{\text{weaker}}}$$

The area of the stronger material is increased by a factor of n. The transformed area is used to calculate the transformed composite area, A_{ct}, or transformed moment of inertia, I_{ct}. For compression and tension members, the stresses in the weaker and stronger materials are

$$\sigma_{\text{weaker}} = \frac{F}{A_{ct}}$$

$$\sigma_{\text{stronger}} = \frac{nF}{A_{ct}}$$

Equation 31.67 and Eq. 31.68: Transformation Method for Beams in Bending

$$\sigma_1 = -nMy/I_T \qquad \text{31.67}$$

$$\sigma_2 = -My/I_T \qquad \text{31.68}$$

Variations

$$\sigma_{\text{weaker}} = \frac{Mc_{\text{weaker}}}{I_{ct}}$$

$$\sigma_{\text{stronger}} = \frac{nMc_{\text{stronger}}}{I_{ct}}$$

Description

For beams in bending, the bending stresses in the stronger and weaker materials, respectively, are given by Eq. 31.67 and Eq. 31.68. The transformed section is composed of a single material. (See Fig. 31.7.)

Figure 31.7 Composite Section Transformation

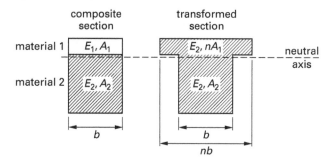

Mechanics of Materials

32 Columns

Nomenclature

A	area	m^2
b	width	m
c	distance to extreme fiber	m
e	eccentricity	m
E	modulus of elasticity	MPa
F	force	N
h	thickness	m
I	moment of inertia	m^4
K	effective length factor	–
ℓ	unbraced length	m
L	column length	m
M	moment	N·m
P	force	N
r	radius of gyration	m
S	strength	MPa

Symbols

δ	deformation	m
σ	normal stress	MPa

Subscripts

c	compressive
cr	critical
col	column
t	tensile
y	yield

1. BEAM-COLUMNS

If a load is applied through the centroid of a tension or compression member's cross section, the loading is said to be *axial loading* or *concentric loading*. *Eccentric loading* occurs when the load is not applied through the centroid. In Fig. 32.1, distance e is known as the *eccentricity*.

If an axial member is loaded eccentrically, it will bend and experience bending stress in the same manner as a beam. Since the member experiences both axial stress and bending stress, it is known as a *beam-column*. Beam-columns may be horizontal or vertical members.

Figure 32.1 *Eccentric Loading of a Beam-Column*

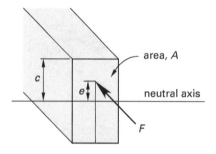

Both the axial stress and bending stress are normal stresses oriented in the same direction; therefore, simple addition can be used to combine them.

$$\sigma_{\text{max,min}} = \frac{F}{A} \pm \frac{Mc}{I}$$
$$= \frac{F}{A} \pm \frac{Fec}{I}$$

$$M = Fe$$

If a vertical pier or column (primarily designed as a compression member) is loaded with an eccentric compressive load, part of the section can still be in tension. Tension will exist when the Mc/I term is larger than the F/A term. It is particularly important to eliminate or severely limit tensile stresses in concrete and masonry piers, since these materials cannot support much tension.

Regardless of the size of the load, there will be no tension as long as the eccentricity is low enough. In a rectangular member, the load must be kept within a rhombus-shaped area formed from the middle thirds of the centroidal axes. This area is known as the *core*, *kern*, or *kernel*. Figure 32.2 illustrates the kernel for various cross sections.

2. LONG COLUMNS

Short columns, called *piers* or *pedestals*, will fail by compression of the material. *Long columns* will *buckle* in the transverse direction that has the smallest radius of gyration. Buckling failure is sudden, often without significant

Figure 32.2 *Kernel for Various Column Shapes*

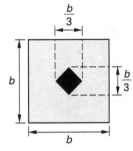

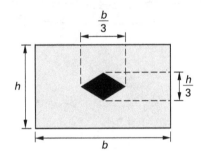

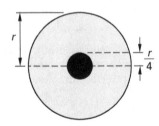

warning. If the material is wood or concrete, the material will usually fracture (because the yield stress is low); however, if the column is made of steel, the column will usually fail by local buckling, followed later by twisting and general yielding failure. Intermediate length columns will usually fail by a combination of crushing and buckling.

Equation 32.1: Euler's Formula for Pinned or Frictionless Ends[1]

$$P_{cr} = \frac{\pi^2 EI}{(K\ell)^2} \qquad \textit{32.1}$$

Variations

$$P_{cr} = \frac{\pi^2 EI}{\ell^2}$$

$$P_{cr} = \frac{\pi^2 EI}{L_{col}^2}$$

Description

The load at which a long column fails is known as the *critical load* or *Euler load*. The Euler load is the theoretical maximum load that an initially straight column can support without transverse buckling. For columns with unrestrained or pinned ends, this load is given by the first variation equation, known as *Euler's formula*.

When a column is not braced along its entire length, the unbraced length is equal to the length (height) of the column: $\ell = L$. As shown in Table 32.1, if the column has pinned or frictionless ends, the effective length factor, K, is 1.00. In that case, the effective length of the column is simply the column length, as presented in the second variation equation.

ℓ is the longest unbraced column length. If a column is braced against buckling at some point between its two ends, the column is known as a *braced column*, and ℓ will be less than the full column height.

Columns do not usually have unrestrained or pinned ends. Often, a column will be fixed at its top and base. In such cases, the *effective length*, $K\ell$, the distance between inflection points on the column, must be used in place of ℓ.

K is the *effective length factor (end-restraint coefficient)*, which theoretically varies from 0.5 to 2.0 according to Table 32.1. For design, values of K should be modified using engineering judgment based on realistic assumptions regarding end fixity.

Example

An ideal rectangular steel bar supports a concentric load of 58.5 kN. Both ends are fixed (i.e., built in).

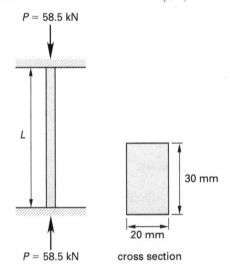

---

[1]The NCEES *FE Reference Handbook* (*NCEES Handbook*) uses ℓ to represent unbraced length, but the symbol L is also used in the structural design parts of the *NCEES Handbook* to represent the same quantity for beams and columns. The effective length may be represented by ℓ_{eff}.

Mechanics of Materials

Table 32.1 *Effective Length Factors*

		K	
illus.	end conditions	theoretical	design
(a)	both ends pinned	1	1.00
(b)	both ends built in	0.5	0.65
(c)	one end pinned, one end built in	0.7	0.8
(d)	one end built in, one end free	2	2.10
(e)	one end built in, one end fixed against rotation but free	1	1.20
(f)	one end pinned, one end fixed against rotation but free	2	2.0

If the modulus of elasticity is 210 GPa, what is most nearly the maximum unbraced length the rod can be without experiencing buckling failure?

(A) 1.3 m

(B) 1.7 m

(C) 4.9 m

(D) 12 m

Solution

Since the column is fixed at the top and base, use the effective length.

$$P_{cr} = \frac{\pi^2 EI}{(K\ell)^2}$$

For an ideal column fixed at both ends, use the design value of $K = 0.5$. For the cross-sectional area of the bar, the smaller dimension is the height. The moment of inertia is

$$
\begin{aligned}
I &= \frac{bh^3}{12} \\
&= \frac{(30 \text{ mm})(20 \text{ mm})^3}{(12)\left(1000 \ \frac{\text{mm}}{\text{m}}\right)^4} \\
&= 2 \times 10^{-8} \text{ m}^4
\end{aligned}
$$

The maximum unbraced length is

$$
\begin{aligned}
P_{cr} &= \frac{\pi^2 EI}{(K\ell)^2} \\
(K\ell)^2 &= \frac{\pi^2 EI}{P_{cr}} \\
(0.5\,\ell)^2 &= \frac{\pi^2 EI}{P_{cr}} \\
&= \frac{\pi^2 (210 \text{ GPa})\left(10^9 \ \frac{\text{Pa}}{\text{GPa}}\right)(2 \times 10^{-8} \text{ m}^4)}{(58.5 \text{ kN})\left(1000 \ \frac{\text{N}}{\text{kN}}\right)} \\
&= 0.709 \text{ m}^2 \\
\ell &= 1.7 \text{ m}
\end{aligned}
$$

The answer is (A).

Equation 32.2 and Eq. 32.3: Critical Column Stress

$$\sigma_{cr} = \frac{P_{cr}}{A} = \frac{\pi^2 E}{(K\ell/r)^2} \qquad \text{32.2}$$

$$r = \sqrt{I/A} \qquad \text{32.3}$$

Description

The column stress corresponding to the Euler load is given by Eq. 32.2. This stress cannot exceed the yield strength of the column material.

The quantity $K\ell/r$ is known as the *effective slenderness ratio*. Long columns have high effective slenderness ratios. The smallest effective slenderness ratio for which Eq. 32.2 is valid is the *critical slenderness ratio*, which can be calculated from the material's yield strength and modulus of elasticity. Typical critical slenderness ratios range from 80 to 120. The critical slenderness ratio becomes smaller as the compressive yield strength increases.

Noncircular columns have two radii of gyration, r_x and r_y, and therefore, have two effective slenderness ratios. The effective slenderness ratio (i.e., the smallest radius of gyration) will govern the design.

Example

The slenderness ratio, $K\ell$, of a column divided by r is one of the terms in the equation for the buckling of a column subjected to compression loads. What does r stand for in the $K\ell/r$ ratio?

(A) radius of the column

(B) radius of gyration

(C) least radius of gyration

(D) maximum radius of gyration

Solution

r is the radius of gyration of the column. For most columns, there are two radii of gyration, and the smallest (least) one is used for the slenderness ratio in design.

The answer is (C).

Diagnostic Exam

Topic IX: Electricity and Magnetism

1. Induction motors on a 13.2 kV circuit draw 10 MVA with a power factor of 0.85 lagging. Most nearly, how much additional capacitive reactive power is needed to correct the power factor to 0.97 lagging?

(A) 2.5 MVAR

(B) 3.1 MVAR

(C) 4.8 MVAR

(D) 5.2 MVAR

2. A transformer circuit is shown.

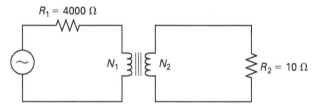

What should be the turns ratio ($N_1{:}N_2$) for maximum power transfer in the circuit?

(A) 1:40

(B) 1:20

(C) 20:1

(D) 40:1

3. Sinusoidal voltage and current waveforms are shown.

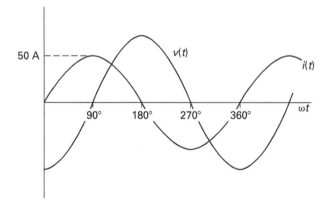

Most nearly, what is the correct phasor (polar) expression for the sinusoidal rms current waveform?

(A) 35 A∠−90°

(B) 35 A∠90°

(C) 50 A∠−90°

(D) 50 A∠90°

4. When the current in a straight wire is 5 A, the current-induced flux passing through an area 3 m from the wire is 30 mWb. The current is decreased to 4 A. The flux passing through that same area will most nearly be

(A) 19 mWb

(B) 20 mWb

(C) 24 mWb

(D) 27 mWb

5. The initial voltage across the capacitor in the circuit shown is 2.0 V. The switch is closed at $t = 0$.

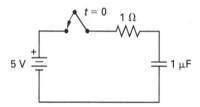

What is most nearly the current immediately after the switch is closed?

(A) 0.2 A

(B) 0.7 A

(C) 1.0 A

(D) 3.0 A

6. The circuit shown is connected across a 120 V, 60 Hz source.

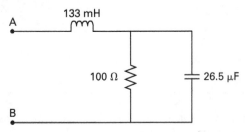

What is most nearly the equivalent input impedance?

(A) $16\ \Omega\angle-33°$

(B) $50\ \Omega\angle0°$

(C) $71\ \Omega\angle-45°$

(D) $110\ \Omega\angle63°$

7. The dielectric material in the capacitor shown has a permittivity of $24\varepsilon_0$ (that is, the permittivity is 24 times that of a vacuum).

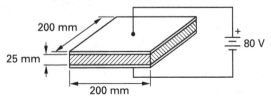

What is most nearly the capacitance?

(A) $3.4 \times 10^{-10}\ \text{F}$

(B) $6.8 \times 10^{-10}\ \text{F}$

(C) $3.4 \times 10^{-7}\ \text{F}$

(D) $6.7 \times 10^{-6}\ \text{F}$

8. A circuit of resistors and batteries is shown.

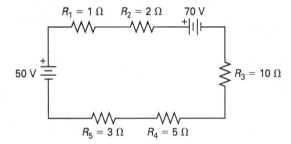

What is most nearly the voltage across the 10 Ω resistor?

(A) 9.5 V

(B) 24 V

(C) 33 V

(D) 57 V

9. A circuit consisting of a battery and resistors is shown.

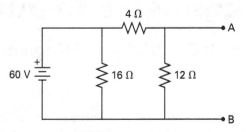

What are most nearly the Thevenin equivalent resistance and voltage, respectively, between terminals A and B?

(A) $R_{\text{Th}} = 3.0\ \Omega$, $V_{\text{Th}} = 45\ \text{V}$

(B) $R_{\text{Th}} = 7.5\ \Omega$, $V_{\text{Th}} = 7.5\ \text{V}$

(C) $R_{\text{Th}} = 7.5\ \Omega$, $V_{\text{Th}} = 60\ \text{V}$

(D) $R_{\text{Th}} = 12\ \Omega$, $V_{\text{Th}} = 5.0\ \text{V}$

10. The capacitor is initially uncharged in the circuit shown.

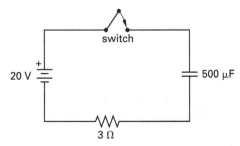

Most nearly, what is the approximate current 3 ms after the switch is closed?

(A) 0.34 A

(B) 0.67 A

(C) 0.82 A

(D) 0.90 A

SOLUTIONS

1. The complex power in polar (phasor) form is $S =$ 10 MVA$\angle\arccos 0.85 = 10$ MVA$\angle 31.79°$. The original real and reactive components are

$$P = S\cos\theta_1 = (10 \text{ MVA})\cos 31.79° = 8.5 \text{ MW}$$
$$Q = S\sin\theta_1 = (10 \text{ MVA})\sin 31.79° = 5.268 \text{ MVAR}$$
$$\mathbf{S} = P + jQ = 8.5 + j5.268$$

To change the power factor, add capacitive kVAR, which affects the reactive component only. The desired power factor, pf, is 0.97.

$$\text{pf} = \cos\theta_2 = 0.97$$
$$\theta_2 = \arccos 0.97$$
$$= 14.07°$$

The power triangles for the current and desired circuits are shown.

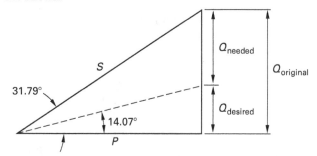

The new reactive power will be

$$Q_{\text{desired}} = P\left(\frac{\sin\theta_2}{\cos\theta_2}\right) = P\tan\theta_2$$
$$= (8.5 \text{ MW})\tan 14.07°$$
$$= 2.13 \text{ MVAR}$$

The capacitive reactive power needed is the difference between the original and desired reactive powers.

$$Q_{\text{needed}} = Q_{\text{original}} - Q_{\text{desired}}$$
$$= 5.268 \text{ MVAR} - 2.13 \text{ MVAR}$$
$$= 3.138 \text{ MVAR} \quad (3.1 \text{ MVAR})$$

The answer is (B).

2. Maximum power transfer occurs in an ideal transformer in which primary and secondary powers are equal.

$$P_P = P_S$$
$$I_P^2 R_P = I_S^2 R_S$$
$$\left(\frac{I_S}{I_P}\right)^2 = \frac{R_P}{R_S}$$

$$a^2 = \frac{R_P}{R_S}$$
$$a = \sqrt{\frac{R_P}{R_S}} = \sqrt{\frac{4000 \text{ }\Omega}{10 \text{ }\Omega}}$$
$$= 20$$
$$N_1 : N_2 = 20 : 1$$

The answer is (C).

3. The rms current is calculated from the peak current.

$$I_{\text{rms}} = \frac{I_{\text{max}}}{\sqrt{2}} = \frac{50 \text{ A}}{\sqrt{2}} = 35.36 \text{ A}$$

The phase angle is referenced to the voltage waveform. The current reaches its peak 90° before the voltage. Leading currents have positive phase shifts.

$$I = I_{\text{rms}}\angle\theta = 35.36 \text{ A}\angle 90° \quad (35 \text{ A}\angle 90°)$$

The answer is (B).

4. The magnetic flux density is

$$B = \mu H = \frac{\mu I}{2\pi r}$$

The flux is calculated from the magnetic flux density.

$$\phi = BA = \frac{\mu I A}{2\pi r}$$

The flux is proportional to the current. The new flux is

$$\phi_{\text{new}} = \phi_{\text{old}}\left(\frac{I_{\text{new}}}{I_{\text{old}}}\right)$$
$$= (30 \text{ mWb})\left(\frac{4 \text{ A}}{5 \text{ A}}\right)$$
$$= 24 \text{ mWb}$$

The answer is (C).

5. At $t = 0^+$, the transient current for an RC circuit is

$$i(t) = \left(\frac{V_{\text{bat}} - v_C(0)}{R} \right) e^{-t/RC}$$

$$i(0^+) = \left(\frac{5 \text{ V} - 2.0 \text{ V}}{1 \text{ } \Omega} \right) e^0$$

$$= 3.0 \text{ A}$$

The answer is (D).

6. The forcing frequency is

$$\omega = 2\pi f = 2\pi (60 \text{ Hz})$$

$$= 377 \text{ rad/s}$$

Find the impedances of the individual elements. For the inductor,

$$Z_L = j\omega L = j \left(377 \text{ } \frac{\text{rad}}{\text{s}} \right) (133 \times 10^{-3} \text{ H})$$

$$= j50 \text{ } \Omega$$

For the resistor,

$$Z_R = R = 100 \text{ } \Omega$$

For the capacitor,

$$Z_C = \frac{1}{j\omega C} = \frac{-j}{\omega C}$$

$$= \frac{-j}{\left(377 \text{ } \frac{\text{rad}}{\text{s}} \right) (26.5 \times 10^{-6} \text{ F})}$$

$$= -j100 \text{ } \Omega$$

Combine the impedances. Use the complex conjugate.

$$Z_{\text{eq}} = \frac{Z_R Z_C}{Z_R + Z_C} + Z_L = \frac{(100 \text{ } \Omega)(-j100 \text{ } \Omega)}{100 \text{ } \Omega - j100 \text{ } \Omega} + j50 \text{ } \Omega$$

$$= \frac{(100 \text{ } \Omega)(-j100 \text{ } \Omega)(100 \text{ } \Omega + j100 \text{ } \Omega)}{(100 \text{ } \Omega - j100 \text{ } \Omega)(100 \text{ } \Omega + j100 \text{ } \Omega)} + j50 \text{ } \Omega$$

$$= \frac{-j10^6 \text{ } \Omega^3 + 10^6 \text{ } \Omega^3}{2 \times 10^4 \text{ } \Omega^2} + j50 \text{ } \Omega$$

$$= -j50 \text{ } \Omega + 50 \text{ } \Omega + j50 \text{ } \Omega$$

$$= 50 \text{ } \Omega \angle 0°$$

The answer is (B).

7. The permittivity of a vacuum is

$$\varepsilon_0 = 8.85 \times 10^{-12} \text{ F/m}$$

The capacitance of the parallel plates is

$$C = \frac{\varepsilon A}{d} = \frac{24\varepsilon_0 A}{d}$$

$$= \frac{(24) \left(8.85 \times 10^{-12} \text{ } \frac{\text{F}}{\text{m}} \right) (200 \times 10^{-3} \text{ m})^2}{25 \times 10^{-3} \text{ m}}$$

$$= 3.4 \times 10^{-10} \text{ F}$$

The answer is (A).

8. The equivalent resistance and equivalent voltage are

$$R_{\text{eq}} = R_1 + R_2 + R_3 + R_4 + R_5$$

$$= 1 \text{ } \Omega + 2 \text{ } \Omega + 10 \text{ } \Omega + 5 \text{ } \Omega + 3 \text{ } \Omega$$

$$= 21 \text{ } \Omega$$

$$V_{\text{eq}} = V_1 + V_2 = 70 \text{ V} + (-50 \text{ V})$$

$$= 20 \text{ V}$$

Use Ohm's law to determine the current through the circuit.

$$V = IR$$

$$I = \frac{V}{R} = \frac{V_{\text{eq}}}{R_{\text{eq}}} = \frac{20 \text{ V}}{21 \text{ } \Omega}$$

$$= 0.952 \text{ A}$$

The voltage across any individual resistor is found from Ohm's law.

$$V = IR = (0.952 \text{ A})(10 \text{ } \Omega) = 9.52 \text{ V} \quad (9.5 \text{ V})$$

The answer is (A).

9. The Thevenin resistance is the resistance between the two terminals with the voltage source short-circuited. With the circuit shorted, the 16 Ω resistor is effectively bypassed, leaving the other two resistors in a simple parallel arrangement in relation to two terminals.

$$R_{\text{Th}} = \frac{(4 \text{ } \Omega)(12 \text{ } \Omega)}{4 \text{ } \Omega + 12 \text{ } \Omega} = 3.0 \text{ } \Omega$$

The Thevenin voltage is the voltage difference between the two terminals, which in this case is equal to the

voltage drop across the 12 Ω resistor. Use Ohm's law to
find the current $I_{12\Omega}$ and to find the voltage across the
resistor.

$$V = IR$$
$$I_{12\Omega} = \frac{V}{R} = \frac{60 \text{ V}}{4 \text{ }\Omega + 12 \text{ }\Omega} = 3.75 \text{ A}$$
$$V_{\text{Th}} = I_{12\Omega}R = (3.75 \text{ A})(12 \text{ }\Omega) = 45 \text{ V}$$

The answer is (A).

10. For an RC circuit transient,

$$i(t) = \left(\frac{V - v_c(0)}{R}\right)e^{-t/RC}$$
$$= \left(\frac{20 \text{ V} - 0 \text{ V}}{3 \text{ }\Omega}\right)e^{-0.003 \text{ s}/(3 \text{ }\Omega)(500\times 10^{-6}\text{ F})}$$
$$= 0.902 \text{ A} \quad (0.90 \text{ A})$$

The answer is (D).

33

Electrostatics

H	magnetic field
L	line or per unit length
S	per unit area, sheet, or surface
V	volume

Nomenclature

A	area	m^2
B	magnetic flux density	T
d	distance	m
E	electric field intensity	N/C or V/m
F	force	N
H	magnetic field strength	A/m
$i(t)$	time-varying current	A
I	constant current	A
J	current density	A/m^2
l	distance moved	m
L	length of a conductor	m
N	number	–
$q(t)$	time-varying charge	C
Q	constant charge	C
r	radius	m
S	surface area	m^2
t	time	s
v	velocity	m/s
v	voltage	V
V	constant voltage or potential difference	V
W	work	J

Symbols

ε	permittivity	F/m or $C^2/N{\cdot}m^2$
μ	permeability	H/m
ρ	flux density	C/m, C/m^2, or C/m^3
ϕ	magnetic flux	Wb
Φ	electric flux	C

Subscripts

0	free space (vacuum)
encl	enclosed

1. INTRODUCTION

Electric charge is a fundamental property of subatomic particles. The charge on an electron is negative one *electrostatic unit* (esu). The charge on a proton is positive one esu. A neutron has no charge. Charge is measured in the SI system in *coulombs* (C). One coulomb is approximately 6.24×10^{18} esu; the charge of one electron is -1.6×10^{-19} C.

Conservation of charge is a fundamental principle or law of physics. Electric charge can be distributed from one place to another under the influence of an electric field, but the algebraic sum of positive and negative charges in a system cannot change.

2. ELECTROSTATIC FIELDS

An *electric field*, E, with units of newtons per coulomb or volts per meter (N/C, same as V/m) is generated in the vicinity of an electric charge. The imaginary lines of force, as illustrated in Fig. 33.1, are called the *electric flux*, Φ. The direction of the electric flux is the same as the force applied by the electric field to a positive charge introduced into the field. If the field is produced by a positive charge, the force on another positive charge placed nearby will try to separate the two charges, and therefore, the lines of force will leave the first positive charge.

Figure 33.1 Electric Field Around a Positive Charge

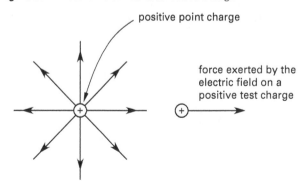

The electric field is a vector quantity having both magnitude and direction. The orientations of the field and flux lines always coincide (i.e., the direction of the electric field vector is always tangent to the flux lines). The total electric flux generated by a point charge is proportional to the charge.

$$\Phi = \frac{Q}{\varepsilon}$$

Equation 33.1 and Eq. 33.2: Forces on Charges

$$\mathbf{F} = Q\mathbf{E} \qquad 33.1$$

$$\mathbf{F}_2 = \frac{Q_1 Q_2}{4\pi\varepsilon r^2}\mathbf{a}_{r12} \qquad 33.2$$

Values

Electric flux does not pass equally well through all materials. It cannot pass through conductive metals at all and is canceled to various degrees by insulating media. The *permittivity* of a medium, ε, determines the flux that passes through the medium. For free space or air, $\varepsilon = \varepsilon_0 = 8.85 \times 10^{-12}$ F/m $= 8.85 \times 10^{-12}$ C²/N·m².

Description

In general, the *force on a test charge Q* in an electric field E is given by Eq. 33.1.

The force experienced by point charge 2, Q_2, in an electric field E created by point charge 1, Q_1, is given by *Coulomb's law*, Eq. 33.2. Because charges with opposite signs attract, Eq. 33.2 is positive for repulsion and negative for attraction. The unit vector $\mathbf{a}_{r12}$ is defined pointing from point charge 1 toward point charge 2. Although the unit vector $\mathbf{a}$ gives the direction explicitly, the direction of force can usually be found by inspection as the direction the object would move when released. Vector addition (i.e., superposition) can be used with systems of multiple point charges.

Example

Two point charges, Q_1 and Q_2, are shown. Q_1 is a charge of 5×10^{-6} C, and Q_2 is a charge of -10×10^{-6} C. The

permittivity of the medium is 8.85×10^{-12} F/m, and the distance between the charges is 10 cm.

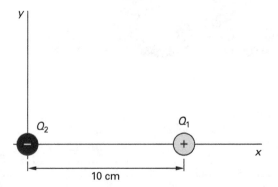

What are most nearly the magnitude and direction of the electrostatic force that acts on Q_2 due to Q_1?

(A) 45 N, from Q_1 to Q_2

(B) 45 N, from Q_2 to Q_1

(C) 89 N, from Q_2 to Q_1

(D) 110 N, from Q_1 to Q_2

Solution

The force is the direction Q_2 would move if unrestrained. Opposite charges attract, so the force is toward Q_1.

Find the magnitude of the force between the point charges using Coulomb's law, Eq. 33.2.

$$
\begin{aligned}
|\mathbf{F}_{21}| &= \frac{Q_1 Q_2}{4\pi\varepsilon r_{12}^2} \\
&= \frac{(5 \times 10^{-6}\ \text{C})(-10 \times 10^{-6}\ \text{C})}{4\pi\left(8.85 \times 10^{-12}\ \dfrac{\text{F}}{\text{m}}\right)\left(\dfrac{10\ \text{cm}}{100\ \dfrac{\text{cm}}{\text{m}}}\right)^2} \\
&= 44.96\ \text{N} \quad (45\ \text{N})
\end{aligned}
$$

The answer is (B).

Equation 33.3: Electric Field Intensity Due to a Point Charge

$$\mathbf{E} = \frac{Q_1}{4\pi\varepsilon r^2}\mathbf{a}_{r12} \qquad 33.3$$

Description

Equation 33.3 is the *electric field intensity* in a medium with permittivity ε at a distance r from a point charge Q_1. The direction of the electric field is represented by the unit vector $\mathbf{a}_{r12}$.

Equation 33.4: Line Charge

$$\mathbf{E}_L = \frac{\rho_L}{2\pi\varepsilon r}\mathbf{a}_r \qquad \textit{33.4}$$

Description

Not all electric fields are radial; the field direction depends on the shape and location of the charged bodies producing the field. For a *line charge* with density ρ_L (C/m), as shown in Fig. 33.2, the electric field is given by Eq. 33.4. *Flux density*, ρ_S (C/m²), is equal to the number of flux lines crossing a unit area perpendicular to the flux. In Eq. 33.4, ρ_L may be interpreted as the *flux density per unit width*. The unit vector $\mathbf{a}_r$ is normal to the line of charge in the cylindrical (radial) coordinate system.

Figure 33.2 Electric Field from a Line Charge

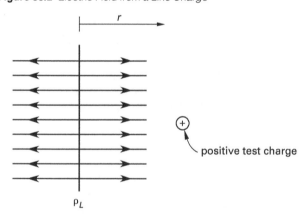

Equation 33.5: Sheet Charge

$$\mathbf{E}_S = \frac{\rho_S}{2\varepsilon}\mathbf{a}_z \quad [z > 0] \qquad \textit{33.5}$$

Description

For a *sheet charge* density of ρ_S (C/m²), as shown in Fig. 33.3, the electric field is given by Eq. 33.5. The unit vector $\mathbf{a}_z$ is normal to the sheet. The lines of flux do not diverge, so the flux density is not dependent on the distance, z, from the sheet.

Figure 33.3 Electric Field from a Sheet Charge

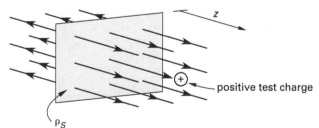

The density of the sheet charge is the total charge divided by the plate area.

$$\rho_S = \frac{Q}{A}$$

The electric field intensity (see Eq. 33.3) usually has an inverse square relationship to r. Equation 33.4 has an inverse relationship to the separation distance, r, but Eq. 33.5 has no relationship to r. This is due to the assumptions that the line length and the sheet area are infinite, and r is small compared to the size of the line or sheet.

Example

A thin metal plate with dimensions of 20 cm × 20 cm carries a total charge of 24 µC. What is most nearly the magnitude of the electric field 2.5 cm away from the center of the plate?

- (A) 1.3×10^3 N/C
- (B) 3.7×10^6 N/C
- (C) 3.4×10^7 N/C
- (D) 4.3×10^8 N/C

Solution

The separation distance is much smaller than the dimensions of the plate, so the plate can be considered infinite. The density of the sheet charge is

$$\rho_S = \frac{Q}{A}$$
$$= \frac{24 \ \mu C}{\left(\dfrac{20 \ cm}{100 \ \dfrac{cm}{m}}\right)^2 \left(10^6 \ \dfrac{\mu C}{C}\right)}$$
$$= 6 \times 10^{-4} \ C/m^2$$

From Eq. 33.5, the sheet charge is

$$|\mathbf{E}_S| = \left|\frac{\rho_S}{2\varepsilon}\mathbf{a}_z\right|$$
$$= \frac{6 \times 10^{-4} \ \dfrac{C}{m^2}}{(2)\left(8.85 \times 10^{-12} \ \dfrac{F}{m}\right)}$$
$$= 3.39 \times 10^7 \ N/C \quad (3.4 \times 10^7 \ N/C)$$

The units F/m are equivalent to C²/N·m².

The answer is (C).

Equation 33.6: Gauss' Law

$$Q_{\text{encl}} = \oiint_S \varepsilon \mathbf{E} \cdot d\mathbf{S} \qquad 33.6$$

Variations

$$\Phi = \frac{\sum q_{\text{encl}}}{\varepsilon} = \frac{Q_{\text{encl}}}{\varepsilon}$$

$$\Phi = \oiint_S \mathbf{E} \cdot d\mathbf{S}$$

Description

Gauss' law states that the total electric flux passing out of an enclosing (closed) surface (i.e., the *Gaussian surface*) is proportional to the total charge within the surface, as shown in the variation equation.

The mathematical formulation of Gauss' law (see Eq. 33.6) states that the total enclosed charge can be determined by summing all of the electric fields on the Gaussian surface, **S**. The variable $d\mathbf{S}$ is a vector that represents an infinitesimal part of the closed surface, the direction of which is perpendicular to the surface.

Equation 33.7 and Eq. 33.8: Work and Energy in Electric Fields

$$W = -Q \int_{p_1}^{p_2} \mathbf{E} \cdot d\mathbf{l} \qquad 33.7$$

$$W_E = (1/2) \iiint_V \varepsilon |\mathbf{E}|^2 \, dV \qquad 33.8$$

Description

The *work*, W, performed by moving a charge Q_1 radially from point p_1 to point p_2 in an electric field is given by Eq. 33.7.[1] (The dot product of two vectors is a scalar.) The energy stored in an electric field is given by Eq. 33.8.

The work, W, performed in moving a point charge Q_B in the radial direction from distance r_1 to r_2 within a field created by a point charge Q_A is given by

$$W = -\int_{r_1}^{r_2} \mathbf{F} \cdot d\mathbf{r} = -\int_{r_1}^{r_2} \frac{Q_A Q_B}{4\pi\varepsilon r^2} \, dr$$

$$= \left(\frac{Q_A Q_B}{4\pi\varepsilon} \right) \left(\frac{1}{r_2} - \frac{1}{r_1} \right)$$

Work is positive if an external force is required to move the charges (e.g., to bring two repulsive charges together or move a charge against an electric field). Work is negative if the field does the work (allowing attracting charges to approach each other, or allowing repulsive charges to separate).

Work is performed only in moving the charges closer or further apart. Moving one point charge around the other in a constant-radius circle performs no work. In general, no work is performed in moving a charged object perpendicular to an electric field.

For a uniform field (as exists between two charged plates separated by a distance d), the work done in moving an object of charge Q a distance l parallel to the uniform field is given by

$$W = -\mathbf{F} \cdot \mathbf{l} = -EQl = \frac{-V_{\text{plates}} Q l}{d}$$

$$= -Q \Delta V$$

Example

What is most nearly the work required to move a positive charge of 10 C for a distance of 5 m in the same direction as a uniform field of 50 V/m?

- (A) $-13\,000$ J
- (B) -2500 J
- (C) -100 J
- (D) -20 J

Solution

From Eq. 33.7, the work required to move a charge in a uniform field is

$$W = -Q \int_{p_1}^{p_2} \mathbf{E} \cdot d\mathbf{l} = -QEl$$

$$= -(10 \text{ C}) \left(50 \, \frac{\text{V}}{\text{m}} \right) (5 \text{ m})$$

$$= -2500 \text{ C} \cdot \text{V} \quad (-2500 \text{ J})$$

The positive charge moves in the direction of the field. Therefore, no external work is required, and the charge returns potential energy to the field.

The answer is (B).

---

[1] In Eq. 33.7, the NCEES *FE Reference Handbook* (*NCEES Handbook*) shows the limits of integration as p_1 and p_2. However, the variable p is not in the equation. Equation 33.7 should not be interpreted too literally, since p is not a variable.

3. VOLTAGE

Voltage is another way to describe the strength of an electric field, using a scalar quantity rather than a vector quantity. The *potential difference*, V, is the difference in electric potential between two points. Potential difference is equal to the work required to move one unit charge from one point to the other. This difference in potential is one volt if one joule of work is expended in moving one coulomb of charge from one point to the other.

Equation 33.9: Electric Field Strength Between Two Parallel Plates

$$E = \frac{V}{d} \qquad \text{33.9}$$

Description

The electric field strength between two parallel plates with potential difference V and separated by a distance d is given by Eq. 33.9.

By convention, the field is directed from the positive plate to the negative plate.

Example

What is most nearly the electric field strength between two plates separated by 0.005 m that are connected across 100 V?

(A) 0.5 kV/m

(B) 2 kV/m

(C) 5 kV/m

(D) 20 kV/m

Solution

Calculate the electric field strength using Eq. 33.9.

$$E = \frac{V}{d} = \frac{100 \text{ V}}{(0.005 \text{ m})\left(1000 \ \dfrac{\text{V}}{\text{kV}}\right)} = 20 \text{ kV/m}$$

The answer is (D).

4. CURRENT

Equation 33.10: Current in Electric Fields

$$i(t) = dq(t)/dt \qquad \text{33.10}$$

Description

Current, $i(t)$, is the movement of charges. By convention, the current moves in a direction opposite to the flow of electrons (i.e., the current flows from the positive terminal to the negative terminal). Current is measured in amperes (A) and is the time rate change of charge (i.e., the current is equal to the number of coulombs of charge passing a point each second). If $q(t)$ is the instantaneous charge, then the current is given by Eq. 33.10.

If the rate of change in charge is constant, the current is denoted as I.

$$I = \frac{dq}{dt}$$

The *areal current density*, J (usually referred to simply as *current density*), is the current per unit surface area. Since current density is charge per unit time, the current can be written as the rate of change of charge surface density.

$$J = \frac{I}{S} = \frac{\dot{\rho}_S S}{S} = \dot{\rho}_S$$

The *volume current density*, J_V, is the current per unit volume. For a conductor with cross-sectional area S and length L, the volume current density can be expressed as the product of the charge surface density and charge velocity, v.

$$J_V = \frac{I}{V} = \frac{\dot{\rho}_S S}{SL} = \rho_S \text{v}$$

The current in the direction perpendicular to a surface, S, can be determined by integrating the current density moving through the surface.

$$i = \int_S \mathbf{J} \cdot d\mathbf{S}$$

Example

The current in a particular DC circuit is numerically equal to one-quarter of the time the current has been running through the circuit. Assuming the circuit starts out carrying no current, what is most nearly the electrical charge delivered by the circuit in 5 s?

(A) 0.2 C

(B) 3 C

(C) 6 C

(D) 30 C

Solution

Rearrange Eq. 33.10 to solve for charge. Because this calculation assumes that $i(t) = t/4$, the calculation is dimensionally inconsistent.

$$i(t) = dq(t)/dt$$

$$\frac{t}{4} = \frac{dq(t)}{dt}$$

$$\int dq(t) = \int_{0\,\text{s}}^{5\,\text{s}} \frac{t}{4}\,dt = \frac{t^2}{8}\Big|_{0\,\text{s}}^{5\,\text{s}}$$

$$= \frac{(5\,\text{s})^2}{8} - \frac{(0\,\text{s})^2}{8}$$

$$= 3.125\,\text{C} \quad (3\,\text{C})$$

The answer is (B).

5. MAGNETIC FIELDS

A magnetic field can exist only with two opposite, equal poles called the *north pole* and *south pole*. This is unlike an electric field, which can be produced by a single charged object. Figure 33.4 illustrates two common permanent magnetic field configurations. It also illustrates the convention that the lines of magnetic flux are directed from the north pole (i.e., the *magnetic source*) to the south pole (i.e., the *magnetic sink*).

Figure 33.4 *Magnetic Fields from Permanent Magnets*

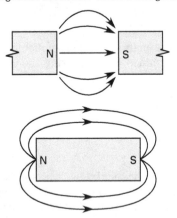

The total amount of magnetic flux in a magnetic field is ϕ, measured in webers (Wb). The flux is given by *Gauss' law* for a magnetic field.

$$\phi = \oint \mathbf{B} \cdot d\mathbf{A} = 0$$

The magnetic flux density, **B**, in teslas (T), equivalent to Wb/m², is one of two measures of the strength of a magnetic field. For this reason, it can be referred to as the *strength of the B-field*. (**B** should never be called the magnetic field strength, as that name is reserved for the variable **H**.) **B** is also known as the *magnetic induction*.

The magnetic flux density is found by dividing the magnetic flux by an area perpendicular to it. Magnetic flux density is a vector quantity, calculated from

$$\mathbf{B} = \frac{\phi}{A}\mathbf{a}$$

The direction of the magnetic field, illustrated in Fig. 33.5, is given by the *right-hand rule*. In the case of a straight wire, the thumb indicates the current direction, and the fingers curl in the field direction; for a coil, the fingers indicate the current flow, and the thumb indicates the field direction.

Figure 33.5 *Right-Hand Rule for the Magnetic Flux Direction in a Coil*

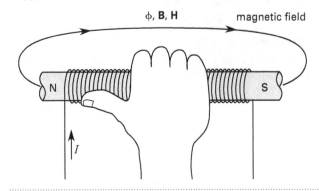

Equation 33.11: Magnetic Field Strength

$$\mathbf{H} = \frac{\mathbf{B}}{\mu} = \frac{I\mathbf{a}_\phi}{2\pi r} \qquad \text{33.11}$$

Values

The *permeability of free space* (air or vacuum) is $\mu_0 = 4\pi \times 10^{-7}$ H/m.

Description

The *magnetic field strength*, **H**, with units of A/m, is derived from the magnetic flux density as in Eq. 33.11.

The magnetic flux density, **B**, is dependent on the *permeability* of the medium much like the electric flux density is dependent on permittivity.

Example

A magnetic field in air has a magnetic flux density of 1×10^{-8} T. What is most nearly the strength of the magnetic field in a vacuum?

(A) 3×10^{-4} A/m

(B) 8×10^{-3} A/m

(C) 3×10^{-2} A/m

(D) 8×10^{-2} A/m

Solution

The permeability of free space is $4\pi \times 10^{-7}$ H/m. The strength of the magnetic field is

$$H = \frac{B}{\mu_0}$$

$$= \frac{1 \times 10^{-8} \text{ T}}{4\pi \times 10^{-7} \frac{\text{H}}{\text{m}}}$$

$$= 7.96 \times 10^{-3} \text{ A/m} \quad (8 \times 10^{-3} \text{ A/m})$$

The answer is (B).

Equation 33.12: Force on a Current-Carrying Conductor in a Uniform Magnetic Field

$$\mathbf{F} = I\mathbf{L}\times\mathbf{B} \qquad\qquad 33.12$$

Description

The analogy to Coulomb's law, where a force is imposed on a stationary charge in an electric field, is that a magnetic field imposes a force on a moving charge. The force on a wire carrying a current I in a uniform magnetic field $\mathbf{B}$ is given by Eq. 33.12. $\mathbf{L}$ is the length vector of the conductor and points in the direction of the current. The force acts at right angles to both the current and magnetic flux density directions.

Equation 33.13: Energy Stored in a Magnetic Field

$$W_H = (1/2) \iiint_V \mu \, |\mathbf{H}|^2 \, dv \qquad\qquad 33.13$$

Variation

$$W_H = \frac{1}{2} \iiint_V \mathbf{B}{\cdot}\mathbf{H}\,dV$$

Description

The energy stored in volume V within a magnetic field, $\mathbf{H}$, can be calculated from Eq. 33.13.[2] Equation 33.13 assumes that the $\mathbf{B}$ and $\mathbf{H}$ fields are in the same direction. Assuming the magnetic field is constant throughout the volume V, Eq. 33.13 reduces further to

$$W_H = \frac{\mu H^2 V}{2} = \frac{B^2 V}{2\mu}$$

The integral over any closed surface of magnetic flux density must be zero. Stated another way, magnetic flux lines must follow a closed path, and no matter how large or small the enclosing surface is, the path must be either entirely inside the surface or it must go out and back in. This law is referred to as the "no isolated magnetic charge" or "no magnetic monopoles" law.

6. INDUCED VOLTAGE

Equation 33.14 and Eq. 33.15: Faraday's Law of Induction

$$v = -N \, d\phi/dt \qquad\qquad 33.14$$

$$\phi = \int_S \mathbf{B}{\cdot}d\mathbf{S} \qquad\qquad 33.15$$

Variation

$$v = -NBL\frac{ds}{dt}$$

Description

Faraday's law of induction states that an induced voltage, v, also called the *electromotive force* or emf, will be generated in a circuit when there is a change in the magnetic flux. Figure 33.6 illustrates one of N series-connected conductors cutting across magnetic flux ϕ, calculated from Eq. 33.15.

The magnitude of the electromagnetic induction is given by *Faraday's law*, Eq. 33.14. The minus sign indicates the direction of the induced voltage, which is specified by *Lenz's law* to be opposite to the direction of the magnetic field.

Figure 33.6 *Conductor Moving in a Magnetic Field*

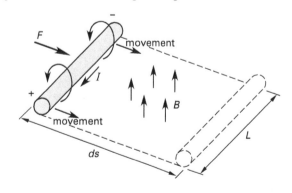

---

[2]The *NCEES Handbook* presents the differential volume in Eq. 33.13 as dv, which is inconsistent with the parallel equation, Eq. 33.8, which uses dV. Since v represents voltage and V is used for volume throughout, the *NCEES Handbook*'s use of dv is considered an error. This section presents Eq. 33.13 with V (not v) and so differs slightly from the *NCEES Handbook*'s equation.

Example

A coil has 100 turns. The magnetic flux in the coil decreases from 20 Wb to 10 Wb in 5 s. What is most nearly the magnitude of the voltage induced in the coil?

(A) 50 V

(B) 100 V

(C) 200 V

(D) 300 V

Solution

Use Faraday's law, Eq. 33.14, to find the voltage induced in the coil.

$$v = -N\, d\phi/dt = \frac{-(100)(20\ \text{Wb} - 10\ \text{Wb})}{5\ \text{s} - 0\ \text{s}}$$
$$= -200\ \text{V} \quad (200\ \text{V})$$

The answer is (C).

34

Direct-Current Circuits

Nomenclature

A	area	m^2
C	capacitance	F
d	diameter	m
d	distance	m
$i(t)$	time-varying current	A
I	constant current	A
l	length	m
L	inductance	H
L	length	m
N	number of turns	–
P	power	W
$q(t)$	time-varying charge	C
Q	constant charge	C
R	resistance	Ω
t	time	s
v	voltage	V
$v(t)$	time-varying voltage	V
V	constant voltage	V

Symbols

ε	permittivity	F/m or $C^2/N \cdot m^2$
μ	permeability	H/m
ρ	resistivity	$\Omega \cdot m$
τ	time constant	s

Subscripts

C	capacitive
eq	equivalent
ext	external
fs	full scale
L	inductive or inductor
N	Norton
oc	open circuit
P	parallel
R	reactive
sc	short circuit
S	series
Th	Thevenin

1. INTRODUCTION

Electrical circuits contain active and passive elements. *Active elements* are elements that can generate electric energy, such as voltage and current sources. *Passive elements*, such as capacitors and inductors, absorb or store electric energy; other passive elements, such as resistors, dissipate electric energy.

An *ideal voltage source* supplies power at a constant voltage, regardless of the current drawn. An *ideal current source* supplies power at a constant current independent of the voltage across its terminals. However, real sources have internal resistances that, at higher currents, decrease the available voltage. Therefore, a real voltage source cannot maintain a constant voltage when currents become large. *Independent sources* deliver voltage and current at their rated values regardless of circuit parameters. *Dependent sources* deliver voltage and current at levels determined by voltages or currents elsewhere in the circuit. The symbols for electrical circuit elements and sources are given in Table 34.1.

Table 34.1 Circuit Element Symbols

symbol	circuit element
$\overset{\text{-\Large\wedge\wedge\wedge-}}{R}$	resistor
$\overset{\text{-\large\vdash\vdash-}}{C}$	capacitor
$\overset{\text{-\large mmm-}}{L}$	inductor
$\overset{-\bigcirc+}{V}$ or $\overset{\vdash\vert\vert\vdash}{V}$	independent voltage source
$\overset{\bigcirc\!\!\leftarrow}{I}$	independent current source
$\overset{+\diamondsuit-}{gV}$	dependent voltage source
$\overset{\diamondsuit\!\!\leftarrow}{gI}$	dependent current source

DC Voltage

Voltage, measured in volts (a combined unit equivalent to W/A, C/F, J/C, A/S, and Wb/s), is used to measure the *potential difference* across terminals of circuit elements. Any device that provides electrical energy is called a *seat of an electromotive force* (emf), and the electromotive force is also measured in volts.

2. RESISTORS

Equation 34.1: Resistance

$$R = \frac{\rho L}{A} \qquad 34.1$$

Description

Resistance, R (measured in ohms, Ω), is the property of a circuit or circuit element to oppose current flow. A circuit with zero resistance is a *short circuit*, whereas an *open circuit* has infinite resistance.

Resistors are usually constructed from carbon compounds, ceramics, oxides, or coiled wire. *Resistance* depends on the *resistivity*, ρ (in $\Omega \cdot m$), which is a material property, and the length and cross-sectional area of the resistor. Resistors with larger cross-sectional areas have more free electrons available to carry charge and have less resistance. Each of the free electrons has a limited ability to move, so the electromotive force must overcome the limited mobility for the entire length of the resistor. The resistance increases with the length of the resistor.

Example

A power line is made of copper (resistivity of 1.83×10^{-6} $\Omega \cdot cm$). The wire diameter is 2 cm. What is most nearly the resistance of 5 km of power line?

(A) $0.0032\ \Omega$

(B) $0.29\ \Omega$

(C) $0.67\ \Omega$

(D) $1.8\ \Omega$

Solution

The wire's resistance is directly proportional to its length and inversely proportional to its cross-sectional area. From Eq. 34.1,

$$
\begin{aligned}
R &= \frac{\rho L}{A} \\
&= \frac{\rho L}{\frac{\pi}{4} d^2} \\
&= \frac{(1.83 \times 10^{-6}\ \Omega \cdot cm)(5\ km)\left(10^5\ \dfrac{cm}{km}\right)}{\left(\dfrac{\pi}{4}\right)(2\ cm)^2} \\
&= 0.29\ \Omega
\end{aligned}
$$

The answer is (B).

Equation 34.2 Through Eq. 34.4: Resistors in Series and Parallel

$$R_S = R_1 + R_2 + \cdots + R_n \qquad 34.2$$

$$R_P = 1/(1/R_1 + 1/R_2 + \cdots + 1/R_n) \qquad 34.3$$

$$R_P = \frac{R_1 R_2}{R_1 + R_2} \qquad 34.4$$

Description

Resistors connected in series share the same current and may be represented by an *equivalent resistance* equal to the sum of the individual resistances. For n resistors in series, the *total resistance*, R_S, is given by Eq. 34.2.

Resistors connected in parallel share the same voltage drop and may be represented by an equivalent resistance equal to the reciprocal of the sum of the reciprocals of the individual resistances. For n resistors in parallel, the total resistance, R_P, is given by Eq. 34.3. The equivalent resistance of two resistors in parallel is given by Eq. 34.4.

Example

For the circuit shown, what is most nearly the equivalent resistance seen by the battery?

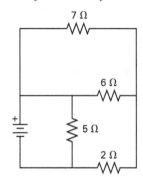

- (A) 0.38 Ω
- (B) 2.2 Ω
- (C) 2.6 Ω
- (D) 6.2 Ω

Solution

Redraw the circuit.

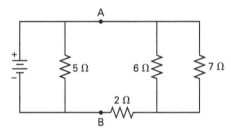

The 7 Ω and 6 Ω resistors are in parallel. The equivalent resistance of terminals A and B is

$$R_{AB} = \frac{(7\ \Omega)(6\ \Omega)}{7\ \Omega + 6\ \Omega} + 2\ \Omega$$
$$= 5.231\ \Omega$$

Using Eq. 34.4, the total resistance seen by the battery is

$$R_P = \frac{R_1 R_2}{R_1 + R_2}$$
$$= \frac{(5.231\ \Omega)(5\ \Omega)}{5.231\ \Omega + 5\ \Omega}$$
$$= 2.556\ \Omega \quad (2.6\ \Omega)$$

The answer is (C).

Equation 34.5: Joule's Law

$$P = VI = \frac{V^2}{R} = I^2 R \qquad 34.5$$

Description

Power is the time rate of energy delivery, usually manifested as a time rate of useful work performed or heat dissipated. In electric circuits, the energy is provided by voltage and/or current sources. In purely resistive circuits, the energy is dissipated in the resistance elements as heat.

In a *direct current* (DC) *circuit*, steady-state voltage and current, V and I respectively, are constant over time.[1] The power dissipated in an individual component with resistance R, or in a circuit with an equivalent resistance R, is given by *Joule's law* (see Eq. 34.5).

Example

A 10 kV power line has a total resistance of 1000 Ω. The current in the line is 10 A. What is most nearly the power lost due to resistive heating?

- (A) 1 kW
- (B) 10 kW
- (C) 100 kW
- (D) 1000 kW

Solution

Use Joule's law, Eq. 34.5.

$$P = I^2 R$$
$$= \frac{(10\ \text{A})^2 (1000\ \Omega)}{1000\ \dfrac{\text{W}}{\text{kW}}}$$
$$= 100\ \text{kW}$$

Check.

$$P = VI$$
$$= \frac{(10\ \text{kV})\left(1000\ \dfrac{\text{V}}{\text{kV}}\right)(10\ \text{A})}{1000\ \dfrac{\text{W}}{\text{kW}}}$$
$$= 100\ \text{kW}$$

The answer is (C).

---

[1]When energy sources are first connected, *unsteady conditions* (*transient conditions*) may develop.

3. CAPACITORS

Equation 34.6 Through Eq. 34.11: Capacitors

$$q_C(t) = C v_C(t) \qquad 34.6$$

$$C = q_C(t)/v_C(t) \qquad 34.7$$

$$C = \frac{\varepsilon A}{d} \qquad 34.8$$

$$i_C(t) = C(dv_C/dt) \qquad 34.9$$

$$v_C(t) = v_C(0) + \frac{1}{C}\int_0^t i_C(\tau)\,d\tau \qquad 34.10$$

$$\text{energy} = Cv_C^2/2 = q_C^2/2C = q_C v_C/2 \qquad 34.11$$

Variation

$$Q = CV \quad [\text{constant } V]$$

Description

A *capacitor* is a device that stores electric charge. Figure 34.1 shows the symbol for a capacitor.[2] A capacitor is constructed as two conducting surfaces separated by an insulator, such as oiled paper, mica, or air. A simple type of capacitor (i.e., the *parallel plate capacitor*) is constructed as two parallel plates. If the plates are connected across a voltage potential, charges of opposite polarity will build up on the plates and create an electric field between the plates. The amount of charge, Q, built up is proportional to the applied voltage. The constant of proportionality, C, is the *capacitance* in farads (F) and depends on the capacitor construction. Capacitance represents the ability to store charge; the greater the capacitance, the greater the charge stored. (See Eq. 34.6 and Eq. 34.7.)

Figure 34.1 *Capacitor Symbol*

Equation 34.8 gives the capacitance of two parallel plates of equal area A separated by distance d. ε is the *permittivity* of the medium separating the plates.

The current passed by a capacitor is the derivative of the voltage times the capacitance. (See Eq. 34.9.) The voltage depends on the amount of charge (number of charged particles) on the capacitor. Since charged particles are matter, they cannot instantaneously change in quantity. Therefore, the voltage cannot instantaneously change. However, the number of charges leaving the capacitor can instantaneously change, so the current can change instantaneously. Any change in charge on a capacitor is manifested as current in the circuit. Equation 34.10 shows that the voltage across a capacitor changes as the current changes.[3]

The total energy (in joules) stored in a capacitor is given by Eq. 34.11.[4]

Unless voltage changes with time, the amount of charge on a capacitor will not change, and accordingly, there will be no current flow. At steady state, the voltage across all circuit elements in a DC circuit is constant, so no current flows through capacitors in the circuit. At steady state, capacitors in DC circuits behave as open circuits and pass no current.

Example

The capacitor shown has a capacitance of 2.5×10^{-10} F.

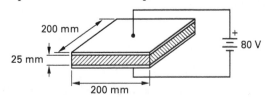

---

[2]The most generic symbol for a capacitor represents the "plates" by two parallel straight lines. This is the symbol used consistently in this book. A flat-plate capacitor has no polarity, and each plate can hold either positive or negative charges. Some capacitors (e.g., electrolytic capacitors) are polarized, requiring the positive capacitor lead to be connected to the more positive part of the circuit. In Fig. 34.1, the NCEES *FE Reference Handbook* (*NCEES Handbook*) shows a *polarized capacitor*.

[3]Not only does the *NCEES Handbook* use the variable reserved for a capacitive time constant, but Eq. 34.10 makes a confusing and unnecessary change of variables in an attempt to differentiate between "real time," t, and "capacitor time," τ. Since the first term, $v_C(0)$, shows that real time starts from $t = 0$ (the same as the lower integration limit of capacitor time), and since real time ends at t (the same as the upper integration limit of capacitor time), t and τ are the same. Equation 34.10 could have been presented as

$$v_C(t) = v_C(0) + \frac{1}{C}\int_0^t i_C(t)\,dt$$

[4]The *NCEES Handbook* is inconsistent in how it represents electrical energy and work terms. The "energy" in Eq. 34.11 and Eq. 34.17 is the same as W_E in Eq. 33.8.

What is most nearly the energy stored in the capacitor?

(A) 0.2 μJ

(B) 0.8 μJ

(C) 1.0 μJ

(D) 20 μJ

Solution

Using Eq. 34.11, the energy stored in the capacitor is

$$\text{energy} = Cv_C^2/2 = \frac{(2.5 \times 10^{-10} \text{ F})(80 \text{ V})^2 \left(10^6 \frac{\mu\text{J}}{\text{J}}\right)}{2}$$

$$= 0.8 \ \mu\text{J}$$

The answer is (B).

Equation 34.12 and Eq. 34.13: Capacitors in Series and Parallel

$$C_S = \frac{1}{1/C_1 + 1/C_2 + \cdots + 1/C_n} \qquad 34.12$$

$$C_P = C_1 + C_2 + \cdots + C_n \qquad 34.13$$

Description

The *total capacitance* of capacitors connected in series, C_S, is given by Eq. 34.12. The total capacitance of capacitors connected in parallel, C_P, is given by Eq. 34.13.

Example

What is most nearly the equivalent capacitance between terminals A and B?

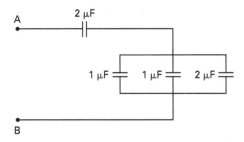

(A) 1.1 μF

(B) 1.3 μF

(C) 2.4 μF

(D) 4.0 μF

Solution

The three capacitors in parallel combine according to Eq. 34.13.

$$C_P = C_1 + C_2 + C_3$$

$$= 1 \ \mu\text{F} + 1 \ \mu\text{F} + 2 \ \mu\text{F}$$

$$= 4 \ \mu\text{F}$$

This equivalent capacitance is in series with the 2 μF capacitor. From Eq. 34.12,

$$C_S = \frac{1}{1/C_1 + 1/C_2} = \frac{1}{\frac{1}{4 \ \mu\text{F}} + \frac{1}{2 \ \mu\text{F}}}$$

$$= 1.33 \ \mu\text{F} \quad (1.3 \ \mu\text{F})$$

The answer is (B).

4. INDUCTORS

Equation 34.14 Through Eq. 34.19: Inductors

$$L = N^2 \mu A/l \qquad 34.14$$

$$v_L(t) = L(di_L/dt) \qquad 34.15$$

$$i_L(t) = i_L(0) + \frac{1}{L} \int_0^t v_L(\tau) d\tau \qquad 34.16$$

$$\text{energy} = Li_L^2/2 \qquad 34.17$$

$$L_P = \frac{1}{1/L_1 + 1/L_2 + \cdots + 1/L_n} \qquad 34.18$$

$$L_S = L_1 + L_2 + \cdots + L_n \qquad 34.19$$

Description

An *inductor* is basically a coil of wire. When connected across a voltage source, current begins to flow in the coil, establishing a magnetic field that opposes current changes. Figure 34.2 shows the symbol for an inductor. Usually, the wire is coiled around a core of magnetic material (high permeability) to increase the inductance. (See Fig. 34.3.) From Faraday's law, the induced voltage across the ends of the inductor is proportional to the change in flux linkage, which in turn is proportional to the current change. The constant of proportionality is the *inductance*, *L*, expressed in henries (H). (See Eq. 34.14.)[5] Equation 34.19 gives the general definition of an inductor. Energy is stored within the magnetic field and the inductor does not dissipate energy.

Figure 34.2 Inductor

Figure 34.3 Inductor

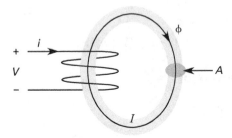

The voltage across an inductor is the derivative of the current times the inductance. (See Eq. 34.15.) The current of inductors cannot change instantaneously, but the voltage can change instantaneously. The current will change as the inductor integrates the voltage to produce a current that opposes the change. (See Eq. 34.16.)

The current depends on the number of charged particles moving through the inductor. Since charged particles are physical matter, they cannot instantaneously change in quantity. Therefore, the current moving in an inductor cannot instantaneously change. However, the voltage across an inductor can instantaneously change. Any change in voltage across an inductor is manifested as a current change in the circuit. Equation 34.16 shows that the current through an inductor changes as the voltage changes.[6]

The total energy (in joules) stored in the electric field of an inductor carrying instantaneous current i_L is given by Eq. 34.17.

The total inductance of inductors connected in parallel, L_P, is given by Eq. 34.18. The total inductance of inductors connected in series, L_S, is given by Eq. 34.19.

5. DC CIRCUIT ANALYSIS

Most circuit problems involve solving for unknown parameters, such as the voltage or current across some element in the circuit. The methods that are used to find these parameters rely on combining elements in series and parallel, and applying Ohm's law or Kirchhoff's laws in a systematic manner.

Equation 34.20: Ohm's Law

$$V = IR \qquad 34.20$$

Description

The *voltage drop*, also known as the *IR drop*, across a circuit with resistance *R* is given by *Ohm's law*, Eq. 34.20.

Using Ohm's law implicitly assumes a *linear circuit* (i.e., one consisting of linear elements and linear sources). A *linear element* is a passive element whose performance can be represented by a linear voltage-current relationship. The output of a linear source is proportional to the first power of a voltage or current in the circuit. Many components used in electronic devices do not obey Ohm's law over their entire operating ranges.

Example

The voltage between nodes B and E in the circuit shown is 300 V.

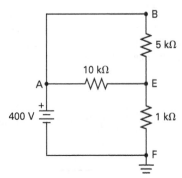

What is most nearly the current flowing between nodes B and E?

(A) 30 mA

(B) 60 mA

(C) 70 mA

(D) 80 mA

---

[5]*L* is the traditional symbol for inductance. However, the *NCEES Handbook* previously used *L* to designate length (see Eq. 34.12 and Eq. 34.1), which is likely the reason for using *l* to represent length in Eq. 34.14.

[6]Not only does the *NCEES Handbook* use the variable reserved for an inductive time constant, but *NCEES Handbook* Eq. 34.16 makes a confusing and unnecessary change of variables in an attempt to differentiate between "real time," *t*, and "inductor time," τ. Since the first term, $i_L(0)$, shows that real time starts from $t = 0$ (the same as the lower integration limit of inductor time), and since real time ends at *t* (the same as the upper integration limit of inductor time), *t* and τ are the same. Equation 34.16 could have been presented as

$$i_L(t) = i_L(0) + \frac{1}{L}\int_0^t v_L(t)dt$$

Solution

The voltage difference between nodes B and E is given. From Ohm's law,

$$V = IR$$

$$I_{BE} = \frac{V_{BE}}{R}$$

$$= \frac{(300 \text{ V})\left(1000 \ \dfrac{mA}{A}\right)}{(5 \text{ k}\Omega)\left(1000 \ \dfrac{\Omega}{k\Omega}\right)}$$

$$= 60 \text{ mA}$$

The answer is (B).

Equation 34.21 and Eq. 34.22: Kirchhoff's Laws

$$\sum I_{in} = \sum I_{out} \qquad 34.21$$

$$\sum V_{rises} = \sum V_{drops} \qquad 34.22$$

Description

Kirchhoff's current law (KCL) (see Eq. 34.21) states that as much current flows out of a node (connection) as flows into it. Electrons must be conserved at any node in an electrical circuit.

Kirchhoff's voltage law (KVL) (see Eq. 34.22) states that the algebraic sum of voltage drops around any closed path within a circuit is equal to the sum of the voltage rises.

Example

In the steady-state circuit shown, all components are ideal.

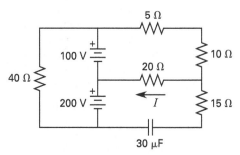

What is most nearly the magnitude of the current through the 20 Ω resistor?

(A)   2.0 A

(B)   2.9 A

(C)   5.0 A

(D)   5.7 A

Solution

Since this is a DC circuit, the capacitor blocks current flow. No current will flow through it.

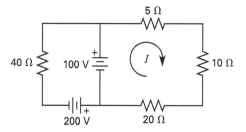

The only voltage source in the loop containing the 5 Ω, 10 Ω, and 20 Ω resistors is the 100 V battery. Write Kirchhoff's voltage law for the loop.

$$\sum V = \sum IR = I\sum R$$

$$100 \text{ V} = I(5 \ \Omega + 10 \ \Omega + 20 \ \Omega)$$

$$I = 2.86 \text{ A} \quad (2.9 \text{ A})$$

The answer is (B).

Rules for Simple Resistive Circuits

In a simple series (single-loop) circuit, such as the circuit shown in Fig. 34.4, the following rules apply.

- The current is the same through all circuit elements.

$$I = I_{R_1} = I_{R_2} = I_{R_3}$$

- The *equivalent resistance* is the sum of the individual resistances.

$$R_{eq} = R_1 + R_2 + R_3$$

- The equivalent applied voltage is the algebraic sum of all voltage sources (polarity considered).

$$V_{eq} = V_1 + V_2$$

- The sum of the voltage drops across all components is equal to the equivalent applied voltage (KVL).

$$V_{eq} = IR_{eq}$$

Figure 34.4 Simple Series Circuit

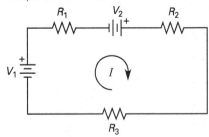

In a series circuit, the voltage across a resistor is the total circuit voltage times the resistance of that particular resistor divided by the total equivalent resistance. This describes the operation of a *voltage divider* circuit. For example, the voltage across resistor R_1 of Fig. 34.4 is given in

$$V_{R_1} = \left(\frac{R_1}{R_{eq}}\right) V_{eq}$$
$$= \left(\frac{R_1}{R_1 + R_2 + R_3}\right)(V_1 + V_2)$$

In a simple parallel circuit with only one active source, such as the circuit shown in Fig. 34.5, the following rules apply.

- The voltage drop is the same across all legs.

$$V = V_{R_1} = V_{R_2} = V_{R_3}$$
$$= I_1 R_1 = I_2 R_2 = I_3 R_3$$

- The reciprocal of the equivalent resistance is the sum of the reciprocals of the individual resistances.

$$\frac{1}{R_{eq}} = \frac{1}{R_1} + \frac{1}{R_2} + \frac{1}{R_3}$$

- The total current is the sum of the leg currents (KCL).

$$I = I_1 + I_2 + I_3$$
$$= \frac{V}{R_1} + \frac{V}{R_2} + \frac{V}{R_3}$$

Figure 34.5 Simple Parallel Circuit

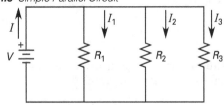

In a parallel circuit, the current through a resistor is the total circuit current times the total circuit resistance divided by the resistor's resistance. This describes the operation of a *current divider circuit*. For example, the current through resistor R_1 of Fig. 34.5 would be given as

$$I_1 = \left(\frac{R_{eq}}{R_1}\right) I = \left(\frac{\dfrac{1}{\dfrac{1}{R_1} + \dfrac{1}{R_2} + \dfrac{1}{R_3}}}{R_1}\right) I$$

6. COMMON DC CIRCUIT ANALYSIS METHODS

The circuit analysis techniques in the following sections show how complicated linear circuits are simplified using circuit reduction and how they are analyzed as a system of n simultaneous equations and n unknowns. Circuit analysis can often be used to directly obtain the current or voltage at a component of interest or to reduce the number of simultaneous equations needed.

Use the following procedure to establish the current and voltage drops in a complicated resistive network. The circuit should be viewed from the perspective of the component of interest. Each step in the reduction should result in a circuit that is simpler.

step 1: Combine series voltage and parallel current sources.

step 2: Combine series resistances to make combinations that more closely resemble a component in parallel with the component of interest.

step 3: Combine parallel resistances to make combinations that more closely resemble a component in series with the component of interest. Lines in the circuit represent zero resistance, and components connected by lines are connected to the same node. The lines can be moved to make parallel combinations more recognizable as long as the components remain connected to the node.

step 4: Repeat steps 2 through 4 as many times as needed.

This principle is only valid for linear circuits or nonlinear circuits that are operating in a linear range. The superposition theorem can be used to reduce a complicated circuit to multiple less-complicated circuits.

Superposition Method

The *superposition method* can be used to reduce a complicated circuit into several simpler circuits. The *superposition theorem* states that the response of (i.e., the voltage across or current through) a linear circuit element fed by two or more independent sources is equal to the combined responses to each source taken individually, with all other sources set to zero (i.e., voltage sources shorted and current sources opened).

The superposition method determines the response of a component to each of the energy sources in a linear circuit separately and then combines the responses. This requires a circuit analysis for each of the energy sources in the circuit. Superposition works equally well for finding unknown currents and unknown voltages. Superposition tends to be more efficient for less-complicated circuits and when there are more loops and nodes than power sources. The superposition method is inefficient for analyzing complicated circuits.

step 1: Choose one of the voltage or current sources, short all other voltage sources, and open all other current sources.

step 2: Make circuit reductions to simplify the circuit and isolate the component of interest.

step 3: Find the voltage or current for the component of interest.

step 4: Repeat steps 1, 2, and 3 for the other voltage and current sources.

step 5: Sum the voltages or currents using the same conventions for voltage polarity and current direction.

Loop-Current Method

The *loop-current method* (also known as the *mesh current method*) is a direct extension of Kirchhoff's voltage law and is particularly valuable in determining unknown currents in circuits with several loops and energy sources. It requires writing $n-1$ simultaneous equations for an n-loop system.

step 1: Select $n-1$ loops (i.e., one less than the total number of loops).

step 2: Assume current directions for the chosen loops. (The choice of current direction is arbitrary, but some currents may end up being negative in step 4.) Show the direction with an arrow.

step 3: Write Kirchhoff's voltage law for each of the $n-1$ chosen loops. A voltage source is positive when the assumed current direction is from the negative to the positive battery terminal. Voltage drops are always positive.

step 4: Solve the $n-1$ equations (from step 3) for the unknown currents.

Node-Voltage Method

The *node-voltage method* is an extension of Kirchhoff's current law. Although currents can be determined with it, it is primarily used to find voltage potentials at various points (nodes) in the circuit. (A *node* is a point where three or more wires connect.)

step 1: (Optional) Convert all current sources to voltage sources.

step 2: Choose one node as the voltage reference (i.e., 0 V) node. Usually, this will be the circuit ground—a node to which at least one negative battery terminal is connected.

step 3: Identify the unknown voltage potentials at all other nodes referred to the reference node.

step 4: Write Kirchhoff's current law for all unknown nodes. (This excludes the reference node.)

step 5: Write all currents in terms of voltage drops.

step 6: Write all voltage drops in terms of the node voltages.

Equation 34.23 and Eq. 34.24: Source Equivalents

$$R_{eq} = \frac{V_{oc}}{I_{sc}} \quad\quad 34.23$$

$$V_{oc} = V_a - V_b \quad\quad 34.24$$

Description

Source equivalents are simplified models of two-terminal networks. They are used to represent a circuit when it is connected to a second circuit. Source equivalents simplify the analysis because the equivalent circuits are much simpler than the originals.

Thevenin's theorem states that a linear, two-terminal network with dependent and independent sources can be represented by a *Thevenin equivalent* circuit consisting of a voltage source in series with a resistor, as illustrated in Fig. 34.6.[7] The *Thevenin equivalent voltage*, or *open-circuit voltage*, V_{oc}, is the open-circuit voltage across terminals A and B. The *Thevenin equivalent resistance*, R_{eq}, is the resistance across terminals A and B when all independent sources are set to zero (i.e., short-circuiting voltage sources and open-circuiting current sources). The equivalent resistance can also be determined by measuring V_{oc} and the current with terminals A and B shorted together, I_{sc}, and using Eq. 34.23.

[7]The *NCEES Handbook* uses lower-case italic subscripts, a and b, to designate the terminals in Eq. 34.24. Since this style convention is not used again in the *NCEES Handbook*, and since that convention is inconsistent with this book's style to designate locations, this book uses uppercase Roman subscripts, A and B, in Fig. 34.6 and in this section.

Figure 34.6 Thevenin Equivalent Circuit

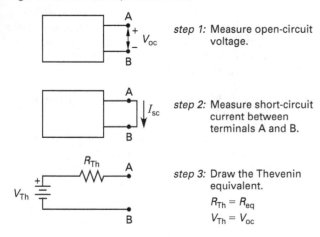

step 1: Measure open-circuit voltage.

step 2: Measure short-circuit current between terminals A and B.

step 3: Draw the Thevenin equivalent.
$R_{Th} = R_{eq}$
$V_{Th} = V_{oc}$

Norton's theorem states that a linear, two-terminal network with dependent or independent sources can be represented by an equivalent circuit consisting of a single current source and resistor in parallel, as shown in Fig. 34.7. The *Norton equivalent current*, I_{sc}, is the *short-circuit current* that flows through a shunt across terminals A and B. The *Norton equivalent resistance*, R_{eq}, is the resistance across terminals A and B when all independent sources are set to zero (i.e., short-circuiting voltage sources and open-circuiting current sources). The *Norton equivalent voltage*, V_{oc}, is measured with terminals open.

Figure 34.7 Norton Equivalent Circuit

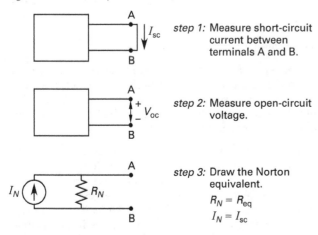

step 1: Measure short-circuit current between terminals A and B.

step 2: Measure open-circuit voltage.

step 3: Draw the Norton equivalent.
$R_N = R_{eq}$
$I_N = I_{sc}$

Norton's equivalent resistance is equal to Thevenin's equivalent resistance.

The conversions from Norton to Thevenin or from Thevenin to Norton can aid in circuit analysis. The Norton equivalent can be easily converted to a Thevenin equivalent and vice versa with the following equations.

$$R_N = R_{Th}$$

$$V_{Th} = I_N R_N$$

$$I_N = \frac{V_{Th}}{R_{Th}}$$

Maximum Power Transfer

Electric circuits are often designed to transfer power from a source (e.g., generator, transmitter) to a load (e.g., motor, light, receiver). There are two basic types of power transfer circuits. In one type of system, the emphasis is on transmitting power with high efficiency. In this power system, large amounts of power must be transmitted in the most efficient way to the loads. In communication and instrumentation systems, small amounts of power are involved. The power at the transmitting end is small, and the main concern is that the maximum power reaches the load.

The *maximum power transfer* from a circuit will occur when the load resistance equals the Norton or Thevenin equivalent resistance of the source.

7. *RC* AND *RL* TRANSIENTS

When a charged capacitor is connected across a resistor, the voltage across the capacitor will gradually decrease and approach zero as energy is dissipated in the resistor. Similarly, when an inductor through which a steady current is flowing is suddenly connected across a resistor, the current will gradually decrease and approach zero. Both of these cases assume that any energy sources are disconnected at the time the resistor is connected. These gradual decreases represent *transient behavior*. Transient behavior is also observed when a voltage or a current source is initially connected to a circuit with capacitors or inductors.

The *time constant*, τ, for a circuit is the time in seconds it takes for the current or voltage to reach $(1 - 1/e$, where e is the base of natural logarithms, approximately 2.718) times the difference between the steady-state value and the original value, or approximately 63.3% of its steady-state value. For a series-*RL* circuit, the time constant is L/R. For a series-*RC* circuit, the time constant is RC. In general, transient variables will have essentially reached their steady-state values after five time constants (99.3% of the steady-state value).

Equation 34.25 through Eq. 34.30 describe *RC* and *RL* transient response for source-free and energizing circuits. Time is assumed to begin when a switch is closed. Decay is a special case of the charging equations where $V = 0$ and either $v_C(0) \neq 0$ or $i_L(0) \neq 0$.

Equation 34.25 Through Eq. 34.27: *RC* Transients

$$v_C(t) = v_C(0)e^{-t/RC} + V(1 - e^{-t/RC})$$
$$[t \geq 0] \qquad 34.25$$

$$i(t) = \{[V - v_C(0)]/R\}e^{-t/RC} \quad [t \geq 0] \qquad 34.26$$

$$v_R(t) = i(t)R$$
$$= [V - v_C(0)]e^{-t/RC} \quad [t \geq 0] \qquad 34.27$$

Description

Equation 34.25 through Eq. 34.27 describe transient behavior in RC circuits.[8] (See Fig. 34.8.) $v_C(0)$ is the voltage across the terminals of the capacitor when the switch is closed.

Figure 34.8 *RC Transient Circuit*

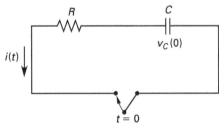

(a) series-*RC*, discharging
(energy source(s) disconnected)

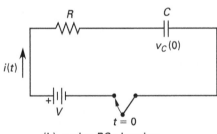

(b) series-*RC*, charging
(energy source(s) connected)

Example

The initial voltage across the capacitor is 5 V. At $t = 0$, the switch is closed.

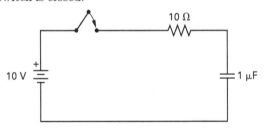

What is most nearly the voltage across the capacitor 10 μs after the switch is closed?

(A)   1.0 V

(B)   5.1 V

(C)   5.4 V

(D)   8.2 V

Solution

When the switch closes, the charge on the capacitor begins to increase. From Eq. 34.25,

$$\frac{t}{RC} = \frac{(10\ \mu s)\left(10^{-6}\ \dfrac{s}{\mu s}\right)}{(10\ \Omega)(1\ \mu F)\left(10^{-6}\ \dfrac{F}{\mu F}\right)} = 1$$

$$\begin{aligned} v_C(t) &= v_C(0)e^{-t/RC} + V(1 - e^{-t/RC}) \\ &= (5\ V)e^{-1} + (10\ V)(1 - e^{-1}) \\ &= 8.16\ V \quad (8.2\ V) \end{aligned}$$

The answer is (D).

Equation 34.28 Through Eq. 34.30: *RL* Transients

$$i(t) = i(0)e^{-Rt/L} + \frac{V}{R}(1 - e^{-Rt/L}) \quad [t \geq 0] \qquad 34.28$$

$$v_R(t) = i(t)R = i(0)Re^{-Rt/L} + V(1 - e^{-Rt/L}) \\ [t \geq 0] \qquad 34.29$$

$$v_L(t) = L(di/dt) = -i(0)Re^{-Rt/L} + Ve^{-Rt/L} \\ [t \geq 0] \qquad 34.30$$

Description

Equation 34.28 through Eq. 34.30 describe transient behavior in RL circuits. (See Fig. 34.9.) $i(0)$ is the current through the inductor when the switch is closed.

---

[8]Generally, parentheses, square brackets, and curly brackets are not combined in presenting mathematical equations. Other than designating a multiplicative combination, there is no significance to the curly brackets used in Eq. 34.26.

Figure 34.9 *RL Transient Circuit*

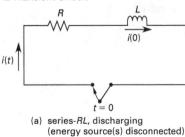

(a) series-*RL*, discharging
(energy source(s) disconnected)

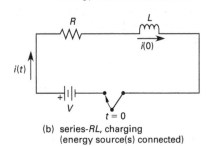

(b) series-*RL*, charging
(energy source(s) connected)

Example

The switch in the circuit shown is closed at $t = 0$.

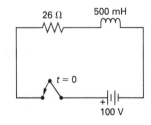

What is the approximate voltage across the inductor at $t = 30$ ms?

   (A)   1.0 V

   (B)   19 V

   (C)   21 V

   (D)   48 V

Solution

Use Eq. 34.30.

$$\frac{Rt}{L} = \frac{(26\ \Omega)(30\ \text{ms})\left(1000\ \dfrac{\text{mH}}{\text{H}}\right)}{(500\ \text{mH})\left(1000\ \dfrac{\text{ms}}{\text{s}}\right)} = 1.56$$

$$v_L(t) = -i(0)Re^{-Rt/L} + Ve^{-Rt/L}$$
$$v_L(30\ \text{ms}) = 0 + (100\ \text{V})e^{-1.56}$$
$$= 21\ \text{V}$$

The answer is (C).

8. DC VOLTMETERS

A *d'Arsonval meter* movement configured to perform as a *DC voltmeter* is shown in Fig. 34.10.

Figure 34.10 *DC Voltmeter*

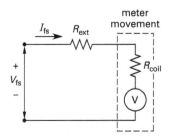

The external resistance is used to limit the current to the full-scale value, I_{fs}, at the desired full-scale voltage, V_{fs}. The electrical relationships in the voltmeter are given by

$$\frac{1}{I_{fs}} = \frac{R_{ext} + R_{coil}}{V_{fs}}$$

The quantity $1/I_{fs}$ is fixed for a given instrument and is called the *sensitivity*. The sensitivity is measured in ohms per volt (Ω/V).

9. DC AMMETERS

A d'Arsonval meter movement configured to perform as a *DC ammeter* is shown in Fig. 34.11.

The *shunt resistance (swamping resistance)* is used to limit the current to the full-scale value, I_{fs}, at the desired full-scale voltage, V_{fs}. For ammeters, the standard full-scale voltage is 50 mV.[9] The electrical relationships in the ammeter are given by

$$I_{design} = \frac{V_{fs}}{R_{shunt}} + I_{fs}$$

Figure 34.11 *DC Ammeter*

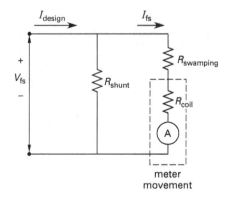

---

[9]The standard ammeter is designed to withstand a 50 mV voltage across the shunt with I_{fs} flowing in the movement at the desired design current flow.

35 Alternating-Current Circuits

Nomenclature

a	turns ratio	–
B	susceptance	S
BW	bandwidth	Hz or rad/s
C	capacitance	H
f	frequency	Hz
G	conductance	S
$i(t)$	time-varying current	A
I	constant current	A
L	inductance	H
N	number of turns	–
pf	power factor	–
P	real power	W
Q	reactive power	VAR
Q	quality factor	–
R	resistance	Ω
S	complex power	VA
t	time	s
T	period	s
$v(t)$	time-varying voltage	V
V	constant voltage	V
x	time-varying general variable	–
X	constant general variable	–
X	reactance	Ω
Y	admittance	S
Z	impedance	Ω

Symbols

θ	phase angle difference	rad
ϕ	offset angle	rad
ω	angular frequency	rad/s

Subscripts

0	at resonance
ave	average
C	capacitive or ideal capacitor
dc	direct current
eff	effective
eq	equivalent
i	imaginary
L	ideal inductor or inductive
max	maximum
P	primary
r	real
rms	effective or root-mean-square
R	ideal resistor
S	secondary

1. ALTERNATING WAVEFORMS

The term *alternating waveform* describes any symmetrical waveform, including square, sawtooth, triangular, and sinusoidal waves, whose polarity varies regularly with time. However, the term *alternating current* (AC) almost always means that the current is produced from the application of a sinusoidal voltage.

Sinusoidal variables can be specified without loss of generality as either sines or cosines. If a sine waveform is used, the instantaneous voltage as a function of time is given by

$$v(t) = V_{\max} \sin(\omega t + \phi)$$

$V_{\max}$ is the maximum value (also known as the *amplitude*) of the sinusoid. If $v(t)$ is not zero at $t = 0$ as in Fig. 35.1, an *offset angle*, ϕ (also known as a *relative phase angle*), must be used.

Figure 35.1 Sinusoidal Waveform with Phase Angle

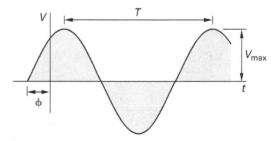

2. SINE-COSINE RELATIONSHIPS

The choice of sine or cosine to represent AC waveforms is arbitrary, with the only distinction being that the relative phase angle, ϕ, differs by $\pi/2$ radians. The phasor form of complex values is shown relative to the cosine form in the trigonometric form, so it may be necessary to convert a sine representation into a cosine representation or vice versa.

Equation 35.1 and Eq. 35.2: Sine-Cosine Relationships

$$\cos(\omega t) = \sin(\omega t + \pi/2) = -\sin(\omega t - \pi/2) \quad \text{35.1}$$

$$\sin(\omega t) = \cos(\omega t - \pi/2) = -\cos(\omega t + \pi/2) \quad \text{35.2}$$

Description

The trigonometric relationships in Eq. 35.1 and Eq. 35.2 are used to solve problems with alternating currents.

Equation 35.3: Frequency

$$f = 1/T = \omega/2\pi \quad \text{35.3}$$

Description

Figure 35.1 illustrates the form of an AC voltage given by $v(t) = V_{max}\sin(\omega t + \phi)$. The *period* of the waveform is T. (Because the horizontal axis corresponds to time and not to distance, the waveform does not have a wavelength.) The *frequency*, f, of the sinusoid is the reciprocal of the period in hertz (Hz), as shown in Eq. 35.3. *Angular frequency*, ω, in radians per second (rad/s) can also be used.

Example

The electric field (in V/m) of a particular plane wave propagating in a dielectric medium is given by

$$\mathbf{E}(t, z) = \mathbf{a_x}\cos\left(10^8 t - \frac{z}{3}\right) - \mathbf{a_y}\sin\left(10^8 t - \frac{z}{3}\right)$$

Time, t, has units of seconds. What is most nearly the field's oscillation frequency?

(A) 6.3 MHz

(B) 7.0 MHz

(C) 16 MHz

(D) 160 MHz

Solution

From the field equation, $\omega = 10^8$ rad/s. From Eq. 35.3,

$$f = \omega/2\pi = \frac{10^8 \, \dfrac{\text{rad}}{\text{s}}}{2\pi\left(10^6 \, \dfrac{\text{Hz}}{\text{MHz}}\right)} = 15.9 \text{ MHz} \quad \text{(16 MHz)}$$

The answer is (C).

3. REPRESENTATION OF SINUSOIDS

There are several equivalent methods of representing a sinusoidal waveform.

*   *trigonometric*

$$V_{max}\cos(\omega t + \phi)$$

*   *polar* (or *phasor*)

$$V_{eff} \angle \phi$$

*   *rectangular*

$$V_r + jV_i = V_{max}(\cos\phi + j\sin\phi)$$

*   *exponential*

$$V_{max}e^{j\phi}$$

In polar, rectangular, or exponential form, the frequency must be specified separately.

When given in polar form, the voltage is usually given as the effective (rms) value (see Sec. 35.5) and not the peak value.[1]

In trigonometric form, ω may be given in either rad/s or deg/s, but rad/s is more common. ϕ is usually given in degrees. This can result in a mismatch in units. (Unfortunately, this is common practice in electrical engineering.) In exponential form, ϕ should always be in radians, but some references use degrees. In polar form and rectangular form, ϕ is usually in degrees.

Equation 35.4 and Eq. 35.5: Trigonometric and Polar (Phasor) Forms

$$P[V_{max}\cos(\omega t + \phi)] = V_{rms} \angle \phi = \mathbf{V} \quad \text{35.4}$$

$$P[I_{max}\cos(\omega t + \theta)] = I_{rms} \angle \theta = \mathbf{I} \quad \text{35.5}$$

---

[1]The convention of using rms values in phasor expressions of sinusoids, as is adopted in the NCEES *FE Reference Handbook* (*NCEES Handbook*), is common but arbitrary. If power is to be calculated from the common $\mathbf{P} = \mathbf{IV}$ (as opposed to from $\mathbf{P} = \frac{1}{2}\mathbf{IV}$), the rms values must be used.

Description

Equation 35.4 and Eq. 35.5 represent different ways to represent sinusoidal voltages and currents.[2]

4. AVERAGE VALUE

Equation 35.6 and Eq. 35.7: Average Value

$$X_{ave} = (1/T) \int_0^T x(t)\, dt \qquad 35.6$$

$$X_{ave} = 2X_{max}/\pi \quad \begin{bmatrix} \text{full-wave} \\ \text{rectified sinusoid} \end{bmatrix} \qquad 35.7$$

Description

Equation 35.6 calculates the *average value* of any periodic variable (e.g., voltage or current).

Waveforms that are symmetrical with respect to the horizontal time axis have an average value of zero, as is shown in Fig. 35.2(a). A full-wave rectified sinusoid is shown in Fig. 35.2(b); the average value of Eq. 35.6 for this waveform is given by Eq. 35.7.

The average value of the half-wave rectified sinusoid as shown in Fig. 35.2(c) is

$$X_{ave} = \frac{X_{max}}{\pi} \quad \begin{bmatrix} \text{half-wave} \\ \text{rectified sinusoid} \end{bmatrix}$$

Figure 35.2 *Average and Effective Values*

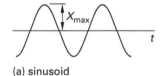

$$X_{ave} = 0$$

$$X_{eff} = \sqrt{\frac{1}{T} \int_0^T x^2(t)\, dt}$$

(a) sinusoid

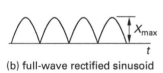

$$X_{ave} = \frac{2X_{max}}{\pi}$$

$$X_{eff} = \frac{X_{max}}{\sqrt{2}}$$

(b) full-wave rectified sinusoid

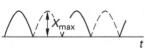

$$X_{ave} = \frac{X_{max}}{\pi}$$

$$X_{eff} = \frac{X_{max}}{2}$$

(c) half-wave rectified sinusoid

Example

The waveform shown repeats every 10 ms.

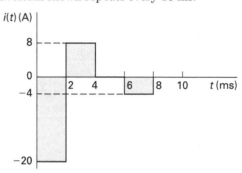

What is most nearly the average value of the waveform?

(A) -20 A

(B) -4.0 A

(C) -3.0 A

(D) 8.0 A

Solution

From Eq. 35.6, the average value of a periodic waveform is

$$I_{ave} = (1/T) \int_0^T i(t)\, dt$$

$$= \left(\frac{1}{10 \text{ ms}}\right) \begin{pmatrix} (-20 \text{ A})(2 \text{ ms}) + (8 \text{ A})(2 \text{ ms}) \\ + (0 \text{ A})(2 \text{ ms}) + (-4 \text{ A})(2 \text{ ms}) \\ + (0 \text{ A})(2 \text{ ms}) \end{pmatrix}$$

$$= -3.2 \text{ A} \quad (-3.0 \text{ A})$$

The answer is (C).

5. EFFECTIVE (rms) VALUES

Equation 35.8 Through Eq. 35.11: Effective Value of Waveforms

$$X_{eff} = X_{rms} = \left[(1/T) \int_0^T x^2(t)\, dt \right]^{1/2} \qquad 35.8$$

---

[2](1) The semantics of using the expression "*P*[*X*]" to designate "the polar form of *X*" is unique to the *NCEES Handbook*. (2) Although the *NCEES Handbook* uses the equals symbol, =, Eq. 35.4 and Eq. 35.5 are not equations. The equivalence symbol, ≡, should have been used to indicate that these are definitions, not mathematical expressions.

$$X_{eff} = X_{rms}$$
$$= X_{max}/\sqrt{2} \quad \begin{bmatrix} \text{full-wave} \\ \text{rectified sinusoid} \end{bmatrix} \quad 35.9$$

$$X_{eff} = X_{rms}$$
$$= X_{max}/2 \quad \begin{bmatrix} \text{half-wave} \\ \text{rectified sinusoid} \end{bmatrix} \quad 35.10$$

$$X_{rms} = \sqrt{X_{dc}^2 + \sum_{n=1}^{\infty} X_n^2} \quad 35.11$$

Description

The voltage level of an alternating waveform changes continuously. For power calculations, an alternating waveform is usually characterized by a single voltage value. This value is equivalent to the DC voltage that would have the same heating effect. This is called the *effective value*, also known as the *root-mean-square*, or *rms* value. A DC current of I produces the same heating effect as an AC current of I_{rms}.

The effective value of a general alternating waveform is given by Eq. 35.8. Use Eq. 35.9 for a full-wave rectified sinusoidal waveform, and use Eq. 35.10 for a half-wave rectified sinusoidal waveform.

Equation 35.11 illustrates how the rms value of a combination of waveforms is calculated. X_{dc} is the *DC biasing voltage* across the entire circuit, while the rms values of the component waveforms are designated as X_n.[3]

In the United States, the effective value of the standard voltage used in households is 115–120 V. The polar form of the voltage is commonly depicted as

$$\mathbf{V} \equiv V_{eff} \angle \phi \equiv \left(\frac{V_{max}}{\sqrt{2}} \right) \angle \phi$$

Household voltages and currents can be considered to be effective values unless otherwise specified.

Example

What is most nearly the effective value of the repeating waveform shown?

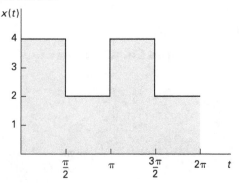

(A) 2.5

(B) 2.8

(C) 3.0

(D) 3.2

Solution

From Eq. 35.8, for an alternating waveform,

$$
\begin{aligned}
X_{rms} &= \left[(1/T) \int_0^T x^2(t)\,dt \right]^{1/2} \\
&= \sqrt{\left(\frac{1}{T} \right) \left(\int_0^{T/2} (4)^2\,dt + \int_{T/2}^T (2)^2\,dt \right)} \\
&= \sqrt{\left(\frac{1}{T} \right) \left(16t \Big|_0^{T/2} + 4t \Big|_{T/2}^T \right)} \\
&= \sqrt{\left(\frac{1}{T} \right) \left(\frac{16\,T}{2} + 4\,T - \frac{4\,T}{2} \right)} \\
&= 3.16 \quad (3.2)
\end{aligned}
$$

The answer is (D).

6. PHASE ANGLES

Ordinarily, the current and voltage sinusoids in an AC circuit do not peak at the same time. A *phase shift* exists between voltage and current, as illustrated in Fig. 35.3.

---

[3](1) Equation 35.8 through Eq. 35.10 use the same symbol as reactance, although X is intended by the *NCEES Handbook* to indicate some generic variable, such as current or voltage. It is not reactance. (2) Unlike Eq. 35.8, Eq. 35.9, and Eq. 35.10, *NCEES Handbook* Eq. 35.11 does not show $X_{eff} = X_{rms}$, although the two terms are still equivalent. (3) The subscript "dc" in Eq. 35.11 is the same as "DC" that the *NCEES Handbook* uses elsewhere to designate direct current. (4) X_{dc} is defined as the "dc component of $x(t)$." $x(t)$ was used in Eq. 35.8 to designate the native waveform. Since there are numerous waveforms being combined in Eq. 35.11, it is taken on faith that $x(t)$ is intended to represent the combined waveform. (5) The *NCEES Handbook* consistently uses n as a summation index (instead of, for instance, the more common i). Usually, n designates the last term in the summation.

Figure 35.3 Leading Phase Angle Difference

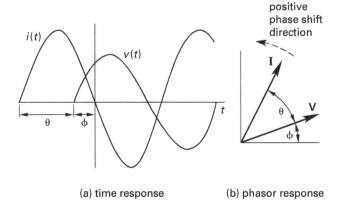

(a) time response (b) phasor response

Figure 35.4 Lagging Impedance Triangle

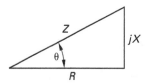

This phase shift is caused by the inductors and capacitors in the circuit. Capacitors and inductors have different effects on the phase angle. In a purely resistive circuit, no phase shift exists between voltage and current, and the current is in phase with the voltage.

It is common practice to use the voltage signal as a reference. In Fig. 35.3, the current *leads* (is ahead of) the voltage. In a purely capacitive circuit, the current leads the voltage by 90°; in a purely inductive circuit, the current *lags* behind the voltage by 90°. In a leading circuit, the phase angle difference is positive and the current reaches its peak before the voltage. In a lagging circuit, the phase angle difference is negative and the current reaches its peak after the voltage.

$$v(t) = V_{\max} \sin(\omega t + \phi) \quad \text{[reference]}$$
$$i(t) = I_{\max} \sin(\omega t + \phi + \theta)$$

Each AC *passive circuit element* (resistor, capacitor, or inductor) is assigned an angle, θ, known as its *impedance angle*, that corresponds to the phase angle shift produced when a sinusoidal voltage is applied across that element alone.

7. IMPEDANCE

The term *impedance*, Z (with units of ohms), describes the combined effect circuit elements have on current magnitude and phase. Impedance is a complex quantity with a magnitude and an associated angle, and it is usually written in polar form. However, it can also be written in rectangular form as the complex sum of its *resistive* (*real part*, R) and *reactive* (*imaginary part*, X) *components*, both having units of ohms. The resistive and reactive components combine trigonometrically in the *impedance triangle*, shown in Fig. 35.4. Resistance is always positive, while reactance may be either positive or negative.

In Fig. 35.4, the impedance is drawn in the complex plane with the real (resistive) part on the horizontal axis and the imaginary (reactive) part on the vertical axis. The impedance in Fig. 35.4 is lagging because the reactive part is positive imaginary. This designation derives from $I = V/Z$ where a positive angle for Z subtracts from the voltage phase angle.

$$\mathbf{Z} \equiv R \pm jX$$

$$R = Z \cos \theta$$

$$X = Z \sin \theta$$

The total resistance is

$$X = X_L - X_C$$

Equation 35.12: Impedance and Ohm's Law

$$\mathbf{Z} = \mathbf{V}/\mathbf{I} \qquad 35.12$$

Description

Ohm's law for AC circuits with linear circuit elements is similar to Ohm's law for DC circuits. The impedance in an AC circuit is derived from Ohm's law, as shown in Eq. 35.12.

V and I can both be either maximum values or effective values, but never a combination of the two. If the voltage source is specified by its effective value, then the current calculated from $I = V/Z$ will be an effective value.

Equation 35.13: Ideal Resistor

$$\mathbf{Z}_R = R \qquad 35.13$$

Variation

$$\mathbf{Z}_R \equiv R \angle 0° \equiv R + j0$$

Description

Equation 35.13 defines the impedance of an ideal resistor. An *ideal resistor* has neither inductance nor capacitance. The magnitude of the impedance is the resistance, R, and the phase angle difference is zero. Current and voltage are in phase in an ideal resistor or in a purely resistive circuit.

Equation 35.14 and Eq. 35.15: Ideal Capacitor

$$\mathbf{Z}_C = \frac{1}{j\omega C} = jX_C \qquad 35.14$$

$$X_C = -\frac{1}{\omega C} \qquad 35.15$$

Variations

$$\mathbf{Z}_C \equiv X_C \angle -90°$$
$$\mathbf{Z}_C = \frac{-j}{\omega C}$$

Description

Equation 35.14 gives the impedance of an *ideal capacitor* with capacitance, C, in farads (F). An ideal capacitor has neither resistance nor inductance. The magnitude of the impedance is the *capacitive reactance*, X_C, with units of ohms, and the phase angle difference is $-\pi/2$ $(-90°)$.[4] Current leads the voltage by $90°$ in a purely capacitive circuit. Some authors casually define X_C as a positive quantity such that Eq. 35.15 does not have a negative sign. The important thing to know is that the impedance of a capacitor is negative imaginary, regardless of how the reactance sign is defined.

Equation 35.16 and Eq. 35.17: Ideal Inductor

$$\mathbf{Z}_L = j\omega L = jX_L \qquad 35.16$$

$$X_L = \omega L \qquad 35.17$$

Variation

$$\mathbf{Z}_L = X_L \angle 90°$$

Description

Equation 35.16 gives the impedance of an ideal inductor with inductance, L, in henries (H). An *ideal inductor* has no resistance or capacitance. The magnitude of the impedance is the *inductive reactance*, X_L, with units of ohms (Ω), and the phase angle difference is $\pi/2$ $(90°)$. Current lags the voltage by $90°$ in a purely inductive circuit.

Some circuits are shown with the capacitor and inductor impedance, rather than the capacitance or inductance, given in ohms. The reactances are at the circuit's operating frequency and can be used for circuit analysis for current dividers and voltage dividers, as with the DC circuits, although analysis must be done with complex algebra.

Example

A simple circuit consists of an inductor in series with a sinusoidal voltage.

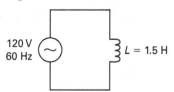

Using the applied voltage as the reference, what is most nearly the current through the inductor?

(A) 0.21 A$\angle -90°$

(B) 0.21 A$\angle 90°$

(C) 1.3 A$\angle -90°$

(D) 1.3 A$\angle 90°$

Solution

From Eq. 35.17, the reactance is

$$\begin{aligned}X_L &= \omega L = 2\pi f L \\ &= 2\pi (60 \text{ Hz})(1.5 \text{ H}) \\ &= 565.5 \ \Omega\end{aligned}$$

From Eq. 35.16, the impedance is

$$\begin{aligned}Z_L &= jX_L \\ &= j565.5 \ \Omega \\ &= 565.5 \ \Omega \angle 90°\end{aligned}$$

The voltage is $V = 120$ V$\angle 0°$. Rearranging Ohm's law, Eq. 35.12, the current through the inductor is

$$\begin{aligned}Z &= V/I \\ I &= \frac{V}{Z_{\text{total}}} \\ &= \frac{120 \text{ V}\angle 0°}{565.5 \ \Omega\angle 90°} \\ &= 0.21 \text{ A}\angle -90°\end{aligned}$$

The answer is (A).

---

[4]Equation 35.15 is derived from Eq. 35.14 and the definition $j^2 = -1$. However, the expression for capacitive reactance is often shown without the negative sign, and capacitive reactance values are normally stated as positive values (e.g., "$X_C = 4 \ \Omega$"). In such cases, the negative impedance angle is understood.

8. ADMITTANCE AND SUSCEPTANCE

The reciprocal of impedance is the complex quantity *admittance*, $\mathbf{Y}$, with units of *siemens* (S). Admittance is particularly useful in analyzing parallel circuits, since admittances of parallel circuit elements add together.

$$\mathbf{Y} = \frac{1}{\mathbf{Z}} = \frac{1}{Z} \angle -\theta$$

The reciprocal of the resistive part of impedance is *conductance*, G. The reciprocal of the reactive part of impedance is *susceptance*, B.

$$G = \frac{1}{R}$$

$$B = \frac{1}{X}$$

By multiplying the numerator and denominator by the *complex conjugate*, admittance can be written in terms of resistance and reactance, and vice versa.

$$\mathbf{Y} = G + jB = \left(\frac{1}{R+jX}\right)\left(\frac{R-jX}{R-jX}\right)$$

$$= \frac{R}{R^2+X^2} - j\left(\frac{X}{R^2+X^2}\right)$$

$$\mathbf{Z} = R + jX = \left(\frac{1}{G+jB}\right)\left(\frac{G-jB}{G-jB}\right)$$

$$= \frac{G}{G^2+B^2} - j\left(\frac{B}{G^2+B^2}\right)$$

Impedances are combined in the same way as resistances: impedances in series are added, while the reciprocals of impedances in parallel are added. For series circuits, the resistive and reactive parts of each impedance element are calculated separately and summed. For parallel circuits, the conductance and susceptance of each element are summed. The total impedance is found by a complex addition of the resistive (conductive) and reactive (susceptive) parts. It is convenient to perform the addition in rectangular form. The given equations represent the magnitude of the combined impedances for series and parallel circuits.

$$Z_{\text{eq}} = \sqrt{\left(\sum R\right)^2 + \left(\sum X_L - \sum X_C\right)^2}$$
[series]

$$Z_{\text{eq}} = \frac{1}{\sqrt{\left(\sum \dfrac{1}{R}\right)^2 + \left(\sum \dfrac{1}{X_L} - \sum \dfrac{1}{X_C}\right)^2}}$$
[parallel]

9. COMPLEX POWER

Equation 35.18: Complex Power Vector

$$\mathbf{S} = \mathbf{V}\mathbf{I}^* = P + jQ \qquad \textit{35.18}$$

Description

The *complex power vector*, $\mathbf{S}$ (also called the *apparent power*), is the vector sum of the real (true, active) power vector, $\mathbf{P}$, and the imaginary reactive power vector, $\mathbf{Q}$. The complex power vector's units are volt-amps (VA). The components of power combine as vectors in the *complex power triangle*, shown in Fig. 35.5.

Figure 35.5 Lagging (Inductive) Complex Power Triangle

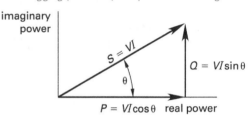

The complex conjugate of the current, $\mathbf{I}^*$, is used in the apparent power, resulting in a positive imaginary part and a positive power angle for a lagging current (which has a negative phase angle compared to the voltage), as shown in Fig. 35.5. For a leading current (which has a positive phase angle compared to the voltage), the power triangle has a negative imaginary part and a negative power angle.

Equation 35.19: Power Factor

$$\text{pf} = \cos\theta \qquad \textit{35.19}$$

Description

The *power factor*, pf (usually given in percent), is $\cos\theta$. The angle θ is called the *power angle* and is the same as the overall impedance angle, or the angle between input voltage and current in the circuit. These are the voltage and current at the source (usually voltage source), which supplies the electric power to the circuit.

The cosine is positive for both positive and negative angles. The descriptions *lagging* (for an inductive circuit) and *leading* (for a capacitive circuit) must be used with the power factor.

For a purely resistive load, pf = 1, and the average real power is given by Eq. 35.24.

The power factor of a circuit, and therefore, the phase angle difference, can be changed by adding either inductance or capacitance. This is known as *power factor correction*.

Example

An industrial complex is fed by a 13 kV (rms) transmission line. The average current delivered during a month is measured as 140 A. The real power consumed within the industrial complex is 1.7 MW. What power factor should be used in determining the month's electrical services invoice?

(A) 0.72

(B) 0.81

(C) 0.86

(D) 0.93

Solution

The apparent power (complex power) is calculated from the voltage and the measured current. The power factor is

$$pf = \cos\theta = \frac{P}{S} = \frac{P}{VI}$$

$$= \frac{(1.7 \text{ MW})\left(10^6 \; \frac{W}{MW}\right)}{(13 \text{ kV})\left(1000 \; \frac{V}{kV}\right)(140 \text{ A})}$$

$$= 0.93$$

The answer is (D).

Example

An ore processing plant with both electrical equipment and coal-fired steam generators has an overall lagging current. In order to reduce electrical costs, what is the best option for the plant to install?

(A) induction motors in parallel with the existing loads

(B) induction motors in series with the existing loads

(C) resistive heater steam generators in place of the coal-fired steam generators

(D) synchronous motors (without anything attached to the output shafts) in parallel with the existing loads

Solution

A lagging power factor indicates that the plant has a predominantly inductive load. Any additional inductive loading, including induction motors, will increase the lagging power factor. Resistive heaters would reduce the lagging power factor but increase electrical costs overall. Unloaded synchronous motors (commonly referred to as *synchronous capacitors*, *synchronous condensers*, and *synchronous compensators*) have leading power factors

and will reduce the power factor, pf, reactive power, Q, and the electrical cost.

The answer is (D).

Equation 35.20 Through Eq. 35.24: Real and Reactive Power

$$P = \left(\frac{1}{2}\right) V_{\max} I_{\max} \cos\theta \quad \text{[sinusoids]} \qquad 35.20$$

$$P = V_{\text{rms}} I_{\text{rms}} \cos\theta \qquad 35.21$$

$$Q = \left(\frac{1}{2}\right) V_{\max} I_{\max} \sin\theta \quad \text{[sinusoids]} \qquad 35.22$$

$$Q = V_{\text{rms}} I_{\text{rms}} \sin\theta \qquad 35.23$$

$$P = V_{\text{rms}} I_{\text{rms}} = V_{\text{rms}}^2 / R = I_{\text{rms}}^2 R \quad \begin{bmatrix} \text{purely} \\ \text{resistive load;} \\ \text{pf} = 1 \end{bmatrix} \qquad 35.24$$

Variations

$$Q = \frac{V_{\text{rms}}^2}{X}$$

$$P_{\text{ave}} = V_{\text{rms}} I_{\text{rms}} \cos 90° = 0$$

$$= V_{\text{rms}} I_{\text{rms}} \cos(-90°) = 0 \quad \begin{bmatrix} \text{purely} \\ \text{reactive load;} \\ \text{pf} = 0 \end{bmatrix}$$

Description

The *real power*, P, with units of watts (W), is given by Eq. 35.20 and Eq. 35.21. Equation 35.20 is only valid for sinusoids, while Eq. 35.21 is valid for all waveforms.

The *reactive power*, Q, in units of volt-amps reactive (VAR), is the imaginary part of **S**. The reactive power is given by Eq. 35.22 and Eq. 35.23. Equation 35.22 is only valid for sinusoids, while Eq. 35.23 is valid for all waveforms.

For a purely resistive load, pf = 1, and the average real power is given by Eq. 35.24.

For a purely reactive load, pf = 0, and the average real power is given by the second variation equation.

Electric energy is stored in a capacitor or inductor during a fourth of a cycle and is returned to the circuit during the next fourth of the cycle. Only a resistance will actually dissipate energy.

The power factor of a circuit, and, therefore, the phase angle difference, can be changed by adding either inductance or capacitance. This is known as *power factor correction*.

Example

A small batch reactor is heated by a two-phase, 240 V (line-to-line) AC resistance heater for five minutes. 3.2 kW are transferred to the reactor contents in an 84% efficient process. Most nearly, what is the resistance of the heater?

(A)   15 Ω

(B)   18 Ω

(C)   21 Ω

(D)   75 Ω

Solution

A 240 V voltage source is obtained by connecting two 120 V phases in series. Since 120 V is an rms (i.e., effective) value, 240 V is the effective value. Use Eq. 35.24.

$$P = V_{\text{rms}}^2/R$$

$$R = \frac{\eta V_{\text{rms}}^2}{P}$$

$$= \frac{(0.84)(240 \text{ V})^2}{(3.2 \text{ kW})\left(1000 \ \dfrac{\text{W}}{\text{kW}}\right)}$$

$$= 15.12 \ \Omega \quad (15 \ \Omega)$$

The answer is (A).

Example

The frequency of the current source in the parallel circuit is adjusted until the circuit is purely resistive (i.e., until the power factor is equal to 1.0).

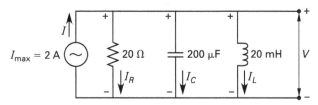

The power dissipated at the adjusted frequency is most nearly

(A)   0 W

(B)   10 W

(C)   20 W

(D)   40 W

Solution

When the circuit is purely resistive, the power factor is equal to 1. Use Eq. 35.24.

$$P = I_{\text{rms}}^2 R = \tfrac{1}{2} I_{\text{max}}^2 R = \left(\frac{1}{2}\right)(2 \text{ A})^2 (20 \ \Omega)$$

$$= 40 \text{ W}$$

The answer is (D).

10. RESONANCE

In a *resonant circuit*, input voltage and current are in phase, and therefore, the phase angle is zero. This is equivalent to saying that the circuit is purely resistive in its response to an AC voltage, although inductive and capacitive elements must be present for resonance to occur. At resonance, the power factor is equal to one, and the reactance, X, is equal to zero, or $X_L + X_C = 0$. The frequency at which the circuit becomes purely resistive, ω_0 or f_0, is the *resonant frequency*.

Equation 35.25 Through Eq. 35.30: Parallel and Series Circuits at Resonant Frequency

$\omega_0 = \dfrac{1}{\sqrt{LC}} = 2\pi f_0 \quad$ [at resonance]	35.25
$Z = R \quad$ [at resonance]	35.26
$\omega_0 L = \dfrac{1}{\omega_0 C} \quad$ [at resonance]	35.27
$\text{BW} = \dfrac{\omega_0}{Q} \quad$ [in rad/s]	35.28
$Q = \dfrac{\omega_0 L}{R} = \dfrac{1}{\omega_0 CR} \quad$ [series-RLC circuit]	35.29
$Q = \omega_0 RC = \dfrac{R}{\omega_0 L} \quad$ [parallel-RLC circuit]	35.30

Variations

$$\text{BW} = f_2 - f_1 = \frac{f_0}{Q} \quad \text{[in Hz]}$$

$$\text{BW} = \omega_2 - \omega_1 \quad \text{[in rad/s]}$$

Description

Equation 35.25 through Eq. 35.27 apply to both parallel and series circuits at the resonant frequency, where $X_L + X_C = 0$ and pf $= 1$.

In a resonant *series-RLC circuit*, impedance is minimized, and the current and power dissipation are maximized. In a resonant *parallel-RLC circuit*, impedance is maximized, and the current and power dissipation are minimized.

For frequencies below the resonant frequency, a series-RLC circuit will be capacitive (leading) in nature. Above the resonant frequency, the circuit will be inductive (lagging) in nature.

For frequencies below the resonant frequency, a parallel-RLC circuit will be inductive (lagging) in nature. Above the resonant frequency, the circuit will be capacitive (leading) in nature.

Circuits can become resonant in two ways. If the frequency of the applied voltage is fixed, the elements must be adjusted so that the capacitive reactance cancels the inductive reactance (i.e., $X_L + X_C = 0$). If the circuit elements are fixed, the frequency must be adjusted.

The behavior of a circuit at frequencies near the resonant frequency is illustrated in Fig. 35.6.

Figure 35.6 *Circuit Characteristics at Resonance*

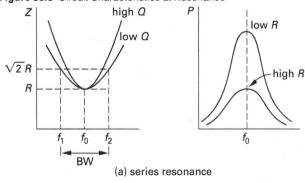

(a) series resonance

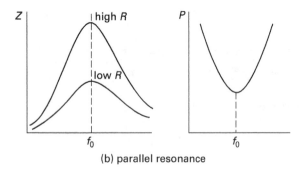

(b) parallel resonance

For both parallel and series resonance, the bandwidth is given by Eq. 35.28.

The half-power points are so named because at those frequencies, the power dissipated in the resistor is half of the power dissipated at the resonant frequency.

$$Z_{f_1} = Z_{f_2} = \sqrt{2}\,R$$

$$I_{f_1} = I_{f_2} = \frac{V}{Z_{f_1}} = \frac{V}{\sqrt{2}\,R} = \frac{I_0}{\sqrt{2}}$$

$$P_{f_1} = P_{f_2} = I^2 R = \left(\frac{I_0}{\sqrt{2}}\right)^2 R = \tfrac{1}{2}P_0$$

The *quality factor*, Q, for a circuit is a dimensionless ratio that compares, for each cycle, the reactive energy stored in an inductor to the resistive energy dissipated. The quality factor indicates the shape of the resonance curve. A circuit with a low Q has a broad and flat curve, while one with a high Q has a narrow and peaked curve. The quality factor for a series-RLC circuit is given by Eq. 35.29, and the quality factor for a parallel-RLC circuit is given by Eq. 35.30.

Assuming a fixed primary impedance, maximum power transfer in an AC circuit occurs when the source and load impedances are complex conjugates (resistances are equal and their reactances are opposite). This is equivalent to having a resonant circuit as shown in Fig. 35.7.

Figure 35.7 *Maximum Power Transfer at Resonance*

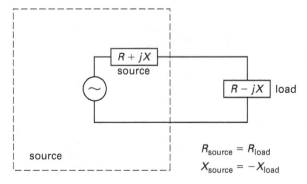

Example

For the circuit shown, what are most nearly the resonant frequency and the quality factor?

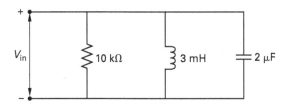

(A) 1.3×10^3 rad/s; 26

(B) 2.0×10^3 rad/s; 0.026

(C) 1.3×10^4 rad/s; 260

(D) 1.5×10^4 rad/s; 2600

Solution

From Eq. 35.25, the resonant frequency is

$$\omega_0 = \frac{1}{\sqrt{LC}}$$
$$= \frac{1}{\sqrt{(3 \times 10^{-3}\ \text{H})(2 \times 10^{-6}\ \text{F})}}$$
$$= 1.29 \times 10^4\ \text{rad/s} \quad (1.3 \times 10^4\ \text{rad/s})$$

From Eq. 35.30, for a parallel-RLC circuit,

$$Q = \frac{R}{\omega_0 L}$$
$$= \frac{10 \times 10^3\ \Omega}{\left(1.29 \times 10^4\ \dfrac{\text{rad}}{\text{s}}\right)(3 \times 10^{-3}\ \text{H})}$$
$$= 258.2 \quad (260)$$

The answer is (C).

11. IDEAL TRANSFORMERS

Transformers are used to change voltages, match impedances, and isolate circuits. They consist of coils of wire wound on a magnetically permeable core. The coils are grouped into primary and secondary windings. The winding connected to the source of electric energy is called the *primary*. The primary current produces a magnetic flux in the core, which induces a current in the *secondary coil*. Core and shell transformer designs are shown in Fig. 35.8.

Figure 35.8 *Core and Shell Transformers*

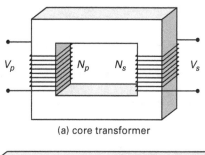

(a) core transformer

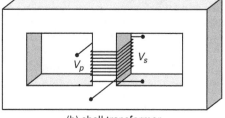

(b) shell transformer

Equation 35.31 Through Eq. 35.33: Turns Ratio

$$a = N_1/N_2 \qquad \qquad 35.31$$

$$a = \left|\frac{\mathbf{V}_P}{\mathbf{V}_S}\right| = \left|\frac{\mathbf{I}_S}{\mathbf{I}_P}\right| \qquad \qquad 35.32$$

$$\mathbf{Z}_P = a^2 \mathbf{Z}_S \qquad \qquad 35.33$$

Variations

$$a = \frac{N_P}{N_S}$$

$$\mathbf{Z}_P = \frac{\mathbf{V}_P}{\mathbf{I}_P} = \mathbf{Z}_1 + a^2 \mathbf{Z}_S \quad \text{[phasor/vector addition]}$$

Description

The ratio of numbers of primary to *secondary windings* is the *turns ratio (ratio of transformation)*, a. If the turns ratio is greater than 1, the transformer decreases voltage and is a *step-down transformer*. If the turns ratio is less than 1, the transformer increases voltage and is a *step-up transformer*.

In a lossless (i.e., 100% efficient) transformer, the power absorbed by the primary winding equals the power generated by the secondary winding, so $I_P V_P = I_S V_S$, and the turns ratio is given by Eq. 35.32.

A lossless transformer is called an *ideal transformer*; its windings are considered to have neither resistance nor reactance.

The impedance seen by the source changes when an impedance is connected to the secondary, as shown in the second variation equation. An impedance of Z_S connected to the secondary of an ideal transformer is equivalent to an impedance of $a^2 Z_S$ connected to the source, as illustrated in Fig. 35.9. It is said that "a secondary impedance of Z_S reflects as $a^2 Z_S$ on the primary side." Real primary circuits have input impedance. Anything attached to the transformer, such as a microphone, will contribute to the input impedance. At a minimum, the transformer's own windings will contribute resistance. The input impedance, $\mathbf{Z}_1$, contributes to the impedance seen by the source (i.e., the primary impedance), as the variation shows.[5]

Figure 35.9 *Equivalent Circuit with Secondary Impedance*

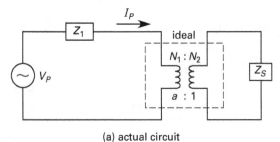

(a) actual circuit

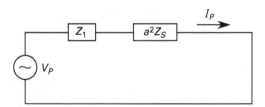

(b) equivalent circuit

Example

In the ideal transformer shown, coil 1 has 500 turns, V_1 is 1200 V, and V_2 is 240 V.

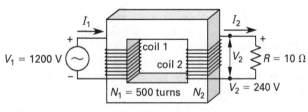

How many turns does coil 2 have?

(A)   100 turns

(B)   200 turns

(C)   500 turns

(D)   1000 turns

Solution

From Eq. 35.31 and Eq. 35.32, the turns ratio is

$$a = N_1/N_2 = \frac{V_1}{V_2}$$

$$N_2 = \frac{N_1 V_2}{V_1} = \frac{(500 \text{ turns})(240 \text{ V})}{1200 \text{ V}}$$

$$= 100 \text{ turns}$$

The answer is (A).

---

[5]Equation 35.33 assumes the input impedance is zero.

36

Rotating Machines

Nomenclature

B	magnetic flux density	T
E	induced voltage	V
f	frequency	Hz
I	current	A
K_a	armature constant (constant of the machine)	V·min/Wb
K_f	field constant	H
L	inductance	H
n	speed	rev/min
p	number of poles	–
P	power	W
R	resistance	Ω
t	time	s
T	torque	N·m
V	voltage	V

Symbols

ϕ	magnetic flux	Wb
ω	angular velocity (electrical)	rad/s
Ω	rotational velocity (mechanical)	rad/s

Subscripts

a	armature
e	electrical
f	field
g	generated
h	heat
m	mechanical or motor
s	synchronous

1. AC MACHINES

Rotating machines are broadly categorized as alternating-current (AC) and direct-current (DC) machines. Both categories include machines that use power (i.e., motors) and those that generate power (alternators and generators). Most AC machines can be constructed in either single-phase or polyphase (usually three-phase) configurations. The rotating part of the machine is called the *rotor*. The stationary part of the machine is called the *stator*. (In AC machines, the rotor is the field and the stator is the

armature if the machine is a generator, and vice versa if the machine is a motor. The terms "armature" and "field" are not commonly used with AC machines.)

For simplicity, Fig. 36.1 shows only one of the poles for each phase. But there is actually a winding on the opposite side from each winding depicted with the voltage in the opposite polarity, such that the magnetic fields produced by the windings have opposite polarities (north and south). When V_a is a maximum value, the field in the a-phase windings will be in the up direction, while the b-phase and c-phase fields will be equal and negative so their net field will be up also. When V_c reaches the maximum negative voltage, the field in the c-phase windings will be in the negative c-direction (60° counterclockwise), while the a-phase and b-phase fields will be equal and positive so their net field will be in the negative c-direction. When V_b is a maximum value, the field in the b-phase windings will be in the positive b-direction (120° counterclockwise), while the a-phase and c-phase fields will be equal and negative so their net field will be in the positive b-direction. The field makes a complete rotation around the stator for one cycle of three-phase voltage.

Figure 36.1 *Three-Pole AC Machine*

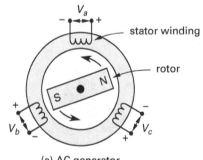

(a) AC generator

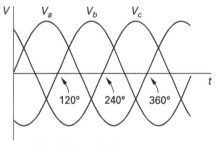

(b) ABC (positive) sequence

In AC machines, the term "pole" refers to a winding in the stationary stator. Each stator winding and its opposite, located directly across the stator, are counted as two poles and constitute a *pole pair*. AC machine stators rarely contain only two poles; a stator may contain 12 or more poles.[1] In an AC generator, each independent pole pair produces a single voltage waveform (i.e., a single phase). The number of independent voltage waveforms produced from an AC generator (one or three, in almost all cases) is equal to the number of independent pole pair sets.

Regardless of the number of phases involved, an AC machine is named according to the number of poles associated with each phase. For example, a single-phase, four-pole AC machine would have four poles arranged around the stator; and a three-phase, two-pole AC machine would have six poles arranged around the stator. The three-phase AC generator shown in Fig. 36.1 is a *two-pole machine* because it has two poles for each phase.

In an AC generator, the number of electrical cycles produced with one mechanical rotation of the rotor depends on the number of poles. With a four-pole machine, one mechanical rotation (360°) of the rotor would produce two electrical cycles (720°) per phase.

Equation 36.1: Synchronous Speed

$$n_s = 120f/p \qquad \qquad 36.1$$

Variation

$$n_s = \frac{60\Omega}{2\pi} = \frac{60\omega}{\pi p} \quad \text{[synchronous speed]}$$

Description

In *synchronous motors* and *induction motors*, the stator magnetic field rotates at a speed known as the *synchronous speed*, n_s, given by Eq. 36.1. f is the electrical frequency of the generated potential. p is the number of poles. The actual rotational speed, n, is known as the *mechanical frequency*. Care must be taken to distinguish between the mechanical rotor speed, n (in rpm), the angular mechanical rotor speed, Ω (in rad/s), and the linear and angular electrical frequencies, f and ω (in Hz and rad/s, respectively).[2]

Example

A two-pole AC motor operates on a three-phase, 60 Hz, line-to-line supply with an rms voltage of 240 V. What is most nearly its synchronous speed?

(A)   1000 rpm

(B)   1800 rpm

(C)   2400 rpm

(D)   3600 rpm

Solution

Since this is a two-pole machine, $p = 2$. From Eq. 36.1,

$$n_s = 120f/p$$

$$= \frac{\left(120 \ \dfrac{\frac{\text{rev}}{\text{min}}}{\text{Hz}}\right)(60 \ \text{Hz})}{2}$$

$$= 3600 \ \text{rpm}$$

The answer is (D).

Synchronous Machines

A *synchronous machine* has a permanent magnet or, more typically, a DC electromagnet that produces a constant magnetic field in the rotor. For the electromagnet, a DC current is provided to windings on the rotor and is transferred by stationary brushes making contact with *slip rings* or *collector rings* on the rotating shaft. The term "slip ring" implies that the conductor is a continuous type and slips under the brush. The term "collector ring" implies that the ring collects current from more than one winding (which is typical). A synchronous machine derives its name from the fact that the rotor turns at the synchronous speed, as determined from Eq. 36.1.

The rotor of a synchronous generator is rotated by a mechanical force. As the rotor rotates, both the current and the magnetic field remain constant, but the angle the magnetic field makes with each of the windings changes as the rotor rotates. For each of the stator windings, the flux lines from the rotor will be perpendicular to the loops at some angles and parallel to them at other angles. The current induced in the loops is greatest when the flux lines are perpendicular to the loops, and is zero when the flux lines are parallel to the loops. In this way, a rotating constant magnetic field induces alternating electrical currents in the stator.

---

[1]Four-pole AC machines are the most common.

[2]The NCEES *FE Reference Handbook* (*NCEES Handbook*) does not distinguish between angular armature and electrical speeds, Ω and ω. Consistent with almost all elementary discussions of two-pole motor construction and performance, the *NCEES Handbook* uses ω to represent the angular armature speed. Since $\Omega = 2\omega/p$, angular armature and electrical speeds are the same only for two-pole devices.

The induced voltage, E, is commonly called the *electro-motive force* (emf). In an elementary generator, emf is the desired end result to the load. In a motor, emf is also produced but is referred to as *back emf* (*counter emf*), since it opposes the input voltage.

A *synchronous motor* is essentially a synchronous generator operating in reverse. There is no difference in the construction of the machine. Alternating current is supplied to the stationary stator windings. A rotating magnetic field is produced when three-phase power is applied to the windings. Direct current is applied to the windings in the rotor through brushes and slip rings, as in the synchronous generators. The rotor current interacts with the stator field, causing the rotor to turn. Since the stator field frequency is fixed, the motor runs only at a single synchronous speed.

Induction Machines

An *induction motor* is essentially a constant-speed device that receives power through induction, without using brushes or slip rings. A motor can be considered to be a rotating transformer secondary (the rotor) with a stationary primary (the stator). Stator construction in an induction motor is the same as that in a synchronous motor. An emf is induced as the stator field moves past the rotor conductors. The stator field rotates at the synchronous speed given by Eq. 36.1. Since the rotor windings have inductive reactance, the rotor field lags the stator field.

Induction motors are commonly used for most industrial applications. They are more common than synchronous motors since they are more rugged, require less maintenance, and are less expensive. Induction motors consume the majority of all electric power generated and come in sizes from a fraction of a horsepower to many thousand horsepower. They are particularly useful in applications that require smooth starting under a load, such as hoists, mixers, or conveyors. Synchronous motors are much better than induction motors in power-generation applications.

Induction generators have few significant commercial uses, although some applications, such as windmills that generate power via induction motors, are gaining popularity. Induction generators are similar in concept to induction motors and are not discussed further in this chapter.

Equation 36.2: Slip

$$\text{slip} = (n_s - n)/n_s \qquad \textit{36.2}$$

Description

For the rotor of an induction motor to have a magnetic field, there must always be a variation in the magnetic flux as a function of time. To have a variation in magnetic flux, the rotor must turn slower than the synchronous speed so that the magnetic fields of the stator and rotor are never in the same direction. The difference in speed is small, but essential. *Percent slip* is the percentage difference in speed between the rotor and stator field. Slip can be expressed as either a decimal or a fraction (e.g., 0.05 slip or 5% slip). A related concept, slip in rpm, is the difference between actual and synchronous speeds.

Induction motor slip is normally 2–5% except for motors designed with a variable rotor resistance that can be increased for speed control.

Example

A three-phase induction motor runs on a 60 Hz power line at 1150 rpm at full load. The motor's stator contains a total of 18 poles. What is most nearly the motor's full-load slip?

(A) 0

(B) 0.042

(C) 0.075

(D) 0.13

Solution

The number of poles per phase is

$$p = \frac{18 \text{ poles}}{3 \text{ phases}} = 6$$

Calculate the synchronous speed of the AC motor from Eq. 36.1.

$$n_s = 120f/p$$

$$= \frac{\left(120 \; \dfrac{\frac{\text{rev}}{\text{min}}}{\text{Hz}}\right)(60 \text{ Hz})}{6}$$

$$= 1200 \text{ rpm}$$

Calculate the slip using Eq. 36.2.

$$\text{slip} = (n_s - n)/n_s$$

$$= \frac{1200 \; \dfrac{\text{rev}}{\text{min}} - 1150 \; \dfrac{\text{rev}}{\text{min}}}{1200 \; \dfrac{\text{rev}}{\text{min}}}$$

$$= 0.042$$

The answer is (B).

2. DC MACHINES

DC machines have a constant magnetic field in the stator (called the *field*). The magnetic field of the rotor (called the *armature*) responds to the stator field. The armature will respond by inducing current if the machine is a generator or by developing torque if the machine is a motor.

Equation 36.3: Magnetic Flux

$$\phi = K_f I_f \quad \text{[in webers]} \qquad 36.3$$

Description

In most DC machines, the magnetic field is provided by electromagnets. (In very small DC machines, it is supplied by permanent magnets.) The stator in a DC machine is composed of windings that produce the machine's field. Field poles are located on the stator and project inward. The poles alternate north and south around the machine and are separated by $360°/p$ around the machine. Each pole has a narrow ferromagnetic (e.g., iron) core around which the winding is wrapped. Each coil may consist of two or more separate windings. The *magnetic flux* produced by the field, Eq. 36.3, is linearly related to the field current, I_f, by a *field constant*, K_f, that depends on the construction of the machine, as long as the current is low enough that saturation does not occur.

The current in the coils creates a magnetic flux in the core that causes currents to circulate in the tiny magnetic domains in the core and reinforces the core's magnetic flux. As the current in the coil increases, the currents in the magnetic domains increase approximately linearly until the currents in the magnetic domains cannot respond fully, and part of the energy in the flux is lost as heat. At this stage, the magnetic material is said to be *saturating*, and the response is no longer linear. As the current in the coil continues to increase, it reaches a point where the currents in the magnetic domains are going as fast as they can, and any additional energy in the flux from the coil is dissipated as heat. At this stage, the magnetic material is said to be *completely saturated*.

The armature circuit and field circuit are actually loops of wire around magnetic materials, but they are each modeled as a resistor in series with an inductor. The variables R_a and L_a are used for the armature resistance and inductance. The variables R_f and L_f are used for the field resistance and inductance. The inductance is usually ignored in DC machines, except for transient conditions.

DC Generators

A *DC generator* is a device that produces DC potential. The actual voltage induced is sinusoidal (i.e., AC). However, brushes on *split-ring commutators* make the connection to the rotating armature and rectify AC potential. The DC generator is, in fact, not DC. Rather, it is rectified AC.

The armature in a simple DC generator consists of a single coil with several turns (loops) of wire. The two ends of the coil terminate at a *commutator*. The commutator consists of a single ring split into two halves known as *segments*. (This arrangement is shown in Fig. 36.2. The field windings and rotor core are omitted for clarity.) The brushes slide on the commutator and make contact with the adjacent segment every half-rotation of the coil. As shown in Fig. 36.2, the coil is nearly perpendicular to the magnetic field, **B**. The magnetic flux through the coil will be at its maximum when the coil is perpendicular to the magnetic field. The magnetic flux through the coil will be zero when the coil is parallel to the magnetic field. The rate of change in the magnetic flux depends on the speed of rotation.

Figure 36.2 Commutator Action

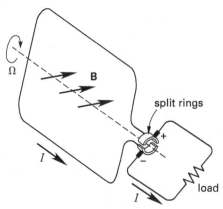

As shown in Fig. 36.2, the current flows from the positive brush to the negative brush. As the coil continues to rotate to be parallel to the magnetic field, the commutator rotates such that the brushes are at the gaps between the commutator segments. As the coil rotates further, the positive brush will touch the commutator segment that the negative brush was previously touching, and vice versa. The current will continue in the same direction. Figure 36.3 shows the full-wave rectified voltage that results from this simple arrangement, which is obviously not a constant voltage.

Figure 36.3 Rectified DC Voltage Induced in a Single Coil

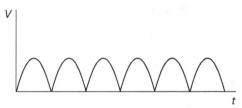

Figure 36.4 shows a simplified DC armature with two coils oriented at 90° to each other. (The field windings and rotor core are omitted for clarity.) Each of the coils

produces a full-wave rectified emf, as in Fig. 36.3. Since the coils are connected in series (in the modern closed-coil winding arrangement), the emf induced is the sum of the emfs induced in the individual coils, as shown in Fig. 36.5. The voltage induced in each coil of a DC generator with multiple coils is still sinusoidal, but the terminal output is nearly constant, not a (rectified) sinusoid. The slight variations in the voltage are known as *ripple*. The more coils there are, the smoother the DC voltage. The output may be filtered or passed through a DC voltage regulator to reduce or eliminate the ripple.

Figure 36.4 Two-Coil, Four-Segment Closed-Coil Armature

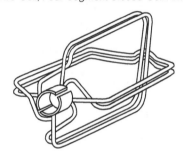

Figure 36.5 Rectified DC Voltage from a Two-Coil, Four-Segment Generator

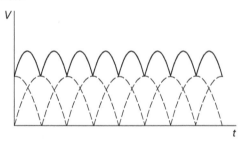

As shown in Fig. 36.6, DC generators can be modeled as an emf, E_g, which represents the part of the voltage induced in the armature circuit by the magnetic flux as the armature rotates in the field, and a resistor, R_a, which represents the resistance in the armature windings.

Figure 36.6 DC Machine Equivalent Circuit

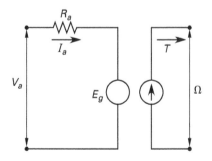

Since the rate of change of the magnetic flux in the armature depends on the speed of rotation, and because the armature is essentially an inductor, the current depends on the magnetic flux. The voltage of an inductor is directly dependent upon the rate of change of the current. Therefore, the induced voltage is directly dependent upon the rotational speed. Also, the greater the magnetic flux, the greater the current induced. Therefore, the induced voltage is directly dependent upon the magnetic flux. The proportionality constant that relates the speed and magnetic flux to the generated voltage is K_a and depends upon the construction of the machine. For the generator model in Fig. 36.6, this results in

$$E_g = K_a n \phi$$

Equation 36.4: Armature Voltage

$$V_a = K_a n \phi \quad \text{[in volts]} \qquad 36.4$$

Description

The *terminal voltage* of the generator model shown in Fig. 36.6 is

$$V_a = E_g + I_a R_a = K_a n \phi + I_a R_a$$

If the armature resistance is disregarded (as in the case of a permanent magnet armature that has no windings), the $I_a R_a$ drop is zero. Only in that case, the terminal and armature voltages are the same, and Eq. 36.4 accurately describes the terminal voltage. K_a is known as the *armature constant (armature winding constant* or *machine constant)*.[3]

Example

A DC generator armature turns at 1200 rpm. The field's magnetic flux is 0.02 Wb. The armature constant is $K_a = 1$ V·min/Wb. Disregarding armature resistance, what is most nearly the output voltage?

    (A)   12 V

    (B)   20 V

    (C)   24 V

    (D)   48 V

---

[3]Although not incorrect, it is not common to specify the armature voltage (or the armature constant) in terms of n in rpm (as opposed to ω in rad/s).

Electricity/
Magnetism

Solution

From Eq. 36.4,

$$V_a = K_a n \phi$$
$$= \left(1 \; \frac{\text{V·min}}{\text{Wb}}\right)\left(1200 \; \frac{\text{rev}}{\text{min}}\right)(0.02 \text{ Wb})$$
$$= 24 \text{ V}$$

The answer is (C).

DC Motors

DC motors are similar in construction and analysis to DC generators. Electrical power is delivered to a motor by applying a voltage to its terminals, resulting in a flow of armature current, I_a, through the armature. Some of that power is dissipated as heat in the armature winding's resistance, and some is converted into mechanical power to turn the armature. The power for the motor model shown in Fig. 36.6 is determined from

$$P_m = P_h + P_e = I_a^2 R_a + I_a E_g$$

Equation 36.5 and Eq. 36.6: Mechanical Power and Torque

$$P_m = V_a I_a \quad \text{[in watts]} \qquad 36.5$$

$$T_m = (60/2\pi) K_a \phi I_a \quad \text{[in newton-meters]} \qquad 36.6$$

Variation

$$P_m = T\Omega$$

Description

Disregarding the power dissipated in armature resistance heating, the motor model power equation can be simplified to Eq. 36.5.

The *torque of the DC motor* is linearly related to the strength of the field and the magnetic field of the armature. The stronger each of these fields is, the stronger the force would need to be to bring them into line (which never happens, due to the commutator). The magnetic field of the armature is linearly related to the current of the armature (ignoring magnetization). The proportionality constant that relates the armature current and magnetic flux to the torque voltage is the same K_a as used in Eq. 36.4 and depends upon the construction of the machine.

The mechanical power can also be expressed in terms of torque, T, and the mechanical rotational velocity, Ω, as shown in the variation equation. This can be derived directly from force-velocity-power relationships.

Example

A DC motor armature draws 100 A while generating a magnetic flux of 0.02 Wb. The armature constant is $K_a = 1$ V·min/Wb. What is most nearly the motor's developed torque?

(A)   19 N·m

(B)   24 N·m

(C)   32 N·m

(D)   51 N·m

Solution

From Eq. 36.6,

$$T_m = (60/2\pi) K_a \phi I_a$$
$$= \left(\frac{60}{2\pi}\right)\left(1 \; \frac{\text{V·min}}{\text{Wb}}\right)(0.02 \text{ Wb})(100 \text{ A})$$
$$= 19 \text{ N·m}$$

The answer is (A).

Diagnostic Exam

Topic X: Dynamics, Kinematics, and Vibrations

1. A projectile is fired from a cannon with an initial velocity of 1000 m/s and at an angle of 30° from horizontal. The point of impact is 1500 m below the point of release.

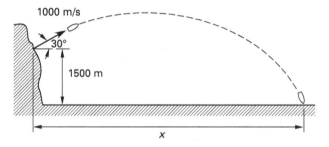

Most nearly, at what distance from the cannon will the projectile strike the ground?

(A) 8200 m

(B) 67 000 m

(C) 78 000 m

(D) 91 000 m

2. A fisherman cuts his boat's engine off as it is entering a harbor. The boat drifts, initially, to a dead stop with its front end touching the dock. The fisherman, with a mass of 80 kg, moves 5 m from his seat in the back to the front of the boat within 5 seconds. As the fisherman is expecting to be able to reach the dock in time before drifting away from the dock's mooring station, the boat moves away from the dock in opposite direction as a reactionary response to the fisherman's immediate movement. If the empty boat has a mass of 300 kg, and disregarding all friction, approximately how far will the boat have moved away from the dock requiring the fisherman to jump the distance?

(A) 1.1 m

(B) 1.3 m

(C) 1.9 m

(D) 5.0 m

3. The elevator in a 12–story building has a mass of 1000 kg. Its maximum velocity and maximum acceleration are 2 m/s and 1 m/s^2, respectively. A passenger with a mass of 75 kg stands on a bathroom scale in the elevator as the elevator ascends at its maximum acceleration. What is most nearly the scale reading just as the elevator reaches its maximum acceleration?

(A) 75 N

(B) 150 N

(C) 810 N

(D) 890 N

4. A 100 kg block is pulled along a smooth, flat surface by an external 500 N force. The coefficient of friction between the block and the surface is 0.15.

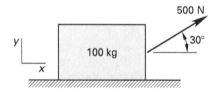

Most nearly what horizontal acceleration is experienced by the block due to the external force?

(A) 3.2 m/s^2

(B) 3.8 m/s^2

(C) 4.3 m/s^2

(D) 5.0 m/s^2

5. A 2000 kg car pulls a 500 kg trailer. The car and trailer accelerate from 50 km/h to 75 km/h at a rate of 1 m/s^2. The linear impulse that the car imparts to the trailer is most nearly

(A) 3500 N·s

(B) 8700 N·s

(C) 13 000 N·s

(D) 17 000 N·s

6. A wheel with a radius of 0.8 m rolls without slipping along a flat surface at 3 m/s. Arc AB on the wheel's perimeter has an interior angle of 90°.

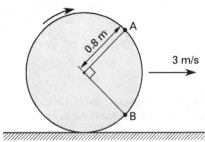

What is most nearly the velocity of point A when point B contacts the ground?

(A) 3.0 m/s

(B) 3.4 m/s

(C) 3.8 m/s

(D) 4.2 m/s

7. A 10 kg block is resting on a horizontal circular disk (e.g., turntable) at a radius of 0.5 m from the center. The coefficient of friction between the block and disk is 0.2. The disk rotates with a uniform angular velocity. What is most nearly the minimum angular velocity of the disk that will cause the block to slip?

(A) 1.4 rad/s

(B) 2.0 rad/s

(C) 3.9 rad/s

(D) 4.4 rad/s

8. A perfect sphere is projected up a frictionless incline by a spring. Which property increases, after the ball loses contact with the spring?

(A) angular velocity

(B) total energy

(C) potential energy

(D) linear momentum

9. A ball is dropped from rest at a point 12 m above the ground into a smooth, frictionless chute. The ball exits the chute 2 m above the ground and at an angle 45° from the horizontal. Air resistance is negligible.

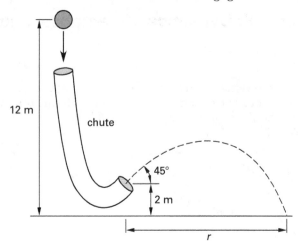

Most nearly, how far will the ball travel in the horizontal direction before hitting the ground?

(A) 12 m

(B) 20 m

(C) 22 m

(D) 24 m

10. A 6 kg sphere moving at 3 m/s collides with a 10 kg sphere traveling at 2.5 m/s in the same direction. The 6 kg sphere comes to a complete stop after the collision. What is most nearly the new velocity of the 10 kg sphere immediately after the collision?

(A) 0.50 m/s

(B) 2.8 m/s

(C) 4.3 m/s

(D) 5.5 m/s

SOLUTIONS

1. $y = -1500$ m since it is below the launch plane.

$$y = v_0 t \sin\theta - \frac{gt^2}{2}$$

$$\frac{g}{2}t^2 - v_0 t \sin\theta + y = 0$$

$$\left(\frac{9.81 \frac{\text{m}}{\text{s}^2}}{2}\right)t^2 - \left(1000 \frac{\text{m}}{\text{s}}\right)t\sin 30° + (-1500 \text{ m}) = 0$$

$$\left(4.905 \frac{\text{m}}{\text{s}^2}\right)t^2 - \left(500 \frac{\text{m}}{\text{s}}\right)t + (-1500 \text{ m}) = 0$$

The time to impact is

$$t = \frac{-b \pm \sqrt{b^2 - 4ac}}{2a} \quad \text{[quadratic formula]}$$

$$= \frac{500 \frac{\text{m}}{\text{s}} \pm \sqrt{\left(-500 \frac{\text{m}}{\text{s}}\right)^2 - (4)\left(4.905 \frac{\text{m}}{\text{s}^2}\right) \times (-1500 \text{ m})}}{(2)\left(4.905 \frac{\text{m}}{\text{s}^2}\right)}$$

$$= +104.85 \text{ s}, -2.9166 \text{ s}$$

The horizontal distance is

$$x = v_0 t \cos\theta$$

$$= \left(1000 \frac{\text{m}}{\text{s}}\right)(104.85 \text{ s})\cos 30°$$

$$= 90\,803 \text{ m} \quad (91\,000 \text{ m})$$

The answer is (D).

2. The velocity of the fisherman relative to the boat is

$$v = \frac{s}{t} = \frac{5 \text{ m}}{5 \text{ s}}$$

$$= 1 \text{ m/s}$$

If the boat moves as the fisherman moves, the velocity of the fisherman relative to the dock is

$$v'_{\text{fisherman}} = 1 \frac{\text{m}}{\text{s}} + v'_{\text{boat}}$$

Use the conservation of momentum.

$$\sum m_i v_i = \sum m_i v'_i$$

$$\begin{array}{c} m_{\text{fisherman}} v_{\text{fisherman}} \\ + m_{\text{boat}} v_{\text{boat}} \end{array} = \begin{array}{c} m_{\text{fisherman}} v'_{\text{fisherman}} \\ + m_{\text{boat}} v'_{\text{boat}} \end{array}$$

However, $v_{\text{fisherman}} = v_{\text{boat}} = 0$ initially, so

$$0 = m_{\text{fisherman}}\left(1 \frac{\text{m}}{\text{s}} + v'_{\text{boat}}\right) + m_{\text{boat}} v'_{\text{boat}}$$

$$v'_{\text{boat}} = \frac{-m_{\text{fisherman}}\left(1 \frac{\text{m}}{\text{s}}\right)}{m_{\text{fisherman}} + m_{\text{boat}}}$$

$$= \frac{-(80 \text{ kg})\left(1 \frac{\text{m}}{\text{s}}\right)}{80 \text{ kg} + 300 \text{ kg}}$$

$$= -0.211 \text{ m/s} \quad \text{[backward]}$$

The direction the fisherman jumps is positive. Therefore, the distance the fisherman will have to jump is

$$s = v'_{\text{boat}} t = \left(0.211 \frac{\text{m}}{\text{s}}\right)(5 \text{ s})$$

$$= 1.06 \text{ m} \quad (1.1 \text{ m})$$

The answer is (A).

3. This is a direct application of Newton's second law. The acceleration of the elevator adds to the gravitational acceleration.

$$F = ma$$

$$= m(g + a)$$

$$= (75 \text{ kg})\left(9.81 \frac{\text{m}}{\text{s}^2} + 1 \frac{\text{m}}{\text{s}^2}\right)$$

$$= 811 \text{ N} \quad (810 \text{ N})$$

The answer is (C).

4. The weight is reduced by the vertical component of the applied force. The frictional force is

Friction

$$F_f = \mu N = \mu(mg - F_y)$$

$$= (0.15)\left((100 \text{ kg})\left(9.81 \frac{\text{m}}{\text{s}^2}\right) - (500 \text{ N})\sin 30°\right)$$

$$= 110 \text{ N}$$

Dynamics/
Vibrations

Use Newton's second law. *[Particle Kinetics]*

$$ma_x = \sum F_x = F_x - F_f$$
$$a_x = \frac{F_x - F_f}{m}$$
$$= \frac{(500 \text{ N})\cos 30° - 110 \text{ N}}{100 \text{ kg}}$$
$$= 3.23 \text{ m/s}^2 \quad (3.2 \text{ m/s}^2)$$

The answer is (A).

5. The impulse delivered to a system is equal to the change in its momentum (the impulse-momentum principle).

$$\text{Imp} = \Delta p = \Delta m \, \text{v} = m(\Delta \text{v})$$
$$= m(\text{v}_2 - \text{v}_1)$$
$$= \frac{(500 \text{ kg})\left(75 \dfrac{\text{km}}{\text{h}} - 50 \dfrac{\text{km}}{\text{h}}\right)\left(1000 \dfrac{\text{m}}{\text{km}}\right)}{3600 \dfrac{\text{s}}{\text{h}}}$$
$$= 3472 \text{ N·s} \quad (3500 \text{ N·s})$$

The answer is (A).

6. The wheel's radius is 0.8 m. Point B becomes the instantaneous center of rotation when it is in contact with the ground.

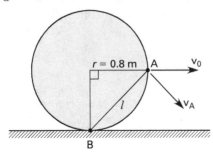

$$l^2 = r^2 + r^2 \quad \text{[Pythagorean theorem]}$$
$$= (0.8 \text{ m})^2 + (0.8 \text{ m})^2$$
$$= 1.28 \text{ m}^2$$
$$l = \sqrt{1.28 \text{ m}^2} = 1.13 \text{ m}$$

The velocity of point A is

$$\text{v}_A = \frac{l \text{v}_0}{r} = \frac{(1.13 \text{ m})\left(3 \dfrac{\text{m}}{\text{s}}\right)}{0.8 \text{ m}}$$
$$= 4.24 \text{ m/s} \quad (4.2 \text{ m/s})$$

The answer is (D).

7. For the block to begin to slip, the centrifugal force must equal the frictional force.

$$F_c = F_f$$
$$mr\omega^2 = \mu N = \mu mg$$
$$\omega^2 = \frac{\mu g}{r}$$
$$\omega = \sqrt{\frac{\mu g}{r}}$$
$$= \sqrt{\frac{(0.2)\left(9.81 \dfrac{\text{m}}{\text{s}^2}\right)}{0.5 \text{ m}}}$$
$$= 1.98 \text{ rad/s} \quad (2.0 \text{ rad/s})$$

The answer is (B).

8. Since the system is frictionless, there is no moment causing the sphere to rotate or stop rotating. Therefore, angular velocity is constant. Since the system is frictionless, total energy is constant. Kinetic energy is converted to potential energy. As the linear velocity decreases, so does the linear momentum.

The answer is (C).

9. The change in elevation between points A and B represents a decrease in the ball's potential energy. The kinetic energy increases correspondingly.

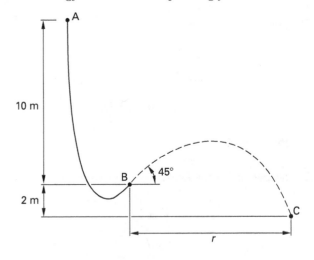

$$mg\Delta h = \frac{m\text{v}^2}{2}$$
$$\text{v}^2 = 2g\Delta h$$
$$\text{v} = \sqrt{2g\Delta h}$$
$$= \sqrt{(2)\left(9.81 \dfrac{\text{m}}{\text{s}^2}\right)(10 \text{ m})}$$
$$= 14.0 \text{ m/s}$$

The ball follows the path of a projectile between points B and C. *[Projectile Motion]*

$$y = \frac{-gt^2}{2} + v_0 \sin(\theta)t$$

$$\left(\frac{g}{2}\right)t^2 - (v_0 \sin\theta)t + y = 0$$

Because the landing point is below the chute exit, $y = -2$ m.

$$\left(\frac{9.81 \, \frac{m}{s^2}}{2}\right)t^2 - \left(14.0 \, \frac{m}{s}\right)(\sin 45°)t + (-2 \text{ m}) = 0$$

$$\left(4.91 \, \frac{m}{s^2}\right)t^2 - \left(9.9 \, \frac{m}{s}\right)t + (-2 \text{ m}) = 0$$

Solve for t using the quadratic formula.

Quadratic Equation

$$t = \frac{-b \pm \sqrt{b^2 - 4ac}}{2a}$$

$$= \frac{9.9 \, \frac{m}{s} \pm \sqrt{\left(9.9 \, \frac{m}{s}\right)^2 - (4)\left(4.91 \, \frac{m}{s^2}\right)(-2 \text{ m})}}{(2)\left(4.91 \, \frac{m}{s^2}\right)}$$

$$= 2.2 \text{ s}, \ -0.2 \text{ s}$$

Calculate the distance traveled from the x-component of the velocity.

$$x = v_0 t \cos\theta$$

$$= \left(14.0 \, \frac{m}{s}\right)(2.2 \text{ s})\cos 45°$$

$$= 21.8 \text{ m} \quad (22 \text{ m})$$

The answer is (C).

10. Use the law of conservation of momentum.

$$m_1 v_1 + m_2 v_2 = m_1 v_1' + m_2 v_2'$$

$$(6 \text{ kg})\left(3 \, \frac{m}{s}\right)$$
$$+ (10 \text{ kg})\left(2.5 \, \frac{m}{s}\right)$$
$$= (6 \text{ kg})\left(0 \, \frac{m}{s}\right) + (10 \text{ kg})v_2'$$

The velocity of the 10 kg sphere is

$$v_2' = \frac{43 \, \frac{\text{kg·m}}{s}}{10 \text{ kg}} = 4.3 \text{ m/s}$$

The answer is (C).

Dynamics/
Vibrations

37 Kinematics

Nomenclature

a	acceleration	m/s^2
f	coefficient of friction	–
f	frequency	Hz
g	gravitational acceleration, 9.81	m/s^2
r	position	m
r	radius	m
s	displacement	m
s	distance	m
s	position	m
t	time	s
v	velocity	m/s
x	horizontal distance	m
y	elevation	m

Symbols

α	angular acceleration	rad/s^2
θ	angular position	rad
ρ	radius of curvature	m
ω	angular velocity	rad/s

Subscripts

0	initial
c	constant
f	final
n	normal
r	radial
t	tangential
x	horizontal
y	vertical
θ	transverse

1. INTRODUCTION TO KINEMATICS

Dynamics is the study of moving objects. The subject is divided into kinematics and kinetics. *Kinematics* is the study of a body's motion independent of the forces on the body. It is a study of the geometry of motion without consideration of the causes of motion. Kinematics deals only with relationships among position, velocity, acceleration, and time.

2. PARTICLES AND RIGID BODIES

A body in motion can be considered a *particle* if rotation of the body is absent or insignificant. A particle does not possess rotational kinetic energy. All parts of a particle have the same instantaneous displacement, velocity, and acceleration.

A *rigid body* does not deform when loaded and can be considered a combination of two or more particles that remain at a fixed, finite distance from each other. At any given instant, the parts (particles) of a rigid body can have different displacements, velocities, and accelerations if the body has rotational as well as translational motion.

Equation 37.1 and Eq. 37.2: Instantaneous Velocity and Acceleration

$$\mathbf{v} = d\mathbf{r}/dt \qquad \text{37.1}$$

$$\mathbf{a} = d\mathbf{v}/dt \qquad \text{37.2}$$

Variation

$$a = \frac{d^2 r}{dt^2}$$

Description

For the position vector of a particle, r, the instantaneous velocity, $\mathbf{v}$, and acceleration, a, are given by Eq. 37.1 and Eq. 37.2, respectively.

Example

The position of a particle moving along the x-axis is given by $r(t) = t^2 - t + 8$, where r is in units of meters and t is in seconds. What is most nearly the velocity of the particle when $t = 5$ s?

(A) 9.0 m/s

(B) 10 m/s

(C) 11 m/s

(D) 12 m/s

Solution

The velocity equation is the first derivative of the position equation with respect to time.

$$\mathbf{v}(t) = dr(t)/dt = \frac{d}{dt}(t^2 - t + 8)$$
$$= 2t - 1$$
$$\mathbf{v}(5) = (2)(5) - 1$$
$$= 9.0 \text{ m/s}$$

The answer is (A).

3. DISTANCE AND SPEED

The terms "displacement" and "distance" have different meanings in kinematics. *Displacement* (or *linear displacement*) is the net change in a particle's position as determined from the position function, $r(t)$. *Distance traveled* is the accumulated length of the path traveled during all direction reversals, and it can be found by adding the path lengths covered during periods in which the velocity sign does not change. Therefore, distance is always greater than or equal to displacement.

$$s = r(t_2) - r(t_1)$$

Similarly, "velocity" and "speed" have different meanings: *velocity* is a vector, having both magnitude and direction; *speed* is a scalar quantity, equal to the magnitude of velocity. When specifying speed, direction is not considered.

4. RECTANGULAR COORDINATES

The position of a particle is specified with reference to a coordinate system. Three coordinates are necessary to identify the position in three-dimensional space; in two dimensions, two coordinates are necessary. A coordinate can represent a linear position, as in the rectangular coordinate system, or it can represent an angular position, as in the polar system.

Consider the particle shown in Fig. 37.1. Its position, as well as its velocity and acceleration, can be specified in three primary forms: vector form, rectangular coordinate form, and unit vector form.

Figure 37.1 Rectangular Coordinates

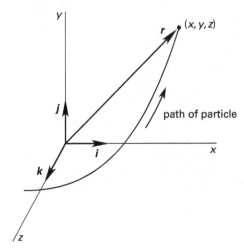

The *vector form* of the particle's position is r, where the vector r has both magnitude and direction. The *Cartesian coordinate system form* (*rectangular coordinate form*) is (x, y, z).

Equation 37.3: Cartesian Unit Vector Form

$$r = xi + yj + zk \qquad \text{37.3}$$

Description

The *unit vector form* of a position vector is given by Eq. 37.3.

Example

The position of a particle in Cartesian coordinates over time is $x = 5t$ in the x-direction, $y = 6t$ in the y-direction, and $z = 5t$ in the z-direction. What is the vector form of the particle's position, r?

(A) $r = 5ti + 6tj + 5tk$

(B) $r = 5ti + 6tj + 6tk$

(C) $r = 6ti + 5tj + 5tk$

(D) $r = 6ti + 5tj + 6tk$

Solution

Using Eq. 37.3, the vector form of the particle's position is

$$r = xi + yj + zk$$
$$= 5ti + 6tj + 5tk$$

The answer is (A).

5. RECTILINEAR MOTION

Equation 37.4 Through Eq. 37.9: Particle Rectilinear Motion

$$a = \frac{dv}{dt} \quad \text{[general]} \qquad 37.4$$

$$v = \frac{ds}{dt} \quad \text{[general]} \qquad 37.5$$

$$a\,ds = v\,dv \quad \text{[general]} \qquad 37.6$$

$$v = v_0 + a_c t \qquad 37.7$$

$$s = s_0 + v_0 t + \frac{1}{2}a_c t^2 \qquad 37.8$$

$$v^2 = v_0^2 + 2a_c(s - s_0) \qquad 37.9$$

Description

A *rectilinear system* is one in which particles move only in straight lines. (Another name is *linear system*.) The relationships among position, velocity, and acceleration for a linear system are given by Eq. 37.4 through Eq. 37.9. Equation 37.4 through Eq. 37.6 show relationships for general (including variable) acceleration of particles.[1] Equation 37.7 through Eq. 37.9 show relationships given constant acceleration, a_c.[2]

When values of time are substituted into these equations, the position, velocity, and acceleration are known as *instantaneous values*.

Equation 37.10 Through Eq. 37.13: Cartesian Velocity and Acceleration

$$v = \dot{x}i + \dot{y}j + \dot{z}k \qquad 37.10$$

$$a = \ddot{x}i + \ddot{y}j + \ddot{z}k \qquad 37.11$$

$$\dot{x} = dx/dt = v_x \qquad 37.12$$

$$\ddot{x} = d^2x/dt^2 = a_x \qquad 37.13$$

Description

The velocity and acceleration are the first two derivatives of the position vector, as shown in Eq. 37.10 and Eq. 37.11.

6. CONSTANT ACCELERATION

Equation 37.14 Through Eq. 37.17: Velocity and Displacement with Constant Linear Acceleration

$$a(t) = a_0 \qquad 37.14$$

$$v(t) = a_0(t - t_0) + v_0 \qquad 37.15$$

$$s(t) = a_0(t - t_0)^2/2 + v_0(t - t_0) + s_0 \qquad 37.16$$

$$v^2 = v_0^2 + 2a_0(s - s_0) \qquad 37.17$$

Variations

$$v(t) = a_0 \int dt$$

$$s(t) = a_0 \iint dt^2$$

Description

Acceleration is a constant in many cases, such as a free-falling body with constant acceleration g. If the acceleration is constant, the acceleration term can be taken out of the integrals shown in Sec. 37.5. The initial distance from the origin is s_0; the initial velocity is a constant, v_0; and a constant acceleration is denoted a_0.

---

[1]Equation 37.6 can be derived from $a\,dt = dv$ and $v\,dt = ds$ by eliminating dt. One scenario where the acceleration depends on position is a particle being accelerated (or decelerated) by a compression spring. The spring force depends on the spring extension, so the acceleration does also.
[2]The NCEES *FE Reference Handbook* (*NCEES Handbook*) is inconsistent in what it uses subscripts to designate. For example, in its Dynamics section, it uses subscripts to designate the location of the accelerating point (e.g., c in a_c for acceleration of the centroid), the direction or related axis (e.g., x in a_x for acceleration in the x-direction), the type of acceleration (e.g., n in a_n for normal acceleration), and the moment in time (e.g., 0 in a_0 for initial acceleration). In Eq. 37.7 through Eq. 37.9, the *NCEES Handbook* uses subscripts to designate the nature of the acceleration (i.e., the subscript c indicates constant acceleration). Elsewhere in the *NCEES Handbook*, the subscript c is used to designate centroid and mass center.

Example

In standard gravity, block A exerts a force of 10 000 N, and block B exerts a force of 7500 N. Both blocks are initially held stationary. There is no friction, and the pulleys have no mass. Block A has an acceleration of 1.4 m/s² once the blocks are released.

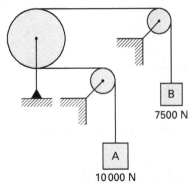

7500 N

A

10 000 N

What is most nearly the velocity of block A 2.5 s after the blocks are released?

   (A) 0 m/s

   (B) 3.5 m/s

   (C) 4.4 m/s

   (D) 4.9 m/s

Solution

Use Eq. 37.15 to solve for the velocity of block A.

$$\mathrm{v_A} = a_\mathrm{A}(t - t_0) + \mathrm{v}_0 = \left(1.4 \; \frac{\mathrm{m}}{\mathrm{s}^2}\right)(2.5 \; \mathrm{s} - 0 \; \mathrm{s}) + 0 \; \frac{\mathrm{m}}{\mathrm{s}}$$

$$= 3.5 \; \mathrm{m/s}$$

The answer is (B).

Equation 37.18 Through Eq. 37.21: Velocity and Displacement with Constant Angular Acceleration

$$\alpha(t) = \alpha_0 \qquad\qquad 37.18$$

$$\omega(t) = \alpha_0(t - t_0) + \omega_0 \qquad\qquad 37.19$$

$$\theta(t) = \alpha_0(t - t_0)^2/2 + \omega_0(t - t_0) + \theta_0 \qquad 37.20$$

$$\omega^2 = \omega_0^2 + 2\alpha_0(\theta - \theta_0) \qquad\qquad 37.21$$

Description

Equation 37.18 through Eq. 37.21 give the equations for constant angular acceleration.

Example

A flywheel rotates at 7200 rpm when the power is suddenly cut off. The flywheel decelerates at a constant rate of 2.1 rad/s² and comes to rest 6 min later. What is most nearly the angular displacement of the flywheel?

   (A) 43×10^3 rad

   (B) 93×10^3 rad

   (C) 140×10^3 rad

   (D) 270×10^3 rad

Solution

From Eq. 37.20, the angular displacement is

$$\theta(t) = \alpha_0(t - t_0)^2/2 + \omega_0(t - t_0) + \theta_0$$

$$= \frac{\left(-2.1 \; \dfrac{\mathrm{rad}}{\mathrm{s}^2}\right)\left(60 \; \dfrac{\mathrm{s}}{\mathrm{min}}\right)^2 (6 \; \mathrm{min} - 0 \; \mathrm{min})^2}{2}$$

$$\quad + \left(7200 \; \frac{\mathrm{rev}}{\mathrm{min}}\right)\left(2\pi \; \frac{\mathrm{rad}}{\mathrm{rev}}\right)(6 \; \mathrm{min} - 0 \; \mathrm{min})$$

$$\quad + 0 \; \mathrm{rad}$$

$$= 135.4 \times 10^3 \; \mathrm{rad} \quad (140 \times 10^3 \; \mathrm{rad})$$

The answer is (C).

7. NON-CONSTANT ACCELERATION

Equation 37.22 and Eq. 37.23: Velocity and Displacement for Non-Constant Acceleration

$$\mathrm{v}(t) = \int_{t_0}^{t} a(t)\,dt + \mathrm{v}_{t_0} \qquad\qquad 37.22$$

$$s(t) = \int_{t_0}^{t} \mathrm{v}(t)\,dt + s_{t_0} \qquad\qquad 37.23$$

Description

The velocity and displacement, respectively, for non-constant acceleration, $a(t)$, are calculated using Eq. 37.22 and Eq. 37.23.

Example

A particle initially traveling at 10 m/s experiences a linear increase in acceleration in the direction of motion as shown. The particle reaches an acceleration of 20 m/s² in 6 seconds.

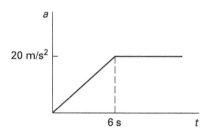

Most nearly, what is the distance traveled by the particle during those 6 seconds?

- (A) 60 m
- (B) 70 m
- (C) 120 m
- (D) 180 m

Solution

The expression for the acceleration as a function of time is

$$a(t) = \left(\frac{20 \, \frac{\text{m}}{\text{s}^2}}{6 \, \text{s}} \right) t = \frac{20 \, \frac{\text{m}}{\text{s}^3}}{6} t$$

From Eq. 37.22, the velocity function is

$$\text{v}(t) = \int a(t)\,dt = \int \frac{20}{6} t \, dt = \frac{20}{12} t^2 + C_1$$

Since $\text{v}(0) = 10$, $C_1 = 10$.

From Eq. 37.23, the position function is

$$s(t) = \int \text{v}(t)\,dt$$
$$= \int \left(\frac{20}{12} t^2 + 10 \right) dt$$
$$= \frac{20}{36} t^3 + 10t + C_2$$

In a calculation of distance traveled, the initial distance (position) is $s(0) = 0$, so $C_2 = 0$. The distance traveled during the first 6 seconds is

$$s(6) = \int_0^6 \text{v}(t)\,dt$$
$$= \frac{20}{36} t^3 + 10t \Big|_0^6$$
$$= 180 \text{ m} - 0 \text{ m}$$
$$= 180 \text{ m}$$

The answer is (D).

Equation 37.24 and Eq. 37.25: Variable Angular Acceleration

$$\omega(t) = \int_{t_0}^{t} \alpha(t)\,dt + \omega_{t_0} \qquad 37.24$$

$$\theta(t) = \int_{t_0}^{t} \omega(t)\,dt + \theta_{t_0} \qquad 37.25$$

Description

For non-constant angular acceleration, $\alpha(t)$, the angular velocity, ω, and angular displacement, θ, can be calculated from Eq. 37.24 and Eq. 37.25.

8. CURVILINEAR MOTION

Curvilinear motion describes the motion of a particle along a path that is not a straight line. Special examples of curvilinear motion include plane circular motion and projectile motion. For particles traveling along curvilinear paths, the position, velocity, and acceleration may be specified in rectangular coordinates as they were for rectilinear motion, or it may be more convenient to express the kinematic variables in terms of other coordinate systems (e.g., polar coordinates).

9. CURVILINEAR MOTION: PLANE CIRCULAR MOTION

Plane circular motion (also known as *rotational particle motion*, *angular motion*, or *circular motion*) is the motion of a particle around a fixed circular path. (See Fig. 37.2.)

Figure 37.2 Plane Circular Motion

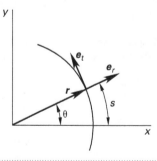

Equation 37.26 Through Eq. 37.31: x, y, z Coordinates

$$\text{v}_x = \dot{x} \qquad 37.26$$

$$\text{v}_y = \dot{y} \qquad 37.27$$

$$v_z = \dot{z} \qquad 37.28$$

$$a_x = \ddot{x} \qquad 37.29$$

$$a_y = \ddot{y} \qquad 37.30$$

$$a_z = \ddot{z} \qquad 37.31$$

Description

Equation 37.26 through Eq. 37.31 give the relationships between acceleration, velocity, and the Cartesian coordinates of a particle in plane circular motion.

Equation 37.32 Through Eq. 37.37: Polar Coordinates

$$v_r = \dot{r} \qquad 37.32$$

$$v_\theta = r\dot{\theta} \qquad 37.33$$

$$v_z = \dot{z} \qquad 37.34$$

$$a_r = \ddot{r} - r\dot{\theta}^2 \qquad 37.35$$

$$a_\theta = r\ddot{\theta} + 2r\dot{\theta} \qquad 37.36$$

$$a_z = \ddot{z} \qquad 37.37$$

Description

In *polar coordinates*, the position of a particle is described by a radius, r, and an angle, θ. Equation 37.32 through Eq. 37.37 give the relationships between velocity and acceleration for particles in plane circular motion in a polar coordinate system.

Equation 37.38 Through Eq. 37.41: Rectilinear Forms of Curvilinear Motion

$$v = \dot{s} \qquad 37.38$$

$$a_t = \dot{v} = \frac{dv}{ds} \qquad 37.39$$

$$a_n = \frac{v^2}{\rho} \qquad 37.40$$

$$\rho = \frac{[1 + (dy/dx)^2]^{3/2}}{\left|\dfrac{d^2y}{dx^2}\right|} \qquad 37.41$$

Description

The relationship between acceleration, velocity, and position in an *ntb coordinate system* is given by Eq. 37.38 through Eq. 37.41.

Equation 37.42 Through Eq. 37.44: Particle Angular Motion

$$\omega = d\theta/dt \qquad 37.42$$

$$\alpha = d\omega/dt \qquad 37.43$$

$$\alpha\, d\theta = \omega\, d\omega \qquad 37.44$$

Variation

$$\alpha = \frac{d^2\theta}{dt^2}$$

Description

The behavior of a rotating particle is defined by its angular position, θ, angular velocity, ω, and angular acceleration, α. These variables are analogous to the s, v, and a variables for linear systems. Angular variables can be substituted one-for-one for linear variables in most equations.

Example

The position of a car traveling around a curve is described by the following function of time (in seconds).

$$\theta(t) = t^3 - 2t^2 - 4t + 10$$

What is most nearly the angular velocity after 3 s of travel?

(A) −16 rad/s

(B) −4.0 rad/s

(C) 11 rad/s

(D) 15 rad/s

Solution

The angular velocity is

$$\omega(t) = \frac{d\theta}{dt}$$
$$= 3t^2 - 4t - 4$$
$$\omega(3) = (3)(3)^2 - (4)(3) - 4$$
$$= 11 \text{ rad/s}$$

The answer is (C).

10. CURVILINEAR MOTION: TRANSVERSE AND RADIAL COMPONENTS FOR PLANAR MOTION

Equation 37.45 Through Eq. 37.49: Polar Coordinate Forms of Curvilinear Motion

$$\boldsymbol{r} = r\boldsymbol{e}_r \qquad 37.45$$

$$\mathbf{v} = \dot{r}\boldsymbol{e}_r + r\dot{\theta}\boldsymbol{e}_\theta \qquad 37.46$$

$$\boldsymbol{a} = (\ddot{r} - r\dot{\theta}^2)\boldsymbol{e}_r + (r\ddot{\theta} + 2\dot{r}\dot{\theta})\boldsymbol{e}_\theta \qquad 37.47$$

$$\dot{r} = dr/dt \qquad 37.48$$

$$\ddot{r} = d^2r/dt^2 \qquad 37.49$$

Variations

$$\mathbf{v} = \mathrm{v}_r\boldsymbol{e}_r + \mathrm{v}_\theta\boldsymbol{e}_\theta$$

$$\boldsymbol{a} = a_r\boldsymbol{e}_r + a_\theta\boldsymbol{e}_\theta$$

Description

The position of a particle in a polar coordinate system may also be expressed as a vector of magnitude r and direction specified by unit vector $\boldsymbol{e}_r$. Since the velocity of a particle is not usually directed radially out from the center of the coordinate system, it can be divided into two components, called *radial* and *transverse*, which are parallel and perpendicular, respectively, to the unit radial vector. Figure 37.3 illustrates the radial and transverse components of velocity in a polar coordinate system, and the unit radial and unit transverse vectors, $\boldsymbol{e}_r$ and $\boldsymbol{e}_\theta$, used in the vector forms of the motion equations.

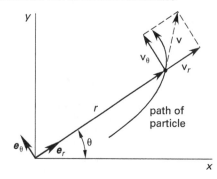

Figure 37.3 *Radial and Transverse Coordinates*

11. CURVILINEAR MOTION: NORMAL AND TANGENTIAL COMPONENTS

Equation 37.50 and Eq. 37.51: Velocity and Resultant Acceleration

$$\mathbf{v} = \mathrm{v}(t)\boldsymbol{e}_t \qquad 37.50$$

$$\boldsymbol{a} = a(t)\boldsymbol{e}_t + (\mathrm{v}_t^2/\rho)\boldsymbol{e}_n \qquad 37.51$$

Variation

$$\boldsymbol{a} = \frac{d\mathrm{v}_t}{dt}\boldsymbol{e}_t + \frac{\mathrm{v}_t^2}{\rho}\boldsymbol{e}_n$$

Description

A particle moving in a curvilinear path will have instantaneous linear velocity and linear acceleration. These linear variables will be directed tangentially to the path, and are known as *tangential velocity*, v_t, and *tangential acceleration*, a_t, respectively. The force that constrains the particle to the curved path will generally be directed toward the center of rotation, and the particle will experience an inward acceleration perpendicular to the tangential velocity and acceleration, known as the *normal acceleration*, a_n. The resultant acceleration, $\boldsymbol{a}$, is the vector sum of the tangential and normal accelerations. Normal and tangential components of acceleration are illustrated in Fig. 37.4. The unit vectors $\boldsymbol{e}_n$ and $\boldsymbol{e}_t$ are normal and tangential to the path, respectively. ρ is the instantaneous *radius of curvature*.

Figure 37.4 *Normal and Tangential Components*

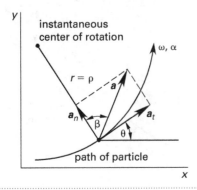

Equation 37.52 Through Eq. 37.56: Vector Quantities for Plane Circular Motion

$$r = re_r \qquad 37.52$$

$$\mathbf{v} = r\omega e_t \qquad 37.53$$

$$a = (-r\omega^2)e_r + r\alpha e_t \qquad 37.54$$

$$\omega = \dot{\theta} \qquad 37.55$$

$$\alpha = \dot{\omega} = \ddot{\theta} \qquad 37.56$$

Description

For plane circular motion, the vector forms of position, velocity, and acceleration are given by Eq. 37.52, Eq. 37.53, and Eq. 37.54. The magnitudes of the angular velocity and angular acceleration are defined by Eq. 37.55 and Eq. 37.56.

12. RELATIVE MOTION

The term *relative motion* is used when motion of a particle is described with respect to something else in motion. The particle's position, velocity, and acceleration may be specified with respect to another moving particle or with respect to a moving frame of reference, known as a *Newtonian* or *inertial frame of reference*.

Equation 37.57 Through Eq. 37.59: Relative Motion with Translating Axis

$$r_A = r_B + r_{A/B} \qquad 37.57$$

$$\mathbf{v}_A = \mathbf{v}_B + \omega \times r_{A/B} = \mathbf{v}_B + \mathbf{v}_{A/B} \qquad 37.58$$

$$\begin{aligned} a_A &= a_B + \alpha \times r_{A/B} + \omega \times (\omega \times r_{A/B}) \\ &= a_B + a_{A/B} \end{aligned} \qquad 37.59$$

Description

The relative position, r_A, velocity, v_A, and acceleration, a_A, with respect to a translating axis can be calculated from Eq. 37.57, Eq. 37.58, and Eq. 37.59, respectively. The angular velocity, ω, and angular acceleration, α, are the magnitudes of the relative position vector, $r_{A/B}$. (See Fig. 37.5.)

Figure 37.5 *Translating Axis*

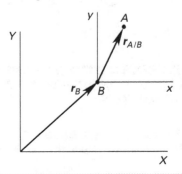

Equation 37.60 Through Eq. 37.62: Relative Motion with Rotating Axis

$$r_A = r_B + r_{A/B} \qquad 37.60$$

$$\mathbf{v}_A = \mathbf{v}_B + \omega \times r_{A/B} + \mathbf{v}_{A/B} \qquad 37.61$$

$$\begin{aligned} a_A &= a_B + \alpha \times r_{A/B} + \omega \times (\omega \times r_{A/B}) \\ &\quad + 2\omega \times \mathbf{v}_{A/B} + a_{A/B} \end{aligned} \qquad 37.62$$

Description

Equation 37.60, Eq. 37.61, and Eq. 37.62 give the relative position, r_A, velocity, v_A, and acceleration, a_A, with respect to a rotating axis, respectively. (See Fig. 37.6.)

Figure 37.6 *Rotating Axis*

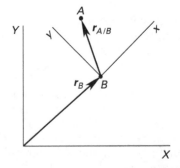

13. LINEAR AND ROTATIONAL VARIABLES

A particle moving in a curvilinear path will also have instantaneous linear velocity and linear acceleration. These linear variables will be directed tangentially to the path and, therefore, are known as *tangential velocity* and *tangential acceleration*, respectively. (See Fig. 37.7.) In general, the linear variables can be obtained by multiplying the rotational variables by the path radius.

Figure 37.7 *Tangential Variables*

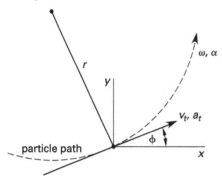

Equation 37.63 Through Eq. 37.66: Relationships Between Linear and Angular Variables

$$v_t = r\omega \qquad 37.63$$

$$a_t = r\alpha \qquad 37.64$$

$$a_n = -r\omega^2 \begin{bmatrix} \text{toward the center} \\ \text{of the circle} \end{bmatrix} \qquad 37.65$$

$$s = r\,\theta \qquad 37.66$$

Variations

$$v_t = r(2\pi f)$$

$$a_t = \frac{dv_t}{dt}$$

$$a_n = \frac{v_t^2}{r}$$

Description

Equation 37.63 through Eq. 37.65 are used to calculate tangential velocity, v_t, tangential acceleration, a_t, and normal acceleration, a_n, respectively, from their corresponding angular variables. If the path radius, r, is constant, as it would be in rotational motion, the linear distance (i.e., the *arc length*) traveled, s, is calculated from Eq. 37.66.

Example

For the reciprocating pump shown, the radius of the crank is 0.3 m, and the rotational speed is 350 rpm. Two

seconds after the pump is activated, the angular position of point A is 35 rad.

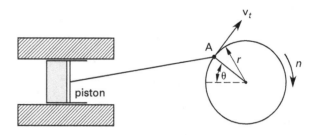

What is most nearly the tangential velocity of point A two seconds after the reciprocating pump is activated?

(A)   0 m/s

(B)   1.1 m/s

(C)   10 m/s

(D)   11 m/s

Solution

Use the relationship between the tangential and angular variables.

ω = angular velocity of the crank in rad/s

$$= \frac{\left(350\ \dfrac{\text{rev}}{\text{min}}\right)\left(2\pi\ \dfrac{\text{rad}}{\text{rev}}\right)}{60\ \dfrac{\text{s}}{\text{min}}}$$

$$= 36.65\ \text{rad/s}$$

Use Eq. 37.63.

$$v_t = r\omega = (0.3\ \text{m})\left(36.65\ \frac{\text{rad}}{\text{s}}\right) = 11\ \text{m/s}$$

The tangential velocity is the same for any point on the crank at $r = 0.3$ m.

The answer is (D).

14. PROJECTILE MOTION

A projectile is placed into motion by an initial impulse. (Kinematics deals only with dynamics during the flight. The force acting on the projectile during the launch phase is covered in kinetics.) Neglecting air drag, once the projectile is in motion, it is acted upon only by the downward gravitational acceleration (i.e., its own weight). Projectile motion is a special case of motion under constant acceleration.

Consider a general projectile set into motion at an angle θ from the horizontal plane and initial velocity, v_0, as shown in Fig. 37.8. The *apex* is the point where the projectile is at

Dynamics/ Vibrations

its maximum elevation. In the absence of air drag, the following rules apply to the case of travel over a horizontal plane.

- The trajectory is parabolic.

- The impact velocity is equal to initial velocity, v_0.

- The range is maximum when $\theta = 45°$.

- The time for the projectile to travel from the launch point to the apex is equal to the time to travel from apex to impact point.

- The time for the projectile to travel from the apex of its flight path to impact is the same time an initially stationary object would take to fall straight down from that height.

Figure 37.8 *Projectile Motion*

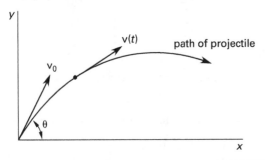

Equation 37.67 Through Eq. 37.72: Equations of Projectile Motion[3]

$a_x = 0$	37.67
$a_y = -g$	37.68
$v_x = v_0 \cos(\theta)$	37.69
$v_y = -gt + v_0 \sin(\theta)$	37.70
$x = v_0 \cos(\theta)t + x_0$	37.71
$y = -gt^2/2 + v_0 \sin(\theta)t + y_0$	37.72

Variations

$$v_y(t) = v_{y,0} - gt$$

$$y(t) = v_{y,0}t - \frac{1}{2}gt^2$$

Description

The equations of projectile motion are derived from the laws of uniform acceleration and conservation of energy.

Example

A golfer on level ground at the edge of a 50 m wide pond attempts to drive a golf ball across the pond, hitting the ball so that it travels initially at 25 m/s. The ball travels at an initial angle of 45° to the horizontal plane. Approximately how far will the golf ball travel?

(A) 32 m

(B) 45 m

(C) 58 m

(D) 64 m

Solution

To determine the distance traveled by the golf ball, the time of impact must be found. At a time of 0 s and the time of impact, the elevation of the ball is known to be 0 m. Rearrange Eq. 37.72 to solve for time, substituting a value of 0 m for the elevation at a time of 0 s and the time of impact.

$$y = -gt^2/2 + v_0 \sin(\theta)t + y_0$$

$$0 \text{ m} = \frac{-gt^2}{2} + v_0 \sin(\theta)t + 0 \text{ m}$$

$$t = \frac{2v_0 \sin \theta}{g}$$

Substitute the expression for the time of impact into Eq. 37.71 and solve. The starting position is 0 m.

$$x = v_0 \cos(\theta)t + x_0$$

$$= v_0 \cos \theta \left(\frac{2v_0 \sin \theta}{g} \right) + x_0$$

$$= \left(25 \ \frac{\text{m}}{\text{s}} \right) \cos 45° \left(\frac{(2)\left(25 \ \frac{\text{m}}{\text{s}} \right) \sin 45°}{9.81 \ \frac{\text{m}}{\text{s}^2}} \right) + 0 \text{ m}$$

$$= 63.7 \text{ m} \quad (64 \text{ m})$$

The answer is (D).

---

[3]As formulated in the *NCEES Handbook*, it is easy to misinterpret the second term in Eq. 37.72. $v_0 \sin(\theta)t$ is the product of three terms: v_0, $\sin \theta$, and t. $\sin(\theta)t$ is not the sine of a function of t. A clearer formulation would have been $v_0 t \sin \theta$.

38 Kinetics

Nomenclature

a	acceleration	m/s^2
F	force	N
g	gravitational acceleration, 9.81	m/s^2
I	mass moment of inertia	$kg \cdot m^2$
m	mass	kg
M	moment	$N \cdot m$
N	normal force	N
p	momentum	$N \cdot s$
R	resultant	N
t	time	s
v	velocity	m/s
W	weight	N
x	displacement or position	m

Symbols

α	angular acceleration	rad/s^2
μ	coefficient of friction	–
ρ	radius of curvature	m
ϕ	angle	deg

Subscripts

0	initial
c	centroidal
f	final or frictional
i	initial
k	dynamic
n	normal
pc	from point p to point c
r	radial
R	resultant
s	static
t	tangential
θ	transverse

1. INTRODUCTION

Kinetics is the study of motion and the forces that cause motion. Kinetics includes an analysis of the relationship between force and mass for translational motion and between torque and moment of inertia for rotational motion. Newton's laws form the basis of the governing theory in the subject of kinetics.

2. MOMENTUM

The vector *linear momentum* (*momentum*), **p**, is defined by the following equation. It has the same direction as the velocity vector from which it is calculated. Momentum has units of force × time (e.g., N·s).

$$\mathbf{p} = m\mathbf{v}$$

Momentum is conserved when no external forces act on a particle. If no forces act on a particle, the velocity and direction of the particle are unchanged. The *law of conservation of momentum* states that the linear momentum is unchanged if no unbalanced forces act on the particle. This does not prohibit the mass and velocity from changing, however. Only the product of mass and velocity is constant.

3. NEWTON'S FIRST AND SECOND LAWS OF MOTION

Newton's first law of motion states that a particle will remain in a state of rest or will continue to move with constant velocity unless an unbalanced external force acts on it.

This law can also be stated in terms of conservation of momentum: If the resultant external force acting on a particle is zero, then the linear momentum of the particle is constant.

Newton's second law of motion (conservation of momentum) states that the acceleration of a particle is directly proportional to the force acting on it and is inversely proportional to the particle mass. The direction of acceleration is the same as the direction of force.

Dynamics/ Vibrations

Equation 38.1 and Eq. 38.2: Newton's Second Law for a Particle

$$\sum \boldsymbol{F} = d(m\mathbf{v})/dt \qquad \text{38.1}$$

$$\sum \boldsymbol{F} = m\,d\mathrm{v}/dt = m\boldsymbol{a} \quad \text{[constant mass]} \qquad \text{38.2}$$

Variation

$$F = \frac{d\mathbf{p}}{dt}$$

Description

Newton's second law can be stated in terms of the force vector required to cause a change in momentum. The resultant force is equal to the rate of change of linear momentum. For a constant mass, Eq. 38.2 applies.

Example

A 3 kg block is moving at a speed of 5 m/s. The force required to bring the block to a stop in 8×10^{-4} s is most nearly

(A)   10 kN

(B)   13 kN

(C)   15 kN

(D)   19 kN

Solution

From Newton's second law, Eq. 38.2, the force required to stop a constant mass of 3 kg moving at a speed of 5 m/s is

$$\sum \boldsymbol{F} = m\,d\mathrm{v}/dt = m(\Delta\mathrm{v}/\Delta t)$$

$$= (3\text{ kg})\left(\frac{5\,\dfrac{\text{m}}{\text{s}} - 0\,\dfrac{\text{m}}{\text{s}}}{(8 \times 10^{-4}\text{ s})\left(1000\,\dfrac{\text{N}}{\text{kN}}\right)}\right)$$

$$= 18.75\text{ kN} \quad (19\text{ kN})$$

The answer is (D).

Equation 38.3 Through Eq. 38.5: Newton's Second Law for a Rigid Body[1]

$$\sum \boldsymbol{F} = m\boldsymbol{a}_c \qquad \text{38.3}$$

$$\sum \boldsymbol{M}_c = I_c\boldsymbol{\alpha} \qquad \text{38.4}$$

$$\sum \boldsymbol{M}_p = I_c\boldsymbol{\alpha} + \boldsymbol{\rho}_{pc} \times m\boldsymbol{a}_c \qquad \text{38.5}$$

Description

A *rigid body* is a complex shape that cannot be described as a particle. Generally, a rigid body is nonhomogeneous (i.e., the center of mass does not coincide with the volumetric center) or is constructed of subcomponents. In those cases, applying an unbalanced force will cause rotation as well as translation. Newton's second law of motion (conservation of momentum) can be applied to a rigid body, but the law must be applied twice: once for linear momentum and once for angular momentum. Equation 38.3 pertains to linear momentum and relates the net (resultant) force, $\boldsymbol{F}$, on an object in any direction to the acceleration, $\boldsymbol{a}_c$, of the object's centroid in that direction.[2] The acceleration is "resisted" by the object's inertial mass, m. Equation 38.4 pertains to angular momentum and relates the net (resultant) moment or torque, $\boldsymbol{M}_c$, on an object about a centroidal axis to the angular rotational acceleration, $\boldsymbol{\alpha}$, around the centroidal axis.[3] The angular acceleration is resisted by the object's centroidal mass moment of inertia, I_c.

In pure rotation, the object rotates about a centroidal axis. The centroid remains stationary as elements of the rigid body. Equation 38.5 pertains to rotation about any particular axis, p, where $\boldsymbol{\rho}_{pc}$ is the perpendicular vector from axis p to the object's centroidal axis.

Example

A net unbalanced torque acts on a 50 kg cylinder that is allowed to rotate around its longitudinal centroidal axis on frictionless bearings. The cylinder has a radius of 40 cm and a mass moment of inertia of 4 kg·m². The cylinder accelerates from a standstill with an angular acceleration of 5 rad/s².

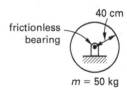

$m = 50$ kg

---

[1]In Eq. 38.3 through Eq. 38.5, the NCEES *FE Reference Handbook* (*NCEES Handbook*) uses bold characters to designate vector quantities (i.e., $\boldsymbol{F}$, $\boldsymbol{M}$, $\boldsymbol{a}$, $\boldsymbol{\alpha}$, and $\boldsymbol{\rho}$). Rectilinear components of vectors may be added; and cross-products are used for multiplication. In most calculations, however, the vector nature of these quantities is disregarded, and only the magnitudes of the quantities are used.

[2]The *NCEES Handbook* is inconsistent in its meaning of a_c. In Eq. 38.3, a_c refers to the acceleration of the centroid, which the *NCEES Handbook* calls "mass center." a_c does not mean constant acceleration as it did earlier in the *NCEES Handbook* Dynamics section.

[3]The *NCEES Handbook* is inconsistent in designating the centroidal parameters. Whereas a_c represents the acceleration of the centroid in Eq. 38.3, and I_c represents the centroidal moment of inertia in Eq. 38.4, the subscript c has been omitted on $\boldsymbol{\alpha}$, the angular acceleration about the centroidal axis, in Eq. 38.5.

What is most nearly the unbalanced torque on the cylinder?

(A) 20 N·m

(B) 40 N·m

(C) 200 N·m

(D) 2000 N·m

Solution

Using Eq. 38.4, the magnitude of the moment acting on the cylinder is

$$\sum M_c = I_c \alpha$$
$$= (4 \text{ kg·m}^2)\left(5 \ \frac{\text{rad}}{\text{s}^2}\right)$$
$$= 20 \text{ N·m}$$

The answer is (A).

Equation 38.6 Through Eq. 38.12: Rectilinear Equations for Rigid Bodies

$$\sum F_x = m a_{xc} \qquad 38.6$$

$$\sum F_y = m a_{yc} \qquad 38.7$$

$$\sum M_{zc} = I_{zc} \alpha \qquad 38.8$$

$$\sum F_x = m (a_G)_x \qquad 38.9$$

$$\sum F_y = m (a_G)_y \qquad 38.10$$

$$\sum M_G = I_G \alpha \qquad 38.11$$

$$\sum M_P = \sum (M_k)_P \qquad 38.12$$

Description

These equations are the scalar forms of Newton's second law equations, assuming the rigid body is constrained to move in an x-y plane. The subscript zc describes the z-axis passing through the body's centroid. Placing the origin at the body's centroid, the acceleration of the body in the x- and y-directions is a_{xc} and a_{yc}, respectively. α is the angular acceleration of the body about the z-axis. Equation 38.6 through Eq. 38.12 are limited to motion in the x-y plane (i.e., two dimensions). Equation 38.11 calculates the sum of moments about a rigid body's center of gravity (mass center, etc.), G. Equation 38.12 calculates the sum of moments about any point, P.[4]

4. WEIGHT

Equation 38.13: Weight of an Object

$$W = mg \qquad 38.13$$

Description

The *weight*, W, of an object is the force the object exerts due to its position in a gravitational field.[5]

Example

A man weighs himself twice in an elevator. When the elevator is at rest, he weighs 713 N; when the elevator

Dynamics/ Vibrations

---

[4](1) Equation 38.6 through Eq. 38.8 are prefaced in the *NCEES Handbook* with, "Without loss of generality, the body may be assumed to be in the x-y plane." This statement sounds as though all bodies can be simplified to planar motion, which is not true. The more general three-dimensional case is not specifically presented, so there is no generality to lose. In fact, Eq. 38.8 represents the sum of moments about any point, so this equation *is* the more general case, not the less general case. (2) Equation 38.9, Eq. 38.10, and Eq. 38.11 are functionally the same as Eq. 38.6, Eq. 38.7, and Eq. 38.8 and are redundant. Both sets of equations are limited to the x-y plane. (3) The subscripts c (centroidal or center of mass) and G (center of gravity) refer to the same thing. The change in notation is unnecessary. (4) The subscripts G and P are not defined. (5) The subscript k is not defined, but probably represents an uncommon choice for the first summation variable, normally i. Since k does not appear in the summation symbol, the meaning of M_k must be inferred. (6) Equation 38.11 specifies the point through which the rotational axis passes, but it does not specify an axis, as does Eq. 38.8. Since the equations are limited to the x-y plane, the rotational axis can only be parallel to the z-axis, as in Eq. 38.8. (7) The subscript c has been omitted on α, the angular acceleration about the center of mass, in Eq. 38.8 and Eq. 38.11.

[5](1) The *NCEES Handbook* introduces Eq. 38.13 with the section heading, "Concept of Weight." Units of weight are specified as newtons. In fact, the concept of weight is entirely absent in the SI system. Only the concepts of mass and force are used. The SI system does not support the concept of "body weight" in newtons. It only supports the concept of the force needed to accelerate a body. In presenting Eq. 38.13, the *NCEES Handbook* perpetuates the incorrect ideas that mass and weight are synonyms, and that weight is a fixed property of a body. (2) The *NCEES Handbook* includes a parenthetical "(lbf)" as the unit of weight for U.S. equations. However, Eq. 38.13 cannot be used with customary and normal U.S. units (i.e., mass in pounds) without including the gravitational constant, g_c. In order to make Eq. 38.13 consistent, the *NCEES Handbook* is forced to specify the unit of mass for U.S. equations as lbf-sec²/ft. This (essentially now obsolete) unit of mass is known as a *slug*, something that is not called out in the *NCEES Handbook*. Since a slug is 32.2 times larger than a pound, an examinee using Eq. 38.13 with customary and normal U.S. units could easily be misdirected by the lbf label.

starts moving upward, he weighs 816 N. What is most nearly the man's actual mass?

(A) 70 kg

(B) 73 kg

(C) 78 kg

(D) 83 kg

Solution

The mass of the man can be determined from his weight at rest.

$$W = mg$$

$$m = \frac{W}{g} = \frac{713 \text{ N}}{9.81 \, \frac{\text{m}}{\text{s}^2}}$$

$$= 72.7 \text{ kg} \quad (73 \text{ kg})$$

The answer is (B).

5. FRICTION

Friction is a force that always resists motion or impending motion. It always acts parallel to the contacting surfaces. If the body is moving, the friction is known as *dynamic friction*. If the body is stationary, friction is known as *static friction*.

The magnitude of the frictional force depends on the normal force, N, and the *coefficient of friction, μ,* between the body and the contacting surface.

$$F_f = \mu N$$

The static coefficient of friction is usually denoted with the subscript s, while the dynamic (i.e., kinetic) coefficient of friction is denoted with the subscript k. μ_k is often assumed to be 75% of the value of μ_s. These coefficients are complex functions of surface properties. Experimentally determined values for various contacting conditions can be found in handbooks.

For a body resting on a horizontal surface, the *normal force*, N, is the weight, W, of the body. If the body rests on an inclined surface, the normal force is calculated as the component of weight normal to that surface, as illustrated in Fig. 38.1. Axes in Fig. 38.1 are defined as parallel and perpendicular to the inclined plane.

$$N = mg \cos \phi = W \cos \phi$$

The frictional force acts only in response to a disturbing force, and it increases as the disturbing force increases. The motion of a stationary body is impending when the disturbing force reaches the maximum frictional force, $\mu_s N$. Figure 38.1 shows the condition of impending

Figure 38.1 *Frictional and Normal Forces*

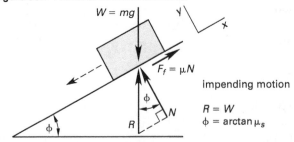

motion for a block on a plane. Just before motion starts, the resultant, R, of the frictional force and normal force equals the weight of the block. The angle at which motion is just impending can be calculated from the coefficient of static friction.

$$\phi = \arctan \mu_s$$

Once motion begins, the coefficient of friction drops slightly, and a lower frictional force opposes movement. This is illustrated in Fig. 38.2.

Figure 38.2 *Frictional Force Versus Disturbing Force*

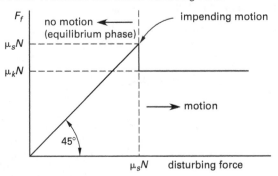

Equation 38.14 Through Eq. 38.17: Laws of Friction

$$F \leq \mu_s N \qquad \text{38.14}$$

$$\boldsymbol{F} < \mu_s \boldsymbol{N} \quad \text{[no slip occurring]} \qquad \text{38.15}$$

$$\boldsymbol{F} = \mu_s \boldsymbol{N} \quad \text{[point of impending slip]} \qquad \text{38.16}$$

$$\boldsymbol{F} = \mu_k \boldsymbol{N} \quad \text{[slip occurring]} \qquad \text{38.17}$$

Values

$$\mu_k \approx 0.75 \mu_s$$

Description

The laws of friction state that the maximum value of the total friction force, $\boldsymbol{F}$, is independent of the magnitude of the area of contact. The maximum total friction force is proportional to the normal force, $\boldsymbol{N}$. For low velocities of sliding, the maximum total frictional force is nearly independent of the velocity. However, experiments show that the force necessary to initiate slip is greater than that necessary to maintain the motion.

Example

A boy pulls a sled with a mass of 35 kg horizontally over a surface with a dynamic coefficient of friction of 0.15. What is most nearly the force required for the boy to pull the sled?

(A) 49 N

(B) 52 N

(C) 55 N

(D) 58 N

Solution

N is the normal force, and μ_k is the dynamic coefficient of friction. The force that the boy must pull with, F_b, must be large enough to overcome the frictional force. From Eq. 38.17,

$$F_b = F_f = \mu_k N = \mu_k m g$$

$$= (0.15)(35 \text{ kg})\left(9.81 \ \frac{\text{m}}{\text{s}^2}\right)$$

$$= 51.5 \text{ kg·m/s}^2 \quad (52 \text{ N})$$

The answer is (B).

6. KINETICS OF A PARTICLE

Newton's second law can be applied separately to any direction in which forces are resolved into components. The law can be expressed in rectangular coordinate form (i.e., in terms of x- and y-component forces), in polar coordinate form (i.e., in tangential and normal components), or in radial and transverse component form.

Equation 38.18: Newton's Second Law

$$a_x = F_x/m \qquad \textit{38.18}$$

Variation

$$F_x = m a_x$$

Description

Equation 38.18 is Newton's second law in rectangular coordinate form and refers to motion in the x-direction. Similar equations can be written for the y-direction or any other coordinate direction. In general, F_x may be a function of time, displacement, and/or velocity.

Example

A car moving at 70 km/h has a mass of 1700 kg. The force necessary to decelerate it at a rate of 40 cm/s^2 is most nearly

(A) 0.68 N

(B) 42 N

(C) 680 N

(D) 4200 N

Solution

Use Newton's second law.

$$a_x = F_x/m$$
$$F_x = m a_x$$

$$= \frac{(1700 \text{ kg})\left(40 \ \dfrac{\text{cm}}{\text{s}^2}\right)}{100 \ \dfrac{\text{cm}}{\text{m}}}$$

$$= 680 \text{ kg·m/s}^2 \quad (680 \text{ N})$$

The answer is (C).

Equation 38.19 Through Eq. 38.21: Equations of Motion with Constant Mass and Force as a Function of Time

$$a_x(t) = F_x(t)/m \qquad \textit{38.19}$$

$$v_x(t) = \int_{t_0}^{t} a_x(t)\,dt + v_{xt_0} \qquad \textit{38.20}$$

$$x(t) = \int_{t_0}^{t} v_x(t)\,dt + x_{t_0} \qquad \textit{38.21}$$

Variation

$$v_x(t) = \int_{t_i}^{t_f} \frac{F_x(t)}{m}\,dt + v_{x,0}$$

Description

If F_x is a function of time only, then the equations of motion are given by Eq. 38.19, Eq. 38.20, and Eq. 38.21.

Equation 38.22 Through Eq. 38.24: Equations of Motion with Constant Mass and Force

$$a_x = F_x/m \qquad \textit{38.22}$$

$$v_x = a_x(t - t_0) + v_{xt_0} \qquad 38.23$$

$$x = a_x(t - t_0)^2/2 + v_{xt_0}(t - t_0) + x_{t_0} \qquad 38.24$$

Variations

$$F_x = ma_x$$

$$v_x(t) = v_{x,0} + \left(\frac{F_x}{m}\right)(t - t_0)$$

$$x(t) = x_0 + v_{x,0}(t - t_0) + \frac{F_x(t - t_0)^2}{2m}$$

Description

If F_x is constant (i.e., is independent of time, displacement, or velocity) and mass is constant, then the equations of motion are given by Eq. 38.22, Eq. 38.23, and Eq. 38.24.

Example

A force of 15 N acts on a 16 kg body for 2 s. If the body is initially at rest, approximately how far is it displaced by the force?

(A) 1.1 m

(B) 1.5 m

(C) 1.9 m

(D) 2.1 m

Solution

The acceleration is found using Newton's second law, Eq. 38.22.

$$a_x = F_x/m = \frac{15\ \text{N}}{16\ \text{kg}} = 0.94\ \text{m/s}^2$$

For a body undergoing constant acceleration, with an initial velocity of 0 m/s, an initial time of 0 s, and a total elapsed time of 2 s, the horizontal displacement is found from Eq. 38.24.

$$x = a_x(t - t_0)^2/2 + v_{xt_0}(t - t_0) + x_{t_0}$$

$$= \frac{\left(0.94\ \frac{\text{m}}{\text{s}^2}\right)(2\ \text{s} - 0\ \text{s})^2}{2} + \left(0\ \frac{\text{m}}{\text{s}}\right)(2\ \text{s} - 0\ \text{s}) + 0\ \text{m}$$

$$= 1.88\ \text{m} \quad (1.9\ \text{m})$$

The answer is (C).

Equation 38.25 and Eq. 38.26: Tangential and Normal Components

$$\sum F_t = ma_t = m\,dv_t/dt \qquad 38.25$$

$$\sum F_n = ma_n = m(v_t^2/\rho) \qquad 38.26$$

Description

For a particle moving along a circular path, the tangential and normal components of force, acceleration, and velocity are related.

Radial and Transverse Components

For a particle moving along a circular path, the radial and transverse components of force are

$$\sum F_r = ma_r$$

$$\sum F_\theta = ma_\theta$$

39 Kinetics of Rotational Motion

Nomenclature

a	acceleration	m/s^2
A	area	m^2
c	number of instantaneous centers	–
d	length	m
F	force	N
g	gravitational acceleration, 9.81	m/s^2
h	height	m
H	angular momentum	N·m·s
I	mass moment of inertia	$kg·m^2$
l	length	m
L	length	m
m	mass*	kg
M	mass[1]	kg
M	moment	N·m
n	quantity	–
r	radius of gyration	m
R	mean radius	m
t	time	s
v	velocity	m/s
W	weight	N

*The NCEES *FE Reference Handbook* (*NCEES Handbook*) is inconsistent in its nomenclature usage. It uses both m and M to designate the mass of a object. It generally uses uppercase M to designate the total mass of non-particles (i.e., cylinders). Care must be taken when solving problems involving both mass and moment, as equations for both quantities use the same symbol.

Symbols

α	angular acceleration	rad/s^2
θ	angular position	rad
μ	coefficient of friction	–
ρ	density	kg/m^3
ω	angular velocity	rad/s

Subscripts

0	initial
c	centrifugal or centroidal
f	frictional
G	center of gravity
m	mass
n	normal
O	origin or center
s	static
t	tangential

1. MASS[1] MOMENT OF INERTIA

Equation 39.1 Through Eq. 39.4: Mass Moment of Inertia

$$I = \int r^2 dm \qquad 39.1$$

$$I_x = \int (y^2 + z^2)\, dm \qquad 39.2$$

$$I_y = \int (x^2 + z^2)\, dm \qquad 39.3$$

$$I_z = \int (x^2 + y^2)\, dm \qquad 39.4$$

Description

The *mass moment of inertia* measures a solid object's resistance to changes in rotational speed about a specific axis. Equation 39.1 shows that the mass moment of inertia is calculated as the second moment of the mass.[2] When the origin of a coordinate system is located at the

---

[1]The NCEES *FE Reference Handbook* (*NCEES Handbook*) is inconsistent in its nomenclature usage. It uses both m and M to designate the mass of a object. It generally uses uppercase M to designate the total mass of non-particles (i.e., cylinders). Care must be taken when solving problems involving both mass and moment, as equations for both quantities use the same symbol.

[2](1) There are two closely adjacent sections in the *NCEES Handbook* labeled "Mass Moment of Inertia," each covering the same topic. (2) The integral shown in Eq. 39.1 is implicitly a triple integral (volume integral), more properly shown as $\int_V$ or $\iiint$.

object's center of mass, the radius, r, to the differential element can be calculated from the components of position as

$$r = \sqrt{x^2 + y^2 + z^2}$$

For a homogeneous body with density ρ, Eq. 39.1 can be written as

$$I = \rho \int_V r^2 dV$$

I_x, I_y, and I_z are the mass moments of inertia with respect to the x-, y-, and z-axes, respectively. They are not components of a resultant value.

Equation 39.5 and Eq. 39.6: Parallel Axis Theorem

$$I_{\text{new}} = I_c + md^2 \hspace{2cm} \textbf{39.5}$$

$$I = I_G + md^2 \hspace{2cm} \textbf{39.6}$$

Variation

$$I = I_{c,1} + m_1 d_1^2 + I_{c,2} + m_2 d_2^2 + \cdots$$

Description

The *centroidal mass moment of inertia*, I_c, is obtained when the origin of the axes coincides with the object's center of gravity.[3] The *parallel axis theorem*, also known as the *transfer axis theorem*, is used to find the mass moment of inertia about any axis. In Eq. 39.5, d is the distance from the center of mass to the new axis.

For a composite object, the parallel axis theorem must be applied for each of the constituent objects, as shown in the variation equation.

Example

The 5 cm long uniform slender rod shown has a mass of 20 g. The centroidal mass moment of inertia is 42 g·cm².

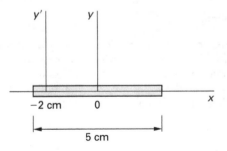

What is most nearly the mass moment of inertia of the rod about the y'-axis 2 cm to the left?

(A)   0.12 kg·cm²

(B)   0.33 kg·cm²

(C)   0.45 kg·cm²

(D)   0.91 kg·cm²

Solution

The y'-axis is 2 cm from the y-axis. The center of gravity of the rod is located halfway along its length. Use Eq. 39.5.

$$I_{y'} = I_c + md^2$$

$$= \frac{42 \text{ g cm}^2 + (20 \text{ g})(2 \text{ cm})^2}{1000 \, \frac{\text{g}}{\text{kg}}}$$

$$= 0.12 \text{ kg cm}^2$$

The answer is (A).

Equation 39.7: Mass Radius of Gyration

$$r_m = \sqrt{I/m} \hspace{2cm} \textbf{39.7}$$

Variation

$$I = r^2 m$$

Description

The *mass radius of gyration*, r_m, of a solid object represents the distance from the rotational axis at which the object's entire mass could be located without changing the mass moment of inertia.

Equation 39.8 Through Eq. 39.19: Properties of Uniform Slender Rods

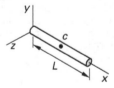

---

[3]Equation 39.5 and Eq. 39.6 both appear on the same page in the *NCEES Handbook* using different notation. The inconsistent subscripts c and G both refer to the same concept: centroidal (center of gravity, center of mass, etc.).

mass and centroid

$$M = \rho L A \qquad \text{39.8}$$

$$x_c = L/2 \qquad \text{39.9}$$

$$y_c = 0 \qquad \text{39.10}$$

$$z_c = 0 \qquad \text{39.11}$$

mass moment of inertia

$$I_x = I_{x_c} = 0 \qquad \text{39.12}$$

$$I_{y_c} = I_{z_c} = ML^2/12 \qquad \text{39.13}$$

$$I_y = I_z = ML^2/3 \qquad \text{39.14}$$

(radius of gyration)^2

$$r_x^2 = r_{x_c}^2 = 0 \qquad \text{39.15}$$

$$r_{y_c}^2 = r_{z_c}^2 = L^2/12 \qquad \text{39.16}$$

$$r_y^2 = r_z^2 = L^2/3 \qquad \text{39.17}$$

product of inertia

$$I_{x_c y_c} = 0 \qquad \text{39.18}$$

$$I_{xy} = 0 \qquad \text{39.19}$$

Description

Equation 39.8 through Eq. 39.19 give the properties of slender rods. The center of mass (center of gravity) is located at (x_c, y_c, z_c), designated point c. M is the total mass; A is the cross-sectional area perpendicular to the longitudinal axis; ρ is the mass density, equal to the mass divided by the volume; I is the mass moment of inertia about the subscripted axis, used in calculating rotational acceleration and moments about that axis; and r is the radius of gyration, a distance from the designated axis from the centroid where all of the

mass can be assumed to be concentrated. I_{xy} is the *product of inertia*, a measure of symmetry, with respect to a plane containing the subscripted axes. The product of inertia is zero if the object is symmetrical about an axis perpendicular to the plane defined by the subscripted axes.

Example

A uniform rod is 2.0 m long and has a mass of 15 kg. What is most nearly the rod's mass moment of inertia?

(A) 5.0 kg·m²

(B) 20 kg·m²

(C) 27 kg·m²

(D) 31 kg·m²

Solution

From Eq. 39.14, the mass moment of inertia of the rod is

$$I_{\text{rod}} = ML^2/3 = \frac{(15 \text{ kg})(2.0 \text{ m})^2}{3}$$

$$= 20 \text{ kg·m}^2$$

The answer is (B).

Equation 39.20 Through Eq. 39.34: Properties of Slender Rings

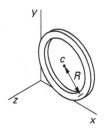

mass and centroid

$$M = 2\pi R \rho A \qquad \text{39.20}$$

$$x_c = R \qquad \text{39.21}$$

$$y_c = R \qquad \text{39.22}$$

$$z_c = 0 \qquad \text{39.23}$$

mass moment of inertia

$$I_{x_c} = I_{y_c} = MR^2/2 \qquad \text{39.24}$$

$$I_{z_c} = MR^2 \qquad \text{39.25}$$

$$I_x = I_y = 3MR^2/2 \qquad \text{39.26}$$

$$I_z = 3MR^2 \qquad \text{39.27}$$

(radius of gyration)^2

$$r_{x_c}^2 = r_{y_c}^2 = R^2/2 \qquad \text{39.28}$$

$$r_{z_c}^2 = R^2 \qquad \text{39.29}$$

$$r_x^2 = r_y^2 = 3R^2/2 \qquad \text{39.30}$$

$$r_z^2 = 3R^2 \qquad \text{39.31}$$

product of inertia

$$I_{x_c y_c} = 0 \qquad \text{39.32}$$

$$I_{y_c z_c} = MR^2 \qquad \text{39.33}$$

$$I_{xz} = I_{yz} = 0 \qquad \text{39.34}$$

Description

Equation 39.20 through Eq. 39.34 give the properties of slender rings. The center of mass (center of gravity) is located at (x_c, y_c, z_c), designated point c, and measured from the mean radius of the ring. M is the total mass; A is the cross-sectional area of the ring; ρ is the mass density, equal to the mass divided by the volume; I is the mass moment of inertia about the subscripted axis, used in calculating rotational acceleration and moments about that axis; and r is the radius of gyration, a distance from the designated axis from the centroid where all of the mass can be assumed to be concentrated. r_{z_c} is the radius of gyration of the ring about an axis parallel to the z-axis and passing through the centroid. I_{xy} is the product of inertia, a measure of symmetry, with respect to a plane containing the subscripted axes. The product

of inertia is zero if the object is symmetrical about an axis perpendicular to the plane defined by the subscripted axes.

Example

The period of oscillation of a clock balance wheel is 0.3 s. The wheel is constructed as a slender ring with its 30 g mass uniformly distributed around a 0.6 cm radius. What is most nearly the wheel's moment of inertia?

(A) 1.1×10^{-6} kg·m^2

(B) 1.6×10^{-6} kg·m^2

(C) 2.1×10^{-6} kg·m^2

(D) 2.6×10^{-6} kg·m^2

Solution

From Eq. 39.25, the wheel's moment of inertia is

$$I = MR^2$$

$$= \left(\frac{30 \text{ g}}{10^3 \frac{\text{g}}{\text{kg}}} \right) \left(\frac{0.6 \text{ cm}}{100 \frac{\text{cm}}{\text{m}}} \right)^2$$

$$= 1.08 \times 10^{-6} \text{ kg·m}^2 \quad (1.1 \times 10^{-6} \text{ kg·m}^2)$$

The answer is (A).

Equation 39.35 Through Eq. 39.46: Properties of Cylinders

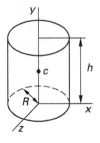

mass and centroid

$$M = \pi R^2 \rho h \qquad \text{39.35}$$

$$x_c = 0 \qquad \text{39.36}$$

$$y_c = h/2 \qquad \text{39.37}$$

$$z_c = 0 \qquad \text{39.38}$$

mass moment of inertia

$$I_{x_c} = I_{z_c} = M(3R^2 + h^2)/12 \qquad 39.39$$

$$I_{y_c} = I_y = MR^2/2 \qquad 39.40$$

$$I_x = I_z = M(3R^2 + 4h^2)/12 \qquad 39.41$$

(radius of gyration)²

$$r_{x_c}^2 = r_{z_c}^2 = (3R^2 + h^2)/12 \qquad 39.42$$

$$r_{y_c}^2 = r_y^2 = R^2/2 \qquad 39.43$$

$$r_x^2 = r_z^2 = (3R^2 + 4h^2)/12 \qquad 39.44$$

product of inertia

$$I_{x_c y_c} = 0 \qquad 39.45$$

$$I_{xy} = 0 \qquad 39.46$$

Description

Equation 39.35 through Eq. 39.46 give the properties of solid (right) cylinders. The center of mass (center of gravity) is located at (x_c, y_c, z_c), designated point c. M is the total mass; ρ is the mass density, equal to the mass divided by the volume; I is the mass moment of inertia about the subscripted axis, used in calculating rotational acceleration and moments about that axis; and r is the radius of gyration, a distance from the designated axis from the centroid where all of the mass can be assumed to be concentrated. r_{y_c} is the radius of gyration of the cylinder about an axis parallel to the y-axis and passing through the centroid. I_{xy} is the product of inertia, a measure of symmetry, with respect to a plane containing the subscripted axes. The product of inertia is zero if the object is symmetrical about an axis perpendicular to the plane defined by the subscripted axes.

Example

A 50 kg solid cylinder has a height of 3 m and a radius of 0.5 m. The cylinder sits on the x-axis and is oriented with its longitudinal axis parallel to the y-axis. What is most nearly the mass moment of inertia about the x-axis?

(A) 4.1 kg·m²

(B) 16 kg·m²

(C) 41 kg·m²

(D) 150 kg·m²

Solution

Find the mass moment of inertia using Eq. 39.41.

$$\begin{aligned} I_x &= M(3R^2 + 4h^2)/12 \\ &= \frac{(50 \text{ kg})\big((3)(0.5 \text{ m})^2 + (4)(3 \text{ m})^2\big)}{12} \\ &= 153.1 \text{ kg·m}^2 \quad (150 \text{ kg·m}^2) \end{aligned}$$

The answer is (D).

**Equation 39.47 Through Eq. 39.58:
Properties of Hollow Cylinders**

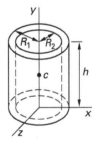

mass and centroid

$$M = \pi(R_1^2 - R_2^2)\rho h \qquad 39.47$$

$$x_c = 0 \qquad 39.48$$

$$y_c = h/2 \qquad 39.49$$

$$z_c = 0 \qquad 39.50$$

mass moment of inertia

$$I_{x_c} = I_{z_c} = M(3R_1^2 + 3R_2^2 + h^2)/12 \qquad 39.51$$

$$I_{y_c} = I_y = M(R_1^2 + R_2^2)/2 \qquad 39.52$$

$$I_x = I_z = M(3R_1^2 + 3R_2^2 + 4h^2)/12 \qquad 39.53$$

(radius of gyration)^2

$$r_{x_c}^2 = r_{z_c}^2 = (3R_1^2 + 3R_2^2 + h^2)/12 \qquad 39.54$$

$$r_{y_c}^2 = r_y^2 = (R_1^2 + R_2^2)/2 \qquad 39.55$$

$$r_x^2 = r_z^2 = (3R_1^2 + 3R_2^2 + 4h^2)/12 \qquad 39.56$$

product of inertia

$$I_{x_c y_c} = 0 \qquad 39.57$$

$$I_{xy} = 0 \qquad 39.58$$

Description

Equation 39.47 through Eq. 39.58 give the properties of hollow (right) cylinders. Due to symmetry, the properties are the same for all axes. R_1 is the outer radius, and R_2 is the inner radius. The center of mass (center of gravity) is located at (x_c, y_c, z_c), designated point c. M is the total mass; ρ is the mass density, equal to the mass divided by the volume; I is the mass moment of inertia about the subscripted axis, used in calculating rotational acceleration and moments about that axis; and r is the radius of gyration, a distance from the designated axis from the centroid where all of the mass can be assumed to be concentrated. r_{y_c} is the radius of gyration of the hollow cylinder about an axis parallel to the y-axis and passing through the centroid. I_{xy} is the product of inertia, a measure of symmetry, with respect to a plane containing the subscripted axes. The product of inertia is zero if the object is symmetrical about an axis perpendicular to the plane defined by the subscripted axes.

Example

A hollow cylinder has a mass of 2 kg, a height of 1 m, an outer diameter of 1 m, and an inner diameter of 0.8 m.

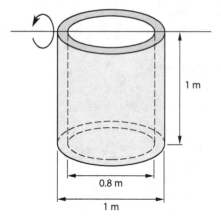

What is most nearly the cylinder's mass moment of inertia about an axis perpendicular to the cylinder's longitudinal axis and located at the cylinder's end?

(A) 0.41 kg·m^2
(B) 0.79 kg·m^2
(C) 0.87 kg·m^2
(D) 1.5 kg·m^2

Solution

The outer radius, R_1, and inner radius, R_2, are

$$R_1 = \frac{1 \text{ m}}{2} = 0.5 \text{ m}$$
$$R_2 = \frac{0.8 \text{ m}}{2} = 0.4 \text{ m}$$

Use Eq. 39.53.

$$I = M(3R_1^2 + 3R_2^2 + 4h^2)/12$$
$$= \frac{(2 \text{ kg})\big((3)(0.5 \text{ m})^2 + (3)(0.4 \text{ m})^2 + (4)(1 \text{ m})^2\big)}{12}$$
$$= 0.87 \text{ kg·m}^2$$

The answer is (C).

Equation 39.59 Through Eq. 39.69: Properties of Spheres

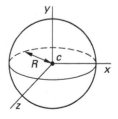

mass and centroid

$$M = \tfrac{4}{3}\pi R^3 \rho \qquad 39.59$$
$$x_c = 0 \qquad 39.60$$
$$y_c = 0 \qquad 39.61$$
$$z_c = 0 \qquad 39.62$$

mass moment of inertia

$$I_{x_c} = I_x = 2MR^2/5 \qquad\qquad 39.63$$

$$I_{y_c} = I_y = 2MR^2/5 \qquad\qquad 39.64$$

$$I_{z_c} = I_z = 2MR^2/5 \qquad\qquad 39.65$$

(radius of gyration)^2

$$r_{x_c}^2 = r_x^2 = 2R^2/5 \qquad\qquad 39.66$$

$$r_{y_c}^2 = r_y^2 = 2R^2/5 \qquad\qquad 39.67$$

$$r_{z_c}^2 = r_z^2 = 2R^2/5 \qquad\qquad 39.68$$

product of inertia

$$I_{x_c y_c} = 0 \qquad\qquad 39.69$$

Description

Equation 39.59 through Eq. 39.69 give the properties of spheres. The center of mass (center of gravity) is located at (x_c, y_c, z_c), designated point c. M is the total mass; ρ is the mass density, equal to the mass divided by the volume; I is the mass moment of inertia about the subscripted axis, used in calculating rotational acceleration and moments about that axis; and r is the radius of gyration, a distance from the designated axis from the centroid where all of the mass can be assumed to be concentrated. The product of inertia for any plane passing through the centroid is zero because the object is symmetrical about an axis perpendicular to that plane.

2. PLANE MOTION OF A RIGID BODY

General rigid body plane motion, such as rolling wheels, gear sets, and linkages, can be represented in two dimensions (i.e., the plane of motion). Plane motion can be considered as the sum of a translational component and a rotation about a fixed axis, as illustrated in Fig. 39.1.

3. ROTATION ABOUT A FIXED AXIS

Instantaneous Center of Rotation

Analysis of the rotational component of a rigid body's plane motion can sometimes be simplified if the location of the body's *instantaneous center* is known. Using the instantaneous center reduces many relative motion problems to simple geometry. The instantaneous center (also known as the *instant center* and IC) is a point at which the body could be fixed (pinned) without

Figure 39.1 Components of Plane Motion

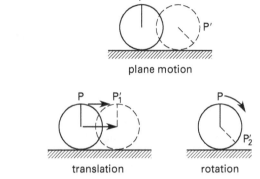

changing the instantaneous angular velocities of any point on the body. For angular velocities, the body seems to rotate about a fixed, instantaneous center.

The instantaneous center is located by finding two points for which the absolute velocity directions are known. Lines drawn perpendicular to these two velocities will intersect at the instantaneous center. (This graphic procedure is slightly different if the two velocities are parallel, as Fig. 39.2 shows.) For a rolling wheel, the instantaneous center is the point of contact with the supporting surface.

Figure 39.2 Graphic Method of Finding the Instantaneous Center

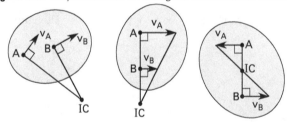

The absolute velocity of any point, P, on a wheel rolling (see Fig. 39.3) with translational velocity, v_O, can be found by geometry. Assume that the wheel is pinned at point C and rotates with its actual angular velocity, $\dot{\theta} = \omega = v_O/r$. The direction of the point's velocity will be perpendicular to the line of length, l, between the instantaneous center and the point.

$$v = l\,\omega = \frac{l v_O}{r}$$

Figure 39.3 Instantaneous Center of a Rolling Wheel

Equation 39.70: Kennedy's Rule

$$c = \frac{n(n-1)}{2} \qquad \text{39.70}$$

Description

The location of the instantaneous center can be found by inspection for many mechanisms, such as simple pinned pulleys and rolling/rotating objects. *Kennedy's rule* (law, theorem, etc.) can be used to help find the instantaneous centers when they are not obvious, such as with slider-crank and bar linkage mechanisms. Kennedy's rule states that any three links (bodies), designated as 1, 2, and 3, of a mechanism (that may have more than three links), and undergoing motion relative to one another, will have exactly three associated instantaneous centers, IC_{12}, IC_{13}, and IC_{23}, and those three instant centers will lie on a straight line. Equation 39.70 calculates the number of instantaneous centers for any number of links. c is the number of instantaneous centers, and n is the number of links.

Example

How many instantaneous centers does the linkage shown have?

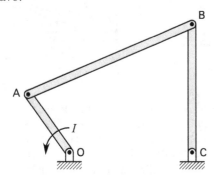

- (A) 3
- (B) 4
- (C) 5
- (D) 6

Solution

This is a four-bar linkage. The fourth bar consists of the fixed link between points O and C. Use Eq. 39.70. The number of instantaneous centers is

$$c = \frac{n(n-1)}{2} = \frac{(4)(4-1)}{2} = 6$$

The answer is (D).

Equation 39.71 Through Eq. 39.73: Angular Momentum

$$\mathbf{H}_0 = \mathbf{r} \times m\mathbf{v} \qquad \text{39.71}$$

$$\mathbf{H}_0 = I_0\,\omega \qquad \text{39.72}$$

$$\sum(\text{syst. } \mathbf{H})_1 = \sum(\text{syst. } \mathbf{H})_2 \qquad \text{39.73}$$

Description

The *angular momentum* taken about a point 0 is the moment of the linear momentum vector. Angular momentum has units of distance × force × time (e.g., N·m·s). It has the same direction as the rotation vector and can be determined from the vectors by use of the right-hand rule (cross product). (See Eq. 39.71.)

For a rigid body rotating about an axis passing through its center of gravity located at point 0, the scalar value of angular momentum is given by Eq. 39.72.[4]

The *law of conservation of angular momentum* states that if no external torque acts upon an object, the angular momentum cannot change. The angular momentum before and after an internal torque is applied is the same. Equation 39.73 expresses the angular momentum conservation law for a system consisting of multiple masses.[5]

Equation 39.74 and Eq. 39.75: Change in Angular Momentum

$$\dot{\mathbf{H}}_0 = d(I_0\,\omega)/dt = \mathbf{M} \qquad \text{39.74}$$

$$\sum(\mathbf{H}_{0i})_{t_2} = \sum(\mathbf{H}_{0i})_{t_1} + \sum\int_{t_1}^{t_2}\mathbf{M}_{0i}\,dt \qquad \text{39.75}$$

---

[4]The *NCEES Handbook* is inconsistent in its representation of the centroidal mass moment of inertia. I_0 and I_c are both used in the Dynamics section for the same concept.

[5]In Eq. 39.73, the nonstandard notation "syst" should be interpreted as the limits of summation (i.e., summation over all masses in the system). This would normally be written as $\sum_{\text{system}}$ or something similar.

Variations

$$\mathbf{M} = \frac{d\mathbf{H}_O}{dt}$$

$$M = I\frac{d\omega}{dt} = I\alpha$$

Description

Although Newton's laws do not specifically deal with rotation, there is an analogous relationship between applied moment (torque) and change in angular momentum. For a rotating body, the moment (torque), $\mathbf{M}$, required to change the angular momentum is given by Eq. 39.74.

The rotation of a rigid body will be about the center of gravity unless the body is constrained otherwise. The scalar form of Eq. 39.74 for a constant moment of inertia is shown in the second variation.

For a collection of particles, Eq. 39.74 may be expanded as shown in Eq. 39.75. Equation 39.75 determines the angular momentum at time t_2 from the angular momentum at time t_1, $\sum (\mathbf{H}_{0i})_{t_1}$, and the angular impulse of the moment between t_1 and t_2, $\sum \int_{t_1}^{t_2} \mathbf{M}_{0i} dt$.

Equation 39.76 Through Eq. 39.86: Rotation About an Arbitrary Fixed Axis

$$\sum M_q = I_q \alpha \qquad \text{39.76}$$

$$\alpha = \frac{d\omega}{dt} \quad \text{[general]} \qquad \text{39.77}$$

$$\omega = \frac{d\theta}{dt} \quad \text{[general]} \qquad \text{39.78}$$

$$\omega \, d\omega = \alpha \, d\theta \quad \text{[general]} \qquad \text{39.79}$$

$$\omega = \omega_0 + \alpha_c t \qquad \text{39.80}$$

$$\theta = \theta_0 + \omega_0 t + \tfrac{1}{2}\alpha_c t^2 \qquad \text{39.81}$$

$$\omega^2 = \omega_0^2 + 2\alpha_c(\theta - \theta_0) \qquad \text{39.82}$$

$$\alpha = M_q / I_q \qquad \text{39.83}$$

$$\omega = \omega_0 + \alpha t \qquad \text{39.84}$$

$$\theta = \theta_0 + \omega_0 t + \alpha t^2 / 2 \qquad \text{39.85}$$

$$I_q \omega^2 / 2 = I_q \omega_0^2 / 2 + \int_{\theta_0}^{\theta} M_q \, d\theta \qquad \text{39.86}$$

Variations

$$\omega = \int \alpha \, dt$$

$$= \omega_0 + \left(\frac{M}{I}\right) t$$

$$\theta = \iint \alpha \, dt^2$$

$$= \theta_0 + \omega_0 t + \left(\frac{M}{2I}\right) t^2$$

Description

The rotation about an arbitrary fixed axis q is found from Eq. 39.76. Equation 39.77 through Eq. 39.79 apply when the angular acceleration of the rotating body is variable. Equation 39.80 through Eq. 39.82 apply when the angular acceleration of the rotating body is constant.[6] Equation 39.83 through Eq. 39.85 apply when the moment applied to the fixed axis is constant. The change in kinetic energy (i.e., the work done to accelerate from ω_0 to ω) is calculated using Eq. 39.86.

Example

A 50 N wheel has a mass moment of inertia of 2 kg·m². The wheel is subjected to a constant 1 N·m torque. What is most nearly the angular velocity of the wheel 5 s after the torque is applied?

- (A) 0.5 rad/s
- (B) 3 rad/s
- (C) 5 rad/s
- (D) 10 rad/s

Solution

Use Eq. 39.83 to find the angular acceleration of the wheel when subjected to a 1 N·m moment.

$$\alpha = M_q / I_q = \frac{1 \text{ N·m}}{2 \text{ kg·m}^2}$$

$$= 0.5 \text{ rad/s}^2$$

---

[6]The use of subscript c in the *NCEES Handbook* Dynamics section to designate a constant angular acceleration is not a normal and customary engineering usage. Since subscript c is routinely used in dynamics to designate centroidal (mass center), the subscript is easily misinterpreted.

From Eq. 39.84, the angular velocity after 5 s is

$$\omega = \omega_0 + \alpha t = 0\ \frac{\text{rad}}{\text{s}} + \left(0.5\ \frac{\text{rad}}{\text{s}^2}\right)(5\ \text{s})$$

$$= 2.5\ \text{rad/s} \quad (3\ \text{rad/s})$$

The answer is (B).

4. CENTRIPETAL AND CENTRIFUGAL FORCES

Newton's second law states that there is a force for every acceleration that a body experiences. For a body moving around a curved path, the total acceleration can be separated into tangential and normal components. By Newton's second law, there are corresponding forces in the tangential and normal directions. The force associated with the normal acceleration is known as the *centripetal force*. The centripetal force is a real force on the body toward the center of rotation. The so-called *centrifugal force* is an apparent force on the body directed away from the center of rotation. The centripetal and centrifugal forces are equal in magnitude but opposite in sign.

The centrifugal force on a body of mass m with distance r from the center of rotation to the center of mass is

$$F_c = ma_n = \frac{mv_t^2}{r} = mr\omega^2$$

5. BANKING OF CURVES

If a vehicle travels in a circular path on a flat plane with instantaneous radius r and tangential velocity v_t, it will experience an apparent centrifugal force. The centrifugal force is resisted by a combination of roadway banking (superelevation) and sideways friction. The vehicle weight, W, corresponds to the normal force. For small banking angles, the maximum frictional force is

$$F_f = \mu_s N = \mu_s W$$

For large banking angles, the centrifugal force contributes to the normal force. If the roadway is banked so that friction is not required to resist the centrifugal force, the superelevation angle, θ, can be calculated from

$$\tan\theta = \frac{v_t^2}{gr}$$

40

Energy and Work

Nomenclature

e	coefficient of restitution	–
E	energy	J
F	force	N
g	gravitational acceleration, 9.81	m/s^2
h	height	m
k	spring constant	N/m
m	mass	kg
M	moment	N·m
p	linear momentum	kg·m/s
P	power	W
r	distance	m
s	position	m
t	time	s
T	kinetic energy	J
U	potential energy	J
v	velocity	m/s
W	work	J
x	displacement	m
y	horizontal displacement	m

Symbols

ε	efficiency	–
θ	angle	deg
ω	angular velocity	rad/s

Subscripts

$1 \rightarrow 2$	moving from state 1 to state 2
c	centroidal or constant
e	elastic
f	final or frictional
F	force
g	gravity
IC	instantaneous center
M	moment
n	normal
s	spring
W	weight

1. INTRODUCTION

The *energy* of a mass represents the capacity of the mass to do work. Such energy can be stored and released. There are many forms that the stored energy can take, including mechanical, thermal, electrical, and magnetic energies. Energy is a positive, scalar quantity, although the change in energy can be either positive or negative. *Work*, W, is the act of changing the energy of a mass. Work is a signed, scalar quantity. Work is positive when a force acts in the direction of motion and moves a mass from one location to another. Work is negative when a force acts to oppose motion. (Friction, for example, always opposes the direction of motion and can only do negative work.) The net work done on a mass by more than one force can be found by superposition.

Equation 40.1 Through Eq. 40.6: Work[1]

$$W = \int \boldsymbol{F} \cdot d\boldsymbol{r} \qquad \text{40.1}$$

$$U_F = \int F \cos \theta \, ds \quad \text{[variable force]} \qquad \text{40.2}$$

$$U_F = (F_c \cos \theta) \Delta s \quad \text{[constant force]} \qquad \text{40.3}$$

$$U_W = -W \Delta y \quad \text{[weight]} \qquad \text{40.4}$$

$$U_s = -\tfrac{1}{2} k (s_2^2 - s_1^2) \quad \text{[spring]} \qquad \text{40.5}$$

$$U_M = M \Delta \theta \quad \text{[couple moment]} \qquad \text{40.6}$$

---

[1]In Eq. 40.2 through Eq. 40.6, the variable for work is given as U for consistency with the NCEES *FE Reference Handbook* (*NCEES Handbook*). Normally, it is given as W.

Description

The work performed by a force is calculated as a dot product of the force vector acting through a displacement vector, as shown in Eq. 40.1. Since the dot product of two vectors is a scalar, work is a scalar quantity. The integral in Eq. 40.1 is essentially a summation over all forces acting at all distances.[2] Only the component of force in the direction of motion does work. In Eq. 40.2 and Eq. 40.3, the component of force in the direction of motion is $F \cos \theta$, where θ represents the acute angle between the force and the direction vectors. For a single constant force (or a force resultant), the integral can be dropped, and the differential ds replaced with Δs, as in Eq. 40.3.[3] Equation 40.4 represents the work done in moving a weight, W, a vertical distance, Δy, against earth's gravitational field.[4] Equation 40.5 represents the work associated with an extension or compression of a spring with a spring constant k.[5] Equation 40.6 is the work performed by a couple (i.e., a moment), M, rotating through an angle θ.[6]

2. KINETIC ENERGY

Kinetic energy is a form of mechanical energy associated with a moving or rotating body.

Equation 40.7: Linear Kinetic Energy[7]

$$T = m\mathrm{v}^2/2 \qquad\qquad 40.7$$

Description

The *linear kinetic energy* of a body moving with instantaneous linear velocity v is calculated from Eq. 40.7.

Example

A 3500 kg car traveling at 65 km/h skids. The car hits a wall 3 s later. The coefficient of friction between the tires and the road is 0.60, and the speed of the car when it hits the wall is 0.20 m/s. What is most nearly the energy that the bumper must absorb in order to prevent damage to the rest of the car?

(A)   70 J

(B)   140 J

(C)   220 J

(D)   360 kJ

Solution

Using Eq. 40.7, the kinetic energy of the car is

$$T = m\mathrm{v}^2/2$$
$$= \frac{(3500 \text{ kg})\left(0.20 \dfrac{\text{m}}{\text{s}}\right)^2}{2}$$
$$= 70 \text{ J}$$

The answer is (A).

---

[2](1) The *NCEES Handbook* attempts to distinguish between work and stored energy. For example, the work-energy principle (called the principle of work and energy in the *NCEES Handbook*) is essentially presented as $U_2 - U_1 = W$. However, there is no energy storage associated with a force, say, moving a box across a frictionless surface, which is one of the possible applications of Eq. 40.3. (2) When denoting work associated with a translating body, the *NCEES Handbook* uses both W and U. (3) The *NCEES Handbook* is inconsistent in its use of the variable U, which has three meanings: work, stored energy, and change in stored energy. (4) The *NCEES Handbook* is inconsistent in the variable used to indicate position or distance. Both r and s are used in this section.

[3]The *NCEES Handbook* is inconsistent in its use of the subscript c. In Eq. 40.3, F_c means a constant force. F_c is not a force directed through the centroid.

[4](1) The subscript W is not associated with work, but rather is associated with the object (i.e., weight) that is moved. (2) The meaning of the negative sign is ambiguous. If Δy is assumed to mean $y_2 - y_1$, then the negative sign would support a thermodynamic first law interpretation (i.e., work is negative when the surroundings do work on the system). However, Eq. 40.1, Eq. 40.2, Eq. 40.3, and Eq. 40.6 do not have negative signs, so these equations do not seem to be written to be consistent with a thermodynamic sign convention. Δy could mean $y_1 - y_2$, and the negative sign may represent mere algebraic convenience.

[5](1) Equation 40.5 is incorrectly presented in the *NCEES Handbook*. The 1/2 multiplier is incorrectly shown inside the parentheses. (2) There is no mathematical reason why the spring constant, k, cannot be brought outside of the parentheses. (3) Whereas the subscripts F, W, and M in Eq. 40.3, Eq. 40.4, and Eq. 40.6 are uppercase, the subscript s in Eq. 40.5 is lowercase. (4) Whereas the subscripts F, W, and M in Eq. 40.3, Eq. 40.4, and Eq. 40.6 are derived from the source of the energy change (i.e., from the item that moves), the subscript s in Eq. 40.5 is derived from the independent variable that changes. If a similar convention had been followed with Eq. 40.3, Eq. 40.4, and Eq. 40.6, the variables in those equations would have been U_r, U_s, and U_θ. (5) For a compression spring acted upon by an increasing force, $s_2 < s_1$, so the negative sign is incorrect for this application from a thermodynamic system standpoint. (6) This equation is shown in a subsequent column of this section of the *NCEES Handbook* as $U_2 - U_1 = k(x_2^2 - x_1^2)/2$, which is not only a different format, but uses x instead of s, and changes the meaning of U from change in energy to stored energy.

[6]The *NCEES Handbook* associates Eq. 40.6 with a "couple moment," an uncommon term. A property of a couple is the moment it imparts, so it is appropriate to speak of the moment of a couple. Similarly, a property of a hurricane is its wind speed, but referring to the hurricane itself as a hurricane speed would be improper. If Eq. 40.6 is meant to describe a pure moment causing rotation without translation, the terms *couple*, *pure moment*, or *torque* would all be appropriate.

[7](1) The *NCEES Handbook* uses different variables to represent kinetic energy. In its section on Units, KE is used. In its Dynamics section, T is used. (2) In its description of Eq. 40.7, the *NCEES Handbook* uses bold **v**, indicating a vector quantity, but subsequently does not indicate a vector quantity in the equation. Kinetic energy is not a vector quantity, and a vector velocity is not required to calculate kinetic energy.

Equation 40.8: Rotational Kinetic Energy

$$T = I_{IC}\omega^2/2 \qquad \text{40.8}$$

Description

The *rotational kinetic energy* of a body moving with instantaneous angular velocity, ω, about an instantaneous center is described by Eq. 40.8. I_{IC} is the mass moment of inertia about the *instantaneous center* of rotation.[8]

Example

A 10 kg homogeneous disk of 5 cm radius rotates on a massless axle AB of length 0.5 m and rotates about a fixed point A. The disk is constrained to roll on a horizontal floor.

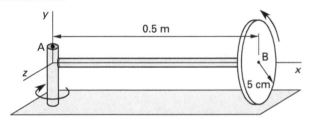

Given an angular velocity of 30 rad/s about the x-axis and -3 rad/s about the y-axis, the kinetic energy of the disk is most nearly

(A) 0.62 J

(B) 17 J

(C) 18 J

(D) 34 J

Solution

Assuming the axle is part of the disk, the disk has a fixed point at A. Since the x-, y-, and z-axes are principal axes of inertia for the disk, the kinetic energy is most nearly

$$
\begin{aligned}
T &= I_{IC}\omega^2/2 \\
&= \frac{I_x\omega_x^2}{2} + \frac{I_y\omega_y^2}{2} + \frac{I_z\omega_z^2}{2} \\
&= \frac{\frac{1}{2}mr^2\omega_x^2}{2} + \frac{\left(mL^2 + \frac{1}{4}mr^2\right)\omega_y^2}{2} + 0
\end{aligned}
$$

$$
\begin{aligned}
&= \frac{\left(\frac{1}{2}\right)(10 \text{ kg})\left(\dfrac{5 \text{ cm}}{100 \frac{\text{cm}}{\text{m}}}\right)^2 \left(30 \frac{\text{rad}}{\text{s}}\right)^2}{2} \\
&\quad + \frac{\left[\begin{array}{l}(10 \text{ kg})(0.5 \text{ m})^2 \\ \quad + \left(\frac{1}{4}\right)(10 \text{ kg})\left(\dfrac{5 \text{ cm}}{100 \frac{\text{cm}}{\text{m}}}\right)^2\end{array}\right]\left(-3 \frac{\text{rad}}{\text{s}}\right)^2}{2} + 0
\end{aligned}
$$

$$= 16.9 \text{ J} \quad (17 \text{ J})$$

The answer is (B).

Equation 40.9 and Eq. 40.10: Kinetic Energy of Rigid Bodies

$$T = m\text{v}^2/2 + I_c\omega^2/2 \qquad \text{40.9}$$

$$T = m(\text{v}_{cx}^2 + \text{v}_{cy}^2)/2 + I_c\omega_z^2/2 \qquad \text{40.10}$$

Description

Equation 40.9 gives the kinetic energy of a rigid body. For general plane motion in which there are translational and rotational components, the kinetic energy is the sum of the translational and rotational forms. Equation 40.10 gives the kinetic energy for motion in the x-y plane.

Example

A uniform disk with a mass of 10 kg and a diameter of 0.5 m rolls without slipping on a flat horizontal surface, as shown.

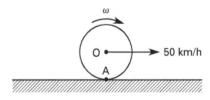

---

[8]Depending on the configuration, in addition to I, the *NCEES Handbook* uses different variables for the mass moment of inertia of bodies with rotational components. For rotation about an arbitrary axis, q, the *NCEES Handbook* uses I_q. For bodies rotating around axes other than their own centroidal axes, it uses I_{IC}. For unconstrained bodies rotating around axes passing through their own centroidal axes, I_{IC} in Eq. 40.8 is the same as I_c in Eq. 40.9 and Eq. 40.10.

When its horizontal velocity is 50 km/h, the total kinetic energy of the disk is most nearly

(A) 1000 J

(B) 1200 J

(C) 1400 J

(D) 1600 J

Solution

The linear velocity is

$$v_0 = \frac{\left(50 \ \frac{km}{h}\right)\left(1000 \ \frac{m}{km}\right)}{\left(60 \ \frac{s}{min}\right)\left(60 \ \frac{min}{h}\right)}$$
$$= 13.89 \ m/s$$

The angular velocity is

$$\omega = \frac{v_0}{r}$$
$$= \frac{13.89 \ \frac{m}{s}}{\frac{0.5 \ m}{2}}$$
$$= 55.56 \ rad/s$$

Using Eq. 40.9, the total kinetic energy is

$$T = mv_0^2/2 + I_c\omega^2/2$$
$$= \frac{mv_0^2}{2} + \frac{\left(\frac{1}{2}mR^2\right)\omega^2}{2}$$
$$= \frac{(10 \ kg)\left(13.89 \ \frac{m}{s}\right)^2}{2}$$
$$+ \frac{\left(\left(\frac{1}{2}\right)(10 \ kg)\left(\frac{0.5 \ m}{2}\right)^2\right)\left(55.56 \ \frac{rad}{s}\right)^2}{2}$$
$$= 1447 \ J \quad (1400 \ J)$$

The answer is (C).

Equation 40.11: Change in Kinetic Energy

$$T_2 - T_1 = m(v_2^2 - v_1^2)/2 \qquad 40.11$$

Description

The change in kinetic energy is calculated from the difference of squares of velocity, not from the square of the velocity difference (i.e., $m(v_2^2 - v_1^2)/2 \neq m(v_2 - v_1)^2/2$).

3. POTENTIAL ENERGY

Equation 40.12: Potential Energy in Gravity Field

$$U = mgh \qquad 40.12$$

Description

Potential energy (also known as *gravitational potential energy*), U, is a form of mechanical energy possessed by a mass due to its relative position in a gravitational field. Potential energy is lost when the elevation of a mass decreases. The lost potential energy usually is converted to kinetic energy or heat.

Equation 40.13: Force in a Spring (Hooke's Law)

$$F_s = kx \qquad 40.13$$

Description

A spring is an energy storage device because a compressed spring has the ability to perform work. In a perfect spring, the amount of energy stored is equal to the work required to compress the spring initially. The stored spring energy does not depend on the mass of the spring.

Equation 40.13 gives the force in a spring, which is the product of the *spring constant* (*stiffness*), k, and the displacement of the spring from its original position, x.

Example

A spring has a constant of 50 N/m. The spring is hung vertically, and a mass is attached to its end. The spring end displaces 30 cm from its equilibrium position. The same mass is removed from the first spring and attached to the end of a second (different) spring, and the displacement is 25 cm. What is most nearly the spring constant of the second spring?

(A) 46 N/m

(B) 56 N/m

(C) 60 N/m

(D) 63 N/m

Solution

The gravitational force on the mass is the same for both springs. From Hooke's law,

$$F_s = k_1 x_1 = k_2 x_2$$

$$k_2 = \frac{k_1 x_1}{x_2}$$

$$= \frac{\left(50 \ \frac{\text{N}}{\text{m}}\right)(30 \ \text{cm})}{25 \ \text{cm}}$$

$$= 60 \ \text{N/m}$$

The answer is (C).

Equation 40.14: Elastic Potential Energy

$$U = kx^2/2 \qquad \qquad 40.14$$

Description

Given a linear spring with spring constant (stiffness), k, the spring's *elastic potential energy* is calculated from Eq. 40.14.

Example

The 40 kg mass, m, shown is acted upon by a spring and guided by a frictionless rail. When the compressed spring is released, the mass stops slightly short of point A. The spring constant, k, is 3000 N/m, and the spring is compressed 0.5 m.

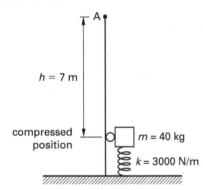

What is most nearly the energy stored in the spring?

(A) 380 J

(B) 750 J

(C) 1500 J

(D) 2100 J

Solution

Using Eq. 40.14, the potential energy is

$$U = kx^2/2$$

$$= \frac{\left(3000 \ \frac{\text{N}}{\text{m}}\right)(0.5 \ \text{m})^2}{2}$$

$$= 375 \ \text{J} \quad (380 \ \text{J})$$

The answer is (A).

Equation 40.15: Change in Potential Energy

$$U_2 - U_1 = k(x_2^2 - x_1^2)/2 \qquad \qquad 40.15$$

Description

The change in potential energy stored in the spring when the deformation in the spring changes from position x_1 to position x_2 is found from Eq. 40.15.[9]

Equivalent Spring Constant

The entire applied load is felt by each spring in a series of springs linked end-to-end. The *equivalent* (*composite*) *spring constant* for springs in series is

$$\frac{1}{k_{eq}} = \frac{1}{k_1} + \frac{1}{k_2} + \frac{1}{k_3} + \cdots \quad \begin{bmatrix} \text{series} \\ \text{springs} \end{bmatrix}$$

Springs in parallel (e.g., concentric springs) share the applied load. The equivalent spring constant for springs in parallel is

$$k_{eq} = k_1 + k_2 + k_3 + \cdots \quad \begin{bmatrix} \text{parallel} \\ \text{springs} \end{bmatrix}$$

Equation 40.16 Through Eq. 40.18: Combined Potential Energy

$$V = V_g + V_e \qquad \qquad 40.16$$

$$V_g = \pm Wy \qquad \qquad 40.17$$

$$V_e = +1/2ks^2 \qquad \qquad 40.18$$

---

[9]The *NCEES Handbook* uses the notation x to denote position, as in Eq. 40.14, and to denote change in length (i.e., a change in position Δx), as in Eq. 40.15. In Eq. 40.5 and Eq. 40.18, the *NCEES Handbook* uses s instead of x as in Eq. 40.15, but the meaning is the same.

Description

In mechanical systems, there are two common components of what is normally referred to as potential energy: gravitational potential energy and strain energy.[10] For a system containing a linear, elastic spring that is located at some elevation in a gravitational field, Eq. 40.16 gives the total of these two components.[11] Equation 40.17 gives the potential energy of a weight in a gravitational field.[12] Equation 40.18 gives the strain energy in a linear, elastic spring.[13]

4. ENERGY CONSERVATION PRINCIPLE

According to the *energy conservation principle*, energy cannot be created or destroyed. However, energy can be transformed into different forms. Therefore, the sum of all energy forms of a system is constant.

$$\sum E = \text{constant}$$

Because energy can be neither created nor destroyed, external work performed on a conservative system must go into changing the systems total energy. This is known as the *work-energy principle*.

$$W = E_2 - E_1$$

Generally, the principle of conservation of energy is applied to mechanical energy problems (i.e., conversion of work into kinetic or potential energy).

Conversion of one form of energy into another does not violate the conservation of energy law. Most problems involving conversion of energy are really special cases. For example, consider a falling body that is acted upon by a gravitational force. The conversion of potential energy into kinetic energy can be interpreted as equating the work done by the constant gravitational force to the change in kinetic energy.

Equation 40.19: Law of Conservation of Energy (Conservative Systems)

$$T_2 + U_2 = T_1 + U_1 \qquad 40.19$$

Description

For *conservative systems* where there is no energy dissipation or gain, the total energy of the mass is equal to the sum of the kinetic and potential (gravitational and elastic) energies.

Example

A projectile with a mass of 10 kg is fired directly upward from ground level with an initial velocity of 1000 m/s. Neglecting the effects of air resistance, what will be the speed of the projectile when it impacts the ground?

(A) 710 m/s

(B) 980 m/s

(C) 1000 m/s

(D) 1400 m/s

Solution

Use the law of conservation of energy.

$$T_2 + U_2 = T_1 + U_1$$

$$\frac{m\mathrm{v}_2^2}{2} + mgh_2 = \frac{m\mathrm{v}_1^2}{2} + mgh_1$$

$$(mgh_1 - mgh_2) + \frac{m\mathrm{v}_1^2 - m\mathrm{v}_2^2}{2} = 0$$

$$0 + \frac{m(\mathrm{v}_1^2 - \mathrm{v}_2^2)}{2} = 0$$

$$\mathrm{v}_2^2 = \mathrm{v}_1^2$$

$$\mathrm{v}_2 = \mathrm{v}_1$$

$$= 1000 \text{ m/s}$$

If air resistance is neglected, the impact velocity will be the same as the initial velocity.

The answer is (C).

---

[10]Equation 40.16 is not limited to mechanical systems. Potential energy storage exists in electrical, magnetic, fluid, pneumatic, and thermal systems also.

[11](1) Although PE is used in the Units section of the *NCEES Handbook* to identify potential energy, and U is defined as energy in the Dynamics section, here the *NCEES Handbook* introduces a new variable, V, for potential energy. Outside of the conservation of energy equation, this new variable does not seem to be used anywhere else in the *NCEES Handbook*. (2) V_g and V_e have previously (in the *NCEES Handbook*) been represented by U_W and U_s, among others. (3) The subscripts g and e are undefined, but gravitational acceleration is implied for g. The meaning of e is unclear but almost certainly refers to an elastic strain energy.

[12](1) The *NCEES Handbook* is inconsistent in the variable used to represent deflection. Equation 40.17 uses y while other equations in the Dynamics section of the *NCEES Handbook* use Δy and h. y is implicitly the distance from some arbitrary elevation for which $y = 0$ is assigned. (2) This use of $\pm$ is inconsistent with a thermodynamic interpretation of energy, as was apparently used in Eq. 40.4. The sign of the energy would normally be derived from the position, which can be positive or negative. By using $\pm$, the implication is that y is always a positive quantity, regardless of whether the mass is above or below the reference datum.

[13](1) Equation 40.18 has previously been presented with different variables in this section as Eq. 40.14. (2) Equation 40.18 uses s while other equations in the Dynamics section of the *NCEES Handbook* use x. (3) The + symbol is ambiguous, but probably should be interpreted as meaning kinetic energy is always positive. The + is redundant, because the s^2 term is always positive. (4) Equation 40.18 should not be interpreted as one over two times ks^2.

Equation 40.20: Law of Conservation of Energy (Nonconservative Systems)

$$T_2 + U_2 = T_1 + U_1 + W_{1\to 2} \qquad 40.20$$

Description

Nonconservative forces (e.g., friction) are accounted for by the work done by the nonconservative forces in moving between state 1 and state 2, $W_{1\to 2}$. If the nonconservative forces increase the energy of the system, $W_{1\to 2}$ is positive. If the nonconservative forces decrease the energy of the system, $W_{1\to 2}$ is negative.

5. LINEAR IMPULSE

Impulse is a vector quantity equal to the change in vector momentum. Units of linear impulse are the same as those for linear momentum: N·s. Figure 40.1 illustrates that impulse is represented by the area under the force-time curve.

$$\mathbf{Imp} = \int_{t_1}^{t_2} \mathbf{F}\,dt$$

Figure 40.1 *Impulse*

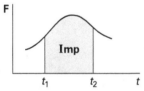

If the applied force is constant, impulse is easily calculated.

$$\mathbf{Imp} = \mathbf{F}(t_2 - t_1)$$

The change in momentum is equal to the impulse. This is known as the *impulse-momentum principle*. For a linear system with constant force and mass,

$$\mathbf{Imp} = \Delta \mathbf{p}$$

Equation 40.21 and Eq. 40.22: Impulse-Momentum Principle for a Particle

$$m\,d\mathbf{v}/dt = \mathbf{F} \qquad 40.21$$

$$m\,d\mathbf{v} = \mathbf{F}\,dt \qquad 40.22$$

Variation

$$\mathbf{F}(t_2 - t_1) = \Delta(m\mathbf{v})$$

Description

The impulse-momentum principle for a constant force and mass demonstrates that the impulse-momentum principle follows directly from Newton's second law.

Example

A 60 000 kg railcar moving at 1 km/h is coupled to a second, stationary railcar. If the velocity of the two cars after coupling is 0.2 m/s (in the original direction of motion) and the coupling is completed in 0.5 s, what is most nearly the average impulsive force on the railcar?

(A)   520 N

(B)   990 N

(C)   3100 N

(D)   9300 N

Solution

The original velocity of the 60 000 kg railcar is

$$v = \frac{\left(1\,\dfrac{\text{km}}{\text{h}}\right)\left(1000\,\dfrac{\text{m}}{\text{km}}\right)}{\left(60\,\dfrac{\text{s}}{\text{min}}\right)\left(60\,\dfrac{\text{min}}{\text{h}}\right)} = 0.2777 \text{ m/s}$$

Use the impulse-momentum principle.

$$F\Delta t = m\Delta v$$

$$\begin{aligned}
F &= \frac{m(v_1 - v_2)}{t_1 - t_2} = \frac{(60\,000\text{ kg})\left(0.2777\,\dfrac{\text{m}}{\text{s}} - 0.2\,\dfrac{\text{m}}{\text{s}}\right)}{0\text{ s} - 0.5\text{ s}} \\
&= -9324 \text{ N} \quad (9300\text{ N}) \quad [\text{opposite original direction}]
\end{aligned}$$

The answer is (D).

Equation 40.23: Impulse-Momentum Principle for a System of Particles

$$\sum m_i(\mathbf{v}_i)_{t_2} = \sum m_i(\mathbf{v}_i)_{t_1} + \sum \int_{t_1}^{t_2} \mathbf{F}_i\,dt \qquad 40.23$$

Description

$\sum m_i(\mathbf{v}_i)_{t_1}$ and $\sum m_i(\mathbf{v}_i)_{t_2}$ are the linear momentum at time t_1 and time t_2, respectively, for a system (i.e., collection) of particles. The impulse of the forces $\mathbf{F}$ from time t_1 to time t_2 is

$$\sum \int_{t_1}^{t_2} \mathbf{F}_i\,dt$$

Dynamics/ Vibrations

6. IMPACTS

According to Newton's second law, momentum is conserved unless a body is acted upon by an external force such as gravity or friction. In an impact or collision, contact is very brief, and the effect of external forces is insignificant. Therefore, momentum is conserved, even though energy may be lost through heat generation and deforming the bodies.

Consider two particles, initially moving with velocities v_1 and v_2 on a collision path, as shown in Fig. 40.2. The conservation of momentum equation can be used to find the velocities after impact, v_1' and v_2'.

Figure 40.2 *Direct Central Impact*

The impact is said to be an *inelastic impact* if kinetic energy is lost. The impact is said to be *perfectly inelastic* or *perfectly plastic* if the two particles stick together and move on with the same final velocity. The impact is said to be an *elastic impact* only if kinetic energy is conserved.

$$m_1 v_1^2 + m_2 v_2^2 = m_1 v_1'^2 + m_2 v_2'^2 \quad \text{[elastic only]}$$

Equation 40.24: Conservation of Momentum

$$m_1 \mathbf{v}_1 + m_2 \mathbf{v}_2 = m_1 \mathbf{v}_1' + m_2 \mathbf{v}_2' \qquad 40.24$$

Description

The *conservation of momentum* equation is used to find the velocity of two particles after collision. $\mathbf{v}_1$ and $\mathbf{v}_2$ are the initial velocities of the particles, and $\mathbf{v}_1'$ and $\mathbf{v}_2'$ are the velocities after impact.

Example

A 60 000 kg railcar moving at 1 km/h is instantaneously coupled to a stationary 40 000 kg railcar. What is most nearly the speed of the coupled cars?

(A) 0.40 km/h

(B) 0.60 km/h

(C) 0.88 km/h

(D) 1.0 km/h

Solution

Use the conservation of momentum principle.

$$m_1 \mathbf{v}_1 + m_2 \mathbf{v}_2 = (m_1 + m_2) \mathbf{v}'$$
$$(60\,000 \text{ kg}) \left(1 \, \frac{\text{km}}{\text{h}} \right)$$
$$+ (40\,000 \text{ kg})(0) = (60\,000 \text{ kg} + 40\,000 \text{ kg}) \mathbf{v}'$$
$$\mathbf{v}' = 0.60 \text{ km/h}$$

The answer is (B).

Equation 40.25: Coefficient of Restitution

$$e = \frac{(v_2')_n - (v_1')_n}{(v_1)_n - (v_2)_n} \qquad 40.25$$

Values

inelastic	$e < 1.0$
perfectly inelastic (plastic)	$e = 0$
perfectly elastic	$e = 1.0$

Description

The *coefficient of restitution*, e, is the ratio of relative velocity differences along a mutual straight line. When both impact velocities are not directed along the same straight line, the coefficient of restitution should be calculated separately for each velocity component.

In Eq. 40.25, the subscript n indicates that the velocity to be used in calculating the coefficient of restitution should be the velocity component normal to the plane of impact.

When an object rebounds from a stationary object (an infinitely massive plane), the stationary object's initial and final velocities are zero. In that case, the *rebound velocity* can be calculated from only the object's velocities.

$$e = \left| \frac{v_1'}{v_1} \right|$$

The value of the coefficient of restitution can be used to categorize the collision as elastic or inelastic. For a perfectly inelastic collision (i.e., a plastic collision), as when two particles stick together, the coefficient of restitution is zero. For a perfectly elastic collision, the coefficient of restitution is 1.0. For most collisions, the coefficient of restitution will be between zero and 1.0, indicating a (partially) inelastic collision.

Example

A 2 kg clay ball moving at a rate of 40 m/s collides with a 5 kg ball of clay moving in the same direction at a rate of 10 m/s. What is most nearly the final velocity of both balls if they stick together after colliding?

(A) 10 m/s

(B) 12 m/s

(C) 15 m/s

(D) 19 m/s

Solution

From the coefficient of restitution definition, Eq. 40.25,

$$e = \frac{(v_2')_n - (v_1')_n}{(v_1)_n - (v_2)_n} = 0$$
$$v_2' = v_1' = v'$$

From the conservation of momentum, Eq. 40.24,

$$m_1 v_1 + m_2 v_2 = (m_1 + m_2)v'$$
$$v' = \frac{m_1 v_1 + m_2 v_2}{m_1 + m_2}$$
$$= \frac{(2 \text{ kg})\left(40 \dfrac{\text{m}}{\text{s}}\right) + (5 \text{ kg})\left(10 \dfrac{\text{m}}{\text{s}}\right)}{2 \text{ kg} + 5 \text{ kg}}$$
$$= 18.6 \text{ m/s} \quad (19 \text{ m/s})$$

The answer is (D).

Equation 40.26 and Eq. 40.27: Velocity After Impact

$$(v_1')_n = \frac{m_2(v_2)_n(1+e) + (m_1 - em_2)(v_1)_n}{m_1 + m_2} \quad 40.26$$

$$(v_2')_n = \frac{m_1(v_1)_n(1+e) - (em_1 - m_2)(v_2)_n}{m_1 + m_2} \quad 40.27$$

Description

If the coefficient of restitution is known, Eq. 40.26 and Eq. 40.27 may be used to calculate the velocities after impact.

41

Vibrations

Nomenclature

a	acceleration	m/s^2
A	amplitude	m
C	coefficient of viscous damping	N·s/m
D	displacement	m
E	modulus of elasticity	Pa
f	frequency	Hz
F	force	N
g	gravitational acceleration, 9.81	m/s^2
G	shear modulus	Pa
I	polar mass moment of inertia	kg·m^2
J	polar area moment of inertia	m^4
k	spring constant	N/m
L	length	m
m	mass	kg
r	radius	m
t	time	s
T	period	s
U	energy	J
v	velocity	m/s
x	displacement	m

Symbols

δ	deflection	m
θ	angular position	rad
τ	period	s
ω	natural frequency	rad/s

Subscripts

0	initial
c	complementary
f	forcing
n	natural
p	particular
st	static
t	torsional

1. TYPES OF VIBRATIONS

Vibration is an oscillatory motion about an equilibrium point. If the motion is the result of a disturbing force that is applied once and then removed, the motion is known as *natural* (or *free*) *vibration*. If a force of impulse is applied repeatedly to a system, the motion is known as *forced vibration*.

Within both of the categories of natural and forced vibrations are the subcategories of damped and undamped vibrations. If there is no *damping* (i.e., no friction), a system will experience free vibrations indefinitely. This is known as *free vibration* and *simple harmonic motion*. (See Fig. 41.1.)

Figure 41.1 *Types of Vibrations*

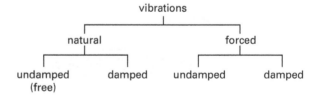

The performance (behavior) of some simple systems can be defined by a single variable. Such systems are referred to as *single degree of freedom* (*SDOF*) *systems*. For example, the position of a mass hanging from a spring is defined by the one variable $x(t)$.[1] Systems requiring two or more variables to define the positions of all parts are known as *multiple degree of freedom* (*MDOF*) *systems*. (See Fig. 41.2.)

---

[1]Although the convention is by no means universal, the variable x is commonly used as the position variable in oscillatory systems, even when the motion is in the vertical (y) direction.

Figure 41.2 *Single and Multiple Degree of Freedom Systems*

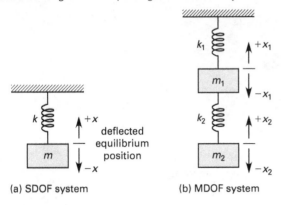

(a) SDOF system   (b) MDOF system

2. IDEAL COMPONENTS

When used to describe components in a vibrating system, the adjectives *perfect* and *ideal* generally imply *linearity* and the absence of friction and damping. The behavior of a *linear component* can be described by a linear equation. For example, the linear equation $F = kx$ describes a linear spring; however, the quadratic equation $F = Cv^2$ describes a nonlinear dashpot. Similarly, $F = ma$ and $F = Cv$ are linear inertial and viscous forces, respectively.

3. STATIC DEFLECTION

An important concept used in calculating the behavior of a vibrating system is the *static deflection*, δ_{st}. This is the deflection of a mechanical system due to gravitational force alone.[2] (The disturbing force is not considered.) In calculating the static deflection, it is extremely important to distinguish between mass and weight. Figure 41.3 illustrates two cases of static deflection.

Figure 41.3 *Examples of Static Deflection*

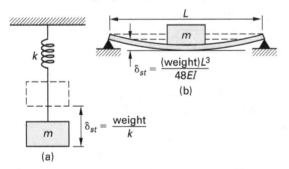

$$\delta_{st} = \frac{(\text{weight})L^3}{48EI}$$

(b)

$$\delta_{st} = \frac{\text{weight}}{k}$$

(a)

4. FREE VIBRATION

The simple mass and ideal spring illustrated in Fig. 41.4 is an example of a system that can experience free vibration. The system is initially at rest. The mass is hanging

on the spring, and the equilibrium position is the static deflection, δ_{st}. After the mass is displaced and released, it will oscillate up and down. Since there is no friction (i.e., the vibration is undamped), the oscillations will continue forever. (See Fig. 41.5.)

Figure 41.4 *Simple Spring-Mass System*

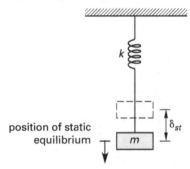

position of static
equilibrium

Figure 41.5 *Free Vibration*

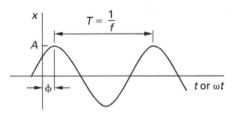

Equation 41.1: System at Rest

$$mg = k\delta_{st} \qquad\qquad 41.1$$

Description

The static deflection, δ_{st}, is the deflection due to the gravitational force alone. m is the mass of the system, g is the gravitational acceleration (9.81 m/s^2), and k is the system's spring constant.

Example

A pump with a mass of 30 kg is supported by a spring with a spring constant of 1250 N/m. The motor is constrained to allow only vertical movement. What is most nearly the static deflection of the spring?

(A) 0.11 m

(B) 0.19 m

(C) 0.24 m

(D) 0.31 m

---

[2]The term *deformation* is used synonymously with *deflection*.

Solution

Calculate the static deflection.

$$mg = k\delta_{st}$$

$$\delta_{st} = \frac{mg}{k}$$

$$= \frac{(30 \text{ kg})\left(9.81 \dfrac{\text{m}}{\text{s}^2}\right)}{1250 \dfrac{\text{N}}{\text{m}}}$$

$$= 0.235 \text{ m} \quad (0.24 \text{ m})$$

The answer is (C).

Equation 41.2 Through Eq. 41.4: Free Vibration Equations of Motion for Simple Spring-Mass System

$$m\ddot{x} = mg - k(x + \delta_{st}) \qquad \text{41.2}$$

$$m\ddot{x} + kx = 0 \qquad \text{41.3}$$

$$\ddot{x} + (k/m)x = 0 \qquad \text{41.4}$$

Variation

$$m\ddot{x} = k\delta_{st} - k(x + \delta_{st})$$

Description

When a simple spring-mass system is disturbed by a downward force (i.e., the mass is pulled downward from its static deflection and released) and the initial disturbing force is removed, the mass will be acted upon by the restoring force $(-kx)$ and the inertial force (mg). Equation 41.2 through Eq. 41.4 are the linear differential equations of motion.

Equation 41.5 Through Eq. 41.8: General Solution to Simple Spring-Mass System

$$x(t) = C_1 \cos(\omega_n t) + C_2 \sin(\omega_n t) \qquad \text{41.5}$$

$$\omega_n = \sqrt{k/m} \qquad \text{41.6}$$

$$\omega_n = \sqrt{g/\delta_{st}} \qquad \text{41.7}$$

$$\tau_n = 2\pi/\omega_n = \frac{2\pi}{\sqrt{\dfrac{k}{m}}} = \frac{2\pi}{\sqrt{\dfrac{g}{\delta_{st}}}} \qquad \text{41.8}$$

Variations

$$f = \frac{\omega}{2\pi} = \frac{1}{\tau}$$

$$\tau = \frac{1}{f} = \frac{2\pi}{\omega}$$

Description

C_1 and C_2 are constants of integration that depend on the initial displacement and velocity of the mass. ω is known as the *natural frequency of vibration* or *angular frequency*. It has units of radians per second. It is not the same as the *linear frequency*, f, which has units of hertz. The *period of oscillation*, τ, is the reciprocal of the linear frequency. The undamped natural frequency of vibration and natural period of vibration are given by Eq. 41.7 and Eq. 41.8, respectively.

Equation 41.7 can be used with a variety of systems, including those involving beams, shafts, and plates.

Example

A mass of 0.025 kg is hanging from a spring with a spring constant of 0.44 N/m. If the mass is pulled down and released, what is most nearly the period of oscillation?

    (A)   0.50 s

    (B)   1.2 s

    (C)   1.5 s

    (D)   2.1 s

Solution

From Eq. 41.8, the period is

$$\tau = \frac{2\pi}{\sqrt{\dfrac{k}{m}}} = \frac{2\pi}{\sqrt{\dfrac{0.44 \dfrac{\text{N}}{\text{m}}}{0.025 \text{ kg}}}} = 1.5 \text{ s}$$

The answer is (C).

Equation 41.9: Specific Solution to Simple Spring-Mass System

$$x(t) = x_0 \cos(\omega_n t) + (v_0/\omega_n)\sin(\omega_n t) \qquad \text{41.9}$$

Description

The initial conditions (i.e., the initial position and velocity) can be used to determine the constants of integration, C_1 and C_2, in Eq. 41.5. Equation 41.9 is the solution to the initial value problem.

Example

A mass is hung from a spring, which causes the spring to be displaced by 2 cm. The mass is then pulled down 6 cm and released. What is most nearly the position of the mass after 0.142 s?

(A) −0.06 m

(B) −0.02 m

(C) 0.04 m

(D) 0.08 m

Solution

From Eq. 41.7, find the natural frequency of the system.

$$\omega_n = \sqrt{g/\delta_{st}}$$

$$= \sqrt{\frac{\left(9.81 \ \frac{\text{m}}{\text{s}^2}\right)\left(100 \ \frac{\text{cm}}{\text{m}}\right)}{2 \ \text{cm}}}$$

$$= 22.15 \ \text{rad/s}$$

The initial velocity of the mass is 0 rad/s, and the initial position of the mass is 6 cm. From Eq. 41.9, the position of the mass is

$$x(t) = x_0 \cos(\omega_n t) + (v_0/\omega_n)\sin(\omega_n t)$$

$$= \left(\frac{6 \ \text{cm}}{100 \ \frac{\text{cm}}{\text{m}}}\right)\cos\left(\left(22.15 \ \frac{\text{rad}}{\text{s}}\right)(0.142 \ \text{s})\right)$$

$$+ \left(\frac{0}{22.1 \ \frac{\text{rad}}{\text{s}}}\right)\sin\left(\left(22.15 \ \frac{\text{rad}}{\text{s}}\right)(0.142 \ \text{s})\right)$$

$$= -0.0599 \ \text{m} \quad (-0.06 \ \text{m})$$

The negative sign indicates that the location is on the opposite side of the neutral (equilibrium) point from where the system was released.

The answer is (A).

5. AMPLITUDE OF OSCILLATION

With natural, undamped vibrations, the initial conditions (i.e., initial position and velocity) do not affect the natural period of oscillation. The amplitude, A, of the oscillations will be affected, as shown. This means, no matter how far the spring is initially displaced before release, the frequency of oscillation and period will be the same. However, the excursions of each oscillation

will depend on the initial displacement. For a perfect lossless system, the mass will return to the point of initial displacement in each oscillation.

$$A = \sqrt{x_0^2 + \left(\frac{v_0}{\omega}\right)^2}$$

6. VERTICAL VERSUS HORIZONTAL OSCILLATION

As long as friction is absent, the two cases of oscillation shown in Fig. 41.6 are equivalent (i.e., will have the same frequency and amplitude). Although it may seem that there is an extra gravitational force with vertical motion, the weight of the body is completely canceled by the opposite spring force when the system is in equilibrium. Therefore, vertical oscillations about an equilibrium point are equivalent to horizontal oscillations about the unstressed point.

Figure 41.6 *Vertical and Horizontal Oscillations*

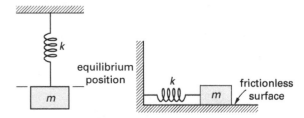

7. NATURAL FREQUENCY

The *conservation of energy* principle requires the kinetic energy at the static equilibrium position to equal the stored elastic energy at the position of maximum displacement. For the spring-mass system shown in Fig. 41.6, the energy conservation equation is

$$U = k$$

$$\frac{kx_{\text{max}}^2}{2} = \frac{mv_{\text{max}}^2}{2}$$

The velocity function is derived by taking the derivative of the position function.

$$x(t) = x_{\text{max}} \sin \omega t$$

$$v(t) = \frac{dx(t)}{dt} = \omega x_{\text{max}} \cos \omega t$$

The previous equation shows that $v_{\text{max}} = \omega x_{\text{max}}$. Substituting this into the energy conservation equation derives the *natural circular frequency of vibration*.

$$\omega^2 = \frac{k}{m}$$

8. TORSIONAL FREE VIBRATION

The *torsional pendulum* shown in Fig. 41.7 can be analyzed in a manner analogous to the spring-mass combination.

Figure 41.7 *Torsional Pendulum*

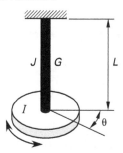

Equation 41.10 and Eq. 41.11: Differential Equation of Motion for Simple Torsional Spring

$$\ddot{\theta} + (k_t/I)\theta = 0 \qquad \textit{41.10}$$

$$\theta(t) = \theta_0\cos(\omega_n t) + (\dot{\theta}_0/\omega_n)\sin(\omega_n t) \qquad \textit{41.11}$$

Description

The differential equation of motion, Eq. 41.10, disregards the mass and moment of inertia of the shaft. The solution to the differential equation, shown in Eq. 41.11, is directly analogous to the solution for the spring-mass system.

Equation 41.12: Torsional Spring Constant

$$k_t = GJ/L \qquad \textit{41.12}$$

Variation

$$k_t = \omega^2 I$$

Description

The *torsional spring constant*, k_t, for a torsional pendulum is found from the shear modulus of elasticity, G, the polar area moment of inertia, J, and the shaft length, L.

Equation 41.13 and Eq. 41.14: Undamped Circular Natural Frequency

$$\omega_n = \sqrt{k_t/I} \qquad \textit{41.13}$$

$$\omega_n = \sqrt{GJ/IL} \qquad \textit{41.14}$$

Description

Equation 41.13 gives the *undamped natural circular frequency*, ω_n, for a solid, round supporting rod used as a torsional spring. Using the relationship from Eq. 41.12, the undamped circular natural frequency can be rewritten as Eq. 41.14. J is the polar area moment of inertia of the vertical support, with units of m^4. I is the polar mass moment of inertia of the oscillating inertial disk, with units of $kg \cdot m^2$. They are not the same.

Example

A torsional pendulum consists of a 5 kg uniform disk with a radius of 0.25 m attached at its center to a rod 1.5 m in length. The torsional spring constant is 0.625 N·m/rad. Disregarding the mass of the rod, what is most nearly the undamped natural circular frequency of the torsional pendulum?

(A) 1.0 rad/s

(B) 1.2 rad/s

(C) 1.4 rad/s

(D) 2.0 rad/s

Solution

The mass moment of inertia of the disk (a cylinder) is

$$I = MR^2/2$$
$$= \frac{(5 \text{ kg})(0.25 \text{ m})^2}{2}$$
$$= 0.1563 \text{ kg} \cdot \text{m}^2$$

Using Eq. 41.13, the undamped natural circular frequency is

$$\omega_n = \sqrt{k_t/I}$$
$$= \sqrt{\frac{0.625 \dfrac{\text{N} \cdot \text{m}}{\text{rad}}}{0.1563 \text{ kg} \cdot \text{m}^2}}$$
$$= 2.0 \text{ rad/s}$$

The answer is (D).

Equation 41.15: Undamped Natural Period

$$\tau_n = 2\pi/\omega_n = \frac{2\pi}{\sqrt{\dfrac{k_t}{I}}} = \frac{2\pi}{\sqrt{\dfrac{GJ}{IL}}} \qquad \textit{41.15}$$

Dynamics/
Vibrations

Description

Similar to the undamped natural period of vibration for a linear system (see Eq. 41.8), the undamped natural period for a torsional system can be calculated from Eq. 41.15.

9. UNDAMPED FORCED VIBRATIONS

When an external disturbing force, $F(t)$, acts on the system, the system is said to be forced. Although the *forcing function* is usually considered to be periodic, it need not be (as in the case of impulse, step, and random functions).[3] However, an initial disturbance (i.e., when a mass is displaced and released to oscillate freely) is not an example of a forcing function. (See Fig. 41.8.)

Figure 41.8 *Forced Vibrations*

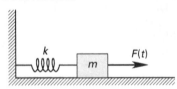

Consider a sinusoidal periodic force with a *forcing frequency* of ω_f and maximum value of F_0.

$$F(t) = F_0 \cos \omega_f t$$

The differential equation of motion is

$$m\frac{d^2x}{dt^2} = -kx + F_0 \cos \omega_f t$$

The solution to the differential equation of motion consists of the sum of two parts: a complementary solution and a particular solution. The *complementary solution* is obtained by setting $F_0 = 0$ (i.e., solving the homogeneous differential equation). As was shown in Eq. 41.5 and Eq. 41.9, the solution is

$$x_c(t) = A \cos \omega t + B \sin \omega t$$

The *particular solution* is

$$x_p(t) = D \cos \omega_f t$$

$$D = \frac{F_0}{m(\omega^2 - \omega_f^2)}$$

The solution of the differential equation of motion is

$$x(t) = A \cos \omega t + B \sin \omega t$$
$$+ \left(\frac{F_0}{m(\omega^2 - \omega_f^2)} \right) \cos \omega_f t$$

10. VIBRATION ISOLATION AND CONTROL

It is often desired to isolate a rotating machine from its surroundings, to limit the vibrations that are transmitted to the supports, and to reduce the amplitude of the machine's vibrations.

The *transmissibility* (i.e., *linear transmissibility*) is the ratio of the transmitted force (i.e., the force transmitted to the supports) to the applied force (i.e., the force from the imbalance). In some cases, the transmissibility may be reported in units of *decibels*.

The magnitude of oscillations in vibrating equipment can be reduced and the equipment isolated from the surroundings by mounting on resilient pads or springs. The isolated system must have a natural frequency less than $1 / \sqrt{2} = 0.707$ times the disturbing (forcing) frequency. That is, the transmissibility will be reduced below 1.0 only if $\omega_f/\omega > \sqrt{2}$. Otherwise, the attempted isolation will actually increase the transmitted force.

The amount of isolation is characterized by the *isolation efficiency*, also known as the *percent of isolation* and *degree of isolation*.

Isolation materials and isolator devices have specific deflection characteristics. If the isolation efficiency is known, it can be used to determine the type of isolator or isolation device used based on the static deflection.

A *tuned system* is one for which the natural frequency of the vibration absorber is equal to the frequency that is to be eliminated (i.e., the forcing frequency). In theory, this is easy to accomplish: the mass and spring constant of the absorber are varied until the desired natural frequency is achieved. This is known as "tuning" the system.

11. ISOLATION FROM ACTIVE BASE

In some cases, a machine is to be isolated from an active base. The base (floor, supports, etc.) vibrates, and the magnitude of the vibration seen by the machine is to be limited or reduced. This case is not fundamentally different from the case of a vibrating machine being isolated from a stationary base.

---

[3]The sinusoidal case is important, since Fourier transforms can be used to model any forcing function in terms of sinusoids.

The concept of transmissibility is replaced by the amplitude ratio (magnification factor or amplification factor). This is the ratio of the transmitted displacement (deflection, excursion, motion, etc.) to the applied displacement. That is, it is the ratio of the maximum mass motion to the maximum base motion.

12. VIBRATIONS IN SHAFTS

A shaft's natural frequency of vibration is referred to as the *critical speed*. This is the rotational speed in revolutions per second that just equals the lateral natural frequency of vibration. Therefore, vibration in shafts is basically an extension of lateral vibrations (e.g., whipping "up and down") in beams. Rotation is disregarded, and the shaft is considered only from the standpoint of lateral vibrations.

The shaft will have multiple modes of vibration. General practice is to keep the operating speed well below the first critical speed (corresponding to the first node). For shafts with distributed or multiple loadings, it may be important to know the second critical speed. However, higher critical speeds are usually well out of the range of operation.

For shafts with constant cross-sectional areas and simple loading configurations, the static deflection due to pulleys, gears, and self-weight can be found from beam formulas. Shafts with single antifriction (i.e., ball and roller) bearings at each end can be considered to be simply supported, while shafts with sleeve bearings or two side-by-side antifriction bearings at each shaft end can be considered to have fixed built-in supports.[4]

A shaft carrying no load other than its own weight can be considered as a uniformly loaded beam. The maximum deflection at midspan can be found from beam tables.

The classical analysis of a shaft carrying single or multiple inertial loads (flywheel, pulley, etc.) assumes that the shaft itself is weightless.

Dynamics/
Vibrations

---

[4]Sleeve bearings (journal bearings) are assumed to be fixed supports, not because they have the mechanical strength to prevent binding, but because sleeve bearings cannot operate and would not be operating with an angled shaft.

Diagnostic Exam

Topic XI: Mechanical Design and Analysis

1. The simple four-bar linkage shown is configured into the open position. Link 1 is 0.57 m long, link 2 is 0.21 m long, link 3 is 0.45 m long, and link 4 is 0.36 m long. Taking link 1 as the reference link, the angle that link 2 makes with the reference link, θ_2, is 62°.

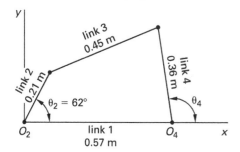

What is most nearly the value of angle θ_4?

(A) 49°

(B) 85°

(C) 99°

(D) 110°

2. Which of the following symptoms or conditions is NOT one of the main causes of pressure vessel failure?

(A) embrittlement

(B) chattering

(C) corrosion

(D) erosion

3. A bolted joint with a joint coefficient of 0.14 experiences a 26 kN tension. The bolt is initially preloaded to 7.5 kN. What is most nearly the maximum bolt load?

(A) 11 kN

(B) 24 kN

(C) 32 kN

(D) 43 kN

4. A bolt has a major-diameter area of 123 mm² and a tensile stress area of 88 mm². The threaded length is 14 mm. The modulus of elasticity is 230 GPa. What is

most nearly the stiffness of the threaded length of the bolt?

(A) 980 kN/mm

(B) 1100 kN/mm

(C) 1400 kN/mm

(D) 1700 kN/mm

5. A 94 N force is applied to a 50 mm long spring made of 2 mm steel wire (shear modulus of 80 GPa). The spring has 7 active coils and a mean diameter of 12 mm. The spring ends are closed. What is most nearly the spring constant?

(A) 2.5 N/mm

(B) 13 N/mm

(C) 27 N/mm

(D) 36 N/mm

6. An 18 tooth straight spur gear transmits a torque of 1300 N·mm. The pitch circle diameter is 2.3 cm, and the pressure angle is 37°. What is most nearly the radial force on the gear?

(A) 43 N

(B) 57 N

(C) 85 N

(D) 110 N

7. A hole has a minimum size of 10.988 mm and a tolerance of 0.011 mm. What is most nearly the nominal size of the hole?

(A) 10.959 mm

(B) 10.967 mm

(C) 10.988 mm

(D) 10.999 mm

8. A shaft has an upper deviation of 0.011 mm and a lower deviation of 0.019 mm. What is most nearly the tolerance of the shaft?

(A) −0.008 mm

(B) 0.008 mm

(C) 0.01 mm

(D) 0.02 mm

9. A particular roller bearing has a life of 3000 h when carrying an equivalent radial load of 9.5 kN and rotating at 500 rpm. What is most nearly the predicted life if the bearing is loaded to 12 kN at the same rotational speed?

(A) 1000 h

(B) 1200 h

(C) 1300 h

(D) 1400 h

10. Two gears are in mesh. Gear 1 has 20 teeth and a radius of 4.6 cm. Gear 2 has 30 teeth and a radius of 7.2 cm. What is most nearly the diametral pitch of these two gears?

(A) 110 m^{-1}

(B) 140 m^{-1}

(C) 180 m^{-1}

(D) 210 m^{-1}

SOLUTIONS

1. Calculate K_1.

$$K_1 = \frac{d}{a} = \frac{0.57 \text{ m}}{0.21 \text{ m}}$$
$$= 2.714$$

Calculate K_2.

$$K_2 = \frac{d}{c} = \frac{0.57 \text{ m}}{0.36 \text{ m}}$$
$$= 1.583$$

Calculate K_3.

$$K_3 = \frac{a^2 - b^2 + c^2 + d^2}{2ac}$$
$$= \frac{(0.21 \text{ m})^2 - (0.45 \text{ m})^2 + (0.36 \text{ m})^2 + (0.57 \text{ m})^2}{(2)(0.21 \text{ m})(0.36 \text{ m})}$$
$$= 1.958$$

Calculate the value of A.

$$A = \cos\theta_2 - K_1 - K_2\cos\theta_2 + K_3$$
$$= \cos 62° - 2.714 - 1.583\cos 62° + 1.958$$
$$= -1.030$$

Calculate the value of B.

$$B = -2\sin\theta_2 = -2\sin 62°$$
$$= -1.766$$

Calculate the value of C.

$$C = K_1 - (K_2 + 1)\cos\theta_2 + K_3$$
$$= 2.714 - (1.583 + 1)\cos 62° + 1.958$$
$$= 3.460$$

For the open position, the value of angle θ_4 is

$$\theta_4 = 2\arctan\left(\frac{-B - \sqrt{B^2 - 4AC}}{2A}\right)$$

$$= 2\arctan\left(\frac{-(-1.766)}{ - \sqrt{\dfrac{(-1.766)^2}{} - (4)(-1.030)(3.460)}}{(2)(-1.030)}\right)$$

$$= 98.77° \quad (99°)$$

The answer is (A).

2. Embrittlement, corrosion, and erosion all compromise material integrity. Chattering is the rapid opening and closing of a pressure relief valve due to some installation or operational valve defect. The resultant vibration can result in failure of the valve and/or associated piping, but valve chattering isn't a cause for pressure vessel failure.

The answer is (B).

3. The maximum bolt load is

$$F_{b,\max} = CP + F_i$$
$$= (0.14)(26 \text{ kN}) + 7.5 \text{ kN}$$
$$= 11.14 \text{ kN} \quad (11 \text{ kN})$$

The answer is (A).

4. The stiffness of the bolt is

$$k_b = \frac{A_d A_t E}{A_d l_t + A_t l_d}$$

$$= \frac{(123 \text{ mm}^2)(88 \text{ mm}^2)(230 \text{ GPa})\left(10^6 \frac{\text{kPa}}{\text{GPa}}\right)}{((123 \text{ mm}^2)(14 \text{ mm}) + (88 \text{ mm}^2)(0 \text{ mm}))}$$
$$\times \left(1000 \frac{\text{mm}}{\text{m}}\right)^2$$
$$= 1446 \text{ kN/mm} \quad (1400 \text{ kN/mm})$$

The answer is (A).

5. The spring constant is

$$k = \frac{d^4 G}{8D^3 N}$$

$$= \frac{(2 \text{ mm})^4(80 \text{ GPa})\left(10^9 \frac{\text{Pa}}{\text{GPa}}\right)}{(8)(12 \text{ mm})^3(7)\left(1000 \frac{\text{mm}}{\text{m}}\right)^2}$$
$$= 13.23 \text{ N/mm} \quad (13 \text{ N/mm})$$

The answer is (A).

6. Calculate the tangential force.

$$W_t = \frac{2T}{d} = \frac{(2)(1300 \text{ N·mm})}{(2.3 \text{ cm})\left(10 \frac{\text{mm}}{\text{cm}}\right)}$$
$$= 113.0 \text{ N}$$

The radial force is

$$W_r = W_t \tan\phi = (113.0 \text{ N})\tan 37°$$
$$= 85.18 \text{ N} \quad (85 \text{ N})$$

The answer is (A).

7. The nominal of the hole is the same as the minimum size $(D_{\min} = D)$. Therefore, the nominal size of the hole is 10.988 mm.

The answer is (C).

8. The tolerance of the shaft is

$$\Delta_d = |\delta_u - \delta_l|$$
$$= |0.011 \text{ mm} - 0.019 \text{ mm}|$$
$$= 0.008 \text{ mm}$$

The answer is (A).

9. Since the bearing is unchanged, its basic load rating, C (typically obtained from a bearing catalog), is unchanged. The bearing life equation is

$$C = P_1 L_1^{1/a} = P_2 L_2^{1/a}$$

The life, L, usually has units of revolutions, but at any

given speed, the duration is proportional to the number of revolutions. So, this can be written in terms of time, t. $a = 10/3$ for roller bearings.

$$t_2 = t_1 \left(\frac{P_1}{P_2} \right)^a$$

$$= (3000 \text{ h}) \left(\frac{9.5 \text{ kN}}{12 \text{ kN}} \right)^{10/3}$$

$$= 1377 \text{ h} \quad (1400 \text{ h})$$

The answer is (A).

10. The diametral pitch is the number of teeth per unit length.

$$r_1 + r_2 = \frac{d_1 + d_2}{2} = \frac{\dfrac{N_1}{P} + \dfrac{N_2}{P}}{2} = \frac{N_1 + N_2}{2P}$$

$$P = \frac{N_1 + N_2}{2(r_1 + r_2)}$$

$$= \frac{(20 + 30)\left(100 \ \dfrac{\text{cm}}{\text{m}}\right)}{(2)(4.6 \text{ cm} + 7.2 \text{ cm})}$$

$$= 211.9 \text{ m}^{-1} \quad (210 \text{ m}^{-1})$$

The answer is (A).

42 Fasteners

Nomenclature

A	area	m^2
A	constant	–
b	constant	–
b	width	m
C	joint coefficient	–
d	diameter	m
d	distance	m
e	eccentricity	m
E	modulus of elasticity	Pa
F	force	N
J	polar moment of inertia	m^4
k	stiffness	N/m
K	stress concentration factor	–
l	length	m
L	length	m
M	moment	N·m
n	number of bolts	–
n_b	bolt load factor	–
n_s	factor of safety against separation	–
p	pressure	Pa
P	load	N
r	radius	m
S	strength	Pa
t	thickness	m
t	throat size	m
T	torque	N·m
y	weld size	m

Symbols

δ	deflection	–
σ	stress	Pa
τ	shear stress	Pa

Subscripts

a	allowable or alternating
b	bolt (fastener)
d	diameter (major) or unthreaded shank
e	effective
i	index or initial (preload)
m	material, mean, or member
max	maximum
min	minimum
p	proof
r	range
s	separation
sep	separation
t	tensile, threaded shank, or torsional
T	torque
v	vertical

1. INTRODUCTION[1]

A *machine* is a combination of stationary and moveable parts that use or generate energy to perform some kind of useful work. The energy produced or consumed can be mechanical, electrical, thermal, or chemical.

Machines are comprised of parts. A *part* is a standalone component of a machine that typically has no usefulness on its own and that cannot be further disassembled. Parts may be assembled into *units* or *elements*, which are capable of independent operation. There are several kinds of standard elements, including mechanisms such as linkages, gears and gear trains, and belts and chain drives, and structural components such as welds, rivets, and bolts.

Machine design is the first step in the creation of a machine and involves the practical application of many disciplines, including kinematics, statics, dynamics, mechanics of materials, and so on. The design stage is

---

[1]Stress and strain are covered in Chap. 29. Some of the material in this topic in the NCEES *FE Reference Handbook* (*NCEES Handbook*) (and, subsequently, in this chapter) is based almost entirely on the conventions (nomenclature, terminology, variables, and equations) in the book *Shigley's Mechanical Engineering Design* (*Shigley's*), Richard G. Budynas and J. Keith Nisbett, various editions, McGraw-Hill, New York, NY.

where the look and functionality of a machine are planned. Common design considerations include material selection and availability; size and weight; production and maintenance costs; adherence to accepted design standards; and life and service needs.

2. BOLTS

There are three leading specifications for bolt thread families: the American National Standards Institute (ANSI), the International Organization for Standardization (ISO) metric, and Deutsches Institut für Normung (DIN) metric.[2] ANSI (essentially identical to SAE International (SAE), ASTM International (ASTM), and ISO-inch standard) is widely used in the United States. DIN fasteners are widely available and broadly accepted.[3] ISO metric fasteners are used in large volume by U.S. car manufacturers. The European Committee for Standardization (CEN) standards promulgated by the European Union (EU) have essentially adopted the ISO standards.

An American National (Unified) thread is specified by the sequence of parameters S(×L)-N-F-A-(H-E), where S is the thread outside diameter (nominal size), L is the optional shank length, N is the number of threads per inch, F is the thread pitch family, A is the class (allowance), and H and E are the optional hand and engagement length designations. The letter R can be added to the thread pitch family to indicate that the thread roots are radiused (for better fatigue resistance). For example, a ⅜ × 1-16UNC-2A bolt has a ⅜ in diameter, a 1 in length, and 16 Unified Coarse threads per inch rolled with a class 2A accuracy.[4] A UNRC bolt would be identical except for radiused roots.

The *grade* of a bolt indicates the fastener material and is marked on the bolt cap.[5] In this regard, the marking depends on whether an SAE grade or ASTM designation is used. The minimum *proof load* (i.e., the maximum stress the bolt can support without acquiring a permanent set) increases with the grade. (The term *proof strength* is less common.) If a bolt is manufactured in the United States, its cap must also show the logo or mark of the manufacturer.

A metric thread is specified by an M or MJ and a diameter and a pitch in millimeters, in that order. For example, M10 × 1.5 is a thread having a nominal major diameter of 10 mm and a pitch of 1.5 mm. The MJ series have rounded root fillets and larger minor diameters.

3. RIVET AND BOLT CONNECTIONS

Figure 42.1 illustrates a tension *lap joint* connection using rivet or bolt connectors.[6] Unless the plate material is very thick, the effects of eccentricity are disregarded. A connection of this type can fail in shear, tension, or bearing. A common design procedure is to determine the number of connectors based on shear stress and then to check the bearing and tensile stresses.

Figure 42.1 *Tension Lap Joint*

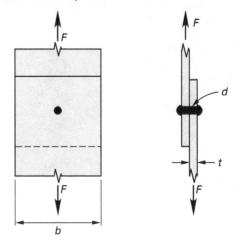

Equation 42.1: Failure by Pure (Single) Shear

$$\tau = F/A \qquad 42.1$$

Variation

$$\tau = \frac{F}{\frac{\pi d^2}{4}}$$

Description

One of the failure modes is shearing of the connectors. In the case of *single shear*, each connector supports its proportionate share of the load. The single shear stress in a bolt or rivet, Eq. 42.1, is calculated from the bolt or rivet's cross-sectional area, A, and the shear load, F.

In *double shear*, each connector has two shear planes, and the stress per connector is halved.[7] (See Fig. 42.2.)

---

[2]Other fastener families include the Italian Organization for Standardization (UNI), Swiss Association of Machinery Manufacturers (VSM), Japanese Industrial Standards (JIS), and United Kingdom's British Standards (BS) series.
[3]To add to the confusion, many DIN standards are identical to ISO standards, with only slight differences in the tolerance ranges. However, the standards are not interchangeable in every case.
[4]Threads are generally rolled, not cut, into a bolt.
[5]The *type* of a structural bolt should not be confused with the *grade* of a structural rivet.
[6]Rivets are no longer used in building construction, but they are still extensively used in manufacturing.
[7]"Double shear" is not the same as "double rivet" or "double butt." *Double shear* means that there are two shear planes in one rivet. *Double rivet* means that there are two rivets along the force path. *Double butt* refers to the use of two backing plates (i.e., "scabs") used on either side to make a tension connection between two plates. Similarly, *single butt* refers to the use of a single backing plate to make a tension connection between two plates.

Figure 42.2 *Single and Double Shear*

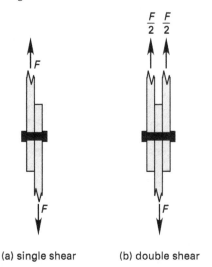

(a) single shear   (b) double shear

The plate can also fail by shear tear-out, as illustrated in Fig. 42.3. The thickness of the piece experiencing tear-out is t. It is not necessary for both assembled pieces to fail simultaneously in shear tear-out. The shear stress on sides of the plug is

$$\tau = \frac{F}{2A} = \frac{F}{2tL}$$

Figure 42.3 *Shear Tear-Out*

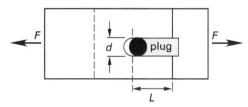

Equation 42.2: Failure by Rupture or by Crushing of a Rivet or Member[8]

$$\sigma = F/A \qquad 42.2$$

Description

The stress in a bolt that would cause it to rupture is found from Eq. 42.2. (See Fig. 42.4.) F is the shear load, and A is the net cross-sectional area of the fastener's thinnest member (for rupture) or is the projected area of a connector (for crushing).

Figure 42.4 *Failure by Rupture*

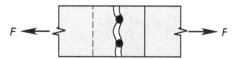

Equation 42.2 can also be used to calculate the stress that would cause a failure due to member or fastener crushing, where A is the projected area of the member or fastener. (See Fig. 42.5.)

Figure 42.5 *Failure by Crushing of Rivet or Member*

4. BOLT PRELOAD[9]

Consider the ungasketed connection shown in Fig. 42.6. The load varies from P_{min} to P_{max}. If the bolt is initially snug but without initial tension, the force in the bolt also will vary from P_{min} to P_{max}. If the bolt is tightened so that there is an initial *preload force*, F_i, greater than P_{max} in addition to the applied load, the bolt will be placed in tension and the parts held together will be in compression.[10] When a load is applied, the bolt tension will increase even more, but the compression in the parts will decrease.

Figure 42.6 *Bolted Tension Joint with Varying Load*

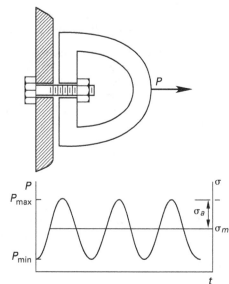

---

[8]Although the *NCEES Handbook* mentions "rivets" in its description, the application is not exclusive to rivets. This equation can be used with bolts and pins.
[9]In the analysis of connector failure modes, the *NCEES Handbook* previously used the variable F to represent the externally applied load. In the following sections covering connector preloading and eccentrically loaded connections, the variable P is used to represent externally applied loads. The variable F is used to represent internal preload force or forces associated with the connectors.
[10]If the initial preload force is less than P_{max}, the bolt may still carry a portion of the applied load.

The amount of compression in the parts, known as the *clamping force* or *clamp load*, will vary as the applied load varies. The clamped members will carry some of the applied load, since this varying load has to "uncompress" the clamped part as well as lengthen the bolt. The net result is the reduction of the variation of the force in the bolt. The initial tension produces a larger mean stress, but the overall result is the reduction of the alternating stress. Preloading is an effective method of reducing the alternating stress in bolted tension connections.

O-ring (metal and elastomeric) seals permit metal-to-metal contact and affect the effective spring constant of the parts very little. However, the seal force tends to separate bolted parts and must be added to the applied force. The seal force can be obtained from the seal deflection and seal stiffness or from manufacturer's literature.

For static loading, recommended amounts of preloading often are specified as a percentage of the *proof load* (or *proof strength*), S_p, in MPa.[11] For bolts, the proof load is slightly less than the yield strength. Traditionally, preload has been specified conservatively as 75% of proof for reusable connectors, and 90% of proof for one-use connectors.[12] Connectors with some ductility can safely be used beyond the yield point, and 100% is now in widespread use.[13] When understood, advantages of preloading to 100% of proof load often outweigh the disadvantages.[14]

If the applied load varies, the forces in the bolt and parts will also vary. In that case, the preload must be determined from an analysis of the Goodman line.

Tightening of a tension bolt will induce a torsional stress in the bolt.[15] Where the bolt is to be locked in place, the torsional stress can be removed without greatly affecting the preload by slightly backing off the bolt. If the bolt is subject to cyclic loading, the bolt will probably slip back by itself, and it is reasonable to neglect the effects of torsion in the bolt altogether. (This is the reason that well-designed connections allow for a loss of 5–10% of the initial preload during routine use.)

Stress concentrations at the beginning of the threaded section are significant in cyclic loading.[16] To avoid a reduction in fatigue life, the alternating stress used in the Goodman line should be multiplied by an appropriate *stress concentration factor*, K. For fasteners with rolled threads, an average factor of 2.2 for SAE grades

0–2 (metric grades 3.6–5.8) is appropriate. For SAE grades 4–8 (metric grades 6.6–10.9), an average factor of 3.0 is appropriate. Stress concentration factors for the fillet under the bolt head are different, but lower than these values. Stress concentration factors for cut threads are much higher.

The stress in a bolt depends on its load-carrying area. This area is typically obtained from a table of bolt properties. In practice, except for loading near the bolt's failure load, working stresses are low, and the effects of threads usually are ignored, so the area is based on the major (nominal) diameter.

$$\sigma_{\text{bolt}} = \frac{KP}{A}$$

A simple (linear, elastic) *stiffness*, k (also referred to as the *stiffness constant*, *spring constant*, *spring rate*, and *rigidity*), can be calculated from basic engineering principles for a single component (e.g., bolt or clamped plate).

$$k = \frac{F}{\delta} = \frac{F}{\dfrac{FL}{AE}} = \frac{AE}{L}$$

The cross-sectional area in tension for a bolt is well-defined. However, the cross-sectional area of a clamped plate that contributes to stiffness is difficult to define and usually must be assumed. The simplest assumption is that the effective area in compression is an annular cylinder with inside diameter equal to the bolt diameter and an outside diameter equal to 2.5 times the bolt diameter. Other non-cylindrical methods (e.g., the *double-cone compression area*) are in widespread use. In order to calculate the compression area, a specific compression area theory must be selected.

If a bolt consists of threaded and unthreaded sections with different lengths and areas, the bolt will behave as two springs in series. The total bolt stiffness can be calculated from the stiffness of each section.

$$\frac{1}{k_{\text{bolt}}} = \frac{1}{k_{\text{threaded}}} + \frac{1}{k_{\text{unthreaded}}}$$

---

[11]This is referred to as a "rule of thumb" specification, because a mathematical analysis is not performed to determine the best preload.

[12]Some U.S. military specifications call for 80% of proof load in tension fasteners and only 30% for shear fasteners. The object of keeping the stresses below yielding is to be able to reuse the bolts.

[13]Even under normal elastic loading of a bolt, local plastic deformation occurs in the bolt-head fillet and thread roots. Since the stress-strain curve is nearly flat at the yield point, a small amount of elongation into the plastic region does not increase the stress or tension in the bolt.

[14]The disadvantages are: (a) Field maintenance probably won't be possible, as manually running up bolts to 100% proof will result in many broken bolts. (b) Bolts should not be reused, as some will have yielded. (c) The highest-strength bolts do not exhibit much plastic elongation and ordinarily should not be run up to 100% proof load.

[15]An argument for the conservative 75% of proof load preload limit is that the residual torsional stress will increase the bolt stress to 90% or higher anyway, and the additional 10% needed to bring the preload up to 100% probably won't improve economic performance much.

[16]Stress concentrations are frequently neglected for static loading.

Similarly, for two or more clamped plates (plus gaskets and washers), the combined stiffness of the members in compression is

$$\frac{1}{k_{\text{members}}} = \frac{1}{k_{\text{plate 1}}} + \frac{1}{k_{\text{plate 2}}} + \frac{1}{k_{\text{washer}}} + \frac{1}{k_{\text{gasket}}}$$

Equation 42.3 Through Eq. 42.9: Threaded Fasteners

$$F_b = CP + F_i \quad [F_m < 0] \qquad 42.3$$

$$F_m = (1 - C)P - F_i \quad [F_m < 0] \qquad 42.4$$

$$C = k_b/(k_b + k_m) \qquad 42.5$$

$$k_b = \frac{A_d A_t E}{A_d l_t + A_t l_d} \qquad 42.6$$

$$k_m = dEA e^{b(d/l)} \qquad 42.7$$

$$\sigma_a = CP/2A_t \qquad 42.8$$

$$\sigma_m = \sigma_a + F_i/A_t \qquad 42.9$$

Values

Table 42.1 *Representative Constants for Joint Member Materials*

material	A	b
steel	0.78715	0.62873
aluminum	0.79670	0.63816
copper	0.79568	0.63553
gray cast iron	0.77871	0.61616

Description

The force carried by the bolt, F_b, and carried by the members, F_m, in a threaded connection are calculated from Eq. 42.3 and Eq. 42.4, respectively.[17] F_i is the bolt preload.

Equation 42.5 calculates the *joint coefficient*, C,[18] from the ratio of the bolt stiffness, k_b, Eq. 42.6, to the sum of the stiffnesses in the bolt and in the members, k_m, Eq. 42.7. Equation 42.7 can be used to calculate the stiffness of two or more members connected by a bolt or rivet as long as all members are of the same material, and the length used is the sum of the member thicknesses.[19] Common values of A and b are given in Table 42.1.[20]

When an externally applied load varies over a range of $P_{\min}$ and $P_{\max}$, the *alternating stress*, σ_a, and *mean stress*, σ_m, are found from Eq. 42.8 and Eq. 42.9. These are shown on Fig. 42.6 for a sinusoidal loading. In Eq. 42.8, C is the fraction of the load, P, carried by the bolt. The *alternating stress* is calculated from one-half of the force excursion.

$$\sigma_a = \frac{P_{\max} - P_{\min}}{2A_t}$$

The *range stress* is defined as twice the alternating stress and represents the entire stress excursion between $\sigma_{\max}$ and $\sigma_{\min}$.

$$\sigma_r = 2\sigma_a = \frac{P_{\max} - P_{\min}}{A_t}$$

The *mean stress* is a function of the bolt preload and the average applied load.

$$\sigma_m = \frac{F_i + \dfrac{P_{\max} - P_{\min}}{2}}{A_t}$$

Example

A bolted joint with a joint coefficient of 0.2 experiences an alternating external tension from 0 kN to 5 kN. The

---

[17]The *NCEES Handbook* qualifies Eq. 42.3 and Eq. 42.4 with the label "$F_m < 0$." The meaning of this label is uncertain. In structural analysis, a compressive force or stress is given a negative sign, so the *NCEES Handbook* probably intends "$F_m < 0$" to indicate that the force in the clamped members is a compressive force. However, a negative value of F_m is inconsistent with and cannot be derived from Eq. 42.4, since both F_i and P are tensile (positive) forces. At a minimum, the label seems to be incompatible with Eq. 42.4.

[18](1) The *NCEES Handbook* uses the term "joint coefficient" to describe the relative stiffness of the connector (i.e., bolt). While this term is consistent with the terminology used in *Shigley's*, the joint coefficient is actually the *relative stiffness* of the connector (i.e., the fraction of the load that is carried by the connector). What the *NCEES Handbook* characterizes as a "joint" property is actually a property of the connector in the connector-member assembly. (2) This parameter is sometimes referred to as the *relative rigidity, relative rigidity ratio, load sharing ratio, load factor,* and *preload efficiency factor* by other authorities. Although the symbol C is used in *Shigley's* and occasionally elsewhere, ϕ and Φ are also common symbols.

[19]The *NCEES Handbook* uses A as a constant in Eq. 42.7 while also using A in Eq. 42.6 to designate "area." These two quantities are not the same, and the A in Eq. 42.7 is not an area.

[20](1) As already mentioned, it is difficult to define the compression area of clamped parts, and, therefore, it is difficult to define the stiffness of those parts. Equation 42.7 circumvents these difficulties by presenting a convenient correlation. The correlation is (presumably) based on observation and curve fitting, but it cannot be derived from engineering fundamentals. (2) The *NCEES Handbook* presents the correlation constants in Table 42.1 without background theory, qualification, limitation, or source authority. These values are for the convenience of the FE exam and are not for design use.

bolt is initially preloaded to 10 kN. What is most nearly the maximum tensile force in the bolt?

(A) 5.0 kN

(B) 11 kN

(C) 12 kN

(D) 15 kN

Solution

From Eq. 42.3, the maximum bolt load is

$$F_{b,\max} = CP + F_i = (0.2)(5 \text{ kN}) + 10 \text{ kN}$$
$$= 11 \text{ kN}$$

The answer is (B).

Equation 42.10 and Eq. 42.11: Threaded Fastener Design Factors

$$n_b = (S_p A_t - F_i)/CP \qquad \text{42.10}$$

$$n_s = F_i/[P(1 - C)] \qquad \text{42.11}$$

Description

There are two requirements for the assembly to be satisfactorily designed: (1) The stress in the bolt must be less than some maximum stress, and (2) the assembly must not separate. Two ratios, n_b and n_s, one for each requirement, can be defined with the requirement that each must be greater than or equal to 1.0 for satisfactory operation.

$$n_b > 1; n_s > 1 \quad \text{[satisfactory operation]}$$

In order to evaluate the first requirement, the maximum allowable stress has to be determined. For this particular case, the bolt's proof strength, S_p, is used. In order to get an equation in terms of stress, all of the force terms in Eq. 42.3 are divided by the tensile stress area of the bolt, A_t.

$$\sigma_b = \frac{F_b}{A_t} = \frac{CP + F_i}{A_t} < S_p$$

Although it makes sense to define a factor of safety against overstress as S_p/σ_b, an alternate decision is to define the factor of safety based on the force margin. If the maximum allowable force in the bolt is $S_p A_t$, and if the bolt is installed with a prestress of F_i, only the force margin of $S_p A_t - F_i$ is available for additional loading. In other words, the maximum external tensile load is $S_p A_t - F_i$. Then, since the actual load carried by the bolt is CP, the ratio of force margin to actual load is given by Eq. 42.10. The *force margin ratio* is[21]

$$n_b = \frac{S_p A_t - F_i}{CP}$$

The clamped members will not separate (i.e., will remain together) as long as they are in compression. The compression force is a direct result of the bolt preload, and if a separating force equal to the preload is applied to the members, separation will occur. At separation, the bolt carries the entire applied load, and assembly stiffness equals the bolt stiffness. The *joint separation ratio* is defined as the ratio of the external load that would cause separation, P_{sep}, to the actual load.[22] This is the basis of Eq. 42.11. The *joint separation ratio* is

$$n_s = \frac{P_{\text{sep}}}{F_{\text{members}}} = \frac{F_i}{P - F_b} = \frac{F_i}{P(1 - C)}$$

Example

A pressure vessel flange has an inside diameter of 25 cm. The flange is connected to the vessel using 8 bolts that have a bolt preload of 14 kN. The joint coefficient is 0.4, and the joint separation safety factor is 4. What is most nearly the maximum design vessel pressure?

(A) 0.73 MPa

(B) 0.95 MPa

(C) 1.3 MPa

(D) 2.3 MPa

---

[21]This book refers to n_b in Eq. 42.10 as the "force margin ratio." The *NCEES Handbook* refers to n_b as the "bolt load factor." That name is consistent with *Shigley's* but is inappropriate. In bolted joints, the term "bolt load factor" generally refers to the relative stiffness ratio, which the *NCEES Handbook* calls the "joint coefficient," C (which is also a *Shigley's* convention). The way that n_b is calculated has been defined specifically by the source document, not by engineering fundamentals. However, even the source document, *Shigley's*, clearly indicates that the name has been concocted by the authors by saying "Here we have called n a load factor...." Unless the name is clarified as "...the load factor as defined by *Shigley's*...," the term "load factor" cannot be recognized as referring to Eq. 42.10. Outside of *Shigley's*, the "load factor" means something else.

[22](1) This book refers to n_s in Eq. 42.11 as the "joint separation ratio," not a factor of safety. (2) The derivation of n_s presented here again follows *Shigley's*. In this case, however, the *NCEES Handbook* uses the term "factor of safety" instead of *Shigley's* "load factor," probably to avoid the ambiguity of having two quantities with the same name, "load factor." (2) There is no significance to the use of square brackets in Eq. 42.11.

Solution

Rearrange Eq. 42.11 to calculate the load on each bolt.

$$n_s = F_i/[P(1 - C)]$$

$$P = \frac{F_i}{n_s(1 - C)} = \frac{14 \text{ kN}}{(4)(1 - 0.4)}$$

$$= 5.83 \text{ kN/bolt}$$

The design vessel pressure is

$$p = \frac{F}{A} = \frac{Pn}{\dfrac{\pi d^2}{4}}$$

$$= \frac{\left(5.83 \; \dfrac{\text{kN}}{\text{bolt}}\right)(8 \text{ bolts})\left(100 \; \dfrac{\text{cm}}{\text{m}}\right)^2}{\dfrac{\pi(25 \text{ cm})^2}{4}}$$

$$= 0.95 \text{ MPa}$$

The answer is (A).

5. BOLT TORQUE TO OBTAIN PRELOAD

During assembly, the preload tension is not monitored directly. Rather, the *torque* required to tighten the bolt is used to determine when the proper preload has been reached. Methods of obtaining the required preload include the standard torque wrench, the *run-of-the-nut method* (e.g., turning the bolt some specific angle past snugging torque), *direct-tension indicating* (DTI) washers, and computerized automatic assembly.

The standard manual torque wrench does not provide precise, reliable preloads, since the fraction of the torque going into bolt tension is variable.[23] Torque-, angle-, and time-monitoring equipment, usually part of an automated assembly operation, is essential to obtaining precise preloads on a consistent basis. It automatically applies the snugging torque and specified rotation, then checks the results with torque and rotation sensors. The computer warns of out-of-spec conditions.

Equation 42.12: Tightening Torque for a Steel Bolt in a Steel Member

$$T = 0.2F_i d \qquad \text{42.12}$$

Variation

$$T = K_T F_i d$$

Description

The *Maney formula* is a simple (and, approximate) relationship between the initial bolt tension, F_i, and the installation torque, T. Equation 42.12 applies only to steel bolts in steel members.[24]

The Maney formula shown in the variation equation uses the *torque coefficient*, K_T (also known as the *bolt torque factor*, *torque-friction coefficient*, and the *nut factor*), to account for the difference in materials and the coefficient of friction, f. The torque coefficient for lubricated bolts generally varies from 0.15 to 0.20, and a value of 0.2 is commonly used.[25] With antiseize lubrication, it can drop as low as 0.12. (The torque coefficient is not the same as the coefficient of friction.)

Example

The initial bolt tension on a 16 mm steel bolt is 45 kN. What is most nearly the approximate torque required to tighten the bolt?

    (A)   85 kN·mm

    (B)   110 kN·mm

    (C)   140 kN·mm

    (D)   180 kN·mm

Solution

The approximate required torque is

$$T = 0.2F_i d = (0.2)(45 \text{ kN})(16 \text{ mm})$$

$$= 144 \text{ kN·mm} \quad (140 \text{ kN·mm})$$

The answer is (A).

6. ECCENTRICALLY LOADED BOLTED CONNECTIONS

An *eccentrically loaded connection* is illustrated in Fig. 42.7. The bracket's natural tendency is to rotate about the centroid of the connector group. The shear stress in the connectors includes both the direct vertical shear and the torsional shear stress. The sum of these

---

[23]Even with good lubrication, about 50% of the torque goes into overcoming friction between the head and collar/flange, another 40% is lost in thread friction, and only the remaining 10% goes into tensioning the connector.

[24](1) As specified in the *NCEES Handbook*, Eq. 42.12 is an approximation limited to steel bolts and members. In addition to those limitations, use of the 0.2 coefficient is further restricted to plain-finished, uncoated, unlubricated (i.e., "dry") bolts. Different values would be used for zinc- or cadmium-plated bolts, and in installations using Teflon™ wrap or molybdenum disulfide grease, for example. (2) Eq. 42.12 is in common use, but it is not derived from engineering principles. It is recognized by engineers to be a crude approximation at best. There are more rigorous methods of relating the tightening torque to the initial preload.

[25]With a coefficient of friction of 0.15, the torque coefficient is approximately 0.20 for most bolt sizes, regardless of whether the threads are coarse or fine.

shear stresses is limited by the shear strength of the *critical connector*, which in turn determines the capacity of the connection, as limited by bolt shear strength.[26] The *critical fastener* is the fastener that is located the farthest from the fastener group's centroid. When fasteners are arranged symmetrically, all fasteners may simultaneously be critical.

Figure 42.7 *Eccentrically Loaded Connection*

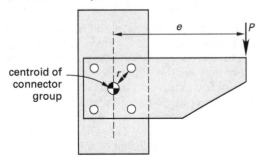

The moment (or torque) on the connector group due to a force, P, acting with an eccentricity, e, is

$$M = Pe$$

Analogous to $\sigma = Mc/I$ for beam bending and $\tau = Tr/J$ for shaft twisting, the torsional shear stress in a fastener due to a moment on a bracket from an eccentric load is $\tau = Mr/J$. Performing an elastic analysis of a connector group often comes down to determining the *polar moment of inertia*, J, of the fastener group.

The polar moment of inertia, J, is calculated from the parallel axis theorem. Since bolts and rivets have little resistance to twisting in their holes, their individual polar moments of inertia are omitted.[27] Only the r^2A terms in the parallel axis theorem are used. r_i is the distance from the fastener group centroid to the centroid (i.e., center) of the ith fastener, which has an area of A_i.

$$J = \sum_i r_i^2 A_i$$

The torsional shear stress is directed perpendicularly to a line between each fastener and the connector group centroid. The direction of the shear stress is the same as the rotation of the connection.

Once the torsional shear stress has been determined in the critical fastener, it is added in a vector sum to the direct vertical shear stress. The direction of the vertical shear stress is the same as that of the applied force.

$$\tau_v = \frac{P}{nA}$$

Typical connections gain great strength from the frictional slip resistance between the two surfaces. By preloading the connection bolts, the normal force between the plates is greatly increased. The connection strength from friction will rival or exceed the strength from bolt shear in connections that are designed to take advantage of preload.

Equation 42.13 Through Eq. 42.16: Fastener Groups[28]

$$\bar{x} = \frac{\sum\limits_{i=1}^{n} A_i x_i}{\sum\limits_{i=1}^{n} A_i} \qquad 42.13$$

$$\bar{y} = \frac{\sum\limits_{i=1}^{n} A_i y_i}{\sum\limits_{i=1}^{n} A_i} \qquad 42.14$$

$$|F_{1i}| = \frac{P}{n} \qquad 42.15$$

$$|F_{2i}| = \frac{Mr_i}{\sum\limits_{i=1}^{n} r_i^2} \qquad 42.16$$

---

[26]This type of analysis is known as an *elastic analysis* of the connection. Although it is traditional, it tends to greatly understate the capacity of the connection.

[27]In spot-welded and welded stud connections, the torsional resistance of each connector can be considered.

[28](1) Subscripts "1" and "2" are used in the *NCEES Handbook* to represent the two components of eccentric connector group force—"direct shear" and "torsional shear," respectively. The subscripts do not refer to connectors 1 and 2. (2) As used by the *NCEES Handbook*, the absolute value bars in Eq. 42.15 and Eq. 42.16 are confusing and mathematically incorrect for the following reasons: (a) As shown in Fig. 42.8, whether the direct and torsional shears add or subtract depends on the fastener. So, unless these two equations are limited to use at the critical fastener where both values add, the signs are important. And, even then, the resulting forces may be directed in the negative direction. (b) Mathematically, because of the absolute values, the left-hand sides of these equations are always positive, while the signs of the right-hand sides are derived from the signs of P and M and may be negative. Therefore, depending on the fastener, the equations could represent "positive = negative." If the intent is to have only positive values of F_1 and F_2, the absolute value of the right-hand sides should be taken. To eliminate any ambiguity, the absolute value of both sides should be taken.

Description

Fastener groups in shear are illustrated in Fig. 42.8.[29] The fastener group's centroid, in coordinate form $(\bar{x}, \bar{y})$, is located using Eq. 42.13 and Eq. 42.14. n is the total number of fasteners, and i is the index number of a given fastener. For an ith fastener, A_i is the cross-sectional area, and x_i and y_i are the x- and y-coordinates, respectively, of the center of the fastener.

Figure 42.8 Fastener Groups in Shear

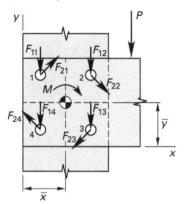

The total shear force on a fastener is the vector sum of the direct shear and the torsional shear caused by the moment. The *direct shear force*, F_1, acts in the direction of the direct shear, P, and is calculated from Eq. 42.15. If all of the connectors have the same area, A, the area term will drop out when distributing the total resisting force to the connectors. In that case, only the ratio $r_i / \sum r_i^2$ is needed, and the shear force, F_2, due to the moment, M, is found from Eq. 42.16. If a line is drawn from the fastener group centroid to the center of a given fastener, the torsional shear force will act perpendicular to that line.

7. FILLET WELDS

The common *fillet weld* is shown in Fig. 42.9. Such welds are used to connect one plate to another. The applied load, F, is assumed to be carried in shear by the *effective weld throat*. The *effective throat size*, t_e, is related to the weld size, y, by

$$t_e = \frac{\sqrt{2}}{2} y$$

Figure 42.9 Fillet Lap Weld and Symbol

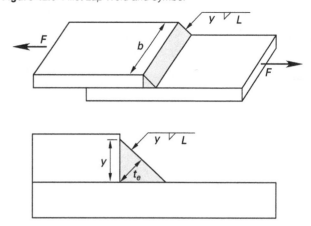

Neglecting any increased stresses due to eccentricity, the shear stress in a fillet lap weld depends on the *effective throat thickness*, t_e, and is

$$\tau = \frac{F}{b t_e}$$

Weld (filler) metal should have a strength equal to or greater than the base material. Properties of filler metals are readily available from their manufacturers and, for standard rated welding rods, from engineering handbooks.

8. ECCENTRICALLY LOADED WELDED CONNECTIONS

The traditional elastic analysis of an eccentrically loaded welded connection is virtually the same as for a bolted connection, with the additional complication of having to determine the polar moment of inertia of the welds.[30] This can be done either by taking the welds as lines or by assuming each weld has an arbitrary thickness, t. After finding the centroid of the weld group, the rectangular moments of inertia of the individual welds are taken about that centroid using the parallel axis theorem. These rectangular moments of inertia are added to determine the polar moment of inertia.

The torsional shear stress, calculated from Mr/J (where r is the distance from the centroid of the weld group to the most distant weld point), is added vectorially to the direct shear to determine the maximum shear stress at the critical weld point.

---

[29](1) Figure 42.8 shows the applied force, P, applied with an eccentricity with respect to the fastener group centroid. In its equivalent figure, the *NCEES Handbook* shows the applied force, P, acting through the centroid of the fastener group, which would be unable to generate the moment-related forces shown. (2) The fasteners in Fig. 42.8 are numbered 1 through 4. Rather than using more descriptive letters or symbols, the *NCEES Handbook* also uses numerical subscripts 1 and 2 to designate the type of reaction generated (i.e., 1 = direct shear, and 2 = torsional shear). This can lead to considerable confusion when trying to determine the meaning of such ambiguous variables as F_{12} and F_{21}.
[30]Steel building design does not use an elastic analysis to design eccentric brackets, either bolted or welded. The design methodology is highly proceduralized and codified.

43 Machine Design

Nomenclature

a	life adjustment factor	–
A	allowance	–
C	basic bearing load rating	N
C	center-to-center distance	m
C	spring index	–
C_0	basic bearing static load rating	N
C_r	basic bearing rating	N
d	diameter	mm
D	diameter	mm
e	eccentricity	mm
e	rolling element bearing factor	–
E	modulus of elasticity	Pa
F	force	N
Fr	moment	N·m
G	shear modulus	Pa
H	power	kW
k	spring constant	N·m/rad
K	correction factor	–
l	lead	m
L	design life	rev
L	length	m
L_{ab}	length of line of action	m
m	module	mm
m_v	velocity ratio	–
n	rotational speed	rev/min
N	number	–
p	circular pitch	mm
p	spring pitch	m
P	diametral pitch	1/m
P	force or load	N
P	power	kW
r	radius	m
RVR	relative velocity ratio	–
S	strength	Pa
T	torque	N·m
v	velocity	m/s
V	rolling element bearing factor	–
VR	velocity ratio	–
w	width	mm
W	force	Pa
W	Wahl correction factor	–
x	deflection	m
X	radial load thrust factor	–
Y	axial load thrust factor	–

Symbols

α	angular acceleration	rad/s^2
η	efficiency	–
θ	angle	deg
θ	deflection	rad
μ	coefficient of friction	–
ν	Poisson's ratio	–
σ	allowable stress	Pa
τ	shear stress	Pa
ϕ	angle	rad
ω	angular velocity	rad/s
ω	rotational speed	rad/s

Subscripts

0	free
a	active or axial
b	base
c	circular, clash, or collar
e	end
eq	equivalent
f	first or frictional

i	inner
L	last or lower
m	mean
o	outer
r	radial or rated
R	raise
s	solid, spring, static, or strength
t	tangential, tensile, or total
T	torque
u	ultimate
v	velocity
w	working
y	yield

1. SPRINGS[1,2]

An *ideal spring* is assumed to be perfectly elastic within its working range. The deflection is assumed to be linear and to follow *Hooke's law* (see Eq. 40.13).[3]

A spring stores energy when it is compressed or extended. By the *work-energy principle*, the energy storage is equal to the work required to displace the spring.

2. SPRING MATERIALS

A wide variety of materials are used for springs, including high-carbon steel, stainless steel and various alloys, nickel-based alloys (e.g., inconel), and copper-based alloys (e.g., phosphor-bronze and silicon-bronze). "Super-alloys" are used for high-temperature and highly corrosive environments. Spring rate, fatigue strength, temperature range, corrosion resistance, magnetic properties, and cost are all considerations.

Springs manufactured from prehardened materials are generally stress-relieved in a low-temperature process by heating to between 200°C and 430°C after forming. Springs with intricate shapes must be manufactured from annealed materials and be subsequently strengthened in high-temperature processes. They are first quenched to full hardness and then tempered. Age-hardenable materials (e.g., beryllium copper) can be strengthened simply by heating after forming.

Most springs are cold-wound. Springs with wire diameters much in excess of 12 mm or 16 mm are wound while red hot. Although the design methods are essentially the same for hot-wound and cold-wound springs, the allowable stresses are reduced approximately 20%, and the

modulus is reduced slightly (approximately 9% for the shear modulus and approximately 5% for the elastic modulus). There are other unique issues and special needs associated with the manufacturing of hot-wound springs, as well.

Materials suitable for fatigue service include music wire (ASTM A228), carbon and alloy valve spring wire (ASTM A230), chrome-vanadium (ASTM A232), beryllium copper (ASTM B197), phosphor bronze (ASTM B159), and, to a lesser degree, type-302 stainless steel (ASTM A313). *Shotpeening* (*stresspeening*) is one of the best methods for increasing a spring's fatigue life.

3. ALLOWABLE SPRING STRESSES: STATIC LOADING

Helical compression and extension springs experience torsional shear stresses. The yield strength in shear is the theoretical maximum stress. There are three common ways of choosing the maximum allowable shear stress for static service.[4]

1. Selecting the allowable stress based on some percentage of the ultimate tensile strength is the most common method. For ferrous materials except for austenitic stainless, the percentage is approximately 45% to 65%. For nonferrous and austenitic stainless, the percentage is approximately 35% to 55%. The lower limit should be used for unconstrained designs (i.e., the spring diameter can be as large as necessary to keep the stresses low). The higher limit is used when space is limited and higher stresses are unavoidable.[5]

2. Selecting the allowable stress based on the yield strength in shear is probably the most theoretically rigorous method. The yield strength in shear can be calculated from the tensile yield strength using either the maximum shear stress or the distortion energy theory.[6] If called for, a factor of safety of approximately 1.5 is appropriate for ferrous springs.

3. Some specifications limit the torsional shear stress to a percentage of the tensile yield strength.

---

[1]Some of the material in this topic in the NCEES *FE Reference Handbook* (*NCEES Handbook*) (and, subsequently, in this chapter) is based almost entirely on the conventions (nomenclature, terminology, variables, and equations) in the book *Shigley's Mechanical Engineering Design* (*Shigley's*), Richard G. Budynas and J. Keith Nisbett, various editions, McGraw-Hill, New York, NY.

[2]The *NCEES Handbook* does not say so, but the equations and values for spring design are specifically limited to springs manufactured from round wire.

[3]A spring can be perfectly elastic even though it does not follow Hooke's law. The deviation from proportionality, if any, occurs at very high loads. The difference in theoretical and actual spring forces is known as the *straight line error*.

[4]These methods apply to helical compression and extension springs. Recommended percentages are different for other types of springs.

[5]For highly precise springs with minimum hysteresis, creep, and drift, the percentages quoted in this section should be reduced.

[6]The tensile yield strength can be estimated for ferrous spring materials as 75% of the ultimate tensile strength.

Some springs (e.g., flat leaf springs and helical torsion springs) experience a bending stress. Such springs are limited by the tensile yield strength of the spring material.

4. HELICAL COMPRESSION SPRINGS: STATIC LOADING

Spring Design

The end treatment shown in Fig. 43.1 affects a spring's solid length and pitch. The exact effects are not always obvious. Table 43.1 contains relationships that are accepted for design use.

Figure 43.1 *End Treatment of Helical Compression Springs*

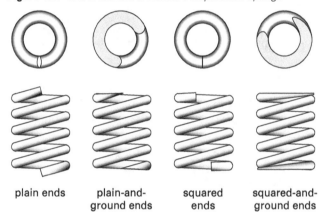

plain ends   plain-and-ground ends   squared ends   squared-and-ground ends

Table 43.1 *Effect of End Treatment on Helical Compression Springs*

term	type of spring ends			
	plain	plain and ground	squared or closed	squared and ground
end coils, N_e	0	1	2	2
total coils, N_t	N	$N+1$	$N+2$	$N+2$
free length, L_0	$pN+d$	$p(N+1)$	$pN+3d$	$pN+2d$
solid length, L_s	$d(N_t+1)$	dN_t	$d(N_t+1)$	dN_t
pitch, p	$(L_0-d)/N$	$L_0/(N+1)$	$(L_0-3d)/N$	$(L_0-2d)/N$

The *solid deflection* is calculated from the free and solid heights.[7]

$$x_s = L_0 - L_s$$

The *spring pitch* (*coil pitch*), p, is the mean coil separation. The *solid height* (*compressed height*) is given in Table 43.1. The *clash allowance*, A_c, is the percentage difference in solid and working deflections. It should be approximately 20%.

$$A_c = \frac{x_s - x_w}{x_w}$$

The *helix direction* for single springs can be either right hand or left hand. If the spring works over a threaded member, the winding direction should be opposite of the thread direction. With two *nested springs* (i.e., one spring inside the other), the winding directions must be opposite to prevent intermeshing. Also for nested springs, the outer spring should support approximately $^2\!/_3$ of the total load. The solid and free heights of both springs should be approximately the same.

Number of Active Coils

The number of *active coils* (i.e., "turns") in a helical spring is less than or equal to the total number of coils, depending on the method of finishing the ends. When a helical compression spring has *plain ends* (i.e., neither squared nor ground), all of the coils contribute to spring force. In that case, the total number of coils, N_t, is equal to the number of active coils, N. However, most designs call for squaring and/or grinding the ends in order to obtain better seating for the spring. The number of end coils, N_e, is given in Table 43.1 for various end treatments. Normally, there should be at least two active coils. At the spring end, if the pitch is reduced such that the space between the wire tip and the next coil is eliminated, the end is referred to as *closed*. If there is no reduction in pitch at the end coils, the end is referred to as *open*. Closing the ends is the most common end treatment for commercial/industrial springs.

The total spring *wire length* is the length of wire in the coils. The *active wire length* is calculated from the number of active coils, N.

$$L_a = \pi D N$$

Example

A spring has 6 active coils, and the ends are squared and ground. What is the total number of coils?

    (A) 4

    (B) 6

    (C) 7

    (D) 8

---

[7]The *NCEES Handbook* uses "length" to describe the free, L_0, and solid, L_s, heights of the spring, as found from Table 43.1. Other sources refer to these dimensions as the free and solid *height*, h_f and h_s, respectively.

Solution

From Table 43.1, for squared and ground spring ends, the total number of coils is

$$N_t = N + N_e = N + 2 = 6 + 2$$
$$= 8$$

The answer is (D).

Equation 43.1: Spring Index

$$C = D/d \qquad 43.1$$

Description

The *spring index*, C, is the ratio of the mean coil diameter, D, to the wire diameter, d.[8] (See Fig. 43.2.) The mean coil diameter can be calculated from the average of the inner diameter, D_i, and outer diameter, D_o, as shown.

$$D = \frac{D_i + D_o}{2} = D_o - d$$

It is difficult to wind springs with small (i.e., less than 4) spring indexes, and the operating stresses will be high. The wire cannot be easily bent to the desired small radius. On the other hand, springs with large indexes (i.e., greater than 12) are flimsy and tend to buckle. Most springs have indexes between 8 and 10, although 5 is a typical value for clutch springs.

Figure 43.2 *Helical Compression Spring*

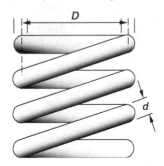

Example

What is most nearly the spring index of the spring shown?

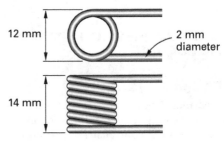

(A) 5

(B) 6

(C) 7

(D) 10

Solution

Use Eq. 43.1 to find the spring index. The mean coil diameter, D, is the outer diameter minus the inner wire diameter.

$$C = D/d = \frac{D_o - d}{d}$$
$$= \frac{12 \text{ mm} - 2 \text{ mm}}{2 \text{ mm}}$$
$$= 5$$

The answer is (A).

Equation 43.2: Spring Constant

$$k = \frac{d^4 G}{8 D^3 N} \qquad 43.2$$

Variations

$$k = \frac{F}{x} = \frac{F_1 - F_2}{x_1 - x_2} \quad \text{[Hooke's law]}$$

$$k = \frac{dG}{8 C^3 N}$$

Description

The *spring constant*, k, is also known as the *stiffness*, *spring rate*, *scale*, and *k-value*. The spring constant is given by the *load-deflection equation*, also called the *spring rate equation*, Eq. 43.2. G is the *shear modulus*. Deflection and force are related by the spring constant, as shown in Hooke's law.

---

[8]This section is only for helical compression springs manufactured from round wire. Springs can also be manufactured from wire with a square or rectangular cross section. The design equations are different in that case.

The shear modulus (also known as the *modulus of rigidity*), G, used in Eq. 43.2, can be calculated from the modulus of elasticity, E, and Poisson's ratio, ν.

$$G = \frac{E}{2(1+\nu)}$$

Example

A 100 N force is applied to a 50 mm long helical compression spring made of 2 mm steel wire (shear modulus of 80 GPa). The spring has 6 active coils and a mean diameter of 10 mm. The spring ends are closed. What is most nearly the spring constant?

(A) 3.0 kN/m

(B) 21 kN/m

(C) 27 kN/m

(D) 35 kN/m

Solution

The spring constant is

$$k = \frac{d^4 G}{8D^3 N}$$

$$= \frac{(2 \text{ mm})^4 (80 \text{ GPa})\left(10^6 \dfrac{\text{kPa}}{\text{GPa}}\right)}{(8)(10 \text{ mm})^3 (6)\left(1000 \dfrac{\text{mm}}{\text{m}}\right)}$$

$$= 26.67 \text{ kN/m} \quad (27 \text{ kN/m})$$

The answer is (C).

Equation 43.3 and Eq. 43.4: Torsional Shear Stress

$$\tau = K_s \frac{8FD}{\pi d^3} \qquad \text{43.3}$$

$$K_s = (2C+1)/(2C) \qquad \text{43.4}$$

Description

The shear stress, τ, is calculated from the force applied to the spring and the wire diameter, d, mean spring diameter, D, and correction factor, K_s. K_s is found from the spring index, C (see Eq. 43.1), and Eq. 43.4.

The maximum shear stress occurs at the inner face of the wire coil where the torsional and direct shear stresses are additive. The factor K_s is known as the *transverse shear factor*. It is not a true stress concentration factor, but rather, represents the theoretical ratio of the maximum and average stresses.[9]

Equation 43.5 Through Eq. 43.7: Maximum Allowable Torsional Stress

$$S_{sy} = \tau = 0.45 S_{ut} \begin{bmatrix} \text{cold-drawn carbon steel} \\ \text{(A227, A228, and A229)} \end{bmatrix} \qquad \text{43.5}$$

$$S_{sy} = \tau = 0.50 S_{ut} \begin{bmatrix} \text{hardened and tempered} \\ \text{carbon and low-alloy steels} \\ \text{(A232 and A401)} \end{bmatrix} \qquad \text{43.6}$$

$$S_{ut} = A/d^m \qquad \text{43.7}$$

Mechanical/
Design/Analysis

---

[9]Equation 43.4 is not the *Wahl correction factor*, which the *NCEES Handbook* does not mention. Although Eq. 43.4 can be derived from basic principles, it does not account for spring wire curvature. Any theoretical stress calculated from Eq. 43.3 and Eq. 43.4 will be 5–20% lower than the actual stress. For static loading, the effect of curvature can be disregarded if it is assumed that local yielding will relieve the effects of overstress at the inner face of the spring. However, it is standard engineering practice to use the Wahl correction factor in the design of helical compression springs to account for both the nonuniform stress distribution and the spring wire curvature. The absence of the Wahl correction factor implies that Eq. 43.4 is only for use with static loading and that local yielding will be used to keep the stress at the yield point. Since the *NCEES Handbook* presents spring wire data only for static loading, that is the implicit limitation of Eq. 43.4.

Values

Table 43.2 Parameters for Calculating Ultimate Tensile Strength

material	ASTM	m	A
music wire	A228	0.163	2060
oil-tempered wire	A229	0.193	1610
hard-drawn wire	A227	0.201	1510
chrome vanadium	A232	0.155	1790
chrome silicon	A401	0.091	1960

Description

The maximum allowable torsional stress of a spring experiencing static loading can be approximated as Eq. 43.5 and Eq. 43.6 using the ultimate tensile strength, S_{ut}. (These equations apply to static applications only.) From Eq. 43.7, the minimum tensile strength, in MPa, is calculated from the wire diameter, d, in millimeters, and two constants, m and A, determined from Table 43.2.[10]

Example

What is most nearly the shear yield strength for 1 mm diameter ASTM A227 hard-drawn wire?

(A)   330 MPa

(B)   680 MPa

(C)   730 MPa

(D)   750 MPa

Solution

From Table 43.2, for hard-drawn wire, $m = 0.201$, and $A = 1510$. The ultimate tensile strength is calculated from Eq. 43.7.

$$S_{ut} = A/d^m = \frac{1510}{(1 \text{ mm})^{0.201}} = 1510 \text{ MPa}$$

From Eq. 43.5, for ASTM A227 steel, the shear yield strength is

$$
\begin{aligned}
S_{sy} &= 0.45 S_{ut} \\
&= (0.45)(1510 \text{ MPa}) \\
&= 679.5 \text{ MPa} \quad (680 \text{ MPa})
\end{aligned}
$$

The answer is (B).

5. HELICAL COMPRESSION SPRINGS: DESIGN

Conventional spring design is an iterative procedure. One or more parameters are varied until the requirements are satisfied. Often one or more parameters are unknown and must be assumed to complete the design.

An important decision is whether the allowable stress is comparable to the maximum working stress or the stress when the spring is compressed solid. Since most helical compression springs will be compressed solid sometime in their lives, it seems logical to use the solid height stress. In the absence of guidance, either interpretation would apply.

6. HELICAL TORSION SPRINGS

Helical torsion springs manufactured from round wire are essentially round cantilever beams.[11] Loading produces a bending stress. Most torsion springs operate over an arbor. A clearance of about 10% between the arbor and spring is generally adequate to prevent binding. The bending stress is largest at the inner radius of the spring. (See Fig. 43.3.)

---

[10](1) The *NCEES Handbook* presents Eq. 43.5 and Eq. 43.6 as fact. The relationships between yield and ultimate strengths presented in the *NCEES Handbook* are not derived from basic principles and should be interpreted as convenient approximations identified with the operator "≈." The yield strength in shear predicted by the maximum shear stress and von Mises theories are $0.5 S_{ut}$ and $0.577 S_{ut}$, respectively, so Eq. 43.5 and Eq. 43.6 have significant degrees of conservatism built in. Although Eq. 43.5 and Eq. 43.6 are clearly identified as equations for allowable stresses, the values calculated are not yield strengths. The notation $S_{sy} = \tau$ should be interpreted as "the maximum allowable stress determined from Joerres' analysis is used as a replacement for the yield strength." (2) Whereas τ was previously used to represent the maximum shear stress in the spring, in Eq. 43.5 and Eq. 43.6, τ is defined by the *NCEES Handbook* as the maximum *allowable* shear stress. Generally, the allowable stress would be differentiated from the actual stress by a subscript (e.g., "a," "al," or "all"). (3) The term "allowable," as used in design, implicitly means that a factor of safety has been incorporated into the value (e.g., $\tau_a = S_{ys}/FS$). Equation 43.5 and Eq. 43.6 imply that it is permissible (allowable) to operate the spring with stresses as high as the yield strength. Good design practice is to limit stresses to the allowable stresses. (4) In Eq. 43.7, d is the wire diameter, but A is not the wire cross-sectional area. (5) The yield strength in shear is normally designated S_{ys}, whereas the *NCEES Handbook* designates it as S_{sy}, consistent with *Shigley's*. This is inconsistent with the order of the subscripts (first for the material behavior, second for the type of stress) used by the *NCEES Handbook* in S_{ut} and S_{uc}, for example. (6) Equation 43.6 is a convenient correlation used to describe the variation in strength with size. The values shown are reported in *Shigley's*, but other researchers have derived different values for the same form of the correlation equation. In any case, each of the correlations is useful only within a range of diameters. The range of useful diameters is different for each material cited, and without the ranges, the parameters cannot reliably be used. Since the parameters are provided without attribution, reliability, or other qualifications, they should not be used for design.

[11]There are two basic types of torsion springs: the *flat coil spring* (also known as a *power spring* or *clock spring*) and the helical torsion spring. Flat coil springs are designed differently and not covered in this section.

Figure 43.3 *Helical Torsion Spring*

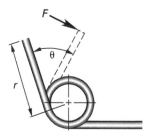

Equation 43.8: Angular Deflection

$$Fr = k\theta \qquad \text{43.8}$$

Description

The relationship between the deflection, θ, and moment, Fr, for a helical torsion spring is shown in Eq. 43.8. The deflection is in units of radians. This is essentially Hooke's law for torsion springs.

Equation 43.9: Torsional Spring Constant

$$k = \frac{d^4 E}{64DN} \qquad \text{43.9}$$

Description

The spring constant, k, for a helical torsion spring is calculated from Eq. 43.9. Since the wire is stressed in bending (not shear), Eq. 43.9 uses the modulus of elasticity, E (not the shear modulus, G). The spring constant has units of N·m/rad.

Equation 43.10 and Eq. 43.11: Torsional Spring Bending Stress

$$\sigma = K_i[32Fr/(\pi d^3)] \qquad \text{43.10}$$

$$K_i = (4C^2 - C - 1)/[4C(C-1)] \qquad \text{43.11}$$

Variation

$$K_o = \frac{4C^2 + C - 1}{4C(C+1)}$$

Description

The bending stress at the inner face of a helical torsion spring is calculated using Eq. 43.10 from the applied force, F, the radius, r, from the center of the coil to the force, the spring index, C (see Eq. 43.1), and the correction factor, K_i, for bending at the inner face, Eq. 43.11.[12] The correction factor is also known as the *Wahl stress correction factor*. The Wahl stress correction factor for bending at the outer face, K_o, is given in the variation equation.

Equation 43.12 and Eq. 43.13: Allowable Stress

$$S_y = \sigma = 0.78 S_{ut} \begin{bmatrix} \text{cold-drawn carbon steel} \\ \text{(A227, A228, and A229)} \end{bmatrix} \qquad \text{43.12}$$

$$S_y = \sigma = 0.87 S_{ut} \begin{bmatrix} \text{hardened and tempered} \\ \text{carbon and} \\ \text{low-alloy steel} \\ \text{(A232 and A401)} \end{bmatrix} \qquad \text{43.13}$$

Description

The allowable bending stress for a torsional spring wire is calculated from Eq. 43.12 and Eq. 43.13.[13] The ultimate tensile strength can be determined using Eq. 43.7.

7. FLAT AND LEAF SPRINGS

Flat springs are constructed as simply supported or cantilever beams. They can be flat, curved, or nested (as in a leaf spring). The traditional beam deflection tables can be used with simple flat springs when the deflections are small.[14]

Since beam bending stress is proportional to the thickness of the beam, stress can be kept low by using several low-thickness springs instead of a single thick spring. *Leaf springs* (*leaf set*), as commonly used in cars, consist of several flat springs, each atop another. The capacity of a leaf set is the sum of the capacities of all springs. The springs slide longitudinally over one another. The effect of this sliding and the resultant friction is difficult to evaluate.

---

[12](1) When a curved beam bends, its neutral axis shifts toward the center of curvature, resulting in a higher compressive stress at the inner face. (Depending on the configuration and loading, such as a U-bolt being pried open, the stresses at the inner and outer faces may be reversed.) The maximum tensile stress occurs at the outer face. In Eq. 43.10, the location of the stress and its sign (compression or tensile) is not identified by subscript (i.e., σ_i) in the *NCEES Handbook*. However, the variable K_i implies that it is associated with the inner face of the spring, and in fact, that is what Eq. 43.10 calculates. (2) There is no significance to the use of square brackets in the denominator of Eq. 43.11. (3) Equation 43.11 is the *Wahl correction factor* that accounts for curvature in helical torsion springs. It is specifically limited to round wires.

[13]Equation 43.12 and Eq. 43.13 are derived from Eq. 43.5 and Eq. 43.6 (by dividing the coefficients by 0.577). Therefore, many of the comments (see Ftn. 10) apply to both sets of equations. Basically, the *NCEES Handbook* confuses yield strength with allowable strength. Although Eq. 43.12 and Eq. 43.13 are clearly identified as equations for allowable stresses, the values calculated are not yield strengths. The notation $S_y = \sigma$ should be interpreted as "the maximum allowable stress determined from Joerres' analysis is used as a replacement for the yield strength."

[14]The common beam equations assume that the deflection is small (i.e., less than a few percent of the length) and that the load remains perpendicular to the beam at all times.

In vehicles, vibrations and impacts produce leaf spring deflections so that potential energy is as strain energy. Increasing the energy storage capability of a leaf spring ensures a more compliant suspension system.

8. SPUR GEAR TERMINOLOGY

Spur gears have the simplest type of teeth. The teeth faces of a spur gear are parallel to the axis of rotation. Figure 43.4 illustrates a typical spur gear and some of the terminology used to describe gear and tooth geometry.

Figure 43.4 Spur Gear Terminology

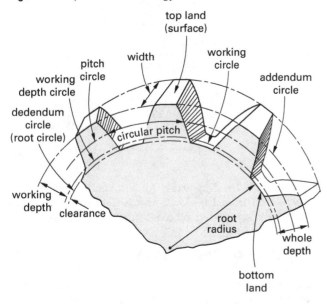

The *pitch circle* is an imaginary circle on which the gear lever arm is based. The *pitch point* is an imaginary point of tangency between the pitch circles of two meshing gears.

The velocity of a pitch point is the *pitch circle velocity* (*pitch velocity*). The pitch velocity can be calculated directly from the pitch diameter.

$$v_t = \pi d n_{\text{rpm}} \quad \text{[consistent units]}$$

The *addendum* is the radial distance from the pitch circle to the top of the tooth. For full-depth gears, it is equal to the reciprocal of the diametral pitch (i.e., $1/P$). The *base circle* is the circle that is tangent to the line of action. The *clearance* is the separation between the dedendum circle of gear 1 and the addendum circle of gear 2 when both gears are in mesh.

The *clearance circle* is the circle that is tangent to the addendum of the meshing gear. The *dedendum* is the radial distance from the pitch circle to the root circle. For full-depth gears, it is equal to either $1.25/P$ or $1.35/P$, depending on the clearance wanted. The *tooth face* is the tooth area between the pitch circle and the

addendum circle. The *face width* is the axial width of the tooth. The *flank* is the tooth area between the pitch circle and the dedendum. The *land* is the flat surface at the top of each tooth.

Whole depth is the distance from the addendum circle to the dedendum circle. It is equal to the working depth plus the clearance. The *working depth* is the distance that a tooth from a meshing gear extends into the space between two teeth.

Most gears in use are *involute gears* (i.e., have involute-cut teeth). An involute of a circle is the curve traced by the end of a taut string that is unwound from the circumference. The base circle is defined as the circle from which the involute is generated.

The *line of action* (also known as the *pressure line* and *generating line*) is a line passing through the pitch point that is tangent to both base circles. It is the distance between the intersections of the pressure line and the addendum circles. In Fig. 43.5, line A-A is tangent to the base circles and is the line of action. Angle ϕ, determined by the points of tangency, is the *pressure angle* (also known as the *angle of obliquity*). This involute is called a "$\phi°$ involute." In the United States, 20°, 22½°, and 25° pressure angles are in common use. The once-used 14½° pressure angle has essentially become obsolete as it produces larger gears.

Figure 43.5 Meshing Gear Terminology

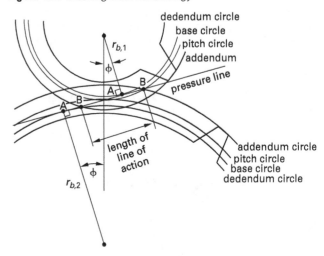

The pressure angle is proportional to the center-to-center distance of the gears, but a small deviation (i.e., error) in center-to-center distance will change the pressure angle slightly. However, changes in center-to-center spacing and backlash don't change the velocity ratio or the general performance of gear sets with involute gears. This is the main reason that involute gearing is widely used.

Figure 43.5 also illustrates the length of the line of contact between teeth on meshing gears. Line B-B is the section of the line of action between the points where it crosses the two addenda circles. This is sometimes called the *length of the line of action*. The length of the line of action is designated L_{ab}.

Equation 43.14 Through Eq. 43.16: Spur Gear Parameters

$$p_c = \pi d/N \quad \text{[circular pitch]} \qquad 43.14$$

$$p_b = p_c \cos \phi \quad \text{[base pitch]} \qquad 43.15$$

$$m = d/N \quad \text{[module]} \qquad 43.16$$

Variations

$$p_c = \frac{\pi}{P} = \pi m \quad \text{[circular pitch]}$$

$$m = \frac{p}{\pi} = \frac{1}{P} \quad \text{[module]}$$

Description

Three meanings for the term "pitch" are used for spur gears. The *diametral pitch*, P, is used with customary U.S. units and is the number of teeth per inch of pitch circle diameter. It is an index of tooth size. The diametral pitch is the same for all meshing teeth.

$$P = \frac{N}{d} = \frac{\pi}{p} = \frac{1}{m} \quad \text{[diametral pitch]}$$

The *circular pitch*, p_c, is the distance between corresponding tooth points along the pitch circle. It is equal to the tooth thickness plus the curved separation distance between teeth. The circular pitch is the same for all meshing teeth. (See Eq. 43.14.)

The *base pitch* (also known as the *normal pitch*), Eq. 43.15, is the distance from a point on one gear to the corresponding point measured along the base circle. It is also the distance from a point to the same corresponding point on the meshing gear tooth.

The *module*, m, of a gear is the ratio of the pitch diameter, d, to the number of teeth, N, as shown in Eq. 43.16. Therefore, the module is the reciprocal of the diametral pitch. The module (with units of mm per tooth) is the common SI index of tooth size.

$$d = \frac{N}{P} = mN \quad \text{[pitch diameter]}$$

Not every diametral pitch is available. To be economical, designs should make use of the standard diametral pitches. Common "coarse" series diametral pitches include 1, $1\frac{1}{4}$, $1\frac{1}{2}$, $1\frac{3}{4}$, 2, $2\frac{1}{4}$, $2\frac{1}{2}$, 3, 4, 6, 8, 10, 12, and 16 teeth/in. Common "fine" series diametral pitches include 20, 24, 32, 40, 48, 80, 96, 120, 150, and 200 teeth/in.

Example

A gear has 15 teeth and a pitch diameter of 5 cm. What is most nearly the circular pitch of the gear?

(A) 1.1 mm

(B) 3.3 mm

(C) 11 mm

(D) 52 mm

Solution

From Eq. 43.14, the circular pitch is

$$p_c = \pi d/N = \frac{\pi(5 \text{ cm})\left(10 \, \dfrac{\text{mm}}{\text{cm}}\right)}{15}$$
$$= 10.47 \text{ mm} \quad (11 \text{ mm})$$

The answer is (C).

9. GEAR TRAIN TERMINOLOGY

An *external gear* is any gear whose teeth "point" away from the axis of rotation, compared to an *internal gear*, whose teeth point in toward the axis of rotation. Figure 43.6 shows both an external and an internal gear.

Figure 43.6 *External and Internal Gears*

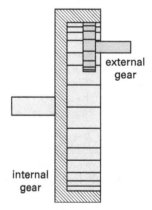

A *simple gear set* (*gear train*) consists of two gears with fixed centers in mesh. The gears turn in opposite directions if both are external gears. If one of the gears is an internal gear, the gears turn in the same direction. Each pair of gears constitutes a *stage*. For multiple gears in mesh, each pair of gears in succession constitute a stage, so that one gear can be part of two stages. An *idler gear*, also known as an *intermediate gear*, is a gear that rotates freely on its bearings and changes the transmission path without changing the gear ratio. (See Fig. 43.7.)

Figure 43.7 *Idler Gear*

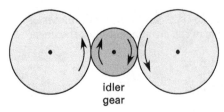

idler
gear

A *compound gear* consists of two gears mounted on a single (usually short) shaft. *Reverted gear sets* are those whose input and output shafts are in-line, usually using one or more compound gears. (See Fig. 43.8.) A reverted gear set always has an even number of stages. Only the gears in mesh need to have the same diametral pitches.

Figure 43.8 *Reverted Gear Set and Compound Gears*

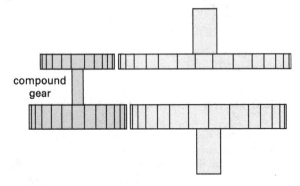

compound
gear

10. GEAR SETS AND GEAR DRIVES

In a simple set of two external gears in contact (referred to as a *mesh* or a *gear set*), one gear drives the other. Often, the smaller gear (which has greater leverage) drives the larger, in which case the smaller gear is referred to as the driving *pinion*. The larger gear in the set is referred to as the driven *gear*. The *center distance* is the distance between the centers of the pinion and gear.

The force between two meshing teeth will be the same. Since the same power ideally will be transmitted by each gear, the product of torque and rotational speed are the same.

$$v_{pinion} = v_{gear}$$

$$F_{pinion} = F_{gear}$$

At times, one pair of teeth will carry all of the force and will transmit all of the power. At other times, two (or more) pairs may be in contact. The average number of tooth pairs in contact is the *contact ratio*, CR. The contact ratio is usually between 1.2:1 and 1.6:1. (1.2:1 means that one pair of teeth is in contact at all times, and a second pair is in contact 20% of the time.) For good design, the contact ratio should be approximately 1.5:1.

A gear set is *prime* when the number of teeth on each meshing gear have no common factor except 1. This is a desirable condition, as all teeth tend to wear evenly.

Equation 43.17 Through Eq. 43.19: Velocity Ratio

$$m_{\text{v}} = \omega_{\text{out}}/\omega_{\text{in}} \qquad 43.17$$

$$m_{\text{v}} = -N_{\text{in}}/N_{\text{out}} \quad \text{[two-gear train]} \qquad 43.18$$

$$m_{\text{v}} = \pm \frac{\text{product of number of teeth on driver gears}}{\text{product of number of teeth on driven gears}} \begin{bmatrix} \text{compound} \\ \text{train} \end{bmatrix} \qquad 43.19$$

Description

The basic *velocity ratio*, m_{v}, for a gear is given by Eq. 43.17 when the input and output speeds, ω_{in} and ω_{out}, respectively, are known.[15] The velocity ratio is also known as the *speed ratio*, *mesh ratio*, *gear ratio*, *transmission ratio*, and *movement ratio*. Its reciprocal is known as the *train value*.

In Eq. 43.17, the symbol ω is used for convenience, but velocity values with units of rev/min and rev/s can be used without converting to rad/s.

The inverse of the velocity ratio is also a *ratio of torques*. Since the tangential force at the pitch circle is the same in a set of engaged gears, the faster-turning gear will transmit a smaller torque because it has a smaller pitch circle radius (i.e., "moment arm").

$$m_{\text{v}} = \frac{\omega_2}{\omega_1} = \frac{T_1}{T_2}$$

$$m_T = \frac{1}{m_{\text{v}}}$$

Equation 43.18 gives the velocity ratio for a two-gear train. In a *two-gear train*, the output and input gears rotate in opposite directions, which is represented by

---

[15](1) The variable m_{v} used by the *NCEES Handbook* for the velocity ratio is unrelated to the module of the gears, m. (2) The variables used by ANSI/AGMA (*Gear Nomenclature, Definition of Terms with Symbols* (ANSI/AGMA 1012-G05) and *Fundamental Rating Factors and Calculation Methods for Involute Spur and Helical Gear Teeth* (ANSI/AGMA 2001-D04)) for gear speed ratio are m_G, always a positive number greater than 1.0, and more recently, u.

the negative sign in Eq. 43.18. N is the number of teeth on the input gear, N_{in}, and output gear, N_{out}, respectively.

The velocity ratio for a compound gear train is given by Eq. 43.19. A *compound gear train* has at least one shaft that carries two or more gears, which rotate at the same speed.

In gear ratio equations, signs can represent direction conventions (e.g., "+" for clockwise, and "−" for counterclockwise) as well as to indicate a change in direction. Equation 43.17 does not have any signs, and the equation is not limited to two gears in mesh (although it applies to two-gear sets), so the velocity ratio can be either positive or negative depending on the directions the gears are turning.

In Eq. 43.19, the "$\pm$" sign is used to indicate that the last gear may turn in the same or opposite direction from the input gear, depending on whether the gear train is made up of an odd or even number of gears.

11. MESH EFFICIENCY

Ideally, the input power is passed through each gear to the next in line.

$$P_{gear} = P_{pinion} \quad \text{[ideal]}$$

$$T_{gear}n_{gear} = T_{pinion}n_{pinion} \quad \text{[ideal]}$$

In reality, each gear set will dissipate some of the input power. This is accounted for by the *efficiency of the gear train* (i.e., the *mesh efficiency*), η_{mesh}.

$$\eta_{mesh} = \frac{P_{output}}{P_{input}}$$

In the case of a pinion driving a gear,

$$P_{gear} = \eta_{mesh}P_{pinion}$$

$$T_{gear}n_{gear} = \eta_{mesh}T_{pinion}n_{pinion}$$

12. FORCE ANALYSIS OF SPUR GEARS

Equation 43.20 Through Eq. 43.22: Forces on Straight Spur Gears

$$W_t = \frac{2T}{d} = \frac{2T}{mN} \qquad \text{43.20}$$

$$W_t = \frac{2H}{d\omega} = \frac{2H}{mN\omega} \qquad \text{43.21}$$

$$W_r = W_t \tan\phi \qquad \text{43.22}$$

Variation

$$W_{t,N} = \frac{P_{kW}\left(1000 \; \dfrac{W}{kW}\right)}{v_{t,m/s}} \qquad \text{[SI only]}$$

Description

The resultant (total, net, etc.) force, W, acting on a gear can be divided into three orthogonal components: tangential, W_t; radial, W_r; and axial, W_a. These are illustrated in Fig. 43.9. For a spur gear with straight-cut teeth, the axial force component is zero. The resultant force can be calculated from the components and the gear pressure angle, ϕ.

$$W = \sqrt{W_t^2 + W_r^2} = \frac{W_t}{\cos\phi} = \frac{W_r}{\sin\phi}$$

Figure 43.9 *Gear Force Components*

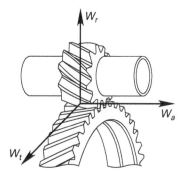

The *tangential force* component, W_t (also known as the *transmitted force* and *peripheral force*), is the only component that causes rotation and transmits power. If the tangential force is known, the transmitted torque, T, can be found from geometry. r is the pitch circle radius. The pitch circle diameter, d, can be found from the module as defined in Eq. 43.16. Any convenient set of units can be used. This is the basis of Eq. 43.20.

$$T = W_tr = \frac{W_td}{2} = \frac{W_tmN}{2}$$

Since power, P, of a force, F, moving at velocity, v, is $P = F$v, the torque can also be found from the transmitted power. This is the basis of Eq. 43.21.[16]

$$P = W_t \text{v}_t = W_t \omega r = \frac{W_t \omega d}{2} = \frac{W_t \omega m N}{2}$$

The radial force does not transmit power. It is the force that tries to separate the gears. It can be found from the tangential force using Eq. 43.22.

13. DESIGN OF GEAR TRAINS

Finding the number of teeth that each gear should have in order to achieve a particular train ratio is time consuming, as a trial-and-error solution may be needed. A particularly desired gear ratio may not exactly be achievable, since each gear must contain an integral number of teeth. Other constraints may be placed on the design, including the minimum and maximum numbers of teeth and the maximum number of stages.

All gears in mesh must have the same diametral pitch. Therefore, for any two gears in mesh, the relationship between the diametral pitch, module, pitch circle diameters, and number of teeth is

$$P_1 = P_2$$

$$m_1 = m_2$$

$$\frac{N_1}{d_1} = \frac{N_2}{d_2}$$

Equation 43.23: Center-to-Center Distance

$$C = (d_1 + d_2)/2 \qquad 43.23$$

Variation

$$C = r_1 + r_2 = \frac{\dfrac{N_1}{P} + \dfrac{N_2}{P}}{2}$$

Description

The *center-to-center distance*, C, is the average of the pitch diameters, d. C can also be calculated as the sum of the two pitch circle radii, r_1 and r_2, as shown in the variation equation. Equation 43.23 can be written for all pairs of meshing gears and solved for unknown quantities. Knowledge of various gear ratios between the meshing gears can be used to simplify the simultaneous equations.

14. EPICYCLIC GEAR SETS

Epicyclic gear sets (also known as *planetary gear sets*) are characterized by one or more gears that do not have fixed axes of rotation. They have two inputs (one of which may be fixed or stationary) and one output. Compared with gear sets where all gears have fixed centers, epicyclic gear sets can have much higher gear ratios, are more compact, have lower tooth loadings and pitch-line velocities, offer in-line input and output shafts, may be easier to lubricate, and are generally less expensive.

The simplest type of epicyclic gear set is shown in Fig. 43.10. It consists of a *sun gear*, *ring gear* (also known as an *annulus gear*), and one or more *planet gears* (also referred to as *planets*, *planet pinions*, and *spider gears*). The rotating bent yoke that connects the planets to their shaft is known as the *planet carrier*, *arm*, and *spider*.

Figure 43.10 *Simple Epicyclic Gear Set*

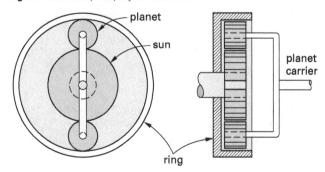

The planets rotate about their own axes and revolve around the sun gear. During rotation, a point on a planet gear traces out epicyclic curves, hence the name. There are generally one to four planets. The number of planets does not affect the output speed, but the maximum power transmission is essentially proportional to the number of planets. The number of planets is limited by space so that the planets do not "overlap." Either the ring gear or the carrier can be fixed. If one is fixed, then the other must rotate.

When the carrier is fixed and the ring gear is the output, the arrangement is known as a *star gear set*. When the sun gear is fixed and the input is the ring gear, the system is called a *solar gear set*.

---

[16](1) The *NCEES Handbook* uses variable H to represent transmitted power in gear sets. This variable is consistent with *Shigley's* and is not unknown in SI documentation, but it is not normal and customary in U.S. engineering practice. It is not the symbol adopted for transmitted power by ANSI/AGMA in ANSI/AGMA 2001-D04 and ANSI/AGMA 1012-G05. (2) Outside of the subject of gear sets, the *NCEES Handbook* uses other variables to designate transmitted power.

15. ANALYSIS OF SIMPLE EPICYCLIC GEAR SETS

Equation 43.24: Velocity Ratio

$$\frac{\omega_L - \omega_{\text{arm}}}{\omega_f - \omega_{\text{arm}}} = \pm m_{\text{v}} \qquad 43.24$$

Description

Using intuition is usually a futile effort with epicyclic gear sets. There are two formal methods (and many combinations thereof) used to analyze epicyclic gear sets: the algebraic method and the methodical tabular method. Even with these methods, special rules and conventions are needed. The algebraic method replaces visualization and imaginary rotation with a formula, so it is arguably the easier of the two methods.

With the algebraic method, analysis first starts by assuming any convenient sign convention for direction, typically "+" for clockwise and "−" for counterclockwise.

Second, the known *gear set velocity ratio* (in this section referred to as "VR") is used to calculate any unknown rotational speeds of the gears connected to the input or output.

$$\text{VR} = \frac{\omega_{\text{out}}}{\omega_{\text{in}}}$$

Third, the "first" and "last" gears are selected. By definition, both the first gear and last gear must mesh with the orbiting planets (the gears that exhibit planetary motion), so the only candidates are the sun gear and ring gear. Skipping all of the justification, it is easiest to just always assign the sun gear to the "first gear" position, leaving the ring gear to be the "last gear."

Fourth, the ratio of numbers of teeth, N, on the last gear and first gear is calculated. This value is also the *relative velocity ratio* (RVR)—the ratio of velocities of the ring and sun gears when the arm is held stationary.[17] The sign of the RVR depends on the directions of the first and last gears. If the first (sun) and last (ring) gears turn in opposite directions when the arm is held stationary, RVR is negative. This will always be the case when the ring gear is an internal gear. So, a convenient rule is that RVR is always negative with internal ring gears.

$$\text{RVR} = \pm \frac{N_{\text{sun (first)}}}{N_{\text{ring (last)}}}$$

Fifth and finally, a second equation for the RVR is written in terms of the rotational speeds of the first gear, last gear, and arm. Any unknown values can be determined from this equation. This is the basis of Eq. 43.24.[18]

$$\text{RVR} = \frac{\omega_{\text{gear (last)}} - \omega_{\text{arm}}}{\omega_{\text{sun (first)}} - \omega_{\text{arm}}}$$

The sequence described may vary depending on whether a problem is analysis or design and depending on what information is missing.

Example

The epicyclic gear set shown has an overall speed reduction of 3:1. The planet carrier is the output gear. The input gear is the sun gear, which turns clockwise at 1000 rpm. The planet has 20 teeth and a diametral pitch of 10.

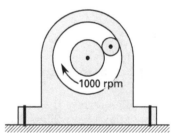

What is the ratio of the number of teeth on the ring gear to the number of teeth on the sun gear?

(A) $\frac{1}{3}$

(B) $\frac{1}{2}$

(C) 1

(D) 2

Solution

Choose clockwise as the positive direction. The sun gear is the input gear. The output element is the arm. The reducing gear set has a velocity ratio of $\text{VR} = \frac{1}{3}$, so the speed of the output arm is

$$\omega_{\text{arm}} = (\text{VR})\omega_{\text{sun}} = \left(\frac{1}{3}\right)\left(1000 \ \frac{\text{rev}}{\text{min}}\right) = 333.3 \ \text{rev/min}$$

---

[17]The *NCEES Handbook* uses the term "is grounded." This is synonymous with "is held stationary" and "is fixed." There is no electrical connotation to "is grounded."

[18]*NCEES Handbook* Eq. 43.24 is misleading, because m_{v} is not the gear set velocity ratio defined in Eq. 43.17. The quantity represented by m_{v} (RVR in this book) is quite different from the ratio of gear set output and input velocities (VR in this book), as the example illustrates in Eq. 43.24. (a) Since the arm angular velocity is subtracted from both the last and first gear angular velocities, m_{v} in Eq. 43.24 is clearly the ratio of last and first gear angular velocities relative (with respect) to the arm when the arm is held stationary. (b) m_{v} in Eq. 43.24 always has the same absolute value, regardless of whether the gear set is speed reducing or speed augmenting.

The ring gear is part of the housing and is stationary, so its speed is zero.

$$\text{RVR} = \frac{\omega_{\text{gear (last)}} - \omega_{\text{arm}}}{\omega_{\text{sun (first)}} - \omega_{\text{arm}}}$$

$$= \frac{0 \; \frac{\text{rev}}{\text{min}} - 333.3 \; \frac{\text{rev}}{\text{min}}}{1000 \; \frac{\text{rev}}{\text{min}} - 333.3 \; \frac{\text{rev}}{\text{min}}}$$

$$= -\frac{1}{2}$$

With an internal ring gear, the relative velocity ratio is negative. The ratio of the numbers of teeth, N, on the ring gear and sun gear is

$$\frac{N_{\text{ring}}}{N_{\text{sun}}} = \frac{-1}{-\text{RVR}} = \frac{-1}{-\frac{1}{2}} = 2$$

The answer is (D).

16. BALL, ROLLER, AND NEEDLE BEARINGS

Ball, roller, and needle bearings (i.e., *anti-friction bearings*) and their variations use rolling-element bearings such as balls or cylinders constrained within *bearing races* to reduce friction. The races, in turn, support and resist the applied loadings. One race is usually fixed, while the other race moves with the rotating element (e. g., a shaft). The balls or rollers themselves rotate as the races rotate relative to each other. *Ball bearings* can support radial and thrust loads, but they are limited in capacity by the compressive contact pressure between them and the races. Therefore, they are used where loads are relatively low. Capacity is a function of the number of balls in play. The balls may be loose or their positions may be constrained with a *cage* (*separator* or *retainer*), in which case the term *caged bearing* or *Conrad bearing* may be used. Caged bearings generally have lower capacities since the number of balls is reduced. Examples of rolling element bearings are shown in Fig. 43.11.

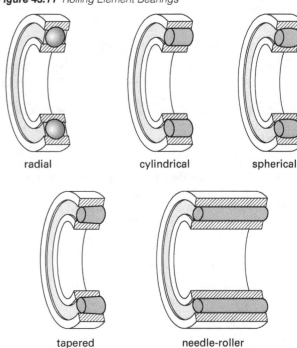

Figure 43.11 Rolling Element Bearings

radial   cylindrical   spherical

tapered   needle-roller

Since the locus of contact points represents a line (as opposed to a ball bearing which has a small contact point), *roller bearings* use rotating cylinders and have greater radial load carrying ability but require greater alignment between the races. Roller bearings cannot normally support thrust loads. *Needle bearings* use small diameter cylinders (needles or pins) and can fit in less space. Since there is no space between the rollers, no cage is required. Although they require less space, needle bearings have greater friction and must run slower than ball and standard roller bearings.

Ball and roller thrust bearings are used with primarily axial loading. Where there is both radial and axial loading, tapered roller bearings are used, often in opposite-facing pairs to support axial loading from both directions.

A *self-aligning bearing* (*Wingquist bearing* or *SKF bearing*, named after the founder and his company that manufactured them first) is useful when there is deflection and angular misalignment of the shaft relative to the housing. (See Fig. 43.12.) Such misalignment is expected with long or flexible shafts. Such a bearing typically has two caged rows of balls that run within a concave spherical raceway in the outer ring. Self-aligning bearings have particularly low axial capacities.

Figure 43.12 *Self-Aligning Bearing*

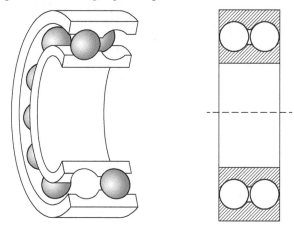

Thrust bearings are used with the largest axial loads, such as propeller shafts and those having substantial vertical weights. Thrust bearings may be simple flat faying pads, be hydrodynamic, or contain ball or roller bearings.

17. BEARING CAPACITY

Bearings are specified by both their static and dynamic load capacities. Bearings are selected (i.e., as from a manufacturer's catalog) so that the equivalent bearing capacity (i.e., the cataloged capacity), C, is greater than the applied or design load (i.e., the cataloged capacity), P. Static capacity can be used if rotational speed is slow, intermittent, and/or subject to shocks. Dynamic capacity is used if the rotational speed is smooth and relatively constant.

The *basic static load rating*, C_0, is determined by the manufacturer and is shown in its catalog. Similarly, for a rotating bearing, the *basic rating*, C_r, is determined by the manufacturer.

Equation 43.25 Through Eq. 43.27: Equivalent Radial Load

$$P_{eq} = XVF_r + YF_a \qquad 43.25$$

$$e = 0.513\left(\frac{F_a}{C_0}\right)^{0.236} \qquad 43.26$$

$$Y = 0.840\left(\frac{F_a}{C_0}\right)^{-0.247} \quad [F_a/VF_r > e] \qquad 43.27$$

Values

parameter	$F_a/VF_r > e$	$F_a/VF_r \le e$
X	0.56	1
Y	see Eq. 43.27	0
V		
inner ring rotates	1	1
outer ring rotates	1.2	1.2

Description

When a bearing is subjected to both a radial loading, F_r, and an axial (thrust) load, F_a, an *equivalent radial load*, P_{eq}, must be calculated in order to select bearings or to calculate bearing life.[19] (The term *equivalent* implies that radial and axial loads have been combined into a single radial parameter.) For a single-row ball bearing, the equivalent radial load can be calculated as shown in Eq. 43.25.

V, X, and Y are factors that are best supplied by the manufacturer, but can be determined from accepted methods. X is the *radial load thrust factor*, and Y is the *axial load thrust factor*. C_0 is the basic static load rating from the manufacturer's catalog. $V = 1$ when the outer ring (raceway) is stationary and the inner ring rotates; $V = 1.2$ when the inner ring is stationary and the outer ring rotates. X and Y depend on the relative ratio of the axial and radial forces. For low axial loading as defined by the following equation, the values of X and Y are given in the values section.

$$\frac{F_a}{VF_r} \le e \quad \text{[low axial loading]}$$

For high axial loading as defined by the following equation, $X = 0.56$, and Y is calculated from Eq. 43.27.

$$\frac{F_a}{VF_r} > e \quad \text{[high axial loading]}$$

Example

A single-row ball bearing is to carry a radial load of 4.4 kN and a thrust load of 6.7 kN. The radial and thrust load factors are 0.63 and 1.25, respectively. If the

---

[19]The *NCEES Handbook* uses F to represent the axial and radial components of the combined (equivalent, resultant, total, etc.) load that is designated by a different variable, P.

inner ring rotates, what is most nearly the equivalent radial load?

(A) 4.4 kN

(B) 9.7 kN

(C) 11 kN

(D) 12 kN

Solution

$V = 1$ if the inner ring rotates. From Eq. 43.25,

$$P_{eq} = XVF_r + YF_a$$
$$= (0.63)(1)(4.4 \text{ kN}) + (1.25)(6.7 \text{ kN})$$
$$= 11.147 \text{ kN} \quad (11 \text{ kN})$$

The answer is (C).

18. ROLLING ELEMENT BEARING LIFE

Lubrication of bearings is provided for the common reasons: (a) reduce friction by separating the surfaces in contact, (b) dissipate heat, (c) prevent corrosion, and (d) remove dirt and contamination. Bearing life is affected by proper lubrication. *Bearing life* (*bearing fatigue life*) is a measure of how long a bearing can be expected to last under standard operating conditions. Bearing life depends primarily on the loading, although care, cleaning, and lubrication are significant external influences on life. The bearing is assumed serviceable as long as 90% of the rolling elements are functional, and the parameter that predicts when 10% of the rolling elements have failed is designated L_{10} and referred to as "L-ten."[20]

Equation 43.28: Minimum Required Basic Load Rating

$$C = PL^{1/a} \qquad \textit{43.28}$$

Values

bearing type	a
ball	3
roller	10/3

Description

The *minimum required basic load rating*, C, is the load under which 90% of the bearings will survive one million revolutions. P is the design radial load, L is the design life in millions of revolutions, and a is a constant equal to 3 for a single row of ball bearings and 10/3 for straight roller bearings, as shown in the values section.

Example

What is most nearly the minimum required basic load rating for a single row of ball bearings with an equivalent radial load of 22 kN and a design life of 340 000 revolutions?

(A) 15 kN

(B) 16 kN

(C) 22 kN

(D) 33 kN

Solution

The constant a is 3 for a single row of ball bearings. The minimum required basic load rating is

$$C = PL^{1/a} = (22 \text{ kN})\left(\frac{340\,000 \text{ rev}}{1\,000\,000 \text{ rev}}\right)^{1/3}$$
$$= 15.355 \text{ kN} \quad (15 \text{ kN})$$

The answer is (A).

19. POWER SCREWS AND SCREW JACKS

A *power screw* changes angular position into linear position (i.e., changes rotary motion into traversing motion). The linear positioning can be horizontal (as in vices and lathes) or vertical, as in jacks. Cross sections of square and Acme threads, both commonly used in power screws, are shown in Fig. 43.13.[21] For square threads, the *thread angle*, ϕ, is zero.

---

[20]In other countries, the designation B_{10} may be used in place of L_{10}.
[21]The 10° modified thread is essentially equivalent to the square thread, but it is more economical to manufacture than the square thread.

Figure 43.13 *Power Screw Threads*

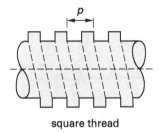

square thread

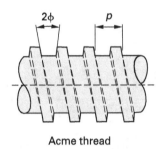

Acme thread

Square power screws are designated by the mean diameter, d_m, pitch, p, and *lead angle*, θ. The *pitch*, p, is the distance between corresponding points on a thread. The *lead*, l, is the distance the screw advances each revolution. Often, double- and triple-threaded screws are used. The lead, l, is one, two, or three times the pitch for single-, double-, and triple-threaded screws, respectively.

$$l = \pi d_m \tan \theta$$

Equation 43.29 and Eq. 43.30: Required Torque

$$T_R = \frac{F d_m}{2}\left(\frac{l + \pi \mu d_m}{\pi d_m - \mu l}\right) + \frac{F \mu_c d_c}{2} \qquad 43.29$$

$$T_L = \frac{F d_m}{2}\left(\frac{\pi \mu d_m - l}{\pi d_m + \mu l}\right) + \frac{F \mu_c d_c}{2} \qquad 43.30$$

Variation

$$T_R = \left(\frac{F d_m}{2}\right)\left(\frac{\tan \theta + \mu}{1 - \mu \tan \theta}\right) \quad \text{[no collar friction]}$$

$$T_L = \left(\frac{F d_m}{2}\right)\left(\frac{\mu - \tan \theta}{1 + \mu \tan \theta}\right) \quad \text{[no collar friction]}$$

Description

The torque required to turn a square screw in motion against an axial force F (i.e., "raise" the load) is given in Eq. 43.29.[22]

The torque required to turn the screw in motion in the direction of the applied axial force (i.e., "lower" the load) is given by Eq. 43.30. If the torque is zero or negative (as it would be if the lead was large or friction was low), then the screw is not self-locking and the load will lower by itself causing the screw to spin (i.e., will "overhaul"). The screw will be self-locking when $\tan \theta \leq \mu$.

Example

A lubricated power screw is used to lower a 1000 N load. The screw has a major diameter of 40 mm, a mean diameter of 37.5 mm, and a lead of 7 mm. The coefficient of friction is 0.15.

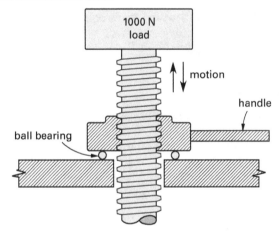

Neglecting collar friction, what is most nearly the torque required to lower the load?

- (A) 1.7 N·m
- (B) 23 N·m
- (C) 160 N·m
- (D) 2200 N·m

---

[22]The relationship is different for Acme and other threads.

Solution

Use Eq. 43.30. Since collar friction can be neglected, the second term can be omitted.

$$
\begin{aligned}
T_L &= \frac{Fd_m}{2}\left(\frac{\pi\mu d_m - l}{\pi d_m + \mu l}\right) \\
&= \left(\frac{(1000\ \text{N})(37.5\ \text{mm})}{(2)\left(1000\ \dfrac{\text{mm}}{\text{m}}\right)}\right) \\
&\quad \times \left(\frac{\pi(0.15)(37.5\ \text{mm}) - 7\ \text{mm}}{\pi(37.5\ \text{mm}) + (0.15)(7\ \text{mm})}\right) \\
&= 1.683\ \text{N·m} \quad (1.7\ \text{N·m})
\end{aligned}
$$

The answer is (A).

Equation 43.31: Power Screw Efficiency

$$
\eta = Fl/2\pi T \qquad \textit{43.31}
$$

Description

The *mechanical efficiency* of the screw can be calculated as the ratio of the ideal work required to raise the jack against the load to the actual work performed. The ideal work is calculated as force × distance. The distance the screw moves for each revolution is the lead, l. The ideal work is

$$
W_{\text{ideal}} = Fl
$$

The actual work is calculated from the actual torque required. Analogous to $W = Fl$, the work of a torque applied for one revolution is

$$
W_{\text{actual}} = T\theta = 2\pi T
$$

The ratio of the ideal to actual work terms is the basis of Eq. 43.31.

The torque calculated in Eq. 43.29 and Eq. 43.30 is required to overcome thread friction and to raise the load (i.e., axially compress the screw). Typically, only 10% to 15% of the torque goes into axial compression of the screw. The remainder is used to overcome friction. The mechanical efficiency of the screw is the ratio of torque without friction to the torque with friction. The torque without friction can be calculated from the two previous equations (depending on the travel direction) using $\mu = 0$.

$$
\eta_m = \frac{T_{\mu=0}}{T}
$$

In the absence of an antifriction ring, an additional torque will be required to overcome friction in the collar. Since the collar is generally flat, the normal force is the jack load, F, for the purpose of calculating the frictional force. (See Fig. 43.14.)

$$
T_{\text{collar}} = F\mu_{\text{collar}} r_{\text{collar}}
$$

Figure 43.14 *Screw With Collar*

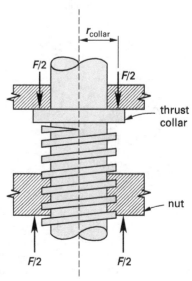

20. FOUR-BAR LINKAGES

The *four-bar linkage* is a simple *mechanism* comprising four *links* (*bars*) that are linked by joints. The linkage is able to rotate within the plane of the mechanism. Four-bar linkages are common components in machine design, and many diverse mechanisms can be analyzed as four-bar linkages. A simple four-bar linkage is shown in Fig. 43.15.

Figure 43.15 *Four-Bar Linkages*

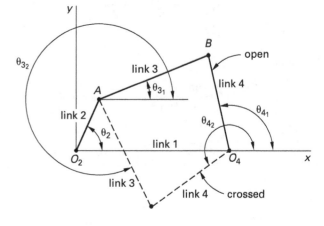

The four-bar linkage in Fig. 43.15 has a *reference link*, link 1; a *crank link* (also known as an *input link*), link 2; a *coupler link*, link 3; and an *output link*, link 4. The reference link is typically fixed (grounded) and is usually taken to coincide with the x-axis. The links are joined by four pivots: two moving pivots, A and B, and two fixed pivots, O_2 and O_4.[23]

The angles of links 2, 3, and 4 with respect to the reference link (i.e., x-axis) are θ_2, θ_3, and θ_4, respectively.[24] The length of links 2, 3, and 4 are a, b, and c, respectively, while link 1 is length d.

The four-bar linkage can be configured into two *positions* (*circuits*), depending on the configuration of links 3 and 4. The *open position* and *crossed position* are illustrated in Fig. 43.15.

Equation 43.32 Through Eq. 43.44: Position Analysis[25,26]

$$\theta_{4_{1,2}} = 2\arctan\left(\frac{-B \pm \sqrt{B^2 - 4AC}}{2A}\right) \qquad 43.32$$

$$\theta_{3_{1,2}} = 2\arctan\left(\frac{-E \pm \sqrt{E^2 - 4DF}}{2D}\right) \qquad 43.33$$

$$A = \cos\theta_2 - K_1 - K_2\cos\theta_2 + K_3 \qquad 43.34$$

$$B = -2\sin\theta_2 \qquad 43.35$$

$$C = K_1 - (K_2 + 1)\cos\theta_2 + K_3 \qquad 43.36$$

$$D = \cos\theta_2 - K_1 + K_4\cos\theta_2 + K_5 \qquad 43.37$$

$$E = -2\sin\theta_2 \qquad 43.38$$

$$F = K_1 + (K_4 - 1)\cos\theta_2 + K_5 \qquad 43.39$$

$$K_1 = \frac{d}{a} \qquad 43.40$$

$$K_2 = \frac{d}{c} \qquad 43.41$$

$$K_3 = \frac{a^2 - b^2 + c^2 + d^2}{2ac} \qquad 43.42$$

$$K_4 = \frac{d}{b} \qquad 43.43$$

$$K_5 = \frac{c^2 - d^2 - a^2 - b^2}{2ab} \qquad 43.44$$

Variations

$$\theta_{4_{1,2}} = 2\arctan\left(\frac{-B - \sqrt{B^2 - 4AC}}{2A}\right) \quad \text{[open position]}$$

$$\theta_{4_{1,2}} = 2\arctan\left(\frac{-B + \sqrt{B^2 - 4AC}}{2A}\right) \quad \text{[closed position]}$$

$$\theta_{3_{1,2}} = 2\arctan\left(\frac{-E - \sqrt{E^2 - 4DF}}{2D}\right) \quad \text{[open position]}$$

$$\theta_{3_{1,2}} = 2\arctan\left(\frac{-E + \sqrt{E^2 - 4DF}}{2D}\right) \quad \text{[closed position]}$$

Description

Position analysis is used to specify the position (orientation) of links with respect to each other. Typically, the lengths of the links are known. If angle θ_2 is known, angle θ_4 can be calculated from Eq. 43.32. Equation 43.32 can be rewritten for either open or crossed position configurations as shown by the variation equations.

If angle θ_2 is known, the angle θ_3 can be calculated from Eq. 43.33. Equation 43.33 can be rewritten for either open or crossed position configurations as shown by the variation equations.

[23]The *NCEES Handbook* uses the term "pivot" to describe what is typically referred to as a "joint," "pin," or "hinge." The technical name for a pin joint is *revolute*.
[24]Although the *NCEES Handbook* uses numbers to designate the links, the *NCEES Handbook* also uses numbers in a second level of subscripts to designate the open ("1") and crossed ("2") positions. So, θ_{3_2} refers to the angle of the crossed position of link 3. The second numerical subscript is unrelated to a link number.
[25]The fundamental engineering principles and theorems used to analyze four-bar linkages are obscured by these equations. The four-bar linkage equations presented in the *NCEES Handbook* can be used to determine position, velocity, and acceleration, but the plug-and-chug calculations do not require or demonstrate engineering knowledge. Other than being aware of their existence and location, there are no engineering fundamentals to learn from these equations.
[26]The *NCEES Handbook* uses "A," "B," "C," and "D" to designate two different concepts: the four joints and four intermediate calculations in Eq. 43.32 through Eq. 43.39. There is no connection between the common designations.

Example

The four-bar linkage system shown is configured into the open position. The values of θ_2, K_1, K_2, and K_3 are $65°$, 0.58, 0.68, and 1.2, respectively.

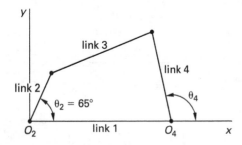

What is most nearly the value of angle θ_4?

(A) $93°$

(B) $98°$

(C) $110°$

(D) $130°$

Solution

From Eq. 43.34,

$$A = \cos\theta_2 - K_1 - K_2\cos\theta_2 + K_3$$
$$= \cos 65° - 0.58 - 0.68\cos 65° + 1.2$$
$$= 0.755$$

From Eq. 43.35,

$$B = -2\sin\theta_2 = -2\sin 65°$$
$$= -1.81$$

From Eq. 43.36,

$$C = K_1 - (K_2 + 1)\cos\theta_2 + K_3$$
$$= 0.58 - (0.68 + 1)\cos 65° + 1.2$$
$$= 1.07$$

From Eq. 43.32, for the open position,

$$\theta_4 = 2\arctan\left(\frac{-B - \sqrt{B^2 - 4AC}}{2A}\right)$$

$$= 2\arctan\left(\frac{-(-1.81) - \sqrt{\begin{array}{c}(-1.81)^2 \\ - (4)(0.755)(1.07)\end{array}}}{(2)(0.755)}\right)$$

$$= 92.65° \quad (93°)$$

The answer is (A).

Equation 43.45 Through Eq. 43.52: Velocity Analysis

$$\omega_3 = \frac{a\omega_2}{b}\frac{\sin(\theta_4 - \theta_2)}{\sin(\theta_3 - \theta_4)} \qquad 43.45$$

$$\omega_4 = \frac{a\omega_2}{c}\frac{\sin(\theta_2 - \theta_3)}{\sin(\theta_4 - \theta_3)} \qquad 43.46$$

$$v_{Ax} = -a\omega_2\sin\theta_2 \qquad 43.47$$

$$v_{BAx} = -b\omega_3\sin\theta_3 \qquad 43.48$$

$$v_{Bx} = -c\omega_4\sin\theta_4 \qquad 43.49$$

$$v_{Ay} = a\omega_2\cos\theta_2 \qquad 43.50$$

$$v_{BAy} = b\omega_3\cos\theta_3 \qquad 43.51$$

$$v_{By} = c\omega_4\cos\theta_4 \qquad 43.52$$

Description

Velocity analysis calculates the angular velocity when the angular velocity of one link is known. The *tangential velocity* (also known as the *peripheral velocity*) of a wheel of radius r rotating about a fixed point is $v_t = r\omega$, and similarly, the tangential velocity of the end of a link of length l rotating about a fixed point is $v_t = l\omega$. If θ is defined as an angle from the horizontal x-axis, the x-component of velocity is $v_x = v_t\sin\theta = l\omega\sin\theta$, and the y-component is $v_y = v_t\cos\theta = l\omega\cos\theta$.

The angular velocity of links 3 and 4, ω_3 and ω_4, can be calculated from Eq. 43.45 and Eq. 43.46, respectively, using the angular velocity of link 2, ω_2. Clockwise and counterclockwise rotational angular velocities and accelerations are distinguished by opposite signs. The most common assumption is that clockwise rotation is positive, but this is an arbitrary decision. Once the angular velocities of all links are known, the velocity in a direction parallel to an axis is calculated as shown in Eq. 43.47 through Eq. 43.52. Although the pivot points of links 2 and 4 are fixed (i.e., stationary), the location of the pivot point for link 3 changes as the linkage moves. So, the linear velocity of link 3 can be specified with respect to either its (moving) pivot point or with respect to the stationary x-y plane. The velocity of a point with respect to another point is designated by a double subscript. For example, v_{BA} is the velocity of point B with respect to point A.

Example

What are most nearly the angular velocities of link 3, ω_3, and link 4, ω_4, of the four-bar mechanism shown?

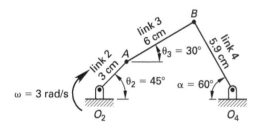

(A) $\omega_3 = 0.78$ rad/s, and $\omega_4 = -0.79$ rad/s

(B) $\omega_3 = 0.78$ rad/s, and $\omega_4 = -0.39$ rad/s

(C) $\omega_3 = 1.4$ rad/s, and $\omega_4 = -0.79$ rad/s

(D) $\omega_3 = 1.4$ rad/s, and $\omega_4 = -0.39$ rad/s

Solution

$\theta_4 = 180° - \alpha = 180° - 60° = 120°$. Calculate the angular velocity of link 3 from Eq. 43.45.

$$\omega_3 = \frac{a\omega_2}{b} \frac{\sin(\theta_4 - \theta_2)}{\sin(\theta_3 - \theta_4)}$$

$$= \frac{(3 \text{ cm})\left(-3 \dfrac{\text{rad}}{\text{s}}\right)\sin(120° - 45°)}{(6 \text{ cm})\sin(30° - 120°)}$$

$$= 1.449 \text{ rad/s} \quad (1.4 \text{ rad/s})$$

Using Eq. 43.46, the angular velocity of link 4 is

$$\omega_4 = \frac{a\omega_2}{c} \frac{\sin(\theta_2 - \theta_3)}{\sin(\theta_4 - \theta_3)}$$

$$= \frac{(3 \text{ cm})\left(-3 \dfrac{\text{rad}}{\text{s}}\right)\sin(45° - 30°)}{(5.9 \text{ cm})\sin(120° - 30°)}$$

$$= -0.3948 \text{ rad/s} \quad (-0.39 \text{ rad/s})$$

The answer is (D).

Equation 43.53 Through Eq. 43.60: Acceleration Analysis

$$\alpha_3 = \frac{CD - AF}{AE - BD} \qquad 43.53$$

$$\alpha_4 = \frac{CE - BF}{AE - BD} \qquad 43.54$$

$$A = c\sin\theta_4 \qquad 43.55$$

$$B = b\sin\theta_3 \qquad 43.56$$

$$C = a\alpha_2\sin\theta_2 + a\omega_2^2\cos\theta_2$$
$$+ b\omega_3^2\cos\theta_3 - c\omega_4^2\cos\theta_4 \qquad 43.57$$

$$D = c\cos\theta_4 \qquad 43.58$$

$$E = b\cos\theta_3 \qquad 43.59$$

$$F = a\alpha_2\cos\theta_2 - a\omega_2^2\sin\theta_2$$
$$- b\omega_3^2\sin\theta_3 + c\omega_4^2\sin\theta_4 \qquad 43.60$$

Description

Acceleration analysis determines the angular acceleration of links when the acceleration of one link, typically the crank link, is known. The tangential acceleration of a wheel of radius r rotating about a fixed point is $a_t = r\alpha$, and similarly, the tangential acceleration of the end of a link of length l rotating about a point is $a_t = l\alpha$. If θ is defined as an angle from the horizontal x-axis, the x-component of acceleration is $a_x = a_t\sin\theta = l\alpha\sin\theta$, and the y-component is $a_y = a_t\cos\theta = l\alpha\cos\theta$. The angular acceleration of links 3 and 4, α_3 and α_4, are calculated from Eq. 43.53 and Eq. 43.54, respectively, when the angular acceleration of link 2, α_2, is known.

44 Hydraulic and Pneumatic Mechanisms

Nomenclature[a]

a	speed of sound	ft/sec	m/s
A	area[b]	ft^2	m^2
B	bulk modulus	lbf/ft^2	Pa
C	capacitance	F	F
C	corrosion allowance	in	mm
C_d	discharge coefficient	–	–
C_f	hydraulic compliance	ft^5/lbf	m^5/N
C_g	pneumatic compliance	lbm-ft^2/lbf	kg·m^2/N
d	inside diameter	ft	m
D	diameter	ft	m
D	outside diameter	ft	m
g	gravitational acceleration, 32.2 (9.81)	ft/sec^2	m/s^2
g_c	gravitational constant, 32.2	lbm-ft/lbf-sec^2	n.a.
h_f	head loss due to friction	ft	m
i	imaginary operator, $\sqrt{-1}$	–	–
I	effective (rms) line current	A	A
I	inertance (inductance)	lbf/ft^4	N/m^4
I_f	hydraulic inertance	lbf-sec^2/ft^5	N·s^2/m^5 (kg/m^4)
I_g	pneumatic inertance	lbf-sec^2/lbm-ft^2	N·s^2/kg·m^2
K	constant	various	various
L	length	ft	m
m	mass	lbm	kg
$\dot{m}$	mass flow rate	lbm/sec	kg/s
n	polytropic exponent	–	–
n	rotational speed	rpm	rpm
p	pressure	lbf/ft^2	Pa
pf	power factor	–	–
P	power	hp (ft-lbf/sec)	W
Q	flow rate (liquids)	gal/min	m^3/min
Q	flow rate (gases)	ft^3/sec	m^3/s
R	electrical resistance	Ω	Ω
R_f	hydraulic resistance	lbf-sec/ft^5	N·s/m^5
R_g	pneumatic resistance	lbf-sec/lbm-ft^2	N·s/kg·m^2
S	maximum allowable tensile stress	lbf/ft^2	Pa
S	strength	lbf/ft^2	Pa
t	nominal thickness	ft	m
t	time	sec	s
t'	design thickness	ft	m
T	torque	ft-lbf	N·m
U	energy	ft-lbf	J
v	velocity	ft/sec	m/s
V	capacity or volume	ft^3	m^3
V	effective (rms) line voltage	V	V
V	voltage	V	V
$\dot{V}$	volumetric flow rate	ft^3/sec	m^3/s
WHF	water hammer factor	–	–
x	distance	ft	m
X	reactance	lbf-sec/ft^5	N·s/m^5
y	temperature derating factor	–	–
Z	impedance	lbf-sec/ft^5	N·s/m^5

[a]Symbols and units consistent with the fluid power industry are used in this chapter.
[b]The symbol S is used in some references to designate surface area.

Symbols

β	compressibility	ft^2/lbf	1/Pa
η	efficiency	–	–
μ	absolute viscosity	lbf-sec/ft^2	Pa·s
ρ	density	lbm/ft^3	kg/m^3

Subscripts

f	hydraulic (liquid)
g	pneumatic (gas)

Mechanical/Design/Analysis

max   maximum
o   characteristic
ut   ultimate tensile

1. INTRODUCTION TO FLUID POWER[1]

Fluid power (*hydraulic power* or *power hydraulic*) *equipment* is hydraulically operating equipment that generates hydraulic pressure at one point in order to perform useful tasks at another. The equipment typically consists of a power source (i.e., an electric motor or internal combustion engine), pump, actuator cylinders or rotary fluid motors, control valves, high-pressure tubing or hose, fluid reservoir, and hydraulic fluid. (See Fig. 44.1.) During operation, the power source pressurizes the hydraulic fluid, and the control valves direct the fluid to the cylinders or hydraulic motors.

Figure 44.1 Typical Fluid Power Circuit

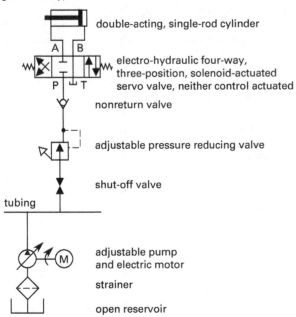

double-acting, single-rod cylinder

electro-hydraulic four-way, three-position, solenoid-actuated servo valve, neither control actuated

nonreturn valve

adjustable pressure reducing valve

shut-off valve

tubing

adjustable pump and electric motor

strainer

open reservoir

2. FLUID POWER SYMBOLS

Most symbols for fluid power equipment are simplified representations of their physical counterparts. Symbols have been standardized by the ANSI and ISO.[2]

3. HYDRAULIC FLUIDS

Petroleum-based oils and fire-resistant fluids are the two general categories of *hydraulic fluids*. Petroleum oils are enhanced with additives intended to inhibit or prevent rust, foam, wear, and oxidation. The largest drawback to petroleum oils, however, is flammability. *Fire-resistant fluids* are categorized as water and oil emulsions,[3] water-glycol mixtures, or straight synthetic fluids (e.g., silicone or phosphate esters, ester blends, and chlorinated hydrocarbon-based fluids).

In addition to cost, the properties most relevant in selecting hydraulic fluids are lubricity (i.e., the ability to reduce friction and prevent wear), viscosity, viscosity index,[4] pour point, flash point, rust resistance, oxidation resistance, and foaming resistance. Relative to petroleum oils, fire resistance is usually achieved to the detriment of the other properties.

Water-oil emulsions are the lowest-cost fire-resistant fluids. They generally perform as well as, or better than, most petroleum fluids.

Due to their similarity to standard antifreeze solutions, water-glycol mixtures are a good choice for low-temperature use. Periodic checking is required to monitor alkalinity and water evaporation. The water content should not be allowed to drop below approximately 35% to 50%.

Synthetic hydraulic fluids are the most costly of the fire-resistant fluids. They have high lubricity. Special formulations may be needed for low-temperature use, and their viscosity indexes are generally lower than those of petroleum oils. A significant factor is that they are not chemically consistent with the seal materials in use for petroleum oils.[5] Therefore, synthetics cannot be used in all existing systems.

The temperature of the hydraulic fluid entering the pump is typically 100°F to 120°F (38°C to 49°C). The temperature is commonly limited by most specifications to 120°F (49°C) for water-based fluids and 130°F (54°C) for all other fluids.

4. DESIGNATIONS OF HYDRAULIC OILS

In hydraulic applications, the type of fluid required is based on many factors, such as type of pump, type of center system (e.g., open/closed), accumulator and cylinder requirements, and use of oil coolers. Hydraulic fluids are identified by both Society of Automotive Engineers (SAE) and/or International Organization for

---

[1]Although the topics of "Hydraulic components" and "Pneumatic components" are included in the NCEES Mechanical CBT exam specifications, there is no content associated with these subjects in the NCEES *FE Reference Handbook* (*NCEES Handbook*).
[2]Refer to ANSI Y32.10 and ISO 1219.
[3]An emulsion of water in oil (as opposed to oil in water) is known as an *invert emulsion*.
[4]*Viscosity index* is the relative rate of change in viscosity with temperature. The viscosities of fluids with high viscosity indexes change less with variations in temperature than those of fluids with low viscosity indexes.
[5]Some of the seal materials that are suitable for use with synthetics include butyl rubber, ethylene-propylene rubber, silicone, Teflon™, and nylon.

Standardization (ISO) designations.[6] Both designations indicate the oil's useful operating range and simplify the selection and identification of an oil with a given viscosity index. The higher the viscosity number, the more viscous is the fluid. The SAE designation is known as the grade or weight.[7] A recommendation of SAE 10W, 20, or 20W is typical in hydraulic applications. An SAE 20 oil (grade 20 or 20 weight) has a viscosity index of approximately 100. Higher viscosity indexes, such as 120 or 160, are used in applications such as manual transmissions, gear driven transfer cases, and front/rear drive axles, but not as hydraulic fluid.

The *ISO viscosity grade* (VG) designation is similar in purpose and is recognized internationally. Designations 32, 46, and 68 are common specifications for hydraulic applications with vane, piston, and gear-type pumps. As shown in Table 44.1, an ISO 32 oil is equivalent to an SAE 10W oil. An ISO 68 oil is equivalent to an SAE 20W oil.

Table 44.1 *Typical Properties of ISO Hydraulic Oils*

ISO viscosity grade	equivalent SAE grade	absolute (dynamic) viscosity*				density	
		(cSt)		reyns × 10⁶ (lbf-sec/in²)			
		40°C	100°C	104°F	212°F	(kg/m³)	(lbm/ft³)
32	10W	32	5.4	4	0.6	857	53.6
46	20	46	6.8	5.7	0.8	861	53.7
68	20W	68	8.7	8.5	1.1	865	54.1
100	30	100	11.4	12.6	1.4	869	54.3
150	40	150	15	19	1.8	872	54.4
220	50	220	19.4	27.7	2.4	875	54.6

(Multiply cSt by 1.0764×10^{-5} to obtain ft²/sec.)
(Multiply lbm/ft³ by 16.018 to obtain kg/m³.)

*For convenience, viscosity in reyns has been increased by 10^6. Multiply table values by 10^{-6}.

5. CONTROL VALVES

Control valves are used to direct the flow of hydraulic fluid. *Pressure reduction valves* are used to reduce the pressure to components that cannot tolerate or do not need the full system pressure. *Pressure relief valves* are used to protect the system from dangerously high pressures.

Although seated poppet (globe, gate, and plunger) valves can be used, the *spool-type valve* is most common for channel selection and directional control.

Control valves are described according to their number of ports, their normal configuration, and their number of positions. The "way" of a control valve is equal to the number of ports. Thus, a three-way valve will have one port for pressurized fluid and two possible discharge ports. A four-way valve will have two ports for pressurized fluid and two discharge ports. If a valve prevents through-flow when de-energized (i.e., when off), it is designated as "normally closed" or "NC." If the valve permits through-flow when de-energized, it is designated as "normally open" or "NO."

In some valves, the fluid can be infinitely split between two discharge ports. In others, there are two distinct *positions*. Thus, a four-way, two-position valve (designated as a "4/2 valve") could switch the discharges completely.

A *three-way control valve* (*single-acting valve*) is commonly used to control a single-acting circuit. A *four-way valve* (*double-acting valve*) is typically used to control a double-acting circuit. There are several ways that a control valve in its neutral position can be designed to function. An *open-center valve* (*tandem-center valve*) is typically used with a fixed-displacement pump. In the neutral position, it allows hydraulic fluid to free-flow back to the tank. Shifting the spool position directs hydraulic fluid to the selected port. An *open-center-power-beyond valve* (*high-pressure carryover valve*) is similar to an open-center valve except that in the neutral position, hydraulic fluid flows to the downstream circuit instead of to the tank. A *closed-center valve* is typically used with a variable-displacement pump. Hydraulic fluid is blocked at the valve until the spool is moved out of the neutral position.

In the neutral position, a *motor-spool valve* (*free-flow valve*) allows hydraulic fluid to flow back to the tank. The operator is able to run a hydraulic motor under load and, when the valve is shifted back to neutral, the motor is allowed to coast to a stop. A *cylinder-spool valve* should be used in applications where a load is to be raised and held aloft with a hydraulic cylinder. With a cylinder-spool valve in its neutral position, fluid is blocked from flowing to the tank. This effectively locks the load in place.

6. TUBING, HOSE, AND PIPE FOR FLUID POWER

Carbon, alloy, and stainless steel fluid power tubings are available, particularly in the smaller sizes (e.g., up to approximately 2 in (50 mm) in diameter).[8] Fluid power

---

[6]In the United States, oils are also designated by their military performance numbers (e.g., MLL-PRF-87257).
[7]The designation "W" in SAE grades stands for "winter," not weight.
[8]Copper pipe may react with some hydraulic fluids and is rarely used.

tubing is available in two different pressure ratings: 0 psi to 1000 psi (0 MPa to 6.89 MPa) and 1000 psi to 2500 psi (6.89 MPa to 17.2 MPa).

Types S (seamless) and F (furnace butt-welded) varieties of A53 and A106 grade B black steel pipe can be used when larger diameter pipes are required.[9] The dimensions are the same as for normal steel pipe of the same schedule.

There are numerous types of flexible hose. Most are reinforced with steel wire, steel braid, or other high strength fiber. Fluid compatibility, bend radius, and operating pressure are selection criteria. The internal diameter of flexible hose is the hose's nominal size. When pressurized to more than 250 psi (1.7 MPa), the working pressure of hose is taken as 25% of the burst pressure.

7. PRESSURE RATING OF PIPE AND TUBING

Allowable working pressure (*pressure rating*) for pipe in fluid power systems is calculated in the same manner as that for pressure piping in other types of power piping systems.[10] The maximum working pressure is

$$p_{max} = \frac{2S(t' - C)}{D - 2y(t' - C)}$$

In the given equation, S is the maximum allowable stress. The maximum allowable stress depends on the metal composition and temperature, but since most fluid power systems run at approximately 100°F (38°C), the maximum stress corresponding to that temperature should be used. By convention, the maximum allowable stress is calculated as the ultimate tensile strength divided by a factor of safety (referred to as a *design factor*) of 3 or, occasionally, 4.[11] Values of 12,500 psi and 17,000 psi (86.1 MPa and 117 MPa) are commonly used for initial studies for A285 carbon steel pipes and tubes, and these values correspond to approximate factors of safety over the ultimate strength of 4 and 3, respectively.

In the given equation, t' is the *design wall thickness* and is calculated as 87.5% of the nominal wall thickness listed in the pipe tables. C is an allowance for bending, production variations, corrosion, threading, and variations in mechanical strength. A value of $C = 0.05$ in (1.27 mm) is appropriate for threaded steel tubes up to

⅜ in (9.525 mm) diameter. For larger threaded steel tubes, C is equal to the depth of the thread in inches (millimeters). $C = 0.05$ in (1.27 mm) for unthreaded steel tubes up to 0.5 in (12.7 mm). $C = 0.065$ in (1.651 mm) for unthreaded steel tubes 1¼ in (31.75 mm) and larger. For both ferritic and austenitic steels, y is 0.4 for operation at temperatures common to fluid power systems, up to 900°F (480°C). For operation at 950°F (510°C), $y = 0.5$. For 1000°F (540°C and above), $y = 0.7$.[12]

The given equation is a code-based approach to calculating the working pressure. Three other theoretical methods are also used, primarily with steel hydraulic tubing connected with flared fittings, to calculate the working pressure.[13] Dimensions used in the Barlow, Boardman, and Lamé formulas are nominal, tabulated values. The *Barlow formula* is the standard thin-wall cylinder formula.

$$p = \frac{2St}{D}$$

The *Boardman formula* is

$$p = \frac{2St}{D - 0.8t}$$

The *Lamé formula* is

$$p = \frac{S(D^2 - d^2)}{D^2 + d^2}$$

Since power fluid systems are subject to rapid valve closures, the pressures calculated from the given equations must be reduced for the effect of water hammer. The amount of reduction for water hammer is calculated from the *water hammer factor*, WHF, the ratio of pressure (in psi) to flow rate (in gpm).[14] The derating in working stress due to water hammer is

$$\Delta p_{psi} = (WHF) Q_{gpm}$$

The working pressure after water hammer may be further reduced for connections and fittings. The amount of the reduction is approximately 25%.

---

[9]The "grade" of a steel is usually its tensile strength in ksi. For example, the tensile strength of A516 grade 60 steel is 60 ksi. The materials, grades, specifications, classes, and types of steel pipes and tubes are easily confused. A285, A515, and A516 are common designations for the carbon steel used in pipes and tubes. The grade of the material may relate to its tensile strength, ductility, or other property. Additional specifications may apply to the manufacturer of the pipe. A285 pipe, for example, is often specified according to the additional specifications A53 and A106. The type (e.g., F or S) relates to how seams are formed.

[10]ASA B31.1.1

[11]The abbreviations SMYS and SMTS stand for "standard minimum yield strength" and "standard minimum tensile strength," respectively.

[12]Values of C and y are specified by Part 2 of ASME's *Code for Power Piping* (ASME B31.1).

[13]Tubing must conform to SAE J524, J525, and J356.

[14]Including an allowance for water hammer should be based on the type of fluid system, not just on the material used for the pipe or tube. Some sources suggest that the allowance for water hammer should be included only with cast-iron pipes. While it is true that most cast irons experience brittle (not ductile) failure, omitting the pressure increase with ductile pipes denies that water hammer actually occurs.

8. BURST PRESSURE

The *burst pressure* is calculated from the following equation, which is derived from the thin-walled cylinder theory. S_{ut} is the ultimate tensile strength.

$$p_{burst} = \frac{2S_{ut}t}{D}$$

9. FLUID POWER PUMPS

Most fluid power pumps are positive displacement pumps. Rotary and reciprocating designs are both used. All of the standard formulas for pump performance (horsepower, torque, etc.) apply. For example, the horsepower needed to drive the pump is given by the following equation. η_{pump} is commonly taken as 0.85.

$$P_{hp} = \frac{p_{psi}Q_{gpm}}{1714\eta_{pump}}$$

The torque on the pump shaft is

$$T_{in\text{-}lbf} = p_{psi}\left(\frac{\text{displacement in }\frac{in^3}{rev}}{2\pi}\right) = \frac{63,025P_{hp}}{n_{rpm}}$$

$$= \frac{36.77Q_{gpm}p_{psi}}{n_{rpm}}$$

The flow rate in pumps is related to the displacement per revolution by

$$Q_{gpm} = \frac{n_{rpm}\left(\text{displacement in }\frac{in^3}{rev}\right)}{231}$$

To prevent cavitation, the flow velocity in suction lines is generally limited by specification to 1 ft/sec to 5 ft/sec (0.3 m/s to 1.5 m/s). The flow velocity in discharge lines is limited to 10 ft/sec to 15 ft/sec (3 m/s to 4.5 m/s).[15] The actual fluid velocity can easily be calculated from

$$v_{ft/sec} = \frac{0.3208Q_{gpm}}{A_{in^2}}$$

When starting a hydraulic pump, the fluid viscosity should be 4000 SSU (870 cS) or less. During steady operation at higher temperaures, viscosity should be above 70 SSU (13 cS).

Pump life is a term that refers to bearing life in hours. Most bearings have a *rated life* at some specific speed and pressure. The rated (bearing) life can be modified for other speeds and pressures with

$$\text{life} = (\text{rated life})\left(\frac{\text{rated speed}}{\text{actual speed}}\right)\left(\frac{\text{rated pressure}}{\text{actual pressure}}\right)^3$$

Bearing life predictions for pump applications are the same as for other applications.

10. ELECTRIC MOTORS

The power needed to drive a hydraulic pump is given by

$$P_{hp} = \frac{p_{psi}Q_{gpm}}{1714\eta_{pump}}$$

Since motors are rated by their developed power, the given equation also specifies the minimum motor size. Most fixed (i.e., not mobile) fluid power pumps are driven by single- or three-phase induction motors. Table 44.2 can be used to solve for typical electrical parameters describing the performance of an induction motor.[16]

Table 44.2 *Electric Motor Variables**

find	given	single-phase	three-phase
I_{amps}	P_{hp}	$\frac{746P_{hp}}{V\eta(pf)}$	$\frac{746P_{hp}}{\sqrt{3}\,V\eta(pf)}$
I_{amps}	P_{kW}	$\frac{1000P_{kW}}{V(pf)}$	$\frac{1000P_{kW}}{\sqrt{3}\,V(pf)}$
I_{amps}	P_{kVA}	$\frac{1000P_{kVA}}{V}$	$\frac{1000P_{kVA}}{\sqrt{3}\,V}$
P_{kW}		$\frac{IV(pf)}{1000}$	$\frac{\sqrt{3}\,IV(pf)}{1000}$
P_{kVA}		$\frac{IV}{1000}$	$\frac{\sqrt{3}\,IV}{1000}$
P_{hp}		$\frac{IV\eta(pf)}{746}$	$\frac{\sqrt{3}\,IV\eta(pf)}{746}$

*η is the motor efficiency.
(Multiply hp by 0.7457 to obtain kW.)

11. STRAINERS AND FILTERS

Although fluid power systems are theoretically closed, they are never free from dirt, grit, and metal particles. Although cold-formed tubes are essentially free of

---

[15]Velocities could be faster—up to 25 ft/sec (7.5 m/s)—but are limited to the lower values in order to prevent excessive friction and noise.
[16]"Line voltage" and "line-to-line voltage" are synonymous terms. There is also a "phase voltage" in three-phase systems. Wye-connected sources are commonly in use, so phase and line voltage are related by $V_{line} = \sqrt{3}\,V_{phase}$.

internal scale, hot-rolled tubes will always have some inside and outside scale. Power systems in daily use should be protected by a 1 μm filter. Backup and occasional-use systems may be able to use a 25 μm filter.

A filter installed in the suction line will protect all components but will contribute to suction pressure loss. For that reason, it is common practice to install the filter after the pump, protecting all components except the pump. The pump is protected by a coarse screen in the suction line.

The maximum permissible pressure drop across a new and clean suction strainer or filter installed below the fluid level (i.e., submerged) is commonly limited by specification to 0.25 psi (1.7 kPa) for fire-resistant fluids and 0.50 psi (3.4 kPa) for all others.

12. ACCUMULATORS

Accumulators store potential energy in the form of pressurized hydraulic fluid. They are commonly used with intermittent duty cycles or to provide emergency power.[17] However, they can also be used to compensate for leakage, act as shock absorbers, and dampen pulsations.

The three basic types of accumulators are weight loaded, mechanical spring loaded, and gas loaded (i.e., hydropneumatic). *Hydropneumatic accumulators*, where pistons, diaphragms, or bladders separate the hydraulic fluid from the gas, are (by far) the most common.[18,19] Most accumulators are high-pressure tanks and, as such, should conform to ASME's *Code for Unfired Pressure Vessels*.

The volume of hydraulic fluid released by or captured in an accumulator is equal to the change in volume of the compressed gas. Compression and expansion of the gas in an accumulator is governed by standard thermodynamic principles. However, calculation of volumetric changes is complicated by the speed of the process, since the gas may heat or cool during the volume change.

13. LINEAR ACTUATORS AND CYLINDERS

Linear actuators (e.g., *hydraulic rams* and *hydraulic cylinders*) are the most common type of fluid power actuators.[20]

14. PNEUMATIC SYSTEMS

Pneumatic systems are fluid power systems that transfer energy using compressed gas (usually, air) as the working fluid.[21] Pneumatic systems require air compressors (instead of fluid pumps) and solenoid valves, but they are otherwise analogous to fluid power systems. Pneumatic systems require *filter-regulator-lubricator* (FRL) components to assure a clean, lubricated supply of air at constant pressure. Compressors and FRL components are rarely shown on pneumatic schematics. Pneumatic systems can be constructed to exhaust the gas (as to the atmosphere) directly without needing to have fluid return systems. Unlike hydraulic fluid applications that operate between 1000 psig and 10,000 psig (6.9 MPa and 69 MPa), most industrial pneumatic applications operate with gas pressures between 80 psig and 1000 psig (550 kPa and 690 kPa). Due to the gas compressibility, pneumatic systems operate more slowly than liquid-based systems using liquid.

Kinetic energy (inertance, inductance) terms are negligible because gas masses are small. Gravimetric (i.e., mass) flow, not volumetric flow, is conserved, since the working fluid is compressible. Gas flow can be laminar, but it is almost always turbulent.[22] Movement of gas within the system may be subsonic or supersonic.

15. MODELING HYDRAULIC AND PNEUMATIC SYSTEMS

In hydraulic and pneumatic systems, work and power are functions of pressure primarily, and as such, pressure is referred to as the *effort variable*. The product of pressure, p, and volumetric flow rate, $\dot{V}$, is fluid power, much like force × velocity in mechanical systems and voltage × current in electrical systems. The power, P, available at a point in a system where the pressure is p is

$$P = pA\,\mathrm{v} = p\dot{V}$$

In addition to using the given equation and continuity of mass and continuity of energy equations, performance of fluid and pneumatic power systems can be analyzed using lumped-parameter models. In a *lumped-parameter model*, a system is divided into small segments (i.e., lumps) that contain one or more components. Although the pressure and velocity can vary with time within the

---

[17]Use of accumulators is becoming less common.
[18]Reactive gases, such as hydrogen and oxygen, should never be used as accumulator gases.
[19]Spring and weight-loaded accumulators are much rarer.
[20]Strictly speaking, a hydraulic motor is a rotary actuator or "linear motor."
[21]Oxygen-free nitrogen (OFN), a compressed gas supplied in bottled form, may be used for convenience or where flammability is an issue. Inert gases, primarily argon, may be used in aerospace applications where minimal chemical reactivity is needed.
[22]If the gas is incompressible and the flow is laminar, the *Hagen-Poiseuille formula* can be used.

$$\dot{V} = \frac{\pi D^4}{128\mu L}\Delta p$$

$$R_f = \frac{\Delta p}{\dot{V}} = \frac{128\mu L}{\pi D^4}$$

system, they are considered instantaneously fixed within the lump. The direction of flow is assumed to be one-dimensional. The concepts of fluid and pneumatic resistance, capacitance, and inductance are easily derived for the lump. Whether all three concepts are used to model a particular system depends on the judgment of the modeller.

In traditional fluid flow analysis of turbulent flow, the relationship between pressure drop and volumetric flow is nonlinear. Specifically, $h_f \propto \mathrm{v}^2$. A relationship similar to $Q = K\sqrt{\Delta p}$ is usually expected. However, for simplicity in fluid power analyses, the relationships are often assumed to be linear over small variations in pressure. This assumption is valid in laminar flow (as in flow through capillary tubes), but it is a convenient simplification otherwise.

Since hydraulic fluid is essentially incompressible, fluid power system component and system models are based on the volumetric flow rate, Q.[23] Gases in pneumatic systems are compressible, so component and system models are based on mass flow rate, $\dot{m} = \rho \dot{V}$. As shown in Table 44.3, the characteristic equations are similar for hydraulic and pneumatic systems except for the use of basic variable.

Table 44.3 Characteristic Equations of Fluid and Pneumatic Power Systems

component	hydraulic fluid power	pneumatic fluid power
resistance, R	$Q = \dfrac{p_1 - p_2}{R_f}$	$\dot{m} = \dfrac{p_1 - p_2}{R_g}$
capacitance (compliance), C	$Q = C_f \dfrac{d}{dt}(p_1 - p_2)$	$Q = C_f \dfrac{d}{dt}(p_1 - p_2)$
inductance (inertance), I	$Q = \dfrac{1}{I_g}\displaystyle\int (p_1 - p_2)\, dt$	$\dot{m} = \dfrac{1}{I_g}\displaystyle\int (p_1 - p_2)\, dt$

16. FLUID RESISTANCE

Dissipation of energy in the form of heat occurs to some extent in all fluid systems. *Fluid resistance* (*hydraulic resistance*) represents the energy-dissipation aspect of a system, corresponding to friction and electrical resistance in mechanical and electrical systems.[24] Analogous to electrical systems ($V_1 - V_2 = IR$), the driving force in hydraulic systems is a pressure difference, and flow, Q, is resisted by hydraulic resistance, R_f. The units of hydraulic resistance are lbf-sec/ft^5 (N·s/m^5).

$$p_1 - p_2 = QR_f$$

Power dissipation in a hydraulic resistance is

$$P = Q\Delta p = Q^2 R_f = \frac{\Delta p^2}{R_f}$$

In pneumatic systems, pressure difference is correlated with mass flow rate. Pressure drops across components in subsonic pneumatic systems are usually small and fluctuate with time about a steady-state value. For turbulent flow, the pressure drop can be predicted by the following equation, where R_g is the *pneumatic resistance to gas flow*. The units of pneumatic resistance are lbf-sec/lbm-ft^2 (N·s/kg·m^2).

$$p_1 - p_2 = \dot{m} R_g$$

Power dissipation, P, in a hydraulic resistance is

$$P = \dot{V}\Delta p = \frac{\dot{m}\Delta p}{\rho} = \frac{\Delta p^2}{R_g}$$

17. FLUID FLOW THROUGH AN ORIFICE

A valve or other flow restriction in a hydraulic system can be modelled as an orifice.[25] Flow through orifices is highly turbulent, and the mass flow rate depends on an experimentally determined *discharge coefficient*, C_d, to account for geometric and frictional effects. The product of the discharge coefficient and the orifice area, $C_d A$, is known as the *effective cross-sectional area*. The common formula for discharge of an incompressible fluid through an orifice is[26]

$$Q = C_d A \sqrt{\frac{2\Delta p}{\rho}}$$

18. FLUID COMPLIANCE

Fluid compliance (*fluid capacitance*) of a pipe, tank, actuator, or other system is the ratio of change in stored volume (for hydraulic systems) or mass (to pneumatic systems) to change in pressure. The units of hydraulic compliance, C_f, are ft^5/lbf (m^5/N). For a hydraulic component, the fluid compliance is defined by

$$C_f = \frac{dV}{dp} = \frac{dV}{dt}\frac{dt}{dp} = Q\frac{dt}{dp}$$

---

[23]Lowercase q is also encountered as the variable for volumetric flow rate in fluid power applications.

[24]Although the term "fluid resistance" is used, both the component and the fluid contribute to resistance.

[25]It will be necessary to determine the discharge coefficient and/or effective area, $C_d A$, of the valve experimentally.

[26]This is the common *Torricelli equation* derived from energy relationships.

The volumetric flow through a component is

$$\Delta Q = Q_1 - Q_2 = C_f \frac{dp}{dt} = C_f \frac{d}{dt}(p_1 - p_2)$$

Fluid compliance is composed of two parts, the *mechanical compliance* from volume change of the container, and the *compressibility compliance* due to fluid's density change.[27] Some compliance derives from the flexibility of the container wall, but even when a pipe or tank is perfectly rigid, the fluid itself has compliance by virtue of its compressibility. This compressibility compliance depends on the fluid's *bulk modulus*, B, and is given by

$$C_{f,\text{compressibility}} = \frac{V}{B} = \frac{AL}{B} = \beta AL$$

A typical bulk modulus for hydraulic fluid is 250,000 psi (1.7 GPa). The reciprocal of bulk modulus is the *compressibility*, β. Compressibility effects are small and are generally disregarded in hydraulic systems.

$$\beta = \frac{1}{B}$$

The compliance of an open tank or reservoir with vertical walls and cross-sectional area, A, whose liquid contents are allowed to change in depth is

$$C_{f,\text{reservoir}} = \frac{A}{\rho g}$$

The energy stored in a hydraulic capacitance by virtue of fluid pressurization is

$$U_f = \tfrac{1}{2} C_f p^2$$

For a pneumatic component with a fixed volume, V, holding a gas with density, ρ, the *pneumatic compliance*, C_g, is defined in terms of the mass, not volume. The compressibility of gases introduces substantial compliance into a system, which adds to the mechanical compliance from variable-volume components such as air bags, bellows, spring-loaded accumulators, and rubber hoses. The compliance is a function of the gas properties and process, as well as the component geometry. The units of pneumatic compliance, C_g, are lbm-ft^2/lbf (kg·m^2/N).

$$C_g = \frac{dm}{dp} = C_{g,\text{mechanical}} + C_{g,\text{compressibility}}$$

For a fixed-volume system, the pneumatic compliance is

$$C_{g,\text{compressibility}} = \frac{dm}{dp} = V\frac{d\rho}{dp} \quad [\text{fixed-volume system}]$$

The mass flow rate through a component with fixed volume is

$$\dot{m} = \frac{dm}{dt} = \frac{dm}{dp}\frac{dp}{dt} = C_g \frac{dp}{dt}$$

The density change depends on the nature of the process. The compliance of a system where a perfect gas in a fixed-volume system experiences a polytropic process is given by the equation below. For a constant pressure process where $n = 0$, pneumatic compliance is infinite. For a constant volume process where $n = \infty$, pneumatic compliance is zero.

$$C_{g,\text{compressibility}} = \frac{m}{np} = \frac{mV}{npV} = \frac{V}{nRT}$$
$$= \frac{kV}{na^2} = \frac{V\rho}{np}$$

Energy, U_g, stored in a pneumatic capacitance by virtue of pressurization is

$$U_g = \frac{C_g p^2}{2\rho}$$

Figure 44.2 illustrates a simple elastic *bellows* of constant cross-sectional area, A, that expands in the longitudinal, x, direction. The mechanical compliance is nonlinear and varies with the displacement, x. The pneumatic compliance is

$$C_{g,\text{mechanical}} = \frac{dm}{dp} = \frac{V}{RT} = \frac{Ax}{RT}$$

Figure 44.2 Pneumatic Bellows

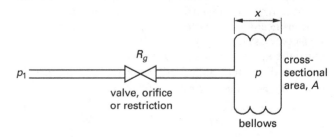

---

[27]Even incompressible fluids may exhibit substantial compliance if they cavitate or contain gas bubbles.

HYDRAULIC AND PNEUMATIC MECHANISMS

19. FLUID INERTANCE

Fluid inertance (also known as *fluid inductance*), I, accounts for the pressure needed to accelerate a lump of gas (fluid).[28] Fluid inertance may be relevant in some systems, particularly those involving transient effects and high frequency behavior, as with sudden on and off valve operation. However, in the simplest models of hydraulic systems, inertance is neglected because the high pressures negate the inertial effects. In pneumatic systems, fluid inertia is neglected due to the low density and low mass of the fluid. The units of hydraulic inertance, I_f, are lbf-sec^2/ft^5 (N·s^2/m^5); the units of *pneumatic inertance*, I_g, are lbf-sec^2/lbm-ft^2 (N·s^2/kg·m^2).

$$I_f = \frac{p_1 - p_2}{\dfrac{dQ}{dt}} \quad \text{[hydraulic]}$$

$$I_g = \frac{p_1 - p_2}{\dfrac{d\dot{m}}{dt}} = \frac{p_1 - p_2}{\dfrac{d\rho\dot{V}}{dt}} \quad \text{[pneumatic]}$$

20. FLUID IMPEDANCE

Fluid impedance, Z, is a complex quantity having both a magnitude and a phase angle derived from the fluid resistance and *fluid reactance*, X. In fluid power systems, the impedance acts in a complicated manner to convert changes in pressure to changes in flow rate. The magnitude portion of the impedance affects the quantity of fluid flow, while the phase angle affects the timing of the fluid flow. For example, the volume of fluid flowing out of an orifice depends on the orifice's resistance, while changes in the flow rate depend on the phase angle and do not instantaneously correspond to changes in pressure.

$$\mathbf{Z} \equiv Z\angle\phi \equiv R + iX$$

Reactance is derived mathematically from the compliance and inertance of the system. Reactance depends on the frequency of energy input. In the absence of specific information about the nature (periodicity, waveform, etc.) of the applied pressure variations, the fluid reactance cannot be evaluated. For fluid power systems that are dominated by fluid resistance (in comparison to fluid compliance and inertance), the magnitude of impedance is simply the fluid resistance, R_f or R_g. Therefore, in all but the most rigorous, complex, and esoteric analyses, the term "resistance" can be substituted for "impedance" in descriptions of fluid power.[29]

The impedance of an infinitely long transmission path (pipe or duct) is referred to as the *characteristic impedance* (or, *surge impedance, hydraulic impedance*), Z_o. The magnitude of the characteristic impedance of a hydraulic system is

$$Z_o = \sqrt{\frac{1}{C}} = \frac{\rho a}{A} = \frac{1}{A}\sqrt{\rho B}$$

Prime movers (pumps and compressors) have their own impedances. For maximum power transfer, the output impedance of a prime mover should be the same as the input impedance of the system it is connected to.

Mechanical/
Design/Analysis

---

[28]L is the common symbol for inductance. In fluid and pneumatic systems, the symbol I is based on the synonym, inertance.
[29]It will be clear when "impedance" is not synonymous with "resistance." Rigorous, complex, and esoteric analyses are those that involve concepts such as transfer functions, differential equations, Laplace transforms, transient analysis, and frequency response curves.

45 Pressure Vessels

Nomenclature

d	diameter	in	mm
D	inside diameter	in	mm
E	efficiency	–	–
h	depth of head	in	mm
h_G	gasket moment arm	in	mm
L	crown radius	in	mm
p	pressure[a][b]	lbf/in²	Pa
r	radius	in	mm
R	inside radius	in	mm
t	thickness	in	mm

[a]The variable for pressure in the *ASME Boiler and Pressure Vessel Code* is uppercase *P*. A lowercase *p* is used in this chapter for consistency with the rest of this book.
[b]All pressures expressed in this chapter are gage pressures.

Symbol

α	one-sided taper angle (half of apex angle)	deg	deg

Subscripts

h	head
k	knuckle

1. INTRODUCTION[1]

The American Society of Mechanical Engineers (ASME) established its Boiler and Pressure Vessel Committee in 1911. The Committee establishes rules governing the design, fabrication, inspection, and repair of boilers and pressure vessels and interprets these rules when questions arise. The rules constitute the *ASME Boiler and Pressure Vessel Code* (BPVC and "Code").

This chapter covers only pressure vessels with curved shells that are under internal pressure and are designed in accordance with Sec. VIII, "Pressure Vessels," Div. 1. BPVC Sec. VIII, Div. 1 covers pressure vessels operating between 15 psig and 3000 psig (103 kPa and 20.7 MPa). BPVC Sec. VIII covers nonnuclear applications.

2. MARKING REQUIREMENTS

Pressure vessels must be permanently marked with information about their construction and type of service. This information may be stamped on the vessel in a conspicuous location (e.g., near an opening or manway) or may be on a permanently attached nameplate as shown in Fig. 45.1.

Figure 45.1 *Typical Nameplate*

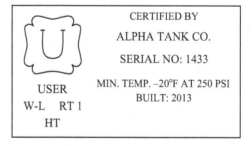

```
              CERTIFIED BY
  ┌─┐
  │U│         ALPHA TANK CO.
  └─┘
              SERIAL NO: 1433

   USER      MIN. TEMP. –20°F AT 250 PSI
                  BUILT: 2013
 W-L   RT 1

   HT
```

A *nameplate* describing a pressure vessel is attached directly to the shell.[2] The nameplate of a pressure vessel designed and constructed in accordance with the BPVC will contain the official "U" stamp and all of the following: manufacturer's name (listed after the words "certified by"), vessel serial number, year built, maximum allowable working pressure and corresponding temperature, and minimum design metal temperature and

---

[1]Although the topic of "Pressure vessels" is included in the NCEES Mechanical CBT exam specifications, there is no content associated with this subject in the NCEES *FE Reference Handbook* (*NCEES Handbook*).
[2]Duplicate nameplates on supports or at other locations must be marked "Duplicate."

corresponding pressure.[3] For pressure vessels that are intended for service below −20°F (−29°C), the minimum allowable temperature is also listed.

The method of construction and type of service must also be listed. One or more of the following abbreviations will be used: W, arc or gas welded; RES, resistance welded; B, brazed; L, lethal service; UB, unfired steam boiler; DF, direct firing; RT-1, fully radiographed; RT-2, some joints partially radiographed; RT-3, spot radiographed; RT-4, radiographed but other categories not applicable; HT, postweld heat treated; or PHT, parts of vessel heat treated.

3. DESIGN ELEMENTS

Figure 45.2 illustrates the various parts of a pressure vessel. The pressure vessel can be divided into shell-type and plate-type elements. A *shell-type element* resists internal pressure through tension (i.e., "membrane action"). A *plate-type element* resists internal pressure through bending. Shell-type elements can be cylindrical, spherical, ellipsoidal, torispherical, or toriconical.

The main body of a pressure vessel is known as the *shell*. A shell can be seamless or seamed. External pipes and equipment are connected to a pressure vessel at *nozzles*. Seamless pipe used for a nozzle is an example of a *seamless shell*.

4. SERVICE APPLICATION

Special restrictions are placed on vessels that contain lethal substances, operate below −20°F (−29°C), are used for steam generation, or are subject to direct firing.

5. MATERIALS

Pressure vessels can be constructed from various materials including carbon steel, low-alloy steel, high-alloy steel, nonferrous metal, cast iron, and integrally clad-plate. The BPVC specifies which materials and at what temperatures these materials can be used. To ensure compatibility in welding, material categories are designated by P-numbers, as shown in Table 45.1.

Table 45.1 *Material Designations*

designation	material
P-1	carbon steels with tensile strengths between 40,000 lbf/in² and 75,000 lbf/in² (276 MPa and 517 MPa)
P-3	alloy steel with up to $\frac{3}{4}$% chromium; alloy steels with up to 2% total alloying ingredients
P-4	alloy steel with chromium between $\frac{3}{4}$% and 2%; alloy steels with more than 2% total alloying ingredients
P-5	alloy steels with up to 10% total alloying ingredients
P-8	austenitic stainless steels
P-9	nickel alloy steels
P-10	other steel alloys

Carbon steels are the most common material chosen for noncorrosive environments between −20°F and 800°F (−29°C and 426°C). However, carbon steel weakens with long exposure to temperatures higher than 785°F (418°C) through a process known as *graphitization*. For service above 800°F (426°C), materials must be selected carefully.

6. HEADS

Heads may be spherical, ellipsoidal, torispherical, conical, or flat, as shown in Fig. 45.3. Ellipsoidal and hemispherical heads are common, while torispherical heads appear more frequently in thin vessels.

Torispherical (i.e., *flanged and dished*) *heads* are specified by their inside diameter, D, crown (dish) radius, L, knuckle radius, r_k, and head thickness, t_h. These variables are shown in Fig. 45.3. An *ASME flanged and dished head* is a torispherical head for which the knuckle radius is 6% of the inside crown radius. *2:1 ellipsoidal heads* have a radius that is twice the height (projection) and are more economical than deeper hemispherical heads.

When a head is no thicker than its shell, the head does not need a flange and may be butt-welded to the shell. In practice, however, most nonhemispherical heads have *straight flanges* (i.e., straight longitudinal necks).

---

[3]It has been common in some metric countries to specify pressure in either bars or kilograms per square cm (kg/cm²). Multiply lbf/in² by 0.06895 to obtain bars. Multiply lbf/in² by 0.07031 to obtain kg/cm².

Figure 45.2 *Parts of a Pressure Vessel*

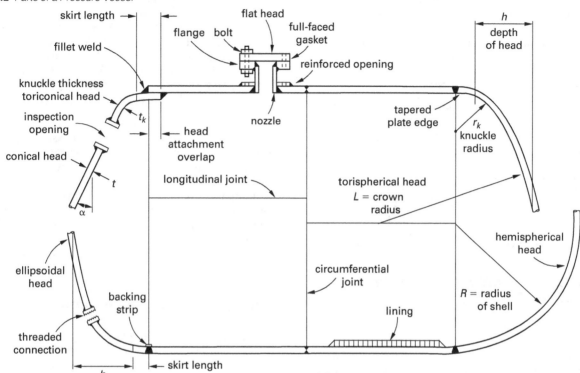

Reproduced from R. Chuse and S. Eber, *Pressure Vessels*, sixth ed., copyright © 1984, with permission of the publisher, McGraw-Hill.

Figure 45.3 *Head Shapes*

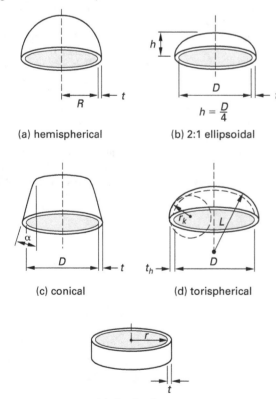

(a) hemispherical

(b) 2:1 ellipsoidal

$h = \frac{D}{4}$

(c) conical

(d) torispherical

(e) circular flat

7. SHAKEDOWN AND RATCHETING

Pressure vessels often experience repeated cycles of pressurization/depressurization and heating/cooling. A vessel's response can be categorized as shakedown or ratcheting, as defined in BPVC Sec. VIII, Div. 2, Part 5.12. (See Fig. 45.4.) Paraphrasing, *shakedown* is caused by cyclic loads or cyclic temperature distributions that produce plastic deformations at a point when the loading or temperature distribution is applied, but upon removal of the loading or temperature distribution, only elastic primary and secondary stresses remain at that point, except in small areas associated with local stress (strain) concentrations. These small areas exhibit a stable hysteresis loop, with no indication of progressive advancement. Further loading and unloading, or applications and removals of the temperature distribution, produce only elastic primary and secondary stresses. Shakedown is not a failure mode, although it does justify using fatigue curve data.

Paraphrasing, *ratcheting* is a progressive, incremental, inelastic deformation or strain that occurs at a point subjected to cycles of thermal stress or cycles of mechanical stress superimposed on a mean stress, or both. (*Thermal stress ratcheting* is partly or wholly caused by thermal stress.) Ratcheting is produced by a sustained load acting over the full cross section at that point, in combination with a strain-controlled cyclic load or temperature distribution that is alternately applied and removed. Ratcheting causes cyclic straining of the material, which can result in failure by fatigue and, at the same time, produces cyclic incremental growth of a failure mechanism, which can ultimately lead to collapse. Ratcheting is a failure mode as it refers to incremental growth in gross dimensions.

Figure 45.4 *Shakedown and Ratcheting*

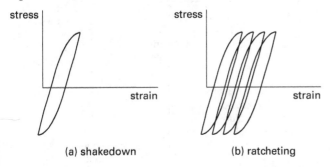

(a) shakedown   (b) ratcheting

8. MAXIMUM ALLOWABLE WORKING PRESSURE

The *maximum allowable working pressure* (MAWP) is specified by the manufacturer. It is the maximum pressure permissible at the top of the vessel in its normal operating position and temperature, in corroded condition, and while under the effects of other expected loadings (e.g., wind and external pressure).[4] MAWP is calculated for different parts of the pressure vessel based on BPVC equations adjusted for static head. The overall MAWP is the smallest of the adjusted values. The maximum allowable working pressure is the design pressure in the thickness equations.

The term *maximum allowable pressure new and cold* (MAWP N&C), is specified by the manufacturer. It is the maximum pressure for the vessel when new (not corroded) and at room temperature.

9. DESIGN PRESSURE AND TEMPERATURE

The BPVC requires that pressure vessels be designed for the most severe combination of pressure and temperature that will be encountered during normal operation, regardless of whether the combination is short term or infrequent.

The maximum design temperature must not be less than the mean metal temperature under expected operating conditions. The *minimum design metal temperature* (MDMT) is the lowest expected service temperature, except where a lower value is allowed by the BPVC. The MDMT marked on the nameplate will correspond to an associated MAWP. As temperature can vary with location and through the thickness, the mean temperature is specified on the nameplate.

The *operating pressure, p,* is the pressure on the top of the vessel at which the vessel normally operates. The maximum difference in pressures between the inside and outside of a vessel or between any two chambers of a combination vessel should also be evaluated. The *design pressure* is the operating pressure plus a reasonable safety margin.[5] Frequently, the design pressure is equal to the MAWP. The design pressure and MDMT are used to determine the minimum allowable thickness of the vessel.

10. CORROSION ALLOWANCE

An optional *corrosion allowance* compensates for any wall thinning expected over the lifetime of the vessel. The BPVC does not provide guidance in determining the allowance.

11. WELD TYPES

The BPVC specified six types of weld joints. Type 1 weld joints are double-welded butt joints. The quality of weld is the same inside and outside of the vessel with double-welded butt joints. Backing strips, if used, are removed after welding. After the weld is made on one side, the second side of the joint is cleaned and rewelded. The weld quality is identical on both sides of the joint. Type 2 welds are single-welded butt joints with backing strips that remain in place after welding. Type 3 welds are single-welded butt joints without backing strips. Type 4 joints are double full-fillet lap joints. Type 5 joints are single full-fillet lap joints with plug welds. Type 6 joints are single full-fillet lap joints without plug welds. The weld types are shown in Fig. 45.5 with their typical welding symbols.[6]

---

[4]A pressure vessel can have more than one operating temperature and hence, more than one MAWP.
[5]A reasonable safety margin is 10% or 25 lbf/in² (170 kPa), whichever is greater.
[6]Standard American Welding Society (AWS) symbols are used.

Figure 45.5 *Types of Welds and Symbols*

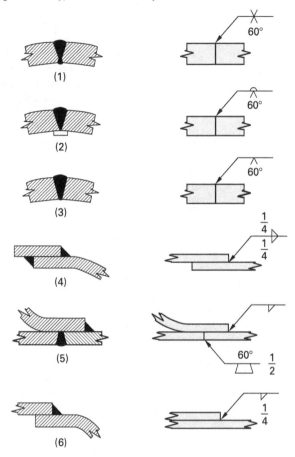

Designations: 1, double-weld butt joint; 2, single-weld butt joint with integral backing strip; 3, single-weld butt joint without backing strip; 4, double-full fillet lap joint; 5, single-full fillet lap joint with plug welds; 6, single-full fillet lap joint without plug welds.

12. JOINT EFFICIENCY

Welded joints are common in the construction of pressure vessels. These joints can be of several different types and subjected to different degrees of radiographic inspection. The type and quality of the weld will affect its ability to reach the strength of the parent material. Consequently, the joint efficiency, E, is used in many calculations as a derating factor. For welded joints subjected to tension, efficiency values depend on the type of weld and inspection (typically radiography) performed.[7] The strongest joints are double-welded butt joints (joint type 1).

13. WELD EXAMINATION

Common methods of *nondestructive examination* (NDE) used on welded joints of pressure vessels are radiography and ultrasonic examination.[8,9] Full radiographic inspection of joints is mandatory for (1) all longitudinal welds and welds at openings when the joint efficiency is taken as 1.0 or 0.9; (2) all butt welds joined by electrogas welding with any single pass greater than $1\frac{1}{2}$ in (38 mm) and all electrogas welds; (3) with some exceptions, all butt welds where the material thickness exceeds $1\frac{1}{2}$ in (38 mm); (4) all butt welds in the head and shells of unfired steam boilers with design pressures exceeding 50 psig (345 kPa); and (5) all butt welds in vessels containing lethal substances.[10]

Spot radiographic inspection can be used to obtain an economical spot check of welding quality.

Radiographic inspection is optional for butt-welded joints that are not required to be fully radiographed, and is not required when the vessel is designed for external pressure or when the joint has been designed (i.e., the joint efficiency value has been chosen) for no inspection.

Full ultrasonic inspection is required for electroslag and electrogas welds in ferritic material.

The *RT marking system* is used to indicate the extent of radiographic examination. "RT-1" means 100% of all longitudinal and circumferential seams were radiographed. It also indicates that 100% of nozzle welds over 1.0 in (25 mm) diameter were radiographed. This level is considered "full radiography" and results in a 1.0 joint efficiency on all welds. RT-1 is mandatory for head/shell thicknesses greater than 1.25 in (32 mm). (Vessels designed to BPVC Sec. I and certain nozzles require 100% RT on circumferential and longitudinal seams.) "RT-2" means 100% of longitudinal weld seams were radiographed, and spot RT was done on circumferential seams. This level is also considered "full radiography" and results in a 1.0 joint efficiency for thickness calculations. No radiographic testing is done on nozzle welds for this level. "RT-3" means, with only a few exceptions, spot radiographic inspection was performed on all longitudinal and circumferential seams. RT-3 results in a 0.85 joint efficiency. No nozzle connection welds were radiographed. "RT-4" means some radiographic examination took place, but the amount can't be described with the RT numbering system. RT-4 results in a 0.70 joint efficiency.

Mechanical/
Design/Analysis

---

[7]The efficiency of a butt weld joint in compression is 100%.

[8]Most other methods of NDE, including eddy current, acoustic emission, liquid penetrant, and magnetic particle testing, are also used with pressure vessels.

[9]Radiography is sometimes referred to as "X-raying." However, radiography can use either X-rays generated from high electrical voltages or gamma rays generated from a radioactive isotope capsule.

[10]Ultrasonic examination may be substituted for radiography for the final closure seam of a pressure vessel if the construction of the vessel does not permit interpretable radiographs in accordance with the BPVC.

14. NOZZLE NECKS

A *nozzle* is an opening in a pressure vessel. The nozzle may connect the vessel to other parts of the piping network, or it may be normally closed off. *Handholes* and larger *manways* are nozzles that are opened for inspection, cleaning, and repair.[11] A nozzle typically ends at a bolted flange plate. The cylindrical section between a pressure vessel and the flange is the *nozzle neck*.

15. FLAT UNSTAYED HEADS

Flat surfaces appear extensively in pressure vessels. Circular surfaces are most common, although other shapes may be used. A flat surface used as the end closure or head of a pressure vessel may be an integral part of the vessel (when formed with the cylindrical shell or welded to it), or it may be a removable plate attached by bolts through a gasket to a flange.[12] Because they are the weakest of head configurations, they may be reinforced with rods, spars, ribs, braces, stiffeners, and so on, known as *stays*, in order to prevent excessive deflection. Flat plates and heads connected around their peripheries but without any other reinforcement are known as *flat unstayed heads*. Unreinforced flat plates are generally two to five times thicker than the surrounding shell. Figure 45.6 illustrates two of the many acceptable ways of attaching flat heads.[13]

Figure 45.6 *Flat Unstayed Heads*

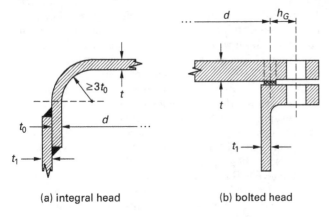

(a) integral head   (b) bolted head

16. FLANGED JOINTS

Flanged joints (with flat cover plates) are needed to disassemble, inspect, and clean pressure vessels. Joints may be bolted or boltless pressure-actuated. *Bolted joints*, where sealing gaskets are compressed by bolt forces, are more common. In boltless joints (which may be of the *axially locked joint* and *pressure-actuated joint* varieties), the internal pressure compresses and seals the gasket. Because of the relative size advantages, a boltless joint may be superior at pressures over 2000 psig (14 MPa) and when the shell diameter is roughly 20 in (510 mm) or when the flange thickness exceeds 1½ in (38 mm).

The three main types of bolted flanges are the ring flange, the tapered hub (also known as *welding neck*) flange, and the lap-joint flange, shown in Fig. 45.7. The *lap-joint flange* is used for low-pressure, low-cost pressure vessels. Joints may be hubbed or hubless. Advantages of this flange type are low cost and ease of bolt hole alignment. The backing ring can be constructed of a different material from the shell and lap ring, an important consideration when expensive alloys are used.

The *ring flange* is suitable for low and moderate pressure. It consists of an annular plate welded to the end of a cylindrical nozzle (shell). Bolts are spaced equidistantly around the bolt circle. The number of bolts is commonly a multiple of four. An unconfined gasket is used between the annular plate and the closure plate. The gasket usually extends to the inner edge of the bolt line so that the bolts can help center the gasket. A full-face gasket may cover the entire flange area and extend beyond the bolt circle, but is typically used for pressure less than 100 psig (700 kPa).[14]

For reliable and safe operation up to a pressure of approximately 5000 psig (35 MPa), the *tapered-hub flange* can be used. This flange is (roughly) L-shaped and is butt-welded to the shell opening.

Depending on the design, the mating area of the flange surfaces and/or cover plate may or may not compress the gasket. An unconfined and prestressed gasket is commonly used with flat-faced ring flanges. Such a gasket can expand inward and outward when tightened. Since the gasket is unconfined, there is no protection against *gasket blowout*.

---

[11]A *davit* (*davit arm*) is a swinging support constructed as part of the vessel, supporting the manway cover when it is unbolted and moved aside.
[12]A toroidal knuckle with a flat head is an example of an integral flat plate head.
[13]BPVC Sec. VIII, Div. 3, Fig. UG-34 shows all of the acceptable standard designs.
[14]In full-face gaskets, the material outside of the bolt ring is not effective in sealing.

Figure 45.7 *Types of Flanges*

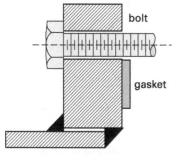

(a) ring flange with flat face

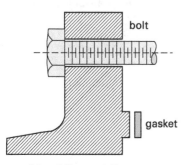

(b) welding neck flange
with tongue facing

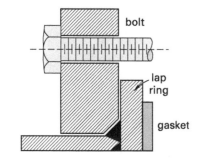

(c) lap joint with raised-face flange

Semiconfined gaskets are confined in single-step male-female types of joints. Gaskets are completely confined in tongue-and-groove, ring, double-step male-female joints. Fully confined gaskets are appropriately chosen when there are significant fluctuations in pressure and temperature.

The major concern in regard to flange and gasket choice is flange leakage. Gaskets chosen for operation under internal pressure are much less effective under vacuum. Sheet gaskets may be "sucked in," though this is countered by specifying a spiral-wound gasket.

17. PRESSURE TESTING

Pressure vessels under internal pressure are normally tested hydrostatically with water.[15] However, vessels that cannot safely be filled with water, that cannot be dried, or that cannot tolerate traces of the test liquid can be tested pneumatically with air.

Most testing is not carried out at the operating temperature. Since material strengths decrease at higher temperatures, the test pressure is increased according to the ratio of the allowable stress at the test temperature to the allowable stress at the design temperature.

According to the ASME Code Sec. VIII, Div. 1, the hydrostatic test pressure is 130% of the MAWP multiplied by the ratio of the allowable stress at the test temperature to the allowable stress at the design temperature. When hydrotesting, it is recommended that the metal temperature is at least 30°F (17°C) above the MDMT, but not greater than 120°F (48°C), to minimize the risk of brittle fracture. For pneumatic tests, the test pressure is 110% of the MAWP multiplied by the ratio of the allowable stress at the test temperature to the allowable stress at the design temperature. The metal temperature during a pneumatic test must be at least 30°F (17°C) above the MDMT to minimize the risk of brittle fracture.

For cast-iron pressure vessels, the test pressure is 200% of the MAWP unless the design working pressure is less than 30 psig (207 kPa), in which case, the test pressure is 60 psig (414 kPa) or 250% of the design working pressure, whichever is less. A corrosion allowance is included when calculating all test pressures.

Following the application of hydrostatic and pneumatic pressures, all joints and connections must be visually inspected. Leakage is not allowed, except for openings intended for welded connections and at temporary test closures. Additionally, for pneumatically tested vessels, the full length of all welds around openings and attachment welds having a throat greater than $1/4$ in (6 mm) must be examined.

Special rules apply to pressure vessels whose operating pressure is limited by flange strength or that have multiple chambers, are subject to external pressure, or operate at below-atmospheric pressures.

18. PRESSURE RELIEF DEVICES

BPVC Sec. VIII, Div. 1, UG-125 through UG-140 require all pressure vessels to be equipped with *overpressure protection devices* such as *rupture disks (burst disks)*, RDs, *pressure relief valves (safety relief valves)*, PRVs, or combinations thereof to prevent catastrophic failure during abnormal conditions. Generally, a PRV is

---

[15]Even pressure vessels that are normally under internal pressure may sometimes draw a vacuum, as during a steamout. Other less predictable instances of vacuum failures occur when the contents of a vessel are being drained while the vent line is closed or blocked, or when a filter element is clogged or under-sized.

a normally closed, spring-actuated device that automatically opens to relieve pressure. When the overpressure situation abates, the PRV closes, preventing further loss of contents.

Two PRVs can be mounted on a *three-way valve* fitting such that either of the PRVs can be removed for maintenance. Only one PRV should be active at any given moment, however. The three-way valve should normally be back-seated to reduce the possibility of leakage through the stem packing.

The set-point pressure, opening pressure, tolerance, overpressure, and accumulation pressure are related concepts. The marked *set-point pressure* (*set pressure*, *setting pressure*) is the value of increasing pressure at which a pressure relief device is intended to (begin to) open. Per UG-134(a), the protection device set point pressure must be at or below the MAWP. The actual *opening pressure* (*popping pressure*, *start-to-leak pressure*, *burst pressure*, or *breaking pressure*) may be slightly different from the set-point pressure due to intrinsic manufacturing batch *tolerances*. *Overpressure* is the pressure above the set pressure, expressed either as an absolute value or as a percentage of the set pressure. "Overpressure" is associated with the device. *Accumulation* is pressure above the maximum MAWP of the vessel, expressed either as an absolute value or a percentage of the MAWP. "Accumulation" is associated with the vessel. (See Fig. 45.8.)

Figure 45.8 *Overpressure and Accumulation*

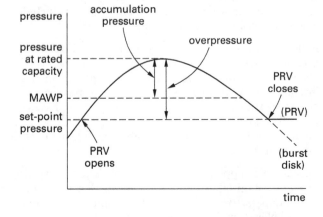

Chattering is a phenomenon where a pressure relief valve repeatedly opens and closes rapidly. In addition to the annoying noise made by the valve, the resulting vibration may cause misalignment and loss of pressure, valve seat damage, and eventual valve spring fatigue failure. Chattering is caused by operating pressures that are too close to the valve's set-point pressure, a too-small line (with subsequently large friction head loss) holding the relief valve, as well as by a too-small line (resulting in an excessive backpressure) into which the relief valve is vented. However, the most common cause is the installation of a pressure relief valve that is too large. A pressure relief valve should be small enough to release the overpressure in a single opening event, bringing the pressure down gradually. If the valve is too large, each time it opens, so much of the local pressurized contents escape that the valve closes before the vessel pressure is suitably reduced.

46 Manufacturability, Quality, and Reliability

Nomenclature

c	number of failures (defects)	–
C	circumference	m
d	shaft diameter	m
D	hole diameter	m
E	modulus of elasticity	Pa
F	force	N
l	length	m
MTBF	mean time between failures	various
MTBFO	mean time before failure outage	various
MTTF	mean time to failure	various
MTTR	mean time to repair	various
n	sample size	–
N	lot size	–
p	pressure	Pa
r	radius	m
t	time	s
T	torque	N·m
Z	objective function	–

Symbols

δ	deviation	–
δ	diametral interference	m
Δ	tolerance	–
ε	strain	–
λ	failure rate	1/time
μ	coefficient of friction	–
μ	mean service (repair) rate	1/time
ν	Poisson's ratio	–
σ	stress	Pa

Subscripts

c	circumferential
d	shaft
D	hole
F	fundamental
i	inner
l	lower
max	maximum
min	minimum
o	outside
r	radial
u	upper

1. MANAGEMENT SCIENCE[1]

Management science, also known as *quantitative business analysis*, *operations research*, and *management systems modeling*, is used to develop mathematical models of real-world situations. This chapter presents various quantitative business analysis techniques used to model and analyze manufacturing and industrial environments. Accordingly, this chapter is more concerned with solutions to problems than with explaining why the problems need to be solved or with listing advantages and disadvantages of solutions. Though they may seem to be obscure, all of the techniques presented in this chapter are commonly taught in operations research (OR), industrial engineering (IE), and MBA curricula.[2]

A *deterministic model* is a mathematical model that is built around a set of fixed rules such that any given input always results in a specific output. If an input can produce a variety of outputs determined by rules of probability, the model is known as a *probabilistic* or *stochastic model*.

---

[1]It is not clear whether the topic of "Quality" included in the NCEES Mechanical CBT exam specifications incorporates the NCEES *FE Reference Handbook* (*NCEES Handbook*) material on statistical quality control (SQC). SQC is generally considered to be an industrial engineering subject. Similarly, the topic of "Reliability" is specifically included in the "Industrial Engineering" section of the *NCEES Handbook*. The content of these two industrial engineering topics is only briefly covered in this chapter.

[2]Operations research developed as a field of its own during World War II when optimizing modeling techniques were used to determine the best way for a submarine to patrol a specific region.

A common aspect of most management science techniques is the goal of arriving at an optimum solution (regardless of whether the goal is actually realized in practice). The process of optimizing is unique to each type of problem. Calculus is not generally used in optimizing.[3] Optimizing real-world problems always requires a computer, though optimization by hand is possible with simple problems.[4]

Some management science methods attempt to optimize a specific mathematical function known as the *objective function*, Z. If Z is a profit function, it is optimized by maximization; if Z is a cost or time function, it is optimized by minimization.[5] Some management science techniques can maximize only, so in cases requiring minimization, the negative of the objective function is maximized.

Objective functions are restricted from increasing without being bound by *constraints* placed on one or more of the function's variables. These constraints are typically mathematical representations of how resources are limited or combined. Non-negativity constraints are common in mathematical programming problems.

If the objective function and its constraints are linear combinations of the independent variables, the model is said to be a *linear model*. Otherwise, the model is nonlinear.

Not all manufacturing management problems need to be solved by complex or obscure procedures. Some problems (e.g., facilities layout) do not have a general solution procedure and must be solved by exhaustive enumeration. Many problems can be solved simply by using common sense and logical thinking to minimize the total cost.

2. MANUFACTURABILITY

The goal of *work methods* (*methods engineering*) is the reduction of fabrication and assembly time, worker effort, and manufacturing cost. This is accomplished in a variety of ways, including initial *design for manufacture and assembly* (DFMA) selection of methods to be used, human factors engineering, work measurement, plant layout, assembly line balancing, and administration of the manufacturing process. Work methods,

which is more worker- and workplace-oriented, goes beyond traditional value engineering, which is product-design oriented.

3. VALUE ENGINEERING

The *value* of an investment is defined as the ratio of its return (performance or utility) to its cost (effort or investment). The basic object of *value engineering* (VE, also referred to as *value analysis*) is to obtain the maximum per-unit value.[6]

Value engineering concepts often are used to reduce the cost of mass-produced manufactured products. This is done by eliminating unnecessary, redundant, or superfluous features, by redesigning the product for a less expensive manufacturing method, and by including features for easier assembly without sacrificing utility and function.[7] However, the concepts are equally applicable to one-time investments, such as buildings, chemical processing plants, and space vehicles. In particular, value engineering has become an important element in all federally funded work.[8]

Typical examples of large-scale value engineering work are using stock-sized bearings and motors (instead of custom manufactured units), replacing rectangular concrete columns with round columns (which are easier to form), and substituting custom buildings with prefabricated structures.

Value engineering is usually a team effort. And, while the original designers may be on the team, usually outside consultants are utilized. The cost of value engineering is usually returned many times over through reduced construction and life-cycle costs.

4. RELIABILITY

A *fault* in a machine or other system is a known cause of breakdown. An *error* is an undesired state within the machine that might lead to improper operation. A *failure* occurs when the machine fails to operate as expected or intended. A *fault-tolerant system* contains provisions to avoid failures after faults occur.

---

[3]One obvious exception is how the economic order quantity is calculated. The economic order quantity (EOQ) formula is derived by taking the derivative of the total cost function.
[4]Some management science techniques, though interesting, are too obtuse, time consuming, or complex for solving by hand. Subjects that have been omitted from or given only a mere mention in this book include nonlinear programming, dynamic programming, and integer programming. Furthermore, most management science subjects have many complicated variations that are omitted from this chapter. Simple forecasting and the EOQ model are also traditional management science subjects.
[5]There is an important difference between *cost* and *price*. Both represent an amount paid, but the distinction depends on who makes the payment and when the payment is made. To one party, the cost of materials incorporated into a manufactured item is the price paid by that party for those materials. That is, there is no difference. However, the cost to one party to acquire or produce an item is much lower than the price at which the item is later sold to a second party.
[6]Value analysis, the methodology that has become today's value engineering, was developed in the early 1950s by Lawrence D. Miles, an analyst at General Electric.
[7]Some people say that value engineering is "the act of going over the plans and taking out everything that is interesting."
[8]U.S. Government Office of Management and Budget Circular A-131 outlines value engineering for federally funded construction projects.

In the most common case, units fail permanently and are neither repaired nor replaced. Reliability of a single item (machine, unit, piece of equipment, etc.) is characterized by its *mean time to failure*, MTTF. The term *mean time between forced outages*, MTBFO, is used with redundant systems in place of MTTF. *Coverage* is the probability of the system reconfiguring itself when a fault occurs. *Redundancy* is the primary tool used to increase reliability and coverage. Systems with two units in parallel are known as *duplex systems*. Systems with three units are known as *triple modular redundancy*, TMR, systems.[9]

The exponential distribution is most frequently used in reliability calculations.[10] The *failure rate*, λ, is the expected number of failures per unit time.

In some cases, failed units are repaired online. The average repair time is the *mean time to repair*, MTTR, and is the reciprocal of the repair rate, μ. The *mean time to failure*, MTTF, is the average time a unit operates before failing. The *mean time between failures*, MTBF, is the length of time between when the original and repaired units start.

Availability is the probability that a system will be operating at any given time. The system *uptime* is calculated by multiplying the availability by the theoretically maximum number of operational hours (e.g., 8760 hours per year).[11] *Unavailability* and *downtime* are similarly calculated.

Repairing a machine as soon as it breaks down is always the preferred course of action. In some cases, however, a faulty machine can be repaired only at regular intervals. This is particularly true for unattended equipment that is inspected only at periodic intervals, often called the *proof test interval*, PTI. A complete failure will occur if the system's redundancy is not adequate to sustain multiple faults during the PTI.

5. PREVENTATIVE MAINTENANCE

The value of *preventative maintenance*, PM, to prevent breakdowns is undisputed.[12] However, it is not as easy to decide on the frequency and timing of PM, the size of maintenance facilities and number of staff, location and centralization issues, and the quantity of spares to be carried. Quantitative business analysis techniques can be used to formulate some of these PM policies.

The general goal in optimizing PM policies is to minimize the total cost of operation, taking into consideration the costs of preventative maintenance, downtime,

and repair. Sometimes the costs are fixed, as when specific penalties must be paid when output is not achieved. At other times, the costs are related to hourly rates and the duration of downtime. The time to failure of a machine and the times for both repair and preventative maintenance are generally not fixed, and they are not always normally distributed either. However, unless simulation is used, it is almost always necessary to work with the average times (e.g., mean time to failure, MTTF).

The following guidelines should be considered when establishing PM policies, particularly for single machines. When there are several identical machines operating in parallel, the problem more closely resembles a waiting-line (queuing) problem. Breakdowns are comparable to arrivals in the line, and repair stations (repair crews) are the stations. The optimum solution takes into consideration the costs of idle maintenance crews.

- PM is more applicable when the time-to-breakdown distribution has low variability because the time before a breakdown can be more accurately predicted.

- PM is only useful when its cost is less than the cost of the breakdown. In the absence of cost information, PM is useful when the average PM time is less than the average repair time.

- PM is more applicable when there is little or no inventory of the item produced by the broken machine.

6. REPLACEMENT

Replacement and *renewal models* determine the most economical time to replace existing equipment. Replacement processes fall into two categories, depending on the life pattern of the equipment, which either deteriorates gradually (becomes obsolete or less efficient) or fails suddenly.

In the case of gradual deterioration, the solution consists of balancing the cost of new equipment against the cost of maintenance or decreased efficiency of the old equipment. Several models are available for cases with specialized assumptions, but no general solution methods exist.

In the case of *sudden failure* (e.g., light bulbs), the solution method consists of finding a replacement frequency that minimizes the costs of the required new items, the

---

[9]With TMR systems, only one unit is required for successful operation. When one unit fails, the system becomes a duplex system until the failed unit is repaired. With logic, software, electronic, and computer systems, failure can be determined by comparing the output of each of the three units. In effect, the two good units "vote" to determine which unit is faulty and should be shut down.

[10]The three-parameter *Weibull distribution* is more descriptive, flexible, and powerful than the negative exponential distribution. It has gained acceptance primarily in the aerospace industry because of its ability to model the failure distribution more exactly. Its complexity, however, makes application to noncritical applications cumbersome.

[11]If the machine does not operate 24 hours per day or 365 days per year, the number of hours will be accordingly reduced.

[12]Maintenance to correct disrepair is known as *remedial maintenance*.

labor for replacement, and the expected cost of failure. The solution is made difficult by the probabilistic nature of the life spans.

The replacement decision criterion with *deterioration models* is the present worth of all future costs associated with each policy. Solution is by trial and error, calculating the present worth of each policy and incrementing the replacement period by one time period for each iteration.

The time between installation and failure is not constant for members in the general equipment population. Therefore, in order to solve a sudden failure model, it is necessary to have the distribution of individual item lives (*mortality curve*). The conditional probability of failure in a small time interval, say from t to $t + \delta t$, is calculated from the mortality curve. This probability is *conditional* since it is conditioned on nonfailure up to time t.

The conditional probability of failure may decrease with time (as with *infant mortality*), remain constant (as with an exponential reliability distribution and failure from random causes), or increase with time (as with items that deteriorate with use). If the conditional probability of failure decreases or remains constant over time, operating items should never be replaced prior to failure.

7. FACILITIES LAYOUT

Facilities layout (*plant layout*) problems are numerous in variety and complexity. Laying out facilities involves locating departments and/or operations with respect to one another. In traditional *process layout*, machines with the same function are grouped together. In *product layout* (product-oriented layout), the layout depends on the sequencing of production operations. If the same equipment is used at two different times, it is duplicated in a product layout.

Some computerized methods exist for exhaustively evaluating alternatives. Manual layout techniques are even more limited. Often, paper-cutting is combined with intuition to come up with a layout. Departments are sized to a particular scale and are cut out of paper. The pieces of paper are slid around until a layout "works."

Except for the artificial case of a small number of equally sized, equally shaped departments or operations whose locations are limited to a rectangular grid, it is unlikely that all possible layouts will be considered.[13] The "optimum" layout may actually be merely the best that could be found given the amount of time available.

An alternate manual method is to construct a graph whose "vertices" (nodes) are the departments or operations. The "edges" (line segments) are drawn between two vertices if adjacent associated departments are desired. The edges may be weighted to indicate the level of traffic between the departments. The goal is to rearrange the vertices so that no edges cross. If this can be done, then the layout can be planar. If the departments are somewhat flexible in terms of size and shape, it is possible to have the desired adjacencies.

Certain simplifying assumptions are usually made with both computerized and manual methods. For example, all layouts may be required to be two dimensional. Departments may be assumed to be square or rectangular. When the locations of specific pieces of equipment within the department are unknown, it is assumed that all movement into and out of the department originates and terminates at the centroid of the departmental area. Also, only highly repetitive movements between departments are considered. Once-in-a-while travel is excluded from the analysis.

Almost all facility layout procedures—manual and computerized, exact, trial-and-error, and heuristic—attempt to minimize the transportation cost, sometimes referred to as *movement*.[14] In simple cases, this may mean minimizing the product of trips between departments and the distances between their centroids. In more complex cases, the product of trips and distances may also be multiplied by volumes, weights, and labor rates.

Nonquantitative factors also need to be considered. Sometimes, as when equipment, records, or personnel are shared, it is absolutely necessary that departments be located next to each other. In other cases, as when safety is compromised, it may be absolutely essential to separate departments. In most cases, the *nearness priorities* characterize the adjacency requirements between being absolutely necessary and being absolutely undesirable.[15] The ways that nonquantitative factors are presented and incorporated into the solution vary from case to case.

8. ASSEMBLY LINE BALANCING

Line balancing determines which tasks will be performed progressively at multiple assembly stations. Some tasks must precede others; some tasks can be performed at any point in the assembly; some tasks (e.g., installation of fasteners and final tightening) can be split between stations. Line balancing can also determine how many stations are needed and which tasks will be performed in parallel to increase throughput.

---

[13]The number of layout variations, including mirror images, with n equally sized square departments is $n!$.
[14]A *trial-and-error method* depends on insight, intuition, and ingenuity to come up with a solution. A *heuristic method* follows a procedure and/or uses rules of thumb to derive an answer. Neither is an optimizing technique.
[15]The *Muther nearness priorities* (developed by Richard Muther in the 1950s) are (1) absolutely necessary, (2) very important, (3) important, (4) OK (ordinary importance), (5) unimportant, and (6) undesirable.

Standard times to perform the various station tasks are used in the balancing process. However, except for robot operators and machine-controlled lines, task times are actually random. Sometimes tasks take longer; sometimes they take less time. This implies that almost every line will be unavoidably unbalanced. If the work is rigidly paced to the cycle time (as it would be if the work were permanently attached to the conveyance system), some work pieces might be left unfinished if the previous part required more time than usual. This scenario introduces what is probably one of the most important requirements for maximizing the line throughput: station inventory.

Line throughput will be maximized if each station has a backlog of unfinished work.[16] In this case, the conveyance system is used merely to bring work to stations rather than to pace the stations. If a station is busy when a new piece of work arrives, the station operator merely places that piece into his or her inventory of unfinished work. If all tasks are finished early, before a new piece of work arrives, the operator begins on a piece from the inventory. The station is never idle.

9. QUALITY CONTROL CHARTS

Statistical quality control, SQC, also known as *statistical process control*, SPC, uses several techniques to ensure that a minimum quality level is consistently obtained from production processes. Typical SQC tasks include routine monitoring of process output, sampling incoming raw materials, and testing finished work.

Monitoring process output and charting the results are often the most visible aspects of SQC. Small samples of work are tested at regular or random intervals, and the results are shown graphically.[17] The graphs are known as *control charts* or *Shewhart control charts* because they show, in addition to the measured values, the *control limits* (i.e., the limits of acceptable values).[18] (See Fig. 46.1.)

Control charts can be prepared for the average value of some process variable (the *x-bar chart*), for the range or other measures of dispersion (*R-chart*, *s-chart*, or *σ-chart*), and for the fraction defective (*p-chart*), the number of defects per unit (*c-chart*), or any combination thereof. Charts that require a measurement of a process variable are known as *variable charts*. The *p*-chart and *c*-chart are examples of *attribute charts*, where only the condition of an item needs to be determined.

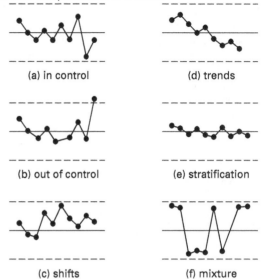

Figure 46.1 *Interpretation of SPC Charts*

(a) in control

(d) trends

(b) out of control

(e) stratification

(c) shifts

(f) mixture

It is a basic assumption that random effects are present in every process. Variation within certain limits is inevitable, and if the magnitudes of the limits or the variation are unacceptable, they must be reduced by changes in manufacturing or product design. If the magnitudes are acceptable, then corrections are required only when the results exceed the magnitude expected on the basis of random effects.

10. QUALITY ACCEPTANCE SAMPLING

Acceptance sampling is the testing of samples taken from a *lot* (batch or process) in order to determine if the entire lot should be accepted or rejected. Acceptance sampling is appropriate when testing is destructive or when 100% testing would be too expensive. To design an *acceptance plan* (also known as a *Dodge-Romig plan*), the number in the sample and the *acceptance number* (i.e., the maximum allowable number of defects in the sample) must be specified.

In *single acceptance plans*, a sample of size n out of a total lot size of N is tested. If the number of defects is equal to or less than c, the lot is accepted. The plan can

Mechanical/
Design/Analysis

---

[16]Measurable increases in line output have been reported by selectively unbalancing the line and ensuring that each station has a backlog of work.
[17]The graphs are often conspicuously posted at the entrances of departments.
[18]Control limits have nothing to do with *specification limits*. Specification limits determine if the product is acceptable to the customer. Control limits determine if the process is statistically in control.

be described graphically by an *operating characteristic* (OC) *curve* (see Fig. 46.2), which plots the *probability of acceptance* (also known as the *producer's acceptance risk*) versus the *lot quality* (i.e., the true fraction or percentage defective).[19] Points on the OC curve are determined from the binomial or, more preferably, from the Poisson approximation to the binomial. In practice, however, acceptance plans are generally designed by referring to tables of predetermined plans.

Figure 46.2 *Acceptance Plan Operation Characteristic Curve*

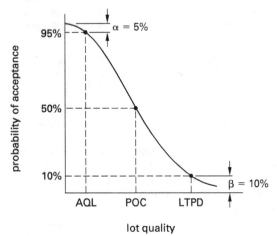

11. LIMITS AND FITS

Exact precision in manufacturing is impossible to achieve. Minimum and maximum values of deviation from the design value, known as *limits*, are boundaries within which a measurement must lie to operate as intended. The *tolerance* for a dimension is the total permissible variation or difference between the acceptable limits. The tolerance for a dimension can be specified in two ways: either as a general rule in the title block (e.g., ±0.001 in unless otherwise specified) or as specific limits that are given with each dimension (e.g., 2.575 in ±0.005 in).

The *fit* describes the assembly of the hole and shaft. A *clearance fit* results in dimensions that assure clearance between mating parts. An *interference fit* (also known as a *force fit* and *shrink fit*) results in dimensions that do not have clearance between mating parts. For example, the shaft diameter will always be larger than the hole through which the shaft must pass. The effect of an interference fit is an almost permanent assembly for two

assembled parts. A *transition fit* might be either a clearance or interference fit. For example, a shaft may be either larger or smaller than the hole in the mating part.

The most common standard of limits and fits is the International Organization for Standardization (ISO) Standard 286, which gives tolerance classes for a wide range of tolerance. Some preferred fits, along with their ISO hole and shaft tolerances, are given in Table 46.1.

Table 46.1 *Some Preferred Fits*

type of fit	fit description	ISO hole/ shaft tolerance
clearance fits	*free running fit:* good for large temperature variations, high running speeds, and heavy journal loads; not used when a high level of accuracy is required	H9/d9
	sliding fit: used where parts do not move freely, but need to move and turn, and locate accurately	H7/g6
	locational fit: snug fit for location of stationary parts; parts can be assembled and disassembled	H7/h6
	loose running fit: used for wide commercial tolerances or allowances on external members	H11/c11
	close running fit: used for running on accurate machines and for accurate location at moderate speeds and journal pressures	H8/f7
transition fits	*locational transition fit:* compromise between clearance and interference fits; provides an accurate location	H7/k6
	locational transition fit: for more accurate location where greater interface is permissible	H7/n6
interference fits	*location interference fit:* for parts requiring rigidity and alignment with prime accuracy of location; parts do not have special bore pressure requirements	H7/p6
	medium drive fit: for ordinary steel parts or shrink fits on light sections; tightest fit usable on cast iron	H7/s6
	force fit: suitable for parts which can be highly stressed or for shrink fits where the heavy pressing forces required are impractical	H7/u6

---

[19]Operating characteristic curves are actually a series of discontinuous points since lot items are finite and discrete. However, they are never drawn in that manner.

12. FITS AND TOLERANCES FOR SHAFTS AND HOLES[20]

The nomenclature used to describe fit parameters related to circular member and circular mating holes is illustrated in Fig. 46.3.[21] The *basic size* (*basic dimension*) is the dimension to which the minimum and maximum tolerances are applied.[22] The basic size of the hole is the basis for all calculations.[23] Uppercase letters are used to identify parameters associated with the hole, while lowercase letters are used for the shaft. The *nominal* (*basic*) *size*, D, is the basic dimension to which the minimum and maximum limits are applied.

Figure 46.3 Limits and Fits

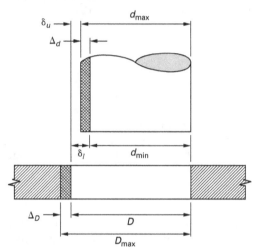

The *tolerance* of the shaft diameter, Δ_d, is the absolute value of the difference between the upper deviation, δ_u, and the lower deviation, δ_l. The International Tolerance (IT) grades are given in Table 46.2. Upper and lower deviations are found from Table 46.3.

$$\Delta_d = |\,\delta_u - \delta_l|$$

Table 46.2 International Tolerance (IT) Grades[*]

basic size	tolerance grade, Δ_D or Δ_d		
	IT6	IT7	IT9
0–3	0.006	0.010	0.025
3–6	0.008	0.012	0.030
6–10	0.009	0.015	0.036
10–18	0.011	0.018	0.043
18–30	0.013	0.021	0.052
30–50	0.016	0.025	0.062

*All values in mm
Source: *Preferred Metric Limits and Fits*, ANSI/ASME B4.2-1978 (R2009)

Equation 46.1 and Eq. 46.2: Minimum and Maximum Hole Sizes

$$D_{\max} = D + \Delta_D \qquad \text{46.1}$$

$$D_{\min} = D \qquad \text{46.2}$$

Description

The *nominal size of the hole*, D, is used to calculate the maximum size, $D_{\max}$, and minimum size, $D_{\min}$, as shown in Eq. 46.1 and Eq. 46.2. The hole's diameter *tolerance*, Δ_D, is the difference between the maximum and minimum limits of the hole.

Example

A hole has a nominal size of 11 mm and a maximum size of 11.016 mm. What are most nearly the tolerance and the minimum diameter of the hole, respectively?

(A) 0.010 mm; 5.0 mm

(B) 0.012 mm; 7.0 mm

(C) 0.014 mm; 9.0 mm

(D) 0.016 mm; 11 mm

[20]The *NCEES Handbook* mentions "the standard," but it does not identify it. There are two standards for fits and tolerances in the United States, one based on U.S. units (ANSI/ASME B4.1-1967 (R2009), *Preferred Limits and Fits for Cylindrical Parts*), and one based on SI units (ANSI/ASME B4.2-1978 (R2009), *Preferred Metric Limits and Fits*). Both have been revised several times since their original releases. The standards contain tables that can be used to find the minimum and maximum diameters of holes and shafts directly, without calculations. The equations listed in the *NCEES Handbook* are found in the appendices of the standards.

[21]Figure 46.3 does not show the basic dimension of the shaft, d, that is used in subsequent equations. If required (as in Eq. 46.6), the basic size of the shaft is taken as the basic size of the hole (i.e., $d = D$).

[22](1) The term "size" is synonymous with "dimension." (2) The *NCEES Handbook* parenthetically indicates that "basic size" and "nominal size" are synonymous terms. However, there is a common, incompatible usage of the term "nominal dimension." A nominal dimension is commonly stated without an attempt to be exact, making "nominal" synonymous with "approximate." For example, a shaft with an actual diameter of 29.7 mm may be referred to as a "30 mm nominal diameter shaft." This usage, however, is inconsistent with Eq. 46.2, which makes the nominal dimension an absolute minimum. For that reason, the terms "basic size" and "basic dimension" are preferred.

[23]There are two parallel fit/tolerance calculation methods presented in each standard: *hole basis* and *shaft basis*. The *NCEES Handbook* presents only the hole basis calculations; it does not mention the alternative shaft basis calculations which are based on the nominal diameter of the shaft, d. Normally, the hole basis is preferred due to the use of standard reamers being used to produce holes, and standard size "go/no-go gauges" used to check holes. However, when a common shaft mates with several holes, the shaft basis system should be used.

Table 46.3 Deviations for Shafts[a,b]

basic size	upper deviation, δ_u					lower deviation, δ_l				
	c	d	f	g	h	k	n	p	s	u
0–3	−0.060	−0.020	−0.006	−0.002	0	0	0.004	0.006	0.014	0.018
3–6	−0.070	−0.030	−0.010	−0.004	0	0.001	0.008	0.012	0.019	0.023
6–10	−0.080	−0.040	−0.013	−0.005	0	0.001	0.010	0.015	0.023	0.028
10–14	−0.095	−0.095	−0.016	−0.006	0	0.001	0.012	0.018	0.028	0.033
14–18	−0.095	−0.050	−0.016	−0.006	0	0.001	0.012	0.018	0.028	0.033
18–24	−0.110	−0.065	−0.020	−0.007	0	0.002	0.015	0.022	0.035	0.041
24–30	−0.110	−0.065	−0.020	−0.007	0	0.002	0.015	0.022	0.035	0.048
30–40	−0.120	−0.080	−0.025	−0.009	0	0.002	0.017	0.026	0.043	0.060
40–50	−0.130	−0.080	−0.025	−0.009	0	0.002	0.017	0.026	0.043	0.070

[a]All values in mm
[b]lower limit < basic size ≤ upper limit
Source: *Preferred Metric Limits and Fits*, ANSI/ASME B4.2-1978 (R2009)

Solution

The tolerance of the hole can be calculated by solving Eq. 46.1 for the tolerance, Δ_D.

$$D_{max} = D + \Delta_D$$
$$\Delta_D = D_{max} - D$$
$$= 11.016 \text{ mm} - 11 \text{ mm}$$
$$= 0.016 \text{ mm}$$

From Eq. 46.2, the minimum diameter of hole, D_{min}, is the same as the nominal diameter, D. Therefore, the minimum diameter is 11 mm.

The answer is (D).

Equation 46.3 and Eq. 46.4: Shaft with Clearance Fits

$$d_{max} = d + \delta_F \qquad 46.3$$

$$d_{min} = d_{max} - \Delta_d \qquad 46.4$$

Description

Equation 46.3 and Eq. 46.4 are used to calculate the maximum, d_{max}, and minimum, d_{min}, nominal sizes of the shaft. These equations apply to shafts with clearance fits d, g, or h only. Δ_d is the tolerance for the shaft. The *fundamental deviation*, δ_F, is the upper deviation, δ_u.

Equation 46.5 and Eq. 46.6: Shaft with Transition or Interference Fits

$$d_{max} = d_{min} + \Delta_d \qquad 46.5$$

$$d_{min} = d + \delta_F \qquad 46.6$$

Description

Equation 46.6 and Eq. 46.5 are used to calculate the maximum and minimum nominal sizes, respectively, of a shaft with a transition or interference fit k, p, s, or u. For interference fits, the fundamental deviation, δ_F, is the upper deviation, δ_u, in Table 46.3.

Example

A carbon-steel gear hub is to be press-fitted to a carbon-steel shaft using a class 25H7/u6 fit. The hub has a nominal thickness of 13 mm. Using hole basis calculations, what are most nearly the loosest and tightest interferences, respectively?

(A) 0.013 mm; 0.021 mm

(B) 0.021 mm; 0.048 mm

(C) 0.027 mm; 0.061 mm

(D) 0.048 mm; 0.061 mm

Solution

The fit is specified as "25H7/u6," which describes a force interference fit with a nominal hole size of 25.000 mm. Since the hole basis is specified, from Eq. 46.2, the minimum hole diameter is

$$D_{min} = D = 25.000 \text{ mm}$$

From Table 46.2, the hole tolerance for an IT grade 7 is $\Delta_D = 0.021$ mm. From Eq. 46.1, the maximum hole diameter is

$$D_{max} = D_{min} + \Delta_D = 25.000 \text{ mm} + 0.021 \text{ mm}$$
$$= 25.021 \text{ mm}$$

From Table 46.3, with a u-class fit for the shaft, the lower deviation of the shaft is $\delta_l = 0.048$ mm. For interference fits, the fundamental deviation is the lower deviation, $\delta_F = \delta_l = 0.048$ mm. From Eq. 46.6, the minimum shaft diameter is

$$d_{\min} = d + \delta_F = 25.000 \text{ mm} + 0.048 \text{ mm}$$
$$= 25.048 \text{ mm}$$

From Table 46.2, the shaft tolerance for an IT grade 6 is $\Delta_d = 0.013$ mm. From Eq. 46.5, the maximum shaft diameter is

$$d_{\max} = d_{\min} + \Delta_d = 25.048 \text{ mm} + 0.013 \text{ mm}$$
$$= 25.061 \text{ mm}$$

The loosest interference is

$$\delta_{\max} = d_{\min} - D_{\max} = 25.048 \text{ mm} - 25.021 \text{ mm}$$
$$= 0.027 \text{ mm}$$

The tightest interference is

$$\delta_{\max} = d_{\max} - D_{\min} = 25.061 \text{ mm} - 25.000 \text{ mm}$$
$$= 0.061 \text{ mm}$$

The answer is (C).

13. MAXIMUM AND LEAST MATERIAL CONDITIONS

The *maximum material condition* (MMC) is the size of the part when it consists of the most material. The *least material condition* (LMC) is the size of the part when it consists of the least material.

A positive δ represents a clearance fit, and a negative δ represents an interference fit. Using that convention and the definitions of MMC and LMC, the maximum amount of space (i.e., clearance) that can exist between the hole and the shaft is

$$\delta_{\max} = \text{LMC}_{\text{hole}} - \text{LMC}_{\text{shaft}}$$

The minimum amount of space (clearance) that can exist between the hole and the shaft is

$$\delta_{\min} = \text{MMC}_{\text{hole}} - \text{MMC}_{\text{shaft}}$$

14. PRESS/SHRINK FITS

When assembling two pieces, interference fitting is often more economical than pinning, keying, or splining. The assembly operation can be performed in a hydraulic press, either with both pieces at room temperature or after heating the outer piece and cooling the inner piece. The former case is known as a *press fit* or *interference fit*; the latter as a *shrink fit*.

If two cylinders are pressed together, the pressure acting between them will expand the outer cylinder (placing it into tension) and will compress the inner cylinder. The *interference*, δ, is the difference in dimensions between the two cylinders. *Diametral interference* and *radial interference* are both used.[24]

$$\delta_{\text{diametral}} = 2\delta_{\text{radial}} = d_{o,\text{inner}} - d_{i,\text{outer}}$$
$$= |\Delta d_{o,\text{inner}}| + |\Delta d_{i,\text{outer}}|$$

The general case is where both cylinders are hollow and have different moduli of elasticity and Poisson's ratios. The outer cylinder is designated as the *hub*; the inner cylinder is designated as the *shaft*. If the shaft is solid, use $r_{i,\text{shaft}} = 0$.

If the two cylinders have the same length, the thick-wall cylinder equations can be used. The materials used for the two cylinders do not need to be the same. Since there is no longitudinal stress from an interference fit and since the radial stress is negative, the strain is

$$\varepsilon = \frac{\Delta d}{d} = \frac{\Delta C}{C} = \frac{\Delta r}{r}$$
$$= \frac{\sigma_c - \nu\sigma_r}{E}$$

The maximum assembly force required to overcome friction during a press-fitting operation is given by

$$F_{\max} = \mu N = 2\pi r_{o,\text{shaft}} \mu p l_{\text{interface}}$$

This relationship is approximate because the coefficient of friction is not known with certainty, and the assembly force affects the pressure, p, through Poisson's ratio. The coefficient of friction, μ, is highly variable. Values in the range of 0.03–0.33 have been reported. In the absence of experimental data, it is reasonable to use 0.12 for lightly oiled connections and 0.15 for dry assemblies.

Most interference fits are designed to keep the contact pressure below a given value. Designs of interference fits limited by strength generally use the distortion energy failure criterion. That is, the maximum shear stress is compared with the shear strength determined from the failure theory.

---

[24]Theoretically, the interference can be given to either the inner or outer cylinder, or it can be shared by both cylinders. However, in the case of a surface-hardened shaft with a standard diameter, all of the interference is usually given to the disk. Otherwise, it may be necessary to machine the shaft and remove some of the hardened surface.

**Mechanical/
Design/Analysis**

Equation 46.7: Interface Pressure

$$p = \frac{0.5\delta}{\dfrac{r}{E_o}\left(\dfrac{r_o^2 + r^2}{r_o^2 - r^2} + \nu_o\right) + \dfrac{r}{E_i}\left(\dfrac{r^2 + r_i^2}{r^2 - r_i^2} - \nu_i\right)} \quad \textit{46.7}$$

Description

The interface pressure, p (also known as the *interfacial pressure*, *contact pressure*, *radial pressure*, and *interference pressure*), caused by a press/shrink fit is calculated from Eq. 46.7. r_i is the inside radius of the inner member, and r_o is the outside radius of the outer member. r is the nominal radius, and δ is the diametral interference.[25] E is the modulus of elasticity (Young's modulus), and ν is Poisson's ratio.

Equation 46.7 has no shaft length or hub thickness terms because these terms are assumed to be the same and equal to the contact length, l. Equal-length components are seldom the case, as the shaft is generally longer than the hub. With unequal-length parts, the pressure is increased at each end (near each exterior face) of the hub. A stress concentration factor generally accounts for this condition. The value of the concentration factor depends upon the contact pressure and the design of the hub, but its theoretical value is seldom greater than 2.0.

Example

A solid shaft has a radius of 5 cm at room temperature, but a radius of 4.950 cm when cooled. The cooled shaft is inserted into a hub having an inside radius of 4.954 cm. After the parts come to room temperature, the shaft radius and hub inside radius are each 4.956 cm, and the outside radius of the hub is 10 cm. The diametral interference is 0.002 cm. The modulus of elasticity and Poisson's ratio of the shaft and hub are 210 kN/mm^2 and 0.3, respectively. What is most nearly the pressure at the interface of the hub and shaft?

(A) 0.98 kN/cm^2

(B) 1.6 kN/cm^2

(C) 2.5 kN/cm^2

(D) 5.3 kN/cm^2

Solution

Using Eq. 46.7,

$$p = \frac{0.5\delta}{\dfrac{r}{E_o}\left(\dfrac{r_o^2 + r^2}{r_o^2 - r^2} + \nu_o\right) + \dfrac{r}{E_i}\left(\dfrac{r^2 + r_i^2}{r^2 - r_i^2} - \nu_i\right)}$$

$$= \frac{(0.5)(0.002 \text{ cm})}{\begin{pmatrix}\dfrac{4.956 \text{ cm}}{\left(210\ \dfrac{\text{kN}}{\text{mm}^2}\right)\left(10\ \dfrac{\text{mm}}{\text{cm}}\right)^2}\end{pmatrix}}$$
$$\times \left(\dfrac{(10 \text{ cm})^2 + (4.956 \text{ cm})^2}{(10 \text{ cm})^2 - (4.956 \text{ cm})^2} + 0.3\right)$$
$$+ \dfrac{4.956 \text{ cm}}{\left(210\ \dfrac{\text{kN}}{\text{mm}^2}\right)\left(10\ \dfrac{\text{mm}}{\text{cm}}\right)^2}$$
$$\times \left(\dfrac{(4.956 \text{ cm})^2 + (0 \text{ cm})^2}{(4.956 \text{ cm})^2 - (0 \text{ cm})^2} - 0.3\right)$$

$$= 1.6 \text{ kN/cm}^2$$

The answer is (B).

Equation 46.8: Maximum Torque

$$T = 2\pi r^2 \mu p l \quad \textit{46.8}$$

Description

The maximum torque that the press-fitted joint can withstand or transmit is found from the length of the hub engagement, l, and the coefficient of friction at the interface, μ, as shown in Eq. 46.8.

Example

A 2 cm diameter solid steel shaft is pressed into a 3 cm long hub. Given an interface pressure of 70 MPa and a coefficient of friction of 0.6, what is most nearly the maximum torque that can be transmitted from the shaft to the hub?

(A) 550 N·m

(B) 630 N·m

(C) 790 N·m

(D) 880 N·m

---

[25]The *NCEES Handbook* defines r as the "nominal interference radius." Since the "interference radius" is ambiguous, this definition should be interpreted as the "nominal radius at the point of interference." The nominal radius is usually referred to as the *transition radius* or *common radius*.

Solution

The radius of the shaft, r, is

$$r = \frac{d}{2} = \frac{2 \text{ cm}}{2} = 1 \text{ cm}$$

Use Eq. 46.8 to calculate the maximum torque that can be transmitted.

$$T = 2\pi r^2 \mu p l$$

$$= \frac{2\pi (1 \text{ cm})^2 (0.6)(70 \text{ MPa})\left(10^6 \, \frac{\text{Pa}}{\text{MPa}}\right)(3 \text{ cm})}{\left(100 \, \frac{\text{cm}}{\text{m}}\right)^3}$$

$$= 792 \text{ N·m} \quad (790 \text{ N·m})$$

The answer is (C).

Measurement/
Instrumentation

Diagnostic Exam

Topic XII: Measurement, Instrumentation, and Controls

1. What power protection device senses abnormal current and voltage levels generated during fault conditions?

(A) fuse

(B) GFCI

(C) thermal disconnect

(D) transducer

2. What is the purpose of a transducer?

(A) signal detection

(B) amplification

(C) voltage reduction

(D) conversion of a physical parameter to an electrical signal

3. What is the difference between transducers and sensors?

(A) Transducers convert impulses from sensors into measurable quantities.

(B) Transducers usually measure physical quantities, while sensors usually measure chemical quantities.

(C) Transducers tend to be much larger than sensors.

(D) Transducers and sensors are basically the same.

4. A unit impulse function at $t = 0$ is the input signal for the transfer function shown.

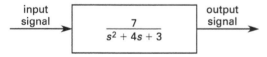

What is the output signal as a function of time?

(A) $y(t) = \left(\dfrac{7}{2}\right)\left(e^{t} + e^{-3t}\right)u(t)$

(B) $y(t) = \left(\dfrac{7}{2}\right)\left(e^{-t} + e^{-3t}\right)u(t)$

(C) $y(t) = \left(\dfrac{7}{2}\right)\left(e^{-3t} - e^{-t}\right)u(t)$

(D) $y(t) = \left(\dfrac{7}{2}\right)\left(e^{-t} - e^{-3t}\right)u(t)$

5. The input signal for the transfer function shown is a step function of height 5 at $t = 0$.

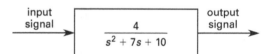

What is the steady-state output?

(A) 0.4

(B) 0.8

(C) 2.0

(D) 2.5

6. A controlled process is shown in block diagram form.

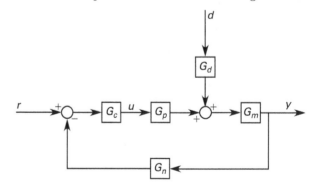

What is the closed-loop transfer function describing the effect of d and r on y?

(A) $y = \left(\dfrac{G_m G_d}{1 + G_m G_p G_c G_n}\right) d + \left(\dfrac{G_m G_p G_c}{1 + G_m G_p G_c G_n}\right) r$

(B) $y = G_m G_d d + G_m G_p G_c (r - G_n)$

(C) $y = G_m G_d d + \left(\dfrac{G_m G_p G_c}{1 + G_m G_p G_c}\right) r$

(D) $y = \left(\dfrac{G_m G_d}{1 + G_m}\right) d + \left(\dfrac{G_m G_p G_c}{1 + G_n}\right) r$

7. A controlled process is described by the closed-loop transfer function $G(s)$.

$$G(s) = \frac{K(s+1)}{2s^2 + (K-1)s + (K-1)}$$

What values of K will stabilize the process?

(A) $K < 1$

(B) $K > 1$

(C) $K > 0.75$

(D) $K \geq 0$

8. Which of the following feedforward transfer function controller equations is realizable?

(A) $G_{ff} = \dfrac{24s(s+1)e^{3s}}{(2s+1)(3s+1)}$

(B) $G_{ff} = \left(-\dfrac{4}{3}\right)\left(\dfrac{3s+1}{2s+1}\right)$

(C) $G_{ff} = \left(+\dfrac{2}{3}\right)\left(\dfrac{(3s+1)e^{2s}}{2s+1}\right)$

(D) $G_{ff} = \left(-\dfrac{1}{9}\right)\left(\dfrac{(2s+1)e^{s}}{s+1}\right)$

9. In the circuit shown, $V_{IN} = 10.00$ V, $V_0 = 0.0125$ V, and $R_1 = R_2 = R_3 = R = 10.00$ kΩ.

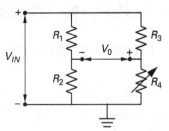

What is most nearly the resistance of R_4?

(A) 10,000 Ω

(B) 10,050 Ω

(C) 10,500 Ω

(D) 15,000 Ω

10. A closed-loop system is shown.

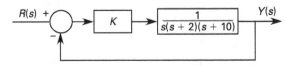

Most nearly, at what gain constant, K, does the system become marginally stable?

(A) 10

(B) 60

(C) 100

(D) 240

SOLUTIONS

1. A transducer is a device used to convert a physical parameter (in this case, a voltage or current) into an electrical signal. For fault conditions, the transducer produces signals that are voltages or currents that are scaled versions of the power system condition, but of much smaller amplitude. Refer to the *NCEES FE Handbook: Instrumentation, Measurement, and Control* for the definition of transducer.

The answer is (D).

2. A transducer is a device used to convert a physical parameter such as temperature, pressure, flow, or light intensity, into an electrical signal (also called a sensor). Transducers are often used in the measurement of voltage or gage displacement.

The answer is (D).

3. The terms "transducer" and "sensor" are used interchangeably, so option (D) is correct. There is a subtle difference. A transducer is anything that converts some physical parameter (such as temperature, pressure, flow, light intensity, etc.) into an electrical parameter (voltage, current, capacitance, etc.). Some transducers are useless for instrumentation because the electrical parameter has a very nonlinear response to the physical parameter. The term "sensor" refers specifically to transducers that are useful for instrumentation. It is also used to refer to systems and components in addition to the transducer that are necessary to use the transducer in an instrumentation application. Page 220 of the FE handbook states: *Transducer* – a device used to convert a physical parameter such as temperature, pressure, flow, light intensity, etc. into an electrical signal (also called a *sensor*).

The answer is (D).

4. The transfer function is

$$\frac{Y(s)}{X(s)} = G(s) = \frac{7}{s^2 + 4s + 3}$$

A unit impulse function at $t=0$ is the input signal, which is also called the Dirac delta function.

$$x(t) = \delta(t)$$

The Laplace transform of the unit impulse function is found in a table of Laplace transform pairs.

$$X(s) = \mathcal{L}(x(t)) = \mathcal{L}(\delta(t)) = 1$$

The output in the Laplace domain is

$$
\begin{aligned}
Y(s) &= G(s)X(s) \\
&= \left(\frac{7}{s^2 + 4s + 3}\right)X(s) \\
&= \frac{7}{s^2 + 4s + 3} \\
&= \frac{7}{(s+1)(s+3)}
\end{aligned}
$$

$Y(s)$ as shown is not in the Laplace transform table. Convert it with partial fractions to an entry that is in the table. Assume $Y(s)$ can be transformed into partial fractions.

$$\frac{7}{(s+1)(s+3)} = \frac{A}{s+1} + \frac{B}{s+3}$$

Multiply by the denominator on the left-hand side to cancel the denominators.

$$7 = \left(\frac{A}{s+1} + \frac{B}{s+3}\right)(s+1)(s+3)$$

This gives the polynomial identity

$$7 = (3A + B) + (A + B)s$$

Since two polynomials are equal if and only if their corresponding coefficients are equal, equate the coefficients of like powers of s. This results in the following set of equations.

$$
\begin{aligned}
3A + B &= 7 \\
A + B &= 0
\end{aligned}
$$

This set of equations has the solutions

$$A = \frac{7}{2}$$

$$B = -\frac{7}{2}$$

The output $Y(s)$ is

$$
\begin{aligned}
Y(s) &= \frac{A}{s+1} + \frac{B}{s+3} \\
&= \left(\frac{7}{2}\right)\left(\frac{1}{s+1} - \frac{1}{s+3}\right)
\end{aligned}
$$

Take the inverse Laplace transform of $Y(s)$ to get the time domain output $y(t)$.

$$y(t) = \mathcal{L}^{-1}(Y(s))$$

$$= \mathcal{L}^{-1}\left(\left(\frac{7}{2}\right)\left(\frac{1}{s+1} - \frac{1}{s+3}\right)\right)$$

$$= \left(\frac{7}{2}\right)\left(\mathcal{L}^{-1}\left(\frac{1}{s+1}\right) - \mathcal{L}^{-1}\left(\frac{1}{s+3}\right)\right)$$

$$= \left(\frac{7}{2}\right)(e^{-t} - e^{-3t}) \quad \left(\left(\frac{7}{2}\right)(e^{-t} - e^{-3t})\,u(t)\right)$$

The answer is (D).

5. The transfer function is

$$\frac{Y(s)}{X(s)} = G(s) = \frac{4}{s^2 + 7s + 10}$$

The input signal is a unit step function of height 5 at $t = 0$.

$$x(t) = 5u(t)$$

The Laplace transform of the unit step function is found from a table of Laplace transform pairs.

$$X(s) = \mathcal{L}(x(t)) = \mathcal{L}(5u(t)) = \frac{5}{s}$$

The output in the Laplace domain is

$$Y(s) = G(s)X(s)$$

$$= \left(\frac{4}{s^2 + 7s + 10}\right)X(s)$$

$$= \left(\frac{4}{s^2 + 7s + 10}\right)\left(\frac{5}{s}\right)$$

$$= \frac{20}{(s^2 + 7s + 10)s}$$

The steady-state output can be obtained from the final value theorem.

$$\lim_{t \to \infty} y(t) = \lim_{s \to 0} sY(s)$$

$$= \lim_{s \to 0} s\frac{20}{(s^2 + 7s + 10)s}$$

$$= \lim_{s \to 0} \frac{20}{(s^2 + 7s + 10)}$$

$$= \lim_{s \to 0} \frac{20}{((0)^2 + (7)(0) + 10)}$$

$$= 2.0$$

The answer is (C).

6. As functions of the input signals, signals y and u are

$$y = G_m(G_d d + G_p u)$$

$$u = G_c(r - G_n y)$$

Combine the two equations.

$$y = G_m\left(G_d d + G_p G_c(r - G_n y)\right)$$

$$= \left(\frac{G_m G_d}{1 + G_m G_p G_c G_n}\right)d + \left(\frac{G_m G_p G_c}{1 + G_m G_p G_c G_n}\right)r$$

The answer is (A).

7. The controlled process is stable if the real part of the roots of the denominator of the closed-loop transfer function is less than 0.

The roots of the denominator of the closed-loop transfer function are

$$s = \frac{-(K-1) \pm \sqrt{K^2 - 2K + 1 - (8)(K-1)}}{4}$$

$$= \frac{1-K}{4} \pm \frac{\sqrt{K^2 - 10K + 9}}{4}$$

Borderline stability will occur when $s = 0$.

$$0 = \frac{1-K}{4} \pm \frac{\sqrt{K^2 - 10K + 9}}{4}$$

$$K = 1$$

As K increases above 1, the roots of the polynomial remain negative, so the process is stable for $K > 1$.

The answer is (B).

8. The e^{3s}, e^{2s}, and e^{s} factors in options (A), (C), and (D) require the controller to know the input (disturbance) 3, 2, and 1 in units of time into the future, respectively. This is not possible. The only transfer function that is realizable is option (B). In addition, option (B) has the same order of polynomial in the numerator and denominator, which is a requirement for realization.

The answer is (B).

9. The circuit is a Wheatstone bridge. If R_4 is close to 10 kΩ, then the quarter bridge approximation can be used.

$$V_0 \approx \frac{\Delta R}{4R} \cdot V_{IN}$$

$$\begin{aligned}
\Delta R &\approx \frac{V_0}{V_{IN}} \cdot 4R \\
&= \left(\frac{0.0125 \text{ V}}{10.00 \text{ V}} \right)(4)(10.0 \times 10^3 \ \Omega) \\
&= 50 \ \Omega \\
R_4 &= R + \Delta R \\
&= 10{,}000 \ \Omega + 50 \ \Omega \\
&= 10{,}050 \ \Omega
\end{aligned}$$

The quarter bridge approximation is valid because

$$\begin{aligned}
R_4 &= 10{,}050 \ \Omega \\
&\approx 10{,}000 \ \Omega \\
&= R
\end{aligned}$$

The answer is (B).

10. The characteristic equation is given by

$$a_n s^n + a_{n-1} s^{n-1} + a_{n-2} s^{n-2} + \cdots + a_0 = 0$$
$$s^3 + 12s^2 + 20s + K = 0$$

Form the Routh table for the coefficients.

s^3	1	20
s^2	12	K
s	$(240 - K)/12$	0
s^0	K	

The Routh-Hurwitz criterion states that the number of sign changes in the first column of the table equals the number of positive, or unstable, roots. If the value of K is between 0 and 240, there are no sign changes, so the system becomes marginally stable at $K = 240$.

The answer is (D).

47 Measurement and Instrumentation

Nomenclature

A	area	m^2
C	concentration	various
E	potential	J
f	frequency	Hz
GF	gage factor	–
I	current	A
L	length	m
n	quantity	–
N	number of resolution steps	–
p	pressure	Pa
P	permeability	C/m^2
R	resistance	Ω
S	proportionality constant	V/pH
t	thickness	m
t	time	s
T	period	s
T	temperature	K
V	voltage	V
w_R	measurement error	various

Symbols

α	temperature coefficient	1/K
β	temperature coefficient	$1/K^2$
ε	strain	–
ε_V	voltage resolution	V

Subscripts

0	reference
a	measured solution
b	balanced
el	electrode
H	high
i	internal buffer (reference solution)
I	of interest
L	low
N	Nyquist
s	sample or sampling
T	at temperature T

1. INSTRUMENTATION

A *transducer* is any device used to convert a physical phenomenon into an electrical signal. For example, a microphone is a transducer that transforms sound energy into electrical signals that can be recorded, amplified, or transmitted. Other transducers sense such phenomena as temperature, pressure, physical movement, and light intensity.

The signal from a transducer may be used in a feedback loop to control the physical phenomenon in some way. For example, a thermostat is a transducer that is sensitive to temperature. When the temperature drops below the set-point temperature, the heater is turned on.

2. SENSITIVITY

Sensitivity is the ratio of the change in electrical signal magnitude to the change in magnitude of the physical parameter being measured. That is, transducer sensitivity is the ratio of the transmitted signal to the sensor signal. If a transducer exhibits a significant change in an electrical characteristic (voltage, current, resistance, capacitance, or inductance) in response to a change in a parameter, then it is sensitive to that parameter. The greater the change in the electrical signal for the same change in the parameter, the greater the sensitivity of the transducer. It is desirable to use transducers that are sensitive to only one parameter and insensitive to all others. For example, an odometer in a car should respond to only the rotation of the car wheels, and the measurement should not depend on other factors like wind speed, temperature, or humidity.

3. LINEARITY

The *linearity* of a transducer is the degree to which the output (e.g., voltage) is in direct proportion to the parameter being measured. Transducers are usually designed and selected to be linear over the range of measurements. This is not always practical, so a second-order term and even a third-order term may be needed.

4. MEASUREMENT ACCURACY

A measurement is said to be *accurate* if it is substantially unaffected by (i.e., is insensitive to) all variations outside of the measurer's control.

For example, suppose a rifle is aimed at a point on a distant target and several shots are fired. The target point represents the "true value" of a measurement—the value that should be obtained. The impact points represent the measured values—what is actually obtained. The distance from the centroid of the points of impact to the target point is a measure of the alignment accuracy between the barrel and the sights. The difference between the true and measured values is known as the *measurement bias*.

5. MEASUREMENT PRECISION

Precision is not synonymous with accuracy. Precision is a function of the repeatability of the measured results. If an experiment is repeated with identical results, the measurement is said to be precise. In the rifle example from Sec. 47.4, the average distance of each impact from the centroid of the impact group is a measure of precision. It is possible to take highly precise measurements and still have a large bias.

Most measurement techniques that are intended to improve accuracy (e.g., taking multiple measurements and refining the measurement methods or procedures) actually increase the precision.

Sometimes, the term *reliability* is used to describe the precision of a measurement. A *reliable measurement* is the same as a *precise estimate*.

6. MEASUREMENT STABILITY

Stability and *insensitivity* are related terms. (Conversely, *instability* and *sensitivity* are also related.) A stable measurement is insensitive to minor changes in the measurement process.

7. SENSORS

While the term "transducer" is commonly used for devices that respond to mechanical input (force, pressure, torque, etc.), the term *sensor* is commonly applied to devices that respond to chemical conditions.[1] For example, an electrochemical sensor might respond to a specific gas, compound, or ion (known as a *target substance* or *species*). Two types of electrochemical sensors are in use today: potentiometric and amperometric. (See Table 47.1.)[2]

Table 47.1 *Examples of Common Chemical Sensors*

sensor type	principle	materials	analyte
semiconducting oxide sensor	conductivity impedance	SnO_2, TiO_2, ZnO_2, WO_3, polymers	O_2, H_2, CO, SO_x, NO_x, combustible hydrocarbons, alcohol, H_2S, NH_3
electrochemical sensor (liquid electrolyte)	amperometric	composite Pt, Au catalyst	H_2, O_2, O_3, CO, H_2S, SO_2, NO_x, NH_3, glucose, hydrazine
ion-selective electrode (ISE)	potentiometric	glass, LaF_3, CaF_2	pH, K^+, Na^+, Cl^-, Ca^2, Mg^{2+}, F^-, Ag^+
solid electrode sensor	amperometric	YSZ, H^+-conductor	O_2, H_2, CO, combustible hydrocarbons
	potentiometric	YSZ, β-alumina, Nasicon	O_2, H_2, CO_2, CO, NO_x, SO_2, H_2S, Cl_2
		Nafion	H_2O, combustible hydrocarbons
piezoelectric sensor	mechanical w/ polymer film	quartz	combustible hydrocarbons, VOCs
catalytic combustion sensor	calorimetric	Pt/Al_2O_3, Pt-wire	H_2, CO, combustible hydrocarbons
pyroelectric sensor	calorimetric	pyroelectric + film	vapors
optical sensors	colorimetric fluorescence	optical fiber/ indicator dye	acids, bases, combustible hydrocarbons, biologicals

Source: *Journal of The Electrochemical Society*, 150(2). ©2003. The Electrochemical Society.

Potentiometric sensors generate a measurable voltage at their terminals. In electrochemical sensors taking advantage of half-cell reactions at electrodes, the generated voltage is proportional to the absolute temperature, T, and is inversely proportional to the number of

---

[1]The categorization is common but not universal. The terms "transducer," "sensor," "sending unit," and "pickup" are often used loosely.
[2](1) By reproducing Table 47.1 directly, the *NCEES Handbook* perpetuated the errors and inconsistencies present in the original source. (2) The table's title, "common chemical sensors," is inaccurate because many of the devices do not respond to chemical species. Semiconducting oxide devices (bias), piezoelectric devices (force), pyroelectric devices (temperature), and optical devices (radiation) are not chemical sensors. (3) All of the entries in the column marked "principle" should list either "amperometric" or "potentiometric." Instead, the column entries are a hodge-podge of response characteristic, sensor type, construction method, and construction material (belonging in the "materials" column). (4) In the "analyte" column for ion-selective electrode, "Ca^2" is an error and should be "Ca^{2+}." (5) For example, the resistance of a nonlinear resistance temperature detector (RTD) (see Sec. 47.8) is frequently modeled as
$R_T = R_0(1 + \alpha T + \beta T^2 + \gamma T^3)$

electrons, n, (i.e., the valence or oxidation number of the ions) taking part in the chemical reaction at the half-cell. In the following equation, p_1 is the partial pressure of the target substance at the measurement electrode; and p_2 is the partial pressure of the target substance at the reference electrode.

$$V \propto \left(\frac{T_{\text{absolute}}}{n}\right)\ln\frac{p_1}{p_2}$$

Amperometric sensors (also known as *voltammetric sensors*) generate a measurable current at their terminals. In conventional electrochemical sensors known as *diffusion-controlled cells*, a high-conductivity acid or alkaline liquid electrolyte is used with a gas-permeable membrane that transmits ions from the outside to the inside of the sensor. A reference voltage is applied to two terminals within the electrolyte, and the current generated at a (third) sensing electrode is measured.

The maximum current generated is known as the *limiting current*. Current is proportional to the concentration, C, of the target substance; the permeability, P; the exposed sensor (membrane) area, A; and the number of electrons transferred per molecule detected, n. The current is inversely proportional to the membrane thickness, t.

$$I \propto \frac{nPCA}{t}$$

Table 47.1 lists types of common chemical sensors.

Equation 47.1: pH Combined Electrode Potential

$$E_{el} = E^0 - S(\text{pH}_a - \text{pH}_i) \qquad 47.1$$

Variation

$$E_{el} = E^0 + 10S(\log[\text{H}_2^+] - \log[\text{H}_1^+])$$
$$= E^0 + 10S\left(\log\frac{[\text{H}_2^+]}{[\text{H}_1^+]}\right)$$

Description

A pH sensor measures the pH of a solution through a probe connected to an electronic meter. The sensor generates an electrode potential, E_{el}, predicted by Eq. 47.1.

The potential generated by a theoretically perfect pH sensor in a neutral (pH of 7) solution is zero. However, a real sensor has an intrinsic potential known as the *standard electrode potential*, E^0. As it is derived from the *Nernst equation* used for analyzing electrolytic reactions, two electrodes are involved, one for each

electrode/solution. In Eq. 47.1, pH_a is the pH of the measured solution as detected by the measurement electrode, and pH_i is the pH of the internal buffer (i.e., reference solution as detected by the reference electrode). (An ideal reference electrode will generate the same reference voltage regardless of the pH.) Simple, uncompensated electrodes that respond directly to solution parameters and that must be used in pairs to obtain the active and reference measurements are known as *single electrodes*. When the two electrodes are combined into a single probe, the term *combination electrode* is used.[3]

Equation 47.1 is the equation of a straight line, so the sensor it describes is implicitly linear in its response over the instrument's pH range, generally between 2 and 11. Since the actual electrical output of a pH sensor is in the millivolt range, the proportionality constant (slope), S, in Eq. 47.1 is in millivolts/pH. The slope is negative because generated potential decreases as pH increases. pH meter scales are usually marked (or, read) directly in pH, not millivolts. Since the Nernst equation (and the proportionality constant, S) is temperature dependent, quality pH measuring devices incorporate temperature probes for internal compensation. In order to use Eq. 47.1, it may be necessary to convert molar hydrogen ion concentrations into pH.

$$\text{pH} = -10\log[\text{H}^+]$$

Example

The potential of a calomel (Hg2Cl2) buffering electrode is 0.241 V. At 25°C, the electrode potential of a silver-AgCl/calomel combined electrode is given by

$$0.558 + 0.059\log[\text{Ag}^+] \quad \text{[volts]}$$

Most nearly, what is the standard electrode potential for the silver reaction, $\text{Ag} \rightleftarrows \text{Ag}^+ + e^-$?

(A)   0.18 V

(B)   0.30 V

(C)   0.35 V

(D)   0.80 V

Solution

Use Eq. 47.1.

$$E_{el} = E^0 - S(\text{pH}_a - \text{pH}_i)$$
$$= E^0 + S(\text{pH}_i) - S(\text{pH}_a)$$
$$= E^0_{\text{Ag}^+} - S(\log_{10}[\text{Hg}^+]) - S(\text{pH}_a)$$

---

[3]pH_a can be interpreted as the pH of the *active sensor* (or, alternatively) the pH of the *acidic* solution, *alkaline* solution, or (in the case of medical sensors) of the *arterial* blood flow. In fact, the subscript is derived from the *activity* of the hydrogen ions in the solution. In general, pH_i is the pH of a reference electrode, so pH_{ref} would be an appropriate variable. However, the *NCEES Handbook* has adopted the subscript specifically for a one-piece, combined sensor having an *inner* buffer reference.

The value of S is not known, but the product of S and $\log_{10}[\mathrm{Hg}^+]$ represents the electrode potential of the calomel reference electrode reaction. This is given as 0.241 V.

$$0.558 \text{ V} = E^0_{\mathrm{Ag}^+} - E^0_{\mathrm{Hg}^+}$$

$$E^0_{\mathrm{Ag}^+} = 0.558 \text{ V} + E^0_{\mathrm{Hg}^+}$$

$$= 0.558 \text{ V} + 0.241 \text{ V}$$

$$= 0.799 \text{ V} \quad (0.80 \text{ V})$$

Since 25°C corresponds to the standardization temperature of electrode potentials, this is the standard electrode potential for the silver reaction.

The answer is (D).

8. RESISTANCE TEMPERATURE DETECTORS

Resistance temperature detectors (RTDs), also known as *resistance thermometers*, change resistance predictably in response to changes in temperature. An RTD is composed of a fine wire wrapped around a form and protected with glass or a ceramic coating. Nickel and copper are commonly used for industrial RTDs. Platinum is often used in RTDs because it is mechanically and electrically stable, is chemically inert, resists contamination, and can be highly refined to a high and consistent purity. RTDs are connected through resistance bridges to compensate for lead resistance.

Equation 47.2: Resistance Versus Temperature

$$R_T = R_0[1 + \alpha(T - T_0)] \qquad \text{47.2}$$

Variations

$$R_T \approx R_0(1 + \alpha\Delta T + \beta\Delta T^2)$$

$$\Delta T = T - T_0$$

Description

With some exceptions, including carbon and silicon, resistance in most conductors increases with temperature. The resistance of RTDs has greater sensitivity and more linear response to temperature than that of standard resistors. The resistance at a given temperature can be calculated from the *coefficients of thermal resistance*, α and β. Higher-order terms —third, fourth, etc.—are used when extreme accuracy is required. The variation of resistance with temperature is nonlinear, though β is small and is often insignificant over short temperature ranges. Therefore, a linear relationship is often assumed and only α is used.[4] In commercial RTDs, α is referred to as the *alpha-value*.

R_0 is the resistance (usually 100 Ω for standard RTDs) at the *reference temperature*, T_0, usually at 0°C (32°F). The first-order approximation in Eq. 47.2 is sufficient in most practical applications.

Similarly to resistors, commercial RTDs are categorized by the precision of their labeled resistance values. RTDs in various classes (e.g., AA, A, B, 1/10 B, etc.) are available, although Class B RTDs are the most common. At 0°C, resistances of Class A RTDs can vary $\pm 0.15\%$ from their nominal values (e.g., 100 Ω), while Class B RTDs can vary $\pm 0.30\%$. The maximum deviations in the as-delivered resistance and the corresponding temperature response are known as *tolerances*. Identifying RTD tolerance classes by their percentages (e.g., "a 0.12% RTD") should be avoided, since tolerances are actually dependent on temperature and resistance wire (or, manufacturing method, in the case of thin-film RTDs) used, and the percentage tolerances are different for resistance and temperature response. Figure 47.1 shows tolerance values for standard 100 Ω RTDs.

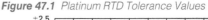
Figure 47.1 Platinum RTD Tolerance Values

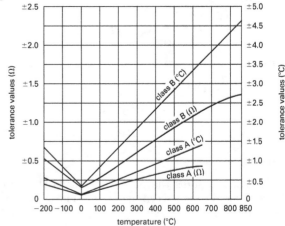

9. STRAIN GAGES

A *bonded strain gage* is a metallic resistance device that is bonded to the surface of the unstressed member. (See Fig. 47.2(a).) The gage consists of a folded

---

[4]Although the *NCEES Handbook* presents Eq. 47.2 as an equality, it is only an approximation. Higher order terms (e.g., the variation equation) may be needed to obtain sufficient accuracy.

metallic conductor (known as the *grid*) on a backing (known as the *substrate*). The grids of strain gages were originally of the folded-wire type. For example, nichrome wire with a total resistance under 1000 Ω was commonly used.

Modern strain gages are generally of the foil type manufactured using printed circuit techniques. Semiconductor gages are used when extreme sensitivity (i.e., a gage factor in excess of 100) is required. However, semiconductor gages are extremely temperature-sensitive.

The substrate and grid experience the same strain as the surface of the member. The resistance of the gage changes as the member is stressed due to changes in conductor cross section and intrinsic changes in resistivity with strain. Temperature effects must be compensated by the circuitry or by using a second unstrained gage as part of the bridge measurement system.

When simultaneous strain measurements in two or more directions are needed, it is convenient to use a commercial *rosette strain gage*. (See Fig. 47.2(b).) A rosette consists of two or more grids properly oriented for application as a single unit.

Table 47.2 at the end of the chapter shows various types of strain gages.

Figure 47.2 Strain Gage

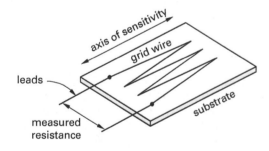

(a) bonded-wire strain gage

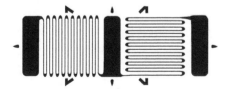

(b) commercial two-element rosette

Equation 47.3: Gage Factor

$$GF = \frac{\Delta R/R}{\Delta L/L} = \frac{\Delta R/R}{\varepsilon} \qquad 47.3$$

Description

The *gage factor* (*strain sensitivity factor*), *GF*, is the ratio of the fractional change in resistance to the fractional change in length (strain) along the detecting axis of the gage. (See Table 47.3.) The gage factor is a function of the gage material. It can be calculated from the grid material's properties and configuration. The higher the gage factor, the greater the sensitivity of the gage. From a practical standpoint, however, the gage factor and gage resistance are provided by the gage manufacturer. Only the change in resistance is measured.

Values

Table 47.3 Approximate Gage Factors

material	*GF*
constantan	2.0
iron, soft	4.2
isoelastic	3.5
manganin	0.47
monel	1.9
nichrome	2.0
nickel	−12*
platinum	4.8
platinum-iridium	5.1

*Value depends on amount of preprocessing and cold working.

Example

A strain gage is to be used in measuring the strain on a test specimen. A strain gage with an initial resistance of 120 Ω exhibits a decrease of 0.120 Ω. The gage factor is 2.00. The initial length of the strain gage was 1.000 cm. What is most nearly the final length of the strain gage?

(A)   0.9995 cm

(B)   1.0000 cm

(C)   1.0005 cm

(D)   1.0050 cm

Solution

From Eq. 47.3,

$$GF = \frac{\Delta R/R}{\Delta L/L}$$

Solve for the change in length.

$$
\begin{aligned}
\Delta L &= \frac{\Delta R/R}{GF/L} \\
&= \frac{\dfrac{0.120\ \Omega}{120\ \Omega}}{\dfrac{2.00}{1.000\ \text{cm}}} \\
&= 0.0005\ \text{cm}
\end{aligned}
$$

The resistance decreased, so the length of the strain gage also decreased.

$$
\begin{aligned}
L_{\text{final}} &= L - \Delta L \\
&= 1.000\ \text{cm} - 0.0005\ \text{cm} \\
&= 0.9995\ \text{cm}
\end{aligned}
$$

The answer is (A).

10. WHEATSTONE BRIDGES

The *Wheatstone bridge* shown in Fig. 47.3 is one type of *resistance bridge*. The Wheatstone bridge can be used to determine the unknown resistance of a resistance transducer (e.g., thermistor or resistance-type strain gage), such as R_1 in Fig. 47.3. The potentiometer, R_4, in Fig. 47.3 and Fig. 47.4, is adjusted (i.e., the bridge is "balanced") until no current flows through the meter or until there is no voltage across the meter, hence the name *null indicator*, or alternatively, *zero-indicating bridge* or *null-indicating bridge*. The unknown resistance can also be determined from the voltage imbalance shown by the meter reading, in which case the bridge is known as a *deflection bridge* rather than a null-indicating bridge. When the bridge is balanced and no current flows through the meter leg, the following equations apply.

$$
\begin{aligned}
I_1 &= I_2 \\
I_4 &= I_3 \\
V_4 + V_3 &= V_1 + V_2 \\
R_1 R_4 &= R_2 R_3 \quad \text{[balanced]}
\end{aligned}
$$

Figure 47.3 Series-Balanced Wheatstone Bridge

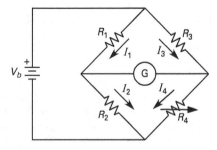

Any one of the four resistances can be the unknown, up to three of the remaining resistances can be fixed or adjustable, and the battery and meter can be connected to either of two diagonal corners. The following bridge law statement can be used to help formulate the proper relationship: *When a series Wheatstone bridge is null-balanced, the ratio of resistance of any two adjacent legs equals the ratio of resistance of the remaining two legs, taken in the same sense.* In this statement, "taken in the same sense" means that both ratios must be formed reading either left to right, right to left, top to bottom, or bottom to top.

Equation 47.4 and Eq. 47.5: Wheatstone Quarter Bridge Equations

$$
\Delta R \ll R \qquad \text{47.4}
$$

$$
V_0 \approx \frac{\Delta R}{4R} \cdot V_{IN} \qquad \text{47.5}
$$

Description

A special case of the Wheatstone bridge circuit is the quarter bridge circuit shown in Fig. 47.4. The quarter bridge circuit has three identical resistors and one resistor with a resistance slightly different from the resistance of the other three. This different resistor is the transducer. The resistance difference, ΔR, can be positive or negative, but it must be relatively small compared to R. (See Eq. 47.4.)

Figure 47.4 *Wheatstone Quarter Bridge*

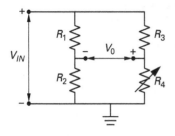

$$R_1 = R_2 = R_3 = R$$

$$R_4 = R + \Delta R$$

Most Wheatstone bridge circuits are difficult analyze if they are not balanced, but the Wheatstone quarter bridge has a simple approximation, given by Eq. 47.5. Equation 47.5 is useful for many instrumentation applications.[5]

Example

In the circuit shown,

$$V_0 = 0.0500 \text{ V}$$
$$R_1 = R_2 = R_3 = R$$
$$= 10.00 \text{ k}\Omega$$
$$R_4 = 10.25 \text{ k}\Omega$$

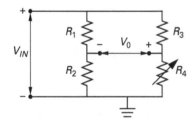

The voltage V_{IN} is most nearly

(A) 2 V

(B) 4 V

(C) 5 V

(D) 8 V

Solution

The circuit is a Wheatstone bridge. Since R_4 is close to 10 kΩ, the quarter bridge approximation can be used.

$$V_0 \approx \frac{\Delta R}{4R} \cdot V_{IN}$$

$$\begin{aligned} V_{IN} &\approx \frac{4R}{\Delta R} V_0 \\ &= \left(\frac{(4)(10 \text{ k}\Omega)}{10.25 \text{ k}\Omega - 10 \text{ k}\Omega} \right) (0.0500 \text{ V}) \\ &= 8 \text{ V} \end{aligned}$$

The answer is (D).

11. SAMPLING

Equation 47.6: Sampling Frequency

$$f_s = \frac{1}{\Delta t} \qquad \text{47.6}$$

Description

As part of the *analog-to-digital conversion* process, continuous-time signals are sampled to produce discrete signals. The analog signal is sampled at regular time intervals designated by Δt. The *sampling frequency* (*sampling rate*) is given by Eq. 47.6.

Equation 47.7: Reproducible Sampling

$$f_s > 2f_N \qquad \text{47.7}$$

Variation

$$f_s > 2f_I$$

Description

Shannon's sampling theorem[6] states that a continuous-time signal is completely defined by (i.e., can be reconstructed from) a sequence of equally spaced values, if the sampling rate is at least twice the highest frequency component, the *frequency of interest*, f_I. Therefore, if the signal is to be reproduced from its samples, the

---

[5]The *NCEES Handbook* is not consistent in its use of subscripts. While upper case letters might have been used to designate a constant DC value, there is probably no distinction between "IN" as used in the "*Instrumentation, Measurement, and Controls*" section and "in" as used in the "*Electrical and Computer Engineering*" section.

[6]Shannon's theorem is also known as the *Nyquist sampling theorem, Nyquist-Shannon theorem, Whittaker-Shannon-Kotelnikov theorem, cardinal theorem of interpolation*, and several other variations.

minimum acceptable sampling rate, known as the *Nyquist rate*, is $2f_I$. Sampling above the Nyquist rate will be sufficient for most practical applications.[7]

If the continuous-time signal is a varying-frequency sinusoid, then sampling at greater than the Nyquist rate will ensure at least one sample in every positive half-cycle and every negative half-cycle. Lower-frequency parts of the signal will be represented by multiple samples.

The signal may also contain frequencies that are higher than twice the sampling rate, a situation that may be acceptable if the frequencies are not of interest. For example, sampling of an audio signal does not need to represent frequencies that are beyond the range that the human ear can hear.

If sampling is done at a lower rate than the Nyquist rate, then the higher frequencies in the measured signal are not accurately represented and will distort the lower frequencies' content in the sampled data. Frequencies greater than the sampling frequencies and at integer multiples of the sampling frequency appear as lower frequencies and are known as *alias frequencies*.

A signal sampling circuit will capture the signal at a fixed sampling frequency. Half of this sampling frequency is known as the *Nyquist frequency*. The Nyquist frequency is a function of the sampling circuit, which doesn't know which frequencies are contained in the signal.

The desired criteria for reproducible sampling are

sampling frequency $\geq 2 \times$ highest signal frequency

sampling frequency $\geq$ Nyquist rate

Nyquist frequency $\geq \frac{1}{2} \times$ Nyquist rate

Impulse sampling refers to taking instantaneous signal measurements at fixed intervals. Figure 47.5 illustrates a continuous, frequency-modulated (FM) signal (part a) that has been sampled at fixed intervals (part b) and reconstructed from the discrete samples (part c). The message function, $m(t)$, is signal voltage or some other measure of signal strength, such as power. The actual *frequency of sampling* (*sampling frequency* or *sampling rate*), f_s, is a feature of the sampling algorithm and/or the equipment setting. The frequency of sampling can be calculated from the *sampling interval* (*sampling period*), T_s, as shown in Eq. 47.8. In order to faithfully reconstruct a signal from the discrete samples, the

actual sampling frequency must be at least the Nyquist rate. (The Nyquist rate for sampling is double the signal's highest frequency of interest, f_I.)

Figure 47.5(c) illustrates how sampling too infrequently can result in reconstructed signals with low frequencies not present in the original signal. Basically, the high-frequency content will alias within the passband (i.e., a false lower frequency component will appear in the reconstructed signal due to an inadequate sampling rate). To prevent aliasing in the passband, a low-pass filter should be used to limit the baseband's frequency content to less than half the sampling rate (i.e., half of the Nyquist rate).

Figure 47.5 *Signal Sampling and Reconstruction*

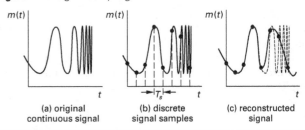

(a) original continuous signal

(b) discrete signal samples

(c) reconstructed signal

Equation 47.8 and Eq. 47.9: Frequency of Sampling (Low-Pass Filter)

$$f_s = 1/T_s \qquad \qquad 47.8$$

$$f_s \geq 2W \quad [M(f) = 0 \text{ for } f > W] \qquad 47.9$$

Variation

$$f_s \geq \text{Nyquist rate} = 2f_I$$

Description

Equation 47.9 shows that in order to reconstruct a low-pass signal faithfully, the sampling frequency should be greater than $2W$ (i.e., twice the message bandwidth).[8] Comparing Eq. 47.9 and the variation equation shows that the message bandwidth, W, and the highest frequency of interest, f_I, are the same for a low-pass filter. In signal processing, the Nyquist rate is two times the bandwidth of a band-limited signal, $2W$.

$$W = f_2 - f_1 \quad [\text{passband}]$$

$$W = f_2 \quad [\text{low-pass}]$$

---

[7]The Nyquist *rate* is a function of the frequencies in the signal and, as such, is better understood as a "signaling rate" (not a sampling rate). The Nyquist *frequency* is a function of the sampling equipment—specifically, half of the actual sampling frequency. Many authorities inaccurately substitute one term for the other. In Eq. 47.7, the *NCEES Handbook* does this and compounds the confusion even more by using the term "Nyquist frequency," f_N, to refer to the highest frequency component (in the "Instrumentation, Measurement, and Controls" section) and to refer to twice the message bandwidth (in the "Electrical and Computer Engineering" section), which is essentially the same as twice the highest frequency component. These are conflicting statements, and both are incorrect.

[8](1) In the *NCEES Handbook*, the expression "where $M(f) = 0$ for $f > W$," which accompanies Eq. 47.9, simply describes a low-pass signal (i.e., "There are no signal components having frequencies greater than $f_2 = W$"). $M(f)$ is the Fourier transform of the signal component. If the signal component has been filtered out, then its Fourier transform will be zero. (2) The *NCEES Handbook* identifies Eq. 47.9 as being applicable to a low-pass signal, but it does not specifically exclude its use for passband signals. Equation 47.9 cannot be used for passband signals. (3) Strictly, the operator ">" in Eq. 47.9 should be "$\geq$."

The message bandwidth, W, can be calculated from the upper and lower limits of the passband. All low-frequency components are present when only a low-pass filter is used, so $f_1 = 0$. There are no frequencies greater than f_2 for a passband signal (and none greater than W for a low-pass signal), so $M(f) = 0$ for frequencies greater than f_2 for a passband signal (and for frequencies greater than W for a low-pass signal).

Example

Human hearing is limited to frequencies that are less than about 20 kHz. Human speech is generally limited to the lower frequencies in a voice band from about 300 Hz to 3000 Hz. Most nearly, what minimum sampling rate should be used to process microphone input signals in order to faithfully process air traffic control voice communications?

(A) 3 kHz

(B) 6 kHz

(C) 8 kHz

(D) 40 kHz

Solution

The only frequencies that need to be transmitted are in the frequency range of 300 Hz to 3000 Hz. For a low-pass filter, the bandwidth is the highest frequency passed, 3000 Hz (3 kHz) in this case. From Eq. 47.9, the minimum sampling rate is 6000 Hz (6 kHz).

The answer is (B).

12. ANALOG-TO-DIGITAL CONVERSION

The resolution of analog-to-digital conversion (ADC) determines the accuracy that is possible for a measured value. The digital number that represents the analog sample does not represent the actual value, but rather it indicates that the actual value is somewhere within a range. That range is the *resolution*.

Equation 47.10: Voltage Resolution

$$\varepsilon_V = \frac{V_H - V_L}{2^n} \qquad 47.10$$

Description

An analog measurement in the range from a high voltage, V_H, to a low voltage, V_L, that is measured by a digital system with n bits has a voltage resolution, ε_V, given by Eq. 47.10.

Example

An analog-to-digital conversion process has a resolution of approximately 1.52588×10^{-4} V. The voltage range is 0–10 V. How many bits are required to represent a sampled voltage digitally?

(A) 4

(B) 8

(C) 16

(D) 32

Solution

Use Eq. 47.10.

$$\varepsilon_V = \frac{V_H - V_L}{2^n}$$

$$2^n = \frac{V_H - V_L}{\varepsilon_V}$$

$$= \frac{10 \text{ V} - 0 \text{ V}}{1.52588 \times 10^{-4} \text{ V}}$$

$$= 65{,}536$$

Solve for n.

$$n \log_{10} 2 = \log_{10} 65{,}536$$

$$n = 16$$

The answer is (C).

Equation 47.11: Analog Voltage Calculated from Digital Representation

$$V = \varepsilon_V N + V_L \qquad 47.11$$

Description

The analog voltage value, V, to be converted in an ADC will be no lower than the *floor voltage*, V_L. Since the voltage resolution of the ADC is ε_V, the number of voltage "steps" between V_L and V is $N = (V - V_L)/\varepsilon_V$. In the ADC, N will be represented as a binary number in the range of 0 to $2^n - 1$. Therefore, the maximum analog value that the ADC can represent is $V_H - \varepsilon_V$ (i.e., one voltage resolution less than the maximum range), which corresponds to the value represented by a binary, N, containing all "1" bits. Using Eq. 47.11, the original analog value, V, can be calculated from the floor voltage, V_L, and the number, N, of resolution steps.

13. MEASUREMENT UNCERTAINTY

The *Kline-McClintock equation*, Eq. 47.12, gives the measurement uncertainty of a function, $R = f(x_1, x_2, x_3, \ldots, x_n)$, whose values have uncertainties $x_1 \pm w_1$, $x_2 \pm w_2$, $x_3 \pm w_3$, and so on.[9]

Equation 47.12: The Kline-McClintock Uncertainty Equation

$$w_R = \sqrt{\left(w_1 \frac{\partial f}{\partial x_1}\right)^2 + \left(w_2 \frac{\partial f}{\partial x_2}\right)^2 + \cdots + \left(w_n \frac{\partial f}{\partial x_n}\right)^2} \quad \text{47.12}$$

Variations

$$w_R = \sqrt{w_1^2 + w_2^2 + \cdots + w_n^2}$$

$$w_R = \sqrt{a_1^2 w_1^2 + a_2^2 w_2^2 + \cdots + a_n^2 w_n^2}$$

Description

The *Kline-McClintock equation* (see Eq. 47.12) is used as a method for estimating the uncertainty, w_R, in a function that depends on more than one measurement. The uncertainties can be caused by anything random. Generally, the measurements will not be at the most extreme value of the inaccuracy (which is known as a *worst-case stack up* of the inaccuracy). Using the Kline-McClintock method gives a result closer to the real inaccuracy than averaging the inaccuracies, in most cases.[10]

If the function R is the sum of the measurements (i.e., $R = x_1 + x_2 + x_3 + \cdots + x_n$), then the Kline-McClintock equation reduces to the first variation equation. This is called the *root-sum-square* (RSS) *value*.

If the function R is a sum of the measurements multiplied by constants (i.e., $R = a_1 x_1 + a_2 x_2 + a_3 x_3 + \cdots + a_n x_n$), then the Kline-McClintock equation reduces to the second variation equation. This is called a *weighted RSS value*.

Example

A calculation is made by combining three measurements, x_1, x_2, and x_3, using the equation shown. The uncertainties of the measurements are ± 0.03, ± 0.05, and ± 0.07, respectively.

$$f = 3x_1 - 5x_2 + 7x_3$$

What is most nearly the estimated uncertainty of the calculation?

(A) 0.34

(B) 0.56

(C) 0.67

(D) 0.79

Solution

Use Eq. 47.12.

$$w_R = \sqrt{\left(w_1 \frac{\partial f}{\partial x_1}\right)^2 + \left(w_2 \frac{\partial f}{\partial x_2}\right)^2 + \cdots + \left(w_n \frac{\partial f}{\partial x_n}\right)^2}$$

$$\frac{\partial f}{\partial x_1} = 3$$

$$\frac{\partial f}{\partial x_2} = -5$$

$$\frac{\partial f}{\partial x_3} = 7$$

$$w_R = \sqrt{\left(w_1 \frac{\partial f}{\partial x_1}\right)^2 + \left(w_2 \frac{\partial f}{\partial x_2}\right)^2 + \left(w_3 \frac{\partial f}{\partial x_3}\right)^2}$$

$$= \sqrt{\left((0.03)(3)\right)^2 + \left((0.05)(-5)\right)^2 + \left((0.07)(7)\right)^2}$$

$$= 0.5574 \quad (0.56)$$

The answer is (B).

---

[9]In Eq. 47.12, "f" is the mathematical notation for "function of." The name of the function, by virtue of the *NCEES Handbook* definition, $R = f(x_1, x_2, x_3)$, is R. This is clear, also, from the left-hand side of Eq. 47.12: "w_R" (NOT w_f) means the "expected error of the relation, R." The "$\partial f/\partial x$" terms on the right-hand side of Eq. 47.12 are nonsensical because they translate into "the partial derivatives of a function of with respect to x." The correct notation would have been either "$\partial R/\partial x$" or "$\partial f(x)/\partial x$."

[10](1) The Kline-McClintock equation suggests a rational way to combine individual measurement uncertainties from pieces of a larger whole. However, as an attempt to come up with a rational measure of uncertainty, it is crude to the point of uselessness. All valuable statistical estimates are associated with confidence limits; however, the Kline-McClintock equation does not guarantee any confidence limit associated with values derived from it. The figure 95% is frequently bantered about when discussing the Kline-McClintock uncertainty, but this is fictitious. The confidence level might be 97%, or it might be 72%. All that can be said is that the Kline-McClintock uncertainty is less than the worst-case stack up. (2) It is clear that the uncertainties of larger measurements will overwhelm the uncertainties of smaller measurements. For example, consider the case where the distance between two points is measured in three legs: one measurement of 1000 ft with an uncertainty of 1 ft; and two measurements of 1 ft with an uncertainty of 0.001 ft. The first leg completely overwhelms the two smaller legs. Whatever the confidence level was for the first leg will determine the confidence level for the combined distance. Nothing in this calculation guarantees a 95% confidence level. (3) The Kline-McClintock equation requires normally distributed (i.e., Gaussian) variables.

Table 47.2 Strain Gages

strain	gage setup	bridge type	sensitivity (mV/V @ 100 $\mu\varepsilon$)*	details
axial		1/4	0.5	Good: Simplest to implement, but must use a dummy gage if compensating for temperature. Also responds to bending strain.
		1/2	0.65	Better: Temperature compensated, but is sensitive to bending strain.
		1/2	1.0	Better: Rejects bending strain, but not temperature. Must use dummy gages if compensating for temperature.
		full	1.3	Best: More sensitive and compensates for both temperature and bending strain.
bending		1/4	0.5	Good: Simplest to implement, but must use a dummy gage if compensating for temperature. Responds equally to axial strain.
		1/2	1.0	Better: Rejects axial strain and is temperature compensated.
		full	2.0	Best: Rejects axial strain and is temperature compensated. Most sensitive to bending strain.
torsional and shear		1/2	1.0	Good: Gages must be mounted at 45° from centerline.
		full	2.0	Best: Most sensitive full-bridge version of previous setup. Rejects both axial and bending strains.

*Although the *NCEES Handbook* defines the variable ε in its *Instrumentation, Measurement, and Controls* section as "strain," the abbreviation "$\mu\varepsilon$" (i.e., "microstrain") is a specific strain value: 10^{-6} (e.g., 10^{-6} mm/mm, etc.).
Adapted from ni.com, 2013, by National Instruments Corporation.

48

Controls

Nomenclature

a	Routh table parameter	–
A	constant	–
$\mathbf{A}$	system matrix	–
b	Routh table parameter	–
$B(s)$	feedback transfer function	–
$\mathbf{B}$	control vector	–
BW	bandwidth	rad/s or Hz
c	Routh table parameter	–
$\mathbf{C}$	output vector	–
$D(s)$	denominator polynomial	–
$\mathbf{D}$	feed-through vector	–
$e(t)$	error function	–
E	error	–
$E(s)$	transform of error function, $\mathcal{L}(e(t))$	–
$F(s)$	transform of forcing function, $\mathcal{L}(f(t))$	various
$G(s)$	forward transfer function	–
GM	gain margin	–

h	magnitude	–
$H(s)$	reverse transfer function	–
$\mathbf{I}$	identity matrix	–
k	spring constant	N/m
K	error constant	–
K	gain constant	–
K	scale factor	–
L	length	m
$L(s)$	load disturbance	–
m	number of zeros	–
M	magnitude	various
n	degrees of freedom	–
$N(s)$	numerator polynomial	–
OS	overshoot	%
p	pole	–
$p(t)$	arbitrary function	–
$P(s)$	transform of arbitrary function, $\mathcal{L}(p(t))$	–
PM	phase margin	–
Q	quality factor	–
r	root or system degree	–
$r(t)$	time-based response function	–
$R(s)$	transform of response function, $\mathcal{L}(r(t))$	–
s	s-domain variable	–
t	time	s
T	system type	–
$T(s)$	transfer function, $\mathcal{L}(t(t))$	–
$u(t)$	unit step function	–
$\mathbf{u}$	unit vector	–
$\mathbf{U}$	r-dimensional control vector	–
$\mathbf{V}$	input vector	–
x	amplitude of oscillation	various
x	position	m
$\mathbf{x}$	state vector	–
X	state variable	–
$\mathbf{X}$	state vector	–
$X(s)$	input transfer function	–
$\mathbf{y}$	output vector	–
$\mathbf{Y}$	output vector	–

Measurement/ Instrumentation

$Y(s)$	output transfer function	–
z	zero	–

Symbols

α	angle on pole-zero diagram	deg
α	termination angle	deg
β	angle on pole-zero diagram	deg
δ	logarithmic decrement	–
ε	a small number	–
ζ	damping ratio	–
σ	asymptote centroid	–
θ	time increment	s
Φ	state transition matrix	–
τ	inverse natural frequency, period of oscillation, or time constant	s
ω	frequency	rad/s

Subscripts

a	acceleration
A	asymptote
B	block
C	compensator or controller
d	damped natural
D	derivative
f	feedback or forcing
ff	feed forward
i	incoming
I	integral
m	number of zeros
n	number of poles or undamped natural
o	out or output
p	peak or position
P	proportional
r	damped resonant
s	settling
ss	steady state
v	velocity
z	zero

1. OPEN-LOOP TRANSFER FUNCTIONS

Equation 48.1: Open-Loop, Linear, Time-Invariant Transfer Function

$$\frac{Y(s)}{X(s)} = G(s) = \frac{N(s)}{D(s)} = K \frac{\displaystyle\prod_{m=1}^{M}(s - z_m)}{\displaystyle\prod_{n=1}^{N}(s - p_n)} \qquad 48.1$$

Description

Equation 48.1 is an open-loop, linear, time-invariant transfer function. This is represented by Fig. 48.1.

A *time-invariant transfer function* simply affects the input in a manner that does not change with time. In a *linear time-invariant system* (LTI), the transfer function can be expressed as a rational fraction of polynomials. In a *proper control system*, the degree of the denominator polynomial is equal to or larger than the degree of the numerator polynomial. (All realizable control systems are proper. An *improper control system* can be imagined or designed, but it cannot be constructed.) In Eq. 48.1, $G(s)$ is a ratio of two polynomials; $N(s)$ is the numerator polynomial; $D(s)$ is the denominator polynomial; K is the *gain constant* (or, just *gain*), a scalar; z_m are the *zeros*, the roots of the numerator polynomial; and p_n are the *poles*, the roots of the denominator polynomial. In a time-invariant system, the numerator and denominator functions do not depend on time (i.e., they are not $N(s,t)$ or $D(s,t)$).[1]

Figure 48.1 Open-Loop, Linear, Time-Invariant Transfer Function

Example

For an open-loop, linear, time-invariant transfer function,

$$X(s) = \frac{A}{s}$$

$$Y(s) = \frac{A(s+1)}{s(s+2)}$$

---

[1]Circuits that contain capacitors or other energy storage devices are usually not time-invariant. However, a system that shifts or delays the input by a fixed amount of time is considered to be time-invariant.

What is most nearly the transfer function?

(A) $G(s) = \dfrac{1}{s+2}$

(B) $G(s) = \dfrac{s+1}{s+2}$

(C) $G(s) = \dfrac{s+2}{s+1}$

(D) $G(s) = \dfrac{1}{s+1}$

Solution

From Eq. 48.1,

$$G(s) = \frac{Y(s)}{X(s)} = \frac{\dfrac{A(s+1)}{s(s+2)}}{\dfrac{A}{s}}$$

$$= \frac{s+1}{s+2}$$

The answer is (B).

2. CLOSED-LOOP FEEDBACK SYSTEMS

A basic feedback system consists of two black-box units (a *dynamic unit* and a *feedback unit*), a pick-off point (take-off point), and a *summing point* (*comparator* or *summer*). The output signal is returned as input in a feedback loop (feedback system). (See Fig. 48.2.) The incoming signal, X_i, is combined with the feedback signal, X_f, to give the *error* (*error signal*), E. Whether addition or subtraction is used depends on whether the summing point is additive (i.e., a positive feedback system) or subtractive (i.e., a negative feedback system), respectively. The summing point is assumed to perform positive addition unless a minus sign is present. $E(s)$ is the *error transfer function* (*error gain*).

$$E(s) = \mathcal{L}(e(t)) = X(s) \pm B(s)$$
$$= X(s) \pm H(s)Y(s)$$

Figure 48.2 *Closed-Loop Feedback System*

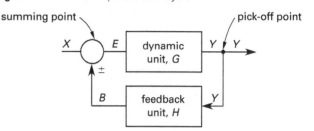

The ratio $E(s)/X(s)$ is the *error ratio* (*actuating signal ratio*).

$$\frac{E(s)}{X(s)} = \frac{1}{1 + G(s)H(s)} \quad \text{[negative feedback]}$$

$$\frac{E(s)}{X(s)} = \frac{1}{1 - G(s)H(s)} \quad \text{[positive feedback]}$$

Since the dynamic and feedback units are black boxes, each has an associated transfer function. The transfer function of the dynamic unit is known as the *forward transfer function* (*direct transfer function*), $G(s)$. In most feedback systems—amplifier circuits in particular—the magnitude of the forward transfer function is known as the *forward gain* or *direct gain*. $G(s)$ can be a scalar if the dynamic unit merely scales the error. However, $G(s)$ is normally a complex operator that changes both the magnitude and the phase of the error.

The *pick-off point* transmits the output signal, Y, from the dynamic unit back to the feedback element. The output of the dynamic unit is not reduced by the pick-off point. The transfer function of the feedback unit is the *reverse transfer function* (*feedback transfer function*, *feedback gain*, etc.), $H(s)$, which can be a simple magnitude-changing scalar or a phase-shifting function. In a *unity feedback system* (*unitary feedback system*), $H(s) = 1$, and $B(s) = Y(s)$.[2]

$$B(s) = H(s)Y(s)$$

The ratio $B(s)/X(s)$ is the *feedback ratio* (*primary feedback ratio*).

$$\frac{B(s)}{X(s)} = \frac{G(s)H(s)}{1 + G(s)H(s)} \quad \text{[negative feedback]}$$

$$\frac{B(s)}{X(s)} = \frac{G(s)H(s)}{1 - G(s)H(s)} \quad \text{[positive feedback]}$$

The *loop transfer function* (*loop gain*, *open-loop gain*, or *open-loop transfer function*), $\pm G(s)H(s)$, is the gain after going around the loop one time.

---

[2]The fact that $B(s)$ can sometimes be the same as $Y(s)$ means that vigilance is required whenever equations containing $Y(s)$ are used. For example, the ratio $Y(s)/X(s)$ refers to the ratio of input to output for all systems, but it can also refer to the primary feedback ratio, $B(s)/X(s)$, in unit feedback systems.

The *overall transfer function* (*closed-loop transfer function*, *control ratio*, *system function*, *closed-loop gain*, etc.), $Y(s)/X(s)$, is the overall transfer function of the feedback system.

$$T(s) = \frac{Y(s)}{X(s)} = \frac{G(s)}{1 + G(s)H(s)} \quad \text{[negative feedback]}$$

$$T(s) = \frac{Y(s)}{X(s)} = \frac{G(s)}{1 - G(s)H(s)} \quad \text{[positive feedback]}$$

Equation 48.2: Characteristic Equation

$$1 + G_1(s)G_2(s)H(s) = 0 \qquad 48.2$$

Description

The quantity $1 + G_1(s)G_2(s)H(s)$ in Eq. 48.2 or $1 + G(s)H(s) = 0$ in the previous sections is the *characteristic equation* and will be a polynomial of the variable s. The *order of the system* is the largest exponent of s in the characteristic equation. (This corresponds to the highest-order derivative in the system equation.) Since the denominator polynomial in a proper control system will always be of a higher degree than the numerator polynomial, the order of the system corresponds to the highest-order term in the denominator polynomial.

Equation 48.2 describes the characteristic equation for a negative feedback system with two forward transfer functions, $G_1(s)$ and $G_2(s)$, in series before the pick-off point. (See Fig. 48.3.)

Figure 48.3 Negative Feedback Control System

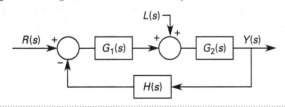

Equation 48.3: Negative Feedback Control System Response

$$Y(s) = \frac{G_1(s)G_2(s)}{1 + G_1(s)G_2(s)H(s)}R(s)$$
$$+ \frac{G_2(s)}{1 + G_1(s)G_2(s)H(s)}L(s) \qquad 48.3$$

Description

In a negative feedback system (see Fig. 48.3), the denominator of Eq. 48.3 will be greater than 1.0. Although the closed-loop transfer function, $Y(s)/X(s)$, will be less than $G(s)$, there may be other desirable effects. Generally, a system with negative feedback will

be less sensitive to variations in temperature, circuit component values, input signal frequency, and signal noise. Other benefits include distortion reduction, increased stability, and impedance matching. (For circuits to be directly connected in series without affecting their performance, all input impedances must be infinite and all output impedances must be zero.)

Although prone to oscillation, positive feedback systems produce high gain. Some circuits, primarily those incorporating op amps, rely on positive feedback to produce bistable states and hysteresis.

Example

How is the output function $Y(s)$ related to the input functions $R(s)$ and $L(s)$ for the feedback control system shown?

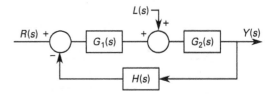

(A) $\quad Y = \dfrac{RG_1G_2}{1 + G_1G_2H} + \dfrac{LG_2}{1 + G_1G_2H}$

(B) $\quad Y = (R + L)\left(\dfrac{G_1G_2}{1 + G_1G_2H} + \dfrac{G_1G_2}{1 + G_1G_2H}\right)$

(C) $\quad Y = \dfrac{RG_1}{1 + G_1G_2H} + \dfrac{LG_2}{1 + G_1G_2H}$

(D) $\quad Y = \dfrac{RG_1G_2}{1 + G_1G_2H} + \dfrac{LG_2}{1 + G_2H}$

Solution

Assume $L(s) = 0$. The feedback is negative.

$$G(s) = G_1(s)G_2(s)$$
$$\frac{Y(s)}{R(s)} = \frac{G(s)}{1 + G(s)H(s)}$$
$$Y(s)_1 = \frac{R(s)G_1(s)G_2(s)}{1 + G_1(s)G_2(s)H(s)}$$

Assume $R(s) = 0$. The feedback into the $L(s)$ summing point is positive, but the output of $H(s)$ is negated, making this a negative feedback system.

$$G(s) = G_2(s)$$
$$H(s) = G_1(s)H(s)$$
$$\frac{Y(s)}{L(s)} = \frac{G(s)}{1 + G(s)H(s)}$$
$$Y(s)_2 = \frac{L(s)G_2(s)}{1 + G_1(s)G_2(s)H(s)}$$

The transfer function is

$$Y(s) = Y(s)_1 + Y(s)_2$$

$$= \frac{R(s)\,G_1(s)\,G_2(s)}{1 + G_1(s)\,G_2(s)H(s)}$$

$$+ \frac{L(s)\,G_2(s)}{1 + G_1(s)\,G_2(s)H(s)}$$

This answer is the same as Eq. 48.3.

The answer is (A).

3. BLOCK DIAGRAM ALGEBRA

The functions represented by several interconnected black boxes (*cascaded blocks*) can be simplified into a single block operation. Some of the most important simplification rules of block diagram algebra are shown in Fig. 48.4. Case 3 represents the standard feedback model.

4. PREDICTING SYSTEM RESPONSE

The transfer function, $T(s)$, is derived without knowledge of the input and is insufficient to predict the response of the system. The system response, $Y(s)$, will depend on the form of the input function, $X(s)$. Since the transfer function is expressed in the s-domain, the forcing and response functions must also be expressed in terms of s.

$$Y(s) = T(s)X(s)$$

The time-based response function, $y(t)$, is found by performing the inverse Laplace transform.

$$y(t) = \mathcal{L}^{-1}\big(Y(s)\big)$$

5. INITIAL AND FINAL VALUES

The initial and final (steady-state) value of any function, $G(s)$, can be found from the *initial* and *final value theorems*, respectively, provided the limits exist. The initial value is found from

$$\lim_{t \to 0^+} g(t) = \lim_{s \to \infty}\big(sG(s)\big) \quad \text{[initial value]}$$

$$\lim_{t \to \infty} g(t) = \lim_{s \to 0}\big(sG(s)\big) \quad \text{[final value]}$$

Figure 48.4 Rules for Simplifying Block Diagrams

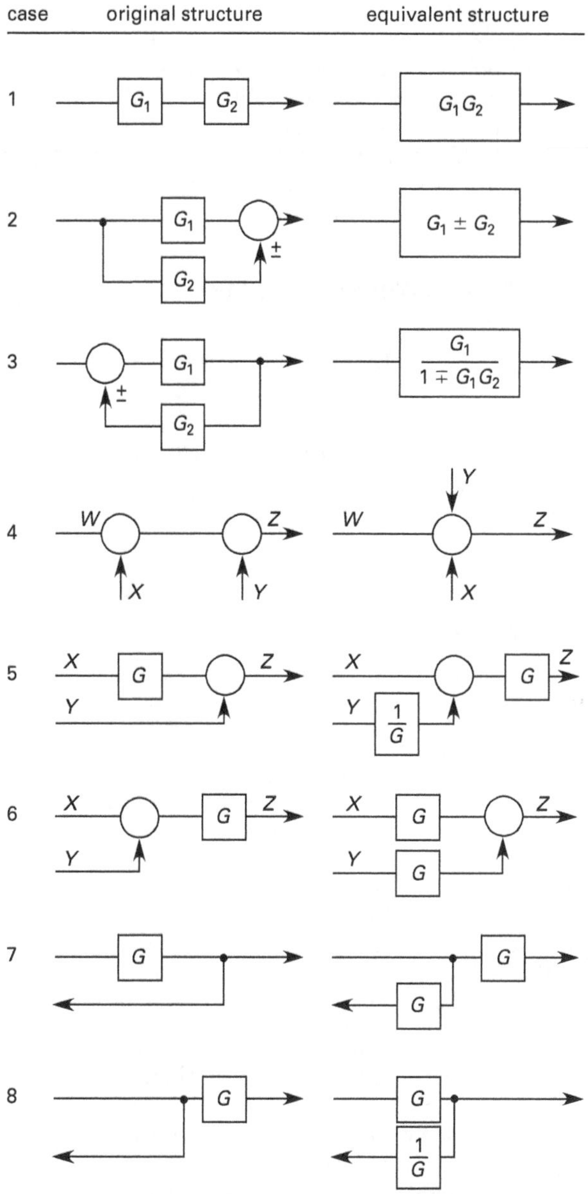

Equation 48.4: DC Gain with Unit Step Input

$$\text{DC gain} = \lim_{s \to 0} G(s) \qquad 48.4$$

Measurement/ Instrumentation

Description

Equation 48.4 can be used to determine the DC gain when all poles of the function $G(s)$ have negative real parts. Equation 48.4 is particularly valuable in determining the steady-state response (substitute $Y(s)$ for $G(s)$) and the steady-state error (substitute $E(s)$ for $G(s)$) for a unit step input. $G(s)$ could be an open-loop or closed-loop transfer function.[3]

6. UNITY FEEDBACK SYSTEM

Equation 48.5: Open-Loop Transfer Function

$$G(s) = \frac{K_B}{s^T} \times \frac{\prod_{m=1}^{M}(1 + s/\omega_m)}{\prod_{n=1}^{N}(1 + s/\omega_n)} \qquad 48.5$$

Variation

$$G(s) = \frac{K_B}{s^T} \times \frac{\prod_{m=1}^{M}(s - z_m)}{\prod_{n=1}^{N}(s - p_n)}$$

Description

Equation 48.5 is used with a unity feedback control system model (see Fig. 48.5). A *unity feedback* loop is a feedback loop with a value of 1.

A unity feedback system can be assumed when the dynamics of $H(s)$ are much faster than that of $G(s)$ (such as when $H(s)$ is merely a filter or scalar) so that the feedback function, $B(s)$, is essentially the same as $Y(s)$. In that case, the control system can be replaced by a unity negative feedback system with an open-loop transfer function of $G(s)H(s)$.

In Eq. 48.5, the exponent T is known as the *system type*. The system type will be an integer greater than or equal to zero. T is the number of *pure integrators* (also known as *free integrators*) in the open transfer function, equal to the number of s variables that can be factored from $D(s)$, the denominator of $G(s)$.

Figure 48.5 *Unity Feedback Control System*

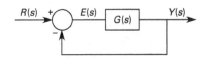

7. SPECIAL CASES OF STEADY-STATE RESPONSE

In addition to determining the steady-state response from the final value theorem (see Sec. 48.5), the steady-state response to a specific input can be easily derived from the transfer function, $T(s)$, in a few specialized cases. For example, the steady-state response function for a system acted upon by an *impulse* is simply the transfer function. That is, a pulse has no long-term effect on a system. Figure 48.6 lists input functions and their Laplace transforms.

Figure 48.6 *Input Functions and their Laplace Transforms*

name	$f(t)$		$F(s)$
impulse	$f(t) = \begin{cases} 1 & t = 0 \\ 0 & t > 0 \end{cases}$		1
step	$f(t) = 1$		$\dfrac{1}{s}$
ramp	$f(t) = t$		$\dfrac{1}{s^2}$
exponential	$f(t) = e^{at}$		$\dfrac{1}{s-a}$
sine	$f(t) = \sin(\omega t)$		$\dfrac{1}{\omega^2 + s^2}$

The steady-state response for a *step input* (often referred to as a *DC input*) is obtained by substituting zero for s everywhere in the transfer function. (If the step has magnitude h, the steady-state response is multiplied by h.)

The steady-state response for a sinusoidal input is obtained by substituting $j\omega_f$ for s everywhere in the transfer function, $T(s)$. The output will have the same frequency as the input. It is particularly convenient to perform sinusoidal calculations using phasor notation.

8. STEADY-STATE ERROR

Another way of determining the long-term performance of a system is to determine the *steady-state error*, e_{ss}. The steady-state error will always have a value of zero,

---

[3]Equation 48.4 is derived from the final value theorem, but gives the appearance of being incorrect. The apparent error derives from the *NCEES Handbook*'s ambiguous and inconsistent use of $G(s)$. In the *NCEES Handbook*'s version of Fig. 48.1, $G(s)$ is the overall transfer function, which is the ratio of the output to the input, regardless of the nature of the feedback system (positive, negative, unity, open, or closed). In Eq. 48.4, $G(s)$ is the ratio of the output to the input, but specifically only with a unit step input (a condition that is not mentioned in the *NCEES Handbook*). Since the transform of a unit step is $1/s$, from the final value theorem, the output of a system with a unit step after the transients have died out is

$$\text{DC gain}\big|_{\text{unit step}} = \lim_{s \to 0} G(s)$$

Equation 48.4 is a derived equation dependent on environment. It is not an engineering "absolute," and it cannot be used with any other form of input.

infinity, or a constant. Ideally, the error $e(t)$ would be zero for both the transient and steady-state cases. Pure gain systems (i.e., ideal linear amplifiers) always have non-zero steady-state errors(i.e., $G(s)$ is a scalar multiplier, K). Integrating systems (i.e., $G(s) = K/s$) can have near-zero steady-state errors.

The steady-state error depends on the type of input, $R(s)$, and the system type. Table 48.1 lists the steady-state errors for unity feedback system types 0, 1, and 2 for unit step, ramp, and parabolic inputs.[4] The system type is the number of pure integrations in the feedforward path, determined as the value of the exponent T (i.e., the "power") of s in the denominator of Eq. 48.5. For a *unit impulse*, $R(s) = 1$; for a *unit step*, $R(s) = 1/s$; for a *unit ramp*, $R(s) = 1/s^2$; and, for a *parabolic input*, $R(s) = 1/s^3$. The values of K_B appearing in Table 48.1 are commonly referred to as *static error constants*. For a unit step, $u(t)$, K_B is known as the *static position error constant*, K_p. For a unit ramp, $tu(t)$, K_B is known as the *static velocity error constant*. For a parabolic input, $\frac{1}{2}t^2 u(t)$, K_B is known as the *static acceleration error constant*, K_a. The steady-state error is found from the final value theorem.

$$e_{ss}(t) = \lim_{t \to \infty} e(t) = \lim_{t \to \infty} \left(r(t) - y(t) \right)$$

$$e_{ss}(s) = \lim_{s \to 0} sE(s) = \lim_{s \to 0} s\left(R(s) - Y(s) \right)$$

$$= \lim_{s \to 0} \frac{sR(s)}{1 - G(s)} \quad \text{[unity feedback]}$$

Table 48.1 *Steady-State Error, e_{ss}, for Unity Feedback*

input	type		
	$T=0$	$T=1$	$T=2$
unit step	$1/(K_B+1)$	0	0
ramp	∞	$1/K_B$	0
acceleration	∞	∞	$1/K_B$

Example

For the feedback control system shown, what is the steady-state error function, $e_{ss}(t)$, for a ramp input function?

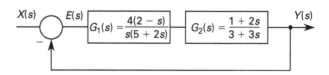

(A) 0

(B) 1/4

(C) 15/8

(D) ∞

Solution

The open-loop transfer function is

$$G(s) = G_1(s)\, G_2(s)$$

$$= \left(\frac{(4)(2-s)}{s(5+2s)} \right)\left(\frac{1+2s}{3+3s} \right)$$

The DC gain, K_B, for a unit ramp is the static velocity error constant, K_v.

$$K_B = K_v = \lim_{s \to 0} sG(s) = \lim_{s \to 0} \frac{4s(2-s)(1+2s)}{s(5+2s)(3+3s)}$$

$$= \frac{(4)(2)(1)}{(5)(3)}$$

$$= 8/15$$

Since s^1 appears in the denominator and no additional factoring is possible, this is a type 1 system.

Using the steady-state error analysis table, the steady-state error function, $e_{ss}(t)$, for a ramp input function is

$$e_{ss}(t) = \frac{1}{K_B}$$

$$= 15/8$$

The answer is (C).

9. DETERMINING THE ERROR CONSTANTS

With a lot of work, the error constant, K_B, in a unity feedback system can be determined by writing the open-loop

---

[4]A parabolic input is also known as an *acceleration input*.

transfer function, $G(s)$, in *canonical form* and factoring out all constants. Alternatively, the error functions can be found directly from limits on $G(s)$.

$$K_p = \lim_{s \to 0} G(s)$$

$$K_v = \lim_{s \to 0} sG(s)$$

$$K_a = \lim_{s \to 0} s^2 G(s)$$

10. POLES AND ZEROS

A *pole* is a value of s that makes a function, $G(s)$, infinite. Specifically, a pole makes the denominator of $G(s)$ zero. (Pole values are the system *eigenvalues*.) A *zero* of the function makes the numerator of $G(s)$ (and $G(s)$ itself) zero. Poles and zeros need not be real or unique; they can be imaginary and repeated within a function.

A *pole-zero diagram* is a plot of poles and zeros in the *s-plane*—a rectangular coordinate system with real and imaginary axes. A zero is represented by $\bigcirc$; a pole is represented by $\times$. Poles off the real axis always occur in conjugate pairs known as *pole pairs*.

Sometimes it is necessary to derive the function $G(s)$ from its pole-zero diagram. This will be only partially successful since repeating identical poles and zeros are not usually indicated on the diagram. Also, scale factors (scalar constants) are not shown.

11. PREDICTING SYSTEM RESPONSE FROM RESPONSE POLE-ZERO DIAGRAMS

A response pole-zero diagram based on $R(s)$ can be used to predict how the system responds to a specific input. (This pole-zero diagram must be based on the product $T(s)F(s)$ since that is how $R(s)$ is calculated. Plotting the product $T(s)F(s)$ is equivalent to plotting $T(s)$ and $F(s)$ separately on the same diagram.)

The system will experience an *exponential decay* when a single pole falls on the real axis. A pole with a value of $-r$, corresponding to the linear term $(s + r)$, will decay at the rate of e^{-rt}. (See Fig. 48.7.) The quantity $1/r$ is the *decay time constant*, the time for the response to achieve approximately 63% of its steady-state value. The farther left the point is located from the vertical imaginary axis, the faster the motion will die out.

Undamped sinusoidal oscillation will occur if a pole pair falls on the imaginary axis. A conjugate pole pair with the value of $\pm j\omega$ indicates oscillation with a natural frequency of ω rad/s.

Pole pairs to the left of the imaginary axis represent *decaying sinusoidal response*. The closer the poles are to the real (horizontal) axis, the slower will be the oscillations. The closer the poles are to the imaginary

(vertical) axis, the slower will be the decay. The *natural frequency*, ω, of undamped oscillation can be determined from a *conjugate pole pair* having values of $r \pm j\omega_f$.

$$\omega = \sqrt{r^2 + \omega_f^2}$$

Figure 48.7 Types of Responses Determined by Pole Location

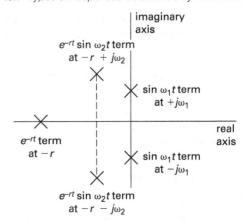

The magnitude and phase shift can be determined for any input frequency from the pole-zero diagram with the following procedure: Locate the angular frequency, ω_f, on the imaginary axis. Draw a line from each pole (i.e., a pole-line) and from zero (i.e., a zero-line) of $T(s)$ to this point. (See Fig. 48.8.) The angle of each of these lines is the angle between it and the horizontal real axis. The overall magnitude is the product of the lengths of the zero-lines, L_z, divided by the product of the lengths of the pole-lines, L_p. (The scale factor, K, must also be included because it is not shown on the pole-zero diagram.) The phase is the sum of the pole-angles less the sum of the zero-angles.

$$|T(s)| = K\frac{\prod_z |L_z|}{\prod_p |L_p|} = K\frac{\prod_z \text{length}}{\prod_p \text{length}}$$

$$\angle T(s) = \sum_p \alpha - \sum_z \beta$$

Figure 48.8 Calculating Magnitude and Phase from a Pole-Zero Diagram

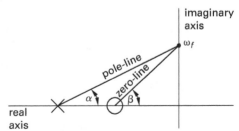

12. FREQUENCY RESPONSE

The gain and phase angle frequency response of a system will change as the forcing frequency is varied. The *frequency response* is the variation in these parameters, always with a sinusoidal input. *Gain* and *phase characteristics* are plots of the steady-state gain and phase angle responses with a sinusoidal input versus frequency. While a linear frequency scale can be used, frequency response is almost always presented against a logarithmic frequency scale.

The steady-state gain response is expressed in decibels, while the steady-state phase angle response is expressed in degrees.

Equation 48.6: Gain Margin

$$\text{If } \angle G(j\omega_{180}) = -180°, \text{ then} \atop \text{GM} = -20\log_{10}(|G(j\omega_{180})|) \qquad 48.6$$

Variation

$$\text{gain} = 20\log|T(j\omega)| \qquad [\text{in dB}]$$

Description

Gain margin is the additional gain required to produce instability in the unity gain feedback control system. The gain is calculated from Eq. 48.6 where $|G(s)|$ is the absolute value of the steady-state response. A doubling of $|G(j\omega)|$ is referred to as an *octave* and corresponds to a 6.02 dB increase. A tenfold increase in $|G(j\omega)|$ is a *decade* and corresponds to a 20 dB increase.

$$\text{no. of octaves} = \frac{\text{gain}_{2,\text{dB}} - \text{gain}_{1,\text{dB}}}{6.02 \text{ dB}}$$
$$= 3.32 \times \text{no. of decades}$$

$$\text{no. of decades} = \frac{\text{gain}_{2,\text{dB}} - \text{gain}_{1,\text{dB}}}{20 \text{ dB}}$$
$$= 0.301 \times \text{no. of octaves}$$

Equation 48.7: Phase Margin

$$\text{If } |G(j\omega)| = 1, \text{ then} \atop \text{PM} = 180° + \angle G(j\omega_{0\text{dB}}) \qquad 48.7$$

Description

Phase margin is the additional phase required to produce instability in the unity gain feedback control system. The *phase margin* of an amplifier's output signal is the difference between its phase angle and 180°.

Example

A control system has an open-loop gain of 1 (0 dB) at the frequency where its phase angle is −200°. What is the phase margin?

(A) −120°

(B) −60°

(C) −20°

(D) −10°

Solution

The phase margin is given by

$$\text{PM} = 180° + \angle G(j\omega_{0\text{dB}})$$
$$= 180° - 200°$$
$$= -20°$$

The answer is (C).

13. GAIN CHARACTERISTIC

The *gain characteristic* (*M-curve* for magnitude) is a plot of the gain as ω_f is varied. It is possible to make a rough sketch of the gain characteristic by calculating the gain at a few points (pole frequencies, $\omega = 0$, $\omega = \infty$, etc.). The curve will usually be asymptotic to several lines. The frequencies at which these asymptotes intersect are *corner frequencies*. The peak gain, M_p, coincides with the natural (resonant) frequency of the system. The gain characteristic peaks when the forcing frequency equals the natural frequency. It is also said that this peak corresponds to the resonant frequency. Strictly speaking, this is true, although the gain may not actually be resonant (i.e., may not be infinite). Large peak gains indicate lowered stability and large overshoots. The *gain crossover point*, if any, is the frequency at which $\log(\text{gain}) = 0$.

The *half-power points* (*cutoff frequencies*) are the frequencies for which the gain is 0.707 (i.e., $\sqrt{2}/2$) times the peak value. This is equivalent to saying the gain is 3 dB less than the peak gain. The *cutoff rate* is the slope of the gain characteristic in dB/octave at a half-power point. The frequency difference between the half-power points is the *bandwidth*, BW. (See Fig. 48.9.) The *closed-loop bandwidth* is the frequency range over which the closed-loop gain falls 3 dB below its value at $\omega = 0$. (The term "bandwidth" often means closed-loop bandwidth.) The *quality factor*, Q, is

$$Q = \frac{\omega_n}{\text{BW}}$$

Figure 48.9 *Bandwidth*

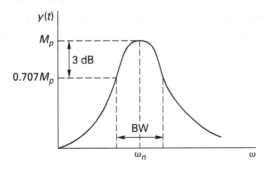

Since a low or negative gain (compared to higher parts of the curve) effectively represents attenuation, the gain characteristic can be used to distinguish between low- and high-pass filters. A *low-pass filter* will have a large gain at low frequencies and a small gain at high frequencies. Conversely, a *high-pass filter* will have a high gain at high frequencies and a low gain at low frequencies.

14. PHASE CHARACTERISTIC

The phase angle response will also change as the forcing frequency is varied. The *phase characteristic* (α *curve*) is a plot of the phase angle as ω_f is varied.

15. STABILITY

A stable system will remain at rest unless disturbed by external influence and will return to a rest position once the disturbance is removed. A pole with a value of $-r$ on the real axis corresponds to an exponential response of e^{-rt}. Since e^{-rt} is a decaying signal, the system is stable. Similarly, a pole of $+r$ on the real axis corresponds to an exponential response of e^{rt}. Since e^{rt} increases without limit, the system is unstable.

Since any pole to the right of the imaginary axis corresponds to a positive exponential, a *stable system* will have poles only in the left half of the *s*-plane. If there is an isolated pole on the imaginary axis, the response is stable. However, a conjugate pole pair on the imaginary axis corresponds to a sinusoid that does not decay with time. Such a system is considered to be unstable.

Passive systems (i.e., the homogeneous case) are not acted upon by a forcing function and are always stable. In the absence of an energy source, exponential growth cannot occur. *Active systems* contain one or more energy sources and may be stable or unstable.

There are several *frequency response (domain) analysis techniques* for determining the stability of a system, including the Bode plot, root-locus diagram, Routh stability criterion, Hurwitz test, and Nichols chart. The term *frequency response* almost always means the steady-state response to a sinusoidal input.

The value of the denominator of $T(s)$ is the primary factor affecting stability. When the denominator approaches zero, the system increases without bound. In the typical feedback loop, the denominator is $1 \pm G(s)H(s)$, which can be zero only if $|G(s)H(s)| = 1$. It is logical, then, that most of the methods for investigating stability (e.g., Bode plots, root-locus diagrams, Nyquist analysis, and the Nichols chart) investigate the value of the open-loop transfer function, $G(s)H(s)$. Since $\log(1) = 0$, the requirement for stability is that $\log(G(s)H(s))$ must not equal 0 dB.

A negative feedback system will also become unstable if it changes to a positive feedback system, which can occur when the feedback signal is changed in phase more than 180°. Therefore, another requirement for stability is that the phase angle change must not exceed 180°.

16. BODE PLOTS

Bode plots are gain and phase characteristics for the open-loop $G(s)H(s)$ transfer function that are used to determine the *relative stability* of a system. In Fig. 48.10, the gain characteristic is a plot of $20\log(|G(s)H(s)|)$ versus ω for a sinusoidal input. (Bode plots, though similar in appearance to the gain and phase frequency response charts, are used to evaluate stability and do not describe the closed-loop system response.)

Figure 48.10 *Gain and Phase Margin Bode Plots*

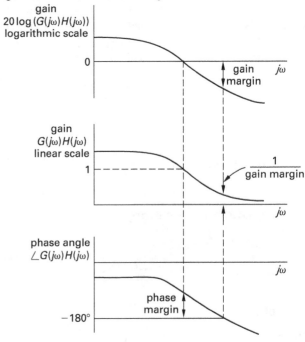

The *gain margin* is the number of decibels that the open-loop transfer function, $G(s)H(s)$, is below 0 dB at the *phase crossover frequency* (i.e., where the phase angle is $-180°$). (If the gain happens to be plotted on a linear scale, the gain margin is the reciprocal of the gain at the phase crossover point.) The gain margin must be positive for a stable system, and the larger it is, the more stable the system will be.

The *phase margin* is the number of degrees the phase angle is above $-180°$ at the *gain crossover point* (i.e., where the logarithmic gain is 0 dB or the actual gain is 1).

In most cases, large positive gain and phase margins will ensure a stable system. However, the margins could have been measured at other than the crossover frequencies. Therefore, a Nyquist stability plot is needed to verify the absolute stability of a system.

17. ROOT-LOCUS DIAGRAMS

A *root-locus diagram* is a pole-zero diagram showing how the poles of $G(s)H(s)$ move when one of the system parameters (e.g., the gain factor) in the transfer function is varied. The diagram gets its name from the need to find the roots of the denominator (i.e., the poles). The locus of points defined by the various poles is a line or curve that can be used to predict *points of instability* or other critical operating points. A point of instability is reached when the line crosses the imaginary axis into the right-hand side of the pole-zero diagram.

A root-locus curve may not be contiguous, and multiple curves will exist for different sets of roots. Sometimes the curve splits into two branches. In other cases, the curve leaves the real axis at *breakaway points* and continues on with constant or varying slopes approaching asymptotes. One branch of the curve will start at each open-loop pole and end at an open-loop zero.

Equation 48.8 Through Eq. 48.10: Poles and Zeros

$$1 + K\frac{(s - z_1)(s - z_2)\cdots(s - z_m)}{(s - p_1)(s - p_2)\cdots(s - p_n)} = 0 \quad [m \le n] \qquad 48.8$$

$$\alpha = \frac{(2k + 1)180°}{n - m} \quad [k = 0, \pm 1, \pm 2, \pm 3, \ldots] \qquad 48.9$$

$$\sigma_A = \frac{\sum_{i=1}^{n}\text{Re}(p_i) - \sum_{i=1}^{m}\text{Re}(z_i)}{n - m} \qquad 48.10$$

Description

In Eq. 48.8, p values are the open-loop poles, and z values are the open-loop zeros. For $m < n$, Eq. 48.9 gives the location at which $n - m$ branches terminate at infinity. This location is the intersection of the real axis with the asymptote angles, or the *asymptote centroid*, and is found by Eq. 48.10, where Re represents the real part.

Example

A control system with negative feedback is shown.

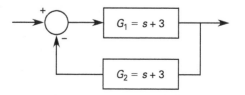

The root-locus diagram of the system has a

(A) pole at $(-2, j0)$ and a zero at $(-3, j0)$

(B) zero at $(-3, j0)$

(C) double zero at $(-3, j0)$

(D) double pole at $(-3, j0)$ and a zero at $(0, 0)$

Solution

The poles and zeros of the root-locus diagram for a control system are the poles and zeros of the open-loop transfer function.

The open-loop transfer function is

$$G(s) = \frac{G_1(s)}{(1 - G_1(s)G_2(s))} = \frac{(s + 3)}{1 - (s^2 + 6s + 9)}$$

There is a pole at $(-2, j0)$ and a zero at $(-3, j0)$.

The answer is (A).

18. PID CONTROLLERS

One widely used control mechanism is the *proportional-integral-derivative controller* (also called a *PID controller* or *three-mode controller*). A PID controller is capable of three modes of control—proportional, integral, and derivative—or a combination of them. These three terms refer to how the controller uses the error (the difference between the set point and the actual value of the process variable) to calculate the adjustment to make to the input.

Proportional control is the simplest method: the adjustment made to the process input is in proportion to the error in the process output. For example, the flow of steam into a system may be increased or decreased in proportion to the difference between the set point and the actual temperature. One disadvantage, however, is that when the set point is changed, proportional control alone cannot bring the process output exactly to the new set point; a small error, called *offset* (also called *proportional-only offset* or *droop*), must persist.

In *integral control* (also called *reset control* or *floating control*), the adjustment made to the process is in proportion to the integral of the error. The adjustment, then, is influenced not only by the magnitude of the error but its duration. Integral control generally moves the process output more quickly toward the set point than proportional control does, and it can also eliminate offset. However, because integral control responds to accumulated past error as well as current error, it does not stop making adjustments at the moment the process variable reaches the set point; this typically causes the process variable to overshoot the set point and reverse direction, making a series of decreasing oscillations around the set point rather than stopping at the set point as soon as it is reached. To reduce this behavior, integral control ($G_c(s) = 1/T_I s$) is typically used in combination with proportional control rather than alone.

In *derivative control* (also known as *rate action control* or *anticipatory control*), the controller calculates the rate at which the process variable is changing and makes adjustments to the process input in proportion to this rate of change. In relatively smooth processes, derivative control can increase stability and hasten recovery from disturbances. If the process is "noisy," however—subject to small, frequent, random fluctuations—derivative control ($G_c(s) = T_D s$) will tend to amplify the fluctuations and make the process less stable, not more.

Equation 48.11: PID Controller Gain

$$G_C(s) = K\left(1 + \frac{1}{T_I s} + T_D s\right) \quad \text{[PID controller]} \qquad 48.11$$

Variation

$$G_C(s) = K_P + \frac{K_I}{s} + K_D s$$

Description

Equation 48.11 gives the gain for a *proportional-integral-derivative controller*, or *PID controller*. In Eq. 48.11, K is the *proportional gain*; K/T_I is the *integral gain* (usually written as K_I); and KT_D is the *derivative gain* (usually written as K_D). T_I and T_D are the *integral time* (also known as *reset time*) and *derivative time* (also known as *rate time*), respectively.

Equation 48.12: Lag or Lead Compensator Gain

$$G_C(s) = K\left(\frac{1 + sT_1}{1 + sT_2}\right) \quad \text{[lag or lead compensator]} \qquad 48.12$$

Variation

$$G_C(s) = K\left(\frac{s - z}{s - p}\right) \quad \text{[first-order compensator]}$$

Description

Phase lead-lag (lag-lead) compensators are common control components placed in a feedback circuit (see Sec. 48.20) to improve the frequency response of a control system.[5] They can also be used to reduce steady-state error, reduce resonant peaks, and improve system response by reducing rise time.

Lead compensators shift the output phase to the left on the time line (i.e., the output leads the input), and *lag compensators* shift the output phase to the right on the time line (i.e., the output lags the input). A lead compensator tends to shift the root-locus toward the complex plane, which improves the system stability and response speed. Lead compensators are associated with derivative (s) terms, while lag compensators are associated with integral ($1/s$) terms. Both lead and lag compensators introduce a single pole-zero pair into the transfer function. A lead compensator will have a pole in the complex plane, while a lag compensator will have a pole on the real line. Figure 48.11 shows the effect of lead compensation on a root-locus diagram.

Stated another way, for a lead compensator, the introduced pole is greater than the introduced zero (i.e., $p > z$), and for a lag compensator, $p < z$. Equation 48.12 can be used for a lag or lead compensator, depending on the ratio of constants T_1/T_2. In Eq. 48.12, the zero is located at $1/T_1$, and the pole is located at $1/T_2$. For a lead compensator, $T_2/T_1 = 1$, and for a lag compensator, $T_2/T_1 > 1$.

19. ROUTH CRITERION

Equation 48.13: Linear Characteristic Equation

$$a_n s^n + a_{n-1} s^{n-1} + a_{n-2} s^{n-2} + \cdots + a_0 = 0 \qquad 48.13$$

Description

From Eq. 48.2, the *characteristic equation* of a control system is $1 + G(s)H(s) = 0$. If any of the linear coefficients, a_n, of the characteristic equation are negative, the system will be marginally stable at best, but more likely, unstable. In a linear system (i.e., with the form of Eq. 48.13), the roots (zeros) will be of the form $z = a + jb$ (i.e., will be a real or a complex number), where $a = \text{Re}(z) = \text{Re}(a + jb)$ is the real part, and $b = \text{Im}(z) = \text{Im}(a + jb)$ is the

---

[5]Compensators may also be referred to as "controllers." The two terms are used interchangeably.

Figure 48.11 *Effect of Lead Compensation on Root-Locus Diagram*

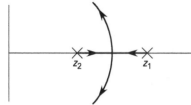

(a) original root-locus diagram

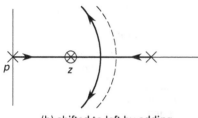

(b) shifted to left by adding
pole *p* and zero *z*

imaginary part. Stable systems will have roots with negative real parts such as $s = -3$, corresponding to decaying exponential terms such as e^{-3t}.

The *Routh-Hurwitz criterion* uses the coefficients of the polynomial characteristic equation, Eq. 48.13, to determine system stability. A table (the *Routh table* or *Hurwitz matrix*) of these coefficients is formed using the conventions in Eq. 48.14 through Eq. 48.18.

Equation 48.14 Through Eq. 48.18: Routh Table

$$\begin{matrix} a_n & a_{n-2} & a_{n-4} & \cdots & \cdots & \cdots \\ a_{n-1} & a_{n-3} & a_{n-5} & \cdots & \cdots & \cdots \\ b_1 & b_2 & b_3 & \cdots & \cdots & \cdots \\ c_1 & c_2 & c_3 & \cdots & \cdots & \cdots \end{matrix} \quad 48.14$$

$$b_1 = \frac{a_{n-1}a_{n-2} - a_n a_{n-3}}{a_{n-1}} \quad 48.15$$

$$b_2 = \frac{a_{n-1}a_{n-4} - a_n a_{n-5}}{a_{n-1}} \quad 48.16$$

$$c_1 = \frac{a_{n-3}b_1 - a_{n-1}b_2}{b_1} \quad 48.17$$

$$c_2 = \frac{a_{n-5}b_1 - a_{n-1}b_3}{b_1} \quad 48.18$$

Description

The *Routh-Hurwitz criterion* states that the number of sign changes in the first column of the Routh table equals the number of positive (unstable) roots. Therefore, a system will be stable if all entries in the first

column have the same sign. The table is organized according to Eq. 48.14. Then, the remaining coefficients are calculated using Eq. 48.15 through Eq. 48.18 until all values are zero.

Special methods are used if there is a zero in the first column but nowhere else in that row. One of the methods is to substitute a small number, represented by ε or δ, for the zero and calculate the remaining coefficients as usual.

The *Routh test* indicates that the necessary conditions for a polynomial to have all its roots in the left-hand plane (i.e., for the system to be stable) are (a) all of the terms must have the same sign; and (b) all of the powers between the highest and the lowest value must have nonzero coefficients, unless all even-power or all odd-power terms are missing. Condition (a) also implies that the coefficient cannot be imaginary.

Example

Which of the following characteristic equations can be stable?

I. $4s^4 + 8s^2 + 3s + 2 = 0$

II. $4s^4 + 2s^3 + 8s^2 + 3s + 2 = 0$

III. $4s^4 + 2s^3 + 8js^2 + 5s + 2 = 0$

IV. $4s^4 + 2s^3 + 8s^2 - 3s + 2 = 0$

(A) I only

(B) II only

(C) I and IV

(D) II and III

Solution

To represent a stable system, according to the Routh test, all consecutive powers of s must be represented. Equation I does not represent a stable system because there is no s^3 term. To be stable, all linear coefficients must be real. Equation III contains the coefficient $8j$, so it does not represent a stable system. Finally, to be stable, all linear coefficients must be positive, so Eq. IV does not represent a stable system. Equation II is the only equation that meets the criteria.

The answer is (B).

Example

A characteristic equation is

$$s^5 + 15s^4 + 185s^3 + 725s^2 - 326s + 120 = 0$$

A Routh table has been constructed as follows.

$$
\begin{array}{llll}
s^5: & 1 & 185 & -326 \\
s^4: & 15 & 725 & 120 \\
s^3: & 136.7 & 334 & \\
s^2: & 761.7 & 120 & \\
s^1: & -355.5 & & \\
s^0: & 120 & &
\end{array}
$$

Which table entry is INCORRECT?

(A) 15

(B) 185

(C) 334

(D) 725

Solution

In this problem,

$$a_n = a_5 = 1$$
$$a_{n-1} = a_4 = 15$$
$$a_{n-2} = a_3 = 185$$
$$a_{n-3} = a_2 = 725$$
$$a_{n-4} = a_1 = -326$$
$$a_{n-5} = a_0 = 120$$

Comparing with Eq. 48.14, values in the s^5 and s^4 rows are all correct. The second s^3 entry should be

$$
\begin{aligned}
b_2 &= \frac{a_{n-1}a_{n-4} - a_n a_{n-5}}{a_{n-1}} \\
&= \frac{a_4 a_1 - a_5 a_0}{a_4} \\
&= \frac{(15)(-326) - (1)(120)}{15} \\
&= -334
\end{aligned}
$$

The answer is (C).

20. APPLICATION TO CONTROL SYSTEMS

A control system monitors a process and makes adjustments to maintain performance within certain acceptable limits. Feedback is implicitly a part of all control systems. The *controller* (*control element*) is the part of the control system that establishes the acceptable limits of performance, usually by setting its own reference inputs. The controller transfer function for a proportional controller is a constant: $G_1(s) = K$. The *plant* (*controlled system*) is the part of the system that responds to the controller. Both of these are in the forward loop. The input signal, $R(s)$,

in Fig. 48.12 is known in a control system as the *command* or *reference value*. Figure 48.12 is known as a *control logic diagram* or *control logic block diagram*. The controller in Fig. 48.12 can be a PID controller or a compensator (see Sec. 48.18).

Figure 48.12 *Typical Feedback Control System*

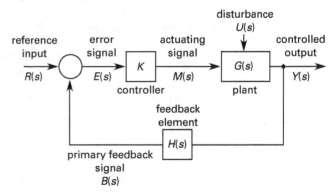

A *servomechanism* is a special type of control system in which the controlled variable is mechanical position, velocity, or acceleration. In many servomechanisms, $H(s) = 1$ (i.e., unity feedback), and it is desired to keep the output equal to the reference input (i.e., maintain a zero-error function). If the input, $R(s)$, is constant, the descriptive terms *regulator* and *regulating system* are used.

21. CONTROL SYSTEM MODELS

Equation 48.19 Through Eq. 48.22: First-Order Control Systems

$$\frac{Y(s)}{R(s)} = \frac{K}{\tau s + 1} \qquad 48.19$$

$$y(t) = y_0 e^{-t/\tau} + KM(1 - e^{-t/\tau}) \qquad 48.20$$

$$\frac{Y(s)}{R(s)} = \frac{K e^{-\theta s}}{\tau s + 1} \qquad 48.21$$

$$y(t) = [y_0 e^{-(t-\theta)/\tau} + KM(1 - e^{-(t-\theta)/\tau})]u(t-\theta) \qquad 48.22$$

Description

Equation 48.19 is the transfer function model for a first-order system, and Eq. 48.20 gives the step response to a step input of magnitude M. Equation 48.21 is used for systems with time delay, such as dead time or transport lag, and Eq. 48.22 gives the step response to a step input of magnitude M, where $u(t)$ is the unit step function.

Equation 48.23 Through Eq. 48.32: Second-Order Control Systems

$$\frac{Y(s)}{R(s)} = \frac{K\omega_n^2}{s^2 + 2\zeta\omega_n s + \omega_n^2} \qquad 48.23$$

$$\omega_d = \omega_n\sqrt{1-\zeta^2} \qquad 48.24$$

$$\omega_r = \omega_n\sqrt{1-2\zeta^2} \qquad 48.25$$

$$t_p = \pi/\left(\omega_n\sqrt{1-\zeta^2}\right) \qquad 48.26$$

$$M_p = 1 + e^{-\pi\zeta/\sqrt{1-\zeta^2}} \qquad 48.27$$

$$\%\text{OS} = 100\, e^{-\pi\zeta/\sqrt{1-\zeta^2}} \qquad 48.28$$

$$\delta = \frac{1}{m}\ln\left(\frac{x_k}{x_{k+m}}\right) = \frac{2\pi\zeta}{\sqrt{1-\zeta^2}} \qquad 48.29$$

$$\omega_d\tau = 2\pi \qquad 48.30$$

$$T_s = \frac{4}{\zeta\omega_n} \qquad 48.31$$

$$\frac{Y(s)}{R(s)} = \frac{K}{\tau^2 s^2 + 2\zeta\tau s + 1} \qquad 48.32$$

Description

Equation 48.23 is the transfer function model for a standard second-order control system, where Eq. 48.24 is the *damped natural frequency*, and Eq. 48.25 is the *damped resonant frequency* or *peak frequency*. Equation 48.26 and Eq. 48.27 are for a normalized, underdamped second-order control system. For one unit step input, Eq. 48.26 gives the time required, t_p, to reach a peak value of M_p, given by Eq. 48.27.

Example

A second-order control system has a control response ratio of

$$\frac{Y(s)}{R(s)} = \frac{1}{s^2 + 0.3s + 1}$$

If the system is acted upon by a unit step, what is most nearly the magnitude of the first oscillatory response peak?

(A) 1.3

(B) 1.6

(C) 2.5

(D) 3.4

Solution

The response transfer function can be written in the form

$$\frac{Y(s)}{R(s)} = \frac{K\omega_n^2}{s^2 + 2\zeta\omega_n s + \omega_n^2}$$

Working with the denominator,

$$\omega_n^2 = 1$$
$$2\zeta = 0.3$$
$$\zeta = 0.15$$

Working with the numerator,

$$K = 1$$

Use Eq. 48.27.

$$M_p = 1 + e^{-\pi\zeta/\sqrt{1-\zeta^2}}$$
$$= 1 + e^{-\pi(0.15)/\sqrt{1-(0.15)^2}}$$
$$= 1.63 \quad (1.6)$$

The answer is (B).

22. STATE-VARIABLE CONTROL SYSTEM MODELS

While the classical methods of designing and analyzing control systems are adequate for most situations, state model representations are preferred for more complex digital sampling cases, particularly those with multiple inputs and outputs or when behavior is nonlinear or varies with time.

The state variables completely define the dynamic state (position, voltage, pressure, etc.), $x_i(t)$, of the system at time t. (In simple problems, the number of state variables corresponds to the number of *degrees of freedom*, n, of the system.) The n state variables are written in matrix form as a state vector, $\mathbf{X}$.

$$\mathbf{X} = \begin{pmatrix} x_1 \\ x_2 \\ x_3 \\ \vdots \\ x_n \end{pmatrix}$$

It is a characteristic of state models that the state vector is acted upon by a first-degree derivative operator, d/dt, to produce a differential term, $\mathbf{X}'$, of order 1,

$$\mathbf{X}' = \frac{d\mathbf{X}}{dt}$$

The previous equations illustrate the general form of a state model representation: $\mathbf{U}$ is an r-dimensional (i.e., an $r \times 1$ matrix) *control vector*; $\mathbf{Y}$ is an m-dimensional (i.e., an $m \times 1$ matrix) *output vector*; $\mathbf{A}$ is an $n \times n$ *system vector*; $\mathbf{B}$ is an $n \times r$ *control vector*; $\mathbf{C}$ is an $m \times n$ *output vector*; and $\mathbf{D}$ is a *feed-through vector*. The actual unknowns are the x_i state variables. The y_i state variables, which may not be needed in all problems, are only linear combinations of the x_i state variables. (For example, x might represent a spring end position; y might represent stress in the spring. Then, $y = k\Delta x$.)

Equation 48.33 and Eq. 48.34: State and Output Equations

$$\dot{\mathbf{x}}(t) = \mathbf{A}\mathbf{x}(t) + \mathbf{B}\mathbf{u}(t) \quad \text{[state equation]} \qquad 48.33$$

$$\mathbf{y}(t) = \mathbf{C}\mathbf{x}(t) + \mathbf{D}\mathbf{u}(t) \quad \text{[output equation]} \qquad 48.34$$

Variations

$$\mathbf{X}' = \mathbf{A}\mathbf{X} + \mathbf{B}\mathbf{U} \quad \text{[state equation]}$$

$$\mathbf{Y} = \mathbf{C}\mathbf{X} \qquad \text{[response equation]}$$

Description

Equation 48.33 is the *state equation*, and Eq. 48.34 is the *output equation* or *response equation*. As is common in transform equations, lowercase letters are used to represent vectors (matrices) containing time-domain values, while uppercase letters are used to represent vectors (matrices) containing s-domain values.

A conventional block diagram can be modified to show the multiplicity of monitored properties in a state model, as shown in Fig. 48.13. (The block $\mathbf{I}/s$ is a diagonal identity matrix with elements of $1/s$. This effectively is an integration operator.) The actual physical system

does not need to be a feedback system. The form of Eq. 48.33 and Eq. 48.34 is the sole reason that a feedback diagram is appropriate.

Figure 48.13 State Variable Diagram

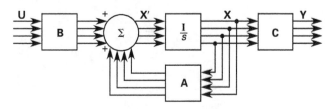

A state variable model permits only first-degree derivatives, so additional x_i state variables are used for higher-order terms (e.g., acceleration).

System controllability exists if all of the system states can be controlled by the inputs, $\mathbf{U}$. In state model language, system controllability means that an arbitrary initial state can be steered to an arbitrary target state in a finite amount of time. *System observability* exists if the initial system states can be predicted from knowing the inputs, $\mathbf{U}$, and observing the outputs, $\mathbf{Y}$. (*Kalman's theorem* based on matrix rank is used to determine system controllability and observability.)

Example

A system is governed by the following differential equations.

$$\dot{x}_2 + a_1\dot{x}_1 + a_0 x_1 = u(t)$$
$$\dot{x}_1 = -x_2$$

The output of the system is

$$y_1(t) = 3x_1$$
$$y_2(t) = 4x_1 - 5\dot{x}_1$$

The output matrix of the state-variable control system model is

(A) $\begin{bmatrix} 3 & 0 \\ 4 & 5 \end{bmatrix}$

(B) $\begin{bmatrix} a_1 \\ a_0 \end{bmatrix}$

(C) $\begin{bmatrix} a_1 & 0 \\ 0 & a_0 \end{bmatrix}$

(D) $\begin{bmatrix} -5 & 3 \\ 4 & 0 \end{bmatrix}$

Solution

The state equation is given by Eq. 48.33 as

$$\dot{\mathbf{x}}(t) = \mathbf{A}\mathbf{x}(t) + \mathbf{B}\mathbf{u}(t)$$

The output equation is given by Eq. 48.34 as

$$\mathbf{y}(t) = \mathbf{C}\mathbf{x}(t) + \mathbf{D}\mathbf{u}(t)$$

Representing the given differentials in this format, the vector notation for the system is

$$y_1(t) = 3x_1$$
$$y_2(t) = 4x_1 - 5\dot{x}_1 = 4x_1 + 5x_2$$
$$\begin{bmatrix} \dot{x}_1 \\ \dot{x}_2 \end{bmatrix} = \begin{bmatrix} 0 & -1 \\ -a_0 & -a_1 \end{bmatrix} \begin{bmatrix} x_1 \\ x_2 \end{bmatrix} + \begin{bmatrix} 0 \\ 1 \end{bmatrix} u(t)$$
$$\begin{bmatrix} y_1 \\ y_2 \end{bmatrix} = \begin{bmatrix} 3 & 0 \\ 4 & 5 \end{bmatrix} \begin{bmatrix} x_1 \\ x_2 \end{bmatrix} + \begin{bmatrix} 0 \\ 0 \end{bmatrix} u(t)$$
$$\mathbf{A} = \begin{bmatrix} 0 & 1 \\ -a_0 & -a_1 \end{bmatrix}$$
$$\mathbf{B} = \begin{bmatrix} 0 \\ 1 \end{bmatrix}$$
$$\mathbf{C} = \begin{bmatrix} 3 & 0 \\ 4 & 5 \end{bmatrix}$$
$$\mathbf{D} = \begin{bmatrix} 0 \\ 0 \end{bmatrix}$$

From the variation equation, because $\mathbf{Y} = \mathbf{C}\mathbf{X}$, the output matrix is $\mathbf{C}$.

The answer is (A).

Equation 48.35 Through Eq. 48.37: Laplace Transform of the State Equation

$$s\mathbf{X}(s) - \mathbf{x}(0) = \mathbf{A}\mathbf{X}(s) + \mathbf{B}\mathbf{U}(s) \qquad 48.35$$

$$\mathbf{X}(s) = \Phi(s)\mathbf{x}(0) + \Phi(s)\mathbf{B}\mathbf{U}(s) \qquad 48.36$$

$$\Phi(s) = [s\mathbf{I} - \mathbf{A}]^{-1} \qquad 48.37$$

Description

Equation 48.35 gives the Laplace transform of the time-invariant state equation, where $\mathbf{X}(s)$ is given by Eq. 48.36, and the Laplace transform of the state transition matrix is found from Eq. 48.37.

Equation 48.38 Through Eq. 48.40: Laplace Transform of the Output Equation

$$\Phi(t) = L^{-1}\{\Phi(s)\} \qquad 48.38$$

$$\mathbf{x}(t) = \Phi(t)\mathbf{x}(0) + \int_0^t \Phi(t-\tau)\mathbf{B}\mathbf{u}(\tau)\, d\tau \qquad 48.39$$

$$\mathbf{Y}(s) = \{\mathbf{C}\Phi(s)\mathbf{B} + \mathbf{D}\}\mathbf{U}(s) + \mathbf{C}\Phi(s)\mathbf{x}(0) \qquad 48.40$$

Description

The state-transition matrix given by Eq. 48.38 can be used in Eq. 48.39. The Laplace transform of the output equation is found from Eq. 48.40. $\{\mathbf{C}\Phi(s)\mathbf{B} + \mathbf{D}\}\mathbf{U}(s)$ represents the output or outputs due to the $\mathbf{U}(s)$ inputs, and $\mathbf{C}\Phi(s)\mathbf{x}(0)$ represents the output or outputs due to the initial conditions.

Diagnostic Exam

Topic XIII: Computational Tools

1. The following flowchart represents an algorithm.

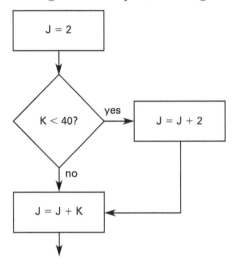

Which of the given structured programming segments correctly translates the algorithm?

(A) J = 2

IF K < 40 THEN J = J + 2

J = J + K

(B) J = 2

IF K < 40 THEN J = J + 2

ELSE J = J + K

(C) J = 2

DO WHILE K < 40

J = J + 2

ENDWHILE

J = J + K

(D) J = 2

DO UNTIL K < 40

ENDUNTIL

J = J + K

2. An operating system is being developed for use in the control unit of an industrial machine. For efficiency, it is decided that any command to the machine will be represented by a combination of four characters, and that only eight distinct characters will be supported. What is the minimum number of bits required to represent one command?

(A)   5

(B)   7

(C)   12

(D)   16

3. For the program segment shown, the input value of X is 5. What is the output value of T?

$$
\begin{aligned}
&\text{INPUT X}\\
&\text{N} = 0\\
&\text{T} = 0\\
&\quad\text{DO WHILE } \text{N} < \text{X}\\
&\quad\text{T} = \text{T} + \text{X} \char`\^ \text{N}\\
&\quad\text{N} = \text{N} + 1\\
&\quad\text{END DO}\\
&\text{OUTPUT T}
\end{aligned}
$$

(A)   156

(B)   629

(C)   781

(D)   3906

4. A spreadsheet has been developed to calculate the cycle time for an assembly line required to meet a given production demand. Cells A1 through A5 contain the task times, cell B1 contains the number of stations, and cell B2 contains the cycle time. The equation for balance delay is

$$\frac{(\text{no. of stations})(\text{cycle time}) - \text{sum of task times}}{(\text{no. of stations})(\text{cycle time})}$$

If cell C1 is to contain the balance delay for the solution, what formula should be put into it?

(A)   (SUM(A1:A5) + B1*B2)/(B1 + B2)

(B)   (B1 − (SUM(A1:A5)/B1*B2))/(SUM(B1:B2))

(C)   (B1*B2 − SUM(A1:A5))/SUM(A1:A5)

(D)   (B1*B2 − SUM(A1:A5))/(B1*B2)

5. The cells in a spreadsheet application are defined as follows.

	A	B	C	D
1	3	12	= SUM(C2:D4)	7
2	5	= AVERAGE(C2:D4)	−1	= C3*2
3	= D2^2	= C1 − B2	= A1 + B4	−10
4	= ABS(B3)	−4	8	= MIN(A1:A3)
5				

What is the value of cell A4?

(A) 0.83

(B) 1.0

(C) 2.5

(D) 8.3

6. What operation is typically represented by the following program flowchart symbol?

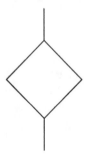

(A) input-output

(B) processing

(C) storage

(D) branching

7. The number 2 is entered into cell A1 in a spreadsheet. The formula A1 + A1 is entered into cell B1. The contents of cell B1 are then copied and pasted into cell C1. The number displayed in cell C1 is

(A) 2

(B) 4

(C) 6

(D) 8

8. Based on the following program segment, what is the final answer?

```
I = 1
J = 2
K = 3
L = 4
ANSWER = C
IF (I > J) OR (K < L) THEN ANSWER = A
IF (I < J) OR (K > L ) THEN ANSWER = B
IF (I > J) OR (K > L) THEN  I = 5
IF (I < L) AND (K < L) THEN ANSWER = D
```

(A) A

(B) B

(C) C

(D) D

9. How many cells are in the range C5:Z30?

(A) 575

(B) 598

(C) 600

(D) 624

10. A subsurface remedial treatment technology cost $245,000 to construct, and the annual operation and maintenance costs are $9000. There is no salvage value at the end of the equipment's 5 yr operational life. Using an annual interest rate of 7%, the annualized cost for the remedial treatment technology is most nearly

(A) $58,000

(B) $60,000

(C) $65,000

(D) $69,000

SOLUTIONS

1. The decision block indicates an IF statement because both outcomes progress toward the end. If the flowchart looped back for one of the outcomes, the chart might indicate a DO WHILE or DO UNTIL loop. The flowchart indicates that the operation $J = J + K$ will occur regardless of the outcome of the IF statement; therefore, there is no ELSE as shown in option B.

The answer is (A).

2. Since $2^3 = 8$, three bits are sufficient to represent 8 characters. Since there are 4 characters per command, a string with a minimum of $4 \times 3 = 12$ bits is needed.

The answer is (C).

3. The program segment defines the series

$$\sum_{0}^{N=X-1} X^N$$

The value of T at the conclusion of the loop can be computed as

N	T	
0	$0 + 5^0$	$= 1$
1	$1 + 5^1$	$= 6$
2	$6 + 5^2$	$= 31$
3	$31 + 5^3$	$= 156$
4	$156 + 5^4$	$= 781$

The answer is (C).

4. The spreadsheet formula is

$$(B1*B2 - SUM(A1:A5))/(B1*B2)$$

The answer is (D).

5. Calculating the value of cell A4 requires the calculation of all of those cells that affect its result, directly or indirectly.

$C3 = A1 + B4 = 3 + (-4) = -1$

$D2 = C3*2 = -1*2 = -2$

$A3 = D2\hat{}2 = (-2)\hat{}2 = 4$

$D4 = MIN(A1 : A3) = MIN(A1, A2, A3) = MIN(3,5,4)$
$\quad = 3$

$C1 = SUM(C2 : D4) = C2 + C3 + C4 + D2 + D3 + D4$
$\quad = -1 + (-1) + 8 + (-2) + (-10) + 3$
$\quad = -3$

$B2 = AVERAGE(C2:D4)$
$\quad = (C2 + C3 + C4 + D2 + D3 + D4)/6 = -3/6$
$\quad = -0.5$

$B3 = C1 - B2 = -3 - (-0.5) = -2.5$

$A4 = ABS(B3) = |-2.5| = 2.5$

The answer is (C).

6. Branching, comparison, and decision operations are typically represented by the diamond symbol.

The answer is (D).

7. When the formula A1 + A1 is copied into cell C1, it becomes A1 + B1. The number displayed in cell B1 is $2 + 2 = 4$. The number displayed in cell C1 is $2 + 4 = 6$.

The answer is (C).

8. The code must be followed all the way from beginning to end. After the first IF, the ANSWER is A; after the second, it is B. The third IF evaluates to "false," so the ANSWER remains B, but the fourth statement is true, so the ANSWER is D.

The answer is (D).

9. A range from m to n, inclusive, has $m - n + 1$ elements, not $m - n$.

$$\text{no. of rows} = (30 - 5) + 1 = 26$$
$$\text{no. of columns} = (Z - C) + 1 = (26 - 3) + 1$$
$$= 24$$
$$\text{no. of cells} = (\text{no. of rows})(\text{no. of columns})$$
$$= (26)(24)$$
$$= 624$$

The answer is (D).

10. From standard interest tables, for an interest rate of 7%, a 5 yr lifespan, and an initial construction cost of $245,000, the annual factor is 0.2439. The annualized cost is

$\text{annualized cost} = \text{maintenance cost} + (\text{annual factor})(\text{capital cost})$
$\quad = \$9000 + (0.2439)(\$245,000)$
$\quad = \$68,756 \quad (\$69,000)$

The answer is (D).

49 Computer Software

1. CHARACTER CODING

Alphanumeric data refers to characters that can be displayed or printed, including numerals and symbols ($, %, &, etc.) but excluding *control characters* (tab, carriage return, form feed, etc.). Since computers can handle binary numbers only, all symbolic data must be represented by binary codes. *Coding* refers to the manner in which alphanumeric data and control characters are represented by sequences of bits.

The *American Standard Code for Information Interchange*, ASCII, is a seven-bit code permitting 128 (2^7) different combinations. It is commonly used in desktop computers, although use of the high order (eighth) bit is not standardized. ASCII-coded magnetic tape and disk files are used to transfer data and documents between computers of all sizes that would otherwise be unable to share data structures.

The *Extended Binary Coded Decimal Interchange Code*, EBCDIC (pronounced eb'-sih-dik), is in widespread use in IBM mainframe computers. It uses eight bits (one byte) for each character, allowing a maximum of 256 (2^8) different characters.

Since strings of binary digits (bits) are difficult to read, the *hexadecimal* (or "packed") format is used to simplify working with EBCDIC data. Each byte is converted into two strings of four bits each. The two strings are then converted to hexadecimal. Since $(1111)_2 = (15)_{10} = (F)_{16}$, the largest possible EBCDIC character is coded FF in hexadecimal.

Example

The American Standard Code for Information Interchange (ASCII) control character "LF" stands for

(A) line feed

(B) large format

(C) limit function

(D) large font

Solution

Lines of text displayed on monitors and printers are often followed by invisible carriage return (CR) and line feed (LF) control characters that determine the location of the next character.

The answer is (A).

2. PROGRAM DESIGN

A *program* is a sequence of computer instructions that performs some function. The program is designed to implement an *algorithm*, which is a procedure consisting of a finite set of well-defined steps. Each step in the algorithm usually is implemented by one or more instructions (e.g., READ, GOTO, OPEN, etc.) entered by the programmer. These original "human-readable" instructions are known as *source code statements*.

Except in rare cases, a computer will not understand source code statements. Therefore, the source code is translated into machine-readable object code and absolute memory locations. Eventually, an executable program is produced.

Programs use variables to store values, which may be known or unknown. A *declaration* defines a variable, specifies the type of data a variable can contain (e.g., INTEGER, REAL, etc.), and reserves space for the variable in the program's memory. *Assignments* give values to variables (e.g., X = 2). *Commands* instruct the program to take a specific action, such as END, PRINT, or INPUT. *Functions* are specific operations (e.g., calculating the SUM of several values) that are grouped into a unit that can be called within the program.

If the executable program is kept on disk or tape, it is normally referred to as *software*. If the program is placed in ROM (read-only memory) or EPROM (erasable programmable read-only memory), it is referred to as *firmware*. The computer mechanism itself is known as the *hardware*.

3. FLOWCHARTS

A *flowchart* is a step-by-step drawing representing a specific procedure or algorithm. Figure 49.1 illustrates the most common flowcharting symbols. The *terminal symbol* begins and ends a flowchart. The *input/output symbol* defines an I/O operation, including those to and from keyboard, printer, memory, and permanent data storage. The *processing symbol* and *predefined process symbol* refer to calculations or data manipulation. The *decision symbol* indicates a point where a decision must be made or two items are compared. The *connector symbol* indicates that the flowchart continues elsewhere. The *off-page symbol* indicates that the flowchart continues on the following page. Comments can be added in an *annotation symbol*.

Figure 49.1 Flowcharting Symbols

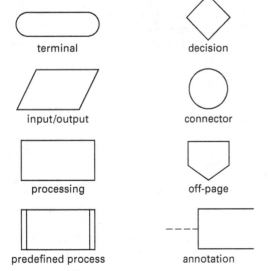

Example

The flowchart shown represents the summer training schedule for a college athlete.

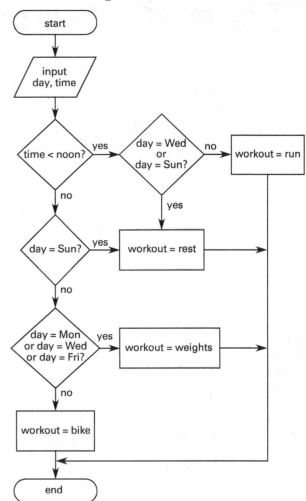

What is the regularly scheduled workout on Wednesday morning?

(A) bike

(B) rest

(C) run

(D) weights

Solution

The day and time being considered are Wednesday morning. At the first decision follow the "yes" branch, which leads to the question "Is the day Wednesday or Sunday?" Again the answer is "yes," so the scheduled workout is actually a resting day.

The answer is (B).

4. LOW-LEVEL LANGUAGES

Programs are written in specific languages, of which there are two general types: low-level and high-level. Low-level languages include machine language and assembly language.

Machine language instructions are intrinsically compatible with and understood by the computer's central processing unit (CPU). They are the CPU's native language. An instruction normally consists of two parts: the operation to be performed (*op-code*) and the operand expressed as a storage location. Each instruction ultimately must be expressed as a series of bits, a form known as *intrinsic machine code*. However, octal and hexadecimal coding are more convenient. In either case, coding a machine language program is tedious and seldom done by hand.

Assembly language is more sophisticated (i.e., is more symbolic) than machine language. Mnemonic codes are used to specify the operations. The operands are referred to by variable names rather than by the addresses. Blocks of code that are to be repeated verbatim at multiple locations in the program are known as *macros* (*macro instructions*). Macros are written only once and are referred to by a symbolic name in the source code.

Assembly language code is translated into machine language by an *assembler* (*macro-assembler* if macros are supported). After assembly, portions of other programs or function libraries may be combined by a *linker*. In order to run, the program must be placed in the computer's memory by a *loader*. Assembly language programs are preferred for highly efficient programs. However, the coding inconvenience outweighs this advantage for most applications.

5. HIGH-LEVEL LANGUAGES

High-level languages are easier to use than low-level languages because the instructions resemble English. High-level statements are translated into machine language by either an interpreter or a compiler. Table 49.1 shows a comparison of a typical ADD command in different computer languages. A *compiler* performs the checking and conversion functions on all instructions only when the compiler is invoked. A true stand-alone executable program is created. An *interpreter*, however, checks the instructions and converts them line by line into machine code during execution but produces no stand-alone program capable of being used without the interpreter. (Some interpreters check syntax as each statement is entered by the programmer. Some languages and implementations of other languages blur the distinction between interpreters and compilers. Terms such as *pseudo-compiler* and *incremental compiler* are used in these cases.)

Table 49.1 Comparison of Typical ADD Commands

language	instruction
intrinsic machine code	1111 0001
machine language	1A
assembly language	AR
high-level language	+

Example

A portion of computer code contains the instructions "LR," "SC," and "JL." Most likely, these are

(A) machine language

(B) assembly language

(C) object code

(D) interpreted code

Solution

Assembly language usually consists of short commands (e.g., "LR" for loading a value into the register, "SC" for storing a result in location C, and "JL" for jumping if the result is less than). Assembly language is translated into binary machine language (also known as "object code") by an interpreter or compiler program.

The answer is (B).

6. RELATIVE COMPUTATIONAL SPEED

Certain languages are more efficient (i.e., execute faster) than others. (Efficiency can also, but seldom does, refer to the size of the program.) While it is impossible to be specific, and exceptions abound, assembly language programs are fastest, followed in order of decreasing speed by compiled, pseudo-compiled, and interpreted programs.

Similarly, certain program structures are more efficient than others. For example, when performing a repetitive operation, the most efficient structure will be a single equation, followed in order of decreasing speed by a stand-alone loop and a loop within a subroutine. Incrementing the loop variables and managing the exit and entry points is known as *overhead* and takes time during execution.

7. STRUCTURE, DATA TYPING, AND PORTABILITY

A language is said to be *structured* if subroutines and other procedures each have one specific entry point and one specific return point. (Contrast this with BASIC, which permits (1) a GOSUB to a specific subroutine

Computational Tools

with a return from anywhere within the subroutine and (2) unlimited GOTO statements to anywhere in the main program.) A language has *strong data types* if integer and real numbers cannot be combined in arithmetic statements.

A *portable language* can be implemented on different machines. Most portable languages either are sufficiently rigidly defined (as in the cases of ADA and C) to eliminate variants and extensions, or (as in the case of Pascal) are compiled into an intermediate, machine-independent form. This so-called *pseudocode* (*p-code*) is neither source nor object code. The language is said to have been "ported to a new machine" when an interpreter is written that converts p-code to the appropriate machine code and supplies specific drivers for input, output, printers, and disk use. (Some companies have produced Pascal engines that run p-code directly.)

8. STRUCTURED PROGRAMMING

Structured programming (also known as *top-down programming*, *procedure-oriented programming*, and *GOTO-less programming*) divides a procedure or algorithm into parts known as subprograms, subroutines, modules, blocks, or procedures. (The format and readability of the source code—improved by indenting nested structures, for example—do not define structured programming.) Internal subprograms are written by the programmer; external subprograms are supplied in a library by another source. Ideally, the mainline program will consist entirely of a series of calls (references) to these subprograms. Liberal use is made of FOR/NEXT, DO/WHILE, and DO/UNTIL commands. Labels and GOTO commands are avoided as much as possible.

Very efficient programs can be constructed in languages that support *recursive calls* (i.e., permit a subprogram to call itself). Recursion requires less code, but recursive calls use more memory. Some languages permit recursion; others do not.

Variables whose values are accessible strictly within the subprogram are *local variables*. *Global variables* can be referred to by the main program and all other subprograms.

Calculations are performed in a specific order in an instruction, with the contents of parentheses done first. The symbols used for mathematical operations in programming are

+	add
−	subtract
*	multiply
/	divide

Raising one expression to the power of another expression depends on the language used. Examples of how X^B might be expressed are

$$X^{**}B$$
$$X^{\wedge}B$$

Example

Two floating point numbers, A and B, are passed to a recursive subroutine. If number A is greater than or equal to 7, the subroutine returns the value of number A to the main program. If number A is less than the smaller of 7 and number B, number A is divided by 2. The subroutine then passes the quotient and number B to itself. Most likely, what condition might this subroutine encounter?

(A) overflow

(B) miscompare

(C) infinite loop

(D) type mismatch

Solution

Consider the case where A = 6 and B = 9. Since 6 is not greater than or equal to 7, control is not returned to the main program. Since 6 is less 7 (the smaller of 7 and 9), 6 is divided by 2, yielding a quotient of 3. The subroutine then passes A = 3 and B = 9 to itself. Since 3 (the new number A) is not greater than or equal to 7, control is not returned to the main program. Since 3 is less 7 (the smaller of 7 and 9), 3 is divided by 2, yielding a quotient of 1.5. The subroutine then passes A = 1.5 and B = 9 to itself. The process repeats indefinitely, since A will never be greater than 7. In some cases, the quotient might become small enough to terminate with an underflow error. (Nothing is said about the data type (variable class) of the number 7 or the comparison rules, so a type mismatch would require additional assumptions.)

The answer is (C).

Conditions and Statements

Following are brief descriptions of some commonly used structured programming functions.

IF THEN statements: In an IF <condition> THEN <action> statement, the condition must be satisfied, or the action is not executed and the program moves on to the next operation. Sometimes an IF THEN statement will include an ELSE statement in the format of IF <condition> THEN <action 1> ELSE <action 2>. If the condition is satisfied, then action 1 is executed. If the condition is not satisfied, action 2 is executed.

DO/WHILE loops: A set of instructions between the DO/WHILE <condition> and the ENDWHILE lines of code is repeated as long as the condition remains true.

The number of times the instructions are executed depends on when the condition is no longer true. The variable or variables that control the condition must eventually be changed by the operations, or the WHILE loop will continue forever.

DO/UNTIL loops: A set of instructions between the DO/UNTIL <condition> and the ENDUNTIL lines of code is repeated as long as the condition remains false. The number of times the instructions are executed depends on when the condition is no longer false. The variable or variables that control the condition must eventually be changed by the operations, or the UNTIL loop will continue forever.

FOR loops: A set of instructions between the FOR <counter range> and the NEXT <counter> lines of code is repeated for a fixed number of loops that depends on the counter range. The counter is a variable that can be used in operations in the loop, but the value of the counter is not changed by anything in the loop besides the NEXT <counter> statement.

GOTO: A GOTO operation moves the program to a number designator elsewhere on the program. The GOTO statement has fallen from favor and is avoided whenever possible in structured programming.

Example

A computer structured programming segment contains the following program segment.

$$\text{Set } G = 1 \text{ and } X = 0$$
$$\text{DO WHILE } G \leq 5$$
$$X = G*X + 1$$
$$G = X$$
$$\text{ENDWHILE}$$

What is the value of G after the segment is executed?

(A) 5

(B) 26

(C) 63

(D) The loop never ends.

Solution

The first execution of the WHILE loop results in

$$G = (1)(0) + 1 = 1$$
$$X = 1$$

The second execution of the WHILE loop results in

$$G = (1)(1) + 1 = 2$$
$$X = 2$$

The third execution of the WHILE loop results in

$$G = (2)(2) + 1 = 5$$
$$X = 5$$

The WHILE condition is still satisfied, so the instruction is executed a fourth time.

$$G = (5)(5) + 1 = 26$$
$$X = 26$$

The answer is (B).

9. HIERARCHY OF OPERATIONS

Operations in an arithmetic statement are performed in the order of exponentiation first, multiplication and division second, and addition and subtraction third. In the event that there are two consecutive operations with the same hierarchy (e.g., a multiplication followed by a division), the operations are performed in the order encountered, normally left to right (except for exponentiation, which is right to left).[1] Parentheses can modify this order; operations within parentheses are always evaluated before operations outside. If nested parentheses are present in an expression, the expression is evaluated outward starting from the innermost pair.

Example

Based on standard processing and hierarchy of operations, what would most nearly be the result of the following calculation?

$$459 + 306 / (6 * 5\,{}^{\wedge}2 + 3)$$

(A) 3

(B) 5

(C) 459

(D) 461

Solution

The standard mathematical processing hierarchy is represented by the acronym "BODMAS": Brackets (parentheses), Order (exponentiation or powers), Division and

---

[1]In most implementations, a statement will be scanned from left to right. Once a left-to-right scan is complete, some implementations then scan from right to left; others return to the equals sign and start a second left-to-right scan. Parentheses should be used to define the intended order of operations.

Multiplication (evaluated left to right), and Addition and Subtraction (evaluated left to right).

Evaluate the quantity in the parentheses first. Within the parentheses, evaluate the powered quantity first: $5^2 = 25$. There are no more powered quantities within the parentheses. Evaluate division and multiplication within the parentheses from left to right: $6*25 = 150$. Evaluate addition and subtraction within the parentheses: $150 + 3 = 153$. This is the value of the parenthetical expression. The original expression is now $459 + 306/153$. There are no brackets. There are no powers. Evaluate the division: $306/153 = 2$. Evaluate the addition: $459 + 2 = 461$.

The answer is (D).

10. SIMULATORS

A *simulator* is a computer program that replicates a real world system. A *digital model* is used in the simulation and incorporates variables representing the physical characteristics and behavioral properties of the system to be simulated (i.e., is a representation of the system itself). The simulator operates a model over a period of time to gain a detailed understanding of the system's characteristics and dynamics. Simulation makes it possible to test and examine multiple design scenarios before selecting or finalizing a design. Simulators can explore various design alternatives that may not be safe, feasible, or economically possible in real life.

Examples of simulators include the response of buildings to seismic forces, stormwater flowing through a drainage structure during a large storm event, automobiles merging onto a freeway during rush hour, and so on. In addition to testing various designs, simulators are used for training, education, and even entertainment.

11. SPREADSHEETS

Spreadsheet application programs (often referred to as *spreadsheets*) are computer programs that provide a table of values arranged in rows and columns and that permit each value to have a predefined relationship to the other values. If one value is changed, the program will also change other related values.

In a spreadsheet, the items are arranged in rows and columns. The rows are typically assigned with numbers (1, 2, 3, ...) along the vertical axis, and the columns are assigned with letters (A, B, C, ...), as is shown in Fig. 49.2.

A *cell* is a particular element of the table identified by an address that is dependent on the row and column assignments of the cell. For example, the address of the shaded cell in Fig. 49.2 is E3. A cell may contain a number, a formula relating its value to another cell or cells, or a label (usually descriptive text).

Figure 49.2 *Typical Spreadsheet Cell Assignments*

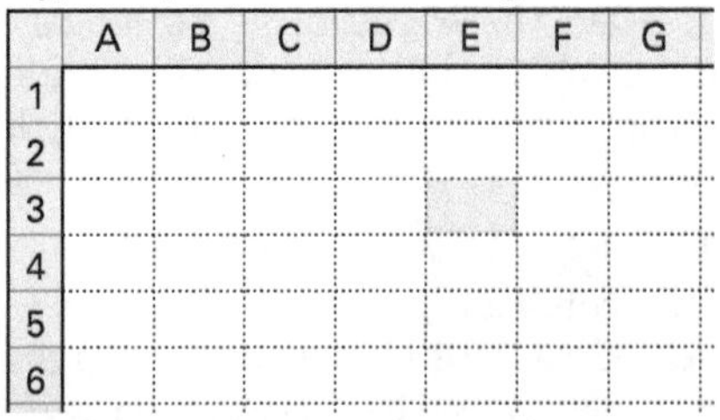

When the contents of one cell are used for a calculation in another cell, the address of the cell being used must be referenced so the program knows what number to use.

When the value of a cell containing a formula is calculated, any cell addresses within the formula are calculated as the values of their respective cells. Cell addressing can be handled one of two ways: relative addressing or absolute addressing. When a cell is copied using *relative addressing*, the row and cell references will be changed automatically. *Absolute addressing* means that when a cell is copied, the row and cell references remain unchanged. Relative addressing is the default. Absolute addressing is indicated by a "$" symbol placed in front of the row or column reference (e.g., $C1 or C$1).

An *absolute cell reference* identifies a particular cell and will have a "$" before both the row and column designators. For example, A1 identifies the cell in the first column and first row, A3 identifies the cell in the first column and third row, and C1 identifies the cell in the third column and first row, regardless of the cell the reference is located in. If the absolute cell reference is copied and pasted into another cell, it continues referring to the exact same cell.

An *absolute column, relative row cell reference* has an absolute column reference (indicated with a "$") and a relative row reference. For example, the cell reference $A1 depends on what row it is entered in; if it is copied into a cell in the final row, it really refers to a cell that is in the first column in the final row.

If this reference is copied and pasted into a cell in the third row, the reference will become $A3. Similarly, a reference of $A3 in the second row refers to a cell in the first column one row below the current row. If this reference is copied and pasted into the third row, it becomes $A4.

A *relative column, absolute row cell reference* has a "$" on the row designator, and the column reference depends on the column it is entered in. For example, a cell reference of B$4 in the fourth column (column D) refers to a cell two columns to the left in the fourth row. If this reference is copied and pasted into the sixth column (column F), it becomes D$4.

A cell reference that does not include a "$" is entirely dependent on the cell in which is it located. For example, a cell reference to B4 in the cell C2 refers to a cell that is one column to the left and two rows below. If this reference is copied and pasted into cell D3, it becomes C5.

The syntax for calculations with rows, columns, or blocks of cells can differ from one brand of spreadsheet to another.

Cells can be called out in square or rectangular blocks, usually for a SUM function. The difference between the row and column designations in the call will define the block. For example, SUM(A1:A3) says to sum the cells A1, A2, and A3; SUM(D3:D5) says to sum the cells D3, D4, and D5; and SUM(B2:C4) says to sum cells B2, B3, B4, C2, C3, and C4.

Example

The cells in a spreadsheet are initialized as shown. The formula B1 + A1*A2 is entered into cell B2 and then copied into cells B3 and B4.

	A	B		
1	3	111		
2	4			
3	5			
4	6			
5				

What value will be displayed in cell B4?

(A) 123

(B) 147

(C) 156

(D) 173

Solution

When the formula is copied into cells B3 and B4, the relative references will be updated. The resulting spreadsheet (with formulas displayed) should look like

	A	B
1	3	111
2	4	B1 + A1*A2
3	5	B2 + A1*A3
4	6	B3 + A1*A4
5		

$$B4 = B3 + (A1)(A4)$$
$$= B2 + (A1)(A3) + (A1)(A4)$$
$$= B1 + (A1)(A2) + (A1)(A3) + (A1)(A4)$$
$$= 111 + (3)(4) + (3)(5) + (3)(6)$$
$$= 156$$

The answer is (C).

12. SPREADSHEETS IN ENGINEERING

Spreadsheets are powerful, widely used computational tools in various engineering disciplines. Their popularity is often attributed to widespread availability, ease of use, and robust functionality. A spreadsheet can be used to collect data, identify and analyze trends within a data set, perform statistical calculations, quickly execute a series of interconnected calculations, and determine the effect of one variable change on other related variables, among other uses.

Applications include calculating open channel flow, scheduling construction activities, determining distribution of moments on a beam, calculating design parameters for a batch reactor, calculating the efficiency of a pump or motor, graphing the relationship between voltages and currents in circuit analysis, and determining costs over time in cost estimation.

Some benefits of using spreadsheets for engineering calculations and applications include the ability to reproduce calculations faithfully, to save and later review input and results, to compare results based on different input values, and to plot results graphically. Drawbacks include the difficulty of programming complex calculations (though many spreadsheets are commercially available), the lack of transparency for how results are calculated, and the resulting challenge of debugging inaccurate results. Spreadsheet calculations can be used in iterative design calculations, but results may need to be validated by some other means.

13. FIELDS, RECORDS, AND FILE TYPES

A collection of *fields* is known as a *record*. For example, name, age, and address might be fields in a personnel record. Groups of records are stored in a *file*.

A *sequential file* structure (typical of data on magnetic tape) contains consecutive records and must be read starting at the beginning. An *indexed sequential file* is one for which a separate index file (see Sec. 49.14) is maintained to help locate records.

With a *random (direct access) file structure*, any record can be accessed without starting at the beginning of the file.

14. FILE INDEXING

It is usually inefficient to place the records of an entire file in order. (A good example is a mailing list with thousands of names. It is more efficient to keep the names in the order of entry than to sort the list each time names are added or deleted.) Indexing is a means of specifying the order of the records without actually changing the order of those records.

An *index* (*key* or *keyword*) file is analogous to the index at the end of this book. It is an ordered list of items with references to the complete record. One field in the data record is selected as the *key field* (*record index*). More than one field can be indexed. However, each field will require its own index file. The sorted keys are usually kept in a file separate from the data file. One of the standard search techniques is used to find a specific key.

15. SORTING

Sorting routines place data in ascending or descending numerical or alphabetical order.

With the method of *successive minima*, a list is searched sequentially until the smallest element is found and brought to the top of the list. That element is then skipped, and the remaining elements are searched for the smallest element, which, when found, is placed after the previous minimum, and so on. A total of $n(n-1)/2$ comparisons will be required. When n is large, $n^2/2$ is sometimes given as the number of comparisons.

In a *bubble sort*, each element in the list is compared with the element immediately following it. If the first element is larger, the positions of the two elements are reversed (swapped). In effect, the smaller element "bubbles" to the top of the list. The comparisons continue to be made until the bottom of the list is reached. If no swaps are made in a pass, the list is sorted. A total of approximately $n^2/2$ comparisons are needed, on the average, to sort a list in this manner. This is the same as for the successive minima approach. However, swapping occurs more frequently in the bubble sort, slowing it down.

In an *insertion sort*, the elements are ordered by rewriting them in the proper sequence. After the proper position of an element is found, all elements below that position are bumped down one place in the sequence. The resulting vacancy is filled by the inserted element. At worst, approximately $n^2/2$ comparisons will be required. On average, there will be approximately $n^2/4$ comparisons.

Disregarding the number of swaps, the number of comparisons required by the successive minima, bubble, and insertion sorts is on the order of n^2. When n is large, these methods are too slow. The *quicksort* is more complex but reduces the average number of comparisons (with random data) to approximately $n \times \log n/\log 2$, generally considered as being on the order of $n \log n$. (However, the quicksort falters, in speed, when the elements are in near-perfect order.) The maximum number of comparisons for a *heap sort* is $n \times \log_2 n = n \times \log n/\log 2$, but it is likely that even fewer comparisons will be needed.

16. SEARCHING

If a group of records (i.e., a list) is randomly organized, a particular element in the list can be found only by a *linear search* (*sequential search*). At best, only one comparison and, at worst, n comparisons will be required to find something (an event known as a *hit*) in a list of n elements. The average is $n/2$ comparisons, described as being on the order of n. (The term *probing* is synonymous with *searching*.)

If the records are in ascending or descending order, a binary search will be superior. (A binary search is unrelated to a binary tree. A binary tree structure (see Sec. 49.18) greatly reduces search time but does not use a sorted list.) The search begins by looking at the middle element in the list. If the middle element is the sought-for element, the search is over. If not, half the list can be disregarded in further searching since elements in that portion will be either too large or too small. The middle element in the remaining part of the list is investigated, and the procedure continues until a hit occurs or the list is exhausted. The maximum number of required comparisons in a list of n elements will be $\log_2 n = \log n/\log 2$ (i.e., on the order of $\log n$).

Example

A binary search is used to determine if a particular test number is present in a sequence of 101 integers derived from a Fibonacci sequence. The numbers are sorted in decreasing magnitude. The smallest number in the sequence is 144. What is the maximum number of comparisons needed to determine if the test number is present?

(A) 6

(B) 7

(C) 11

(D) 49

Solution

A binary search looks at half of an active list at a time. Comparing continues until the active list contains only a single value. The index of the middle integer in a sorted list of 101 integers is at index $(1 + 101)/2 = 51$. The first comparison is to integer 51.

The active list now contains 50 integers. The second comparison is to the middle integer at index $(1 + 50)/2 = 25$. The active list now contains a maximum of 25 items. The third comparison is to the integer at index $(26 + 50)/2 = 38$. The active list now contains 12 items. The fourth comparison is to the integer at index $(26 + 37)/2 = 31$. The active list now contains a maximum of 6 items. The fifth comparison is to the integer at index $(32 + 37)/2 = 35$. The active list now contains a maximum of 3 items. The sixth comparison is to the integer at index $(32 + 34)/2 = 33$. The active list now contains 1 item, which is used in the seventh and final comparison.

Since $\log_2 128 = 7$ (i.e., $2^7 = 128$), up to 128 integers can be searched with 7 comparisons.

The answer is (B).

17. HASHING

An index file is not needed if the record number (i.e., the storage location for a read or write operation) can be calculated directly from the key, a technique known as *hashing*. The procedure by which a numeric or nonnumeric key (e.g., a last name) is converted into a record number is called the *hashing function* or *hashing algorithm*. Most hashing algorithms use a remaindering modulus—the remainder after dividing the key by the number of records, n, in the list. Excellent results are obtained if n is a prime number; poor results occur if n is a power of 2. (Finding a record in this manner requires it to have been written in a location determined by the same hashing routine.)

Not all hashed record numbers will be valid. A *collision* occurs when an attempt is made to use a record number that is already in use. Chaining, linear probing, and double hashing are techniques used to resolve such collisions.

18. DATABASE STRUCTURES

Databases can be implemented as indexed files, linked lists, and tree structures; in all three cases, the records are written and remain in the order of entry.

An *indexed file* such as that shown in Fig. 49.3 keeps the data in one file and maintains separate index files (usually in sorted order) for each key field. The index file must be recreated each time records are added to the field. A *flat file* has only one key field by which records can be located. Searching techniques (see Sec. 49.16) are used to locate a particular record. In a *linked list* (*threaded list*), each record has an associated *pointer* (usually a record number or memory address) to the next record in key sequence. Only two pointers are changed when a record is added or deleted. Generally, a linear search following the links through the records is used. Figure 49.4(a) shows an example of a linked list structure.

Pointers are also used in *tree structures*. Each record has one or more pointers to other records that meet certain criteria. In a binary tree structure, each record has two pointers—usually to records that are lower and higher, respectively, in key sequence. In general, records in a tree structure are referred to as *nodes*. The first record in a file is called the *root node*. A particular node will have one node above it (the *parent* or *ancestor*) and one or more nodes below it (the *daughters* or *offspring*).

Figure 49.3 Key and Data Files

key file

key	record
ADAMS	3
JONES	2
SMITH	1
THOMAS	4

data file

record	last name	first name	age
1	SMITH	JOHN	27
2	JONES	WANDA	39
3	ADAMS	HENRY	58
4	THOMAS	SUSAN	18

Figure 49.4 Database Structures

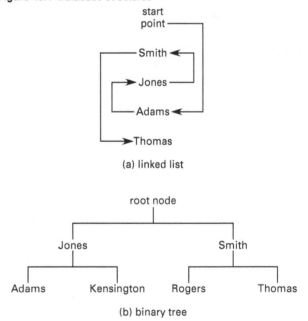

(a) linked list

(b) binary tree

Records are found in a tree by starting at the root node and moving sequentially according to the tree structure. The number of comparisons required to find a particular element is $1 + (\log n/\log 2)$, which is on the order of $\log n$. Figure 49.4(b) shows an example of a binary tree structure.

19. HIERARCHICAL AND RELATIONAL DATA STRUCTURES

A *hierarchical database* contains records in an organized, structured format. Records are organized according to one or more of the indexing schemes. However, each field within a record is not normally accessible. Figure 49.5 shows an example of a hierarchical structure.

Figure 49.5 *A Hierarchical Personnel File*

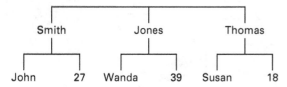

A *relational database* stores all information in the equivalent of a matrix. Nothing else (no index files, pointers, etc.) is needed to find, read, edit, or select information. Any information can be accessed directly by referring to the field name or field value. Figure 49.6 shows an example of relational structure.

Figure 49.6 *A Relational Personnel File*

rec. no.	last	first	age	
1	Smith	John	27	
2	Jones	Wanda	39	
3	Thomas	Susan	18	

20. ARTIFICIAL INTELLIGENCE

Artificial intelligence (AI) in a machine implies that the machine is capable of absorbing and organizing new data, learning new concepts, reasoning logically, and responding to inquiries. AI is implemented in a category of programs known as *expert systems* that "learn" rules from sets of events that are entered whenever they occur. (The manner in which the entry is made depends on the particular system.) Once the rules are learned, an expert system can participate in a dialogue to give advice, make predictions and diagnoses, or draw conclusions.

Computational Tools

Diagnostic Exam

Topic XIV: Engineering Economics

1. Cost estimates for a proposed municipal facility are being evaluated. Initial construction cost is anticipated to be $120,000, and annual maintenance expenses are expected to be $6500 for the first 20 years and $2000 for every year thereafter. The facility is to be used and maintained for an indefinite period of time. Using an interest rate of 10% per year, the present worth of the cost of this facility is most nearly

(A) $140,000

(B) $160,000

(C) $180,000

(D) $220,000

2. A machine has an initial cost of $18,000 and operating costs of $2500 each year. The salvage value decreases by $3000 each year. The machine is now three years old. Assuming an effective annual interest rate of 12%, the cost of owning and operating the machine for one more year is most nearly

(A) $5500

(B) $6100

(C) $6600

(D) $7100

3. A chemical plant purchased a $140,000 machine that has a useful life of seven years. If the machine has a salvage value of $20,000 at the end of its life, and straight line depreciation is used, the book value at the end of year 4 is most nearly

(A) $20,000

(B) $50,000

(C) $60,000

(D) $70,000

4. Calculate the approximate rate of return for an investment with the following characteristics.

initial cost	$20,000
project life	10 yr
salvage value	$5000
annual receipts	$7500
annual disbursements	$3000

(A) 20%

(B) 21%

(C) 23%

(D) 25%

5. On January 1, $5000 is deposited into a high-interest savings account that pays 8% interest compounded annually. If all of the money is withdrawn in five equal end-of-year sums beginning December 31 of the first year, most nearly how much will each withdrawal be?

(A) $1010

(B) $1150

(C) $1210

(D) $1250

6. If you needed to have $800 in savings at the end of four years and your savings account yielded 5% interest paid annually, most nearly how much would you need to deposit today?

(A) $570

(B) $600

(C) $660

(D) $770

Engineering
Economics

7. At the end of each year for five years, $500 is deposited into a credit union account. The credit union pays 5% interest compounded annually. At the end of five years (immediately following the fifth deposit), most nearly, how much will be in the account?

(A) $640

(B) $1800

(C) $2800

(D) $3600

8. $5000 is put into an empty savings account with a nominal interest rate of 5%. No other contributions are made to the account. With monthly compounding, approximately how much interest will have been earned after five years?

(A) $1250

(B) $1380

(C) $1400

(D) $1420

9. An investment currently costs $28,000. If the current inflation rate is 6% and the effective annual return on investment is 10%, approximately how long will it take for the investment's future value to reach $40,000?

(A) 1.8 yr

(B) 2.3 yr

(C) 2.6 yr

(D) 3.4 yr

10. The purchase price of a car is $25,000. Mr. Smith makes a down payment of $5000 and borrows the balance from a bank at 6% nominal annual interest, compounded monthly. Most nearly, what is the required monthly payment to pay off the loan in 5 years?

(A) $350

(B) $400

(C) $450

(D) $500

SOLUTIONS

1. The cost that continues indefinitely is converted to a present cost using the capitalized cost factor, which is defined as the limit of the $(P/A, 10\%, n)$ factor as n approaches infinity. The capitalized cost factor is equal to one divided by the interest rate.*[Engineering Economics: Factor Table]*

In this problem, there is a one-time cost of $120,000. As stated in the problem, the maintenance costs are two fold: $6500 for the first 20 years, and $2000 thereafter. In order to simplify the calculations, we can rearrange the maintenance cost to become $4500 (that is $6500-$2000) for the first 20 years as well as $2000 starting at the present time and continues indefinitely (this covers $2000 that we removed from the first 20 years as well as the $2000 for ever year thereafter).*[Interest Rate Tables]*

$$P = \$120,000 + A_1(P/A, i, n) + A_2(\text{captitalized cost factor}, i)$$
$$= \$120,000 + (\$6500 - \$2000)(P/A, 10\%, 20) + (\$2000)(1/i, 10\%)$$
$$= \$120,000 + (\$4500)(8.5136) + (\$2000)\left(\frac{1}{0.10}\right)$$
$$= \$178,311 \quad (\$180,000)$$

The answer is (C).

2. The cost of owning and operating the machine one more year is equal to the operating costs plus the lost salvage value. The value of having the cash one year earlier must also be considered. After three years, the machine's salvage value is $9000, and after another year it will be $6000.

The cost of one more year of ownership and operation is

$$C = \text{operating cost} + \text{lost salvage value} + \text{opportunity cost}$$
$$= \$2500 + (\$9000 - \$6000) + (0.12)(\$9000)$$
$$= \$6580 \quad (\$6600)$$

The answer is (C).

3. The straight-line depreciation is

$$D = \frac{C - S_n}{n}$$
$$= \frac{\$140{,}000 - \$20{,}000}{7 \text{ yr}}$$
$$= \$17{,}143/\text{yr}$$

The book value at the end of year 4 is

$$\text{BV}_j = C - \sum D_j$$
$$\text{BV}_4 = \$140{,}000 - (4)(\$17{,}143)$$
$$= \$71{,}428 \quad (\$70{,}000)$$

The answer is (D).

4. For the investment,

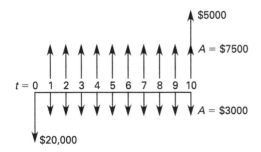

$$P = 0 = -\$20{,}000 + (\$5000)(P/F, i\%, 10)$$
$$+(\$7500)(P/A, i\%, 10)$$
$$-(\$3000)(P/A, i\%, 10)$$
$$\$20{,}000 = (\$5000)(P/F, i\%, 10)$$
$$+(\$4500)(P/A, i\%, 10)$$
$$= (\$5000)(1 + i)^{-10}$$
$$+(\$4500)\left[\frac{(1 + i)^{10} - 1}{i(1 + i)^{10}}\right]$$

By trial and error, $i = 19.5\%$ (20%).

The answer may also be obtained by linear interpolation of values from the discount factor tables, but this will not give an exact answer.

The answer is (A).

5. Use the uniform series capital recovery factor to solve for disbursements.

Engineering Economics: Factor Table

$$A = P(A/P, i\%, n) = P\left[\frac{i(1 + i)^n}{(1 + i)^n - 1}\right]$$
$$= (\$5000)\left[\frac{(0.08)(1 + 0.08)^5}{(1 + 0.08)^5 - 1}\right]$$
$$= \$1252 \quad (\$1250)$$

The answer is (D).

6. Use the single payment present worth formula.

$$P = F(P/F, i\%, n) = F\left[\frac{1}{(1 + i)^n}\right]$$
$$= (\$800)\left[\frac{1}{(1 + 0.05)^4}\right]$$
$$= \$658.16 \quad (\$660)$$

The answer is (C).

7. Use the uniform series compound amount formula.

$$F = A(F/A, i\%, n) = A\left[\frac{(1 + i)^n - 1}{i}\right]$$
$$= (\$500)\left[\frac{(1 + 0.05)^5 - 1}{0.05}\right]$$
$$= \$2762.82 \quad (\$2800)$$

The answer is (C).

8. 5% is the nominal rate per year. The effective annual interest rate is

Non-Annual Compounding

$$i_e = \left(1 + \frac{r}{m}\right)^m - 1$$
$$= \left(1 + \frac{0.05}{12}\right)^{12} - 1$$
$$= 0.05116$$

The total future value after five years is

Engineering Economics: Factor Table

$$F = P(F/P, i\%, n) = P(1 + i)^n$$
$$= (\$5000)(1 + 0.05116)^5$$
$$= \$6417$$

The interest earned is

$$I_{\text{earned}} = F - P = \$6417 - \$5000$$
$$= \$1417 \quad (\$1420)$$

(This problem can also be solved by calculating the effective interest rate per month and compounding for 60 months.)

The answer is (D).

9. The combined interest rate adjusted for inflation is

$$d = i + f + (i \times f)$$
$$= 0.10 + 0.06 + (0.10)(0.06)$$
$$= 0.166$$

Use the present worth factor to determine the number of periods, n.

$$P = F(1 + d)^{-n}$$
$$\$28,000 = (\$40,000)(1 + 0.166)^{-n}$$
$$0.7 = (1 + 0.166)^{-n}$$

Take the log of both sides.

$$\log 0.7 = \log(1.166)^{-n}$$
$$= -n \log 1.166$$
$$-0.1549 = -n(0.0667)$$
$$n = 2.32 \quad (2.3 \text{ yr})$$

The answer is (B).

10. The present worth, P, of the loan is

$$P = \$25,000 - \$5000 = \$20,000$$

The effective rate per month is

$$i = \frac{6\%}{12} = 0.5\%$$
$$n = (5 \text{ yr})\left(12 \ \frac{\text{mo}}{\text{yr}}\right) = 60 \text{ mo}$$

Use the capital recovery factor.

$$A = (\$20,000)(A/P, 0.5\%, 60)$$
$$= (\$20,000)(0.0193)$$
$$= \$386 \quad (\$400)$$

The answer is (B).

50

Engineering Economics

Nomenclature

A	annual amount or annual value	$
B	present worth of all benefits	$
BV	book value	$
C	initial cost, or present worth of all costs	$
d	interest rate per period adjusted for inflation	decimal or %
D	depreciation	$
f	inflation rate per period	decimal or %
F	future worth (future value)	$
G	uniform gradient amount	$
i	interest rate per period	decimal or %
j	number of compounding periods or years	–
m	number of compounding periods per year	–
n	total number of compounding periods or years	–
P	present worth (present value)	$
r	nominal rate per year (rate perannum)	decimal or %
S	salvage value	$
t	time	yr

Subscripts

0	initial
e	effective
j	jth year or period
n	final year or period

1. INTRODUCTION

In its simplest form, an *engineering economic analysis* is a study of the desirability of making an investment.[1] The decision-making principles in this chapter can be applied by individuals as well as by companies. The nature of the spending opportunity or industry is not important. Farming equipment, personal investments, and multimillion dollar factory improvements can all be evaluated using the same principles.

Similarly, the applicable principles are insensitive to the monetary units. Although *dollars* are used in this chapter, it is equally convenient to use pounds, yen, or euros.

Finally, this chapter may give the impression that investment alternatives must be evaluated on a year-by-year basis. Actually, the *effective period* can be defined as a day, month, century, or any other convenient period of time.

2. YEAR-END AND OTHER CONVENTIONS

Except in short-term transactions, it is simpler to assume that all receipts and disbursements (cash flows) take place at the end of the year in which they occur.[2] This is known as the *year-end convention*. The exceptions to the year-end convention are initial project cost (purchase cost), trade-in allowance, and other cash flows that are associated with the inception of the project at $t = 0$.

---

[1]This subject is also known as *engineering economics* and *engineering economy*. There is very little, if any, true economics in this subject.
[2]A *short-term transaction* typically has a lifetime of five years or less and has payments or compounding that are more frequent than once per year.

On the surface, such a convention appears grossly inappropriate since repair expenses, interest payments, corporate taxes, and so on seldom coincide with the end of a year. However, the convention greatly simplifies engineering economic analysis problems, and it is justifiable on the basis that the increased precision associated with a more rigorous analysis is not warranted (due to the numerous other simplifying assumptions and estimates initially made in the problem).

There are various established procedures, known as *rules* or *conventions*, imposed by the Internal Revenue Service on U.S. taxpayers. An example is the *half-year rule*, which permits only half of the first-year depreciation to be taken in the first year of an asset's life when certain methods of depreciation are used. These rules are subject to constantly changing legislation and are not covered in this book. The implementation of such rules is outside the scope of engineering practice and is best left to accounting professionals.

3. CASH FLOW

The sums of money recorded as receipts or disbursements in a project's financial records are called *cash flows*. Examples of cash flows are deposits to a bank, dividend interest payments, loan payments, operating and maintenance costs, and trade-in salvage on equipment. Whether the cash flow is considered to be a receipt or disbursement depends on the project under consideration. For example, interest paid on a sum in a bank account will be considered a disbursement to the bank and a receipt to the holder of the account.

Because of the time value of money, the timing of cash flows over the life of a project is an important factor. Although they are not always necessary in simple problems (and they are often unwieldy in very complex problems), *cash flow diagrams* can be drawn to help visualize and simplify problems that have diverse receipts and disbursements.

The following conventions are used to standardize cash flow diagrams.

- The horizontal (time) axis is marked off in equal increments, one per period, up to the duration of the project.

- *Receipts* are represented by arrows directed upward. *Disbursements* are represented by arrows directed downward. The arrow length is approximately proportional to the magnitude of the cash flow.

- Two or more transfers in the same period are placed end to end, and these may be combined.

- Expenses incurred before $t = 0$ are called *sunk costs*. Sunk costs are not relevant to the problem unless they have tax consequences in an after-tax analysis.

For example, consider a mechanical device that will cost $20,000 when purchased. Maintenance will cost $1000 each year. The device will generate revenues of $5000 each year for five years, after which the salvage value is expected to be $7000. The cash flow diagram is shown in Fig. 50.1(a), and a simplified version is shown in Fig. 50.1(b).

Figure 50.1 Cash Flow Diagrams

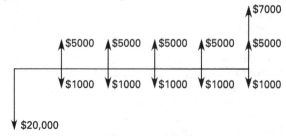

(a) cash flow diagram

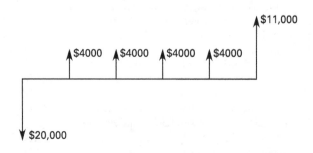

(b) simplified cash flow diagram

In order to evaluate a real-world project, it is necessary to present the project's cash flows in terms of standard cash flows that can be handled by engineering economic analysis techniques. The standard cash flows are single payment cash flow, uniform series cash flow, and gradient series cash flow.

A *single payment cash flow* can occur at the beginning of the time line (designated as $t = 0$), at the end of the time line (designated as $t = n$), or at any time in between.

The *uniform series cash flow*, illustrated in Fig. 50.2, consists of a series of equal transactions starting at $t = 1$ and ending at $t = n$. The symbol A (representing an *annual amount*) is typically given to the magnitude of each individual cash flow.

Figure 50.2 Uniform Series

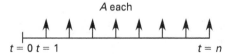

Notice that the cash flows do not begin at the beginning of a year (i.e., the year 1 cash flow is at $t = 1$, not $t = 0$). This convention has been established to accommodate the timing of annual maintenance and other cash flows for which the *year-end convention* is applicable. The year-end convention assumes that all receipts and disbursements take place at the end of the year in which they occur. The exceptions to the year-end convention are *initial project cost* (purchase cost), *trade-in allowance*, and other cash flows that are associated with the inception of the project at $t = 0$.

The *gradient series cash flow*, illustrated in Fig. 50.3, starts with a cash flow (typically given the symbol G) at $t = 2$ and increases by G each year until $t = n$, at which time the final cash flow is $(n-1)G$. The value of the gradient at $t = 1$ is zero.

Figure 50.3 Gradient Series

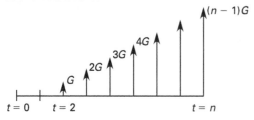

4. TIME VALUE OF MONEY

Consider $100 placed in a bank account that pays 5% effective annual interest at the end of each year. After the first year, the account will have grown to $105. After the second year, the account will have grown to $110.25.

The fact that $100 grows to $105 in one year at 5% annual interest is an example of the *time value of money* principle. This principle states that funds placed in a secure investment will increase in value in a way that depends on the elapsed time and the interest rate.

The interest rate that is used in calculations is known as the *effective interest rate*. If compounding is once a year, it is known as the *effective annual interest rate*. However, effective quarterly, monthly, or daily interest rates are also used.

5. DISCOUNT FACTORS

Assume that there will be no need for money during the next two years, and any money received will immediately go into an account and earn a 5% effective annual interest rate. Which of the following options would be more desirable?

option a: receive $100 now

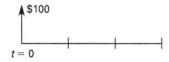

option b: receive $105 in one year

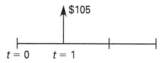

option c: receive $110.25 in two years

None of the options is superior under the assumptions given. If the first option is chosen, $100 will be immediately placed into a 5% account, and in two years the account will have grown to $110.25. In fact, the account will contain $110.25 at the end of two years regardless of which option is chosen. Therefore, these alternatives are said to be *equivalent*.

The three options are equivalent only for money earning a 5% effective annual interest rate. If a higher interest rate can be obtained, then the first option will yield the most money after two years. So, equivalence depends on the interest rate, and an alternative that is acceptable to one decision maker may be unacceptable to another who invests at a higher rate. The procedure for determining the equivalent amount is known as *discounting*.

Table 50.1: Discount Factors

Table 50.1 Discount Factors for Discrete Compounding

factor name	converts	symbol	formula
single payment compound amount	P to F	$(F/P, i\%, n)$	$(1+i)^n$
single payment present worth	F to P	$(P/F, i\%, n)$	$(1+i)^{-n}$
uniform series sinking fund	F to A	$(A/F, i\%, n)$	$\dfrac{i}{(1+i)^n - 1}$
capital recovery	P to A	$(A/P, i\%, n)$	$\dfrac{i(1+i)^n}{(1+i)^n - 1}$
uniform series compound amount	A to F	$(F/A, i\%, n)$	$\dfrac{(1+i)^n - 1}{i}$
uniform series present worth	A to P	$(P/A, i\%, n)$	$\dfrac{(1+i)^n - 1}{i(1+i)^n}$
uniform gradient present worth	G to P	$(P/G, i\%, n)$	$\dfrac{(1+i)^n - 1}{i^2(1+i)^n} - \dfrac{n}{i(1+i)^n}$
uniform gradient future worth*	G to F	$(F/G, i\%, n)$	$\dfrac{(1+i)^n - 1}{i^2} - \dfrac{n}{i}$
uniform gradient uniform series	G to A	$(A/G, i\%, n)$	$\dfrac{1}{i} - \dfrac{n}{(1+i)^n - 1}$

*See Eq. 50.9.

Description

The discounting factors are listed in symbolic and formula form. For more detail on individual factors, see the commentary accompanying Eq. 50.1 through Eq. 50.10. Normally, it will not be necessary to calculate factors from these formulas. Values of these cash flow (discounting) factors are tabulated in Table 50.4 through Table 50.13 (at the end of this chapter) for various combinations of i and n. For intermediate values, computing the factors from the formulas may be necessary, or linear interpolation can be used as an approximation. The interest rate used must be the effective rate per period for all discounting factor formulas. The basis of the rate (annually, monthly, etc.) must agree with the type of period used to count n. It would be incorrect to use an effective annual interest rate if n was the number of compounding periods in months.

6. SINGLE PAYMENT EQUIVALENCE

The equivalent future amount, F, at $t = n$, of any *present amount*, P, at $t = 0$ is called the *future worth*. The equivalence of any future amount to any present amount is called the *present worth*. Compound amount factors may be used to convert from a known present amount to a future worth or vice versa.

Equation 50.1: Single Payment Future Worth

$$F = P(1 + i)^n \qquad 50.1$$

Variation

$$F = P(F/P, i\%, n)$$

Description

The factor $(1 + i)^n$ is known as the *single payment compound amount factor*. Rather than actually writing the formula for the compound amount factor (which converts a present amount to a future amount), it is common convention to substitute the standard functional notation of $(F/P, i\%, n)$, as shown in the variation equation. This notation is interpreted as, "Find F, given P, using an interest rate of $i\%$ over n periods."

Example

A 40-year-old consulting engineer wants to set up a retirement fund to be used starting at age 65. $20,000 is invested now at 6% compounded annually. The amount of money that will be in the fund at retirement is most nearly

(A) $84,000

(B) $86,000

(C) $88,000

(D) $92,000

Solution

Determine the future worth of $20,000 in 25 years. From Eq. 50.1,

$$F = P(1 + i)^n = (\$20{,}000)(1 + 0.06)^{25}$$
$$= \$85{,}837 \quad (\$86{,}000)$$

The answer is (B).

Equation 50.2: Single Payment Present Worth

$$P = F(1 + i)^{-n} \qquad 50.2$$

Variations

$$P = F(P/F, i\%, n)$$

$$P = \frac{F}{(1 + i)^n}$$

Description

The factor $(1 + i)^{-n}$ is known as the *single payment present worth factor*.

Example

$2000 will become available on January 1 in year 8. If interest is 5%, what is most nearly the present worth of this sum on January 1 in year 1?

(A) $1330

(B) $1350

(C) $1400

(D) $1420

Solution

From January 1 in year 1 to January 1 in year 8 is seven years. From Eq. 50.2, the present worth is

$$P = F(1 + i)^{-n}$$
$$= (\$2000)(1 + 0.05)^{-7}$$
$$= \$1421 \quad (\$1420)$$

The answer is (D).

7. UNIFORM SERIES EQUIVALENCE

A cash flow that repeats at the end of each year for n years without change in amount is known as an *annual amount* and is given the symbol A. (This is shown in Fig. 50.2.)

Although the equivalent value for each of the n annual amounts could be calculated and then summed, it is more expedient to use one of the uniform series factors.

Equation 50.3: Uniform Series Future Worth

$$F = A\left[\frac{(1+i)^n - 1}{i}\right]$$
50.3

Variation

$$F = A(F/A, i\%, n)$$

Description

Use the *uniform series compound amount factor* to convert from an annual amount to a future amount.

Example

$20,000 is deposited at the end of each year into a fund earning 6% interest. At the end of ten years, the amount accumulated is most nearly

(A) $150,000

(B) $180,000

(C) $260,000

(D) $280,000

Solution

The amount accumulated at the end of ten years is

$$F = A\left[\frac{(1+i)^n - 1}{i}\right]$$

$$= (\$20,000)\left[\frac{(1+0.06)^{10} - 1}{0.06}\right]$$

$$= \$263,616 \quad (\$260,000)$$

The answer is (C).

Equation 50.4: Uniform Series Annual Value of a Sinking Fund

$$A = F\left[\frac{i}{(1+i)^n - 1}\right]$$
50.4

Variation

$$A = F(A/F, i\%, n)$$

Description

A *sinking fund* is a fund or account into which annual deposits of A are made in order to accumulate F at $t = n$ in the future. Because the annual deposit is calculated as $A = F(A/F, i\%, n)$, the (A/F) factor is known as the *sinking fund factor*.

Example

At the end of each year, an investor deposits some money into a fund earning 7% interest. The same amount is deposited each year, and after six years the account contains $1600. The amount deposited each time is most nearly

(A) $190

(B) $220

(C) $240

(D) $250

Solution

Use the sinking fund factor from Eq. 50.4 to find the annual value.

$$A = F\left[\frac{i}{(1+i)^n - 1}\right] = (\$1600)\left[\frac{0.07}{(1+0.07)^6 - 1}\right]$$

$$= \$224 \quad (\$220)$$

The answer is (B).

Equation 50.5: Uniform Series Present Worth

$$P = A\left[\frac{(1+i)^n - 1}{i(1+i)^n}\right]$$
50.5

Variation

$$P = A(P/A, i\%, n)$$

Description

An *annuity* is a series of equal payments, A, made over a period of time. Usually, it is necessary to "buy into" an investment (a bond, an insurance policy, etc.) in order to fund the annuity. In the case of an annuity that starts at the end of the first year and continues for n years, the purchase price, P, is calculated using the *uniform series present worth factor*.

Engineering Economics

Example

A sum of money is deposited into a fund at 5% interest. $400 is withdrawn at the end of each year for nine years, leaving nothing in the fund at the end. The amount originally deposited is most nearly

(A) $2600

(B) $2800

(C) $2900

(D) $3100

Solution

Find the present worth using the present worth factor.

$$P = A\left(\frac{(1+i)^n - 1}{i(1+i)^n}\right) = (\$400)\left(\frac{(1+0.05)^9 - 1}{(0.05)(1+0.05)^9}\right)$$

$$= \$2843 \quad (\$2800)$$

The answer is (B).

Equation 50.6: Uniform Series Annual Value Using the Capital Recovery Factor

$$A = P\left(\frac{i(1+i)^n}{(1+i)^n - 1}\right) \qquad 50.6$$

Variation

$$A = P(A/P, i\%, n)$$

Description

The *capital recovery factor* is often used when comparing alternatives with different lifespans. A comparison of two possible investments on the simple basis of their present values may be misleading if, for example, one alternative has a lifespan of 11 years and the other has a lifespan of 18 years. The capital recovery factor can be used to convert the present value of each alternative into its equivalent annual value, using the assumption that each alternative will be renewed repeatedly up to the duration of the longest-lived alternative.

8. UNIFORM GRADIENT EQUIVALENCE

A common situation involves a uniformly increasing cash flow. If the cash flow has the proper form (see Fig. 50.3), its present worth can be determined by using the *uniform gradient factor*, also called the *uniform gradient present worth factor*. The uniform gradient factor, $(P/G, i\%, n)$, finds the present worth of a uniformly increasing cash flow. By definition of a uniform gradient, the cash flow starts in year 2, not in year 1. Similar factors can be used to find the cash flow's future worth and annual worth.

There are three common difficulties associated with the form of the uniform gradient. The first difficulty is that the first cash flow starts at $t = 1$. This convention recognizes that annual costs, if they increase uniformly, begin with some value at $t = 1$ (due to the year-end convention), but do not begin to increase until $t = 2$. The tabulated values of (P/G) have been calculated to find the present worth of only the increasing part of the annual expense. The present worth of the base expense incurred at $t = 1$ must be found separately with the (P/A) factor.

The second difficulty is that, even though the $(P/G, i\%, n)$ factor is used, there are only $n - 1$ actual cash flows. n must be interpreted as the *period number* in which the last gradient cash flow occurs, not the number of gradient cash flows.

Finally, the sign convention used with gradient cash flows can be confusing. If an expense increases each year, the gradient will be negative, since it is an expense. If a revenue increases each year, the gradient will be positive. In most cases, the sign of the gradient depends on whether the cash flow is an expense or a revenue.

Equation 50.7: Uniform Gradient Present Worth

$$P = G\left(\frac{(1+i)^n - 1}{i^2(1+i)^n} - \frac{n}{i(1+i)^n}\right) \qquad 50.7$$

Variation

$$P = G(P/G, i\%, n)$$

Description

Equation 50.7 is used to find the present worth, P, of a cash flow that is increasing by a uniform amount, G. This factor finds the value of only the increasing portion of the cash flow; if the value at $t = 1$ is anything other than zero, its present worth must be found separately and added to get the total present worth.

Equation 50.8 and Eq. 50.9: Uniform Gradient Future Worth

$$F = G\left(\frac{(1+i)^n - 1}{i^2} - \frac{n}{i}\right) \qquad 50.8$$

$$F/G = (F/A - n)/i = (F/A) \times (A/G) \qquad 50.9$$

Variation

$$F = G(F/G, i\%, n)$$

Description

Equation 50.8 is used to find the future worth, F, of a cash flow that is increasing by a uniform amount, G. This factor finds the value of only the increasing portion of the cash flow; if the value at $t=1$ is anything other than zero, its future worth must be found separately and added to get the total future worth.

Equation 50.9 shows how the future worth factor, $(F/G, i\%, n)$, is closely related to (and, therefore, can be calculated quickly from) the factor $(F/A, i\%, n)$, or from the factors $(F/A, i\%, n)$ and $(A/G, i\%, n)$.

Equation 50.10: Uniform Gradient Uniform Series Factor

$$A = G\left(\frac{1}{i} - \frac{n}{(1+i)^n - 1}\right) \qquad 50.10$$

Variation

$$A = G(A/G, i\%, n)$$

Description

Equation 50.10 is used to find the equivalent annual worth, A, of a cash flow that is increasing by a uniform amount, G. This factor finds the value of only the increasing portion of the cash flow; if the value at $t=1$ is anything other than zero, its annual worth must be found separately and added to get the total annual worth.

Example

The maintenance cost on a house is expected to be $1000 the first year and to increase $500 per year after that. Assuming an interest rate of 6% compounded annually, the maintenance cost after 10 years is most nearly equivalent to an annual maintenance cost of

(A) $1900

(B) $3000

(C) $3500

(D) $3800

Solution

Use the uniform gradient uniform series factor to determine the effective annual cost, remembering that the first year's cost, $A_1 = \$1000$, must be added separately.

The annual increase is $G = \$500$. The effective annual cost of the increasing portion of the costs alone is

$$
\begin{aligned}
A &= G\left(\frac{1}{i} - \frac{n}{(1+i)^n - 1}\right) \\
&= (\$500)\left(\frac{1}{0.06} - \frac{10}{(1+0.06)^{10} - 1}\right) \\
&= \$2011
\end{aligned}
$$

The total effective annual cost is

$$
\begin{aligned}
A_{\text{total}} &= A_1 + A \\
&= \$1000 + \$2011 \\
&= \$3011 \quad (\$3000)
\end{aligned}
$$

The answer is (B).

9. FUNCTIONAL NOTATION

There are several ways of remembering what the functional notation means. One method of remembering which factor should be used is to think of the factors as *conditional probabilities*. The conditional probability of event A given that event B has occurred is written as $P\{A|B\}$, where the given event comes after the vertical bar. In the standard notational form of discounting factors, the given amount is similarly placed after the slash. The desired factor (i.e., A) comes before the slash. (F/P) would be a factor to find F given P.

Another method of remembering the notation is to interpret the factors algebraically. The (F/P) factor could be thought of as the fraction F/P. The numerical values of the discounting factors are consistent with this algebraic manipulation. The (F/A) factor could be calculated as $(F/P)(P/A)$. This consistent relationship can be used to calculate other factors that might be occasionally needed, such as (F/G) or (G/P).

10. NONANNUAL COMPOUNDING

If $100 is invested at 5%, it will grow to $105 in one year. If only the original principal accrues interest, the interest is known as *simple interest*, and the account will grow to $110 in the second year, $115 in the third year, and so on. Simple interest is rarely encountered in engineering economic analyses.

More often, both the principal and the interest earned accrue interest, and this is known as *compound interest*. If the account is compounded yearly, then during the second year, 5% interest continues to be accrued, but on $105, not $100, so the value at year end will be $110.25. The value after the third year will be $115.76, and so on.

The interest rate used in the discount factor formulas is the *interest rate per period*, i (called the *yield* by banks). If the interest period is one year (i.e., the interest is compounded yearly), then the interest rate per period, i, is equal to the *effective annual interest rate*, i_e. The effective annual interest rate is the rate that would yield the same accrued interest at the end of the year if the account were compounded yearly.

The term *nominal interest rate*, r (*rate per annum*), is encountered when compounding is more than once per year. The nominal rate does not include the effect of compounding and is not the same as the effective annual interest rate.

Equation 50.11: Effective Annual Interest Rate

$$i_e = \left(1 + \frac{r}{m}\right)^m - 1 \qquad \textit{50.11}$$

Description

The effective annual interest rate, i_e, can be calculated if the nominal rate, r, and the number of compounding periods per year, m, are known. If there are m compounding periods during the year (two for semiannual compounding, four for quarterly compounding, twelve for monthly compounding, etc.), the *effective interest rate per period*, i, is r/m. The effective annual interest rate, i_e, can be calculated from the effective interest rate per period by using Eq. 50.11.

Example

Money is invested at 5% per annum and compounded quarterly. The effective annual interest rate is most nearly

(A) 5.1%

(B) 5.2%

(C) 5.4%

(D) 5.5%

Solution

The rate per annum is the nominal interest rate. Use Eq. 50.11 to calculate the effective annual interest rate.

$$i_e = \left(1 + \frac{r}{m}\right)^m - 1$$
$$= \left(1 + \frac{0.05}{4}\right)^4 - 1$$
$$= 0.05095 \quad (5.1\%)$$

The answer is (A).

11. DEPRECIATION

Tax regulations do not generally allow the purchase price of an asset or other property to be treated as a single deductible expense in the year of purchase. Rather, the cost must be divided into portions, and these artificial expenses are spread out over a number of years. The portion of the cost that is allocated to a given year is called the *depreciation*, and the period of years over which these portions are spread out is called the *depreciation period* (also known as the *service life*).

When depreciation is included in an engineering economic analysis problem, it will increase the asset's after-tax present worth (profitability). The larger the depreciation is, the greater the profitability will be. For this reason, it is desirable to make the depreciation in each year as large as possible and to accelerate the process of depreciation as much as possible.

The *depreciation basis* of an asset is that part of the asset's purchase price that is spread over the depreciation period. The depreciation basis may or may not be equal to the purchase price.

A common depreciation basis is the difference between the purchase price and the expected salvage value at the end of the depreciation period (i.e., depreciation basis = $C - S_n$).

In the *sum-of-the-years' digits* (SOYD) method of depreciation, the digits from 1 to n inclusive are added together. An easy way to calculate this sum is the formula

$$\sum_{j=1}^{n} j = \frac{n(n+1)}{2}$$

The depreciation in year j is found from

$$D_j = \frac{n+1-j}{\sum_{j=1}^{n} j}(C - S_n)$$

Using this method, the depreciation from one year to the next decreases by a constant amount.

Equation 50.12: Straight Line Method

$$D_j = \frac{C - S_n}{n} \qquad \textit{50.12}$$

Description

With the *straight line method*, depreciation is the same each year. The depreciation basis $(C - S_n)$ is divided uniformly among all of the n years in the depreciation period.

Example

A computer will be purchased at $3900. The expected salvage value at the end of its service life of 10 years is $1800. Using the straight line method, the annual depreciation for this computer is most nearly

(A) $210

(B) $230

(C) $260

(D) $280

Solution

From Eq. 50.12, the annual depreciation using the straight line method is

$$D_j = \frac{C - S_n}{n}$$
$$= \frac{\$3900 - \$1800}{10}$$
$$= \$210$$

The answer is (A).

Equation 50.13: Modified Accelerated Cost Recovery System (MACRS)

$$D_j = (\text{factor})C \qquad \textit{50.13}$$

Values

Table 50.2 Representative MACRS Depreciation Factors

| year j | \multicolumn{4}{c}{recovery period (years)} |
| | 3 | 5 | 7 | 10 |
	\multicolumn{4}{c}{recovery rate (percent)}
1	33.33	20.00	14.29	10.00
2	44.45	32.00	24.49	18.00
3	14.81	19.20	17.49	14.40
4	7.41	11.52	12.49	11.52
5		11.52	8.93	9.22
6		5.76	8.92	7.37
7			8.93	6.55
8			4.46	6.55
9				6.56
10				6.55
11				3.28

Description

In the United States, property placed into service in 1981 and thereafter must use the *Accelerated Cost Recovery System* (ACRS), and property placed into service after 1986 must use the *Modified Accelerated Cost Recovery System* (MACRS) or another statutory method. Other methods, including the straight line method, cannot be used except in special cases.

Under ACRS and MACRS, the cost recovery amount in a particular year is calculated by multiplying the initial cost of the asset by a factor. (This initial cost is not reduced by the asset's salvage value.) The factor to be used varies depending on the year and on the total number of years in the asset's cost recovery period. These factors are subject to continuing legislation changes. Representative MACRS depreciation factors are shown in Table 50.2.

Example

A groundwater treatment system costs $2,500,000. It is expected to operate for a total of 130,000 hours over a period of 10 years, and then have a $250,000 salvage value. During the system's first year in service, it is operated for 6500 hours. Using the MACRS method, its depreciation in the third year is most nearly

(A) $160,000

(B) $250,000

(C) $360,000

(D) $830,000

Solution

MACRS depreciation depends only on the original cost, not on the salvage cost or hours of operation. From Table 50.2, the factor for the third year of a 10-year recovery period is 14.40%. From Eq. 50.13,

$$D_j = (\text{factor})C$$
$$D_3 = (0.1440)(\$2,500,000)$$
$$= \$360,000$$

The answer is (C).

12. BOOK VALUE

The difference between the original purchase price and the accumulated depreciation is known as the *book value*, BV. The book value is initially equal to the purchase price, and at the end of each year it is reduced by that year's depreciation.

Engineering Economics

Figure 50.4 compares how the ratio of book value to initial cost changes over time under the straight line and the MACRS methods.

Figure 50.4 *Book Value with Straight Line and MACRS Methods*

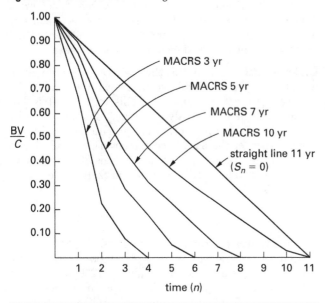

Equation 50.14: Book Value

$$BV = \text{initial cost} - \sum D_j \qquad 50.14$$

Description

In Eq. 50.14, BV is the book value at the end (not the beginning) of the jth year—that is, after j years of depreciation have been subtracted from the original purchase price.

Example

A machine initially costing $25,000 will have a salvage value of $6000 after five years. Using MACRS depreciation, its book value after the third year will be most nearly

(A) $5500

(B) $7200

(C) $10,000

(D) $14,000

Solution

Book value is the initial cost less the accumulated depreciation; the salvage value is disregarded. Use Eq. 50.14 and the MACRS factors for a five-year recovery period.

$$
\begin{aligned}
BV &= \text{initial cost} - \sum D_j \\
&= \text{initial cost} - (D_1 + D_2 + D_3) \\
&= \text{initial cost} - \left(\begin{array}{l} (\text{factor}_1)(\text{initial cost}) \\ \quad + (\text{factor}_2)(\text{initial cost}) \\ \quad + (\text{factor}_3)(\text{initial cost}) \end{array} \right) \\
&= (1 - \text{factor}_1 - \text{factor}_2 - \text{factor}_3)(\text{initial cost}) \\
&= (1 - 0.20 - 0.32 - 0.192)(\$25{,}000) \\
&= \$7200
\end{aligned}
$$

The answer is (B).

13. EQUIVALENT UNIFORM ANNUAL COST

Alternatives with different lifespans will generally be compared by way of *equivalent uniform annual cost*, or EUAC. An EUAC is the annual amount that is equivalent to all of the cash flows in the alternative.

The EUAC differs in sign from all of the other cash flows. Costs and expenses expressed as EUACs, which would normally be considered negative, are considered positive. Conversely, benefits and returns are considered negative. The term *cost* in the designation EUAC serves to make clear the meaning of a positive number.

14. CAPITALIZED COST

The present worth of a project with an infinite life is known as the *capitalized cost*. Capitalized cost is the amount of money at $t = 0$ needed to perpetually support the project on the earned interest only. Capitalized cost is a positive number when expenses exceed income.

Normally, it would be difficult to work with an infinite stream of cash flows since most discount factor tables do not list factors for periods in excess of 100 years. However, the (A/P) discount factor approaches the interest rate as n becomes large. Since the (P/A) and (A/P) factors are reciprocals of each other, it is possible to divide an infinite series of annual cash flows by the interest rate in order to calculate the present worth of the infinite series.

Equation 50.15: Capitalized Costs for an Infinite Series

$$\text{capitalized costs} = P = \frac{A}{i} \qquad 50.15$$

Description

Equation 50.15 can be used when the annual costs are equal in every year. If the operating and maintenance costs occur irregularly instead of annually, or if the costs vary from year to year, it will be necessary to somehow determine a cash flow of equal annual amounts that is equivalent to the stream of original costs (i.e., to determine the EUAC).

Example

The construction of a volleyball court will cost $1200, and annual maintenance cost is expected to be $300. At an effective annual interest rate of 5%, the project's capitalized cost is most nearly

(A) $2000

(B) $3000

(C) $7000

(D) $20,000

Solution

The cost of the project consists of two parts: the construction cost of $1200 and the annual maintenance cost of $300. The maintenance cost is an infinite series of annual amounts, so use Eq. 50.15 to find its present worth.

$$P_{\text{maintenance}} = \frac{A}{i} = \frac{\$300}{0.05}$$
$$= \$6000$$

Add the present worth of the initial construction cost to get the total present worth (i.e., the capitalized cost) of the project.

$$P_{\text{total}} = P_{\text{construction}} + P_{\text{maintenance}} = \$1200 + \$6000$$
$$= \$7200 \quad (\$7000)$$

The answer is (C).

15. INFLATION

To be meaningful, economic studies must be performed in terms of constant-value dollars. Several common methods are used to allow for *inflation*. One alternative is to replace the effective annual interest rate, i, with a value adjusted for inflation, d.

Equation 50.16: Interest Rate Adjusted for Inflation

$$d = i + f + (i \times f) \quad \text{50.16}$$

Description

In Eq. 50.16, f is a constant *inflation rate* per year. The inflation-adjusted interest rate, d, can be used to compute present worth.

Example

An investment of $20,000 earns an effective annual interest of 10%. The value of the investment in five years, adjusted for an annual inflation rate of 6%, is most nearly

(A) $27,000

(B) $32,000

(C) $42,000

(D) $43,000

Solution

The interest rate adjusted for inflation is

$$d = i + f + (i \times f) = 0.10 + 0.06 + (0.10)(0.06)$$
$$= 0.166$$

To determine the future worth of the investment, adjusted for inflation, use d instead of i in Eq. 50.1.

$$F = P(1 + d)^n = (\$20,000)(1 + 0.166)^5$$
$$= \$43,105 \quad (\$43,000)$$

The answer is (D).

16. CAPITAL BUDGETING (ALTERNATIVE COMPARISONS)

In the real world, the majority of engineering economic analysis problems are alternative comparisons. In these problems, two or more mutually exclusive investments compete for limited funds. A variety of methods exists for selecting the superior alternative from a group of proposals. Each method has its own merits and applications.

Present Worth Analysis

When two or more alternatives are capable of performing the same functions, the economically superior alternative will have the largest present worth. The *present worth method* is restricted to evaluating alternatives that are mutually exclusive and that have the same lives. This method is suitable for ranking the desirability of alternatives.

Engineering Economics

Annual Cost Analysis

Alternatives that accomplish the same purpose but that have unequal lives must be compared by the *annual cost method*. The annual cost method assumes that each alternative will be replaced by an identical twin at the end of its useful life (i.e., infinite renewal). This method, which may also be used to rank alternatives according to their desirability, is also called the *annual return method* or *capital recovery method*.

The alternatives must be mutually exclusive and repeatedly renewed up to the duration of the longest-lived alternative. The calculated annual cost is known as the *equivalent uniform annual cost* (EUAC) or *equivalent annual cost* (EAC). Cost is a positive number when expenses exceed income.

Rate of Return Analysis

An intuitive definition of the *rate of return* (ROR) is the effective annual interest rate at which an investment accrues income. That is, the rate of return of an investment is the interest rate that would yield identical profits if all money was invested at that rate. Although this definition is correct, it does not provide a method of determining the rate of return.

The present worth of a $100 investment invested at 5% is zero when $i = 5\%$ is used to determine equivalence. Therefore, a working definition of rate of return would be the effective annual interest rate that makes the present worth of the investment zero. Alternatively, rate of return could be defined as the effective annual interest rate that makes the benefits and costs equal.

A company may not know what effective interest rate, i, to use in engineering economic analysis. In such a case, the company can establish a minimum level of economic performance that it would like to realize on all investments. This criterion is known as the *minimum attractive rate of return*, or MARR.

Once a rate of return for an investment is known, it can be compared with the minimum attractive rate of return. If the rate of return is equal to or exceeds the minimum attractive rate of return, the investment is qualified (i.e., the alternative is viable). This is the basis for the rate of return method of alternative viability analysis.

If rate of return is used to select among two or more investments, an *incremental analysis* must be performed. An incremental analysis begins by ranking the alternatives in order of increasing initial investment. Then, the cash flows for the investment with the lower initial cost are subtracted from the cash flows for the higher-priced alternative on a year-by-year basis. This produces, in effect, a third alternative representing the costs and benefits of the added investment. The added expense of the higher-priced investment is not warranted unless the rate of return of this third alternative exceeds the minimum attractive rate of return as well.

The alternative with the higher initial investment is superior if the incremental rate of return exceeds the minimum attractive rate of return.

Finding the rate of return can be a long, iterative process, requiring either interpolation or trial and error. Sometimes, the actual numerical value of rate of return is not needed; it is sufficient to know whether or not the rate of return exceeds the minimum attractive rate of return. This comparative analysis can be accomplished without calculating the rate of return simply by finding the present worth of the investment using the minimum attractive rate of return as the effective interest rate (i.e., $i = \text{MARR}$). If the present worth is zero or positive, the investment is qualified. If the present worth is negative, the rate of return is less than the minimum attractive rate of return and the additional investment is not warranted.

The present worth, annual cost, and rate of return methods of comparing alternatives yield equivalent results, but they are distinctly different approaches. The present worth and annual cost methods may use either effective interest rates or the minimum attractive rate of return to rank alternatives or compare them to the MARR. If the incremental rate of return of pairs of alternatives are compared with the MARR, the analysis is considered a rate of return analysis.

17. BREAK-EVEN ANALYSIS

Break-even analysis is a method of determining when the value of one alternative becomes equal to the value of another. It is commonly used to determine when costs exactly equal revenue. If the manufactured quantity is less than the *break-even quantity*, a loss is incurred. If the manufactured quantity is greater than the break-even quantity, a profit is made.

An alternative form of the break-even problem is to find the number of units per period for which two alternatives have the same total costs. Fixed costs are spread over a period longer than one year using the EUAC concept. One of the alternatives will have a lower cost if production is less than the break-even point. The other will have a lower cost if production is greater than the break-even point.

The *pay-back period*, PBP, is defined as the length of time, n, usually in years, for the cumulative net annual profit to equal the initial investment. It is tempting to introduce equivalence into pay-back period calculations, but the convention is not to.

18. BENEFIT-COST ANALYSIS

The *benefit-cost ratio method* is often used in municipal project evaluations where benefits and costs accrue to different segments of the community. With this method, the present worth of all benefits (irrespective of the beneficiaries), B, is divided by the present worth of all costs, C. If the benefit-cost ratio, B/C, is greater than or equal to 1.0, the project is acceptable. (Equivalent uniform annual costs can be used in place of present worths.)

When the benefit-cost ratio method is used, disbursements by the initiators or sponsors are *costs* and added to C. Disbursements by the users of the project are known as *disbenefits* and subtracted from B. It is often difficult to decide whether a cash flow should be regarded as a cost or a disbenefit. The placement of such cash flows can change the value of B/C, but cannot change whether B/C is greater than or equal to 1.0. For this reason, the benefit-cost ratio alone should not be used to rank competing projects.

If ranking is to be done by the benefit-cost ratio method, an incremental analysis is required, as it is for the rate-of-return method. The incremental analysis is accomplished by calculating the ratio of differences in benefits to differences in costs for each possible pair of alternatives. If the ratio exceeds 1.0, alternative 2 is superior to alternative 1. Otherwise, alternative 1 is superior.

Equation 50.17: Analysis Criterion

$$B - C \geq 0 \text{ or } B/C \geq 1 \qquad 50.17$$

Description

A project is acceptable if its benefit-cost ratio equals or exceeds 1 (i.e., $B/C \geq 1$). This will be true whenever $B - C \geq 0$.

Example

A large sewer system will cost \$175,000 annually. There will be favorable consequences to the general public equivalent to \$500,000 annually, and adverse consequences to a small segment of the public equivalent to \$50,000 annually. The benefit-cost ratio is most nearly

(A) 2.2

(B) 2.4

(C) 2.6

(D) 2.9

Solution

The adverse consequences worth \$50,000 affect the users of the project, not its initiators, so this is a disbenefit. The benefit-cost ratio is

$$B/C = \frac{\$500,000 - \$50,000}{\$175,000}$$
$$= 2.57 \quad (2.6)$$

The answer is (C).

19. SENSITIVITY ANALYSIS, RISK ANALYSIS, AND UNCERTAINTY ANALYSIS

Data analysis and forecasts in economic studies require estimates of costs that will occur in the future. There are always uncertainties about these costs. However, these uncertainties are an insufficient reason not to make the best possible estimates of the costs. Nevertheless, a decision between alternatives often can be made more confidently if it is known whether or not the conclusion is sensitive to moderate changes in data forecasts. *Sensitivity analysis* provides this extra dimension to an economic analysis.

The sensitivity of a decision to various factors is determined by inserting a range of estimates for critical cash flows and other parameters. If radical changes can be made to a cash flow without changing the decision, the decision is said to be *insensitive* to uncertainties regarding that cash flow. However, if a small change in the estimate of a cash flow will alter the decision, that decision is said to be very *sensitive* to changes in the estimate. If the decision is sensitive only for a limited range of cash flow values, the term *variable sensitivity* is used. Figure 50.5 illustrates these terms.

Figure 50.5 *Types of Sensitivity*

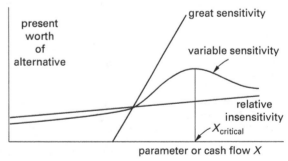

An established semantic tradition distinguishes between risk analysis and uncertainty analysis. *Risk* is the possibility of an unexpected, unplanned, or undesirable event occurring (i.e., an occurrence not planned for or predicted in risk analysis). *Risk analysis* addresses variables that have a known or estimated probability distribution. In this regard, statistics and probability theory can be used to determine the probability of a cash flow varying between given limits. On the other hand, *uncertainty analysis* is concerned with situations in which there is not enough information to determine the probability or frequency distribution for the variables involved.

As a first step, sensitivity analysis should be performed one factor at a time to the dominant factors. Dominant cost factors are those that have the most significant impact on the present value of the alternative.[3] If warranted, additional investigation can be used to determine the sensitivity to several cash flows varying simultaneously. Significant judgment is needed, however, to successfully determine the proper combinations of cash flows to vary. It is common to plot the dependency of the present value on the cash flow being varied in a two-dimensional graph. Simple linear interpolation is used (within reason) to determine the critical value of the cash flow being varied.

20. ACCOUNTING PRINCIPLES

Basic Bookkeeping

An accounting or *bookkeeping system* is used to record historical financial transactions. The resultant records are used for product costing, satisfaction of statutory requirements, reporting of profit for income tax purposes, and general company management.

Bookkeeping consists of two main steps: recording the transactions, followed by categorization of the transactions.[4] The transactions (receipts and disbursements) are recorded in a *journal* (*book of original entry*) to complete the first step. Such a journal is organized in a simple chronological and sequential manner. The transactions are then categorized (into interest income, advertising expense, etc.) and posted (i.e., entered or written) into the appropriate *ledger account*.[5]

Together, the ledger accounts constitute the *general ledger* or *ledger*. All ledger accounts can be classified into one of three types: *asset accounts*, *liability accounts*, and *owners' equity accounts*. Strictly speaking, income and expense accounts, kept in a separate journal, are included within the classification of owners' equity accounts.

Together, the journal and ledger are known simply as "the books" of the company, regardless of whether bound volumes of pages are actually involved.

Balancing the Books

In a business environment, *balancing the books* means more than reconciling the checkbook and bank statements. All accounting entries must be posted in such a way as to maintain the equality of the *basic accounting equation*,

$$\text{assets} = \text{liability} + \text{owners' equity}$$

In a *double-entry bookkeeping system*, the equality is maintained within the ledger system by entering each transaction into two balancing ledger accounts. For example, paying a utility bill would decrease the cash account (an asset account) and decrease the utility expense account (a liability account) by the same amount.

Transactions are either *debits* or *credits*, depending on their sign. Increases in asset accounts are debits; decreases are credits. For liability and equity accounts, the opposite is true: Increases are credits, and decreases are debits.[6]

Cash and Accrual Systems[7]

The simplest form of bookkeeping is based on the *cash system*. The only transactions that are entered into the journal are those that represent cash receipts and disbursements. In effect, a checkbook register or bank deposit book could serve as the journal.

During a given period (e.g., month or quarter), expense liabilities may be incurred even though the payments for those expenses have not been made. For example, an invoice (bill) may have been received but not paid. Under the *accrual system*, the obligation is posted into the appropriate expense account before it is paid.[8] Analogous to expenses, under the accrual system, income will be claimed before payment is received. Specifically, a sales transaction can be recorded as income when the customer's order is received, when the outgoing invoice is generated, or when the merchandise is shipped.

---

[3]In particular, engineering economic analysis problems are sensitive to the choice of effective interest rate, i, and to accuracy in cash flows at or near the beginning of the horizon. The problems will be less sensitive to accuracy in far-future cash flows, such as subsequent generation replacement costs.

[4]These two steps are not to be confused with the *double-entry bookkeeping method*.

[5]The two-step process is more typical of a *manual bookkeeping system* than a computerized *general ledger system*. However, even most computerized systems produce reports in journal entry order, as well as account summaries.

[6]There is a difference in sign between asset and liability accounts. An increase in an expense account is actually a decrease. The accounting profession, apparently, is comfortable with the common confusion that exists between debits and credits.

[7]There is also a distinction made between cash flows that are known and those that are expected. It is a *standard accounting principle* to record losses in full, at the time they are recognized, even before their occurrence. In the construction industry, for example, losses are recognized in full and projected to the end of a project as soon as they are foreseeable. Profits, on the other hand, are recognized only as they are realized (typically, as a percentage of project completion). The difference between cash and accrual systems is a matter of *bookkeeping*. The difference between loss and profit recognition is a matter of *accounting convention*. Engineers seldom need to be concerned with the accounting principles and conventions.

[8]The expense for an item or service might be accrued even *before* the invoice is received. It might be recorded when the purchase order for the item or service is generated, or when the item or service is received.

Financial Statements

Each period, two types of corporate financial statements are typically generated: the *balance sheet* and *profit and loss* (P&L) *statement*.[9] The profit and loss statement, also known as a *statement of income and retained earnings*, is a summary of sources of *income* or *revenue* (interest, sales, fees charged, etc.) and *expenses* (utilities, advertising, repairs, etc.) for the period. The expenses are subtracted from the revenues to give a *net income* (generally, before taxes).[10] Figure 50.6 illustrates a simplified profit and loss statement.

Figure 50.6 Simplified Profit and Loss Statement

revenue		
interest	2000	
sales	237,000	
returns	(23,000)	
net revenue		216,000
expenses		
salaries	149,000	
utilities	6000	
advertising	28,000	
insurance	4000	
supplies	1000	
net expenses	188,000	
period net income	28,000	
beginning retained earnings	63,000	
net year-to-date earnings		91,000

The *balance sheet* presents the *basic accounting equation* in tabular form. The balance sheet lists the major categories of assets and outstanding liabilities. The difference between asset values and liabilities is the *equity*. This equity represents what would be left over after satisfying all debts by liquidating the company.

Figure 50.7 is a simplified balance sheet.

There are several terms that appear regularly on balance sheets.

- *current assets:* cash and other assets that can be converted quickly into cash, such as accounts receivable, notes receivable, and merchandise (inventory). Also known as *liquid assets.*

- *fixed assets:* relatively permanent assets used in the operation of the business and relatively difficult to convert into cash. Examples are land, buildings, and equipment. Also known as *nonliquid assets.*

- *current liabilities:* liabilities due within a short period of time (e.g., within one year) and typically paid out of current assets. Examples are accounts payable, notes payable, and other accrued liabilities.

Figure 50.7 Simplified Balance Sheet

ASSETS

current assets			
cash	14,000		
accounts receivable	36,000		
notes receivable	20,000		
inventory	89,000		
prepaid expenses	3000		
total current assets		162,000	
plant, property, and equipment			
land and buildings	217,000		
motor vehicles	31,000		
equipment	94,000		
accumulated depreciation	(52,000)		
total fixed assets		290,000	
total assets			452,000

LIABILITIES AND OWNERS' EQUITY

current liabilities			
accounts payable	66,000		
accrued income taxes	17,000		
accrued expenses	8000		
total current liabilities		91,000	
long-term debt			
notes payable	117,000		
mortgage	23,000		
total long-term debt		140,000	
owners' and stockholders' equity			
stock	130,000		
retained earnings	91,000		
total owners' equity		221,000	
total liabilities and owners' equity			452,000

- *long-term liabilities:* obligations that are not totally payable within a short period of time (e.g., within one year).

Analysis of Financial Statements

Financial statements are evaluated by management, lenders, stockholders, potential investors, and many other groups for the purpose of determining the *health of the company*. The health can be measured in terms of *liquidity* (ability to convert assets to cash quickly), *solvency* (ability to meet debts as they become due), and *relative risk* (of which one measure is *leverage*—the portion of total capital contributed by owners).

The analysis of financial statements involves several common ratios, usually expressed as percentages. The following are some frequently encountered ratios.

---

[9]Other types of financial statements (*statements of changes in financial position*, *cost of sales statements*, *inventory and asset reports*, etc.) also will be generated, depending on the needs of the company.
[10]Financial statements also can be prepared with percentages (of total assets and net revenue) instead of dollars, in which case they are known as *common size financial statements*.

- *current ratio:* an index of short-term paying ability.

$$\text{current ratio} = \frac{\text{current assets}}{\text{current liabilities}}$$

- *quick* (or *acid-test*) *ratio:* a more stringent measure of short-term debt-paying ability. The *quick assets* are defined to be current assets minus inventories and prepaid expenses.

$$\text{quick ratio} = \frac{\text{quick assets}}{\text{current liabilities}}$$

- *receivable turnover:* a measure of the average speed with which accounts receivable are collected.

$$\text{receivable turnover} = \frac{\text{net credit sales}}{\text{average net receivables}}$$

- *average age of receivables:* number of days, on the average, in which receivables are collected.

$$\text{average age of receivables} = \frac{365}{\text{receivable turnover}}$$

- *inventory turnover:* a measure of the speed, on the average, with which inventory is sold.

$$\text{inventory turnover} = \frac{\text{cost of goods sold}}{\text{average unit cost of inventory}}$$

- *days supply of inventory on hand:* number of days, on the average, that the current inventory would last.

$$\text{days supply of inventory on hand} = \frac{365}{\text{inventory turnover}}$$

- *book value per share of common stock:* number of dollars represented by the balance sheet owners' equity for each share of common stock outstanding.

$$\text{book value per share of common stock} = \frac{\text{common shareholders' equity}}{\text{number of outstanding shares}}$$

- *gross margin:* gross profit as a percentage of sales. (Gross profit is sales less cost of goods sold.)

$$\text{gross margin} = \frac{\text{gross profit}}{\text{net sales}}$$

- *profit margin ratio:* percentage of each dollar of sales that is net income.

$$\text{profit margin} = \frac{\text{net income before taxes}}{\text{net sales}}$$

- *return on investment ratio:* shows the percent return on owners' investment.

$$\text{return on investment} = \frac{\text{net income}}{\text{owners' equity}}$$

- *price-earnings ratio:* an indication of the relationship between earnings and market price per share of common stock; useful in comparisons between alternative investments.

$$\text{price-earnings} = \frac{\text{market price per share}}{\text{earnings per share}}$$

21. ACCOUNTING COSTS AND EXPENSE TERMS

The accounting profession has developed special terms for certain groups of costs. When annual costs are incurred due to the functioning of a piece of equipment, they are known as *operating and maintenance* (O&M) *costs*. The annual costs associated with operating a business (other than the costs directly attributable to production) are known as *general, selling, and administrative* (GS&A) *expenses*.

Direct labor costs are costs incurred in the factory, such as assembly, machining, and painting labor costs. *Direct material costs* are the costs of all materials that go into production.[11] Typically, both direct labor and direct material costs are given on a per-unit or per-item basis. The sum of the direct labor and direct material costs is known as the *prime cost*.

There are certain additional expenses incurred in the factory, such as the costs of factory supervision, stock-picking, quality control, factory utilities, and miscellaneous supplies (cleaning fluids, assembly lubricants, routing tags, etc.) that are not incorporated into the final product. Such costs are known as *indirect manufacturing expenses* (IME) or *indirect material and labor costs*.[12] The sum of the per-unit indirect manufacturing expense and prime cost is known as the *factory cost*.

Research and development (R&D) *costs* and *administrative expenses* are added to the factory cost to give the *manufacturing cost* of the product.

---

[11]There may be complications with pricing the material when it is purchased from an outside vendor and the stock on hand derives from several shipments purchased at different prices.
[12]The *indirect material and labor costs* usually exclude costs incurred in the office area.

Additional costs are incurred in marketing the product. Such costs are known as *selling expenses* or *marketing expenses*. The sum of the selling expenses and manufacturing cost is the *total cost* of the product. Figure 50.8 illustrates these terms.[13] Typical classifications of expenses are listed in Table 50.3.

Figure 50.8 *Costs and Expenses Combined*

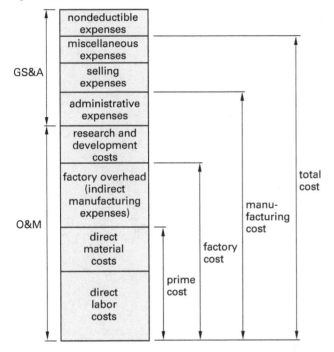

The distinctions among the various forms of cost (particularly with overhead costs) are not standardized. Each company must develop a classification system to deal with the various cost factors in a consistent manner. There are also other terms in use (e.g., *raw materials*, *operating supplies*, *general plant overhead*), but these terms must be interpreted within the framework of each company's classification system. Table 50.3 is typical of such classification systems.

22. COST ACCOUNTING

Cost accounting is the system that determines the cost of manufactured products. Cost accounting is called *job cost accounting* if costs are accumulated by part number or contract. It is called *process cost accounting* if costs are accumulated by departments or manufacturing processes.

Cost accounting is dependent on historical and recorded data. The unit product cost is determined from actual expenses and numbers of units produced. Allowances (i.e., budgets) for future costs are based on these historical figures. Any deviation from historical figures is called a

variance. Where adequate records are available, variances can be divided into *labor variance* and *material variance.*

When determining a unit product cost, the direct material and direct labor costs are generally clear-cut and easily determined. Furthermore, these costs are 100% variable costs. However, the indirect cost per unit of product is not as easily determined. Indirect costs (*burden, overhead*, etc.) can be fixed or semivariable costs. The amount of indirect cost allocated to a unit will depend on the unknown future overhead expense as well as the unknown future production (*vehicle size*).

A typical method of allocating indirect costs to a product is as follows.

step 1: Estimate the total expected indirect (and overhead) costs for the upcoming year.

step 2: Determine the most appropriate vehicle (basis) for allocating the overhead to production. Usually, this vehicle is either the number of units expected to be produced or the number of direct hours expected to be worked in the upcoming year.

step 3: Estimate the quantity or size of the overhead vehicle.

step 4: Divide expected overhead costs by the expected overhead vehicle to obtain the unit overhead.

step 5: Regardless of the true size of the overhead vehicle during the upcoming year, one unit of overhead cost is allocated per unit of overhead vehicle.

Once the prime cost has been determined and the indirect cost calculated based on projections, the two are combined into a *standard factory cost* or *standard cost*, which remains in effect until the next budgeting period (usually a year).

During the subsequent manufacturing year, the standard cost of a product is not generally changed merely because it is found that an error in projected indirect costs or production quantity (vehicle size) has been made. The allocation of indirect costs to a product is assumed to be independent of errors in forecasts. Rather, the difference between the expected and actual expenses, known as the *burden (overhead) variance*, experienced during the year is posted to one or more *variance accounts*.

Burden (overhead) variance is caused by errors in forecasting both the actual indirect expense for the upcoming year and the overhead vehicle size. In the former case, the variance is called *burden budget variance*; in the latter, it is called *burden capacity variance*.

---

[13]*Total cost* does not include income taxes.

Table 50.3 *Typical Classification of Expenses*

direct labor expenses
  machining and forming
  assembly
  finishing
  inspection
  testing
direct material expenses
  items purchased from other vendors
  manufactured assemblies
factory overhead expenses (indirect manufacturing expenses)
  supervision
  benefits
    pension
    medical insurance
    vacations
  wages overhead
    unemployment compensation taxes
    social security taxes
    disability taxes
  stock-picking
  quality control and inspection
  expediting
  rework
  maintenance
  miscellaneous supplies
    routing tags
    assembly lubricants
    cleaning fluids
    wiping cloths
    janitorial supplies
  packaging (materials and labor)
  factory utilities
  laboratory
  depreciation on factory equipment
research and development expenses
  engineering (labor)
  patents
  testing
  prototypes (material and labor)
  drafting
  O&M of R&D facility

administrative expenses
  corporate officers
  accounting
  secretarial/clerical/reception
  security (protection)
  medical (nurse)
  employment (personnel)
  reproduction
  data processing
  production control
  depreciation on nonfactory equipment
  office supplies
  office utilities
  O&M of offices
selling expenses
  marketing (labor)
  advertising
  transportation (if not paid by customer)
  outside sales force (labor and expenses)
  demonstration units
  commissions
  technical service and support
  order processing
  branch office expenses
miscellaneous expenses
  insurance
  property taxes
  interest on loans
nondeductible expenses
  federal income taxes
  fines and penalties

Table 50.4 *Factor Table i = 0.50%*

n	P/F	P/A	P/G	F/P	F/A	A/P	A/F	A/G
1	0.9950	0.9950	0.0000	1.0050	1.0000	1.0050	1.0000	0.0000
2	0.9901	1.9851	0.9901	1.0100	2.0050	0.5038	0.4988	0.4988
3	0.9851	2.9702	2.9604	1.0151	3.0150	0.3367	0.3317	0.9967
4	0.9802	3.9505	5.9011	1.0202	4.0301	0.2531	0.2481	1.4938
5	0.9754	4.9259	9.8026	1.0253	5.0503	0.2030	0.1980	1.9900
6	0.9705	5.8964	14.6552	1.0304	6.0755	0.1696	0.1646	2.4855
7	0.9657	6.8621	20.4493	1.0355	7.1059	0.1457	0.1407	2.9801
8	0.9609	7.8230	27.1755	1.0407	8.1414	0.1278	0.1228	3.4738
9	0.9561	8.7791	34.8244	1.0459	9.1821	0.1139	0.1089	3.9668
10	0.9513	9.7304	43.3865	1.0511	10.2280	0.1028	0.0978	4.4589
11	0.9466	10.6670	52.8526	1.0564	11.2792	0.0937	0.0887	4.9501
12	0.9419	11.6189	63.2136	1.0617	12.3356	0.0861	0.0811	5.4406
13	0.9372	12.5562	74.4602	1.0670	13.3972	0.0796	0.0746	5.9302
14	0.9326	13.4887	86.5835	1.0723	14.4642	0.0741	0.0691	6.4190
15	0.9279	14.4166	99.5743	1.0777	15.5365	0.0694	0.0644	6.9069
16	0.9233	15.3399	113.4238	1.0831	16.6142	0.0652	0.0602	7.3940
17	0.9187	16.2586	128.1231	1.0885	17.6973	0.0615	0.0565	7.8803
18	0.9141	17.1728	143.6634	1.0939	18.7858	0.0582	0.0532	8.3658
19	0.9096	18.0824	160.0360	1.0994	19.8797	0.0553	0.0503	8.8504
20	0.9051	18.9874	177.2322	1.1049	20.9791	0.0527	0.0477	9.3342
21	0.9006	19.8880	195.2434	1.1104	22.0840	0.0503	0.0453	9.8172
22	0.8961	20.7841	214.0611	1.1160	23.1944	0.0481	0.0431	10.2993
23	0.8916	21.6757	233.6768	1.1216	24.3104	0.0461	0.0411	10.7806
24	0.8872	22.5629	254.0820	1.1272	25.4320	0.0443	0.0393	11.2611
25	0.8828	23.4456	275.2686	1.1328	26.5591	0.0427	0.0377	11.7407
30	0.8610	27.7941	392.6324	1.1614	32.2800	0.0360	0.0310	14.1265
40	0.8191	36.1722	681.3347	1.2208	44.1588	0.0276	0.0226	18.8359
50	0.7793	44.1428	1,035.6966	1.2832	56.6452	0.0227	0.0177	23.4624
60	0.7414	51.7256	1,448.6458	1.3489	69.7700	0.0193	0.0143	28.0064
100	0.6073	78.5426	3,562.7934	1.6467	129.3337	0.0127	0.0077	45.3613

Table 50.5 *Factor Table i = 1.00%*

n	P/F	P/A	P/G	F/P	F/A	A/P	A/F	A/G
1	0.9901	0.9901	0.0000	1.0100	1.0000	1.0100	1.0000	0.0000
2	0.9803	1.9704	0.9803	1.0201	2.0100	0.5075	0.4975	0.4975
3	0.9706	2.9410	2.9215	1.0303	3.0301	0.3400	0.3300	0.9934
4	0.9610	3.9020	5.8044	1.0406	4.0604	0.2563	0.2463	1.4876
5	0.9515	4.8534	9.6103	1.0510	5.1010	0.2060	0.1960	1.9801
6	0.9420	5.7955	14.3205	1.0615	6.1520	0.1725	0.1625	2.4710
7	0.9327	6.7282	19.9168	1.0721	7.2135	0.1486	0.1386	2.9602
8	0.9235	7.6517	26.3812	1.0829	8.2857	0.1307	0.1207	3.4478
9	0.9143	8.5650	33.6959	1.0937	9.3685	0.1167	0.1067	3.9337
10	0.9053	9.4713	41.8435	1.1046	10.4622	0.1056	0.0956	4.4179
11	0.8963	10.3676	50.8067	1.1157	11.5668	0.0965	0.0865	4.9005
12	0.8874	11.2551	60.5687	1.1268	12.6825	0.0888	0.0788	5.3815
13	0.8787	12.1337	71.1126	1.1381	13.8093	0.0824	0.0724	5.8607
14	0.8700	13.0037	82.4221	1.1495	14.9474	0.0769	0.0669	6.3384
15	0.8613	13.8651	94.4810	1.1610	16.0969	0.0721	0.0621	6.8143
16	0.8528	14.7179	107.2734	1.1726	17.2579	0.0679	0.0579	7.2886
17	0.8444	15.5623	129.7834	1.1843	18.4304	0.0643	0.0543	7.7613
18	0.8360	16.3983	134.9957	1.1961	19.6147	0.0610	0.0510	8.2323
19	0.8277	17.2260	149.8950	1.2081	20.8109	0.0581	0.0481	8.7017
20	0.8195	18.0456	165.4664	1.2202	22.0190	0.0554	0.0454	9.1694
21	0.8114	18.8570	181.6950	1.2324	23.2392	0.0530	0.0430	9.6354
22	0.8034	19.6604	198.5663	1.2447	24.4716	0.0509	0.0409	10.0998
23	0.7954	20.4558	216.0660	1.2572	25.7163	0.0489	0.0389	10.5626
24	0.7876	21.2434	234.1800	1.2697	26.9735	0.0471	0.0371	11.0237
25	0.7798	22.0232	252.8945	1.2824	28.2432	0.0454	0.0354	11.4831
30	0.7419	25.8077	355.0021	1.3478	34.7849	0.0387	0.0277	13.7557
40	0.6717	32.8347	596.8561	1.4889	48.8864	0.0305	0.0205	18.1776
50	0.6080	39.1961	879.4176	1.6446	64.4632	0.0255	0.0155	22.4363
60	0.5504	44.9550	1,192.8061	1.8167	81.6697	0.0222	0.0122	26.5333
100	0.3697	63.0289	2,605.7758	2.7048	170.4814	0.0159	0.0059	41.3426

Table 50.6 *Factor Table i = 1.50%*

n	P/F	P/A	P/G	F/P	F/A	A/P	A/F	A/G
1	0.9852	0.9852	0.0000	1.0150	1.0000	1.0150	1.0000	0.0000
2	0.9707	1.9559	0.9707	1.0302	2.0150	0.5113	0.4963	0.4963
3	0.9563	2.9122	2.8833	1.0457	3.0452	0.3434	0.3284	0.9901
4	0.9422	3.8544	5.7098	1.0614	4.0909	0.2594	0.2444	1.4814
5	0.9283	4.7826	9.4229	1.0773	5.1523	0.2091	0.1941	1.9702
6	0.9145	5.6972	13.9956	1.0934	6.2296	0.1755	0.1605	2.4566
7	0.9010	6.5982	19.4018	1.1098	7.3230	0.1516	0.1366	2.9405
8	0.8877	7.4859	26.6157	1.1265	8.4328	0.1336	0.1186	3.4219
9	0.8746	8.3605	32.6125	1.1434	9.5593	0.1196	0.1046	3.9008
10	0.8617	9.2222	40.3675	1.1605	10.7027	0.1084	0.0934	4.3772
11	0.8489	10.0711	48.8568	1.1779	11.8633	0.0993	0.0843	4.8512
12	0.8364	10.9075	58.0571	1.1956	13.0412	0.0917	0.0767	5.3227
13	0.8240	11.7315	67.9454	1.2136	14.2368	0.0852	0.0702	5.7917
14	0.8118	12.5434	78.4994	1.2318	15.4504	0.0797	0.0647	6.2582
15	0.7999	13.3432	89.6974	1.2502	16.6821	0.0749	0.0599	6.7223
16	0.7880	14.1313	101.5178	1.2690	17.9324	0.0708	0.0558	7.1839
17	0.7764	14.9076	113.9400	1.2880	19.2014	0.0671	0.0521	7.6431
18	0.7649	15.6726	126.9435	1.3073	20.4894	0.0638	0.0488	8.0997
19	0.7536	16.4262	140.5084	1.3270	21.7967	0.0609	0.0459	8.5539
20	0.7425	17.1686	154.6154	1.3469	23.1237	0.0582	0.0432	9.0057
21	0.7315	17.9001	169.2453	1.3671	24.4705	0.0559	0.0409	9.4550
22	0.7207	18.6208	184.3798	1.3876	25.8376	0.0537	0.0387	9.9018
23	0.7100	19.3309	200.0006	1.4084	27.2251	0.0517	0.0367	10.3462
24	0.6995	20.0304	216.0901	1.4295	28.6335	0.0499	0.0349	10.7881
25	0.6892	20.7196	232.6310	1.4509	30.0630	0.0483	0.0333	11.2276
30	0.6398	24.0158	321.5310	1.5631	37.5387	0.0416	0.0266	13.3883
40	0.5513	29.9158	524.3568	1.8140	54.2679	0.0334	0.0184	17.5277
50	0.4750	34.9997	749.9636	2.1052	73.6828	0.0286	0.0136	21.4277
60	0.4093	39.3803	988.1674	2.4432	96.2147	0.0254	0.0104	25.0930
100	0.2256	51.6247	1,937.4506	4.4320	228.8030	0.0194	0.0044	37.5295

Table 50.7 *Factor Table i = 2.00%*

n	P/F	P/A	P/G	F/P	F/A	A/P	A/F	A/G
1	0.9804	0.9804	0.0000	1.0200	1.0000	1.0200	1.0000	0.0000
2	0.9612	1.9416	0.9612	1.0404	2.0200	0.5150	0.4950	0.4950
3	0.9423	2.8839	2.8458	1.0612	3.0604	0.3468	0.3268	0.9868
4	0.9238	3.8077	5.6173	1.0824	4.1216	0.2626	0.2426	1.4752
5	0.9057	4.7135	9.2403	1.1041	5.2040	0.2122	0.1922	1.9604
6	0.8880	5.6014	13.6801	1.1262	6.3081	0.1785	0.1585	2.4423
7	0.8706	6.4720	18.9035	1.1487	7.4343	0.1545	0.1345	2.9208
8	0.8535	7.3255	24.8779	1.1717	8.5830	0.1365	0.1165	3.3961
9	0.8368	8.1622	31.5720	1.1951	9.7546	0.1225	0.1025	3.8681
10	0.8203	8.9826	38.9551	1.2190	10.9497	0.1113	0.0913	4.3367
11	0.8043	9.7868	46.9977	1.2434	12.1687	0.1022	0.0822	4.8021
12	0.7885	10.5753	55.6712	1.2682	13.4121	0.0946	0.0746	5.2642
13	0.7730	11.3484	64.9475	1.2936	14.6803	0.0881	0.0681	5.7231
14	0.7579	12.1062	74.7999	1.3195	15.9739	0.0826	0.0626	6.1786
15	0.7430	12.8493	85.2021	1.3459	17.2934	0.0778	0.0578	6.6309
16	0.7284	13.5777	96.1288	1.3728	18.6393	0.0737	0.0537	7.0799
17	0.7142	14.2919	107.5554	1.4002	20.0121	0.0700	0.0500	7.5256
18	0.7002	14.9920	119.4581	1.4282	21.4123	0.0667	0.0467	7.9681
19	0.6864	15.6785	131.8139	1.4568	22.8406	0.0638	0.0438	8.4073
20	0.6730	16.3514	144.6003	1.4859	24.2974	0.0612	0.0412	8.8433
21	0.6598	17.0112	157.7959	1.5157	25.7833	0.0588	0.0388	9.2760
22	0.6468	17.6580	171.3795	1.5460	27.2990	0.0566	0.0366	9.7055
23	0.6342	18.2922	185.3309	1.5769	28.8450	0.0547	0.0347	10.1317
24	0.6217	18.9139	199.6305	1.6084	30.4219	0.0529	0.0329	10.5547
25	0.6095	19.5235	214.2592	1.6406	32.0303	0.0512	0.0312	10.9745
30	0.5521	22.3965	291.7164	1.8114	40.5681	0.0446	0.0246	13.0251
40	0.4529	27.3555	461.9931	2.2080	60.4020	0.0366	0.0166	16.8885
50	0.3715	31.4236	642.3606	2.6916	84.5794	0.0318	0.0118	20.4420
60	0.3048	34.7609	823.6975	3.2810	114.0515	0.0288	0.0088	23.6961
100	0.1380	43.0984	1,464.7527	7.2446	312.2323	0.0232	0.0032	33.9863

Table 50.8 *Factor Table i = 4.00%*

n	P/F	P/A	P/G	F/P	F/A	A/P	A/F	A/G
1	0.9615	0.9615	0.0000	1.0400	1.0000	1.0400	1.0000	0.0000
2	0.9246	1.8861	0.9246	1.0816	2.0400	0.5302	0.4902	0.4902
3	0.8890	2.7751	2.7025	1.1249	3.1216	0.3603	0.3203	0.9739
4	0.8548	3.6299	5.2670	1.1699	4.2465	0.2755	0.2355	1.4510
5	0.8219	4.4518	8.5547	1.2167	5.4163	0.2246	0.1846	1.9216
6	0.7903	5.2421	12.5062	1.2653	6.6330	0.1908	0.1508	2.3857
7	0.7599	6.0021	17.0657	1.3159	7.8983	0.1666	0.1266	2.8433
8	0.7307	6.7327	22.1806	1.3686	9.2142	0.1485	0.1085	3.2944
9	0.7026	7.4353	27.8013	1.4233	10.5828	0.1345	0.0945	3.7391
10	0.6756	8.1109	33.8814	1.4802	12.0061	0.1233	0.0833	4.1773
11	0.6496	8.7605	40.3772	1.5395	13.4864	0.1141	0.0741	4.6090
12	0.6246	9.3851	47.2477	1.6010	15.0258	0.1066	0.0666	5.0343
13	0.6006	9.9856	54.4546	1.6651	16.6268	0.1001	0.0601	5.4533
14	0.5775	10.5631	61.9618	1.7317	18.2919	0.0947	0.0547	5.8659
15	0.5553	11.1184	69.7355	1.8009	20.0236	0.0899	0.0499	6.2721
16	0.5339	11.6523	77.7441	1.8730	21.8245	0.0858	0.0458	6.6720
17	0.5134	12.1657	85.9581	1.9479	23.6975	0.0822	0.0422	7.0656
18	0.4936	12.6593	94.3498	2.0258	25.6454	0.0790	0.0390	7.4530
19	0.4746	13.1339	102.8933	2.1068	27.6712	0.0761	0.0361	7.8342
20	0.4564	13.5903	111.5647	2.1911	29.7781	0.0736	0.0336	8.2091
21	0.4388	14.0292	120.3414	2.2788	31.9692	0.0713	0.0313	8.5779
22	0.4220	14.4511	129.2024	2.3699	34.2480	0.0692	0.0292	8.9407
23	0.4057	14.8568	138.1284	2.4647	36.6179	0.0673	0.0273	9.2973
24	0.3901	15.2470	147.1012	2.5633	39.0826	0.0656	0.0256	9.6479
25	0.3751	15.6221	156.1040	2.6658	41.6459	0.0640	0.0240	9.9925
30	0.3083	17.2920	201.0618	3.2434	56.0849	0.0578	0.0178	11.6274
40	0.2083	19.7928	286.5303	4.8010	95.0255	0.0505	0.0105	14.4765
50	0.1407	21.4822	361.1638	7.1067	152.6671	0.0466	0.0066	16.8122
60	0.0951	22.6235	422.9966	10.5196	237.9907	0.0442	0.0042	18.6972
100	0.0198	24.5050	563.1249	50.5049	1,237.6237	0.0408	0.0008	22.9800

Table 50.9 *Factor Table i = 6.00%*

n	P/F	P/A	P/G	F/P	F/A	A/P	A/F	A/G
1	0.9434	0.9434	0.0000	1.0600	1.0000	1.0600	1.0000	0.0000
2	0.8900	1.8334	0.8900	1.1236	2.0600	0.5454	0.4854	0.4854
3	0.8396	2.6730	2.5692	1.1910	3.1836	0.3741	0.3141	0.9612
4	0.7921	3.4651	4.9455	1.2625	4.3746	0.2886	0.2286	1.4272
5	0.7473	4.2124	7.9345	1.3382	5.6371	0.2374	0.1774	1.8836
6	0.7050	4.9173	11.4594	1.4185	6.9753	0.2034	0.1434	2.3304
7	0.6651	5.5824	15.4497	1.5036	8.3938	0.1791	0.1191	2.7676
8	0.6274	6.2098	19.8416	1.5938	9.8975	0.1610	0.1010	3.1952
9	0.5919	6.8017	24.5768	1.6895	11.4913	0.1470	0.0870	3.6133
10	0.5584	7.3601	29.6023	1.7908	13.1808	0.1359	0.0759	4.0220
11	0.5268	7.8869	34.8702	1.8983	14.9716	0.1268	0.0668	4.4213
12	0.4970	8.3838	40.3369	2.0122	16.8699	0.1193	0.0593	4.8113
13	0.4688	8.8527	45.9629	2.1239	18.8821	0.1130	0.0530	5.1920
14	0.4423	9.2950	51.7128	2.2609	21.0151	0.1076	0.0476	5.5635
15	0.4173	9.7122	57.5546	2.3966	23.2760	0.1030	0.0430	5.9260
16	0.3936	10.1059	63.4592	2.5404	25.6725	0.0990	0.0390	6.2794
17	0.3714	10.4773	69.4011	2.6928	28.2129	0.0954	0.0354	6.6240
18	0.3505	10.8276	75.3569	2.8543	30.9057	0.0924	0.0324	6.9597
19	0.3305	11.1581	81.3062	3.0256	33.7600	0.0896	0.0296	7.2867
20	0.3118	11.4699	87.2304	3.2071	36.7856	0.0872	0.0272	7.6051
21	0.2942	11.7641	93.1136	3.3996	39.9927	0.0850	0.0250	7.9151
22	0.2775	12.0416	98.9412	3.6035	43.3923	0.0830	0.0230	8.2166
23	0.2618	12.3034	104.7007	3.8197	46.9958	0.0813	0.0213	8.5099
24	0.2470	12.5504	110.3812	4.0489	50.8156	0.0797	0.0197	8.7951
25	0.2330	12.7834	115.9732	4.2919	54.8645	0.0782	0.0182	9.0722
30	0.1741	13.7648	142.3588	5.7435	79.0582	0.0726	0.0126	10.3422
40	0.0972	15.0463	185.9568	10.2857	154.7620	0.0665	0.0065	12.3590
50	0.0543	15.7619	217.4574	18.4202	290.3359	0.0634	0.0034	13.7964
60	0.0303	16.1614	239.0428	32.9877	533.1282	0.0619	0.0019	14.7909
100	0.0029	16.6175	272.0471	339.3021	5638.3681	0.0602	0.0002	16.3711

Engineering Economics

Table 50.10 *Factor Table i = 8.00%*

n	P/F	P/A	P/G	F/P	F/A	A/P	A/F	A/G
1	0.9259	0.9259	0.0000	1.0800	1.0000	1.0800	1.0000	0.0000
2	0.8573	1.7833	0.8573	1.1664	2.0800	0.5608	0.4808	0.4808
3	0.7938	2.5771	2.4450	1.2597	3.2464	0.3880	0.3080	0.9487
4	0.7350	3.3121	4.6501	1.3605	4.5061	0.3019	0.2219	1.4040
5	0.6806	3.9927	7.3724	1.4693	5.8666	0.2505	0.1705	1.8465
6	0.6302	4.6229	10.5233	1.5869	7.3359	0.2163	0.1363	2.2763
7	0.5835	5.2064	14.0242	1.7138	8.9228	0.1921	0.1121	2.6937
8	0.5403	5.7466	17.8061	1.8509	10.6366	0.1740	0.0940	3.0985
9	0.5002	6.2469	21.8081	1.9990	12.4876	0.1601	0.0801	3.4910
10	0.4632	6.7101	25.9768	2.1589	14.4866	0.1490	0.0690	3.8713
11	0.4289	7.1390	30.2657	2.3316	16.6455	0.1401	0.0601	4.2395
12	0.3971	7.5361	34.6339	2.5182	18.9771	0.1327	0.0527	4.5957
13	0.3677	7.9038	39.0463	2.7196	21.4953	0.1265	0.0465	4.9402
14	0.3405	8.2442	43.4723	2.9372	24.2149	0.1213	0.0413	5.2731
15	0.3152	8.5595	47.8857	3.1722	27.1521	0.1168	0.0368	5.5945
16	0.2919	8.8514	52.2640	3.4259	30.3243	0.1130	0.0330	5.9046
17	0.2703	9.1216	56.5883	3.7000	33.7502	0.1096	0.0296	6.2037
18	0.2502	9.3719	60.8426	3.9960	37.4502	0.1067	0.0267	6.4920
19	0.2317	9.6036	65.0134	4.3157	41.4463	0.1041	0.0241	6.7697
20	0.2145	9.8181	69.0898	4.6610	45.7620	0.1019	0.0219	7.0369
21	0.1987	10.0168	73.0629	5.0338	50.4229	0.0998	0.0198	7.2940
22	0.1839	10.2007	76.9257	5.4365	55.4568	0.0980	0.0180	7.5412
23	0.1703	10.3711	80.6726	5.8715	60.8933	0.0964	0.0164	7.7786
24	0.1577	10.5288	84.2997	6.3412	66.7648	0.0950	0.0150	8.0066
25	0.1460	10.6748	87.8041	6.8485	73.1059	0.0937	0.0137	8.2254
30	0.0994	11.2578	103.4558	10.0627	113.2832	0.0888	0.0088	9.1897
40	0.0460	11.9246	126.0422	21.7245	259.0565	0.0839	0.0039	10.5699
50	0.0213	12.2335	139.5928	46.9016	573.7702	0.0817	0.0017	11.4107
60	0.0099	12.3766	147.3000	101.2571	1253.2133	0.0808	0.0008	11.9015
100	0.0005	12.4943	155.6107	2199.7613	27,484.5157	0.0800	–	12.4545

Table 50.11 Factor Table i = 10.00%

n	P/F	P/A	P/G	F/P	F/A	A/P	A/F	A/G
1	0.9091	0.9091	0.0000	1.1000	1.0000	1.1000	1.0000	0.0000
2	0.8264	1.7355	0.8264	1.2100	2.1000	0.5762	0.4762	0.4762
3	0.7513	2.4869	2.3291	1.3310	3.3100	0.4021	0.3021	0.9366
4	0.6830	3.1699	4.3781	1.4641	4.6410	0.3155	0.2155	1.3812
5	0.6209	3.7908	6.8618	1.6105	6.1051	0.2638	0.1638	1.8101
6	0.5645	4.3553	9.6842	1.7716	7.7156	0.2296	0.1296	2.2236
7	0.5132	4.8684	12.7631	1.9487	9.4872	0.2054	0.1054	2.6216
8	0.4665	5.3349	16.0287	2.1436	11.4359	0.1874	0.0874	3.0045
9	0.4241	5.7590	19.4215	2.3579	13.5735	0.1736	0.0736	3.3724
10	0.3855	6.1446	22.8913	2.5937	15.9374	0.1627	0.0627	3.7255
11	0.3505	6.4951	26.3962	2.8531	18.5312	0.1540	0.0540	4.0641
12	0.3186	6.8137	29.9012	3.1384	21.3843	0.1468	0.0468	4.3884
13	0.2897	7.1034	33.3772	3.4523	24.5227	0.1408	0.0408	4.6988
14	0.2633	7.3667	36.8005	3.7975	27.9750	0.1357	0.0357	4.9955
15	0.2394	7.6061	40.1520	4.1772	31.7725	0.1315	0.0315	5.2789
16	0.2176	7.8237	43.4164	4.5950	35.9497	0.1278	0.0278	5.5493
17	0.1978	8.0216	46.5819	5.5045	40.5447	0.1247	0.0247	5.8071
18	0.1799	8.2014	49.6395	5.5599	45.5992	0.1219	0.0219	6.0526
19	0.1635	8.3649	52.5827	6.1159	51.1591	0.1195	0.0195	6.2861
20	0.1486	8.5136	55.4069	6.7275	57.2750	0.1175	0.0175	6.5081
21	0.1351	8.6487	58.1095	7.4002	64.0025	0.1156	0.0156	6.7189
22	0.1228	8.7715	60.6893	8.1403	71.4027	0.1140	0.0140	6.9189
23	0.1117	8.8832	63.1462	8.9543	79.5430	0.1126	0.0126	7.1085
24	0.1015	8.9847	65.4813	9.8497	88.4973	0.1113	0.0113	7.2881
25	0.0923	9.0770	67.6964	10.8347	98.3471	0.1102	0.0102	7.4580
30	0.0573	9.4269	77.0766	17.4494	164.4940	0.1061	0.0061	8.1762
40	0.0221	9.7791	88.9525	45.2593	442.5926	0.1023	0.0023	9.0962
50	0.0085	9.9148	94.8889	117.3909	1163.9085	0.1009	0.0009	9.5704
60	0.0033	9.9672	97.7010	304.4816	3,034.8164	0.1003	0.0003	9.8023
100	0.0001	9.9993	99.9202	13,780.6123	137,796.1234	0.1000	–	9.9927

Engineering
Economics

Table 50.12 *Factor Table i = 12.00%*

n	P/F	P/A	P/G	F/P	F/A	A/P	A/F	A/G
1	0.8929	0.8929	0.0000	1.1200	1.0000	1.1200	1.0000	0.0000
2	0.7972	1.6901	0.7972	1.2544	2.1200	0.5917	0.4717	0.4717
3	0.7118	2.4018	2.2208	1.4049	3.3744	0.4163	0.2963	0.9246
4	0.6355	3.0373	4.1273	1.5735	4.7793	0.3292	0.2092	1.3589
5	0.5674	3.6048	6.3970	1.7623	6.3528	0.2774	0.1574	1.7746
6	0.5066	4.1114	8.9302	1.9738	8.1152	0.2432	0.1232	2.1720
7	0.4523	4.5638	11.6443	2.2107	10.0890	0.2191	0.0991	2.5515
8	0.4039	4.9676	14.4714	2.4760	12.2997	0.2013	0.0813	2.9131
9	0.3606	5.3282	17.3563	2.7731	14.7757	0.1877	0.0677	3.2574
10	0.3220	5.6502	20.2541	3.1058	17.5487	0.1770	0.0570	3.5847
11	0.2875	5.9377	23.1288	3.4785	20.6546	0.1684	0.0484	3.8953
12	0.2567	6.1944	25.9523	3.8960	24.1331	0.1614	0.0414	4.1897
13	0.2292	6.4235	28.7024	4.3635	28.0291	0.1557	0.0357	4.4683
14	0.2046	6.6282	31.3624	4.8871	32.3926	0.1509	0.0309	4.7317
15	0.1827	6.8109	33.9202	5.4736	37.2797	0.1468	0.0268	4.9803
16	0.1631	6.9740	36.3670	6.1304	42.7533	0.1434	0.0234	5.2147
17	0.1456	7.1196	38.6973	6.8660	48.8837	0.1405	0.0205	5.4353
18	0.1300	7.2497	40.9080	7.6900	55.7497	0.1379	0.0179	5.6427
19	0.1161	7.3658	42.9979	8.6128	63.4397	0.1358	0.0158	5.8375
20	0.1037	7.4694	44.9676	9.6463	72.0524	0.1339	0.0139	6.0202
21	0.0926	7.5620	46.8188	10.8038	81.6987	0.1322	0.0122	6.1913
22	0.0826	7.6446	48.5543	12.1003	92.5026	0.1308	0.0108	6.3514
23	0.0738	7.7184	50.1776	13.5523	104.6029	0.1296	0.0096	6.5010
24	0.0659	7.7843	51.6929	15.1786	118.1552	0.1285	0.0085	6.6406
25	0.0588	7.8431	53.1046	17.001	133.3339	0.1275	0.0075	6.7708
30	0.0334	8.0552	58.7821	29.9599	241.3327	0.1241	0.0041	7.2974
40	0.0107	8.2438	65.1159	93.0510	767.0914	0.1213	0.0013	7.8988
50	0.0035	8.3045	67.7624	289.0022	2,400.0182	0.1204	0.0004	8.1597
60	0.0011	8.3240	68.8100	897.5969	7,471.6411	0.1201	0.0001	8.2664
100	–	8.3332	69.4336	83,522.2657	696,010.5477	0.1200	–	8.3321

Engineering Economics

Table 50.13 *Factor Table i = 18.00%*

n	P/F	P/A	P/G	F/P	F/A	A/P	A/F	A/G
1	0.8475	0.8475	0.0000	1.1800	1.0000	1.1800	1.0000	0.0000
2	0.7182	1.5656	0.7182	1.3924	2.1800	0.6387	0.4587	0.4587
3	0.6086	2.1743	1.9354	1.6430	3.5724	0.4599	0.2799	0.8902
4	0.5158	2.6901	3.4828	1.9388	5.2154	0.3717	0.1917	1.2947
5	0.4371	3.1272	5.2312	2.2878	7.1542	0.3198	0.1398	1.6728
6	0.3704	3.4976	7.0834	2.6996	9.4423	0.2859	0.1059	2.0252
7	0.3139	3.8115	8.9670	3.1855	12.1415	0.2624	0.0824	2.3526
8	0.2660	4.0776	10.8292	3.7589	15.3270	0.2452	0.0652	2.6558
9	0.2255	4.3030	12.6329	4.4355	19.0859	0.2324	0.0524	2.9358
10	0.1911	4.4941	14.3525	5.2338	23.5213	0.2225	0.0425	3.1936
11	0.1619	4.6560	15.9716	6.1759	28.7551	0.2148	0.0348	3.4303
12	0.1372	4.7932	17.4811	7.2876	34.9311	0.2086	0.0286	3.6470
13	0.1163	4.9095	18.8765	8.5994	42.2187	0.2037	0.0237	3.8449
14	0.0985	5.0081	20.1576	10.1472	50.8180	0.1997	0.0197	4.0250
15	0.0835	5.0916	21.3269	11.9737	60.9653	0.1964	0.0164	4.1887
16	0.0708	5.1624	22.3885	14.1290	72.9390	0.1937	0.0137	4.3369
17	0.0600	5.2223	23.3482	16.6722	87.0680	0.1915	0.0115	4.4708
18	0.0508	5.2732	24.2123	19.6731	103.7403	0.1896	0.0096	4.5916
19	0.0431	5.3162	24.9877	23.2144	123.4135	0.1881	0.0081	4.7003
20	0.0365	5.3527	25.6813	27.3930	146.6280	0.1868	0.0068	4.7978
21	0.0309	5.3837	26.3000	32.3238	174.0210	0.1857	0.0057	4.8851
22	0.0262	5.4099	26.8506	38.1421	206.3448	0.1848	0.0048	4.9632
23	0.0222	5.4321	27.3394	45.0076	244.4868	0.1841	0.0041	5.0329
24	0.0188	5.4509	27.7725	53.1090	289.4944	0.1835	0.0035	5.0950
25	0.0159	5.4669	28.1555	62.6686	342.6035	0.1829	0.0029	5.1502
30	0.0070	5.5168	29.4864	143.3706	790.9480	0.1813	0.0013	5.3448
40	0.0013	5.5482	30.5269	750.3783	4,163.2130	0.1802	0.0002	5.5022
50	0.0003	5.5541	30.7856	3,927.3569	21,813.0937	0.1800	–	5.5428
60	0.0001	5.5553	30.8465	20,555.1400	114,189.6665	0.1800	–	5.5526
100	–	5.5556	30.8642	15,424,131.91	85,689,616.17	0.1800	–	5.5555

Engineering
Economics

Diagnostic Exam

Topic XV: Ethics and Professional Practice

1. Seventeen years ago, Susan designed a corrugated steel culvert for a rural road. Her work was accepted and paid for by the county engineering department. Last winter, the culvert collapsed as a loaded logging truck passed over. Although there were no injuries, there was damage to the truck and roadway, and the county tried unsuccessfully to collect on Susan's company's bond. The judge denied the claim on the basis that the work was done too long ago. This defense is known as

(A) privity of contract

(B) duplicity of liability

(C) statute of limitations

(D) caveat emptor

2. Ethics requires you to take into consideration the effects of your behavior on which group(s) of people?

I. your employer

II. the nonprofessionals in society

III. other professionals

(A) II only

(B) I and II

(C) II and III

(D) I, II, and III

3. Which of the following terms is NOT related to ethics?

(A) integrity

(B) honesty

(C) morality

(D) profitability

4. What actions can be taken by a state regulating agency against a design professional who violates one or more of its rules of conduct?

I. the professional's license may be revoked or suspended

II. notice of the violation may be published in the local newspaper

III. the professional may be asked to make restitution

IV. the professional may be required to complete a course in ethics

(A) I and II

(B) I and III

(C) I and IV

(D) I, II, III, and IV

5. An engineering, architectural design, and construction consulting company with worldwide business has adopted and routinely uses the phrase, "Building for Your Future" to distinguish itself from other companies. Most likely, how should that phrase be marked in order to prevent other companies from using it?

(A) "©"

(B) "All rights reserved."

(C) "TM"

(D) "SM"

6. An engineer working for a big design firm has decided to start a consulting business, but it will be a few months before she leaves. How should she handle the impending change?

(A) The engineer should discuss her plans with her current employer.

(B) The engineer may approach the firm's other employees while still working for the firm.

(C) The engineer should immediately quit.

(D) The engineer should return all of the pens, pencils, pads of paper, and other equipment she has brought home over the years.

7. During the day, an engineer works for a scientific research laboratory doing government research. During the night, the engineer uses some of the lab's equipment to perform testing services for other consulting engineers. Why is this action probably unethical?

(A) The laboratory has not given its permission for the equipment use.

(B) The government contract prohibits misuse and misappropriation of the equipment.

(C) The equipment may wear out or be broken by the engineer and the replacement cost will be borne by the government contract.

(D) The engineer's fees to the consulting engineers can undercut local testing services' fees because the engineer has a lower overhead.

8. An engineer spends all of his free time (outside of work) gambling illegally. Is this a violation of ethical standards?

(A) No, the engineer is entitled to a life outside of work.

(B) No, the engineer's employer, his clients, and the public are not affected.

(C) No, not as long as the engineer stays debt-free from the gambling activities.

(D) Yes, the engineer should associate only with reputable persons and organizations.

9. During routine inspections, a field engineer discovers that one of the company's pipelines is leaking hazardous chemicals into the environment but less than the reportable threshold. The engineer recommends that the line be shut down so that seals can be replaced and the pipe can be inspected more closely. His supervisor commends him on his thoroughness, and says the report will be passed on to the company's maintenance division. The engineer moves on to his next job, assuming things will be taken care of in a timely manner. While working in the area again several months later, the engineer notices that the problem hasn't been corrected and is in fact getting worse. What should the engineer do?

(A) Give the matter some more time. In a large corporate environment, it is understandable that some things take longer than people would like them to.

(B) Ask the supervisor to investigate what action has been taken on the matter.

(C) Personally speak to the director of maintenance and insist that this project be given high priority.

(D) Report the company to the EPA for allowing the situation to worsen without taking any preventative measures.

10. An engineering firm receives much of its revenue from community construction projects. Which of the following activities would it be unethical for the firm to participate in?

(A) Contribute to the campaigns of local politicians.

(B) Sponsor the American Society of Civil Engineers (ASCE) local chapter events

(C) Encourage employees to volunteer in community organizations.

(D) Rent billboards to increase the company's name recognition.

SOLUTIONS

1. Most states have statutes of limitations. Unless a crime or fraudulent act has been committed, defects appearing after a certain amount of time are not actionable.

The answer is (C).

2. Ethical behavior places restrictions on behavior that affect you, your employer, other engineers, your clients, and society as a whole.

The answer is (D).

3. Ethical actions may or may not be profitable.

The answer is (D).

4. All four punishments are commonly used by state engineering licensing boards.

The answer is (D).

5. The company is a service company. The phrase would probably be considered a service mark, and it should be identified by "SM."

The answer is (D).

6. There is nothing wrong with wanting to go into business for oneself. The ethical violation occurs when one of the parties does not know what is going on. Even if the engineer acts ethically, takes nothing, and talks to no one about her plans, there will still be the appearance of impropriety if she leaves later. The engineer should discuss her plans with her current employer. That way, there will be minimal disruption to the firm's activities. The engineer shouldn't quit unless her employer demands it. (Those pencils, pens, and pads of paper probably shouldn't have been brought home in the first place.)

The answer is (A).

7. Options (A), (B), (C), and (D) may all be valid. However, the rationale for specific ethical prohibitions on using your employer's equipment for a second job is economic. When you don't have to pay for the equipment, you don't have to recover its purchase price in your fees for services.

The answer is (D).

8. The gambling is illegal. Engineers should do nothing that brings them and their profession into disrepute. It is impossible to separate people from their professions. When engineers participate in disreputable activities, it casts the entire profession in a bad light.

The answer is (D).

9. While it is true that corporate bureaucracy tends to slow things down, several months is too lengthy a period for an environmental issue. On the other hand, it is by no means clear that the company is ignoring the situation. There could have been some action taken that the engineer is unaware of, or extenuating circumstances that are delaying the repair. To go outside the company or even over the head of his supervisor would be premature without more information. The engineer should ask his previous supervisor to look into the issue, and should only take further measures if he is dissatisfied with the response.

The answer is (B).

10. Contributing to local politics, either to individual campaigns or in the form of a gift to the city, would be seen as an attempt to gain political favor. Encouraging the company's employees to volunteer their own time to the community is acceptable because the company is unlikely to get any specific benefit from it. Sponsoring local industry trade events (ASCE or any other group) as well as the renting of billboards are considered standard practice both to achieve name recognition as well as for networking and recruiting.

The answer is (A).

51 Professional Practice

1. AGREEMENTS AND CONTRACTS

General Contracts

A *contract* is a legally binding agreement or promise to exchange goods or services.[1] A written contract is merely a documentation of the agreement. Some agreements must be in writing, but most agreements for engineering services can be verbal, particularly if the parties to the agreement know each other well.[2] Written contract documents do not need to contain intimidating legal language, but all agreements must satisfy three basic requirements to be enforceable (binding).

- There must be a clear, specific, and definite *offer* with no room for ambiguity or misunderstanding.

- There must be some form of conditional future *consideration* (i.e., payment).[3]

- There must be an *acceptance* of the offer.

There are other conditions that the agreement must meet to be enforceable. These conditions are not normally part of the explicit agreement but represent the conditions under which the agreement was made.

- The agreement must be *voluntary* for all parties.

- All parties must have *legal capacity* (i.e., be mentally competent, of legal age, not under coercion, and uninfluenced by drugs).

- The purpose of the agreement must be *legal*.

For small projects, a simple *letter of agreement* on one party's stationery may suffice. For larger, complex projects, a more formal document may be required. Some clients prefer to use a *purchase order*, which can function as a contract if all basic requirements are met.

Regardless of the format of the written document—letter of agreement, purchase order, or standard form—a contract should include the following features.[4]

- introduction, preamble, or preface indicating the purpose of the contract

- name, address, and business forms of both contracting parties

- signature date of the agreement

- effective date of the agreement (if different from the signature date)

- duties and obligations of both parties

- deadlines and required service dates

- fee amount

- fee schedule and payment terms

- agreement expiration date

- standard boilerplate clauses

- signatures of parties or their agents

- declaration of authority of the signatories to bind the contracting parties

- supporting documents

---

[1]Not all agreements are legally binding (i.e., enforceable). Two parties may agree on something, but unless the agreement meets all of the requirements and conditions of a contract, the parties cannot hold each other to the agreement.
[2]All states have a *statute of frauds* that, among other things, specifies what types of contracts must be in writing to be enforceable. These include contracts for the sale of land, contracts requiring more than one year for performance, contracts for the sale of goods over $500 in value, contracts to satisfy the debts of another, and marriage contracts. Contracts to provide engineering services do not fall under the statute of frauds.
[3]Actions taken or payments made prior to the agreement are irrelevant. Also, it does not matter to the courts whether the exchange is based on equal value or not.
[4]*Construction contracts* are unique unto themselves. Items that might also be included as part of the *contract documents* are the agreement form, the general conditions, drawings, specifications, and addenda.

Example

Which feature is NOT a standard feature of a written construction contract?

- (A) identification of both parties
- (B) specific details of the obligations of both parties
- (C) boilerplate clauses
- (D) subcontracts

Solution

A written contract should identify both parties, state the purpose of the contract and the obligations of the parties, give specific details of the obligations (including relevant dates and deadlines), specify the consideration, state the boilerplate clauses to clarify the contract terms, and leave places for signatures. Subcontracts are not required to be included, but may be added when a party to the contract engages a third party to perform the work in the original contract.

The answer is (D).

Agency

In some contracts, decision-making authority and right of action are transferred from one party (the owner, or *principal*) who would normally have that authority to another person (the *agent*). For example, in construction contracts, the engineer may be the agent of the owner for certain transactions. Agents are limited in what they can do by the scope of the agency agreement. Within that scope, however, an agent acts on behalf of the principal, and the principal is liable for the acts of the agent and is bound by contracts made in the principal's name by the agent.

Agents are required to execute their work with care, skill, and diligence. Specifically, agents have *fiduciary responsibility* toward their principal, meaning that the agent must be honest and loyal. Agents are liable for damages resulting from a lack of diligence, loyalty, and/or honesty. If the agents misrepresented their skills when obtaining the agency, they can be liable for breach of contract or fraud.

Standard Boilerplate Clauses

It is common for full-length contract documents to include important *boilerplate clauses*. These clauses have specific wordings that should not normally be changed, hence the name "boilerplate." Some of the most common boilerplate clauses are paraphrased here.

- Delays and inadequate performance due to war, strikes, and acts of God and nature are forgiven (*force majeure*).
- The contract document is the complete agreement, superseding all prior verbal and written agreements.
- The contract can be modified or canceled only in writing.
- Parts of the contract that are determined to be void or unenforceable will not affect the enforceability of the remainder of the contract (*severability*). Alternatively, parts of the contract that are determined to be void or unenforceable will be rewritten to accomplish their intended purpose without affecting the remainder of the contract.
- None (or one, or both) of the parties can (or cannot) assign its (or their) rights and responsibilities under the contract (*assignment*).
- All notices provided for in the agreement must be in writing and sent to the address in the agreement.
- Time is of the essence.[5]
- The subject headings of the agreement paragraphs are for convenience only and do not control the meaning of the paragraphs.
- The laws of the state in which the contract is signed must be used to interpret and govern the contract.
- Disagreements shall be arbitrated according to the rules of the American Arbitration Association.
- Any lawsuits related to the contract must be filed in the county and state in which the contract is signed.
- Obligations under the agreement are unique, and in the event of a breach, the defaulting party waives the defense that the loss can be adequately compensated by monetary damages (*specific performance*).
- In the event of a lawsuit, the prevailing party is entitled to an award of reasonable attorneys' and court fees.[6]
- Consequential damages are not recoverable in a lawsuit.

Example

An engineering consultant has signed a standard owner-engineer contract to build a scale model of a bridge in time for the owner to present the proposal to a financing committee. After the scale model has been built, it is destroyed in a building fire that consumes the consultant's building. The consultant is unable to rebuild the model in time. A breach of contract judgment against

[5]Without this clause in writing, damages for delay cannot be claimed.
[6]Without this clause in writing, attorneys' fees and court costs are rarely recoverable.

the consultant is most likely NOT obtainable due to which legal argument?

- (A) caveat emptor
- (B) privity of contract
- (C) force majeure
- (D) strict liability in tort

Solution

Standard contracts have force majeure clauses that excuse nonperformance due to "acts of God" and other unforeseen events such as weather and acts of terrorism.

The answer is (C).

Subcontracts

When a party to a contract engages a third party to perform the work in the original contract, the contract with the third party is known as a *subcontract*. Whether or not responsibilities can be subcontracted under the original contract depends on the content of the *assignment clause* in the original contract.

Parties to a Construction Contract

A specific set of terms has developed for referring to parties in consulting and construction contracts. The *owner* of a construction project is the person, partnership, or corporation that actually owns the land, assumes the financial risk, and ends up with the completed project. The *developer* contracts with the architect and/or engineer for the design and with the contractors for the construction of the project. In some cases, the owner and developer are the same, in which case the term *owner-developer* can be used.

The *architect* designs the project according to established codes and guidelines but leaves most stress and capacity calculations to the *engineer*.[7] Depending on the construction contract, the engineer may work for the architect, or vice versa, or both may work for the developer.

Once there are approved plans, the developer hires *contractors* to do the construction. Usually, the entire construction project is awarded to a *general contractor*. Due to the nature of the construction industry, separate

subcontracts are used for different tasks (electrical, plumbing, mechanical, framing, fire sprinkler installation, finishing, etc.). The general contractor who hires all of these different *subcontractors* is known as the *prime contractor* (or *prime*). (The subcontractors can also work directly for the owner-developer, although this is less common.) The prime contractor is responsible for all acts of the subcontractors and is liable for any damage suffered by the owner-developer due to those acts.

Construction is managed by an agent of the owner-developer known as the *construction manager*, who may be the engineer, the architect, or someone else.

Standard Contracts for Design Professionals

Several professional organizations have produced standard agreement forms and other standard documents for design professionals.[8] Among other standard forms, notices, and agreements, the following standard contracts are available.[9]

- standard contract between engineer and client
- standard contract between engineer and architect
- standard contract between engineer and contractor
- standard contract between owner and construction manager

Besides completeness, the major advantage of a standard contract is that the meanings of the clauses are well established, not only among the design professionals and their clients but also in the courts. The clauses in these contracts have already been litigated many times. Where a clause has been found to be unclear or ambiguous, it has been rewritten to accomplish its intended purpose.

Consulting Fee Structure

Compensation for consulting engineering services can incorporate one or more of the following concepts.

- *lump-sum fee:* This is a predetermined fee agreed upon by client and engineer. This payment can be used for small projects where the scope of work is clearly defined.

---

[7]On simple small projects, such as wood-framed residential units, the design may be developed by a *building designer*. The legal capacities of building designers vary from state to state.
[8]There are two main sources of standardized construction and design agreements: the *Engineers Joint Contract Documents Committee* (EJCDC) and American Institute of Architects (AIA). Consensus documents, known as *ConsensusDOCS*, for every conceivable situation have been developed by EJCDC. EJCDC includes the American Society of Civil Engineers (ASCE), the American Council of Engineering Companies (ACEC), National Society of Professional Engineers' (NSPE's) Professional Engineers in Private Practice Division, Associated General Contractors of America (AGC), and more than fifteen other participating professional engineering design, construction, owner, legal, and risk management organizations, including the Associated Builders and Contractors; American Subcontractors Association; Construction Users Roundtable; National Roofing Contractors Association; Mechanical Contractors Association of America; and National Plumbing-Heating-Cooling Contractors Association. The AIA has developed its own standardized agreements in a less collaborative manner. Though popular with architects, AIA provisions are considered less favorable to engineers, contractors, and subcontractors who believe the AIA documents assign too much authority to architects, too much risk and liability to contractors, and too little flexibility in how construction disputes are addressed and resolved.
[9]The Construction Specifications Institute (CSI) has produced standard specifications for materials. The standards have been organized according to a UNIFORMAT structure consistent with ASTM Standard E1557.

- *unit price:* Contract fees are based on estimated quantities and unit pricing. This payment method works best when required materials can be accurately identified and estimated before the contract is finalized. This payment method is often used in combination with a lump-sum fee.

- *cost plus fixed fee:* All costs (labor, material, travel, etc.) incurred by the engineer are paid by the client. The client also pays a predetermined fee as profit. This method has an advantage when the scope of services cannot be determined accurately in advance. Detailed records must be kept by the engineer in order to allocate costs among different clients.

- *per diem fee:* The engineer is paid a specific sum for each day spent on the job. Usually, certain direct expenses (e.g., travel and reproduction) are billed in addition to the per diem rate.

- *salary plus:* The client pays for the employees on an engineer's payroll (the salary) plus an additional percentage to cover indirect overhead and profit plus certain direct expenses.

- *retainer:* This is a minimum amount paid by the client, usually in total and in advance, for a normal amount of work expected during an agreed-upon period. Usually, none of the retainer is returned, regardless of how little work the engineer performs. The engineer can be paid for additional work beyond what is normal, however. Some direct costs, such as travel and reproduction expenses, may be billed directly to the client.

- *incentive:* This type of fee structure is based on established target costs and fees and lists minimum and maximum fees and an adjustment formula. The formula may be based on performance criteria such as budget, quality, and schedule. Once the project is complete, payment is calculated based on the formula.

- *percentage of construction cost:* This method, which is widely used in construction design contracts, pays the architect and/or the engineer a percentage of the final total cost of the project. Costs of land, financing, and legal fees are generally not included in the construction cost, and other costs (plan revisions, project management labor, value engineering, etc.) are billed separately.

Example

Which fee structure is a nonreturnable advance paid to a consultant?

(A) per diem fee

(B) retainer

(C) lump-sum fee

(D) cost plus fixed fee

Solution

A *retainer* is a (usually) nonreturnable advance paid by the client to the consultant. While the retainer may be intended to cover the consultant's initial expenses until the first big billing is sent out, there does not need to be any rational basis for the retainer. Often, a small retainer is used by the consultant to qualify the client (i.e., to make sure the client is not just shopping around and getting free initial consultations) and as a security deposit (to make sure the client does not change consultants after work begins).

The answer is (B).

Mechanic's Liens

For various reasons, providers of material, labor, and design services to construction sites may not be promptly paid or even paid at all. Such providers have, of course, the right to file a lawsuit demanding payment, but due to the nature of the construction industry, such relief may be insufficient or untimely. Therefore, such providers have the right to file a *mechanic's lien* (also known as a *construction lien, materialman's lien, supplier's lien,* or *laborer's lien*) against the property. Although there are strict requirements for deadlines, filing, and notices, the procedure for obtaining (and removing) such a lien is simple. The lien establishes the supplier's security interest in the property. Although the details depend on the state, essentially the property owner is prevented from transferring title of (i.e., selling) the property until the lien has been removed by the supplier. The act of filing a lawsuit to obtain payment is known as "perfecting the lien." Liens are perfected by forcing a judicial foreclosure sale. The court orders the property sold, and the proceeds are used to pay off any lienholders.

Discharge of a Contract

A contract is normally discharged when all parties have satisfied their obligations. However, a contract can also be terminated for the following reasons:

- mutual agreement of all parties to the contract

- impossibility of performance (e.g., death of a party to the contract)

- illegality of the contract

- material breach by one or more parties to the contract

- fraud on the part of one or more parties

- failure (i.e., loss or destruction) of consideration (e.g., the burning of a building one party expected to own or occupy upon satisfaction of the obligations)

Some contracts may be dissolved by actions of the court (e.g., bankruptcy), passage of new laws and public acts, or a declaration of war.

Extreme difficulty (including economic hardship) in satisfying the contract does not discharge it, even if it becomes more costly or less profitable than originally anticipated.

2. PROFESSIONAL LIABILITY

Breach of Contract, Negligence, Misrepresentation, and Fraud

A *breach of contract* occurs when one of the parties fails to satisfy all of its obligations under a contract. The breach can be *willful* (as in a contractor walking off a construction job) or *unintentional* (as in providing less than adequate quality work or materials). A *material breach* is defined as nonperformance that results in the injured party receiving something substantially less than or different from what the contract intended.

Normally, the only redress that an *injured party* has through the courts in the event of a breach of contract is to force the breaching party to provide *specific performance*—that is, to satisfy all remaining contract provisions and to pay for any damage caused. Normally, *punitive damages* (to punish the breaching party) are unavailable.

Negligence is an action, willful or unwillful, taken without proper care or consideration for safety, resulting in damages to property or injury to persons. "Proper care" is a subjective term, but in general it is the diligence that would be exercised by a reasonably prudent person.[10] Damages sustained by a negligent act are recoverable in a tort action. (See "Torts.") If the plaintiff is partially at fault (as in the case of *comparative negligence*), the defendant will be liable only for the portion of the damage caused by the defendant.

Punitive damages are available, however, if the breaching party was fraudulent in obtaining the contract. In addition, the injured party has the right to void (nullify) the contract entirely. A *fraudulent act* is basically a special case of *misrepresentation* (i.e., an intentionally false statement known to be false at the time it is made). Misrepresentation that does not result in a contract is a tort. When a contract is involved, misrepresentation can be a breach of that contract (i.e., *fraud*).

Unfortunately, it is extremely difficult to prove *compensatory fraud* (i.e., fraud for which damages are available). Proving fraud requires showing *beyond a reasonable doubt* (a) a reckless or intentional

misstatement of a material fact, (b) an intention to deceive, (c) it resulted in misleading the innocent party to contract, and (d) it was to the innocent party's detriment.

For example, if an engineer claims to have experience in designing steel buildings but actually has none, the court might consider the misrepresentation a fraudulent action. If, however, the engineer has some experience, but an insufficient amount to do an adequate job, the engineer probably will not be considered to have acted fraudulently.

Example

The owner of a construction site is aware that the state driving license of one of its heavy machinery operators has been suspended for multiple driving under the influence (DUI) violations. In order to secure a desirable standing and contract with an abstinence-based commune, the owner misrepresents the non-drinking status of the construction crew. A serious injury occurs when the operator drives a loader over the leg of a member of the commune while intoxicated. Most likely, the commune will be able to obtain a judgment against the operator based on

(A)   negligence

(B)   breach of contract

(C)   misrepresentation

(D)   fraud

Solution

All elements necessary to obtain a judgement against the owner based on fraud are present in this scenario. The operator is, most likely, guilty only of negligence.

The answer is (A).

Torts

A *tort* is a civil wrong committed by one person causing damage to another person or person's property, emotional well-being, or reputation.[11] It is a breach of the rights of an individual to be secure in person or property. In order to correct the wrong, a civil lawsuit (*tort action* or *civil complaint*) is brought by the alleged injured party (the *plaintiff*) against the *defendant*. To be a valid *tort action* (i.e., lawsuit), there must have been

---

[10]Negligence of a design professional (e.g., an engineer or architect) is the absence of a *standard of care* (i.e., customary and normal care and attention) that would have been provided by other engineers. It is highly subjective.
[11]The difference between a *civil tort* (*lawsuit*) and a *criminal lawsuit* is the alleged injured party. A *crime* is a wrong against society. A criminal lawsuit is brought by the state against a defendant.

injury (i.e., damage). Generally, there will be no contract between the two parties, so the tort action cannot claim a breach of contract.[12]

Tort law is concerned with compensation for the injury, not punishment. Therefore, tort awards usually consist of general, compensatory, and special damages and rarely include punitive and exemplary damages. (See "Damages" for definitions of these damages.)

Strict Liability in Tort

Strict liability in tort means that the injured party wins if the injury can be proven. It is not necessary to prove negligence, breach of explicit or implicit warranty, or the existence of a contract (*privity of contract*). Strict liability in tort is most commonly encountered in product liability cases. A defect in a product, regardless of how the defect got there, is sufficient to create strict liability in tort.

Case law surrounding defective products has developed and refined the following requirements for winning a strict liability in tort case. The following points must be proved.

- The product was defective in manufacture, design, labeling, and so on.

- The product was defective when used.

- The defect rendered the product unreasonably dangerous.

- The defect caused the injury.

- The specific use of the product that caused the damage was reasonably foreseeable.

Manufacturing and Design Liability

Case law makes a distinction between *design professionals* (architects, structural engineers, building designers, etc.) and manufacturers of consumer products. Design professionals are generally consultants whose primary product is a design service sold to sophisticated clients. Consumer product manufacturers produce specific product lines sold through wholesalers and retailers to the unsophisticated public.

The law treats design professionals favorably. Such professionals are expected to meet a *standard of care* and skill that can be measured by comparison with the conduct of other professionals. However, professionals are not expected to be infallible. In the absence of a contract provision to the contrary, design professionals are not held to be guarantors of their work in the strict sense of legal liability. Damages incurred due to design errors are recoverable through tort actions, but proving a breach of contract requires showing negligence (i.e., not meeting the standard of care).

On the other hand, the law is much stricter with consumer product manufacturers, and perfection is (essentially) expected of them. They are held to the standard of strict liability in tort without regard to negligence. A manufacturer is held liable for all phases of the design and manufacturing of a product being marketed to the public.[13]

Prior to 1916, the court's position toward product defects was exemplified by the expression *caveat emptor* ("let the buyer beware").[14] Subsequent court rulings have clarified that "... a manufacturer is strictly liable in tort when an article [it] places on the market, knowing that it will be used without inspection, proves to have a defect that causes injury to a human being."[15]

Although all defectively designed products can be traced back to a design engineer or team, only the manufacturing company is usually held liable for injury caused by the product. This is more a matter of economics than justice. The company has liability insurance; the product design engineer (who is merely an employee of the company) probably does not. Unless the product design or manufacturing process is intentionally defective, or unless the defect is known in advance and covered up, the product design engineer will rarely be punished by the courts.[16]

Example

An engineer designs and self-manufactures a revolutionary racing bicycle. The engineer uses finite element analysis (FEA) software to perfect the design, has the design checked by a reputable authority, and subjects the major components that he manufactures to nondestructive testing. After three years of heavier-than-anticipated usage,

---

[12]It is possible for an injury to be both a breach of contract and a tort. Suppose an owner has an agreement with a contractor to construct a building, and the contract requires the contractor to comply with all state and federal safety regulations. If the owner is subsequently injured on a stairway because there was no guardrail, the injury could be recoverable both as a tort and as a breach of contract. If a third party unrelated to the contract was injured, however, that party could recover only through a tort action.

[13]The reason for this is that the public is not considered to be as sophisticated as a client who contracts with a design professional for building plans.

[14]1916, *MacPherson v. Buick*. MacPherson bought a Buick from a car dealer. The car had a defective wheel, and there was evidence that reasonable inspection would have uncovered the defect. MacPherson was injured when the wheel broke and the car collapsed, and he sued Buick. Buick defended itself under the ancient *prerequisite of privity* (i.e., the requirement of a face-to-face contractual relationship in order for liability to exist), since the dealer, not Buick, had sold the car to MacPherson, and no contract between Buick and MacPherson existed. The judge disagreed, thus establishing the concept of *third-party liability* (i.e., manufacturers are responsible to consumers even though consumers do not buy directly from manufacturers).

[15]1963, *Greenman v. Yuba Power Products*. Greenman purchased and was injured by an electric power tool.

[16]The engineer can expect to be discharged from the company. However, for strategic reasons, this discharge probably will not occur until after the company loses the case.

one of the engineer's bicycles disintegrates in a race, killing its rider. In his defense, the engineer may claim

- (A) privity of contract
- (B) standard of care
- (C) statute of limitations
- (D) contributory negligence

Solution

The scenario does not contain information about initial and ongoing testing, but the engineer has done everything described in a competent manner. While the engineer may still be held responsible in some manner, he has met a normal standard of care in the design and manufacturing of his bicycles.

The answer is (B).

Damages

An injured party can sue for *damages* as well as for specific performance. Damages are the award made by the court for losses incurred by the injured party.

- *General* or *compensatory damages* are awarded to make up for the injury that was sustained.

- *Special damages* are awarded for the direct financial loss due to the breach of contract.

- *Nominal damages* are awarded when responsibility has been established but the injury is so slight as to be inconsequential.

- *Liquidated damages* are amounts that are specified in the contract document itself for nonperformance.

- *Punitive* or *exemplary damages* are awarded, usually in tort and fraud cases, to punish and make an example of the defendant (i.e., to deter others from doing the same thing).

- *Consequential damages* provide compensation for indirect losses incurred by the injured party but not directly related to the contract.

Insurance

Most design firms and many independent design professionals carry *errors and omissions insurance* to protect them from claims due to their mistakes. Such policies are costly, and for that reason, some professionals choose to "go bare."[17] Policies protect against inadvertent mistakes only, not against willful, knowing, or conscious efforts to defraud or deceive.

---

[17]Going bare appears foolish at first glance, but there is a perverted logic behind the strategy. One-person consulting firms (and perhaps, firms that are not profitable) are "judgment-proof." Without insurance or other assets, these firms would be unable to pay any large judgments against them. When damage victims (and their lawyers) find this out in advance, they know that judgments will be uncollectable. So the lawsuit often never makes its way to trial.

52 Ethics

1. CODES OF ETHICS

Creeds, Rules, Statutes, Canons, and Codes

It is generally conceded that an individual acting on his or her own cannot be counted on to always act in a proper and moral manner. Creeds, rules, statutes, canons, and codes all attempt to complete the guidance needed for an engineer to do "...the correct thing."

A *creed* is a statement or oath, often religious in nature, taken or assented to by an individual in ceremonies. For example, the *Engineers' Creed* adopted by the National Society of Professional Engineers (NSPE) is[1]

> As a Professional Engineer, I dedicate my professional knowledge and skill to the advancement and betterment of human welfare.
>
> I pledge...
>
> ⋯ to give the utmost of performance;
>
> ⋯ to participate in none but honest enterprise;
>
> ⋯ to live and work according to the laws of man and the highest standards of professional conduct;
>
> ⋯ to place service before profit, the honor and standing of the profession before personal advantage, and the public welfare above all other considerations.
>
> In humility and with need for Divine Guidance, I make this pledge.

A *rule* is a guide (principle, standard, or norm) for conduct and action in a certain situation, or a regulation governing procedure. A *statutory rule*, or statute, is enacted by the legislative branch of state or federal government and carries the weight of law. Some U.S. engineering registration boards have statutory *rules of professional conduct*.

A *canon* is an individual principle or body of principles, rules, standards, or norms. A *code* is a system of principles or rules. For example, the code of ethics of the American Society of Civil Engineers (ASCE) contains the following seven canons.

1. Engineers shall hold paramount the safety, health, and welfare of the public and shall strive to comply with the principles of sustainable development in the performance of their professional duties.

2. Engineers shall perform services only in areas of their competence.

3. Engineers shall issue public statements only in an objective and truthful manner.

4. Engineers shall act in professional matters for each employer or client as faithful agents or trustees and shall avoid conflicts of interest.

5. Engineers shall build their professional reputation on the merit of their services and shall not compete unfairly with others.

6. Engineers shall act in such a manner as to uphold and enhance the honor, integrity, and dignity of the engineering profession and shall act with zero tolerance for bribery, fraud, and corruption.

7. Engineers shall continue their professional development throughout their careers and shall provide opportunities for the professional development of those engineers under their supervision.

Example

Relative to the practice of engineering, which one of the following best defines "ethics"?

(A) application of United States laws

(B) rules of conduct

(C) personal values

(D) recognition of cultural differences

---

[1]The *Faith of an Engineer* adopted by the Accreditation Board for Engineering and Technology (ABET) is a similar but more detailed creed.

Solution

Ethics are the rules of conduct recognized in respect to a particular class of human actions or governing a particular group, culture, and so on.

The answer is (B).

Purpose of a Code of Ethics

Many different sets of *codes of ethics* (*canons of ethics, rules of professional conduct*, etc.) have been produced by various engineering societies, registration boards, and other organizations.[2] The purpose of these ethical guidelines is to guide the conduct and decision making of engineers. Most codes are primarily educational. Nevertheless, from time to time they have been used by the societies and regulatory agencies as the basis for disciplinary actions.

Fundamental to ethical codes is the requirement that engineers render faithful, honest, professional service. In providing such service, engineers must represent the interests of their employers or clients and, at the same time, protect public health, safety, and welfare.

There is an important distinction between what is legal and what is ethical. Many legal actions can be violations of codes of ethical or professional behavior. For example, an engineer's contract with a client may give the engineer the right to assign the engineer's responsibilities, but doing so without informing the client would be unethical.

Ethical guidelines can be categorized on the basis of who is affected by the engineer's actions—the client, vendors and suppliers, other engineers, or the public at large. (Some authorities also include ethical guidelines for dealing with the employees of an engineer. However, these guidelines are no different for an engineering employer than they are for a supermarket, automobile assembly line, or airline employer. Ethics is not a unique issue when it comes to employees.)

Example

Complete the sentence: "Guidelines of ethical behavior among engineers are needed because

(A) engineers are analytical and they don't always think in terms of right or wrong."

(B) all people, including engineers, are inherently unethical."

(C) rules of ethics are easily forgotten."

(D) it is easy for engineers to take advantage of clients."

Solution

Untrained members of society are at the mercy of the professionals (e.g., doctors, lawyers, engineers) they employ. Even a cab driver can take advantage of a new tourist who doesn't know the shortest route between two points. In many cases, the unsuspecting public needs protection from unscrupulous professionals, engineers included, who act in their own interest.

The answer is (D).

2. SUSTAINABILITY

Many professional societies' codes of ethics stress the importance of incorporating sustainability into engineering design and development. *Sustainability* (also known as *sustainable development* or *sustainable design*) encompasses a wide range of concepts and strategies. However, a general definition of sustainability is any design or development that seeks to minimize negative impacts on the environment so that the present generation's resource needs do not compromise the resource needs of a future generation. Examples of sustainable design principles include using renewable energy sources, conserving water, and using *sustainable materials* (materials sourced, manufactured, and transported with sustainability in mind).

3. NCEES MODEL LAW

Introduction[3]

Engineering is considered to be a "profession" rather than an occupation because of several important characteristics shared with other recognized learned professions, law, medicine, and theology: special knowledge, special privileges, and special responsibilities. Professions are based on a large knowledge base requiring extensive training. Professional skills are important to the well-being of society. Professions are self-regulating, in that they control the training and evaluation processes that admit new persons to the field. Professionals have autonomy in the workplace; they are expected to utilize their independent judgment in carrying out their professional responsibilities. Finally, professions are regulated by ethical standards.

The expertise possessed by engineers is vitally important to public welfare. In order to serve the public effectively, engineers must maintain a high level of technical competence. However, a high level of technical expertise without adherence to ethical guidelines is as much a

[2]All of the major engineering technical and professional societies in the United States (ASCE, IEEE, ASME, AIChE, NSPE, etc.) and throughout the world have adopted codes of ethics. Most U.S. societies have endorsed the *Code of Ethics of Engineers* developed by the Accreditation Board for Engineering and Technology (ABET), formerly the Engineers' Council for Professional Development (ECPD). The National Council of Examiners for Engineering and Surveying (NCEES) has developed its *Model Rules* as a guide for state registration boards in developing guidelines for the professional engineers in those states.
[3]Adapted from C. E. Harris, M. S. Pritchard, and M. J. Rabins, *Engineering Ethics: Concepts and Cases*, copyright © 1995 by Wadsworth Publishing Company, pg. 27–28.

threat to public welfare as is professional incompetence. Therefore, engineers must also be guided by ethical principles.

The ethical principles governing the engineering profession are embodied in codes of ethics. Such codes have been adopted by state boards of registration, professional engineering societies, and even by some private industries. An example of one such code is the NCEES Rules of Professional Conduct, found in Section 240 of *Model Rules* and presented here. As part of his/her responsibility to the public, an engineer is responsible for knowing and abiding by the code. Additional rules of conduct are also included in *Model Rules.*

The three major sections of Model Rules address (1) Licensee's Obligation to Society, (2) Licensee's Obligation to Employers and Clients, and (3) Licensee's Obligation to Other Licensees. The principles amplified in these sections are important guides to appropriate behavior of professional engineers.

Application of the code in many situations is not controversial. However, there may be situations in which applying the code may raise more difficult issues. In particular, there may be circumstances in which terminology in the code is not clearly defined, or in which two sections of the code may be in conflict. For example, what constitutes "valuable consideration" or "adequate" knowledge may be interpreted differently by qualified professionals. These types of questions are called *conceptual issues*, in which definitions of terms may be in dispute. In other situations, *factual issues* may also affect ethical dilemmas. Many decisions regarding engineering design may be based upon interpretation of disputed or incomplete information. In addition, *trade-offs* revolving around competing issues of risk vs. benefit, or safety vs. economics, may require judgments that are not fully addressed simply by application of the code.

No code can give immediate and mechanical answers to all ethical and professional problems that an engineer may face. Creative problem solving is often called for in ethics, just as it is in other areas of engineering.

Example

Which organizations typically do NOT enforce codes of ethics for engineers?

- (A)   technical societies (e.g., ASCE, ASME, IEEE)

- (B)   national professional societies (e.g., the National Society of Professional Engineers)

- (C)   state professional societies (e.g., the Michigan Society of Professional Engineers)

- (D)   companies that write, administer, and grade licensing exams

Solution

Companies that write, administer, and grade licensing exams typically do not enforce codes of ethics for engineers.

The answer is (D).

Licensee's Obligation to Society[4]

1.   Licensees, in the performance of their services for clients, employers, and customers, shall be cognizant that their first and foremost responsibility is to the public welfare.

2.   Licensees shall approve and seal only those design documents and surveys that conform to accepted engineering and surveying standards and safeguard the life, health, property, and welfare of the public.

3.   Licensees shall notify their employer or client and such other authority as may be appropriate when their professional judgment is overruled under circumstances where the life, health, property, or welfare of the public is endangered.

4.   Licensees shall be objective and truthful in professional reports, statements, or testimony. They shall include all relevant and pertinent information in such reports, statements, or testimony.

5.   Licensees shall express a professional opinion publicly only when it is founded upon an adequate knowledge of the facts and a competent evaluation of the subject matter.

6.   Licensees shall issue no statements, criticisms, or arguments on technical matters which are inspired or paid for by interested parties, unless they explicitly identify the interested parties on whose behalf they are speaking and reveal any interest they have in the matters.

7.   Licensees shall not permit the use of their name or firm name by, nor associate in the business ventures with, any person or firm which is engaging in fraudulent or dishonest business of professional practices.

8.   Licensees having knowledge of possible violations of any of these Rules of Professional Conduct shall provide the board with the information and assistance necessary to make the final determination of such violation.

Example

While working to revise the design of the suspension for a popular car, an engineer discovers a flaw in the design currently being produced. Based on a statistical

[4]Adapted from *NCEES FE Reference Handbook* (*NCEES Handbook*), 9th Ed., pg. 3–4, © 2013 by the National Council of Examiners for Engineering and Surveying® (ncees.org).

analysis, the company determines that although this mistake is likely to cause a small increase in the number of fatalities seen each year, it would be prohibitively expensive to do a recall to replace the part. Accordingly, the company decides not to issue a recall notice. What should the engineer do?

(A) The engineer should go along with the company's decision. The company has researched its options and chosen the most economic alternative.

(B) The engineer should send an anonymous tip to the media, suggesting that they alert the public and begin an investigation of the company's business practices.

(C) The engineer should notify the National Transportation Safety Board (NTSB), providing enough details for them to initiate a formal inquiry.

(D) The engineer should resign from the company. Because of standard nondisclosure agreements, it would be unethical as well as illegal to disclose any information about this situation. In addition, the engineer should not associate with a company that is engaging in such behavior.

Solution

The engineer's highest obligation is to the public's safety. In most instances, it would be unethical to take some public action on a matter without providing the company with the opportunity to resolve the situation internally. In this case, however, it appears as though the company's senior officers have already reviewed the case and made a decision. The engineer must alert the proper authorities, the NTSB, and provide them with any assistance necessary to investigate the case. To contact the media, although it might accomplish the same goal, would fail to fulfill the engineer's obligation to notify the authorities.

The answer is (C).

Licensee's Obligation to Employer and Clients

1. Licensees shall undertake assignments only when qualified by education or experience in the specific technical fields of engineering or surveying involved.

2. Licensees shall not affix their signatures or seals to any plans or documents dealing with subject matter in which they lack competence, nor to any such plan or document not prepared under their direct control and personal supervision.

3. Licensees may accept assignments for coordination of an entire project, provided that each design segment is signed and sealed by the licensee responsible for preparation of that design segment.

4. Licensees shall not reveal facts, data, or information obtained in a professional capacity without the prior consent of the client or employer except as authorized or required by law. Licensees shall not solicit or accept gratuities, directly or indirectly, from contractors, their agents, or other parties in connection with work for employers or clients.

5. Licensees shall make full prior disclosures to their employers or clients of potential conflicts of interest or other circumstances which could influence or appear to influence their judgment or the quality of their service.

6. Licensees shall not accept compensation, financial or otherwise, from more than one party for services pertaining to the same project, unless the circumstances are fully disclosed and agreed to by all interested parties.

7. Licensees shall not solicit or accept a professional contract from a governmental body on which a principal or officer of their organization serves as a member. Conversely, licensees serving as members, advisors, or employees of a government body or department, who are the principals or employees of a private concern, shall not participate in decisions with respect to professional services offered or provided by said concern to the governmental body which they serve.

Example

Plan stamping is best defined as the

(A) legal action of signing off on a project you didn't design but are taking full responsibility for

(B) legal action of signing off on a project you didn't design or check but didn't accept money for

(C) illegal action of signing off on a project you didn't design but did check

(D) illegal action of signing off on a project you didn't design or check

Solution

It is legal to stamp (i.e., sign off on) plans that you personally designed and/or checked. It is illegal to stamp plans that you didn't personally design or check, regardless of whether you got paid. It is legal to work as a "plan checker" consultant.

The answer is (D).

Licensee's Obligation to Other Licensees

1. Licensees shall not falsify or permit misrepresentation of their, or their associates', academic or professional qualifications. They shall not misrepresent or exaggerate their degree of responsibility in prior assignments nor the complexity of said assignments. Presentations incident to the solicitation of employment or business shall not misrepresent pertinent facts concerning employers, employees, associates, joint ventures, or past accomplishments.

2. Licensees shall not offer, give, solicit, or receive, either directly or indirectly, any commission, or gift, or other valuable consideration in order to secure work, and shall not make any political contribution with the intent to influence the award of a contract by public authority.

3. Licensees shall not attempt to injure, maliciously or falsely, directly or indirectly, the professional reputation, prospects, practice, or employment of other licensees, nor indiscriminately criticize other licensees' work.

Example

Without your knowledge, an old classmate applies to the company you work for. Knowing that you recently graduated from the same school, the director of engineering shows you the application and resume your friend submitted and asks your opinion. It turns out that your friend has exaggerated his participation in campus organizations, even claiming to have been an officer in an engineering society that you are sure he was never in. On the other hand, you remember him as being a highly intelligent student and believe that he could really help the company. How should you handle the situation?

(A) You should remove yourself from the ethical dilemma by claiming that you don't remember enough about the applicant to make an informed decision.

(B) You should follow your instincts and recommend the applicant. Almost everyone stretches the truth a little in their resumes, and the thing you're really being asked to evaluate is his usefulness to the company. If you mention the resume padding, the company is liable to lose a good prospect.

(C) You should recommend the applicant, but qualify your recommendation by pointing out that you think he may have exaggerated some details on his resume.

(D) You should point out the inconsistencies in the applicant's resume and recommend against hiring him.

Solution

Engineers are ethically obligated to prevent the misrepresentation of their associates' qualifications. You must make your employer aware of the incorrect facts on the resume. On the other hand, if you really believe that the applicant would make a good employee, you should make that recommendation as well. Unless you are making the hiring decision, ethics requires only that you be truthful. If you believe the applicant has merit, you should state so. It is the company's decision to remove or not remove the applicant from consideration because of this transgression.

The answer is (C).

4. ETHICAL CONSIDERATIONS

Ethical Priorities

There are frequently conflicting demands on engineers. While it is impossible to use a single decision-making process to solve every ethical dilemma, it is clear that ethical considerations will force engineers to subjugate their own self-interests. Specifically, the ethics of engineers dealing with others need to be considered in the following order from highest to lowest priority.

- society and the public
- the law
- the engineering profession
- the engineer's client
- the engineer's firm
- other involved engineers
- the engineer personally

Example

To whom/what is a registered engineer's foremost responsibility?

(A) client

(B) employer

(C) state and federal laws

(D) public welfare

Solution

The purpose of engineering registration is to protect the public. This includes protection from harm due to conduct as well as competence. No individual or organization may legitimately direct a registered engineer to harm the public.

The answer is (D).

Ethics/ Prof. Prac.

Dealing with Clients and Employers

The most common ethical guidelines affecting engineers' interactions with their employer (the *client*) can be summarized as follows.[5]

- Engineers should not accept assignments for which they do not have the skill, knowledge, or time to complete.

- Engineers must recognize their own limitations. They should use associates and other experts when the design requirements exceed their abilities.

- The client's interests must be protected. The extent of this protection exceeds normal business relationships and transcends the legal requirements of the engineer-client contract.

- Engineers must not be bound by what the client wants in instances where such desires would be unsuccessful, dishonest, unethical, unhealthy, or unsafe.

- Confidential client information remains the property of the client and must be kept confidential.

- Engineers must avoid conflicts of interest and should inform the client of any business connections or interests that might influence their judgment. Engineers should also avoid the *appearance* of a conflict of interest when such an appearance would be detrimental to the profession, their client, or themselves.

- The engineers' sole source of income for a particular project should be the fee paid by their client. Engineers should not accept compensation in any form from more than one party for the same services.

- If the client rejects the engineer's recommendations, the engineer should fully explain the consequences to the client.

- Engineers must freely and openly admit to the client any errors made.

All courts of law have required an engineer to perform in a manner consistent with normal professional standards. This is not the same as saying an engineer's work must be error-free. If an engineer completes a design, has the design and calculations checked by another competent engineer, and an error is subsequently shown to have been made, the engineer may be held responsible, but will probably not be considered negligent.

Example

You are an engineer in charge of receiving bids for an upcoming project. One of the contractors bidding the job is your former employer. The former employer laid you off in a move to cut costs. Which of the following should you do?

    I.   say nothing

   II.   inform your present employer of the situation

  III.   remain objective when reviewing the bids

  (A) II only

  (B) I and II

  (C) I and III

  (D) II and III

Solution

Registrants should remain objective at all times and should notify their employers of conflicts of interest or situations that could influence the registrants' ability to make objective decisions.

The answer is (D).

Dealing with Suppliers

Engineers routinely deal with manufacturers, contractors, and vendors (*suppliers*). In this regard, engineers have great responsibility and influence. Such a relationship requires that engineers deal justly with both clients and suppliers.

An engineer will often have an interest in maintaining good relationships with suppliers since this often leads to future work. Nevertheless, relationships with suppliers must remain highly ethical. Suppliers should not be encouraged to feel that they have any special favors coming to them because of a long-standing relationship with the engineer.

The ethical responsibilities relating to suppliers are listed as follows.

- The engineer must not accept or solicit gifts or other valuable considerations from a supplier during, prior to, or after any job. An engineer should not accept discounts, allowances, commissions, or any other indirect compensation from suppliers, contractors, or other engineers in connection with any work or recommendations.

- The engineer must enforce the plans and specifications (i.e., the *contract documents*) but must also interpret the contract documents fairly.

- Plans and specifications developed by the engineer on behalf of the client must be complete, definite, and specific.

---

[5]These general guidelines contain references to contractors, plans, specifications, and contract documents. This language is common, though not unique, to the situation of an engineer supplying design services to an owner-developer or architect. However, most of the ethical guidelines are general enough to apply to engineers in the industry as well.

- Suppliers should not be required to spend time or furnish materials that are not called for in the plans and contract documents.

- The engineer should not unduly delay the performance of suppliers.

Example

In dealing with suppliers, an engineer may

(A) unduly delay vendor performance if the client agrees

(B) spend personal time outside of the contract to ensure adequate performance

(C) prepare plans containing ambiguous design-build references as cost-saving measures

(D) enforce plans and specifications to the letter, without regard to fairness

Solution

An engineer not only may, but is required to, ensure performance consistent with plans and specifications. If a job is intentionally or unintentionally underbid, the engineer will have to use personal time to complete the project.

The answer is (B).

Dealing with Other Engineers

Engineers should try to protect the engineering profession as a whole, to strengthen it, and to enhance its public stature. The following ethical guidelines apply.

- An engineer should not attempt to maliciously injure the professional reputation, business practice, or employment position of another engineer. However, if there is proof that another engineer has acted unethically or illegally, the engineer should advise the proper authority.

- An engineer should not review someone else's work while the other engineer is still employed unless the other engineer is made aware of the review.

- An engineer should not try to replace another engineer once the other engineer has received employment.

- An engineer should not use the advantages of a salaried position to compete unfairly (i.e., moonlight) with other engineers who have to charge more for the same consulting services.

- Subject to legal and proprietary restraints, an engineer should freely report, publish, and distribute information that would be useful to other engineers.

Dealing with (and Affecting) the Public

In regard to the social consequences of engineering, the relationship between an engineer and the public is essentially straightforward. Responsibilities to the public demand that the engineer place service to humankind above personal gain. Furthermore, proper ethical behavior requires that an engineer avoid association with projects that are contrary to public health and welfare or that are of questionable legal character.

- Engineers must consider the safety, health, and welfare of the public in all work performed.

- Engineers must uphold the honor and dignity of their profession by refraining from self-laudatory advertising, by explaining (when required) their work to the public, and by expressing opinions only in areas of their knowledge.

- When engineers issue a public statement, they must clearly indicate if the statement is being made on anyone's behalf (i.e., if anyone is benefitting from their position).

- Engineers must keep their skills at a state-of-the-art level.

- Engineers should develop public knowledge and appreciation of the engineering profession and its achievements.

- Engineers must notify the proper authorities when decisions adversely affecting public safety and welfare are made (a practice known as *whistle-blowing*).

Example

Whistle-blowing is best described as calling public attention to

(A) your own previous unethical behavior

(B) unethical behavior of employees under your control

(C) secret illegal behavior by your employer

(D) unethical or illegal behavior in a government agency you are monitoring as a private individual

Solution

"Whistle-blowing" is calling public attention to illegal actions taken in the past or being taken currently by your employer. Whistle-blowing jeopardizes your own good standing with your employer.

The answer is (C).

Competitive Bidding

The ethical guidelines for dealing with other engineers presented here and in more detailed codes of ethics no longer include a prohibition on *competitive bidding*. Until 1971, most codes of ethics for engineers considered competitive bidding detrimental to public welfare, since cost cutting normally results in a lower quality design. However, in a 1971 case against the National Society of Professional Engineers that went all the way to the U.S. Supreme Court, the prohibition against competitive bidding was determined to be a violation of the Sherman Antitrust Act (i.e., it was an unreasonable restraint of trade).

The opinion of the Supreme Court does not *require* competitive bidding—it merely forbids a prohibition against competitive bidding in NSPE's code of ethics. The following points must be considered.

- Engineers and design firms may individually continue to refuse to bid competitively on engineering services.

- Clients are not required to seek competitive bids for design services.

- Federal, state, and local statutes governing the procedures for procuring engineering design services, even those statutes that prohibit competitive bidding, are not affected.

- Any prohibitions against competitive bidding in individual state engineering registration laws remain unaffected.

- Engineers and their societies may actively and aggressively lobby for legislation that would prohibit competitive bidding for design services by public agencies.

Example

Complete the sentence: "The U.S. Department of Justice's successful action in the 1970s against engineering codes of ethics that formally prohibited competitive bidding was based on the premise that

(A) competitive bidding allowed minority firms to participate."

(B) competitive bidding was required by many government contracts."

(C) the prohibitions violated antitrust statutes."

(D) engineering societies did not have the authority to prohibit competitive bidding."

Solution

The U.S. Department of Justice's successful challenge was based on antitrust statutes. Prohibiting competitive bidding was judged to inhibit free competition among design firms.

The answer is (C).

53 Licensure

1. ABOUT LICENSING

Engineering licensing (also known as *engineering registration*) in the United States is an examination process by which a state's *board of engineering licensing* (typically referred to as the "engineers' board" or "board of registration") determines and certifies that an engineer has achieved a minimum level of competence.[1] This process is intended to protect the public by preventing unqualified individuals from offering engineering services.

Most engineers in the United States do not need to be licensed.[2] In particular, most engineers who work for companies that design and manufacture products are exempt from the licensing requirement. This is known as the *industrial exemption*, something that is built into the laws of most states.[3]

Nevertheless, there are many good reasons to become a licensed engineer. For example, you cannot offer consulting engineering services in any state unless you are licensed in that state. Even within a product-oriented corporation, you may find that employment, advancement, and managerial positions are limited to licensed engineers.

Once you have met the licensing requirements, you will be allowed to use the titles *Professional Engineer* (PE), *Structural Engineer* (SE), *Registered Engineer* (RE), and/or *Consulting Engineer* (CE) as permitted by your state.

Although the licensing process is similar in each of the 50 states, each has its own licensing law. Unless you offer consulting engineering services in more than one state, however, you will not need to be licensed in the other states.

2. THE U.S. LICENSING PROCEDURE

The licensing procedure is similar in all states. You will take two examinations. The full process requires you to complete two applications, one for each of the two examinations. The first examination is the *Fundamentals of Engineering* (FE) *examination*, formerly known (and still commonly referred to) as the *Engineer-In-Training* (EIT) *examination*.[4] This examination is designed for students who are close to finishing or have recently finished an undergraduate engineering degree. Seven versions of the exam are offered: chemical, civil, electrical and computer, environmental, industrial, mechanical, and other disciplines. Examinees are encouraged to take the module that best corresponds to their undergraduate degree. In addition to the discipline-specific topics, each exam covers subjects that are fundamental to the engineering profession, such as mathematics, probability and statistics, ethics, and professional practice.

The second examination is the *Professional Engineering* (PE) *examination*, also known as the *Principles and Practices* (P&P) *examination*. This examination tests your ability to practice competently in a particular engineering discipline. It is designed for engineers who have gained at least four years' post-college work experience in their chosen engineering discipline.

The actual details of licensing qualifications, experience requirements, minimum education levels, fees, and examination schedules vary from state to state. Contact your state's licensing board for more information. You will find contact information (websites, telephone numbers, email addresses, etc.) for all U.S. state and territorial boards of registration at **ppi2pass.com**.

---

[1]Licensing of engineers is not unique to the United States. However, the practice of requiring a degreed engineer to take an examination is not common in other countries. Licensing in many countries requires a degree and may also require experience, references, and demonstrated knowledge of ethics and law, but no technical examination.

[2]Less than one-third of the degreed engineers in the United States are licensed.

[3]Only one or two states have abolished the industrial exemption. There has always been a lot of "talk" among engineers about abolishing it, but there has been little success in actually doing so. One of the reasons is that manufacturers' lobbies are very strong.

[4]The terms *engineering intern* (EI) and *intern engineer* (IE) have also been used in the past to designate the status of an engineer who has passed the first exam. These uses are rarer but may still be encountered in some states.

Ethics/
Prof. Prac.

3. NATIONAL COUNCIL OF EXAMINERS FOR ENGINEERING AND SURVEYING

The *National Council of Examiners for Engineering and Surveying* (NCEES) in Seneca, South Carolina, writes, publishes, distributes, and scores the national FE and PE examinations.[5] The individual states administer the exams in a uniform, controlled environment as dictated by NCEES.

4. UNIFORM EXAMINATIONS

Although each state has its own licensing law and is, theoretically, free to administer its own exams, none does so for the major disciplines. All states have chosen to use the NCEES exams. The exams from all the states are graded by NCEES. Each state adopts the cut-off passing scores recommended by NCEES. These practices have led to the term *uniform examination*.

5. RECIPROCITY AMONG STATES

With minor exceptions, having a license from one state will not permit you to practice engineering in another state. You must have a professional engineering license from each state in which you work. Most engineers do not work across state lines or in multiple states, but some do. Luckily, it is not too difficult to get a license from every state you work in once you have a license from one of them.

All states use the NCEES examinations. If you take and pass the FE or PE examination in one state, your certificate or license will be honored by all of the other states. Upon proper application, payment of fees, and proof of your license, you will be issued a license by the new state. Although there may be other special requirements imposed by a state, it will not be necessary to retake the FE or PE examinations.[6] The issuance of an engineering license based on another state's licensing is known as *reciprocity* or *comity*.

---

[5]National Council of Examiners for Engineering and Surveying, 280 Seneca Creek Road, Seneca, SC 29678, (800) 250-3196, ncees.org.
[6]For example, California requires all civil engineering applicants to pass special examinations in seismic design and surveying in addition to their regular eight-hour PE exams. Licensed engineers from other states only have to pass these two special exams. They do not need to retake the PE exam.

Index

input, and Laplace transform (fig), 48-6
loop transfer, 48-3
objective, 46-2
of formation, Gibbs, 13-6
open-loop transfer, 48-3
open-loop, linear, time-invariant transfer function (fig), 48-2
path, 14-20
point, 14-20
potential, Laplace, 3-11
probability density, 6-10, 6-11
probability distribution, 6-11
probability distribution, continuous random variable, 6-11
probability distribution, discrete random variable, 6-11
probability mass, 6-10
reciprocal, 1-13
scalar, 3-10
shear, 31-2
state, 13-3
step, 4-4
system, 48-4
time-invariant transfer, 48-2
trigonometric, 1-12, 1-13
work, 26-7
Functional notation, 50-7
Functionality, mer, 27-7
Fund, sinking, 50-5
Fundamental
constants (tbl), xl
deviation, 46-8
frequency, 4-5
theorem of integral calculus, 3-7
Fundamentals of Engineering exam, 53-1
Fusion
metals, 28-9
weld (fig), 28-9
Future
worth, 50-4
worth (tbl), 50-3

G

Gage
bonded strain, 47-4
factor, 47-5
pressure, 7-2
setup (tbl), 47-11
strain, rosette, 47-5
Gain
characteristic, 48-9
closed-loop, 48-4
constant, 48-2
crossover, 48-9
crossover point, 48-9, 48-11
derivative, 48-12
direct, 48-3
error, 48-3
feedback, 48-3
forward, 48-3
heat, 18-3
instantaneous heat, 18-3
integral, 48-12
internal heat, 18-3
loop, 48-3
margin, 48-10
PID (*see also* type), 48-12
proportional, 48-12
system, 4-4
Galvanic
action, 27-14
cell, 27-14
series, 27-14
series in seawater (tbl), 27-15
Galvanizing, 28-11
Gamma
function, 6-15
-iron, 27-19
Gap, energy, 26-6
Gas
acetylene, 28-9
constant, specific, 11-1, 13-11

constant, universal, 11-1, 13-11
dynamics, 11-1
high-velocity, 11-1
ideal, 11-1, 13-2, 13-11
ideal, criteria, 13-12
ideal, law, 11-1
ideal, properties, 13-12
law, ideal, 13-11
MAPP, 28-9
metal arc welding, 28-10
methyacetylene propadiene, 28-9
mixture, 13-2, 16-5
perfect, 13-2, 13-12
perfect (*see also* Gas, ideal), 11-1
perfect, properties, 13-12
real, 13-2, 13-13
turbine cycle, 15-10
-vapor mixture, 13-2
welding, 28-1, 28-9
Gasket blowout, 45-6
Gauss-Jordan elimination, 2-10
Gauss' law, 33-4
Gauss' law, 33-6
Gaussian
distribution, 6-13
surface, 33-4
Gear, 43-10
annulus, 43-12
axial force, 43-11
compound, 43-10
drive, 43-1, 43-10
external, 43-9
idler, 43-9
intermediate, 43-9
internal, 43-9
involute, 43-8
module, 43-9
parameters, spur, 43-9
peripheral force, 43-11
planet, 43-12
radial force, 43-12
ratio, 43-10
ring, 43-12
set, 43-1, 43-9, 43-10
set velocity ratio, 43-13
set, epicyclic, 43-12
set, planetary, 43-12
set, prime, 43-10
set, reverted, 43-10
set, simple, 43-9
set, solar, 43-12
set, star, 43-12
spider, 43-12
spur, 43-8
spur, pitch circle velocity, 43-8
stage, 43-9
sun, 43-12
tangential force, 43-11
terminology, 43-1, 43-9
train, 43-9
train design, 43-1, 43-12
train value, 43-10
train, compound, 43-11
train, efficiency, 43-11
train, two-, 43-10
transmitted force, 43-11
transmitted power, 43-12
General
contractor, 51-3
damages, 51-7
expense, 50-16
form, conic section, 1-4
form, straight-line, 1-2
ledger, 50-14
ledger system (ftn), 50-14
selling, and administrative selling (GS&A) expense, 50-16
solution, simple spring-mass system, 41-3
spandrel, 25-13
spandrel, area moment of inertia, 25-13
spandrel, centroid, 25-13

strain, 29-8
triangle, 1-15
Generalized compressibility, 13-14
factors (fig), 13-19
Generating line, 43-8
Generator
DC, 36-4
two-pole, 36-2
Geometric
angle of attack, 9-22
mean, 6-7
progression, 2-15
sequence, 2-15
similarity, 10-6
Gibbs function, 13-6
of formation, 13-6
Gibbs'
energy, 16-5
phase rule, 13-3, 27-20
rule, 16-5
theorem, 16-5
Glass, 27-9
behavior (fig), 27-10
common, 27-10
fibers, chopped, 27-8
transition temperature, 27-10
Global variable, 49-4
GMAW, 28-10
Goodman theory, modified, 29-10
Goodness of fit, 6-21
Gooseneck, 28-7
GOTO, 49-5
-less programming, 49-4
Government, bronze, 27-5
Grade
bolt, 42-2
of steel (ftn), 44-4
rivet, 42-2
viscosity, oil, 44-3
Gradient, 3-10
identity, 3-11
scalar function, 3-10
series cash flow, 50-3
temperature, 19-4
thermal, 19-4
vector field, 3-10
velocity, 7-5
Grain
boundary defect, 27-15
-boundary surface area, 27-23
in standard area, 27-23
size number, ASTM, 27-23
size, ASTM, 27-23
size, metal, 27-23
unit of mass, 16-8
Graphitic iron, compacted, 27-5
Graphitization, 45-2
Grashof number (ftn), 20-4
Gravimetric
component fraction, 27-18
fraction, 16-2
Gravitational
constant, xxxiii, xxxiv
potential energy, 40-4
Gravity
acceleration, xxxiii, xxxiv
center of, 3-8, 25-4
die casting, 28-6
drop hammer, 28-6
flow, 9-8
molding, 28-6
specific, 7-2
Gray
body, 21-2
body, net heat transfer, 21-4
cast iron, 27-4
Greenman v. Yuba Power (ftn), 51-6
Grid, 47-5
Grinding, 28-3
centerless, 28-4
centerless (fig), 28-4
electrochemical, 28-4

INDEX - K

INDEX - M

INDEX - R